P9-CNH-939

MAGRUDER'S

AMERICAN GOVERNMENT

Daniel M. Shea

Boston, Massachusetts
Chandler, Arizona
Glenview, Illinois
New York, New York

Social Studies Reimagined

[To start, download the free **Pearson BouncePages** app on your smartphone or tablet. Simply search for the Pearson BouncePages app in your mobile app store. The app is available for Android and IOS (iPhone®/iPad®).]

Make your book come alive!

Activate your digital course interactivities directly from the page.

To launch the myStory video look for this icon. 

To activate more interactivities look for this icon. **Interactive**

1. **AIM** the camera over the image so it is easily viewable on your screen.
2. **TAP** the screen to scan the page.
3. **BOUNCE** the page to life by clicking the icon.

Cover Images: The Ronald Reagan Presidential Library and Museum. Buttons, badges, and watches from the Reagan-Bush presidential campaign in the 80's are on display at the Ronald Reagan Presidential Library and Museum. Ruaridh Stewart/ZUMA/ Corbis. Vintage American patriotic and political pins. Comstock/Stockbyte/Getty Images

Acknowledgements of third-party content appear at the end of the book, which constitute an extension of this copyright page.

PEARSON

ISBN-13: 978-01-3330699-6
ISBN-10: 0-13-330699-2

12 18

Authors, Consultants, Partners

[Authors]

Daniel M. Shea

Daniel M. Shea is a Professor of Political Science and Director of the Goldfarb Center for Public Affairs and Civic Engagement at Colby College. He earned his Ph.D. from the University of Albany, State University of New York. An award-winning teacher, Shea has spearheaded numerous initiatives at Colby and other institutions designed to help young Americans better appreciate their potential to affect democratic change. The author or editor of nearly twenty books and dozens of articles and chapters on the American political process, Shea's research focuses on campaigns and elections, political parties, the politics of scandal, and grassroots activism. His coauthored volume *The Fountain of Youth* (2007) garnered national attention for its findings on how local party organizations often neglect young citizens. His work on civility and compromise led to the publication of a co-edited volume, *Can We Talk? The Rise of Rude, Nasty, Stubborn Politics* (2012). Other works authored by Shea include *Let's Vote: The Essentials of the American Electoral Process* and the college text *Living Democracy*.

Magruder's American Government, first published in 1917, is a testament to the authors' faith in American ideals and American institutions. Frank Abbott Magruder's life and work serve as an outstanding example of American patriotism. After Magruder's death in 1949, his student, Bill McClenaghan, authored the text for the next sixty years and poured his own passion for American government into his work. The torch has now been passed to a new author, but the legacies of the previous authors live on through all the students and future readers of *Magruder's American Government*.

[Program Consultant]

Dr. Kathy Swan is an Associate Professor of Curriculum and Instruction at the University of Kentucky. Her research focuses on standards-based technology integration, authentic intellectual work, and documentary-making in the social studies classroom. Swan has been a four-time recipient of the National Technology Leadership Award in Social Studies Education. She is also the advisor for the Social Studies Assessment, Curriculum, and Instruction Collaborative (SSACI) at CCSSO.

[Program Partners]

NBC LEARN

NBC Learn, the educational arm of NBC News, develops original stories for use in the classroom and makes archival NBC News stories, images, and primary source documents available on demand to teachers, students, and parents. NBC Learn partnered with Pearson to produce the myStory videos that support this program.

Constitutional Rights Foundation is a nonprofit, nonpartisan organization focused on educating students about the importance of civic participation in a democratic society. Constitutional Rights Foundation is the lead contributor to the development of the Civic Discussion Topic Inquiries for this program. Constitutional Rights Foundation is also the provider of the Civic Action Project (CAP) for the *Economics* and *Magruder's American Government* programs. CAP is a project-based learning model for civics, government, and economics courses.

Reviewers & Academic Consultants

Pearson Magruder's American Government was developed especially for you and your students. The story of its creation began with a three-day Innovation Lab in which teachers, historians, students, and authors came together to imagine our ideal Social Studies teaching and learning experiences. We refined the plan with a series of teacher roundtables that shaped this new approach to ensure your students' mastery of content and skills. A dedicated team, made up of Pearson authors, content experts, and social studies teachers, worked to bring our collective vision into reality. Kathy Swan, Professor of Education and architect of the new College, Career, and Civic Life (C3) Framework, served as our expert advisor on curriculum and instruction.

Pearson would like to extend a special thank you to all of the teachers who helped guide the development of this program. We gratefully acknowledge your efforts to realize Next Generation Social Studies teaching and learning that will prepare American students for college, careers, and active citizenship.

[Program Advisors]

Campaign for the Civic Mission of Schools is a coalition of over 70 national civic learning, education, civic engagement, and business groups committed to improving the quality and quantity of civic learning in American schools. The Campaign served as an advisor on this program.

Buck Institute for Education is a nonprofit organization dedicated to helping teachers implement the effective use of Project-Based Learning in their classrooms. Buck Institute staff consulted on the Project-Based Learning Topic Inquiries for this program.

[Program Academic Consultants]

Barbara Brown
Director of Outreach
College of Arts and Sciences
African Studies Center
Boston University
Boston, Massachusetts

William Childs
Professor of History Emeritus
The Ohio State University
Columbus, Ohio

Jennifer Giglielmo
Associate Professor of History
Smith College
Northhampton, Massachusetts

Joanne Connor Green
Professor, Department Chair
Political Science
Texas Christian University
Fort Worth, Texas

Ramdas Lamb, Ph.D.
Associate Professor of Religion
University of Hawaii at Manoa
Honolulu, Hawaii

Huping Ling
Changjiang Scholar Chair Professor
Professor of History
Truman State University
Kirksville, Missouri

Jeffery Long, Ph.D.
Professor of Religion and Asian Studies
Elizabethtown College
Elizabethtown, Pennsylvania

Gordon Newby
Professor of Islamic, Jewish and Comparative Studies
Department of Middle Eastern and South Asian Studies
Emory University
Atlanta, Georgia

Mark Peterson
Associate Professor
Department of Asian and Near Eastern Languages
Brigham Young University
Provo, Utah

William Pitts
Professor, Department of Religion
Baylor University
Waco, Texas

Benjamin Ravid
Professor Emeritus of Jewish History
Department of Near Eastern and Judaic Studies
Brandeis University
Waltham, Massachusetts

Harpreet Singh
College Fellow
Department of South Asian Studies
Harvard University
Cambridge, Massachusetts

Christopher E. Smith, J.D., Ph.D.
Professor
Michigan State University
MSU School of Criminal Justice
East Lansing, Michigan

John Voll
Professor of Islamic History
Georgetown University
Washington, D.C.

Michael R. Wolf
Associate Professor
Department of Political Science
Indiana University-Purdue University Fort Wayne
Fort Wayne, Indiana

Social Studies Reimagined

Social studies is more than dots on a map or dates on a timeline. It's where we've been and where we're going. It's stories from the past and our stories today. And in today's fast-paced, interconnected world, it's essential.

Welcome to the next generation of social studies!

Pearson's new social studies program was created in collaboration with educators, social studies experts, and students. The program is based on Pearson's Mastery System. The System uses tested best practices, content expectations, technology, and a four-part framework—Connect, Investigate, Synthesize, and Demonstrate—to prepare students to be college-and-career ready.

The System includes:

- Higher-level content that gives support to access complex text, acquire core content knowledge, and tackle rigorous questions.
- Inquiry-focused Projects, Civic Discussions, and Document Analysis activities that develop content and skills mastery in preparation for real-world challenges;
- Digital content on Pearson Realize that is dynamic, flexible, and uses the power of technology to bring social studies to life.
- The program uses essential questions and stories to increase long-term understanding and retention of learning.

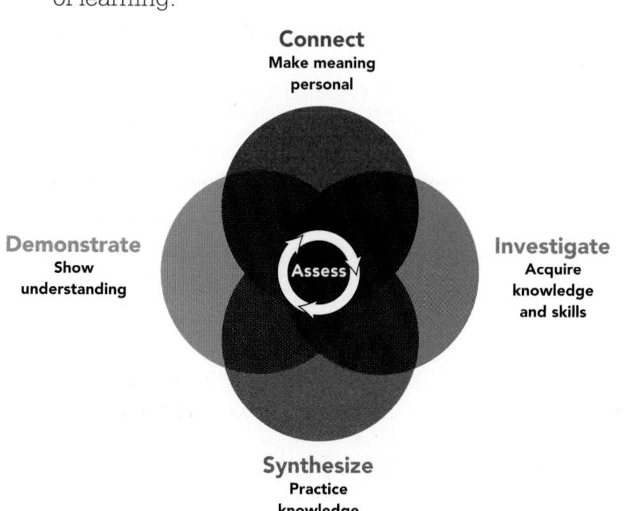

» Go online to learn more and see the program overview video.

PEARSON realize™

The digital course on Realize!

The program's digital course on Realize puts rich and engaging content, embedded assessments with instant data, and flexible tools at your fingertips.

CONNECT! Begin the Pearson Mastery System by engaging in the topic story and connecting it to your own lives.

Preview—Each Topic opens with the Enduring Understandings section, allowing you to preview expected learning outcomes.

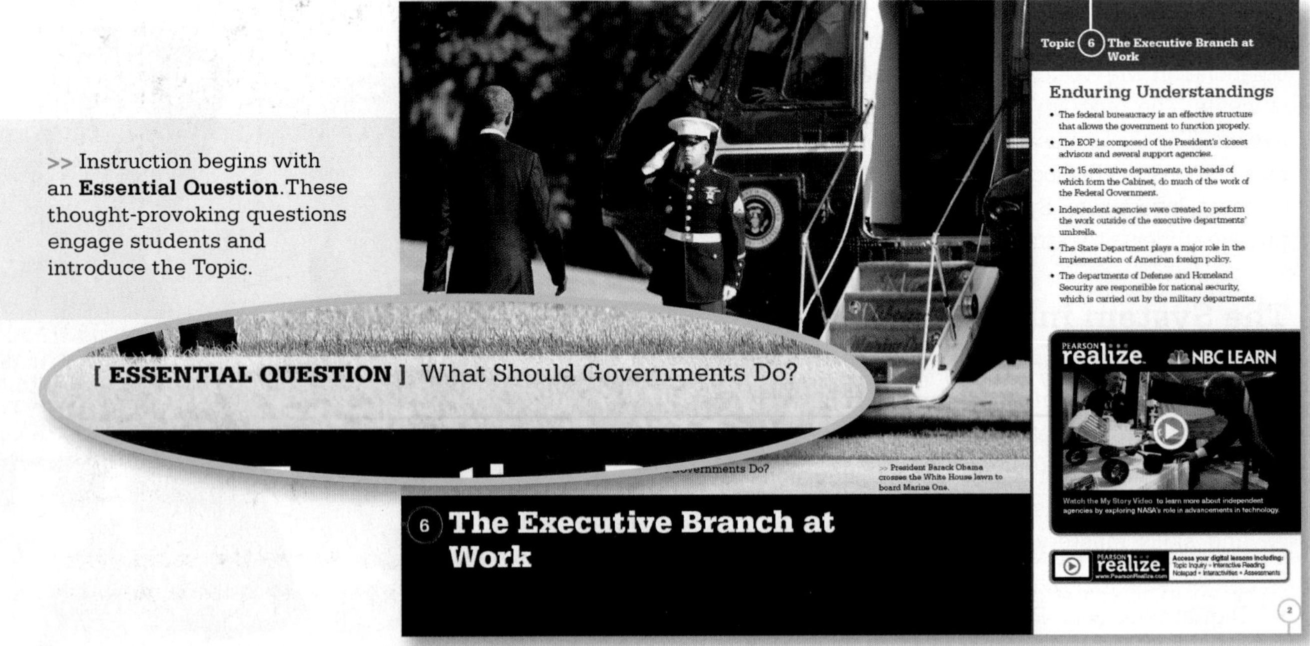

PEARSON realize
NBC LEARN
Watch the My Story Video to learn more about independent agencies by exploring NASA's role in advancements in technology.

Developed in partnership with NBCLearn, the **My Story** videos help students connect to the Topic content by hearing the personal story of an individual whose life is related to the content students are about to learn.

INVESTIGATE! Step two of the Mastery System allows you to investigate the topic story through a number of engaging features as you learn the content.

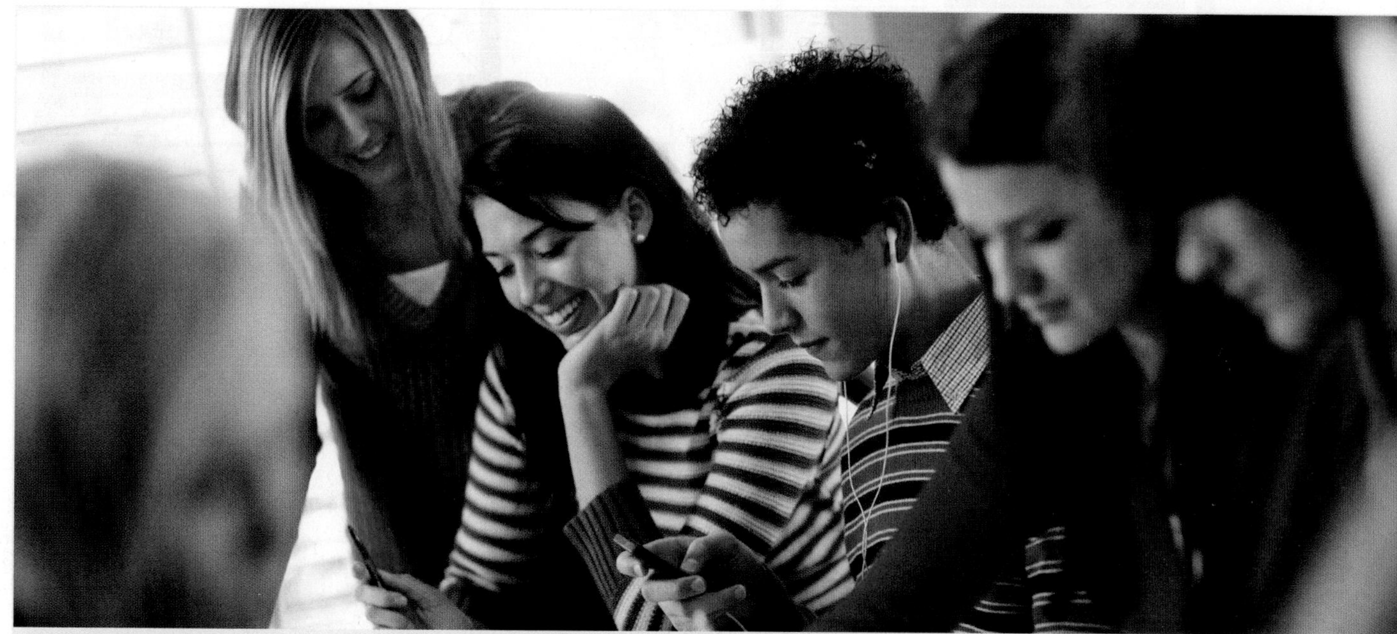

>> **Active Classroom Strategies** integrated in the daily lesson plans help to increase in-class participation, raise energy levels and attentiveness, all while engaging in the story. These 5-15 minute activities have you use what you have learned to draw, write, speak, and decide.

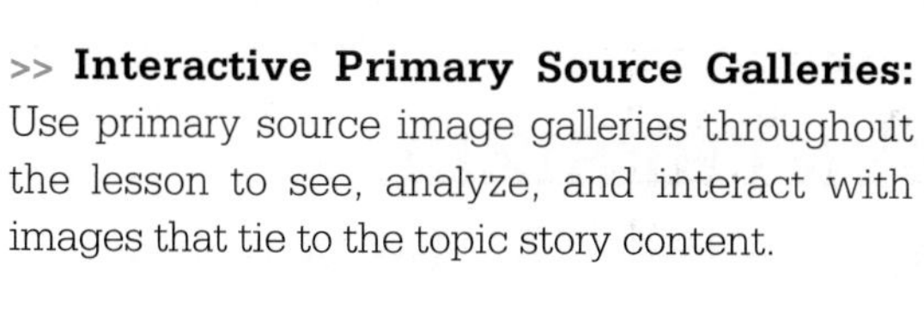

>> **Interactive Primary Source Galleries:** Use primary source image galleries throughout the lesson to see, analyze, and interact with images that tie to the topic story content.

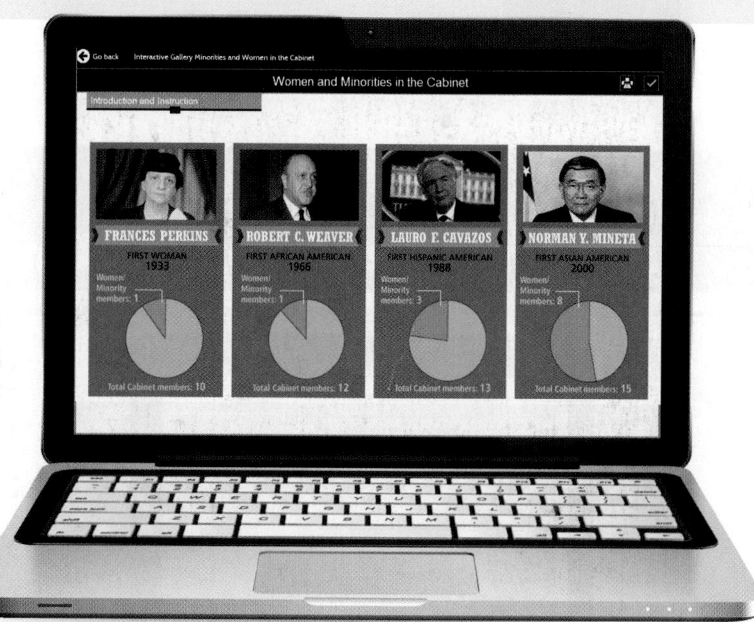

Investigate

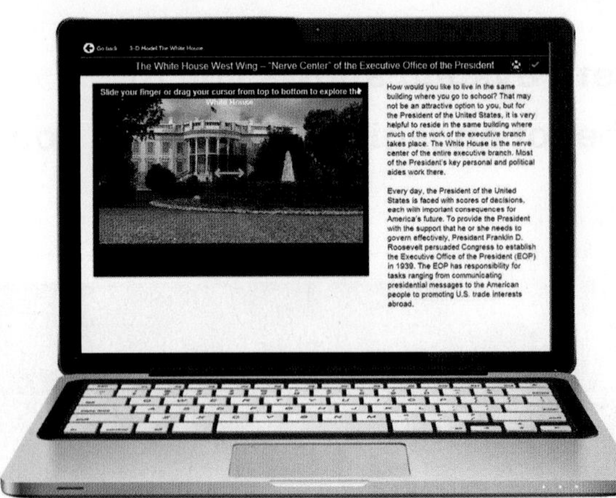

>> Feel like you are a part of the story with **interactive 3-D models**.

>> Continue to investigate the topic story through **dynamic interactive charts, graphs, and timelines**. Build rigorous analytical skills while covering the essential standards.

>> Learn content by reading narrative text online or in a printed Student Edition.

Synthesize: Practice Knowledge and Skills

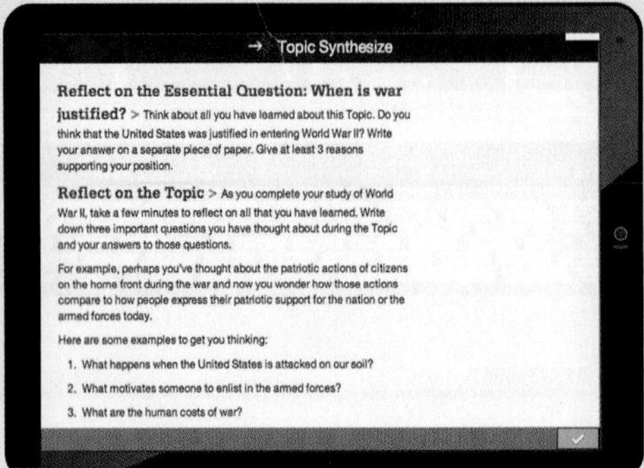

SYNTHESIZE!

In step three of the Mastery System, pause to reflect on what you learn and revisit an essential question.

DEMONSTRATE! The final step of the Mastery System is to demonstrate understanding of the text.

PEARSON realize™

>> **The digital course on Realize!** The program's digital course on Realize puts engaging content, embedded assessments, instant data, and flexible tools at your fingertips.

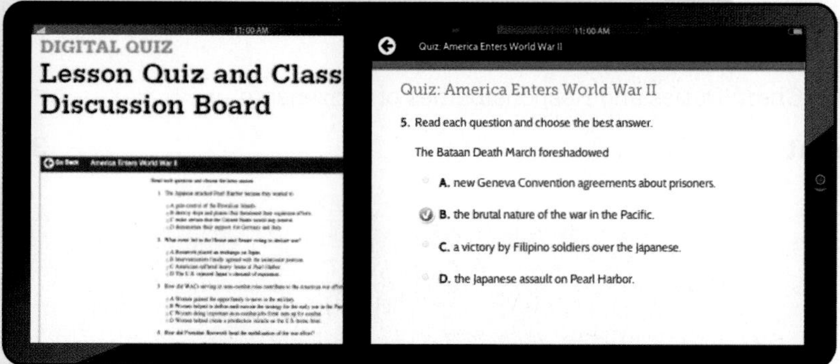

>> **Assessment**. At the end of each lesson and topic, demonstrate understanding through Lesson Quizzes, Topic Tests, and Topic Inquiry performance assessments. The System provides remediation and enrichment recommendations based on your individual performance towards mastery.

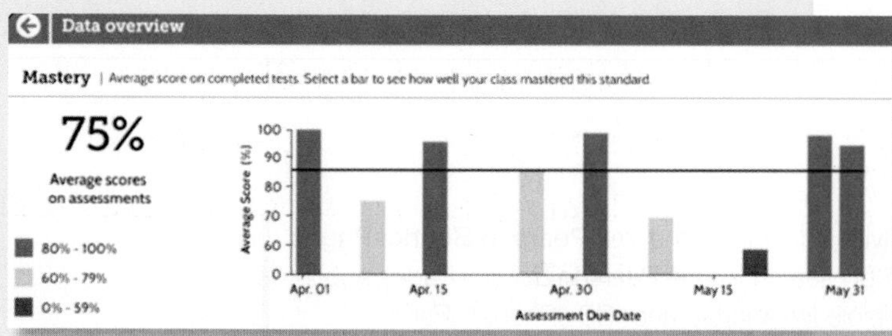

>> **Class and Data** features on Realize make it easy to see your mastery data.

Table of Contents

TOPIC 1 Foundations of Government 2

To activate your digital course interactivities download the free **Pearson BouncePages** app on your smartphone or tablet. Simply search for the Pearson BouncePages app in your mobile app store. The app is available for Android and IOS (iPhone®/iPad®).

TOPIC 2 The Beginnings of American Government 38

Table of Contents

TOPIC 3 The Constitution 76

www.PearsonRealize.com
Access your Digital Resources

TOPIC 4 The Legislative Branch 126

Table of Contents

TOPIC 5 The Executive Branch—The Presidency and Vice Presidency 198

TOPIC 6 The Executive Branch at Work 234

Table of Contents

TOPIC 7 The Judicial Branch 296

PEARSON realize www.PearsonRealize.com Access your Digital Resources

MR. PRESIDENT
HOW LONG
MUST
WOMEN WAIT
FOR LIBERTY
MR. PRESIDENT
WHAT
WILL YOU DO
FOR
WOMAN SUFFRAGE

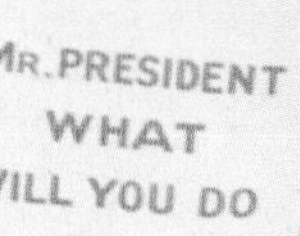
MR. PRESIDENT
WHAT
WILL YOU DO

TOPIC 8 Protecting Civil Liberties 324

Table of Contents

TOPIC 9 Citizenship and Civil Rights 388

TOPIC 10 Government by the People 422

Table of Contents

TOPIC 11 Elections 500

TOPIC 12 Government and the Economy 560

TOPIC 14 Comparative Political Systems 674

Digital Resources

Many types of digital resources help you investigate the topics in this course. You'll find biographies, primary sources, maps, and more. These resources will help bring the topics to life.

Core Concepts

Culture

- What Is Culture?
- Families and Societies
- Language
- Religion
- The Arts
- Cultural Diffusion and Change
- Science and Technology

Economics

- Economics Basics
- Economic Process
- Economic Systems
- Economic Development
- Trade
- Money Management

Geography

- The Study of Earth
- Geography's Five Themes
- Ways to Show Earth's Surface
- Understanding Maps
- Earth in Space
- Time and Earth's Rotation
- Forces on Earth's Surface
- Forces Inside Earth
- Climate and Weather
- Temperature
- Water and Climate
- Air Circulation and Precipitation
- Types of Climate
- Ecosystems
- Environment and Resources
- Land Use
- People's Impact on the Environment
- Population
- Migration
- Urbanization

Government and Civics

- Foundations of Government
- Political Systems
- Political Structures
- Conflict and Cooperation
- Citizenship

History

- How Do Historians Study History?
- Measuring Time
- Historical Sources
- Archaeology and Other Sources
- Historical Maps

Personal Finance

- Your Fiscal Fitness: An Introduction
- Budgeting
- Checking
- Investments
- Savings and Retirement
- Credit and Debt
- Risk Management
- Consumer Smarts
- After High School
- Taxes and Income

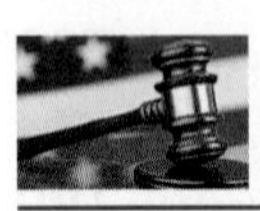

Landmark Supreme Court Cases

- *Korematsu* v. *United States*
- *Marbury* v. *Madison*
- *McCulloch* v. *Maryland*
- *Gibbons* v. *Ogden*
- *Worcester* v. *Georgia*
- *Dred Scott* v. *Sandford*
- *Plessy* v. *Ferguson*
- *Schenck* v. *United States*
- *Brown* v. *Board of Education*
- *Engel* v. *Vitale*
- *Sweatt* v. *Painter*
- *Mapp* v. *Ohio*
- *Hernandez* v. *Texas*
- *Gideon* v. *Wainwright*
- *Wisconsin* v. *Yoder*
- *Miranda* v. *Arizona*
- *White* v. *Regester*
- *Tinker* v. *Des Moines School District*
- *Roe* v. *Wade*
- *Baker* v. *Carr*
- *Grutter* v. *Bollinger*
- *Edgewood* v. *Kirby*
- *Texas* v. *Johnson*
- *National Federation of Independent Businesses et al.* v. *Sebelius et al.*
- *Mendez* v. *Westminster* and *Delgado* v. *Bastrop*

Interactive Primary Sources

- Code of Hammurabi
- Psalm 23
- The Republic, Plato
- Politics, Aristotle
- Edicts, Asoka
- Analects, Confucius
- First Letter to the Corinthians, Paul
- The Quran
- The Magna Carta
- Travels, Ibn Battuta
- The Destruction of the Indies, Bartolomé de Las Casas
- Mayflower Compact
- English Petition of Right
- English Bill of Rights
- Two Treatises of Government, John Locke
- The Spirit of Laws, Baron de Montesquieu
- The Social Contract, Jean-Jacques Rousseau
- The Interesting Narrative of the Life of Olaudah Equiano
- "Give Me Liberty or Give Me Death," Patrick Henry
- "Remember the Ladies," Abigail Adams
- Common Sense, Thomas Paine
- Declaration of Independence
- Virginia Declaration of Rights
- Virginia Statute for Religious Freedom, Thomas Jefferson
- "To His Excellency, General Washington," Phillis Wheatley
- Articles of Confederation
- Anti-Federalist Papers
- Federalist No. 10, James Madison
- Federalist No. 39, James Madison
- Federalist No. 51
- Federalist No. 78, Alexander Hamilton
- Northwest Ordinance
- Iroquois Constitution
- Declaration of the Rights of Man and the Citizen
- Farewell Address, George Washington
- Mexican Federal Constitution of 1824
- State Colonization Law of 1825
- Law of April 6, 1830
- Debate Over Nullification, Webster and Calhoun
- Turtle Bayou Resolutions
- Democracy in America, Alexis de Tocqueville
- 1836 Victory or Death Letter from the Alamo, Travis
- Texas Declaration of Independence
- Declaration of Sentiments and Resolutions
- "Ain't I a Woman?," Sojourner Truth
- Uncle Tom's Cabin, Harriet Beecher Stowe
- "A House Divided," Abraham Lincoln
- First Inaugural Address, Abraham Lincoln
- Declaration of Causes: February 2, 1861
- Emancipation Proclamation, Abraham Lincoln
- Gettysburg Address, Abraham Lincoln
- Second Inaugural Address, Abraham Lincoln
- "I Will Fight No More Forever," Chief Joseph
- How the Other Half Lives, Jacob Riis
- The Pledge of Allegiance
- Preamble to the Platform of the Populist Party
- Atlanta Exposition Address, Booker T. Washington
- The Jungle, Upton Sinclair
- Hind Swaraj, Mohandas Gandhi
- The Fourteen Points, Woodrow Wilson
- Two Poems, Langston Hughes
- Four Freedoms, Franklin D. Roosevelt
- Anne Frank: The Diary of a Young Girl, Anne Frank
- Charter of the United Nations
- Universal Declaration of Human Rights
- Autobiography, Kwame Nkrumah
- Inaugural Address, John F. Kennedy
- Silent Spring, Rachel Carson
- "I Have a Dream," Martin Luther King, Jr.
- "Letter From Birmingham Jail," Martin Luther King, Jr.
- "Tear Down This Wall," Ronald Reagan
- "Freedom From Fear," Aung San Suu Kyi
- "Glory and Hope," Nelson Mandela

 Biographies

- Abigail Adams
- John Adams
- John Quincy Adams
- Samuel Adams
- James Armistead
- Crispus Attucks
- Moses Austin
- Stephen F. Austin
- James A. Baker III
- William Blackstone
- Simón Bolívar
- Napoleon Bonaparte
- Chief Bowles
- Omar Bradley
- John C. Calhoun
- César Chávez
- Wentworth Cheswell
- George Childress
- Winston Churchill
- Henry Clay
- Bill Clinton
- Jefferson Davis
- Martin De León
- Green DeWitt
- Dwight Eisenhower
- James Fannin
- James L. Farmer, Jr.
- Benjamin Franklin
- Milton Friedman
- Betty Friedan
- Bernardo de Gálvez
- Hector P. Garcia
- John Nance Garner
- King George III
- Henry B. González
- Raul A. Gonzalez, Jr.
- Mikhail Gorbachev
- William Goyens
- Ulysses S. Grant
- José Gutiérrez de Lara
- Alexander Hamilton
- Hammurabi
- Warren Harding
- Friedrich Hayek
- Jack Coffee Hays
- Patrick Henry
- Adolf Hitler
- Oveta Culp Hobby
- James Hogg
- Sam Houston
- Kay Bailey Hutchison
- Andrew Jackson
- John Jay
- Thomas Jefferson
- Lyndon B. Johnson
- Anson Jones
- Barbara Jordan
- Justinian
- John F. Kennedy
- John Maynard Keynes
- Martin Luther King, Jr.
- Marquis de Lafayette
- Mirabeau B. Lamar
- Robert E. Lee
- Abraham Lincoln
- John Locke
- James Madison
- John Marshall
- George Marshall
- Karl Marx
- George Mason
- Mary Maverick
- Jane McCallum
- Joseph McCarthy
- James Monroe
- Charles de Montesquieu
- Edwin W. Moore
- Moses
- Benito Mussolini
- José Antonio Navarro
- Chester A. Nimitz
- Richard M. Nixon
- Barack Obama
- Sandra Day O'Connor
- Thomas Paine
- Quanah Parker
- Rosa Parks
- George Patton
- John J. Pershing
- John Paul II
- Sam Rayburn
- Ronald Reagan
- Hiram Rhodes Revels
- Franklin D. Roosevelt
- Theodore Roosevelt
- Lawrence Sullivan Ross
- Haym Soloman
- Antonio Lopez de Santa Anna
- Phyllis Schlafly
- Erasmo Seguín
- Juan N. Seguín
- Roger Sherman
- Adam Smith
- Joseph Stalin
- Raymond L. Telles
- Alexis de Tocqueville
- Hideki Tojo
- William B. Travis
- Harry Truman
- Lech Walesa
- Mercy Otis Warren
- George Washington
- Daniel Webster
- Lulu Belle Madison White
- William Wilberforce
- James Wilson
- Woodrow Wilson
- Lorenzo de Zavala
- Mao Zedong

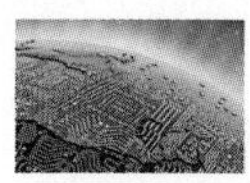

21st Century Skills

- Identify Main Ideas and Details
- Set a Purpose for Reading
- Use Context Clues
- Analyze Cause and Effect
- Categorize
- Compare and Contrast
- Draw Conclusions
- Draw Inferences
- Generalize
- Make Decisions
- Make Predictions
- Sequence
- Solve Problems
- Summarize
- Analyze Media Content
- Analyze Primary and Secondary Sources
- Compare Viewpoints
- Distinguish Between Fact and Opinion
- Identify Bias
- Analyze Data and Models
- Analyze Images
- Analyze Political Cartoons
- Create Charts and Maps
- Create Databases
- Read Charts, Graphs, and Tables
- Read Physical Maps
- Read Political Maps
- Read Special-Purpose Maps
- Use Parts of a Map
- Ask Questions
- Avoid Plagiarism
- Create a Research Hypothesis
- Evaluate Web Sites
- Identify Evidence
- Identify Trends
- Interpret Sources
- Search for Information on the Internet
- Synthesize
- Take Effective Notes
- Develop a Clear Thesis
- Organize Your Ideas
- Support Ideas With Evidence
- Evaluate Existing Arguments
- Consider & Counter Opposing Arguments
- Give an Effective Presentation
- Participate in a Discussion or Debate
- Publish Your Work
- Write a Journal Entry
- Write an Essay
- Share Responsibility
- Compromise
- Develop Cultural Awareness
- Generate New Ideas
- Innovate
- Make a Difference
- Work in Teams
- Being an Informed Citizen
- Paying Taxes
- Political Participation
- Serving on a Jury
- Voting

Atlas

- United States: Political
- United States: Physical
- World Political
- World Physical
- World Climate
- World Ecosystems
- World Population Density
- World Land Use
- North Africa and Southwest Asia: Political
- North Africa and Southwest Asia: Physical
- Sub-Saharan Africa: Political
- Sub-Saharan Africa: Physical
- South Asia: Political
- South Asia: Physical
- East Asia: Political
- East Asia: Physical
- Southeast Asia: Political
- Southeast Asia: Physical
- Europe: Political
- Europe: Physical
- Russia, Central Asia, and the Caucasus: Political
- Russia, Central Asia, and the Caucasus: Physical
- North America: Political
- North America: Physical
- Central America and the Caribbean: Political
- Central America and the Caribbean: Physical
- South America: Political
- South America: Physical
- Australia and the Pacific: Political
- Australia and the Pacific: Physical

Celebrate Freedom

> "We hold these Truths to be self-evident, that all Men are created equal, that they are endowed by their Creator with certain unalienable Rights, that among these are Life, Liberty and the Pursuit of Happiness. That to secure these Rights, Governments are instituted among Men, deriving their just Powers from the Consent of the Governed."
>
> — Declaration of Independance

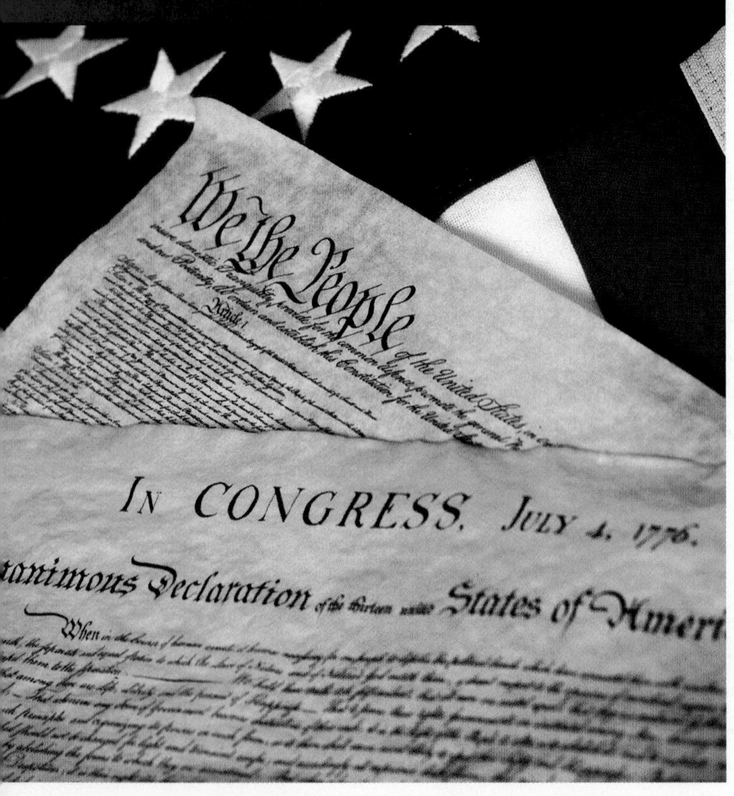

Declaration of Independence

When the Continental Congress issued the Declaration of Independence in 1776, they did more than announce their separation from Great Britain. They also summed up the most basic principles that came to underlie American government. This section is sometimes called the "social contract" section. You can read the words at left.

These ideas have had significant effect on later developments in American history. You will notice the relationship of the ideas behind the Declaration of Independence to the American Revolution, the writing of the U.S. Constitution, including the Bill of Rights, and the movements to end slavery and to give women the right to vote. You'll see how the United States became a nation of immigrants, with its rich diversity of people, and the ways this development relates to the ideas of the Declaration of Independence.

Read the first three paragraphs of the Declaration of Independence. Then recite words from the Declaration of Independence quoted at left. Consider their meaning and then answer these questions.

ASSESSMENT

1. **Identify Central Idea** This part of the Declaration is sometimes called the "social contract" section. Based on these statements, what is a social contract? Who benefits from it?
2. **Contrast** How does the idea of government based on a "social contract" differ from the idea behind a monarchy? A dictatorship?
3. **Apply Information** Identify two ways that your federal, state, or local government protect the rights to life, liberty, or the pursuit of happiness.

Constitution Day Assembly

September 17 is Constitution Day, and your school may hold an assembly or other celebration in honor of the day. As part of this celebration, your teacher may ask you to participate in planning and holding a Constitution Day assembly.

Organize As a class, create the basic plan for your assembly. Discuss the following:

1. When and where should the assembly take place?
2. How long should it take? Should you plan on a short program taking a single class period, or a longer program?
3. Who should be involved? Will other classes or other grades take part? Will you invite outsiders, such as parents or people from the community?
4. What activities might be included?

Plan After your discussion, divide the class into committees to complete jobs such as getting permission from the school administration, preparing a program, inviting any guests, advertising the plan beforehand, and blogging about it afterward.

Give thought to the types of activities that might be included in the assembly. You might invite a guest speaker from your community. You might run an essay contest among students and have the winners read their essays during the assembly. Some students might prepare a video presentation about the Bill of Rights. Others might write and perform a skit about what the Declaration of Independence or U.S. Constitution mean to them.

You might start your assembly by asking everyone to rise to say the Pledge of Allegiance to the United States flag. One student might give a brief speech about how the pledge reflects the ideas of the Declaration of Independence and the U.S. Constitution.

>> Your school may hold a Constitution Day assembly like the one shown here.

Communicate Present your Constitution Day assembly. After the assembly is over, discuss the event with the class. Ask yourselves questions such as these:

1. How well was the assembly planned and organized? What imporvements could we have made?
2. How would you rate each of the presentations or other activities of the assembly?
3. Was the audience engaged?
4. How effectively did the class work together?

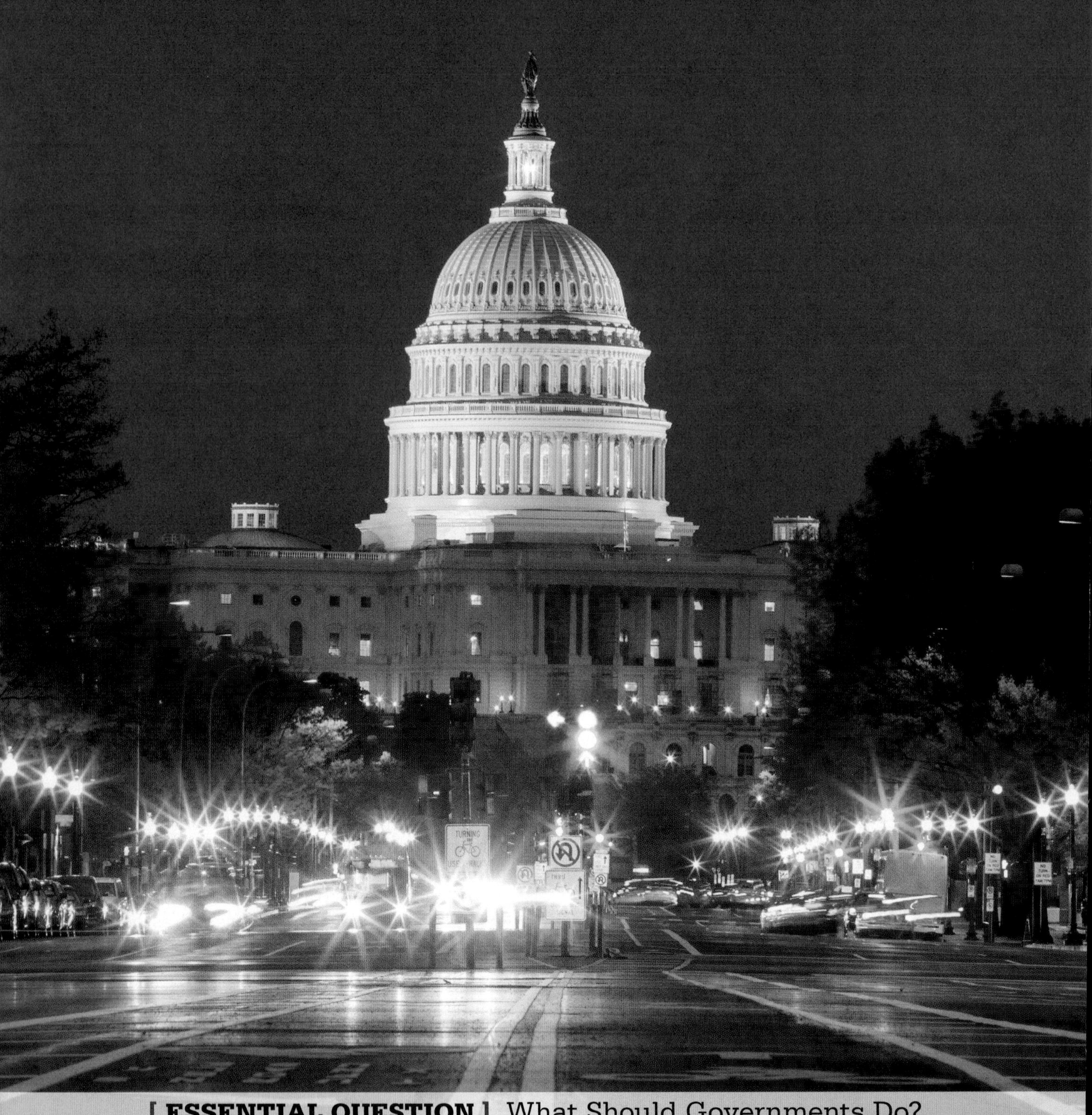

[**ESSENTIAL QUESTION**] What Should Governments Do?

1 Foundations of Government and Citizenship

>> United States Capitol building in Washington, D.C.

Topic 1 Foundations of Government and Citizenship

Enduring Understandings

- Government is the institution through which a society makes and enforces its public policies, and is made up of those who exercise its powers, and have power and authority over the people.
- Governments are classified by who can participate, the distribution of power, and the relationship between lawmakers and those who execute the laws.
- The origins of modern democratic government lie in the ideas of ancient Greece, Rome, and the Enlightenment.
- A democracy is based upon recognizing the worth and dignity of all, equality, majority rule balanced with minority rights, compromise, and individual freedom.

Watch the My Story Video for an introduction to the principles that helped inspire American independence.

Access your digital lessons including: Topic Inquiry • Interactive Reading Notepad • Interactivities • Assessments

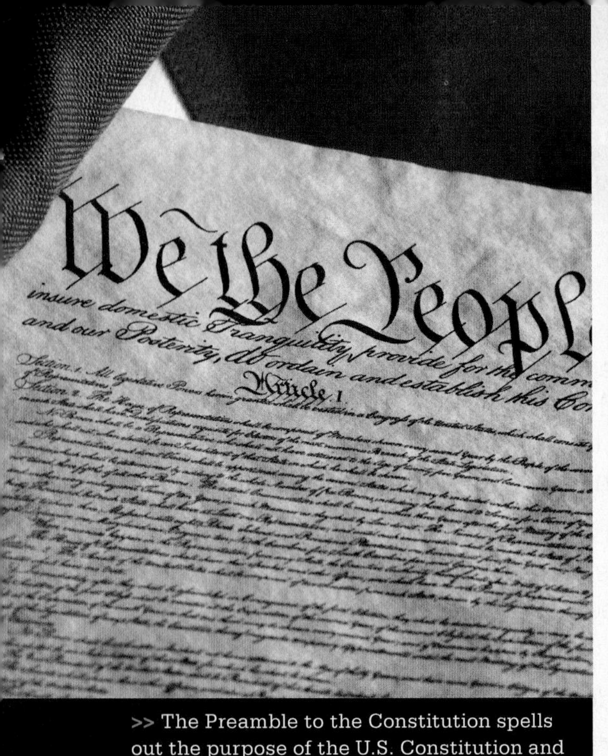

>> The Preamble to the Constitution spells out the purpose of the U.S. Constitution and identifies the values and principles of the government.

Interactive Flipped Video

1.1

This is a course about government—and, more particularly, about government in the United States. The Preamble to the U.S. Constitution begins with the phrase, "We the People of the United States." As a citizen, you are an important member of the "We." For that reason alone, you should know as much as you possibly can about government. Government affects you in an uncountable number of very important ways. It does so today, it did so yesterday, and it will do so every day for the rest of your life.

>> Objectives

Define government and the basic powers every government holds.

Describe the four defining characteristics of a state.

Identify the four theories that attempt to explain the origin of the state.

Understand the purpose of government in the United States and other countries.

>> Key Terms

government
public policies
legislative power
executive power
judicial power
dictatorship
democracy
Aristotle
state
sovereign
Thomas Hobbes
John Locke

Principles of Government

Government–We the People

Think of the point in this light: What would your life be like *without* government? Who would protect you, and all of the rest of us, against terrorist attacks and against other threats from abroad? Who would provide for education, guard the public's health, and protect the environment? Who would pave the streets, regulate traffic, punish criminals, and respond to fires and other human-made and natural disasters? Who would protect civil rights and care for the elderly, the poor, and those who cannot care for themselves? Who would protect consumers and property owners?

The Need for Government Government does all of these things, of course—and much more. In short, if government did not exist, we would have to invent it.

Government is the institution through which a society makes and enforces its public policies. Government is made up of those people who exercise its powers, all those who have authority and control over people.

The **public policies** of a government are, in short, all of those things a government decides to do. Public policies cover matters ranging from taxation, defense, education, crime, and healthcare to transportation, the environment, civil rights, and working conditions. Indeed, the list of public policy issues handled by government is nearly endless.

Basic Powers of Government Governments must have power in order to make and carry out public policies. Power is the ability to command or prevent action, the ability to achieve a desired end.

Every government has and exercises three basic kinds of power: (1) **legislative power**—the power to make laws and to frame public policies; (2) **executive power**—the power to execute, enforce, and administer laws; and (3) **judicial power**—the power to interpret laws, to determine their meaning, and to settle disputes that arise within the society. These powers of government are often outlined in a country's constitution. A constitution is the body of fundamental laws setting out the principles, structures, and processes of a government.

The ultimate responsibility for the exercise of these powers may be held by a single person or by a small group, as in a **dictatorship**. In this form of government, those who rule cannot be held responsible to the will of the people. When the responsibility for the exercise of these powers rests with a majority of the people, that form of government is known as a democracy. In a **democracy**, supreme authority rests with the people.

>> Many governments carry out their work through legislative bodies. Today in the U.S. Congress, legislators decide matters of public policy as they did in ancient Rome or Greece.

Interactive Chart

>> When the emerging Roman republic was threatened by war with neighboring Sabine tribes, the Roman senate appointed Lartius as a dictator to defeat the enemy.

Government as Human Invention Government is among the oldest of all human inventions. Its origins are lost in the mists of time. But, clearly, government first appeared when human beings realized that they could not survive without some way to regulate their own actions, as well as those of their neighbors.

The appearance of major political ideas began early in history. The earliest known evidences of government date from ancient Egypt and the sixth century B.C. More than 2,300 years ago, the Greek philosopher **Aristotle** observed that "man is by nature a political animal." When he wrote those words, Aristotle was only recording a fact that, even then, had been obvious for thousands of years.

What did Aristotle mean by "political"? That is to say, what is "politics"? Although people often equate the two, politics and government are very different things. Politics is a process, while government is an institution.

More specifically, politics is the process by which a society decides how power and resources will be distributed within that society. Politics enables a society to decide who will reap the benefits, and who will pay the reap costs, of its public policies. The word *politics* is sometimes used in a way that suggests that it is somehow immoral or something to be avoided. But, again, politics is the means by which government is conducted. It is neither "good" nor "bad," but it is necessary. Indeed, it is impossible to conceive of government without politics.

EXPLAIN What are public policies?

The State

The state has developed from major political ideas in history. The **state** can be defined as a body of people, living in a defined territory, organized politically (that is, with a government), and with the power to make and enforce law without the consent of any higher authority.

There are more than 200 states in the world today. They vary greatly in size, military power, natural resources, and economic importance. Still, each of them possesses all four of the characteristics of a state. That is, each of them has population, territory, sovereignty, and government.

Note that the word *state* describes a legal entity. In popular usage, a state is often called a "nation" or a "country." In a strict sense, however, the word *nation* is an ethnic term, referring to races or other large groups of people. The word *country* is a geographic term, referring to a particular place, region, or area of land.

Population Clearly, a state must have people—a population. The size of that population, however, has nothing directly to do with the existence of a state. One of the world's smallest states, in population terms, is San Marino. Bound on all sides by Italy, it has only some 30,000 people. The People's Republic of China is the world's most populous state, with more than 1.3 billion people—just about one fifth of all of the world's population. The more than 310 million people who live in the United States make it the world's third-most-populous state, after China and India.

The people who make up a state may or may not be homogeneous. The adjective *homogeneous* describes members of a group who share customs, a common language, and ethnic background. Today, the population of the United States includes people from a wide variety of backgrounds. Still, most Americans think of themselves as exactly that: Americans.

Territory Just as a state cannot exist without people, so must it have land—territory—with known and recognized boundaries. The states in today's world vary as widely in terms of territory as they do in population. Here, too, San Marino ranks among the world's smallest states. It covers less than 24 square miles, and so is smaller than thousands of cities and towns in the United States. The United States also recognizes the

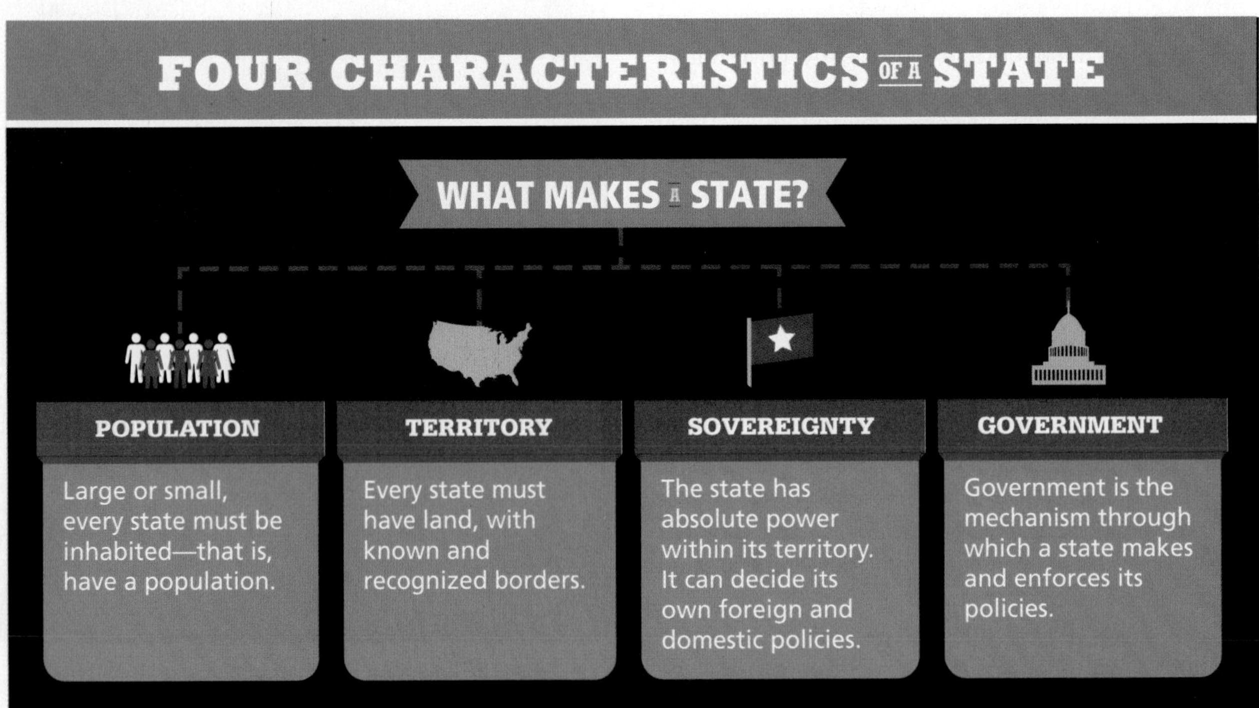

FOUR CHARACTERISTICS OF A STATE
WHAT MAKES A STATE?
POPULATION
Large or small, every state must be inhabited—that is, have a population.
TERRITORY
Every state must have land, with known and recognized borders.
SOVEREIGNTY
The state has absolute power within its territory. It can decide its own foreign and domestic policies.
GOVERNMENT
Government is the mechanism through which a state makes and enforces its policies.

>> Every state in the world has four characteristics. **Analyze Charts** How does the sovereignty of a State in the U.S. compare to the national sovereignty of the U.S. as a whole?

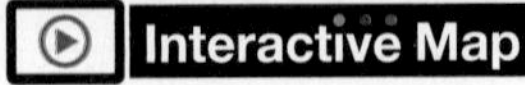

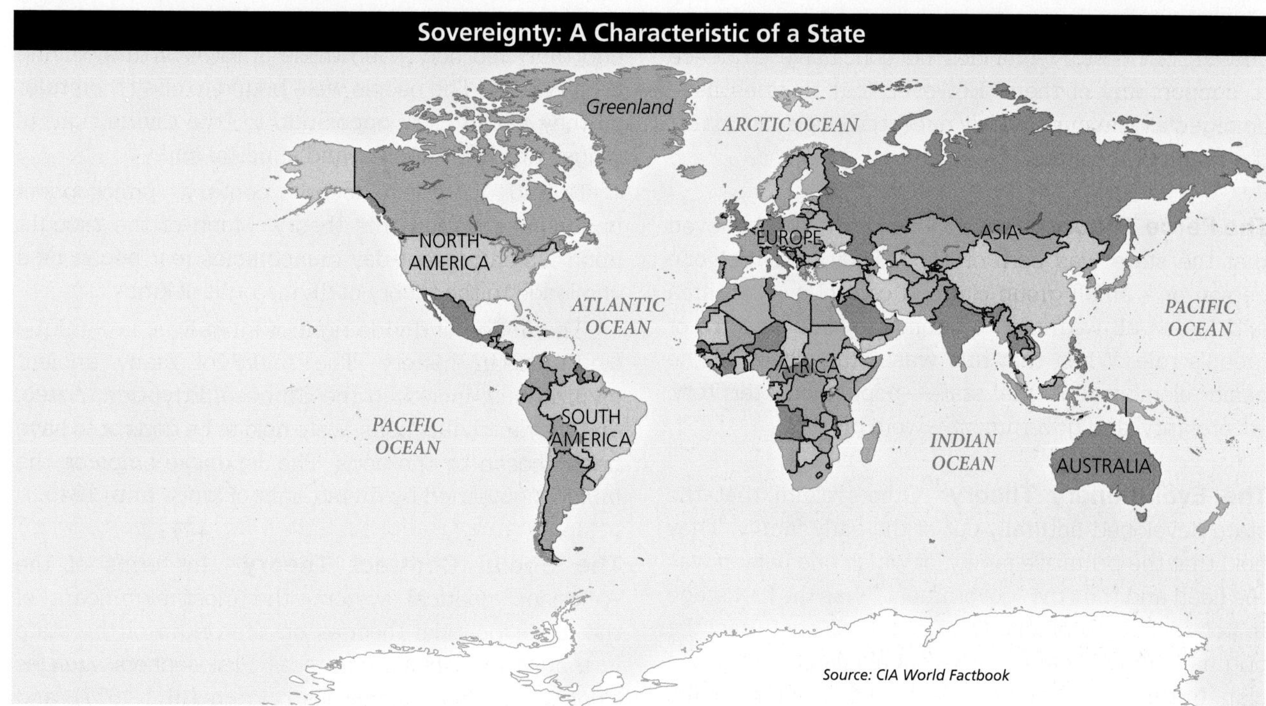

>> Sovereignty is one of the four characteristics possessed by every state in the world.
Analyze Maps How many sovereign states are in the United States?

state of Vatican City, which is completely surrounded by the city of Rome. It has a permanent population of less than 900 and an area of only 109 acres.

Russia, the world's largest state, stretches across some 6.6 million square miles. The total area of the United States is slightly less than 3.8 million square miles.

Sovereignty Every state is **sovereign**—that is, it has supreme and absolute power within its own territory and can decide its own foreign and domestic policies. It is neither subordinate nor responsible to any other authority. Sovereignty is the one characteristic that distinguishes the state from all other, lesser political units in the world.

Thus, as a sovereign state, the United States can determine its form of government, frame its own economic system, and shape its own foreign policies. The States within the United States are not sovereign and so are not states in the international, legal sense. Each State is subordinate to the Constitution of the United States. At the United States' international borders, citizens observe the laws and serve the public good of countries on both sides of the border by showing passports and other identification in compliance with the rules of each state.

Government Every state is politically organized. That is, every state has a government. Recall, a government is the institution through which society makes and enforces its public policies. A government is the agency through which the state exerts its will and works to accomplish its goals. Government includes the machinery and the personnel by which the state is ruled.

Government is necessary to avoid what the English philosopher **Thomas Hobbes** (1588–1679) called "the war of every man against every man." Without government, said Hobbes, there would be "continual fear and danger of violent death and the life of man [would be] solitary, poor, nasty, brutish, and short." Indeed, in Lebanon, Bosnia, Somalia, and many other places over recent years, the world has seen a number of sobering examples of what happens when government disappears.

DESCRIBE How would you describe the concept of sovereignty?

How States Arose

For centuries, historians, philosophers, and others have pondered the question of the origin of the state. What major political ideas in history resulted in the emergence of states?

Over time, many different answers have been offered, but history provides no conclusive evidence to support any of them. However, four theories have emerged as the most widely accepted explanations for the origin of the state.

The Force Theory Many scholars have long believed that the state was born of force. They hold that one person or a small group claimed control over an area and forced all within it to submit to that person's or group's rule. When that rule was established, all the basic elements of the state—population, territory, sovereignty, and government—were present.

The Evolutionary Theory Others claim that the state developed naturally out of the early family. They hold that the primitive family, of which one person was the head and thus the "government," was the first stage in political development. Over countless centuries, the original family became a network of related families, a clan. In time, the clan became a tribe. When the tribe first turned to agriculture and gave up its nomadic, wandering ways, tying itself to the land, the state was born.

The Divine Right of Kings Theory The theory of divine right of kings was widely accepted in much of the Western world from the fifteenth through the eighteenth centuries. It held that God created the state and that God had given those of royal birth a "divine right" to rule. The people were bound to obey their ruler as they would God; opposition to "the divine right of kings" was both treason and a mortal sin.

During the seventeenth century, philosophers began to question this theory. Much of the thought upon which present-day democracies rest began as a challenge to the theory of divine right of kings.

The notion of divine right of kings was not unique to European history. The rulers of many ancient civilizations, including the Chinese, Egyptian, Aztec, and Mayan civilizations, were held to be gods or to have been chosen by the gods. The Japanese emperor, the *mikado,* governed by divine right of kings until 1945.

The Social Contract Theory In terms of the American political system, the most significant of the major political theories on the origin of the state is that of the "social contract." Philosophers such as Thomas Hobbes, James Harrington (1611–1677), and **John Locke** (1632–1704) in England and Jean Jacques Rousseau (1712–1778) in France developed this theory in the seventeenth and eighteenth centuries.

Hobbes wrote that in earliest history humans lived in unbridled freedom, that is in a "state of nature," in which no government existed and no person was subject to any superior power. That which people could

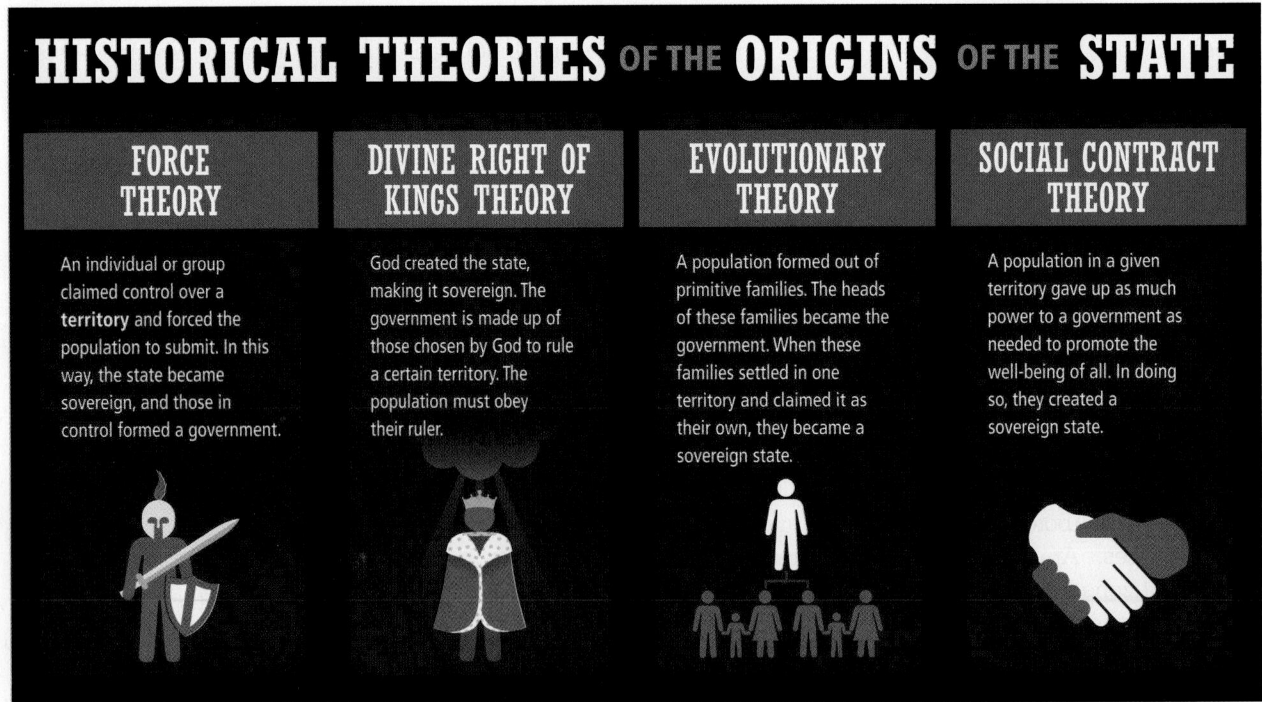

HISTORICAL THEORIES OF THE ORIGINS OF THE STATE
FORCE THEORY
An individual or group claimed control over a territory and forced the population to submit. In this way, the state became sovereign, and those in control formed a government.
DIVINE RIGHT OF KINGS THEORY
God created the state, making it sovereign. The government is made up of those chosen by God to rule a certain territory. The population must obey their ruler.
EVOLUTIONARY THEORY
A population formed out of primitive families. The heads of these families became the government. When these families settled in one territory and claimed it as their own, they became a sovereign state.
SOCIAL CONTRACT THEORY
A population in a given territory gave up as much power to a government as needed to promote the well-being of all. In doing so, they created a sovereign state.

>> There are four theories as to how the state came to be. **Analyze Charts** Which of the theories best describes the origins of the United States? Why?

take by force belonged to them. However, all people were similarly free in that state of nature. No authority existed to protect one person from the aggressive actions of another. Thus, individuals were only as secure as their own physical strength and intelligence could make them.

Human beings overcame their unpleasant condition, says the social contract theory, by agreeing with one another to create a state. By contract, people within a given area agreed to give up to the state as much power as was needed to promote the safety and well-being of all. In the contract (that is, through a constitution), the members of the state created a government to exercise the powers they had voluntarily given to the state.

People Agree to Form a State In short, the social contract theory argues that the state arose out of a voluntary act of free people. It holds that the state exists only to serve the will of the people, that they are the sole source of political power, and that they are free to give or to withhold that power as they choose from the government. The theory may seem somewhat far-fetched today. The great concepts that this theory promoted, however—popular sovereignty, limited government, and individual rights—were immensely important to the shaping of the American governmental system.

The Declaration of Independence justified its revolution through the social contract theory, arguing that King George III and his ministers had violated the contract. Thomas Jefferson called the document "pure Locke." In the Declaration of Independence, Jefferson also included justification based on the "laws of nature and nature's God," meaning that the colonists' right to have an equal voice in their government was given by nature and could not be taken away by the king.

>> Locke believed that the powers of governments are based on the powers of the governed. The signers of the Declaration of Independence (shown here) embraced this idea as one of the self-evident truths.

INFER How does the divine right of kings theory relate to the Declaration of Independence?

What Government Does

What does government do? You can find a very meaningful answer to that question in the Constitution of the United States. The American system of government was created to serve the purposes set out there.

> We the People of the United States, in Order to form a more perfect Union, establish Justice, insure domestic Tranquility, provide for the common defence, promote the general Welfare, and secure the Blessings of Liberty to ourselves and our Posterity, do ordain and establish this Constitution for the United States of America.
>
> —Preamble to the Constitution

Form a More Perfect Union The United States, which had just won its independence from Great Britain, faced an altogether uncertain future in the postwar 1780s. In 1781, the Articles of Confederation, the nation's first constitution, created "a firm league of friendship" among the 13 States. That league soon proved to be neither very firm nor very friendly. The government created by the Articles was powerless to overcome the intense rivalries and jealousies among the States that marked the times.

The Constitution of today was written in 1787. The original States adopted it in order to link themselves, and the American people, more closely together. That Constitution was built in the belief that in union there is strength. A written constitution is important as an official record of governing principles.

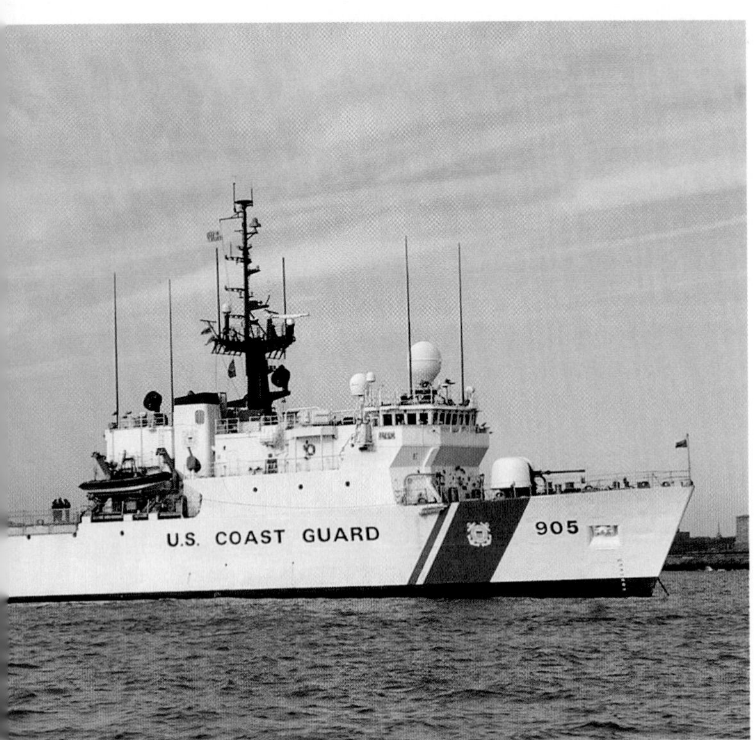

>> The U.S. Coast Guard, part of the U.S. Department of Homeland Security, serves the public good by carrying out such functions as rescues at sea and patrolling the nation's coastlines.

>> National Guard troops can be called upon to serve in military actions and in domestic emergencies such as patrolling Penn Station after 9/11.

Establish Justice To provide justice, said Thomas Jefferson, is "the most sacred of the duties of government." No purpose, no goal of public policy, can be of greater importance in a democracy.

But what is justice? The term is difficult to define, for justice is a concept—an idea, an invention of the human mind. Like other concepts, such as truth, liberty, and fairness, justice means what people want it to mean.

As the concept of justice has developed over time in American thought and practice, it has come to mean this: The law, in both its content and its administration, must be reasonable, fair, and impartial. Those standards of justice have not always been met in this country. We have not attained our professed goal of "equal justice for all." However, this must be said: The history of this country can be told largely in terms of our continuing attempts to reach that goal.

"Injustice anywhere," said Martin Luther King, Jr., "is a threat to justice everywhere." You will encounter this idea again and again in this course.

Insure Domestic Tranquility Order is essential to the well-being of any society, and keeping the peace at home has always been a prime function of government. Most people can only imagine what it would be like to live in a state of anarchy—without government, law, or order. In fact, people do live that way in some parts of the world today. For years now, Somalia, located on the eastern tip of Africa, has not had a permanent functioning government; rival warlords control different parts of the country.

In *The Federalist* No. 51, James Madison observed: "If men were angels, no government would be necessary." Madison, who was perhaps the most thoughtful of the Framers of the Constitution, knew that most human beings fall far short of that standard.

Provide for the Common Defense Defending the nation against foreign enemies has always been one of government's major responsibilities. You can see its importance in the fact that defense is mentioned far more often in the Constitution than any of the other functions of government.

The nation's defense and its foreign policies are but two sides of the same coin: the security of the United States. To provide this security, the nation maintains an army, navy, air force, and coast guard where people are serving in the military. Departments such as the Department of Homeland Security keep watch for threats to the country and its people.

The United States has become the world's most powerful nation, but the world remains a dangerous place. This country must maintain its vigilance and its armed strength. Just a glance at today's newspapers or at one of this evening's television news programs will furnish abundant proof of that fact.

Promote the General Welfare Few people realize the extent to which government acts as the servant of its citizens, yet you can see examples everywhere. Public schools are one illustration of government's work to promote the general welfare. So, too, are its efforts to protect the quality of the air you breathe, the water you drink, and the food you eat. The list of tasks government performs for your benefit goes on and on.

Some governmental functions that are common in other countries—operating steel mills, airlines, and coal mines, for example—are not carried out by government in this country. In general, the services that government provides in the United States are those that benefit all or most people. Many of them are the services that are not very likely to be provided by the voluntary acts of private individuals or groups.

Secure the Blessings of Liberty This nation was founded by those who loved liberty and prized it above all earthly possessions. They believed with Thomas Jefferson that "the God who gave us life gave us liberty at the same time." They subscribed to Benjamin Franklin's maxim: "They that can give up essential liberty to obtain a little temporary safety deserve neither liberty nor safety."

The American dedication to freedom for the individual recognizes that liberty cannot be absolute. It is, instead, a relative matter. Among the responsibilities, duties, and obligations of citizenship are observing the laws and serving the public good. No one can be free to do whatever he or she pleases, that behavior would interfere with the freedoms of others. As Clarence Darrow, the great defense lawyer, once said: "You can only be free if I am free."

Both the Federal Constitution and the State constitutions set out many guarantees of rights and liberties for the individual in this country. That does not mean that those guarantees are so firmly established that they exist forever, however. To preserve and protect them, each generation must learn and understand them anew, and be willing to stand up for them when necessary.

For many people, the inspiration to protect our rights and liberties arises from deep feelings of patriotism. Many would argue that it is a citizen's responsibility, duty, and obligation to foster their individual patriotism.

Patriotism is the love of one's country; the passion that drives one to serve one's country, either by defending it from invasion or by protecting its rights and maintaining its laws and institutions. Patriotism is the defining characteristic of a good citizen, the noblest passion that animates a man or a woman in the character of a citizen. As a good citizen, you, too, must agree with Thomas Jefferson: "Eternal vigilance is the price of liberty."

? EXPLAIN Why is it important to have a written constitution?

ASSESSMENT

1. **Distinguish** Distinguish between the three basic types of power that many governments have.
2. **Infer** Explain why the phrase "the laws of nature and nature's God" was included in the Declaration of Independence?
3. **Summarize** Summarize the divine right of kings and the social contract theories of the origin of the state.
4. **Make Generalizations** How can people demonstrate their understanding of the responsibilities, duties, and obligations of citizenship?
5. **Apply Concepts** How does the Federal Government serve the purposes set forth in the Preamble to the Constitution?

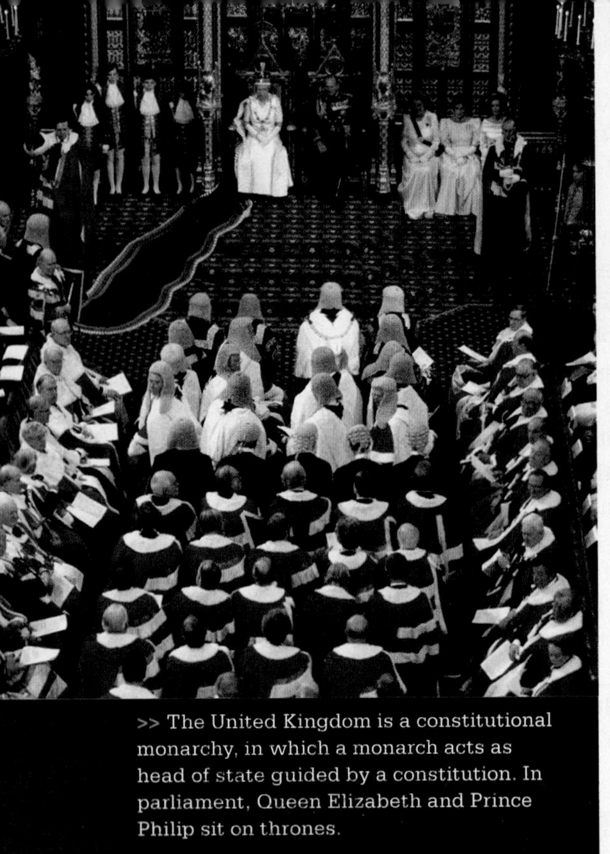

>> The United Kingdom is a constitutional monarchy, in which a monarch acts as head of state guided by a constitution. In parliament, Queen Elizabeth and Prince Philip sit on thrones.

Interactive Flipped Video

1.2 **Does the form a government takes, the way in which it is structured, have any importance? Political scientists, historians, and other social commentators have long argued that question. The English poet Alexander Pope wrote a couplet about the issue in 1733.**

>> Objectives

Classify governments according to three sets of characteristics.

Define systems of government based on who can participate.

Identify ways that power can be distributed, geographically, within a state.

Describe a government by the distribution of power between the legislative branch and executive branch.

>> Key Terms

autocracy
oligarchy
unitary government
federal government
division of powers
confederation
presidential government
parliamentary
Abraham Lincoln
Alexander Pope
autocracy

Types of Government

Classifying Governments

For Forms of Government let fools contest;
Whate'er is best adminster'd is best. . . ."

—*Essay on Man*

Was Pope right? Does it matter what form a government takes? Pope thought not. You can form your own opinion as you read this section.

No two governments are, or ever have been, exactly alike, for governments are the products of human needs and experiences. All governments can be classified according to one or more of their basic features, however. Over time, political scientists have developed many bases upon which to classify (and so to describe, compare, and analyze) governments.

Three of those classifications are especially important and useful. These are classifications according to (1) who can participate in the governing process, (2) the geographic distribution of governmental power within the state, and (3) the relationship between the legislative (lawmaking) and the executive (law-executing) branches of the government.

SUMMARIZE Restate in your own words the three most important characteristics that political scientists use to classify governments.

Who Can Participate?

To many people, the most meaningful of these classifications is the one that depends on the number of persons who can take part in the governing process. Here there are two basic forms to consider: democracies and dictatorships.

Democracy In a democracy, supreme political authority rests with the people. The people hold the sovereign power, and government is conducted only by and with the consent of the people.

Abraham Lincoln gave immortality to this definition of democracy in his Gettysburg Address in 1863: "government of the people, by the people, for the people." Nowhere is there a better, more concise statement of the American understanding of democracy.

A democracy can be either direct or indirect in form. A direct democracy, also called a pure democracy, exists where the will of the people is translated into public policy (law) directly by the people themselves, in mass meetings. Such was the case in Ancient Greece and Rome. Clearly, direct democracy can work only in small communities, where the citizenry can meet in a central place, and where the problems of government are few and relatively simple.

Direct Democracy and Indirect Democracy Direct democracy does not exist at the national level anywhere in the world today. However, the New England town meeting and the *Landsgemeinde* in a few of the smaller Swiss cantons are excellent examples of direct democracy in action.

Americans are more familiar with the indirect form of democracy—that is, with a constitutional republic or representative democracy. In a representative democracy, a small group of persons, chosen by the people to act as their representatives, expresses the popular will. These agents of the people are responsible for carrying out the day-to-day conduct of government—the making and executing of laws and so on. They are held accountable to the people for that conduct, especially at periodic elections.

At these elections, the people have an opportunity to express their approval or disapproval of their representatives by casting ballots for or against them. To put it another way, representative democracy is government by popular consent—government with the consent of the governed.

Republic Some people insist that the United States is more properly called a republic rather than a democracy. They hold that in a republic the sovereign power is held by those eligible to vote, while the political power is exercised by representatives chosen by and held responsible to those citizens. For them, democracy can be defined only in terms of a direct democracy.

Many Americans use the terms *democracy, republic, representative democracy,* and *republican form of government* interchangeably, although they are not the same. Whatever the term used, remember that in a democracy the people are sovereign. They are the only source for any and all of government's power. In other words, the people rule.

Dictatorship Authoritarian forms of government such as a dictatorship exists where those who rule

Direct And Indirect Democracy

WHO GOVERNS?	
Direct Democracy	**Indirect Democracy**
• Also called pure democracy • The people themselves formulate public policy • Works only at a small, local level	• Also called representative democracy • A group of persons chosen by the people formulates public policy • Widely used at the national, State, and local levels

>> Democratic government derives its power from the people but can be either direct or indirect democracy. **Analyze Charts** Why might indirect democracy be better for a larger population?

cannot be held responsible to the will of the people. The government is not accountable for its policies, nor for how they are carried out. Dictatorship is probably the oldest, and it is certainly the most common, form of government known to history.

Dictatorships are sometimes identified as either autocracies or oligarchies. An **autocracy** is a government in which a single person holds unlimited political power. An **oligarchy** is a government in which the power to rule is held by a small, usually self-appointed elite.

Modern Dictatorships All dictatorships are authoritarian; those in power hold absolute and unchallengeable authority over the people. Modern dictatorships have tended to be totalitarian, as well. That is, they exercise complete power over nearly every aspect of human affairs. Their power embraces all matters of human concern.

The leading examples of dictatorship in the modern era have been those in Fascist Italy (from 1922 to 1943), in Nazi Germany (from 1933 to 1945), in the Soviet Union (from 1917 until the late 1980s), and one that still exists in the People's Republic of China (where the present regime came to power in 1949).

Although they do exist, one-person dictatorships are not at all common today. A few close approaches to such a regime can be found in North Korea, led by Kim Jong-un (who succeeded his father, Kim Jong-il, in 2011), and in some Arab and African states.

Most present-day dictatorships are not nearly so absolutely controlled by a single person or by a small group as may appear to be the case. Outward appearances may hide the fact that several groups—the army, religious leaders, industrialists, and others—compete for power in the political system.

Dictatorships often present the outward appearance of control by the people. The people often vote in popular elections, but the vote is closely controlled, and ballots usually contain the names of candidates of only one political party. An elected legislative body often exists, but its only purpose is to rubber-stamp the policies of the dictatorship.

Typically, dictatorial regimes are militaristic in character. They usually gain power by force. The military holds many of the major posts in the government. After crushing all effective opposition at home, these regimes may turn to foreign aggression to enhance the country's military power, political control, and prestige.

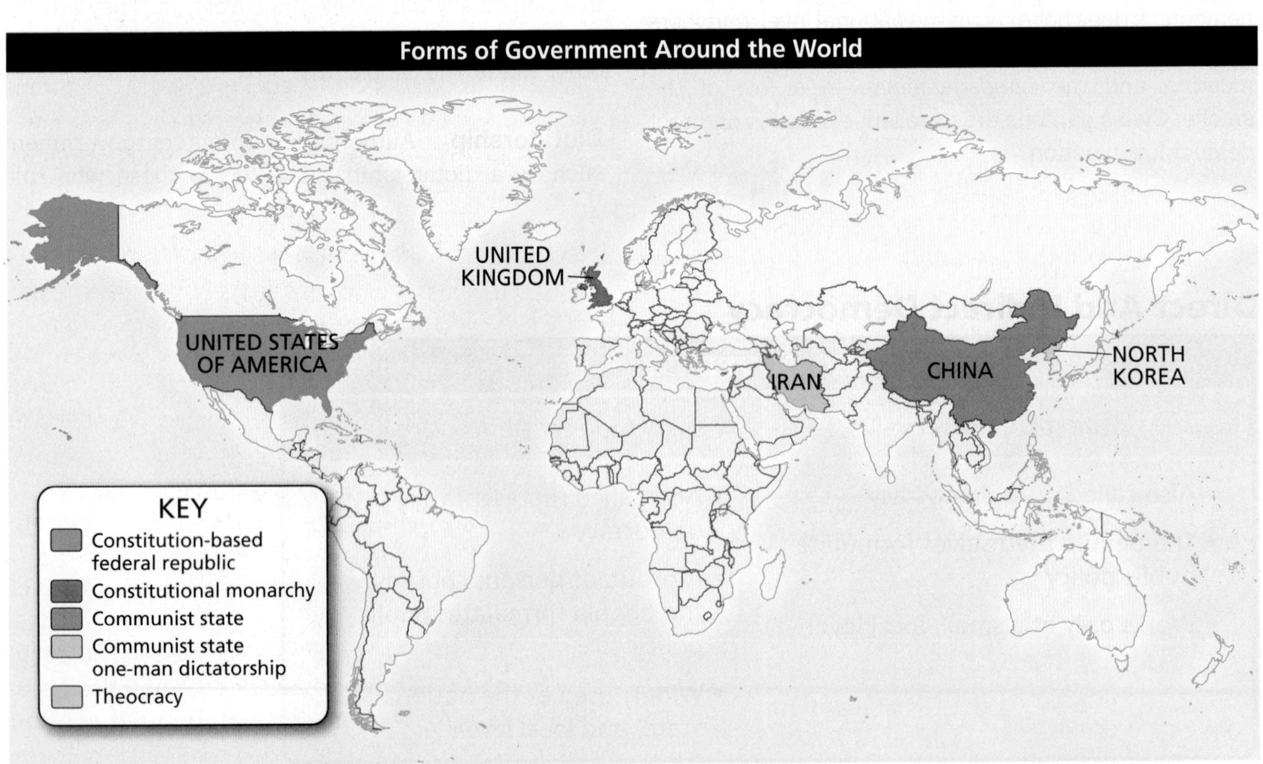

>> There are different forms of government all over the world. People express their will differently in each. **Analyze Maps** How does each government's reaction differ to expressions of will?

Interactive Map

Theocracy A theocracy exists where the legal system of a state is based on religious law. Theocracies were more common in early civilizations, but have become rare in modern times. Iran is a present-day theocracy, often referred to as a theocratic Islamic republic.

Iran's government resembles a parliamentary democracy, based upon their 1979 constitution, and holds elections to fill many of its governmental posts. However, most scholars agree that Iran is a theocracy because the Supreme Leader, who is appointed by an Islamic religious advisory board, is the highest state authority and has the final say in all matters. All laws passed by the government must also be compatible with Sharia, the moral code and religious law of Islam.

Tribal and Other Republics The Vandals were one of many Germanic tribes in Europe during the Roman Empire. Their original leader was a central chief, a member of the royal clan, who was elected for life and held religious and military responsibilities. This type of military chieftainship was replaced when the Vandals established their kingdom in North Africa. Government officials replaced the old tribal aristocracy, and later, a monarchy was created that allowed only the royal family to succeed to the throne. This new kingdom helped to bring about the fall of the Roman Empire.

Another type of republic was the Venetian republic. Its capital was Venice, a center of industry, trade, and culture. The Venetian republic existed from the late 7th century to the late 18th century and was one of the most successful city-states. The republic was ruled by the Doge, elected by representatives of the rich and noble families, and the Great Council who managed the state's affairs. During its later years Venice began to lose its position as the center of trade to other empires surrounding the Mediterranean Sea, such as the Ottoman Empire. The state eventually came to an end with the outbreak of the French Revolution. Napoleon Bonaparte, a military reformer of the revolution, was determined to destroy the Venetian republic. Venice was without an ally in the conflict and was forced to depose of its last Doge and become a part of the state of Austria.

? IDENTIFY MAIN IDEAS What is the most important feature of a democracy?

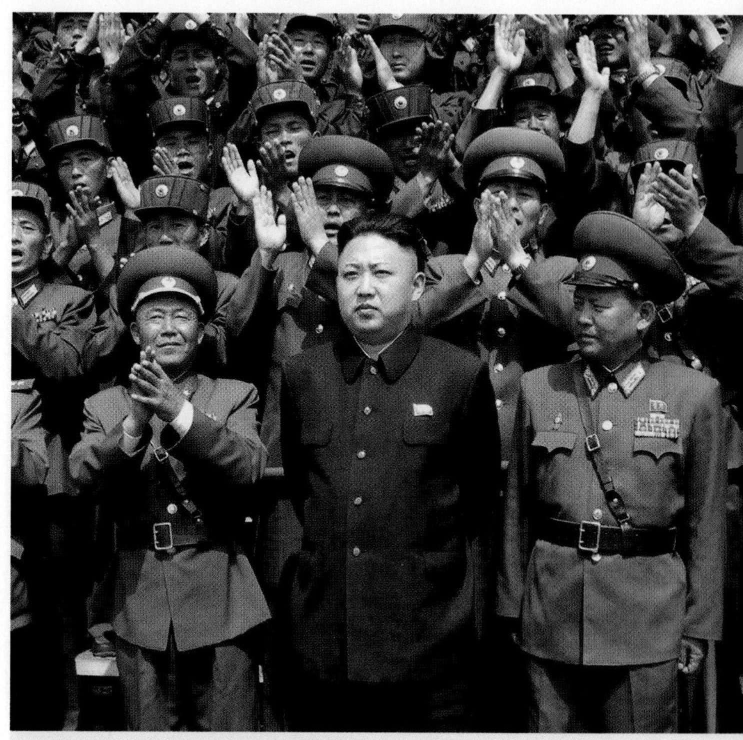

>> North Korean dictator Kim Jong-un observes a military procession. Kim has the same "military first" policy as his father, the previous dictator.

Geographic Distribution of Power

In every system of government, the power to govern is located in one or more places geographically. From this standpoint, three basic forms of government exist: unitary, federal, and confederate.

Centralized Government A **unitary government** is often described as a centralized government. All powers held by the government belong to a single, central agency. The central (national) government creates local units of government for its own convenience. Those local governments have only those powers that the central government chooses to give them.

Great Britain Most governments in the world are unitary in form. Great Britain is a classic illustration. A single central organization, the Parliament, holds all of the government's power. Local governments do exist—but solely to relieve Parliament of burdens it could perform only with much difficulty and inconvenience. Though unlikely, Parliament could do away with all local government in Britain at any time. This is one of the disadvantages of unitary governments.

Be careful not to confuse the unitary form of government with a dictatorship. In the unitary form, all of the powers held by the government are concentrated in the central government.

That government might not hold all power, however. In Great Britain, for example, the powers held by the government are limited. British government is unitary and, at the same time, democratic.

>> In the United States, local, State, and federal agencies often work together during domestic disasters. Local police in Boston conferred with federal agents after the Boston Marathon bombings.

Central and Local Governments A **federal government** is one in which the powers of government are divided between a central government and several local governments. An authority superior to both the central and local governments makes this **division of powers** on a geographic basis; that division cannot be changed by either the local or national level acting alone. Both levels of government act directly on the people through their own sets of laws, officials, and agencies.

United States In the United States, for example, the National Government has certain powers, and the 50 States have others. This division of powers is set out in the Constitution of the United States. The Constitution stands above both levels of government; it cannot be changed unless the people, acting through both the National Government and the States, agree to the change. A clear disadvantage of the federal system of government is that each of the 50 states can have its own policy on the same issue.

Other States Australia, Canada, Mexico, Switzerland, Germany, India, and some 20 other states also have federal forms of government today. In the United States, the phrase "the Federal Government" is often used to identify the National Government, the government headquartered in Washington, D.C. Note, however, that each of the 50 State governments in this country is unitary, not federal, in form.

>> About 180 currencies are in circulation today. The use of a common currency in one area eliminates the need for exchanging money within that area, but establishing a common currency is expensive.

Alliance of Independent States A **confederation** is an alliance of independent states. A central organization, the confederate government has the power to handle only those matters that the member states have assigned to it. Typically, confederate governments have had limited powers and only in such fields as defense and foreign affairs.

Most often, confederate governments have not had the power to make laws that apply directly to individuals, at least not without some further action by the member states. A confederate structure of government makes it possible for the several states to cooperate in matters of common concern and, at the same time, retain their separate identities.

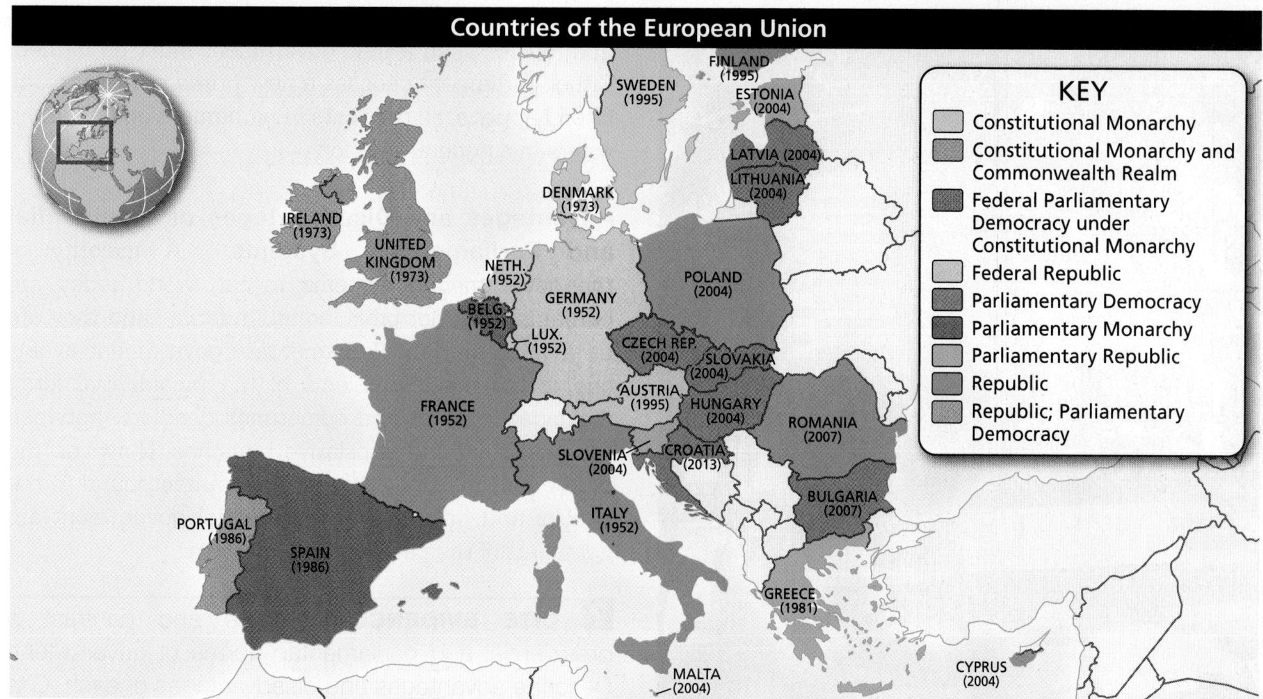

>> Countries with many different types of government are part of the European Union. **Analyze Maps** Based on this map, what generalization can you make about these governments?

Confederate States In our own history, the United States under the Articles of Confederation (1781–1789) and the Confederate States of America (1861–1865) also provide examples of this form of government.

The European Union Confederations are rare today. The European Union (EU), formed by 12 countries in 1993, is the closest approach to one in modern times. It has established free trade among its 28 member-nations (the southeastern European nation of Croatia was the latest to join in 2013). The EU has also launched a common currency and seeks to coordinate its members' foreign and defense policies.

? IDENTIFY MAIN IDEAS How is power distributed in a Federal government?

Legislative and Executive Branches

Political scientists also classify governments based on the relationship between their legislative (law-making) and executive (law- executing) agencies. This classification yields two basic forms of government, known as parliamentary and presidential.

Separation of Powers Between Branches of Government A **presidential government** features a separation of powers between the executive and the legislative branches of the government. The two branches are independent of one another and coequal. The chief executive (the President) is chosen by the people, independently of the legislature. He or she holds office for a fixed term and has a number of significant powers that are not subject to the direct control of the legislative branch.

Written Constitution The details of this separation of the powers of these two branches are almost always spelled out in a written constitution—as they are in the United States. Each of the branches is regularly given several powers with which it can block actions of the other branch.

The United States is the world's leading example of presidential government. In fact, the United States invented the form. Nearly all of the other presidential systems that exist in the world today are also found in the Western Hemisphere.

Parliamentary Government In a **parliamentary** government, the executive branch is made up of the prime minister or premier, and that official's cabinet. The prime minister and cabinet are themselves

>> Members of the South African parliament are sworn into office. A voter-elected National Assembly and a National Council of Provinces comprises the South African Parliament.

Interactive Chart

members of the legislative branch, the parliament. The prime minister is the leader of the majority party or of a like-minded group of parties (a coalition) in parliament and is chosen by that body. With parliament's approval, the prime minister selects the members of the cabinet from among the members of parliament. The executive is thus chosen by the legislature, is a part of it, and is subject to its direct control.

The prime minister and the cabinet (often called "the government") remain in office only as long as their policies and administration have the support of a majority in parliament. If the parliament defeats the prime minister and cabinet on an important matter, the government may receive a "vote of no confidence," and the prime minister and his cabinet must resign from office. Then a new government must be formed. Either parliament chooses a new prime minister or, as often happens, all the seats in parliament go before the voters in a general election.

Advantages and Disadvantages of Presidential and Parliamentary Systems A majority of the governmental systems in the world today are parliamentary, not presidential, in form—and they are by a wide margin. Parliamentary government avoids one of the major problems of the presidential form: prolonged conflict and sometimes deadlock between the executive and legislative branches. However, the protections against arbitrary government found in the checks and balances of presidential government are not a part of the parliamentary system.

CITE EVIDENCE Compare and contrast a presidential and parliamentary forms of government. Describe advantages and disadvantages of each. Cite evidence in the text to support your answer.

ASSESSMENT

1. **Compare** How does a direct democracy differ from an indirect democracy?
2. **Determine Central Ideas** What do the unitary, federal, and confederate forms of government have in common?
3. **Draw Conclusions** Explain why it is possible that a unitary government might be either democratic or dictatorial in form.
4. **Compare Points of View** Should democracies take action to help prevent dictatorships? Why or why not?
5. **Cite Evidence** How is the executive branch related to the legislative branch in a presidential government?

1.3

As you know, government is among the oldest of all human inventions. It emerged long before the dawn of recorded history, when human beings first realized that they could not survive without it—that is, without some means by which they could regulate their own and their neighbors' behavior. The earliest evidences of government date back some 3,000 years, but clearly the institution is much older than that.

>> The U.S. Supreme Court building, completed in 1935, was designed to resemble the classic Greek and Roman temples and to reflect the same values and significance.

Interactive Flipped Video

Origins of the Modern Democratic State

>> **Objectives**

Identify the ancient foundations of the state in Athens, in Rome and in the Feudal system.

Analyze the rise of sovereign states.

Explain how governments can achieve legitimacy.

Understand why European nations turned to colonialism.

Understand how Enlightenment ideas helped influence the expansion of popular sovereignty.

>> **Key Terms**

patricians
plebeians
feudalism
sovereignty
legitimacy
divine right of kings
colonialism
mercantilism
William Blackstone
François-Marie Arouet

American Government–Building on the Past

An uncountable number of governments of various forms have appeared, and disappeared, through the centuries in Europe, Asia, Africa, and the Americas. Those that survived for any length of time were those that could adapt to major changes in their environments.

The roots of democratic government in today's world—including government in the United States—lie deep in human history. They reach back most particularly to ancient Greece and Rome, and also to elements of Judeo-Christian philosophy and later beliefs and practices that emerged elsewhere in Europe.

Those who built a governmental system for the newly independent United States in the late 1700s were, on the whole, well educated. They were quite familiar with the political institutions of their day and, importantly, those of ancient Greece and Rome, as well.

Athens: The First Democracy Greek civilization began to develop some 700 to 800 years before the birth of Christ, and it reached its peak in the fourth century B.C. The Greece of that time was a loose collection of many small, independent, and somewhat isolated city-states—a pattern dictated by the geography of the region, where every island, valley, and plain is cut off from its neighbors by the sea or by mountain ranges.

The concept of democracy was born in those city-states, most notably in Athens. Like the other city-states, Athens began as a monarchy. By the sixth century B.C., however, the Athenians had overthrown monarchical rule, and they soon replaced it with what they called *demokratia*—literally, "rule by the people."

Athenian democracy was, at base, direct democracy. Its central feature was an Assembly (the *Ecclesia*) open to all male citizens at least 18 years of age. The Assembly met 40 times a year to debate public matters and make law. Decisions in the Assembly were made by majority vote.

The Assembly's agenda was set by a Council of Five Hundred (the *boule*). That body was composed of 500 citizens who were chosen randomly, served one-year terms, and did the routine day-to-day work of government. Courts (*dikasteria*) were staffed by volunteers who were at least 30 years of age. They, too, were chosen randomly, served one-year terms, and settled both public and private disputes.

>> Power in the ancient Athenian government came from the people, not from a single ruler. Demosthenes, an ancient Greek statesman, spoke against Philip II, the king of Macedonia.

Athens reached the peak of its glory in art, literature, and philosophy in the fifth century B.C., but it had been severely weakened by the long Peloponnesian War (431–404 B.C.) and later conquest by the Macedonians. What remained of Athenian democracy was extinguished by the Romans who overran Greece in 146 B.C.

The Roman Republic At about the time that glimmers of democracy first appeared in Greece, they began to emerge as well in Rome on the Italian peninsula. Rome was founded in 753 B.C. and, like Athens, was originally a city-state ruled by a monarchy. Monarchical rule was overthrown in 509 B.C. and was soon replaced by a crude form of popular government. The Romans referred to their new system as *res publica*, a republic.

The Roman Republic was to last for some 400 years, until it became the Roman Empire at the end of the first century B.C. Over that period, Rome, involved in almost continuous military conflict, expanded its domain to include most of the lands surrounding the Mediterranean Sea and nearly all of Western Europe.

The Republic was far from democratic in the modern sense. It did introduce the concept of representation, however. Much of the political history of the republican period revolved around an often violent struggle between two social classes: the **patricians**, mostly rich upper-class, landowning aristocrats; and the **plebeians**, the common folk. The Romans did hold elections to choose some public officials, but women, slaves, and the foreign-born could not participate.

Government was centered in the Senate, composed of some 300 members, and two consuls chosen by the Senate. Senators were elected by the citizenry. The patricians dominated that body, but, over time, an increasing number of plebeians were elected to the Senate and to a number of lesser assemblies. The consuls were, effectively, the heads of state. They commanded the army and conducted foreign affairs. The consuls also presided over the Senate and enforced its decrees. Interestingly, each consul had the power to veto the other's decisions. In times of crisis, the Senate could appoint a dictator to serve in place of the consuls and exercise absolute power, but for no longer than six months.

Feudalism The decline and fall of the Roman Empire in the fifth century A.D. marked the beginning of the Middle Ages—the period from that epochal event on to the 16th century. It also marked the collapse of centralized authority and organized government over vast stretches of the western world. For more than a

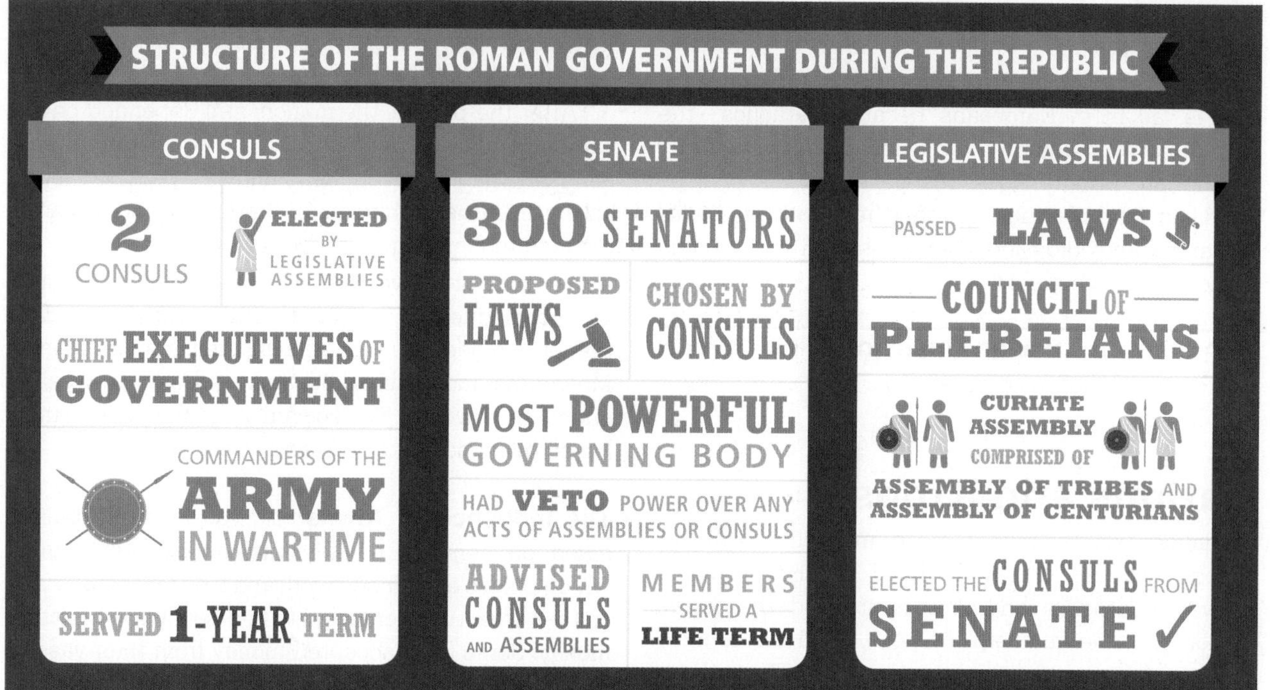

STRUCTURE OF THE ROMAN GOVERNMENT DURING THE REPUBLIC
CONSULS
2 CONSULS
ELECTED BY LEGISLATIVE ASSEMBLIES
CHIEF EXECUTIVES OF GOVERNMENT
COMMANDERS OF THE ARMY IN WARTIME
SERVED 1-YEAR TERM
SENATE
300 SENATORS
PROPOSED LAWS
CHOSEN BY CONSULS
MOST POWERFUL GOVERNING BODY
HAD VETO POWER OVER ANY ACTS OF ASSEMBLIES OR CONSULS
ADVISED CONSULS AND ASSEMBLIES
MEMBERS SERVED A LIFE TERM
LEGISLATIVE ASSEMBLIES
PASSED LAWS
COUNCIL OF PLEBEIANS
CURIATE ASSEMBLY
COMPRISED OF
ASSEMBLY OF TRIBES AND ASSEMBLY OF CENTURIANS
ELECTED THE CONSULS FROM SENATE

>> During the Roman republic, Plebeians (commoners) were part of the legislative assembly. **Analyze Charts** What kind of power was available to Roman Plebians?

thousand years, that world would know little or nothing of government in the modern sense of the term.

The feudal system was born in response to that chaos and disorder. It developed in fits and starts and came to hold sway over much of Europe from the ninth through the twelfth centuries. **Feudalism** was a loosely organized system in which powerful lords divided their lands among other, lesser lords. Those with land and power agreed to protect others in exchange for their loyalty, their military service, and a share of the crops they produced. The basic economic units in the feudal system were the lords' manors. Each manor contained all of a lord's land holdings, which often included a town or village, as well.

The Structure of the Feudal System The primary relationship in the feudal chain was that between a lord and his vassals, lesser lords who pledged their loyalty to the ranking lord—who was, in some places, a monarch. The lord ruled and the vassals served him, watching over the lands in their section of the manor.

The lord did perform some functions of the state in the modern world. He provided protection for his vassals and administered a rough form of justice. In return, the vassals supported the lord's decisions and served under his military command when necessary. The lord-vassal relationship was but one part of a large complex of relationships. Often, a vassal was himself a lord to other, less powerful vassals, and a lord was sometimes a vassal under an even more powerful lord.

Serfs, the bulk of the population, lived at the bottom of the chain of feudal relationships. They were peasants, bound to the land they farmed. The serfs gave a share of what they grew to their vassals in return for protection in times of war. They led harsh lives. None could leave the land without the lord's permission, and their children inherited their ties and responsibilities to the lord. Most died young, never having journeyed more than a few miles from the lord's manor.

The Roman Catholic Church As the Roman Empire had spread across Western Europe, so had Roman Catholicism. The Church survived the collapse of imperial rule and now, in concert with feudalism, it provided some measure of government-like order to life in the Europe of the Middle Ages.

The Roman Catholic Church, now nearly 2,000 years old, traces its origins to the birth of Christianity and to the death of Jesus in Jerusalem, in the Roman province of Judea, in A.D. 33. Its teachings drew from Biblical texts, including the book of Exodus, in which Moses is described as bringing the Ten Commandments to the people of Israel. Catholicism managed to overcome three centuries of often violent persecution by a succession of hostile emperors. In A.D. 380, the Roman

Catholic Church became the official church of the Roman Empire.

As most of Europe was converted to Christianity—that is, as most Europeans became Catholics—the Roman Catholic Church became increasingly powerful. By the late Middle Ages, the pope and his bishops ruled vast land holdings, and they frequently vied with monarchs and lords for political as well as religious influence over people's lives.

POSE AND ANSWER QUESTIONS How long did the Roman Republic operate?

Nations and Kings

Feudalism was, at best, a loose, makeshift basis for government. As cracks emerged in the system—between Catholics and Protestants and the feudal manor and the marketplace—the need for a more structured arrangement became apparent. The outlines of the modern, sovereign nation-state began to emerge.

The Commercial Revolution By the end of the Middle Ages, a commercial revolution began to change the ways in which people lived and did business. A horrific plague, the Black Plague of the 1340s, was a major catalyst of that revolution. In all, it killed a third of Western Europe's population. The Plague itself did not destroy the feudal system. Rather its far-reaching effects undercut that system.

After the plague, the manors still depended on the same amount of work, but from the smaller number of serfs who had survived. Serfs and free peasants found strength in the high value of their labor and began to demand higher wages and better conditions.

Because of the vast decrease in population caused by the plague, the prices of food crops fell, and so the lords made less money from their manorial lands. Merchants and artisans became increasingly wealthy and more powerful. The economy became increasingly based on money and trade, rather than land.

The Influence of Towns As you know, feudalism relied on personal relationships and agreements in which people exchanged work and food for security and justice. Over time, lords had to find new ways to gather money. Some lords accepted money from their vassals in place of military service. Others allowed free people to set up towns on their land for a fee under a charter. In this way, towns began to spring up across Europe. Those towns were centers of trade and freedom that tested the limits of feudalism.

The most important of these towns were found in northern Italy, northern Germany, and the Netherlands.

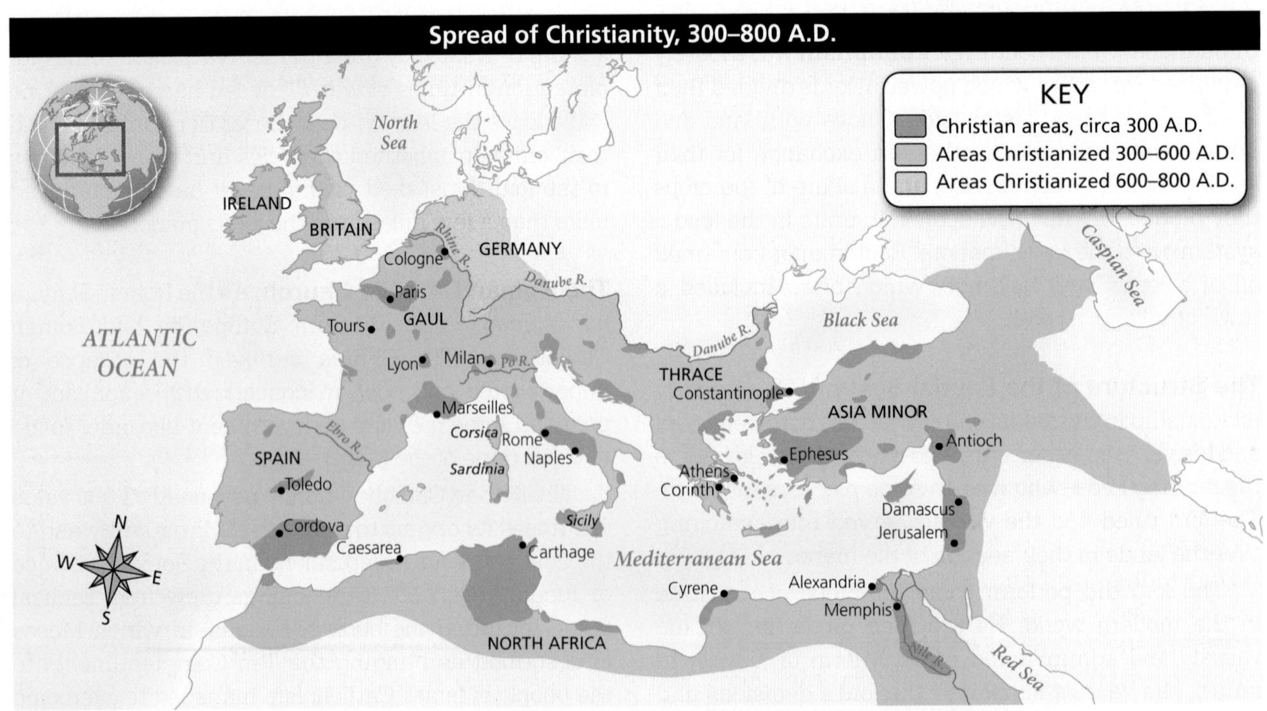

>> Christianity began in the Middle East and diffused across widely settled lands.
Analyze Maps According to the map, how far had Christianity spread by about 800 A.D.?

Monarchical Government During the Middle Ages

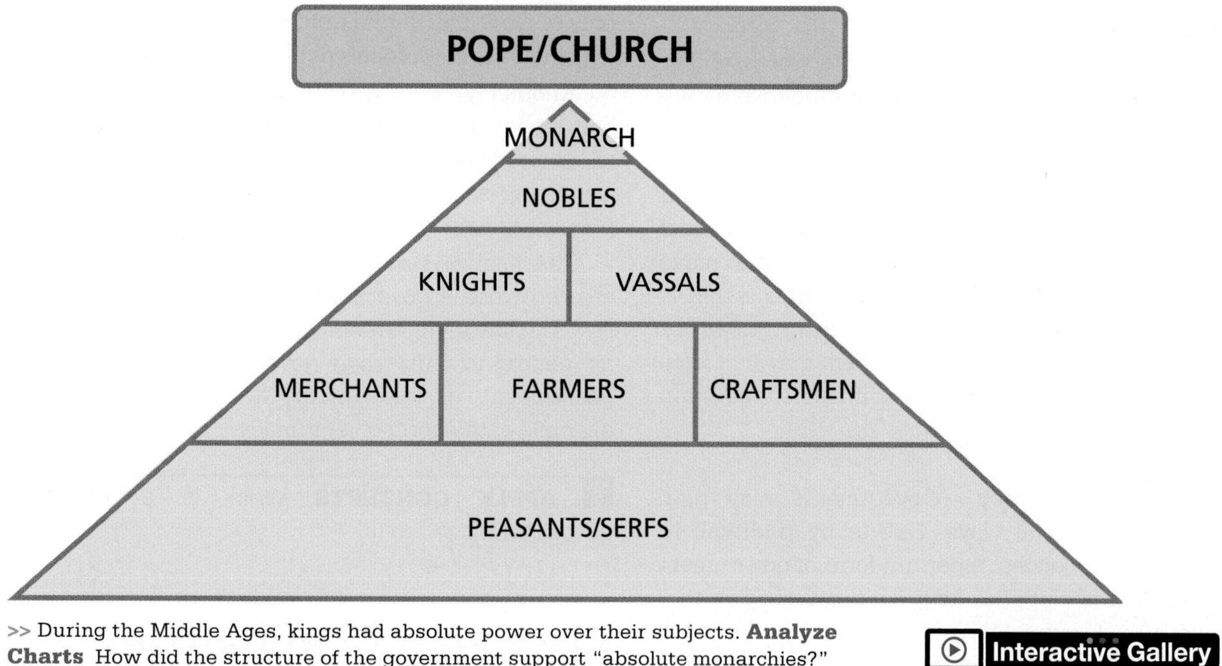

>> During the Middle Ages, kings had absolute power over their subjects. **Analyze Charts** How did the structure of the government support "absolute monarchies?"

Their income came from trade with Central Europe and Asia. The merchants in these towns had uneasy relationships with the lords. Although the merchants were free, they had to pay money to lords for protection, duties on their trade goods, and the right to use roads, rivers, and bridges. Many lords tried to extend their system of justice to the towns. They often failed because they depended on the merchants and bankers of the towns for loans. Trade guilds also developed in the cities and towns, and their members demanded a say in government.

The Rise of Monarchies All of these factors began to undermine the feudal system, weakening the power of the lords. At the same time, the leaders of the towns began to appreciate the benefits of supporting a central authority and they allied themselves with monarchs. The monarchs, in turn, saw the towns as a source of wealth that could free them from dependence on their vassals.

Therefore, by the late 1400s the power of the monarchs was expanding, and feudalism was fast disappearing. In nations such as England, Spain, and France, rulers centralized power, establishing national governments with national legal systems, national identities, and, most important for the monarchs, national taxes. Warfare now was between national armies, not between powerful nobles. Monarchs, whose power was absolute or nearly so, no longer needed the lords to support them and could also ignore popular representative assemblies, if they wished, for long periods of time.

The Power of Absolute Monarchs To help manage the national government, monarchs hired loyal civil servants typically born in the towns and educated at local universities. Their perspectives were national, not regional. The state, in the person of the monarch, now had **sovereignty**, or the utmost authority in decision making and in maintaining order. Everyone, including the nobles, was subordinate to that authority. This form of ultimate power is often referred to as "absolute monarchy."

Because monarchs already existed within the feudal system, they enjoyed the benefits and respect of tradition. A monarch was now recognized as the strongest individual who could best govern a state and protect the people from harm. With sovereignty, the monarch now had the right to make laws for the entire nation and all its people.

? CHECK UNDERSTANDING Which form of government had become most prevalent in Europe in 1490?

Power, Authority, and Legitimacy

The development of the sovereign state was useful in creating political organization, but claiming sovereignty alone does not establish government. All governments must have legitimacy to rule.

Rulers have strong reasons to seek consent for their rule. This consent is known as **legitimacy**, the belief of the people that a government has the right to make public policy. A legitimate government is one that is accepted by its people and other governments as the sovereign authority of a nation. Leaders may use force to keep power. However, force is difficult to maintain over time.

Forms of Legitimacy Governments may gain legitimacy in several ways. One is by tradition. In this case, people accept a certain form of government because their society has long been governed in that way, and people expect their institutions and traditions to be carried on into the future. One type of traditional legitimacy is known as the **divine right of kings**. For hundreds of years, European monarchs based their right to rule on this belief that God had granted them that authority. To disobey a monarch was to deny the natural order of society and to commit a sin against God. In theory, monarchs who ruled by divine right did not have to answer to parliaments or to the people, only to God. The divine right of kings drew its claim to legitimacy from Europe's deep-rooted Christian values.

Another way for a government, and in particular one leader, to win legitimacy is through the power of personality. A charismatic person with strong leadership skills can often win popular support. The people agree to allow this person to rule them.

The final and most durable form of legitimacy is created when a government binds itself to the rule of law. The law must be seen as fair and effective in order for people to trust their government. Constitutional government in the United States is an excellent example of this form of legitimacy.

APPLY CONCEPTS What is a legitimate government?

European Colonialism

Beginning in the late 1400s and early 1500s, several European monarchies embarked on a policy of **colonialism**—the control of one nation over lands abroad. European settlers, laws, and religious beliefs spread around the world as rival nations competed for colonial possessions.

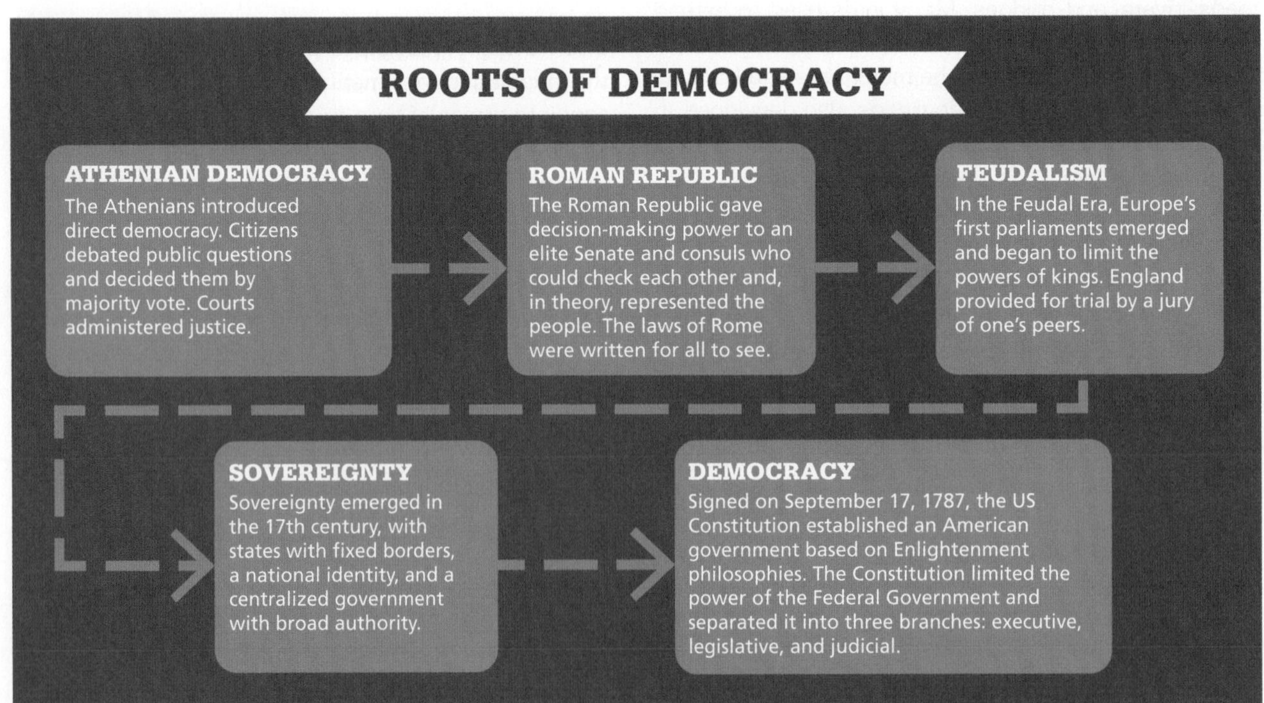

ROOTS OF DEMOCRACY
ATHENIAN DEMOCRACY
The Athenians introduced direct democracy. Citizens debated public questions and decided them by majority vote. Courts administered justice.
ROMAN REPUBLIC
The Roman Republic gave decision-making power to an elite Senate and consuls who could check each other and, in theory, represented the people. The laws of Rome were written for all to see.
FEUDALISM
In the Feudal Era, Europe's first parliaments emerged and began to limit the powers of kings. England provided for trial by a jury of one's peers.
SOVEREIGNTY
Sovereignty emerged in the 17th century, with states with fixed borders, a national identity, and a centralized government with broad authority.
DEMOCRACY
Signed on September 17, 1787, the US Constitution established an American government based on Enlightenment philosophies. The Constitution limited the power of the Federal Government and separated it into three branches: executive, legislative, and judicial.

>> Democracy has its roots in governments from ancient Greece to the 1700s. **Analyze Charts** How did prior forms of sovereignty lead to the development of the United States and its Constitution?

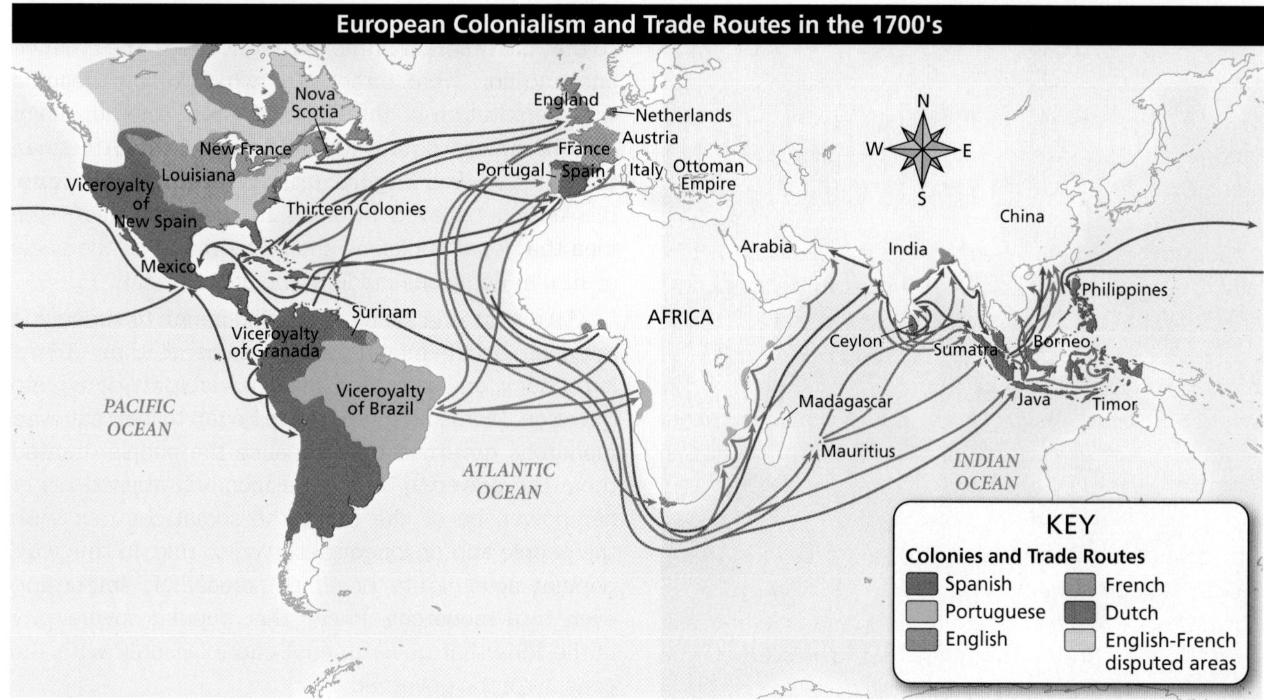

>> By the 1700s many trade routes were established from Europe across the oceans.
Analyze Maps How did trade routes help spread European colonies?

Colonial trade and its wealth brought newfound power to merchants, and monarchs adopted mercantilism to control and profit from that situation. **Mercantilism** is an economic and political theory emphasizing money as the chief source of wealth to increase the absolute power of the monarchy and the nation. The policy stressed the accumulation of precious metals, like gold and silver. It also called for the establishment of colonies and a merchant marine and the development of industry and mining to build a favorable balance of trade with other countries.

Mercantilist policies brought the monarchy and the state deep into the economy. Monarchs taxed imports heavily to protect locally produced goods. Foreigners were required to buy licenses from the state in order to trade with local merchants. Monarchs sought to fill their treasuries and enhance their own and their nations' power.

The High Cost of Colonial Trade Mercantilism expanded when European explorers reached the Western Hemisphere. Their explorations there opened new opportunities for trade and farming, but only monarchs had the wealth and power to establish and control new colonies.

The high cost of exploration allowed monarchs to control overseas commerce by setting up companies to monopolize trade with the new regions. The company system allowed monarchs to tap new sources of wealth from distant gold and silver mines and from far-flung trade.

European colonization brought about new developments in modern government. Britain's colonial efforts led to the American Revolution and the creation of the United States and its constitutional government. The experiences of other countries originally colonized by Spain, France, Portugal, and even Great Britain, however, differed in several ways from the American experience.

APPLY CONCEPTS Why were monarchs able to monopolize overseas commerce?

Power Comes from the People

By the beginning of the eighteenth century, scientific discoveries and new thinking had led to an intellectual movement based on reason and known as the Enlightenment. Some of the most important ideas about modern government, economics, and society were developed at the time, as people began to discuss the rights of individuals to control their own fates and to have a meaningful say in their governance.

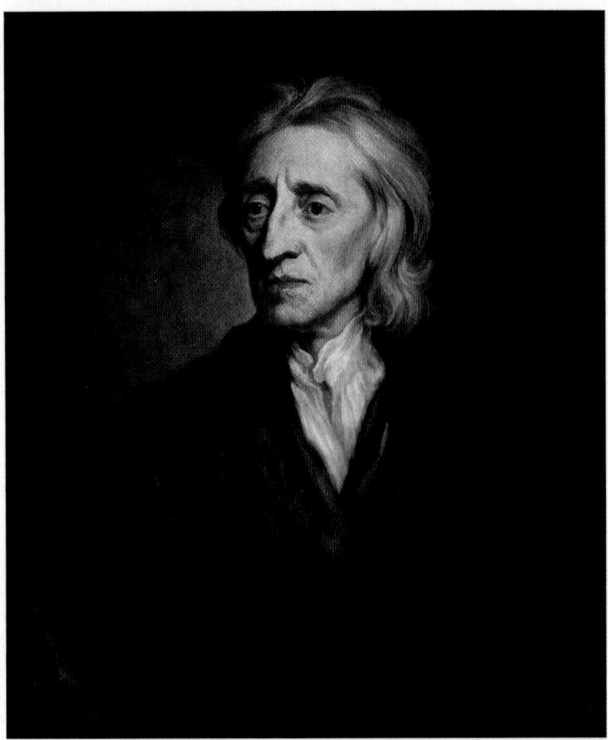

>> John Locke believed "the end of law is not to abolish or restrain, but to preserve and enlarge freedom."

Interactive Gallery

Major Enlightenment Figures Early in the movement, English political theorist John Locke (1632–1704) put forth the notion of the natural rights of all human beings, including the rights to life, liberty, and property—ideas that later formed the basis for the Declaration of Independence. He built on the view of fellow Englishman Thomas Hobbes (1588–1679): that the people and their rulers are parties to a social contract that defines the rights and powers of each. Economists, including Adam Smith (1723–1790) and David Ricardo (1772–1823), criticized those economic policies that had helped monarchs grow wealthier while most of their subjects became steadily poorer and less free.

In France, the philosopher **François-Marie Arouet** (1694–1778), known as Voltaire, advocated reason, freedom of religion, the importance of scientific observation, and the idea of human progress. The ideas of the Baron de Montesquieu (1689–1755) were crucial to political theory during the Enlightenment. His theories about the separation of powers of government, so that the different branches might check and balance one another, were integral to what was to become the Constitution of the United States. Another major Enlightenment figure who influenced the American Constitution was English jurist **William Blackstone**. Blackstone believed strongly in "common law"—the idea that legal decisions should be made on the basis of similar decisions made in the past.

As reason and secular thinking began to supersede religious belief, monarchs lost some of their divine legitimacy, and their God-given sovereignty came into question. More and more people began to feel that even monarchs governed only because the people granted them the power to do so. If a monarch abused his or her power, he or she broke the social contract with the people and no longer deserved to rule. In this way, popular sovereignty became increasingly important, even in a monarchy. Recall that popular sovereignty is the idea that governments can exist only with the consent of the governed.

Popular sovereignty would eventually form the basis for the many republics and democracies in the world today. Since the eighteenth century, almost every government has had to address issues of popular sovereignty in one way or another.

? APPLY CONCEPTS What is the purpose of a "social contract"?

ASSESSMENT

1. **Contrast** How is feudalism different from popular sovereignty?
2. **Hypothesize** How might Europe be different if the Black Plague had never occurred?
3. **Identify Cause and Effect** What events were influential in the development of the Enlightenment?
4. **Apply Concepts** How did the Catholic Church support the claims of monarchs?
5. **Support Ideas with Examples** Provide an example of how the rise of monarchs led to colonialism.

1.4 What do you make of this assessment of democracy by British statesman James Bryce: "No government demands so much from the citizen as Democracy, and none gives so much back"? What does democratic government demand from you? What does it give you in return?

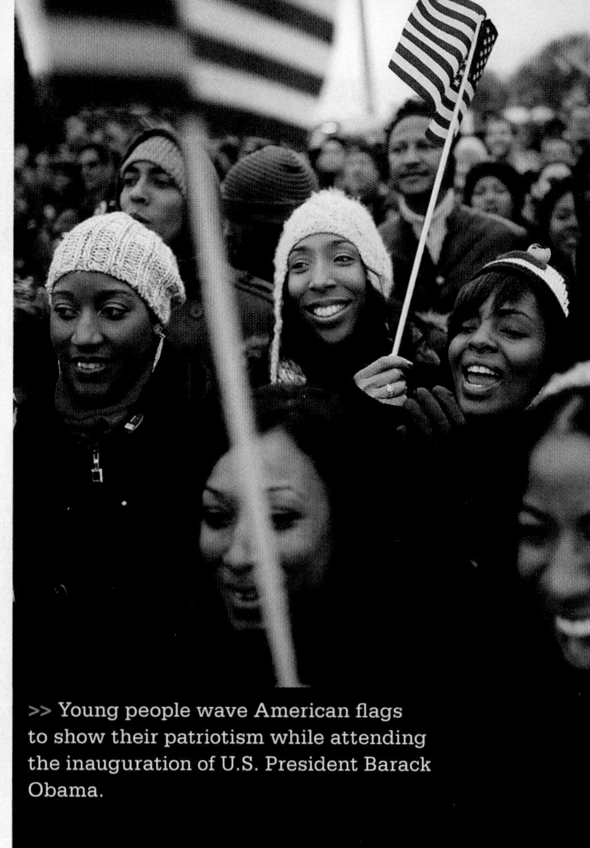

>> Young people wave American flags to show their patriotism while attending the inauguration of U.S. President Barack Obama.

Interactive Flipped Video

The Basics of Democracy

>> **Objectives**

Understand the foundations of democracy.

Analyze the connections between democracy and the free enterprise system.

>> **Key Terms**

majority rule
compromise
citizen
free enterprise system
James Bryce
Winston Churchill
Oliver Wendell Holmes
Theodore Roosevelt
George Washington

Foundations of Democracy

Democracy is not inevitable. It does not exist in the United States simply because Americans regard it as the best of all possible political systems. Rather, democracy exists in this country because the American people believe in its basic concepts. It will continue to exist only for as long as we, the people, continue to subscribe to and practice those concepts.

Sir **Winston Churchill** (1874–1965) once put the argument for democracy this way: "No one pretends that democracy is perfect or all-wise. Indeed, it has been said that democracy is the worst form of government except all those other forms that have been tried from time to time."

The American concept of democracy—what we believe democracy means—rests on these basic notions:

1. Recognition of the fundamental worth and dignity of every person; 2. Respect for the equality of all persons; 3. Faith in majority rule and an insistence upon minority rights; 4. Acceptance of the necessity of compromise; and 5. Insistence upon the widest possible degree of individual freedom.

>> A first-time voter casts a ballot in a presidential election. To work, democracy requires an educated and informed population of voters who participate in the election process.

Of course, these concepts can be worded in other ways. No matter what the wording, however, they form the very minimum with which anyone who professes to believe in democracy must agree.

Worth of the Individual Democracy is firmly based upon a belief in the fundamental importance of the individual. Each individual, no matter what his or her station in life, is a separate and distinct being.

This concept of the dignity and worth of the individual is of overriding importance in democratic thought. At various times, of course, the welfare of one or a few individuals is subordinated to the interests of the many in a democracy. People can be forced to do certain things whether they want to or not. Examples range from paying taxes to registering for the draft to stopping at a stop sign.

When a democratic society forces people to pay a tax or obey traffic signals, it is serving the interests of the many. However, it is not simply serving the interests of the many who as a mass of people happen to outnumber the few. Rather, it is serving the many who, as individuals, together make up that society.

The distinction we are trying to make here between *an* individual and *all* individuals may be difficult to grasp. It is, however, critically important to a real understanding of the meaning of democracy.

>> Elizabeth Eckford was an African American who enrolled at Central High School, an all-white school in Arkansas, after the Supreme Court ruled that segregation denied African Americans their guaranteed equality.

Interactive Gallery

Equality of All Persons Hand in hand with the belief in the worth of the individual, democracy stresses the equality of all individuals. It holds, with Jefferson, that "all men are created equal."

Certainly, democracy does not imply an equality of condition for all persons. Thus, it does not claim that all are born with the same mental or physical abilities. Nor does it hold that all persons have a right to an equal share of worldly goods.

Rather, the democratic concept of equality means that every person is entitled to (1) equality of opportunity and (2) equality before the law. That is, the democratic concept of equality holds that no person should be held back for any such arbitrary reasons as those based on race, color, religion, or gender. It states that each person must be free to develop himself or herself as fully as he or she wishes to, and that each person should be treated as the equal of all other persons under the law.

We have come a great distance toward the goal of equality for all in this country. It is clear, however, that we are still a considerable distance from a genuine, universally recognized and respected equality for all of America's people.

Majority Rule, Minority Rights In a democracy, the will of the people and not the dictate of the ruling few determines public policy. What is the popular will, and how is it determined? Some device must exist by which these crucial questions can be answered. The only satisfactory device democracy knows is that of **majority rule**. Democracy holds that a majority will be right more often than it will be wrong, and that the majority will also be right more often than any one person or small group will.

Democracy can be described as an experiment or a trial-and-error process designed to find satisfactory ways to order human relations. Democracy does not dictate that the majority will always arrive at the best decisions on public matters. In fact, the democratic process is not meant to come up with "right" or "best" answers. Rather, the democratic process is a search for *satisfactory* solutions to public problems.

Of course, in a democracy the majority's decisions will usually be more, rather than less, satisfactory. Democracy does admit the possibility of mistakes; there is the possibility that "wrong" or less satisfactory answers will sometimes be found. Democracy also recognizes that seldom is any solution to a public problem so satisfactory that it cannot be improved upon, and that circumstances can change over time. So, the process of experimentation, of seeking answers to public questions, is a never-ending one.

Certainly, a democracy cannot work without the principle of majority rule. Unchecked, however, a majority could destroy its opposition and, in the process, destroy democracy itself. Thus, democracy requires majority rule restrained by minority rights. The majority must always recognize the right of any minority to become, if it can by fair and lawful means, the majority. The majority must always be willing to listen to a minority's argument, to hear its objections, to bear its criticisms, and to welcome its suggestions.

>> Politics involves an element of compromise. **Analyze Political Cartoons** Who do the chefs represent in this cartoon?

Necessity of Compromise In a democracy, public decision making must be largely a matter of give-and-take among the various competing interests. It is a matter of compromise in order to find the position most acceptable to the largest number. **Compromise** is the process of blending and adjusting competing views and interests.

Compromise is an essential part of the democratic concept for two major reasons. First, remember that democracy puts the individual first and, at the same time, insists that each individual is the equal of all others. In a democratic society made up of many individuals and groups with many different opinions and interests, how can the people make public decisions except by compromise?

Second, few public questions have only two sides. Most can be answered in several ways. Take the apparently simple question of how a city should pay for the paving of a public street. Should it charge those who own property along the street? Or should the costs be paid from the city's general treasury? Or should the city and the adjacent property owners share the costs? What about those who will use the street but do not live in the city? Should they have to pay a toll?

Remember, compromise is a process, a way of achieving majority agreement. It is never an end in itself. Not all compromises are good, and not all are necessary.

Insistence upon Individual Freedom It should be clear by this point that democracy can thrive only in an atmosphere of individual freedom. However, democracy does not and cannot insist on complete freedom for the individual. Absolute freedom can exist only in a state of anarchy—the total absence of government. Anarchy can only lead, inevitably and quickly, to rule by the strong and ruthless.

Democracy does require that each individual must be as free to do as he or she pleases as far as the freedom of all will allow. Justice **Oliver Wendell Holmes** once had this to say about the relative nature of each individual's rights: "The right to swing my fist ends where the other man's nose begins."

Drawing a line between the rights of one individual and those of another is not easy. Still, the drawing of that line is a continuous and vitally important function of democratic government.

Striking the proper balance between freedom for the individual and the rights of society as a whole is similarly difficult—and vital. Abraham Lincoln described democracy's problem by asking a question.

> Must a government, of necessity, be too strong for the liberties of its own people, or too weak to maintain its own existence?
>
> —Message to Congress, July 4, 1861

Human beings desire both liberty and authority. Democratic government must work constantly to strike the proper balance between the two. The authority of government must be adequate to the needs of society. At the same time, that authority must never be allowed to become so great that it restricts the individual beyond what is absolutely necessary.

? SUMMARIZE To what are citizens entitled under the democratic concept of equality?

>> As John F. Kennedy, the 35th President of the United States said, "The rights of every man are diminished when the rights of one man are threatened."

Interactive Chart

Responsibilities, Duties, and Obligations of Citizenship

Over the centuries, any number of statesmen, philosophers, and others have told us that citizenship carries with it both duties and responsibilities. **Theodore Roosevelt** put that point this way in 1902: "The first requisite of a good citizen in our republic is that he should be able and willing to pull his weight."

Being a "Good Citizen" In a democratic society, the *duties* of "a good citizen" all revolve around his or her commitment to obey the law—a point long accepted in this country. In his Farewell Address in 1796, **George Washington** put that obligation this way: "the very idea of the power and right of the People to establish Government presupposes the duty of every individual to obey the established Government."

The several *responsibilities* of "a good citizen" in a free society all come down to this: an abiding respect for each of the core beliefs on which democracy is based in this country. A **citizen** is one who holds both rights and responsibilities in a state. Ask yourself this question: Do I understand and am I committed to honoring the basic concepts of American democracy?

What is the difference between personal and civic responsibilities? Personal responsibilities encompass taking care of yourself — being responsible for your own behavior, taking care of your family, being considerate of others. Civic responsibilities, on the other hand, involve your role as a citizen of a larger community. They include obeying the law, paying taxes, being informed and voting, respecting the rights of others, serving as a juror, and serving in the armed forces. All of these civic responsibilities serve to strengthen and support the community.

In a democracy, part of every citizen's responsibility is to serve the public good. This involves caring for the welfare of the community including its environment, safety, and education. Volunteering, participating in public service organizations, and seeking opportunities to serve the community are all ways to meet this important obligation.

Making a Difference How effective are the various methods of political participation at local, state, and national levels? The answer to that question depends largely on each individual. For many, however, the most effective form of participation in a democracy is to seek elected office. The decisions being made, the compromises necessary, are all made by individuals who have been selected by their fellow citizens to guide the hand of authority in the ways that best serve

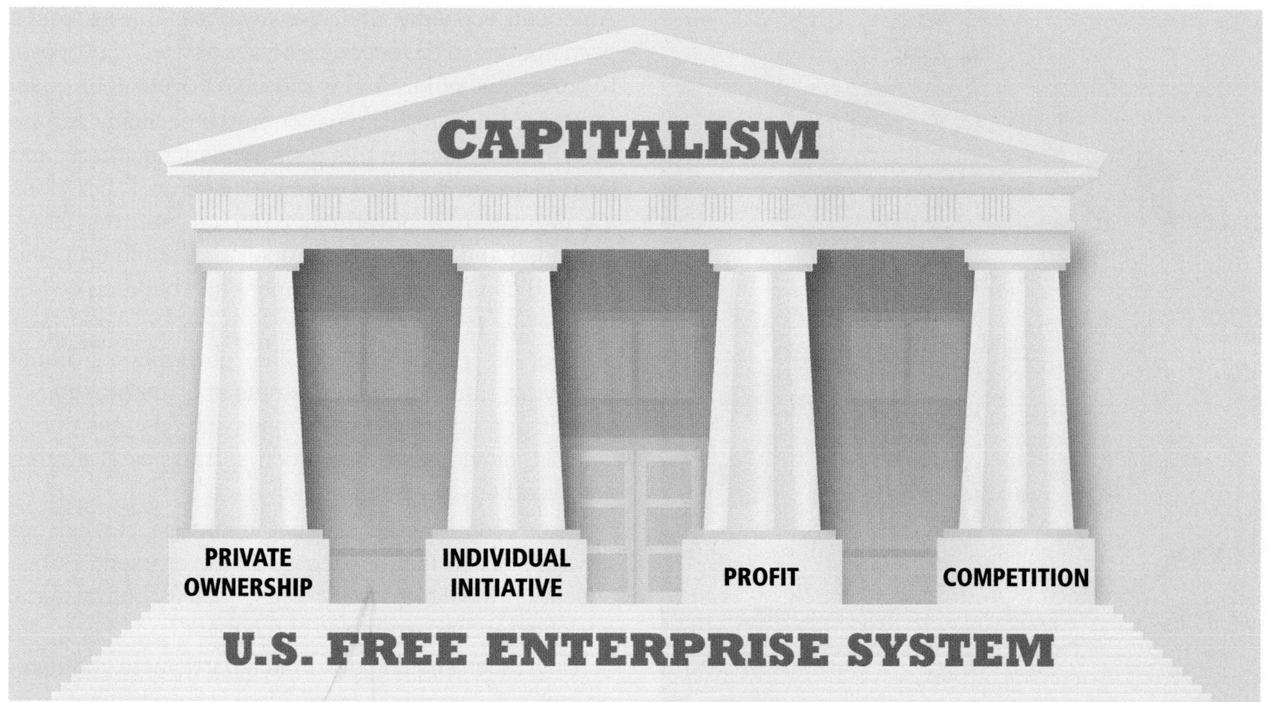

>> The four pillars are the basis for free enterprise, or capitalism, in the United States. **Analyze Charts** What are some examples of each pillar, such as home ownership or starting a business?

their country. Another effective method is to take part in the working of the government itself. From the smallest towns and villages to the grand scope of an entire nation, there must be those who implement the decisions being made.

Similarly, those who draw up petitions or form action groups to address issues can have a very real effect on public policy. Letters can be written to government leaders including city council members, state legislators, and national Congressmen and -women. Joining political parties, working on campaigns, and contributing time and money towards political causes can also be useful ways to participate, because working to make a party stronger or get a certain candidate elected can have a real impact on laws and policies at all levels of government.

The simplest way to participate in politics is to vote, to exercise the right to speak and be heard. Voting at every level, from national to local, helps to ensure that the needs of the people are being heard and addressed. Being informed and participating are rights and responsibilities of every citizen.

INTERPRET What is the most basic duty of a U.S. citizen?

Democracy and the Free Enterprise System

The American commitment to freedom for the individual is deep-rooted, and it is as evident in the nation's economic system as it is in the political system. The American economic system is often called the **free enterprise system**. It is an economic system characterized by the private ownership of capital goods; investments made by private decision, not by government directive; and success or failure determined by competition in the marketplace. The free enterprise system is based on four fundamental factors: private ownership, individual initiative, profit, and competition.

How the System Works The free enterprise system is often called capitalism. It is also known as the private enterprise system and as a market-based system. It does not rely on government to decide what items are to be produced, how much of any particular item should be produced, or how much any item is to sell for. Rather, those decisions are made in the marketplace. Millions of producers and consumers obey the unwritten law of supply and demand: When supplies of goods and services become plentiful, prices will tend to drop; when, on the other hand, supplies become scarce, prices will very likely rise.

>> This cartoon shows two trains sidetracked by a monopoly. **Analyze Political Cartoons** Why might there be tension in the economy between the government and private enterprise?

Democracy and the free enterprise system are not the same thing. One is a political system, and the other is an economic system. However, both are firmly based on the concept of individual freedom. America's experience with both systems clearly suggests that the two reinforce one another in practice.

That is not to say that the American free enterprise system is without flaws. Many Americans believe that society as a whole benefits through the continuous creation of new businesses, new jobs, and increased wealth when individuals can pursue their own interests and have opportunities to use private property to create jobs and generate income. Yet, this American ideal is not always fulfilled in practice. Historically, racial and gender discrimination have limited opportunities for many Americans to find good jobs or start their own businesses. Growing disparities between the rich and poor have led to occasional calls for a change in the American economic system. For the most part, however, criticisms are focused on revising specific aspects of capitalism, rather than attempting to replace that system entirely.

Government and the Free Enterprise System The basis of the American economic system is the free market. However, government does play a role in the American economy, and it always has. Government's participation in the economy serves a two-fold purpose: to protect the public and to preserve private enterprise.

Government's participation in the economy can be seen at every level in this country: national, State, and local. Here are but a few examples: Economic activities are regulated by government through antitrust laws, pure food and drug laws, antipollution standards, and city and county zoning ordinances and building codes.

The nation's economic life is promoted in a great number of public ways. The government grants money for transportation systems and the growing of particular food crops, builds roads and operates public schools, provides services such as the postal system and weather reports, and much more.

Thus, some activities that might be carried out privately are in fact conducted by government. Public education, local fire departments, and city bus systems are longstanding examples of the point.

How much should government participate, regulate, promote, police, and serve? Many heated debates in American politics center on that question, and we are often reminded of Abraham Lincoln's advice about the object of government.

> The legitimate object of government, is to do for a community of people, whatever they need to have done, but can not do, at all, or can not, so well do, for themselves—in their separate, and individual capacities.
>
> —Abraham Lincoln

? LIST What are the four factors of the free enterprise system?

ASSESSMENT

1. **Draw Conclusions** Why is democracy the political system of the U.S. government?
2. **Apply Concepts** Explain the ideas behind majority rule and minority rights.
3. **Interpret** What does it mean to be a good citizen?
4. **Draw Conclusions** What might be the consequences if citizens were not required to serve on a jury?
5. **Apply Concepts** How does supply and demand work?

TOPIC 1 ASSESSMENT

1. **What Government Does**
   - Form a More Perfect Union
   - Establish Justice
   - Insure Domestic Tranquility
   - Provide for the Common Defense
   - Promote the General Welfare
   - Secure the Blessings of Liberty

   Explain the Major Responsibilities of the Federal Government Use the chart above to write a paragraph explaining what the federal government does in domestic policy and in foreign policy. Give an example of something the government is responsible for in each of the categories, and explain how it is related to domestic or foreign policy.

2. **Explain Major Political Ideas** Write a paragraph explaining social contract theory. Consider the following questions to support your response: What is social contract theory? How does social contract theory explain why governments are created? What political thinkers are associated with social contract theory?

3. **Identify Traditions That Informed the American Founding** Write a paragraph explaining the influence of the Enlightenment on the founding of the United States. Consider the following questions in your response: What was the Enlightenment? What philosophies did Enlightenment figures support and encourage? What affect did the Enlightenment have on the concepts of liberty, rights, and the responsibilities of individuals? What Enlightenment principles can be seen in the Declaration of Independence and the U.S. Constitution?

4. **Explain a Written Constitution** Explain the importance of a written constitution. Refer to valid primary and secondary sources to support your ideas.

5. **Identify Individuals That Informed the American Founding Documents** Write a paragraph identifying William Blackstone's influence on the American founding documents. Consider the following questions in your response: With what school of thought and time period was William Blackstone associated? What concept is Blackstone credited with arguing for? Explain this concept. Which branch of the U.S. government reflects Blackstone's concept?

6. **Evaluate Constitutional Provisions** Write a paragraph explaining how separation of power outlined in the U.S. Constitution limits the role of government. Consider the following questions in your response: What is separation of powers? How can the separation of powers limit the role of government? How is separation of powers reflected in the U.S. Constitution?

7. **Analyze the Functions of the Legislative Branch of Government** Create an oral presentation analyzing the functions of the bicameral Congress. Consider the following questions in your presentation: What are the two houses of Congress, and what function does each serve? How are each house's members chosen? What does each house do as a part of the U.S. government? Why are there two branches of Congress?

8. **Analyze the Functions of the Executive Branch of Government** Create a presentation focusing on the issue of the growth of presidential power and analyzing the function of the executive branch. Consider the following questions: What is the executive branch of government? What are the powers of the executive branch of government as outlined in the U.S. Constitution? How have the powers of the President grown since the founding of the United States? Why have presidential powers grown?

9. **Compare the Structures of Governments** Create a chart or other visual presentation comparing the structures of national, state, and local governments. Consider the following questions: What are the branches found within each? What are the titles of the political figures that lead each? Who chooses the members of each branch? How are the powers of each type of government split and organized? How is each type of government involved in the economy?

10. **Compare the U.S. Constitutional Republic** Write a paragraph comparing the U.S. government to socialist governments. Consider the following questions: What is a socialist government? How is the structure of a socialist government different from that of the U.S. constitutional republic? How are the leaders of each government chosen? How do the powers of each government differ?

TOPIC 1 ASSESSMENT

11. **Analyze Unitary Government** Write a paragraph analyzing the advantages and disadvantages of a unitary government. Consider the following questions: What is a unitary government? What structures within a unitary government hold the power? How does a unitary government help its citizens? How does a unitary government limit its citizens?

12. **Identify Significant Individuals** Use the information from the text quoted below to write a paragraph identifying Abraham Lincoln and analyzing his comment to infer his sentiments about government.

"Must a government, of necessity, be too strong for the liberties of its own people, or too weak to maintain its own existence?"

—Abraham Lincoln, Message to Congress, July 4, 1861

13. **Explain Personal and Civic Responsibilities** Write a paragraph explaining the difference between personal and civic responsibilities. Consider the following questions: What are personal responsibilities? Include examples. What are civic responsibilities? Include examples. How are personal responsibilities different from civic responsibilities?

14. **Understand the Rule of Law** Using the following quote, write a paragraph on how the rule of law protects individual rights. Consider the following questions: What is the rule of law? What defines individual rights? How does the quote from the Magna Carta relate to the rule of law? How does the rule of law protect individual rights?

"No freemen shall be taken or imprisoned or disseised or exiled or in any way destroyed, nor will we go upon him nor send upon him, except by the lawful judgment of his peers or by the law of the land."

—Article 39, Magna Carta (1215)

15. **Analyze a Presidential Government** Write a paragraph analyzing the advantages and disadvantages of a presidential government. Consider the following questions: What is a presidential government? What structures within it have more power? How does it help its citizens? What are the disadvantages of a presidential government?

16. **Understand Government Regulation** In the U.S., the interaction between the government and private enterprise is commonly referred to as the "free enterprise system." This system in turn provides the base which supports capitalism. Use the graphic below to write a paragraph explaining how government regulation can restrict private enterprise. Consider the following questions: What is private enterprise? How is private enterprise related to capitalism? What is government regulation? How can government regulation restrict private enterprise?

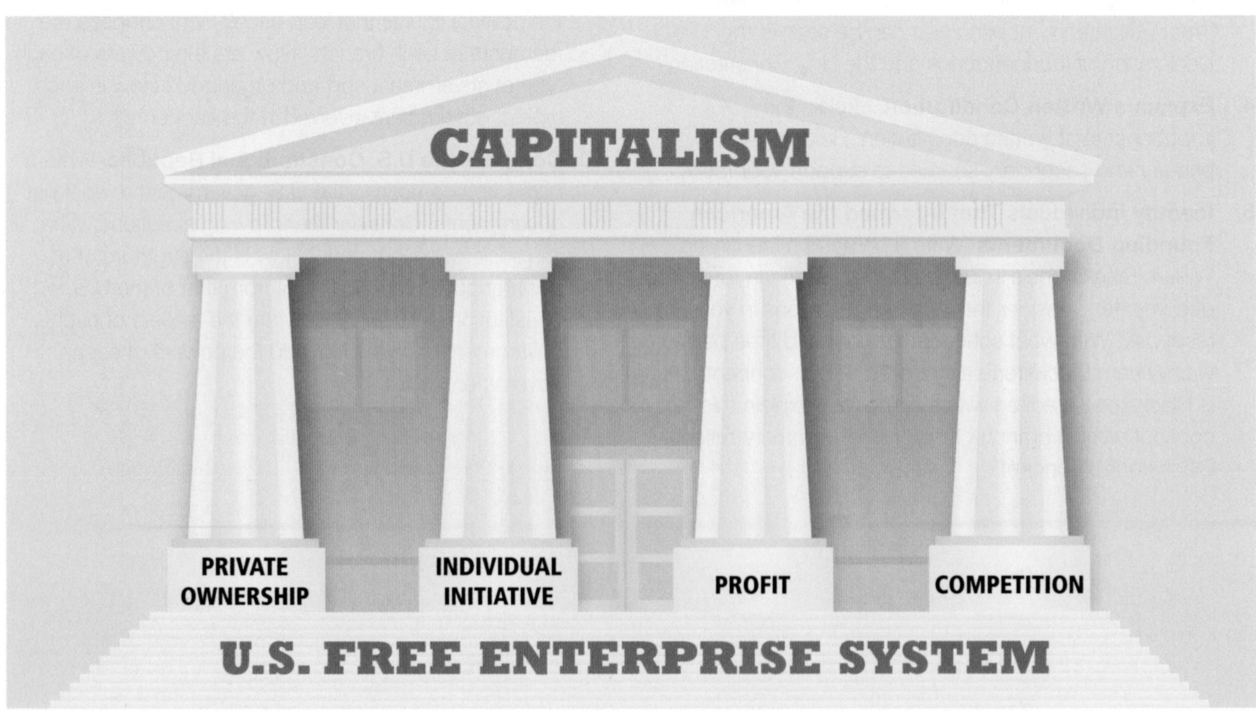

17. Understand Citizenship Write a paragraph explaining the obligations of citizenship. Consider the following questions: What are obligations as they refer to citizenship? How are obligations different from responsibilities and duties? What are some obligations of citizenship? Why are the obligations of citizenship important to the health of democracy?

18. Evaluate the Obligations of Citizenship Use the cartoon below to write a paragraph evaluating the compromises made between personal desires and the public good in a democratic society. Consider the following questions: What is the public good? Does citizenship ever require that the public good come before personal interests? When? Why is compromise relevant to the public good and personal desires?

19. Analyze the Functions of the Judicial Branch of Government Use the quotation below to write a paragraph analyzing judicial powers, including the federal court system. Consider the following questions: What are the role and powers of the judicial branch of the U.S. government? Which court is defined in the Constitution? According to the quote, how long do you interpret the term of a federal judge to be? Why might the founders have chosen that term of office?

"The judicial Power of the United States, shall be vested in one supreme Court, and in such inferior Courts as the Congress may from time to time ordain and establish. The Judges, both of the supreme and inferior Courts, shall hold their Offices during good Behavior, and shall, at stated Times, receive for their Services a Compensation which shall not be diminished during their Continuance in Office."

20. Identify Beliefs and Principles Use the information from the text below to write a paragraph identifying how American beliefs and principles are demonstrated in the current United States.

"According to the text, the American concept of democracy—what we believe democracy means—rests on these basic notions:

1. *Recognition of the fundamental worth and dignity of every person;*
2. *Respect for the equality of all persons;*
3. *Faith in majority rule and an insistence upon minority rights;*
4. *Acceptance of the necessity of compromise; and*
5. *Insistence upon the widest possible degree of individual freedom."*

21. **Analyze Participation in the Political Process** Write a paragraph analyzing and categorizing which political actions are most effective in state politics. Consider the following questions: How can you participate in the political process? What is state government? Which ways of participation in the political process would make the greatest difference at the state level? Why?

22. **Analyze the Federalist Papers** Using the quote below, write a paragraph analyzing how *Federalist* No. 51 explains the principles of the American government. Consider the following questions: Which principle of the U.S. government is discussed below? Why does the author think this principle is important to a republic and, specifically, to the U.S. system of government?

 "In a single republic, all the power surrendered by the people is submitted to the administration of a single government; and the usurpations are guarded against by a division of the government into distinct and separate departments. In the compound republic of America, the power surrendered by the people is first divided between two distinct governments, and then the portion allotted to each subdivided among distinct and separate departments. Hence a double security arises to the rights of the people. The different governments will control each other, at the same time that each will be controlled by itself."

 —Federalist No. 51

23. **Evaluate Purposes and Analyze Information** Use the information from the text quoted below to write a paragraph explaining and analyzing how the U.S. government meets the goals set out by the Preamble to the Constitution. Consider the following questions: What does the Preamble set out as the goals for the government described in the Constitution? Which branches of government address each of the goals in the Preamble? Are all of the goals in the Preamble met by the federal government? How?

 "We the People of the United States, in Order to form a more perfect Union, establish Justice, insure domestic Tranquility, provide for the common defence, promote the general Welfare, and secure the Blessings of Liberty to ourselves and our Posterity, do ordain and establish this Constitution for the United States of America."

 —Preamble to the Constitution of the United States

24. **Understand Citizenship** Write a short essay explaining why obeying the law and paying taxes are required of citizens. Consider the following questions: Why must people obey the law and pay taxes? What happens if people do not obey the law and pay taxes?

Countries of the European Union

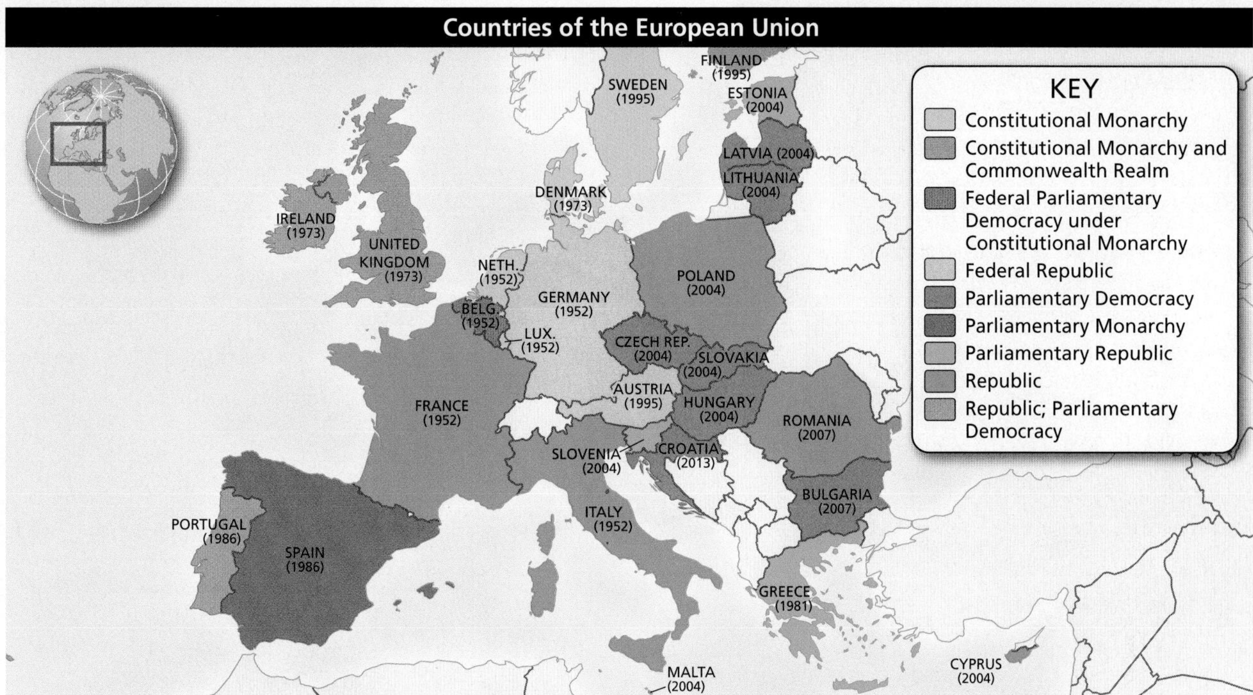

25. **Analyze a Confederate Government** Use the map of the European Union above to write a paragraph analyzing the advantages and disadvantages of a confederate government. Consider the following questions: What is a confederate government? What structures within a confederacy have more power? How does a confederacy help its members? How does a confederacy limit its members? Look at the map above. Why might the nations of Europe have formed a confederacy?

26. **Analyze Participation in the Political Process** Write a paragraph analyzing and categorizing which political actions are most effective in local politics. Consider the following questions: How can you participate in the political process? What is local government? Which ways of participation in the political process would make the greatest difference at the local level? Why?

27. **Understand Citizenship** Write a short essay explaining how jury duty is an obligation. Consider the following questions: Why is it an obligation to serve if you are called for jury duty? What happens if people do not participate in jury duty?

28. **Write About the Essential Question Write an essay on the Essential Question: What should governments do?** Use evidence from your study of this Topic to support your answer.

[ESSENTIAL QUESTION] How Much Power Should a Government Have?

2 The Beginnings of American Government

>> Painting of George Washington, the first President of the United States

Enduring Understandings

- Government in the thirteen colonies was influenced by British ideas, laws, customs, documents, and institutions.
- Reaction to British policies and growing colonial unity led to a revolutionary war and ultimately to American independence in the late 1700s.
- The government established under the Articles of Confederation had several weaknesses that seriously threatened the future of the new United States.
- In 1787, State delegates wrote a new Constitution for the United States that outlined the structure and functions of the government; after vigorous debate and compromises, the new plan of government was ratified.

PEARSON realize NBC LEARN

Watch the My Story Video to learn about one of the most important political thinkers in U.S. history, James Madison.

Access your digital lessons including:
Topic Inquiry • Interactive Reading Notepad • Interactivities • Assessments

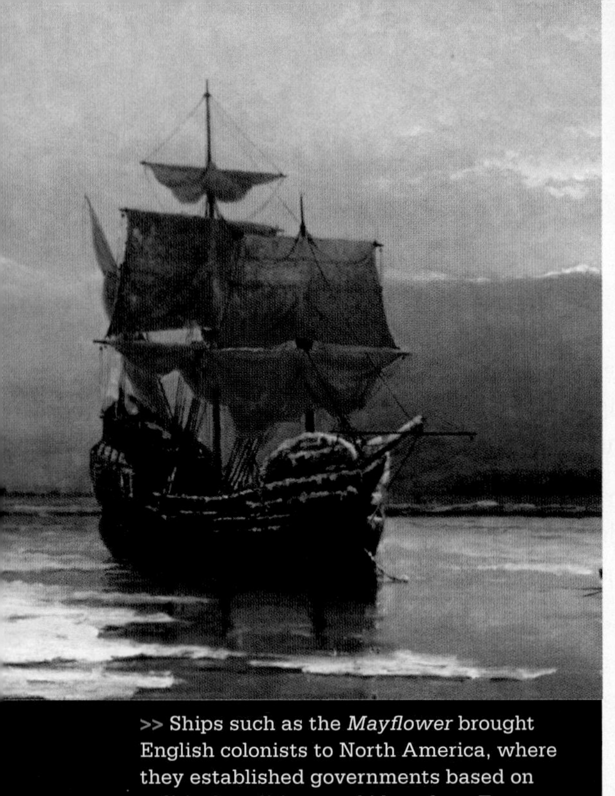

>> Ships such as the *Mayflower* brought English colonists to North America, where they established governments based on political traditions and ideas from Europe and elsewhere.

Interactive Flipped Video

2.1 **The American system of government did not suddenly spring into being with the signing of the Declaration of Independence in 1776. Nor was it created by the Framers of the Constitution in 1787. Instead, the beginnings of what was to become the United States can be found in the mid-sixteenth century, when explorers, traders, and settlers first made their way to North America.**

>> Objectives

Explain how constitutional government in the United States has been influenced by centuries of political ideas and traditions from England and elsewhere.

Analyze the significance of three landmark historical documents to the American system of government.

Describe the three types of colonies that the English established in North America and explain why they are important to the study of American government.

>> Key Terms

limited government
representative government
Magna Carta
due process
Petition of Right
English Bill of Rights
charter
bicameral
proprietary
unicameral
Jamestown
King John
King Charles I
William and Mary of Orange
Glorious Revolution
King George II
London
George Calvert, Lord Baltimore
William Penn

Origins of American Political Ideals

Origins of American Constitutional Government

The French, Dutch, Spanish, Swedes, and others came to explore and settle what would become this nation—and, in the process, to dominate those Native Americans who were here for centuries before the arrival of the first Europeans. It was the English, however, who came in the largest numbers. And it was the English who soon controlled the 13 colonies that stretched for some 1,300 miles along the Atlantic seaboard.

The earliest English settlers brought with them knowledge of a political system that had been developing in England for centuries. That system included customs, practices, and government institutions. English common law, for example, which is unwritten, judge-made law developed over centuries, was one integral part of that system. English constitutionalism, the notion that government leaders are subject to the limitations of the law, had also been developing for hundreds of years in England. These traditions of common law and constitutionalism, like many other major intellectual, philosophical, political, and religious traditions, would later influence the founding of America.

PEARSON realize www.PearsonRealize.com Access your Digital Lesson.

The origins of many of these fundamental ideas stretch back into ancient times and across many lands. Thus, the concept of the rule of law that influenced English political ideas, for example, has roots in the early civilizations of Africa and Asia.

King Hammurabi of Babylonia, for example, developed a system of laws known as Hammurabi's Code around 1750 B.C. Jewish legal concepts relating to individual worth, fair trial, and the rule of law were detailed in the Hebrew Bible. The English were quite familiar with and devoutly attracted to the biblical concept of the rule of law, the idea that government is always subject to, never above, the law.

Even more directly, the ancient Romans occupied much of England from A.D. 43 to 410. They left behind a legacy of law, religion, and custom. From this rich political history, the English colonists brought to North America three basic notions that were to loom large in the shaping of government in the United States.

Ordered Government The English colonists saw the need for an orderly regulation of their relationships with one another—that is, a need for government. They created local governments, based on those they had known in England. Many of the offices and units of government they established are with us yet today: the offices of sheriff and justice of the peace, the grand jury, counties, and several others.

Limited Government The colonists also brought with them the idea that government is restricted in what it may do. This concept is called **limited government**, and it was deeply rooted in English belief and practice by the time the first English ships set sail for America.

The colonists also believed firmly that every individual has certain rights—unalienable rights—that government cannot take away. These concepts had been planted in England centuries earlier and had been developing there for nearly 400 years before **Jamestown** was settled in 1607.

Representative Government The early English settlers carried another important concept across the Atlantic: **representative government**. This idea that government should serve the will of the people had also been developing in England for several centuries. With it had come a growing insistence that the people should have a voice in deciding what government should and should not do. As with the concept of limited government, the idea of "government of, by, and for the people" flourished in America.

? IDENTIFY CENTRAL ISSUES In what way did the local governments established by the English colonists reflect major political ideas and traditions in history?

Influential Documents and Ideas

These basic notions of ordered, limited, and representative government can be traced to ideas that began to emerge hundreds of years before the English reached North America, as well as to several landmark documents in English history.

The Magna Carta A group of determined barons forced **King John** to sign the **Magna Carta**—the Great Charter—at Runnymede in 1215. Weary of John's military campaigns and heavy taxes, the barons who prompted the Magna Carta were seeking protection against heavy-handed and arbitrary acts by the king.

The Magna Carta included guarantees of such fundamental rights as trial by jury and **due process** of law (protection against the arbitrary taking of life, liberty, or property). Those protections against the

Basic Concepts of Government

Ordered	• Government regulates affairs among people. • Government maintains order and predictability.
Limited	• Government is restricted in what it may do. • Every individual has certain rights government cannot take away.
Representative	• Government should serve the will of the people. • People should have a voice in deciding what government can and cannot do.

>> The English settlers brought ideas about government with them to North America. **Analyze Charts** How is representative government practiced in the United States today?

absolute power of the king were originally intended for the privileged classes only. Over time, however, they became the rights of all English people and were incorporated into other documents. The Magna Carta established the critical idea that the monarchy's power was not absolute.

The Petition of Right The Magna Carta was respected by some monarchs and ignored by others for 400 years. Over that period, England's Parliament slowly grew in influence. In 1628, when **Charles I** asked Parliament for more money in taxes, Parliament refused until he agreed to sign the **Petition of Right**.

The Petition of Right limited the king's power in several ways. Most importantly, it demanded that the king no longer imprison or otherwise punish any person but by the lawful judgment of his peers or by the law of the land. The document also insisted that the king may not impose martial law, or military rule, in times of peace, or require homeowners to shelter the king's troops without their consent. The Petition declared that no man should be

> compelled to make or yield any gift, loan, benevolence, tax, or such like charge, without common consent by act of parliament.
>
> —Petition of Right

>> The English Bill of Rights, presented to William and Mary in 1689, is still in force today. A century later, it influenced a similar declaration of rights in the newly formed United States.

Interactive Timeline

The Petition challenged the idea of the divine right of kings, declaring that even a monarch must obey the law of the land.

The English Bill of Rights In 1689, after years of revolt and turmoil, Parliament offered the crown to **William and Mary of Orange**. The events surrounding their ascent to the throne are known as the **Glorious Revolution**. To prevent abuse of power by William and Mary and all future monarchs, Parliament that same year drew up a list of provisions to which William and Mary had to agree.

This document, the **English Bill of Rights**, prohibited a standing army in peacetime, except with the consent of Parliament, and required that all parliamentary elections be free. In addition, the document declared

> that the pretended power of suspending the laws, or the execution of laws, by regal authority, without consent of Parliament is illegal . . . that levying money for or to the use of the Crown . . . without grant of Parliament . . . is illegal . . . that it is the right of the subjects to petition the king . . . and that prosecutions for such petitioning are illegal . . .
>
> —English Bill of Rights

The English Bill of Rights also included such guarantees as the right to a fair trial, as well as freedom from excessive bail and from cruel and unusual punishment.

Our nation has built upon, changed, and added to those ideas and institutions that settlers brought here from England. Still, much in American government and politics today bears the stamp of those early English ideas. Surely, this is not so strange when you recall that the colonial period of American history lasted for some 170 years and that the United States has existed as an independent nation for only a slightly longer period.

? DESCRIBE Explain the ways in which the English Bill of Rights limited the power of the monarch.

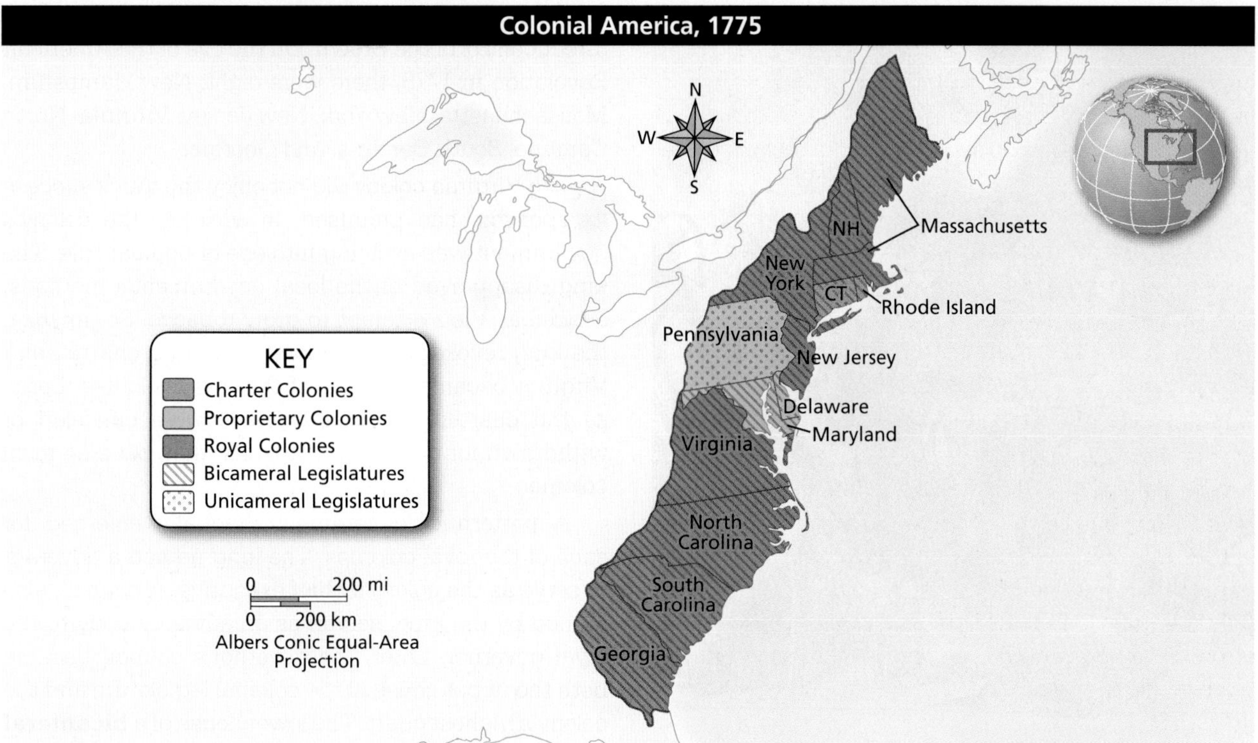

>> Despite the varying government systems of the colonies, they were all influenced by their English roots. **Analyze Maps** How were the legislatures of the proprietary colonies structured?

Three Types of Colonies

England's colonies in North America have been described as "schools of government," because they were the settings in which Americans first began to learn the difficult art of government. Later, the lessons learned by the colonists would help inform the development of the government of the new United States.

The English and other Europeans did not introduce the idea of government to the Americas, however. Several Native American societies already had developed complex systems. For example, five Native American groups in what is now New York State—the Seneca, Cayuga, Oneida, Onondaga, and Mohawk—formed a confederation known as the Iroquois League. The League was originally created to end conflicts among the tribes. It proved so successful as a form of government that it lasted for some 200 years.

Thirteen of England's North American colonies would eventually break away from Great Britain and the other colonies. These 13 were established, separately, over a span of some 125 years. During that long period, outlying trading posts and isolated farm settlements developed into organized communities. The first of these colonies, Virginia, was founded with the first permanent English settlement in North America at Jamestown in 1607. Georgia was the last to be formed, with the settlement of Savannah in 1733.

Each of the colonies was born out of a particular set of circumstances. Virginia was originally organized as a commercial venture. Its first colonists were employees of the Virginia Company of London (also called the London Company), a private trading corporation. Massachusetts was first settled by people who came to North America in search of greater personal and religious freedom. **King George II** granted Georgia to 21 trustees, who governed the colony.

But the differences among the colonies are of little importance. Of much greater significance is the fact that all of them were shaped by their English origins. The many similarities among these colonies far outweighed their differences.

Each colony was established on the basis of a **charter**, a written grant of authority from the king. This grant gave colonists or companies a grant of land and some governing rights, while the Crown retained a certain amount of power over a colony. Over time, these instruments of government led to the development of three different types of colonies: royal, proprietary, and charter.

>> In 1619, Virginia's colonial legislature became the first representative body to meet in the North American English colonies. Its lower house was called the House of Burgesses.

>> After receiving a charter from Charles II, William Penn (right) came to North America in 1682 and established the Pennsylvania colony as a haven for Quakers and other religious minorities.

Royal Colonies The royal colonies were subject to the direct control of the Crown. On the eve of the American Revolution in 1775, there were eight: New Hampshire, Massachusetts, New York, New Jersey, Virginia, North Carolina, South Carolina, and Georgia.

The Virginia colony did not enjoy the quick success its sponsors had promised. In addition, the colony's government was evolving into one of popular rule. The king disapproved of the local government's methods, as well as their attempt to grow tobacco. So, in 1624, the king revoked the London Company's charter, and Virginia became the first of the royal colonies. Later, as the charters of other colonies were canceled or withdrawn for a variety of reasons, they became royal colonies.

A pattern of government gradually emerged for each of the royal colonies. The king named a governor to serve as the colony's chief executive. A council, also named by the king, served as an advisory body to the royal governor. Later, the governor's council became both the upper house of the colonial legislature and the colony's highest court. The lower house of a **bicameral** (two-house) legislature was elected by those property owners qualified to vote. It owed much of its influence to the fact that it shared with the governor and his council the power of the purse—the power to tax and spend. The governor, advised by the council, appointed judges for the colony's courts.

The laws passed by the legislatures in the royal colonies had to be approved by the governor and the Crown. Royal governors often ruled with a stern hand, following instructions from London. Much of the resentment that finally flared into revolution was fanned by their actions.

The Proprietary Colonies By 1775, there were three **proprietary** colonies: Maryland, Pennsylvania, and Delaware. These colonies were organized by a proprietor, a person to whom the king had made a grant of land. By charter, that land could be settled and governed much as the proprietor chose. In 1632, the king granted Maryland to **George Calvert, Lord Baltimore**, which was intended as a haven for Catholics. In 1681, Pennsylvania was granted to **William Penn**. In 1682, Penn also acquired Delaware.

The governments of these three colonies were much like those in the royal colonies. The governor, however, was appointed by the proprietor. In Maryland and Delaware, the legislatures were bicameral. In Pennsylvania, the legislature was a **unicameral** body. The Frame of Government, a constitution that William Penn drew up for that colony in 1682, was, for its time, exceedingly democratic. As in the royal colonies, appeals of decisions in the proprietary colonies could be carried to the king in London.

The Charter Colonies The Massachusetts Bay Colony was established as the first charter colony in 1629. Its charter was later revoked, and Massachusetts became a royal colony in 1691.

Connecticut and Rhode Island were charter colonies founded by religious dissidents from Massachusetts. Connecticut was founded in 1633, and granted a charter in 1662. Rhode Island was founded in 1636 and granted a charter in 1663. Both colonies were largely self-governing.

The governors of Connecticut and Rhode Island were elected each year by the white, male property owners in each colony. Although the king's approval was required before the governor could take office, it was not often asked. Laws made by their bicameral legislatures were not subject to the governor's veto, nor was the Crown's approval needed. Judges in the charter colonies were appointed by the legislature, but appeals could be taken from the colonial courts to the king.

The Connecticut and Rhode Island charters were so liberal for their time that, after independence, they were kept with only minor changes as State constitutions until 1818 and 1843, respectively. In fact, many historians say that if Britain had allowed the other colonies the same freedoms and self-government found in the charter colonies, the Revolution might never have occurred.

>> Legend has it that colonists hid Connecticut's royal charter in this oak tree to protect it from confiscation by the English governor general. The tree later became known as the Charter Oak.

? CONNECT In what way did the different types of governments present in the English colonies influence the political ideas and institutions of the United States?

ASSESSMENT

1. **Apply Concepts** How was the concept of representive government reflected in the royal colonies? What aspects of these governments did NOT reflect the concept of representative government?
2. **Cite Evidence** The Petition of Right challenged the traditional idea of the divine right of kings. Give at least one specific example that supports this statement, and explain how its underlying message weakened the divine right theory.
3. **Connect** How did the barons who forced King John to sign the Magna Carta in 1215 have an impact on the governments established in the English colonies founded centuries later?
4. **Compare and Contrast** In what ways were the charter colonies more democratic than either the royal or proprietary colonies?
5. **Draw Conclusions** In the royal colonies, why might the colonists resent the "stern hand" of a royal governor?

>> The Second Continental Congress met just weeks after the battles of Lexington and Concord. One of their first tasks was to appoint George Washington as commander in chief of the new army.

2.2

"We must all hang together, or assuredly we shall all hang separately." Benjamin Franklin is said to have spoken these words on July 4, 1776, as he and the other members of the Second Continental Congress approved the Declaration of Independence. Those who heard him may have chuckled, but they also may have felt a shiver, for Franklin's humor carried a deadly serious message. In this section, you will follow the events that led to the momentous decision to break with Great Britain. You will also consider the new State governments that were established with the coming of independence.

Interactive Flipped Video

>> Objectives

Explain how Britain's colonial policies contributed to the growth of self-government in the colonies.

Identify the major steps that led to growing feelings of colonial unity.

Consider the ways the colonists organized to protest British policies, and the contributions of significant individuals, including Thomas Jefferson, Samuel Adams, John Adams, Roger Sherman, John Jay, and George Washington.

Examine the debates and compromises that impacted the creation of the Declaration of Independence.

Understand the major ideas of the Declaration of Independence, including unalienable rights, the social contract theory, and the right of resistance to illegitimate government.

>> Key Terms

Albany Plan of Union
Benjamin Franklin
popular sovereignty
duty
John Jay
John Adams
Samuel Adams
Thomas Jefferson
George Washington
Roger Sherman
John Locke
James Wilson
confederation
delegates
duty

Independence

British Colonial Policies

Much of British political history can be told in terms of the century-long struggle for supremacy between the monarch and Parliament. That conflict was largely settled by England's Glorious Revolution of 1688, but it did continue through the American colonial period and into the nineteenth century.

In the midst of this struggle, Parliament paid little attention to the American colonies until late in the colonial period. Instead, they were separately controlled under the king, largely through the Privy Council and the Board of Trade in London. Although Parliament did become increasingly interested in matters of trade, it often left administrative matters to the Crown.

Over the century and a half that followed the first settlement at Jamestown, the colonies developed within that framework of royal control. In theory, they were governed from London. But London was more than 3,000 miles away, and it took nearly two months to sail that distance. The colonists became used to a large measure of self-government.

Each colonial legislature began to assume broad lawmaking powers. Many found the power of the purse to be an effective way to circumvent the king's appointed officers. They often bent a royal governor to their will by not voting the money for his salary until he came to terms with them. As one member of New Jersey's assembly put it: "Let us keep the dogges poore, and we'll make them do as we please."

By the mid-1700s, the relationship between Britain and the colonies had become, in fact if not in form, federal. This meant that the central government in London was responsible for colonial defense and for foreign affairs. It also provided a uniform system of money and credit and a common market for colonial trade. Beyond that, the colonies were allowed a fairly wide amount of self-rule. Little was taken from them in direct taxes to pay for the central government. The few regulations set by Parliament, mostly about trade, were largely ignored.

Shortly after George III came to the throne in 1760, however, Britain began to deal more firmly with its colonies. New taxes were levied to help pay the heavy costs incurred by the British during the French and Indian War (1754–1763). Since the war had been fought to protect the colonies, Parliament and King George III reasoned that the colonists should have to pay a share of those costs. In addition to the new taxes, restrictive trading acts were expanded and enforced.

Many colonists took strong exception to those policies. They objected to taxes imposed on them from afar. Because the colonies had no representatives in Parliament, they claimed such taxes amounted to "taxation without representation." They saw little need for the costly presence of British troops on North American soil, since the French had been defeated. Yet at the same time, the colonists still considered themselves British subjects loyal to the Crown.

The king's ministers were poorly informed and stubborn. They pushed ahead with their policies, despite the resentments they stirred in America. Within a few years, the colonists faced a fateful choice: submit or revolt.

? **DEFINE** What does the term *taxation without representation* mean?

Growing Colonial Unity

A decision to revolt was not one to be taken lightly—or alone. The colonies would need to learn to work together if they wanted to succeed. Indeed, long before the 1770s, several attempts had been made to promote cooperation among the colonies.

Early Attempts In 1643, the Massachusetts Bay, Plymouth, New Haven, and Connecticut settlements formed the New England **Confederation**, a "league of friendship" for defense against Native American tribes. As the danger passed and frictions among the settlements grew, the confederation lost importance and finally dissolved in 1684.

In 1696, William Penn offered an elaborate plan for intercolonial cooperation, largely in trade, defense, and

British Colonial Policies, 1761–1774

YEAR	ACT
1761	**Writs of Assistance** allowed British officials to search homes and businesses for smuggled goods.
1763	**Proclamation of 1763** restricted white settlers from land west of Appalachian mountains and required a license for trade with Native Americans.
1764	**Sugar Act** required and heavily enforced taxes on sugar and other goods imported into America.
1765	**Stamp Act** taxed printed paper, including legal documents, newspapers, and playing cards.
1767	**Townshend Acts** taxed glass, lead, paint, paper, and tea.
1773	**Tea Act** manipulated the tax on tea to favor the East India Company, giving them a monopoly and undercutting local merchants.
1774	**"Intolerable Acts,"** so named by the colonists, included closing the port of Boston until colonists paid for the tea dumped during the Boston Tea Party, restricting town meetings in Massachusetts, and allowed for British soldiers to be housed in private homes.

>> During the latter 1700s, the British began to implement new policies in its North American colonies. **Analyze Charts** Who benefited from these British policies?

>> Members of a New England Confederation militia return home after responding to a false alarm of a Native American attack.

>> This famous political cartoon was published by Benjamin Franklin in 1754. **Analyze Political Cartoons** What does it suggest about the importance of colonial unity?

criminal matters. It received little attention and was very quickly forgotten.

The Albany Plan In 1754, the British Board of Trade called a meeting of seven of the northern colonies at Albany. The main purpose of the meeting was to discuss the problems of colonial trade and the danger of attacks by the French and their Native American allies. Here, Benjamin Franklin offered what came to be known as the **Albany Plan of Union**.

In his plan, Franklin proposed the creation of an annual congress of **delegates** from each of the 13 colonies. That body would have the power to raise military and naval forces, make war and peace with the Native Americans, regulate trade with them, tax, and collect customs **duties**.

Franklin's plan was ahead of its time. It was agreed to by the representatives attending the Albany meeting, but it was turned down by the colonies and by the Crown.

The Stamp Act Congress Britain's harsh tax and trade policies fanned resentment in the colonies. Parliament had passed a number of new laws, among them the Stamp Act of 1765. That law required the use of tax stamps on all legal documents, on certain business agreements, and on newspapers.

The new taxes were widely denounced, in part because the rates were perceived as severe, but largely because they amounted to "taxation without representation." In October of 1765, nine colonies—all except Georgia, New Hampshire, North Carolina, and Virginia—sent delegates to a meeting in New York, the Stamp Act Congress. There, they prepared a strong protest, called the Declaration of Rights and Grievances, against the new British policies and sent it to the king. The Stamp Act Congress marked the first time a significant number of the colonies had joined to oppose the British government.

Parliament repealed the Stamp Act, but new laws and policies tied the colonies more closely to London. Colonists showed their anger by completely evading the laws. Mob violence erupted at several ports, and many colonists supported a boycott of English goods. On March 5, 1770, British troops in Boston fired on a jeering crowd, killing five, in what came to be known as the Boston Massacre.

Organized resistance was carried on through Committees of Correspondence, which had grown out of a group formed by political leader **Samuel Adams** in Boston in 1772. Those committees soon spread throughout the colonies, providing a network for cooperation and the exchange of information among the patriots.

Protests multiplied. The Boston Tea Party took place on December 16, 1773. A group of men, disguised as Native Americans, boarded three tea ships in Boston Harbor. They broke open the chests and dumped the ship's cargo into the sea to protest British control of the tea trade.

SEQUENCE What did the Stamp Act Congress accomplish? In what way did it mark a turning point in colonial-British relations?

The First Continental Congress

In the spring of 1774, Parliament passed yet another set of laws, this time to punish the colonists for the troubles in Boston and elsewhere. These new laws, denounced in America as the Intolerable Acts, prompted widespread calls for a meeting of the colonies.

Delegates from every colony except Georgia met in Philadelphia on September 5, 1774. Many of the ablest men of the day were there: Samuel Adams of Massachusetts; **Roger Sherman** of Connecticut; Stephen Hopkins of Rhode Island; John Dickinson and Joseph Galloway of Pennsylvania; **John Jay** and Philip Livingston of New York; and John Rutledge of South Carolina.

Virginia sent **George Washington**, Richard Henry Lee, and Patrick Henry. At the time, Washington, a former colonel in the French and Indian War, was serving as a Virginia legislator. He had voted against British policies, defied royal orders for the legislature to stop meeting, and helped organize a boycott of British trade in Virginia.

John Adams, a rising lawyer in Boston, was also present. Adams had defended the British officers accused of murder in the Boston Massacre, despite his opposition to British colonial policies. By the time of the First Continental Congress, he had become a staunch supporter of independence as well as a brilliant political analyst.

Lawyer **James Wilson** was one of Pennsylvania's delegates. His essay, *Considerations on the Nature and Extent of the Legislative Authority of the British Parliament*, circulated among the other delegates. In it, Wilson proposed the idea that the British government had no authority to govern the colonies.

For nearly two months, these and other members of that First Continental Congress discussed the worsening situation and debated plans for action. Most of the delegates, many of whom would later be considered Founding Fathers of the United States, were opposed to independence. There was still great hope that a compromise could be reached. To this end, the delegates sent a Declaration of Rights, protesting Britain's colonial policies, to King George III. In it, they wrote:

>> The 340 chests of tea destroyed during the Boston Tea Party would be worth about $1.7 million today. The colonists took great care, however, not to harm the crew or damage other property.

Interactive Timeline

> Resolved, . . . That our ancestors, who first settled these colonies, were at the time of their emigration from the mother country, entitled to all the rights, liberties, and immunities of free and natural-born subjects, within the realm of England.
>
> Resolved, . . . That by such emigration they by no means forfeited, surrendered, or lost any of those rights. . . .
>
> —The Declaration of Rights and Grievances, 1774

The term "natural-born subjects" relates to the ideas of English philosopher Thomas Hobbes (1588–1679). Hobbes wrote that, according to the laws of nature, humans live freely and without authority, leaving weak people vulnerable to the aggression of others. They voluntarily create governments to promote their safety and well-being.

The delegates also urged the colonies to refuse all trade with England until the hated taxes and trade regulations were repealed. Finally, the delegates called for the creation of local committees to enforce that boycott.

The meeting adjourned on October 26, 1774, with a call for a second congress to be convened the following May. Over the next several months, all 13 colonial legislatures gave their support to the actions of the First Continental Congress.

? GENERATE EXPLANATIONS Why do you think the delegates to the First Continental Congress believed that refusing to buy British goods would help their cause?

The Second Continental Congress

During the fall and winter of 1774–1775, the British government continued to refuse to compromise, let alone reverse, its colonial policies. It reacted to the Declaration of Rights as it had to other expressions of colonial discontent—with even stricter and more repressive measures.

The Second Continental Congress met in Philadelphia on May 10, 1775. By then, the Revolution had begun. The "shot heard 'round the world" had been fired. The battles of Lexington and Concord had been fought three weeks earlier, on April 19. With this bloodshed, many delegates believed that compromise with Great Britain was no longer possible.

The Nation's Founding Fathers Each of the 13 colonies sent representatives to the Congress. Most of those who had attended the First Continental Congress were again present. Notable among the newcomers were Benjamin Franklin of Pennsylvania and John Hancock of Massachusetts.

Hancock was chosen president of the Congress. In just over a month, a continental army was created, and George Washington appointed its commander-in-chief. Thirty-two-year-old **Thomas Jefferson** joined the Virginia delegation in June 1775. New York lawyer John Jay favored a course of moderation, and drafted an early version of an Olive Branch petition as a last attempt to make peace with Great Britain. John Dickinson of Pennsylvania wrote the final draft, which Jay signed. John Hancock also signed it, as did John Adams, Roger Sherman, Benjamin Franklin, and Thomas Jefferson. When King George III rejected the petition, the delegates began discussing other strategies for responding to England.

Key Delegates to Second Continental Congress, 1775

COLONY	DELEGATES	KEY CONTRIBUTIONS
Massachusetts	**John Hancock** **John Adams**	President of the Continental Congress Nominated George Washington to command Continental Army; served on committee that drafted the Declaration of Independence
Connecticut	**Roger Sherman**	Served on the committee that drafted the Declaration of Independence
New York	**John Jay**	Favored a course of moderation toward Great Britain; helped draft the Olive Branch petition
Virginia	**Thomas Jefferson** **Richard Henry Lee**	Primary author of the Declaration of Independence Made motion calling for independence
Pennsylvania	**James Wilson** **Benjamin Franklin**	Argued passionately for independence Served on the committee that drafted the Declaration of Independence

>> This chart shows just a few of the key delegates to the Second Continental Congress. **Analyze Charts** What qualifications did these men have to suit them to the task of leading the colonies?

First Government The Second Continental Congress became, by force of circumstance, the nation's first national government. However, it rested on no constitutional base. It was condemned by the British as an unlawful assembly and a den of traitors. But it was supported by the force of public opinion and practical necessity.

The Second Continental Congress served as the first government of the United States for five fateful years, from the formal adoption of the Declaration of Independence in July 1776 until the Articles of Confederation went into effect on March 1, 1781. During that time, the Second Continental Congress fought a war, raised armies and a navy, borrowed funds, bought supplies, created a money system, made treaties with foreign powers, and did other things that any government would have had to do in those circumstances.

The unicameral Congress had both legislative and executive powers. In legislative matters, each colony—later, State—had one vote. Executive functions were handled by committees of delegates.

? ANALYZE Why did the British call the Second Continental Congress "a den of traitors"?

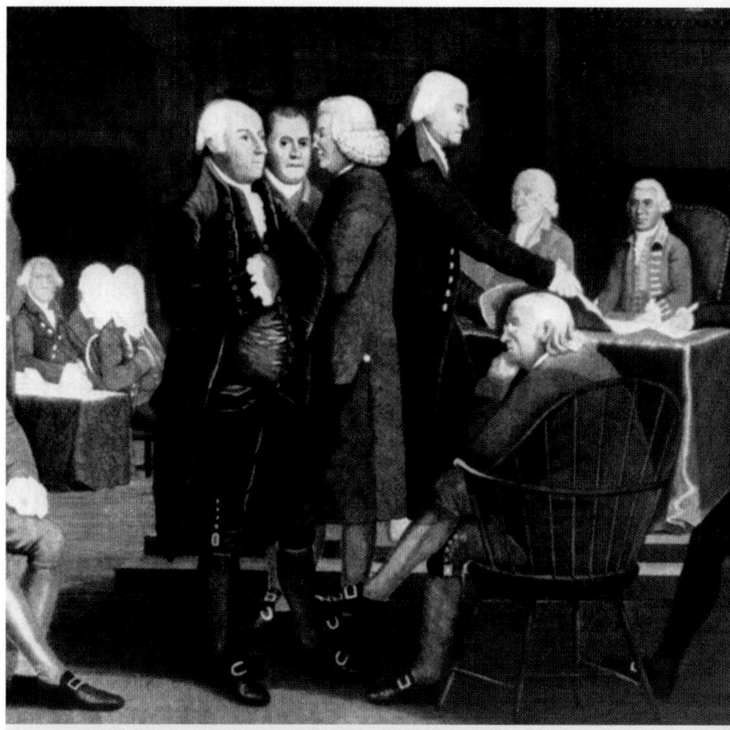

>> Congressional delegates thought the move for independence should be unanimous, so they delayed the final vote until 12 colonial delegations favored it. New York abstained.

The Declaration of Independence

Slightly more than a year after the Revolution began, Virginia's Richard Henry Lee proposed to the Congress:

> Resolved, That these United Colonies are, and of right ought to be, free and independent States, that they are absolved from all allegiance to the British Crown, and that all political connection between them and the State of Great Britain is, and ought to be, totally dissolved.
>
> —Resolution of June 7, 1776

As debate on Lee's resolution began, Congress named a committee of five—Benjamin Franklin, John Adams, Roger Sherman, Robert Livingston, and Thomas Jefferson—to prepare a proclamation of independence. Their momentous product, the Declaration of Independence, was very largely the work of Jefferson.

Jefferson's Work Thomas Jefferson was a young delegate, well-respected though shy. As a lawyer, he had gained early notoriety through an essay he wrote in 1774 in which he argued for colonial independence. As a member of the Second Continental Congress, he spoke rarely but nonetheless impressed his colleagues with his passionate belief in the cause of independence. The document he crafted drew from the political philosophies of Enlightenment thinker **John Locke**, in particular the ideas of natural rights and the social contract theory.

Locke believed that people have natural rights—rights that belong to them simply because they are human, not because kings or governments have granted them these rights. He also put forward his own view of the social contract theory. According to Locke, people form governments to protect their natural rights, but they do not surrender control over their government. If a government fails to act in the best interests of the people, the people have the right to revolt and replace that government with a new one.

Debates and Compromises As Thomas Jefferson worked, the delegates continued to debate Lee's resolution. Many of them had serious doubts about the wisdom of a complete separation from England. Could the colonies survive on their own? Others had grave reservations about remaining British subjects. They believed that the British government clearly did not have the best interests of the colonies at heart. On July 2, the delegates finally reached a decision. They agreed to Lee's resolution and quickly took up consideration of Jefferson's work.

Spirited debate again ensued. Should Jefferson's lines criticizing the English people remain? Many delegates feared that such language would offend those they still considered friends, and it was removed from the first draft. So too were the lines condemning the slave trade, in deference to the southern States. The debates continued for more than two days, but on July 4, 1776, in one of the most historic votes of all time, the Congress adopted the revised Declaration of Independence.

At its heart, the Declaration proclaims:

> We hold these truths to be self-evident, that all men are created equal, that they are endowed by their Creator with certain unalienable Rights, that among these are Life, Liberty and the pursuit of Happiness. That to secure these rights, Governments are instituted among Men, deriving their just powers from the consent of the governed; That whenever any Form of Government becomes destructive of these ends it is the Right of the People to alter or to abolish it, and to institute new Government, laying its foundations on such principles and organizing its powers in such form, as to them shall seem most likely to effect their Safety and Happiness.
>
> —The Unanimous Declaration of the Thirteen United States of America

>> The Second Continental Congress adopted the Declaration of Independence on July 4, 1776, but the document wasn't actually signed until the first week of August.

Revolutionary Ideas With the adoption of the Declaration of Independence, the United States was born. The 13 colonies became free and independent States, and the American Revolution became more than a war for independence. Indeed, the Declaration ushered in groundbreaking notions of human rights and limited government.

No political system had ever been founded on the notion that the people should rule instead of being ruled. None had ever rested on the idea that every person is important as an individual, "created equal," and endowed with "certain unalienable rights," meaning rights that the government could not take away.

The Declaration was also revolutionary because it was founded on the concept of "the consent of the governed," rather than divine right or tradition as the basis for the exercise of power. Central to this concept was the notion that "the Laws of nature and of nature's God" entitle people to certain rights. Governments exist only to serve the will of the people.

Almost immediately, these ideas created a new *national* identity that set the United States apart from all other nations and united Americans behind a core set of beliefs. As the ideals of the Declaration were put into practice, they also contributed to creating a *federal* identity, in which certain rights were protected by the National Government and others by State governments.

It would be State governments that would protect the public safety, provide aid during times of natural disasters, and set up institutions such as hospitals and schools. All these ideals are embodied in the United States today in countless ways, including representative

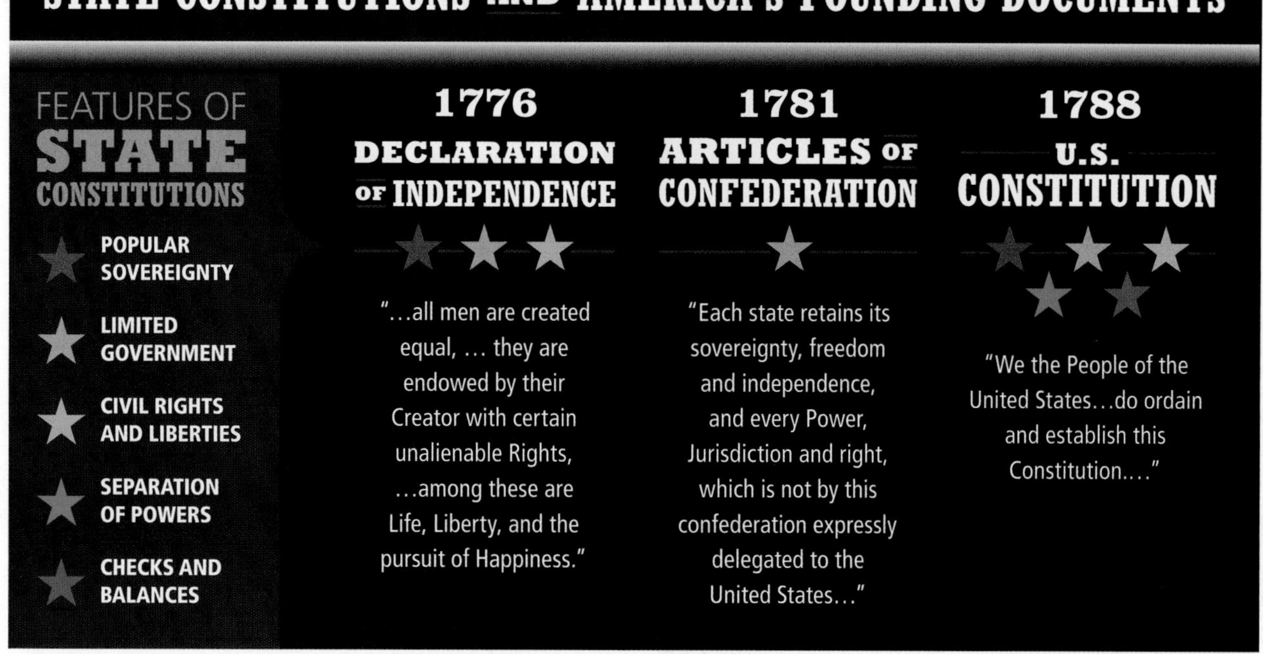

STATE CONSTITUTIONS AND AMERICA'S FOUNDING DOCUMENTS
FEATURES OF STATE CONSTITUTIONS
POPULAR SOVEREIGNTY
LIMITED GOVERNMENT
CIVIL RIGHTS AND LIBERTIES
SEPARATION OF POWERS
CHECKS AND BALANCES
1776 DECLARATION OF INDEPENDENCE
"...all men are created equal, ... they are endowed by their Creator with certain unalienable Rights, ...among these are Life, Liberty, and the pursuit of Happiness."
1781 ARTICLES OF CONFEDERATION
"Each state retains its sovereignty, freedom and independence, and every Power, Jurisdiction and right, which is not by this confederation expressly delegated to the United States..."
1788 U.S. CONSTITUTION
"We the People of the United States...do ordain and establish this Constitution...."

>> The initial State constitutions had several features in common with America's founding documents. **Analyze Charts** What features were most common?

government, federalism, popular sovereignty, and limited government.

SUMMARIZE. What gave the signers of the Declaration of Independence the authority to dissolve their status as a British colony and create a new government?

The First State Constitutions

In January 1776, New Hampshire adopted a constitution to replace its royal charter. Less than three months later, South Carolina followed suit. Then, on May 10, nearly two months before the adoption of the Declaration of Independence, the Congress urged each of the colonies to adopt "such governments as shall, in the opinion of the representatives of the people, best conduce to the happiness and safety of their constituents."

Drafting State Constitutions In 1776 and 1777, most of the States adopted written constitutions—bodies of fundamental laws setting out the principles, structures, and processes of their governments. Assemblies or conventions were commonly used to draft and then adopt these new documents.

Massachusetts set a lasting example in the constitution-making process. There, a popularly elected convention submitted its work to the voters for ratification. The Massachusetts constitution of 1780, authored by John Adams, is the oldest of the present-day State constitutions. It also is the oldest written constitution in force in the world today. John Jay helped draft New York's State constitution.

Common Features The first State constitutions differed, sometimes widely, in their details. Yet they were on the whole more alike than not. The most common features were the principles of **popular sovereignty**, limited government, civil rights and liberties, separation of powers, and checks and balances. Most importantly, the basic principles set out in the earliest of those documents were, within a very few years, to have a marked impact on the drafting of the Constitution of the United States.

Popular Sovereignty. Everywhere, the people were recognized as the only source of governmental authority. In the new United States, government could be conducted only with the consent of the governed.

Limited Government. The new State governments could exercise only those powers granted to them by the people through the constitution. The powers that were given were hedged with many restrictions to protect the rights of individual citizens.

>> In order to vote in the United States following the Revolutionary War, a person had to be a white male who owned property.

Civil Rights and Liberties. In every State, it was made clear that the sovereign people held certain rights that government must at all times respect. Seven of the new documents began with a bill of rights, setting out the "unalienable rights" held by the people.

Separation of Powers, Checks and Balances. The powers granted to the new State governments were divided among three distinct branches: executive, legislative, and judicial. Each branch was given powers with which to check, or restrain the actions of, the other branches of the government.

Beyond those basics, the new State constitutions were rather brief documents. They were, for the most part, declarations of principle and statements of limitation on governmental power. Memories of the royal governors were fresh, and State governors were given little real power. Most of the authority that was granted to government was placed in the legislature. Elective terms of office were made purposely short, seldom more than one or two years. The right to vote was limited to those adult white males who could meet rigid qualifications, including property ownership.

? GENERATE EXPLANATIONS Why were elective terms of office made purposely short, seldom more than one or two years?

ASSESSMENT

1. **Analyze Information** How did "taxation without representation" conflict with John Locke's social contract idea of government?
2. **Identify Central Ideas** Who was Thomas Jefferson, and what was his contribution toward the development of the United States government?
3. **Sequence Events** The Declaration of Independence was issued *after* the Revolutionary War had already started. What was the focus of debate about the war at the Second Continental Congress?
4. **Infer** The ideas in the Declaration of Independence created a new national identity that united colonists behind a core set of beliefs and set the new nation apart from other countries throughout the world. Why else was it significant that the ideas in the Declaration of Independence created a new national identity?
5. **Draw Conclusions** How was the Revolutionary War much more than just a war for independence?

2.3 The First and Second Continental Congresses rested on no legal base. They were called in haste to meet an emergency, and they were intended to be temporary. Something more regular and permanent was clearly needed. In this reading, you will look at the first attempt to establish a lasting government for the new nation.

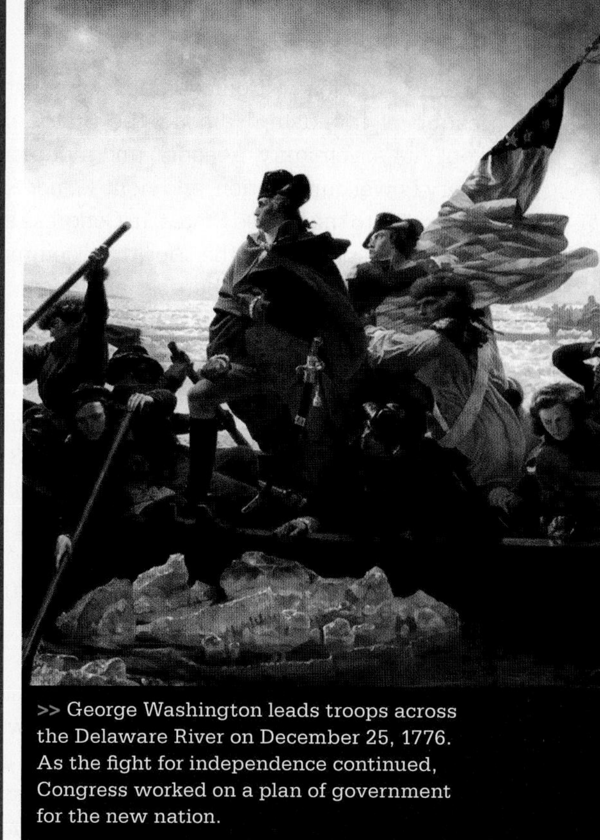

>> George Washington leads troops across the Delaware River on December 25, 1776. As the fight for independence continued, Congress worked on a plan of government for the new nation.

Interactive Flipped Video

First Steps

>> **Objectives**

Describe the debates that impacted the creation of the Articles of Confederation, the structure of the government set up under the Articles, and how that government was influenced by ideas, people, and historical documents.

Explain why the weaknesses of the Articles led to a critical period for the country in the 1780s.

Describe how a growing need for a stronger national government led to plans for a Constitutional Convention.

>> **Key Terms**

Articles of Confederation
ratification
full faith and credit
Shays' Rebellion
Daniel Shays
Alexander Hamilton
James Madison

The Articles of Confederation

Richard Henry Lee's resolution that led to the Declaration of Independence also called on the Second Continental Congress to propose "a plan of confederation" to the States. Off and on, for 17 months, Congress debated the best organization for the new government.

One widely discussed issue centered around the amount of money each State should pay into a common treasury. The northern States proposed that the sum should be in proportion to a State's total population, which they said should include enslaved people but not untaxed Native Americans. The southern States objected to this proposal because they considered enslaved people to be "property, not persons," and they were attempting to limit their required contribution to the treasury. After much debate, Congress decided to base contributions not on population, but instead on the value of land within each State.

A second area of debate involved the voting power of the States in Congress. The original plan provided that each State would have one vote. Some delegates proposed instead that on financial questions, each State should have votes in proportion to its population. This amendment eventually failed, and the original article was accepted. Finally, on November 15, 1777, after various other issues were resolved, the **Articles of Confederation** were approved at last.

The Articles of Confederation established "a firm league of friendship" among the States. Each State kept "its sovereignty, freedom, and independence, and every Power, jurisdiction, and right . . . not . . . expressly delegated to the United States, in Congress assembled." The States came together "for their common defense, the security of their Liberties, and their mutual and general welfare. . . ." In effect, the Articles created a structure that more closely resembled an alliance of independent states than a government "of the people."

The Articles did not go into effect immediately, however. The **ratification** of each of the 13 States was needed first. Eleven States approved the document within a year. Delaware added its approval in February 1779. Maryland did not ratify until March 1, 1781. The Second Continental Congress declared the Articles effective on that date.

A Simple Structure The government set up by the Articles was quite simple. A Congress was the sole body created. It was unicameral, made up of delegates chosen yearly by the States in whatever way their legislatures might direct. Each State had only one vote in the Congress, regardless of its population or wealth.

The Articles established no executive or judicial branch. These functions were to be handled by committees of the Congress. Each year, the Congress would choose one of its members as its president. That person would be its presiding officer, but not the President of the United States. Civil officers such as postmasters were to be appointed by the Congress.

Congressional Powers Several important powers were given to the Congress. It could make war and peace, send and receive ambassadors, make treaties, borrow money, set up a money system, establish post offices, build a navy, raise an army by asking the States for troops, fix uniform standards of weights and measures, and settle disputes among the States.

The States Under the Articles By agreeing to the Articles, the States pledged to obey both the Articles and acts of the Congress. They promised to provide the funds and troops requested by Congress; treat citizens of other States fairly and equally within their own borders; and give **full faith and credit** to the public acts, records, and judicial proceedings of every other State. In addition, the States agreed to surrender fugitives from justice to one another, submit their disputes to Congress for settlement, and allow open travel and trade among the States.

Beyond those few obligations, the States retained those powers not explicitly given to the Congress. They, not the Congress, were primarily responsible for protecting life and property, and for promoting "the safety and happiness of the people."

Major Weaknesses Surface The powers of the Congress appear, at first glance, to have been considerable. Several important powers were missing, however. Their omission, together with other weaknesses, soon proved the Articles inadequate for the needs of the time.

The Congress did not have the power to tax. It could raise money only by borrowing and by asking the States for funds. Borrowing was, at best, a poor source. The Second Continental Congress had borrowed heavily to support the Revolution, and many of those debts had not been paid. And, while the Articles remained in force, not one State came close to meeting the financial requests made by the Congress.

Nor did the Congress have the power to regulate trade among the States. This lack of a central mechanism to regulate the young nation's growing commerce was one of the major factors that soon led to the adoption of the Constitution.

The Congress was further limited by a lack of power to make the States obey the Articles of Confederation or the laws it made. Congress could exercise the powers it did have only with the consent of 9 of the 13 State

ARTICLES
OF
CONFEDERATION
AND
PERPETUAL UNION
BETWEEN THE
STATES
OF
NEW-HAMPSHIRE, MASSACHUSETTS-BAY, RHODE-ISLAND AND PROVIDENCE PLANTATIONS, CONNECTICUT, NEW-YORK, NEW-JERSEY, PENNSYLVANIA, DELAWARE, MARYLAND, VIRGINIA, NORTH CAROLINA, SOUTH CAROLINA AND GEORGIA.

WILLIAMSBURG:
Printed by J. DIXON & W. HUNTER.
M,DCC,LXXVIII.

>> The Articles of Confederation sought to unify the former colonies, while balancing States' rights and the powers of the federal government.

Interactive Chart

delegations. Finally, the Articles themselves could be changed only with the consent of all 13 of the State legislatures.

SUMMARIZE What two main issues were debated that impacted the creation of the Articles of Confederation?

>> Many State legislatures forgave debt and printed more money during the 1780s, but not Massachusetts. Shays' Rebellion was a desperate protest against high taxes and unresponsive government.

A Time of Troubles, the 1780s

The long Revolutionary War finally ended on October 19, 1781. America's victory was confirmed by the signing of the Treaty of Paris in 1783. Peace, however, brought the new nation's economic and political weaknesses into sharp focus.

Problems, made even more difficult by the weaknesses of the Articles, soon surfaced. With a central government unable to act, the States bickered among themselves. They grew increasingly jealous and suspicious of one another. They often refused to support the new central government, financially and in almost every other way. Several of them made agreements with foreign governments without the approval of the Congress, even though that was forbidden by the Articles. Most organized their own military forces. George Washington complained, ". . . we are one nation today and 13 tomorrow. Who will treat with us on such terms?"

The States taxed one another's goods and even banned some trade. They printed their own money, often with little backing. Economic chaos spread throughout the colonies as prices soared and sound credit vanished. Debts, public and private, went unpaid. Violence broke out in a number of places.

The most spectacular of these events played out in western Massachusetts in a series of incidents that came to be known as **Shays' Rebellion**. As economic conditions worsened there, property holders, many of them small farmers, began to lose their land and possessions for lack of payment on taxes and other debts.

In the fall of 1786, **Daniel Shays**, who had served as an officer in the War for Independence, led an armed uprising that forced several State judges to close their courts. Early the next year, Shays mounted an unsuccessful attack on the federal arsenal at Springfield. State forces finally moved to quiet the rebellion and Shays fled to Vermont. In response to

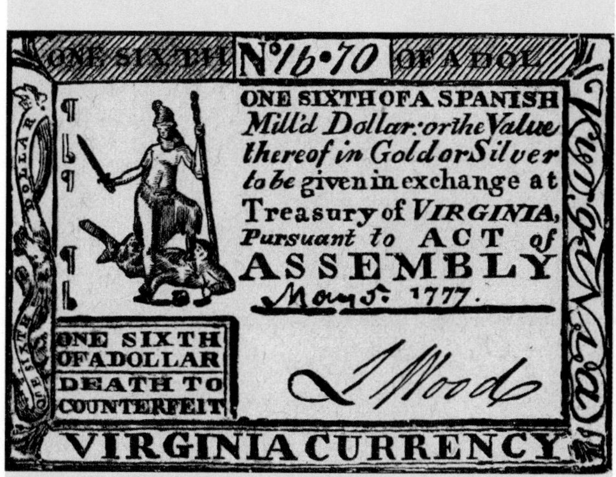

>> States often printed their own money, which was not backed by silver or gold and did not hold its value. Banks and merchants often refused to accept this money, leading to economic chaos.

the violence, the Massachusetts legislature eventually passed laws to ease the burden of debtors.

? INTERPRET What did George Washington mean when he said ". . . we are one nation today and 13 tomorrow"?

A Demand for Stronger Government

The Articles had created a government unable to deal with the nation's troubles. Inevitably, demand grew for a stronger, more effective national government. Those who were most threatened by economic and political instability—large property owners, merchants, traders, and other creditors—soon took the lead in efforts to that end. The movement for change began to take concrete form in 1785.

First Steps Toward Change Maryland and Virginia, plagued by bitter trade disputes, took the first step in the movement for change. Ignoring the Congress, the two States agreed to a conference to resolve conflicts over commerce and navigation on the Potomac River and Chesapeake Bay.

>> Representatives from Virginia and Maryland moved their discussions to Mount Vernon (shown here) in 1785. This Mount Vernon Conference began a new era of interstate cooperation.

Representatives from the two States met at Alexandria, Virginia, in March 1785. At George Washington's invitation, they moved their sessions to his home at nearby Mount Vernon. Their negotiations proved so successful that on January 21, 1786, the Virginia General Assembly called for "a joint meeting of [all of] the States to consider and recommend a federal plan for regulating commerce."

A Call for Action That joint meeting opened at Annapolis, Maryland, on September 11, 1786. Turnout was poor, with representatives from only 5 of the 13 States attending: New York, New Jersey, Pennsylvania, Delaware, and Virginia. Although New Hampshire, Massachusetts, Rhode Island, and North Carolina had appointed delegates, none attended the Annapolis meeting. Disappointed but still hopeful, **Alexander Hamilton**, a delegate from New York, and Virginia's **James Madison** persuaded the gathering to call for yet another meeting of the States.

By mid-February of 1787, seven of the States had named delegates to the Philadelphia meeting: Delaware, Georgia, New Hampshire, New Jersey, North Carolina, Pennsylvania, and Virginia. On February 21, the Congress, which had been hesitating, also called upon the States to send delegates to Philadelphia

> . . . for the sole and express purpose of revising the Articles of Confederation and reporting to Congress and the several legislatures such alterations and provisions therein as shall when agreed to in Congress and confirmed by the States render the [Articles] adequate to the exigencies of Government and the preservation of the Union.
>
> —The United States in Congress Assembled, February 21, 1787

That Philadelphia meeting became known as the Constitutional Convention. What began as an assembly to revise the existing Articles of Confederation soon evolved into a meeting dedicated to a different purpose—the creation of an entirely new kind of government for the United States of America. This government would derive its power from a constitution.

? DRAW CONCLUSIONS What weakness in the Articles of Confederation led to conflicts regarding trade and navigation between Virginia and Maryland?

ASSESSMENT

1. **Identify Central Issues** Describe the major debates that impacted the creation of the Articles of Confederation.
2. **Make Generalizations** How did the government structure set up under the Articles of Confederation reflect the ideas and experiences of the English colonists who had so recently been embroiled in a fight for independence?
3. **Infer** Why did Congress refrain from including the power to tax in the Articles of Confederation?
4. **Identify Cause and Effect** In what ways was Shays' Rebellion a result of weaknesses in the Articles of Confederation?
5. **Support Ideas with Evidence** When the States ratified the Articles, they agreed to obey the Articles and all acts of Congress. Did the States honor that agreement? Give evidence to support your answer.

>> This painting, *The Signing of the Constitution,* by Howard Chandler Christy, depicts the scene on the day the U.S. Constitution was signed after four long months of debate and compromise.

Interactive Flipped Video

2.4

Picture the scene. It is hot—sweltering, in fact. Yet all of the windows of the State House are closed and shuttered to discourage eavesdroppers. Outside, soldiers keep curious onlookers and others at a distance. Inside, the atmosphere is frequently tense, as fifty or so men exchange sometimes heated views. Indeed, some who are there become so upset that they threaten to leave the hall, and a few actually do so.

>> Objectives

Identify the Framers of the Constitution, the individuals, principals, and ideas that influenced them, how they organized the Constitutional Convention, and their contributions to the creation of the United States Constitution.

Compare and contrast the Virginia and New Jersey plans for the new government.

Examine the convention's major debates and compromises.

Identify the opposing sides in the fight for ratification and describe the major arguments for and against the proposed Constitution.

>> Key Terms

Framers
Virginia Plan
New Jersey Plan
Three-Fifths Compromise
Commerce and Slave Trade Compromise
Federalists
Anti-Federalists
quorum
veto
George Mason
Charles de Montesquieu
Jean Jacques Rousseau
William Blackstone
Connecticut Compromise

Creating and Ratifying the Constitution

The Framers Meet

This was often the scene at the Philadelphia meeting, which finally began on May 25, 1787. Over the long summer months, until mid-September, the Framers of what was to become the Constitution worked to build a new government that could meet the needs of the nation. In this section, you will consider that meeting and its outcome.

The Delegates Many of the men attending the meeting had read the enlightened philosophers of the 17th and 18th centuries. They had studied the writings of John Locke, **Baron de Montesquieu**, **Jean Jacques Rousseau**, and **William Blackstone**. Like these great thinkers, the Framers of the Constitution believed that government should exist only by the consent of the governed. They also subscribed to such Enlightenment ideas as natural rights, the social contract, separation of powers, and checks and balances. It is no surprise, then, that these principles formed the basis of their new plan of government.

Twelve of the thirteen States, all but Rhode Island, sent delegates to Philadelphia. In total, 74 delegates were chosen by the legislatures in those 12 States. For a number of reasons, however, only 55 of them actually attended the convention.

Of that 55, this much can be said: Never, before or since, has so remarkable a group been brought together in this country. Thomas Jefferson, who was not among them, later called the delegates "an assembly of demigods."

A New Generation in American Politics The delegates who attended the Philadelphia Convention, known as the **Framers** of the Constitution, included many outstanding individuals. These were men of wide knowledge and public experience.

Many of the Framers had fought in the Revolution; 46 had been members of the Continental Congress or the Congress of the Confederation, or both. Eight had served in constitutional conventions in their own States, and seven had been State governors. Eight had signed the Declaration of Independence. Thirty-four of the delegates had attended college in a day when there were but a few colleges in the land. Two were to become Presidents of the United States, and one a Vice President. Nineteen later served in the Senate and thirteen in the House of Representatives.

Is it any wonder that the product of such a gathering was described by the English statesman William E. Gladstone, nearly a century later, as "the most wonderful work ever struck off at a given time by the brain and purpose of man"?

Remarkably, the average age of the delegates was only 42, and most of the leaders were in their thirties—James Madison, arguably the principal architect of the Constitution, was 36, Gouverneur Morris was 35, Edmund Randolph was 34, and Alexander Hamilton was 30. At 81, Benjamin Franklin was the oldest, and although his health was failing, he nonetheless managed to attend many of the meetings. George Washington, at 55, was one of the few older members who played a key role at the convention. Jonathan Dayton of New Jersey was, at 26, the youngest delegate.

James Wilson of Pennsylvania was 45 when the convention began. He was one of the most active delegates at the meeting, arguing for a strong central government and other provisions he thought would best guarantee a government by the people.

By and large, the Framers of the Constitution were of a new generation in American politics. Several of the leaders of the Revolutionary period were not in Philadelphia. Patrick Henry said he "smelt a rat" and refused to attend. Samuel Adams, John Hancock, and Richard Henry Lee were not selected as delegates by their States. Thomas Paine was in Paris. So was Thomas Jefferson, as American minister to France.

Selected Framers of the Constitution

VIRGINIA	CONNECTICUT	NEW YORK	VIRGINIA	VIRGINIA
George Washington	**Roger Sherman**	**Alexander Hamilton**	**James Madison**	**George Mason**
• Planter • Commander of the Continental Army • Continental Congress • Presence lent respectability to the Convention	• Merchant • Continental Congress; Confederation Congress • Member of Declaration of Independence and Articles of Confederation committees	• Soldier in the Revolutionary War; lawyer • Continental Congress; Confederation Congress • Favored a strong national government	• Involved in state and local politics • Continental Congress; Confederation Congress • Leading figure in movement to replace Articles of Confederation	• Planter • Author of Virginia's Declaration of Rights • Concerned with the absence of a declaration of rights in the Constitution

>> The Framers of the Constitution were accomplished men who came from different backgrounds. **Analyze Charts** How might their experiences have helped the Framers to create the Constitution?

John Adams was the envoy to England and Holland at the time.

? ASSESS CREDIBILITY Suppose you lived in 1787 and wanted to defend the delegates to the Constitutional Convention in terms of their suitability for the job of drafting a new Constitution. What facts might you use to back up your argument?

The Delegates Adopt Rules of Procedure

The Framers met in the Pennsylvania State House (now Independence Hall), probably in the same room in which the Declaration of Independence had been signed 11 years earlier. Not enough States were represented on the date Congress had set, May 14, to begin the meeting. The delegates who were present met until the 25th, when a **quorum** of the States was finally on hand.

On that date, the delegates unanimously elected George Washington president of the convention. Then, and at the second session on Monday, May 28, they adopted several rules of procedure. A majority of the States would be needed to conduct business. Each State delegation was to have one vote on all matters, and a majority of the votes cast would carry any proposal.

The Framers met on 92 of the 116 days from May 25 through their final meeting on September 17. They did most of their work on the floor of the convention. They handled some matters in committees, but the full body ultimately settled all questions.

Remember, Congress had called the Philadelphia Convention "for the sole and express purpose" of recommending revisions to the Articles of Confederation. However, almost at once the delegates agreed that they were meeting to create an entirely new government for the United States. On May 30 they adopted this proposal:

> Resolved, . . . that a national Government ought to be established consisting of a supreme Legislative, Executive and Judiciary.
>
> —Edmund Randolph, Delegate from Virginia

With this momentous decision, the Framers redefined the purpose of the convention. From that point on, they set about writing a new constitution, intended to replace the Articles of Confederation. (However, much that would go into this new constitution would come directly from the Articles of Confederation.) Their debates were spirited, even bitter. At times the convention seemed near collapse. Once they had passed Randolph's resolution, however, the resolve of most of the delegates never wavered.

>> Independence Hall, often referred to as the birthplace of the United States, was originally home to all three branches of Pennsylvania's colonial government.

? SUMMARIZE How did the goal of the Philadelphia meeting change from the time the meeting was called to the first week of the convention?

Two Plans of Government

Once the Framers resolved to replace the Articles of Confederation, two major plans were offered for the new government, the Virginia Plan and the New Jersey Plan.

The Virginia Plan No State had more to do with the calling of the convention than Virginia. It was not surprising, then, that its delegates should offer the first plan for a new constitution. On May 29, the **Virginia Plan**, largely the work of James Madison, was presented by Edmund Randolph.

The Virginia Plan called for a new government with three separate branches: legislative, executive, and judicial. The legislature—Congress—would be bicameral. Representation in each house was to

HIGHLIGHTS OF THE VIRGINIA PLAN

CREATED A NEW GOVERNMENT WITH THREE SEPARATE BRANCHES: EXECUTIVE, LEGISLATIVE, JUDICIAL

CONGRESS COULD TAKE CONTROL OF INDIVIDUAL STATES IN EXTREME CASES

MEMBERS OF THE LOWER HOUSE WOULD BE ELECTED BY POPULAR VOTE

REPRESENTATION BASED ON POPULATION OR THE AMOUNT OF MONEY EACH STATE GAVE TOWARD THE CENTRAL GOVERNMENT

CONGRESS WOULD BE BICAMERAL

MEMBERS OF THE SENATE WOULD BE CHOSEN BY THE HOUSE FROM A LIST SUGGESTED BY THE STATE LEGISLATURES

A NATIONAL EXECUTIVE AND A NATIONAL JUDICIARY, CHOSEN BY CONGRESS, WOULD HAVE THE POWER TO VETO CONGRESSIONAL ACTS

>> Edmund Randolph proposed the Virginia Plan to the convention, but it was written largely by James Madison. **Analyze Charts** How many branches would the government have under the Virginia Plan?

be based either on each State's population or on the amount of money it gave for the support of the Federal Government. The members of the lower house, the House of Representatives, were to be popularly elected in each State. Those of the upper house, the Senate, were to be chosen by the House from lists of persons nominated by the State legislatures.

Congress was to be given all of the powers it held under the Articles. In addition, it would have the power "to legislate in all cases to which the separate States are incompetent" to act, to veto any State law in conflict with national law, and to use force if necessary to make a State obey national law.

Under the proposed Virginia Plan, Congress would choose a "National Executive" and a "National Judiciary." Together, these two branches would form a "Council of revision." They could **veto** acts passed by Congress, but a veto could be overridden by the two houses. The executive would have "a general authority to execute the National laws." The judiciary would "consist of one or more supreme tribunals [courts], and of inferior tribunals."

The Virginia Plan also provided that all State officers should take an oath to support the Union, and that each State be guaranteed a republican form of government. Under the plan, Congress would have the exclusive power to admit new States to the Union.

The Virginia Plan, then, would create a new constitution by thoroughly revising the Articles. Its goal was the creation of a truly national government with greatly expanded powers and, importantly, the power to enforce its decisions.

The Virginia Plan set the agenda for much of the convention's work. Its major support came from the three most populous States: Virginia, Pennsylvania, and Massachusetts. But some delegates—especially those from New York (then only the fifth most populous State) and the smaller States of Delaware, Maryland, and New Jersey—found it too radical. Soon they developed their counter proposals. On June 15, William Paterson of New Jersey presented the position of the smaller States.

The New Jersey Plan Paterson and his colleagues offered several amendments to the Articles, but not nearly so thorough a revision as that proposed by the Virginia Plan. The **New Jersey Plan** retained the unicameral Congress of the Confederation, with each of the States equally represented. In addition to those powers Congress already had, the plan would add closely limited powers to tax and to regulate trade between the States.

The New Jersey Plan also called for a "federal executive" of more than one person. This plural executive would be chosen by Congress and could be removed by it at the request of a majority of the States' governors. The "federal judiciary" would be composed of a single "supreme Tribunal," appointed by the executive.

Among their several differences, the major point of disagreement between the two plans centered on this question: How should the States be represented in Congress? Would it be on the basis of their populations or financial contributions, as in the Virginia Plan? Or would it be on the basis of State equality, as in the Articles and the New Jersey Plan?

For weeks the delegates returned to this conflict, debating the matter again and again. The lines were sharply drawn. Several delegates on both sides of the issue threatened to withdraw. Finally, the dispute was settled by one of the key compromises the Framers were to make as they built the Constitution.

? COMPARE AND CONTRAST Explain the major difference between the Virginia Plan and the New Jersey Plan.

Debates and Compromises

The disagreement over representation in Congress was critical. The larger States expected to dominate the new government. The smaller States feared that they would not be able to protect their interests. Tempers flared on both sides. The debate became so intense that Benjamin Franklin was moved to suggest that "henceforth prayers imploring the assistance of Heaven . . . be held in this Assembly every morning before we proceed to business."

The Connecticut Compromise The Connecticut delegates—Roger Sherman, Oliver Ellsworth, and William Samuel Johnson—presented their compromise to the convention as a means to end the deadlock between the supporters of the rival New Jersey and Virginia plans. Roger Sherman had been one of the most active members of the Continental Congress and, during the convention, he actively defended the rights of the smaller States. He was also the main architect of the **Connecticut Compromise**.

The compromise proposed that Congress should be composed of two houses. In the smaller Senate, the States would be represented equally. In the House, the representation of each State would be based upon its population.

HIGHLIGHTS OF THE NEW JERSEY PLAN
SUGGESTED CHANGES TO THE ARTICLES OF CONFEDERATION BUT NOT AS COMPLETE A REVISION AS THE VIRGINIA PLAN
CONGRESS WOULD GAIN THE POWERS TO TAX AND REGULATE TRADE BETWEEN THE STATES
EACH STATE EQUALLY REPRESENTED IN CONGRESS
RETAINED THE UNICAMERAL CONGRESS SET UP IN THE ARTICLES OF CONFEDERATION
FEDERAL EXECUTIVE OF MORE THAN ONE PERSON CHOSEN BY CONGRESS, AND WHO COULD BE REMOVED AT THE REQUEST OF A MAJORITY OF THE STATES' GOVERNORS
FEDERAL JUDICIARY WOULD BE APPOINTED BY THE FEDERAL EXECUTIVE

>> The smaller States proposed that the New Jersey Plan be substituted for the plan proposed by Randolph. **Analyze Charts** How many branches would the government have under this plan?

By combining basic features of the plans, the convention's most serious dispute was resolved. The agreement satisfied the smaller States in particular, allowing them to support the creation of a strong central government. The Connecticut Compromise was so pivotal to the writing of the Constitution that it has often been called the Great Compromise.

>> The Connecticut Compromise established a legislature with a population-based House of Representatives per the Virginia Plan and a Senate with equal representation per the New Jersey Plan.

The Three-Fifths Compromise Once it had been agreed to base the seats in the House on each State's population, this question arose: Should enslaved people be counted in figuring the populations of the States?

Most delegates from the southern States argued that enslaved people should be counted. Most of the northerners took the opposing view. All could see the contradictions between slavery and the sentiments expressed in the Declaration of Independence, but slavery was legal in every State except Massachusetts. The slave population was concentrated in the southern States, however, therefore those States stood to gain or lose the most.

Again, debate on the issue was fierce. Finally, the Framers agreed to the **Three-Fifths Compromise**. It provided that all "free persons" should be counted, and so, too, should "three fifths of all other persons" (Article I, Section 2, Clause 3; by "all other persons," the delegates meant "slaves.") For the three-fifths won by the southerners, the northerners exacted a price. That formula was also to be used in fixing the amount of money to be raised in each State by any direct tax levied by Congress. In short, the southerners could count the enslaved members of their population, but they would have to pay for them.

This odd compromise disappeared from the Constitution with the adoption of the 13th Amendment, abolishing slavery, in 1865. For nearly 150 years, there have been no "all other persons" in this country.

>> The South relied on labor provided by enslaved people. Therefore, the Three-Fifths Compromise was a critical step towards a Constitution all delegates would sign.

The Commerce and Slave Trade Compromise The Framers generally agreed that Congress must have the power to regulate foreign and interstate trade. To many southerners, that power carried a real danger, however. They worried that Congress, likely to be controlled by northern commercial interests, would act against the interests of the agricultural South.

They were particularly fearful that Congress would try to pay for the new government out of export duties, and southern tobacco was the major American export of the time. They also feared that Congress would interfere with the slave trade.

Before they would agree to the commerce power, the southerners insisted on certain protections. So, according to the **Commerce and Slave Trade Compromise**, Congress was forbidden the power to tax the export of goods from any State. It was also forbidden the power to act on the slave trade for a period of at least 20 years. It could not interfere with "the migration or importation of such persons as any State now existing shall think proper to admit," except for a small head tax, at least until the year 1808.

A "Bundle of Compromises" The convention spent much of its time, said Franklin, "sawing boards to make them fit." The Constitution drafted at Philadelphia has often been called a "bundle of compromises." Those descriptions are apt, if they are properly understood.

There were differences of opinion among the delegates, certainly. After all, the delegates came from 12 different States widely separated in geographic and economic terms, and the delegates often reflected the particular interests of their own States. Bringing those interests together did require compromise. Indeed, final decisions on issues such as the selection of the President, the treaty-making process, the structure of the national court system, and the amendment process were all reached as a result of compromise.

But by no means did all, or even most, of what shaped the document come from compromises. The Framers were agreed on many of the basic issues they faced. Thus, nearly all the delegates were convinced that a new national government, a federal government, had to be created, and that it had to have the powers necessary to deal with the nation's grave social and economic problems. The Framers were also dedicated to the concepts of popular sovereignty and limited government. None questioned for a moment the wisdom of representative government. The principles of separation of powers and of checks and balances were accepted almost as a matter of course.

Many disputes did occur, and the compromises by which they were resolved came only after hours, days, and even weeks of heated debate. The point here, however, is that the differences were not over the most fundamental of questions. They involved, instead, such vital but lesser points as these: the details of the structure of Congress, the method by which the President was to be chosen, and the practical limits that should be put on the several powers to be given to the new central government.

The Constitution in its Final Form For several weeks, through the hot Philadelphia summer, the delegates took up resolution after resolution. On September 8, a committee was named "to revise the stile of and arrange the articles which had been agreed to" by the convention. That committee, the Committee of Stile and Arrangement, put the Constitution into its final form.

Finally, on September 17, the convention approved its work and 39 names were placed on the finished

Major Compromises of the Constitutional Convention

COMPROMISE	ISSUE TO RESOLVE	COMPROMISE REACHED	PROS/CONS
The Connecticut Compromise	How should the States be represented in Congress?	Congress should have two houses. In the Senate, States would be represented equally. In the House, representation would be based on population.	Enabled the small States to support the creation of a strong central government
The Three-Fifths Compromise	Should the enslaved be counted when figuring the populations of the States?	All free persons in each State would be counted, and "three fifths of all other persons" would also be counted. "Three fifths of all other persons" was generally recognized to be referring to those who were enslaved.	The southern States were able to count a portion of their slaves, but they also had to count them when figuring any direct tax that was levied by Congress.
The Commerce/ Slave Trade Compromise	Should Congress have the power to regulate foreign and interstate trade?	Congress could not tax the export of goods from any State or interfere with the slave trade for at least 20 years.	Southerners agreed to the inclusion of the commerce power, but northerners had to wait 20 years to ban the slave trade.

>> During the Constitutional Convention, the delegates made many compromises. **Analyze Charts** Why were these compromises important in creating the Constitution?

document. Three of the 41 delegates present on the last day refused to sign the proposed Constitution: Edmund Randolph of Virginia, who later supported ratification and served as Attorney General and then Secretary of State under President Washington; Elbridge Gerry of Massachusetts, who later became Vice President under Madison; and **George Mason** of Virginia, who opposed the Constitution because he believed it did not give enough attention to citizens' rights.

George Read of Delaware signed both for himself and for his absent colleague John Dickinson. Because not all of the delegates were willing to sign the Constitution, its final paragraph was very carefully worded to give the impression of unanimity: "Done in Convention by the Unanimous Consent of the States present. . . ."

Perhaps none of the Framers was completely satisfied with their work. Nevertheless, wise old Benjamin Franklin put into words what many of them must have thought on that final day:

> Sir, I agree with this Constitution with all its faults, if they are such; because I think a general Government necessary for us . . . I doubt . . . whether any other Convention we can obtain, may be able to make a better Constitution. For when you assemble a number of men to have the advantage of their joint wisdom, you inevitably assemble with those men, all their prejudices, their passions, their errors of opinion, their local interests, and their selfish views. From such an assembly can a perfect production be expected? It therefore astonishes me, Sir, to find this system approaching so near to perfection as it does...
>
> —*Notes* of Debates in the Federal Convention of 1787, James Madison

On Franklin's motion, the Constitution was signed. Madison tells us that

> . . . Doctor Franklin, looking towards the President's chair, at the back of which a rising sun happened to be painted, observed to a few members near him, that painters had found it difficult to distinguish in their art a rising sun from a setting sun. 'I have,' said he, 'often and often in the course of the Session . . . looked at that behind the President without being able to tell whether it was rising or setting: But now at length I have the happiness to know that it is a rising and not a setting Sun.'
>
> —*Notes* of Debates in the Federal Convention of 1787, James Madison

>> Benjamin Franklin is called the "First American" for many reasons, including his qualities of industriousness, self-reliance, and commitment to the vision of an independent America.

? MAKE GENERALIZATIONS Why was it said that the Constitution was a "bundle of compromises"? Was this aspect of the document positive or negative for the nation?

The Fight for Ratification

Today, the Constitution of the United States is the object of unparalleled admiration and respect, both here and abroad. But in 1787 and 1788, it was widely criticized, and in every State there were many who opposed its adoption. The battle over the ratification of the document was not easily decided.

Remember, the Articles of Confederation provided that changes could be made to them only if *all* of the State legislatures agreed. But the Framers had determined that the new Constitution would replace, not amend, the Articles. They had seen how crippling the requirement of unanimity could be. So, the new Constitution provided that

> The ratification of the conventions of nine States shall be sufficient for the establishment of this Constitution between the States so ratifying the same.
>
> —Article VII

The Congress of the Confederation agreed to this irregular procedure. On September 28, 1787, it sent copies of the new document to the States.

Federalists and Anti-Federalists The Constitution circulated widely and was debated vigorously. Two groups quickly emerged in each of the States: the **Federalists**, who favored ratification, and the **Anti-Federalists**, who opposed it.

The Federalists were led by many of those who attended the Philadelphia Convention. Among the most active were James Madison and Alexander Hamilton. The opposition was headed by such well-known Revolutionary War figures as Patrick Henry, Richard Henry Lee, John Hancock, and Samuel Adams.

The Federalists stressed the weaknesses of the Articles. They argued that the many difficulties facing the Republic could be overcome only by the creation of a new government based on the Constitution.

The Anti-Federalists attacked nearly every part of the document. Many objected to the ratification process. Several worried that the presidency could become a monarchy and that Congress would become too powerful. In Massachusetts, Amos Singletary, a delegate to the ratifying convention, condemned the Federalists:

> These lawyers, and men of learning, and monied men, that talk so finely and gloss over matters so smoothly, to make us poor illiterate people, swallow down the pill, expect to get into Congress themselves; they expect to . . . get all the power and all the money into their own hands, and then they will swallow up all us little folks . . . just as the whale swallowed up Jonah.
>
> —Amos Singletary

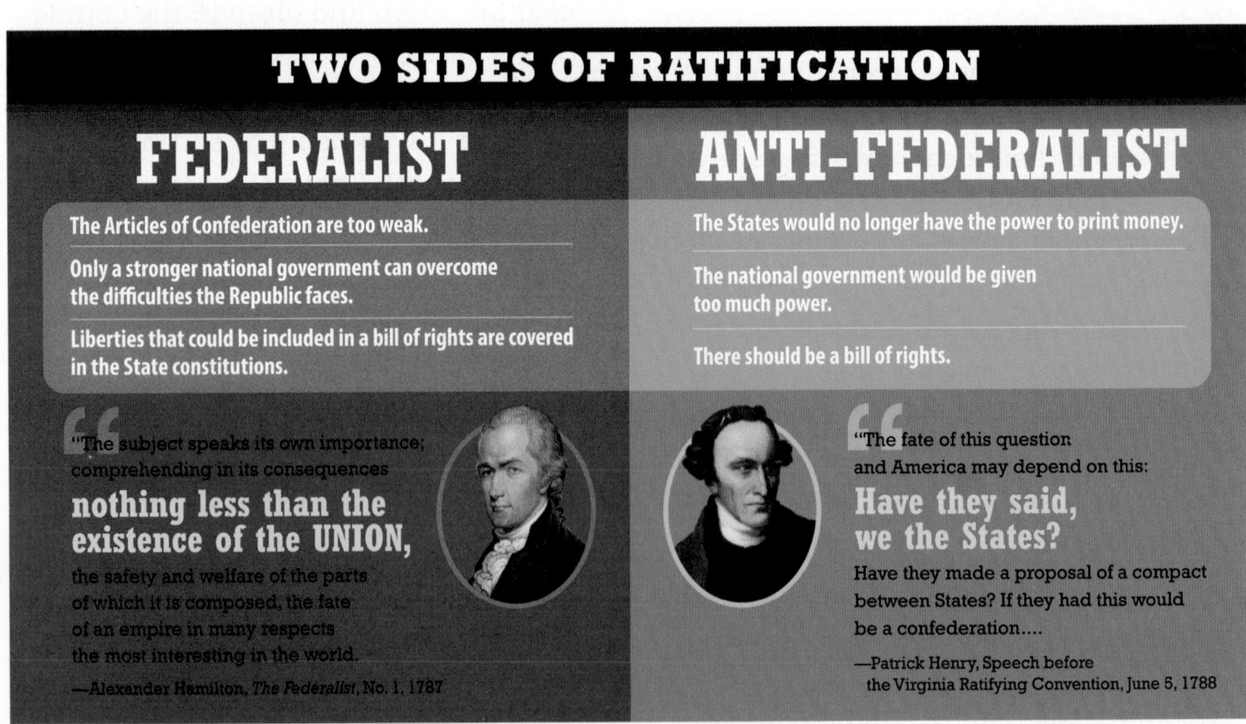

TWO SIDES OF RATIFICATION
FEDERALIST
The Articles of Confederation are too weak.
Only a stronger national government can overcome the difficulties the Republic faces.
Liberties that could be included in a bill of rights are covered in the State constitutions.
"The subject speaks its own importance; comprehending in its consequences
nothing less than the existence of the UNION,
the safety and welfare of the parts of which it is composed, the fate of an empire in many respects the most interesting in the world.
—Alexander Hamilton, The Federalist, No. 1, 1787
ANTI-FEDERALIST
The States would no longer have the power to print money.
The national government would be given too much power.
There should be a bill of rights.
"The fate of this question and America may depend on this:
Have they said, we the States?
Have they made a proposal of a compact between States? If they had this would be a confederation....
—Patrick Henry, Speech before the Virginia Ratifying Convention, June 5, 1788

>> Both the Federalists and Anti-Federalists felt strongly about the proposed Constitution. **Analyze Charts** What do these comments reveal about the sentiments of the time?

Ratification of the Constitution

STATE	DATE	VOTE	STATE	DATE	VOTE
Delaware	Dec. 7, 1787	30–0	South Carolina	May 23, 1788	149–73
Pennsylvania	Dec. 12, 1787	46–23	New Hampshire	June 21, 1788	57–46
New Jersey	Dec. 18, 1787	38–0	Virginia	June 25, 1788	89–79
Georgia	Jan. 2, 1788	26–0	New York	July 26, 1788	30–27
Connecticut	Jan. 9, 1788	128–40	North Carolina*	Nov. 21, 1789	195–77
Massachusetts	Feb. 6, 1788	187–168	Rhode Island	May 29, 1790	34–32
Maryland	April 28, 1788	63–11	* Second vote; ratification was originally defeated on August 4, 1788, by a vote of 184–84.		

>> The battle between Federalists and Anti-Federalists continued throughout the ratification process. **Analyze Charts** In which States was ratification won by only a narrow margin?

The lack of one major feature of the proposed Constitution drew the heaviest fire: a bill of rights. The new document did contain some protections of individual rights—for example, a provision for the writ of habeas corpus, which is a protection against arbitrary arrest. The Framers had made no provision for such basic liberties as freedom of speech, press, and religion, however—largely because those matters were covered by the existing State constitutions. They also believed that because the powers to be granted to the new government would be fragmented among three branches, no branch of the government could become powerful enough to threaten the rights of the people.

Everywhere, the Anti-Federalists bore down on the absence of a bill of rights. At Virginia's ratifying convention, Patrick Henry said of the proposed Constitution, "I look on that paper as the most fatal plan that could possibly be conceived to enslave a free people." Stung by the criticism, the Federalists promised that the Constitution, once adopted, would be amended to overcome this fault.

The Battle on Paper Over the course of the struggle for ratification, an extraordinary number of essays, speeches, letters, and other commentaries were printed. Of them all, the most remarkable were a series of 85 essays that first appeared in various newspapers in New York in the fall of 1787 on into the spring of 1788.

Those essays, supporting the Constitution, were written by Alexander Hamilton, James Madison, and John Jay, and they were soon published in book form as *The Federalist: A Commentary on the Constitution of the United States*. All of the essays bore the pen name "Publius" (Latin for "Public Man"), and they were reprinted throughout the 13 States. They remain an excellent commentary on the Constitution and rank among the finest of all political writings in the English language.

The Anti-Federalists' attacks were also published widely. Among the best of their works were several essays usually attributed to Robert Yates, who had been one of New York's delegates to the Philadelphia Convention; they were signed by "Brutus" and appeared in the *New York Journal* at the same time that the paper carried several of the *Federalist* essays. The Anti-Federalists' views were also presented in pamphlets and letters written by Richard Henry Lee of Virginia, who used the pen name "The Federal Farmer."

Nine States Ratify Ratification came fairly quickly in a few States and only after a bitter struggle in others. Delaware was the first to approve the Constitution, on December 7. Pennsylvania followed five days later. In Pennsylvania, however, where the legislature had been slow to call a ratifying convention, several Federalists, angered by Anti-Federalist delays, took matters into their own hands. They broke into a Philadelphia boarding house, seized two legislators hiding there, and forcibly marched them to the State house so the assembly could vote to schedule the convention.

The contest for ratification was close in several States, but the Federalists finally prevailed in all of

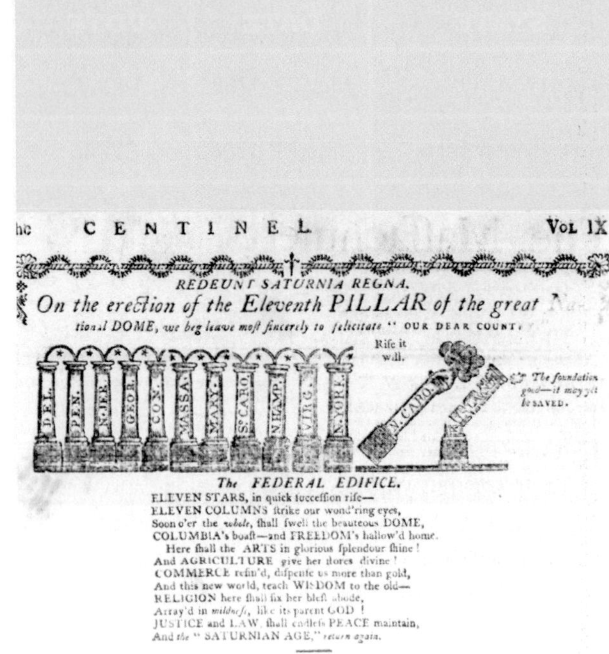

>> Columns representing the States that had ratified the Constitution are placed in a row by the hand of God. **Analyze Political Cartoons** Is this a Federalist or Anti-Federalist cartoon?

>> New Yorkers welcomed ratification with celebrations. This parade float celebrates the key role played by Alexander Hamilton in the ratification process.

them. On June 21, 1788, New Hampshire brought the number of ratifying States to nine.

Under Article VII, New Hampshire's ratification should have brought the Constitution into effect, but it did not. Neither Virginia nor New York had yet ratified. Without either of those key States the new government could not hope to succeed.

Virginia's Ratification Virginia's vote for ratification followed New Hampshire's by just four days. The brilliant debates in its convention were followed closely throughout the State. The Federalists were led by Madison, John Marshall, and Governor Edmund Randolph (even though he had refused to sign the Constitution at Philadelphia). Patrick Henry, leading the opposition, was joined by James Monroe, Richard Henry Lee, and George Mason (another of the nonsigners).

Although George Washington was not one of the delegates to Virginia's convention, his strong support for ratification proved vital. With Madison, he was able to get a reluctant Thomas Jefferson to support the document. Had Jefferson fought as did other Anti-Federalists, Virginia might never have ratified the Constitution.

New York, The Last Key State In New York, the ratifying convention was bitterly divided. The Anti-Federalists were led by Governor George Clinton and two of the State's three delegates to the Philadelphia convention: Robert Yates and John Lansing, who had quit Philadelphia in late July, claiming that the convention had gone beyond its authority.

New York's approval of the Constitution was absolutely necessary, for that large commercial State effectively separated New England from the rest of the nation. Its ratification of the Constitution, on July 26, brought the number of ratifying States to 11. The victory there was largely won by Alexander Hamilton.

Inauguration of the New Government On September 13, 1788, with 11 of the 13 States "under the federal roof," the Congress of the Confederation paved the way for its successor. It chose New York City as the temporary capital. It set the first Wednesday in January as the date on which the States would choose presidential electors. The first Wednesday in February was set as the date on which those electors would vote, and the first Wednesday in March as the date for the inauguration of the new government.

The new Congress convened on March 4, 1789. It met in Federal Hall, on Wall Street in New York City. But because it lacked a quorum, it could not count the electoral votes until April 6. Finally, on that day, it found that George Washington had been elected President by a unanimous vote. John Adams was elected Vice President by a large majority.

On April 30, after a historic trip from Mount Vernon to New York, Washington took the oath of office as the first President of the United States.

? IDENTIFY CENTRAL ISSUES On what main point did the Anti-Federalists focus their arguments against ratification of the Constitution?

ASSESSMENT

1. **Summarize** How did the writings of philosophers of the seventeenth and eighteenth centuries inspire the delegates attending the Constitutional Convention?
2. **Determine Relevance** What was the Connecticut Compromise, and why was it so important to the future of the new government?
3. **Make Generalizations** In what way did the principles of Enlightenment thinkers John Locke, Baron de Montesquieu, Jean Jacques Rousseau, and William Blackstone influence the American founding documents?
4. **Identify Supporting Details** What was a common element in the two key debates at the convention—one regarding representation in Congress and the other regarding slavery? Give details to support your answer.
5. **Support Ideas with Evidence** Read the following quotation: "Six years is a long period for a man to be absent from his home, it would have a tendency to wean him from his constituents." What is this quotation referring to and what does it mean? Do you believe this quotation came from a Federalist or an Anti-Federalist? Support your answer with evidence.

TOPIC 2 ASSESSMENT

1. **Examine Debates and Analyze the Validity of Information** Write a paragraph examining the debates surrounding the writing of the U.S. Constitution, and how the reality of those debates compares with the depiction of the delegates shown in the painting above. Consider the following questions: What was the general atmosphere during much of the Constitutional Convention? How does the atmosphere shown in the painting compare with the reality? Do you think the artist is showing bias in his painting? Why or why not?
2. **Explain Major Political Ideas** Write a paragraph explaining the divine right of kings. Include the following: comparison of a monarch's rule before and after the Petition of Right; description of how the Petition of Right limited the power of the monarch and challenged the idea of the divine right of kings.
3. **Explain Major Political Ideas in History** Write a paragraph comparing and contrasting the social contract theory with the divine right of kings theory. In your paragraph, make sure to define both theories before comparing and contrasting them.
4. **Identify Contributions of Founding Fathers** Write a paragraph comparing John Adams's and John Jay's views on independence from England. In your paragraph, briefly explain both delegates' stances on independence and how their philosophies influenced the development of the U.S. government.
5. **Examine Impacts on Founding Documents** Write a paragraph summarizing which issues caused the most debate during the creation of the Articles of Confederation, and the compromises that resulted. Explain how "a firm league of friendship" was eventually established among the States. Consider such things as: the different roles of the national and state governments in the new nation and the ratification of the Articles of Confederation. In your paragraph, explain how the debates led to compromises and how these events impacted one founding document.

6. **Identify Significant Individuals** Write a paragraph describing Thomas Jefferson's role in the drafting of the Declaration of Independence. Consider the following questions: Why was Jefferson chosen to be part of the committee to draft the Declaration of Independence? What part did Jefferson take in drafting the Declaration of Independence? What philosophies and ideas influenced Jefferson?

7. **Identify Contributions of the Founding Fathers** Give a brief oral presentation that compares and contrasts Alexander Hamilton and James Madison and how their political philosophies influenced the development of the U.S. government. Make sure your oral presentation includes clear main and supporting ideas by: clearly stating the similarities and differences you are trying to identify; providing several pieces of evidence in the form of primary or secondary sources to support your claims; and identifying the ways that these two philosophies helped shape the U.S. government.

8. **Analyze the Structure and Functions of the Legislative Branch** Prepare and give a brief presentation that explains why the Framers agreed on a bicameral Congress. Make sure your presentation answers the following questions: What does *bicameral* mean? Explain the bicameral structure of Congress. Why did the Founding Fathers agree to make Congress bicameral? What other options did they consider?

9. **Evaluate Constitutional Provisions** Write a paragraph defining the concept of popular sovereignty and examining how it was reflected in the first State constitutions.

10. **Examine Debates That Impacted the Founding Documents and Analyze the Validity of Arguments and Counterarguments** Use the following quotations to write a paragraph analyzing the arguments and counterarguments made by Jonathan Smith and Amos Singletary regarding the ratification of the U.S. Constitution. Consider such things as: Jonathan Smith's point of view; Amos Singletary's point of view; Smith's and Singletary's bias for or against the U.S. Constitution.

> *"I had been a member of the convention to form our own state constitution, and had learnt something of the checks and balances of power; and I found them all here."*
>
> *—Speech by Jonathan Smith, Massachusetts farmer, 1788*

> *"We contended with Great Britain–some said for a three-penny duty on tea, but it was not that. It was because they claimed a right to tax us and bind us in all cases whatever. And does not this Constitution do the same? Does it not take away all we have–all our property? Does it not lay all taxes, duties, imposts, and excises? And what more have we to give?"*
>
> *—Speech by Amos Singletary at Massachusetts convention on ratification of the Constitution, 1788*

11. **Analyze the Federalist Papers** Analyze how the *Federalist Papers* Number 10, Number 39, and Number 51 explain the principles of the American constitutional system of government. In your paragraphs, identify why the *Federalist Papers* were written, summarize the main idea of each of these three *Federalist Papers*, and explain how these three essays helped defend the principles of the American constitutional system of government.

12. **Identify American Beliefs and Principles** Write a paragraph identifying how the core beliefs and principles of democracy can be seen in America today. Consider the following questions in your response: What are the principles outlined in the Declaration of Independence and the U.S. Constitution? How are the ideas expressed in these documents visible in the government institutions and democratic practices seen in United States today?

13. **Identify and Define Unalienable Rights and Use** Write a paragraph in which you identify and define the concept of "unalienable rights" and answer the following questions: What are unalienable rights? Which unalienable rights are outlined in the Declaration of Independence? Which other rights may be considered to be "unalienable"? Why?

14. **Understand the Role of Limited Government** Write a paragraph describing how an individual's rights are protected in a limited government. Consider the following questions in your response: What is limited government? How does limited government protect the rights of individuals?

15. **Give Examples of Processes Used to Affect Policy** Write a paragraph explaining how the actions of colonial leaders affected public support of the ratification of the Constitution. Consider the following question: How did the Federalists and Anti-Federalists try to sway public opinion regarding the ratification of the Constitution?

16. **Understand the Rule of Law and Analyze Information** Use the quotation below to write a paragraph describing the main idea of the Mayflower Compact and how the document reflects the idea of the rule of law. When writing the paragraph, try to rephrase the language of the Mayflower Compact into modern English.

"IN THE NAME OF GOD, AMEN. We, whose names are underwritten, the Loyal Subjects of our dread Sovereign Lord King James, by the Grace of God, of Great Britain, France, and Ireland, King, Defender of the Faith. . . . Having undertaken for the Glory of God, and Advancement of the Christian Faith, and the Honour of our King and Country, a Voyage to plant the first Colony in the northern Parts of Virginia; Do by these Presents, solemnly and mutually, in the Presence of God and one another, covenant and combine ourselves together into a civil Body Politick, for our better Ordering and Preservation, and Furtherance of the Ends aforesaid: And by Virtue hereof do enact, constitute, and frame, such just and equal Laws, Ordinances, Acts, Constitutions, and Officers, from time to time, as shall be thought most meet and convenient for the general Good of the Colony; unto which we promise all due Submission and Obedience."

—*Mayflower Compact*

17. **Explain Major Political Ideas in History** Write a paragraph analyzing Britain's financial problems following the French and Indian War, and how this led to colonists' viewing the king and Parliament as an illegitimate government. Consider the following questions: How did Britain plan to pay its debts after the French and Indian War? What is "taxation without representation"? How did the colonists resist the policies enforced by Britain? Was it reasonable for Britain to tax the colonists in order to pay for the French and Indian War? Why or why not?

18. **Identify Major Traditions** Use the information from the English Bill of Rights below to explain the concepts of English common law and constitutionalism. Consider the following in your response: How is the English Bill of Rights related to the concepts of English common law and constitutionalism?

"The said Lords [Parliament] . . . do in the first place . . . declare
that the pretended power of suspending the laws, or the execution of laws, by regal authority, without consent of Parliament is illegal . . .
that levying money for or to the use of the Crown . . . without grant of Parliament, . . . is illegal . . .
that it is the right of the subjects to petition the king, . . . and prosecutions for such petitioning are illegal. . . ."

—*English Bill of Rights*

19. **Analyze Information for Bias and Point of View** Use the quotation below to write a paragraph analyzing Cato's point of view regarding the ratification of the U.S. Constitution. How valid is his argument? Consider such things as: Cato's attitude toward the executive branch and the facts Cato offers to support his point of view.

". . . [T]he great powers of the President, connected with his duration in office would lead to oppression and ruin. That he would be governed by favorites and flatterers, or that a dangerous council would be collected from the great officers of state. . . ."

—*Letter V by "Cato," The New York Journal, November 22, 1787*

20. **Write About the Essential Question Write an essay on the Essential Question: How much power should a government have?** Use evidence from your study of this Topic to support your answer.

PEARSON realize™ www.PearsonRealize.com Access your Digital Lesson

Go online to PearsonRealize.com and use the texts, quizzes, interactivities, Interactive Reading Notepads, Flipped Videos, and other resources from this Topic to prepare for the Topic Test.

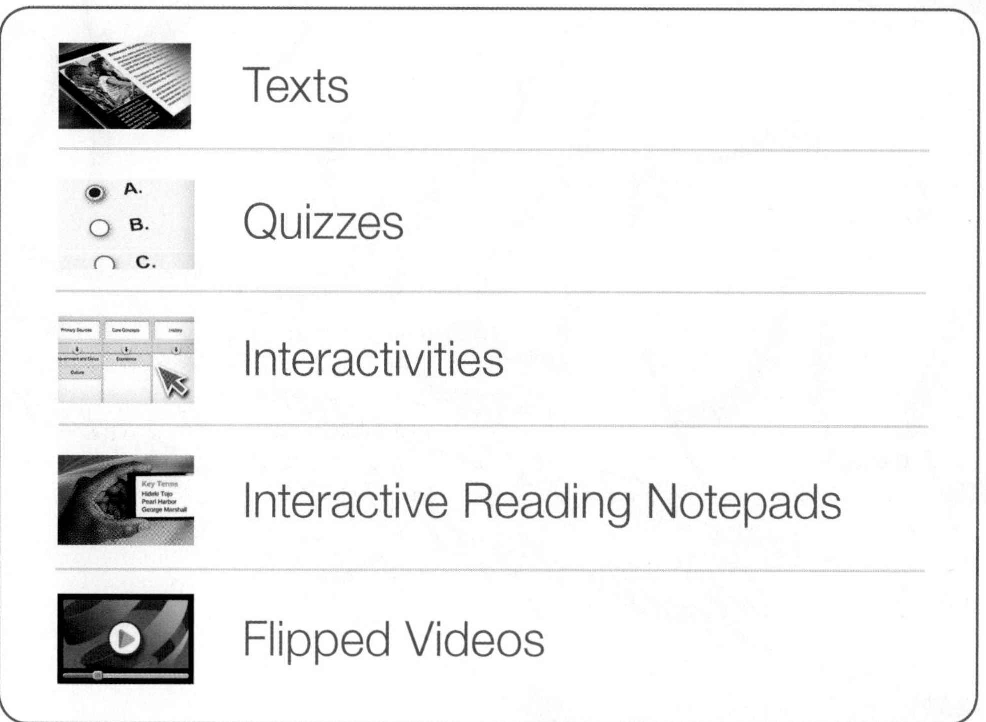

While online you can also check the progress you've made learning the topic and course content by viewing your grades, test scores, and assignment status.

[ESSENTIAL QUESTION] What Is the Right Balance of Power in Good Government?

3 The Constitution

>> Opening line of the Preamble of the United States Constitution

Enduring Understandings

- The U.S. Constitution provides the basic principles upon which the government is constructed and operates.
- The Constitution is built around six basic principles: popular sovereignty, limited government, separation of powers, checks and balances, judicial review, and federalism.
- The Constitution also provides the methods required to propose and ratify amendments, allowing for changes in its laws and procedures.
- The U.S. system of government is federalism, wherein the powers are divided between the National Government, with a set of powers given to it explicitly by the Constitution, and the States.

PEARSON realize™ NBC LEARN

MR. PRESIDENT
WHAT
WILL YOU DO
FOR
WOMAN SUFFRAGE
LELAND STANFORD
U of MO.

Watch the My Story Video to learn more about the long battle to win the right to vote for American women.

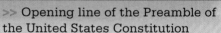

PEARSON realize™
www.PearsonRealize.com

Access your digital lessons including:
Topic Inquiry • Interactive Reading Notepad • Interactivities • Assessments

>> The U.S. Constitution is on display in the Rotunda of the National Archives Building in Washington, D.C. At night, it is stored in a highly secure underground vault.

3.1 **The Articles of Confederation had provided the new nation with domestic and international legitimacy, at the price of a weak general government. The new Constitution created a stronger federal government with a chief executive, the power to tax, and a court system.**

Interactive Flipped Video

>> Objectives

Understand the basic outline of the Constitution.

Understand the basic principles of the Constitution: popular sovereignty, limited government, and separation of powers.

Understand the basic principles of the Constitution: checks and balances, judicial review, and federalism.

>> Key Terms

bicameral
Executive Article
inferior courts
popular sovereignty
limited government
constitutionalism
rule of law
separation of powers
checks and balances
veto
judicial review
unconstitutional
federalism
James Madison
Alexander Hamilton
Andrew Johnson
Barack Obama
Donald Trump

An Overview of the Constitution

An Outline of the U.S. Constitution

The Constitution of the United States begins with the Preamble.

> "We the People of the United States, in Order to form a more perfect Union, establish Justice, insure domestic Tranquility, provide for the common defence, promote the general Welfare, and secure the Blessings of Liberty to ourselves and our Posterity, do ordain and establish this Constitution for the United States of America."
>
> —United States Constitution

The Constitution of the United States dates from the latter part of the eighteenth century. Written in 1787, it took effect in 1789. The fact that it is more than 220 years old does not mean, however, that in the twenty-first century, it is only an interesting historical artifact, best left to museums and dusty shelves. On the contrary, it remains a vitally important and vibrant document.

The Constitution is this nation's fundamental law. It is, by its own terms, "the supreme Law of the Land"—the highest form of law in the United States.

Sets the Rules The Constitution sets out the basic principles upon which government in the United States was built and operates today. The document lays out the ways in which the Federal Government is organized, how the leaders of that government are selected, and many of the procedures those leaders must follow as they perform their duties. Of utmost importance, it sets out the limits within which government must conduct itself.

The Constitution also lays out the basic rules of American politics. By doing so, it helps to determine who wins and who loses in the political arena. To really understand government and politics in this country, we must know a good deal about the Constitution and how it has been interpreted and applied throughout our history.

Amendments Even with its 27 amendments, the Constitution is a fairly brief document. Its little more than 7,000 words can be read in half an hour. Remember that this document has successfully guided this nation through more than two centuries of tremendous growth and change. One of the Constitution's greatest strengths is that it deals largely with matters of basic principle. Unlike most other constitutions—those of the 50 States and those of other nations—the Constitution of the United States is not weighted down with detailed and cumbersome provisions.

As you read the Constitution, you will also see that it is organized in a simple and straightforward way. It begins with a short introduction, the Preamble. The balance of the original document is divided into seven numbered sections called articles.

The first three articles deal with the three branches of the National Government: Congress, the presidency, and the federal court system. These articles outline the basic organization and powers of each branch, and the methods by which the members of Congress, the President and Vice President, and federal judges are chosen.

Article IV deals mostly with the place of the States in the American Union and their relationships with the National Government and with one another. Article V indicates how formal amendments may be added to the document. Article VI declares that the Constitution is the nation's supreme law; Article VII provided for the ratification of the Constitution.

Articles of the Constitution

SECTION	SUBJECT
Preamble	States the purpose of the Constitution
Article I	Creates the Legislative branch
Article II	Creates the Executive branch
Article III	Creates the Judicial branch
Article IV	Relations among the States
Article V	Amending the Constitution
Article VI	National debts, supremacy of national law, and oaths of office
Article VII	Ratifying the Constitution

>> The body of the Constitution is made up of seven articles. These articles set out the basic shape of the Federal Government. **Analyze Charts** What is the purpose of the first three articles?

The 7 articles of the original document are followed by 27 amendments, printed in the order in which each provision was adopted.

CATEGORIZE Describe the basic organization of the Constitution and why this organization was used by the Framers.

Article I

Immediately, the Constitution establishes a **bicameral** legislature—that is, a legislature made up of two houses. It does so for historical, practical, and theoretical reasons.

Historical The British Parliament had consisted of two houses since the 1300s. The Framers and most other Americans knew the British system of bicameralism quite well. Most of the colonial assemblies and, in 1787, all but two of the new State legislatures were also bicameral. Among the original 13 colonies, only Georgia and Pennsylvania had unicameral colonial and then State legislatures. Georgia's legislature became bicameral in 1789 and Pennsylvania's in 1790. (Only one State, Nebraska, has a unicameral legislature today.)

Practical The Framers had to create a two-chambered body to settle the conflict between the Virginia and the New Jersey Plans at Philadelphia in 1787. Recall, the most populous States wanted to distribute the seats in Congress in proportion to the population of each State, while the smaller States demanded an equal voice in Congress.

Bicameralism is a reflection of federalism. Each of the States is equally represented in the Senate and each is represented in line with its population in the House.

Theoretical The Framers favored a bicameral Congress in order that one house might act as a check on the other.

A leading constitutional historian recounts a conversation between Thomas Jefferson and George Washington at Mount Vernon. Jefferson, who had just returned from France, told Washington that he was opposed to a two-chambered legislature. As he made his point, he poured his tea into his saucer, and Washington asked him why he did so. "To cool it," replied Jefferson. "Even so," said Washington, "we pour legislation into the senatorial saucer to cool it."

As a whole, the Framers were convinced that the legislature would dominate the new National Government. As **Madison** observed,

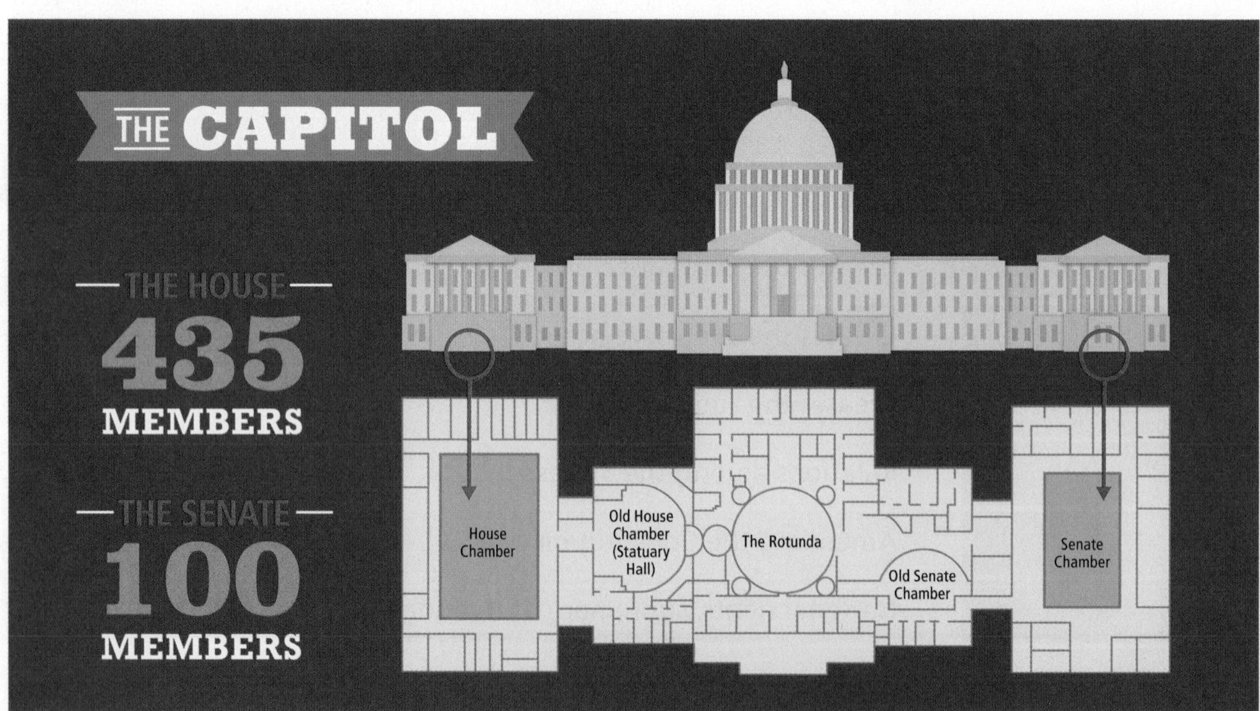

>> Congress meets in the Capitol, which has undergone several additions as both the nation and Congress have grown. **Analyze Maps** Why are both chambers in the same building?

> In republican government, the legislative authority necessarily predominates. The remedy for this inconveniency is to divide the legislature into different branches.
>
> —*The Federalist* No. 51

The Framers saw bicameralism as a way to diffuse the power of Congress and so prevent it from overwhelming the other two branches of government.

For more than 200 years now, some people have argued that equal representation of the States in the Senate is undemocratic and should be eliminated. They often point to the two extremes to make their case. The State with the least population, Wyoming, has only some 560,000 residents. The most populous State, California, now has a population of more than 37 million. Yet each of these States has two senators.

Those who object to State equality in the Senate ignore a vital fact. The Senate was purposely created as a body in which the States would be represented as coequal members and partners in the Union. Remember, if the Framers had been unable to agree that the States would be equally represented in the Senate, the Constitution might never have been written.

>> Patricia Schroeder (D., Colorado) was the first woman from Colorado to be elected to Congress. She served in the House of Representatives from 1973 to 1997.

SYNTHESIZE What practical problem did the Framers solve by creating a bicameral legislature?

Article II

Article II of the Constitution is known as the **Executive Article**, which in only a few words established the presidency. It begins this way:

> The executive Power shall be vested in a President of the United States of America.
>
> —Article II, Section 1

With this one sentence, the Framers laid the basis for the vast power and influence that the nation's chief executive possesses today.

The Constitution also sets out other, somewhat more specific grants of presidential power. Thus, the President is given the power to command the armed forces, to make treaties, to approve or veto acts of Congress and call special sessions of that body, to send and receive diplomatic representatives, and to "take Care that the Laws be faithfully executed."

Still, the Constitution lays out the powers of the presidency in a very sketchy fashion. Article II reads

>> Mount Rushmore in South Dakota features four U.S. Presidents—George Washington, Thomas Jefferson, Theodore Roosevelt, and Abraham Lincoln—representing the first 130 years of U.S. history.

almost like an outline. It has been called "the most loosely drawn chapter" in the nation's fundamental law. It does not define "the executive Power," and the other grants of presidential power are couched in similarly broad terms.

Much of our political history can be told in terms of the struggle over the meaning of the constitutional phrase "executive Power"—that is, over the extent of presidential power. That struggle has pitted those who have argued for a weaker presidency, subordinate to Congress, against those who have pressed for a stronger, independent, coequal chief executive.

That never-ending contest began at the Philadelphia Convention in 1787. There, several of the Framers agreed with Roger Sherman of Connecticut, who, according to James Madison,

> considered the Executive Magistracy as nothing more than an institution for carrying the will of the legislature into effect, that the person or persons [occupying the presidency] ought to be appointed by and accountable to the Legislature only, which was the depository of the supreme will of the Society.
>
> —James Madison, *Notes of Debates in the Federal Convention of 1787*

>> Until the late 1700s, U.S. laws were interpreted by State courts. In a 1735 trial, Andrew Hamilton's successful defense of John Peter Zenger set a precedent for freedom of the press.

As you know, those delegates who argued for a stronger executive carried the day. The Framers established a single executive, chosen independently of Congress and with its own distinct field of powers.

COMPARE POINTS OF VIEW What two points of view of the presidency were debated by the Framers?

Article III

During the years the Articles of Confederation were in force (1781–1789), there was no provision for federal courts or a national judiciary. The laws of the United States were interpreted and applied as each State saw fit, and sometimes not at all. Disputes between States and between persons who lived in different States were decided, if at all, by the courts in one of the States involved. Often, decisions by the courts in one State were ignored by courts in the other States.

Alexander Hamilton spoke to the point in *The Federalist* No. 22. He described "the want of a judiciary power" as a "circumstance which crowns the defects of the Confederation." Arguing the need for a federal court system, he added, "Laws are a dead letter without courts to expound and define their true meaning and operation." The Framers created a national judiciary for the United States in a single sentence in the Constitution:

> The judicial Power of the United States shall be vested in one supreme Court, and in such inferior Courts as the Congress may from time to time ordain and establish.
>
> —Article III, Section 1

Congress also is given the expressed power "to constitute Tribunals inferior to the supreme Court"—that is, create the rest of the federal court system—in Article I, Section 8, Clause 9.

Keep in mind this important point: There are *two* separate court systems in the United States. On one hand, the national judiciary spans the country with its more than 100 courts. On the other hand, each of the 50 States has its own system of courts. Their numbers run well into the thousands, and most of the cases that are heard in court today are heard in those State, not the federal, courts.

The Constitution establishes the Supreme Court and leaves to Congress the creation of the **inferior courts**—the lower federal courts under the Supreme Court. Over the years, Congress has created two distinct types of federal courts: (1) the constitutional courts, and (2) the special courts.

The constitutional courts are those federal courts that Congress has formed under Article III to exercise "the judicial Power of the United States." Together with the Supreme Court, they now include the courts of appeals, the district courts, and the U.S. Court of International Trade. The constitutional courts are also called the regular courts and, sometimes, Article III courts.

The special courts do not exercise the broad "judicial Power of the United States." Rather, they have been created by Congress to hear cases arising out of some of the expressed powers given to Congress in Article I, Section 8. The special courts hear a much narrower range of cases than those that may come before the constitutional courts.

These special courts are also called the legislative courts and, sometimes, Article I courts. Today, they include the U.S. Court of Appeals for the Armed Forces, the U.S. Court of Appeals for Veterans Claims, the U.S. Court of Federal Claims, the U.S. Tax Court, the various territorial courts, and the courts of the District of Columbia.

>> Lillian Sing is a judge at the Community Justice Center of the Superior Court of California, San Francisco. This center has both a courtroom and a social-service center to help those in need.

EXPRESS PROBLEMS CLEARLY Why did the Framers see a need for the creation of a national judiciary?

Basic Principles

The Constitution is built around six basic principles. The first three are popular sovereignty, limited government, and separation of powers.

Popular Sovereignty In the United States, all political power resides in the people, a concept known as **popular sovereignty**. The people are the *only* source for any and all governmental power. Government can govern only with the consent of the governed.

The principle of popular sovereignty is woven throughout the Constitution. In its opening words—the Preamble—that document declares: "We the People of the United States . . . do ordain and establish this Constitution for the United States of America."

Thus, the people have given the United States Government whatever powers it has, through the Constitution. That government exercises those powers through popularly elected leaders who are chosen

>> The principle of popular sovereignty was set out in the Constitution. **Analyze Political Cartoons** According to the cartoon, what is citizens' role in the government?

by the people to represent them in the exercise of the people's power, which is essentially what James Madison referred to as republicanism.

>> Another basic principle of the Constitution is that of limited government. **Analyze Political Cartoons** How are limited government and popular sovereignty related?

Interactive Cartoon

Limited Government The principle of **limited government** holds that no government is all-powerful. That government may do *only* those things that the people have given it the power to do.

In effect, the principle of limited government is the other side of the coin of popular sovereignty. It is that principle stated the other way around: The people are the only source of any and all of government's authority; and government has only that authority the people have given to it.

The concept of limited government can be put another way: Government must obey the law. Stated this way, the principle is often called **constitutionalism**—that is, government must be conducted according to constitutional principles. The concept of limited government is also frequently described as the **rule of law**, which holds that government and its officers, in all that they do, are always subject to—never above—the law.

In large part, the Constitution is a statement of limited government. Much of it reads as prohibitions of power to government. For example, notice the Constitution's guarantees of freedom of expression. Those great guarantees—of freedom of religion, of speech, of the press, of assembly, and of petition—are vital to democratic government. They are enshrined in the 1st Amendment, which begins with the words: "Congress shall make no law. . . ."

>> The Constitution also specifies the separation of powers. **Analyze Political Cartoons** How does the separation of powers keep government from becoming too powerful?

Separation of Powers Recall that in a parliamentary system, the legislative, executive, and judicial powers of government are all gathered in the hands of a single agency. British government is a leading example of the form. In a presidential system, these basic powers are distributed—separated—among three distinct and independent branches of the government.

This concept is known as **separation of powers**. The idea had been written into each of the State constitutions adopted during the Revolution. A classic expression of the doctrine can be found in the Massachusetts constitution written in 1780:

> "In the government of this commonwealth, the legislative department shall never exercise the executive and judicial powers, or either of them: The executive shall never exercise the legislative and judicial

powers, or either of them: The judicial shall never exercise the legislative and executive powers, or either of them: to the end it may be a government of laws and not of men."

—Part the First, Article XXX

The Constitution of the United States distributes the powers of the National Government among the Congress (the legislative branch), the President (the executive branch), and the courts (the judicial branch). This separation of powers is clearly set forth in the opening words of each of the first three Articles of the Constitution.

Article I, Section 1 declares: "All legislative Powers herein granted shall be vested in a Congress of the United States. . . ." Thus, Congress is the lawmaking branch of the National Government.

Article II, Section 1 declares: "The executive Power shall be vested in a President of the United States of America." Thus, the President is given the law-executing, law enforcing, and law-administering powers of the National Government.

Article III, Section 1 declares: "The judicial Power of the United States shall be vested in one supreme Court, and in such inferior Courts as the Congress may from time to time ordain and establish." Thus, the federal courts, and most importantly the Supreme Court, interpret and apply the laws of the United States in cases brought before them.

Remember, the Framers intended to create a stronger central government for the United States. Yet they also intended to limit the powers of that government. The doctrine of separation of powers was designed to accomplish just that.

In *The Federalist,* No. 47, James Madison wrote of this arrangement: "The accumulation of all powers, legislative, executive, and judiciary, in the same hands, whether of one, a few, or many . . . may justly be pronounced the very definition of tyranny."

The earliest of the State constitutions provided for a separation of powers among the legislative, executive, and judicial branches of the new governments they established. This was a reflection of the mistrust and suspicion toward any government common to the people of the new United States in the late 1700s. Thus, the inclusion of the doctrine of separation of powers was both natural and inevitable in the writing of the Constitution.

? EXPRESS IDEAS CLEARLY Explain the concept of popular sovereignty in your own words.

>> The legislative, executive, and judicial branches are connected by a system of checks and balances. **Analyze Political Cartoons** What is one way the President can check the powers of Congress?

More Basic Principles

The remaining three basic principles of the Constitution are checks and balances, judicial review, and federalism.

Check and Balances The National Government is organized around three separate branches. As you have just seen, the Constitution gives to each branch its own field of governmental authority: legislative, executive, and judicial.

These three branches are not entirely separated nor completely independent of one another. Rather, they are tied together by a complex system of **checks and balances**. This means that each branch is subject to a number of constitutional checks, or restraints, by the other branches. In other words, each branch has certain powers with which it can check the operations of the other two.

Congress has the power to make laws, but the President may **veto** (reject) any act of Congress. In its turn, Congress can override a presidential veto by a two-thirds vote in each house. Congress can refuse to provide funds requested by the President, or the Senate may refuse to approve a treaty or an appointment made by the chief executive. The President is the commander in chief of the armed forces, but Congress provides that military force; and so on.

The system of checks and balances links the judicial branch to the legislative and the executive branches. The President has the power to name all federal judges. Each appointment, however, must be approved by a majority vote in the Senate. At the same time, the courts have the power to determine the constitutionality of acts of Congress and of presidential actions, and to strike down those they find unconstitutional.

Head-on clashes between the branches of government do not often happen. The check-and-balance system operates all the time, however, and in routine fashion. The very fact that it exists affects much of what happens in Washington, D.C.

For example, when the President picks someone to serve in some important office in the executive branch—as, say, secretary of state or director of the Office of National Intelligence—the President is quite aware that the Senate must confirm that appointment. So, the chief executive is apt to pick someone who very likely will be approved by the Senate. In a similar sense, when Congress makes a law, it does so with a careful eye on both the President's veto power and the power of the courts to review its actions.

Spectacular clashes—direct applications of the check-and-balance system—do sometimes occur, of course. The President does veto some acts of Congress. On rare occasions, Congress does override a veto. And, even more rarely, the Senate does reject a presidential appointee. Twice in our history, the House of Representatives has impeached (brought charges against) a President, seeking his removal: **Andrew Johnson** in 1868 and Bill Clinton in 1998. On both occasions the President was acquitted by the Senate.

But, again, these and other direct confrontations are not common. Congress, the President, and even the courts try to avoid them. The check-and-balance system makes compromise necessary—and, remember, compromise is a vital part of democratic government.

Over time, the checks-and-balances system has worked well. It has done what the Framers intended it to do; it has prevented "an unjust combination of a majority." At the same time, the system of checks and balances has not often forestalled a close working relationship between the executive and legislative branches of the Federal Government.

Note, however, that working relationship runs more smoothly when the President and a majority in both houses of Congress are of the same political party. When the other party controls one or both houses, partisan friction and conflict play a larger-than-usual part in that relationship.

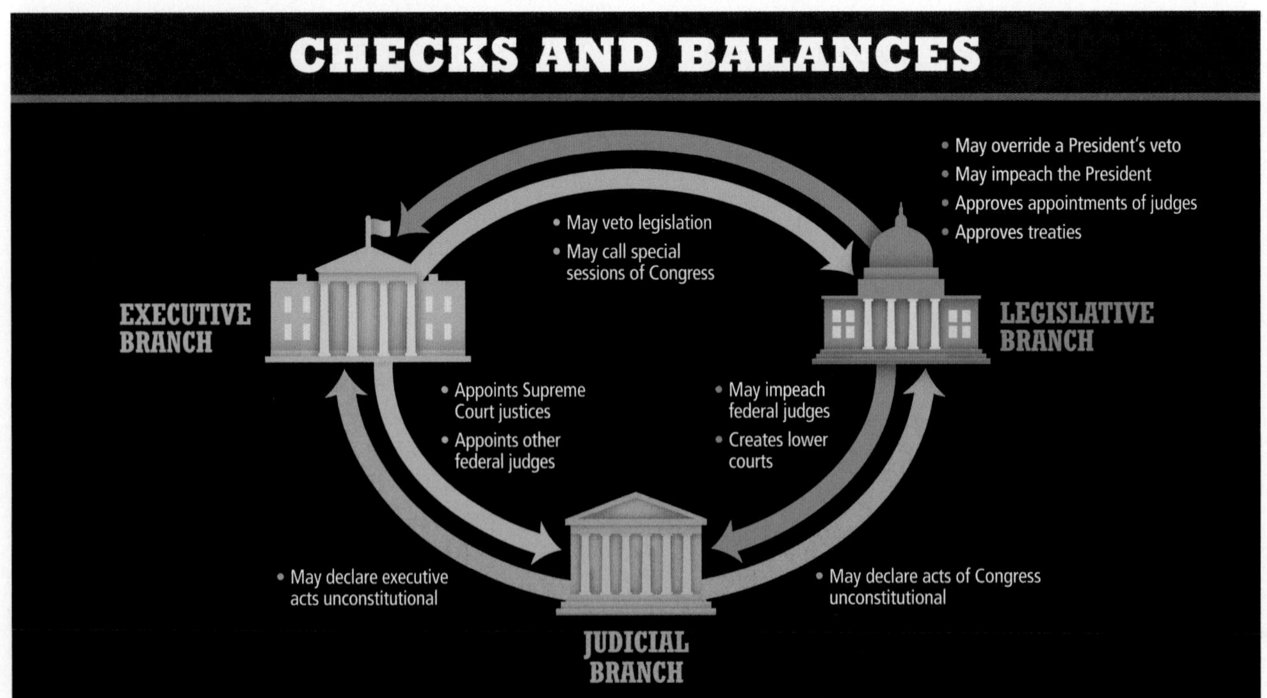

CHECKS AND BALANCES
• May override a President's veto
• May impeach the President
• Approves appointments of judges
• Approves treaties
• May veto legislation
• May call special sessions of Congress
EXECUTIVE BRANCH
LEGISLATIVE BRANCH
• Appoints Supreme Court justices
• Appoints other federal judges
• May impeach federal judges
• Creates lower courts
• May declare executive acts unconstitutional
• May declare acts of Congress unconstitutional
JUDICIAL BRANCH

>> The system of checks and balances allows each branch of government to limit the actions of the others. **Analyze Diagrams** How can the executive branch be checked by the other two branches?

Interactive Chart

Through most of our history, the President and a majority of the members of both houses of Congress have been of the same party. Over the past 50 years or so, however, the American people have become quite familiar with divided government—that is, a political environment in which one party occupies the White House and the other controls one or both houses of Congress.

Democrat **Barack Obama** had a divided government for most of his presidency. That was not the case when Republican President **Donald Trump** took office in 2017, however. The Republicans had captured control of the House in 2010 and of the Senate in 2014. The GOP kept their majorities in the 2016 elections, giving their party control of both the executive and legislative branches.

Judicial Review One aspect of the principle of checks and balances is of such importance in the American constitutional system that it stands by itself, as one of that system's basic principles. The power of **judicial review** may be defined as the power of a court to determine the constitutionality of a governmental action.

In part, then, judicial review is the power to declare **unconstitutional**—to declare illegal, null and void, of no force and effect—a governmental action found to violate some provision in the Constitution. The power of judicial review is held by all federal courts and by most State courts, as well.

The Constitution does not provide for judicial review in so many words. Yet it seems clear that the Framers intended that the federal courts, and in particular the Supreme Court, should have that power. In *The Federalist* No. 51, James Madison described the judicial power as one of the "auxiliary precautions" against the possible domination of one branch of the government over another.

In *The Federalist* No. 78, Alexander Hamilton wrote:

"The interpretation of the laws is the proper and peculiar province of the courts. A constitution is, in fact, and must be regarded by the judges as a fundamental law. It therefore belongs to them to ascertain its meaning, as well as the meaning of any particular act proceeding from the legislative body. If there should happen to be an irreconcilable variance between the two, that which has the superior obligation and validity ought, of course, to be preferred; or, in other words, the Constitution ought to be preferred to the statute...."

—*The Federalist* No. 78

>> Judicial review is one of the six principles of government established by the Constitution. **Analyze Political Cartoons** According to this cartoon, what is the role of the judicial branch?

In practice, the Supreme Court established the power of judicial review in the landmark case of *Marbury* v. *Madison* in 1803. Since *Marbury*, the Supreme Court and other federal and State courts have used the power in thousands of cases. For the most part, those courts have upheld challenged governmental actions. That is, in most cases in which the power of judicial review is exercised, the actions of government are found to be constitutional.

That is not always the case, however. To date, the Supreme Court has decided some 150 cases in which it has found an act or some part of an act of Congress to be unconstitutional. It has struck down several presidential and other executive branch actions as well. The Court has also voided hundreds of actions of the States and their local governments, including some 1,200 State laws and local ordinances.

Federalism As you know, the American governmental system is federal in form. The powers held by government are distributed on a territorial basis. The National Government holds some of those powers, which it uses to fulfill responsibilities for domestic policy, such as healthcare, education, and business, and foreign policy, which includes international trade and alliances with other countries. Other powers belong to the 50 States.

The principle of **federalism**—the division of power among a central government and several regional governments—came to the Constitution out of both experience and necessity. At Philadelphia, the Framers faced a number of difficult problems, not the least of them: How to build a new, stronger, more effective National Government while preserving the existing States and the concept of local self-government.

The colonists had rebelled against the harsh rule of a powerful and distant central government. They had fought for the right to manage their own local affairs without the meddling and dictation of the king and his ministers in far-off London. Surely, the colonists would not now agree to another such government.

The Framers found their solution in federalism. In short, they constructed the federal arrangement, with its division of powers, as a compromise. It was an alternative to both the system of nearly independent States, loosely tied to one another in the weak Articles of Confederation, and to a much feared, too powerful central government.

Keep in mind that federalism is an important part of the Constitution's web of protections of individual freedom. Remember, the Framers were dedicated to the concept of limited government. They were convinced (1) that governmental power poses a threat to individual liberty, (2) that, therefore, the exercise of governmental power must be restrained, and (3) that to divide governmental power, as federalism does, is to curb it and so prevent its abuse. James Madison addressed this point in this passage from *The Federalist Papers:*

> In the compound republic of America, the power surrendered by the people is first divided between two distinct governments, and then the portion allotted to each is subdivided among distinct and separate departments. Hence a double security arises to the rights of the people. The different governments will control each

Who has the Power?

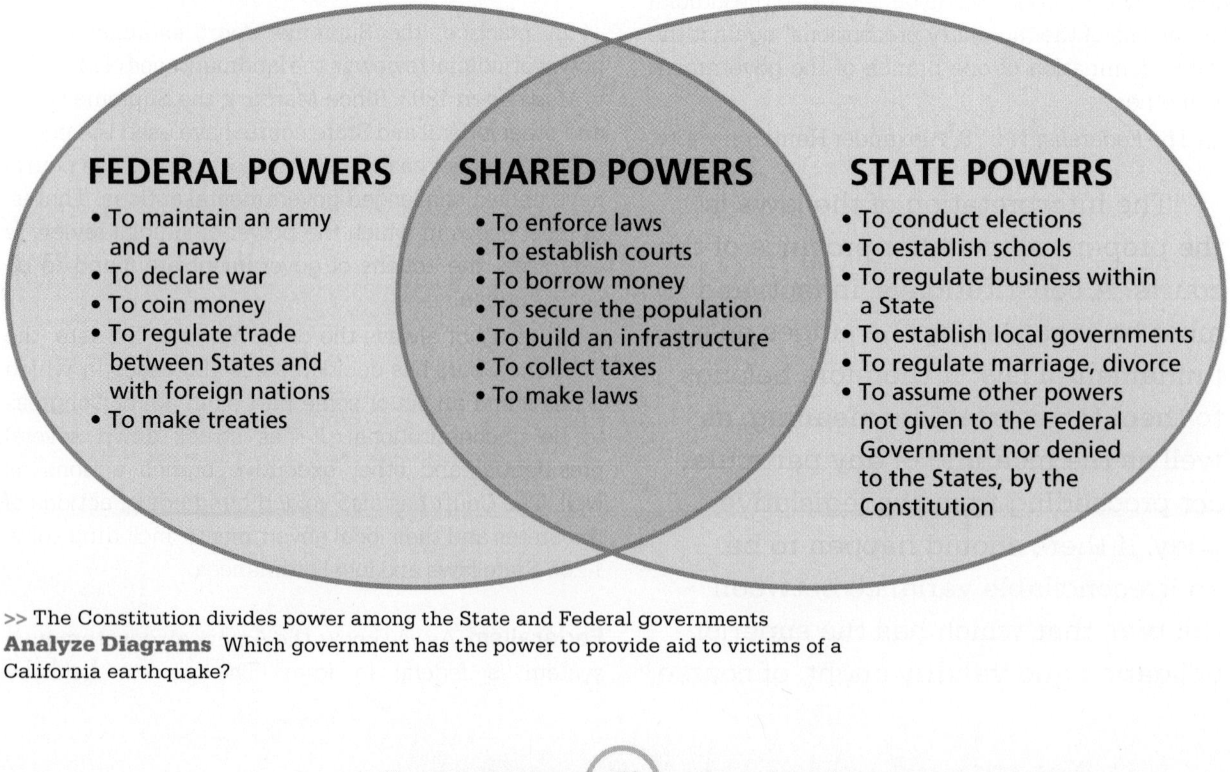

FEDERAL POWERS
- To maintain an army and a navy
- To declare war
- To coin money
- To regulate trade between States and with foreign nations
- To make treaties

SHARED POWERS
- To enforce laws
- To establish courts
- To borrow money
- To secure the population
- To build an infrastructure
- To collect taxes
- To make laws

STATE POWERS
- To conduct elections
- To establish schools
- To regulate business within a State
- To establish local governments
- To regulate marriage, divorce
- To assume other powers not given to the Federal Government nor denied to the States, by the Constitution

>> The Constitution divides power among the State and Federal governments
Analyze Diagrams Which government has the power to provide aid to victims of a California earthquake?

other, at the same time that each will be controlled by itself.

—*The Federalist* No. 51

? EXPRESS IDEAS CLEARLY Explain the concept of judicial review and why it is important.

ASSESSMENT

1. **Evaluate Arguments** Why might some argue that the organization of the Senate is undemocratic?
2. **Draw Conclusions** In 2006, the Supreme Court struck down President Bush's plan to use military tribunals to prosecute persons captured in the war against terrorism, deciding that only Congress has the power to provide for the creation of such court-like bodies. On what constitutional principle was this decision based?
3. **Interpret** Suppose two people who live in adjoining states are having a land dispute. Identify the article of the Constitution that addresses this issue, and explain how it addresses the problem.
4. **Infer** Why is it in the President's best interest to nominate federal judges favored by most Senators?
5. **Synthesize** How did the principle of federalism resolve the issue of national versus States' rights?

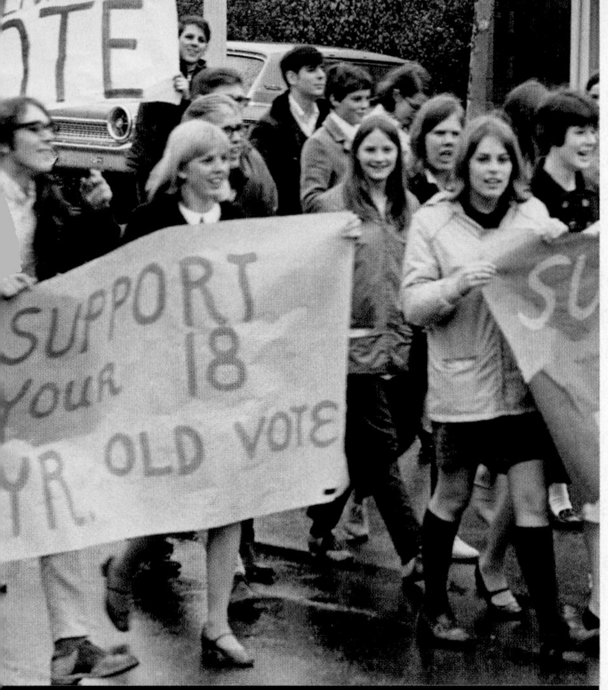

>> Students in Seattle march in a rally in support of the 26th Amendment. Congress passed the amendment in March 1971, and the States ratified it in just four months.

3.2 The Constitution of the United States has now been in force for more than 200 years—longer than the written constitution of any other nation in the world.

Interactive Flipped Video

>> **Objectives**

Describe the constitutionally prescribed procedures by which the Constitution may be formally changed.

Explain how the formal amendment process illustrates the principles of federalism and popular sovereignty.

Understand the 27 amendments that have been added to the Constitution, and that several amendments have been proposed but not ratified.

Identify how basic legislation has added to our understanding of the Constitution over time.

Analyze how interpretation of the Constitution has changed over the years through the actions of the executive and judicial branches, and by party practices and customs.

>> **Key Terms**

amendment
ratification
formal amendment
Bill of Rights
executive agreement
treaty
electoral college
Cabinet
senatorial courtesy
Thomas Jefferson
Franklin D. Roosevelt
James Madison
George Washington
Lyndon Johnson

Amending the Constitution

Formal Amendment Process

When the Constitution became effective in 1789, the United States was a small agricultural nation of fewer than four million people. That population was scattered for some 1,300 miles along the eastern edge of the continent. The 13 States, joined together mostly by travel on horseback and sailing ships, struggled to stay alive in a generally hostile world.

An Enduring Document Today, well over 300 million people live in the United States. The now 50 States stretch across the continent and beyond, and the country has many far-flung commitments. The United States is the most powerful nation on Earth, and its modern, highly industrialized and technological society has produced a standard of living that has long been the envy of many other countries.

How has the Constitution, written in 1787, endured and kept pace with that astounding change and growth? The answer lies in this highly important fact: The Constitution of today is, and at the same time is not, the document of 1787. Many of its words are the same, and much of their meaning remains the same. But some of its words have been changed, some have been eliminated, and some have been added. And, very importantly, the meanings of many of its provisions have been modified, as well.

This process of constitutional change, of modification and growth, has come about in two basic ways: (1) by formal amendment and (2) by other, informal means. In this section, you will look at the first of them: the addition of formal amendments to the Constitution.

The Framers knew that even the wisest of constitution makers cannot build for all time. Thus, the Constitution provides for its own **amendment**—that is, for changes in its written words.

Methods of Formal Amendment Article V sets out two methods for the proposal and two methods for the **ratification** of amendments. So, there are four possible methods of **formal amendment**—changes or additions that become part of the written language of the Constitution itself.

First, an amendment may be proposed by a two-thirds vote in each house of Congress and ratified by three fourths of the State legislatures. Today, at least 38 State legislatures must approve an amendment to make it a part of the Constitution. Of the Constitution's 27 amendments, 26 were adopted in this manner.

Second, an amendment may be proposed by Congress and ratified by conventions, called for that purpose, in three fourths of the States. Only the 21st Amendment (1933) was adopted in this way.

When Congress proposes an amendment, it chooses the method of ratification. State conventions were used to ratify the 21st Amendment, largely because the lawmakers felt that the conventions' popularly elected delegates would be more likely to reflect public opinion on the question of the repeal of nationwide prohibition than would State legislators.

Third, an amendment may be proposed by a national convention, called by Congress at the request of two thirds of the State legislatures—today, 34. It must then be ratified by three fourths of the State legislatures. To this point, Congress has not called such a convention.

And fourth, an amendment may be proposed by a national convention and then ratified by conventions in three fourths of the States. Remember, the Constitution itself was adopted in much this same way.

IDENTIFY MAIN IDEAS How does the formal amendment process reflect the concept of federalism?

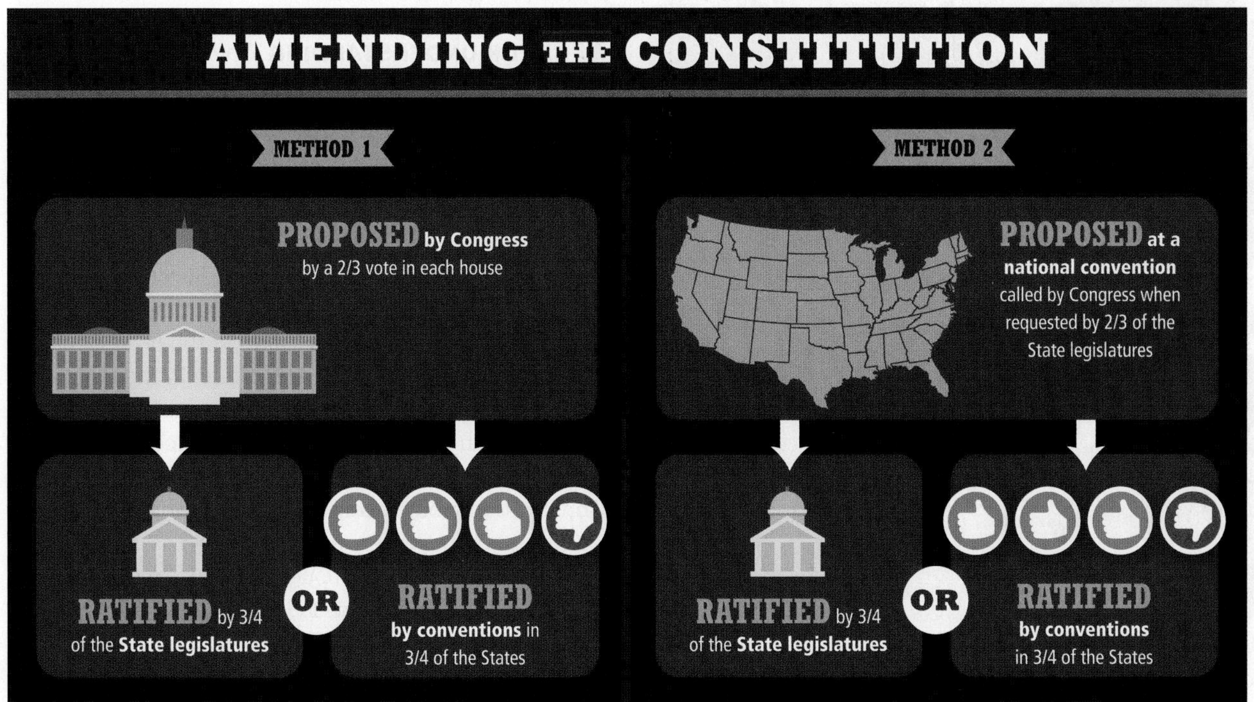
AMENDING THE CONSTITUTION
METHOD 1
PROPOSED by Congress
by a 2/3 vote in each house
RATIFIED by 3/4
of the State legislatures
OR
RATIFIED
by conventions in
3/4 of the States
METHOD 2
PROPOSED at a
national convention
called by Congress when
requested by 2/3 of the
State legislatures
RATIFIED by 3/4
of the State legislatures
OR
RATIFIED
by conventions
in 3/4 of the States

>> The President does not have a role in the formal amendment process. **Analyze Charts** Why do you think the Constitution outlines amendment methods involving Congress and State legislatures?

Interactive Gallery

>> A senator stands atop a pyramid of the groups that got him elected. **Analyze Political Cartoons** How might each group have contributed to his election?

>> Inez Milholland was a labor lawyer and activist who rode in the Woman Suffrage Parade in 1913 as part of her fight to amend the Constitution to give women the right to vote.

Federalism and Popular Sovereignty

Note that the formal amendment process emphasizes the federal character of the governmental system. Proposal takes place at the national level and ratification is a State-by-State matter. Also note that when the Constitution is amended, that action represents the expression of the people's sovereign will.

Some criticize the practice of sending proposed amendments to the State legislatures rather than to ratifying conventions, especially because it permits a constitutional change without a clear-cut expression by the people.

The critics point out that State legislators, who do the ratifying, are elected to office for a mix of reasons, including party membership, name familiarity, and their stands on certain issues. They are almost never chosen because of their stand on a proposed amendment. On the other hand, the delegates to a ratifying convention would be chosen by the people on the basis of only one factor: a yes-or-no stand on the proposed amendment.

The Supreme Court has held that a State cannot require an amendment proposed by Congress to be approved by a vote of the people of the State before it can be ratified by that State's legislature. It made that ruling in *Hawke* v. *Smith*, in 1920. However, a State legislature can call for an advisory vote by the people before it acts, as the Court held in *Kimble* v. *Swackhamer*, in 1978.

CHECK UNDERSTANDING Why have some people criticized sending proposed amendments to the State legislatures rather than to ratifying conventions?

Proposing an Amendment

The Constitution places only one restriction on the subjects with which a proposed amendment may deal. Article V declares that "no State, without its Consent, shall be deprived of its equal Suffrage in the Senate."

When both houses of Congress pass a resolution proposing an amendment, Congress does not send it to the President to be signed or vetoed, though the Constitution would seem to require it—because when Congress proposes an amendment, it is not making law (not legislating). Although the chief executive has no formal role in the amendment process, his or her political influence can affect the success or failure of any attempt to amend the Constitution, of course.

If a State rejects a proposed amendment, it is not forever bound by that action. It may later reconsider and ratify the proposal. Most constitutional scholars

The Bill of Rights

1	• Freedom of religion, speech and the press • Freedom to peaceably assemble and to petition the government	**6**	The right to: • a speedy trial by an impartial jury • be informed of the charges, to cross-examine witnesses, and to present favorable witnesses • an attorney
2	• The right to maintain a militia • The right to bear arms	**7**	The right to trial by jury in any civil case where the amount of money involved is $20 or more
3	Protection from having to quarter (house) soldiers in a time of peace without the consent of the owner, nor in a time of war except as provided by law	**8**	Protection from: • excessive bail or fines • cruel and unusual punishment
4	Protection against arbitrary searches and seizures without a proper warrant	**9**	The fact that the Constitution spells out a number of civil rights does not mean that there are not other, unwritten, rights held by the people.
5	Protection from: • prosecution without an indictment • being tried for the same crime twice • having to testify against oneself • the loss of life, liberty, or property without due process of law • loss of property without just compensation	**10**	The powers not delegated to the Federal Government may be exercised by the States, as long as they are not prohibited by the Constitution.

>> The first ten amendments protect many fundamental rights held by the people. **Generate Explanations** Why is it important to spell out these rights?

agree that the reverse is not true, however. Once a State has approved an amendment, that action cannot be undone; and no governor's veto power extends to the ratification of a proposed amendment.

Proposed Amendments Some 12,000 joint resolutions calling for amendments to the Constitution have been proposed in Congress since 1789. Only 33 of them have been sent on to the States. Of those, only 27 have been finally ratified. One of the unratified amendments had been offered by Congress in 1789—along with 10 other proposals that became the Bill of Rights in 1791, and another that became the 27th Amendment in 1992.

The unratified amendment of 1789 dealt with the distribution of seats in the House of Representatives. A second, proposed in 1810, would have voided the citizenship of anyone accepting any foreign title or other honor. Another, in 1861, would have prohibited forever any amendment relating to slavery. A fourth, in 1924, was intended to give Congress the power to regulate child labor. A fifth one, proclaiming the equal rights of women (ERA), was proposed in 1972; it fell three States short of ratification and died in 1982. An amendment to give the District of Columbia seats in Congress was proposed in 1978; it died in 1985.

Reasonable Time Limit When Congress proposed the 18th Amendment in 1917, it set a seven-year deadline for its ratification. The Supreme Court held that Congress can place "a reasonable time limit" on the ratification process in a case from California, *Dillon* v. *Gloss*, in 1921. Congress has set a similar limit on the ratification period for each of the amendments (except the 19th) that it has proposed since then. It also granted a three-year extension of the deadline for the Equal Rights Amendment in 1979.

? DESCRIBE How can the chief executive impact the formal amendment process?

The 27 Amendments

As you read about the Constitution's amendments, consider that they are quite significant, but they have not been responsible for the extraordinary vitality of the Constitution. That is to say, they have not been a major part of the process by which the Constitution has kept pace with more than two centuries of change.

The Bill of Rights The first ten amendments were added to the Constitution less than three years after it became effective. They were proposed by the first session of the First Congress in 1789 and were ratified by the States in late 1791. Each of these amendments arose out of the controversy surrounding the ratification of the Constitution itself. Many people, including Thomas Jefferson, had agreed to support the

Constitution only if a listing of the basic rights held by the people were added to it, immediately.

Collectively, the first ten amendments are known as the **Bill of Rights**. They set out the great constitutional guarantees of freedom of belief and expression, of freedom and security of the person, and of fair and equal treatment before the law.

The first ten amendments were added to the Constitution so quickly that, for all intents and purposes, they might just as well be regarded as a part of the original Constitution. In point of fact, they were not. We shall look at the 1st through the 9th amendments at some length in later readings. The 10th Amendment does not deal with civil rights, as such. Rather, it spells out the concept of reserved powers held by the States in the federal system.

The Later Amendments Each of the other amendments that have been added to the Constitution over the past 200 years also grew out of some particular, and often interesting, set of circumstances. For example, the 11th Amendment declares that no State may be sued in the federal courts by a citizen of another State or by a citizen of any foreign state. It was proposed by Congress in 1794 and ratified in 1795, after the State of Georgia had lost a case in the United States Supreme Court. The case (*Chisholm* v. *Georgia*, decided by the Court in 1793) arose out of a dispute over the ownership of some land in Georgia. It had been brought to the brand new federal court system by a man who lived in South Carolina.

>> The Buffalo Soldiers were members of the first all-black regiments to serve in the U.S. Army during peacetime. Because of the 13th and 14th Amendments, they were free men and U.S. citizens.

The 12th Amendment was added in 1804 after the electoral college had failed to produce a winner in the presidential election of 1800. **Thomas Jefferson** became the third President of the United States in 1801, but only after a long, bitter fight in the House of Representatives. The 13th Amendment, added in 1865, provides another example. It abolished slavery in the United States and was a direct result of the Civil War.

Slaves freed under the 13th Amendment were legally in limbo in regards to their rights. The 14th Amendment, adopted in 1868, defined citizenship as "all persons born or naturalized in the United States," granting the former slaves citizenship.

Passage of the 14th Amendment was bitterly contested by the southern States, who were forced to ratify it in order to regain representation in Congress. The 15th Amendment later prohibited denying the vote based on a citizen's "race, color, or previous condition of servitude," which granted the freed slaves the right to vote.

The 18th Amendment, establishing a nationwide prohibition of alcohol, was ratified in 1919. Known as "the noble experiment," it lasted fewer than 14 years. The 18th Amendment was repealed by the 21st in 1933.

The 22nd Amendment (1951), limiting the number of terms in which a President may serve to two, was proposed in 1947, soon after the Republican Party had gained control of Congress for the first time in 16 years. Over that period, **Franklin D. Roosevelt**, a Democrat, had won the presidency four times.

The 26th Amendment was added in 1971. It lowered the voting age to 18 in all elections in the United States. Many who backed the amendment began to work for its passage during World War II, creating the slogan "Old enough to fight, old enough to vote." Its ratification was spurred by the war in Vietnam.

The most recent amendment, the 27th, was written by **James Madison** and was among the first to be offered by Congress, in 1789. It forbids members of Congress from raising their own pay during that term. It finally became a part of the Constitution in 1992, when the 38th State, Michigan, ratified it.

? SYNTHESIZE Many of the 27 current amendments were proposed in response to legal disputes, social conflicts, or perceived constitutional problems. What problem was resolved by the 12th Amendment?

Change by Other Means

Surely, the Framers would be surprised to learn that only 17 amendments have been added to their handiwork since the adoption of the Bill of Rights more than two centuries ago. That so few formal changes have been made is, in part, a tribute to the wisdom of the Framers. But it is also due, in no small part, to the fact that many of the Constitution's provisions are cast in almost outline-like form; they are brief and seldom very detailed or specific. In short, their skeletal nature virtually guarantees interpretation.

So, to understand the Constitution, you must grasp this key point: There is much in that document—in fact, a great deal—that cannot be seen with the naked eye.

To put this essential point another way: Over time, many interpretations have been made in the Constitution that have not involved any changes in its written words.

This vital process of constitutional change by means other than formal amendment has taken place—and continues to occur—in five key ways: through (1) the passage of basic legislation by Congress; (2) actions taken by the President; (3) key decisions of the Supreme Court; (4) the activities of political parties; and (5) custom and usage.

>> Gun control advocates and opponents protest outside the U.S. Supreme Court. The role of the Court is to interpret the Constitution and determine the constitutionality of federal laws.

Basic Legislation Congress has been a major agent of constitutional change in two important ways. First, it has passed a number of laws to clarify several of the Constitution's brief provisions. That is, Congress has added flesh to the bones of those sections of the Constitution that the Framers left purposely skeletal—provisions they left for Congress to detail as circumstances required.

Take the structure of the federal court system as an example. In Article III, Section 1, the Constitution provides for "one supreme Court, and . . . such inferior Courts as the Congress may from time to time ordain and establish." Beginning with the Judiciary Act of 1789, all of the federal courts, except the Supreme Court, have been created by acts of Congress. Or, similarly, Article II creates only the offices of President and Vice President. The many departments, agencies, and offices in the now huge executive branch have been created by acts of Congress.

As an additional example, the Constitution deals with the matter of presidential succession, but only up to a point. The 25th Amendment says that if the presidency becomes vacant, the Vice President automatically succeeds to the office. Who becomes President if both the presidency and the vice presidency are vacant? Thus, the Constitution leaves the answer to that question to Congress.

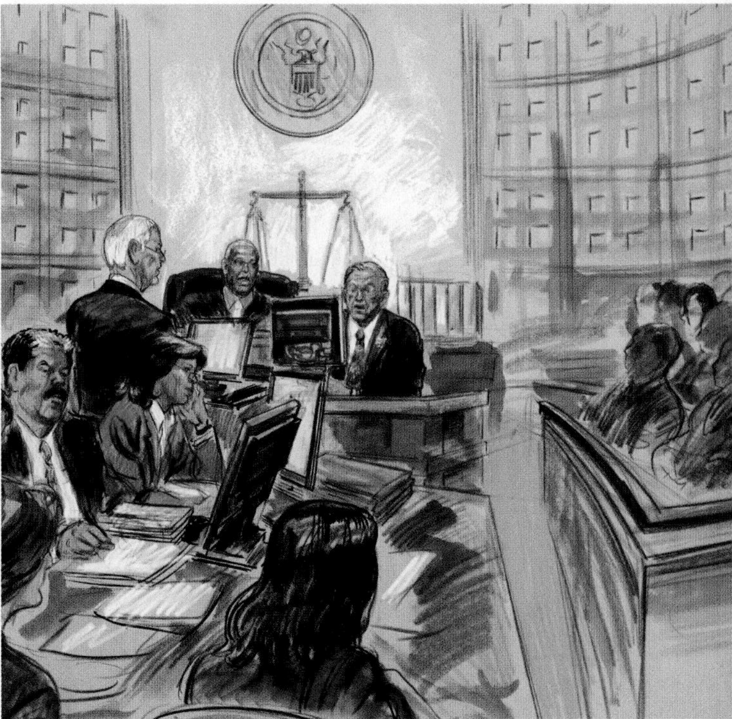

>> The Judiciary Act of 1789 established the federal court system and gave Congress the power to create the courts.

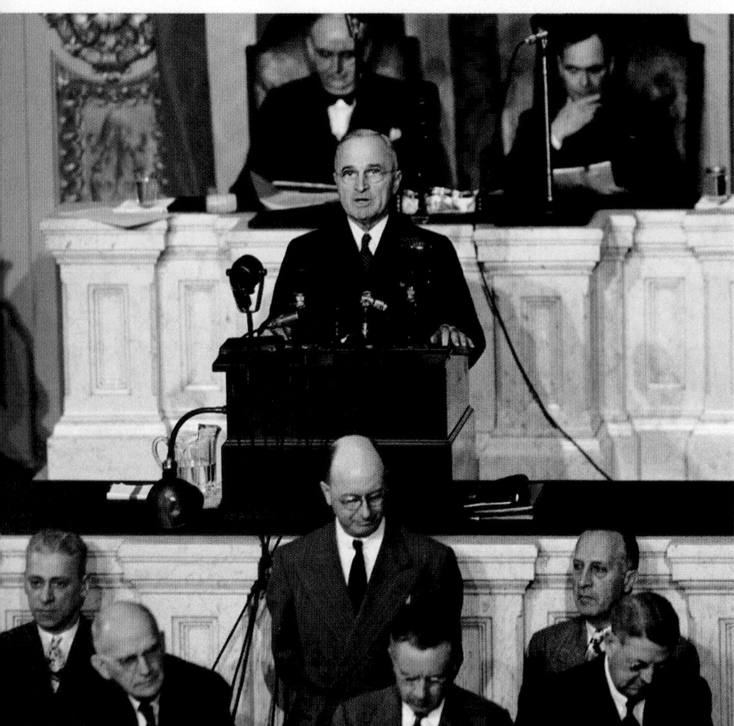

>> In 1947, President Harry S. Truman signed the Presidential Succession Act, which designated the Speaker of the House to succeed the President and Vice President if neither is able to serve.

>> President Obama meets in the Situation Room to plan for the war in Afghanistan. As commander in chief, the President can send U.S. troops into combat without an official declaration of war.

Second, Congress has added to the Constitution by the way in which it has used many of its powers. The Constitution gives to Congress the expressed power to regulate foreign and interstate commerce. But what is "foreign commerce" and "interstate commerce"? What, exactly, does Congress have the power to regulate? The Constitution does not say. Congress has done much to define those words, however, by exercising its commerce power with the passage of literally thousands of laws. As it has done so, Congress has, in a very real sense, expanded the Constitution.

Executive Action The manner in which various Presidents, especially the more vigorous ones, have used their powers has also contributed to the growth of the Constitution. For example, the document says that only Congress can declare war. But the Constitution also makes the President the commander in chief of the nation's armed forces. Acting under that authority, several Presidents have made war without a declaration of war by Congress. In fact, Presidents have used the armed forces abroad in combat without such a declaration on several hundred occasions in our history.

Take the use of executive agreements in the conduct of foreign affairs as another example. An **executive agreement** is a pact made by the President directly with the head of a foreign state. A **treaty**, on the other hand, is a formal agreement between two or more sovereign states.

The principal difference between agreements and treaties is that executive agreements need not be approved by the Senate. They are as legally binding as treaties, however. Recent Presidents have often used them in our dealings with other countries, instead of the much more cumbersome treaty-making process outlined in Article II, Section 2 of the Constitution.

Additionally, most Presidents have insisted that the phrase "executive power" in Section 1 of Article II includes much more than the particular presidential powers set out in that article. Thus, Thomas Jefferson engineered the Louisiana Purchase in 1803, doubling the size of the United States—even though the Constitution does not say that the President has the power to acquire territory.

Court Decisions The nation's courts, most tellingly the United States Supreme Court, interpret and apply the Constitution in many of the cases they hear. You have already encountered several of these instances of constitutional interpretation by the Court, most notably in *Marbury* v. *Madison*, 1803.

Recall that the Court established the power of judicial review—which is not specifically mentioned in the Constitution. You will find many more instances of constitutional interpretation—for the Supreme Court is, as Woodrow Wilson once put it, "a constitutional convention in continuous session."

Party Practices The nation's political parties have been a major agent of constitutional change over the course of our political history, despite the fact that the Constitution makes no mention of them. In fact, most of the Framers were opposed to political parties. In his Farewell Address in 1796, **George Washington** warned the people against what he called "the baneful effects of the spirit of party."

He and many others feared the divisive effect of party politics on government. Yet, even as he spoke, parties were developing. They have had a major place in the shaping of government and its processes ever since. Illustrations of that point are almost endless.

Neither the Constitution nor any law provides for the nomination of candidates for the presidency. From the 1830s on, however, the major parties have held national conventions to do just that. The parties have converted the **electoral college**, the body that makes the formal selection of the nation's President, from what the Framers intended into a "rubber stamp" for each State's popular vote in presidential elections. Both houses of Congress are organized and conduct much of their business on the basis of party. The President makes appointments to office with an eye to party politics. In short, government in the United States is in many ways government through party.

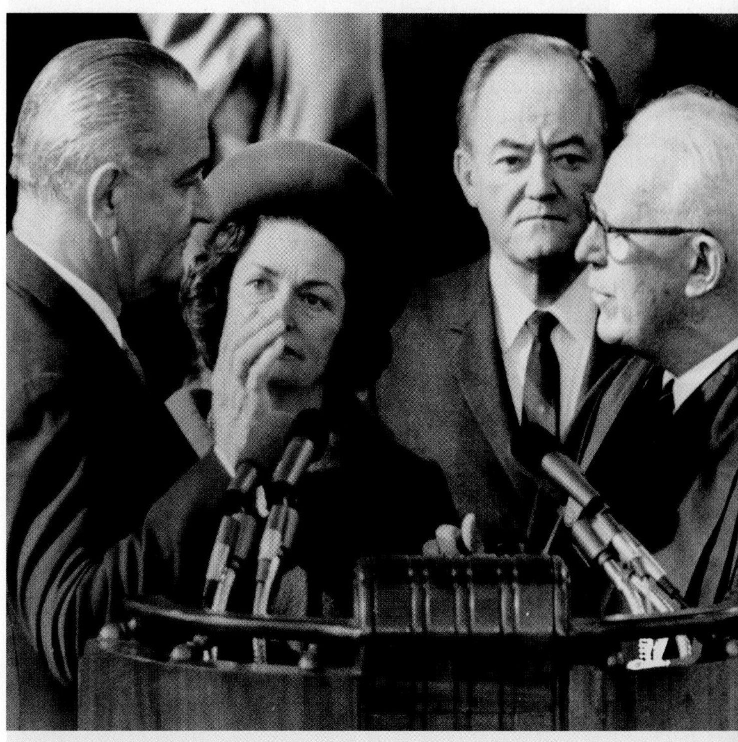

>> After succeeding to the office of President after John F. Kennedy's 1963 assassination, Lyndon Johnson was elected President in his own right in 1964.

Custom and Usage Unwritten customs may be as strong as written law, and many of them have developed in our governmental system. Again, there are many examples. By custom, not because the Constitution says so, the heads of the 15 executive departments make up the **Cabinet**, an advisory body to the President.

On each of the eight occasions when a President died in office, the Vice President succeeded to that office—most recently **Lyndon Johnson**, following John Kennedy's assassination in 1963. Yet, the written words of the Constitution did not provide for this practice until the adoption of the 25th Amendment in 1967. Until then, the Constitution said only that the powers and duties of the presidency—but *not* the office itself—"shall devolve on" (be transferred to) the Vice President.

It is a long-established custom that the Senate will approve only those presidential appointees, such as a federal judge or a United States marshal, who are acceptable to the senator or senators of the President's party from the State involved. This practice is known as **senatorial courtesy**, and it amounts to an unwritten rule that is closely followed in the Senate. Notice that its practical effect is to shift a portion of the appointing power from the President, where the formal wording of the Constitution puts it, to certain members of the Senate.

Both the strength and the importance of unwritten customs can be seen in the reaction to the rare circumstances in which one of them has not been observed. For nearly 150 years, the "no-third-term tradition" was a closely followed rule in presidential politics. The tradition began in 1796, when George Washington refused to seek a third term as President, and several later Presidents followed that lead. In 1940, and again in 1944, however, Franklin Roosevelt broke the no-third-term custom. He sought and won a third and then, four years later, a fourth term in the White House. As a direct result, the 22nd Amendment was added to the Constitution in 1951, limiting the President to two terms. What had been an unwritten custom, an informal rule, became part of the written Constitution itself.

IDENTIFY CAUSE AND EFFECT How has the general way the Framers laid out the provisions of the Constitution eased change throughout the last two centuries?

ASSESSMENT

1. **Make Generalizations** How do the constitutionally prescribed procedures by which the U.S. Constitution can be changed reflect the concepts of federalism and sovereignty?
2. **Draw Conclusions** What is the purpose of the Bill of Rights?
3. **Synthesize** Woodrow Wilson called the Supreme Court "a constitutional convention in continuous session." What did Wilson mean by this?
4. **Generate Explanations** Why do you think only 27 amendments have been added to the Constitution since its ratification, even though thousands have been proposed?
5. **Cite Evidence** The Framers wrote the Constitution knowing that needs and customs would change over time. What techniques did they use to ensure that the Constitution would, in fact, be relevant for hundreds of years?

3.3 You know that federal law requires young men to register for military service at age 18, that most employers must pay their workers at the least a minimum wage set by act of Congress, and that no person can be denied a job on the basis of his or her race or ethnicity.

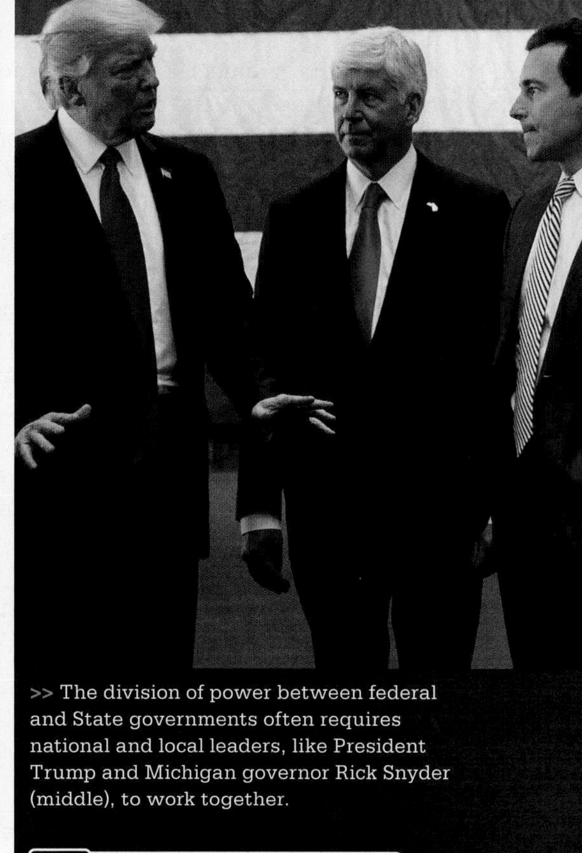

>> The division of power between federal and State governments often requires national and local leaders, like President Trump and Michigan governor Rick Snyder (middle), to work together.

Interactive Flipped Video

Federalism: Powers Divided

>> **Objectives**

Define federalism and explain why the Framers adopted a federal system instead of a unitary system.

Categorize powers delegated to and denied to the National Government, and powers reserved for and denied to the States, and the difference between exclusive and concurrent powers.

Summarize the obligations that the Constitution, as the "the supreme Law of the Land," places on the National Government with regard to the States.

>> **Key Terms**

federalism
division of powers
delegated powers
expressed powers
implied powers
inherent powers
reserved powers
exclusive powers
concurrent powers
Supremacy Clause
John Marshall

The Founders Choose Federalism

You also know that State law says that you must have a driver's license in order to drive a car, that it is illegal for anyone under 21 to buy alcoholic beverages, and that only those persons who can satisfy certain requirements can buy or own firearms.

Those three examples illustrate a very complex matter: the division of the powers of government in this country between the National Government, on the one hand, and the 50 States on the other. This section will help you to better understand that sometimes complicated, but very important, arrangement.

Balancing National and State Powers When the Framers of the Constitution met at Philadelphia in 1787, they faced a number of difficult questions. Not the least of them: How could they possibly create a new central government that would be strong enough to meet the needs of the day and would, at the same time, preserve the already existing States? Even those founders who, like Thomas Jefferson, were not part of the Constitutional writing process, took an active interest in designing the document to meet the needs of a growing nation.

Few of the Framers favored a strong central government based on the British model, and all of them knew that the Revolution had been fought in the name of local self-government. They also knew that the government established under the Articles of Confederation had proved too weak to deal with the new nation's many problems.

While the Framers favored a stronger national government, they also knew firsthand the importance of limiting federal powers. They were convinced that (1) governmental power inevitably poses a threat to individual liberty, (2) that therefore the exercise of governmental power must be restrained, and (3) that to divide governmental power, as federalism does, is to prevent its abuse.

SUMMARIZE What set of contradictions made the development of a Constitution so complex?

What Is Federalism?

Federalism Defined **Federalism** is a system of government in which a written constitution divides the powers of government on a territorial basis, between a central government and several regional governments, usually called states or provinces. Each of those basic levels of government has its own substantial set of powers. Neither level, acting alone, can change the basic division of powers the Constitution has created. Additionally, each level of government operates through its own agencies and acts directly through its own officials and laws.

>> The American Revolution was fought for freedom from British control, fueling the desire of the Framers of the Constitution to create the right balance between local and central government.

The American system of government stands as a prime example of federalism. The basic design of that system is set out in the Constitution. The document provides for a **division of powers** between the National Government and the governments of the 50 States. That is, it assigns certain powers to the National Government and reserves others to the States. This division of powers was implied in the original Constitution and then spelled out in the 10th Amendment.

In effect, federalism produces a dual system of government. That is, it provides for two basic levels of government, each with its own field of authority, and each operating over the same people and the same territory at the same time.

In the American federal system, each of the two basic levels of government can make certain decisions and do certain things that the other level cannot. For example, only the Federal Government can regulate interstate commerce—that is, trade conducted between and among the various States. On the other hand, each of the States decides for itself whether those who commit certain crimes in that State can be put to death.

Strengths of Federalism Federalism's major strength lies in this central fact: It allows local action in matters of local concern and national action in matters of wider concern. Local traditions, needs, and desires vary from one State to another, and federalism allows for differing circumstances among the States. In addition, geographic differences can have a significant impact on States' policies.

States located in earthquake zones, for example, may need to enact laws regarding earthquake-resistant building codes, while States located along the coasts may need to enact policies related to flooding, fisheries, or maritime commerce.

Illustrations of this point are nearly endless. For example, in 48 States most gas stations are self-service; in New Jersey and Oregon, the law forbids motorists to pump their own gas. Only one State—North Dakota—does not require voters to register in order to cast their ballots. Only Nebraska has a unicameral (one-house) legislature. Oregon and Washington are the only States that have legalized physician-assisted suicide.

The Role of State and Federal Governments in Welfare Reform

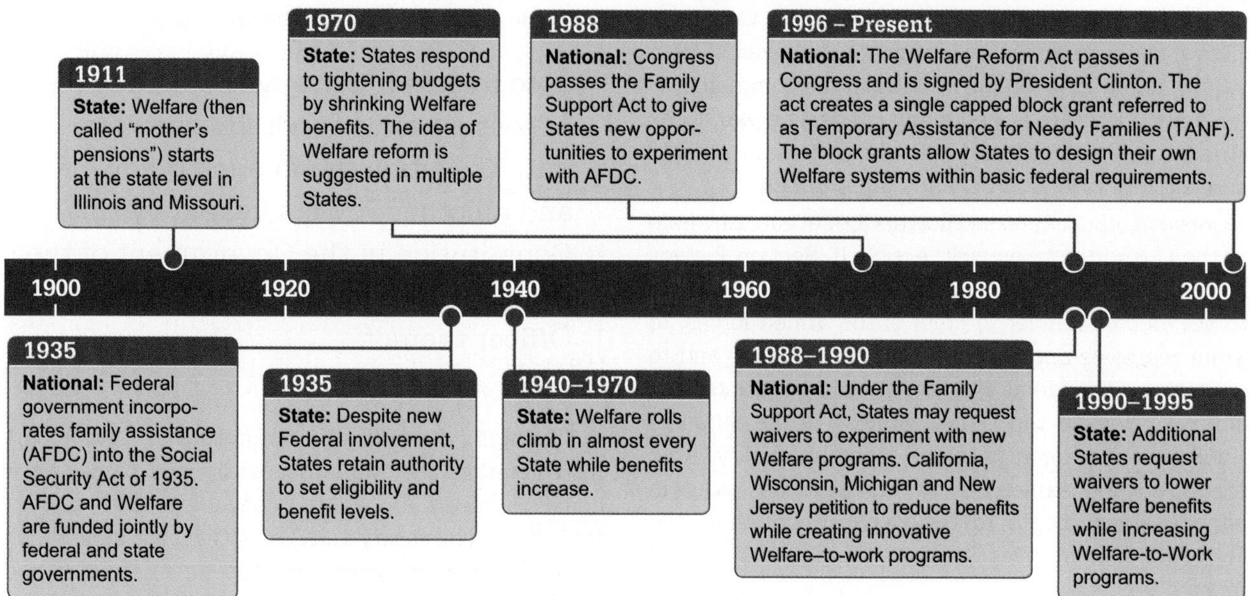

1911
State: Welfare (then called "mother's pensions") starts at the state level in Illinois and Missouri.
1970
State: States respond to tightening budgets by shrinking Welfare benefits. The idea of Welfare reform is suggested in multiple States.
1988
National: Congress passes the Family Support Act to give States new opportunities to experiment with AFDC.
1996 – Present
National: The Welfare Reform Act passes in Congress and is signed by President Clinton. The act creates a single capped block grant referred to as Temporary Assistance for Needy Families (TANF). The block grants allow States to design their own Welfare systems within basic federal requirements.
1900
1920
1940
1960
1980
2000
1935
National: Federal government incorporates family assistance (AFDC) into the Social Security Act of 1935. AFDC and Welfare are funded jointly by federal and state governments.
1935
State: Despite new Federal involvement, States retain authority to set eligibility and benefit levels.
1940–1970
State: Welfare rolls climb in almost every State while benefits increase.
1988–1990
National: Under the Family Support Act, States may request waivers to experiment with new Welfare programs. California, Wisconsin, Michigan and New Jersey petition to reduce benefits while creating innovative Welfare–to-work programs.
1990–1995
State: Additional States request waivers to lower Welfare benefits while increasing Welfare-to-Work programs.

>> Welfare reform has alternated between State and National governments for many years. **Analyze Charts** How are welfare programs now managed at both levels of government?

Only five States—Alaska, Delaware, New Hampshire, Montana, and Oregon—do not impose a general sales tax.

Federalism also allows for experimentation and innovation in solving public policy problems. Indeed, the several States have long been described as so many "laboratories of government." New approaches to difficult matters may originate in one State and then be adopted in another or even be put in place at the national level.

The Welfare Reform Act passed by Congress in 1996 affords a useful illustration of the point. That landmark statute revolutionized the Federal Government's approach to providing welfare assistance to millions of Americans on the lower rungs of the nation's economic ladder—and its basic features were first suggested by welfare administrators in the States of Wisconsin, California, and Michigan.

In its most noteworthy provisions, the law abolished the Aid to Families with Dependent Children (AFDC) program, replacing it with block grants to the States. The several States now have wide discretion in the determination of eligibility for financial assistance.

While federalism allows individual States to handle State and local matters, it also provides for the strength that comes from union. National defense and foreign affairs offer useful illustrations of this point. So, too, do domestic affairs. Take, for example, a natural disaster. When a flood, drought, hurricane, or other catastrophe hits a particular State, the resources of the National Government and all of the other States can be mobilized to aid the stricken area. However, a disadvantage of federalism is the redundancy that can occur due to overlapping jurisdictions, as evidenced by the handling of Hurricane Katrina. In this instance, the National Government's efforts and the State's efforts were not coordinated.

APPLY CONCEPTS Why are the States sometimes described as "laboratories of government?"

Three Types of Federal Powers

The National Government is a government of **delegated powers**. That is, that government has only those powers delegated (granted) to it in the Constitution. There are three distinct types of delegated powers: expressed, implied, and inherent.

The Expressed Powers The **expressed powers** are those powers delegated to the National Government in so many words—spelled out, expressly, in the Constitution. Those powers are also sometimes called the "enumerated powers."

You can find most of the expressed powers in Article I, Section 8. There, in 18 separate clauses, the Constitution expressly gives 27 powers to Congress. They include the power to lay and collect taxes, to coin money, to regulate foreign and interstate commerce, to raise and maintain armed forces, to declare war, to fix standards of weights and measures, to grant patents and copyrights, and to do many other things.

Several other expressed powers are set out elsewhere in the Constitution, as well. Article II, Section 2 gives several powers to the President—including the power to act as commander in chief of the armed forces, to grant reprieves and pardons, to make treaties, and to appoint major federal officials. Article III grants "the judicial Power of the United States" to the Supreme Court and other courts in the federal judiciary. And, finally, several expressed powers also are found in various amendments to the Constitution; thus, the 16th Amendment gives Congress the power to levy an income tax.

The Implied Powers The **implied powers** are not expressly stated in the Constitution, but they are reasonably suggested—implied—by the expressed powers. The constitutional basis for the implied powers is found in one of the expressed powers. Article I, Section 8, Clause 18 gives Congress the "necessary and proper power." The Necessary and Proper Clause says that Congress has the power

> to make all Laws which shall be necessary and proper for carrying into Execution the foregoing Powers and all other Powers vested by this Constitution in the Government of the United States, or in any Department or Officer thereof.
>
> —Article I, Section 8, Clause 18

Through decades of congressional and court interpretation, the words *necessary and proper* have come to mean, in effect, "convenient and useful." Indeed, the Necessary and Proper Clause is sometimes called the Elastic Clause, because, over time, it has been stretched to cover so many different situations.

Here are but a few of the thousands of examples of the exercise of implied powers: Congress has provided for the regulation of labor-management relations, the building of hydroelectric power dams, and the building of the 42,000-mile interstate highway system. It has made federal crimes of such acts as moving stolen goods, gambling devices, and kidnapped persons across State lines. It has prohibited racial discrimination in granting all people access to such places as restaurants, theaters, hotels, and motels. Congress has taken these actions, and many more, because the power to do so is reasonably implied by just one of the expressed powers: the power to regulate interstate commerce.

The Inherent Powers The **inherent powers** are those powers that belong to the National Government because it is the national government of a sovereign state in the world community. Although the Constitution does not expressly provide for them, they are powers that, over time, all national governments have come to possess. It stands to reason that the Framers of the Constitution intended the National Government they created would also hold those several constitutional powers.

The inherent powers are few in number. The major ones include the power to regulate immigration, to deport aliens, to acquire territory, to grant diplomatic recognition to other states, and to protect the nation against rebellion or other attempts to overthrow the government by force or violence.

One can argue that most of the inherent powers really are implied by one or more of the expressed powers. For example, the power to regulate immigration is

>> President Woodrow Wilson walking with other world leaders while negotiating the Treaty of Versailles. The Constitution gives the Federal Government the power to negotiate and sign treaties.

Interactive Chart

Examples of Powers Expressly Denied to the Federal Government

POWER DENIED	EXAMPLE OF ILLEGAL USE OF POWER
Levy taxes on exports	The Federal Government levies a tax on coal exports from Pennsylvania to Canada.
Take private property for public use without payment of compensation	The Federal Government appropriates a farmer's land to build a highway, and offers him no compensation.
Prohibit freedom of religion, speech, press, or assembly	The Federal Government enacts a law stating that no one may make a speech outside of public buildings.
Conduct illegal search or seizure	The Federal Government sends an agent without a warrant to find and confiscate a business's financial records.
Deny a speedy trial to an accused person	The Federal Government holds a suspected criminal in jail without trial for two years.

>> The powers denied to the National Government are varied and extensive. **Analyze Charts** How is federalism preserved by the denial of these powers?

suggested by the expressed power to regulate foreign trade. The power to acquire territory can be drawn from the treaty-making power and the several war powers. But the doctrine of inherent powers holds that it is not necessary to go to these lengths to find these powers in the Constitution. In short, these powers exist because the United States exists.

DRAW CONCLUSIONS Why would it be unacceptable for a State to deport illegal aliens?

Powers Denied to the Federal Government

Although the Constitution delegates certain powers to the National Government, it also *denies* certain powers to that level of government in order to keep federalism intact. It does so in three distinct ways.

First, the Constitution denies some powers to the National Government in so many words—*expressly.* Among them are the powers to levy duties on exports; to take private property for public use without the payment of just compensation; to prohibit freedom of religion, speech, press, or assembly; to conduct illegal searches or seizures; and to deny to any person accused of a crime a speedy and public trial or a trial by jury.

Second, several powers are denied to the National Government because of the *silence* of the Constitution. Recall that the National Government is a government of delegated powers; it has only those powers the Constitution gives to it.

Among the many powers not granted to the National Government are the powers to do such things as create a public school system for the nation, enact uniform marriage and divorce laws, and set up units of local government. The Constitution says nothing that would give the National Government the power to do any of those things, expressly, implicitly, or inherently. In short, the lack of any such provision—the silence of the Constitution—denies power to the National Government.

Third, some powers are denied to the National Government because of the federal system itself. Clearly the Constitution does not intend that the National Government should have the power to take any action that would threaten the existence of that system. For example, in the exercise of its power to tax, Congress cannot tax any of the States or any of their local units in the conduct of their various governmental functions. If it could, it would have the power to destroy—tax out of existence—one or more, or all, of the States.

APPLY CONCEPTS Explain why the U.S. Government cannot break into your home to search for stolen goods without a warrant.

Powers of the Fifty States

The 50 States are the other half of the very complicated equation we call federalism. Their many-sided role in the American federal system is no less important than that of the National Government.

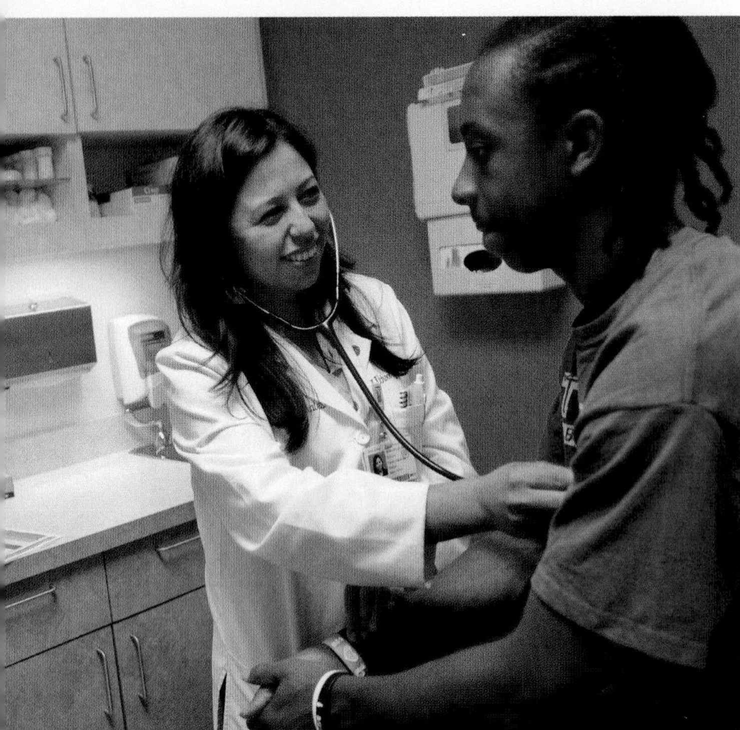

>> One reserved State power is the right to issue licenses to various professionals, such as nurses and physicians. Such a license is required to practice in that particular State.

Interactive Gallery

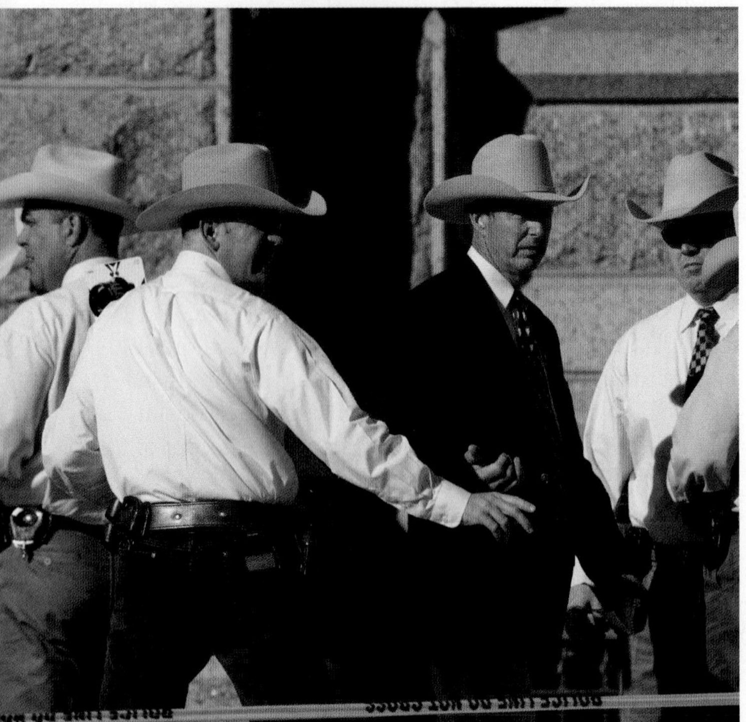

>> The Texas Ranger Division is the oldest State law enforcement agency in the country and is an example of a State's right to enforce order among its own people.

Powers Reserved to the States Recall, the 10th Amendment states that the States are governments of **reserved powers**. The reserved powers are those powers that the Constitution does not grant to the National Government and does not, at the same time, deny to the States.

Thus, any State can forbid persons under 18 to marry without parental consent. It can ban the sale of pornography, outlaw prostitution, and permit some forms of gambling and prohibit others. A State can require that doctors, lawyers, hairdressers, and plumbers be licensed in order to practice in the State. It can confiscate automobiles and other property used in connection with such illicit activities as drug trafficking. It can establish public schools, enact land use laws, regulate the services and restrict the profits of such public utilities as natural gas, oil, electric power, and telephone companies, and do much, much more.

In short, the sphere of powers held by each State—the scope of the reserved powers—is huge. The States can do all of those things just mentioned, because the Constitution does not give the National Government the power to do those things, and it does not deny the States the power to do them.

How broad the reserved powers really are can be understood from this fact: Most of what government does in this country today is done by the States (and their local governments), not by the National Government. The point can also be seen from this fact: The reserved powers include the vitally important police power—the power of a State to protect and promote the public health, the public morals, the public safety, and the general welfare.

The Constitution does not grant expressed powers to the States, with one notable exception. Section 2 of the 21st Amendment gives the States a virtually unlimited power to regulate the manufacture, sale, and consumption of alcoholic beverages.

Powers Denied to the States Just as the Constitution denies many powers to the National Government, so it denies many powers to the States. Some of those powers are denied to the States in so many words. For example, no State can enter into any treaty, alliance, or confederation. Nor can a State print or coin money or deprive any person of life, liberty, or property without due process of law.

Some powers are denied to the States inherently—that is, by the existence of the federal system. Thus, no State (and no local government) can tax any of the agencies or functions of the National Government.

Remember, too, each State has its own constitution. Those documents also deny many powers to the States.

CHECK UNDERSTANDING Describe the breadth of powers provided to the States.

The Exclusive and the Concurrent Powers

Exclusive Powers Most of the powers that the Constitution delegates to the National Government are **exclusive powers**. That is, they can be exercised only by the National Government; they cannot be exercised by the States under any circumstances.

Some of these powers are expressly denied to the States—for example, the power to coin money, to make treaties with foreign states, and to lay duties (taxes) on imports. Some of them are not expressly denied to the States but are, nonetheless, among the exclusive powers of the Federal Government because of the nature of the particular power involved. The power to regulate interstate commerce is a leading example of this point. If the States could exercise that power, trade between and among the States would be at best chaotic and at worst impossible.

>> The 1897 Dingly Tariff Act is an example of the exclusive power to lay duties on imports. **Analyze Political Cartoons** What was the impact of this act according to this cartoon?

Concurrent Powers Some of the powers delegated to the National Government are **concurrent powers**. That is, they are powers that both the National Government and the States possess and exercise. Those powers include the power to levy and collect taxes, to define crimes and set punishments for them, and to condemn (take) private property for public use.

The concurrent powers are held and exercised separately and simultaneously by the two basic levels of government. That is, the concurrent powers are those powers that the Constitution does not grant exclusively to the National Government and that, at the same time, does not deny to the States. The concurrent powers, in short, are those powers that make it possible for a federal system of government to function.

Although government in the United States is often discussed in terms of three levels—national, State, and local—there are, in fact, only two basic levels in the federal system: the National Government and the State governments. The more than 87,000 units of local government in the United States today are subunits of the various State governments. Local governments can provide services, regulate activities, collect taxes, and do many other things only because the State has given them the power to do so. In short, when local

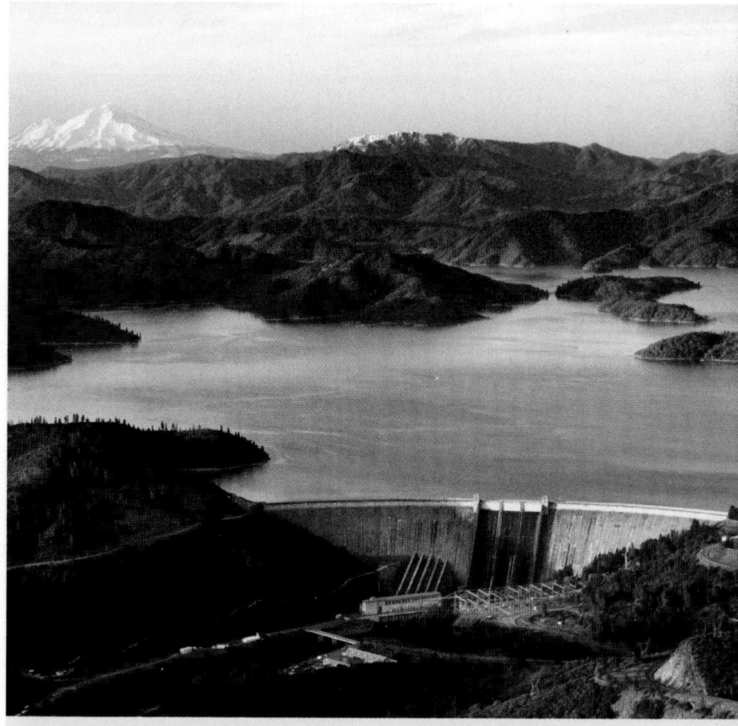
>> Some reservoirs, such as Shasta Lake in California, were created on land with existing homes. The land was claimed through eminent domain, a power shared by federal and State governments.

governments exercise their powers, they are actually exercising State powers.

Another way of putting all of this is to remind you of a point that we first made in Chapter 1. Each of the 50 States has a *unitary* form of government—an arrangement in which a central government that creates local units of government for its own convenience.

? EXPRESS IDEAS CLEARLY How do local governments relate to State governments?

The Constitution Reigns Supreme

As you have just seen, the division of powers in the American federal system produces a dual system of government, one in which two basic levels of government operate over the same territory and the same people at the same time. Such an arrangement is bound to result in conflicts between national and State law.

The Supremacy Clause The Framers anticipated those conflicts—and so they wrote the **Supremacy Clause** into the Constitution. That provision declares that

>> Local governments can collect taxes and provide some local services like fire departments, but their authority comes from the State.

> This Constitution, and the Laws of the United States which shall be made in Pursuance thereof; and all Treaties made, or which shall be made, under the Authority of the United States, shall be the supreme Law of the Land; and the Judges in every State shall be bound thereby, anything in the Constitution or Laws of any State to the Contrary notwithstanding.
>
> —Article VI, Section 2

The Constitution and the laws and treaties of the United States are "the supreme Law of the Land." This means that the Constitution ranks above all other forms of law in the United States. Acts of Congress and treaties stand immediately beneath the Constitution.

The Supremacy Clause has been called the "linchpin of the Constitution" because it joins the National Government and the States into a single governmental unit, a federal government. In other words, the Supremacy Clause is the provision in the Constitution that makes the complex federal system a working reality.

Our political history is studded with challenges to the concept of national supremacy. Recall that this nation fought a horrific Civil War in part over that very matter in the years 1861 to 1865. Those who have rejected the concept of national supremacy have insisted that the Constitution is, at base, a compact among sovereign States, rather than one between and among "We the People of the United States." They believe that the powers that compact does give to the National Government are to be very narrowly defined and applied. Echoes of that view can still be found in contemporary American politics.

The Supreme Court and Federalism The Supreme Court is the umpire in the federal system. One of its chief duties is to apply the Constitution's Supremacy Clause to the conflicts that the dual system of government inevitably produces.

The Court was first called to settle a clash between a national and a State law in 1819. The case, *McCulloch* v. *Maryland,* involved the controversial Second Bank of the United States. The bank had been chartered by Congress in 1816. In 1818, the Maryland legislature, hoping to cripple the bank, placed a tax on all notes issued by its Baltimore branch. James McCulloch, the branch cashier, refused to pay the tax, and the Maryland courts convicted him for that refusal. The

Supreme Court unanimously reversed the Maryland courts.

Speaking for the Court, Chief Justice **John Marshall** based the decision squarely on the Constitution's Supremacy Clause:

> [If] any one proposition could command the universal assent of mankind, we might expect it would be this—that the government of the Union, though limited in its powers, is supreme within its sphere of action.
>
> . . . [T]he states have no power . . . to retard, impede, burden, or in any manner control, the operations of the constitutional laws enacted by Congress. . . .
>
> —***McCulloch*** v. ***Maryland,*** 1819

Marshall, a strong Federalist, served on the Supreme Court for more than 30 years, and he believed strongly in the importance of the Supreme Court as a force in determining the law of the land. Since the decision in this landmark case, it has been impossible to overstate the significance of the role of the Court as the umpire of the federal system.

Had the Court not assumed this role, the American federal system and probably the United States itself could not have survived its early years. Justice Oliver Wendell Holmes once made that point in these words:

> I do not think the United States would come to an end if we [the Court] lost our power to declare an Act of Congress void. I do think the Union would be imperiled if we could not make that declaration as to the laws of the several States.
>
> —Collected Legal Papers

The Supreme Court first held a State law to be unconstitutional in a case from Georgia, *Fletcher* v. *Peck,* in 1810. The Court found that a Georgia law passed in 1794 that sold some 35 million acres

> [If] any one proposition could command the universal assent of mankind, we might expect it would be this—that the government of the Union, though limited in its powers, is supreme within its sphere of action.
>
> —*McCulloch* v. *Maryland,* 1819

>> Chief Justice John Marshall established that the Constitution grants the Federal Government implied powers for implementing its express powers, and that States cannot impede those powers.

of public land for 1.5 cents an acre amounted to a contract between the State and Peck and other buyers. Despite the obvious corruption involved, it found that the legislature's later (1796) repeal of the law violated the Constitution's Contract Clause (Article I, Section 10, Clause 1). That provision prohibits the States the power to pass any "Law impairing the Obligation of Contracts." Over the centuries since then, the High Court has found thousands of State laws and local ordinances unconstitutional, but it has upheld the constitutionality of thousands of others.

? **RECALL** Why is the Supremacy Clause often called the "linchpin" of the Constitution?

ASSESSMENT

1. **Connect** How does the Supremacy Clause impact disputes among States or between States and the National Government?
2. **Compare** How do the powers of the National Government compare in breadth to the powers of the States?
3. **Identify** How would President Lyndon Johnson be able to justify the use of federal troops to manage riots during the summer of 1967?
4. **Apply** Anna wanted to apply for a license to become a lawyer in the State of Alabama. Would she apply to the federal or State government for the license? Why?
5. **Check Understanding** What approach did the Framers of the Constitution use to limit the powers of the National Government, and why was that approach successful?

3.4 Have you ever really focused on the words *United States*, and what those two words say? The United States is a union of States, the several States joined together, the States united.

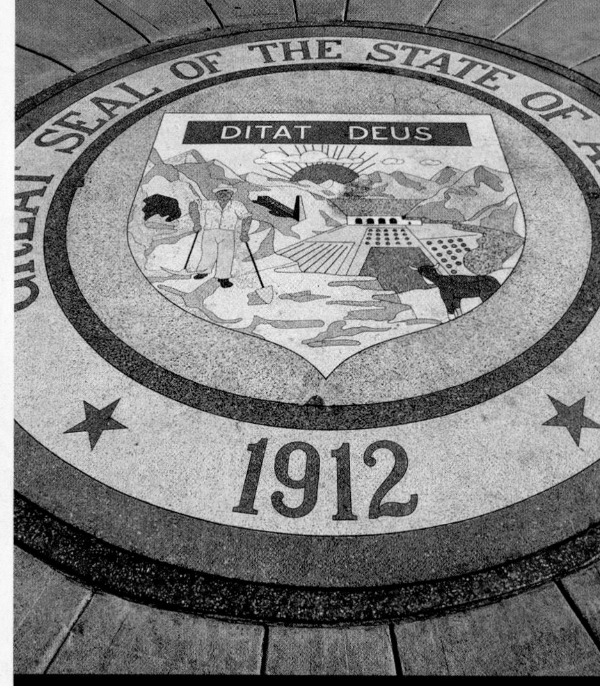

>> Arizona's journey to statehood took more than two years. After changing a provision in its constitution, the State was finally admitted as the 48th State on February 14, 1912.

Interactive Flipped Video

The National Government and the States

>> **Objectives**

Explain the process for admitting new States to the Union.

Examine the many and growing areas of cooperative federalism.

Explain why States make interstate compacts.

Understand the purpose of the Full Faith and Credit Clause, the Extradition Clause, and the Privileges and Immunities Clause.

>> **Key Terms**

reserved powers
enabling act
act of admission
grants-in-aid programs
categorical grants
block grants
project grants
interstate compacts
Full Faith and Credit Clause
extradition
Privileges and Immunities Clause
William Howard Taft

The Nation's Obligations Under the Constitution

The Framers of the Constitution created that union of States, and they intended to preserve it. To that end, the Constitution (1) requires the National Government to guarantee certain things to the States and (2) makes it possible for the National Government to do certain things for the States.

The Constitution places several obligations on the National Government for the benefit of the States. Most of them are found in Article IV.

Republican Form of Government The Constitution requires the National Government to "guarantee to every State in this Union a Republican Form of Government." The Constitution does not define "Republican Form of Government," and the Supreme Court has regularly refused to do so. The term is generally understood to mean a "representative government."

"Take it quietly UNCLE ABE and I will draw it closer than ever"!!
"A few more stitches ANDY and the good old UNION will be mended"!
INDIANA
ILLINOIS
IOWA
GEORGIA
FLORIDA
LOUISIANA
THE "RAIL SPLITTER" AT WORK REPAIRING THE UNION.

>> President Lincoln planned to quickly reunite the nation after the Civil War. **Analyze Political Cartoons** How might his assassination have affected reconciliation?

Interactive Cartoon

>> The Constitution guarantees the Federal Government will assist States that are attacked. U.S. Army soldiers helped patrol New York City after the 2001 attack on the World Trade Center.

The Supreme Court has held that the question of whether a State has a republican form of government is a "political question." That is, it is one to be decided by the political branches of the government—the President and Congress—and not by the courts.

The only extensive use ever made of the republican-form guarantee came in the years immediately following the Civil War. Congress declared that several southern States did not have governments of a republican form, and refused to admit senators and representatives from those States until they had ratified the 13th, 14th, and 15th amendments and broadened their laws to recognize the voting and other rights of African Americans.

The Constitution states that the National Government must also

> protect each of them [the States] against Invasion; and on Application of the Legislature, or of the Executive (when the Legislature cannot be convened) against domestic Violence.
>
> —Article IV, Section 4

Making War, Keeping Peace Today it is clear that an invasion of any one of the States would be met as an attack on the United States itself. This constitutional guarantee is therefore now of little significance.

That was not the case in the late 1780s. Then it was not at all certain that all 13 States would stand together if a foreign power attacked one of them. So, before the States agreed to give up their war-making powers, each demanded that an attack on any one of the States would be met as an attack on all of them.

The federal system assumes that each of the 50 States will keep the peace within its own borders. Thus, the primary responsibility for curbing insurrection, riot, or other internal disorder rests with the individual States. However, the Constitution does recognize that a State might not be able to control some situations. It therefore guarantees protection against internal disorder, or what the Constitution calls "domestic Violence."

The use of federal force to restore order within a State has been a rare event historically. Several instances did occur in the 1960s, however. When racial unrest exploded into violence in Detroit during the "long, hot summer" of 1967, President Lyndon Johnson ordered units of the United States Army into the city. He acted at the request of the governor of Michigan, George Romney, and only after Detroit's police and firefighters, supported by State police and National

Guard units, could not control riots, arson, and looting in the city.

In 1968, again at the request of the governors involved, federal troops were sent into Chicago and Baltimore to help put down the violence that erupted following the assassination of Martin Luther King, Jr. In 1992, President George H.W. Bush ordered members of the National Guard, the Army, and the Marines to Los Angeles to restore order after three days of rioting. The violence was sparked by the acquittal of four white officers charged with beating Rodney King, a black motorist, after he led them on a highspeed chase.

Normally, a President has sent troops into a State only in answer to a request from its governor or legislature. If national laws are being broken, national functions interfered with, or national property endangered, however, a President does not need to wait for such a plea.

President Grover Cleveland ordered federal troops to end rioting in the Chicago rail yards during the Pullman Strike in 1894 despite the objections of Illinois Governor William Altgeld. The Supreme Court upheld his actions in *In re Debs* (1895). The Court found that rioters had threatened federal property and impeded the flow of the mail and interstate commerce. Thus, more than "domestic Violence" was involved. Since then, several Presidents have acted without a request from the State involved. President Dwight Eisenhower did so at Little Rock, Arkansas, in 1957, and President John Kennedy did so at the University of Mississippi in 1962 and at the University of Alabama in 1963. In each of those instances, the President acted to halt the unlawful obstruction of school integration orders issued by the federal courts.

The ravages of nature—storms, floods, drought, forest fires, and the like—can be far more destructive than human violence. Here, too, acting to protect the States against "domestic Violence," the Federal Government stands ready to aid stricken areas.

Respect for Territorial Integrity The National Government is constitutionally bound to respect the territorial integrity of each of the States. That is, the National Government must recognize the legal existence and the physical boundaries of each State.

The basic scheme of the Constitution imposes this obligation. Several of its provisions do so, as well. For example, Congress must include, in both of its houses, members chosen in each one of the States. Recall, too, that Article V of the Constitution declares that no State can be deprived of its equal representation in the United States Senate without its own consent.

>> In 1963, President Kennedy sent federal troops to intervene when Governor George Wallace blocked the door of the University of Alabama to prevent African American students from entering.

INFER What compromise made it possible for States to agree to give up their power to make war?

Admitting New States

That new States would soon join the original 13 as members of the new United States was generally accepted as fact in the 1780s. To that end, the Congress of the Confederation, meeting as the Framers were drafting what was to become the Constitution, enacted the Northwest Ordinance of 1787—clearly, the most important measure passed by that body in its eight years as the government of the United States.

The ordinance anticipated the creation of new States in what was then known as the Northwest Territory—a roughly defined area lying north of the Ohio River and west of New York, Pennsylvania, and Virginia. The measure provided for the eventual Statehood of any sector in that region that acquired a population of at least 60,000 persons. Understanding that geographical differences would require unique laws and policies, it made provisions for local self-government, for civil and political rights, and for the support of education. An earlier measure, the Ordinance of 1785, had created the township system for the dividing of land for the support of local schools. Its provisions were folded into the 1787 enactment.

The Northwest Ordinance was re-adopted by the new Congress under the Constitution in 1790, and it served as the basis for later legislation regarding the nation's territorial possessions. It established that those territories were not to be kept in a second-class status but were to be groomed for Statehood on an equal footing with the existing States.

Congress and New States Only Congress has the power to admit new States to the Union, and the Constitution places only one restriction on that power: A new State cannot be created by taking territory from one or more of the existing States without the consent of the legislature(s) of the State(s) involved.

Congress has admitted 37 States since the original 13 formed the Union, as the map shows. Four States (Kentucky, Tennessee, Maine, and West Virginia) were created from parts of already existing States. Texas and Vermont were independent republics before admission. California was admitted shortly after being ceded to the United States by Mexico. Each of the other 30 States entered the Union only after a longer period of time, frequently more than 15 years, as an organized territory.

Admission Procedure The process of admission to the Union is usually simple. The area desiring Statehood first asks Congress for admission. If and when Congress chooses, it passes an **enabling act**, an act directing the people of the territory to frame a proposed State constitution. A territorial convention prepares the constitution, which is then put to a popular vote in the proposed State. If the voters approve the document, it is submitted to Congress for its consideration. If Congress still agrees to Statehood after reviewing the proposed constitution, it passes an **act of admission**, an act creating the new State. If the President signs the act, the new State enters the Union.

The two newest States, Alaska and Hawaii, shortened the usual admission process. Each adopted a proposed constitution without waiting for an enabling act, Hawaii in 1950 and Alaska in 1956. Both became States in 1959.

Conditions for Admission Before finally admitting a new State, Congress has often set certain conditions. For example, in 1896, Utah was admitted on condition that its constitution outlaw polygamy, the practice of having more than one spouse at a time. In admitting

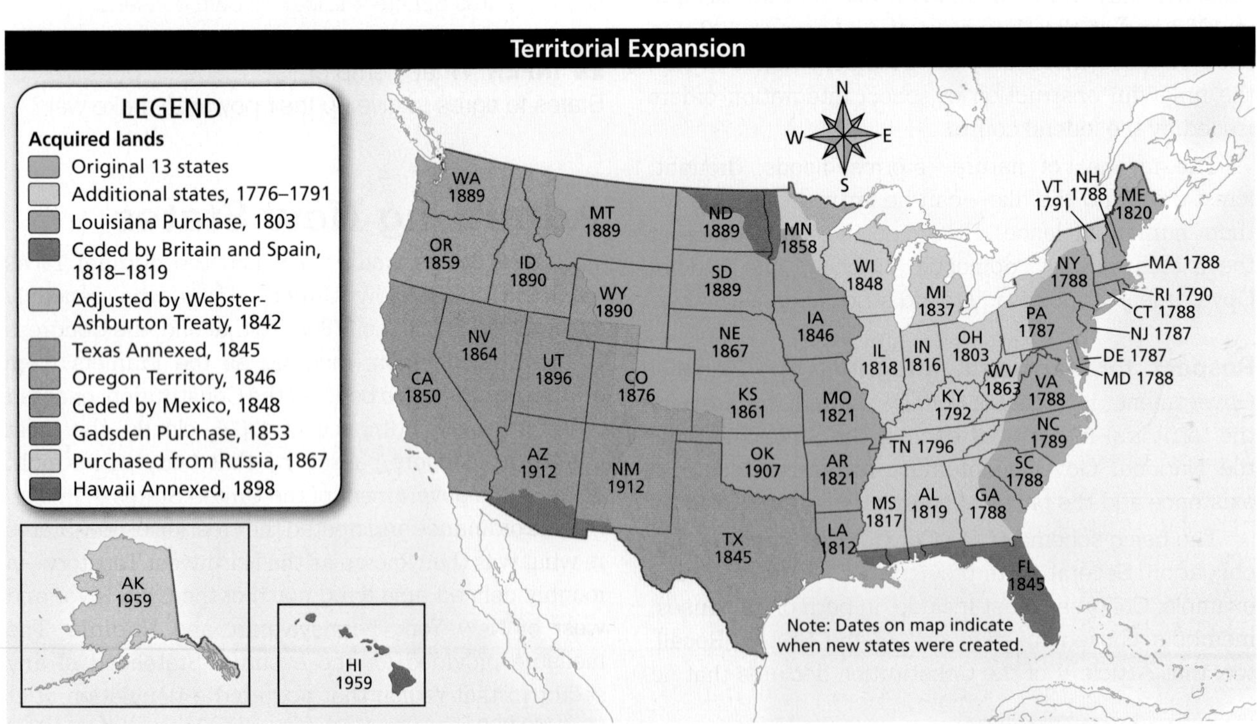

>> From 1776 to 1898, the U.S. acquired the land from which new States were eventually formed. **Analyze Maps** From which acquisition were the most States formed?

Interactive Map

Alaska to the Union, Congress forever prohibited that State from claiming title to any lands legally held by any Native American.

Each State enters the Union on an equal footing with each of the other States. Thus, although Congress can set certain conditions like those just described, it cannot impose conditions of a political nature. For example, when Oklahoma was admitted to the Union in 1907, Congress said the State could not move its capital from Guthrie to any other place before 1913. In 1910, however, the Oklahoma legislature moved the State's capital to Oklahoma City. When that step was challenged, the Supreme Court held, in *Coyle* v. *Smith* (1911) that Congress can set conditions for a prospective State's admission, but those conditions cannot be enforced if they compromise the independence of a State to manage its own internal affairs.

Consider one more example: President **William Howard Taft** vetoed a resolution to admit Arizona to the Union in 1911. He did so because Arizona's proposed constitution provided that members of the State's judiciary could be recalled (removed from office) by popular vote. This provision meant, said Taft, that in deciding cases a judge would have to keep one eye on the law and the other on public opinion. In response to the President's concern, Arizona removed the recall section from the document. In 1912 Congress passed, and the President signed, another act of admission for Arizona. Almost immediately after admission, however, the new State amended its new constitution to provide for the recall of judges. That provision remains a valid part of Arizona's constitution today.

>> Passed in 1971, the Alaska Native Claims Settlement Act gave Alaska Natives title to lands they had used for generations. The United States paid them to give up claims to other lands.

? IDENTIFY STEPS IN A PROCESS What are the usual steps required to admit a new State to the United States of America?

States and Federal Government Sharing Resources

Remember, federalism produces a dual system of government, one in which *two* basic levels operate over the same people and the same territory at the same time. As a result of this complex arrangement, competition, tensions, and conflict are a regular and ongoing part of American federalism. In short, the American federal system is much like a tug-of-war, a continuing power struggle between the National Government and the States.

The American federal system also involves a broad area of *shared* powers. That is, in addition to the two separate spheres of power held and exercised by the

"Sorry, but all my power's been turned back to the states."

>> A superhero, representing the Federal Government, is ineffective due to a shift in power to the States. **Analyze Political Cartoons** How does the Constitution prevent this from happening?

>> In 1984, the Federal Government withheld partial funding for highway maintenance to encourage States to raise the minimum drinking age to 21. States depend on federal funds for road repairs.

>> The Morrill Act established land-grant colleges, such as Texas A & M, to provide a practical education to students. Classes originally covered agriculture, military science, and engineering.

two basic levels of government, there are large and growing areas of cooperation between them.

Federal Grants-in-Aid Perhaps the best known examples of this intergovernmental cooperation are the many federal **grants-in-aid programs**—grants of federal money or other resources to the States and their cities, counties, and other local units. Many of these governments are regularly strapped for funds; these grants often help them perform a large share of their everyday functions.

The history of grants-in-aid goes back more than 200 years, to the period before the Constitution. In the Northwest Ordinance, the Congress under the Articles of Confederation provided for the government of the territory beyond the Ohio River and set aside sections of land for the support of public education in those future States.

On through the nineteenth century, most States received grants of federal lands for a number of purposes: schools and colleges, roads and canals, flood control work, and several others. A large number of the major State universities, for example, were founded as land-grant colleges. These schools were built with the money that came from the sale of public lands given to the States by the Morrill Act of 1862.

Congress began to make grants of federal money quite early, too. In 1808, it gave the States $200,000 to support the militia, the forerunner of the present-day National Guard. Cash grants did not play a large role, however, until the Depression years of the 1930s. Many of the New Deal programs aimed at bringing the nation out of its economic crisis were built around grants of money.

Since then, Congress has set up hundreds of grants-in-aid programs. In fact, more than 500 are now in operation. Dozens of programs function in a variety of areas: in education, mass transit, highway construction, healthcare, and many others.

Grants-in-aid are based on the National Government's taxing power. The Constitution gives Congress that power in order

> to pay the Debts and provide for the common Defense and general Welfare of the United States. . . .
>
> —Article I, Section 8, Clause 1

Today, these grants total about $400 billion, and account for about a third of all State and local government spending each year.

In effect, grants-in-aid blur the division-of-powers line in the federal system. They make it possible for the

TYPES OF FEDERAL GRANTS TO STATES

BLOCK

Funds used for **BROAD PURPOSES** where States have freedom to decide how to spend the money.

EXAMPLES
- Social Services
- Transportation
- Education

CATEGORICAL

Funds used for **CLOSELY DEFINED PURPOSES** with conditions set by Federal Government.

EXAMPLES
- Construction of airports
- Distribution of school lunches
- Construction of wastewater plants
- Support for senior centers

PROJECT

Funds used for **INDIVIDUAL PROJECTS** that States, localities, and private agencies compete for.

EXAMPLES
- Research into diabetes treatments
- Implementation of an innovative educational program
- Digitization of a local library

>> Congress has the implied power to make grants-in-aid to States and their local governments. **Analyze Charts** What kinds of organizations might receive a block grant?

Federal Government to operate in many policy areas in which it would otherwise have no constitutional authority—for example, in such fields as education, low-income housing, local law enforcement, and mental health.

Critics of grants-in-aid have long made this point. They also argue that the grants, which usually come with strings attached, often give Washington a major—and, they say, an unwarranted—voice in the making of public policy at the State and local levels. Conversely, proponents of grants-in-aid maintain that the many programs and projects made possible by grants-in-aid offset any negatives associated with the funds.

Types of Federal Grants Today, Congress appropriates money for three types of grants-in-aid: categorical grants, block grants, and project grants.

Over time, most grants have been categorical. **Categorical grants** are made for some specific, closely defined purpose—for school lunches or for the construction of airports or wastewater treatment plants, for example. Categorical grants are usually made with conditions attached. These "strings" require the State to (1) use the federal monies only for the specific purpose involved; (2) make its own monetary contribution, often a matching amount but sometimes much less; (3) provide an agency to administer the grant; and (4) obey a set of guidelines tailored to the particular purpose for which the monies are given.

Block grants have come into wide use over the last several years. They are made for much more broadly defined purposes than are categorical grants—for healthcare, social services, or welfare, for example. They are also made with fewer strings attached, so State and local governments have greater freedom in deciding just how and on what to spend block grant dollars. From the 1980s on, many programs once supported by separate and fragmented categorical grants have been merged into broader block grants.

Congress also provides money for **project grants**. These are grants made to States, localities, and sometimes private agencies that apply for the grants. The Department of Health and Human Services makes many project grants—through its National Institutes of Health, for example, to support scientists engaged in research on cancer, diabetes, neurological disease, and other medical issues. Many State and local governments also apply for these grants to fund their job training and employment programs.

Other Forms of Federal Aid The National Government aids the States in several other important ways. For example, the FBI gives extensive help to State and local police. The army and the air force equip and train each State's National Guard units. The Census Bureau's data are essential to State and local school, housing, and transportation officials as they plan for the future.

Many other forms of aid are not nearly so visible. "Lulu payments," for example, are federal monies that go to local governments in those areas in which there are large federal landholdings. These direct payments are made in lieu of (to take the place of) the property taxes that those local governments cannot collect from the National Government. These payments are also known as PILTs (payment in lieu of taxes).

State Aid to the National Government Intergovernmental cooperation is a two-way street. That is, the States and their local governments also aid the National Government in many ways. Thus, State and local election officials conduct national elections. These elections are financed with State and local funds, and they are regulated largely by State laws.

The legal process by which aliens can become citizens, called naturalization, takes place most often in State courts. The examples go on and on.

? INTERPRET In what way is the American government like a "tug of war?"

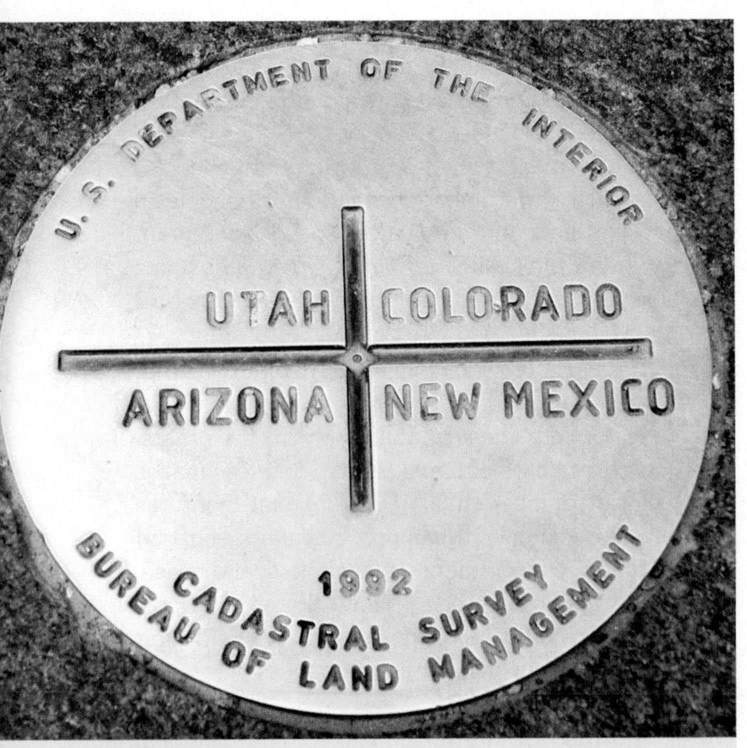

>> The Four Corners monument marks the legally accepted intersection of Arizona, New Mexico, Utah and Colorado. The location was surveyed in 1868 and was upheld by the Supreme Court in 1925.

Agreements Among States

The Constitution Reduces Interstate Frictions You know that rivalries, conflicts, and jealousies among the newly independent States was a principal reason for the writing and the adoption of the Constitution. The fact that the new document strengthened the hand of the National Government, especially with regard to trade among the States, reduced many of those frictions. So, too, did several of the new Constitution's provisions dealing with the States' relationships with one another.

Interstate Compacts No State can enter into any treaty, alliance, or confederation, says the Constitution. However, the States can, with the consent of Congress, enter into **interstate compacts**—agreements among themselves and with foreign states.

The States made few of these agreements for several decades—only 36 of them by 1920. The number has grown steadily since then, however. New York and New Jersey led the way in 1921 with a pact creating what is now the Port Authority of New York and New Jersey to manage the harbor facilities bordering both States. More than 200 compacts are now in force, and many involve several States.

There are several interstate compacts that all 50 States have signed onto, such as the Compact for the Supervision of Parolees and Probationers and the Compact on Juveniles. These two compacts enable States to share important law-enforcement data.

Other agreements cover a widening range of subjects. They include pacts that coordinate the development and conservation of such resources as water, oil, wildlife, and fish; counter the effects of global climate change; and encourage the cooperative use of public universities.

? ANALYZE INFORMATION For what purpose have all fifty States joined together in interstate compacts?

How the Law Crosses State Lines

In Article IV, Section 1, the Constitution commands that: "Full Faith and Credit shall be given in each State to the public Acts, Records, and judicial Proceedings of every other State."

The term *public acts* refers to the laws of a State. *Records* refers to such documents as birth certificates, marriage licenses, deeds to property, car registrations, and the like. The words *judicial proceedings* relate to the outcome of court actions: damage awards, the probating of wills, divorce decrees, and so forth.

The **Full Faith and Credit Clause** most often comes into play in court matters. Take this example: Allen sues Bill in Florida, and the Florida court awards Allen $50,000 in damages.

Bill cannot escape payment of the damages by moving to Georgia, because Allen could simply ask the Georgia courts to enforce the damage award. Nor would the case have to be retried in Georgia. Instead, the Georgia courts would have to give full faith and credit to—recognize and respect the validity of—the judgment made by the Florida court.

In a similar vein, a person can prove age, place of birth, marital status, title to property, and similar facts by securing the necessary documents from the State where the record was made. The validity of these documents will be recognized in each of the 50 States.

>> When Richard and Mildred Loving were married in 1958, interracial marriage was illegal in some States. In 1967, the Supreme Court ruled that all States must recognize interracial marriage.

Exceptions The Full Faith and Credit Clause is regularly observed, and it usually operates routinely between the States. There are two notable exceptions to the rule, however. First, it applies only to *civil,* not *criminal,* matters. One State cannot enforce another State's criminal law. Second, full faith and credit need not be given to certain divorces granted by one State to residents of another State.

On the second exception, the key question is always this: Was the person who obtained the divorce in fact a resident of the State that granted it? If so, the divorce will be accorded full faith and credit in other States. If not, the State granting the divorce did not have the authority to do so, and another State can refuse to recognize it.

Marriage and Divorce The matter of interstate "quickie" divorces has been troublesome for decades, and especially since the Supreme Court's decision in a 1945 case, *Williams* v. *North Carolina.* In that case, a man and a woman traveled to Nevada, where each wanted to obtain a divorce so they could marry one another. They lived in Las Vegas for six weeks, the minimum period of State residence required by Nevada's divorce law. The couple were granted their divorces, were married, and returned to North Carolina the next day.

Problems arose when that State's authorities refused to recognize their Nevada divorces. North Carolina brought the couple to trial and a jury convicted each of them of the crime of bigamous cohabitation (marrying and living together while a previous marriage is still legally in effect).

On appeal, the Supreme Court upheld North Carolina's denial of full faith and credit to the Nevada divorces. It ruled that the couple had not in fact established *bona fide*—good faith, valid—residence in Nevada. Rather, the Court held that the couple had remained legal residents of North Carolina. In short, it found that Nevada lacked the authority to grant their divorces.

A divorce granted by a State court to a *bona fide* resident of that State must be given full faith and credit in all other States. To become a legal resident of a State, a person must intend to reside there permanently, or at least indefinitely. Clearly, the Williamses had not intended to do so.

The *Williams* case, and later ones like it, have cast dark clouds of doubt over the validity of thousands of other interstate divorces. The later marriages of people involved in these divorces, and the frequently tangled estate problems produced by their deaths, suggest the serious nature of the matter.

Even the legality of some marriages differs among the States. Today, most States and the District of Columbia allow same-sex unions within their borders. However, 14 States have constitutional or statutory provisions prohibiting such marriages.

In 2003, Massachusetts' Supreme Judicial Court held that the State's constitutional equal rights guarantees mean that same-sex couples have exactly the same marriage rights as those enjoyed by male-female couples in Massachusetts. Soon after, nearby Connecticut (2005) and then New Jersey (2007) came to the same position.

The movement gradually gained momentum over the following years, culminating in the legalization of same-sex marriages by 17 States in 2014 alone. Today, by court decision, legislation, or (in Maine) ballot initiative, 36 States and the District of Columbia have legalized same-sex marriages within their borders. The most recent State to do so was Florida, where a district judge ruled the State's ban on same-sex unions to be unconstitutional in early 2015. Shortly afterward, the Supreme Court agreed to hear a case that would decide the issue on the national level. That historic case will be decided by the early summer of 2015.

If a same-sex couple, legally married to one another in one State, moves to a State where those unions are outlawed, does the Full Faith and Credit Clause require the second State to recognize the validity of that couple's marriage? That thorny question reached the Supreme Court in 2013, in the case of *United States* v. *Windsor*. In a 5–4 decision, the justices ruled that States need not allow same-sex marriage, but same-sex couples who are legally married will be treated as married by the Federal Government-even if they live in a State which does not recognize same-sex marriage. In other words, anyone who is legally married in any State will receive federal tax, health, and pension benefits.

The decision overturned part of the existing Defense of Marriage Act (DOMA), which had been enacted in 1996. That law declared that only those marriages that unite a man and a woman are legal in the United States. It also provided that no State can be required to give full faith and credit to any same-sex marriage performed in any other State.

State and National governments and agencies are still working to understand just what the 2013 ruling really implies. There are implications for tax codes, health care, pensions, and many other issues that are indirectly associated with laws surrounding marriage. Meanwhile, many States are unhappy with the Supreme Court decision and are discussing how best to respond.

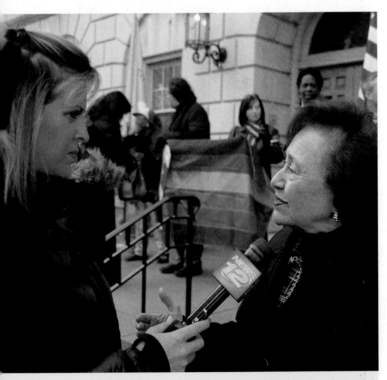

>> Congresswoman Nita Lowey (D., NY) speaks to a reporter about DOMA. The Supreme Court's decision in the case affected the way benefits and taxes were managed at State and federal levels.

? APPLY CONCEPTS Barnaby stole a car in one State and fled to another. The State in which he stole the car demanded that the State in which he now resides must enforce its law against auto theft. Does the Full Faith and Credit Clause apply in this situation?

Extradition

Definition of Extradition The Constitution makes provisions for those who flee to another State to avoid punishment for a crime:

> A Person charged in any State with Treason, Felony, or other Crime, who shall flee from Justice, and be found in another State, shall on Demand of the executive Authority of the State from which he fled, be delivered up, to be removed to the State having Jurisdiction of the Crime.
>
> —Article IV, Section 2, Clause 2

This clause refers to **extradition**, the legal process by which a fugitive from justice in one State can be returned to that State. Extradition is designed to prevent a person from escaping justice by fleeing a State.

Changes in Extradition Law The return of a fugitive from justice is usually a routine matter; governors regularly approve the extradition requests they receive from other States' chief executives. Some of those requests, however, are contested. This is especially true in cases with strong racial or political overtones, and in cases of parental kidnapping of children involved in custody disputes.

Until the 1980s, governors could, and on occasion did, refuse to return fugitives. In *Kentucky* v. *Dennison* (1861) the Supreme Court had held that the Constitution did not give the Federal Government any power with which to compel a governor to act in an extradition case. So, for more than a century, the Constitution's word *shall* in the Extradition Clause had to be read as "may."

The Court overturned that ruling in 1987, however. In *Puerto Rico* v. *Branstad,* a unanimous Court held that the federal courts can indeed order an unwilling governor to extradite a fugitive.

SUPPORT IDEAS WITH EXAMPLES Provide an example of a situation in which the return of a fugitive from justice might be contested.

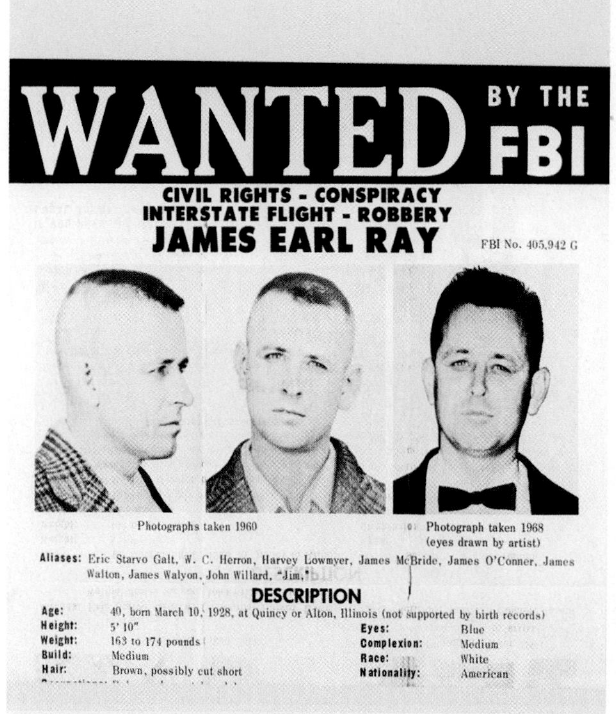

>> James Earl Ray assassinated Martin Luther King, Jr., in June of 1968. Less than two months later, he was caught in England with a fake Canadian passport and extradited to the United States.

Privileges and Immunities

The Constitution also protects citizens who move between the States.

> The Citizens of each State shall be entitled to all Privileges and Immunities of Citizens in the several States.
>
> —Article IV, Section 2, Clause 1

This clause, known as the **Privileges and Immunities Clause**, means that no State can draw unreasonable distinctions between its own residents and those persons who happen to live in another State.

Each State must recognize the right of any American to travel in or become a resident of that State. It must also allow any citizen, no matter where he or she lives, to use its courts and make contracts; buy, own, rent, or sell property; or marry within its borders.

Unreasonable Distinctions However, a State cannot do such things as try to relieve its unemployment problems by requiring employers to hire in-State residents first. Thus, the Supreme Court struck down an Alaskan law requiring employers to prefer Alaskan workers to construct that State's oil and gas pipelines (*Hicklin* v. *Orbeck,* 1978). The Court overturned a California law that set the welfare benefits for newly arrived residents from States with lower welfare benefit levels at a lower level than those paid to long-term residents (*Saenz* v. *Roe,* 1999).

>> Convicted murderer Chadrick Fulks being escorted from Indiana to West Virginia by U.S. Marshals in 2013, in order to assist the FBI in their search for the body of one of his victims.

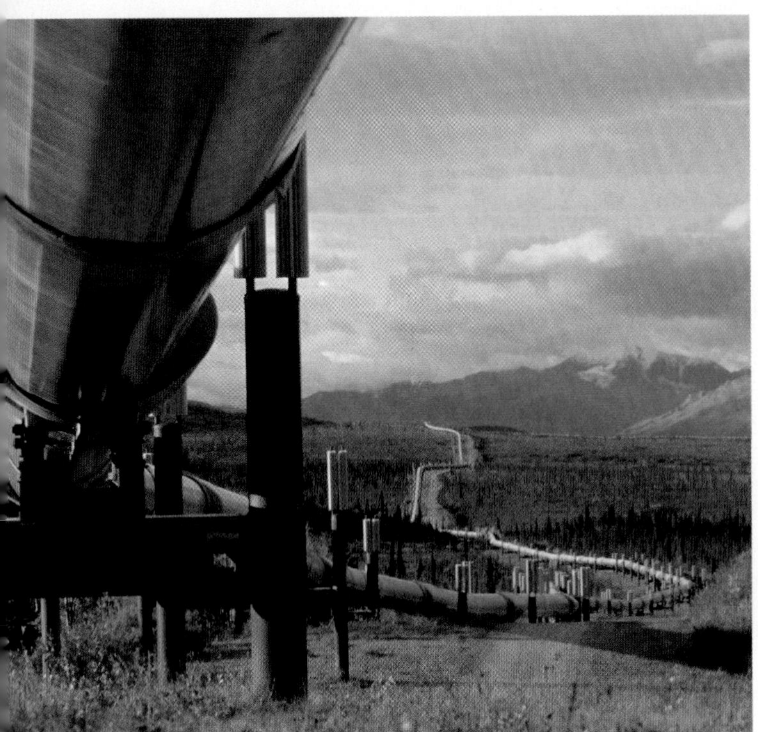

>> In the three years it took to complete the Trans-Alaska pipeline, workers on the project from Alaska and other States earned high salaries and endured brutal conditions.

Reasonable Distinctions However, the Privileges and Immunities Clause does allow States to draw *reasonable* distinctions between its own residents and those of other States. Thus, any State can require that a person live within the State for some time before he or she can vote or hold public office. It also can require some period of residence before one can be licensed to practice law, medicine, dentistry, and so on.

In another example, the wild fish and game in a State are considered the common property of the people of that State. So, a State can require nonresidents to pay higher fees for fishing or hunting licenses than those paid by residents—who pay taxes to provide fish hatcheries, enforce game laws, and so on. By the same token, State colleges and universities regularly set higher tuition rates for out-of-State students.

APPLY CONCEPTS Describe an example of reasonable distinction under the Privileges and Immunities Clause.

ASSESSMENT

1. **Generate Explanations** The Constitution requires the National Government to "guarantee to every State in this Union a Republican Form of Government," but the Supreme Court has refused to define the term "Republican Form of Government." Why is this the case?
2. **Infer** Would it be legal for Congress to allow a territory of the United States to become a full State on the condition that it choose a new governor? Why or why not?
3. **Identify Cause and Effect** While federal grants of land were common during the 19th century, cash grants-in-aid were not made until the mid-20th century. What was the reason for this change?
4. **Infer** What might keep a State from accepting a categorical grant-in-aid?
5. **Apply Concepts** When Wilma moved from Tennessee to Michigan, she expected no legal obstacles to buying or renting a home in Michigan. Was Wilma correct? Why?

TOPIC 3 ASSESSMENT

1. **Create a Visual Presentation** Create a visual presentation describing how the painting above of James Madison delivering the final draft of the U.S. Constitution to George Washington serves as propaganda for the new United States of America. Consider the following information in the presentation: What was involved in the process of creating the Constitution? Who are the individuals shown in the painting and what were their stances on the issues surrounding the Constitution? How are the Founders and delegates presented in the painting? How does the painting serve as a piece of propaganda?
2. **Identify the Contributions** Write a paragraph describing the contributions of Alexander Hamilton's ideas about judicial review. Include the following information in your paragraph: an explanation of the power of judicial review as established by *Marbury* v. *Madison*; a description of Hamilton's beliefs about the Constitution as expressed in *The Federalist* No. 78 and how those beliefs relate to the power of judicial review; an explanation of the importance of judicial review to the workings of the U.S. government.
3. **Analyze Legislative Branch** Write a paragraph that explains the role committees play in the amendment process. Consider such questions as: What are legislative committees? How are committees structured? What are the functions of committees? How are committees involved with the amendment process?
4. **Analyze the Functions of the Executive Branch** Write a paragraph in which you analyze the constitutional powers of the President. Consider the following: the powers granted by the Constitution; why the Framers established each of these as presidential powers in the Constitution; and how these powers differ from those of a despot or monarch.
5. **Create a Presentation Evaluating How the Government Fulfills the Preamble** Create an oral presentation evaluating how the federal government serves the purposes set forth in the Preamble to the U.S. Constitution. When creating the presentation, answer the following questions: Are each of the principles as relevant to our government today as when they were written? Why or why not? What are some of the specific ways in which the principles are upheld by our government? How are these principles meaningful in your own life?

"We the People of the United States, in Order to form a more perfect Union, establish Justice, insure domestic Tranquility, provide for the common defence, promote the general Welfare, and secure the Blessings of Liberty to ourselves and our Posterity, do ordain and establish this Constitution for the United States of America."

—Preamble to the Constitution

6. **Identify Major Intellectual, Philosophical, Political, and Religious Traditions** Write a paragraph identifying how English common law and constitutionalism informed the founding of America and form the basis of American government. Consider the following questions: What is constitutionalism? How are constitutionalism and limited government connected? How do constitutionalism and English common law form the basis of the concepts of liberty, rights, and responsibilities of individuals?
7. **Understand the Role** Analyze the rule of law created by the Framers of the U.S. Constitution. Then write a paragraph and answer the following questions: What is the rule of law? How does the rule of law protect individual rights? How does the rule of law uphold the principle of limited government?
8. **Create a Visual Presentation** Create a visual presentation that categorizes government powers as national, state, or shared. Answer the following questions: What powers does the national government have in the United States? What powers do the individual states have in the United States? What powers are shared by the national and state governments?
9. **Understand the Limits on the National Government** Write a paragraph about the limits on United States government at the national and state levels. Consider the following questions: How does the U.S. Constitution limit the powers of both the national and state governments? Why is limited government a fundamental idea of the U.S. Constitution?
10. **Compare the Functions and Processes** Write a paragraph describing the functions and processes of federal, state, and local governments. Consider the following questions: What are some functions and processes of the federal government as laid out in the Constitution? What are some of the functions and processes reserved for state and local governments as laid out in the Constitution? In general, how do the functions and processes of the federal government compare to the functions and processes of state and local governments?
11. **Explain the Major Responsibilities** Write a paragraph describing the federal government's responsibilities in regard to the states. Consider the following in the paragraph: insurrection, riots, and other internal disorder; natural disasters; why the national government has these responsibilities.
12. **Describe the Constitutionally Prescribed Procedures** Write a paragraph describing the methods by which an amendment may be proposed and ratified as described in Article V of the U.S. Constitution. Why do you think the amendment process was created to be so complicated?
13. **Recall the Conditions** Write a paragraph describing the conditions that led to the 14th Amendment. Consider the following questions: Why was the 14th Amendment needed? What did the 14th Amendment guarantee? What was the significance of the 14th Amendment?
14. **Evaluate Constitutional Provisions** Use the political cartoon below to write a paragraph analyzing the cartoonist's viewpoint about popular sovereignty. Consider the following questions: What is popular sovereignty? What is the cartoonist suggesting about how popular sovereignty affects government? How would you describe the bias shown, if any, by the cartoonist? Is the information expressed in the cartoon valid?

15. **Create a Project** Create an annotated timeline, Web site, poster, or other type of project on the role of the amendment process in a constitutional government. Choose an amendment that has been proposed in the twenty-first century and research why the amendment was proposed, who proposed it, and the process of the amendment. Use the following process: Ask questions about the circumstances that led to the amendment proposal and explore the issues. Plan the project by outlining goals and objectives. Research the amendment proposal using primary and secondary sources. Create the project. Improve the project by editing and reevaluating the goals and objectives. Draw a conclusion about the role of the amendment process in a constitutional government. Present the project.

16. **Explain the Importance** Write a paragraph explaining why having a written constitution is important. Consider the following questions: Why is a written constitution important for individuals? Why is a written constitution important for the government? Can a country function without a written constitution? Why or why not? Consider documents such as the U.S. Constitution and the Bill of Rights when writing your response.

17. **Identify American Beliefs and Principles** Write a paragraph describing how the U.S. Constitution reflects American beliefs and principles and establishes a both a national and a federal identity. Consider such things as: what American beliefs and principles are; the details in the Constitution that relate to the nation as a whole; and the details in the Constitution regarding the relationship between the national government and the states.

18. **Explain How Political Divisions Are Crafted** Write a paragraph explaining how political divisions formed through the process of admitting states into the Union. Make sure to: describe the political division crafted in this process; explain the role of the Northwest Ordinance of 1787 in establishing the process; and describe the relationship between the existing states and a newly admitted state.

19. **Analyze Information** Use the following quote to write a paragraph to describe the circumstances leading to the formation of a national judiciary. Consider the following: the provisions for a federal court system in the Articles of Confederation; the reasons why a federal court system was necessary; and the effect of filling that need.

"The judicial Power of the United States shall be vested in one supreme Court, and in such inferior Courts as the Congress may from time to time ordain and establish."

—Article III, Section 1

20. **Explain Why the Founding Fathers Adopted a Federal System** Write a paragraph explaining why the Founders chose a federal system of government. Consider the following questions: What is a federal system of government? What is a unitary system of government? What factors played a role in influencing the Founders' choice of system? Why did the Founders choose a federal system over a unitary system?

21. **Explain Certain Provisions of the U.S. Constitution** Review the checks-and-balances system established by the U.S. Constitution. Then write a paragraph that answers the following question: How does the system of checks and balances established by the U.S. Constitution make compromise necessary?

22. **Analyze the Functions of the Judicial Branch** Write a paragraph analyzing the structure and functions of the federal court system. Consider the following questions: What are the two types of courts that make up the inferior courts? How are they structured within the judicial branch of the federal government? List one example of each type of inferior court and describe its function. Why is a federal court system necessary?

23. **Analyze the Federal System of Government** Analyze advantages and disadvantages of a federal system of government. Write a paragraph expressing your opinion on the effectiveness of the United States' federal system as a form of government. Consider such things as: division of power; how each level operates; conflicts between national and state governments.

24. **Create a Written Presentation** Create a written presentation about the conflict between the national and state governments on the issue of same-sex marriage. Consider the following questions: What is the legality of same-sex marriage among the states? What is DOMA? How did the case of *United States* v. *Windsor* influence the recognition of same-sex marriage? Which level of government do you think should have jurisdiction over this issue?

25. **Create a Written or Oral Presentation** Select one of the *Federalist Papers* (No. 10, 39, or 51) and analyze it and its Anti-Federalists' counterargument on the governmental principle it addresses. Also identify elements within the essays that could be viewed as propaganda. Consider the following: the views of the Federalists and Anti-Federalists; the *Federalist Papers* No. 10, No. 39, or No. 51; Anti-Federalist counterarguments made in Centinel No. 1 or Brutus No. 1; the ratification process of the U.S. Constitution; and how these arguments were used as propaganda during the ratification process.

26. **Identify Freedoms and Rights** Use the Amendment below to write a paragraph describing the freedoms protected by the 5th Amendment. Make sure to: identify the five protections guaranteed by the 5th Amendment; explain how these protections place limits on the government.

"No person shall be held to answer for a capital, or otherwise infamous crime, unless on a presentment or indictment of a Grand Jury, except in cases arising in the land or naval forces, or in the Militia, when in actual service in time of War or public danger; nor shall any person be subject for the same offence to be twice put in jeopardy of life or limb; nor shall be compelled in any criminal case to be a witness against himself, nor be deprived of life, liberty, or property, without due process of law; nor shall private property be taken for public use, without just compensation."

—Amendment V, Bill of Rights

27. **Write About the Essential Question Write an essay on the Essential Question: What is the right balance of power in good government?** Use evidence from your study of this Topic to support your answer.

Go online to PearsonRealize.com and use the texts, quizzes, interactivities, Interactive Reading Notepads, Flipped Videos, and other resources from this Topic to prepare for the Topic Test.

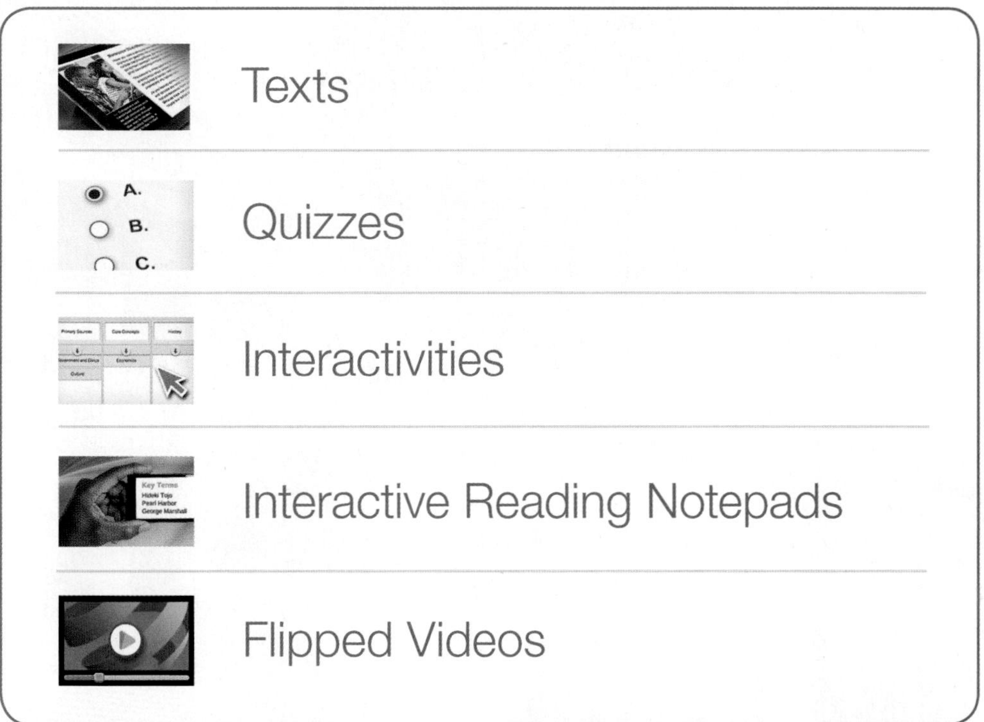

While online you can also check the progress you've made learning the topic and course content by viewing your grades, test scores, and assignment status.

[ESSENTIAL QUESTION] How should government meet the needs of its people?

4 The Legislative Branch

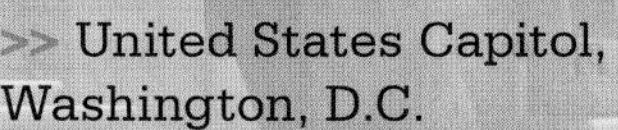

>> United States Capitol, Washington, D.C.

Enduring Understandings

- The Constitution establishes Congress as a bicameral legislature, with two houses—the Senate and the House of Representatives—acting as checks on one another.
- The House has 435 seats, apportioned by population. Members respresent a specific State district and serve two-year terms.
- The Senate has 100 members, two from each State, who serve 6-year terms.
- The Constitution grants Congress a number of expressed and implied powers and some non-legislative duties.
- A bill is a proposed law presented to either house. If passed by both, a bill is presented to the President. Vetoes can be overturned with a 2/3 vote.

PEARSON realize™ NBC LEARN

Watch the My Story Video to explore the unusual success story of lawmaker Loretta Sanchez.

PEARSON realize™ www.PearsonRealize.com

Access your digital lessons including: Topic Inquiry • Interactive Reading Notepad • Interactivities • Assessments

>> The freshman class of the 113th Congress included 65 men, 19 women, the first openly gay senator, the first Buddhist, and the first Asian American woman.

Interactive Flipped Video

4.1 The Framers of the Constitution were well versed in the history of government. They knew that throughout world history, heads of state—usually kings—often abused their power. Indeed, the "list of grievances" in the Declaration of Independence was aimed squarely at King George III. "The history of the present King of Britain," wrote Thomas Jefferson, "is a history of repeated injuries and usurpations. . . ."

>> Objectives

Explain the role of Congress and the job of its members.

Explain the difference between a term and a session of Congress.

Describe a situation in which the President may convene or end a session of Congress.

Identify the personal and political backgrounds of members of Congress.

Describe the duties performed by those who serve in Congress.

Describe the compensation and privileges of members of Congress.

>> Key Terms

delegates
trustees
partisans
politicos
bills
floor consideration
oversight function
term
session
convene
adjourn
recess
prorogue
special session
franking privilege
Luther Patrick
Nancy Pelosi
Harry Truman

National Legislature Overview

The Role of Congress in a Democracy

Representative Assemblies Because of this distrust of a powerful executive, coupled with an emerging view that just governments derive their powers from the will of the people, the colonists put great stock in representative assemblies. As alarms about oppression by the British government grew, sentiments like "no taxation without representation" reflected this belief. The nation's first such assembly was the Second Continental Congress, which governed the nation from the Declaration of Independence until the Confederation Congress convened in 1781, and was composed of delegates from every colony.

National Government The individual colonies (and later, States) put their faith in this representative body to guide them through both war with Great Britain and the United States' early days as a sovereign nation. Even so, the Framers worried about vesting too much power in a body chosen directly by the people. The average citizen can be overly passionate and driven by self-interest, they argued. So, they designed a National Government that couched the legislature's powers within both a broader system of checks and balances and a federal system where a good deal would be left to the States. It would be the job of each representative to "enlarge and refine the public views," as suggested by James Madison in *The Federalist* No. 10. That is, to help citizens look beyond their immediate interest to the national interest.

? MAKE GENERALIZATIONS The Framers distrusted a powerful executive, putting great trust in representative assemblies, but they were also concerned about vesting too much power in a body chosen directly by the people. Does this idea still hold true today?

Congress: The Job

One leading commentary on American politics describes Congress and the job of a member of Congress this way:

> Congress has a split personality. On the one hand, it is a lawmaking institution and makes policy for the entire nation. In this capacity, all the members are expected to set aside their personal ambitions and perhaps even the concerns of their constituencies. Yet Congress is also a representative assembly, made up of 535 elected officials who serve as links between their constituents and the National Government. The dual roles of making laws and responding to constituents' demands forces members to balance national concerns against the specific interests of their States or districts.
>
> —James M. Burns, et al., ***Government by the People***

Members of both houses of Congress fulfill five major roles. They are most importantly (1) legislators and (2) representatives of their constituents. Beyond those roles, they are also (3) committee members, (4) servants of their constituents, and (5) politicians. Here, we consider their representative, committee member, and servant functions.

"Congress has a split personality. On the one hand, it is a lawmaking institution and makes policy for the entire nation. In this capacity, all the members are expected to set aside their personal ambitions and perhaps even the concerns of their constituencies. Yet Congress is also a representative assembly, made up of 535 elected officials who serve as links between their constituents and the National Government. The dual roles of making laws and responding to constituents' demands forces members to balance national concerns against the specific interests of their States or districts.

—James M. Burns, et al., *Government by the People*

>> House Speaker Paul Ryan and President Donald Trump shake hands on the floor of the House. The Framers envisioned Congress as a body "whose wisdom may best discern the true interest of their country."

Interactive 3-D Model

Representatives of the People Senators and representatives are elected to represent the people. What does that really mean? The members of both houses cast hundreds of votes during each session of Congress. Many of those votes involve quite routine, relatively unimportant matters; for example, a bill to designate a week in May as National Wildflower Week. But many of those votes, including some on matters of organization and procedure, do involve questions of far reaching importance.

Therefore, no questions about the lawmaking branch can be more vital than these: How do the people's representatives represent the people? On what basis do they cast their votes?

In broadest terms, each lawmaker has four voting options. He or she can vote as a delegate, a trustee, a partisan, or a politico.

Delegates see themselves as the agents of the people who elected them. They believe that they should discover what "the folks back home" think about an issue and vote that way. They are often willing to suppress their own views, ignore those of their party's leadership, and turn a deaf ear to the arguments of their colleagues and of special interests from outside their constituencies.

Trustees believe that each question they face must be decided on its merits. Conscience and judgment are their guides. They reject the notion that they must act as robots or rubber stamps. Instead, they call issues as they see them, regardless of the views held by a majority of their constituents or by any of the other groups that seek to influence their decisions.

Partisans believe that they owe their first allegiance to their political party. They feel duty-bound to cast their votes in line with the party platform and the views of their party's leaders. Most studies of legislators' voting behavior indicate that partisanship is the leading factor influencing lawmakers' votes on most important questions.

Politicos attempt to combine the basic elements of the delegate, trustee, and partisan roles. They try to balance these often conflicting factors: their own view of what is best for their constituents and/or the nation as a whole, the political facts of life, and the peculiar pressures of the moment.

Current Trends Which model is the most popular today? Scholars generally agree that a growing number of legislators adhere to the delegate model. This fact is largely due to the marvels of modern-day polling, which gives legislators, the media, and voters a much clearer picture of "the will of the people" than was possible in the past. In addition, the Internet has given constituents the ability to check the voting records of their legislators with a few quick clicks, making lawmakers much more accountable to the public than in earlier times. Finally, today's senators and representatives often enter Congress with the goal of remaining in Washington for years to come. Throughout the nation's early history, a stint in the House or Senate was viewed as a public service, and legislators returned to private life after a few terms. Today, however, lawmakers often

Roles of Members of Congress

ROLES	DUTIES
Legislator	• Study proposals and draft legislation • Frame public policies
Agent of Constituents	• Be the people's representative on important matters
Committee Member	• Serve on committees that screen proposals for floor consideration
Servant of Constituents	• Assist constituents with bureaucratic and ceremonial tasks
Politician	• Balance interests of constituents and political party

>> Members of both houses of Congress have many roles to play. **Analyze Charts** Why are the legislative and agent of constituent roles the most important?

view membership in Congress as a long-term career, giving rise to a new era that has been dubbed the "rise of career legislators." And of course, the surest way to stay in office is to rarely, if ever, buck public opinion. This fact makes voting as a delegate of the people much more important than it was in the past.

Committee Members In every session of Congress, proposed laws, known as **bills,** are referred to the various committees in each chamber. As committee members, senators and representatives must screen those proposals. They decide, in committee, which measures will go on to **floor consideration**—that is, be considered and acted upon by the full membership of the House or Senate.

Although Congress enacts laws and appropriates the money to implement them, the Constitution assigns the task of executing those laws to the executive branch. Congress must see that executive agencies carry out those laws faithfully and spend that money properly. It does so through the exercise of its critically important **oversight function,** the process by which Congress, through its committees, checks to see that the executive branch agencies are carrying out the policies that Congress has set by law.

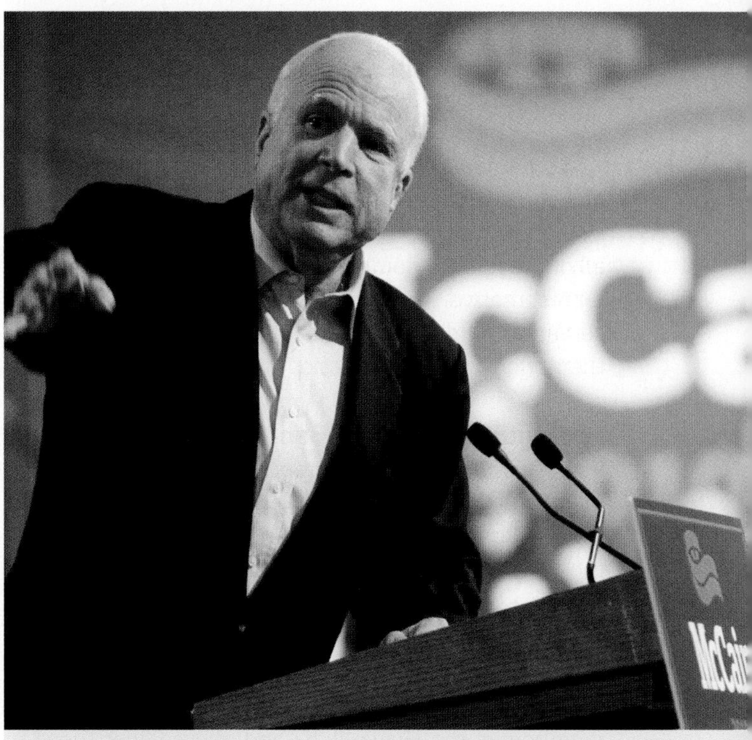

>> U.S. Senator John McCain speaks at a campaign rally during the 2010 Senate race. Today, most senators and representatives view Congress as a career rather than a short public service stint.

Servants of the People Members of both the House and the Senate act as servants of their constituents. Most often, they do this as they (and their staff aides) try to help people in various dealings with the federal bureaucracy. Those interactions may involve a Social Security benefit, a passport application, a small business loan, or any one of a thousand other matters.

Some of "the folks back home" seem to think that members of Congress are sent to Washington mostly to do favors for them. Most members are swamped with constituent requests from the moment they take office. The range of these requests is almost without limit—everything from help in securing a government contract or an appointment to a military academy, to asking for a free sightseeing tour of Washington or even a personal loan. Consider this job description offered only half-jokingly by a former representative:

> A Congressman has become an expanded messenger boy, an employment agency, getter-outer of the Navy, Army, Marines, ward heeler, wound healer, trouble shooter, law explainer, bill finder, issue translator, resolution interpreter, controversy oil pourer, gladhand extender, business promoter, convention goer, civil ills skirmisher, veterans' affairs adjuster, ex-serviceman's champion, watchdog for the underdog, sympathizer with the upper dog, namer and kisser of babies, recoverer of lost luggage, soberer of delegates, adjuster for traffic violators, voter straying into Washington and into toils of the law, binder up of broken hearts, financial wet nurse, Good Samaritan, contributor to good causes—there are so many good causes—cornerstone layer, public building and bridge dedicator, ship christener—to be sure he does get in a little flag waving—and a little constitutional hoisting and spread-eagle work, but it is getting harder every day to find time to properly study legislation—the very business we are

primarily here to discharge, and that must be done above all things.

—Rep. Luther Patrick (D., Alabama)

Most members of Congress know that to deny or fail to respond to most of these requests would mean to lose votes in the next election. This is a key fact, for all of the roles a member of Congress plays—legislator, representative, committee member, constituent servant, and politician—are related, at least in part, to their efforts to win reelection.

Personal and Political Background Can you name your two senators? Your representative? Regrettably, most Americans cannot—let alone tell you much about the backgrounds, qualifications, or voting records of those who represent them in Congress.

Whatever else they may be, the 535 members of Congress are *not* a representative cross section of the American people. Rather, the "average" member is a white male in his late 50s. The average age of the members of the House is 57 and about 62 for those in the Senate.

The composition of Congress is gradually becoming more diverse. For example, the 113th Congress included the largest number of women in history. Eighty-one women served in the House of Representatives, up from 23 only 25 years before. **Nancy Pelosi** (D., California), who became the first woman Speaker of the House in 2007, was elected Minority Leader. Twenty women sat in the Senate, whereas only 39 women had served in all previous years *combined*. The 113th Congress was also notable for its inclusion of the first two women combat veterans to be elected to office.

>> House Minority Leader Nancy Pelosi was the first woman to be elected Minority Whip, and the first woman elected Speaker of the House of Representatives.

In addition, the Congress included 42 African Americans and 35 Hispanics in the House, as well as 11 Asian Americans, 2 Native Americans, and one Pacific Islander. Three Hispanics and one Asian sat in the Senate, including the first ever Asian American woman. One African American served in the upper house, but only six had ever held seats in that body.

Nearly all members were married, a few were divorced, and they had, on average, two children. Only a very few members said they had no religious affiliation. Over half were Protestants, nearly three in ten were Roman Catholics, less than one in ten were Jewish, three were Buddhists, two were Muslims, one was a Quaker, and one was Hindu.

Well over a third of the members of the House and over half the senators were lawyers. Ninety-four percent had a college degree and two thirds had advanced degrees. Most senators and representatives were born in the States they represented.

Only a handful were born outside the United States. Sprinkled among the members of Congress were several millionaires. A surprisingly large number of the men and women who sat in the House depended on their congressional salaries as their major source of income, however.

Most members of Congress have had considerable political experience. The average senator is serving a second term, and the typical representative has served four terms. Approximately one-half of the senators once sat in the House. Several senators are former governors. A few senators have held Cabinet seats or other high posts in the executive branch of the Federal Government. The House includes a large number of former State legislators and prosecuting attorneys among its members.

Again, Congress is not an accurate cross section of the nation's population. Rather, it is made up of upper-middle-class Americans, who are, on the whole, quite able and hardworking people.

? DISTINGUISH A representative is preparing to vote on a bill that includes some benefits for her State, but also results in greater deficit spending. She is aware that most of her constituents support the bill. Under what circumstances do you think she would choose to

Terms and Sessions of Congress

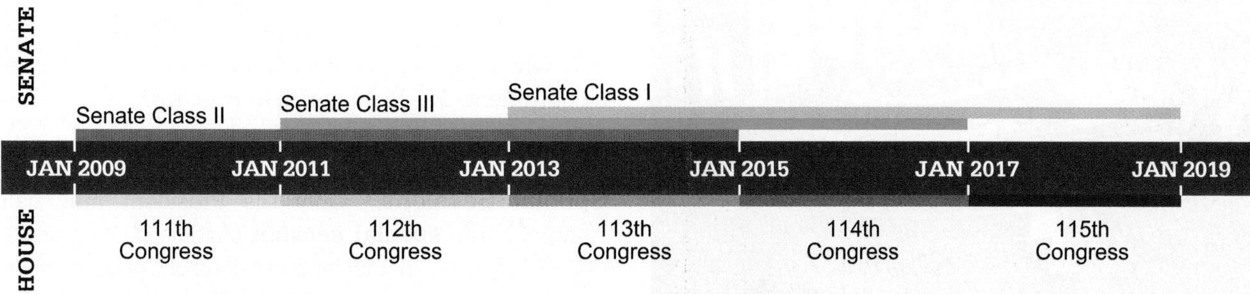

>> The Senate is divided into three equal classes so that only a third of the Senate seats may change hands in an election. **Analyze Charts** How does the Senate arrangement differ from the House?

vote as a partisan or a trustee, rather than a delegate, on this bill?

Terms and Sessions of Congress

It is said that a woman, incensed at something her senator had done, said to him, "You know, the 535 of you people in Congress meet every two years. Well, Senator, there are some of us who think that it would be much better if just two of you met every 535 years."

Whether that story is true or not, that woman's advice has never been followed. Ever since 1789, Congress has met for two-year terms.

Terms of Congress Each **term** of Congress lasts for two years, and each of those two-year terms is numbered consecutively (Article I, Section 2, Clause 1). Congress began its first term on March 4, 1789. That term ended two years later, on March 3, 1791.

The date for the start of each new term was changed by the 20th Amendment in 1933. In an earlier era, the several months from election to March 4 allowed for delays in communicating election results, and it gave newly chosen lawmakers time to arrange their affairs and travel to Washington. The March date gave Congress less time to accomplish its work each year, however, and by the 1930s travel and communications were no longer an issue. The start of each new two-year term is now "noon of the 3d day of January" of every odd-numbered year. So the scheduled term of the 113th Congress runs for two years—from noon on January 3, 2013, to noon on January 3, 2015.

Sessions of Congress A **session** of Congress is that period of time during which, each year, Congress assembles and conducts business. There are two sessions to each term of Congress—one session each year. The Constitution provides that:

> The Congress shall assemble at least once in every year, and such meeting shall begin at noon on the 3d day of January, unless they shall by law appoint a different day.
>
> —20th Amendment, Section 2

In fact, Congress often does "appoint a different day." The second session of each two-year term frequently **convenes** a few days or even a few weeks after the third of January.

Congress **adjourns,** or suspends until its next session, each regular session as it sees fit. Until World War II, the nation's lawmakers typically met for four or five months each year. Today, the many pressing issues facing Congress force it to remain in session through most of each year. Both houses do **recess** for several short periods during a session. That is, they temporarily suspend business.

Neither house may adjourn *sine die* (finally, ending a session) without the other's consent. The Constitution provides that

> Neither House . . . shall, without the Consent of the other, adjourn for more than three days, nor to any other Place

than that in which the two Houses shall be sitting.

—Article I, Section 5, Clause 4

>> When Congress is not in session, the House of Representatives is empty and legislators may be working in their home States. The 2014 schedule called for Congress to be in session 113 days.

>> During a special joint session of Congress the day after the Japanese attack on Pearl Harbor, President Franklin D. Roosevelt asked Congress to declare war on Japan.

Article II, Section 3 of the Constitution does give the President the power to **prorogue** a session, but only when the two houses cannot agree on a date for adjournment. No President has ever had to use that power.

Special Sessions Only the President may call Congress into **special session** (Article II, Section 3). Only 27 of these special joint sessions of Congress have ever been held. President **Harry Truman** called the most recent one in 1948, to consider anti-inflation and welfare measures in the aftermath of World War II.

Note that the President can call Congress or either of its houses into a special session. The Senate has been called alone on 46 occasions, to consider treaties or presidential appointments, but not since 1933. The House has never been called alone.

Of course, the fact that Congress now meets nearly year-round reduces the likelihood of special sessions. That fact also lessens the importance of the President's power to call one. Still, as Congress nears the end of a session, the President sometimes finds it useful to threaten a special session if the two chambers do not act on some measure high on the administration's legislative agenda.

? DRAW CONCLUSIONS What option does the Constitution give the President if Congress adjourns without an approved budget?

Congressional Compensation

The Constitution says that members of Congress "shall receive a Compensation for their Services, to be ascertained by Law. . . (Article I Section 6, Clause 1)." That is, the Constitution says that Congress fixes its own pay. The late Senator Russell Long (D., Louisiana) once characterized this provision as one that gives to members of Congress "a power that no good man would want and no bad man should have." The 27th Amendment modified this pay-setting authority. It declares that no increase in members' pay can take effect until after the next congressional election—that is, not until after voters have had an opportunity to react to the pay raise.

Salary Today senators and representatives are paid $174,000 per year. A few members are paid somewhat

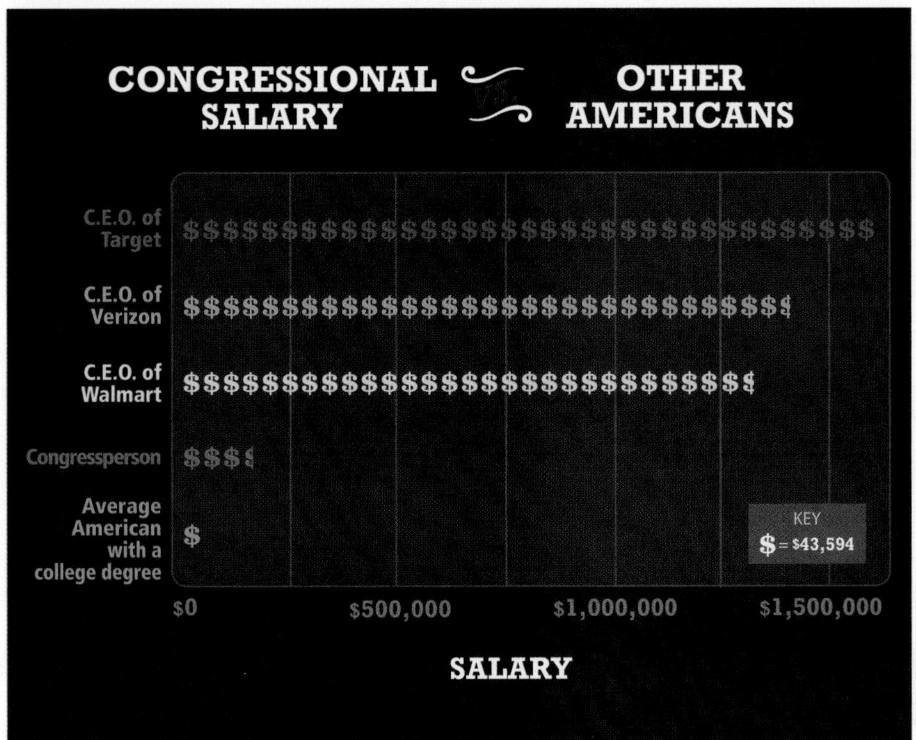

>> This chart shows the salaries of members of Congress from a different perspective. **Analyze Charts** How do congressional salaries compare to the salaries of C.E.O.s and the average American?

more. The Speaker of the House makes $223,500 per year. The Vice President makes $230,700 per year. The Senate's president pro tem and the floor leaders in both houses receive $193,400 per year.

Nonsalary Compensation Members receive a number of "fringe benefits," and some are quite substantial. For example, each member has a special tax deduction. That deduction recognizes the fact that most members of Congress must maintain two residences, one in his or her home State and one in Washington.

Generous travel allowances offset the cost of several round trips each year between home and Washington. Members pay relatively small amounts for life and health insurance and for outpatient care by a medical staff on Capitol Hill; they can get full medical care, at very low rates, at any military hospital. They also have a generous retirement plan, to which they contribute. The plan pays a pension based on years of service in Congress, and longtime members can retire with an income of $150,000 or more per year. The lawmakers are also covered by Social Security's retirement and Medicare programs.

Members are also provided with offices in one of the several Senate and House office buildings near the Capitol and allowances for offices in their home State or district. Each member is given funds for hiring staff and for the operating costs related to running those offices. The **franking privilege** is a well-known benefit that allows them to mail letters and other materials postage-free by substituting their facsimile signature (frank) for the postage.

Congress has also provided its members with the free printing—and through franking, the free distribution—of speeches, newsletters, and the like. Radio and television tapes can be produced at very low cost. Each member can choose among several fine restaurants and two first-rate gymnasiums. Members receive still more privileges, including such things as the help of the excellent services of the Library of Congress and free parking in spaces reserved for them at the Capitol and also at Washington's major airports.

Why Serve? Despite these many fringe benefits, few citizens choose to run for Congress. In addition to the costs such a venture entails, the reluctance to serve can be traced to the enormous challenges of the job, weighed against the relatively modest compensation enjoyed by the nation's lawmakers. While it is true that millions of Americans would view $174,000 as a hefty salary, the fact is that many of the men and women who

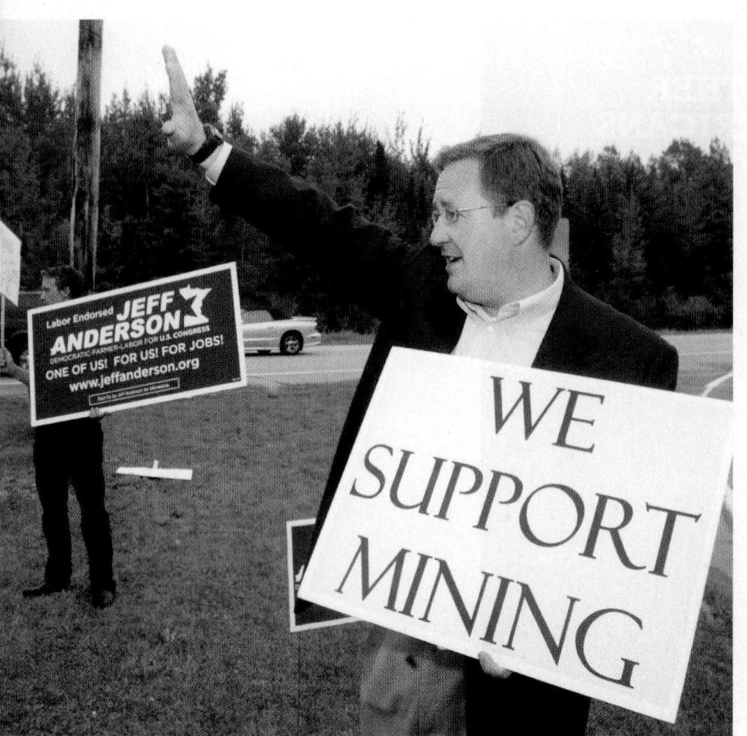

>> Jeff Anderson (right) campaigned for Minnesota's 8th U.S. Congressional seat in 2012, though few people think the compensation for being in Congress is adequate for the work and scrutiny.

serve in Congress are at the top of their professions and actually take a pay cut to serve. Several are also already millionaires. The work entails long hours and intense public scrutiny. Additionally, running for office can be expensive and exhausting and can sometimes draw a candidate's family into the fray. So why *does* anyone serve in Congress?

Many members of Congress are anxious to make a difference—to bring about changes they care about and to help their communities. In addition, the prestige of office is also an appealing part of the job. Congress, as an institution, is sometimes held in low regard, but individual members are well respected. Not everyone in office cares about being a "big shot," but many do. In fact, some speculate that Congress is filled with a disproportionately large number of folks who care about prestige. But that might not be a bad thing. Even the Framers knew that the desire to be held in high regard by constituents can serve to keep legislators, as they say, "on task."

The Politics of Pay There are only two real limits on the level of congressional pay. One is the President's veto power. The other and more potent limit is the fear of voter backlash, an angry reaction by constituents at the ballot box. That fear of election-day fallout has always made most members reluctant to vote to raise their own salaries.

Congress has often tried to skirt the politically sensitive pay question. It has done so by providing for such fringe benefits as a special tax break for those who must maintain two residences, a liberal pension plan, more office and travel funds, and other perquisites, or "perks"—items of value that are much less apparent to "the folks back home."

? IDENTIFY CENTRAL ISSUES The Constitution specifies that Congress has the power to fix its own pay. Why was it important to modify this authority with the 27th Amendment?

ASSESSMENT

1. **Identify Central Issues** A poll showed voters prefer that members of Congress act as delegates. How might we expect the effect of this to differ between senators and representatives?
2. **Make Generalizations** What is the *most likely* reason that the Constitution placed limits on the President's power to convene and dismiss Congress?
3. **Interpret** In what way does Congress's oversight function provide a process of checks and balances?
4. **Support Ideas with Examples** What aspects of the National Government exemplify the Framers' plan to have representatives focused on national, rather than personal, interests?
5. **Identify Cause and Effect** Lawmakers often view membership in Congress today differently than during the nation's early history. How and why might this be reflected in the way today's members of Congress vote?

4.2 Article I of the Constitution directs that "All legislative Powers herein granted shall be vested in a Congress of the United States, which shall consist of a Senate and House of Representatives." Thus, Congress is bicameral, meaning it has two houses. In election years, candidates for both houses try to win votes on social media, on Web sites, and with yard signs, billboards, flyers, buttons, and radio and television spots.

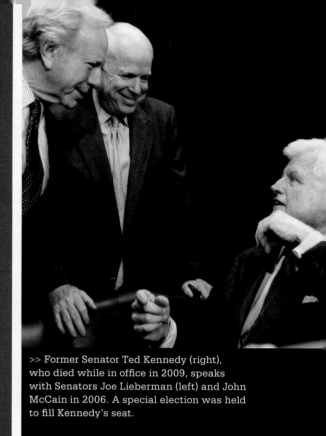

>> Former Senator Ted Kennedy (right), who died while in office in 2009, speaks with Senators Joe Lieberman (left) and John McCain in 2006. A special election was held to fill Kennedy's seat.

Interactive Flipped Video

The Two Houses

>> **Objectives**

Explain how House seats are distributed and describe the length of a term in the House.

Explain how House seats are reapportioned among the States after each census.

Describe a typical congressional election and congressional district.

Analyze the formal and informal qualifications for election to the House and the Senate.

Compare the size of the Senate to the size of the House of Representatives.

Explain how and why a senator's term differs from a representative's term.

>> **Key Terms**

apportioned
reapportion
single-member district
at-large
gerrymandering
off-year elections
incumbent
continuous body
constituencies
James Madison
Woodrow Wilson
Robert C. Byrd

The House

Size of House The exact size of the House of Representatives—today, 435 members—is not fixed by the Constitution. Rather, it is set by Congress. The Constitution provides that the total number of seats in the House of Representatives shall be **apportioned** among the States on the basis of their respective populations (Article I, Clause 3). Each State is guaranteed at least one seat no matter what its population. Today, seven States only have one representative apiece: Alaska, Delaware, Montana, North Dakota, South Dakota, Vermont, and Wyoming.

Voters in the District of Columbia, Guam, the Virgin Islands, and American Samoa each elect a delegate to represent them in the House, and Puerto Rico chooses a resident commissioner. Those officials are not, however, full-fledged members of the House of Representatives and do not vote on bills.

Terms for Representatives Article I, Section 2, Clause 1 of the Constitution provides that "Representatives shall be . . . chosen every second Year"—that is, they are elected for two-year terms. This rather short term means that, for House members, the next election is always just around the corner. That fact tends to make them pay close attention to "the folks back home."

There is no constitutional limit on the number of terms any member of Congress may serve. A considerable effort was made in the 1990s to persuade Congress to offer a constitutional amendment to limit congressional terms. Most versions of such an amendment would have put a three- or four-term limit on service in the House and a two-term limit for the Senate.

IDENTIFY CENTRAL ISSUES Why did the Constitution provide that the total number of seats in the House of Representatives should be apportioned among the States based on population, rather than being set at a fixed number?

Reapportionment of Congress

Article I of the Constitution directs Congress to **reapportion** the seats in the House every ten years, after each census (Article I, Section 2, Clause 3). Until a first census could be taken, the Constitution set the size of the House at 65 seats. That many members served in the First and Second Congresses (1789–1793). The census of 1790 showed a national population of 3,929,214 persons; so in 1792, Congress increased the number of House seats by 41, to 106.

A Growing Nation As the nation's population grew over the decades, and as the number of States also increased, so did the size of the House. It went to 142 seats after the census of 1800, to 182 seats 10 years later, and so on. By 1912, following the census of 1910 and the admission of Arizona and then New Mexico to the Union, the House had grown to 435 seats.

With the census of 1920, Congress found itself in a difficult political position. The House had long since grown too large for effective floor action. To reapportion without adding more seats, however, would mean that some States would have to lose seats.

Congress met the problem by doing nothing. So, despite the Constitution's command, there was no reapportionment on the basis of the 1920 census.

Reapportionment Act of 1929 Faced with the 1930 census, Congress avoided repeating its earlier lapse by passing the Reapportionment Act of 1929. That law, still on the books, sets up what is often called an "automatic reapportionment." It provides:

1. The "permanent" size of the House is 435 members. Of course, that figure is permanent only so long as Congress does not decide to change it. Congress did enlarge the House temporarily in 1959 when Alaska and then Hawaii became States. Today each of the 435 seats in the House represents an average of over 700,000 persons.

2010 Congressional Reapportionment

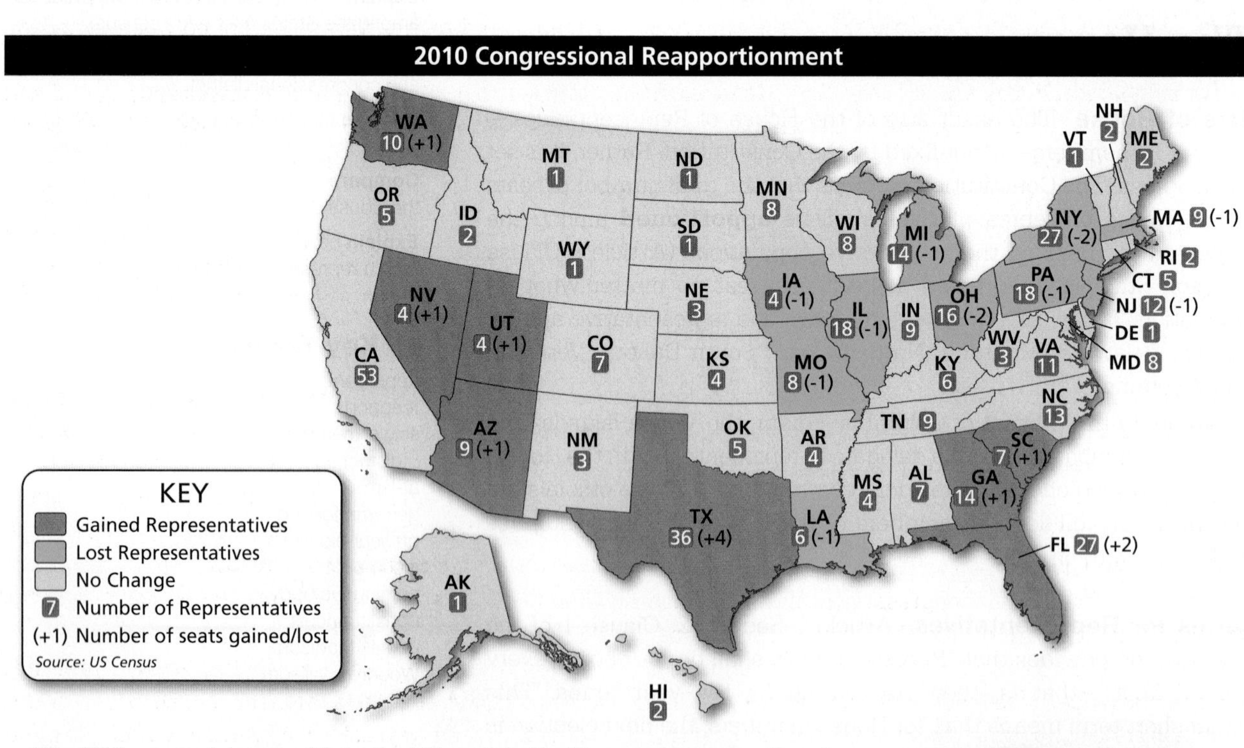

>> The 2010 census determined how the 435 seats in the House were reapportioned among the States. **Analyze Maps** What regions gained or lost population?

Interactive Chart

2. Following each census, the Census Bureau is to determine the number of seats each State should have.

3. When the Bureau's plan is ready, the President must send it to Congress.

4. If, within 60 days of receiving it, neither house rejects the Census Bureau's plan, it becomes effective.

The plan set out in the 1929 law has worked quite well through eight reapportionments. The law leaves to Congress its constitutional responsibility to reapportion the House, but it gives to the Census Bureau the mechanical chores and the political "heat" that go with that task.

Congressional Districts The 435 members of the House are chosen by the voters in 435 separate congressional districts across the country. Recall that seven States each have only one seat in the House. There are, then, 428 congressional districts within the other 43 States.

The Constitution makes no mention of congressional districts. For more than half a century, Congress allowed each State to decide whether to elect its members by a general ticket system or on a **single-member district** basis. Under the single-member district arrangement, the voters in each district elect one of the State's representatives from among a field of candidates running for a seat in the House from that district.

Most States quickly set up single-member districts. However, several States used the general ticket system. Under that arrangement, all of the State's seats were filled **at-large**—that is, elected from the State as a whole, rather than from particular districts. Every voter could vote for a candidate for each one of the State's seats in the House.

At-large elections proved grossly unfair. A party with even a very small plurality of voters statewide could win all of a State's seats in the House. Congress finally did away with the general ticket system in 1842. Thereafter, all of the seats in the House were to be filled from single-member districts in each State. Since the seven States with the fewest residents each have only one representative in the House, these representatives are said to be elected "at-large." Although each of them does represent a single-member district, that district covers the entire State.

The 1842 law gave each State legislature the responsibility for drawing congressional districts within its own State. It also required that each congressional district be made up of "contiguous territory." That is, it must be one piece, not several scattered pieces. In 1872, Congress added the command that the districts within each State have "as nearly as practicable an equal number of inhabitants." In 1901, it further directed that all the districts be of "compact territory"—in other words, a comparatively small area.

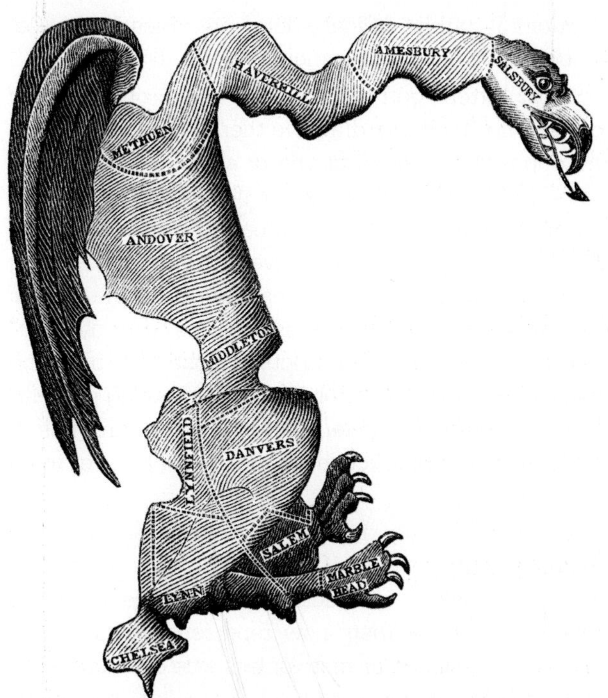

>> Gerrymandering got its name from Massachusetts Governor Elbridge Gerry, who redrew state voting districts to favor his party. **Analyzing Political Cartoons** What point does the drawing make?

Interactive Map

These requirements of contiguity, population equality, and compactness were often disregarded by State legislatures, and Congress made no real effort to enforce them. The requirements were left out of the Reapportionment Act of 1929. In 1932, the Supreme Court held (in *Wood* v. *Broom*) that they had therefore been repealed. Over time, then, and most notably since 1929, the State legislatures have drawn many districts with very peculiar geographic shapes. Moreover, until fairly recently, many districts were also of widely varying populations.

Gerrymandering Congressional district maps in several States show one and sometimes several districts of very odd shapes. Some look like the letters S or Y, some resemble a dumbbell or a squiggly piece of spaghetti, and some defy description. Those districts have usually been **gerrymandered**. That is, they have been drawn to the advantage of the political party that controls the State's legislature.

Gerrymandering is widespread today—and not just at the congressional district level. Districts for the election of State legislators are regularly drawn for the advantage of one party. In fact, gerrymandering can be found in most places where lines are drawn for the election of public officeholders—in cities, counties, school districts, and elsewhere.

Most often gerrymandering takes one of two forms. The lines are drawn either (1) to concentrate the opposition's voters in one or a few districts, thus leaving the other districts comfortably safe for the dominant party; or (2) to spread the opposition as thinly as possible among several districts, limiting the opposition's ability to win anywhere in the region. Gerrymandering's main goal is to create as many "safe" districts as possible—districts almost certain to be won by the party in control of the line-drawing process. And the computer-driven map-making techniques of today make the practice more effective than ever in its storied past.

Gerrymandering is the principle reason why, presently, only a handful of seats in the House are actually at risk in an election. In most elections, no more than 40 members now represent districts that cannot be classified as more or less safe districts.

For decades, gerrymandering led to congressional districts that differed widely in the number of people they included. State legislatures were responsible for this situation, of course. A number of them regularly drew district lines on a partisan basis—with the Republicans gouging the Democrats in those States where the GOP controlled the legislature, and the Democrats doing the same thing to the Republicans where they held sway. In fact, that circumstance exists in several States today. Historically, most States were carved up on a rural versus urban basis as well as a partisan one—because, through much of history, the typical State legislature was dominated by the less-populated (and over-represented) rural areas of the State.

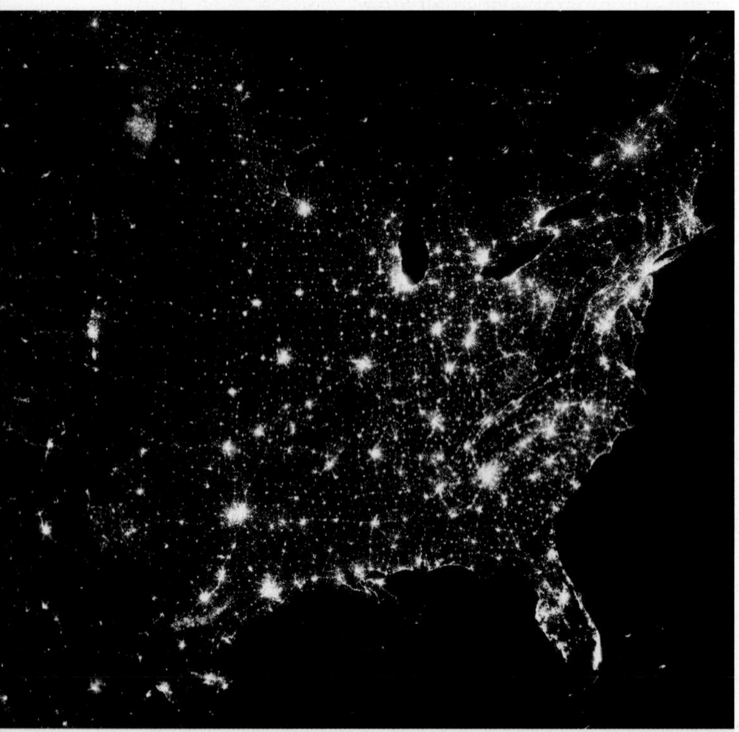

>> A view of the United States at night shows the differences in regional populations. Urban and rural populations have different needs and interests, which Congress struggles to balance.

Wesberry v. _Sanders_, 1964 The long-standing pattern of congressional districts of widely varying populations and, as a result, the long-standing fact of rural overrepresentation in the House came to an abrupt end in the mid to late 1960s. That dramatic change was the product of an historic Supreme Court decision in 1964. In a case from Georgia, *Wesberry* v. *Sanders*, the Supreme Court held that the Constitution demands that the States draw congressional districts of substantially equal populations.

The Court's "one person, one vote" decision in *Wesberry* had an immediate and extraordinary impact on the makeup of the House, on the content of public policy, and on the shape of electoral politics in general. The nation's cities and suburbs now speak with a much louder voice in Congress than they did before that decision. But notice, it remains quite possible for States to draw their congressional (or any other) district lines in accord with the "one person, one vote" rule and, at the same time, gerrymander those districts.

Gerrymandering based solely on race, however, is a violation of the 15th Amendment, *Gomillion* v. *Lightfoot*, 1960. So-called "majority-minority districts" were drawn in some States following the census in 1990 and again in 2000. Those districts were crafted to include a majority of African Americans and/or Latinos and so were likely to send African Americans and Latinos to Congress. The Supreme Court struck down those race-based districts in several cases—most notably in two cases from Texas, *Bush* v. *Vera,* 1996 and *United Latin American Citizens* v. *Perry*, 2006.

However, the Court has also held this: While race cannot be the controlling factor in drawing district lines, race can be one of the mix of factors that shape that process. It did so in a case from North Carolina, *Hunt* v. *Cromartie*, in 2001.

Partisan Gerrymandering The Court has said that under some circumstances, which it has never spelled out, excessively partisan gerrymandering might be unconstitutional. It did so for the first time in a 1986 case, *Davis* v. *Bandemer*. In 2003, Texas became the first State to redistrict between censuses, with the purpose of increasing the number of Republican-held

Texas seats in the U.S. House of Representatives. In a dramatic showdown, the Republican governor called a special session of the legislature. Democratic legislators fled the State, but ultimately they were unable to stop the redistricting.

In a 2006 decision, a bare majority of the Court ruled that neither the Constitution nor any act of Congress prevents a State from redrawing its district lines whenever the party in control of the legislature believes that it might be to its advantage to do so (*United Latin American Citizens* v. *Perry*).

DRAW CONCLUSIONS What was the effect of the 1932 Supreme Court case *Wood* v. *Broom* on the Constitution's goal of equal representation in the House?

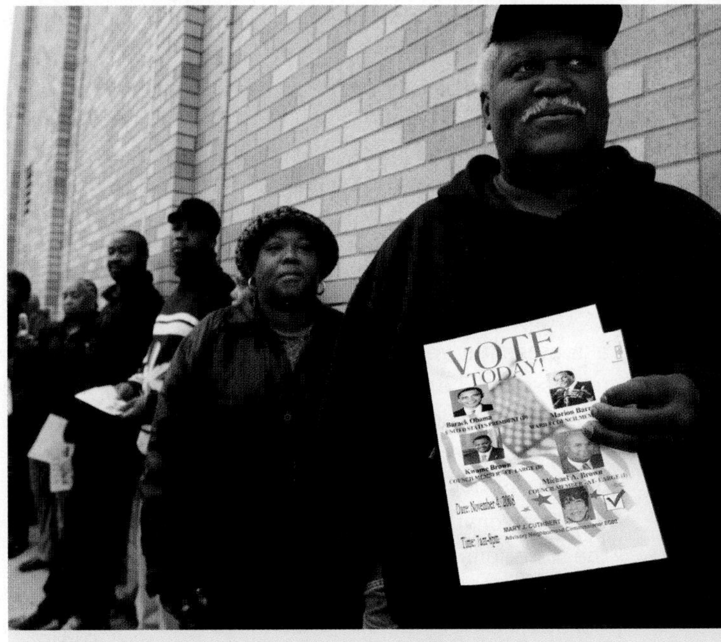

>> People line up to vote in 2008. Gerrymandering affects the political influence of a group of people by putting them in a single district, or by splitting them among several districts.

House Elections

According to the Constitution, any person whom a State allows to vote for members of "the most numerous Branch" of its own legislature is qualified to vote in congressional elections (Article I, Section 2, Clause 1). The Constitution also provides that

> The Times, Places and Manner of holding [Congressional] Elections . . . shall be prescribed in each State by the Legislature thereof; but the Congress may at any time by Law make or alter such Regulations. . . .
>
> —Article I, Section 4, Clause 1

Setting the Date Elections for Congress are held on the same day in every State. Since 1872 Congress has required that those elections be held on the Tuesday following the first Monday in November of each even-numbered year. Congress has made an exception for Alaska, which may hold its election in October. To date, however, Alaskans have chosen to use the November date.

In that same 1872 law, Congress directed that representatives be chosen by written or printed ballots. The use of voting machines was approved in 1899. Today, most votes cast in congressional elections are cast on some type of (usually electronic) voting device.

Off-Year Elections Those congressional elections that occur in nonpresidential years—that is, between presidential elections—are called **off-year elections.** The next ones will occur in 2014 and 2018.

Far more often than not, the party that holds the presidency loses seats in the off-year elections. The most recent exception occurred in 2002, in the first election to be held after the terrorist attacks on September 11, 2001. The Republicans, sparked by the campaign efforts of President Bush, regained control of the Senate and padded their slim majority in the House. The party in power lost seats in the 2010 off-year elections, however. The Republicans, riding a wave of popular dissatisfaction with a stubbornly sluggish economy, captured control of the House, while the Democrats retained their hold on the Senate.

INFER The author has stated that "far more often than not, the party that holds the presidency loses seats in the off-year elections." What can you infer causes this loss?

Qualifications for Office in the House

You know that there are 435 members of the House of Representatives, and that each one of them had to win an election to get there. Each one of them also had to meet two quite different sets of qualifications to win office: the formal qualifications for membership in the House set out in the Constitution and a number of informal qualifications imposed by the realities of politics.

Formal Qualifications The Constitution says that a member of the House must (1) be at least 25 years of age, (2) have been a citizen of the United States for at least 7 years, and (3) be an inhabitant of the State from which he or she is elected (Article I, Section 2, Clause 2; see also Article I, Section 6, Clause 2).

Custom, not the Constitution, also requires that a representative must live in the district he or she represents. The custom is based on the belief that the legislator should be familiar with the locale he or she represents, its people, and its problems. Rarely, then, does a district choose an outsider to represent it.

The Constitution makes the House "the Judge of the Elections, Returns and Qualifications of its own Members" (Article I, Section 5, Clause 1) Thus, when the right of a member-elect to be seated is challenged, the House has the power to decide the matter. Challenges are rarely successful.

The House may refuse to seat a member-elect by majority vote. It may also "punish its Members for disorderly Behavior" by majority vote, and "with the Concurrence of two thirds, expel a Member"(Article 1, Section 5, Clause 2).

>> Victor Berger won two separate elections to the House in 1919, but was denied his seat because he opposed U.S. participation in World War I. He later served three terms in Congress.

Imposing Additional Standards For decades, the House viewed its power to judge the qualifications of members-elect as the power to impose additional standards. It did so several times. In 1900, it refused to seat Brigham H. Roberts of Utah because he was a polygamist—that is, he had more than one wife. In 1919 and again in 1920, the House excluded Victor L. Berger of Wisconsin, the first Socialist Party candidate to win a House seat. During World War I, Mr. Berger wrote several newspaper articles denouncing America's participation in that conflict. In 1919, he was convicted of sedition for obstructing the war effort and sentenced to 20 years in prison. The Supreme Court reversed that conviction in 1921. Mr. Berger was reelected to the House three more times and seated each time without challenge. In *Powell* v. *McCormack*, 1969, however, the Supreme Court held that the House could not exclude a member-elect who meets the Constitution's standards of age, citizenship, and residence. The House has not excluded anyone since that decision.

Over more than 200 years, the House has expelled only 5 members. Three were ousted in 1861 for their "support of rebellion." Michael Myers (D., Penn.) was expelled for corruption in 1980. James Traficant (D., Ohio) was ejected after his conviction for bribery, fraud, and tax evasion in 2002. Over time, a few members have resigned to avoid almost certain expulsion. Thus, Randy "Duke" Cunningham (R., Calif.) resigned after pleading guilty to bribery charges in 2005. The House has not often punished a member for "disorderly Behaviour," but such actions are not nearly so rare as expulsions. For example, the House voted to reprimand Laura Richardson (D., California) in 2012 for improperly using House resources for campaign, personal, and nonofficial purposes, requiring her staff to work on her reelection campaign, and other charges.

Informal Qualifications The realities of politics produce a number of informal qualifications for membership in the House, beyond those requirements set out in the Constitution. Those informal yardsticks vary from time to time, sometimes from State to State, and even from one congressional district to another within the same State. Clearly, some of those factors that attract or repel voters in a heavily urbanized district differ from some of those that influence how voters see candidates in a largely rural setting.

These informal qualifications have to do with a candidate's vote-getting abilities. They include such considerations as party identification, name familiarity, gender, ethnic characteristics, and political experience. Being the **incumbent,** the person who currently holds the office, almost always helps. Regularly, well over

Growth of Seats in Congress 1815–2013

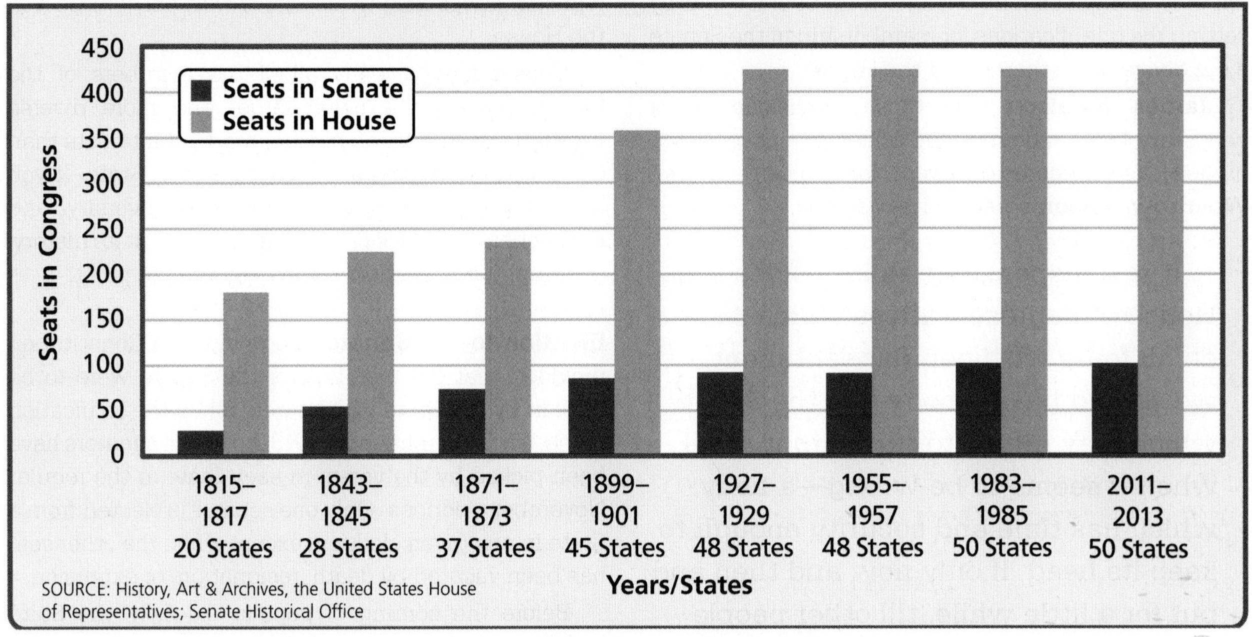

>> The number of seats in the House grew rapidly until 1929. The number of seats in the Senate grew more slowly and then leveled off. **Analyze Graphs** What are the reasons for these trends?

90 percent of those members of the House who seek reelection do so successfully.

Much more so today than in the past, a candidate's fundraising abilities also figure into the mix of informal qualifications. Like all other races, congressional campaigns have become very expensive. The average amount spent on a winning bid for the House topped $1.4 million in 2010. Several winners, and some losers, spent a good deal more than that.

The "right" combination of these informal measurements will help a candidate win nomination and then election to the House of Representatives. The "wrong" mix will almost certainly spell defeat.

MAKE GENERALIZATIONS What is the significance of the 1969 Supreme Court's decision in *Powell* v. *McCormack* to uphold the Constitution's formal qualifications of age, citizenship, and residency for a member of the House?

The Senate: Size, Election, and Terms

You should not be very surprised by these facts: Nearly a third of the present members of the Senate once served in the House of Representatives; none of the current members of the House has ever served in the Senate. Indeed, many of the men and women who now serve in the House look forward to the day when, they hope, they will sit in the Senate. As you read, you will come to see why the Senate is often called the "upper house."

Why are there 100 members of the United States Senate? Have the members of the Senate always been elected by the voters of their States? Why do senators serve six-year terms? What qualifications must candidates for the Senate meet? Read on to find the answers to these and other questions.

Senate Size The Constitution says that the Senate "shall be composed of two senators from each State," and so the Senate is a much smaller body than the House of Representatives (Article I, Section 3, Clause 1 and the 17th Amendment). Today, however, the Senate is a much larger body than the Framers imagined. The Senate had only 22 members when it held its first session in March of 1789, and 26 members by the end of the 1st Congress in 1791. Like the House, the size of the upper chamber has grown with the country. Today, 100 senators represent the 50 States. The Framers hoped that the smaller Senate would be a more enlightened and responsible body than the House. Many of them thought that the House would be too often swayed by the immediate impact of events and by the passions of the moment, mostly because of the short term of office for members of the lower chamber. They reinforced that hope by giving senators a longer term of office and by setting the qualifications for membership in the Senate a cut above those they set for the House.

James Madison saw those provisions as "a necessary fence" against the "fickleness and passion" of the House of Representatives. Nearly a century later, **Woodrow Wilson** agreed with Madison:

> It is indispensable that besides the House of Representatives which runs on all fours with popular sentiment, we should have a body like the Senate which may refuse to run with it at all when it seems to be wrong—a body which has time and security enough to keep its head, if only now and then and but for a little while, till other people have had time to think.
>
> —Woodrow Wilson, Congressional Government

Each one of the 100 members of the upper house represents an entire State. That same thing can be said of only a few members of the lower house—the seven representatives from those States with only one seat in the House.

>> President Woodrow Wilson once argued, "Just what is it that America stands for? If she stands for one thing more than another, it is for the sovereignty of self-governing people."

Consequently, nearly all of the members of the Senate represent a much larger and more diverse population and a much broader range of interests than do the several representatives from their State. If you look at your own State—at the size, diversity, and major characteristics of its population and at its history, geography, and economy—you will see the point.

Election to the Senate Originally, the Constitution provided that the members of the Senate were to be chosen by the State legislatures. Since the ratification of the 17th Amendment in 1913, however, senators have been picked by the voters in each State at the regular November elections. Only one senator is elected from a State in any given election, except when the other seat has been vacated by death, resignation, or expulsion.

Before the coming of popular election, the State legislatures often picked well-liked and qualified men to be senators. On other occasions, however, their choice was the result of maneuvering and infighting among the leaders of various factions in the State. These personalities all spent a great deal of energy trying to gain (and sometimes buy) enough legislators' votes to win a seat in the United States Senate. In fact, by the late 1800s, the Senate was often called the "Millionaires' Club," because so many wealthy party and business leaders sat in that chamber.

The Senate twice defeated House-passed amendments to provide for popular election. In 1912, it finally bowed to public opinion and agreed to what became the 17th Amendment the next year. The Senate was also persuaded by the fact that several States had already devised ways to ensure that their legislatures would choose senators who were supported by the people of the State.

Each senator is elected from the State at-large. The 17th Amendment declares that all persons whom the State allows to vote for members of "the most numerous Branch" (the larger house) of its legislature are automatically qualified to vote for candidates for the U.S. Senate.

Term of Office Senators serve for six-year terms, three times the length of those for which members of the House are chosen (Article I, Section 3, Clause 1). The Constitution puts no limit on the number of terms any senator may serve. The late **Robert C. Byrd** was first elected to the upper house in 1958 and holds the all-time record for length of service there—more than 51 years.

Senators' terms are staggered. Only a third of them—33 or 34 terms—expire every two years. The Senate is, then, a **continuous body.** That is, all of its seats are never up for election at the same time.

The six-year term gives senators somewhat greater job security than that enjoyed by members of the lower house. Those six years give senators some insulation from the rough-and-tumble of day-to-day politics. The six-year term also tends to make senators less subject to the pressures of public opinion and less susceptible to the pleas of special interests than their colleagues in the House.

The larger size and the geographic scope of their **constituencies**—the people and interests the senators represent—are designed to have much the same effect. That is to say, senators are supposed to be less concerned with the interests of some particular small locality and more focused on the "big picture" of national concerns. Indeed, senators are much more likely to be regarded as national political leaders than are most House members.

The large size of the House generally prevents representatives from gaining as much notice and public exposure as most members of the Senate attract. Senators, and especially those who have presidential ambitions, are better able to capture national media attention. Over the past several elections, the Senate has emerged as a prime source of contenders for the presidential nomination in both parties. Senators also find it easier to establish themselves as the champions of public policies that appeal to large segments of the American people—for example, social security or national health care.

Senators are also more likely to be covered by the media in their States. And they tend to have more clout in their State's politics than that enjoyed by members of the House of Representatives.

>> Texas Senator Ted Cruz talks with the press after speaking out against the Affordable Care Act. The Senate provides aspiring presidential candidates with media exposure and name recognition.

? IDENTIFY CAUSE AND EFFECT Representative Jones, acting as a delegate, votes for a spending bill favored by his constituents, even though he is not in favor of the bill. Senator Miller votes against it as a partisan, even though his constituents favor the bill. What effect does each Congressman's term length have on their voting decision?

Qualifications for Office in the Senate

A senator must meet a higher level of qualifications for office than those the Constitution sets for a member of the House. A senator must (1) be at least 30 years of age, (2) have been a citizen of the United States for at least nine years, and (3) be an inhabitant of the State from which he or she is elected (Article I, Section 3, Clause 3. Note that a senator need not have lived in the State for any particular period of time).

Senators must satisfy a number of informal qualifications for office—various extralegal yardsticks based on such factors as party, name familiarity, gender, ethnic characteristics, and political experience. Both incumbency and a talent for fundraising are also major assets in Senate races.

The Senate can also judge the qualifications of its members when and if they are challenged, and it may exclude a member-elect by a majority vote (Article I, Section 5, Clause 1). The upper house has refused to seat someone on three occasions. It has not exercised that power since 1867, however. The chamber may also "punish its Members for disorderly Behaviour" by majority vote and "with the Concurrence of two thirds, expel a Member" (Article 1, Section 5, Clause 2).

Fifteen members of the Senate have been expelled by that body, one in 1797 and 14 during the Civil War. Senator William Blount of Tennessee was expelled in 1797 for conspiring to lead two Native American tribes, supported by British warships, in attacks on Spanish Florida and Louisiana. The 14 senators ousted in 1861

>> Congresswomen and staff members who accused Senator Bob Packwood of making inappropriate advances hold a press conference urging women to speak out about sexual harassment.

and 1862 were all from States of the Confederacy and had supported secession.

Over time, a few senators have resigned in the face of almost certain expulsion. In 1995, the Senate's Ethics Committee found that four-term Senator Bob Packwood (R., Oregon) had been involved in several instances of blatant sexual harassment, and it urged his dismissal. Senator Packwood fought the charges for a time but resigned when it became apparent that his colleagues had had more than enough of his behavior.

The punishing of a senator for "disorderly Behaviour" has also been rare. In the most recent case, in 1990, the Senate formally "denounced" Senator David Durenberger (R., Minnesota). The Ethics Committee had found him guilty on several counts of financial misconduct. The Senate called Senator Durenberger's conduct "reprehensible" and declared that he had "brought the Senate into dishonor and disrepute." Senator Durenberger chose not to seek reelection to a third term in 1994.

? INTERPRET What did the Constitution intend when it provided procedures for the Senate to judge the conduct of its members?

ASSESSMENT

1. **Predict Consequences** How did the 17th Amendment effect a change that more closely matched the original goals of the Framers?
2. **Support Ideas with Examples** In what way might gerrymandering thwart the purpose of members being elected on a single-member district basis?
3. **Make Predictions** What effect would you expect the 1964 Supreme Court case, *Wesberry* v. *Sanders,* to have on the likelihood of a group of small rural farmers being heard in Congress and why?
4. **Support a Point of View with Evidence** James Madison saw the organization of Congress as "a necessary fence" against the "fickleness and passion" of the House of Representatives. How does this view compare with that of the Framers?
5. **Test Conclusions** The 2010 census showed that population growth has increased in the South and West, and decreased in the Northeast and Midwest regions of the country. How do provisions in the Constitution address the shifting population?

4.3 A typical day in either chamber of Congress might suggest that there is no limit to what Congress can do. On any given day, the House might consider bills dealing with such varying matters as the interstate highway system, an increase in the minimum wage, and grazing on public lands. Meanwhile, the Senate might be considering aid to a famine-stricken country in Africa, the President's nomination of someone to fill a vacancy on the Supreme Court, or any number of other matters.

>> Members of Congress head to their next meeting. The majority of a Congress member's time—about two thirds—is actually spent on constituent issues, fundraising, and media relations.

Interactive Flipped Video

The Expressed Powers

>> Objectives

Describe the three types of powers delegated to Congress.

Understand the expressed powers of Congress, including the commerce, taxing, bankruptcy, and borrowing powers, and explain why the Framers gave Congress the power to issue currency.

Identify the key sources of the foreign relations powers of Congress.

Describe the power-sharing arrangement between Congress and the President on the issues of war and national defense.

List other key domestic powers exercised by Congress.

>> Key Terms

expressed powers
implied powers
inherent powers
commerce power
tax
public debt
deficit financing
bankruptcy
legal tender
copyright
patent
territory
eminent domain
naturalization
District of Columbia
Bill Clinton
Boston
Philadelphia
Benjamin Franklin
Lyndon Johnson
Richard Nixon
Hudson River
John Marshall

Types of Congressional Powers

Still, there are very real limits on what Congress can do. It is important to note that (1) the government in the United States is a limited government, and (2) the American system of government is federal in form. These two fundamental facts work to shape and also to limit the powers of Congress.

The Delegated Powers Congress has only those powers delegated (granted, given) to it by the Constitution. Large areas of power are denied to Congress (1) in so many words in the Constitution, (2) by the Constitution's silence on many matters, and (3) because the Constitution creates a federal system.

There is much that Congress cannot do. It cannot create a national public school system, require people to vote or attend church, or set a minimum age for marriage or drivers' licenses. It cannot abolish jury trials, confiscate all handguns, or authorize the censorship of newspapers or radio or television broadcasts. Congress cannot do these and a great many other things because the Constitution does not delegate to it any power to do so.

Still, Congress does have the power to do many things. The Constitution grants it a number of specific powers—and, it delegates those powers in three different ways: (1) explicitly, in its specific wording—the **expressed powers;** (2) by reasonable deduction from the expressed powers—the **implied powers;** and (3) by creating a national government for the United States—the **inherent powers.**

The Framers very purposefully created a limited government. Given that fact, it is understandable that the existence and the scope of both the implied and the inherent powers have been the subject of dispute ever since the adoption of the Constitution.

The Expressed Powers Most, but not all, of the expressed powers of Congress are found in Article I, Section 8 of the Constitution. There, in 18 separate clauses, 27 different powers are explicitly given to Congress.

These grants of power are brief. What they do and do not allow Congress to do often cannot be discovered by merely reading the few words involved. Rather, their meaning is found in the ways in which Congress has exercised its powers since 1789, and in scores of Supreme Court cases arising out of the measures Congress has passed.

As a case in point, take the Commerce Clause, in Article I, Section 8, Clause 3. It gives Congress the power "to regulate Commerce with foreign Nations, and among the several States, and with the Indian Tribes." What do these words mean? Over the past two centuries, Congress and the Court have had to answer hundreds of questions about the scope of the Commerce Clause. Here are but a few examples: Does "commerce" include people crossing State lines or entering or leaving the country? What about business practices? Working conditions? Radio and television broadcasts? The Internet? Does Congress have the power to ban the shipment of certain goods from one State to another? To prohibit discrimination? What trade is "foreign" and what is "interstate"? And what trade is neither?

In answering these and dozens of other questions arising out of this one provision, Congress and the Court have defined—and are still defining—the meaning of the Commerce Clause. So it is with most of the other constitutional grants of power to Congress.

The commerce power and, with it, the expressed power to tax have provided much of the basis upon which Congress and the courts have built nearly all of the implied powers. Most of what the Federal Government does, day to day and year to year, it does as the result of legislation enacted by Congress in the exercise of those two powers.

DESCRIBE Explain why the Constitution limits the powers of Congress.

The Commerce Power

Commerce, generally, is the buying and selling of goods and services. The **commerce power**—the power of Congress to regulate interstate and foreign trade—is vital to the welfare of the nation. Its few words have prompted the growth of the greatest open market in the world. The Commerce Clause proved to be more

The Delegated Powers

INHERENT	EXPRESSED	IMPLIED
Inherent powers are those that belong to all sovereign nations—for example, the power to control a nation's borders.	Expressed powers are those stated in the Constitution—for example, the power to regulate both foreign and interstate commerce.	Implied powers are not stated in the Constitution, but drawn from the expressed powers. Based on the expressed power to regulate commerce, Congress has set a minimum wage for hourly workers.

>> This chart gives an example of each type of congressional power. **Analyze Charts** How do these powers help to create a limited government?

>> New technologies, such as the steamboat, brought with them new legal issues and implications for the growing nation in the 1800s.

useful for the building of a strong and *United* States out of a weak confederation than any other provision in the Constitution.

***Gibbons* v. *Ogden*, 1824** The first case involving the Commerce Clause to reach the Supreme Court, *Gibbons* v. *Ogden,* was decided in 1824. The case arose out of a clash over the regulation of steamboats by the State of New York, on the one hand, and the Federal Government, on the other. In 1807, Robert Fulton's steamboat, the *Clermont,* had made its first successful run up the **Hudson River**, from New York City to Albany. The State legislature then gave Fulton an exclusive, long-term grant to navigate the waters of the State by steamboat. Fulton's monopoly then gave Aaron Ogden a permit for steamboat navigation between New York City and New Jersey.

Thomas Gibbons, operating with a coasting license from the Federal Government, began to carry passengers on a competing line. Ogden sued, and the New York courts ruled in his favor, holding that Gibbons could not sail by steam in New York waters.

Gibbons appealed that ruling to the Supreme Court. He claimed that the New York grant conflicted with the congressional power to regulate interstate commerce. The Court agreed. It rejected Ogden's argument that "commerce" should be defined narrowly, as simply "traffic" or the mere buying and selling of goods. Instead, the Court read the Commerce Clause in very broad terms. Chief Justice **John Marshall,** speaking for the majority, wrote:

> Commerce, undoubtedly, is traffic, but it is something more; it is intercourse. It describes the commercial intercourse between nations, and parts of nations, in all its branches, and is regulated by prescribing rules for carrying on that intercourse.
>
> —*Gibbons* v. *Ogden,* 1824

The Court's ruling was widely popular at the time because it dealt a death blow to steamboat monopolies. Freed from restrictive State regulation, many new steamboat companies came into existence. As a result, steam navigation developed rapidly. Within a few years, the railroads were similarly freed, which revolutionized transportation within the United States.

Over the decades, the Court's sweeping definition of commerce has brought an extension of federal authority into many areas of American life—a reach of federal power beyond anything the Framers could have imagined.

As another of the many examples of the point, note this: It is on the basis of the commerce power that the Civil Rights Act of 1964 prohibits discrimination in access to or service in hotels, motels, theaters, restaurants, and in other public accommodations on grounds of race, color, religion, or national origin.

The Supreme Court upheld this use of the commerce power in *Heart of Atlanta Motel* v. *United States* in 1964. The unanimous Court noted that there was "overwhelming evidence of the disruptive effect that racial discrimination has had on commercial intercourse."

Limits on the Commerce Power The congressional power to regulate commerce is not unlimited. It, too, must be exercised in accord with all other provisions in the Constitution. As but one example: the Supreme Court struck down the Gun-Free School Zone Act of 1990 in *United States* v. *Lopez,* 1995. That act had made it a federal crime for anyone other than a police officer to possess a firearm in or around a school. The Court could find no useful connection between interstate commerce and guns at school. It held that Congress had in this case invaded the reserved powers of the States.

In more specific terms, the Constitution places four explicit limits on the use of the commerce power. The Constitution declares that Congress

1. cannot tax exports (Article I, Section 9, Clause 5);
2. cannot favor the ports of one State over those of any other in the regulation of trade (Article I, Section 9, Clause 6);
3. cannot require that "Vessels bound to, or from, one State be obliged to enter, clear, or pay Duties in another" (Article I, Section 9, Clause 6); and finally,
4. could not interfere with the slave trade until at least the year 1808 (Article I, Section 9, Clause 1). This last limitation, part of the curious Slave-Trade Compromise the Framers struck at Philadelphia, has been a dead letter for more than two centuries.

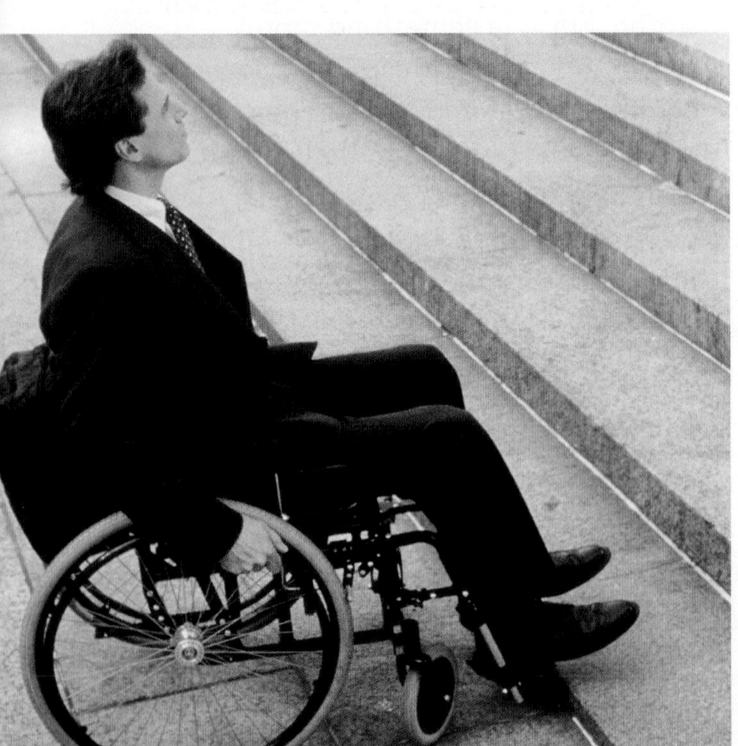

>> Because of the Court's broad interpretation of the Commerce Clause, Congress can regulate practices that disrupt commerce, such as lack of accessibility.

? ANALYZE INFORMATION What was the long-term impact of *Gibbons* v. *Ogden* on the commerce power of Congress?

The Money Powers

Congress has several expressed powers related to money, including the power to tax, the power to borrow, the power to establish laws on bankruptcy, and the power to coin money. These congressional powers have played an important role in the forming of our nation.

The Power to Tax The Constitution gives Congress the power

> To lay and collect Taxes, Duties, Imposts and Excises, to pay the Debts and provide for the common Defense and general Welfare of the United States. . . .
>
> —Article I, Section 8, Clause 1

The Articles of Confederation had not given Congress the power to tax. Congress did have the power to requisition funds from the States; that is, Congress could ask (in reality, beg) each of the 13 States for money.

But, through the 1780s, not a single State came even remotely close to meeting the few requests that Congress made, and a number of them paid nothing at all. The government was impotent, and the lack of a power to tax was a leading cause for the creation of the Constitution.

The Purpose of Taxes Here are a number of important points regarding the taxing power: The Federal Government will take in some $2.1 trillion in fiscal year 2013, and almost certainly an even larger sum in 2014. Most of that money—well over 95 percent of it—will come from the various taxes levied by Congress.

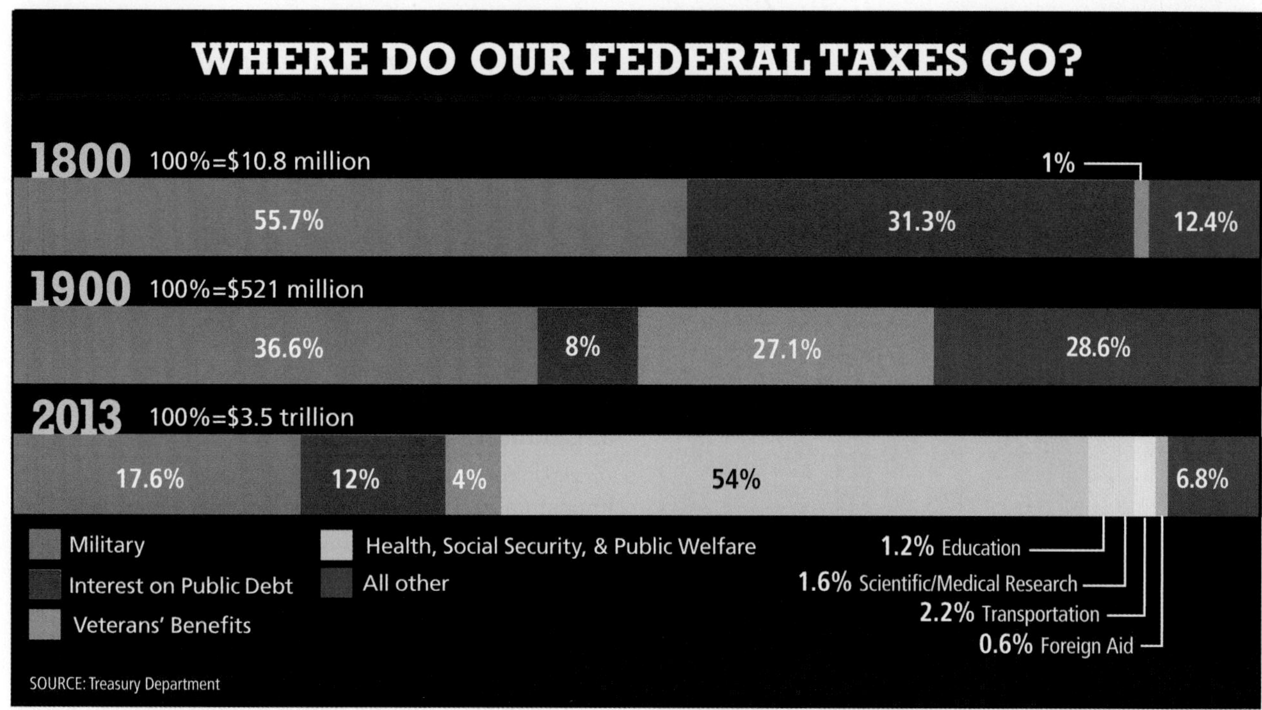

>> The way the Federal Government spends tax revenues has changed over time.
Analyze Charts What 2015 category(ies) of spending did not exist in 1800 or 1900?

A **tax** is a charge levied by government on persons or property to raise money to meet public needs. But notice, Congress does sometimes impose taxes for other purposes as well. The protective tariff is perhaps the oldest example of this point. Although it does bring in some revenue every year, its real goal is to "protect" domestic industry against foreign competition by increasing the cost of imported goods.

Taxes are also sometimes levied to protect the public health and safety. The Federal Government's regulation of narcotics is a case in point. Only those who have a proper federal license can legally manufacture, sell, or deal in those drugs—and licensing is a form of taxation.

Limits on the Taxing Power Congress does not have an unlimited power to tax. As with all other powers, the taxing power must be used in accord with all other provisions of the Constitution. Thus, Congress cannot lay a tax on church services, for example—because such a tax would violate the 1st Amendment. Nor could it lay a poll tax as a condition for voting in federal elections, for that would violate the 24th Amendment.

More specifically, the Constitution places four explicit limitations on the congressional power to tax:

1. Congress may tax only for public purposes, not for private benefit. Article I, Section 8, Clause 1 says that taxes may be levied only "to pay the Debts and provide for the common Defence and general Welfare of the United States. . . ."

2. Congress may not tax exports. Article I, Section 9, Clause 5 declares "[n]o Tax or Duty shall be laid on Articles exported from any State." Thus, customs duties (tariffs), which are taxes, can be levied only on goods brought into the country (imports), not on those sent abroad (exports).

3. Direct taxes must be apportioned among the States, according to their populations:

> No Capitation, or other direct, Tax shall be laid, unless in Proportion to the Census of enumeration herein before directed to be taken.
>
> —Article I, Section 9, Clause 4

A direct tax is one that must be paid directly to the government by the person on whom it is imposed—for example, a tax on the ownership of land or buildings, or a capitation (head or poll) tax.

An income tax is a direct tax, but it may be laid without regard to population:

> The Congress shall have power to lay and collect taxes on incomes, from whatever source derived, without

apportionment among the several States, and without regard to any census or enumeration.

—16th Amendment

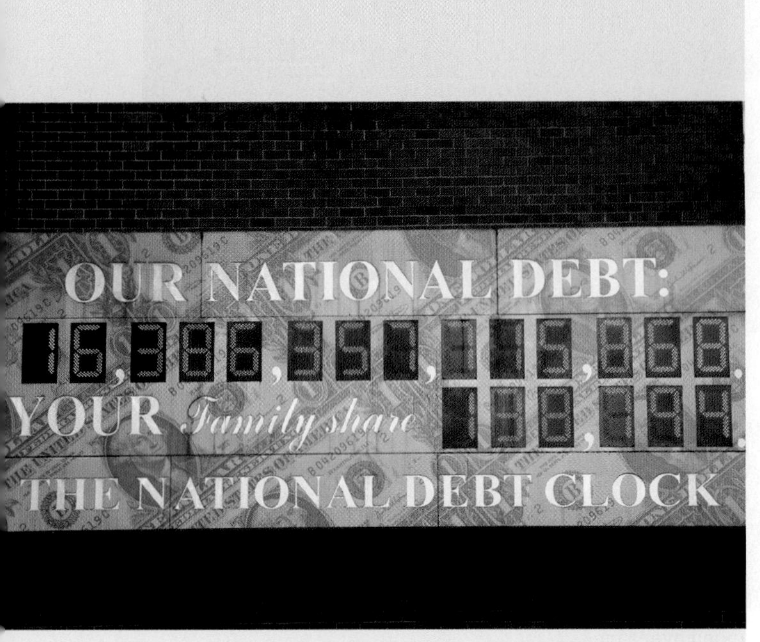

OUR NATIONAL DEBT:
16,386,351,115,868
YOUR Family share
138,194
THE NATIONAL DEBT CLOCK

>> The National Debt Clock in New York City shows a real-time estimate of the total United States debt, as well as each family's share.

"I assure you, Madam, that every penny you pay in taxes goes straight into the government's pocket."

>> An IRS agent assures a taxpayer that every cent she pays "goes straight into the government's pockets." **Analyze Political Cartoons** What is ironic about his statement?

Wealth (which translates to the ability to pay taxes) is not evenly distributed among the States. So, a direct tax levied in proportion to population would fall more heavily on the residents of some States than it would on others—and would, therefore, be grossly unfair. Consequently, Congress has not levied any direct tax—except for the income tax—outside the **District of Columbia** since 1861.

Article I, Section 8, Clause 1 provides that "all Duties, Imposts and Excises shall be uniform throughout the United States." That is, all indirect taxes levied by the Federal Government must be levied at the same rate in every part of the country. Those indirect taxes include the federal levies on gasoline, alcoholic beverages, and tobacco products.

As a general rule, an indirect tax is one first paid by one person but then passed on to another. It is indirectly paid by that second person. Take, for example, the federal tax on cigarettes. It is paid to the Treasury by the tobacco company but is then passed on through the wholesaler and retailer to the person who finally buys the cigarettes.

The Borrowing Power Article I, Section 8, Clause 2 gives Congress the power "[t]o borrow Money on the credit of the United States." There are no constitutional limits on the amount of money Congress may borrow and no restrictions on the purposes for borrowing.

The Treasury does the actual borrowing. Usually, it issues Treasury Notes (T-bills) for short-term borrowing and bonds for long-term purposes. Those securities are, in effect, promissory notes—IOUs—for which the government agrees to pay investors a certain sum plus interest on a certain date.

Congress has put a statutory ceiling on the public debt, however. The **public debt** is all of the money borrowed by the Federal Government over the years and not yet repaid, plus the accumulated interest on that money. That legal ceiling has never amounted to much more than a political gesture, however. Congress regularly raises the limit whenever the debt threatens to overtake it. The public debt is approximately $16 trillion.

For decades, the Federal Government has practiced **deficit financing.** That is, it regularly spends more than it takes in each year and then borrows to make up the difference. Thus, the government has relied on deficit financing—on borrowing—to deal with the economic Depression of the 1930s, to meet the extraordinary costs of World War II, and to pay for wars and social programs over the decades since then.

In fact, the government's books showed a deficit in all but seven years from 1930 to 1969. And they were in the red *every* year from 1969 to 1998. As a result, the public debt climbed to more than $5.5 trillion at the beginning of fiscal year 1998. A concerted effort by a Republican-controlled Congress and President **Bill Clinton** did curb the soaring debt. In fact, it produced four straight years of budget surpluses from 1998 to 2002.

Deficits are once again the order of the day, however. The Treasury has reported a deficit for every fiscal year since 2002. The shortfall reached some $1.1 trillion in 2012.

>> Cooperation between the Clinton-Gore administration and Republican senators like Bob Dole (left) and Newt Gingrich (right) helped keep the national debt in check for four years.

The Bankruptcy Power Article I, Section 8, Clause 4 gives Congress the power "[t]o establish . . . uniform Laws on the subject of Bankruptcies throughout the United States." A bankrupt individual or company or other organization is one a court has found to be insolvent—that is, unable to pay debts in full. **Bankruptcy** is the legal proceeding in which the bankrupt's assets—however much or little they may be—are distributed among those to whom a debt is owed. That proceeding frees the bankrupt from legal responsibility for debts acquired before bankruptcy.

The States and the National Government have concurrent power to regulate bankruptcy. Today, however, federal bankruptcy law is so broad that it all but excludes the States. Nearly all bankruptcy cases are now heard in federal district courts.

The Currency Power Article I, Section 8, Clause 5 gives Congress the power "[t]o coin Money [and] regulate the Value thereof." The States are expressly denied that power. (Article I, Section 10, Clause 1)

Until the Revolution, the English money system, built on the shilling and the pound, was in general use in the colonies. With independence, that stable currency system collapsed. The Second Continental Congress and then the Congress under the Articles issued paper money. Without sound backing, and with no taxing power behind it, however, the money was practically worthless. Each of the 13 States also issued its own currency. Adding to the confusion, people still used English coins, and Spanish money circulated freely in the southern States.

Nearly all the Framers agreed on the need for a single, national system of "hard" money. So the Constitution gave the currency power to Congress, and it all but excluded the States from that field. Currency is money in any form when it is in use as a medium of exchange. From 1789 on, among the most important of all of the many tasks performed by the Federal Government has been that of providing the nation with a uniform, stable monetary system.

From the beginning, the U.S. has issued coins in gold, silver, and other metals. Congress chartered the first Bank of the United States in 1791 and gave it the power to issue bank notes—that is, paper money. Those notes were not legal tender, however. **Legal tender** is any kind of money that a creditor must by law accept in payment for debts.

Congress did not create a national paper currency, and make it legal tender, until 1862. Its new national notes, known as Greenbacks, had to compete with other paper currencies already in the marketplace. Although the States could not issue paper money themselves, State governments could and did charter (license) private banks, whose notes did circulate as money. When those private bank notes interfered with the new national currency, Congress (in 1865) laid a ten percent tax on their production. The private bank notes soon disappeared. The Supreme Court upheld the 1865 law as a proper exercise of the taxing power in *Veazie Bank* v. *Fenno,* 1869.

At first, the Greenbacks could not be redeemed for gold or silver. Their worth fell to less than half their face

> To promote the Progress of Science and useful Arts, by securing for limited Times to Authors and Inventors the exclusive Right to their respective Writings and Discoveries.
>
> —Article I, Section 8, Clause 8

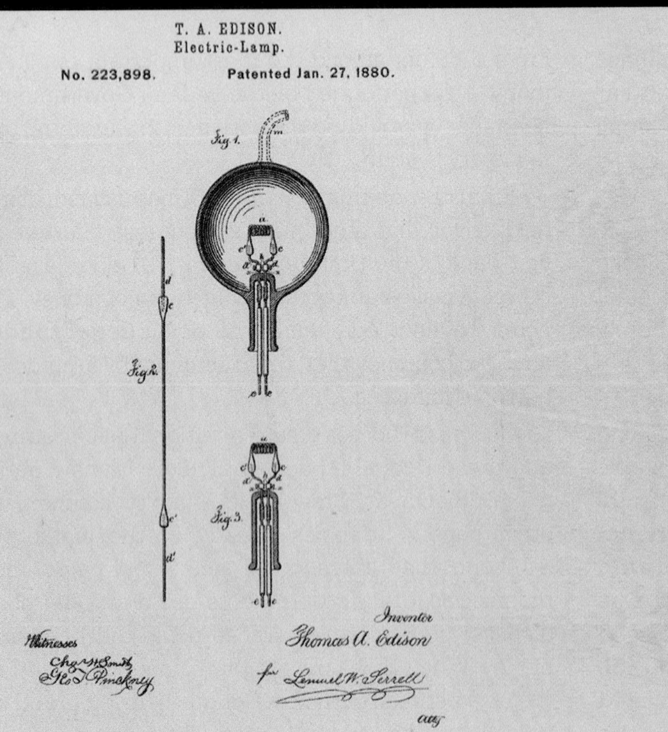

>> A patent drawing by Thomas Edison for an improvement to electric lamps. By assigning rights to intellectual property, patents and copyrights encourage creativity and progress.

Interactive Gallery

value on the open market. Then, in 1870, the Supreme Court held their issuance to be unconstitutional. In *Hepburn* v. *Griswold* it said "to coin" meant to stamp metal and so the Constitution did not authorize the National Government to issue paper money.

The Court soon changed its mind, however, in the *Legal Tender Cases* in 1871 and again in *Juliard* v. *Greenman* in 1884. In both cases, it held the issuing of paper money as legal tender to be a proper use of the currency power. The Court also declared this a power properly implied from both the borrowing and the war powers.

IDENTIFY STEPS IN A PROCESS What steps would you expect that President Clinton and a Republican-controlled Congress took in order to produce four years of budget surpluses from 1998 to 2002?

Other Domestic Powers

The other expressed powers relate to domestic matters. Each of them has a direct and a considerable effect on the daily lives of the American people.

Copyrights and Patents The Constitution gives Congress the power

> To promote the Progress of Science and useful Arts, by securing for limited Times to Authors and Inventors the exclusive Right to their respective Writings and Discoveries.
>
> —Article I, Section 8, Clause 8

A **copyright** is the exclusive right of an author to reproduce, publish, and sell his or her creative work. That right may be assigned—transferred by contract—to another, as to a publishing firm by mutual agreement between the author and the other party.

Copyrights are registered by the Copyright Office in the Library of Congress. Under present law, they are good for the life of the author plus 70 years.

They cover a wide range of creative efforts: books, magazines, newspapers, musical compositions and lyrics, dramatic works, paintings, sculptures, cartoons, maps, photographs, motion pictures, sound recordings, and much more. The Office registers more than 500,000 copyrights each year.

The Copyright Office does not enforce the protections of a copyright. If the holder thinks a copyright has been violated, he or she may bring a suit for damages in the federal courts.

A **patent** grants a person the sole right to manufacture, use, or sell "any new and useful process, machine, manufacture, or composition of matter, or any new and useful improvement thereof." A patent is good for up to twenty years. The term of a patent may be extended only by a special act of Congress. The Patent and Trademark Office in the Department of Commerce administers patent laws.

Patent protection has played an important role in fostering competition and entrepreneurship. Having a patent often increases the value of an invention, scientific discovery, or technological advancement. Many industries, particularly pharmaceuticals, have grown and experienced economic success due to the patents that they hold. A patent can also increase the value of a company and gives that company a competitive advantage for a period of time. In short, the patent system produces monetary incentives to pursue inventions and to make important scientific discoveries.

>> Benjamin Franklin served as the country's first Postmaster General at this Philadelphia post office, establishing the foundations of the postal system that continues to operate today.

The Postal Powers Article I, Section 8, Clause 7 gives Congress the power "[t]o establish Post Offices and Post roads"—in effect, the power to provide for the carrying of the mail. "Post roads" are all postal routes, including rail lines, airways, and waters within the United States, during the time mail is being carried on them.

Carrying the mail is among the oldest of all governmental functions. Its origins date back at least to Egyptian practice before 4000 B.C. The first post office in America was established in **Boston** in 1639, by the General Court of the Massachusetts Bay Colony. The first successful postal system in the colonies, the Penn Post, was begun by William Penn in 1683. He established a post office in **Philadelphia** and provided a regular weekly service along a 30-mile route from there to New Castle, Delaware.

The United States Postal Service traces its history back to the early colonial period. The remarkable **Benjamin Franklin** is generally recognized as the father of the present-day postal system. He served as Co-Deputy Postmaster of the British Colonies in North America from 1753 to 1774, when the British removed him from office because of his political activities. In 1775, he became, by unanimous choice of the Second Continental Congress, the first Postmaster General of the United States.

Today, the Postal Service functions as an independent agency in the executive branch. It serves the nation through some 32,000 post offices. The 546,000 career employees of the Postal Service handle nearly 170 billion pieces of mail every year. These figures reflect drops in recent years as the agency has struggled to maintain its financial footing in an era dominated by Internet communications and private mail carriers.

Congress has established a number of crimes based on the postal power. It is, for example, a federal crime for anyone to obstruct the mails or to use the mails to commit any criminal act. It has also prohibited the mailing of many items, among them poisons, explosives, intoxicating liquors, some live animals, libelous or obscene matter, lottery tickets, and any dangerous articles. Any article prohibited by a State's laws—for example, switchblade knives or firecrackers—cannot be sent into that State by mail.

The States and their local governments cannot interfere with the mails in any unreasonable way. Nor can they require licenses for Postal Service vehicles, tax the gas they use, or tax post offices or any other property of the United States Postal Service.

Territories and Other Areas In two places—in Article I, Section 8, Clause 17 and in Article IV, Section 3, Clause 2—the Constitution delegates to Congress the power to acquire, manage, and dispose of various federal areas. That power relates to the District of Columbia and to the several federal **territories,** parts of the United States that are not admitted as States and that have their own systems of government, including Puerto Rico, Guam, and the Virgin Islands. It also covers hundreds of military and naval installations, arsenals, dockyards, post offices, prisons, parks and forest preserves, and many other federal holdings.

The Federal Government may acquire property by purchase or gift. It may also do so through the exercise of the power of **eminent domain,** the inherent power to take private property for public use. Notice that the Taking Clause in the 5th Amendment restricts the Federal Government's use of the power with these words: "nor shall private property be taken for public use, without just compensation." Private property may be taken by eminent domain only (1) for a public use, (2) with proper notice to the owner, and (3) for a fair price. What in fact constitutes a public use, proper notice, or a fair price often becomes a matter for courts to decide.

Territory may also be acquired from a foreign state as the result of the exercise of the power of Congress to admit new States (in Article IV), the war powers, or the President's treaty-making power (in Article II). Under international law, any sovereign state may acquire unclaimed territory by discovery.

Weights and Measures Article I, Section 8, Clause 5 gives Congress the power to "fix the Standard of Weights and Measures" throughout the United States. The power reflects the absolute need for accurate, uniform gauges of time, distance, area, weight, volume, and the like.

In 1838, Congress set the English system of pound, ounce, mile, foot, gallon, quart, and so on, as the legal standards of weights and measures in this country. In 1866, Congress also legalized the use of the metric system of gram, meter, kilometer, liter, and so on.

In 1901, Congress created the National Bureau of Standards in the Commerce Department. Now known as the National Institute of Standards and Technology, the agency keeps the original standards for the United States. It is these standards by which all other measures in the United States are tested and corrected.

>> The first atomic clock, invented by Professor Townes (left) and Dr. Gordon, was funded by the government. The weights and measures clause lets Congress set standards for measuring time.

Naturalization Citizens of one country become citizens of another through a process called **naturalization.** Article I, Section 8, Clause 4 gives Congress the exclusive power "[t]o establish an uniform Rule of Naturalization." Today, the nation's population includes more than 14 million naturalized citizens.

Judicial Powers As a part of the system of checks and balances, the Constitution gives Congress several judicial powers. Thus, it has the power to create all of the federal courts below the Supreme Court and otherwise provide for the organization and composition of the federal judiciary.

Congress also has the power to define federal crimes and set the punishments that may be imposed on those who violate federal law. The Constitution mentions only four offenses. Three are found in Article I, Section 8: counterfeiting, piracies and felonies committed on the high seas, and offenses against international law. Treason is listed in Article III, Section 3. In addition to these, Congress has used its implied powers to establish more than 100 other federal crimes.

? APPLY CONCEPTS How do copyrights and patents "promote the Progress of Science and useful Arts?" Why do you think the Framers granted this power to Congress?

Congress and Foreign Policy

The Federal Government has greater powers in the field of foreign affairs than it does in any other area of public policy. The 50 States that comprise the Union are not sovereign, so they have no standing in international law. In short, the Constitution does not allow them to take part in foreign relations. (See Article I, Section 10, Clauses 1 and 3.)

The Constitution gives the President primary responsibility for the conduct of American foreign policy. As the Supreme Court put that point in a leading case, *United States* v. *Curtiss-Wright Export Corp.* in 1936, the chief executive is "the sole organ of the Federal Government in the field of international relations."

Still, the Constitution does give Congress a significant place in the field of foreign affairs. Its authority in that area arises from two sources: (1) from a number of the expressed powers, most especially the spending, the commerce, and the war powers; and (2) from the fact that the United States is a sovereign state in the world community. As the lawmaking body of the sovereign United States, Congress has the inherent power to act on matters affecting the security of the nation—for example, the regulation of immigration and the enactment of measures to combat terrorism here and abroad.

SUPPORT IDEAS WITH EVIDENCE How do the foreign policy powers of the legislative and executive branches establish a system of checks and balances between these two branches of government?

>> In *United States* v. *Curtiss-Wright Export Corp.*, an American plane builder was charged with illegally selling arms to Bolivia after President Franklin D. Roosevelt had declared an embargo.

The War Powers

Six of the 27 expressed powers set out in Article I, Section 8 deal explicitly with the subject of war and national defense. Remember that here, too, Congress shares power with the chief executive. The Constitution makes the President commander in chief of the nation's armed forces, (Article II, Section 2, Clause 1) and, as such, the President dominates the field.

The congressional war powers are, however, both extensive and substantial. Only Congress can declare war. It alone has the power to raise and support armies, to provide and maintain a navy, and to make rules for the governing of the nation's military forces. Congress also has the power to provide for "calling forth the Militia" (today, the National Guard), and for the organizing, arming, and disciplining of that force. And Congress is also given the power to grant letters

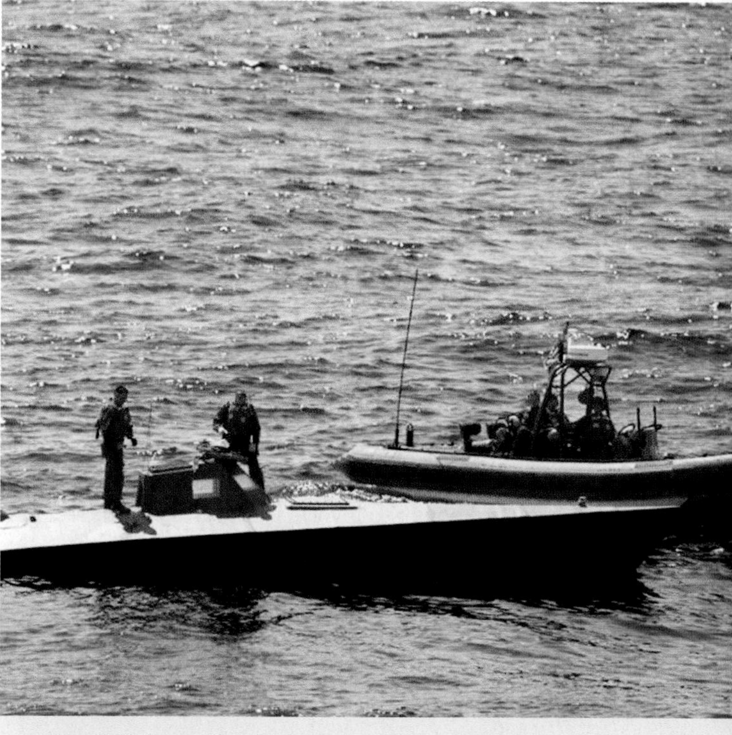

>> The U.S. Coast Guard inspects a boat suspected of smuggling illegal drugs. Administration of the Coast Guard falls under the war powers granted to Congress by Article I, Section 8.

>> President Lyndon Johnson gives the Medal of Honor to Army Staff Sergeant Jennings in 1968. Congress gave Johnson power to use military force in Vietnam, later reversed in 1973.

of marque and reprisal, and to make rules concerning captures on land and water.

As you think about congressional war powers, consider this question: Does the Constitution give the President the power to make war in the absence of a declaration of war by Congress? Many argue that it does not, but more than 200 years of American history argue otherwise. Indeed, most Presidents have used the armed forces of the United States abroad, in combat, without a congressional declaration of war.

In today's world, no one can doubt that the President must have the power to respond, rapidly and effectively, to any threat to the nation's security. Still, many people have long warned of the dangers inherent in a presidential power to involve the country in undeclared wars.

The War Powers Resolution In the context of the war powers of Congress, we must examine the War Powers Resolution, a statute enacted by Congress in 1973.

The war-making power as it was exercised by Presidents **Johnson** and **Nixon** during the undeclared war in Vietnam (1964–1973) moved Congress to enact the War Powers Resolution. That law provides that the chief executive can commit American military forces to combat abroad only (1) if Congress has declared war, or (2) when Congress has specifically authorized a military action, or (3) when an attack on the United States or any of its armed forces has occurred.

If troops are ordered into combat in the third circumstance, the President is directed to report that fact to Congress within 48 hours. Any such commitment of military forces must end within 60 days, unless Congress agrees to a longer involvement. And Congress can end a commitment at any time.

The constitutionality of the War Powers Resolution remains in dispute. A determination of the question must await a situation in which Congress demands that its provisions be obeyed but the President refuses to do so.

? ANALYZE INFORMATION How is the balance of power between Congress and the President reinforced through the limits placed on the President's war powers?

ASSESSMENT

1. **Describe** Describe how the meanings of the constitutional clauses that grant powers to Congress have been defined.
2. **Compare and Contrast** Compare *Gibbons* v. *Ogden*, 1824 and *United States* v. *Lopez*, 1995, and how the Commerce Clause has been interpreted by the Supreme Court in these two cases.
3. **Analyze Information** Why did the Framers explicitly grant the powers of currency, borrowing, and bankruptcy to Congress? What might be the outcome if these powers had not been granted to Congress?
4. **Apply Concepts** Describe the manner in which Congress and the President share power in the fields of foreign affairs, war, and national defense. Is the division of power reasonable?
5. **Interpret** Why did the Framers grant Congress sole power to declare war? What tensions may arise from the division of the war powers?

4.4 What does the Constitution have to say about education? Nothing, not a word. Still, Congress provides tens of billions of dollars every year for the United States Department of Education to spend in a variety of ways throughout the country. Look around you. What indications of these federal dollars can you find in your local school? If you attend a public school anywhere in the United States, that evidence should not be hard to spot.

>> Senator Joseph McCarthy and his aide listen to proceedings at a Senate investigation in 1954 into alleged attempts to obtain an Army reserve officer commission for McCarthy's political ally.

Interactive Flipped Video

The Implied and Nonlegislative Powers

>> Objectives

Explain how the Necessary and Proper Clause gives Congress flexibility in lawmaking.

Compare the strict construction and liberal construction positions on the scope of congressional power.

Describe the ways in which the implied powers have been applied.

Describe the investigatory powers of Congress.

Identify the executive powers of Congress.

Describe the power of Congress to impeach, and summarize presidential impeachment cases.

Describe the role of Congress in amending the Constitution and its electoral duties.

>> Key Terms

Necessary and Proper Clause	Thomas Jefferson
strict constructionist	Alexander Hamilton
liberal constructionist	Barack Obama
consensus	Samuel Alito
appropriate	George W. Bush
impeach	Andrew Johnson
acquit	Abraham Lincoln
perjury	Richard Nixon
censure	John Quincy Adams
subpoena	
successor	

The Necessary and Proper Clause

How can this be? Congress has only those powers delegated to it by the Constitution, and that document says nothing about education. The answer to that question lies in the implied powers of Congress.

Implied powers are those powers that are not set out in so many words in the Constitution but are, rather, implied by (drawn from) those that are. The constitutional basis for the existence of the implied powers is found in one of the expressed powers. The **Necessary and Proper Clause,** the final clause in the lengthy Section 8 of Article I in the Constitution, gives to Congress the expressed power

> To make all Laws which shall be necessary and proper for carrying into Execution the foregoing Powers, and all other Powers vested by this Constitution in the Government of the United States, or in any Department or Officer thereof.
>
> —Article I, Section 8, Clause 18

Much of the vitality and adaptability of the Constitution can be traced directly to this provision, and even more so to the ways in which both Congress and the Supreme Court have interpreted and applied it over the years. In effect, the Necessary and Proper Clause allows Congress to choose the means "for carrying into Execution" the many powers given to it by the Constitution.

The manner in which Congress has viewed the concept, together with the supporting decisions of the Supreme Court, have made the final clause in Article I, Section 8, truly the "Elastic Clause." It has earned that name, for it has been stretched so far and made to cover so much over the years.

Strict vs. Liberal Construction The Constitution had barely come into force when the meaning of the Elastic Clause became the subject of one of the most important disputes in American political history. The Framers of the Constitution intended to create a new and stronger National Government. The ratification of their plan was opposed by many, and that opposition was not stilled by the adoption of the Constitution. Rather, the conflict between the Federalists and the Anti-Federalists continued into the early years of the Republic. Much of that conflict centered on the powers of Congress and the meaning of the Elastic Clause. Just how broad, in fact, were those powers?

The **strict constructionists,** led by **Thomas Jefferson**, continued to argue the Anti-Federalist position from the ratification period. They insisted that Congress should be able to exercise (1) its expressed powers and (2) only those implied powers absolutely necessary to carry out those expressed powers. They maintained that the States should keep as much power as possible. They agreed with Jefferson that "that government is best which governs least."

Most of these Jeffersonians did acknowledge a need to protect interstate trade, and they recognized the need for a strong national defense. At the same time, they feared the consequences of a strong National Government. They believed, for instance, that the interests of the people of Connecticut were not the same as those of South Carolinians or Marylanders or Pennsylvanians. They argued that only the States—not the far-off National Government—could protect and preserve those differing interests.

The **liberal constructionists,** led by **Alexander Hamilton**, had led the fight to adopt the Constitution. Now they favored a liberal interpretation of that document, a broad construction of the powers it gives to Congress. They believed that the country needed, as

THE IMPLIED POWERS OF CONGRESS
THE EXPRESSED POWER TO
IMPLIES THE POWER TO
LAY AND COLLECT TAXES
• Punish tax evaders
• Regulate some commodities and outlaw the use of others
• Set conditions to qualify for federal funding
BORROW MONEY
• Establish the Federal Reserve System of banks
CREATE NATURALIZATION LAW
• Regulate and limit immigration
RAISE ARMIES AND A NAVY
• Draft Americans into the military
REGULATE COMMERCE
• Establish a minimum wage
• Ban discrimination in workplaces and public facilities
• Pass laws protecting the disabled
• Regulate banking
ESTABLISH POST OFFICES
• Prohibit mail fraud and obstruction of the mails
• Bar the shipping of certain items through the mail

>> Modern lawmakers must try to interpret the Framers' intent in light of modern circumstances. **Analyze Charts** Without its implied powers, how effectively could Congress address new situations?

Strict vs. Liberal Constructionists

STRICT CONSTRUCTIONISTS	LIBERAL CONSTRUCTIONISTS
 Thomas Jefferson	 Alexander Hamilton
• Favored a very limited role for the new government created by the Constitution • Majority of power would remain with the States and the people • Based on a strict reading of the Necessary and Proper Clause in the Constitution to prevent the government from gaining too much power	• Favored a powerful government that could exercise implied powers • Favored vigorous executive leadership • Based on a liberal interpretation of the Constitution because the Constitution did not specifically grant the government these powers

>> Strict constructionists battled with liberal constructionists over congressional powers. **Analyze Charts** How would each want Congress to address new situations not originally anticipated?

Hamilton put it in *The Federalist* No. 70, "an energetic government."

The strict constructionists were sorely troubled by that broad view of the powers of Congress. They were sure that it would all but destroy the reserved powers of the States.

Liberal Construction Prevails The Supreme Court upheld the concept of implied powers in *McCulloch* v. *Maryland* in 1819. At the time, a Maryland law required all banks not chartered by the State to print their currency on special paper stamped by the State, which amounted to a tax. James McCulloch, the cashier of the Baltimore branch of the Second Bank of the United States, refused to use the paper, claiming that States could not tax the Federal Government. The Court declared the Maryland law unconstitutional.

That victory for the liberal constructionists set a pattern that, in general, has been followed ever since. Over the years, the powers wielded by the National Government have grown to a point that even the most ardent supporters of liberal construction could not have imagined. It is impossible to see how the United States could have developed as it has over the past two centuries had the Court not ruled as it did in *McCulloch*.

Several factors, working together with the liberal construction of the Constitution, have been responsible for that marked growth in national power. They have included wars, economic crises, and other national emergencies. Spectacular advances, especially in transportation and communication, have also had a real impact on the size and the scope of government. Equally important have been the demands of the people for more and still more services from government.

Congress has been led by these and other factors to view its powers in broader and broader terms. Most Presidents have regarded their powers in like fashion. The Supreme Court has generally taken a similar position in its decisions in cases involving the powers of the National Government.

Moreover, the American people have generally agreed with a broader rather than a narrow reading of the Constitution. This **consensus,** or general agreement, has prevailed even though our political history has been marked, and still is, by controversies over the proper limits of national power.

? APPLY CONCEPTS How has the doctrine of implied powers increased the powers of Congress?

The Doctrine in Practice

The ways in which the Necessary and Proper Clause has been construed (interpreted) and applied over the last 200 years has enabled the National Government to meet the changing needs of the times. As a result, it has virtually eliminated the need for frequent amendment of the Constitution.

Instances of the exercise of the doctrine of implied powers are almost too numerous to count. The concept of implied powers has made it possible for the Government of the United States to meet any number of problems that could not possibly have been foreseen by the Framers. It does not stretch matters too much to say that, today, the Constitution's words "necessary and proper" really mean "convenient and useful."

Every exercise of implied powers must be based on at least one of the expressed powers. Thus, in *McCulloch* v. *Maryland* the Supreme Court found that the creation of the Bank of the United States was "necessary and proper" to the execution of four expressed powers held by Congress: the taxing, borrowing, currency, and commerce powers.

Over the years, Congress has most often found a basis for the exercise of implied powers in (1) the commerce power, (2) its power to tax and spend, and (3) the war powers.

The Commerce Clause The Commerce Clause gives Congress the power to regulate both foreign and interstate trade. The Supreme Court's hugely expansive reading of that provision began in 1824 with *Gibbons* v. *Ogden* when the Court found in favor of Gibbons, ruling that the State of New York could not prevent him from carrying passengers on his steamboat between New York and New Jersey. The word "commerce" has been held to include the production and the buying and selling of goods as well as the transportation of people and commodities.

Commerce has been defined so broadly that it encompasses virtually every form of economic activity today. Congress has the authority to regulate manufacturing, wages and hours, labor-management relations, foods and drugs, air travel, and much more. It can provide for the building of interstate highways, consumer protection, the protection of the environment—the list goes on and on.

Recently, many had assumed that if the Supreme Court were to uphold the individual mandate provision of the Affordable Care Act, a health care reform measure promoted by President **Barack Obama** and Democrats in Congress in 2012, it would once again be on the grounds of commerce. This provision stated that every American citizen must have health insurance or else be required to pay a fine. To the surprise of many, however, the Court upheld the law by linking it to a different enumerated power—the power to lay and collect taxes.

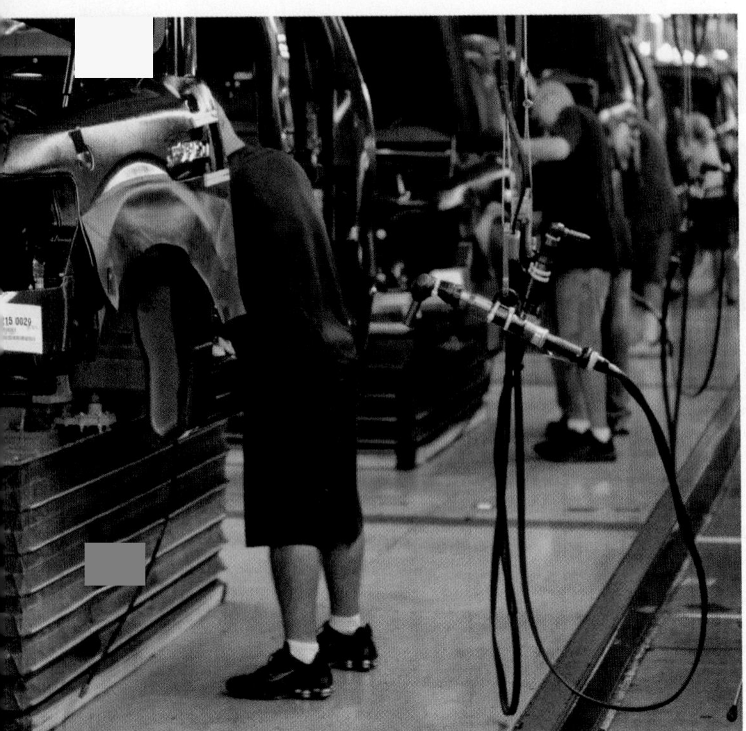

>> The 2009 government bailout and subsequent takeover of failing automotive companies Chrysler, Ford, and General Motors was an example of the exercise of the doctrine of implied powers.

Get out! New York gave me the exclusive right to operate steamships in New York waters.

Wrong. New York gave the United States the exclusive right to regulate interstate commerce.

stus.com

>> An illustration of the conflict over interstate commerce in the case of *Gibbons* v. *Ogden*. **Analyze Political Cartoons** Did that Supreme Court ruling reflect strict or liberal constructionist views?

Constitutional Limits on the Commerce Power

Constitutional Limits on the Commerce Power
Congress cannot tax exports. (Article I, Section 9, Clause 5)
Congress cannot favor the ports of one State over those of any other in the regulation of trade. (Article I, Section 9, Clause 6)
Congress cannot require that "Vessels bound to, or from, one State, be obliged to enter, clear, or pay Duties in another." (Article I, Section 9, Clause 6)
Congress could not interfere with the slave trade, at least not until the year 1808 (Article I, Section 9, Clause 1). This last limitation, part of the curious Slave-Trade Compromise the Framers struck at Philadelphia, has been a dead letter for more than two centuries.

>> Congress' expressed and implied use of the commerce power is not unlimited.
Analyze Charts Why are limits on the commerce power important?

Limits on the Commerce Power Still, Congress is not free to use the Commerce Clause to do whatever it chooses. The Constitution places four explicit limitations on the exercise of the commerce power. And the Supreme Court does, at least on occasion, find that the lawmaking branch has overstepped its authority under that provision. Congress cannot pass a law based solely on the grounds that a measure will somehow promote "the general Welfare of the United States." But it can and does levy taxes and provide for the spending of money for that purpose. Thus, for example, as discussed earlier, Congress **appropriates**—assigns to a particular use—tens of billions of dollars per year to support education. And, similarly, it does so to provide for such things as farm subsidies, unemployment compensation, Social Security, Medicare, and a host of other programs.

The War Powers The several war powers reflect the fact that the National Government is responsible for the protection of this country against aggression and, when necessary, for the waging of war. As with its other expressed powers, Congress has the authority to do whatever is necessary and proper for the execution of its war power—with the exception that, in doing so, it cannot violate any other provision of the Constitution. Among many other examples of the point, Congress has the power to provide for compulsory military service—a draft—because Article I, Section 8 gives it the expressed power "[t]o raise and support Armies" (in Clause 12) and "[t]o provide and maintain a Navy" (in Clause 13). The Supreme Court originally upheld the constitutionality of a draft in a series of cases challenging the Selective Service Act of 1917 (*Selective Draft Law Cases,* 1918).

SUMMARIZE Explain how Congress has used each of the following expressed powers as a basis for the exercise of implied powers: the commerce powers, the tax powers, the war powers.

The Power to Investigate

Congress has the power to investigate—to inquire into, or inform itself on—any matter that falls within the scope of its lawmaking authority. The authority to do so is implied by the Constitution's grant of the legislative power to Congress, in Article I, Section 1. Both the House and Senate exercise that power through the standing committees and their subcommittees and often through special committees, as well.

Both houses may choose to conduct investigations for any one or a number of reasons. Most often, those inquiries are held to (1) gather information necessary to the framing of legislation, (2) oversee the operations of various agencies in the executive branch, (3) focus public attention on some particular matter, (4) expose the questionable activities of some public official or private person or group, and/or (5) promote the particular interests of some members of Congress.

Notice that the second of these motives, oversight, is a little-noted but quite important aspect of the constitutional system of checks and balances. Note, too, that Congress is more inclined to exercise its oversight function when one or both of its chambers is controlled by the party that does not hold the presidency, most recently in 2013 and 2014.

Recent Investigations Over recent years, Congress has improved its ability both to inform itself and to perform its oversight responsibilities by increasing the staff resources available to the standing committees of both houses. The three little-known agencies in the legislative branch which also add to that capability are:

1. the Congressional Budget Office, which committees of both houses rely on quite heavily in taxing, spending, and other budget-related matters;
2. the Congressional Research Service, in the Library of Congress, whose several hundred staff specialists provide members with factual information on virtually any subject; and
3. the Government Accountability Office, also called Congress' watchdog because it has broad authority to monitor the work of the Federal Government and report its findings to Congress.

Recently, we have seen an increase in congressional investigations during President Barack Obama's presidency, particularly during his second term. These have included an investigation into the attack on a diplomatic building in Benghazi, Libya, and the way the administration released details about the attack. This investigation was led by Representative Darrell Issa (R., California) as chairman of the House Oversight and Government Reform committee. Another recent congressional investigation included an examination of the manner in which the IRS reviewed tax exemptions by allegedly non-political groups self-identified as "Patriots," including some associated with the Tea Party movement.

? APPLY CONCEPTS From what source does Congress get its investigative powers? List the five main reasons that committees in Congress conduct investigations.

Executive Powers

The Constitution gives two executive powers to the Senate. One of those powers has to do with appointments to office, and the other with treaties made by the President. (Article II, Section 2, Clause 2)

Appointments All major appointments made by the President must be confirmed by the Senate by majority vote. Each of the President's nominations is referred to the appropriate standing committee of the Senate. That committee may then hold hearings to decide whether or not to make a favorable recommendation to the full Senate for that appointment. When the committee's recommendation is brought to the floor of the Senate, it

Examples of Senate Rejections of Cabinet Nominees

PRESIDENT	NOMINEE, YEAR	POSITION	REASON FOR REJECTION
Andrew Jackson	Roger B. Taney, 1834	Secretary of the Treasury	The pro-bank majority in the Senate rejected Taney, who planned to dismantle the Second Bank of the United States.
John Tyler	Caleb Cushing, 1843	Secretary of the Treasury	The Senate Whig majority opposed President Tyler and rejected his nominations in contentious and partisan voting.
	David Henshaw, 1844	Secretary of the Navy	
	James M. Porter, 1844	Secretary of War	
	James S. Green, 1844	Secretary of the Treasury	
Dwight Eisenhower	Lewis L. Strauss, 1959	Secretary of Commerce	Rejected due to Strauss's antagonistic treatment of the Senate Commerce Committee members during his confirmation hearings.
George H. W. Bush	John G. Tower, 1989	Secretary of Defense	Allegations of misconduct led to Tower's rejection.

SOURCE: Senate.gov

>> Even though it has not occurred often, Congress has rejected several presidential cabinet nominees. **Analyze Charts** How does the political climate play a role in the reason for rejection?

may be, but seldom is, considered in executive (secret) session.

The appointment of a Cabinet officer or of some other top member of the President's "official family" is rarely rejected by the Senate. The Senate has rejected only nine Cabinet appointments in the country's history. The most recent rejection came in 1989, when the Senate refused President **George W. Bush's** nomination of John Tower as secretary of defense. More commonly, the President will withdraw a nomination if the Senate sends signals that it will reject the nominee. In 2005, for example, President George W. Bush withdrew the nomination of Harriet Miers, his White House Counsel, to the Supreme Court. He later nominated **Samuel Alito**, who was confirmed by the Senate.

In the current era of divided government, the confirmation process has been characterized by partisanship. Democrat President Obama, for example, chose Merrick Garland to replace Justice **Antonin Scalia** on the Supreme Court, but the Republican-led Senate refused even to hold hearings on his nomination.

Republican President **Donald Trump**, too, saw his share of confirmation troubles when Democrats in the Senate filibustered his Supreme Court nominee, **Neil Gorsuch**. Justice Gorsuch was confirmed only after the Senate resorted to the so-called "nuclear option"—a rule change to allow confirmation with only a simple majority, rather than the 60 votes needed to end a filibuster. In addition, the President's pick for Labor secretary, Andrew Puzder, was forced to withdraw amid controversy surrounding his business dealings and personal conduct.

It is with the President's appointment of federal officers who serve in the various States (for example, U.S. attorneys and federal marshals) that the unwritten rule of "senatorial courtesy" comes into play. The Senate will turn down such a presidential appointment if it is opposed by a senator of the President's party from the State involved. The Senate's observance of this unwritten rule has a significant impact on the President's exercise of the power of appointment; in effect, this rule means that some senators virtually dictate certain presidential appointments.

Treaties The President makes treaties "by and with the Advice and Consent of the Senate, . . . provided two thirds of the Senators present concur" (Article II, Section 2, Clause 2). For a time after the adoption of the Constitution, the President asked the advice of the Senate when a treaty was being negotiated and prepared. Now the President most often consults the members of the Senate Foreign Relations Committee and other influential senators of both parties.

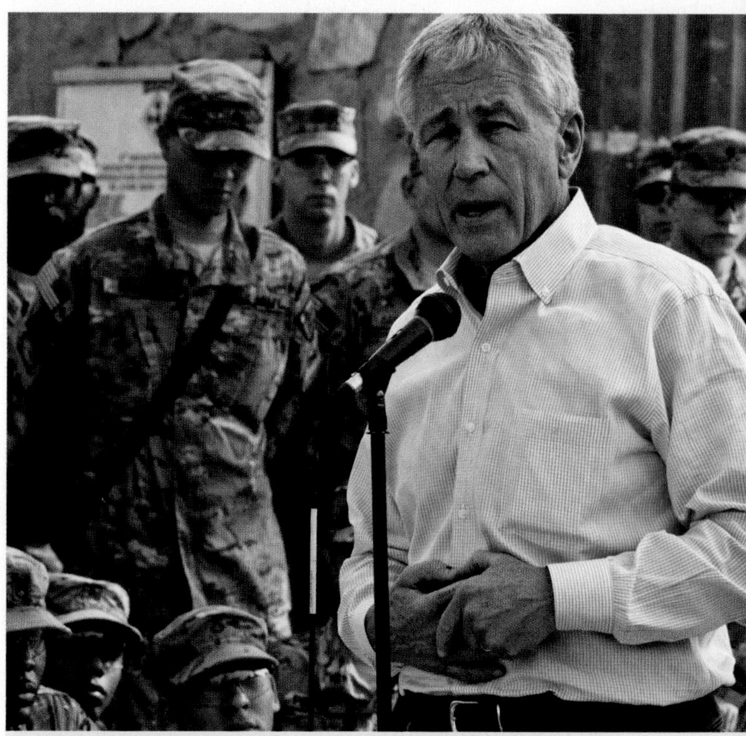

>> Defense secretary Charles "Chuck" Hagel speaks to troops during a visit to Afghanistan. He faced a Senate filibuster during his confirmation hearings in 2013, but was eventually confirmed.

The Senate may accept or reject a treaty as it stands, or it may decide to offer amendments, reservations, or understandings to it. Treaties are sometimes considered in executive session. Because the House has a hold on the public purse strings, influential members of that body are often consulted in the treaty-making process, too.

? SUMMARIZE What is the unwritten rule of senatorial courtesy and how does it affect the President's power of appointments?

Impeachment

The Constitution provides that the President, Vice President, and all civil officers of the United States may "be removed from Office on Impeachment for, and Conviction of, Treason, Bribery, or other high Crimes and Misdemeanors." (Article II, Section 4) A close reading of those words suggests that the Framers expected that only serious criminal offenses, not political disagreements, would lead to impeachment. Politics has, nevertheless, been at the root of most impeachment controversies.

The House has the sole power to **impeach**—to accuse, bring charges. The Senate has the sole power to try—to judge, to sit as a court—in impeachment cases. (Article I, Section 2, Clause 5; Section 3, Clause 6)

Impeachment requires only a majority vote in the House; conviction requires a two-thirds vote in the Senate. The Chief Justice presides over the Senate when a President is to be tried. The penalty for conviction is removal from office. The Senate may also prohibit a convicted person from ever holding federal office again; and he or she can be tried in the regular courts for any crime involved in the events that led to the impeachment. To date, there have been 19 impeachments and eight convictions; all eight persons removed by the Senate were federal judges.

Two Presidents have been impeached by the House: **Andrew Johnson** in 1868 and Bill Clinton in 1998. The Senate voted to **acquit** both men—that is, it found them not guilty.

Andrew Johnson The unsuccessful attempt to remove Andrew Johnson grew out of the turmoil that followed the Civil War. Mr. Johnson had become the nation's 17th President when **Abraham Lincoln** was assassinated in April of 1865, and he soon became enmeshed in a series of disputes with the Radical Republicans who controlled both houses of Congress. Many of those disagreements centered around the treatment of the defeated Southern States in the immediate post-war period.

President Johnson tried to carry out the conciliatory Reconstruction policies favored by Abraham Lincoln—policies that Mr. Lincoln has summarized in these memorable words in his Second Inaugural Address on March 4, 1865: "With malice toward none, with charity for all... " The Radical Republicans supported a much harsher approach to Reconstruction.

Matters came to a head when Congress passed the Tenure of Office Act, over the President's veto, in 1867. President Johnson's violation of that law triggered his impeachment by a House bent on political revenge. The Senate fell just one vote short of removing him from office.

Bill Clinton Bill Clinton was impeached by the House in 1998. In proceedings steeped in partisanship, the House voted two articles of impeachment against him on December 19. Both articles arose out of the President's admitted "inappropriate relationship" with a White House intern. The first article charged the President with **perjury**—that is, lying under oath. The second article accused him of obstruction of justice because he had withheld information about his affair with the intern.

Members of the House who supported the articles of impeachment contended that the acts of lying under oath and of withholding evidence were within the meaning of the Constitution's phrase "other high Crimes and Misdemeanors." Therefore, they argued, the President's immediate removal from office was justified.

Judges Removed by Impeachment

YEAR	JUDGE	REASONS	YEAR	JUDGE	REASONS
1804	John Pickering	mental instability; intoxication on the bench	1986	Harry E. Claiborne	income tax evasion; remaining on the bench following criminal conviction
1862	West H. Humphreys	refusal to hold court; waging war against the U.S. government	1989	Alcee Hastings	perjury; conspiring to solicit a bribe
1913	Robert Archbald	improper business relationship with litigants	1989	Walter Nixon	perjury before a federal grand jury
1936	Halsted Ritter	Showing favoritism in appointments; practicing law while sitting as a judge	2010	G. Thomas Porteous, Jr.	accepting bribes; making false statements under penalty of perjury

SOURCE: Federal Judicial Center

>> Congress has impeached and removed eight judges from the bench since 1804.
Analyze Charts Why does Congress need this impeachment power over judges?

Their opponents argued that the facts involved in the case did not justify either charge. They insisted that, while the President's conduct was deplorable and should be condemned, that conduct did not rise to the level of an impeachable offense. Many of them pressed, instead, for a resolution to **censure** the President—that is, for a formal condemnation of his behavior.

The Senate received the articles of impeachment when the new Congress convened in 1999, and it began to sit in judgment of the President on January 7.

Richard Nixon A few officeholders have resigned in the face of almost certain impeachment—most notably, **Richard Nixon**, who resigned the presidency in mid-1974. President Nixon's second term in office was cut short by the Watergate scandal.

The term *Watergate* comes from a June 1972 attempt by Republican operatives to break into the Democratic Party's national headquarters in the Watergate office complex in Washington, D.C. The investigation of that incident, by the *Washington Post* and then by other media, led to official investigations by the Department of Justice and by the Senate's Select Committee on Presidential Campaign Activities, popularly known as the Senate Watergate Committee.

The probes unearthed a long list of illegal acts, including bribery, perjury, income tax fraud, and illegal campaign contributions. They also revealed the use of the Federal Bureau of Investigation, the Internal Revenue Service, and other government agencies for personal and partisan purposes.

The House Judiciary Committee voted three articles of impeachment against President Nixon in late July 1974. He was charged with obstruction of justice, abuse of power, and failure to respond to the Judiciary Committee's **subpoenas.** A committee's subpoena is a legal order directing one to appear before that body and/or to produce certain evidence. Mr. Nixon had ignored the committee's subpoena of several tape recordings of Watergate-related conversations in the Oval Office.

It was quite apparent that the full House would impeach the President and that the Senate would convict him. Those facts prompted Mr. Nixon to resign the presidency on August 9, 1974.

Beyond doubt, the Watergate scandal involved the most extensive and the most serious violations of public trust in the nation's history. Among its other consequences, several Cabinet officers, presidential assistants, and others were convicted of various

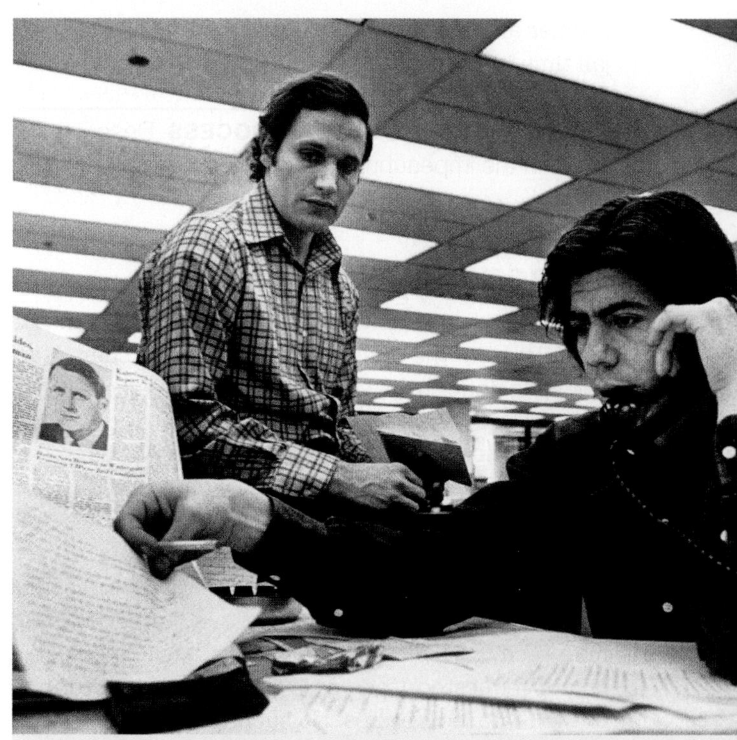

>> *Washington Post* reporters Bob Woodward (left) and Carl Bernstein uncovered the Watergate scandal, prompting Congress to investigate, and leading President Richard Nixon to resign.

>> Richard Nixon made a hand sign for victory following his 1974 resignation. He first used the trademark gesture after his nomination as the 1968 Republican presidential candidate.

Interactive Gallery

felonies and misdemeanors—and many of them served jail time.

IDENTIFY STEPS IN A PROCESS Describe the steps in the impeachment process.

Other Powers

Congress is a legislative body; its primary function is to make law. But the Constitution does give it some other chores to perform as well.

Constitutional Amendments Article V says that Congress may propose amendments to the Constitution by a two-thirds vote in each house. All 27 of the amendments thus far added to the document have been proposed by Congress. Article V also provides that Congress may call a national convention of delegates from each of the States to propose an amendment—but only if requested to do so by at least two thirds (34) of the State legislatures. No such convention has ever been called.

In recent years, several State legislatures have petitioned Congress for amendments—among them measures that would require Congress to balance the federal budget each year, prohibit flag burning, permit prayer in public schools, outlaw abortions, impose term limits on members of Congress, and prohibit same-sex marriages.

Electoral Duties The Constitution gives certain electoral duties to Congress. But they are to be exercised only in very unusual circumstances.

The House may be called on to elect a President. The 12th Amendment says that if no one receives a majority of the electoral votes for President, the House, voting by States, is to decide the issue. It must choose from among the three highest contenders in the electoral college balloting. Each State has but one vote to cast, and a majority of the States is necessary for election.

The Senate must choose a Vice President if no candidate wins a majority of the electoral votes for that office. In that situation, the vote is by individual senators, with a majority of the full Senate necessary for election.

The House has had to choose a President twice: Thomas Jefferson in 1801 and **John Quincy Adams** in 1825. The Senate has had to pick a Vice President only once: Richard M. Johnson in 1837.

The 25th Amendment provides for the filling of a vacancy in the vice presidency. When one occurs, the President nominates a **successor**—a replacement, someone to fill the vacancy, subject to a majority vote in both houses of Congress. That process has also

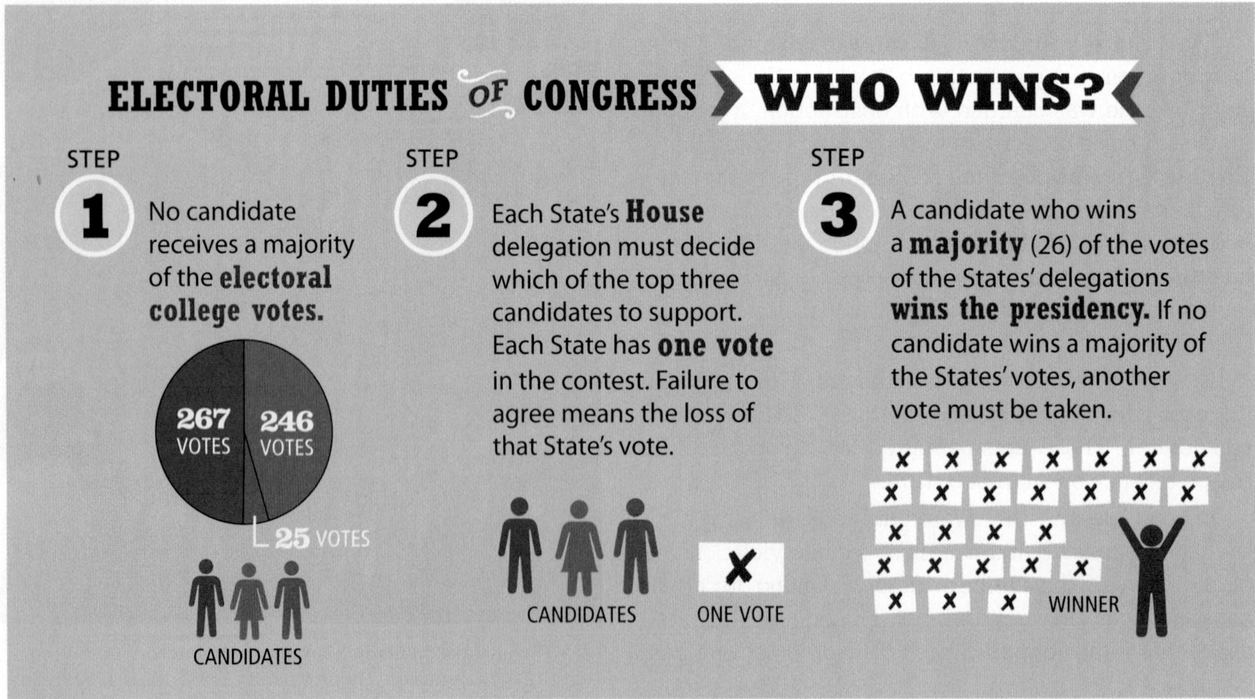

ELECTORAL DUTIES OF CONGRESS
WHO WINS?
STEP 1
No candidate receives a majority of the electoral college votes.
267 VOTES
246 VOTES
25 VOTES
CANDIDATES
STEP 2
Each State's House delegation must decide which of the top three candidates to support. Each State has one vote in the contest. Failure to agree means the loss of that State's vote.
CANDIDATES
ONE VOTE
STEP 3
A candidate who wins a majority (26) of the votes of the States' delegations wins the presidency. If no candidate wins a majority of the States' votes, another vote must be taken.
WINNER

>> One presidential candidate must receive the majority of the electoral college votes. **Analyze Charts** What is an example of a situation that might prevent any candidate from winning a majority?

★ VICE-PRESIDENTIAL VACANCY ★

"The 25th Amendment provides, in part: Whenever there is a vacancy in the office of the Vice President, the President shall nominate a Vice President who shall take office upon confirmation by a majority vote of both Houses of Congress."
—25th Amendent, Section 2

A vacancy occurs.

The President selects a successor.

Both Houses of Congress vote to confirm or reject the nominee. A majority vote is required.

VICE PRESIDENT SPIRO AGNEW **RESIGNS** AFTER A CONVICTION FOR INCOME TAX EVASION.

PRESIDENT NIXON **NOMINATES** HOUSE MINORITY LEADER GERALD FORD (R., MI) TO SUCCEED SPIRO AGNEW AS VICE PRESIDENT.

CONGRESS CONFIRMS GERALD FORD TO SUCCEED SPIRO AGNEW AS **VICE PRESIDENT.**

>> Congress' electoral duties include selecting a successor if the vice presidency becomes vacant. **Analyze Charts** Why is it important that Congress is involved in filling such a vacancy?

been used twice: Gerald Ford was confirmed as Vice President in 1973 and Nelson Rockefeller in 1974.

? SUMMARIZE Summarize the processes Congress may take to amend the Constitution and discuss how each has been used.

ASSESSMENT

1. **Compare and Contrast** How do strict constructionists and liberal constructionists differ in their attitude toward congressional power?
2. **Interpret** What is the significance of the court's decision in *McCulloch* v. *Maryland*, 1819?
3. **Analyze Information** How do each of the nonlegislative powers of Congress illustrate the principle of checks and balances?
4. **Apply Concepts** What is the Necessary and Proper Clause? Why has it been called the Elastic Clause?
5. **Draw Conclusions** Why is the Commerce Clause, written in 1787, still adequate to meet the needs of the nation in the 21st century?

>> Senate Watergate Committee chairman Sam Ervin confers with colleagues during the 1974 hearings. Ervin also chaired the committee that investigated Senator Joe McCarthy in 1954.

Interactive Flipped Video

4.5

What comes to mind when you hear the word *Congress*? The Capitol? Your members of Congress? Some particular bill? Those senators and representatives you often see on the evening news? Of course, you know that the nation's lawmaking body is much more than that. It is, in fact, a very complex enterprise, and much larger than most people realize. Some 30,000 men and women work for the legislative branch today, and Congress appropriates some $5 billion every year to finance its own many-sided operations.

>> Objectives

Describe how and when Congress convenes.

Compare the roles of the presiding officers in the Senate and the House.

Identify the duties of the party officers in each house.

Describe how committee chairman are chosen and explain their role in the legislative process.

Explain how standing committees function.

Describe the responsibilities and duties of the House Rules Committee.

Describe the role of select committees.

Compare the functions of joint and conference committees.

>> Key Terms

Speaker of the House
president of the Senate
president pro tempore
party caucus
floor leaders
majority leader
minority leader
whips
committee chair
seniority rule
standing committee
subcommittee
select committee
joint committee
conference committee
John Boehner
Joe Biden
Patrick Leahy

Congress at Work—Organization and Committees

Congress Convenes

Congress convenes—begins a new term—every two years, on January 3 of every odd-numbered year. Each new term follows the general elections in November.

Opening Day in the House Every other January, the 435 men and women who have been elected to the House come together at the Capitol to begin a new term. At that point, they are, in effect, just so many representatives-elect. Because all 435 of its seats are up for election every two years, the House technically has no sworn members, no rules, and no organization until its opening-day ceremonies are held.

Senator Sherrod Brown (D., Ohio) sat in the House for seven terms before he won election to the Senate in 2006. He remembers his first opening day, in 1993, this way:

> Walking around the chamber the first day, I was awed and nervous. . . . [Q]uestions gnawed

at me when I walked into that august [grand] room, when I met several members about whom I had read and whom I had seen on television. And then I thought about the President of the United States coming to address us— 'Do I deserve to be here with all these people? How did I get here? Will I measure up? How was I chosen for this privilege?'

—Sherrod Brown, *Congress From the Inside*

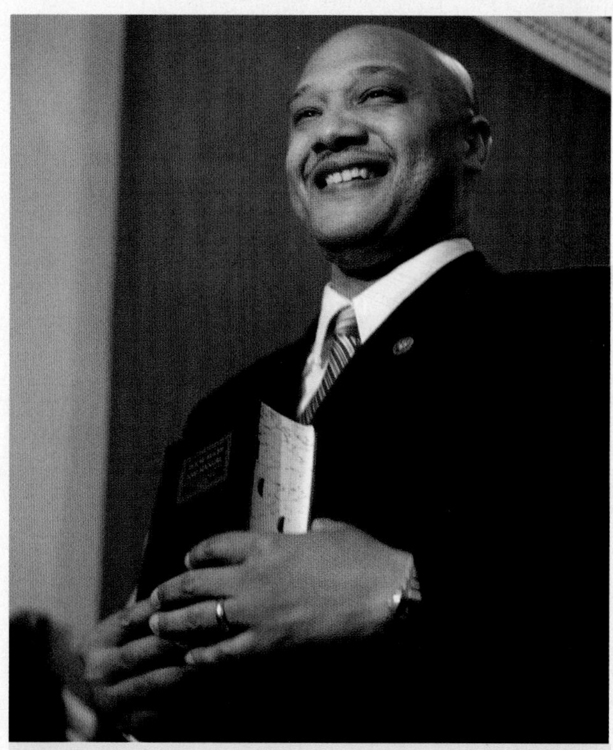

>> Newly elected Indiana Representative Andre Carson used the *House Rules and Manual* for his ceremonial swearing-in, which followed his official swearing-in held earlier in the day.

The clerk of the House in the preceding term presides at the beginning of the first day's session. The clerk calls the chamber to order and checks the roll of representatives elect. Those members-to-be then choose a Speaker, who will be their permanent presiding officer. By custom, the Speaker is a long-standing member of the majority party, and election on the floor is only a formality. The majority party's members in the House have settled the matter beforehand.

The Speaker then takes the oath of office. By tradition, the oath is administered by the Dean of the House, the member-elect with the longest record of service in the House. With that accomplished, the Speaker swears in the rest of the members, as a body. The Democrats take their seats to the right of the center aisle; the Republicans, to the left.

Next, the House elects its clerk, parliamentarian, sergeant at arms, chief administrative officer, and chaplain. None of these people are members of the House, and their elections are also a formality. The majority party has already decided the matter.

Then, the House adopts the rules that will govern its proceedings through the term. The rules of the House have been developing for over 200 years, and they are contained in a volume of about 400 pages. They are readopted, most often with little or no change, at the beginning of each term, though they are occasionally and sometimes extensively amended during a term. Thus, in 2009, the rules were amended to repeal a limit on the number of terms any member can chair any House committee. That controversial limit (of three terms, six years) had been adopted by a newly elected Republican majority at the beginning of the 104th Congress in 1995.

Finally, members of the 20 permanent committees of the House are appointed by a floor vote. With that, the House is organized.

>> A long-standing tradition in the House of Representatives, the chaplain is one of its officers. In addition to leading opening prayers, the chaplain performs ceremonial and pastoral duties.

Opening Day in the Senate The Senate is a continuous body. It has been organized without

He shall from time to time give to the Congress Information of the State of the Union, and recommend to their Consideration such Measures as he shall judge necessary and expedient . . .

—Article II, Section 3

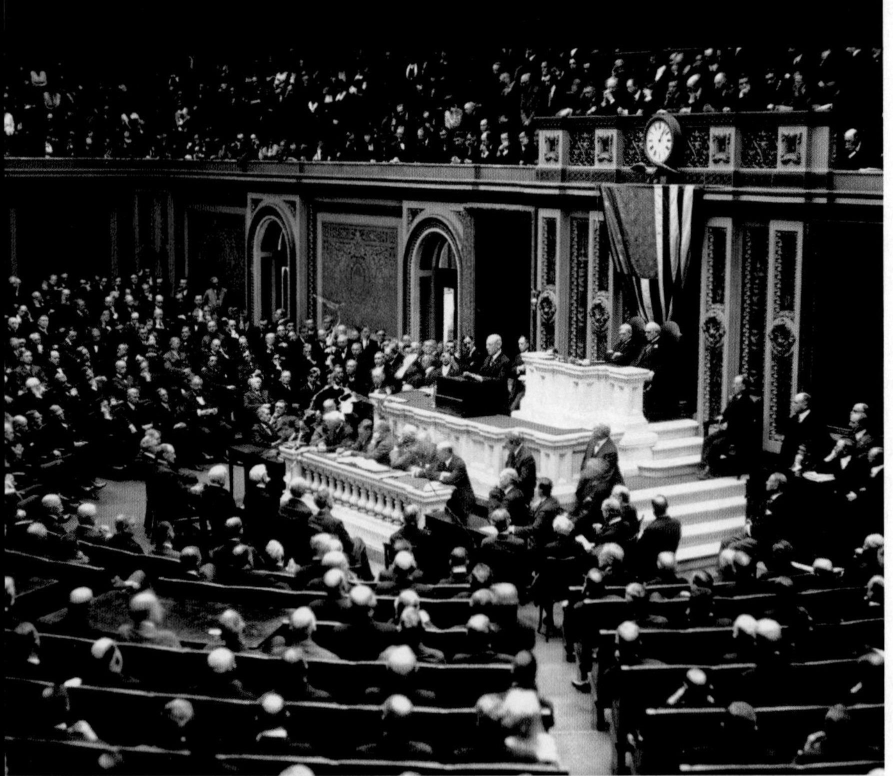

>> Woodrow Wilson gives his State of the Union address to a joint session of Congress in 1918. Before Wilson's first 1913 address, the reports were always delivered in writing.

interruption since its first session in 1789. Recall that only one third of the seats are up for election every two years. Two thirds of the Senate's membership is carried over from one term to the next. As a result, the Senate does not face large organizational problems at the beginning of a term. Its first-day session is nearly always fairly short and routine, even when the elections have brought a change in the majority party. Newly elected and reelected members must be sworn in, vacancies in Senate organization and on committees must be filled, and a few other details attended to.

State of the Union Message When the Senate is notified that the House of Representatives is organized, a joint committee of the two chambers is appointed and instructed "to wait upon the President of the United States and inform him that a quorum of each House is assembled and that the Congress is ready to receive any communication he may be pleased to make."

Within a few weeks—in late January or early February—the President delivers the annual State of the Union message to a joint session of Congress. The speech is a major political event and is based on this constitutional command:

> He shall from time to time give to the Congress Information of the State of the Union, and recommend to their Consideration such Measures as he shall judge necessary and expedient . . .
>
> —Article II, Section 3

From Woodrow Wilson's first message in 1913, the President has almost always presented his annual assessment in person. Members of Congress, together with the members of the Cabinet, the justices of the Supreme Court, the foreign diplomatic corps, and other dignitaries, assemble in the House chamber to hear him.

In the address, the President reports on the state of the nation as he or she sees it, in both domestic and foreign policy terms. The message is widely covered by the news media, and it is very closely followed both here and abroad. In fact, the chief executive's speech is as much a message to the American people, and to the world, as it is an address to Congress. In it, the President lays out the broad shape of the policies the administration expects to follow and the course the chief executive has charted for the nation. The message regularly includes a number of specific legislative recommendations, along with a plea that Congress will enact them. Its presentation is soon followed by scores of bills drawn up in the executive branch and introduced in the House and Senate by various members of the President's party.

With the conclusion of the speech, the joint session is adjourned. Each house then separately turns to the legislative business that will come before it.

INFER What is the purpose of the organization of the House, where all 435 seats are up for election every two years, and the Senate, which is a continuous body?

>> House Speaker John Boehner of Ohio displays his gavel during the first session of the 112th Congress. The House of Representatives elects the Speaker on the first day of every new Congress.

Interactive Chart

The Presiding Officers

The Constitution provides for the presiding officers of each house of Congress—the Speaker of the House and the president of the Senate. Article I, Section 2, Clause 5 directs that "The House of Representatives shall choose their Speaker and other Officers. . . ." And Article I, Section 3, Clause 4 declares: "The Vice President of the United States shall be President of the Senate. . . ."

The Speaker of the House Of the two positions, the **Speaker of the House** is by far the more important and more powerful within the halls of Congress. This is particularly so because the Speaker is both the elected presiding officer of the House and the acknowledged leader of its majority party.

Although neither the Constitution nor its own rules require it, the House has always chosen the Speaker from among its own members. Today, the post is held by **John Boehner** (R., Ohio). He was first elected to the House in 1990 and became Speaker in 2011.

The Speaker is expected to preside in a fair and judicious manner and regularly does. The Speaker is also expected to aid the fortunes of the majority party and its legislative goals, and regularly does that, too.

Nearly all of the Speaker's powers revolve around two duties: to preside and to keep order. The Speaker chairs most sessions of the House but often appoints another member as temporary presiding officer. No member may speak until he or she is recognized by the Speaker. The presiding officer also interprets and applies the rules, refers bills to committee, rules on points of order (questions of procedure raised by members), puts motions to a vote, and decides the outcome of most votes taken on the floor of the House. (The Speaker can be overridden by a vote of the House, but that almost never happens.) The Speaker also names the members of all select and conference committees and must sign all bills and resolutions passed by the House.

As an elected member of the House, the Speaker may debate and vote on any matter before that body. That seldom happens, but when it does, the Speaker appoints another member as the temporary presiding officer and he or she then occupies the Speaker's chair. The Speaker does not often vote, and the House rules say only that the Speaker *must* vote to break a tie. Notice then, that because a tie vote defeats a question, the Speaker occasionally votes to cause a tie and so defeat a proposal.

The Speaker of the House follows the Vice President in the line of succession to the presidency. That fact is a considerable testimony to the power and importance of both the office and the person who holds it.

The President of the Senate The Constitution makes the Vice President the **president of the Senate,** the Senate's presiding officer. This means that (1) unlike the House, the Senate does not choose its own presiding officer and (2) unlike the Speaker of the House, the Senate's presiding officer is not in fact a member of that body. Indeed, the Vice President might not even be a member of the party that controls the Senate.

All of this adds up to the major reason why the Vice President plays a much less powerful role in the Senate than that played by the Speaker in the House. Also note this important point: the Vice President's career path, the route traveled to the post, is a much different path than the one the Speaker has followed. The Vice President has not become the Senate's presiding officer out of long service in that body. He has, instead, come to the post out of a much different process.

>> Whatever influence the president of the Senate has comes from a personal relationship with other senators. Vice President Dan Quayle once represented Indiana in the Senate.

The president of the Senate does have the usual powers of a presiding officer: to recognize members, put questions to a vote, and so on. However, the Vice President cannot take the floor to speak or debate and may vote *only* to break a tie.

Any influence a Vice President may have in the Senate is largely the result of personal abilities and relationships. Several of the more recent Vice Presidents came to that office from the Senate: Harry Truman, Alben Barkley, Richard Nixon, Lyndon Johnson, Hubert Humphrey, Walter Mondale, Dan Quayle, Al Gore, and **Joe Biden**. Each was able to build at least some power into the position out of that earlier experience.

The Senate does have another presiding officer, the **president pro tempore** who serves in the Vice President's absence. The president *pro tempore,* or president pro tem for short, is elected by the Senate itself and is always a leading member of the majority party—usually its longest-serving member. In 2013, the post was occupied by Senator **Patrick Leahy** (D., Vermont). Senator Leahy, who was elected to his first term in the upper house in 1974, became president *pro tempore* in 2012.

>> Vice President Biden swore in Senator Patrick Leahy as president *pro tempore* of the Senate in 2012. Leahy was unanimously elected following the death of Senator Daniel Inouye.

The president pro tem follows the Speaker of the House in the line of presidential succession. Other senators do frequently preside over the Senate, on a temporary basis; newly elected members regularly do so early in their terms.

? INFER The Constitution specifies that the Senate's presiding officer is not a member of that body. In what ways does this affect his or her influence in the Senate?

Party Officers

Congress is a *political* body. This is so for two leading reasons: (1) Congress is the nation's central *policy*-making body, and (2) Congress is *partisan*. Reflecting

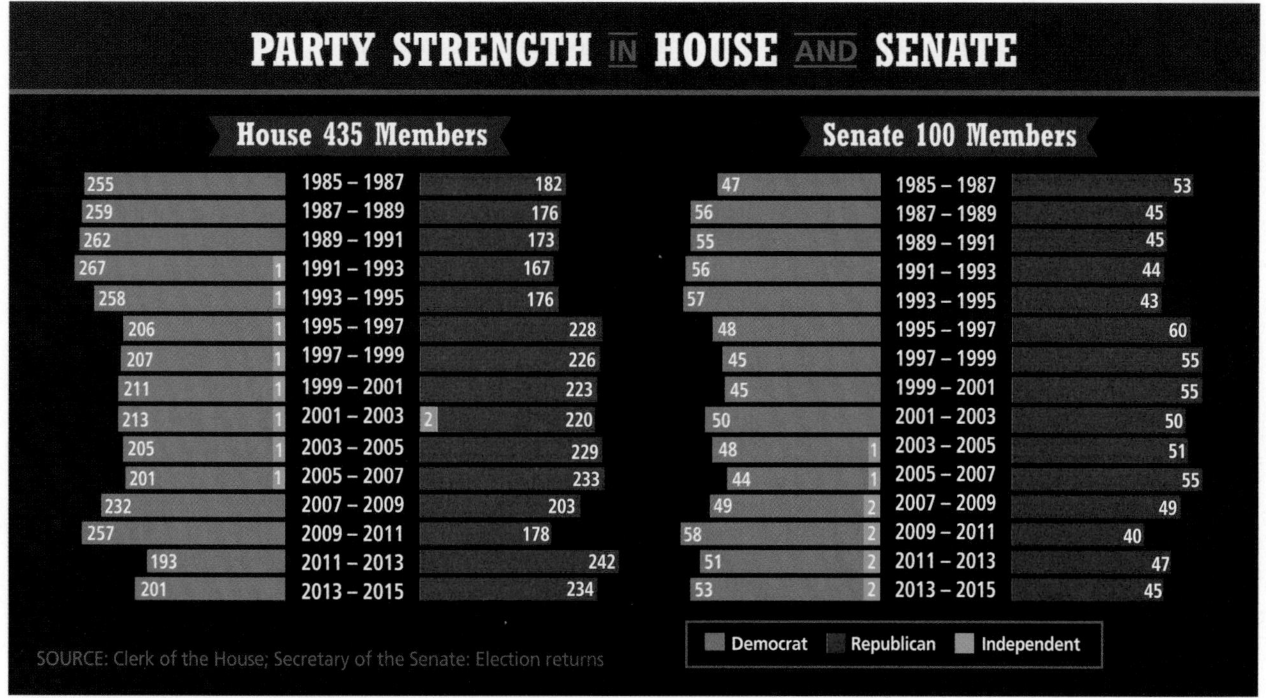

>> This chart shows party strength at the start of the past 15 terms of Congress.
Analyze Charts What is the largest majority each party has held in each house over the past 30 years?

its political character, both houses of Congress are organized along party lines.

The Party Caucus The **party caucus** is a closed meeting of the members of each party in each house. These meetings are regularly held just before Congress convenes in January and occasionally during a session. In recent years the Republicans have called their caucus in each house the *party conference*, and the Democrats now use this term in the Senate, too.

A caucus deals mostly with matters related to party organization, such as the selection of the party's floor leaders and questions of committee membership. It sometimes takes stands on particular bills, but neither party tries to force its members to follow its caucus decisions, nor can it.

The policy committee is composed of the party's top leadership. It acts as an executive committee for the party caucus. That body is known as the *policy committee* in each party's structure in the Senate and in the Republicans' organization in the House. However, it is called the *steering and policy committee* by the Democrats in the lower chamber.

The Floor Leaders Next to the Speaker, the **floor leaders** in the House and Senate are the most important officers in Congress. They do not hold official positions in either chamber. Rather, they are party officers, picked for their posts by their party colleagues.

The floor leaders are legislative strategists. Assisted by paid staff, they try to carry out the decisions of their parties' caucuses and steer floor action to their parties' benefit. Each of them is also the chief spokesman for his party in his chamber. All of that calls for political skills of a high order. Senator Howard Baker (R., Tennessee), one of the Senate's most effective floor leaders, often likened his job to that of "herding cats."

The floor leader of the party that holds the majority of seats in each house of Congress is known as the **majority leader.** The floor leader of the party that holds the minority of seats in each house is the **minority leader.** The majority leader is the more powerful in each house—for the obvious reason that the majority party has more seats (more votes) than the other party has. And, the majority leader very largely controls the order of business on the floor in his or her chamber.

The two floor leaders in each house are assisted by party **whips.** The majority whip and the minority whip are, in effect, assistant floor leaders. Each of them is chosen at the party caucus, almost always at the floor leader's recommendation. A number of assistant whips serve in the House.

Whips serve as a liaison—a two-way link—between the party's leadership and its rank-and-file members.

The term *whip* was borrowed from British politics. There, it came from the "whipper-in" in a fox hunt, the rider who is supposed to keep the hounds bunched in a pack. The whips check with party members and tell the floor leader which members, and how many votes, can be counted on in any particular matter. The whips also see that all members of the party are present for important votes and that they vote with the party leadership. If a member must be absent for some reason, a whip sees that that member is paired with a member of the other party who will also be absent that day or who agrees not to vote on certain measures at that day's session—so one non-vote cancels out another.

? DRAW CONCLUSIONS Why can't a party force its members to take a particular stand on a bill during the party's caucus?

Committee Chairs

The bulk of the work of Congress, especially in the House, is really done in committee. Thus, **committee chairmen**—those members who head the standing committees in each chamber—hold very strategic posts. The chairman of each of these permanent committees is chosen from the majority party by the majority party caucus. Note the title *chairman* is used here because this is the form historically used in Congress, although some committees have moved to *chair* or *chairwoman* when led by a woman. These men and women are always ranking members of the majority party.

Although committee chairmen are less powerful now than in years past, they still have a major say in such matters as which bills a committee will consider and in what order and at what length, whether public hearings are to be held, and what witnesses the committee will call. When a committee's bill has been reported—approved for consideration—to the floor, the chairman usually manages the debate and tries to steer it to final passage.

We shall take a closer look at committees and their chairs in a moment. But, first, consider the seniority rule.

The Seniority Rule The **seniority rule** is, in fact, an unwritten custom. It dates from the late 1800s, and is still more or less closely followed in both houses today. The seniority rule provides that the most important posts in Congress, in both the formal and the party organizations, will be held by those party members with the longest records of service. (Notice that seniority rule does not apply to the presiding officers or

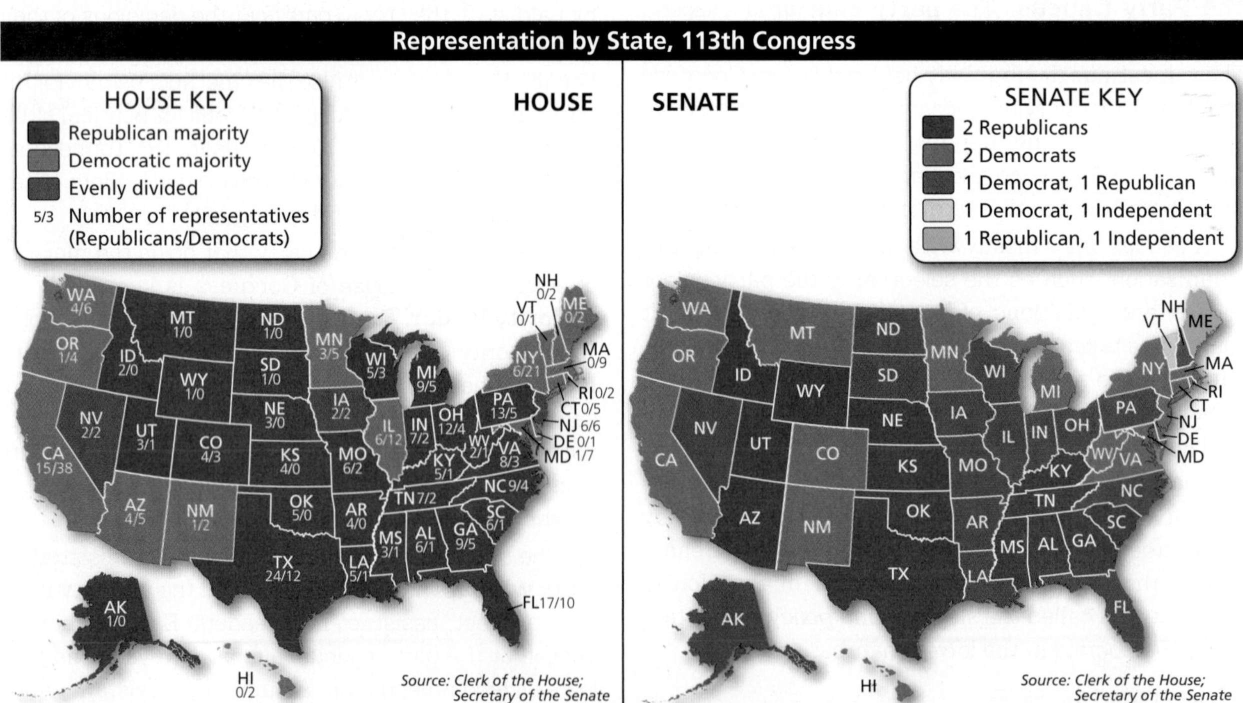

>> The colors on these maps indicate the party composition of each State's delegation in the House and Senate. **Analyze Maps** Which States are the same color on both maps?

Interactive Map

to the floor leaders in either chamber. As you've seen, their selection is otherwise provided for.)

The rule is applied most strictly to the choice of committee chairmen. The head of each committee is almost always the longest-serving majority party member of that committee. The rule is also followed quite closely in the selection of those members who chair the several subcommittees into which nearly all the standing committees are divided.

Criticism of the Seniority Rule Critics of the seniority rule are many, and they do make a strong case. They insist that the seniority system ignores ability, rewards mere length of service, and works to discourage younger members. Its opponents also note that the rule means that a committee head often comes from a "safe" constituency—a State or district in which one party regularly wins the seat. With no play of fresh and conflicting forces in those places, critics claim, the chairman of a committee is often out of touch with current public opinion.

Defenders of the seniority rule argue that it ensures that a powerful and experienced member will head each committee. They also say that the rule encourages members to stay on a particular committee and so, over time, gain a wide-ranging knowledge of matters that fall within that committee's jurisdiction. In addition, they note that the rule is fairly easy to apply and that it very nearly eliminates the possibility of fights within the party.

The rule's opponents have gained some ground in recent years. Thus, the House Republican Conference (caucus) now picks several GOP members of House committees by secret ballot. House Democrats use secret ballots to choose a committee chairman whenever 20 percent of their caucus requests that procedure.

Whatever the arguments against the seniority rule, it is unlikely to be eliminated. Those members with the real power to abolish the rule are also the ones who reap the largest benefits from it.

IDENTIFY CAUSE AND EFFECT In what ways do seniority practices within Congressional committees minimize the impact of changes in voters' choices?

Standing Committees

Do you know the phrase "a division of labor"? It means dividing the work to be done, assigning the several parts of the overall task to various members of the group. The House and the Senate are both so large, and their agendas are so crowded with so many different matters, that both chambers must rely on a division of labor. That is to say, much of the work that Congress does is in fact done by committees. Indeed, Representative Clem Miller (D., California) once described Congress as "a collection of committees that come together in a chamber periodically to approve of one another's actions."

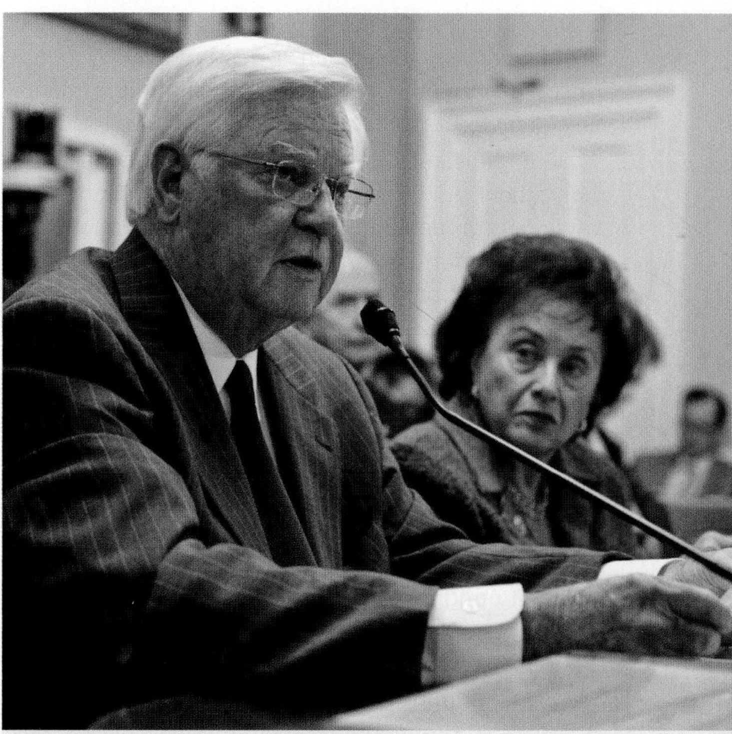

>> House Appropriations Committee chairman Hal Rogers and Representative Nita Lowey testify in a 2013 meeting related to an aid package for victims of Superstorm Sandy.

In 1789, the House and Senate each adopted the practice of naming a special committee to consider each bill as it was introduced. By 1794, there were more than 300 committees in each chamber. Each house then began to set up permanent panels, **standing committees**, to which all similar bills can be sent. The number of these committees has varied over the years. In 2014, there were 20 standing committees in the House and 16 in the Senate. Each House committee has from 10 to as many as 75 members, and each Senate committee has from 14 to 28. Representatives are normally assigned to one or two standing committees and senators to three or four.

The pivotal role these committees play in the lawmaking process cannot be overstated. Most bills receive their most thorough consideration in these bodies. Members of both houses regularly respect the decisions and follow the recommendations they make. Thus, the fate of most bills is usually decided in the various standing committees, not on the floor of either house. More than a century ago, Woodrow Wilson described "Congress in its committee rooms" as "Congress at work," and that remains true today.

Some panels are more prominent and more influential than others. As you would expect, most members try to win assignments to one of these major panels. The leading committees in the House are the Rules, Ways and Means, Appropriations, Armed Services, Judiciary, Foreign Affairs, and Agriculture committees. In the Senate, senators usually compete for places on the Foreign Relations; Appropriations; Finance; Judiciary; Armed Services; and Banking, Housing, and Urban Affairs committees.

Of course, some of the other committees are particularly attractive to some members. Thus, a representative whose district lies wholly within a major city might want to sit on the House Committee on Education and the Workforce. A senator from one of the western States might angle for assignment to the Senate's Committee on Energy and Natural Resources.

Most of the standing committees review bills dealing with particular policy matters—say, public lands, taxes, or veterans' affairs. However, there are four standing committees that are not organized as subject-matter bodies: in the House, the Rules Committee, the Committee on House Administration, and the Committee on Standards of Official Conduct, and in the Senate, the Committee on Rules and Administration.

When a bill is introduced in either house, the Speaker or the president of the Senate refers the measure to the appropriate standing committee. Thus, the Speaker sends all tax measures to the House Ways and Means Committee; in the Senate, tax measures go to the Finance Committee. A bill dealing with the creation of additional federal district judgeships will be sent to the Judiciary Committee in both chambers, and so on.

Recall that the chairman of each of the standing committees is chosen according to the seniority rule. As a consequence, most committee chairmen have served in Congress for at least 12 years and some much longer. The seniority rule is also closely applied in each house when it elects the other members of each of its committees.

The members of each standing committee are formally elected by a floor vote at the beginning of each term of Congress. In fact, each party has already drawn up its own committee roster before that vote, and the floor vote merely ratifies those party choices. The majority party always holds a majority of the seats on each standing committee. The other party is well represented, however.

Subcommittees Most standing committees are divided into **subcommittees**—divisions of standing

Senate Standing Committee Chairs, 2017–2018

COMMITTEE	NAME, PARTY, STATE, YEAR ELECTED*	COMMITTEE	NAME, PARTY, STATE, YEAR ELECTED*
Agriculture, Nutrition, and Forestry	Pat Roberts (R., KS), 1996	**Finance**	Orrin Hatch (R., UT), 1976
		Foreign Relations	Bob Corker (R., TN), 2006
Appropriations	Thad Cochran (R., MS), 1978	**Health, Education, Labor, and Pensions**	Lamar Alexander (R., TN), 2002
Armed Services	John McCain (R., AZ), 1986		
Banking, Housing, and Urban Affairs	Michael Crapo (R., ID), 1998	**Homeland Security and Governmental Affairs**	Ron Johnson (R., WI), 2010
Budget	Mike Enzi (R., WY), 1996		
Commerce, Science, and Transportation	John Thune (R., SD), 2004	**Judiciary**	Chuck Grassley (R., IA), 1980
		Rules and Administration	Richard Shelby (R., AL), 1986
Energy and Natural Resources	Lisa Murkowski (R., AK), 2002	**Small Business and Entrepreneurship**	James Risch (R., ID), 2008
Environment and Public Works	John Barrasso (R., WY), 2008	**Veterans' Affairs**	Johnny Isakson (R., GA), 2004

SOURCE: senate.gov *to Senate

>> Chairing a committee is viewed as a powerful role and a badge of honor. **Analyze Charts** What conclusions can you draw about committees' jurisdictions based on their titles?

House Standing Committee Chairs, 2017–2018

COMMITTEE	NAME, PARTY, STATE, YEAR ELECTED*	COMMITTEE	NAME, PARTY, STATE, YEAR ELECTED*
Agriculture	Mike Conaway (R., TX), 2004	Judiciary	Robert W. Goodlatte (R., VA), 1992
Appropriations	Rodney Frelinghuysen (R., NJ), 1994	Natural Resources	Rob Bishop (R., UT), 2002
Armed Services	Mac Thornberry (R., TX), 1994	Oversight and Government Reform	Jason Chaffetz (R., UT), 2008
Budget	Diane Black (R., TN), 2010	Rules	Pete Sessions (R., TX), 1996
Education and the Workforce	Virginia Foxx (R., NC), 2004	Science, Space, and Technology	Lamar Smith (R., TX), 1986
Energy and Commerce	Greg Walden (R., OR), 1998	Small Business	Steve Chabot (R., OH), 1994
Ethics	Susan W. Brooks (R., IN), 2012	Transportation and Infrastructure	Bill Shuster (R., PA), 2000
Financial Services	Jeb Hensarling (R., TX), 2002	Veterans' Affairs	Phil Roe (R., TN), 2008
Foreign Affairs	Ed Royce (R., CA), 1992	Ways and Means	Kevin Brady (R., TX), 1996
Homeland Security	Michael McCaul (R., TX), 2004		
House Administration	Gregg Harper (R., MS), 2008		

SOURCE: house.gov/committees *to House

>> House committees consider bills that fall within their jurisdictions. **Analyze Charts** Why does the House have more committees than the Senate?

committees that do most of the committees' work. Each subcommittee is responsible for a portion of the committee's workload. There are now more than 150 subcommittees in the two houses—nearly 70 in the Senate and about 100 in the House.

Take a look at the Senate's 18-member Judiciary Committee (currently composed of 10 Democrats and 8 Republicans). It does most of its work in its seven subcommittees. Each member serves on at least two, and their titles describe their focuses: Administrative Oversight and the Courts; Antitrust, Competition Policy and Consumer Rights; The Constitution, Civil Rights, and Human Rights; Crime and Terrorism; Human Rights and the Law; Immigration, Refugees and Border Security; and Privacy, Technology, and the Law.

The House Rules Committee The House Committee on Rules is the Speaker's "right arm." It controls the flow of bills to the floor and sets the conditions for their consideration there. The panel is often described as the "traffic cop" in the lower house. So many measures are introduced in the House each term that some sort of screening device is absolutely necessary.

Most bills die in the committees to which they are referred. Still, several hundred are reported out every year. So, before most of these bills can reach the floor of the House, they must also clear the Rules Committee.

Normally, a bill gets to the floor only if it has been granted a rule—been scheduled for floor consideration—by the Rules Committee. The committee decides whether and under what conditions the full House will consider a measure. As you will see, this means that the powerful 12-member Rules Committee can speed, delay, or even prevent House action on a measure. In the smaller Senate, where the process is not so closely regulated, the majority leader controls the appearance of bills on the floor.

INFER How can party control of the Legislature impact the passage of a bill through committee to floor consideration?

Select Committees

At times, each house finds a need for a **select committee,** sometimes called special committees. They are panels set up for some specific purpose and, most often, for a limited time. The Speaker of the House or the president of the Senate appoints the members of these special committees, with the advice of the majority and minority leaders.

The congressional power to investigate is an essential part of the lawmaking function. Congress must decide on the need for new laws and gauge the adequacy of those already on the books. It also must exercise its vital oversight function, to ensure that federal agencies are following the laws it has already passed. At times, too, a committee may conduct an investigation of an issue—for example, the threat of domestic terrorism—in order to focus public attention on that matter. Most investigations are conducted by standing committees, or by their subcommittees.

However, select committees are sometimes formed to investigate a current issue, as the Senate's Select Committee on Indian Affairs recently did. That 14-member panel spent nearly three years investigating the behavior of a number of well-connected lobbyists who represented several Native American tribes as they sought to establish gambling casinos. The committee's extensive probe uncovered massive instances of fraud, bribery, tax evasion, and other illegal activities for which several offenders began to serve long prison sentences in 2006 and 2007. The most prominent of those miscreants were Washington-based lobbyist Jack Abramoff and a member of Congress, Representative Robert Ney (R., Ohio), who had been chairman of the House Committee on Administration.

At times, select committees have been spectacularly important. This happened, for example, with the Senate's Select Committee on Presidential Campaign Activities, popularly known as the Senate Watergate Committee. As the Watergate scandal began to unfold in 1973, the Senate created that committee. Chaired by Senator Sam Ervin (D., North Carolina), its job was to investigate "the extent, if any, to which illegal, improper, or unethical activities were engaged in by any persons . . . in the presidential election of 1972." Its sensational hearings riveted the nation for months. Eventually, they formed a key link in the chain of events that led to President Richard Nixon's resignation from office in mid-1974.

Another notable instance came in 1987, with the work of two panels: the Senate's Select Committee on Secret Military Assistance to Iran and the Nicaraguan Opposition, and the House Select Committee to Investigate Covert Arms Transactions with Iran. These twin committees, often referred to jointly as the Iran-Contra Committee, probed the Reagan administration's conduct of two highly secret projects abroad: the sale of arms to Iran and efforts to give military aid to the Contra rebels in Nicaragua.

The operation in Iran was intended, at least in part, as an arms-for-hostages deal, and it failed. The aid to the Contras was funded in part with money from the Iranian arms sales, despite an act of Congress that expressly prohibited such aid by the United States.

Most congressional investigations are not nearly so visible, nor so historic. Their more usual shape can be seen when, for example, the House Committee on Agriculture probes the spruce budworm problem (an infestation affecting trees in the Pacific Northwest) or the Senate's Armed Services Committee looks at the Army's recruiting programs.

>> A group of Contras on patrol in northern Nicaragua. Congress later formed a committee to investigate weapon sales to the Contras.

? INFER Why would a select committee need to focus public attention on a particular issue?

Joint and Conference Committees

A **joint committee** is one composed of members of both houses. Some of these are select committees set up to serve some temporary purpose. Most are permanent groups that serve on a regular basis. Because the standing committees of the two houses often duplicate one another's work, many have long urged that Congress make much greater use of the joint committee device.

Some joint committees are investigative in nature and issue periodic reports to the House and Senate—for example, the Joint Committee on Taxation. It conducts in depth studies of the federal tax system and presents its findings to the House Ways and Means Committee and the Senate's Finance Committee. Most often, those committees perform more routine duties—for example, the Joint Committee on the Library oversees the administration of that remarkable institution, the Library of Congress.

Before a bill may be sent to the President, each house must pass it in identical form. Sometimes, the two houses pass differing versions, and the first house will not agree to the changes the other has made. When this happens, a **conference committee**—a temporary, joint body—is created to iron out the differences in the bill. Its job is to produce a compromise bill that both houses will accept—as you will see shortly.

? GENERATE EXPLANATIONS What is the purpose of having both the House of Representatives and the Senate debate the same bill?

ASSESSMENT

1. **Describe** Describe how and when Congress convenes.
2. **Compare and Contrast** Compare the roles of the Speaker of the House and the president of the Senate.
3. **Identify** Identify the party officers in each house and what their roles are.
4. **Compare** Compare the functions of a standing committee, the House Rules Committee, a select committee, a joint committee, and a conference committee.
5. **Describe** Describe how committee chairs are chosen and their role in the legislative process.

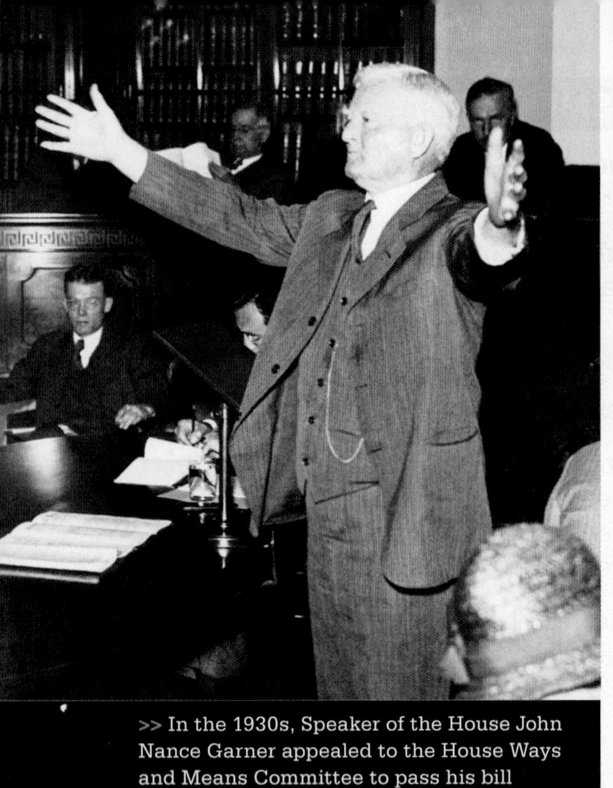

>> In the 1930s, Speaker of the House John Nance Garner appealed to the House Ways and Means Committee to pass his bill providing relief for the unemployed.

Interactive Flipped Video

4.6

These numbers may surprise you: From 6,000 to 9,000 bills and resolutions are introduced in the House and Senate during each session of Congress. Fewer than ten percent become law. Where do all those measures come from? Why are so few of them passed? How, by process, does Congress make law?

>> Objectives

Identify the first steps in the introduction of a bill to the House.

Describe what happens to a bill once it is referred to a committee.

Explain how House leaders schedule debate on a bill.

Explain what happens to a bill on the House floor, and identify the final step in the passage of a bill in the House.

Describe how a bill is introduced in the Senate.

Compare the Senate's rules for debate with those in the House.

Describe the role of conference committees in the legislative process.

Evaluate the actions the President can take after both houses have passed a bill.

>> Key Terms

bill
joint resolution
concurrent resolution
resolution
rider
pigeonholed
discharge petition
quorum
engrossed
filibuster
cloture
veto
pocket veto
Huey Long
Strom Thurmond
George Norris
omnibus measure

Congress at Work—Making Laws

The First Steps

A **bill** is a proposed law presented to the House or Senate for consideration. Most of the bills introduced in either house do not originate with members themselves. Instead, however, many of the most important bills are born somewhere in the executive branch. Business, labor, agriculture, and other special interest groups often draft measures, as well. And some bills, or at least the ideas for them, come from private citizens who think "there ought to be a law. . . ." Many others are born in the standing committees of Congress.

According to Article I, Section 7, Clause 1 of the Constitution, "bills for raising Revenue shall originate in the House." In other words, tax bills must first be acted upon by the House. Measures dealing with any other matter may be introduced in either chamber. Only members can introduce bills in the House, and they do so by dropping them into the hopper, a box hanging on the edge of the clerk's desk.

Often, before a member introduces a bill, he or she will circulate a letter informing other members about the measure and why its sponsor thinks it should become law. That is, he or she hopes to persuade several other members to become cosponsors, thereby increasing the chances that the bill will be passed. By the time many measures are introduced, in either house, a number of members are listed on them as cosponsors.

Public and Private Bills The thousands of measures—bills and resolutions—Congress considers take several forms. To begin with, there are two types of bills: public bills and private bills.

Public bills are measures applying to the nation as a whole—for example, a tax measure. Private bills are measures that apply to certain persons or places rather than to the entire nation. As an example, Congress once passed an act to give a sheep rancher $85,000 for his losses resulting from attacks by grizzly bears. The bears had been moved from Yellowstone National Park to other public lands on which the rancher grazed his flock.

Joint resolutions are similar to bills, and, when passed, have the force of law. They most often deal with unusual or temporary matters—for example, to appropriate money for the presidential inauguration ceremonies. Joint resolutions are used as well to propose constitutional amendments, and they have also been used to annex territories.

Concurrent resolutions deal with matters in which the House and Senate must act jointly. However, they do not have the force of law and do not require the President's signature. Concurrent resolutions are used most often by Congress to state a position on some matter—for example, in foreign affairs.

Resolutions, often called "simple resolutions," deal with matters concerning either house alone and are taken up only by that body. They are regularly used for such matters as the adoption of a new rule of procedure or the amendment of some existing rule. Like concurrent resolutions, a resolution does not have the force of law and is not sent to the President for approval.

A bill or resolution usually deals with a single subject, but sometimes a rider dealing with an unrelated matter is included. A **rider** is a provision not likely to pass on its own merit that is attached to an important measure certain to pass. Its sponsors hope that it will "ride" through the legislative process on the strength of the main measure.

Most riders are tacked onto appropriations measures, and are often called "earmarks." In fact, some money bills have so many riders attached that they are called "Christmas trees." The opponents of those "decorations" and the President are almost always forced to accept them if they want the bill's major provisions to become law.

Introduction and First Reading The clerk of the House numbers each bill as it is introduced. Thus, H.R. 3410 would be the 3,410th measure introduced in the

>> House Doorkeeper Ralph Roberts shows freshman Congressman Richard Nixon the hopper where new House bills are placed. The role of Doorkeeper was abolished in 1995; the hopper was not.

Interactive Chart

>> In politics, "pork" refers to benefits a politician arranges for his or her home district. **Analyze Political Cartoons** What does this cartoon imply about the military spending bill?

House during the congressional term. Bills originating in the Senate receive the prefix S.—such as S. 210. Resolutions are similarly identified in each house in the order of their introduction.

The clerk also gives each bill a short title—a brief summary of its principal contents. Having received its number and title, the bill is then entered in the House *Journal* and in the *Congressional Record* for the day.

The *Journal* contains the minutes, the official record, of the daily proceedings in the House or Senate. The *Congressional Record* is a voluminous account of the daily proceedings (speeches, debates, other comments, votes, motions, etc.) in each house. The *Record* is not quite a word-for-word account, however. Members have five days in which to make changes in each temporary edition. They often insert speeches that were in fact never made, reconstruct "debates," and revise thoughtless or inaccurate remarks.

With these actions the bill has received its first reading. All bills are printed immediately after introduction and distributed to all members of the House.

Each bill that is finally passed in either house is given three readings along the legislative route. In the House, second reading comes during floor consideration, if the measure gets that far. Third reading takes place just before the final vote on the measure. Each reading is usually by number and title only: "H.R. 3410, A bill to provide. . . ." However, the more important or controversial bills are read in full and taken up line by line, section by section, at second reading.

>> The term "pigeonholed" originally referred to the practice of shelving items in the pigeonholes of a desk.

The three readings, an ancient parliamentary practice, are intended to ensure careful consideration of bills. Today, the readings are little more than way stations along the legislative route. They were quite important in the early history of Congress, however, when some members could not read.

After the first reading, the Speaker refers the bill to one or more of the standing committees. A bill's content largely determines where it will go. The Speaker does have some discretion, however, particularly over complex measures with provisions covering a number of subjects. Which committee gets a bill can matter. For example, a controversial provision in the bill might receive a more favorable welcome in one committee than it might in another.

CHECK UNDERSTANDING Would a rider be likely to be attached to a bill proposing abolishing the federal income tax and the Internal Revenue Service? Why or why not?

The Bill in Committee

The Constitution makes no mention of standing committees. These bodies do play an absolutely essential role in the lawmaking process, however—and in both houses of Congress. Indeed, their place is so pivotal that they are sometimes called "little legislatures."

The standing committees act as sieves. They sift through all of the many bills referred to them—rejecting most, considering and reporting only those they find to be worthy of floor consideration. In short, the fate of most bills is decided in these committees rather than on the floor of either house.

Most of the thousands of bills introduced in each session of Congress are **pigeonholed.** That is, they are buried; they die in committee. They are simply put away, never to be acted upon. The term comes from the old-fashioned rolltop desks with pigeonholes—slots into which papers were put and often soon forgotten. Most "by request" bills are routinely pigeonholed; they are the measures that members introduce but only because some constituent or some interest group has asked them to do so.

Most pigeonholed bills do deserve their fate. On occasion, however, a committee buries a measure that a majority of the members of the House want to consider. When that happens, the bill can be blasted out of the committee with a discharge petition.

A **discharge petition** enables members to force a bill that has remained in committee 30 days (7 in the Rules Committee) onto the floor for consideration. Any member may file a discharge motion. If that motion is signed by a majority (218) of House members, the committee has seven days to report the bill. If it does not, any member who signed the motion may, on the second and fourth Mondays of each month, move that the bill be discharged from the committee—that is, sent to the floor. If the motion carries, the rules require the House to consider the bill at once. This maneuver is not often tried, and it seldom succeeds.

The process was most recently successful in 2002, however. What went on to become the Bipartisan Campaign Reform Act of 2002 was blasted out of the Committee on House Administration—where the House leadership had managed to bury it for several years. That measure marked the first major change in federal campaign finance law in 23 years.

>> House Foreign Affairs Committee member and Republican chairman of the European and Euroasian Subcommittee Dan Burton speaks at a wreath-laying ceremony in Hungary.

A Subcommittee's Work Once a bill reaches a committee, the chairman almost always refers it to one of several subcommittees. For an important or controversial measure, a committee, or most often one of its subcommittees, holds public hearings. Interested parties, including the representatives of interest groups, public officials, and others, are invited to testify at these information-gathering sessions. If necessary, a committee can issue a subpoena, forcing a witness to testify. A subpoena is an order compelling one to testify and/or produce evidence. Failure to obey a subpoena may lead the House or Senate to cite the offender for contempt of Congress—a federal crime punishable by fine and/or imprisonment.

Occasionally, a subcommittee will make a trip to locations affected by a measure. Thus, several members of the House Foreign Affairs Committee's Subcommittee on the Western Hemisphere may visit Rio de Janero for a firsthand look at Brazil's successful efforts to reduce that country's dependence on foreign oil.

These trips are made at public expense, and members of Congress are sometimes criticized for taking them. Some of these junkets deserve criticism. But an on-the-spot investigation often proves to be among the best ways a committee can inform itself.

Committee Actions When a subcommittee has completed its work on a bill, the measure goes to the full committee. At the chairman's direction, that body may do one of several things. It may:

1. Report the bill favorably, with a "do pass" recommendation. It is then the chairman's job to steer the bill through debate on the floor.

2. Refuse to report the bill—that is, pigeonhole it. Again, this is the fate suffered by most measures in both houses.

3. Report the bill in amended form. Many bills are changed in committee, and several bills on the same subject may be combined into a single measure.

4. Report the bill with an unfavorable recommendation. This does not often happen. Occasionally, however, a committee feels that the full House should have a chance to consider a bill or does not want to take the responsibility for killing it.

5. Report a committee bill. The panel produces a substantially rewritten measure as a substitute for one or several of the bills referred to it.

? DRAW CONCLUSIONS The U.S. Constitution does not state that Congress needs to form committees to handle business. Why did the House add them?

Scheduling Floor Debate

Before it goes to the floor for consideration, a bill reported by a standing committee is placed on one of several calendars in the House. A calendar is a schedule of the order in which bills will be taken up on the floor.

The Purpose of Five Calendars There are five calendars in the lower house. The *Calendar of the Committee of the Whole House on the State of the Union,* commonly known as the *Union Calendar,* is for all bills having to do with revenues, appropriations, or government property. The *House Calendar* is for all other public bills. The *Private Calendar* is for all private bills. The *Corrections Calendar* is for all bills from the Union or House Calendar taken out of order by unanimous consent of the House of Representatives. These are most often minor bills to which there is no opposition. The *Discharge Calendar* is for petitions to discharge bills from committee.

Under the rules of the House, bills are taken from each of these calendars for consideration on a regularly scheduled basis. For example, bills from the Corrections Calendar are supposed to be considered on the second and fourth Tuesdays of each month. Measures relating to the District of Columbia can be taken up on the second and fourth Mondays, and private bills on the first and third Tuesdays. On "Calendar Wednesdays," the various committee chairmen may each call up one bill from the House or Union calendars that has cleared their committees.

>> The House Appropriations Committee calendar for the 105th Congress as it hung on the wall in the Appropriations Committee office, ready to be filled in with scheduled meetings.

The Powerful Rules Committee None of these arrangements is followed too closely, however. What most often happens is even more complicated. Remember that the Rules Committee plays a critical role in the legislative process in the House.

It must grant a rule before most bills can in fact reach the floor. That is, before most measures can be taken from a calendar, the Rules Committee must approve that step and set a time for its appearance on the floor.

By not granting a rule for a bill, the Rules Committee can effectively kill it. Or, when the Rules Committee does grant a rule, it may be a special rule—one setting conditions under which the members of the House will consider the measure. A special rule often sets a time limit on floor debate. It may even prohibit amendments to certain, or even to any, of the bill's provisions.

Then, too, certain bills are privileged. That is, they may be called up at almost any time, ahead of any other business before the House. The most privileged measures include major appropriations (spending) and general revenue (tax) bills, conference committee reports, and special rules granted by the Rules Committee.

On certain days, the House may suspend its rules. A motion to that effect must be approved by a two-thirds vote of the members present. When that happens, as it sometimes does, the House moves so far away from its established operating procedures that a measure can go through all the many steps necessary to enactment in a single day.

All of these—the calendars, the role of the Rules Committee, and the other complex procedures—have developed over time to help members of the House manage their heavy workload. Because of the large size of the House and the sheer number and variety of bills its members introduce, no one member could possibly know the contents, let alone the merits, of every bill on which he or she has to vote.

? INTERPRET Does the Rules Committee or a standing committee have more influence on whether a bill is debated on the floor of the House?

The Bill on the House Floor

If a bill finally reaches the floor, it receives its second reading in the House. Many bills the House passes are minor ones, with little or no opposition. Most of these less important measures are called from the Corrections Calendar, get their second reading by title only, and are quickly disposed of.

Nearly all of the more important measures are dealt with in a much different manner. They are considered in the Committee of the Whole, an old parliamentary device for speeding business on the floor.

The Committee of the Whole includes all the members of the House, sitting as one large committee of the House, not as the House itself. The rules of the Committee of the Whole are much less strict than the rules of the House, and floor action moves along at a faster pace. For example, a **quorum,** which is a majority of the full membership (218), must be present in order for the House to do business. Only 100 members need be present in the Committee of the Whole.

When the House resolves itself into the Committee of the Whole, the Speaker steps down because the full House of Representatives is no longer in session. Another member presides. General debate begins, and the bill receives its second reading, section by section. As each section is read, amendments may be offered. Under the five-minute rule, supporters and opponents of each amendment have just that many minutes to make their cases. Votes are taken on each section and its amendment as the reading proceeds.

When the bill has been gone through—and many run to dozens and sometimes hundreds of pages—the Committee of the Whole has completed its work. It then rises, that is, dissolves itself. Presto! The House is now back in session. The Speaker resumes the chair, and the House formally adopts the committee's work.

Debate Its large size has long since forced the House to impose severe limits on floor debate. A rule first adopted in 1842 forbids any member from holding the floor for more than one hour without unanimous consent to speak for a longer time. Since 1880, the Speaker has had the power to force any member who strays from the subject at hand to give up the floor.

The majority and minority floor leaders generally decide in advance how they will split the time to be spent on a bill. But at any time, any member may "move the previous question." That is, any member can demand a vote on the issue before the House. If that motion is adopted, debate ends. An up-or-down vote must be taken. This device is the only motion that can be used in the House to close (end) debate, but it can be a very effective one.

>> Although the Committee of the Whole, a concept taken from Great Britain's Parliament, is still used in the House, it is no longer used in the Senate.

Voting A bill may be the subject of several votes on the floor. If amendments are offered, as they frequently are, members must vote on each of them. Then, too, a number of procedural motions may be offered, for example, one to table the bill (lay it aside), another for the previous question, and so on. The members must vote on each of these motions. These several other votes are very often a better guide to a bill's friends and foes than is the final vote itself. Sometimes, a member votes for a bill that is now certain to pass, even though he or she had supported amendments to it that, had they been adopted, would have in fact defeated the measure.

The House uses four different methods for taking floor votes:

Voice votes are the most common. The Speaker calls for the "ayes" and then the "noes," the members answer in chorus, and the Speaker announces the result.

If any member thinks the Speaker has erred in judging a voice vote, he or she may demand a standing vote, also known as a division of the House. All in favor, and then all opposed, stand and are counted by the clerk.

>> In the House, members vote by inserting their voting cards into a slot and pressing the appropriate button. The machines record the votes and tally the results.

>> An electronic tally board shows votes made in the House of Representatives. The first electronic roll-call vote, in January 1973, took fifteen minutes, compared to 30 to 45 minutes previously.

One fifth of a quorum (44 members in the House or 20 in the Committee of the Whole) can demand a teller vote. When this happens, the Speaker names one teller from each party. The members pass between the tellers and are counted, for and against. Teller votes are rare today. The practice has been replaced by electronic voting.

A roll-call vote, also known as a record vote, may be demanded by one fifth of the members present.

In 1973, the House installed a computerized voting system for all quorum calls and record votes to replace the roll call by the clerk. Members now vote at any of the 48 stations on the floor by inserting a personalized plastic card in a box and then pushing one of three buttons: "Yea," "Nay," or "Present." The "Present" button is most often used for a quorum call—a check to make sure that a quorum of the members is in fact present. Otherwise, it is used when a member does not wish to vote on a question but still wants to be recorded as present. A "present" vote is not allowed on some questions, however—for example, a vote to override a veto.

A large master board above the Speaker's chair shows instantly how each member has voted. The House rules allow the members 15 minutes to answer quorum calls or cast record votes. Voting ends when the Speaker pushes a button to lock the electronic system, producing a permanent record of the vote at the same time. Under the former roll-call process, it took the clerk up to 45 minutes to call each member's name and record his or her vote. Before 1973, roll calls took up about three months of House floor time each session.

Voting procedures are much the same in the Senate. The upper house uses voice, standing, and roll-call votes, but does not take teller votes or use an electronic voting process. Only six or seven minutes are needed for a roll-call vote in the smaller upper chamber.

Final Steps Once a bill has been approved at second reading, it is **engrossed,** or printed in its final form. Then it is read a third time, by title, and a final vote is taken. Invariably, a bill is approved at third reading, and then the Speaker signs it. A page—a legislative aide—then carries it to the Senate side of the Capitol and places it on the Senate president's desk.

INTERPRET Once a bill reaches the House for debate, what can a representative do to try to prevent that bill from passing? Should the rules be changed to prevent this kind of last-minute maneuvering?

The Bill on the Senate Floor

The House and the Senate really are two quite different places. Overall, however, the basic steps in the lawmaking process are much the same in the two chambers. Still, there are a few critical differences in their processes.

The chief differences between House and Senate procedures involve the consideration of measures on the floor. With introduction by a senator formally recognized for the purpose, a measure is given a number, read twice, and then referred to a standing committee, where it is dealt with much as are bills in the House. The Senate's proceedings are less formal and its rules less strict than those in the much larger lower house. For example, the Senate has only one calendar for all bills reported out of its committees. (Recall, there are five of these schedules in the House.) Bills are called to the Senate floor by the majority leader, usually, but not always, in consultation with the minority leader.

Where debate in the House is strictly limited, it is almost unrestrained in the Senate. Indeed, most members of the Senate are intensely proud of belonging to what has often been called "the greatest deliberative body in the world."

As a general matter, a senator may speak on the floor for as long as he or she pleases. Unlike the House, the Senate has no rule that requires a member to speak only to the measure before the chamber. In short, a senator can talk about anything he or she wants to. And the Senate's rules do not allow any member to move the previous question.

Many bills, and particularly the most important pieces of legislation, come to the Senate floor under a unanimous consent agreement. The majority leader regularly negotiates these agreements with the minority leader, and they become effective only if no senator objects. Unanimous consent agreements usually limit the amount of floor time to be devoted to a particular measure and the number and content of amendments that may be offered to it.

The Senate does have a "two-speech rule." No senator may speak more than twice on a given question on the same legislative day. By recessing rather than adjourning a day's session, the Senate can prolong a "legislative day" indefinitely. Thus, the two-speech rule can successfully limit the amount of time the Senate spends on some matters.

The Senate's dedication to freedom of debate is almost unique among modern legislative bodies. That freedom is intended to encourage the fullest possible discussion of matters on the floor. But, notice, the great latitude it allows also gives rise to the filibuster.

>> Speaker of the House Nancy Pelosi hands the College Cost Reduction Act of 2007 to House Clerk Lorraine Miller after signing it, for delivery to the Senate for consideration.

The Filibuster Essentially, a **filibuster** is an attempt to "talk a bill to death." It is a stalling tactic by which a minority of senators seeks to delay or prevent Senate action on a measure. The filibusterers try to monopolize the Senate floor and its time so that the Senate must either drop the bill or change it in some manner acceptable to the minority.

Talk—and more talk—is the filibusterers' major weapon. In addition, senators may use time-killing motions, quorum calls, and other parliamentary maneuvers. Indeed, anything to delay or obstruct is grist for the minority's mill as it works to block a bill that would very likely pass if brought to a vote.

Among the many better-known filibusterers, Senator **Huey Long** (D., Louisiana) spoke for more than 15 hours in 1935. He stalled by reading from the Washington telephone directory and giving his colleagues his recipes for "pot-likker," corn bread, and turnip greens. Senator **Strom Thurmond** (R., South Carolina) set the current filibuster record for an individual. He held the floor for 24 hours and 18 minutes in an unsuccessful, one-person effort against what, despite his arguments, became the Civil Rights Act of 1957.

A few later efforts have come close to Senator Thurmond's record. In 1986, for example, Senator Alfonse D'Amato (R., New York) staged a successful

23-1/2-hour filibuster against a military spending bill that would have cut funding for a warplane built by a company in his district. Well over 300 measures have been killed by filibusters. Just the *threat* of a filibuster has resulted in the Senate's failure to consider a number of bills and the amending of many others.

The Senate often tries to beat off a filibuster with lengthy, even day-and-night, sessions to wear down the participants. At times, some little-observed rules are strictly enforced. Among them are the requirements that senators stand—not sit, lean on their desks, or walk about—as they speak and that they not use "unparliamentary language" on the floor. These countermeasures seldom work.

The Cloture Rule The Senate's real check on the filibuster is its Cloture Rule, Rule XXII in the Standing Rules of the Senate. It was first adopted in 1917, after one of the most notable of all filibusters in Senate history. That filibuster, which lasted for three weeks, took place less than two months before the United States entered World War I.

German submarines had renewed their attacks on shipping in the North Atlantic, so President Wilson asked Congress to permit the arming of American merchant vessels. The bill, widely supported in the country, quickly passed the House, by a vote of 403–13. The measure died in the Senate, however, because twelve senators filibustered it until the end of the congressional term on March 4th.

The public was outraged. President Wilson declared: "A little group of willful men, representing no opinion but their own, has rendered the great Government of the United States helpless and contemptible." The Senate passed the Cloture Rule at its next session.

Rule XXII provides for **cloture**—limiting debate. The rule is not in regular, continuing force; it can be brought into play only by a special procedure. A vote to invoke the rule must be taken two days after a petition calling for that action has been submitted by at least 16 members of the Senate. If at least 60 senators—three fifths of the full Senate—vote for the motion, the rule becomes effective. From that point, no more than another 30 hours of floor time may be spent on the measure. Then it *must* be brought to a final vote.

Of more than 1,700 attempts to invoke the rule, less than a third have been successful. Many senators hesitate to vote for cloture because (1) they honor the tradition of free debate and/or (2) they worry that frequent use of cloture will undercut the value of the filibuster that they may someday want to use.

Modern Uses of the Filibuster Filibusters have become much more common in recent years because, for more than a decade, party control of the upper house has been a very narrow thing. Between 2011 and 2014, the Democratic Party had only a small majority of votes in the Senate, and they did not have the 60 votes needed to invoke cloture. By 2015, the shoe was on the other foot—Republicans held a majority in the 114th Congress, but also did not have enough votes to stop a filibuster.

During these years, the minority party, at times the Republicans, currently the Democrats, made frequent use of the filibuster to block legislation backed by the majority party. And their filibusters were regularly

The Longest Filibusters

NAME OF SENATOR	YEAR	TOPIC	LENGTH OF FILIBUSTER
Strom Thurmond	1957	opposed Civil Rights Act of 1957	24 h, 18 m
Alfonse D'Amato	1986	opposed military spending bill	23 h, 30 m
Wayne Morse	1953	opposed Tidelands oil bill	22 h, 26 m
Robert LaFollette	1908	opposed a currency bill	18 h, 23 m
William Proxmire	1981	opposed a debt ceiling increase	16 h, 12 m

SOURCE: Washingtonpost.com

>> In a filibuster, a senator speaks at length until a cloture vote passes or until the senator runs out of energy. **Analyze Charts** How does the filibuster protect the rights of the minority?

More Filibusters, More Cloture

CONGRESS	YEAR	CLOTURE MOTIONS FILED	CLOTURE INVOKED
85	1957–1958	0	0
95	1977–1978	23	3
100	1987–1988	54	12
110	2007–2008	139	61
112	2011–2012	115	41
113	2013–2014	253	187
114	2015–2016	128	61

SOURCE: Senate.gov

>> Since the Senate adopted the cloture rule in 1917, its use has grown as filibusters have become more common. **Analyze Charts** Though filed often, why do you think cloture is invoked so rarely?

successful. This is because, given the Cloture Rule, the minimum number of votes necessary to pass an important bill in the Senate today is not 51 or a simple majority of the members present and voting. It is, instead, 60, the minimum number of votes necessary to invoke cloture (end debate).

In 2013, frustrated with the large number of Republican filibusters of President Obama's appointees, Democrats changed longstanding rules. Under the new procedures, nominees for all executive branch positions and lower court vacancies can be approved by a simple majority of 51 votes. The Republicans took this a step further in 2017, allowing even Supreme Court nominees to be approved with a simple majority.

These changes effectively eliminate senators' ability to filibuster nearly all presidential nominations. Most legislation, however, still must pass the 60-vote threshold.

? COMPARE AND CONTRAST Name the differences between House and Senate rules on debate.

House-Senate Conference Committees

As you have seen, a bill must survive any number of challenges in order to become a law. Most don't. A measure can be killed, or simply buried, in a subcommittee, in the full committee, in the House Rules Committee, or in any of the parallel committees in the Senate. The remainder must make it through votes on the floor in both houses.

Any measure that does survive the legislative process *must* be passed by both houses in identical form. Most often, a bill approved by one house and then the other is left unchanged by the second. When the House and Senate do pass different versions of the same bill, the first house usually concurs in the other's amendments, and congressional action is completed.

When one house will not accept the other's version of a bill, the measure is sent to a conference committee—a temporary joint committee of the two chambers. It seeks to produce a compromise bill acceptable to both houses. Conferees—managers—are named by the respective presiding officers. Mostly, they are leading members of the standing committee that first handled the measure.

Both chambers' rules say that a conference committee can consider only those parts of a bill on which the two houses have disagreed. In practice, however, conferees often add provisions never considered in either the House or Senate.

Once the conferees agree, their report, the compromise bill, is submitted to both houses. It must be accepted or rejected without amendment. Only rarely does either house turn down a conference committee's work. This is not surprising, for two major reasons: (1) the powerful membership of the typical conference committee, and (2) the fact that its report usually comes in the midst of the rush to adjournment at the end of a congressional session.

The conference committee stage is a most strategic step. A number of major legislative decisions and compromises are often made at that point. Indeed, the late Senator **George Norris** (R., Nebraska) once quite aptly described conference committees as "the third house of Congress."

GENERATE EXPLANATIONS Why do members of a House and Senate conference committee sometimes add provisions to a bill as they work on it?

The President Acts on a Bill

The Constitution requires that bills and resolutions be sent to the President after they have passed both houses of Congress. The President has four options at this point:

The President may sign the bill, and it then becomes law.

The President may **veto**—refuse to sign—the bill. The measure must then be returned to the house in which it originated, together with the President's objections (a veto message). Although it seldom does, Congress may then pass the bill over the President's veto, by a two-thirds vote of the full membership of each house.

The President may allow the bill to become law without signing it—by not acting on it within 10 days, not counting Sundays, of receiving it.

The fourth option is a variation of the third, called the **pocket veto.** If Congress adjourns its session within 10 days of submitting a bill to the President, and the President does not act, the measure dies. (Sundays are not counted.) Congress added another element to the President's veto power with the passage of the Line Item Veto Act of 1996. That law gave the chief executive the power to reject individual items in appropriations bills. The Supreme Court held the law unconstitutional, however, in *Clinton* v. *City of New York,* 1998.

Because Congress can seldom muster enough votes to override a veto, the power can play an extremely effective part in the President's dealings with Congress. The weight of that power in the executive-legislative relationship is underscored by this fact: The mere threat of a veto is often enough to defeat a bill or to prompt changes in its provisions as it moves through the legislative process.

INFER Why might a President use a pocket veto instead of a regular veto for bill?

HOW A BILL BECOMES A LAW

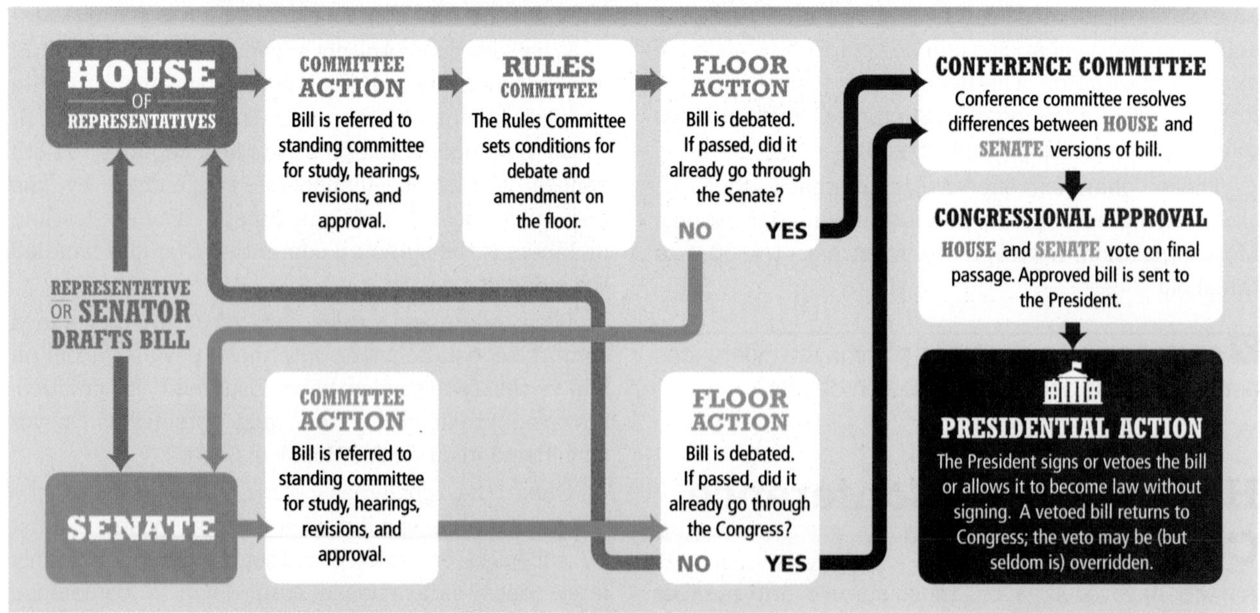

>> A bill may be introduced first in either the House or the Senate. **Analyze Sequence** In what ways does the lawmaking process in the House differ from that in the Senate?

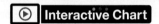

Interactive Chart

Unorthodox Lawmaking and Emergency Legislation

The steps outlined by the Constitution explain the process used throughout most of our nation's history for a bill to become law. However, a number of adjustments in recent decades have continued to transform the lawmaking process. For example, it is increasingly common for each chamber to pass generic bills, knowing that the true details of the legislation will be ironed-out in conference committee. Another approach to reconciling differences, often called "ping-ponging," is for each chamber to take turns adding amendments until disagreements are resolved. On occasion, particularly at the end of the legislative session, when there is a push to tie up loose ends, bills can "ping-pong" back and forth between the House and Senate on an hourly basis. **Omnibus measures**, where one bill contains numerous issues and topics, have also become much more common.

Why have these changes to the traditional lawmaking process occurred? Simply stated, the two major parties have found less and less common ground in recent years. In addition, majority party leaders have been granted greater leeway from their members to insert themselves more directly into key stages of the process, with an eye toward producing results. There is no question that both parties are using unorthodox approaches to advance their initiatives in the modern Congress.

Occasionally, emergencies arise during which the legislature is called upon to act quickly and to condense the process into a few days. With such events, Congress does not have the luxury to follow every step strictly by the book.

Such was the case with the Emergency Economic Stabilization Act of 2008, the so-called "Wall Street Bailout Bill," passed in response to the economic crisis in September of that year when a number of large banks and other financial institutions began to fail in rapid succession. President George W. Bush's advisors proposed a plan by which the U.S. Treasury would acquire up to $700 billion worth of mortgage-backed securities. By doing so, they argued, banks would again start lending money. Congress acted quickly, but not as fast as the Bush administration had hoped. On the one hand, many legislators understood that a massive governmental intervention was the only hope to stave off a financial collapse. On the other hand, many also knew that average citizens saw the proposed measure as helping the business elite. As a result, the plan was very unpopular back in many lawmakers' home districts, leading to some minor delays in its passage.

>> Despite frequent "ping-ponging", Congress may have difficulty reaching consensus on a bill. **Analyze Political Cartoons** What does the cartoon tell you about passing the Farm Bill?

>> President George W. Bush signs the Patriot Act Anti-Terrorism bill on October 26, 2001. The bill was introduced on October 23, passed the House on October 24, and the Senate on October 25.

In short, when emergencies arise, Congress can move quickly, but not nearly as rapidly as the executive branch can. This is exactly what the Framers envisioned—immediate action from the executive branch, but slower deliberations in the legislature. Also, unlike Presidents, members of Congress face direct constituencies, and what is good for the nation might be unpopular back home.

? ANALYZE INFORMATION Why did the Framers of the Constitution envision immediate action from the executive branch but slower deliberation in the legislature? What is one advantage and one disadvantage of each type of decision making?

ASSESSMENT

1. **Synthesize** Does the Rules Committee influence the outcome of a bill more than its sponsor?
2. **Explain** Why would government observers complain that the filibuster allows a minority to control the Senate?
3. **Check Understanding** The House of Representatives uses five calendars to schedule bills, yet the schedule is often ignored. What is the purpose of special procedures to bring bills to the floor?
4. **Compare and Contrast** Explain the similarities and differences between pigeonholing a bill and exercising a pocket veto.
5. **Synthesize** Who is most important in the passage of a law—the bill's sponsor, the committee chairman who considers the bill, or the President? Explain your answer.

TOPIC 4 ASSESSMENT

1. **Explain Federal Responsibilities** Write a paragraph explaining the major responsibilities of Congress regarding foreign policy. Consider the following questions to support your response: What role does Congress play in the creation of treaties? How does Congress influence U.S. foreign policy? What checks and balances are provided by Congress's war powers?
2. **Compare Methods of Filling Public Offices** Write a paragraph comparing how members of the Senate and the House of Representatives are chosen. Consider the following questions to support your response: Who did the Constitution originally call to elect members of the House and Senate? How are the members of the House and Senate chosen now? What is the difference in how they are chosen?
3. **Analyze the 17th Amendment** Analyze the impact of the passage of the 17th Amendment. Write a paragraph about the amendment, and consider the following questions to support your analysis: When was the 17th Amendment to the U.S. Constitution passed? What change did the 17th Amendment make to the Constitution? What was the impact of the 17th Amendment?
4. **Explain Political Divisions** Write a paragraph explaining the impact that the Supreme Court decision in *Wesberry* v. *Sanders* had on the boundaries of congressional districts. What has the Supreme Court said about race-based districts?
5. **Identify Significant Individuals** Write a paragraph about Ronald Reagan. Consider the following questions to support your response: Who was Ronald Reagan? How were select committees used for investigations related to the Reagan administration?
6. **Identify the Contributions of the Founding Fathers** Use the chart below to write a paragraph identifying Thomas Jefferson and his contributions. Consider the following questions to support your response: Who was Thomas Jefferson? How did Jefferson's position as a strict constructionist influence the Constitution and the founding of the United States?

Strict vs. Liberal Constructionists

STRICT CONSTRUCTIONISTS	LIBERAL CONSTRUCTIONISTS
 Thomas Jefferson	 Alexander Hamilton
• Favored a very limited role for the new government created by the Constitution • Majority of power would remain with the States and the people • Based on a strict reading of the Necessary and Proper Clause in the Constitution to prevent the government from gaining too much power	• Favored a powerful government that could exercise implied powers • Favored vigorous executive leadership • Based on a liberal interpretation of the Constitution because the Constitution did not specifically grant the government these powers

7. **Analyze the Functions of the Legislative Branch** Write a paragraph about the legislative branch's procedure for enacting laws about bankruptcy. Consider the following questions to support your response: What is bankruptcy? What are Congress's bankruptcy powers? How does the Congress pass a law related to the bankruptcy powers?

8. **Understand the Role of Limited Government** Write a paragraph explaining how limited government protects individual rights related to taxation. Consider the following questions to support your response: What is a tax? What limits did the Constitution place on Congress's ability to tax? Why?

9. **Understand Constitutional Protections** Write a paragraph explaining how constitutional protections have fostered competition among business by explaining the case of *Gibbons* v. *Ogden*.

10. **Understand Government Taxation** Write a brief report explaining how government taxation can restrict private enterprise. Consider the following questions: How does Congress address the issue of the impact of taxes on private enterprise? What do you believe Congress should do? Why?

11. **Analyze How the *Federalist Papers* Explain American Government** Use the following quote and valid primary and secondary sources about *Federalist* Number 10 to write a paragraph explaining how it supports the principles of the American system of government. Consider the following questions to support your response: What was Madison responding to in writing the *Federalist* Number 10? What counterarguments does Madison make about dealing with special interests that are held by a minority of citizens? A majority? How do Congressional powers relating to electoral duties play into Madison's concerns about "factions"?

"If a faction consists of less than a majority, relief is supplied by the republican principle, which enables the majority to defeat its sinister views by regular vote. It may clog the administration, it may convulse the society; but it will be unable to execute and mask its violence under the forms of the Constitution. When a majority is included in a faction, the form of popular government, on the other hand, enables it to sacrifice to its ruling passion or interest both the public good and the rights of other citizens."

—James Madison, Federalist Number 10

12. **Analyze the Functions of the Legislative Branch** Write a paragraph analyzing the functions of Congressional committees. Research a recent Congressional investigation, and choose a point of view to defend. Make sure to include which committees were involved in the investigation and why.

13. **Explain Cultural Changes** Write a paragraph explaining how the GI Bill helped to change American culture. Consider the following questions to support your response: What was the Servicemen's Readjustment Act of 1944? How did Congress use its implied powers to create the policy? How did the GI Bill change American culture?

14. **Evaluate Constitutional Provisions for Limiting Government** Write a paragraph explaining how checks and balances help to limit the role of government. Consider the following questions to support your response: How does Congress provide a check on the executive branch when passing laws? How does the executive branch provide a check on Congress when passing laws?

15. **Explain How Provisions Provide for Checks and Balances** Write a paragraph explaining how the Constitution provides checks and balances between the judicial branch and the legislative branch.

16. **Identify the Contributions of the Founders** Use the following quote to write a paragraph identifying James Madison's contributions to the development of the U.S. government. In your paragraph, analyze and evaluate his point of view based on primary documents such as the quotation. Consider the following questions to support your response: Who was James Madison? Why did James Madison advocate for a longer term of office in the Senate and the appointment of Senators by state legislatures? What does the quotation tell you about Madison's goals for the formation of the legislative branch?

"It is a misfortune incident to republican government, though in a less degree than to other governments, that those who administer it may forget their obligations to their constituents, and prove unfaithful to their important trust. In this point of view, a senate, as a second branch of the legislative assembly, distinct from, and dividing the power with, a first, must be in all cases a salutary check on the government. It doubles the security to the people, by requiring the concurrence of two distinct bodies in schemes of usurpation or perfidy, where the ambition or corruption of one would otherwise be sufficient."

—*James Madison, Federalist No. 62*

17. **Analyze the Functions of the Legislative Branch** Use the graph and the questions below to write a paragraph analyzing the legislative branch of Congress: What does *reapportion* mean? How is Congress reapportioned? What does the graph tell you about the reapportionment of congressional seats?

18. **Write About the Essential Question Write an essay on the Essential Question: How should government meet the needs of its people?** Use evidence from your study of this Topic to support your answer.

Reappropriation of Congressional Seats

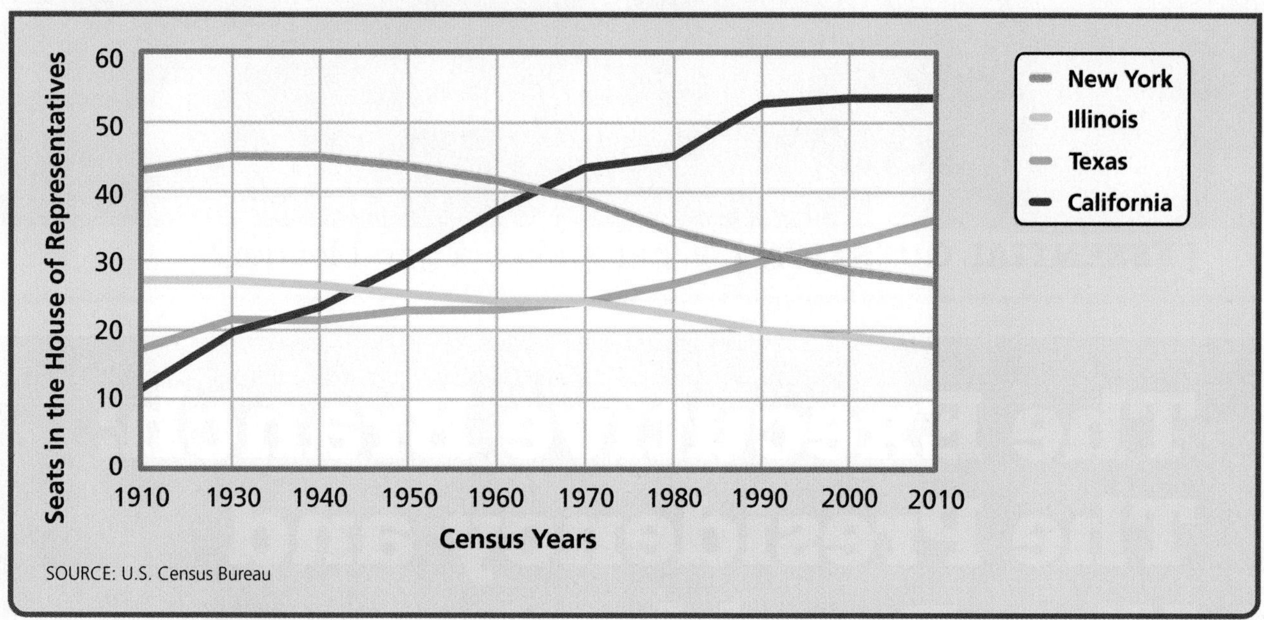

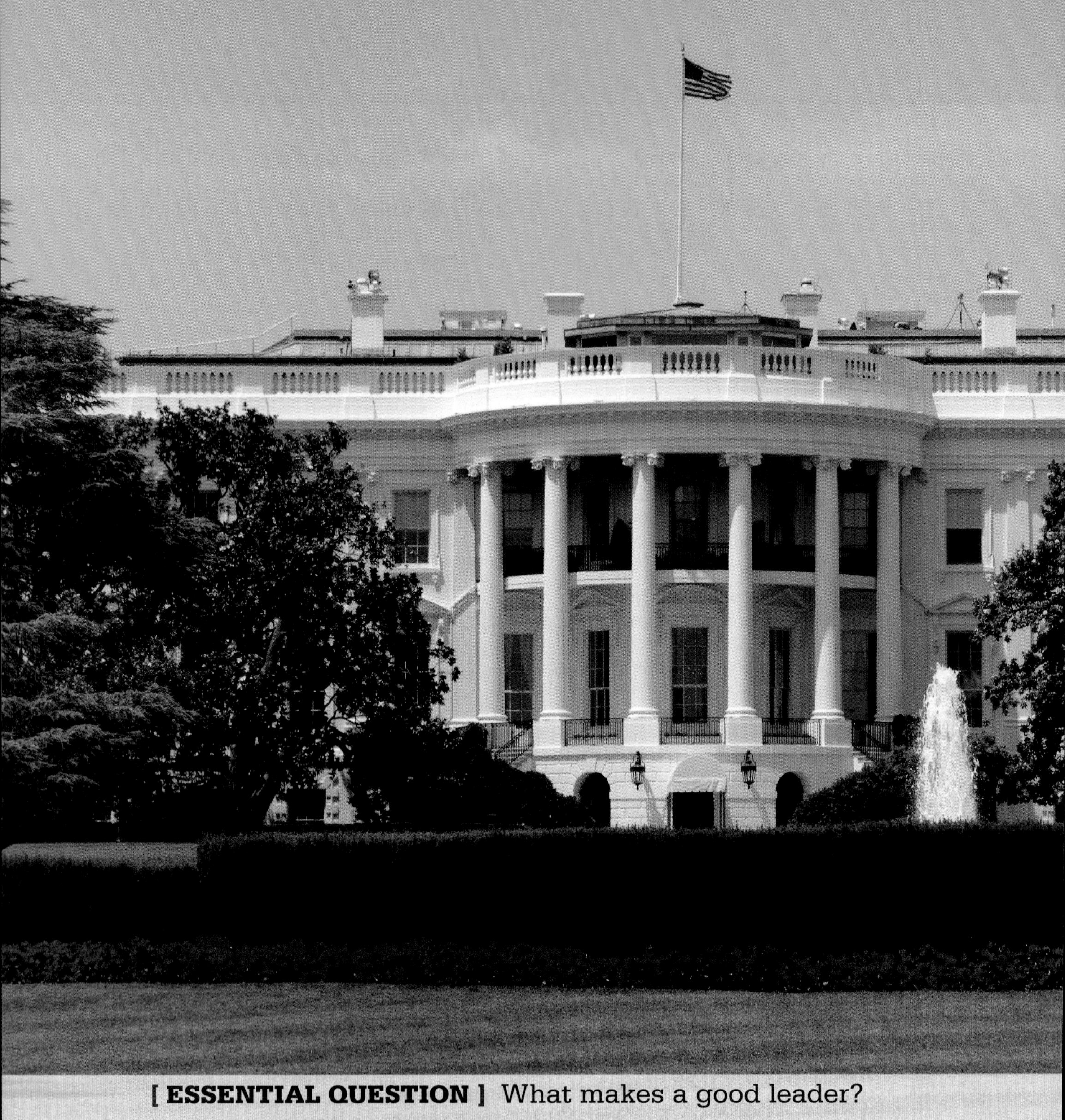

[**ESSENTIAL QUESTION**] What makes a good leader?

5 The Executive Branch: The Presidency and Vice Presidency

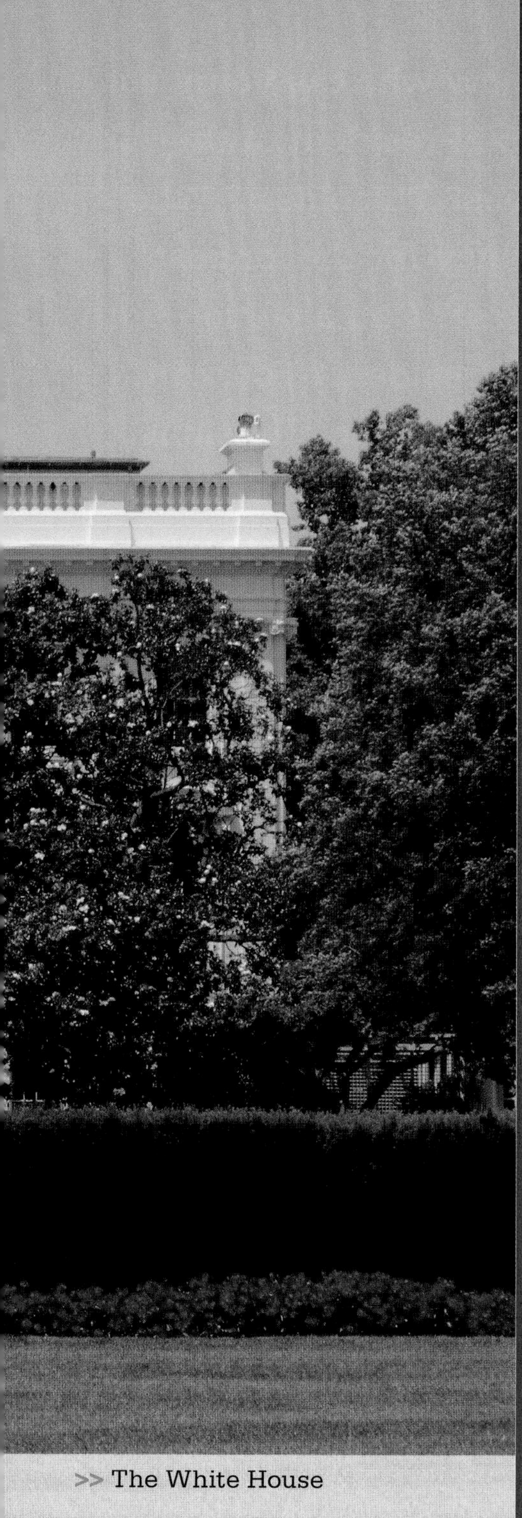
>> The White House

Enduring Understandings

- A person seeking to be President of the United States must meet certain requirements and be able to balance many roles simultaneously.
- The Constitution lays out the order of presidential succession, with the Vice President being first in that order.
- There is ongoing debate about the growth of presidential power; however, certain constitutional provisions provide for checks by the other two branches.
- The President is essential to the conduct of foreign relations; however, the system of checks and balances requires the President to share military and diplomatic powers with Congress.

Watch the My Story Video to examine the qualities that make a good President by exploring the presidencies of Theodore Roosevelt and Ronald Reagan.

Access your digital lessons including:
Topic Inquiry • Interactive Reading Notepad • Interactivities • Assessments

>> The moment he takes the oath of office, the President must immediately assume many different roles. Here, Donald J. Trump is sworn in as the 45th President in 2017.

5.1 **Do you know who the youngest person ever to be President of the United States was? The oldest? Who held the presidency for the longest time? The shortest? Can a person born abroad become President? You will find the answers to these questions, and much more, in this section, which provides a basic overview of the presidential office.**

Interactive Flipped Video

>> Objectives

Describe the President's many roles.

Understand the formal qualifications necessary to become President.

Explain how the number of terms for which a President may serve has changed over time and the roles played by Presidents George Washington and Franklin D. Roosevelt in that evolution.

>> Key Terms

chief of state
chief executive
domestic affairs
foreign affairs
chief administrator
chief diplomat
chief legislator
commander in chief
chief economist
chief of party
chief citizen
presidential succession
impeachment
Presidential Succession Act of 1947
president pro tempore
William Howard Taft
Harry Truman
Franklin D. Roosevelt
Lyndon B. Johnson
Richard Nixon
John F. Kennedy
Theodore Roosevelt
Bill Clinton
Barack Obama
Donald Trump
Ronald Reagan
Herbert Hoover
Dwight Eisenhower
Alexander Hamilton
George Washington
George H.W. Bush
William Henry Harrison
Woodrow Wilson
George W. Bush

The Presidency—An Overview

The President's Many Roles

At any given time, of course, only one person is the President of the United States. The office, with all of its awesome powers and duties, belongs to that one individual. Whoever that person may be, he—and most likely someday she—must fill several different roles, and all of them at the same time. The President is simultaneously (1) chief of state, (2) chief executive, (3) chief administrator, (4) chief diplomat, (5) chief legislator, (6) commander in chief, (7) chief economist, (8) chief of party, and (9) chief citizen.

Chief of State To begin with, the President is **chief of state**, the ceremonial head of the government of the United States. He or she is, then, the symbol of all of the people of the nation—in President **William Howard Taft's** words, "the personal embodiment and representative of their dignity and majesty."

In many countries, the chief of state reigns but does not rule. That is certainly true of the queens of England, Denmark, and the Netherlands; the kings of Norway, Sweden, and Belgium; the emperor of Japan; and the presidents of Italy and Germany. It is just as certainly *not* true of

PEARSON realize. www.PearsonRealize.com Access your Digital Lesson.

the President of the United States. The President both reigns and rules.

Chief Executive The President is the nation's **chief executive**, vested by the Constitution with "the executive Power" of the United States. That power is immensely broad in **domestic affairs** as well as **foreign affairs**. Indeed, the American presidency is often described as "the most powerful office in the world."

But remember, the President is not all-powerful. He or she lives in an environment filled with constitutional checks and balances in which there are many practical limits on what he or she can and cannot do.

Chief Administrator The President is also the **chief administrator**, the director of the huge executive branch of the Federal Government. He or she heads one of the largest governmental machines the world has ever known. Today, the President directs an administration that employs some 2.7 million civilians and spends some $3.8 trillion a year.

Managing the sprawling executive branch is only one of the President's several jobs. **Harry Truman** complained that he had to spend too much of his time "flattering, kissing, and kicking people to get them to do what they were supposed to do anyway."

>> President George W. Bush wears a traditional jacket at a meeting with Chinese President Jiang Zemin. As chief diplomat, the U.S. President meets with world leaders and shapes foreign policy.

Chief Diplomat Every President is also the nation's **chief diplomat**, the main architect of American foreign policy and the nation's chief spokesman to the rest of the world. "I make foreign policy," President Truman once said—and he did. Everything the President says and does is closely followed, both here and abroad.

Chief Legislator The President is also the nation's **chief legislator**, the principal author of its public policies. Most often, it is the President who sets the overall shape of the congressional agenda—initiating, suggesting, requesting, insisting, and demanding that Congress enact most of the major pieces of legislation that it does.

The President and Congress do sometimes clash, and the President does not always get his or her way on Capitol Hill. Still, working with Congress occupies a major part of the President's time.

These six presidential roles all come directly from the Constitution. Yet they do not complete the list. The President has still other vital roles to play.

Commander in Chief In close concert with his or her role in foreign affairs, the Constitution also makes the President the **commander in chief** of the nation's armed forces. The 1.5 million men and women

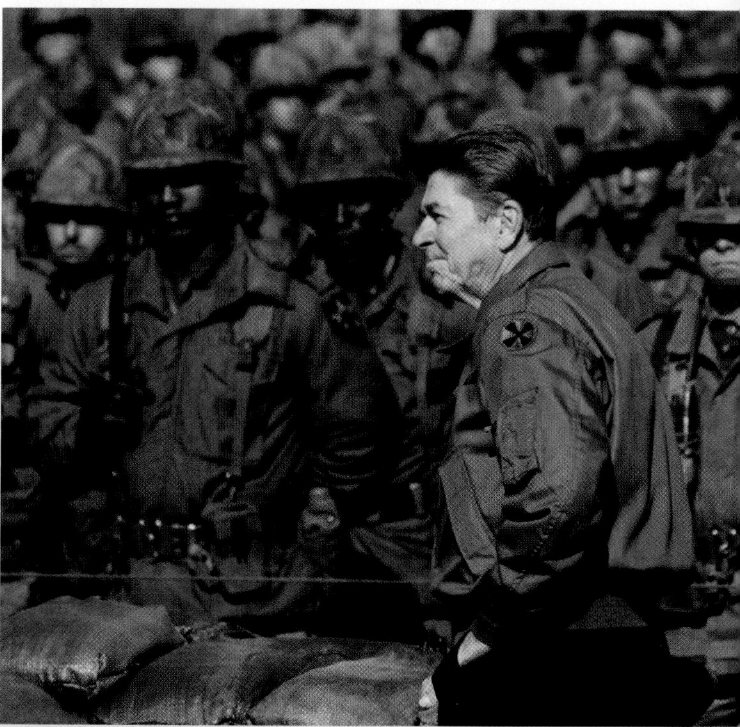

>> In his role as commander in chief of U.S. forces, President Ronald Reagan speaks to U.S. Army troops stationed in South Korea in 1983.

Interactive Chart

in uniform and all of the nation's military might are subject to the President's direct and immediate control. The Constitution does give Congress some significant powers in foreign affairs and over the military, but the President has long since become dominant in both fields.

Chief Economist Some observers have suggested that modern Presidents must also be the nation's **chief economist**. That is, the President is expected to keep a close eye on the nation's economy and to take immediate and effective action when conditions dictate. Since the collapse of communism in the Soviet Union and Eastern Europe in 1989, and paralleling the rapid expansion of Asian economies (especially those of China and India), the management of America's trade relationships has been an expanding aspect of presidential responsibilities. This change has created unique challenges for the President. Opening foreign markets for American goods requires lowering or removing trade restrictions and tariffs on goods imported into the United States.

As chief economist, the President must constantly balance many conflicting demands, including those of consumers, labor unions, and manufacturers. At the same time, the President must remain ever sensitive to the effect that American economic policies can have on our relationships with countries around the world.

>> President Obama comforts a New Jersey resident as he and Governor Chris Christie survey hurricane damage in 2012. As chief citizen, the President fights for the people's best interests.

Chief of Party The President is, automatically, the **chief of party**, the acknowledged leader of the political party that controls the executive branch—and is virtually unchallengeable in that role. As you know, parties are not mentioned in the Constitution, but they do have a vital place in the workings of the American governmental system. Much of the real power and influence of the President depends on his or her ability to play this critical role.

Chief Citizen The office also automatically makes its occupant the nation's **chief citizen**. The President is expected to be "the representative of all the people." He or she is expected to take the high road and champion the public interest against the many different and competing private interests. "The presidency," said **Franklin Roosevelt**, "is not merely an administrative office. That is the least of it. It is, preeminently, a place of moral leadership."

Listing the President's roles is a useful way to describe the President's job. But, remember, the President must juggle all of these roles simultaneously, and they are all interconnected. In addition, as presidential power has grown over time, so has the number and scope of the roles he or she must fulfill. Note, too, that none of them can be performed in isolation. The manner in which a President plays any one role can effect on his or her ability to execute the others.

As but two illustrations of the point, take the experiences of Presidents **Lyndon Johnson** and **Richard Nixon**. Each was a strong and relatively effective President during his first years in office. But Mr. Johnson's actions as commander in chief during the agonizing and increasingly unpopular war in Vietnam seriously damaged his stature and effectiveness in the White House. In fact, the damage was so great that it helped persuade LBJ not to run for reelection in 1968.

The many-sided and sordid Watergate scandal brought President Nixon's downfall. The manner in which he filled the roles of party leader and chief citizen so destroyed Mr. Nixon's presidency that he was forced to leave office in disgrace in 1974.

? IDENTIFY MAIN IDEAS The President fills several different roles simultaneously. Analyze how the roles of chief of state, chief diplomat, and commander in chief are related.

Selected Presidential Ages

PRESIDENT	DATES OF PRESIDENCY	AGE ON TAKING OATH OF OFFICE	METHOD OF ATTAINING PRESIDENCY	AGE ON LEAVING OFFICE
George Washington	1789–1797	57	Elected	65
Theodore Roosevelt	1901–1909	42 (Youngest to hold office)	Succession	51
Franklin D. Roosevelt	1933–1945	51	Elected	63 (Died in office)
John F. Kennedy	1961–1963	43 (Youngest elected)	Elected	46 (Assassinated)
Donald Trump	2017–	70 (Oldest elected)	Elected	

>> The Framers set the minimum age requirement for President at 35. **Analyze Charts** Why do you think the Framers set a minimum age? Do you think there should be a maximum age limit? Why?

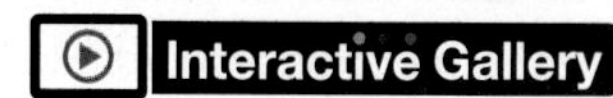

Qualifications for the Presidency

Whatever else a President must be, the Constitution says that he—and likely one day, she—must meet three formal qualifications for office (Article II, Section 1, Clause 5). These qualifications are related to a candidate's citizenship, age, and residency.

Citizenship Any man or woman who seeks the presidency must first be "a natural born Citizen . . . of the United States." But what exactly do the words "natural born" mean? Do they refer to being "native born"—that is, born in the United States? By law, a person born abroad to an American-citizen parent becomes an American citizen at birth. That law leads many to argue that it is therefore possible for a person born outside the United States to become President. Some dispute that view, however. The question of what the Constitution means here cannot be answered until someone born a citizen, but born abroad, does in fact seek the presidency.

Age The Constitution also states that in order to serve as President, a person must "have attained . . . the Age of 35 years." **John F. Kennedy**, at 43, was the youngest person ever elected to the office. **Theodore Roosevelt** reached the White House by succession at age 42. Only seven other chief executives took the oath of office before age 50, most recently, **Bill Clinton** in 1993, and **Barack Obama** in 2009.

Donald Trump, who was 70 when he was elected in 2016, was the oldest candidate ever to win the office. **Ronald Reagan** was 77 when he left office, making him the oldest person ever to hold the presidency. Most chief executives have been in their 50s when they resided in the White House.

Residency Finally, to hold the office of President of the United States, a person must "[H]ave . . . been fourteen years a Resident within the United States." Given the elections of **Herbert Hoover** (in 1928) and **Dwight Eisenhower** (in 1952), we know that here the Constitution means any 14 years in a person's life. Both Mr. Hoover and General Eisenhower spent several years outside the country before winning the White House.

While these formal qualifications do have some importance, they are really not very difficult to meet. Indeed, well over 100 million Americans do so today. Several other *informal* and important qualifications for the presidency exist as well, however. These include such requirements as political experience and speaking ability.

DRAW CONCLUSIONS Why do you think the Framers chose to provide formal qualifications for the office of the President?

The Presidential Term of Office

The Framers considered a number of different limits on the length of the presidential term. Most of their debate centered on a four-year term, with the President eligible for reelection, versus a single six-year or seven-year term without being eligible for reelection. They finally settled on a four-year term (Article II, Section 1, Clause 1). They agreed, as **Alexander Hamilton** wrote in *The Federalist* No. 71, that four years was a long enough period for a President to have gained experience, demonstrated his abilities, and established stable policies.

Until 1951, the Constitution placed no limit on the number of terms a President might serve. Several Presidents, beginning with **George Washington**, refused to seek more than two terms, however. Soon, the "no-third term tradition" became an unwritten rule.

Franklin D. Roosevelt broke the tradition by seeking and winning a third term in 1940, and then a fourth in 1944. To prevent this from recurring, the 22nd Amendment made the unwritten custom limiting presidential terms a part of the written Constitution.

Each President may now serve a maximum of two full terms—eight years—in office. A President who succeeds to the office after the midpoint in a term could possibly serve for more than eight years. In that case, the President may finish out the predecessor's term and then seek two full terms of his or her own. However, no President may serve more than ten years in the office.

Many people, including Presidents Truman, Eisenhower, and Reagan, have called for the repeal of the 22nd Amendment. They insist that the two-term rule is undemocratic because it places an arbitrary limit on the people's right to decide who should be President. Critics also say that it undercuts the authority of a two-term President, especially in the latter part of a second term. Supporters of the amendment defend it as a reasonable safeguard against "executive tyranny."

Several Presidents have urged a single six-year term. They and others have argued that a single, nonrenewable term would free a President from the pressures of a campaign for a second term—and so would allow the chief executive to focus on the pressing demands of the office.

>> After Franklin Roosevelt was elected President four times, Congress passed the 22nd Amendment to limit the number of presidential terms. **Infer** What are the pros and cons of term limits?

? IDENTIFY CAUSE AND EFFECT Who was Franklin D. Roosevelt, and what effect did he have on the development of the 22nd Amendment?

Presidential Succession and Disability

Consider these facts. To this point, 48 people have served as Vice President. Of these, 14 have reached the Oval Office—most recently, **George H.W. Bush** in 1989. Indeed, 5 of the last 12 Presidents were once Vice President.

Methods of Filling Vacancies **Presidential succession** is the scheme by which a presidential vacancy is filled. If a President dies, resigns, or is removed from office by **impeachment**, the Vice President succeeds to the office. Originally, the Constitution did not provide for the succession of a Vice President. Rather, it declared that "the powers and duties" of the office—not the office itself—were to "devolve on [transfer to] the Vice President" (read carefully Article II, Section 1, Clause 6).

In practice, however, the Vice President did succeed to the office when it became vacant. Vice President John Tyler was the first to do so. He set the precedent in 1841 when he succeeded President **William Henry Harrison**, who died of pneumonia just one month after taking office. What had been practice became a part of the written Constitution with the 25th Amendment in 1967, which states, "In case of the removal of the

The Line of Succession

1	Vice President	**10**	Secretary of Commerce
2	Speaker of the House	**11**	Secretary of Labor
3	President pro tempore of the Senate	**12**	Secretary of Health and Human Services
4	Secretary of State	**13**	Secretary of Housing and Urban Development
5	Secretary of the Treasury	**14**	Secretary of Transportation
6	Secretary of Defense	**15**	Secretary of Energy
7	Attorney General	**16**	Secretary of Education
8	Secretary of the Interior	**17**	Secretary of Veterans Affairs
9	Secretary of Agriculture	**18**	Secretary of Homeland Security

>> By tradition, one of the people in the line of succession does not attend the President's State of the Union address with the others. **Analyze Charts** Why do you think this is done?

President from office or of his death or resignation, the Vice President shall become President."

Order of Succession According to Article II, Section 1, Clause 6 of the Constitution, Congress fixes the order of succession following the Vice President. The present law on the matter is the **Presidential Succession Act of 1947**. By its terms, the Speaker of the House and then the **president pro tempore** of the Senate are next in line. They are followed, in turn, by the secretary of state and then by each of the other 14 heads of the Cabinet departments, in order of each position's precedence—that is, the order in which their offices were created by Congress.

Disability of the President Until the 25th Amendment was adopted in 1967, the arrangement for presidential succession had serious gaps. Neither the Constitution nor Congress had made any provision for deciding when a President was so disabled that he could not perform the duties of the office. Nor was there anything to indicate by whom such a decision was to be made.

For nearly 180 years, then, the nation played with fate. President Eisenhower suffered three serious but temporary illnesses while in office: a heart attack in 1955, ileitis in 1956, and a mild stroke in 1957. Two other Presidents were disabled for much longer periods. James Garfield lingered for 80 days before he died from an assassin's bullet in 1881. **Woodrow Wilson** suffered a paralytic stroke in September of 1919 and was an invalid for the rest of his second term. In fact, he was so ill that he could not meet with his Cabinet for seven months after his stroke. And, in 1981, Ronald Reagan was gravely wounded in an assassination attempt.

Filling the Disability Gap Sections 3 and 4 of the 25th Amendment fill the disability gap, and in detail. The Vice President is to become Acting President if (1) the President informs Congress, in writing, "that he is unable to discharge the powers and duties of his office," or (2) the Vice President and a majority of the members of the Cabinet inform Congress, in writing, that the President is so incapacitated.

The President may resume the powers and duties of the office by informing Congress by "written declaration" that no inability exists. However, the Vice President and a majority of the Cabinet may challenge the President on this score. If they do, Congress has 21 days in which to decide the matter.

Transferring Power Thus far, the disability provisions of the 25th Amendment have come into play on three occasions: In 1985, Ronald Reagan transferred the powers of the presidency to Vice President George H.W. Bush for nearly eight hours, while surgeons removed a tumor from Mr. Reagan's large intestine. In 2002, and again in 2007, President **George W. Bush** conveyed his powers to Vice President Dick Cheney for some two hours, while Mr. Bush was anesthetized during a routine medical procedure.

? INFER Why do you think the nation felt it was necessary to add the 25th Amendment to the Constitution when the practice of succession had already been established by Vice President Tyler?

ASSESSMENT

1. **Apply Concepts** In what way is the President's effectiveness as chief economist dependent on his or her expertise as chief diplomat?
2. **Draw Conclusions** Who were Ronald Reagan and Franklin D. Roosevelt, and what viewpoint did they share about the presidential term of office?
3. **Identify Cause and Effect** Who was Theodore Roosevelt, and how was he affected by succession?
4. **Make Generalizations** Why was the 25th Amendment necessary?
5. **Interpret** At the national level, public offices can be filled by election or appointment. Why do you think the Constitution does not provide for the presidency to be filled by appointment if the office becomes vacant?

5.2 "I am Vice President. In this I am nothing, but I may be everything." So said John Adams, the nation's first Vice President. Those words could have been repeated, very appropriately, by each of the men who held that office through the first 150 years of the nation's history. After World War II, however, the status of the vice presidency began to change.

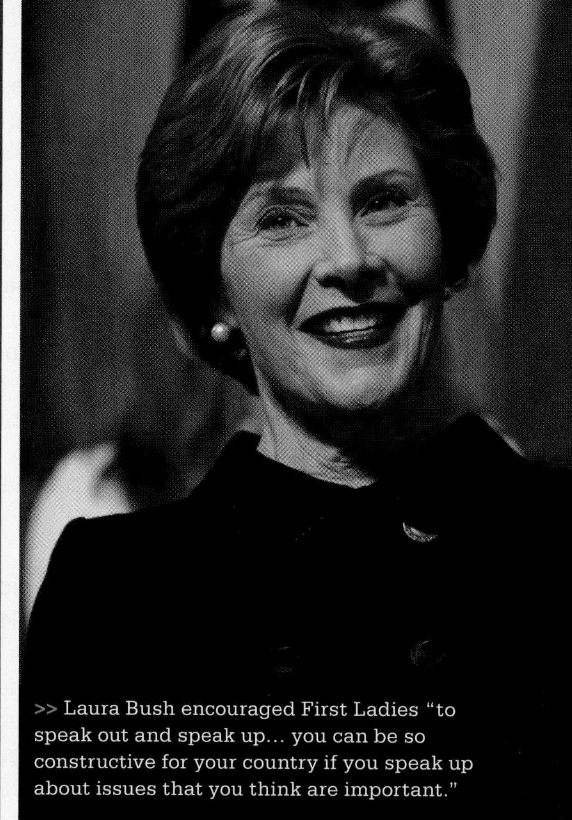

>> Laura Bush encouraged First Ladies "to speak out and speak up... you can be so constructive for your country if you speak up about issues that you think are important."

Interactive Flipped Video

The Vice President and the First Lady

>> **Objectives**

Analyze the functions of the executive branch of government in terms of the formal duties the Constitution assigns to the Vice President.

Describe how the role of the Vice President has changed over time.

Explain the part played by First Ladies throughout the nation's history.

>> **Key Terms**

balance the ticket
First Lady

The Structure and Function of the Vice Presidency

Early Vice Presidents The Constitution pays little attention to the office of the Vice President. It assigns the position only two formal duties. Article I, Section 3, Clause 4 says that the Vice President will preside over the Senate, and the 25th Amendment directs him or her to help decide the question of presidential disability. Beyond those duties, the Constitution makes the Vice President, in effect, a "President-in-waiting," ready to step into that office should the President become unable to fulfill his duties.

Despite the fact that the Vice President is literally "only a heartbeat away from the presidency," the office has been treated as one of little real consequence throughout much of the nation's history. Benjamin Franklin once quipped that the Vice President should be addressed as "your Superfluous Excellency." Thomas Marshall, Vice President under Woodrow Wilson, once told a story of two brothers: "One ran away to sea; the other was elected Vice President. And nothing was heard of either of them again."

Much of the blame for the low status of the vice presidency can be laid on the two major parties and the way they have chosen their candidates for the office. Traditionally, each national convention names the handpicked choice of its just-nominated presidential candidate. Usually, the newly minted presidential candidate picks someone who will **"balance the ticket."** That is, the nominee chooses a running mate who can strengthen his or her chance of being elected by virtue of certain ideological, geographic, racial, ethnic, gender, or other characteristics. In short, fate—presidential succession—does not very often have a high priority in the vice presidential candidate selection process.

The Transformation of the Vice Presidency With the advent of the cold war in the late 1940s and the proliferation of nuclear weapons, concerns grew about the Vice President's readiness to take the helm at a moment's notice, fully abreast of world and military developments. Harry Truman, who became President following Franklin Roosevelt's sudden death in April 1945, had been kept in the dark about the American project to build an atomic bomb. He was also not fully apprised of the rapidly mounting tension between the United States and its ally, the Soviet Union, as World War II drew to a close. On President Roosevelt's death, Harry Truman was forced to step into the presidency with little preparation for handling the grave issues confronting the nation at that time.

By the 1950s, in a new age of nuclear missiles, many Americans believed that such a situation should never be allowed again. Dwight Eisenhower remarked, "Even if [Vice President] Nixon and I were not good friends, I would still have him in every important conference of government, so that if the Grim Reaper [death] would find it time to remove me from the scene, he is ready to slip in without any interruption." Thus began a move toward bringing Vice Presidents into the inner circle of the administration. As a result of this shift, the job of the Vice President changed.

By the 1990s, Al Gore, Vice President under Bill Clinton, was given several important responsibilities, including studying the Federal Government to pinpoint wasteful areas. Vice President Gore also had full access to the President, including weekly one-on-one lunch meetings. Dick Cheney, who served with George W. Bush from 2001 to 2009, also played a central role in the White House; in fact, some have suggested that he has been the most influential Vice President in American history. Barack Obama's Vice President, Joe Biden, has also played a key role in the President's administration. He attends most strategy sessions in the Oval Office, and is known to be one of Barack Obama's most trusted advisors.

>> The vice presidency changed significantly during the cold war as the nuclear arms race made Americans aware of the importance of an involved and informed Vice President.

Filling a Vice-Presidential Vacancy The vice presidency has been vacant 18 times thus far: nine times by succession to the presidency, seven times by death, and twice by resignation. John C. Calhoun resigned to become a senator from South Carolina in 1832, and Spiro T. Agnew resigned in 1973, after a conviction for income tax evasion.

Yet not until 1967 and the 25th Amendment did the Constitution deal with the matter of vice presidential vacancies. The amendment provides, in part:

> Whenever there is a vacancy in the office of the Vice President, the President shall nominate a Vice President who shall take office upon confirmation by a majority vote of both Houses of Congress.
>
> —25th Amendment, Section 2

This provision was first implemented in 1973. In that year, President Richard Nixon selected and Congress confirmed Gerald R. Ford to succeed Spiro Agnew as Vice President. It came into play again in

1974 when, following Mr. Nixon's resignation, President Ford named and Congress approved Nelson Rockefeller for the post.

? SUMMARIZE Summarize how the overall nature of the vice presidency has changed over time.

The First Lady

First Lady is the official title for the President's wife or the White House hostess. Not all First Ladies were wives of a President; one such example is Harriet Lane, First Lady for her uncle, President James Buchanan.

First Ladies are not elected by the American people, which means they do not have a direct role in the President's administration. From Martha Washington to Michelle Obama, these women have made their mark on American history, however, by providing informal advice, advocating for particular policies, and undertaking a host of symbolic (yet important) functions. They have lobbied lawmakers, met with foreign dignitaries, coaxed members of their husband's Cabinet, spoken at national conventions, and cultivated public sympathies. Today, First Ladies even have their own staff within the White House Office, called The Office of the First Lady.

>> In recent years, Vice Presidents have often taken on a larger role and become close presidential advisors. Here, President Bush and Vice President Dick Cheney confer over lunch.

Interactive Gallery

Champions for Many Causes During the early part of our nation's history, First Ladies limited their work to informal, behind-the-scenes advice and social functions. Abigail Adams was a prime example, serving as a trusted friend and confidant to her husband John throughout his long, distinguished political career, including his term as President.

As time went on, First Ladies began to take on a more public role. Edith Wilson, for example, spoke on her husband Woodrow's behalf and filtered all communications after he was left partially paralyzed by a stroke in 1919. Jacqueline Kennedy undertook an historic restoration of the White House and used her position to support the arts in general, hosting opera, ballet, Shakespeare, and other White House performances. President Nixon's First Lady, Pat Nixon, spent up to five hours a day responding to letters from voters, promoted a national volunteer program, and championed the cause of those with special needs. More recently, First Lady Laura Bush helped buttress support for military personnel and their families during wars in Iraq and Afghanistan, and she also promoted education reform.

Beginning with Eleanor Roosevelt, more First Ladies have become openly involved in political issues. Mrs. Roosevelt, the wife of Franklin D. Roosevelt, traveled extensively and spoke on behalf of her husband's

>> The First Lady is a very visible national figure. Here, First Lady Michelle Obama appears with former First Ladies Laura Bush, Hillary Clinton, Barbara Bush, and Rosalynn Carter.

Interactive Gallery

>> First Ladies Melania Trump and Michelle Obama discuss raising children in the White House over tea in the Yellow Oval Room. Melania Trump, born in Slovenia, is only the second First Lady to be born outside the United States.

policies, as well as her own concerns. She wrote a weekly newspaper column and worked tirelessly for Democratic candidates.

The Evolving Role of First Ladies Many First Ladies since Mrs. Roosevelt have played important roles in American society. Betty Ford was known for her support of equal rights for women, while Barbara Bush launched a national effort to end illiteracy. In the 1990s, First Lady Hillary Clinton spearheaded the Clinton administration's efforts to overhaul the nation's healthcare system. First Lady Michelle Obama was an outspoken advocate for programs and policies that support healthy eating and lifestyles. And First Lady Melania Trump pledged to focus her efforts on ending cyberbullying among the nation's youth.

Clearly, the role of presidential spouses will continue to evolve in the coming years. As more and more women move into positions of authority and lead high-profile professional lives, the role of behind-the-scenes advisor and ceremonial figure will almost certainly become a thing of the past. In fact, the real question in today's society is this: What role will the nation's "first gentlemen" perform in the future?

? SUMMARIZE Summarize how the role of First Ladies has changed over time.

ASSESSMENT

1. **Identify** Do you think it is a positive or negative development that the responsibilities of the Vice President have increased from the original responsibilities listed in the Constitution?
2. **Evaluate Arguments** Do you think an attempt to "balance the ticket" is an acceptable method of selecting a Vice President? Why or why not?
3. **Identify Steps in a Process** Suppose that it is 2007 and Dick Cheney is Vice President. He resigns to become a senator from Wyoming. Describe the steps that would be taken to fill this vacancy.
4. **Identify Cause and Effect** Explain the impact of the nuclear arms race on the role of the Vice President.
5. **Compare and Contrast** Compare and contrast the way Abigail Adams handled the role of First Lady to the way Eleanor Roosevelt approached it.

5.3 **The presidency is regularly called "the most powerful office in the world," and it is. However, is this what the Framers had in mind when they created the post in 1787? In Philadelphia, they purposely created a single executive with very broadly stated powers. Still, they agreed with the sentiment expressed by Thomas Jefferson in the Declaration of Independence: a Tyrant "is unfit to be the ruler of a free people."**

>> President Johnson signs a bill to create the Department of Housing and Urban Development in 1965. Multiple pens are used to sign important bills because they often become historical artifacts.

Interactive Flipped Video

The President's Domestic Powers

>> Objectives

List the reasons for the growth of presidential power and explain how the systems of checks and balances limits that growth.

Understand the constitutional powers of the President, including the President's power to execute the law and issue executive orders.

Explain how certain provisions of the Constitution provide for checks and balances among the three branches of government, including the appointment and removal powers of the President.

Examine the powers of executive privilege and clemency, and consider notable examples of their use over time.

Explain the legislative powers and how they are an important part of the system of checks and balances.

>> Key Terms

executive order
ordinance power
executive privilege
pocket veto
line-item veto
reprieve
pardon
clemency
commutation
amnesty
Abraham Lincoln
James Madison
Andrew Jackson
Gerald Ford
Andrew Johnson
James Monroe
Ulysses S. Grant
veto
Thomas Jefferson

The Growth of Presidential Power

The Framers Debate Indeed, few issues took up more time at the Constitutional Convention than shaping the office of the presidency. The first debate centered around whether there should even be a President. If so, should the office consist of one person or a small group of leaders? Should the President be subordinate to the legislature or have the power to check congressional actions? How much influence should the President have in military matters?

In the end, the Framers created a one-person executive. Presidential powers would be broad in some respects, particularly foreign affairs, but limited in other areas. Even so, the very idea of a "chief executive" sent shivers down the spines of many citizens during the ratification period. Had it not been generally understood that George Washington, who had voluntarily resigned from his post as commander of the Continental Army, would be the first President, it is quite possible that this issue might have seriously derailed the ratification of the new Constitution.

The Constitution's formal grants of power to the President have not been changed since those early years. Yet presidential power has

BORN TO COMMAND.

OF VETO MEMORY.

HAD I BEEN CONSULTED.

KING ANDREW THE FIRST.

>> This political cartoon depicts President Jackson as a power-hungry tyrant. **Analyze Political Cartoons** What symbols does the cartoonist use to convey this point?

>> Theodore Roosevelt (left) and his eventual successor, William Howard Taft, disagreed on how much power the President should have.

Interactive Gallery

grown remarkably over the past two centuries. Today, that change represents one of the most significant developments in the American political system.

The Whig Theory Throughout the nineteenth century, most Presidents took a restrained approach to leadership. This was called the Whig theory, which assumed that Congress would lead the policy process, while Presidents were limited to the powers expressly granted to them in the Constitution.

While this was the general approach to the office, a few exceptions can be noted. **Andrew Jackson**, first elected in 1828, regularly became involved in important policy questions, and he used the veto much more often than prior Presidents. During the tumultuous political climate of the Civil War, **Abraham Lincoln**, first elected in 1860, took bold, far-reaching steps that stretched the limits of presidential power. His 1863 Emancipation Proclamation is a prime example. It freed Confederate slaves but scholars still debate whether it rested on any firm constitutional foundation.

The Stewardship Theory The restrained approach to presidential power also was challenged by President Theodore Roosevelt, who served from 1901 to 1908. He believed that Presidents should be allowed to do everything except what the Constitution prohibited. According to Roosevelt's "stewardship theory," Presidents should not merely carry out the will of Congress but instead should lead the nation and build public support for particular policy agendas. According to Roosevelt,

> "My view was that every executive officer . . . was a steward of the people bound actively and affirmatively to do all that he could for the people. . . . My belief was that it was not only [a President's] right but his duty to do anything that the needs of the Nation demanded unless such action was forbidden by the Constitution or by the laws. . . . I did not usurp power, but I did greatly broaden the use of executive power.."
>
> —Theodore Roosevelt, *Theodore Roosevelt: An Autobiography*, 1913

Not everyone agreed with Roosevelt's approach. Ironically, the most strongly worded presidential statement of the opposing view came from Roosevelt's handpicked successor in the office, William Howard

Taft. Looking back on his years in the White House, Mr. Taft had this to say:

> "The true view of the Executive function is, as I conceive it, that the President can exercise no power which cannot be fairly and reasonably traced to some specific grant of power. . . . Such specific grant must be either in the Federal Constitution or in an act of Congress. . . . There is no undefined residuum of power which he can exercise because it seems to him to be in the public interest. . . . My judgment is that the view of . . . Mr. Roosevelt, ascribing an undefined residuum of power to the President, is an unsafe doctrine."
>
> —William Howard Taft, *Our Chief Magistrate and His Powers*, 1916

It was not until Teddy Roosevelt's cousin, Franklin D. Roosevelt, was elected in 1932 that the limited approach to the presidency was shattered for good. FDR came into office during the Great Depression and immediately set in motion aggressive government programs in an attempt to lift the nation from its economic woes. By doing so, he forever changed the nature of the presidency.

Reasons for the Expansion There are several reasons for the dramatic expansion of presidential powers. First, these changes were due, in no small part, to Presidents themselves, and especially the stronger ones—Abraham Lincoln and the two Roosevelts, for example. The Constitution is rather vague on certain aspects of presidential powers, so certain Presidents simply filled the void as they saw fit.

Also, as each chief executive inserted himself into policy disputes, subsequent Presidents were expected to do the same. Conversely, those Presidents who remained on the sidelines were deemed poor leaders.

Second, the ability for Presidents to exert their power has grown due to the expansion of the executive branch. Beginning with FDR and the creation of the Executive Office of the President, the number and size of support agencies and office personnel has mushroomed. Because Presidents have so many agencies, offices, and staff working on their behalf, they have been able to exert more control over nearly all aspects of domestic and foreign policy.

>> This cartoon depicts Theodore Roosevelt and William Howard Taft as bickering schoolchildren. **Analyze Political Cartoons** How did Taft's view of the presidency differ from Roosevelt's?

>> The Works Progress Administration (WPA) was one of President Roosevelt's New Deal programs. At its peak, the WPA put some three million Americans back to work during the Great Depression.

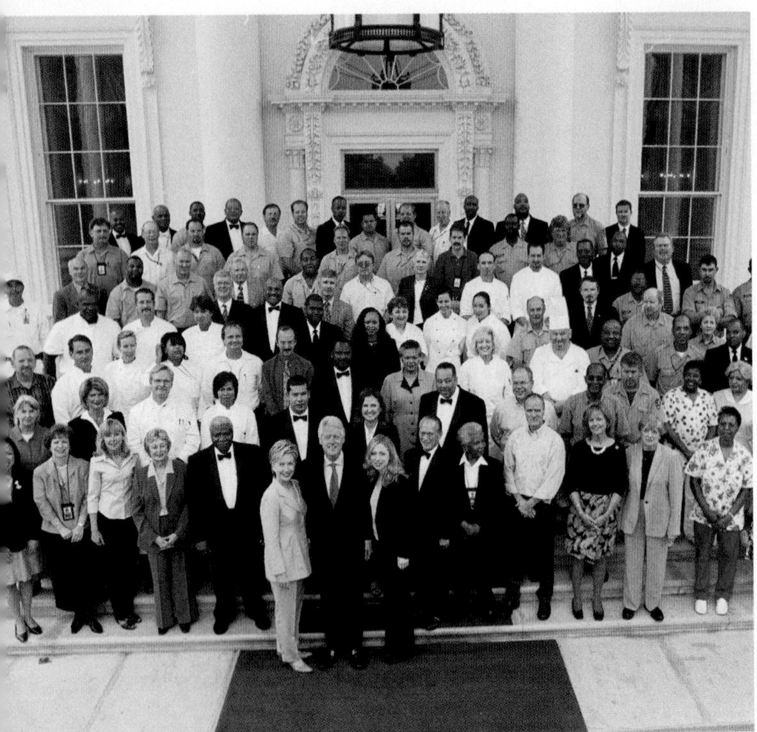

>> President Bill Clinton, with Hillary and Chelsea Clinton, pose with White House staff members. Unlike earlier Presidents, today's chief executive has a huge staff at his or her disposal.

>> Presidential power is not unlimited. An attempt by President Truman to prevent a strike during the Korean War by seizing control of steel mills was ruled unconstitutional by the Supreme Court.

Third, the nation's increasingly complex economy and society have also had a telling effect on presidential power. As the United States has become more industrialized and technologically advanced, many citizens wanted the Federal Government to take a larger and larger role in transportation, communications, health, welfare, employment, education, civil rights, and a host of other fields. And they have looked especially to the President for leadership in those matters.

Fourth, the need for immediate and decisive action in times of crisis, and most notably in times of war, has also had a major impact here. The ability of the President—the single, commanding chief executive—to act in those situations has done much to strengthen "the executive Power."

Finally, Congress has also been involved, as it has passed the thousands of laws that have been a key part of the historic growth of the Federal Government, especially since the 1930s. Congress has neither the time nor the specialized knowledge to provide much more than basic outlines of public policy. Out of necessity, it has delegated substantial authority to the executive branch to carry out the laws it has enacted.

Limits to Power Despite the expanded scope of the presidency, no President can become all-powerful. The Constitution, which grants much power to the President, also provides for a number of restraints on the exercise of that power. Here are just two illustrations of that crucial point.

In 1952, at the height of the Korean War, a labor dispute threatened to shut down the nation's steel industry and imperil the war effort. To avert a strike, President Harry Truman, acting as commander in chief, ordered the Secretary of Commerce to seize and operate several steel mills.

The Supreme Court found that the President had overstepped his constitutional authority. It held that only Congress, acting under its commerce power, could authorize the seizure of private property in time of war, and it had not done so.

More recently, President Barack Obama tried to get around the increasingly contentious Senate confirmation process for three appointees to the National Labor Relations Board in 2013. He chose to use what is referred to as "recess appointments," a mechanism occasionally used by Presidents to fill posts when senators are away from Washington. The federal courts, however, ruled that Obama's move was unconstitutional. They said that recess appointments are limited to breaks between sessions of Congress, not breaks within sessions or merely vacation adjournments.

Congressional Oversight In addition, congressional oversight can be a powerful check on executive power. Congressional oversight occurs as Congress keeps a close watch over the executive branch to ensure that it acts in compliance with previously passed laws and appropriations. The ability of Congress to limit presidential actions through oversight can be real and significant—and quite frustrating to Presidents at times.

By the end of Barack Obama's first term of office, for example, Congress began flexing its oversight muscles. A failed operation to curb gun-running from the United States to Mexico—a scheme organized by the Bureau of Alcohol, Tobacco, Firearms and Explosives (ATF)—drew congressional attention. As part of the plan, dubbed Operation Fast and Furious, ATF agents allowed 2,000 guns to be smuggled across the border in an attempt to learn how guns were getting to drug cartels.

Agents lost track of the guns, however, and many were later found at crime scenes in Mexico and the United States. Two turned up at the scene of a shoot-out in which a U.S. Border Patrol agent was killed. Congressional oversight hearings and investigations were initiated to understand how the plan got botched, who was to blame, and whether any sort of cover-up had been attempted.

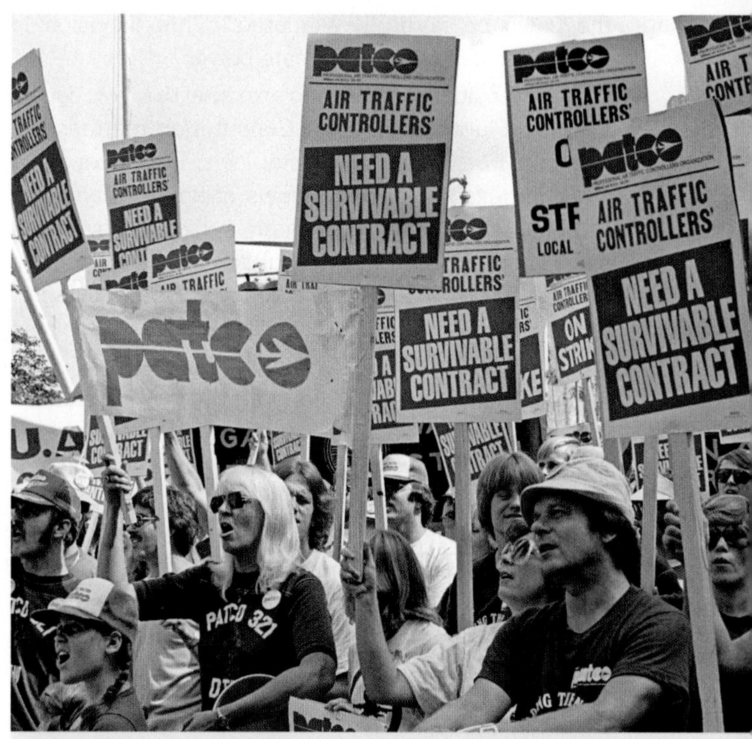

>> President Ronald Reagan exercised his power to enforce federal laws in 1981 by firing striking air traffic controllers. The strike was illegal according to a 1955 law passed by Congress.

Critics and Supporters In recent times, critics of what they see as a too-powerful chief executive have condemned what has been called "the imperial presidency." The term paints a picture of the President as a strong-willed emperor, taking various actions without consulting Congress or seeking its approval—sometimes acting in secrecy to evade or even deceive Congress. Critics of the imperial presidency worry that Presidents have shifted the balance of power between the executive and legislative branches.

On the other side of the debate are those who believe that in today's complex and globally interconnected world, the President must be able to react quickly to events at home and abroad, in consultation with advisors and members of Congress. Supporters of a strong presidency say the chief executive must have the power to shepherd the country through the challenges and opportunities of the 21st century.

DESCRIBE In 2006, President George W. Bush ordered the formation of military tribunals to prosecute suspected terrorists held at Guantanamo Bay. This action might be seen as an example of which approach to the presidency?

The Power to Execute the Law

Thomas Jefferson wrote this to a friend in 1789: "The execution of the laws is more important than the making of them." Whether Jefferson was right about that or not, in this section you will see that the President's power to execute the law endows the chief executive with extraordinary authority.

As chief executive, the President executes (enforces, administers, carries out) the provisions of federal law. The power to do so rests on two brief constitutional provisions. The first of them is the oath of office sworn by the President on the day he or she takes office:

> I do solemnly swear (or affirm) that I will faithfully execute the Office of President of the United States, and will to the best of my Ability, preserve, protect and defend the Constitution of the United States.
>
> —Article II, Section 1, Clause 8

The other provision is the Constitution's command in Article II, Section 3 that "he shall take Care that the Laws be faithfully executed." This provision is sometimes called the "take care power."

The President's power to execute the law covers all federal laws. In fact, the Constitution requires the President to execute *all* federal laws, no matter what the chief executive's own views of any of them may be. Their number, and the many subjects they cover, nearly boggle the mind. Social security, gun control, affirmative action, immigration, minimum wages, terrorism, environmental protection, taxes—these only begin the list. There are scores of others.

The President—and, importantly, the President's subordinates—have much to say about the meaning of laws, as do Congress and the courts. In executing and enforcing law, the executive branch also interprets it.

To look at the point more closely: Many laws that Congress enacts are written in fairly broad terms. Congress sets out the basic policies and standards to be followed. The specific details—much of the fine print necessary to the actual, day-to-day administration of the law—are usually left to be worked out by the executive branch.

For example, immigration laws require that all immigrants seeking permanent admission to this country must be able to "read and understand some dialect or language." But what does this broadly worded requirement mean in day-to-day practice? How well must an alien be able to "read and understand"? The law does not say. Rather, the details come from within the executive branch—from the U.S. Citizenship and Immigration Services in the Department of Homeland Security.

IDENTIFY CENTRAL IDEAS In what way does the executive branch influence the laws passed by Congress?

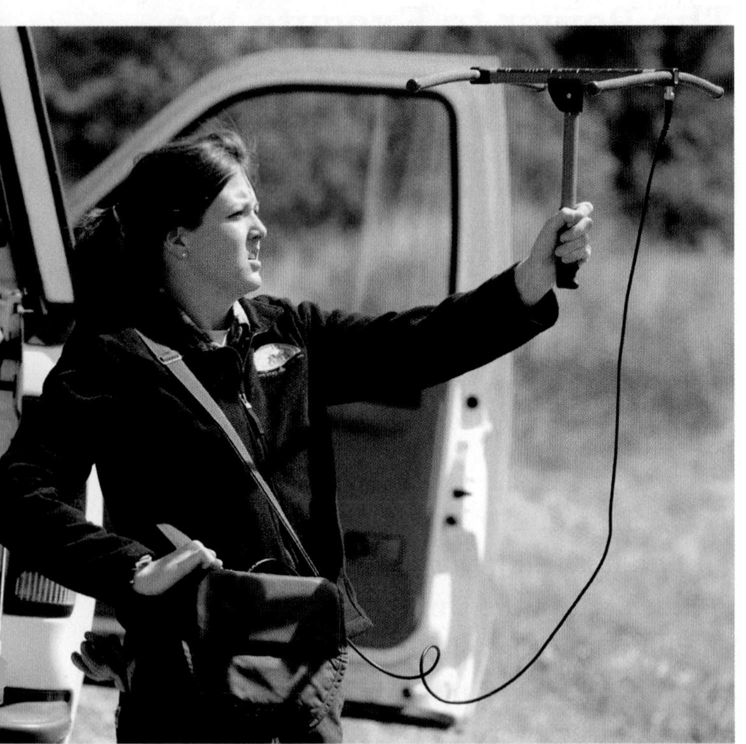

>> Executive orders can be used for such purposes as increasing federal job opportunities for college graduates. This graduate is scanning for a black bear as part of a federal study.

Executive Orders and Executive Privilege

The job of administering and applying most federal law is the day-to-day work of all of the many departments, commissions, and other agencies of the Federal Government. All of the some 2.7 million civilian men and women who staff those agencies are subject to the President's control and direction.

The chief executive has the power to issue **executive orders**, which are directives, rules, or regulations that have the effect of law. The power to issue these orders, the **ordinance power**, arises from two sources: the Constitution and acts of Congress.

The Constitution does not mention the ordinance power in so many words, but that power is clearly intended. In granting certain powers to the President, the Constitution obviously anticipates their use. In order to exercise those powers, the chief executive must have the power to issue the necessary orders, and, as well, the power to implement them.

The number, the scope, and the complexity of the problems that face the government of the United States have grown over the course of more than two centuries. Because of this fact, Congress has found it necessary to delegate more and yet more discretion to the President and to top-level subordinates in the executive branch to spell out the policies and programs it has approved. As a result, presidential executive orders deal with a dizzying array of subjects, from establishing a White House Council on Women and Girls, to setting out medical countermeasures to be taken in the event of a biological weapons attack.

The Power of Executive Privilege Beginning with George Washington in 1796, the nation's chief executives have at times insisted that the Constitution gives the President the inherent power to refuse to disclose certain information to Congress or to the federal courts. That is, they have claimed the power of **executive privilege**. Most often, a claim of executive privilege has been made with regard to conversations and other communications between Presidents and their closest advisors.

The chief executive must, of necessity, rely on the information and advice received from key staff and their ability to speak with utmost candor, which depends on the confidential nature of their relationship with the President. These officials must be sure that what they say will become known publicly only if and when the President chooses to disclose that information.

Congress has never recognized executive privilege. It has often tried to compel executive officials to testify at congressional committee hearings, and Presidents have frequently resisted those efforts, citing executive privilege.

The federal courts have been reluctant to become involved in this dispute between the executive and legislative branches. However, the Supreme Court has recognized both the existence of and the need for executive privilege in a historic case, *United States* v. *Nixon*, in 1974. There, a unanimous Court said that although the President might legitimately claim executive privilege in matters involving national security, that privilege cannot be used to prevent evidence from being heard in a criminal proceeding. This decision was a key factor in Mr. Nixon's resignation.

>> President Obama nominated Sonia Sotomayor to the Supreme Court in 2009. Supreme Court judges have an impact on how the nation's laws are interpreted long after a President leaves office.

MAKE GENERALIZATIONS How has the growth of the nation affected the President's ordinance power?

The Powers of Appointment and Removal

A President cannot hope to succeed without loyal subordinates who support the policies of the President's administration. To that end, the Constitution says that the President

> by and with the Advice and Consent of the Senate . . . shall appoint Ambassadors, other public Ministers and Consuls, Judges of the supreme Court, and all other Officers of the United States, whose Appointments are not herein otherwise provided for . . .but the Congress may by Law vest the Appointment of such inferior Officers, as they think proper, in the President alone, in the Courts of Law, or in the Heads of Departments.
>
> —Article II, Section 2, Clause 2

Those "Officers of the United States whose Appointments are . . . otherwise provided for" are the Vice President, members of Congress, and presidential electors.

Acting alone, the President names fewer than 1,000 of the 2.7 million civilians who work for the Federal Government. The vast majority of the rest of the federal work force is hired under the civil service laws.

Appointees The President names most of the top-ranking officers of the Federal Government. Among them are (1) ambassadors and other diplomats; (2) Cabinet members and their top aides; (3) the heads of independent agencies; (4) all federal judges, U.S. marshals, and attorneys; and (5) all officers in the armed forces. When the President makes one of these appointments, the nomination is sent to the Senate. There, the support of a majority of the senators present and voting is needed for confirmation.

The unwritten rule of senatorial courtesy plays an important part in this process. That rule applies to the choice of those federal officers who serve within a State—a federal district judge or a U.S. marshal, for example. The rule holds that the Senate will approve only those federal appointees acceptable to the senator or senators of the President's party from the State involved. The practical effect of this custom, which is closely followed in the Senate, is to place a meaningful part of the President's appointing power in the hands of particular senators.

Recess Appointments The Constitution does allow the President to make "recess appointments," that is, appointments "to fill up all Vacancies that may happen during the Recess of the Senate" (Article II, Section 2, Clause 3). Over time, the words "may happen" have come to mean "may happen to exist." Any such appointment automatically expires at the end of the congressional term in which it is made.

Recess appointments have often been a matter of contention—in particular, because they make it possible for the President to bypass the Senate confirmation process. So, as a rule, Presidents have not usually given these appointments to highly controversial personalities or to someone whom the Senate has previously rejected. Over time, Presidents have made very few recess appointments. The number tends to increase when the President's party does not control the Senate.

The Removal Power The power to remove is the other side of the appointment coin, and is as important to presidential success as is the power to appoint. Yet, except for mention of the little-used impeachment process, the Constitution says nothing about how, by whom, or why an appointed officer may be dismissed.

The matter was hotly debated in the first session of Congress, in 1789. Several members argued that, if an appointment required Senate approval, Senate consent should also be required for removal. They insisted that this restriction on presidential authority was essential to congressional supervision (oversight) of the executive branch. But others argued that the President could not "take Care that the Laws be faithfully executed" without a free hand to dismiss those who were incompetent or otherwise unsuited to office.

The latter view prevailed. The First Congress gave the President the power to remove any officer he appointed, except federal judges. Over the years since then, Congress has sometimes tried, with little success, to restrict the President's freedom to dismiss.

One notable instance occurred in 1867. Locked with **Andrew Johnson** in the fight over Reconstruction, Congress passed the Tenure of Office Act. That law's plain purpose was to prevent President Johnson from removing several top officers in his administration, in particular the secretary of war, Edwin M. Stanton. The law provided that any person holding an office by presidential appointment with Senate consent

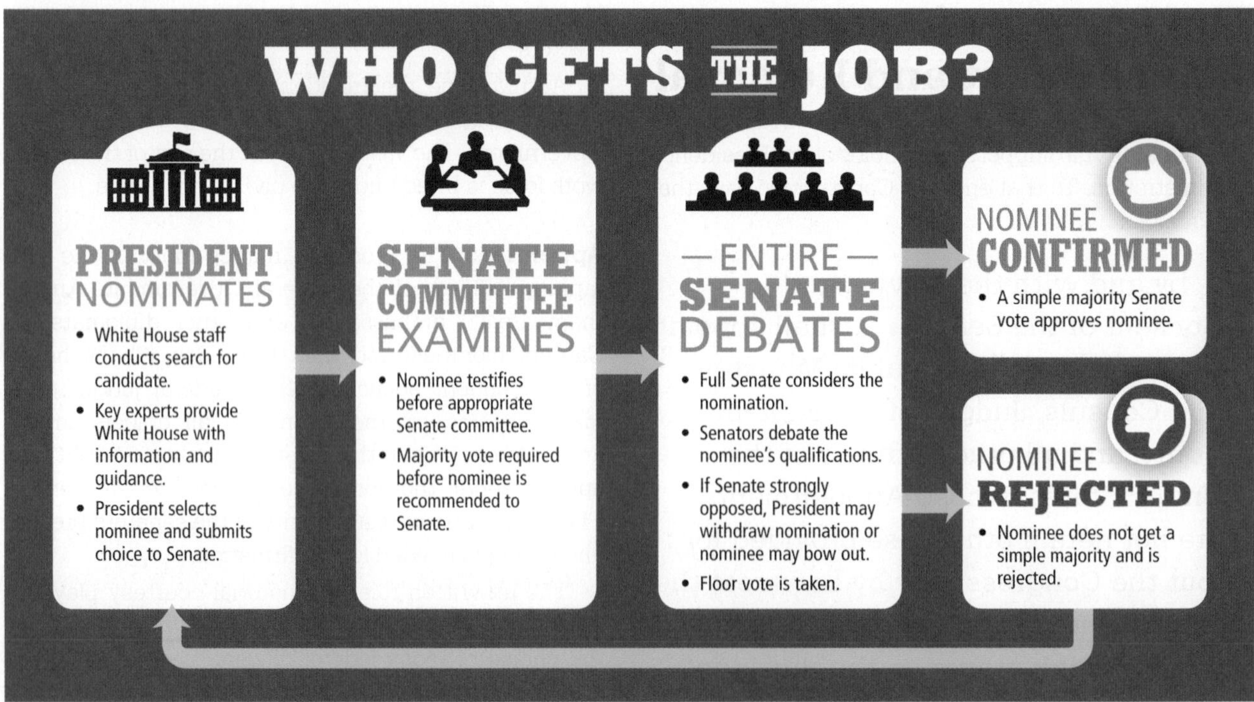

WHO GETS THE JOB?
PRESIDENT NOMINATES
• White House staff conducts search for candidate.
• Key experts provide White House with information and guidance.
• President selects nominee and submits choice to Senate.
SENATE COMMITTEE EXAMINES
• Nominee testifies before appropriate Senate committee.
• Majority vote required before nominee is recommended to Senate.
— ENTIRE — SENATE DEBATES
• Full Senate considers the nomination.
• Senators debate the nominee's qualifications.
• If Senate strongly opposed, President may withdraw nomination or nominee may bow out.
• Floor vote is taken.
NOMINEE CONFIRMED
• A simple majority Senate vote approves nominee.
NOMINEE REJECTED
• Nominee does not get a simple majority and is rejected.

>> The Senate must approve most presidential nominations. This process can be long and, at times, grueling for the nominee. **Analyze Charts** Why is this multi-step process necessary?

should remain in that office until a successor had been confirmed by the Senate.

The President vetoed the bill, charging that it was an unconstitutional invasion of executive authority. The veto was overridden, but Mr. Johnson ignored Congress and fired Stanton anyway. The veto and Stanton's removal sparked the move for Johnson's impeachment. Ultimately, the President was acquitted, and the law was ignored in practice. It was finally repealed in 1887.

Removal and the Court The question of the President's removal power did not reach the Supreme Court until *Myers* v. *United States*, 1926. In 1876, Congress had passed a law requiring Senate consent before the President could dismiss any first-class, second-class, or third-class postmaster.

In 1920, without consulting the Senate, President Woodrow Wilson removed Frank Myers as the postmaster at Portland, Oregon. The deposed postmaster then sued for the salary for the rest of his four-year term. He based his claim on the point that he had been removed in violation of the 1876 law.

The Court, led by a former President, Chief Justice Taft, found the law unconstitutional. It held that the removal power was an essential part of executive power, clearly necessary to the faithful execution of the laws.

The Supreme Court did place some limits on the President's removal power in 1935, in *Humphrey's Executor* v. *United States*. President Herbert Hoover had appointed William Humphrey to a seven-year term on the Federal Trade Commission (FTC) in 1931. When Franklin D. Roosevelt took office in 1933, he found Commissioner Humphrey to be in sharp disagreement with many of his policies. He asked the commissioner to resign, saying that his administration would be better served with someone else on the FTC. When Mr. Humphrey refused, President Roosevelt removed him. Humphrey soon died, but his heirs filed a suit for back salary.

The Supreme Court upheld the heirs' claim. It based its decision on the act creating the FTC. That law provides that a member of the commission may be removed only for "inefficiency, neglect of duty, or malfeasance in office."

The Court further held that Congress does have the power to set the conditions under which a member of the FTC and other such agencies might be removed by the President. It did so because those agencies, the independent regulatory commissions, are not purely executive agencies.

As a general rule, the President may remove those whom the President appoints. Occasionally, a presidential appointee does have to be fired. Most often, however, what was in fact a dismissal is called a "resignation."

"Do you have any 'Congratulations on Your Presidential Pardon' cards?"

>> Presidents receive thousands of requests for clemency during their time in office. **Analyze Political Cartoons** What does this cartoon imply about the number of pardons given by Presidents?

INTEGRATE INFORMATION What is the significance of the Supreme Court decision *Humphrey's Executor* v. *United States*?

The Powers of Clemency

The President has been given certain judicial powers. Specifically, the Constitution gives the President the power to

> . . . Grant Reprieves and Pardons for Offenses against the United States, except in Cases of Impeachment.
>
> —Article II, Section 2, Clause 1

A **reprieve** is the postponement of the execution of a sentence. A **pardon** is legal forgiveness of a crime.

The President's power to grant reprieves and pardons is absolute, except in cases of impeachment, where they may never be granted. These powers of **clemency** (mercy or leniency) may be used only in cases involving *federal* offenses.

Presidential pardons are usually granted after a person has been convicted in court. Yet the President may pardon a federal offender before that person is tried, or even before that person has been formally charged.

Notable Pardons Pardons in advance of a trial or charge are rare. The most noteworthy pardon, by far, was granted in 1974. In that year, President **Gerald Ford** gave "a full, free and absolute pardon unto Richard Nixon for all offenses against the United States which he . . . has committed or may have committed or taken part in during the period from January 20, 1969, through August 9, 1974." Of course, that pardon referred to the Watergate scandal.

To be effective, a pardon must be accepted by the person to whom it is granted. When a pardon is granted prior to a charge or conviction, as in the Nixon case, its acceptance is regularly seen as an admission of guilt by the person to whom it is given.

Nearly all pardons are accepted, of course, and usually gratefully. A few have been rejected, however. One of the most dramatic refusals led to a Supreme Court case, *Burdick* v. *United States,* 1915. George Burdick, a New York newspaper editor, had refused to testify before a federal grand jury regarding the sources for certain news stories his paper had printed.

>> Do journalists have to reveal their sources to the courts? Journalist George Burdick said "no" and emphasized his point by rejecting President Wilson's pardon.

Those stories reported fraud in the collection of customs duties. He invoked the 5th Amendment, claiming that his testimony could incriminate him. President Woodrow Wilson then granted Burdick "a full and unconditional pardon for all offenses against the United States" that he might have committed in obtaining material for the news stories.

Interestingly, Burdick refused to accept the pardon, and he continued to refuse to testify. With that, the federal judge in that district fined and jailed him for contempt. The judge ruled that (1) the President's pardon was fully effective, with or without Burdick's acceptance and (2) there was, therefore, no basis for Burdick's continued claim of protection against self-incrimination.

The Supreme Court overturned the lower court's action. It unanimously upheld the rule that a pardon must be accepted in order to be effective, and it ordered Burdick's release from jail.

Commutation and Amnesty The pardoning power includes the power to grant conditional pardons, provided the conditions are reasonable. It also includes the power of **commutation**, or the power to reduce a fine or the length of a sentence imposed by a court.

The pardoning power also includes the power of **amnesty**, which is in effect a blanket pardon offered to a group of law violators. Thus, in 1893, President Benjamin Harrison issued a proclamation of amnesty forgiving all Mormons who had violated the antipolygamy (multiple marriage) laws in the federal territories. And in 1977, President Jimmy Carter granted amnesty to those who evaded the draft during the war in Vietnam.

? SUPPORT A POINT OF VIEW WITH EVIDENCE
Give one reason why a President might grant amnesty to a group that has broken the law. Use evidence from the reading to support your answer.

The Power to Recommend Legislation

In *The Federalist* No. 51, **James Madison** analyzes the Constitution's elaborate system of checks and balances. Its "constant aim," he says, "is to divide and arrange the several [branches] in such a manner as that each may be a check on the other." And, he adds, "the great security against a gradual concentration of the several powers in the same department consists in giving to those who administer each department the necessary constitutional means and personal motives to resist encroachments of the others. . . . "

The Constitution gives the President certain legislative powers. They are, in Madison's phrase, "the constitutional means" that make it possible for the President to check the actions of Congress.

The President's legislative powers, exercised in combination with a skillful playing of the roles of chief of party and chief citizen, have made the President, in effect, the nation's chief legislator. It is the President who initiates, suggests, and demands that Congress enact much of the major legislation that it produces. However, a President whose party controls both houses on Capitol Hill may have an easier time of it than one who faces a hostile Congress.

The Message Power Article II of the Constitution gives the President what is often called the message power. This provision says that the President

> shall from time to time give to the Congress Information of the State of the Union, and recommend to their Consideration such Measures as he shall judge necessary and expedient. . . .
>
> —Article II, Section 3

The chief executive regularly sends three major messages to Capitol Hill each year. The first is the State of the Union message, a speech almost always delivered in person to a joint session of Congress. The President's budget message and then the annual Economic Report soon follow. The President often sends the lawmakers a number of other messages on a wide range of topics.

Other Legislative Powers According to Article II, Section 3 of the Constitution, only the President can call Congress into special session. The fact that Congress is now in session through most of each year practically eliminates the likelihood of special sessions and also lessens the importance of the President's power to call one. Still, as Congress nears the end of a regular session, Presidents have sometimes found it useful to threaten a special session if lawmakers do not act on some particular measure. President Harry Truman called the most recent special session in 1948, in an effort to force Congress to consider anti-inflation and welfare measures in the post-World War II period.

The same constitutional provision also gives the chief executive the power to prorogue (adjourn) Congress in the event the two houses cannot agree on a date for their adjournment. That has never happened.

>> President James Madison praised the Constitution's system of checks and balances as a way of preventing any one branch of government from wielding too much power.

CHECK UNDERSTANDING Why might a President whose party controls Congress have an easier time as "chief legislator" than a President who does not have support in Congress?

The Power of the Veto

The Constitution says that "Every Bill" and "Every Order, Resolution, or Vote to which the Concurrence of the Senate and House of Representatives may be necessary (except on a question of Adjournment) shall be presented to the President" (Article I, Section 7, Clauses 2 and 3). Remember, the Constitution presents the President with four options once a measure has been approved by Congress.

First, he or she may sign the bill, making it law, which is what usually happens. Or the President can **veto** the bill, and the measure must then be returned to Congress. The word *veto* comes from the Latin meaning "I forbid." Congress can then override that veto, by a two-thirds vote in each of its two chambers, but it seldom does.

As a third option, the President may allow a bill to become law by not acting on it, neither signing nor vetoing it, within ten days (excluding Sundays). This rarely happens.

The fourth option, the **pocket veto**, can be used only at the end of a congressional session. If Congress adjourns within ten days (not counting Sundays) of sending a bill to the White House and the chief executive does not act on it, the measure dies.

The veto power is an exceedingly valuable tool in the President's dealings with the legislative branch. Even the mere *threat* of a veto can defeat a bill or, at the least, prompt changes in its provisions as it moves through the legislative mill. When the chief executive makes such a threat, congressional leaders must do the math: Can they find enough votes in both houses to overcome a presidential veto?

George Washington rejected only two measures in his eight years in the presidency, and for nearly seven decades his successors also used their veto pens infrequently. But from Andrew Johnson in the 1860s onward, most chief executives have been much more willing to reject measures.

Signing Statements From **James Monroe** in the 1820s to today, various Presidents have issued "signing statements" as they approved some measures. On occasion, those statements were used to point out constitutional or other problems the President saw in a newly enacted law. More often, the statements have been used to do such things as to direct the manner in which a new law is to be enforced.

President George W. Bush stirred controversy by issuing signing statements more often than any of his predecessors, attaching them to more than 700 of the bills he signed. In doing so, he claimed a power, on one hand, to refuse to enforce those provisions or, on the other, to interpret them "in a manner consistent with" his view of "the constitutional authority of the President."

His critics claim that Mr. Bush, in effect, used these statements as a substitute for the veto power, deciding which new laws he would execute and how those laws would be interpreted and applied. Defenders argue that signing statements have been used by Presidents throughout the nation's history, that they are an important means for the President to express his reservations about a piece of legislation, and that the national security issues that arose during the Bush administration warranted any increased use.

President Obama has generally rejected his predecessor's view of signing statements. He has used them sparingly, in much the same way that earlier chief executives have.

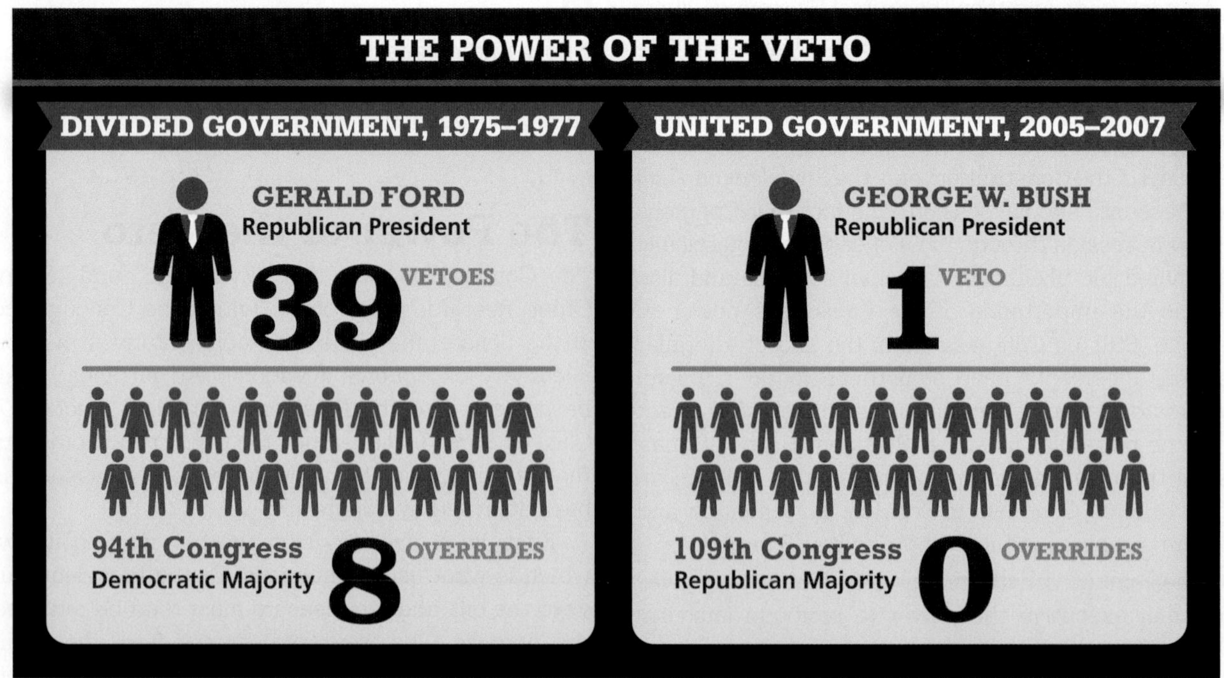

>> When the President and the majority of Congress are of the same party, vetoes tend to be rare. **Analyze Charts** How can Congress check the President's veto power?

The Line-Item Veto If the President decides to veto a bill, he must reject the *entire* measure. He cannot veto only a portion of it.

Since **Ulysses S. Grant's** day, most Presidents have favored expanding the veto power to include a **line-item veto**. That is, they have sought the power to cancel out some provisions in a measure while approving others. Most often, those who have proposed this device would restrict its application to specific dollar amounts (line items) in spending bills enacted by Congress. Many supporters argue that the line-item veto would be a potent weapon against wasteful and unnecessary federal spending.

Opponents of the line-item veto have long argued that the move would bring a massive and dangerous shift of power from the legislative branch to the executive branch. To this point, efforts to persuade Congress to propose a line-item veto amendment to the Constitution have failed.

In 1996, Congress did pass a Line-Item Veto Act. The Supreme Court struck it down, however, holding that Congress lacked the power to give the President a line-item veto, in *Clinton* v. *New York City*, 1998. If the chief executive is to have that authority, said the Court, it can come only as the result of an amendment to the Constitution.

THE 8,000 EARMARKS IN THIS BILL ARE OFFICIALLY LAST YEAR'S BUSINESS.
W
OMNIBUS SPENDING BILL
SIGNING STATEMENT
©MATSON
ROLL CALL

>> This cartoon plays on the meaning of "signing statements" to make a point. **Analyze Political Cartoons** Why might a President issue a signing statement rather than simply vetoing a measure?

? INTERPRET What are the pros and cons of signing statements?

ASSESSMENT

1. **Compare Points of View** How are Theodore Roosevelt and the idea of the "imperial presidency" related?
2. **Infer** The number and scope of the executive orders issued by the President have increased dramatically. What does this suggest about the presidency?
3. **Apply Concepts** In what way are presidential appointments an example of the system of checks and balances?
4. **Draw Conclusions** Given what you know about George Washington, why do you think he rarely used the veto power?
5. **Make Generalizations** Which branch of the government has often been charged with interpreting the proper extent of presidential powers? Give one example.

>> U.S. involvement overseas can last a long time. U.S. troops have been stationed in South Korea since 1950. Here, President Obama looks from South Korea across the border to North Korea.

5.4 In a 1961 radio broadcast, John F. Kennedy described the pressures of the presidency this way: "When I ran for the presidency . . . I knew the country faced serious challenges, but I could not realize—nor could any man who does not bear the burdens of this office—how heavy and constant would be those burdens."

Interactive Flipped Video

>> Objectives

Explain how treaties are negotiated by the President, approved by the Senate, and ratified by the President under the system of checks and balances.

Explain why and how executive agreements are made.

Summarize how the power of recognition is used by the President.

Describe the President's constitutional powers as commander in chief.

>> Key Terms

treaty
executive agreement
recognition
persona non grata
John Tyler
William McKinley

The President's Foreign Affairs Powers

The President's Diplomatic Powers

When President Kennedy made that comment, he had in mind the subject of this section: the President's awesome responsibilities as chief diplomat and commander in chief.

The Constitution does not say, in so many words, that the President is the nation's chief diplomat. Rather, Presidents have come to dominate the field of foreign affairs through the use of the powers of the office. In major part, they were able to do so because the Constitution makes the President the commander in chief of the nation's armed forces—and several centuries of relationships between sovereign states tells us that military force is the ultimate language of diplomacy.

The Power to Make Treaties A **treaty** is a formal agreement between two or more sovereign states. The President, usually acting through the secretary of state, negotiates these international agreements. The Senate must give its approval by a two-thirds vote of the members present before a treaty made by the President can become effective. Recall, the Constitution, in Article VI, makes treaties a part of "the supreme Law of the Land."

Contrary to popular belief, the Senate does not ratify treaties. The Constitution requires the Senate's "Advice and Consent" to a treaty made by the President. Once the Senate has given its consent, the President ratifies a treaty by the exchange of formal notifications with the other party or parties to the agreement.

Treaties have the same legal standing as acts of Congress, and their provisions are enforceable in the courts. Congress may abrogate (repeal) a treaty by passing a law contrary to its provisions, and an existing law may be repealed by the terms of a treaty. When the provisions of a treaty and an act of Congress conflict, the courts consider the latest enacted to be the law (*The Head Money Cases*, 1884). The terms of a treaty cannot conflict with any provision in the Constitution (*Missouri* v. *Holland*, 1920); but the Supreme Court has never found a treaty provision to be unconstitutional.

>> The President's words and actions related to the leaders of other nations carry great weight, both in the U.S. and around the world. Here, President Trump meets with the emir of Qatar, a small country in the Middle East.

Checks and Balances: Treaties and the Senate The Framers considered the Senate—with, originally, only 26 members—a suitable council to advise the President in foreign affairs. Secrecy was thought to be necessary and was seen as an impossibility in a body as large as the House.

The two-thirds rule for treaty approval creates the possibility that a relatively small Senate minority can kill an international agreement. For example, in 1920, the Senate rejected the Treaty of Versailles, the general peace agreement negotiated by Woodrow Wilson to end World War I. The treaty included provisions for the League of Nations. Forty-nine senators voted for the pact and 35 against, but the vote was 7 short of the necessary two thirds. More than once, a President has been forced to bow to the views of a few senators in order to get a treaty approved, even when this has meant making concessions opposed by the majority.

At times, a President has had to turn to roundabout methods in order to achieve his goals. When a Senate minority defeated a treaty to annex Texas, President **John Tyler** was able to bring about annexation in 1845 by encouraging passage of a joint resolution—a move that required only a majority vote in each house. In 1898, President **William McKinley** used the same tactic to annex Hawaii, again after a treaty his administration had negotiated failed in the Senate.

>> During his presidency, Ronald Reagan (right) negotiated and signed—with the approval of the Senate—an arms control treaty with Soviet leader Mikhail Gorbachev.

Interactive Chart

Executive Agreements Recent Presidents have relied more heavily on executive agreements than on formal treaties in their dealings with foreign governments, especially in routine matters. An **executive**

agreement is a pact between the President and the head of a foreign state, or their subordinates. Unlike treaties, these agreements do not have to be approved by the Senate.

These pacts have the same standing as treaties in the relationships between sovereign states, but they do not supersede federal law or the laws of any State. However, they are otherwise binding on the United States.

Most executive agreements flow out of legislation already passed by Congress or out of treaties to which the Senate has agreed. However, the President can make these agreements without any congressional action. Treaties, once made, become a permanent part of American law. Executive agreements do not. When a change of administrations occurs, only those the new President agrees to remain in force.

A few executive agreements have been extraordinary, most notably the destroyers-for-bases deal of 1940. Under its terms, the United States gave Great Britain 50 "over-age" U.S. destroyers, naval vessels that the British needed to combat German submarine attacks in the North Atlantic. In return, the United States received 99-year leases to a string of air and naval bases extending from Newfoundland to the Caribbean.

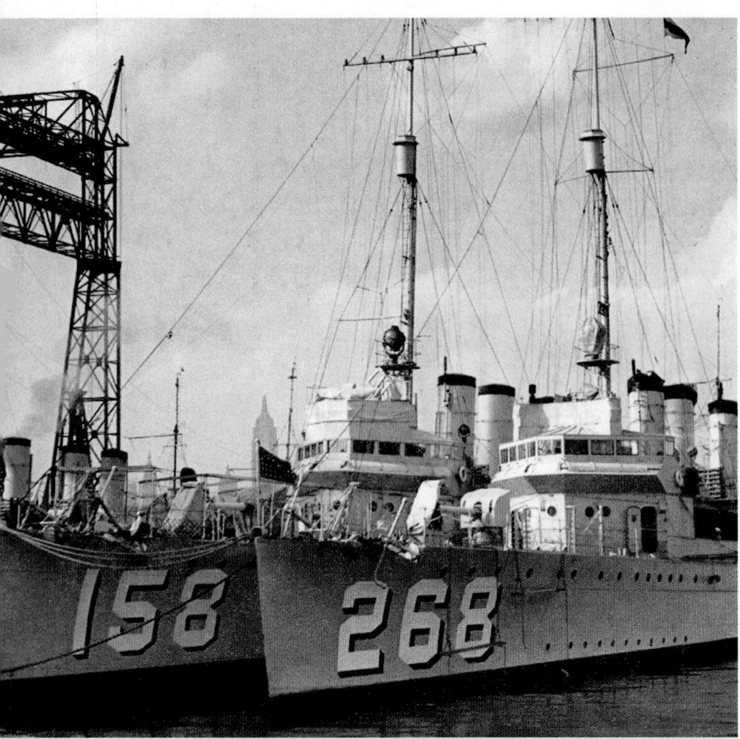

>> In 1940, President Franklin Roosevelt negotiated the destroyers-for-bases deal with Great Britain, which he accomplished through the use of an executive agreement.

The Power of Recognition When the President receives the diplomatic representatives of another sovereign state, the President exercises the power of **recognition**. That is, the chief executive, acting for the United States, acknowledges the legal existence of that country and its government. The President's action indicates that the United States accepts that country as an equal member of the family of nations. Sovereign states generally recognize one another through the exchange of diplomatic representatives. Recognition also may be accomplished by other means, such as proposing to negotiate a treaty, since in international law only sovereign states can make such agreements.

Recognition does not mean that one government approves the character or the conduct of another. The United States recognizes several governments about which it has serious misgivings. Among the most notable examples today is the People's Republic of China. The facts of life in world politics make relations with these governments necessary.

Recognition can be used to gain some advantage in world affairs. President Theodore Roosevelt's quick recognition of Panama in 1903 is a classic example of that point. He recognized the new state less than three days after the Panamanians had begun a revolt against Colombia, of which Panama had been a part. Roosevelt's action guaranteed their success. Similarly, President

>> President Theodore Roosevelt used the power of recognition to legitimize and support Panama's independence from Colombia in 1903, thus paving the way for U.S. control of the Panama Canal.

Harry Truman's dramatic recognition of Israel, within minutes of its creation in 1948, helped that new state to survive among its hostile Arab neighbors.

The President may show American displeasure with the conduct of another country by asking for the recall of that nation's ambassador or other diplomatic representatives in this country. The official recalled is declared to be **persona non grata**, an unwelcome person. The same point can be made by the recalling of an American diplomat from a post in another country. The withdrawal of recognition is the sharpest diplomatic rebuke one government may give to another and has often been a step on the way to war.

POSE AND ANSWER QUESTIONS The system of checks and balances is part of the treaty-making process. In order to avoid clashes with the legislative or judicial branches, what questions might a President ask advisors prior to negotiating a treaty? What answers might convince the President to proceed with the negotiations?

>> As commander in chief, President Lincoln often visited soldiers in the field and was known for taking a personal interest in the men. Here, he meets with officers at Antietam in 1862.

Commander in Chief

The Constitution makes the chief executive the commander in chief of the nation's armed forces (Article II, Section 2, Clause 1), although Congress does have extensive war powers. However, the President dominates the field of military policy. In fact, the President's powers as commander in chief have often been the source of conflict between the legislative and executive branches.

Consider this illustration of the point: In 1907, Theodore Roosevelt sent the Great White Fleet around the world. He did so partly as a training exercise for the Navy but mostly to impress other nations with America's naval might. Several members of Congress objected to the cost and threatened to block funds for the President's project. To this, Roosevelt is said to have replied, "Very well, the existing appropriation will carry the Navy halfway around the world and if Congress chooses to leave it on the other side, all right." Congress was forced to give in.

Presidents delegate much of their command authority to military subordinates. They are not required to do so, however. George Washington actually took command of federal troops and led them into Pennsylvania during the Whiskey Rebellion of 1794. Abraham Lincoln often visited the Army of the Potomac and his generals in the field during the Civil War.

Most Presidents have not become so directly involved in military operations. Still, the President has the final authority over and responsibility for all military matters, and the most critical decisions are invariably made by the commander in chief.

Making Undeclared War Does the Constitution give the President the power to make war without a declaration of war by Congress? Although many argue that it does not, 200 years of American history argue otherwise. Presidents have often used the armed forces abroad, in combat, without a declaration of war. In fact, most Presidents have done so, and on several hundred occasions.

John Adams was the first to do so, in 1798. At his command, the Navy fought and won a number of battles with French warships harassing American merchantmen in the Atlantic and the Caribbean. There have been a great many other foreign adventures since then. The long military conflicts in Korea, Vietnam, and now in Afghanistan and Iraq stand as the most extensive of these "undeclared wars."

Congressional Resolutions to Balance Executive Power Congress has not declared war since World War II. On eight occasions since then, however, it has enacted joint resolutions to authorize the President to meet certain international crises with military force.

President Dwight Eisenhower sought the first of these measures in 1955, to block the designs the People's Republic of China had (and still has) on Taiwan. That show of American resolve, and the presence of American warships, defused the situation.

The most recent authorization of force occurred in 2002, when Congress agreed that President George W. Bush should take those measures "necessary and appropriate" to eliminate the threat posed by Saddam Hussein and his Iraqi dictatorship. Operation Iraqi Freedom lasted nearly nine years and sacrificed the lives of nearly 4,500 American troops. At a cost of some $820 billion, the mission ousted Hussein from power and oversaw the installation of a fledgling democracy in Iraq.

Continued violence and unrest plague the nation, however. Further complicating matters, a new threat arose in 2013 in the form of the Islamic militant group ISIS (Islamic State of Iraq and Syria; also known as ISIL—Islamic State of Iraq and the Levant). The Iraqi army began fighting a full-fledged war against ISIS, which seized major areas of the country. The U.S. military, along with allies, joined the fight when it began conducting airstrikes on key targets within Iraq in 2014.

Other Uses of Military Power Since the end of World War II, there have been many other dire situations in which Presidents have deployed the nation's armed forces without a congressional resolution. Certainly, the Korean War stands as the foremost illustration of that fact. Among other notable instances: the 1983 attack on Grenada to frustrate a military coup, ordered by Ronald Reagan; the 1989 invasion of Panama, at the command of George H.W. Bush, to oust dictator General Manuel Noriega and protect American interests; the dispatch of U.S. forces to the Balkans in 1995 and 1999 by Bill Clinton as part of NATO's response to a vicious civil war and Serbian President Slobodan Milosevic's horrific "ethnic cleansing" campaign; and most recently, President Obama's 2011 use of the American military, in conjunction with other NATO forces, to support democratic uprisings in the North African nation of Libya; and most recently, the U.S. airstrikes against ISIS in Iraq and Syria and those against the Syrian military, ordered in 2017 by President Trump after evidence emerged that the Syrian government had used chemical weapons against civilians.

Limiting Presidential War Powers The war-making power as it was exercised by Presidents Johnson and Nixon during the undeclared war in Vietnam moved Congress to enact (over President Nixon's veto) the War Powers Resolution of 1973. That statute provides that the President can commit American military forces to combat only (1) if Congress has declared war, (2) if Congress has authorized that action, or (3) when an attack on the nation or its armed forces has occurred.

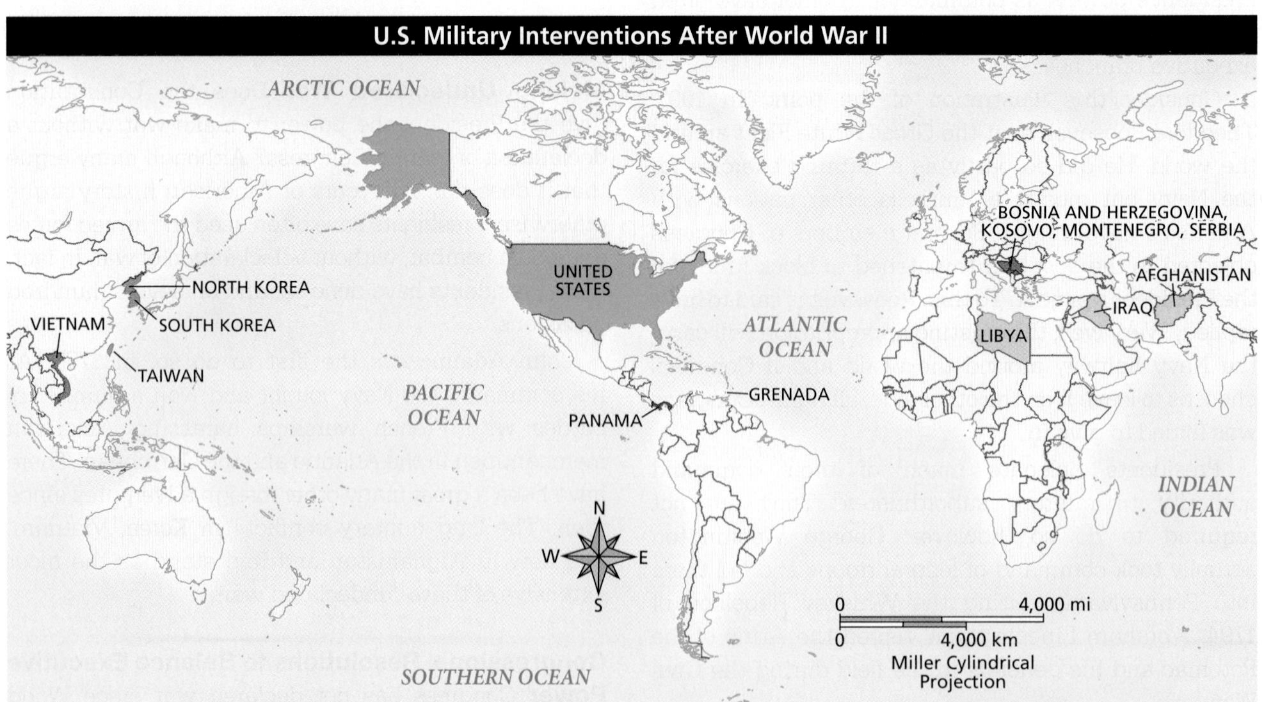

>> All of the conflicts shown on this map took place without a congressional declaration of war. **Analyze Maps** Why does military power sometimes shift from Congress to the President?

Interactive Map

If troops are ordered into combat in the third circumstance, the President must report it to Congress within 48 hours. Any such commitment of American forces must end within 60 days, unless Congress agrees to a longer involvement. At any time, Congress can end a commitment by the passage of a concurrent resolution (which is not subject to veto). The constitutionality of the War Powers Resolution remains in dispute.

? SYNTHESIZE Since the founding of the United States, Congress has declared war against other nations 11 times, most recently during World War II. Yet the United States has entered into hundreds of armed conflicts. What power allows the President to enter into a military conflict without congressional approval? Give an example of how a President has used this power.

ASSESSMENT

1. **Explain** A President has signed an arms control treaty approved by the Senate, but 20 years later, a different President thinks the terms are not stringent enough. What, if anything, can the new President do to change the situation?
2. **Sequence** When Panama was created in 1903, why did President Theodore Roosevelt use his power to recognize the new nation so quickly?
3. **Interpret** How does President Theodore Roosevelt's comment, "speak softly and carry a big stick" relate to the President's powers as a diplomat and as commander in chief? Do you agree with this approach? Why or why not?
4. **Determine Author's Purpose** When President Nixon vetoed the War Powers Resolution in 1973, he noted: "If the [War Powers] resolution had been in operation, America's effective response to a variety of challenges in recent years would have been vastly complicated or even made impossible. We may well have been unable to respond in the way we did during the Berlin crisis of 1961, the Cuban missile crisis of 1962, the Congo rescue operation in 1964, and the Jordanian crisis of 1970—to mention just a few examples." How do the examples given by President Nixon support his decision to veto the War Powers Act?
5. **Analyze** Reflect on the power of the President as the commander in chief. Why do you think the Framers gave this power to the President, rather than Congress?

1. **Identify Contributions of the Founding Fathers** Use the quotation below, and other primary and secondary sources, such as *Federalist* No. 71, to write a paragraph describing the contributions of Alexander Hamilton to the development of the office of President. Consider the following questions: Who was Alexander Hamilton? What does the Constitution say about the presidential term of office? Why did Hamilton advocate for that length of term?

   "The executive Power shall be vested in a President of the United States of America. He shall hold his Office during the Term of four Years, and, together with the Vice President, chosen for the same Term, be elected . . ."

   —Article II, Section 1, Clause 1

2. **Analyze Functions of the Executive Branch** Write a paragraph summarizing the Cabinet's role in determining presidential disability. Consider the Cabinet, vice presidential, and presidential roles and duties in your response.

3. **Analyze the Functions of the Executive Branch** Create an oral presentation describing the powers of the President that are not expressed in the U.S. Constitution. The presentation should also explain how presidential power has grown through the years. Consider the following presidential responsibilities: Chief Economist; Chief of Party; Chief Citizen.

4. **Compare Methods of Filling Public Offices** Use the chart below to write a short paper. Your paper should review the process of appointment and confirmation at the national level and then compare that process to the process at the state level. Consider the following questions: Why is the Senate involved in the appointment process? How is the process different at the state level? What would be the concerns if the Senate were not involved in the appointment process?

5. **Analyze Information by Comparing** Compare the method(s) by which the offices of President and Vice President are filled. Then write a paragraph that answers the following questions: What role does a presidential candidate play in the selection of a Vice President? Are Presidents and Vice Presidents elected in the same way or in different ways?

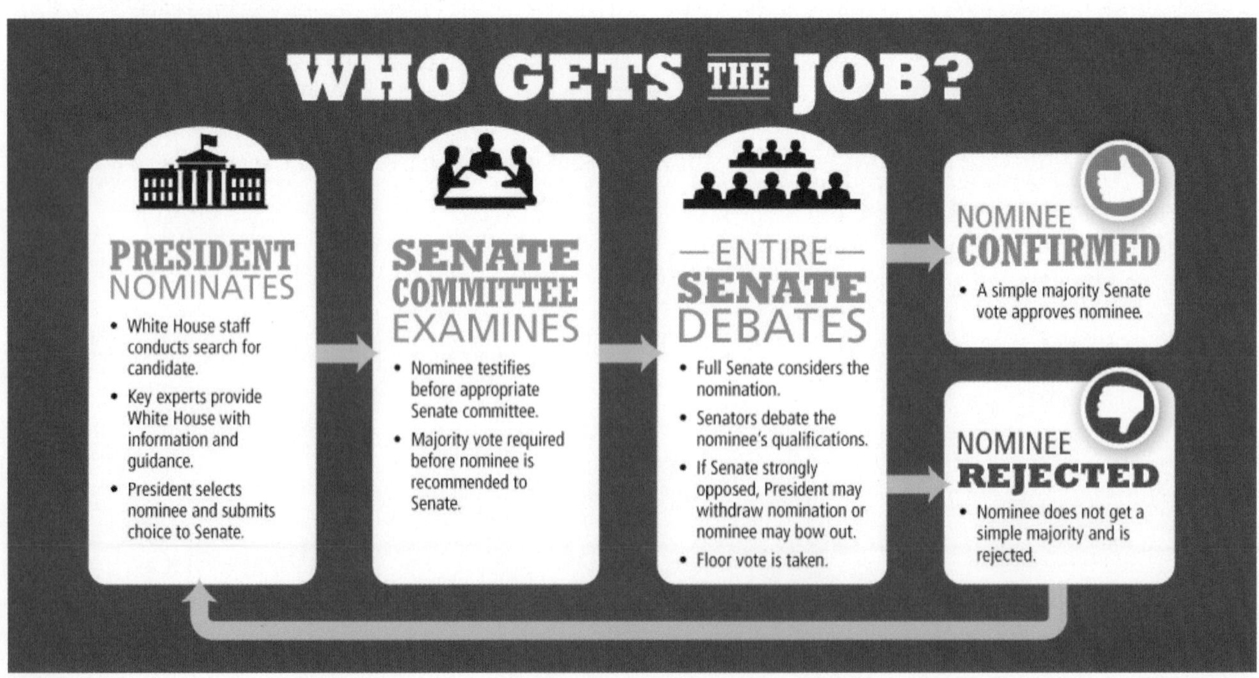

WHO GETS THE JOB?
PRESIDENT NOMINATES
• White House staff conducts search for candidate.
• Key experts provide White House with information and guidance.
• President selects nominee and submits choice to Senate.
SENATE COMMITTEE EXAMINES
• Nominee testifies before appropriate Senate committee.
• Majority vote required before nominee is recommended to Senate.
— ENTIRE — SENATE DEBATES
• Full Senate considers the nomination.
• Senators debate the nominee's qualifications.
• If Senate strongly opposed, President may withdraw nomination or nominee may bow out.
• Floor vote is taken.
NOMINEE CONFIRMED
• A simple majority Senate vote approves nominee.
NOMINEE REJECTED
• Nominee does not get a simple majority and is rejected.

6. **Explain Provisions of the U.S. Constitution** Write a paragraph describing the role of the President's veto power in the system of checks and balances among the three branches of government. Consider the following questions: What is a veto? What happens when a bill is vetoed? Why is the power of a veto a valuable tool for the President? How is a veto an example of checks and balances at work?
7. **Analyze U.S. Foreign Policy** Write a paragraph examining the power of recognition and the political impact recognition can have on a nation. Consider the following questions: In foreign policy terms, what is recognition? What role did recognition have in countries such as Panama and Israel? What political impact can a U.S. foreign policy such as recognition have on a nation?
8. **Analyze the Impact of Political Changes** Write a paragraph describing the role the First Lady plays in bringing about political changes and how that role has transformed over time. Consider the following questions: How has the role of the First Lady changed over time? What is the impact First Ladies have had on politics and government? How have the causes advocated by First Ladies led to changes in U.S. society or government? Give an example.
9. **Identify the Significance of Global Places** Create a written presentation that identifies the importance to the United States of the location of North and South Korea. Consider the following questions: Why did the United States commit forces to the Korean peninsula? Does the United States continue to have an interest in North and South Korea?
10. **Analyze the *Federalist Papers* and Evaluate Constitutional Provisions** Use the following quotation to write a paragraph analyzing James Madison's viewpoint on the reason the Constitution gives the President certain legislative and judicial powers. Consider the following questions: What point is Madison making in this quotation from *Federalist* Number 51? What constitutional provisions help the President limit the roles of the other two branches of government? Give at least three examples.

[The] constant aim [of checks and balances], is to divide and arrange the several [branches] in such a manner as that each may be a check on the other. . . ."
". . . the great security against a gradual concentration of the several powers in the same department consists in giving to those who administer each department the necessary constitutional means and personal motives to resist encroachments of the others. . . .

—Federalist No. 51

11. **Explain Major Foreign Policy Responsibilities** Write a paragraph describing the President's foreign policy powers. Consider the following questions: What is the difference between an executive agreement and a treaty? What other foreign affairs powers does the President have?
12. **Compare Methods of Filling Public Offices** Write a paragraph comparing different methods of filling the office of President, including election and succession. Consider the following questions: What is the Presidential Succession Act, and how is it a method for filling the office of President? How does this method compare with the way the presidency is normally filled? According to the act, who becomes President should the Vice President be unable to do so?
13. **Understand the Responsibilities, Duties, and Obligations of Citizenship** Write a paragraph that explains how First Ladies throughout the nation's history have worked to serve the public good. Consider the following questions: What specific causes have particular First Ladies chosen to support? Give at least three examples. How have these causes served the public good?

14. **Analyze U.S. Foreign Policy** Research the President's foreign affairs powers with regard to China. How has the exercise of those powers affected that nation? Choose one of these contemporary issues related to China: trade or human rights. Then, research the President's position on this issue using at least three different sources. Review each source carefully, considering the author's point of view and frame of reference and looking for evidence of bias. Finally, use the information from these sources to write a research report explaining the President's policy on the issue, which of the President's foreign affairs powers is most relevant in this case, and how the President's policy affects China. Make sure to list your sources.

15. **Identify Significant Individuals in Government and Politics** Use the quotation below to write a paragraph identifying Theodore Roosevelt and explaining his Stewardship Theory of the presidency. Consider the following questions: Based on the quotation below, what was Roosevelt's Stewardship Theory? How did this theory influence the office of the President?

    "My view was that every executive officer . . . was a steward of the people bound actively and affirmatively to do all that he could for the people. . . . My belief was that it was not only [a President's] right but his duty to do anything that the needs of the Nation demanded unless such action was forbidden by the Constitution or by the laws. . . . I did not usurp power, but I did greatly broaden the use of executive power. . . ."

    —*Theodore Roosevelt, Theodore Roosevelt: An Autobiography, 1913*

16. **Compare Methods of Filling Public Offices** Describe how someone becomes Vice President. Consider the following questions: How is a presidential candidate chosen? How is a vice presidential candidate chosen? What attributes does a presidential hopeful look for when choosing a running mate?

17. **Write About the Essential Question Write an essay on the Essential Question: What makes a good leader?** Use evidence from your study of this Topic to support your answer.

Go online to PearsonRealize.com and use the texts, quizzes, interactivities, Interactive Reading Notepads, Flipped Videos, and other resources from this Topic to prepare for the Topic Test.

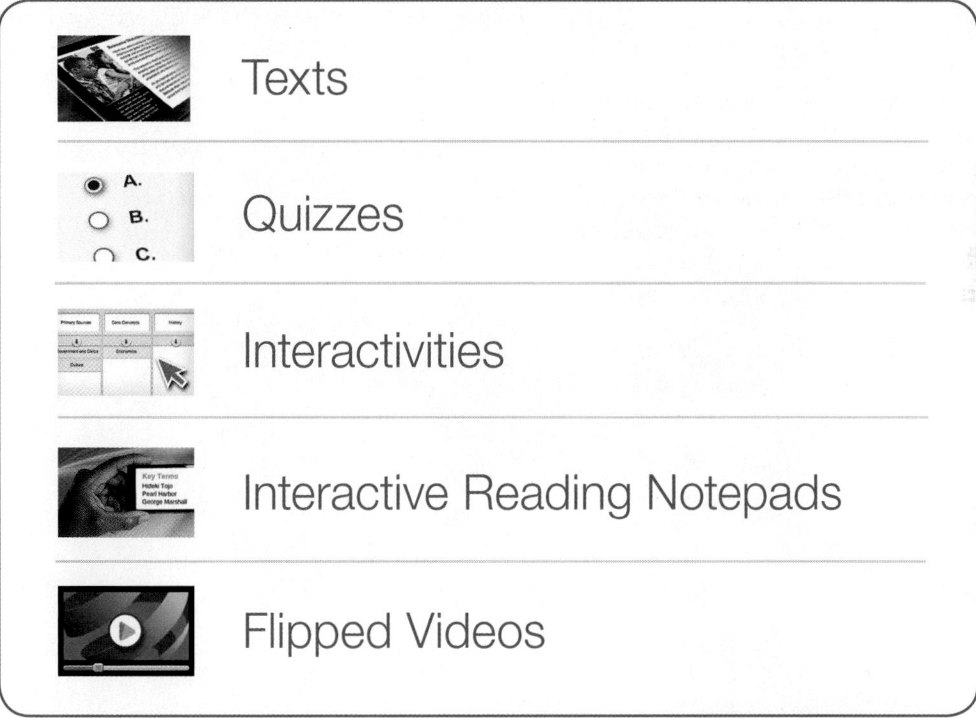

While online you can also check the progress you've made learning the topic and course content by viewing your grades, test scores, and assignment status.

[ESSENTIAL QUESTION] What Should Governments Do?

6 The Executive Branch at Work

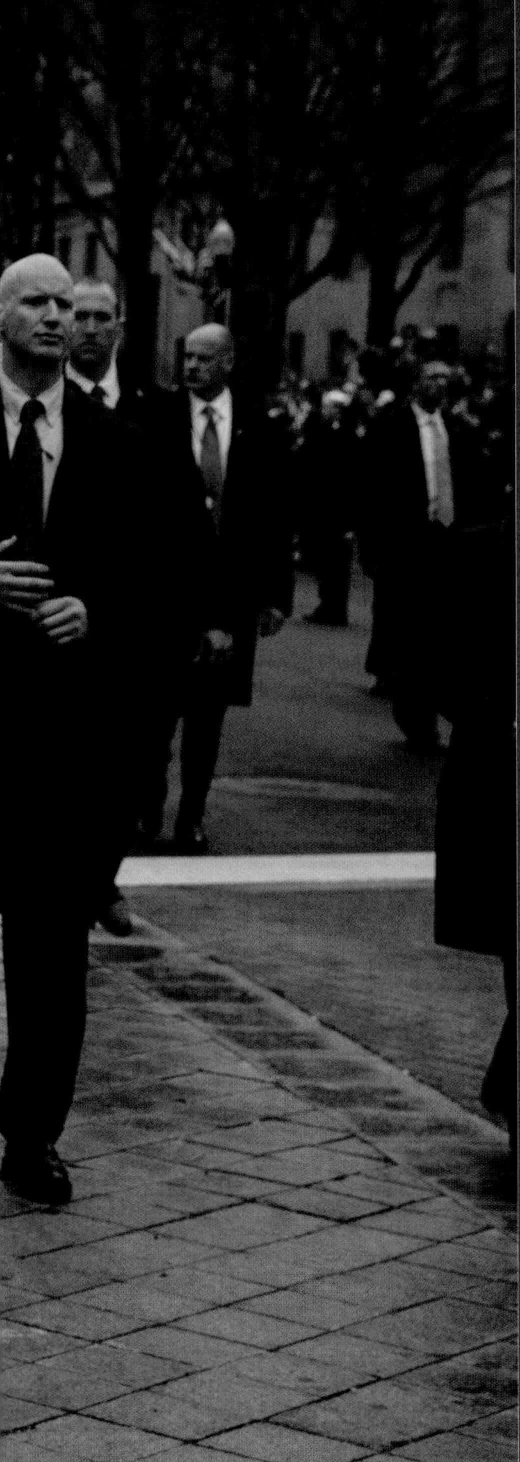

>> President Donald Trump walks with First Lady Melania Trump in his inaugural parade.

Enduring Understandings

- The federal bureaucracy is an effective structure that allows the government to function properly.
- The EOP is composed of the President's closest advisors and several support agencies.
- The 15 executive departments, the heads of which form the Cabinet, do much of the work of the Federal Government.
- Independent agencies were created to perform the work outside of the executive departments' umbrella.
- The State Department plays a major role in the implementation of American foreign policy.
- The departments of Defense and Homeland Security are responsible for national security, which is carried out by the military departments.

PEARSON realize™ NBC LEARN

Watch the My Story Video to learn more about independent agencies by exploring NASA's role in advancements in technology.

Access your digital lessons including:
Topic Inquiry • Interactive Reading Notepad • Interactivities • Assessments

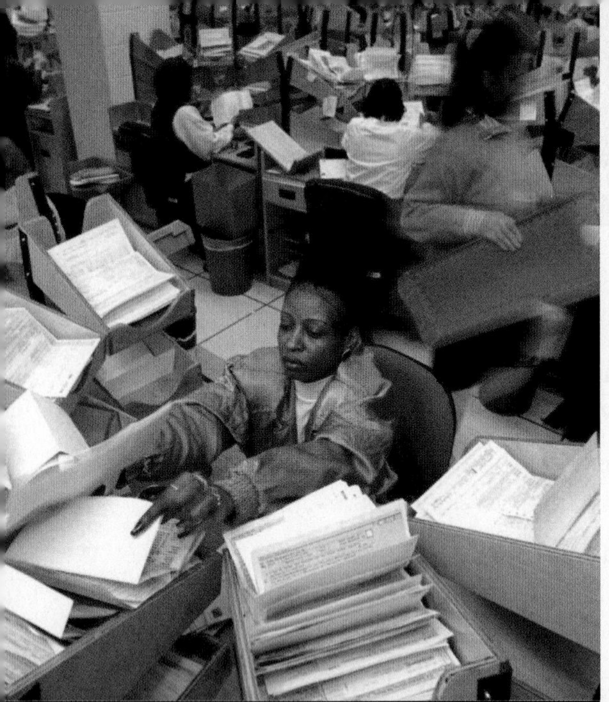

>> The Internal Revenue Service is part of the huge executive branch bureaucracy, responsible for processing all federal tax returns. The agency handles millions of pages of paperwork each year.

Interactive Flipped Video

6.1 **The Federal Government is an immense organization. Its employees deliver the mail, regulate business practices, collect taxes, defend the nation, administer Social Security programs, manage the national forests, explore outer space, and do dozens of other things every day. Indeed, you cannot live through a single day without somehow encountering the federal bureaucracy.**

>> Objectives

Define a bureaucracy.

Identify the major elements of the federal bureaucracy.

Explain how groups within the federal bureaucracy are named.

Describe the difference between a staff agency and a line agency.

>> Key Terms

bureaucracy
bureaucrat
administration
staff agency
line agency
James Madison

The Federal Bureaucracy

What Is a Bureaucracy?

A **bureaucracy** is a large, complex administrative structure that handles the everyday business of an organization. To many Americans, the word *bureaucracy* suggests such things as waste, red tape, and delay. While that image is not altogether unfounded, it is quite lopsided. Basically, at its best, bureaucracy can be an efficient and effective way to organize people (bureaucrats) to do work.

Bureaucracies are found wherever there are large organizations, in both the public and the private sectors of this country. Thus, the United States Air Force, McDonald's, the Social Security Administration, MTV, your city government, Yahoo!, the Boy Scouts of America, Twitter, and the Roman Catholic Church are all bureaucracies. Even your school is a bureaucracy.

Defining Bureaucracy By definition, a bureaucracy is a system of organization built on three principles: hierarchical authority, job specialization, and formalized rules.

Hierarchical authority. The word *hierarchical* describes any organization structured as a pyramid, with a chain of command running from the top of the pyramid on down to its base. The few officials and units at the top of the structure have authority over those officials and units at the larger middle level, who in turn direct the activities of the many at the bottom level.

Job specialization. Each **bureaucrat,** each person who works for the organization, has certain defined duties and responsibilities. There is, then, a precise division of labor within the organization.

Formalized rules. The bureaucracy does its work according to a number of established regulations and procedures. Those rules are set out in written form and so can be known by all who are involved in that work.

The Benefits and Drawbacks of Bureaucracy
Those three principles—hierarchical authority, job specialization, and formalized rules—can make bureaucracy the most effective way for people to work together on large and complex tasks, whether public or private.

The hierarchy can speed action by reducing conflicts over who has the power and the appropriate authority to make decisions. The higher a person's rank in the organization, the greater the decision-making power he or she has.

Job specialization promotes efficiency because each person in the organization is required to focus on one particular job. Each worker thus gains a set of specialized skills and knowledge.

Formalized rules mean that workers can act with some speed and precision because decisions are based on a set of known standards, not on someone's likes, dislikes, or inclinations. Those rules also enable work to continue with little interruption even as some workers leave an organization and new workers are hired to replace them.

At the same time, however, bureaucracies can suffer from several important flaws. Among them are the inefficiency and waste that can result from too many levels in the hierarchy or unnecessarily complex procedures that result from formalized rules. In addition, it is important to recognize this very important point about public bureaucracies: their bureaucrats hold appointive offices. Bureaucrats are *unelected* makers and implementers of public policy. This is not to say that bureaucracies are undemocratic. However, in a democracy, much depends on how effectively the bureaucracy is controlled by those whom the people *do* elect—the President and Congress. Listen to **James Madison** on the point:

> In framing a government which is to be administered by men over men, the great difficulty lies in this: you must

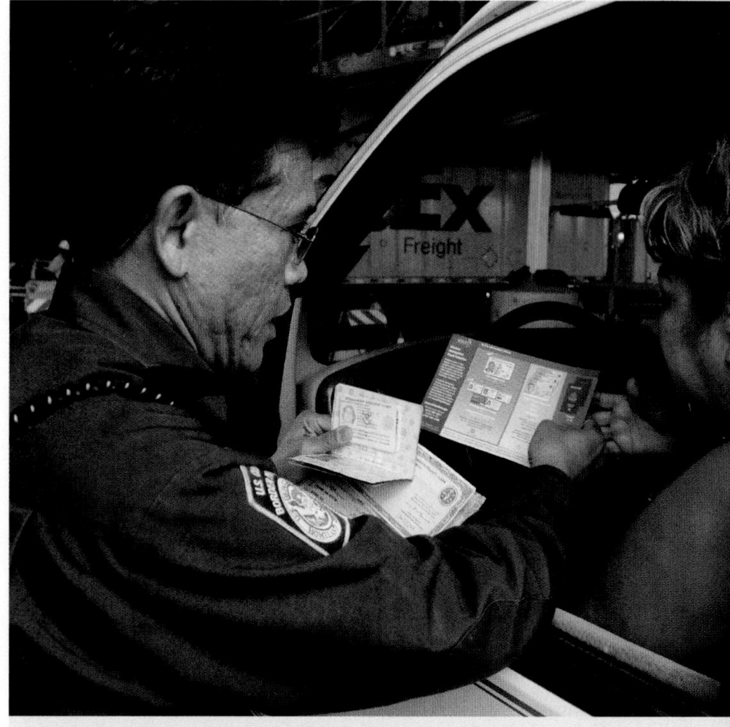

>> A U.S. border patrol officer checks a driver's documents. He is one of more than 2.7 million people who work for the agencies and organizations that make up the federal bureaucracy.

>> Bureaucracy and its sometimes convoluted procedures are often criticized as an inefficient way to run the government. **Analyze Political Cartoons** How does the cartoon illustrate this point?

> first enable the government to control the governed; and in the next place oblige it to control itself.
>
> —The *Federalist Papers,* No. 51

GENERATE EXPLANATIONS If a furniture manufacturer with a bureaucratic organization undergoes a large turnover of employees from one year to the next, what feature of the bureaucratic structure enables that organization to continue to produce furniture, despite the changes to its staff? Explain your answer.

Executive Branch Bureaucracy

The federal bureaucracy is all of the agencies, people, and procedures through which the Federal Government operates. It is the means by which the government makes and administers public policy—the sum of all of its decisions and actions. Nearly all of that huge bureaucracy is located in the executive branch. Not all of it, however, because both Congress and the federal court system are bureaucracies, as well.

The Constitution makes the President the chief administrator of the Federal Government. Article II, Section 3 declares that "he shall take Care that the Laws be faithfully executed." But the Constitution makes only the barest mention of the administrative machinery (the bureaucracy) through which the President is to exercise that power.

Article II does suggest executive departments by giving to the President the power to "require the Opinion, in writing, of the principal Officer in each of the executive Departments" (Article II, Section 2, Clause 1). A reference to "Heads of Departments" is in Clause 2, and to "any Department or Officer" of the government is in Article I, Section 8, Clause 18.

Article II anticipates two departments in particular, one for military and one for foreign affairs. It does so by making the President the "Commander in Chief of the Army and Navy," and by giving the chief executive both the power to make treaties and to appoint "Ambassadors, other public Ministers, and Consuls" (Article II, Section 2, Clauses 1 and 2).

Beyond those references, the Constitution is silent on the organization of the executive branch. The Framers certainly intended that administrative agencies be created, however. They understood that no matter how wise the President and Congress, their decisions still had to be carried out in order to be effective. Without an **administration**—the government's many administrators and agencies—even the best policies would amount to just so many words and phrases. The President and Congress need millions of men and women to put policies into action in Washington, D.C., and in offices all around the country and the world.

The chief organizational feature of the federal bureaucracy is its division into areas of specialization. The executive branch is composed of three broad groups of agencies: (1) the Executive Office of the President, (2) the 15 Cabinet departments, and (3) a large number of independent agencies.

>> President Reagan is saluted by members of the U.S. Navy. The Constitution suggests the creation of a federal military by making the President the commander in chief of the army and navy.

ANALYZE INFORMATION On what basis has the federal bureaucracy been established?

How Units Are Named

The titles given to the many units that make up the executive branch vary a great deal. The name *department* is reserved for agencies of Cabinet rank. Beyond the title of *department*, however, there is little standardized use of titles among the agencies.

The Executive Branch

EXECUTIVE OFFICE OF THE PRESIDENT	EXECUTIVE DEPARTMENTS		SELECTED INDEPENDENT AGENCIES
• White House Office • Office of the Vice President • Council of Economic Advisors • Council on Environmental Quality • National Security Council • Office of Administration • Office of Management and Budget • Office of National Drug Control Policy • Office of Science and Technology Policy • Office of the United States Trade Representative	• State • Treasury • Defense • Justice • The Interior • Agriculture • Commerce • Labor • Health and Human Services	• Housing and Urban Development • Transportation • Energy • Education • Veterans Affairs • Homeland Security	• Amtrak • Central Intelligence Agency • Environmental Protection Agency • Federal Reserve System • National Aeronautics and Space Administration • National Endowment for the Arts • National Science Foundation • Peace Corps • Social Security Administration • United States Postal Service

>> Each executive branch agency is created by act of Congress to execute the nation's laws. **Analyze Charts** Why do you think the executive branch is the largest part of the federal bureaucracy?

Common Names The most commonly used titles for units in the executive branch include *agency, administration, commission, corporation, authority, bureau, service, office, branch*, and *division*. The term *agency* is often used to refer to any governmental body. It is sometimes used to identify a major unit headed by a single administrator of near-cabinet status, such as the Environmental Protection Agency. But so, too, is the title *administration*; for example, the National Aeronautics and Space Administration and the General Services Administration.

The name *commission* is usually given to agencies charged with the regulation of business activities, such as the Federal Communications Commission and the Securities and Exchange Commission. Top-ranking officers called commissioners head these units. The same title, however, is given to some investigative, advisory, and reporting bodies, including the U.S. Commission on Civil Rights and the Federal Election Commission.

Either *corporation* or *authority* is the title most often given to those agencies that conduct businesslike activities. Corporations and authorities are regularly headed by a board and a manager—as is the case with the Federal Deposit Insurance Corporation, the Commodity Credit Corporation, and the Tennessee Valley Authority.

Irregular Names Within each major agency, the same confusing lack of uniformity in the use of names is common. *Bureau* is the name often given to the major elements in a department, but *service, administration, office, branch,* and *division* are often used for the same purpose. For example, the major units within the Department of Justice include the Federal Bureau of Investigation, the United States Marshals Service, the Drug Enforcement Administration, the Office of the Pardon Attorney, the Criminal Division, and the National Drug Intelligence Center.

Acronyms as Names Many federal agencies are often referred to by their initials. The EPA, IRS, FBI, CIA, FCC, NASA, and TVA are but a few of the dozens of familiar examples we hear and read about every day. A few are also known by nicknames. For example, the Government National Mortgage Association is often called "Ginnie Mae," and the National Railroad Passenger Corporation is better known to us as Amtrak.

The use of acronyms can sometimes cause problems. When the old Bureau of the Budget was reorganized in 1970, it was also renamed. It is now the Office of Management and Budget (OMB). However, it was for a time slated to be known as the Bureau of Management and Budget (BOMB).

CONNECT Unlike the numerous other titles given to various units in the executive branch, the name *department* is reserved for a special use. What is that use?

Staff and Line Agencies

The units that make up any administrative organization can be classified as either staff or line agencies. The Federal Government units are also described as such.

Staff agencies serve in a support capacity. They aid the chief executive and other administrators by offering advice and assistance in the management of the organization. **Line agencies,** on the other hand, actually perform the tasks for which the organization exists.

Congress and the President give the line agencies goals to meet, and the staff agencies help the line agencies meet these goals as effectively as possible through advising, budgeting, purchasing, planning, and management. The general public is much more aware of the work of line agencies than it is of that of most of the staff units. It is for a rather obvious reason: it is the line agencies that carry out public policies and, in doing so, deal directly with the public.

Two illustrations of the distinction here can be found in the several agencies that make up the Executive Office of the President and, in contrast, the Environmental Protection Agency. The agencies that make up the Executive Office of the President (The White House, the National Security Council, the Office of Management and Budget, the Office of Policy Development, and others) each exist as staff support to the President. Their primary mission is to assist the President in the exercise of the executive power and in the overall management of the executive branch. They are not operating agencies. That is, they do not actually administer public programs.

The Environmental Protection Agency (EPA), on the other hand, has an altogether different mission. It is responsible for the day-to-day enforcement of the many antipollution laws Congress has enacted over the years. The EPA operates "on the line," where the action is.

This difference between staff agencies and line agencies can help you find your way through the complex federal bureaucracy. The distinction between the two can be oversimplified, however. For example, most line agencies do have staff units to aid them in their line operations. Thus, the Environmental Protection Agency's Office of Civil Rights is a staff unit. Its job is to ensure that the agency's hiring and other personnel practices do not violate the Federal Government's anti-discrimination policies.

CONTRAST When the Department of Education conducts research on learning styles, is it functioning as a staff or a line agency? Explain your answer.

Staff and Line Agencies

STAFF AGENCIES

- Serve in support capacity
- Offer advice and management assistance

Both

- Form the federal administrative organizations
- Work together to meet goals

LINE AGENCIES

- Perform specific tasks
- Meet goals set by Congress and the President
- Administer public policy

>> The federal bureaucracy is made up of both staff and line agencies. **Analyze Charts** What are some examples of each type of agency?

ASSESSMENT

1. **Analyze Information** Explain how the defining features of a bureaucracy both help and hurt the effectiveness and efficiency of the Federal Government.
2. **Synthesize** Why does the bottom level of the bureaucratic hierarchy have the most employees?
3. **Infer** Why does the Federal Government need an administration, despite the fact that the Constitution says little about it?
4. **Generate Explanations** Why do some people argue that the federal bureaucracy is undemocratic? What is the opposing argument?
5. **Apply Concepts** The Council of Economic Advisors is a staff agency in the Executive Office of the President. Based on its title and the definition of a staff agency, what do you think this group does?

>> President Obama poses with his first Cabinet. Today, presidential Cabinet choices are scrutinized for how well they represent American diversity.

Interactive Flipped Video

6.2 **Thomas Jefferson performed his presidential duties with the help of two aides, one a messenger and the other his secretary. Like other early Presidents, he paid their salaries out of his own pocket. Indeed, Congress did not provide any money for presidential staff until 1857, when it gave President James Buchanan $2,500 for one clerk.**

>> Objectives

Analyze the structure and functions of the executive branch of government.

Describe the Executive Office of the President.

Explain the duties of the White House, the National Security Council, and the Office of Management and Budget.

Identify other agencies that make up the Executive Office of the President.

Describe the role of the Cabinet and executive departments in the executive branch.

>> Key Terms

Executive Office of the President
federal budget
fiscal year
domestic affairs
executive departments
secretary
attorney general
civilian
George Washington
Abraham Lincoln

The EOP and the Executive Departments

Structure of the Executive Office of the President

President Jefferson presided over an executive branch that employed, altogether, only some 2,100 people. The situation is remarkably different today. Approximately 2.7 million men and women work in the Obama administration. Two institutions—the Executive Office of the President and the President's Cabinet—are at the center of today's huge executive branch.

Every officer, every employee, and every agency in the executive branch of the Federal Government is legally subordinate to the President. They all exist to help the President—the chief executive—in the exercise of the executive power.

The President's right arm, however, is the **Executive Office of the President** (the EOP). The Executive Office of the President is, in fact, an umbrella agency, a complex organization of several separate agencies staffed by more than 1,800 of the President's key advisers and assistants. President Franklin Roosevelt persuaded Congress to establish the EOP in 1939. It has been reorganized in every administration since then, including the Obama Administration.

The Role of the White House The EOP's nerve center—in fact, the nerve center of the entire executive branch—is an agency now called the White House. Most of the President's key personal and political aides work there.

The two wings on either side of the White House hold the offices of most of the President's staff. These presidential assistants occupy much of the crowded West Wing, which the public seldom sees and where the legendary Oval Office and the Cabinet Room are located.

The White House chief of staff to the President directs all of the operations of the EOP and is among the most influential presidential aides. The counselor to the President and a number of senior advisers are also key members of the President's inner circle.

Several top officials work in the White House Office. A number of assistants and deputy assistants to the President aid the chief executive in such vital areas as foreign policy, defense, homeland security, the economy, political affairs, congressional relations, speech writing, and contacts with the news media and the public.

The staff of the White House Office also includes such major presidential aides as the press secretary, the appointments and scheduling assistant, and the President's physician. The First Lady's very visible place in public life today is reflected by the fact that one of the assistants to the President serves as her chief of staff and one of the several deputy assistants is her press secretary.

The staff of the White House Office now includes more than 450 men and women. The titles of some of the subunits they work for indicate the scope of their responsibilities: The Office of Digital Strategy, Oval Office Operations, the Office of the First Lady, the Office of Cabinet Affairs, the Office of Urban Affairs, and the Office of the Press Secretary.

The National Security Council Most of the President's major steps in foreign affairs are taken in close consultation with the National Security Council (NSC). It meets at the President's call, often on short notice, to advise him in all domestic, foreign, and military matters that relate to the nation's security.

The President chairs the Council. Its other members include the Vice President and the secretaries of state, treasury, and defense. The Director of National Intelligence and the chairman of the Joint Chiefs of Staff regularly attend its meetings. The NSC has a

>> President Obama consults with two key aides aboard Air Force One: Chief of Staff Denis McDonough (right) and Deputy National Security adviser for Strategic Communications Ben Rhodes (left).

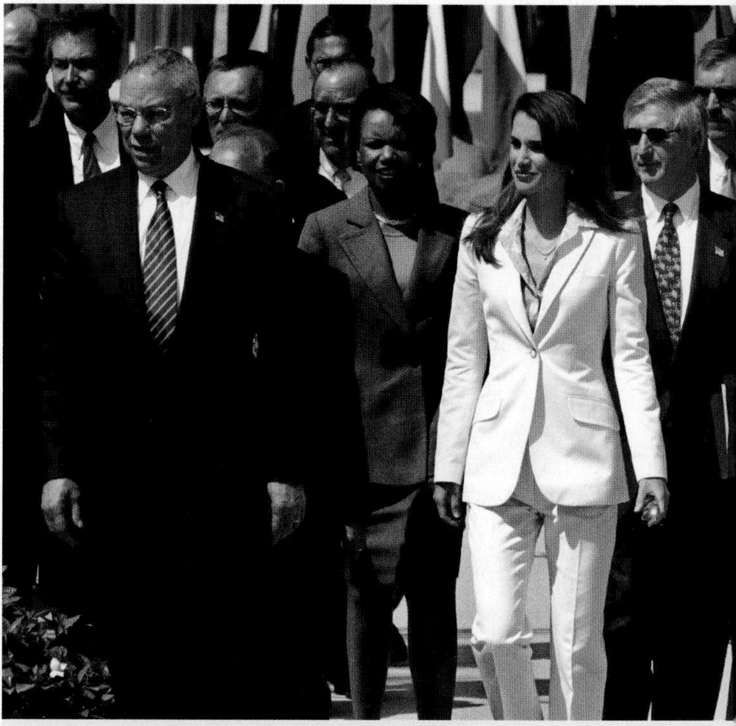

>> A U.S. delegation in Jordan in 2003. From left: Secretary of State Colin Powell, National Security adviser Condoleezza Rice, Jordanian Queen Rania Al Abdullah, and chief of staff Andy Card.

Interactive Gallery

small staff of foreign and military policy experts. They work under the direction of the President's national security adviser. The government's several intelligence agencies do much of their often super-secret work at the direction of the National Security Council.

The National Security Council is a staff agency. That is, its job is to advise the President in all matters affecting the nation's security. However, during the Reagan administration in the 1980s, the NSC's staff actually conducted a number of secret operations, including the sale of arms to Iran. The disclosure of the NSC's role in this sale led to the Iran-Contra scandal of the mid-1980s.

The Office of Management and Budget The Office of Management and Budget (OMB) is the largest and, after the White House, the most influential unit in the Executive Office. The OMB is headed by a director who is appointed by the President and confirmed by the Senate. The OMB's major task is the preparation of the federal budget, which the President must submit to Congress every year.

The **federal budget** is a very detailed estimate of receipts and expenditures, an anticipation of federal income and outgo, during the next fiscal year. A **fiscal year** is the 12-month period used by government and business for record keeping, budgeting, and other financial management purposes. The Federal Government's fiscal year runs from October 1 through September 30.

The budget is more than just a financial document. It is a plan—a carefully drawn, closely detailed work plan for the conduct of government. It is an annual statement of the public policies of the United States, expressed in dollar terms.

The creation of each fiscal year's budget is a lengthy process that begins more than a year before the start of the fiscal year for which it is intended. Each federal agency prepares detailed estimates of its spending needs for that 12-month period. The OMB reviews those proposals and gives agency officials the opportunity to defend their dollar requests. Following that agency-by-agency review, the revised (and usually lowered) spending estimates are fitted into the President's overall program before it is sent to Congress. The OMB then monitors the spending of the funds Congress appropriates.

Beyond its budget chores, the OMB is a sort of presidential "handy-man" agency. It makes continuing studies of the organization and management of the executive branch and keeps the President up to date on the work of all its agencies. The OMB checks and clears agency stands on all legislative matters to make certain they agree with the President's policy positions. It also helps prepare the hundreds of executive orders the President must issue each year and the veto messages the chief executive occasionally sends to Congress.

The Office of National Drug Control Policy The EOP's umbrella covers several other—and quite

The OMB and the Budget

FACTORS THE OMB CONSIDERS WHEN CREATING THE PRESIDENT'S BUDGET PROPOSAL	
What can the government spend?	The OMB must estimate how much income, principally from taxes, the government will receive in an upcoming fiscal year. Much of that sum must be spent for purposes and at levels previously set by Congress (mandatory spending).
What do the people want?	The people expect the Federal Government to maintain most existing programs. Only about 20 percent of all federal spending can be directed to expanding these programs and/or the creation of new ones (discretionary spending).
What does the President want?	Some spending has a higher priority in the give-and-take of the budget-making process than others—in particular, spending for those programs which are, for whatever reason, important to the President.

>> The Office of Management and Budget considers many factors when creating the President's final budget proposal. **Analyze Charts** Which of these factors might be the most difficult to quantify?

FROM THE OFFICE OF NATIONAL DRUG CONTROL POLICY

COST OF DRUG ABUSE

$120 billion lost productivity

$11 billion healthcare costs

$61 billion criminal justice costs

— Office of National Drug Control Policy EOP

"ONDCP seeks to foster healthy individuals and safe communities by effectively leading the Nation's effort to reduce drug use and its consequences."

— Executive Office of the President
Office of National Drug Control Policy

>> The Office of National Drug Control Policy provides resources such as community-based prevention programs and interventions to help recovering drug offenders and to promote public safety.

important—agencies. Each of those agencies provides essential staff help to the chief executive.

The Office of National Drug Control Policy was established in 1988. It is headed by a director who is appointed by the President, with Senate approval. The Office prepares an annual national drug control strategy, which the President sends on to Congress. The director also coordinates the ongoing efforts of the more than 50 federal agencies that participate in the continuing war on drugs.

The Council of Economic Advisers Three of the country's leading economists, chosen by the President with Senate consent, make up the Council of Economic Advisers. This Council is the chief executive's major source of information and advice on the state of the nation's economy. It also helps the President prepare the annual Economic Report to Congress, which goes to Capitol Hill in late January or early February each year.

The Roles of Other EOP Units A number of other agencies in the Executive Office house key presidential aides. These men and women make it possible for the President to meet the many-sided responsibilities of the presidency.

The Domestic Policy Council advises the chief executive on all matters relating to the nation's **domestic affairs**—that is, all matters not directly connected to the realm of foreign affairs.

The Council on Environmental Quality aids the President in environmental policy and in writing the annual "state of the environment" report to Congress. It sees that federal agencies comply with presidential policy and the nation's environmental laws. The President, with Senate consent, appoints the three members of the council.

The Office of the Vice President houses the now more than fifty men and women who help the Vice President perform the duties of that office. The marked growth in the size of that staff in recent years illustrates the increase in the importance and political clout of the vice presidency.

The Office of United States Trade Representative advises the chief executive in all matters of foreign trade. The trade representative, appointed by the President and confirmed by the Senate, carries the rank of ambassador and represents the President in foreign trade negotiations.

The Office of Science and Technology Policy is the President's major adviser in all scientific, engineering, and other technological matters. Its director is drawn from the nation's scientific community.

The Office of Administration is the general housekeeping agency for all the other units in the Executive Office. It provides them with the many support services they must have in order to do their jobs.

? ANALYZE INFORMATION Analyze the reasons for creating different offices within the EOP.

The Executive Departments

In *The Federalist* No. 76, Alexander Hamilton declared that "the true test of a good government is its aptitude and tendency to produce a good administration." Given that comment, it seems strange that Hamilton and the other Framers of the Constitution spent so little time on the organization of the executive branch of the government they were creating. Instead, the machinery of federal administration has been built over time to meet the changing needs of the country.

Much of the work of the Federal Government is done by the 15 **executive departments.** Often called the Cabinet departments, they employ nearly two thirds of the Federal Government's **civilian** workforce. They are the traditional units of federal administration, and each of them is built around some broad field of activity.

>> President Trump congratulates retired United States Marine General James Mattis after naming him Defense Secretary. Mattis is one of 15 executive department secretaries.

The First Congress created three of these departments in 1789: the Departments of State, Treasury, and War. As the size and the workload of the Federal Government grew, Congress added new departments. Some of the newer ones took over various duties originally assigned to older departments, and gradually assumed new functions, as well. Over time, Congress has also created and later combined or abolished some departments.

The work done by the executive departments is diverse, covering a vast array of responsibilities. Above all, however, note this: These departments are the major mechanism through which the domestic and foreign policies crafted by Congress and the President are carried out. Domestic policies are those concerned with matters at home, while foreign policies are concerned with matters abroad.

Executive Officers and Their Staffs Each department is headed by a **secretary,** except for the Department of Justice, whose work is directed by the **attorney general.** As you will see, those department heads serve in the President's Cabinet. Their duties as the chief officers of their specific department take up most of their time, however.

Each department head is the primary link between presidential policy and his or her own department. Just as importantly, each of them also strives to promote and protect his or her department with the White House, with Congress and its committees, with the rest of the federal bureaucracy, and with the media and the public.

An under secretary or deputy secretary and several assistant secretaries aid the secretary in his or her multidimensional role. These officials are also named by the President and confirmed by the Senate. Staff support for the secretary comes from assistants and aides with a wide range of titles in such areas as personnel, planning, legal advice, budgeting, and public relations.

Subunits in the Executive Departments Each department is made up of a number of subunits, both staff and line. Each of these subunits, or agencies, is usually further divided into smaller working units. Thus, the Occupational Safety and Health Administration (OSHA) in the Department of Labor is composed of a number of sections, including, for example, the Standards and Guidance Section and the Whistleblower Protection Programs. OSHA is the main federal agency charged with the enforcement of the safety and health legislation passed by Congress. Approximately 80

The Executive Departments Over Time

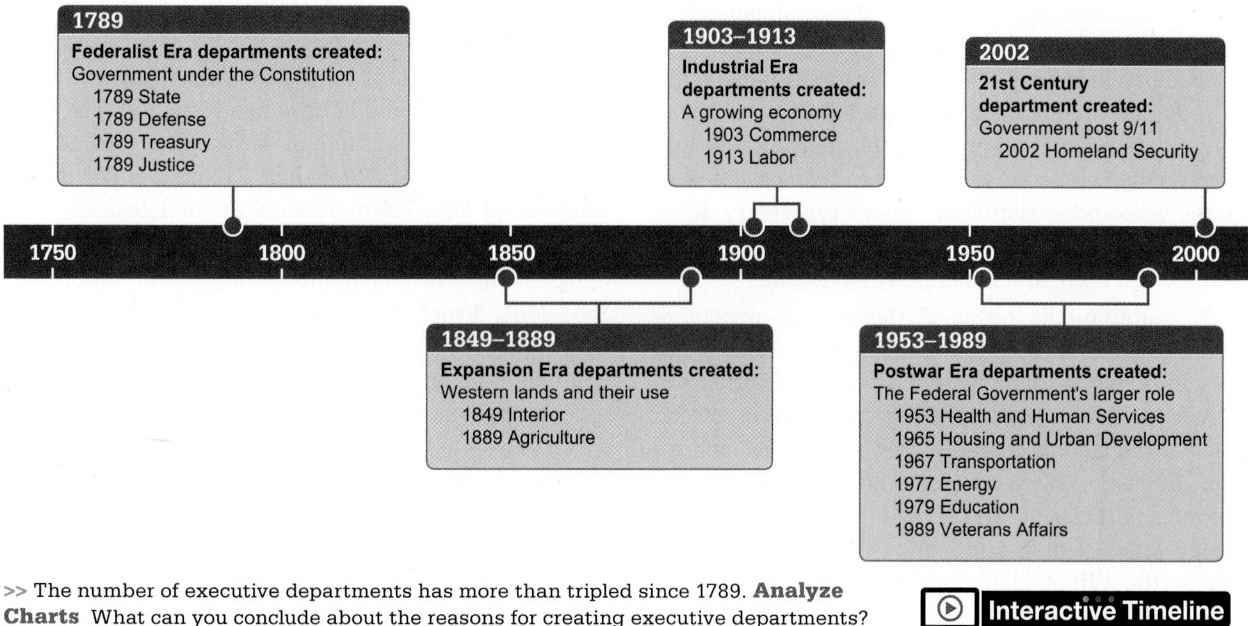

>> The number of executive departments has more than tripled since 1789. **Analyze Charts** What can you conclude about the reasons for creating executive departments?

Interactive Timeline

percent of the men and women who head OSHA, as well as all the other bureaus, divisions, and major units within each of the executive departments, are career people, not political appointees.

Many of the agencies in the executive departments are structured geographically. Much of their work is done through regional and district offices, which, in turn, direct the activities of the agency's employees in the field. In fact, some 90 percent of all of the men and women who work as civilian employees of the Federal Government are stationed outside the nation's capital.

Like any other government entity, the work of the executive departments and their various subunits can sometimes be controversial. Some people, for example, strongly believe that OSHA is necessary to protect the health and safety of American workers. Others, however, believe just as strongly that the agency's rules are confusing, its policies too rigid, and its penalties unreasonable. Still others think that the agency does not do enough to protect workers' rights.

The Executive Departments Today Today, the executive departments vary a great deal in terms of visibility, size, and importance. The Department of State is the oldest and the most prestigious department; but it is also among the smallest, with only some 30,000 employees. The Department of Defense is the largest, with nearly 700,000 civilian workers, and another 1.4 million men and women in the military services.

The Department of Health and Human Services (HHS) has the largest budget; it accounts for just about a fourth of all federal spending each year. In contrast, the Department of Commerce has the smallest budget and contributes to less than one percent of all federal expenditures.

The Department of Homeland Security became the newest of the executive departments when Congress created it in 2002. The department was formed by combining all or part of 22 existing federal agencies into one unit. It currently employs more than 240,000 people.

IDENTIFY MAIN IDEAS Analyze the reasons why the executive departments have changed over time.

The Cabinet and Its Functions

The Cabinet is an informal advisory body brought together by the President to serve his needs. The Constitution makes no mention of this group of advisors, nor did Congress create it.

The closest approach to it is in Article II, Section 2, Clause 1, where the President is given the power to "require the Opinion, in writing, of the principal Officer in each of the executive Departments, upon any Subject relating to the duties of their respective Offices." The

Cabinet was first mentioned in an act of Congress in 1907, well over a century after its birth.

At its first session in 1789, Congress established four top-level executive posts: secretary of state, secretary of the treasury, secretary of war, and attorney general. By his second term, President **George Washington** was regularly seeking the advice of the four outstanding people he had named to those offices: Thomas Jefferson (State), Alexander Hamilton (Treasury), Henry Knox (War), and Edmund Randolph (attorney general). So the Cabinet was born, and it has grown over time.

By tradition, the heads of the now 15 executive departments form the Cabinet. Each of the last several Presidents has regularly added a number of other top officials to the group, including the director of the Office of Management and Budget and the President's chief domestic policy advisor. The Vice President is a regular participant, and several other major figures usually attend Cabinet meetings. Those others often include the White House chief of staff, the United States trade representative, the director of the Office of National Drug Control Policy, the administrators of the Environmental Protection Agency and the Small Business Administration, and the representative to the United Nations.

>> George Washington's 1789 Cabinet consisted of just the secretaries of state, treasury, and war, and the attorney general. The modern-day presidential Cabinet is nearly four times that size.

How the President Chooses Cabinet Members The President appoints the head of each of the 15 executive departments. Each of these appointments is subject to confirmation by the Senate. Rejections have been exceedingly rare. Of more than 600 appointments made since 1789, only 12 have been rejected. The most recent rejection occurred in 1989, when the Senate refused to confirm President George H.W. Bush's selection of John Tower as secretary of defense.

Many factors influence the President's Cabinet choices. Party is almost always important. Republican Presidents do not often pick Democrats, and vice versa. One or more of a new President's appointees invariably come from among those who played a major role in the recent presidential campaign.

Of course, professional qualifications and practical experience are also taken into account in the selection of Cabinet secretaries. Geography plays a part as well. Each President tries to give some regional balance to the Cabinet. Thus, the secretary of the interior regularly comes from the West, where most of that department's wide-ranging work is carried out. The secretary of agriculture usually comes from one of the farm States in the Midwest and the secretary of housing and urban development often comes from one of the nation's major metropolitan centers.

Interest groups care about Cabinet appointments, and they influence some choices. The secretary of the treasury regularly comes out of the financial world, the secretary of commerce from the ranks of business, the secretary of education from among professional educators, the attorney general from the legal community, and so on.

Other considerations also guide the President's choices: gender and race, management abilities and experience, personal characteristics—these and a host of other factors play a part in the process.

Cabinets Today Today, most Presidents make Cabinet choices with an eye to racial, ethnic, and gender balance, in an effort to ensure that the nation's diverse population has a voice at the top levels of government. Thirty-one Presidents had named more than 300 Cabinet officers, however, before Franklin Roosevelt appointed the first woman to that body: Frances T. ("Ma") Perkins, who served as secretary of labor from 1933 to 1945. In 1966, the first African American, Robert C. Weaver, was selected by Lyndon Johnson to head the Department of Housing and Urban Development. Ronald Reagan named the first Hispanic Cabinet officer, Lauro F. Cavazos, as secretary of education in 1988.

By the early 2000s, Barack Obama had appointed the most diverse Cabinets in American history. All told, his Cabinets included eight women, five African Americans, four Hispanic Americans, three Asian Americans, and one Arab American.

Donald Trump's Cabinet includes one Asian American woman (Elaine Chao, Transportation), one white woman (Betsy DeVos, Education), and one African American (Ben Carson, Housing and Urban Development). Dr. Carson is a retired neurosurgeon who ran against President Trump for the Republican nomination in 2016.

The Trump Cabinet is notable for the fact that many of its members hail from the business community. In addition, it originally included three former military officers—four-star general James Mattis (Defense), John Kelly (Homeland Security), and ex-Navy SEAL commander Ryan Zinke (Interior).

Service members must ordinarily wait seven years before they are eligible to serve as secretary of defense, because civilian control of the military is a pillar of American democracy. General Mattis, who had only been retired for three years at the time of his nomination, was granted a waiver by Congress in order to serve. This was only the second time in American history that this special exemption was given. The other was for one of President Eisenhower's appointments—General George Marshall following World War II.

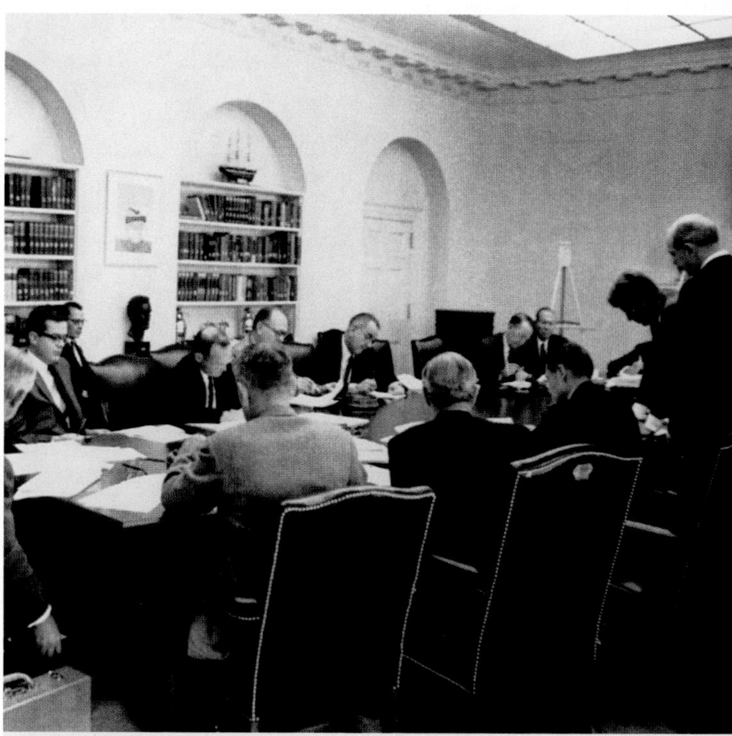

>> President John Kennedy meets with his Cabinet during the Cuban missile crisis of 1962. The Cabinet is often called together in times of crisis to advise the President.

Interactive 3-D Model

The Role of the Cabinet Cabinet members have two major responsibilities. Individually, each is the head of one of the executive departments. Collectively, they are advisors to the President.

Once a central cog in presidential government, the overall importance of the Cabinet has declined. Through much of our history, the Cabinet was a principal source of presidential advice. It met frequently, sometimes as often as twice a week, to offer counsel to the chief executive, and its influence could be seen in virtually all areas of public policy.

The growth of other presidential resources—particularly the vast amount of staff assistance centered in the Executive Office of the President—began to eclipse the Cabinet's role, however. Indeed, during his presidency, John Kennedy said that he could see no need to discuss, say, Defense Department matters with his secretaries of labor and agriculture, and he found Cabinet meetings to be "a waste of time."

This trend continued under President Johnson and was fully embraced by President Nixon, who centralized control in the White House and regularly declined to involve his Cabinet in key decisions. Since Nixon's time, every President has relied more fully on White House staff and advisors than they have on their Cabinets.

Given the limited number of hours in the day and the seemingly limitless number of issues that need to be addressed, should policy experts trump political strategists, or the other way around? It is often a mix, but there is evidence to suggest that the political strategists are winning out. Many reasons can be cited for this state of affairs, but chief among them is the belief that policy experts—i.e., Cabinet secretaries—often do a poor job of promoting or sticking to the President's political agenda. Additionally, the President has more control over the White House staff than the Cabinet, and that staff can respond much more quickly to issues than the executive departments can. Finally, Cabinet secretaries can be seen as causing trouble for the President—when they propose a controversial new rule, for example, or make a proposal that contradicts administration goals or raises a firestorm of unwanted media attention.

After leaving his post as secretary of labor in the Clinton administration, Robert Reich wrote a 1997 book that spoke to this point, aptly titled *Locked in the Cabinet*. Even though Reich had been friends with both Bill and Hillary Clinton, as a member of the Cabinet he found it difficult to get even a few minutes of the President's time.

>> President George H.W. Bush speaks to reporters in Kennebunkport, Maine, in 1990, with members of his Cabinet, including Vice President Dan Quayle (left) and Defense Secretary Dick Cheney (far right).

Still, Presidents do continue to call Cabinet meetings, though certainly not nearly as frequently as was once the case. More often than not, those sessions are held to do such things as show the administration's unified support for some particular presidential policy, rather than to thrash out the details of that matter. Cabinet members still do offer their advice—which need not be taken, of course—to the chief executive. President **Abraham Lincoln** once laid a proposition he favored before his seven-member Cabinet.

Each member opposed it, whereupon Lincoln, who was for it, declared: "Seven nays, one aye: the ayes have it."

William Howard Taft put the role of the President's Cabinet in its proper light nearly a century ago:

> The Constitution . . . contains no suggestion of a meeting of all the department heads, in consultation over general governmental matters. The Cabinet is a mere creation of the President's will. . . . It exists only by custom. If the President desired to dispense with it, he could do so.
>
> —William Howard Taft, *Our Chief Magistrate and His Powers*

No President has ever suggested eliminating the Cabinet. However, several Presidents have leaned on other, unofficial advisory groups and sometimes depended upon them more heavily than on the Cabinet. Andrew Jackson began the practice when he became President in 1829. Several of his close friends often met with him in the kitchen at the White House and, inevitably, came to be known as the Kitchen Cabinet.

Franklin Roosevelt's Brain Trust of the 1930s and Harry Truman's Cronies in the late 1940s were in the same mold.

? GENERATE EXPLANATIONS Is it appropriate for the President to pick Cabinet members with an eye toward racial, ethnic, and gender diversity? Why or why not?

ASSESSMENT

1. **Cite Evidence** At different times in history, the National Security Council has acted as both a line and a staff agency. Give evidence to support this statement.
2. **Explain** The President wishes to consult with a member of his staff regarding the possibility of expanding trade with Indonesia. Which agency in the EOP would the President consult and why?
3. **Support Ideas with Examples** Given the past history of Presidents and their Cabinets, what do you predict might be the role of the Cabinet under the next President? Is the past an accurate predictor of the future relationship between the President and the Cabinet? Explain your answer, citing details from the text.
4. **Generate Explanations** Why is it important for the President to select the heads of the executive departments?
5. **Compare** How is the Cabinet of today similar to the Cabinet during the presidency of George Washington?

6.3 Until the 1880s, nearly all the Federal Government did was done through its Cabinet departments. Since then, however, Congress has created a large number of additional agencies—the independent agencies—located outside the departments. Today, they number more than 150. In addition to the executive departments, these agencies are the major mechanism through which the Federal Government carries out the nation's domestic policies.

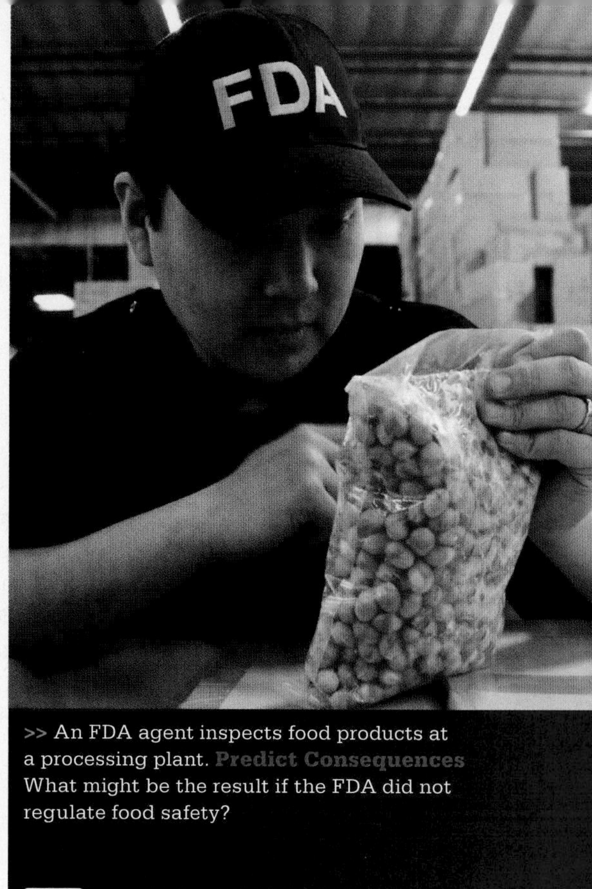

>> An FDA agent inspects food products at a processing plant. **Predict Consequences** What might be the result if the FDA did not regulate food safety?

Interactive Flipped Video

The Independent Agencies

The Purpose of Independent Agencies

Several independent agencies administer programs similar to those of the Cabinet departments. The work of the National Aeronautics and Space Administration (NASA), for example, is not unlike that of a number of agencies in the Department of Defense. NASA's responsibilities are also not very far removed from those of the Department of Transportation.

Neither the size of an independent agency's budget nor the number of its employees provides a good way to distinguish these agencies from the executive departments. For example, the Social Security Administration (SSA) is the largest of the independent agencies today. Only one Cabinet department, Health and Human Services, has a larger budget. The SSA now employs over 65,000 people—more than work for several Cabinet departments.

The Reasons Congress Created Independent Agencies The reasons these agencies exist outside of the Cabinet departments are nearly as many as the agencies themselves. A few major reasons stand out, however. Some have been set up outside the regular departmental

>> Objectives

Explain why Congress created the independent agencies.

Identify the characteristics of independent executive agencies.

Describe the history, purpose, and effect on private enterprise of selected independent executive agencies and regulatory commissions, including NASA and the EPA.

Explain the structure and function of government corporations.

>> Key Terms

independent agencies
independent executive agencies
civil service
patronage
spoils system
draft
independent regulatory commissions
government corporations
Chester Arthur
James Garfield
Theodore Roosevelt
Jimmy Carter
Andrew Jackson

structure simply because they do not fit well within any of the departments.

The General Services Administration (GSA) is a leading example of the point. The GSA is the Federal Government's major housekeeping agency. Its main chores include the construction and operation of public buildings, purchase and distribution of supplies and equipment, management of real property, and a host of similar services to most other federal agencies.

Congress has given some agencies, such as the Social Security Administration, the Federal Election Commission, and the U.S. Commission on Civil Rights, an independent status to protect them from the influence of both partisan and pressure politics. But, notice, this point can be turned on its head: Congress has located some of these agencies outside any of the Cabinet departments because that is exactly where certain special interest groups want them.

Some agencies were born as independents largely by accident. In short, no thought was given to the problems of administrative confusion when they were created. Finally, some agencies are independent because of the peculiar and sensitive nature of their functions. This is especially true of the independent regulatory commissions.

The Independent Agency Umbrella The label *independent agency* is really a catchall. Most of these agencies are independent only in that they are not located within any of the 15 Cabinet departments. They are not independent of the President and the executive branch. A handful of them are independent in a much more concrete way, however. For most purposes, they do lie outside the executive branch and are largely free of presidential control.

Perhaps the best way to understand all of these many independent agencies is to divide them into three main groups: (1) the independent executive agencies, (2) the independent regulatory commissions, and (3) the government corporations.

? INFER Why would certain special interest groups want particular independent agencies located outside of the Cabinet departments? Why might Congress concede to their wishes?

Independent Executive Agencies

The **independent executive agencies** include most of the non-Cabinet agencies. Some are huge, with thousands of employees, multimillion-dollar or even multibillion-dollar budgets, and extremely important public tasks to perform.

Types of Independent Agencies

	INDEPENDENT EXECUTIVE AGENCIES	INDEPENDENT REGULATORY COMMISSIONS	GOVERNMENT CORPORATIONS
DESCRIPTION	Non-Cabinet agencies with specialized functions	Agencies that regulate various aspects of the economy; outside presidential control	Agencies that operate like businesses but are financed with public funds and subject to congressional and presidential oversight
EXAMPLES	• National Aeronautics and Space Administration (NASA) • Environmental Protection Agency (EPA) • Food and Drug Administration (FDA) • Peace Corps • Office of Personnel Management (OPM)	• Federal Communications Commission (FCC) • Securities and Exchange Commission (SEC) • Consumer Financial Protection Bureau (CFPB) • Federal Reserve System • Consumer Product Safety Commission	• Federal Deposit Insurance Corporation (FDIC) • Export-Import Bank of the United States • U.S. Postal Service (USPS) • National Railroad Passenger Corporation (AMTRAK) • Tennessee Valley Authority (TVA)

>> The three types of independent agencies are distinctly different, but they do share some common features. **Analyze Charts** What features do these three types of agencies share?

The GSA, NASA, and the Environmental Protection Agency (EPA) are, for example, three of the largest of the independent executive agencies. They are organized much like the Cabinet departments: they are headed by a single administrator with subunits operating on a regional basis, and so on. The most important difference between these independent executive agencies and the 15 executive departments is simply in the fact that they do not have Cabinet status.

These larger agencies, such as the EPA and the Food and Drug Administration (FDA) play a large role in American life today. The EPA establishes and enforces pollution and other standards in order to protect the environment. Similarly, the FDA protects citizens by regulating safety standards for food, drugs, medical devices, vaccines, veterinary supplies, tobacco, and cosmetics. While many Americans see the work done by these agencies as valuable and necessary, they are not without their critics. Some people argue that the standards and regulations imposed by the EPA and the FDA place too heavy a burden on private businesses, thereby restricting economic growth.

Most independent executive agencies operate far from the limelight. They have few employees, comparatively small budgets, and rarely attract any attention. The American Battle Monuments Commission, the Citizens' Stamp Advisory Committee, and the National Indian Gaming Commission are typical of the dozens of these seldom seen or heard public bodies.

Neither the scope nor the effects of the many tasks performed by a number of these independent bureaucracies can be overstated. To make the point, take a quick look at a few specific examples.

>> Members of the Citizens' Stamp Advisory Committee unveil art for a new stamp honoring baseball great Willie Stargell. The CSAC is one of many independent agencies in the executive branch.

The National Science Foundation: Scientific Discoveries and Technological Innovations The National Science Foundation (NSF) is an independent federal agency created by Congress in 1950. Some of the scientific discoveries and technological innovations the NSF has helped to fund include the bar codes used at checkout counters, magnetic resonance imaging (MRI) technology, air bags in vehicles, touch-screen technology, and biometric identification.

The potential impact has yet to be realized for some recent scientific discoveries. For example, scientists are studying the purple sea fan, a type of coral, to discover how it fights pathogens and how it repairs injured tissue. What these scientists discover could hold clues for all of us about fighting and recovering from disease. Scientists have also discovered a bacterium in the hot springs at Yellowstone National Park that allows them to more quickly and easily study DNA. Among other uses, improved DNA technology helps law enforcement officials identify a suspect's involvement in a crime or demonstrate his or her innocence.

Many technological innovations also have a potentially great future impact for society. For example, 3-D printing is being used to make a variety of custom-made objects from metal, ceramics, and other materials. Some researchers are starting to use the technology to create custom medical implants to fix complicated injuries that can't be helped by conventional implants.

Another example of a recent innovation with a potentially large impact is nanogrids. These are large metal grids that, when activated by sunlight, break down oil from a spill, leaving behind only biodegradable compounds. This technology has the potential to avoid the devastating consequences on wildlife and local economies that have resulted from recent oil spills.

NASA—An Independent Executive Agency The National Aeronautics and Space Administration (NASA) was created by Congress in 1958 to handle this nation's space programs. Today, the scope of those programs is truly astounding. NASA's work ranges from basic scientific research focusing on the origin, evolution, and structure of the universe, to ongoing explorations of outer space.

The military importance of NASA's work can hardly be exaggerated. Still, Congress has directed the space agency to bend its efforts "to peaceful purposes for the benefit of all humankind," as well. Its wide-ranging research and development efforts have opened new frontiers in a great many areas: in astronomy, physics, and the environmental sciences; in communication, medicine, and weather forecasting; and many more. Many scientific advances, pioneered by NASA, have been put to productive use in the civilian realm.

For example, lifesaving heart and other computer monitoring systems were originally created to observe the effects of space travel on astronauts. Similarly, weather forecasters use NASA-based technology to monitor the weather using 3-D maps in real-time, and firefighters regularly use two-way radios that incorporate NASA's technology to communicate with each other during fire emergencies.

NASA's Space Shuttle Program In the 1980s, NASA developed the space shuttle program. This program was so successful that NASA spaceflights and other extraterrestrial projects became fairly routine and attracted little public notice. That changed in 1986, however, following the shocking and tragic explosion of the shuttle *Challenger*. NASA's space activities were put on hold for several years, extended when another tragedy, involving the shuttle *Columbia*, shook the nation in 2003.

For 30 years, shuttles have delivered personnel and supplies to the international space station. Rotating three-member international crews have lived aboard the outpost since late 2000.

By 2020, in addition to the completion of this advanced research laboratory in space, NASA plans to have more robotic missions exploring Mars and other planets in the solar system and eventually return to the moon as well. The potential future impact of these efforts will likely be seen in advances in medicine, disaster relief, and many other areas.

The Office of Personnel Management (OPM) The Federal Government is the nation's largest employer. Some 2.8 million civilians now work for Uncle Sam, including all branches of the government (and, recall, another 1.4 million men and women serve in the military today). Their ranks include computer programmers, forest rangers, electricians, chemists, physicists, FBI agents, security guards, engineers, librarians, truck drivers, botanists, and men and women in literally hundreds of other occupations.

Most of the civilians who work for the Federal Government are members of the **civil service.** That is, they are career employees who were hired, and who

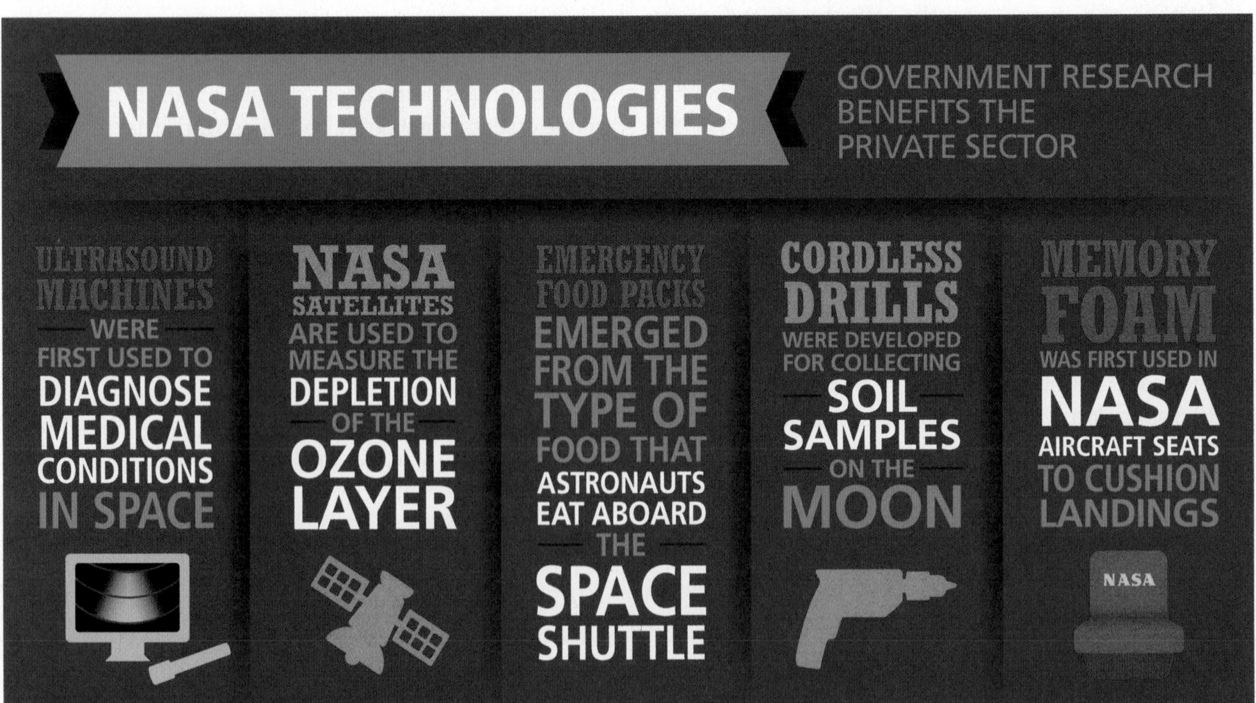

>> NASA's technological advances have ensured successful space travel and benefited the general public. **Analyze Information** How have each of these NASA innovations benefited civilians?

are paid and promoted, in accord with acts of Congress administered by an independent agency, the Office of Personnel Management.

>> This cartoon shows former President Hayes leaving a baby on President Garfield's doorstep. **Analyze Political Cartoons** What symbol does the cartoonist use to represent civil service reform? Why?

The Spoils System For most of the first century following the adoption of the Constitution, federal employees were hired according to the **patronage** system. That practice, often called the **spoils system**, was expanded by President **Andrew Jackson.** In fact, the phrase comes from a comment made by Senator William Learned Marcy of New York in 1832, as he defended President Jackson's appointment of an ambassador. Speaking from the floor of the Senate, Marcy declared: "To the victor belongs the spoils of the enemy."

Every change of administration brought a new round of patronage-based rewards and punishments. Inefficiency, even corruption, became the order of the day. Able people, in and out of government, pressed for reform, but little came of their efforts.

The Pendleton Act Unfortunately, it was a tragedy that at last brought about fundamental changes. In 1881, President **James Garfield** was fatally shot by a disappointed office seeker, Charles J. Guiteau. Garfield had rejected the mentally unstable Guiteau's request that he be appointed to a high diplomatic post. Congress, pushed hard by Garfield's successor, **Chester Arthur**, passed the Pendleton Act—the Civil Service Act of 1883.

The Pendleton Act laid the foundation for the present federal civil service system. The law set up two categories of employment in the executive branch: the classified and the unclassified services. All hiring for positions in the classified service was to be based on merit. That quality was to be measured by "practical" examinations given by an independent agency, the Civil Service Commission (since 1978, the OPM).

The Pendleton Act placed only about 10 percent of the Federal Government's then 130,000 employees in the classified service; it did give the President the power to extend that coverage, however. **Theodore Roosevelt** championed the merit system, and by the end of his term in 1909, the classified umbrella covered two thirds of the federal workforce. Today, not counting the United States Postal Service and a few other federal agencies, nearly 90 percent of all the men and women who work for the executive branch agencies are covered by the merit system.

Today's Civil Service The first goal of civil service reform—the elimination of the spoils system—was largely achieved in the early years of the last century. Gradually, a new purpose emerged: recruiting and keeping the best available people in the federal workforce. On the whole, efforts to reach that newer goal have succeeded. Today, most federal employees are hired through a competitive process. They are paid and promoted on the basis of written evaluations by their superiors. They are generally protected from disciplinary actions or dismissal for partisan reasons.

Still, the federal civil service is not perfect. Critics often claim that not enough attention is paid to merit in the merit system. Another independent agency, the Merit Systems Protection Board, actually enforces the merit principle in the federal bureaucracy. The Board is bipartisan—that is, its five members, appointed by the President and Senate, must include members of both major political parties. It hears appeals from those federal workers who have complaints about personnel actions—for example, denials of pay increases, demotions, or firings.

The Selective Service System Through most of our history, the nation's armed forces have depended on voluntary enlistments to fill their ranks. From 1940 to 1973, however, the **draft**—also called conscription, or compulsory military service—was a major source of military manpower.

Conscription has a long history in this country. Several colonies and later nine States required all able-bodied males to serve in their militias. However, in the 1790s, Congress rejected proposals for national compulsory military service.

Both the North and the South did use limited conscription programs during the Civil War. It was not until 1917, however, that a national draft was first used in this country, even in wartime. More than 2.8 million of the 4.7 million men who served in World War I were drafted under the terms of the Selective Service Act of 1917.

The nation's first peacetime draft came with the Selective Training and Service Act of 1940, as World War II raged in Europe but before the United States entered the war. Eventually, more than 10 million of the 16.3 million Americans in uniform during World War II entered the service under that law.

The World War II draft ended in 1947. The crises of the postwar period, however, quickly moved Congress to revive the draft, which was reestablished by the Selective Service Act of 1948. From 1948 through 1973, nearly 5 million young men were drafted.

The Draft Today Mounting criticisms of compulsory military service, fed by opposition to our Vietnam policy, led many Americans to call for an end to the draft in the late 1960s. By 1972, fewer than 30,000 men were being drafted per year, and selective service was suspended in 1973. Nevertheless, the draft law is still on the books, and is administered by an independent agency, the Selective Service System.

The draft law places a military obligation on all males in the United States between the ages of 18 and 26. During the years in which the draft operated, it was largely conducted through hundreds of local selective service boards. All young men had to register for service at age 18. The local boards then selected those who were to enter the armed forces.

In 1980, President **Jimmy Carter** reactivated the registration requirement, and his executive order is still in force. All young males are required to sign up soon after they reach their 18th birthday. The President's power to order the actual induction of men into the armed forces expired on June 30, 1973, however. If the draft is ever to be reactivated, Congress must first renew that presidential authority.

CONNECT Why do you think the draft was suspended instead of cancelled? Describe the steps that could be taken to increase the number of troops using the draft.

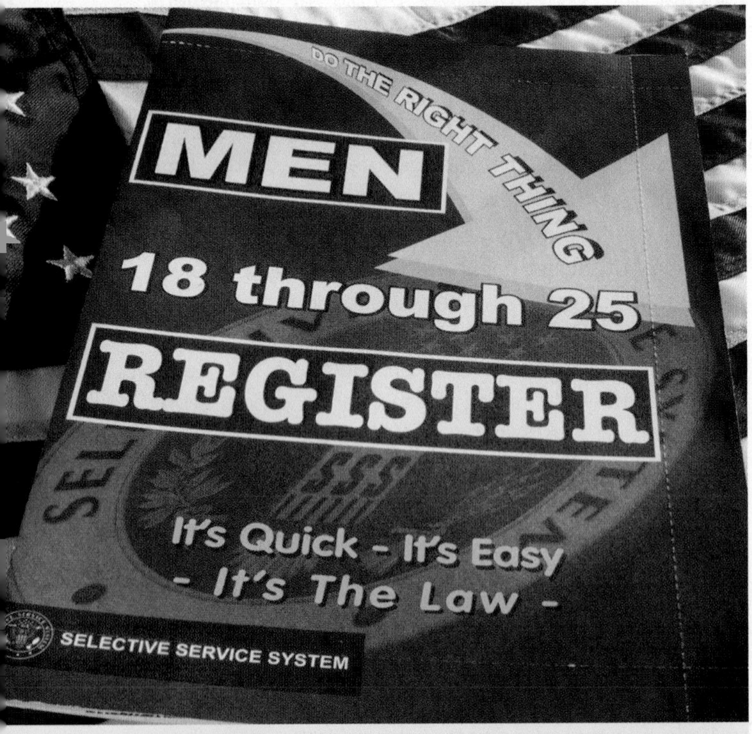

>> When young men turn eighteen, they are required to register for the draft. Although females can serve in the U.S. military, they are not required to register with the Selective Service.

Independent Regulatory Commissions

The **independent regulatory commissions** stand out among the independent agencies because they are largely beyond the reach of presidential direction and control. There are 12 of these agencies today, each created to regulate—monitor, police—important aspects of the nation's economy. A notable example is the Federal Communications Commission (FCC). It regulates interstate and international communications by radio, television, wire, satellite, and cable while ensuring reasonable rates.

Structured for Independence The independent regulatory commissions' large measure of independence from the White House comes mainly from the way in which Congress has structured them. Each is headed by a board or commission made up of five to seven members appointed by the President with Senate consent; those officials have terms of such length that it is unlikely a President will gain control over any of these agencies through the appointment process, at least not in a single presidential term.

Several other features of these boards and commissions put them beyond the reach of presidential control. No more than a bare majority of the members of each board or commission may belong to the same political party. Thus, several of those officers must belong to the party out of power.

Moreover, the appointed terms of the members are staggered so that the term of only one member on each board or commission expires in any one year. In addition, the officers of five of these agencies can be removed by the President only for those causes Congress has specified.

Executive, Legislative, and Judicial Powers As with the other independent agencies, the regulatory commissions are executive bodies. That is, Congress has given them the power to administer the programs for which they were created. However, unlike other independent agencies, the regulatory commissions are also quasi-legislative and quasi-judicial bodies. That is, Congress has also given these agencies certain legislative-like and judicial-like powers.

These agencies exercise their quasi-legislative powers when they make rules and regulations. Those rules and regulations have the force of law. They implement and spell out the details of the laws that Congress has directed these regulatory bodies to enforce.

>> A radio station host talks to listeners on the air. The radio waves, as well as any content transmitted over them, are regulated by the Federal Communications Commission (FCC).

Securities and Exchange Commission To illustrate the point: Congress has said that those who want to borrow money by issuing stocks, bonds, or other securities must provide a "full and fair disclosure" of all pertinent information to prospective investors. The Securities and Exchange Commission (SEC) makes that requirement effective and indicates how those who offer securities are to meet it by issuing rules and regulations.

The regulatory commissions exercise their quasi-judicial powers when they decide disputes in those fields in which Congress has given them policing authority. For example, if an investor in Iowa thinks a local stockbroker has cheated him, he may file a complaint with the SEC's regional office in Chicago. SEC agents will investigate and report their findings, and the agency will judge the merits of the complaint much as a court would do. Decisions made by the SEC, and by the other independent regulatory bodies, can be appealed to the United States courts of appeals.

>> Traders at work on the floor of the New York Stock Exchange. The Securities and Exchange Commission sets and enforces regulations for individuals and companies involved in stock trading.

Filling In for Congress In a sense, Congress has created these agencies to act in its place. Congress could hold hearings and set interest rates, license radio and TV stations and nuclear reactors, check on business practices, and do the many other things it has directed the regulatory commissions to do. These activities are complex and time-consuming, however, and they demand constant and expert attention. If Congress were to do all of this work, it would have no time for its other important legislative work.

Note that because these regulatory bodies possess all three of the basic governmental powers—executive, legislative, and judicial—they are exceptions to the principle of separation of powers. Technically, they should not be grouped with the other independent agencies. Instead, they should be located somewhere between the executive and legislative branches, and between the executive and judicial branches, as well.

How Much Regulation Is Necessary? Several authorities, and most recent Presidents, have urged that at least some of the administrative functions of the independent regulatory bodies be given to executive department agencies. Critics have raised other serious questions about these regulatory commissions and many think that they should be abolished or, at the least, redesigned.

Many critics specify that government taxation and regulation serve as significant restrictions to private enterprise. Governmental goals, such as ensuring competition, protecting consumers, maintaining fair prices, and overseeing industrial safety, are viewed by some private business owners as stumbling blocks to growth and a hindrance to the free enterprise system.

These critics say that government regulations can limit the start-up of new businesses and negatively affect the nation's economy. This is true not only at the national level. Federal regulations affect businesses at the State and local levels, as well. So, too, do additional regulations imposed by State and local governments. While some maintain that these safeguards are necessary to protect consumers and the environment and ensure fairness in the marketplace, others note that the many layers of rules and regulations have become unnecessarily complex.

Some other troubling questions are these: Have some of the regulatory commissions been unduly influenced by the special interests they are expected to regulate? Are all of the many and detailed rules created by these agencies really needed? Do some of those regulations have the effect of stifling legitimate competition in the free enterprise system? Do some of them add unreasonably to the costs of doing business and therefore to the prices that consumers must pay?

Congress sets the basic policies of these agencies, and so it has a major responsibility to answer these questions. It has done so in recent years, particularly by deregulating much of the transportation industry. Airlines, bus companies, truckers, and railroads have greater freedom to operate today than they did only a few years ago. The same trend can be seen in the field of communications, notably with regard to cable television.

While some industries require less regulation today, problems in others have led to more government regulation. The severe recession that struck the nation's economy in 2007–2008 prompted the passage of the Dodd-Frank Wall Street Reform and Consumer Protection Act in 2010.

In addition to the most sweeping financial reforms since the Great Depression, the law established a new independent regulatory commission, the Consumer Financial Protection Bureau (CFPB). As a "watchdog for the American consumer," the CFPB has the authority to make rules and regulations for all institutions that offer consumer financial services or products, as well as the task of educating consumers on financial matters. The commission is funded by the Federal Reserve, rather than by Congress, in an effort to keep it free from the influence of special interests.

HYPOTHESIZE In what ways might the Federal Communications Commission (FCC) use its legislative and judicial powers?

>> The Dodd-Frank Act was passed to try to help avoid another financial crisis like the one that occurred in 2008. **Analyzing Political Cartoons** What point does the cartoon make about the act?

Government vs. Private Corporations

GOVERNMENT CORPORATIONS	PRIVATE CORPORATIONS
Produces income that goes back into the agency's programs	Makes a profit beyond what is invested back into the business
Congress decides agency's purpose and functions	Investors decide purpose and function of the corporation
Officers and workers are public employees	Executives and other employees are private individuals, not government workers
President selects top officers with Senate approval	Investors or directors choose top officers
Financed by public funds	Financed by private investors
Federal Government owns stock	Shareholders own stock

>> Government corporations blur the line between public and private businesses. **Analyze Charts** What are some ways that government and private corporations are similar?

Government Corporations

A number of independent agencies are **government corporations.** They, too, are located within the vast executive branch and are subject to presidential direction and control. Unlike the other independent agencies, however, they were set up by Congress to carry out certain businesslike activities.

Congress established the first government corporation when it chartered the Bank of the United States in 1791. However, government corporations were little used until World War I and then during the Great Depression. In both periods, Congress set up dozens of corporations to carry out emergency programs. Several still exist—among them, the Federal Deposit Insurance Corporation (FDIC), which insures bank deposits, and the Export-Import Bank of the United States (Eximbank), which makes loans to help the export and sale of American goods abroad.

There are now more than 50 of these corporations. They do such things as provide intercity rail passenger service (the National Railroad Passenger Corporation, Amtrak); protect pension benefits (the Pension Benefit Guaranty Corporation); and generate, sell, and distribute electric power (the Tennessee Valley Authority).

Differences Between Government and Private Corporations The typical government corporation is set up much like a corporation in the private sector. It is run by a board of directors, with a general manager who directs the corporation's operations according to the policies laid down by the board. Most government corporations produce income that is plowed back into the agency's programs.

There are several differences between government and private corporations, however. Congress decides the purpose for which the public agencies exist and the functions they perform. Their officers are public officers; in fact, all who work for these corporations are public employees. The President selects most of the top officers of government corporations with Senate approval.

In addition, these public agencies are financed by public funds appropriated by Congress, not by private investors. The Federal Government, representing the American people, owns the stock.

The advantage most often claimed for these agencies is their flexibility. It is said that the government corporation, freed from the controls of regular departmental organization, can carry on its activities with the incentive, efficiency, and ability to experiment that make many private concerns successful. Whether that claim is valid or not is open to question. At the very least, it raises this complex issue: Is a public corporation's need for flexibility compatible with the basic democratic requirement that all public agencies be held responsible and accountable to the people?

>> Operated by the Army Corps of Engineers, the Center Hill Hydroelectric Dam in Tennessee features the ACOE's second largest flood control reservoir. The TVA operates 47 similar dams in the area.

Varying Levels of Independence The degree of independence and flexibility government corporations have varies considerably. In fact, some corporations are not independent at all. They are attached to an executive department.

The Commodity Credit Corporation (CCC), for example, is the government's major crop-loan and farm-subsidy agency. It is located within the Department of Agriculture, and the secretary of agriculture chairs its seven-member board. The CCC carries out most of its functions through a line agency in the Department of Agriculture—the Farm Service Agency—which is also subject to the direct control of the secretary.

Some corporations do have considerable independence, however. The Tennessee Valley Authority (TVA) is a case in point. It operates under a statute that gives it considerable discretion over its own programs. Although its budget is subject to review by the OMB, the President, and Congress, the TVA has a large say in the uses of the income its several operations produce.

? **COMPARE** Explain how independent regulatory commissions and government corporations are similar.

ASSESSMENT

1. **Connect** What is the relationship between independent agencies and partisan politics?
2. **Make Generalizations** Make one generalization that is true of *all* independent executive agencies.
3. **Synthesize** How does the Office of Personnel Management help the federal bureaucracy serve the American people?
4. **Apply Concepts** Identify the ways in which the independent regulatory commissions are an exception to both the principle of checks and balances and the principle of separation of powers.
5. **Integrate Information** Describe the several ways that Congress is involved with government corporations.

6.4 In *The Federalist* No. 72, Alexander Hamilton noted that the "actual conduct" of America's foreign affairs would be in the hands of "the assistants or deputies of the chief magistrate," the President. Today, most of the President's "assistants or deputies" in the field of foreign affairs are located within the Department of State.

>> U.S. soldiers in Afghanistan board a helicopter that will transport them to their next mission.

Interactive Flipped Video

Foreign Policy Overview

>> **Objectives**

Explain the major responsibilities of the Federal Government for foreign policy.

Summarize U.S. foreign policy during the first 150 years of its history, including its adherence to isolationism.

Show how World War II finally ended America's traditional policy of isolationism, giving way to internationalism and the principles of collective security and deterrence.

Analyze how today's U.S. foreign policy affects selected places and regions, as well as the significance to the United States of the location and key natural resources of selected global places or regions.

>> **Key Terms**

domestic affairs
foreign affairs
isolationism
foreign policy
collective security
deterrence
cold war
containment
détente
Isthmus of Panama
Pearl Harbor
Dwight Eisenhower
John F. Kennedy
Lyndon Johnson
Ronald Reagan
Harry Truman

What Is Foreign Policy?

Foreign affairs have been of prime importance from the nation's very beginnings, more than a dozen years before Hamilton penned his comment in *The Federalist*. Indeed, it is important to remember that the United States would have been hard pressed to win its independence without the aid of a foreign ally, France.

Every nation's **foreign policy** is actually many different policies on many different topics. It is made up of all of the stands and actions that a nation takes in every aspect of its relationships with other countries—diplomatic, military, commercial, and all others. To put the point another way, a nation's foreign policy includes everything that that nation's government says and everything that it does in world affairs.

Thus, American foreign policy consists of all of the Federal Government's official statements and all of its actions as it conducts this nation's foreign relations. It involves treaties and alliances, international trade, the defense budget, foreign economic and military aid, the United Nations and other international organizations, nuclear weapons testing, and disarmament negotiations.

It also includes the American position on oil imports and grain exports. Human rights, immigration, climate change, space exploration, fishing rights, cultural exchange programs, economic sanctions, computer technology exports, and a great many other matters are also subjects that fall under the heading "foreign policy."

Bedrock Principles Some aspects of foreign policy remain largely unchanged over time. For example, an insistence on freedom of the seas has been a basic part of American policy from the nation's beginnings. Other policies are more flexible. Two decades ago, resisting the ambitions of the Soviet Union was a basic part of American foreign policy. Since the fall of the Soviet Union, the United States and Russia have built close, if not always friendly, political, military, and economic ties; the United States has also developed close relations with several other former Soviet republics.

The location and key natural resources of various places or regions also has a bearing on American foreign policy. Neighboring countries, such as Canada and Mexico, have been a major focus of U.S. policy goals because their proximity makes it essential that the relationship with these countries is on good terms. By the same token, those countries that possess natural resources important to the United States, such as Middle Eastern oil or gold from China, are also focal points of U.S. foreign policy.

>> Japanese prime minister Shinzo Abe and President Trump shake hands at the start of their talks in Italy, prior to the Group of Seven industrialized nations' summit.

One other important point should be noted here: Because the United States is the world's only "superpower," American foreign policy has a dramatic effect on places and regions around the world. Thus, when that policy includes, for example, sanctions against a particular country due to human rights abuses, those sanctions are likely to have a crippling effect on the target country's economy.

The President is both the nation's chief diplomat and the commander in chief of its armed forces. Constitutionally and by tradition, the President bears the major responsibility for both making and conducting foreign policy. The President depends on a number of officials and agencies—Hamilton's "assistants or deputies"—to meet the immense responsibilities that come with this dual role.

CONNECT Why is studying a nation's foreign policy important? Give one example to support your answer.

Beginnings Through World War I

The basic purpose of American foreign policy has always been to protect the security and well-being of the United States—and so it is today. It would be impossible to present a full-blown, detailed history of America's foreign relations in this course. But we can review its major themes and highlights here.

With the coming of independence, and then for more than 150 years, the American people were chiefly concerned with **domestic affairs**—with events at home. **Foreign affairs,** this nation's relationships with other nations, were of little or no concern to them. Through that period, America's foreign relations were very largely shaped by a policy of **isolationism**—a purposeful refusal to become generally involved in the affairs of the rest of the world.

Isolationism arose in the earliest years of this nation's history. In his Farewell Address in 1796, George Washington declared that "our true policy" was "to steer clear of permanent alliances with any portion of the foreign world." Our "detached and distant situation," Washington said, made it desirable for us to have "as little political connection as possible" with other nations.

At the time, and for decades to come, isolationism seemed a wise policy to most Americans. The United States was a new and relatively weak nation with a great many problems, a huge continent to explore and settle, and two oceans to separate it from the rest of the world.

The policy of isolationism did not demand a *complete* separation from the rest of the world, however. From the first, the United States developed ties abroad by exchanging diplomatic representatives with other nations, making treaties with many of them, and building an extensive foreign commerce. In fact, isolationism was, over time, more a statement of our desire for non-involvement outside the Western Hemisphere than a description of United States policy within our own hemisphere.

The Monroe Doctrine James Monroe gave the policy of isolationism a clearer shape in 1823. In a historic message to Congress, he proclaimed what has been known ever since as the Monroe Doctrine.

A wave of revolutions had swept Latin America, destroying the old Spanish and Portuguese empires there. The United States viewed the prospect that other European powers would now help Spain and Portugal to take back their lost possessions as a threat to this country's security and a challenge to its economic interests.

In his message, President Monroe restated America's intentions to stay out of European affairs. He also warned the nations of Europe to stay out of the affairs of both North and South America. He declared that the United States would look on

> any attempt on their part to extend their system to any portion of this hemisphere as dangerous to our peace and safety.
>
> —Speech by President James Monroe to Congress, December 2, 1823

At first, most Latin Americans took little notice of this doctrine. They knew that it was really the Royal Navy and British interest in Latin American trade that protected them from European domination. But in 1867, the Monroe Doctrine got its first real test. While Americans were immersed in the Civil War, France invaded Mexico. The French leader, Napoleon III, installed Archduke Maximilian of Austria as Mexico's puppet emperor. In 1867, the United States backed the Mexicans in forcing the French to withdraw, and the Maximilian regime fell.

Later, as the United States became more powerful, many Latin Americans came to view the Monroe Doctrine differently. They saw it as a selfish policy designed to protect the political and economic interests of the United States, not the independence of other nations in the Western Hemisphere.

>> President Monroe (standing) is shown with key members of his Cabinet, including John Quincy Adams, who helped draft the Monroe Doctrine. **Describe** What was the intent of the Monroe Doctrine?

Expanding Influence Following its victory in the Revolutionary War, the United States began to expand across the continent almost at once. The Louisiana Purchase in 1803 doubled the nation's size in a single stroke and the Florida Purchase Treaty in 1819 completed its expansion to the south.

Through the second quarter of the nineteenth century, the United States pursued what most Americans believed was this nation's "Manifest Destiny": the mission to expand its boundaries across the continent to the Pacific Ocean. By 1900, the nation had not only accomplished that task, it had spread its influence beyond the continental boundaries to become both a colonial and a world power. The nation's interests now extended to Alaska, to the tip of Latin America, and across the Pacific to the Philippines.

Latin America in the 1900s The threat of European intervention in the Western Hemisphere that troubled President Monroe declined in the second half of the nineteenth century. That threat was replaced by problems within the hemisphere. Political instability, revolutions, unpaid foreign debts, and injuries to citizens and property of other countries plagued Central and South America.

Under what came to be known as the Roosevelt Corollary to the Monroe Doctrine, the United States began to police Latin America in the early 1900s. Several times, the marines were used to quell revolutions and other unrest in Nicaragua, Haiti, Cuba, and elsewhere in Latin America.

In 1903, Panama revolted and became independent of Colombia, with America's blessing. In the same year, the United States gained the right to build a canal across the **Isthmus of Panama**. The canal was significant, because it dramatically shortened the time required to sail between the East and West coasts of the United States, thus making global shipping much cheaper. The canal indirectly affected Panama by providing jobs and a bustling trade in the region around the canal.

In 1917, the United States purchased the Virgin Islands from Denmark to help guard the canal. Many in Latin America resented these and other steps. They complained of "the Colossus of the North," of "Yankee imperialism," and of "dollar diplomacy"—and many still do.

This country's Latin American policies took a dramatic turn in the 1930s. Theodore Roosevelt's Corollary was replaced by Franklin Roosevelt's Good Neighbor Policy, a conscious attempt to win friends to the south by reducing this nation's political and military interventions in the region.

Today, the central provision of the Monroe Doctrine—the warning against foreign encroachments in the Western Hemisphere—is set out in the Inter-American Treaty of Reciprocal Assistance (the Rio Pact) of 1947. Still, the United States is, without question, the dominant power in the Western Hemisphere, and the Monroe Doctrine remains a vital part of American foreign policy.

A FAIR FIELD AND NO FAVOR!
UNCLE SAM: "I'M OUT FOR COMMERCE, NOT CONQUEST!"

>> This 1899 political cartoon refers to the Open Door policy, which denounced trade barriers in China. **Analyzing Political Cartoons** What point does the cartoon make about U.S. goals in China?

The United States and China Historically, American foreign-policy interests have centered on Europe and Latin America. But America has also been involved in Asia since the mid-1800s. Forty-five years before the United States acquired territory in the Pacific, the U.S. Navy's Commodore Matthew Perry had opened Japan to American trade.

By the late nineteenth century, however, America's thriving trade in Asia was being seriously threatened. The British, French, Germans, and Japanese were each ready to take slices of the Chinese coast as their own exclusive trading preserves. In 1899, Secretary of State John Hay announced this country's insistence on an Open Door policy in China. That doctrine promoted equal trade access for all nations, and demanded that China's independence and sovereignty over its own territory be preserved.

The other major powers came to accept the American position, however reluctantly. Relations between the United States and Japan worsened from that point on, up to the climax at Pearl Harbor in 1941. Over the same period, the United States built increasingly strong ties with China; but those ties were cut when communists won control of the Chinese mainland in 1949. For nearly 30 years, the United States and the People's Republic of China refused diplomatic recognition of one another.

World War I Germany's submarine campaign against American shipping in the North Atlantic forced the United States out of its isolationist cocoon in 1917. America entered World War I "to make the world safe for democracy."

With the defeat of Germany and the Central Powers, however, America pulled back from the involvements brought on by the war. The United States refused to join the League of Nations, and many Americans were determined to avoid future entanglement in problems in Europe and the rest of the world.

? APPLY CONCEPTS Why did the direction of American foreign policy change in Latin America?

World War II to the End of the Cold War

America's historic commitment to isolationism was finally ended by World War II. The United States became directly involved in the war when the Japanese attacked the American naval base at **Pearl Harbor** in Hawaii on December 7, 1941. From that point on—along with the British, the Russians, the Chinese, and our other Allies—the United States waged an all-out effort to defeat the Axis Powers (Germany, Italy, and Japan).

Under the direction and leadership of President Franklin Roosevelt, the United States became the "arsenal of democracy." American resources and industrial capacity supplied most of the armaments and other materials we and our Allies needed to win World War II. Within a very short time, the United States was transformed into the mightiest military power in the world—and it has remained so ever since.

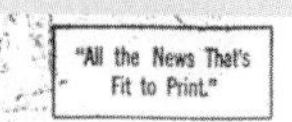

"All the News That's Fit to Print."

The New York Times.

THE WEATHER

VOL. LXIV...NO. 20,923. NEW YORK, SATURDAY, MAY 8, 1915.—TWENTY-FOUR PAGES. ONE CENT

LUSITANIA SUNK BY A SUBMARINE, PROBABLY 1,000 DEAD; TWICE TORPEDOED OFF IRISH COAST; SINKS IN 15 MINUTES; AMERICANS ABOARD INCLUDED VANDERBILT AND FROHM... WASHINGTON BELIEVES THAT A GRAVE CRISIS IS AT H...

SHOCKS THE PRESIDENT

Washington Deeply Stirred by Disaster and Fears a Crisis.

BULLETINS AT WHITE HOUSE

Wilson Reads Them Closely, but is Silent on the Nation's Course.

HINTS OF CONGRESS CALL

Loss of Lusitania Recalls Firm Tone of Our First Warning to Germany.

CAPITAL FULL OF RUMORS

SOME DEAD...

STEWARDTE...

SHIP LISTS

ATTACKED

The Lost Cunard Steamship Lusitania

Cunard Office Here Besieged for News; Fate of 1,918 on Lusitania Long in Doubt

Loss of the Lusitania Fills London With Horror and Utter Amazement

>> The sinking of the *Lusitania*, a British liner outfitted for war but carrying civilian passengers, turned public opinion against Germany and ultimately led the United States to enter World War I.

Collective Security The coming of World War II brought a historic shift from a position of isolationism to one of internationalism. This nation's foreign policy has been cast in that newer direction for more than 60 years now. Even so, the overall objective of that policy remains what it has always been: the protection of the security and well-being of the United States.

Following World War II, the United States and most of the rest of a war-weary world looked to the principle of **collective security** to keep international peace and order. America hoped to forge a world community in which at least most nations would agree to act together against any nation that threatened the peace.

To that end, this country took the lead in creating the United Nations in 1945. The organization's charter declares that the UN was formed to promote international cooperation and so "to save succeeding generations from the scourge of war . . . and to maintain international peace and security."

It soon became clear, however, that the UN would not shape the future of the world. Rather, international security would depend largely on the nature of the relations between the two superpowers, the United States and the Soviet Union. Those relations, never very close, quickly deteriorated—and for the next 40 years, American foreign policy was built around that fact.

With the breakup of the Soviet Union, the United States became the only superpower in today's world. Still, collective security remains a cornerstone of American policy. The United States has supported the United Nations and other efforts to further international cooperation. This country has also taken another path

>> The attack on Pearl Harbor, which President Roosevelt called "unprovoked and dastardly," left 2,403 Americans dead and the U.S. fleet decimated. It also led to a U.S. declaration of war.

Interactive Timeline

to collective security: the building of a network of regional security alliances.

Deterrence The principle of deterrence has also been a part of American foreign policy since World War II. Basically, **deterrence** is the strategy of maintaining military might at so great a level that that very strength will deter—discourage, prevent—an attack on this country by any hostile power.

President **Harry Truman** initiated deterrence as U.S.–Soviet relations worsened after World War II. Every President since President Truman's day has reaffirmed the strategy, and deterrence was a key factor in the collapse of the Soviet Union.

The Cold War One cannot hope to understand either recent or current American foreign policy without a knowledge of the long years of the cold war. The **cold war** was a period of more than 40 years during which relations between the two superpowers were at least tense and, more often than not, distinctly hostile. It was, for the most part, not a "hot war" of military action, but rather a time of threats, posturing, and military buildup.

At the Yalta Conference in early 1945, Soviet Premier Josef Stalin had agreed with President Franklin Roosevelt and British Prime Minister Winston Churchill to promote the establishment of "democratic governments" by "free elections" in the liberated countries of Eastern Europe. Instead, the Soviets imposed dictatorial regimes on those countries. The Soviets also looked to exploit postwar chaos in other nations, as well. In 1946, Churchill declared that "an iron curtain" had descended across the continent.

The Truman Doctrine The United States began to counter the aggressive actions of the Soviet Union in the early months of 1947. Both Greece and Turkey were in danger of falling under Soviet control. At President Harry Truman's urgent request, Congress approved a massive program of economic and military aid, and both countries remained free. In his message to Congress, the President declared that it was now

> the policy of the United States to support free peoples who are resisting attempted subjugation by armed minorities or by outside pressures.
>
> —Speech by President Harry S Truman to Congress, March 12, 1947

The Truman Doctrine soon became part of a broader American plan for dealing with the Soviet Union. From mid-1947 through the 1980s, the United States followed

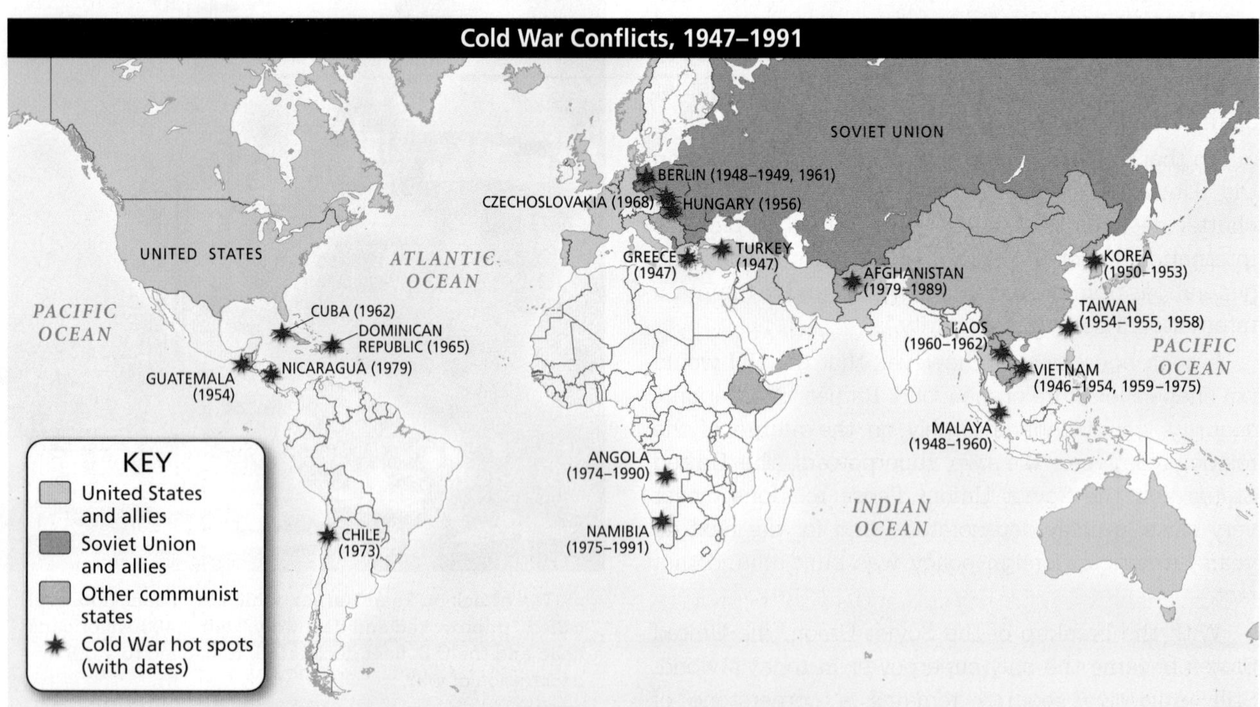

>> Competition between the two superpowers became a source of political tension; nations allied themselves with one or the other. **Analyze Maps** What do most of these locations have in common?

the policy of **containment.** That policy was rooted in the belief that if communism could be kept within its existing boundaries, it would collapse under the weight of its own internal weaknesses.

The United States and the Soviet Union confronted one another often during the cold war years. Two of those confrontations were of major, near-war proportions. The first, the Berlin blockade, occurred in 1948–1949, when the Soviets tried to force the United States and its allies to abandon the German city of Berlin to Soviet domination. The other major incident, the Cuban missile crisis, arose in 1962. The United States threatened war over the placement of Soviet nuclear missiles on the island of Cuba. In both cases, the Soviets backed down in the face of determined American resistance.

Not all cold war conflicts ended peacefully, however. During the postwar period, the United States fought two hot wars against communist forces in Asia.

Conflict in Korea The Korean War began on June 25, 1950. Communist North Korea (the People's Democratic Republic of Korea) attacked South Korea (the UN-sponsored Republic of Korea). Immediately, the UN's Security Council called on all UN members to help South Korea repel the invasion.

The war lasted for more than three years. It pitted the United Nations Command, largely made up of American and South Korean forces, against Soviet-trained and Soviet-equipped North Korean and communist Chinese troops. Cease-fire negotiations began in July 1951, but fighting continued until an armistice was signed on July 27, 1953.

The long and bitter Korean conflict did not end in a clear-cut UN victory. Still, the invasion was turned back, and the Republic of Korea remained standing. For the first time in history, armed forces of several nations fought under an international flag against aggression. There is no telling how far the tide of that aggression might have been carried had the United States not come to the aid of South Korea.

The Vietnam War In the years following World War II, a nationalist movement arose in French Indochina—today, Vietnam. Vietnamese nationalists were seeking independence from their French colonial rulers. Made up mostly of communist forces led by Ho Chi Minh, the nationalists fought and defeated the French in a lengthy conflict. Under truce agreements signed in 1954, the country was divided into two zones. The communist-dominated North Vietnam, with its capital in Hanoi, and an anticommunist South Vietnam, with its capital in Saigon.

>> In 1948, the people of Berlin were faced with starvation due to a Soviet blockade of their city. In response, the U.S. airlifted food and other supplies to the city for 11 months.

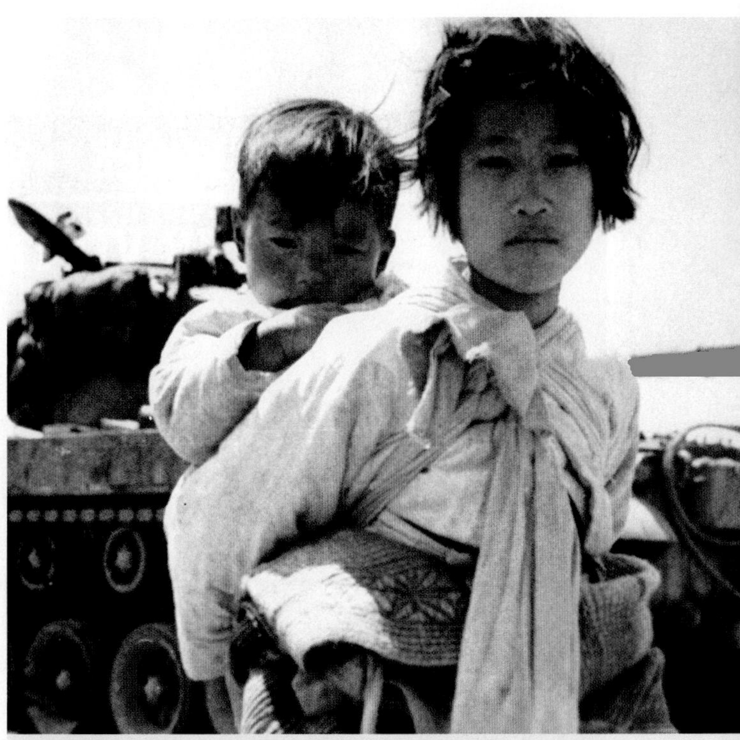

>> After World War II, Soviet forces occupied North Korea and U.S. forces occupied South Korea (shown here). Political tension between them led to UN intervention in 1950.

Almost at once, communist guerrillas (the Viet Cong), supported by the North Vietnamese, began a civil war in South Vietnam. Because President **Dwight Eisenhower** and other foreign policy experts believed that South Vietnam was critical to the security of all of Southeast Asia, the Eisenhower administration responded with economic and then military aid to Saigon. President **John F. Kennedy** increased that aid, and President **Lyndon Johnson** committed the United States to full-scale war in early 1965.

In 1969, President Richard Nixon began what he called the "Vietnamization" of the war. Over the next four years, the United States gradually pulled troops out of combat. Finally, the two sides reached a cease-fire agreement in early 1973, and the United States withdrew its last units. In 1975, South Vietnam fell to the communist North.

The ill-fated war in Vietnam cost the United States more than 58,000 American lives. As the war dragged on, millions of Americans came to oppose American involvement in Southeast Asia—and traces of the divisiveness of that period can still be seen in the politics of today.

Détente: Successes and Failures As the United States withdrew from Vietnam, the Nixon administration embarked on a policy of **détente.** In this case, the policy of détente included a purposeful attempt to improve relations with the Soviet Union and, separately, with China.

President Richard Nixon flew to Beijing in 1972 to begin a new era in American-Chinese relations. His visit paved the way for further contacts and, finally, for formal diplomatic ties between the United States and the People's Republic of China. Less than three months later, Mr. Nixon journeyed to Moscow. There, he and Soviet Premier Leonid Brezhnev signed the first Strategic Arms Limitations Talks agreement, SALT I—a five-year pact in which both sides agreed to a measure of control over their nuclear weapons.

Relations with mainland China have improved in fits and starts since the 1970s. Efforts at détente with the Soviets, however, proved less successful. Moscow continued to apply its expansionist pressures and provided economic and military aid to revolutionary movements around the world.

In 1979, an effort by the Soviet Union to impose a communist regime in Afghanistan was met by unexpectedly stiff resistance of armed groups of Afghans and their supporters around the region. The United States, acting largely in secret through the CIA, provided support to some of the groups resisting communist expansion. This type of war by proxy between the United States and the Soviet

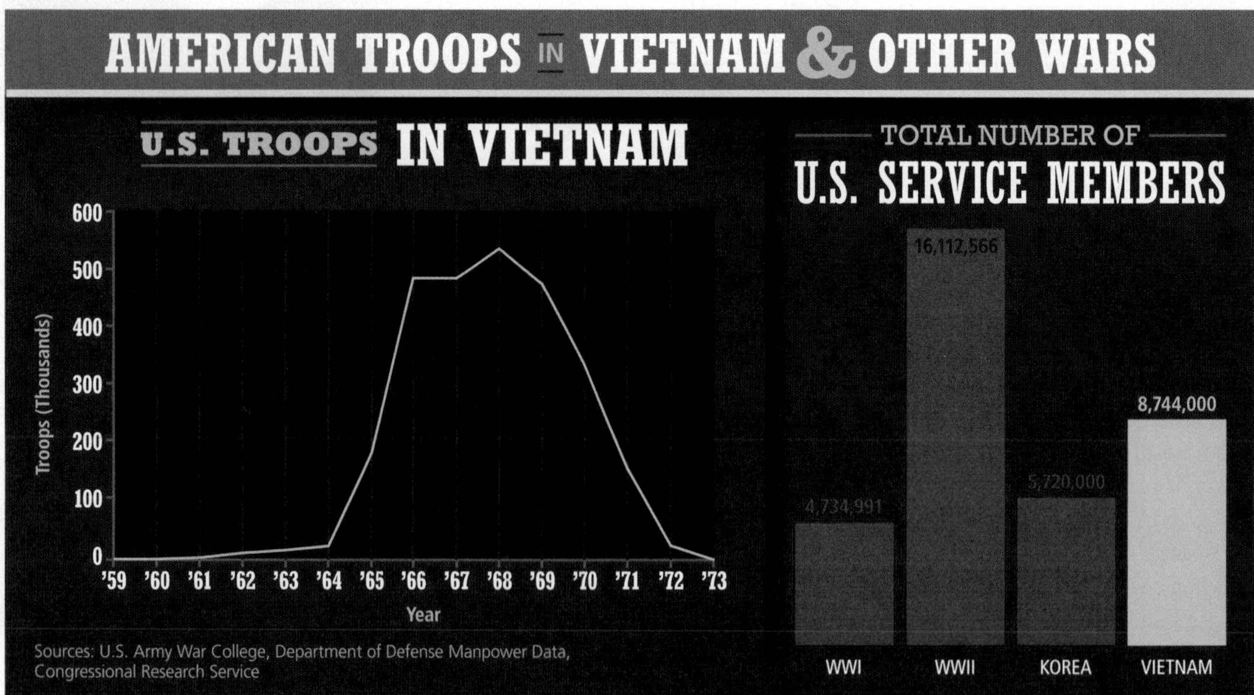

>> The U.S. committed to full-scale war in Vietnam in 1965 and began to end that involvement in 1969. **Analyze Charts** According to the bar graph, how many total troops served in the wars shown?

Union became common during the cold war. After the aggression against Afghanistan, the Carter and then the Reagan administrations placed a renewed emphasis on the containment of Soviet power.

The Cold War Ends Relations between the United States and the USSR improved remarkably after Mikhail Gorbachev came to power in Moscow in 1985. He and President **Ronald Reagan** met in a series of summit conferences that helped pave the way to the end of the cold war. Those meetings, focused on arms limitations, eased long-standing tensions.

Certainly, Mikhail Gorbachev deserves much credit for the fundamental change in the Soviets' approach to world affairs. But, just as certainly, that historic change was prompted by deepening political and economic chaos in Eastern Europe and within the Soviet Union itself—by conditions that ultimately brought the collapse of the Soviet Union in late 1991.

The fact that the cold war is now a matter of history should also be seen in this light: The American policies of deterrence and containment, first put in place in 1947, finally realized their goals.

>> At this summit meeting in Geneva, Switzerland, in 1985, President Reagan and Soviet leader Gorbachev agreed "that a nuclear war cannot be won and must never be fought."

? DRAW CONCLUSIONS How were the U.S policies of deterrence and containment used during the Cold War?

Today's Foreign Policy Challenges

The period from the 1940s onward has been marked by a profound change in the place of the United States in world affairs. The coming of World War II finally convinced the American people that neither they nor anyone else can live in isolation—that, in many ways, and whether we like it or not, the world of today is indeed "one world." The well-being of everyone in this country—in fact, the very survival of the United States—is affected by much that happens elsewhere on the globe. If nothing else, the realities of ultra-rapid travel and instantaneous communications make it clear that we now live in a "global village."

>> The presence of U.S.-owned businesses in the Yuyuan Temple Bazaar, in Shanghai, China, is evidence of America's ever-growing presence in the global economy.

Economic conditions elsewhere in the world, for example, have a direct and often immediate effect on and in this country. The American economy has become an intertwined part of a truly global economy, linked by international banking, multinational corporations, and worldwide investments that transcend national boundaries.

Wars and other political upheavals abroad also have an impact on the United States and on the daily lives of the American people. Five times over the past century, the United States fought major wars abroad; and in several other instances, it has committed its armed forces to lesser, but significant, foreign conflicts. The ongoing war in Afghanistan, terrorists' plots in Europe, Asia, and at home, the continuing Arab-Israeli disputes in the Middle East—these and other circumstances around the globe threaten the security of the United States.

Other sobering situations include the fact that the volatile country of North Korea appears bent on becoming a nuclear power. Iran, too, has failed to convince the international community that its nuclear program has only peaceful purposes, although late 2013 saw encouraging signs of progress in that regard. Seemingly endless upheavals elsewhere in today's world also pose challenges to foreign policymakers—not the least of them the civil war in Syria and the rising influence of China. In our own neighborhood, the instability of Mexico and tensions with Venezuela and its President, Nicolás Maduro, are also cause for concern.

The Middle East The Middle East is both oil rich and conflict ridden. America's foreign policy interests in the Middle East have, for decades, been torn in two quite opposite directions: by its long-standing support of Israel and by the critical importance of Arab oil.

>> In 1948, David Ben-Gurion became the first prime minister of the newly established state of Israel.

The United Nations created Israel as an independent state on May 14, 1948, and the United States recognized the new Jewish state within a matter of minutes. Since that time, this country has been Israel's close ally while also attempting to strengthen its ties with most of the Arab states in the volatile Middle East.

With the active involvement of President Jimmy Carter, Israel and Egypt negotiated the historic Camp David Accords in 1979. That agreement led to the end of more than 30 years of hostilities between those two countries. Israel and Jordan signed a similar pact in 1994.

In 1993, Israel and the Palestinian Liberation Organization (PLO) signed the Oslo Accords. In them, the two nations officially recognized one another and Israel agreed to limited Palestinian self-rule. Beyond those first steps, however, the promise of the Oslo Accords has yet to be realized, despite both UN and United States efforts to bring the two sides together.

The "Arab Spring" revolutions that swept through the Middle East and North Africa in 2010 and 2011 further complicated matters, causing widespread instability in the region and rising hostility to Israel. The uprisings toppled authoritarian governments in a dizzying number of countries, including Egypt, Libya, Yemen, Tunisia, and others.

The worst incarnation of the perilous political environment could be seen in the country of Syria. There, protests against dictator Bashar al-Assad led to the outbreak of civil war in 2012. The ongoing fighting sent massive waves of refugees pouring into neighboring countries and threatened to ignite a larger, regional conflict. In 2013, the United States charged the Syrian government with unleashing a chemical weapons attack against its own people. After threats of military strikes by the United States, Assad finally agreed to comply with a UN resolution calling for the destruction of Syria's chemical weapons stockpiles.

Afghanistan and Iraq The Soviet Union's invasion of Afghanistan in 1979 introduced an era of war and devastation to that Central Asian country. Although the Soviets left Afghanistan in defeat in 1989, the occupation led to civil war. By the late 1990s, an ultraconservative political and religious faction, the Taliban, had gained control over most of Afghanistan. Under the Taliban, Afghanistan became a haven for Islamist militants, including Osama bin Laden, the leader of the Al Qaeda militant organization.

On September 11, 2001, the Al Qaeda Islamist terrorist group hijacked four commercial passenger airplanes and crashed two of them into the World Trade Center in New York City and one into the Pentagon in northern Virginia. A fourth plane, aimed at the

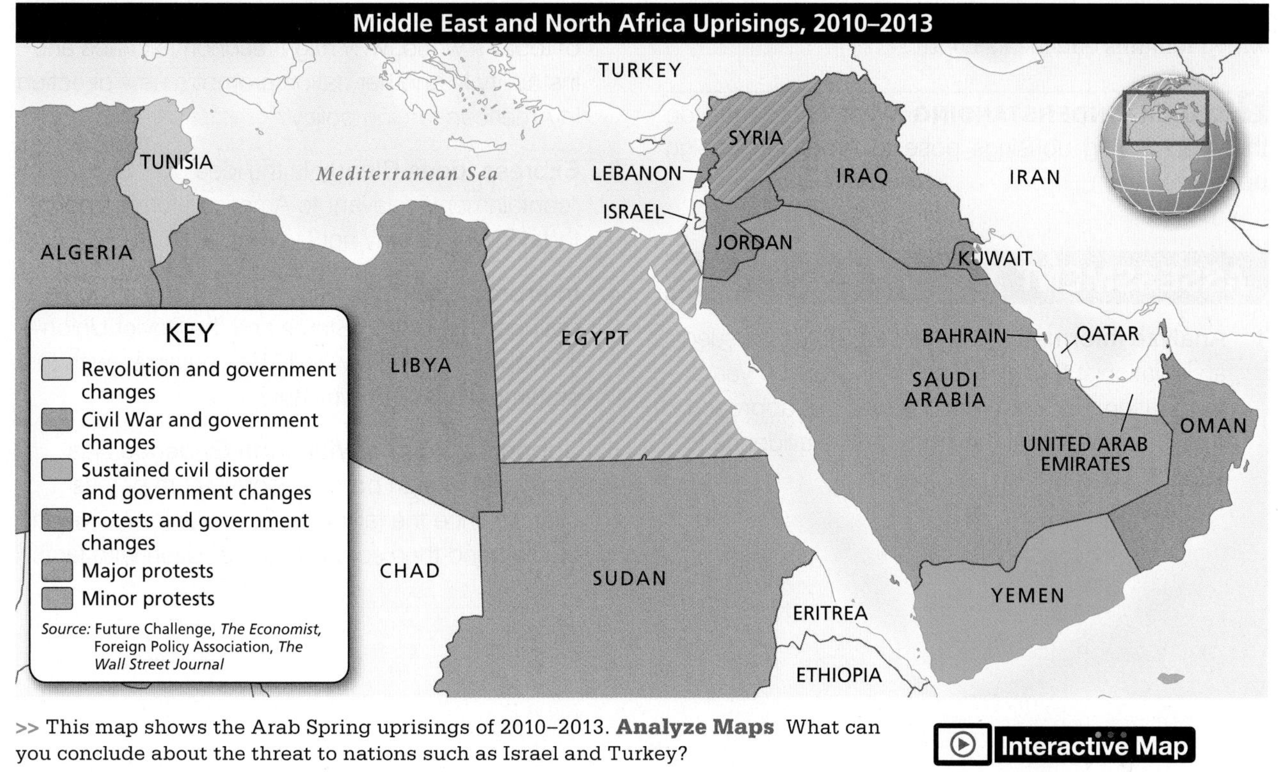

>> This map shows the Arab Spring uprisings of 2010–2013. **Analyze Maps** What can you conclude about the threat to nations such as Israel and Turkey?

Interactive Map

White House, crashed into a Pennsylvania field after passengers rushed the hijackers in the cockpit. Nearly 3,000 people died in the attacks. In response, the United States and its NATO allies toppled the Taliban regime, which had sheltered leader Osama bin Laden and Al Qaeda.

The Taliban reemerged in subsequent years, however, leading to a protracted U.S. military campaign in Afghanistan. Troop withdrawals began in late 2012, but the persistent Taliban threat prompted military and government leaders to plan to keep some American troops in Afghanistan until 2014 and likely beyond.

During the early 2000s, the U.S. waged a second war in Iraq. After the first Gulf War (1991), Iraq's president Saddam Hussein agreed to destroy his country's stock of chemical and biological weapons. By 2003, however, he had failed to convince the international community that he had honored that promise. Consequently, a coalition led by the United States and Great Britain launched the second Gulf War. Iraq was conquered and Saddam Hussein's regime toppled in less than six weeks. Hussein was captured, tried, and executed in 2006.

Subsequent efforts to establish a democracy in Iraq proved difficult, however. As a result, United States troops remained in the country until the end of 2011. The war cost the United States some $1 trillion and more than 4,400 American lives. In the wake of the U.S. withdrawal, the international community was troubled by what appeared to be Prime Minister Nuri Kamal al-Maliki's slide toward dictatorship. Today, Iraq's fate—and history's assessment of the success or failure of the American intervention there—rests in the hands of Iraq's leaders, its security forces, and its people.

Libya Since 1969, Muammar al-Qaddafi ruled the North African country of Libya with an iron hand. Inspired by other Arab Spring uprisings, rebels challenged his control in 2011. Qaddafi responded with brutal force, prompting the United Nations to authorize military action against the dictator's regime. In early 2012, the United States joined a multinational coalition that unleashed a devastating hailstorm of air strikes on pro-Qaddafi targets in Libya. The intervention turned the tide of war in favor of the rebels. By August, they had taken the capital city of Tripoli. Qaddafi himself was captured and killed in October.

Democratic elections were held in mid-2012, but it soon became all too apparent that problems remained. On September 11, 2012—the anniversary of the 2001 attacks on the World Trade Center and Pentagon—an assault on the U.S. embassy in Benghazi led to the deaths of four Americans, including ambassador J. Christopher Stevens. The attacks were believed to have been carried out by local militia groups. Today, the Libyan government struggles to gain control over these groups and to stabilize the country, much of which remains outside its control.

? CHECK UNDERSTANDING What challenges do the Arab Spring uprisings pose to American foreign policy?

ASSESSMENT

1. **Analyze Information** The United States pursued an isolationist foreign policy for its first 150 years as a nation. For what reasons was this approach a reasonable one at the time? ? Give evidence to support your answer.
2. **Apply Concepts** Given the interconnected nature of today's world, why might economic chaos and instability in another nation prompt a new direction in American foreign policy?
3. **Express Ideas Clearly** Is the idea of "containment" relevant to American foreign policy today? Why or why not?
4. **Interpret** "The Cold War was not just a struggle between the United States and the Soviet Union—it involved the entire world." Do you agree with this statement? Why or why not?
5. **Support a Point of View with Evidence** Has American foreign policy become more or less difficult since the fall of the Soviet Union? Give an opinion and then support your position with facts.

6.5 **The State Department, headed by the secretary of state, is the President's right arm in foreign affairs. The President names the secretary of state, subject to confirmation by the Senate. It is to the secretary of state and to the Department of State that the President looks for advice and assistance in both the formulation and the conduct of the nation's foreign policy.**

>> Secretary of State Rex Tillerson, appointed by President Trump, is greeted upon arrival in Beijing, China. The secretary of state is responsible for helping to carry out the President's foreign policy.

Interactive Flipped Video

Diplomacy

America's Representatives to the World

The Secretary of State The secretary of state ranks first among the members of the President's Cabinet. That ranking speaks to the importance of the office, and also to the fact that the State Department was the first of the now 15 executive departments that Congress created.

A Department of Foreign Affairs had first been created in 1781 under the Articles of Confederation. Congress re-created it in 1789 as the first major unit in the executive branch under the Constitution. Later that year, its name was changed to the Department of State.

President George Washington appointed **Thomas Jefferson** as the nation's first secretary of state, in 1789. Bill Clinton appointed the first woman to hold the post, **Madeleine Albright**, in 1997. **Colin Powell**, who served as secretary of state in George W. Bush's first term (2001 to 2005), became the first African American to occupy the office; and his successor, **Condoleezza Rice**, who is both a woman and an African American, served from 2005 to 2009. She was replaced by another major personality—former First Lady and former senator from New York, **Hillary Rodham Clinton**, who held the post from

>> Objectives

Describe the functions, components, and organization of the State Department and its overseas representatives.

Examine how the U.S. government uses economic resources in foreign policy, including foreign aid.

Describe the major regional security alliances developed by the United States.

Examine the history, structure, and work of the United Nations and its relationship with the United States.

>> Key Terms

right of legation
ambassador
diplomatic immunity
passport
visa
foreign aid
regional security alliances
NATO
United Nations
Security Council
Trusteeship Council
Thomas Jefferson
Madeleine Albright
Colin Powell
Condoleezza Rice
Hillary Rodham Clinton
John Kerry
Ayatollah Khomeini
George C. Marshall
Balkans
Slobodan Milosevic
Franklin D. Roosevelt
Winston Churchill

2009 to 2013. In 2013, Hillary Clinton stepped down, and former senator from Massachusetts **John Kerry** became secretary of state.

Today, the duties of the secretary relate almost entirely to foreign affairs. That is, they center on the making and conduct of policy and on the management of the department, its many overseas posts, and its workforce of more than 40,000 men and women.

Some Presidents—most famously, Woodrow Wilson and Franklin Roosevelt—have tended to ignore their secretaries of state and have handled many foreign policy matters personally and quite often directly. Others, notably Richard Nixon, Gerald Ford, and both Bushes, have chosen instead to rely on their national security advisors. Some chief executives—in particular, the earlier ones—have chosen to delegate a large share of the responsibility for matters of foreign policy to the secretary. President Obama, for example, made it clear that he considered Secretary Clinton to be a major player in both the formation and the conduct of American foreign policy.

State Department Organization The State Department is organized along both geographic and functional lines. Some of its agencies, such as the Bureau of African Affairs and the Bureau of Near Eastern Affairs, deal with matters involving particular regions of the world.

Other agencies have broader missions—for example, the Bureau of International Narcotics and Law Enforcement Affairs, sometimes called "Drugs 'n' Thugs." Most bureaus are headed by an assistant secretary and include several offices. Thus, both the Office of Passport Services and the Office of Visa Services are found in the Bureau of Consular Affairs.

>> Secretary of State Henry Kissinger (left) met with Communist leader Leonid Brezhnev in 1973, the same year Kissinger received the Nobel Peace Prize for his efforts to end the Vietnam War.

The Right of Legation Some 12,000 men and women now represent the United States as members of the Foreign Service, many of them serving abroad. Under international law, every nation has the **right of legation**—the right to send and receive diplomatic representatives. International law consists of those rules and principles that guide sovereign states in their dealings with one another and in their treatment of foreign nationals (private persons and groups). Its sources include treaties, decisions of international courts, and custom. Treaties are the most important source today. The right of legation is an ancient practice. Its history can be traced back to the Egyptian civilization of 6,000 years ago.

The Second Continental Congress named this nation's first foreign service officer in 1778. That year, it chose Benjamin Franklin to be America's minister to France. He served in that capacity for nearly eight years.

American Ambassadors An **ambassador** is the official representative of a sovereign state in the conduct of its foreign affairs. For some five centuries now, most of the formal contacts between sovereign nations—that is, most of their diplomatic relationships—have been conducted through their duly appointed ambassadors.

In this country, ambassadors are appointed by the President, with Senate consent, and they serve at his pleasure. Today, the United States is represented by an ambassador stationed at the capital of each sovereign state this nation recognizes. Thus, American embassies are now located in more than 180 countries around the world.

The United States now maintains over 260 diplomatic and consular offices abroad as well. There, Foreign Service officers promote American interests in a multitude of ways—for example, encouraging trade, gathering intelligence data, advising persons who seek to enter this country, and aiding American citizens who are abroad and in need of legal advice or other help.

Some ambassadorships are much desired political plums, and whenever a new President moves into the White House, he typically makes many new appointments. Too often, Presidents have appointed

THE IRAN HOSTAGE CRISIS

U.S. EMBASSIES

- Embassies serve diplomatic functions, and are also symbols of the U.S. abroad.
- Tensions between nations have led to attacks on U.S. embassies at times.

AMERICAN HOSTAGES

- In 1979, Iranian students attacked the American embassy in Tehran.
- They held U.S. embassy staff hostage for 444 days.
- The Iran hostage crisis was an unusual assault against both the U.S. and international law.

An American hostage is paraded in front of the media by Iranian militants in 1979.

YELLOW RIBBONS

- During the crisis, yellow ribbons were tied to trees to symbolize public support for the hostages.

>> International law requires the "receiving state" to protect the safety of diplomats and treat them with respect. **Analyze Charts** How did the Iran hostage crisis breach international law?

people to ambassadorships and other major diplomatic posts as a reward for those individuals' support—financial and otherwise—of the President's election to office. However, in many cases these ranks are filled with career diplomats in the Foreign Service.

President Harry Truman named the first African American, Edward R. Dudley, as an ambassador to Liberia, in 1949. Later that same year President Truman also appointed the first woman, Eugenie Anderson, as our ambassador to Denmark.

Special Diplomats Those persons whom the President names to certain other top diplomatic posts also carry the rank of ambassador. Examples include the United States representative to the UN and the American member of the North Atlantic Treaty Council. The President also often assigns the personal rank of ambassador to those diplomats who take on special assignments abroad—for example, representing the United States in the ongoing efforts to resolve Arab-Israeli differences.

Diplomatic Privileges In international law, every sovereign state is supreme within its own boundaries. All persons or things found within that state's territory are subject to its jurisdiction.

As a major exception to that rule, ambassadors are regularly granted **diplomatic immunity**—they are not subject to the laws of the state to which they are accredited. They cannot be arrested, sued, or taxed. Their official residences (embassies) cannot be entered or searched without their consent, and all official communications and other properties are protected. All other embassy personnel and their families receive this same immunity.

Diplomatic immunity is essential to the ability of every nation to conduct its foreign relations. The practice assumes that diplomats will not abuse their privileged status. If a host government finds a diplomat's conduct unacceptable, that official may be declared *persona non grata* and expelled from the country. The mistreatment of diplomats is considered a major breach of international law.

Diplomatic immunity is a generally accepted practice. There are exceptions, however. The most serious breach in modern times occurred in Iran in late 1979. Militant followers of the **Ayatollah Khomeini** seized the American embassy in Tehran on November 4 of that year; 66 Americans were taken hostage and 52 were held for 444 days. The Iranians finally released the hostages moments after Ronald Reagan became President on January 20, 1981.

Passports and Visas A **passport** is a legal document issued by a state that identifies a person as a citizen of that state. It grants that person a right of protection while traveling abroad and the right to return to the homeland. Passports entitle their holders to the privileges accorded to them by international custom and treaties. Few countries will admit persons who do not hold valid passports.

The State Department's Office of Passport Services now issues more than ten million passports to Americans each year. Do not confuse passports with visas. A **visa** is a permit to enter another state and must be obtained from the country one wishes to enter. Trips to most foreign countries require visas today. Most visas to enter this country are issued at American consulates abroad.

? APPLY CONCEPTS To what degree do the Constitution or acts of Congress require that the secretary of state take charge of important international diplomacy?

American Foreign Aid

Do you know this ancient saying: "Those who help others help themselves"? You will see that that maxim underlies two basic elements of present-day American foreign policy: foreign aid and regional security alliances.

What Is Foreign Aid? **Foreign aid**—the economic and military aid given to other countries—has been a basic feature of American foreign policy for about seventy years. It began with the Lend-Lease program of the early 1940s, through which the United States gave nearly $50 billion in food, munitions, and other supplies to its allies in World War II. Since then, this country has sent about more than $900 billion in aid to more than 180 countries around the world.

Foreign aid became an important part of the containment policy beginning with American aid to Greece and Turkey in 1947. The United States also helped its European allies rebuild after the devastation of World War II. Under the Marshall Plan, named for its author, Secretary of State **George C. Marshall**, the United States poured some $13 billion into 16 nations in Western Europe between 1948 and 1952.

Purposes of Foreign Aid Over the years, foreign aid has taken several different directions. Immediately after World War II, American aid was primarily economic. Since that time, however, military assistance has assumed a larger role in aid policy. Until the mid-1950s, Europe received the lion's share of American help. Today, the largest amounts have gone to nations in Asia, the Middle East, and Africa.

Most aid, which makes up some one percent of the federal budget, has been sent to those nations regarded as the most critical to the realization of American foreign policy objectives. In recent years, Afghanistan, Iraq, Israel, Pakistan, Haiti, and various African countries have been the major recipients of American help, both economically and militarily. These countries are all of strategic importance to the United States, in some cases due to their location or natural resources, and in others, due to military or economic ties.

Most foreign aid money must be used to buy American goods and services. So, most of the billions spent for that aid amounts to a substantial subsidy to both business and labor in this country. The

Travel Documents

PASSPORTS	VISAS
• Issued by a government and identifies the bearer as a citizen or national of the issuing country • Entitles the bearer to consular protection abroad and to return to his or her country of citizenship • Valid for 10 years • Three types: diplomatic, official, tourist	• Issued by the country the individual requests permission to enter • Permits the traveler to remain in a country for a specified period of time, but does not guarantee entry • Valid only for the time period stated • Of many types, including: transit, tourist, business, and student

>> In the past, a valid passport was all one needed to travel abroad and enter most countries. Today, a visa is often required as well. **Analyze Charts** Why do you think this is now the case?

Distribution of Aid, 1992 vs. 2012

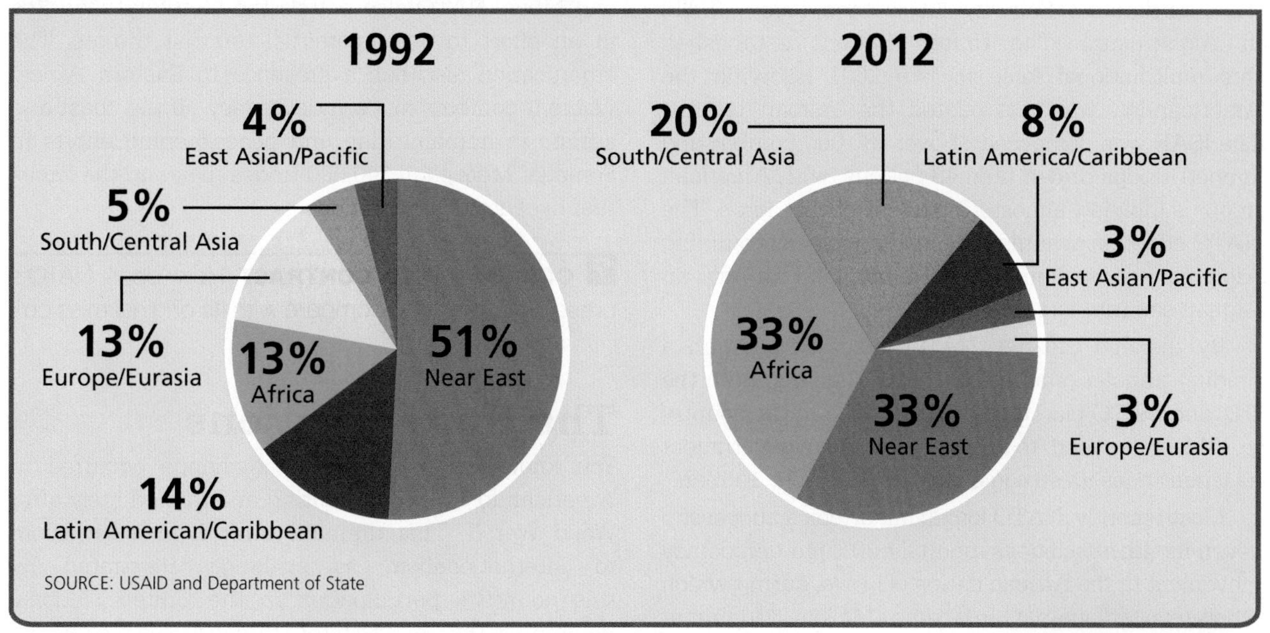

>> Foreign aid includes economic, humanitarian, and military assistance. **Analyze Charts** What conclusions can you draw from the changes in aid distribution between 1992 and 2012?

independent United States Agency for International Development (USAID) administers most of the economic aid programs, in close cooperation with the Departments of State and Agriculture. Most military aid is channeled through the Defense Department.

APPLY CONCEPTS Do you think foreign aid is necessary today?

NATO

Since World War II, the United States has constructed a large network of **regional security alliances** built on mutual defense treaties. In each of those agreements, the United States and the other countries involved have agreed to act to meet any aggression in a particular part of the world. Among these many alliances, the North Atlantic Treaty Organization (NATO) ranks as one of the most significant.

History of NATO The North Atlantic Treaty, signed in 1949, established **NATO,** the North Atlantic Treaty Organization. The alliance was formed initially to promote the collective defense of Western Europe, particularly against the threat of Soviet aggression. NATO was originally composed of the United States and 11 other countries (see map).

With the collapse of the Soviet Union, NATO's mutual security blanket was extended to cover much of Eastern Europe. Though it has grown in size, the alliance remains dedicated to the basic goal of protecting the freedom and security of its members through political and military action. Each of the now 28 member countries has agreed that "an armed attack against one or more of them in Europe or in North America shall be considered an attack against them all."

What has changed with NATO since its founding? NATO was formed for defensive purposes and—if defense includes military intervention in conflicts that may destabilize Europe, and with it, the prevention of humanitarian disasters—defense remains its basic charge.

Increasingly, however, NATO is focused on what it calls "crisis management and peacekeeping." Its involvement in the **Balkans** provides a leading illustration of this role. First in Bosnia in 1995 and then in Kosovo in 1999, NATO forces, drawn mostly from the United States, Great Britain, and Canada, ended years of vicious civil war in what was once Yugoslavia. Those military interventions also put an end to the horrific campaigns of "ethnic cleansing," directed by Serbia's President **Slobodan Milosevic**. NATO troops continue to maintain a fragile peace in the Balkans today.

NATO Today In 2003, NATO took command of the International Security Assistance Force (ISAF) in Afghanistan. The United Nations established this multinational force in late 2001 following the American-led war that ousted the Taliban regime. The ISAF was composed of over 130,000 combat and support troops drawn from 48 nations, with American troops supplying almost 70 percent of that force. The NATO coalition assumed the leading role in rebuilding Afghanistan, weakening the Taliban, and training an Afghan security force.

By the end of 2011, NATO forces had begun a gradual transfer of authority to the Afghans. Both the U.S. and NATO plan to keep a presence in the country to 2014 and beyond, to support the Afghan government as it continues its struggle against a resilient Taliban.

Most recently, NATO forces undertook a successful seven-month mission to support the 2011 pro-democracy movement in the African nation of Libya, during which rebels revolted against the regime of Colonel Muammar al-Qaddafi. The Libyan movement was part of the so-called "Arab Spring"—a wave of revolutions that swept across the Arab world beginning in 2010. In an operation initially led by the United States, NATO used air strikes and sea power to enforce a United Nations-imposed arms embargo and no-fly zone against Libya. The mission ended with the death of Qaddafi and the installation of a transitional government.

In addition to its roles in Kosovo, Afghanistan, and Libya, NATO also patrols the Mediterranean Sea in an effort to deter potential terrorist threats. The organization also has a presence in Eastern Africa, where it combats modern-day piracy off the coast and assists in humanitarian and peacekeeping efforts in Somalia. More than 140,000 troops make up the forces that execute those missions.

COMPARE AND CONTRAST How does NATO's present-day mission compare with its original mission?

The United Nations

You know that a fundamental change occurred in American foreign policy during and immediately after World War II. That dramatic shift from isolationism to internationalism, is strikingly illustrated by this country's participation in the United Nations. Remember, the United States refused to join the League of Nations after World War I. With the end of World War II, however, the American people realized that America was a world power with worldwide interests and responsibilities.

The **United Nations** (UN) came into being at the United Nations Conference on International Organization, which met in San Francisco from April 25 to June 26, 1945. There, the representatives of 50 nations—the victorious allies of World War II—drafted

ISAF Top Troop-Contributing Nations 2013

COUNTRY	TROOPS	COUNTRY	TROOPS
United States	60,000	Georgia	1,560
United Kingdom	7,900	Poland	1,553
Germany	4,400	Turkey	1,041
Italy	2,826	Australia	1,029
Total troops from all 49 contributing nations			86,834

SOURCE: International Security Assistance Force, NATO; December 2013 data

>> The United States has provided the bulk of NATO troops in Afghanistan. **Analyze Charts** What are the advantages of a NATO coalition in Afghanistan?

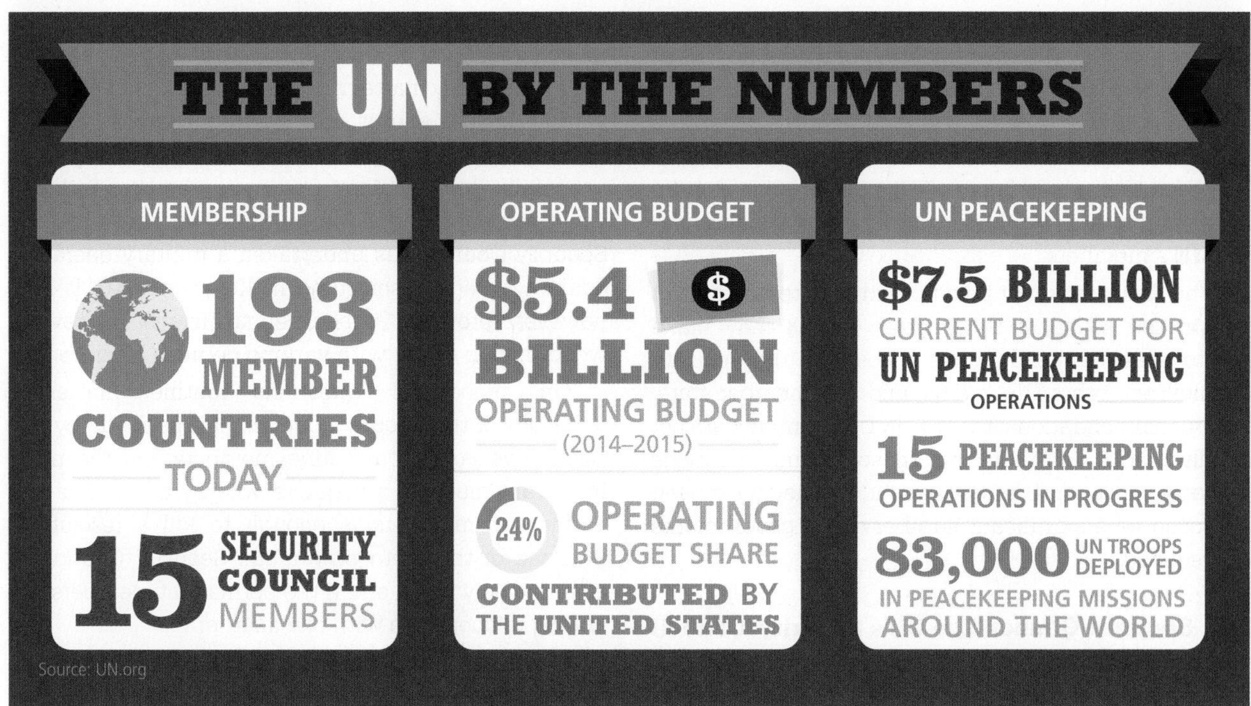

>> Data can provide a great deal of insight into the nature of an organization. **Analyze Charts** What does this information tell you about the UN?

the United Nations Charter. The charter is a treaty among all of the UN's member-states, and it serves as the body's constitution.

The United States became the first nation to ratify the UN Charter. The Senate approved it by an overwhelming vote, 89–2, on July 24, 1945. The other states that had taken part in the San Francisco Conference then ratified the charter in quick order, and it went into force on October 24, 1945. The UN held the first session of its General Assembly in London on January 10, 1946.

The United Nations Charter The UN's charter is a lengthy document. It opens with an eloquent preamble, which reads in part:

> We, the peoples of the United Nations
>
> Determined to save succeeding generations from the scourge of war, which twice in our lifetime has brought untold sorrow to mankind, and . . .
>
> To practice tolerance and live together in peace with one another as good neighbors, and
>
> To unite our strength to maintain international peace and security . . .
>
> Have resolved to combine our efforts to accomplish these aims.
>
> —Charter of the United Nations

The body of the document begins in Article I, with a statement of the organization's purposes: the maintenance of international peace and security, the development of friendly relations between and among all nations, and the promotion of justice and cooperation in the solution of international problems.

The UN has 193 members today. Membership is open to those "peace-loving states" that accept the obligations of the charter and are, in the UN's judgment, able and willing to carry out those obligations. New members may be admitted by a two-thirds vote of the General Assembly, upon recommendation by the Security Council.

The charter sets forth the complicated structure of the UN. It is built around six principal bodies: the General Assembly, the Security Council, the Economic and Social Council, the Trusteeship Council (which exists in name only today), the International Court of Justice, and the Secretariat.

The General Assembly The UN's General Assembly has been called "the town meeting of the world." Each of the UN's members has a seat and a vote in the Assembly. It meets once a year, and sessions take place at the UN's permanent headquarters in New York City. The secretary-general may call special sessions, at the request of either the Security Council or a majority of the UN's members.

The Assembly may take up and debate any matter within the scope of the charter, and it may make whatever recommendation it chooses to the Security Council, the other UN organs, and any member-state. The recommendations it makes to UN members are not legally binding on them, but these recommendations do carry some considerable weight, for they have been approved by a significant number of the governments of the world.

The Security Council The UN's **Security Council** is made up of 15 members. Five—the United States, Britain, France, Russia (originally the Soviet Union's seat), and China—are permanent members. The General Assembly chooses the 10 non-permanent members for 2-year terms; they cannot be immediately reelected. The council meets in continuous session.

The Security Council bears the UN's major responsibility for maintaining international peace. It may take up any matter involving a threat to or a breach of that peace, and it can adopt measures ranging from calling on the parties to settle their differences peacefully to placing economic and/or military sanctions on an offending nation. The only time the Security Council has undertaken a military operation against an aggressor came in Korea in 1950. It has, however, provided peacekeeping forces in several world trouble spots, with varying degrees of success.

On procedural questions—routine matters—decisions of the Security Council can be made by the affirmative vote of any nine members. On the more important matters, a negative vote by any one of the permanent members is enough to kill a resolution. Because of that veto power, the Security Council is effective only when and if the permanent members are willing to cooperate with one another.

The veto does not come into play in a situation in which one or more of the permanent members abstains. When, on June 25, 1950, the Security Council called on all UN members to aid South Korea in repelling the North Korean invasion, the Soviet delegate was boycotting sessions of the Security Council and so was not present to veto that action.

>> The UN Security Council must come to a consensus to act on all substantive measures. If one permanent member casts a negative vote, the General Assembly can take up the issue.

Economic and Social Council The Economic and Social Council (ECOSOC) is made up of 54 members elected by the General Assembly to three-year terms. It is responsible to the Assembly for carrying out the UN's many economic, cultural, educational, health, and related activities. It coordinates the work of the UN's specialized agencies—a number of independent international bodies that have a working relationship with the world organization. There are now 15 of these independent bodies—among the most notable: the World Health Organization (WHO), the International Monetary Fund (IMF), the World Bank Group, and the Food and Agriculture Organization (FAO).

International Court of Justice The International Court of Justice (ICJ), also known as the World Court, is the UN's judicial arm. A UN member may agree to accept the court's jurisdiction over cases in which it may be involved either unconditionally or with certain reservations (exceptions that may not conflict with the ICJ Statute).

The ICJ is made up of 15 judges selected for 9-year terms by the General Assembly and the Security Council. It sits in permanent session at the Peace Palace in The Hague, the Netherlands, and handles cases brought to it voluntarily by both members and nonmembers of the UN.

UN Secretary-Generals

NAME	COUNTRY / TERM OF OFFICE
Trygve Lie	Norway / 1946–1953
Dag Hammarskjöld	Sweden / 1953–1961
U Thant	Burma / 1961–1971
Kurt Waldheim	Austria / 1972–1981
Javier Perez de Cuellar	Peru / 1982–1991
Boutros Boutros-Ghali	Egypt / 1992–1996
Kofi Annan	Ghana / 1997–2006
Ban Ki-moon	South Korea / 2007–Present

SOURCE: United Nations

>> The secretary-general must act as the spokesperson for the people of the world. **Analyze Charts** How do the nationalities of the secretaries-general reflect the UN's mission?

The Secretariat The civil service branch of the UN is the Secretariat. It is headed by the secretary-general, who is elected to a five-year term by the General Assembly on the recommendation of the Security Council.

The secretary-general heads a staff of some 40,000 men and women who conduct the day-to-day work of the UN in New York and elsewhere around the globe. Beyond administrative chores, the Charter gives this vital power to the secretary-general to bring before the Security Council any matter that he or she believes poses a serious threat to international peace and security.

The secretary-general prepares the UN's two-year budget, which must be approved by the General Assembly. For 2014–2015, the operating budget came to $5.4 billion. The Assembly apportions the UN's expenses for each two-year period among its member states.

Early on, the secretary-general was seen as little more than the UN's chief clerk. The post amounts to much more than that, however, because the eight men who have thus far held it transformed the office into a major channel for the negotiated settlement of international disputes.

CHECK UNDERSTANDING What world events persuaded the United States to join the United Nations? How did this differ from its previous stance regarding American involvement in an international organization for peace?

The UN's Work

The purpose of the United Nations can be summed up this way: to make the world a better place. To that end, the UN is involved in a wide variety of activities.

Peacekeeping is a primary function of the United Nations. Nearly 117,000 military and civilian personnel provided by some 120 member countries are currently engaged in 15 UN global peacekeeping operations.

The UN's specialized agencies spend some several billion dollars a year for economic and social programs to help the world's poorest nations. Those monies are beyond that loaned by the World Bank, the International Monetary Fund, and the other UN agencies that further development in poorer countries.

Health is the major concern of several UN agencies. A joint program of UNICEF and WHO has immunized 80 percent of the world's children against six killer diseases, and it is estimated that this program saves the lives of more than two million children a year. Smallpox, which plagued the world for centuries, has now been all but eliminated by a WHO-led campaign. Today, that organization coordinates a massive global effort to control the spread of AIDS.

The health of the environment is also a significant concern of the world organization. United Nations environmental conventions have helped reduce acid rain, lessened marine pollution, and phased out the production of gases that destroy the ozone layer. The UN also helped establish the Intergovernmental Panel on Climate Change. That body was created to examine the large volume of information about climate change generated by the scientific community and to help provide government decision-makers with accurate, balanced analysis of this data.

Human rights have long been a leading priority for the United Nations. In 1948, the UN drafted the Universal Declaration of Human Rights, and it has sponsored more than 80 treaties that help protect specific rights. Various United Nations agencies work to aid and protect refugees and displaced persons, and the international organization raises more than $1 billion a year for assistance to victims of war and natural disasters.

The UN and Nongovernmental Organizations The UN also works closely with nongovernmental organizations, NGOs, around the world. As the name suggests, NGOs are independent of governments, and the list of issues and topics that they exist to address is nearly endless. On issues ranging from public health to the environment to the status of women, these groups perform valuable work around the world. The United Nations actively seeks to partner with those organizations as a means of achieving its goals. A prime example is the International Committee of the Red Cross, a humanitarian NGO with which the UN works to assist victims of disasters ranging from military conflicts to those inflicted by Mother Nature.

The UN–U.S. Relationship The United States has a long and close relationship with the UN. It was President **Franklin D. Roosevelt** who, with Britain's **Winston Churchill**, first proposed the formation of the UN. The United States occupies a permanent place on the Security Council. Although the United States is one of 193 members of the UN, it funds some 22 percent of the UN budget. (Each member's contribution is roughly equal in proportion to its share of the world's gross domestic product.)

The relationship with the UN is complex, however. The United States has at times been critical of the UN. In fact, the United States has even withheld payment of funds to the institution. Also, the United States has not always agreed with some formal policy positions taken by the UN. In 2003, for example, the Bush administration was frustrated in its efforts to win UN support for military action against Iraq.

Yet, the United States often works closely with the UN on a variety of issues to further policies that are important to both, including environmental and humanitarian causes. For example, in 2014 the UN

UN Millennium Development Goals

1	Eradicate extreme poverty and hunger
2	Achieve universal primary education
3	Promote gender equality and empower women
4	Reduce child mortality
5	Improve maternal health
6	Combat HIV/AIDS, malaria and other diseases
7	Ensure environmental sustainability
8	Develop a global partnership for economic development

SOURCE: United Nations, un.org

>> The UN's Millenium Development Goals are a blueprint to which all member countries have committed. **Analyze Charts** Which of these goals reflect the UN's human rights objective?

was closely involved with American efforts to destroy Syria's chemical weapons stockpiles and bring about a peaceful resolution to the conflict there.

? APPLY CONCEPTS In some circumstances, the United Nations lacks the resources to provide sufficient aid after a major disaster. How might the UN cope with such a situation?

>> Afghan girls take classes at a school funded by American actress Angelina Jolie, a goodwill ambassador for the UN High Commissioner for Refugees.

ASSESSMENT

1. **Compare and Contrast** Compare and contrast the significance of foreign affairs to the United States at the time of its founding with its significance today.
2. **Describe** How and to what degree does the international community ensure the safety and welfare of representatives abroad?
3. **Infer** How does United States foreign aid affect the American economy?
4. **Analyze Information** How has the fall of the Soviet Union affected NATO's work?
5. **Apply Concepts** The UN General Assembly voted in favor of a measure that required action by several member nations. What action, if any, are those nations now likely to take?

>> The Salute to Our Troops parade in Hawaii features representatives of the five active duty services—the Army, Marines, Navy, Air Force, and Coast Guard.

 Interactive Flipped Video

6.6 **How many federal agencies, in addition to the Department of State, are involved with the nation's foreign affairs? Dozens of them. Thus, the FBI combats terrorism and espionage here and abroad. The Public Health Service works with the United Nations and foreign governments to conquer diseases and meet other health problems in many parts of the world. The United States Agency for International Development (USAID) provides economic help to foreign countries. The Office of the United States Trade Representative promotes this country's interests in international trade.**

>> Objectives

Summarize the functions, components, and organization of the Defense Department and its military departments.

Explain how the Director of National Intelligence and the Department of Homeland Security contribute to national security.

>> Key Terms

espionage
terrorism

National Security

The Department of Defense

A recitation of this sort could go on and on. But, as you will see, this section deals with those agencies most directly involved in the areas of foreign and defense policy.

Congress established what is today called the Department of Defense (DoD) in the National Security Act of 1947. It is the present-day successor to two historic Cabinet-level agencies: the War Department, created by Congress in 1789, and the Navy Department, created in 1798.

Congress created the Defense Department in order to unify the nation's armed forces. It wished to bring the then-separate Army (including the Air Force) and the Navy under the control of a single Cabinet department. Today, there are nearly 1.4 million men and women on active duty in the military, over one million in the National Guard and Reserves, and some 788,000 civilians employed by the Defense Department.

The Framers and the Military The authors of the Constitution understood the importance of the nation's defense. They emphasized that fact clearly in the Preamble, and they underscored it in the body of the Constitution by mentioning defense more frequently than any other governmental function.

The Framers also recognized the dangers inherent in military power and the potential of its abuse. They knew that its very existence can pose a threat to free government. Therefore, the Constitution is studded with provisions to make sure that the military is always subject to the control of the nation's civilian authorities. Thus, the Constitution makes the elected President the commander in chief of the armed forces. To the same end, it gives broad military powers to Congress—that is, to the elected representatives of the people.

The principle of civilian control has always been a major factor in the making of defense policy and in the creation and staffing of the various agencies responsible for the execution of that policy. The importance of civilian control is clearly illustrated by this fact: The National Security Act of 1947 provides that the secretary of defense cannot have served on active duty in any of the armed forces for at least 10 years before being named to that post.

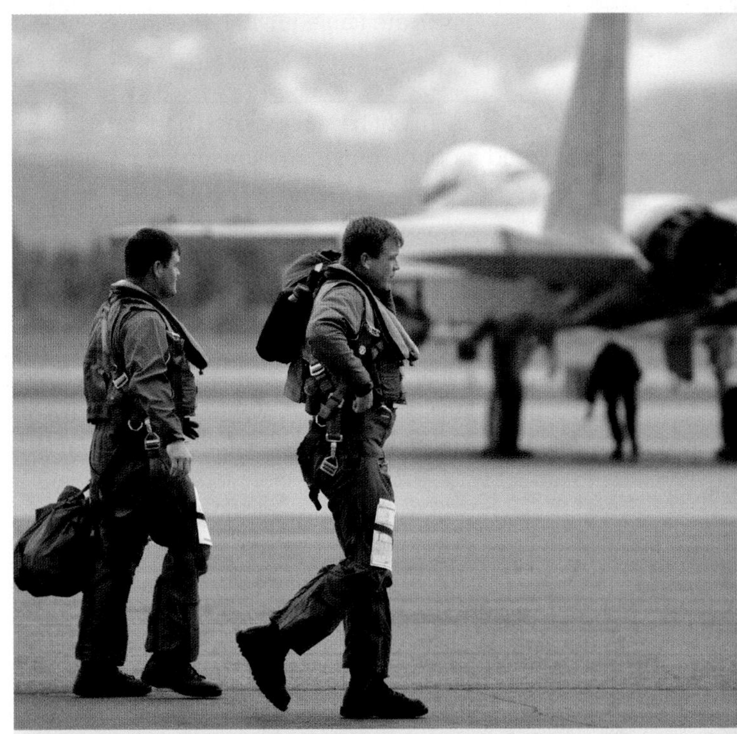

>> The Department of Defense is America's oldest and largest government agency. Service members, like these Air Force fighter pilots, serve in more than 150 countries around the world.

The Secretary of Defense The Department of Defense is headed by the secretary of defense, whose appointment by the President is subject to confirmation by the Senate. The secretary, who serves at the President's pleasure, is charged with two major responsibilities. He is simultaneously (1) the President's chief aide and advisor in making and carrying out defense policy, and (2) the operating head of the Defense Department.

The secretary's huge domain is often called the Pentagon—because of its massive five-sided headquarters building in Virginia, across the Potomac River from the Capitol. Its operations have regularly taken a large slice of the federal budget every year for more than 70 years—and about a fifth of all federal spending today. The global war on terrorism has forced vast increases in expenditures for the military. The Department of Defense spent nearly $300 billion in fiscal year 2001, the year of the September 11 attacks. It spent over twice that amount in fiscal year 2013.

>> Secretary of defense Chuck Hagel is welcomed to South Korea. The secretary of defense often visits allies of the United States, especially countries where U.S. troops are stationed.

The Joint Chiefs of Staff The six members of the Joint Chiefs of Staff serve as the principal military advisers to the secretary of defense, and to the President and the National Security Council. This collective body is made up of the chairman of the Joint Chiefs, the vice chairman, the Army chief of staff, the chief of naval operations, the commandant of the Marine Corps, and the Air Force chief of staff. The highest ranking uniformed officers in the armed services, the members of the Joint Chiefs are named by the President, subject to Senate approval.

INFER What might have happened had the Framers not placed control of the military in the hands of civilians?

Branches of the Military

The three military departments—the Departments of the Army, the Navy, and the Air Force—are major units and sub-Cabinet departments within the Department of Defense. A civilian secretary, named by the President and directly responsible to the secretary of defense, leads each military department. The nation's armed forces—the Army, the Navy, and the Air Force—operate within that unified structure.

The Army The Army is the largest of the armed services, and the oldest. The American Continental Army, now the United States Army, was established by the Second Continental Congress on June 14, 1775—more than a year before the Declaration of Independence.

The Army is essentially a ground-based force, and it is responsible for military operations on land. It must be ready (1) to defeat any attack on the United States itself, and (2) to take swift and forceful action to protect American interests in any other part of the world. To these ends, it must organize, train, and equip its active duty forces—the Regular Army, the Army National Guard, and the Army Reserve.

Over 550,000 Army National Guard soldiers and reservists have been called to service since September 11, 2001, many of them for the wars in Afghanistan and Iraq. All of the Army's active duty personnel are under the direct command of the Army's highest ranking officer, the Army chief of staff.

The Regular Army is the nation's standing Army, the heart of its land forces. There are now some 1.5 million soldiers on active duty—officers and enlisted personnel, professional soldiers, and volunteers. The Army has been downsized in the post–cold war era, however. At the time of the collapse of the Soviet Union in 1991, there were more than 700,000 men and women on active duty.

Women make up about 14 percent of the Army and now serve in all Regular Army units, except the Special Forces. Over recent years, women's roles have come to include many combat-related duties in the Army and in each of the other armed services, as well.

The Army trains and equips its combat units to fight enemy forces. The infantry takes, holds, and defends land areas. The artillery supports the infantry, seeks to destroy enemy concentrations with its heavier guns, and gives anti-aircraft cover. The armored cavalry also supports the infantry, using armored vehicles and

Women in the Military

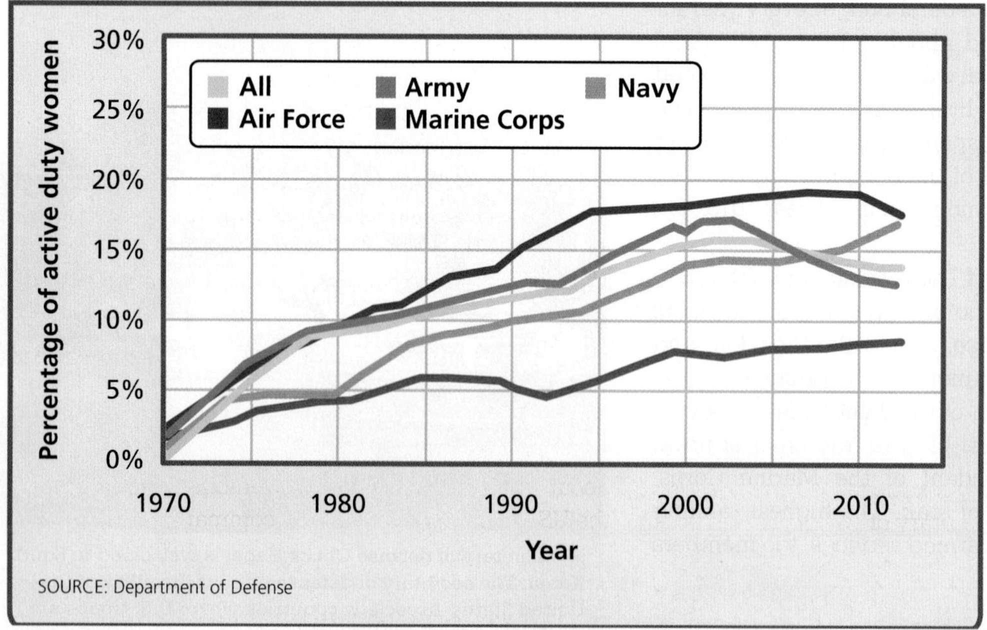

>> The percentage of women in the military has increased dramatically since the 1970s. **Analyze Graphs** Which branch has seen the greatest increase?

U.S. Armed Forces Overseas: Major Military Deployments

	COUNTRY	TOTAL	ARMY	NAVY	MARINE CORPS	AIR FORCE
EUROPE	Germany	43,280	27,768	484	828	14,200
EUROPE	Italy	10, 958	3,450	3,488	15	4,005
MIDDLE EAST/ EAST ASIA	Japan	50,159	2,439	19,597	15,468	12,655
MIDDLE EAST/ EAST ASIA	Afghanistan, Iraq, Kuwait, South Korea	36,158	22,316	341	4,317	9,184

SOURCE: Defense Manpower Data Center, August 7, 2013

>> Protecting the nation's security does not end at the nation's borders. **Analyze Charts** Why is it necessary to post the armed forces overseas in order to protect national security?

helicopters to spearhead assaults and oppose enemy counteroffensives.

Other units of the Army provide the many services and supplies in support of combat troops. Those soldiers could not fight without the help of members of the engineer, quartermaster, signal, ordnance, transportation, military police, and medical corps.

The Navy The United States Navy was first formed as the Continental Navy—a fledgling naval force created by the Second Continental Congress on October 13, 1775. Ever since, its major responsibility has been sea warfare.

The chief of naval operations is the Navy's highest ranking officer and is responsible for its preparations and readiness for war and for its use in combat. Similar to the Army, the Navy's ranks also have been thinned in the post–cold war period. Today, some 320,000 officers and enlisted personnel serve in the Navy, with women making up about 16 percent of the force.

The Second Continental Congress established the United States Marine Corps (USMC) on November 10, 1775. Today, it operates as a separate armed service within the Navy Department, but it is not under the control of the chief of naval operations. Its commandant answers directly to the secretary of the Navy.

The Marines are a combat-ready land force for the Navy. They have two major combat missions: (1) to seize or defend land bases from which the ships of the fleet and the air power of the Navy and Marines can operate, and (2) to carry out other land operations essential to a naval campaign. Today, some 200,000 men and women serve in the USMC. The proportion of women in the Marines is lower than it is in the other service branches—about 7 percent.

The Air Force The Air Force is the youngest of the military services. Congress established the United States Air Force (USAF) and made it a separate branch of the armed forces in the National Security Act of 1947. However, its history dates back to 1907, when the Army assigned an officer and two enlisted men to a new unit called the Aeronautical Division of the Army Signal Corps. Those three men were ordered to take "charge of all matters pertaining to military ballooning, air machines and all kindred subjects."

Today, the USAF is the nation's first line of defense. It has primary responsibility for military air and aerospace operations. In time of war, its major duties are to defend the United States; attack and defeat enemy air, ground, and sea forces; strike military and other war-related targets in enemy territory; and provide transport and combat support for land and naval operations.

Reduced by 180,000 since 1991, the Air Force now has about 330,000 officers and enlisted personnel, about 19 percent of whom are women. All who serve in the USAF are under the direct command of the chief of staff of the Air Force.

? DRAW CONCLUSIONS Why do you think the text makes a particular point of listing the percentage of women involved in various branches of the military?

>> The operations center of the National Counterterrorism Center investigates threat reports and coordinates and shares real-time intelligence on terrorism.

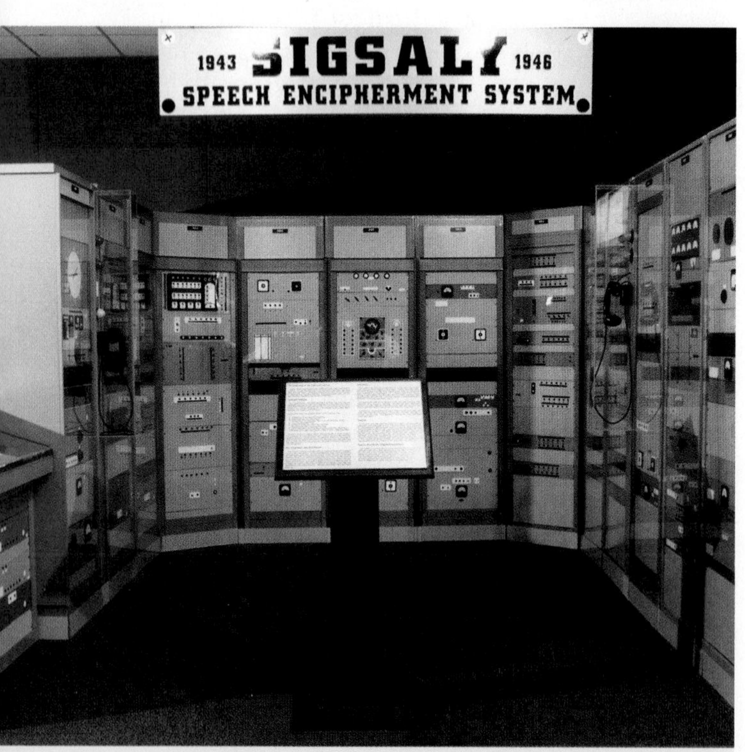

>> This photo shows SIGSALY, a voice encryption system first used during World War II to protect communications between London and Washington, D.C.

The Director of National Intelligence

The Director of National Intelligence (DNI) heads the Office of the Director of National Intelligence, established in 2005. The Office was born out of the pre-9/11 failure of the government's several intelligence agencies to collect and share information that might have warned of al Qaeda's coming attacks.

The Work of the DNI The President, with Senate approval, appoints the DNI, who is now the President's chief advisor in all matters relating to intelligence. The DNI supervises the operations of the 16 separate agencies that make up the federal intelligence community and directs the work of the National Counterterrorism Center (NCTC). The NCTC's hundreds of specialists receive and evaluate all information gathered by the intelligence community and relay it to all those who have "the need to know." As the first DNI, John Negroponte, put it: "Our job is to integrate foreign, military, and domestic intelligence in defense of the homeland and of United States interests abroad."

Agencies Controlled by the DNI Some of the agencies controlled by the DNI are fairly well known, among them the FBI, the DEA, and the CIA. Indeed, for more than half a century, one of them, the Central Intelligence Agency, was—as its title suggests—the government's principal, its central, intelligence gathering organization. The CIA remains a major "cloak and dagger" agency, but the DNI now holds its once leading role in the intelligence community.

Some of the agencies in the intelligence community are little known, however, including the National Geospatial Agency, the Defense Intelligence Agency, and the world's largest spy organization, the National Security Agency. Much of their work involves **espionage**—spying—and is shrouded in deepest secrecy. Even Congress has generally shied away from more than a passing check on their activities, and their operating funds are disguised at several places in the federal budget each year.

Balancing Security and Liberty Most Americans agree that the work of the several agencies that comprise the intelligence community is absolutely essential to the security of the United States. At the same time, however, both government leaders and the American people recognize the potential dangers of a group of government agencies whose operations are conducted in utmost secrecy.

Combat Terrorism or Protect Privacy: Which Is More Important?

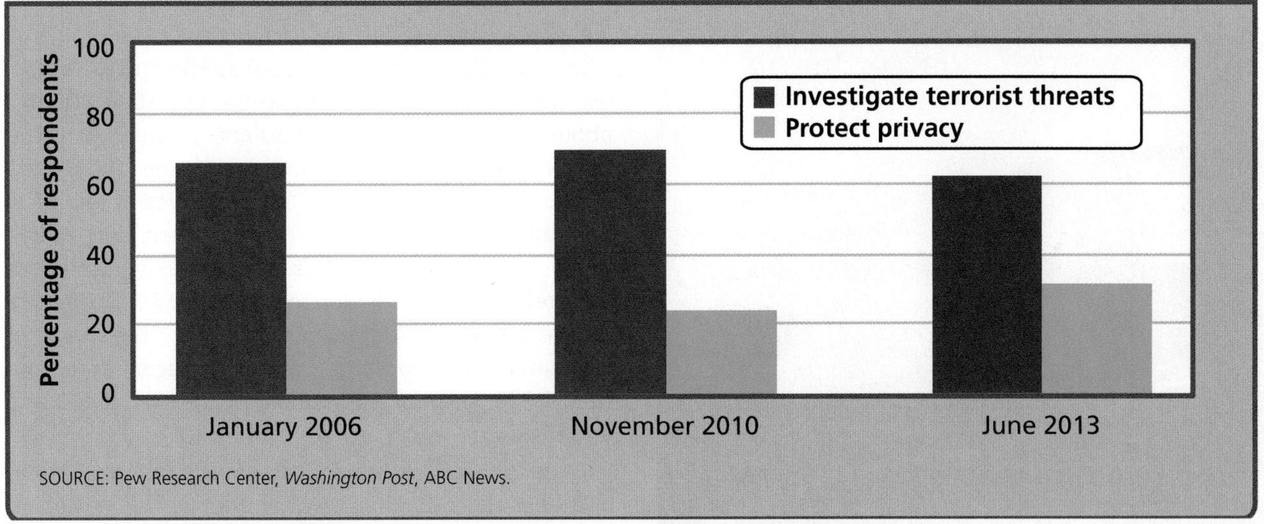

>> After the attacks by the Al Qaeda Islamist terrorist group, polling data on security and privacy heavily favored security. **Analyze Charts** How have these preferences changed over the years?

The American people expect the government, through agencies such as the National Security Agency (NSA), to collect and analyze a vast array of information and to keep the country safe from terrorist attacks. At the same time, however, Americans expect a right to privacy. In fact, the Constitution speaks to this issue in several places, including the 3rd Amendment, which prohibits the quartering of soldiers in times of peace, and the 4th Amendment, which bars unreasonable searches of persons or property. Numerous Supreme Court decisions have also found privacy to be a fundamental right.

The issue of the tricky balance between national security and individual rights came to the fore in 2013, when Edward Snowden, a computer specialist and a former CIA and NSA employee, disclosed classified, top-secret information regarding government surveillance to the press. According to Snowden, he leaked the information because it showed that government intelligence agencies were illegally invading the privacy of innocent Americans. Specifically, his information revealed a secret court order allowing the Federal Government to access the phone records of millions of Americans.

President Obama and others in the administration defended the court order. They argued that the information was not only consistent with laws passed by Congress, but also necessary for national security.

The Snowden controversy underscored the sensitive nature of the work of the DNI and its agencies. It also stressed the need for vigilance on the part of the American people. Democracy requires that citizens are informed about what government is doing, that they participate in discussions about government policies and actions, and that they take the right to vote seriously, so that only the most trustworthy and qualified individuals serve in government. Only in this way can the delicate balance between security and liberty be maintained.

COMPARE POINTS OF VIEW What are some of the arguments for and against secret intelligence agencies?

The Department of Homeland Security

The Department of Homeland Security (DHS) is charged with the awesome and complex task of protecting the United States against terrorism. **Terrorism** is the use of violence to intimidate a government or a society, usually for political or ideological reasons.

Congress created the department in 2002, and it became operational in 2003. It is responsible for the coordination and the direction of all anti-terrorist activities of all of the public agencies that operate in the field of domestic security—including thousands of police departments, fire departments, emergency medical and search and rescue units, and other disaster response agencies across the country.

>> Many federal agencies, including customs, immigration, and border patrol, as well as State troopers and private security organizations, work to protect the Trans-Alaska pipeline from terrorist attack.

Interactive Gallery

The Work of the Department of Homeland Security The Homeland Security Act of 2002 gives the department major operating responsibilities in five specific areas:

- border and transportation security
- infrastructure protection
- emergency preparedness and response
- chemical, biological, radiological, and nuclear defense
- information analysis (intelligence)

The department was built mostly of agencies transferred to it from other Cabinet departments. Those agencies include the Secret Service and the newly entitled U.S. Immigration and Customs Enforcement (ICE), from the Treasury Department; the Coast Guard and the Transportation Security Administration, from the Transportation Department; the renamed U.S. Citizenship and Immigration Services, from the Justice Department; and the independent Federal Emergency Management Agency (FEMA).

A Daunting Task The threat of bioterrorism—the use of such biological agents as smallpox or anthrax as weapons—dramatizes the immensity of the problems facing the Department of Homeland Security. So, too, do these facts: There are more than 600,000 bridges, about 155,000 water systems, and more than 6,000 power plants (with 104 nuclear reactors) in the United States. There are also some 140,000 miles of rail lines, 2.1 million miles of natural gas pipelines, and 25,000 miles of inland waterways. Additionally, there are hundreds of skyscrapers, more than 13,000 airports (including some 300 major facilities), thousands of stadiums and other large gathering places, and more than 7,000 miles of international border with Canada and Mexico.

Add to those fundamental facts such critical matters as the nation's food and water supply, its healthcare system, and its communications networks, and this point becomes clear: The task of protecting the United States against terrorist acts is a daunting one. Despite the enormity of that task, the DHS is charged with (1) preventing most—if not all—terrorist attacks, and (2) bringing those responsible for any attempted attacks to justice.

? INFER Why is the threat of bioterrorism such an immense issue for the Department of Homeland Security?

ASSESSMENT

1. **Interpret** How did the Framers of the Constitution address the importance of the military?
2. **Analyze Information** A vast increase in defense spending in recent years may be attributed to what events or changes?
3. **Apply Concepts** What is a potential benefit and a potential negative impact of the work of the DNI?
4. **Connect** Why does the author consider the work of the Department of Homeland Security to be such a daunting task?
5. **Compare** Compare the United States Army and Air Force in terms of responsibilities and size.

Top Ten U.S. Foreign Aid Recipients, 2014

RANK	COUNTRY	AMOUNT OF AID
1	Israel	$3,100,000,000
2	Afghanistan	$2,193,950,000
3	Egypt	$1,559,326,000
4	Pakistan	$1,162,570,000
5	Nigeria	$692,695,000
6	Jordan	$670,500,000
7	Iraq	$573,162,000
8	Kenya	$563,753,000
9	Tanzania	$552,488,000
10	Uganda	$456,327,000

SOURCE: foreignassistance.gov

1. **Examine Economic Resources in Foreign Policy** Use the chart above and a world map to write a paragraph examining how the U.S. government distributes foreign aid. Consider the following questions: Which three countries received the most U.S. foreign aid in 2014? Locate each country on a world map. In which part(s) of the world are they located? Why did those countries receive more aid? How much aid did the countries in sub-Saharan Africa receive? Why might these countries be in the top ten nations receiving U.S. aid?

2. **Explain Government Regulatory Policies** Write a paragraph explaining how regulation impacts the economy. Consider the following questions: What is the function of regulatory commissions concerning the economy at the state and national levels? What are some criticisms of regulatory commissions concerning the economy? Are regulatory commissions necessary? Explain.

3. **Understand Responsibilities of Citizenship** Write a paragraph that shows an understanding of the responsibilities of serving in the military. Consider the following questions: What is conscription, and how does it differ from voluntary enlistment in the military? At what times in American history has the draft been important? What is the Selective Service System? What is the responsibility of citizens today regarding serving in the military?

4. **Explain Major Responsibilities of Government** Explain the major responsibilities of the Director of National Intelligence and his or her importance to national defense. Consider the following questions: Why was the Office of the Director of National Intelligence established? What is the role of the Director of National Intelligence (DNI)? How do all of the agencies in the DNI work together to provide national defense?

5. **Analyze the Federalist Papers** Use the quotation below to write a paragraph analyzing the role of bureaucracy in American constitutional government. Consider the following questions: What is bureaucracy? What are the pros and cons of bureaucracy? According to James Madison, what makes a bureaucracy effective?

> *"In framing a government which is to be administered by men over men, the great difficulty lies in this: you must first enable the government to control the governed; and in the next place oblige it to control itself."*
>
> —*Federalist, No. 51*

6. **Examine Resources in Foreign Policy** Write a paragraph that examines how the U.S. government uses economic resources in foreign policy. Consider the following questions: What are economic resources used in foreign policy called? How does the United States determine the allocation of these economic resources? How do you think the use of economic resources advances U.S. foreign policy goals?

7. **Understand Government Regulations and Identify the Purpose** Write a paragraph that examines the purpose of the EPA and how its regulations can serve as a restriction to private enterprise. Consider the following questions: What is the purpose of the EPA? How do the EPA's regulations affect private businesses? How can EPA regulations restrict private businesses?

8. **Compare Methods of Filling Public Offices** Analyze the Cabinet and how members are appointed to the Cabinet. Consider the following questions: What is the Cabinet? Traditionally, who makes up the Cabinet? How does a President choose his Cabinet members? Compare how a President chooses his Cabinet to how a mayor fills public offices.

9. **Compare Staff and Line Agencies** Use the chart below to evaluate the difference between staff agencies and line agencies. Then write a paragraph that answers the following questions: What are the responsibilities of staff agencies? What are the responsibilities of line agencies? What characteristics do staff and line agencies share? What are some examples of staff and line agencies and their functions?

10. **Identify the Purpose of Regulatory Commissions** Create a written or oral presentation identifying the purpose of selected regulatory commissions, including the Occupational Safety and Health Administration (OSHA). Consider the following information: purpose of OSHA; subsections of OSHA; controversies surrounding OSHA.

Staff and Line Agencies

STAFF AGENCIES
• Serve in support capacity
• Offer advice and management assistance
• Form the federal administrative organizations
• Work together to meet goals
LINE AGENCIES
• Perform specific tasks
• Meet goals set by Congress and the President
• Administer public policy

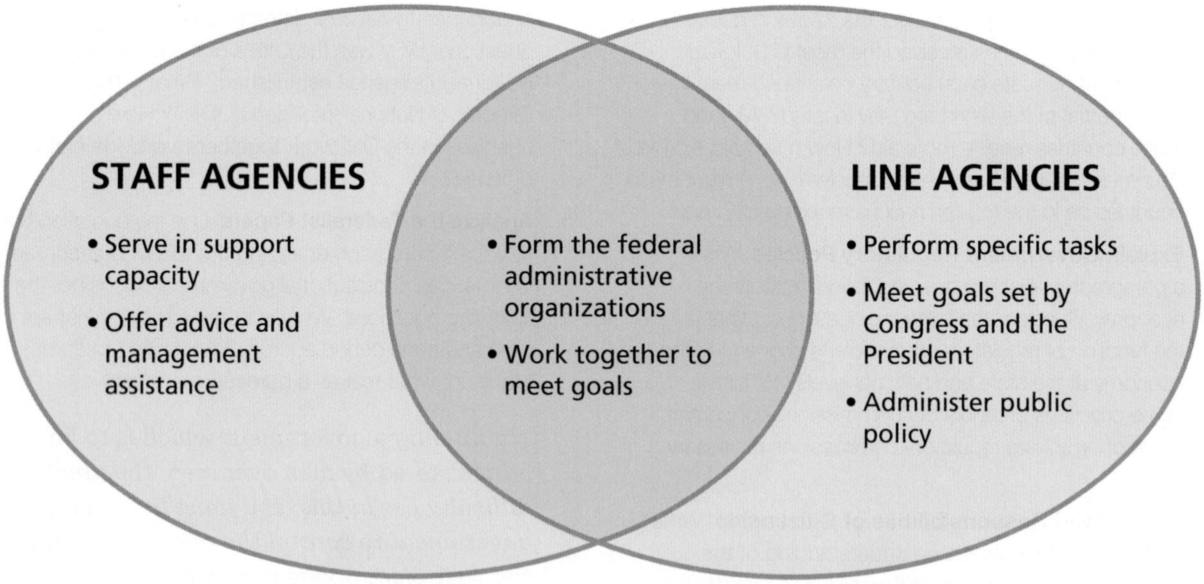

11. **Understand Impact of Scientific Discoveries** Create a visual presentation explaining the potential impact on society of recent scientific discoveries. Include the following in your visual presentation: one or more recent scientific discoveries such as those made by the National Science Foundation; the impact of one or more recent scientific discoveries on society; at least one chart or graph that helps explain a scientific discovery and/or its impact on society.

12. **Identify Research that Improved Products** Write a paragraph identifying examples of government-assisted research that have resulted in improved consumer products. Consider the following computer technologies: 3-D printing; touchscreen technology; magnetic resonance imaging.

13. **Identify the Purpose of Executive Agencies** Create a brochure, newsletter, blog, poster, or other product that identifies the purpose of NASA or another independent executive agency and explores a contemporary issue connected with that agency. Use the following process: Ask a question about the issue or topic you want to learn more about. Plan the project by outlining goals and objectives. Research information using primary and secondary sources. Create the project. Improve the project by editing and reevaluating your goals and objectives. Present your project.

14. **Explain Major Foreign Policy Responsibilities** Create a written or oral presentation analyzing and evaluating the role of ambassadors in carrying out the foreign policy responsibilities of the nation. Consider the following questions: What are the key duties and responsibilities of an ambassador? What are the implications of the selection process on the role? When and how have particular ambassadors been important to U.S. foreign policy? How can the position of ambassador best serve U.S. foreign policy interests?

15. **Identify Individuals in Government and Politics** Use the following quotation to write a paragraph identifying George Washington's significance in terms of U.S. foreign policy during the nation's first 100 years. Consider the following questions: Considering the quotation provided, what stand on foreign affairs did George Washington advise in his 1796 Farewell Address? How did this influence American foreign policy during the 1800s?

"It is our true policy to steer clear of permanent alliances with any portion of the foreign world; so far, I mean, as we are now at liberty to do it; for let me not be understood as capable of patronizing infidelity to existing engagements. I hold the maxim no less applicable to public than to private affairs, that honesty is always the best policy. I repeat it, therefore, let those engagements be observed in their genuine sense. But, in my opinion, it is unnecessary and would be unwise to extend them."

—George Washington, Farewell Address, 1796

16. **Identify the Significance of Key Natural Resources** Review United States foreign policy interests in the Middle East, including the importance of resources such as oil. Then write a paragraph and consider the following: United States dependence on oil from the Middle East; the volatility of politics in the Middle East; possible solutions to dependence on a key resource from such a volatile region.

17. **Understand the Role** Write a paragraph examining the Office of United States Trade Representative and the role it plays in setting international trade policy. Consider the following questions: What are the responsibilities of the Office of United Trade Representative? What official role does the trade representative have? What duties and responsibilities come with this role?

18. **Analyze U.S. Foreign Policy** Create a visual timeline that displays the expansion of NATO using sequential data. Include a short paragraph explaining the importance of each date and why these locations were important to U.S. foreign policy. Consider the following: establishment of NATO; Bosnia and Kosovo; Afghanistan; Libya.

19. **Explain Domestic Policy** Research a domestic policy problem facing the executive branch. For example, choose a problem related to the executive branch's involvement in the budget. Then share your findings in the form of a research report.

20. **Analyze the Functions of the Executive Branch** Analyze the structure and function of the current Executive Office of the President (EOP) and how it reflects the growth of presidential power. Consider the following questions: How has the EOP staff changed since the time of the nation's first Presidents? What is the relationship of the White House Office to the Executive Office of the President? What functions does the White House staff perform? How do these functions enhance presidential power?

21. **Write About the Essential Question Write an essay on the Essential Question: What should governments do?** Use evidence from your study of this Topic to support your answer.

Go online to PearsonRealize.com and use the texts, quizzes, interactivities, Interactive Reading Notepads, Flipped Videos, and other resources from this Topic to prepare for the Topic Test.

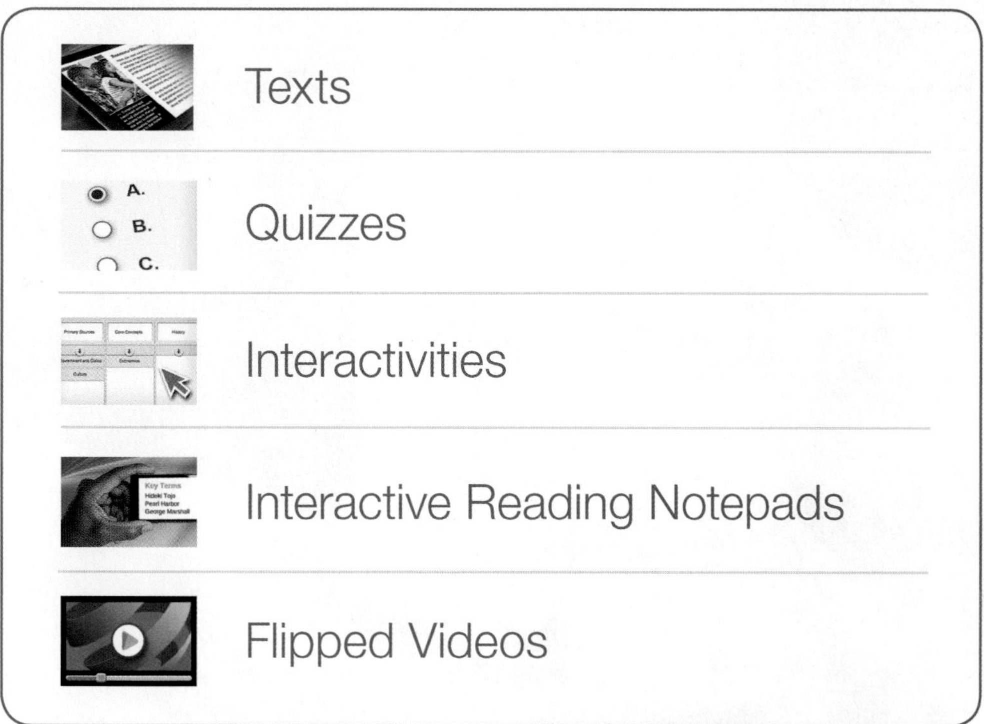

While online you can also check the progress you've made learning the topic and course content by viewing your grades, test scores, and assignment status.

[**ESSENTIAL QUESTION**] How Should We Handle Conflict?

7 The Judicial Branch

Topic 7 The Judicial Branch

>> Contemplation of Justice sits on the west side of the U.S. Supreme Court building

Enduring Understandings

- The Constitution created the Supreme Court, its jurisdiction, and the manner and terms of federal judicial appointments.
- The power of judicial review established the key role of the judicial branch.
- The Supreme Court is the final authority on questions arising under the Constitution, an act of Congress, or a U.S. treaty.
- Laws are put in place to provide order, protect society, and settle conflicts. Law officers enforce the laws and the courts interpret them.
- The inferior constitutional courts form the core of the federal judicial system, but special courts were created to handle specific types of cases.

Watch the My Story Video to explore the Supreme Court's role in the fight for civil rights and equality.

Access your digital lessons including:
Topic Inquiry • Interactive Reading Notepad • Interactivities • Assessments

>> Sandra Day O'Connor, nominated to the Supreme Court by President Ronald Reagan, was rejected by 40 law firms because she was a woman following her graduation from law school.

Interactive Flipped Video

7.1 As the ideas of self-government and fundamental civil liberties began to emerge in colonial America, colonists cast a critical eye on the courts. Corrupt, tyrannical leaders throughout history had used many tactics to maintain control, including exerting undue influence on the legal process. Those who acted against these rulers would be arrested and jailed without a trial, for example, quite often without ever being charged with a crime. Even for those lucky enough to stand before the court, a guilty verdict was inevitable. By controlling the court system, corrupt leaders could control the people.

>> Objectives

Explain why the Constitution created a national judiciary, and analyze its structure and functions.

Identify the criteria that determine whether a case is within the jurisdiction of a federal court, and compare the types of jurisdiction.

Outline the process for appointing federal judges, and list their terms of office.

Understand the impact of judicial philosophy, and analyze issues raised by judicial activism and judicial restraint.

Examine the roles of court officers.

>> Key Terms

inferior courts
jurisdiction
concurrent jurisdiction
plaintiff
defendant
original jurisdiction
appellate jurisdiction
judicial restraint
precedent
judicial activism
Sandra Day O'Connor
Ruth Bader Ginsburg
Sonia Sotomayor
Elena Kagan
Thurgood Marshall
Clarence Thomas
District of Columbia

The National Judiciary

The Courts and Democracy

It is telling that one of the earliest struggles between the colonists and the British involved the court system. In 1733, the British governor of New York, William Cosby, replaced a popular judge with a friend, a person alleged to be both corrupt and incompetent. This caused great indignation among the colonists in New York, and soon a newspaper, the *New York Weekly Journal,* began running a series of articles critical of the governor. Cosby responded by putting the editor of the paper, Peter Zenger, in jail. A colonial jury found Zenger not guilty because the stories he had printed were based on fact. The trial of Peter Zenger was widely followed and is still important today, not only because it dealt with freedom of the press, but also because it highlights the importance the colonists placed on an impartial court system.

It is also notable that much of the Bill of Rights addresses the rights of the accused. The 4th Amendment, for example, forbids illegal searches and establishes the need for probable cause; the 6th Amendment speaks to jury trials. These safeguards were put in place to ensure that leaders in the United States could not maintain power by manipulating the courts.

Finally, the Framers of the Constitution thought it essential that federal judges be separated from public pressures, as well as from coercion from the other branches of government. This is why it is stipulated that federal judges be appointed, rather than elected, and that they serve for life. Judges are to make decisions based on the law, without facing the prospect of removal for issuing an unpopular decision. Put in another way, the Framers of our system believed that in a functioning democracy, the law would rule—not tyrants or popular opinion.

? INTERPRET How did the trial of Peter Zenger in 1733 demonstrate the need for an impartial court system?

Creation of a National Judiciary

During the years the Articles of Confederation were in force (1781–1789), there were no national courts and no national judiciary. The laws of the United States were interpreted and applied as each State saw fit, and sometimes not at all. Disputes between States and between persons who lived in different States were decided, if at all, by the courts in one of the States involved. Often, decisions by the courts in one State were ignored by courts in the other States.

Alexander Hamilton spoke to the point in *The Federalist* No. 22. He described "the want of a judiciary power" as a "circumstance which crowns the defects of the Confederation." Arguing the need for a federal court system, he added, "Laws are a dead letter without courts to expound and define their true meaning and operation."

The Framers created a national judiciary for the United States in the following single sentence in the Constitution.

> The judicial Power of the United States shall be vested in one supreme Court, and in such inferior Courts as the Congress may from time to time ordain and establish.
>
> —Article III, Section 1

Congress also is given the expressed power "to constitute Tribunals inferior to the supreme Court"—that is, create the rest of the federal court system—in Article I, Section 8, Clause 9.

A Dual Court System: Federal Courts and State Courts Keep in mind this important point about the structure of the court systems in the United States: There are *two* separate court systems. On the one hand, the federal court system spans the country with its more than 100 courts. On the other hand, each of the 50 States has its own system of courts. Their numbers run well into the thousands, and most of the cases that are heard in court today are heard in those States, not the federal, courts.

The First Type of Federal Court: Constitutional Courts The Constitution establishes the Supreme Court and leaves to Congress the creation of the **inferior courts**—the lower federal courts, those beneath the Supreme Court. Over the years, Congress has created two distinct types of federal courts: (1) the constitutional courts, and (2) the special courts. See the diagram "Types of Federal Courts."

The constitutional courts are those federal courts that Congress has formed under Article III to exercise "the judicial Power of the United States." Together with the Supreme Court, they now include the courts of appeals, the district courts, and the U.S. Court of International Trade. The constitutional courts are also

>> Alexander Hamilton favored a federal judiciary with the power to settle State disputes and override State laws. He advocated a strong federal court system in several of his *Federalist* essays.

Interactive Chart

called the regular courts and, sometimes, Article III courts.

The Second Type of Federal Court: Special Court The special courts do not exercise the broad "judicial Power of the United States." Rather, they have been created by Congress to hear cases arising out of some of the expressed powers given to Congress in Article I, Section 8. The special courts hear a much narrower range of cases than those that may come before the constitutional courts.

These special courts are also called the legislative courts and, sometimes, Article I courts. Today, they include the U.S. Court of Appeals for the Armed Forces, the U.S. Court of Appeals for Veterans Claims, the U.S. Court of Federal Claims, the U.S. Tax Court, the various territorial courts, and the courts of the District of Columbia.

HYPOTHESIZE Why did the Framers see a need for a federal court system?

>> A ship capsizes, sending its cargo into the sea. Problems caused by accidents, such as oil spills and the recovery of goods and wreckage, fall under the federal umbrella of admiralty law.

Jurisdiction in the Federal Court System

The constitutional courts hear most of the cases tried in the federal courts. That is to say, those courts have jurisdiction over most federal cases. **Jurisdiction** is defined as the authority of a court to hear (to *try* and to *decide*) a case. The term means, literally, the power "to say the law."

The Constitution gives federal courts jurisdiction over only certain cases. Recall, most cases heard in court in the United States are heard in State, not federal, courts. Article III, Section 2 provides that the federal courts may hear cases either because of (1) the *subject matter* or (2) the *parties* involved in those cases.

Subject Matter In terms of subject matter, the federal courts may hear a case if it involves a "federal question"—that is, the interpretation and application of a provision in the Constitution or in any federal statute or treaty—or a question of admiralty or maritime law.

Admiralty law related to matters that arise on the high seas of the navigable waters of the United States, such as a collision at sea or a crime committed aboard a ship. Maritime law relates to matters that arise on land but are directly related to the water, such as a contract to deliver ship supplies and dockside.

The Framers purposefully gave the federal courts exclusive jurisdiction in all admiralty and maritime cases in order to ensure national supremacy in the regulation of all waterborne commerce.

Parties A case falls within the jurisdiction of the federal courts if one of the parties involved in the case is (1) the United States or one of its officers or agencies; (2) an ambassador, consul, or other official representative of a foreign government; (3) one of the 50 States suing another State, a resident of another State, or a foreign government or one of its subjects; (4) a citizen of one State suing a citizen of another State; (5) an American citizen suing a foreign government or one of its subjects; or (6) a citizen of a State suing another citizen of that same State where both claim title to land under grants from different States.

These criteria for determining which cases can be heard in the federal courts may seem quite complicated, and they are. But the matter is also a reflection of Federalism and, so, of the dual system of courts in this country. To put the whole point of the jurisdiction of the federal courts the other way around: those cases

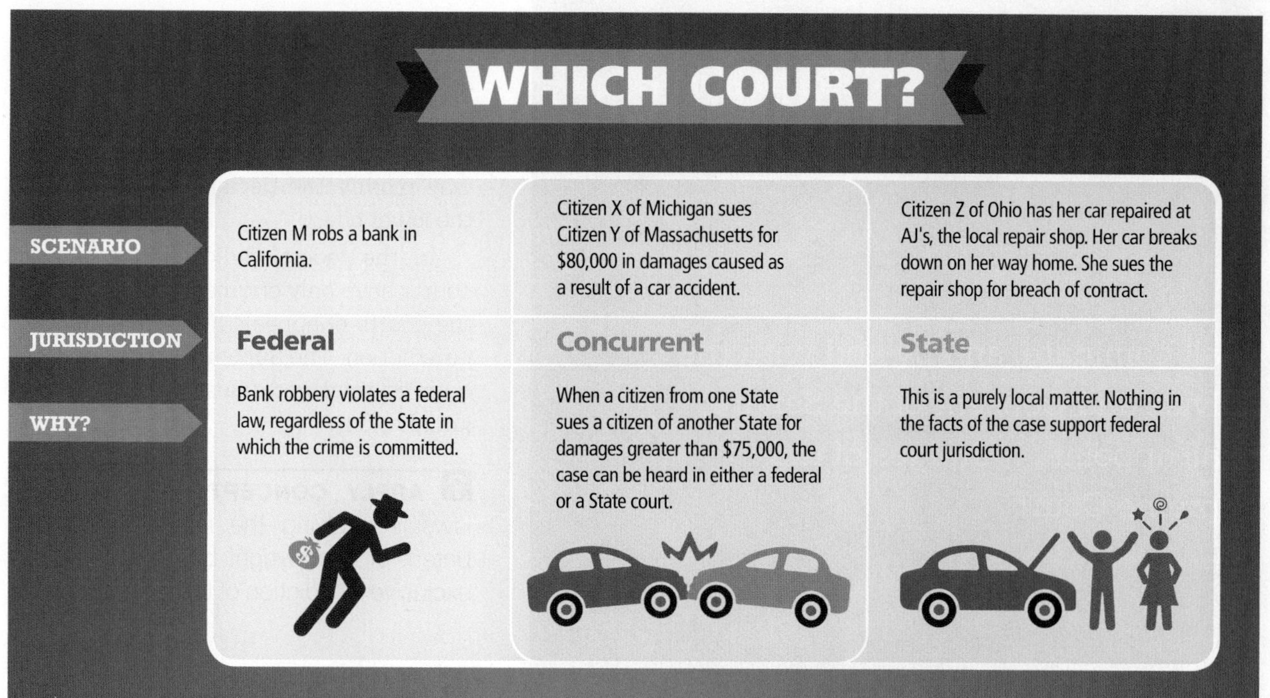

WHICH COURT?
SCENARIO
JURISDICTION
WHY?
Citizen M robs a bank in California.
Federal
Bank robbery violates a federal law, regardless of the State in which the crime is committed.
Citizen X of Michigan sues Citizen Y of Massachusetts for $80,000 in damages caused as a result of a car accident.
Concurrent
When a citizen from one State sues a citizen of another State for damages greater than $75,000, the case can be heard in either a federal or a State court.
Citizen Z of Ohio has her car repaired at AJ's, the local repair shop. Her car breaks down on her way home. She sues the repair shop for breach of contract.
State
This is a purely local matter. Nothing in the facts of the case support federal court jurisdiction.

>> Two separate court systems, federal and State, hear cases in the United States. **Analyze Information** What does this infographic tell you about the jurisdictions of these two court systems?

that are not heard by the federal courts fall within the jurisdiction of the State courts.

APPLY CONCEPTS How is the matter of federal court jurisdiction a reflection of federalism in the United States?

Types of Jurisdiction

Still more must be said on this quite complex matter of federal court jurisdiction. The federal courts exercise both *exclusive* and *concurrent* jurisdiction and, also, original and appellate jurisdiction.

Exclusive Jurisdiction Most of the cases that can be heard in the federal courts fall within their exclusive jurisdiction. That is, they can be tried *only* in the federal courts. Thus, a case involving an ambassador or some other official of a foreign government cannot be heard in a State court; it *must* be tried in a federal court. The trial of a person charged with a federal crime, or a suit involving the infringement of a patent or a copyright, or one involving any other matter arising out of an act of Congress is also within the exclusive (sole) jurisdiction of the federal courts.

Concurrent Jurisdiction Some cases may be tried in either a federal *or* a State court. Then, the federal and State courts have **concurrent jurisdiction,** meaning they share the power to hear these cases. Disputes involving citizens of different States are fairly common examples of this type of case. Such cases are known in the law as cases in diverse citizenship.

Congress has provided that a federal district court may hear a case of diverse citizenship only when the amount of money involved in that case is at least $75,000. In such a case, the **plaintiff**—the person who files the suit—may bring the case in the proper State or federal court, as he or she chooses. If the plaintiff brings the case in a State court, the **defendant**—the person against whom the complaint is made—can have the trial moved, under certain circumstances, to the federal district court.

Original and Appellate Jurisdiction A court in which a case is first heard is said to have **original jurisdiction** over that case. That court, the trial court, is often described as "the court of first instance." A court that hears a case on appeal from a lower court exercises **appellate jurisdiction** over that case. Appellate comes from the word *appellare,* "meaning to speak to, to call upon, to appeal to."

shall nominate, and by and with the Advice and Consent of the Senate, shall appoint . . . Judges of the supreme Court . . .

—Article II, Section 2, Clause 2

>> In 2009, President Barack Obama nominated Sonia Sotomayor to serve as an associate justice of the Supreme Court.

Interactive Illustration

Appellate courts do not retry cases. Rather, they determine whether a trial court has acted in accord with applicable law. The higher court—the appellate court—may uphold, overrule, or in some way modify the decision appealed from the lower court.

In the federal judiciary, the district courts have only original jurisdiction, and the courts of appeals have only appellate jurisdiction. The Supreme Court exercises both original and (most often) appellate jurisdiction.

? APPLY CONCEPTS Why would a lawsuit involving the infringement of a patent or a copyright be considered the exclusive jurisdiction of the federal courts?

Federal Judges and Court Officers

The manner in which federal judges are chosen, the terms for which they serve, and even the salaries they are paid are vital parts of the Constitution's design of an independent judicial branch. The Constitution declares that the President

> shall nominate, and by and with the Advice and Consent of the Senate, shall appoint . . . Judges of the supreme Court . . .
>
> —Article II, Section 2, Clause 2

First, in the Judiciary Act of 1789, and ever since, Congress has provided the same procedure for the selection of all federal judges.

Selection of Judges The Senate has a major part in the selection of every federal judge. In effect, the Constitution says that the President can name to the federal bench anyone whom the Senate will confirm. The practice of senatorial courtesy gives great weight to the wishes of the senators from a State in which a federal judge is to serve. In short, that unwritten rule means that the President almost always selects someone the senators from that State recommend.

The Constitution sets no age, residence, or citizenship requirements for federal judges. Nor does it require that a judge have a professional background in the law.

Influences on the Selection of Judges The President's closest legal and political aides, especially the Attorney General, take the lead in selecting federal judges. Influential senators—especially those from the nominee's home State and members of the Judiciary Committee, the President's allies and supporters in the legal profession, and various other personalities in the President's political party also play a major role in selecting judges. Several interest groups are also quite influential in the process.

Today, an increasing number of those persons who are appointed to the federal bench have had prior judicial experience. Most federal judges are drawn from the ranks of leading attorneys, legal scholars and law school professors, former members of Congress, and State court judges. Elective office (in particular, a seat in the U.S. Senate) was once a well-traveled path to the Supreme Court; now, most justices reach the High Court from the courts of appeals.

>> Steamships like the *Cornelius Vanderbilt* and the *Bay State* might not have been seen in New York harbor in 1849 if the Supreme Court had ruled differently in *Gibbons* v. *Ogden*, 1824.

History Concerning Judgeships To this point (2013), only 4 of the now 112 Supreme Court justices have been women: **Sandra Day O'Connor** was the first, appointed in 1981. The other three now sit on the Court: **Ruth Bader Ginsburg** (1993), **Sonia Sotomayor** (2009), and **Elena Kagan** (2010). Justice Sotomayor is also the Court's first Hispanic member. Only two African Americans have thus far become justices: **Thurgood Marshall** (appointed in 1967) and **Clarence Thomas** (1991).

From George Washington's day, Presidents have looked to their own political party to fill judgeships. Republican Presidents usually choose Republicans; Democrats consistently pick Democrats. Every President knows that judges may serve for decades. So chief executives regularly look for jurists who tend to agree with their own views.

The Judicial Philosophy of Judicial Restraint Another major impact on the judicial selection process is judicial philosophy—in particular, the concepts of judicial restraint and judicial activism. All federal judges make decisions in which they must interpret and apply provisions in the Constitution and acts of Congress. That is, they often decide questions of public policy—and, in doing so, they inevitably *shape* public policy.

Although the line between the two judicial philosophies can become blurred, the proponents of **judicial restraint** believe that judges should decide cases on the basis of (1) the original intent of the Framers or those who enacted the statute(s) involved in a case, and (2) **precedent**—a judicial decision that serves as a guide for settling later cases of a similar nature. They say that the courts should defer to policy judgments made in the legislative and executive branches of the government and, in so doing, honor the basic premise of self-government: the right of the majority to determine public policy. In short, they argue that elected legislators, not appointed judges, should make law.

The Judicial Philosophy of Judicial Activism Those who support **judicial activism** take a much broader view of judicial power. They argue that provisions in the Constitution and in statute law should be interpreted and applied in the light of ongoing changes in conditions and values—especially in cases involving civil rights and social welfare issues.

They, too, insist on the fundamental importance of majority rule and the value of precedents, but they believe that the courts should not be overly deferential to existing legal principles or to the judgments of elected officials.

Terms of Judges Article III, Section 1 of the Constitution reads, in part: "The Judges, both of the supreme and inferior Courts, shall hold their Offices during good Behaviour. . . . " This means that the judges of the constitutional courts are appointed for life; they serve until they resign, retire, or die in office. The Framers provided for what amounts to life tenure for these judges quite purposefully, to ensure the independence of the federal judiciary.

The very next words of the Constitution are directed to that same purpose. Article III, Section 1 of the Constitution deals with compensation for federal judges: "and [they] shall, at stated Times, receive for their Services, a Compensation, which shall not be diminished during their Continuance in Office."

Federal judges may be removed from office only through the impeachment process. In 180 years, only 15 have ever been impeached. Of that number, seven were convicted and removed by the Senate, including three in the recent past.

Those judges who sit on the special courts are not appointed for life. They are named, instead, to terms of 8 to 15 years—and may be, but seldom are, reappointed. In the **District of Columbia**, Superior Court judges are chosen for four-year terms; those who sit on the district's Court of Appeals are chosen for a period of eight years.

Salaries and Duties of Federal Judges Congress sets the salaries of federal judges and has provided a generous retirement for them. They may retire at age 70, and if they have served for at least 10 years, receive full salary for the rest of their lives. Or, they may retire at full salary at age 65, after at least 15 years of service. The Chief Justice may call any retired judge back to temporary duty in a lower federal court at any time.

Today, federal judges have little involvement in the day-to-day administrative operations of the courts over which they preside. Their primary mission is to hear and decide cases. A clerk, several deputy clerks, bailiffs, court reporters and stenographers, probation officers, and others provide support services.

The judges of each of the 94 district courts appoint one or more United States magistrates, of which there are now more than 400. They are appointed to eight-year terms and handle a number of legal matters once dealt with by the judges themselves. They issue warrants of arrest, and often hear evidence to decide whether or not a person who has been arrested on a federal charge should be held for action by a grand jury. They also set bail in federal criminal cases, and even have the power to try those who are charged with certain minor offenses.

Other Federal Judges and Appointments Each federal judicial district also has at least one bankruptcy judge. These judges handle bankruptcy cases under the direction of the district court to which they are

Types of Inferior Federal Courts

	CONSTITUTIONAL COURTS				SPECIAL COURTS					
Courts	District Courts	U.S. Courts of Appeals	U.S. Court of Appeals for the Federal Circuit	U.S. Court of International Trade	U.S. Court of Federal Claims	U.S. Tax Court	Territorial Courts	U.S. Court of Appeals for the Armed Forces	Courts of the District of Columbia	U.S. Court of Appeals for Veterans Claims
Year Created	1789	1891	1982	1890	1855	1969	n/a	1951	1970s	1988
Number of Courts	94	13	1	1	1	1	3	1	4	1
Number of Judges	678	179	18	9	17	34	n/a	5	n/a	9
Terms of Judges	Life	Life	Life	Life	8–15 years	8–15 years	8–15 years	8–15 years	8–15 years	8–15 years

SOURCES: United States Courts online, United States Tax Court online, United States Court of Appeals for the Armed Forces online, Encyclopedia Britannica Online

>> The inferior courts include the constitutional and the special courts. **Analyze Charts** What events in U.S. history might have contributed to the need for the Court of International Trade?

assigned. There are now some 300 bankruptcy judges, all of them appointed to 14-year terms by the judges of each federal court of appeals.

The President and the Senate appoint a United States Attorney for each federal judicial district. The U.S. Attorneys and their many deputies are the government's prosecutors. They work closely with the FBI and other law enforcement agencies, and they bring to trial those persons charged with federal crimes. They also represent the United States in all civil actions brought by or against the Federal Government in their districts.

The President and Senate also select a United States marshal to serve each of the district courts. These marshals, and their several deputy U.S. marshals, perform duties much like those of a county sheriff.

The marshals make arrests in federal criminal cases, hold accused persons in custody, secure jurors, serve legal papers, keep order in courtrooms, and execute court orders and decisions. They also respond to such emergency situations as riots, mob violence, and other civil disturbances, as well as terrorist incidents. All United States Attorneys and marshals are appointed to four-year terms.

>> There are 875 federal judges: 9 on the Supreme Court, 179 on courts of appeals, 678 on district courts, and 9 on the Court of International Trade. Their trials follow similar formats.

DRAW CONCLUSIONS Why did the Framers create a system of judicial selection that requires the cooperation of the President and the Senate?

ASSESSMENT

1. **Support Ideas with Examples** Why did the Framers of the Constitution stipulate that federal judges be appointed, rather than elected, and serve for life?
2. **Infer** Why did the Framers believe that an independent judiciary was so important?
3. **Infer** What are the two general principles that determine whether the federal courts have jurisdiction over a case? Do you think these principles are broad enough? Why or why not?
4. **Analyze Information** What could happen if it is a concurrent jurisdiction situation and the plaintiff files in the State court, rather than in a federal court?
5. **Compare and Contrast** Explain the difference between judicial restraint and judicial activism.

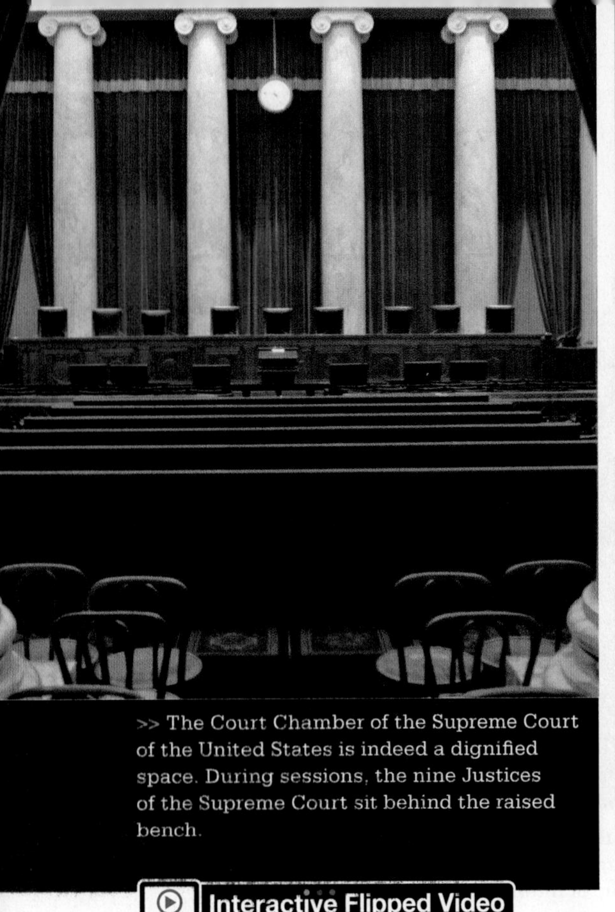

>> The Court Chamber of the Supreme Court of the United States is indeed a dignified space. During sessions, the nine Justices of the Supreme Court sit behind the raised bench.

Interactive Flipped Video

7.2 The eagle, the flag, Uncle Sam—you almost certainly recognize these symbols. They are used widely to represent the United States. You probably also know the symbol for justice: the blindfolded woman holding a balanced scale. She represents what is perhaps this nation's loftiest goal: equal justice under the law. Indeed, those words are chiseled in marble above the entrance to the Supreme Court building in Washington, D.C.

>> Objectives

Define the concept of judicial review, and identify the roles played by Thomas Jefferson, James Madison, and John Marshall in the case in which the Court first asserted its power of judicial review.

Outline the types of jurisdiction that apply to the Supreme Court.

Explain how cases reach the Supreme Court.

Summarize the way the Supreme Court operates.

>> Key Terms

judicial review
writ of certiorari
certificate
brief
majority opinion
concurring opinion
dissenting opinions
James Madison
John Marshall
Thomas Jefferson
William Marbury

The Supreme Court

What Is Judicial Review?

Composition of the Court The Supreme Court of the United States is the only court specifically created by the Constitution, in Article III, Section 1. The Court is made up of the Chief Justice of the United States, whose office is also established by the Constitution (Article I, Section 3, Clause 6), and eight associate justices.

Congress sets the number of associate justices and thus the size of the Supreme Court. The Judiciary Act of 1789 created a Court of six justices, including the Chief Justice. The Court was reduced to five members in 1801 but increased to seven in 1807, to nine in 1837, and to 10 in 1863. It was reduced to seven in 1866 and increased to the present size of nine in 1869.

The Third Branch of Government The Framers quite purposely placed the Court on an equal plane with the President and Congress. As the highest court in the land, it stands as the court of last resort in all questions of federal law. That is, the Supreme Court of the United States is the final authority in any case involving any question arising under the Constitution, an act of Congress, or a treaty of the United States.

Remember, most courts in this country, both federal and State, may exercise the critically important power of **judicial review**. They have the extraordinary power to decide the constitutionality of an act of government, whether executive, legislative, or judicial.

The ultimate exercise of that power rests with the Supreme Court of the United States. That single fact makes the Supreme Court the final authority on the meaning of the Constitution.

The Constitution does not, in so many words, provide for the power of judicial review. Nevertheless, there is little doubt that the Framers intended that the federal courts—and, in particular, the Supreme Court—should have this power. (See Article III, Section 2, setting out the Court's jurisdiction, and Article VI, Section 2, the Supremacy Clause.)

Marbury* v. *Madison The Court first asserted its power of judicial review in *Marbury* v. *Madison* in 1803. Recall that the case arose in the aftermath of the stormy elections of 1800. **Thomas Jefferson** had won the presidency and control of both houses of Congress. The outgoing Federalists, stung by their defeat, then tried to pack the judiciary with loyal party members. Congress created several new federal judgeships in the early weeks of 1801, and President John Adams quickly filled those posts with Federalists.

William Marbury had been appointed a justice of the peace for the District of Columbia. The Senate had promptly confirmed his appointment, and late on the night of March 3, 1801, President Adams signed the commissions of office for Marbury and a number of other new judges. The next day, Jefferson became President and discovered that Marbury's commission and several others had not been delivered.

Angered by the Federalists' attempted court-packing scheme, President Jefferson instructed **James Madison**, the new secretary of state, not to deliver those commissions. William Marbury then went to the Supreme Court, seeking a writ of mandamus to force delivery. A writ of mandamus is a court order compelling an officer of government to perform an act that the officer has a clear legal duty to perform.

Overturning an Act of Congress Marbury based his suit on the Judiciary Act of 1789, in which Congress had created the federal court system. That law gave the Supreme Court the right to hear such suits in its original jurisdiction (not on appeal from a lower court).

In a unanimous opinion written by Chief Justice **John Marshall**, the Court refused Marbury's request. It did so because it found the section of the Judiciary Act on which Marbury had based his case to be in conflict with Article III of the Constitution and, therefore, void.

How the *Marbury* Decision Affects the Supreme Court Today With the Court's decision, Chief Justice Marshall claimed for the Supreme Court the right to

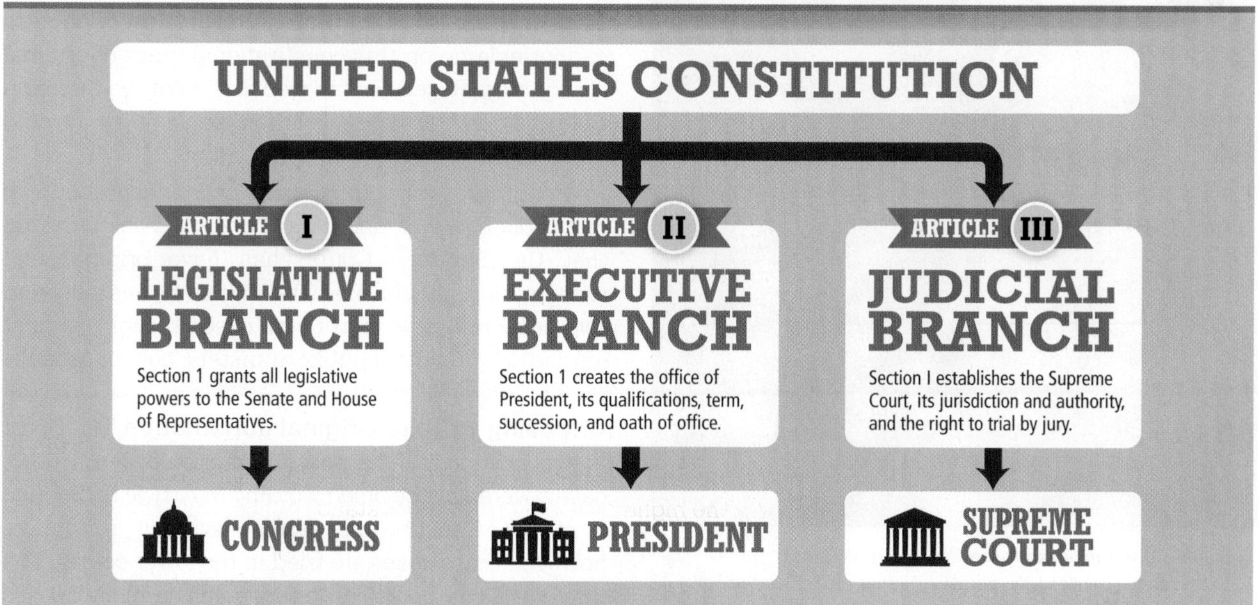
THE THREE BRANCHES OF GOVERNMENT
UNITED STATES CONSTITUTION
ARTICLE I
LEGISLATIVE BRANCH
Section 1 grants all legislative powers to the Senate and House of Representatives.
CONGRESS
ARTICLE II
EXECUTIVE BRANCH
Section 1 creates the office of President, its qualifications, term, succession, and oath of office.
PRESIDENT
ARTICLE III
JUDICIAL BRANCH
Section I establishes the Supreme Court, its jurisdiction and authority, and the right to trial by jury.
SUPREME COURT

>> The U.S. Constitution created three branches of government: legislative, executive, and judicial. **Analyze Information** Why do you think the Framers created the three branches to be equal?

>> Chief Justice John Marshall wrote the Court's opinion in *Marbury* v. *Madison,* saying, "A law repugnant to the Constitution is void."

>> The U.S. ambassador to Colombia, William Brownfield (center left, pointing), was reprimanded by the Supreme Court in 2009 for interfering in Colombia's civil matters.

declare acts of Congress unconstitutional, and so laid the foundation for the judicial branch's key role in the development of the American system of government.

The dramatic and often far-reaching effects of the Supreme Court's exercise of the power of judicial review tend to overshadow much of its other work. Each year, the Supreme Court hears dozens of cases in which questions of constitutionality are not raised, but in which federal law is interpreted and applied. Thus, many of the more important statutes that Congress has passed have been brought to the Supreme Court time and again for decisions. So, too, have many of the lesser ones. In interpreting those laws and applying them to specific situations, the Court has had a real impact on both their meaning and their effect.

? **COMPARE** How does the Supreme Court's power of judicial review differ from the power of a district court to determine guilt or innocence in a criminal case?

Jurisdiction of the Supreme Court

The Supreme Court has both original and appellate jurisdiction. Most of its cases, however, come on appeal—from the lower federal courts and from the highest State courts. Article III, Section 2 of the Constitution spells out two classes of cases that may be heard by the High Court in its original jurisdiction: (1) those to which a State is a party, and (2) those affecting ambassadors, other public ministers, and consuls.

Two Types of Original Jurisdiction Congress cannot enlarge on this constitutional grant of original jurisdiction. Recall, that is precisely what the Supreme Court held in *Marbury.* If Congress could do so, it would in effect be amending the Constitution.

Congress can implement the constitutional provision, however, and it has done so. It has provided that the Supreme Court shall have original and exclusive jurisdiction over (1) all controversies involving two or more States, and (2) all cases brought against ambassadors or other public ministers, but not consuls.

Choosing to Take Original Jurisdiction The Court may choose to take original jurisdiction over any other case covered by the broad wording in Article III, Section 2 of the Constitution. Almost without exception, however, those cases are tried in the lower courts. The Supreme Court hears only a very small number of cases in its original jurisdiction—in fact, no more than a case or two each term.

INTEGRATE INFORMATION In 2013, the Supreme Court agreed to hear a case challenging Environmental Protection Agency (a federal agency) regulations related to greenhouse gases. The case had previously been heard in federal court—most recently, by the United States Court of Appeals for the District of Columbia Circuit in 2012. What type of jurisdiction did the Supreme Court have in this case, and why?

Appealing to the Supreme Court

More than 10,000 cases are now appealed to the Supreme Court each term. Of these, the Court accepts only a few hundred for decision. In most cases, petitions for review are denied, usually because most of the justices agree with the decision of the lower court or believe that the case involves no significant point of law.

In short, the High Court is in the somewhat enviable position of being able to set its own agenda. It decides what it wants to decide. The Court selects those cases that it does hear according to "the rule of four": At least four of its nine justices must agree that a case should be put on the Court's docket.

More than half the cases decided by the Court are disposed of in brief orders. For example, an order may remand (return) a case to a lower court for reconsideration in light of some other recent and related case decided by the High Court. All told, the Court now decides, after hearing arguments and with full opinions, fewer than 80 cases per term.

Writs of Certiorari Most cases reach the Supreme Court by **writ of certiorari** (from the Latin, meaning "to be made more certain"). This writ is an order by the Court directing a lower court to send up the record in a given case for its review. Either party to a case can petition the Court to issue a writ. But, again, "cert" is granted in only a very limited number of instances—typically, only when a petition raises some important constitutional question or a serious problem in the interpretation of a statute.

When certiorari is denied, the decision of the lower court stands in that particular case. Note, however, that the denial of cert is not a decision on the merits of a case. All a denial means is that, for whatever reason, four or more justices could not agree that the Supreme Court should accept that particular case for review.

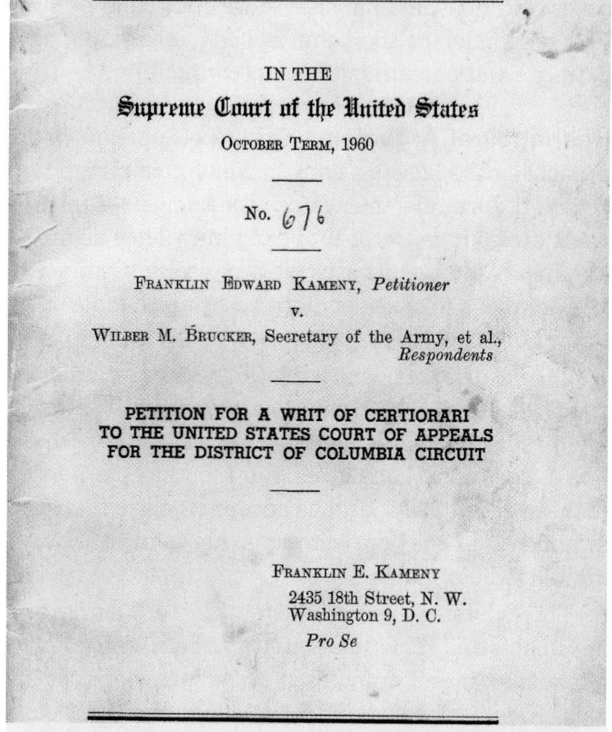

IN THE

Supreme Court of the United States

October Term, 1960

No. 676

Franklin Edward Kameny, *Petitioner*

v.

Wilber M. Brucker, Secretary of the Army, et al., *Respondents*

PETITION FOR A WRIT OF CERTIORARI TO THE UNITED STATES COURT OF APPEALS FOR THE DISTRICT OF COLUMBIA CIRCUIT

Franklin E. Kameny
2435 18th Street, N. W.
Washington 9, D. C.
Pro Se

>> A petition for a writ of certiorari can be issued by either party to a case to the Supreme Court. If the Court issues a writ, it means that the Court has agreed to accept the case.

Interactive Chart

Certifying Answers to Specific Questions A few cases do reach the Court in yet another way: by **certificate.** This process is used when a lower court is not clear about the procedure or the rule of law that should apply in a case. The lower court asks the Supreme Court to certify the answer to a specific question in the matter.

Most cases that reach the Court do so from the highest State courts and the federal courts of appeals. A very few do come from the federal district courts and an even smaller number from the Court of Appeals for the Armed Forces.

CONTRAST How does the procedure for obtaining a writ of certiorari differ from the procedure for obtaining a certificate?

Hearing a Supreme Court Case

A Supreme Court terms lasts from the first Monday in October to the first Monday in October of the following year. During that time, the Court actually sits—hears cases and delivers opinions—only until June or July. The remainder of the term is spent analyzing new petitions and preparing for the following term.

Hearing Oral Arguments Once the Supreme Court accepts a case, it sets a date on which that matter will be heard. As a rule, the justices consider cases in two-week cycles from October to early May. They hear oral arguments in several cases for two weeks; then recess for two weeks to consider those cases and handle other Court business.

On those days on which the Court hears arguments, it convenes at 10:00 a.m. on Mondays, Tuesdays, Wednesdays, and sometimes Thursdays. At those public sessions, the lawyers, representing the parties of those cases the Court has accepted, make their oral arguments. Their presentations are almost always limited to 30 minutes.

The justices usually listen to an attorney's arguments and sometimes interrupt them with pointed questions. After 25 minutes, a white light flashes at the lectern from which an attorney addresses the Court. Five minutes later, a red light signals the end of the presentation and it must stop, even if the lawyer is in mid-sentence.

>> President Barack Obama meets with Donald Verrilli (second from left) and other advisors in the Oval Office. Verrilli was the 46th solicitor general of the United States.

Filing Briefs Each party files detailed written statements—**briefs**—with the Court before they present their oral arguments. These detailed statements spell out the party's legal position and are built largely on relevant facts and the citation of precedents. Briefs often run to hundreds of pages.

The Court may also receive *amicus curiae* (friend of the court) briefs. These are briefs filed by persons or groups who are not actual parties to a case but who nonetheless have a substantial interest in its outcome.

Thus, for example, cases involving such highly charged matters as abortion or affirmative action regularly attract a large number of *amicus* briefs. Notice, however, that these briefs can be filed only with the Court's permission or at its request.

The Solicitor General The solicitor general, a principal officer in the Department of Justice, is often called the Federal Government's chief trial lawyer. He or she represents the United States in all cases to which it is a party in the Supreme Court and may appear and argue for the government in any federal or State court.

The solicitor general also has another extraordinary responsibility. He decides which cases the government should ask the Supreme Court to review and what position the United States should take in those cases it brings before the High Court.

Meeting in Conference On most Fridays through a term, the justices meet in conference. There, in closest secrecy, they consider the cases in which they have heard oral arguments; and there, too, they decide which new cases they will accept for decision.

Only the Chief Justice, who presides, and the eight other members of the Court are present at the conference. The Chief Justice leads the discussion of each case to be considered—stating the facts, summarizing the questions of law involved, and usually indicating how he thinks the Court should dispose of that case. Then each of the associate justices, in order of seniority, present their views and conclusions. A majority must decide which party wins or loses a case and whether a lower court's decision in that matter is to be affirmed or reversed.

About a third of the Court's decisions are unanimous, but most find the Court divided. The High Court is sometimes criticized for its split decisions. However, most of the cases it hears pose difficult and complicated questions, and many present questions on which lower courts have disagreed. In short, most of the Court's cases excite controversy; the easy cases seldom get that far.

The Power of Precedent

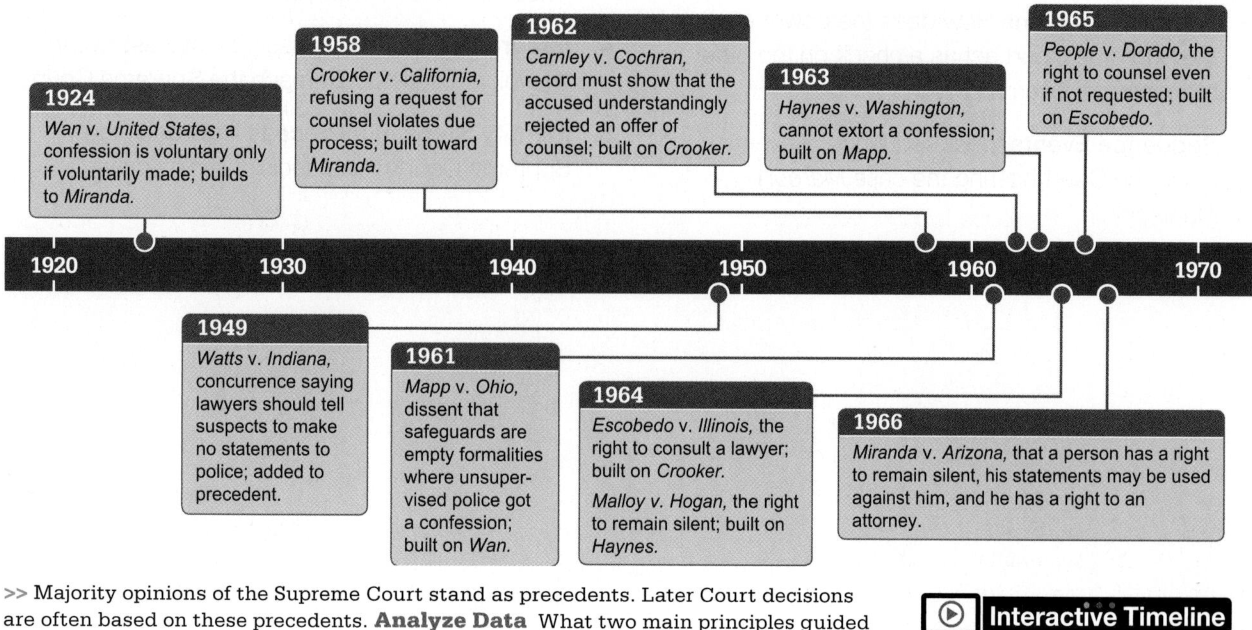
1924
Wan v. United States, a confession is voluntary only if voluntarily made; builds to Miranda.
1958
Crooker v. California, refusing a request for counsel violates due process; built toward Miranda.
1962
Carnley v. Cochran, record must show that the accused understandingly rejected an offer of counsel; built on Crooker.
1963
Haynes v. Washington, cannot extort a confession; built on Mapp.
1965
People v. Dorado, the right to counsel even if not requested; built on Escobedo.
1920
1930
1940
1950
1960
1970
1949
Watts v. Indiana, concurrence saying lawyers should tell suspects to make no statements to police; added to precedent.
1961
Mapp v. Ohio, dissent that safeguards are empty formalities where unsupervised police got a confession; built on Wan.
1964
Escobedo v. Illinois, the right to consult a lawyer; built on Crooker.
Malloy v. Hogan, the right to remain silent; built on Haynes.
1966
Miranda v. Arizona, that a person has a right to remain silent, his statements may be used against him, and he has a right to an attorney.

>> Majority opinions of the Supreme Court stand as precedents. Later Court decisions are often based on these precedents. **Analyze Data** What two main principles guided the Court in *Miranda*?

Interactive Timeline

Announcing a Decision Once a case has been considered and decided in conference, the Court announces its decision in the matter and, with it, issues one or more written opinions. The decision indicates which party has won the dispute and by what margin among the justices. Where the decision is unanimous, the Chief Justice most often writes the Court's opinion. If there has been a split decision, the Chief Justice may write the majority opinion, or he may assign that task to another justice in the majority. When the Chief Justice is in the minority, the senior justice in the majority makes that assignment.

The Majority Opinion The **majority opinion,** officially called "the Opinion of the Court," sets out the facts in a case, identifies the issues it presents, and details the reasons that underpin the majority's decision.

Most majority opinions, and many concurring and dissenting opinions, run to dozens of pages. Some Supreme Court decisions are issued with very brief, unsigned opinions. These *per curiam* (for the court) opinions seldom run more than a paragraph or two and usually dispose of relatively uncomplicated cases. All of the High Court's opinions in every case are published online and in the United States Reports, the official printed record of the decisions.

The Power of Precedent The Court's opinions are exceedingly valuable. Its majority opinions stand as precedents. The lower courts, both federal and State, are expected to follow precedent—that is, decide cases of like nature in a manner consistent with previous rulings.

The doctrine of precedent is often identified as *stare decisis*—Latin for "let the decision stand," or adhere to decided cases.

Concurring Opinions One or more of the justices on the majority side may write a **concurring opinion,** usually to make some point not made or not emphasized in the majority opinion. In effect, a justice who writes a concurring opinion agrees with (concurs in) the majority decision as to the winner of a case but offers different reasons for reaching that conclusion.

Dissenting Opinions One or more **dissenting opinions** may be written by those justices who do not agree with the Court's majority decision. Those dissents do not become precedent. They are, instead, expressions of opposition to the majority's views in a case. Chief Justice Charles Evans Hughes once described dissenting opinions as "an appeal to the brooding spirit of the law, to the intelligence of a future day." Rarely, the High Court does reverse itself—and so minority opinion of today could become the Court's majority position on some distant tomorrow.

? MAKE GENERALIZATIONS Why would a justice refer to precedent while writing an opinion on a case?

ASSESSMENT

1. **Draw Conclusions** How does the power of the Supreme Court act as a check on the other branches of government?
2. **Sequence Events** What sequence of events led to the Court hearing the case *Marbury* v. *Madison*?
3. **Compare** Compare the Supreme Court's original jurisdiction with its appellate jurisdiction.
4. **Integrate Information** Describe at least two ways by which a case could reach the Supreme Court.
5. **Identify Steps in a Process** How does the Supreme Court reach decisions in its cases?

7.3 You know that the particular meaning of a word often depends on the context—the setting—in which it is used. Thus, *pitch* can be either a baseball term or a musical term; it can also refer to setting up a tent or to a high-pressure sales talk. The word *inferior* also has various meanings. Here, it describes the lower federal courts, those courts created by an act of Congress to function beneath the Supreme Court. The inferior courts handle nearly all of the cases tried in the federal courts.

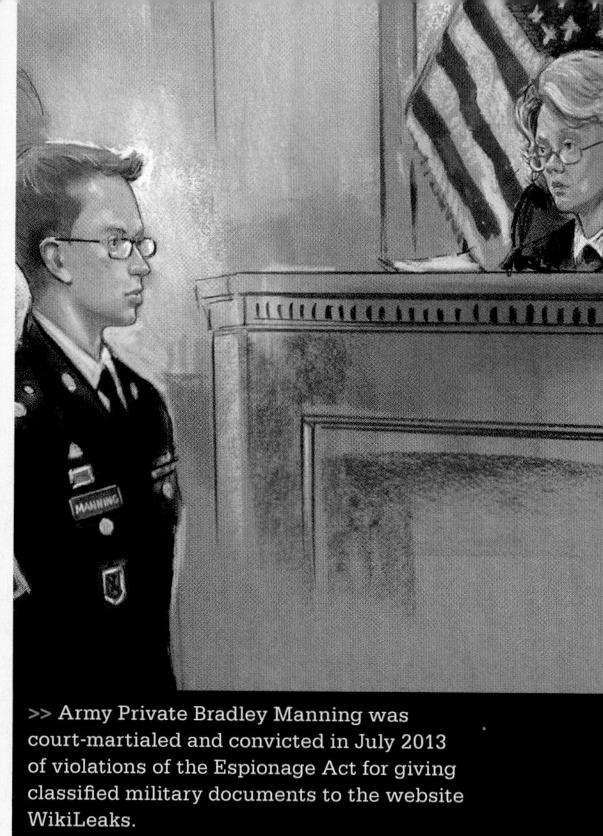

>> Army Private Bradley Manning was court-martialed and convicted in July 2013 of violations of the Espionage Act for giving classified military documents to the website WikiLeaks.

Interactive Flipped Video

The Inferior Courts and the Special Courts

>> Objectives

Describe the structure and jurisdiction of the federal district courts, the federal courts of appeals, and other constitutional courts.

Contrast the jurisdiction of the Court of Appeals for the Armed Forces and the Court of Appeals for Veterans Claims.

Explain how a citizen may sue the United States government in the Court of Federal Claims.

Examine the roles of the territorial courts and those of the District of Columbia courts.

Explain what types of cases are brought to the Tax Court.

>> Key Terms

criminal case
civil case
docket
record
courts-martial
civilian tribunal
redress
Guantanamo Bay, Cuba

The Structure and Role of the Federal District Courts

The United States district courts are the federal trial courts. Their judges handle more than 350,000 cases per year, about 80 percent of the federal caseload. The district courts were first created by Congress in the Judiciary Act of 1789. There are now 94 of them.

Federal Judicial Districts and Judges The 50 States are divided into 89 federal judicial districts. There are also federal district courts for Washington, D.C., Puerto Rico, the Virgin Islands, Guam, and the Northern Mariana Islands. Each State forms at least one judicial district. Some are divided into two or more districts, however—usually because of the larger amount of judicial business there. At least two judges are assigned to each district, but many districts have several. Thus, New York is divided into four judicial districts; one of them, the United States Judicial District for Southern New York, now has 44 judges.

Cases tried in the district courts are most often heard by a single judge. However, certain cases may be heard by a three-judge panel. Chiefly, these are cases that involve congressional districting or State legislative apportionment questions; those arising under the Civil Rights Act of 1964 or the Voting Rights Acts of 1965, 1970, 1975, and 1982; and certain antitrust actions.

Courts Focused on Terrorism Two little-known multi-judge panels—made up entirely of judges drawn from the district courts—play a key role in ongoing efforts to combat terrorism in this country and abroad. Both are shrouded in secrecy. One is the Foreign Intelligence Surveillance Court, created by Congress in 1978. It is often called the "FISA court" and is composed of 11 federal district court judges, who are appointed to seven-year terms by the Chief Justice of the United States. The court, which meets in secret, has the power to issue secret search warrants—court orders that allow the FBI and other federal law enforcement agencies to conduct covert surveillance of persons suspected of being spies or members of terrorist organizations.

The other is the Alien Terrorist Removal Court, created by Congress in 1996. It is made up of five district court judges, appointed by the Chief Justice to five-year terms. This court has the power to decide whether those persons identified as "alien terrorists" by the Attorney General of the United States should be expelled from this country.

District Court Jurisdiction The district courts have original jurisdiction over more than 80 percent of the cases that are heard in the federal court system. The only federal cases that do not begin in the district courts are those few that fall within the original jurisdiction of the Supreme Court, as well as those cases heard by the Court of International Trade or by one of the special courts. Thus, the district courts are the principal trial courts, the "courts of first instance," in the federal judiciary.

District Court Cases District court judges hear a wide range of both criminal cases and civil cases. In the federal courts, a **criminal case** is one in which a defendant is tried for committing some action that Congress has declared by law to be a federal crime. A federal **civil case** involves some noncriminal matter—say, a dispute over the terms of a contract or a suit in which the plaintiff seeks damages (money) for some harm done by the defendant.

The United States is always a party to a federal criminal case, as the prosecutor. Most civil cases are disputes between private parties, but here, too, the

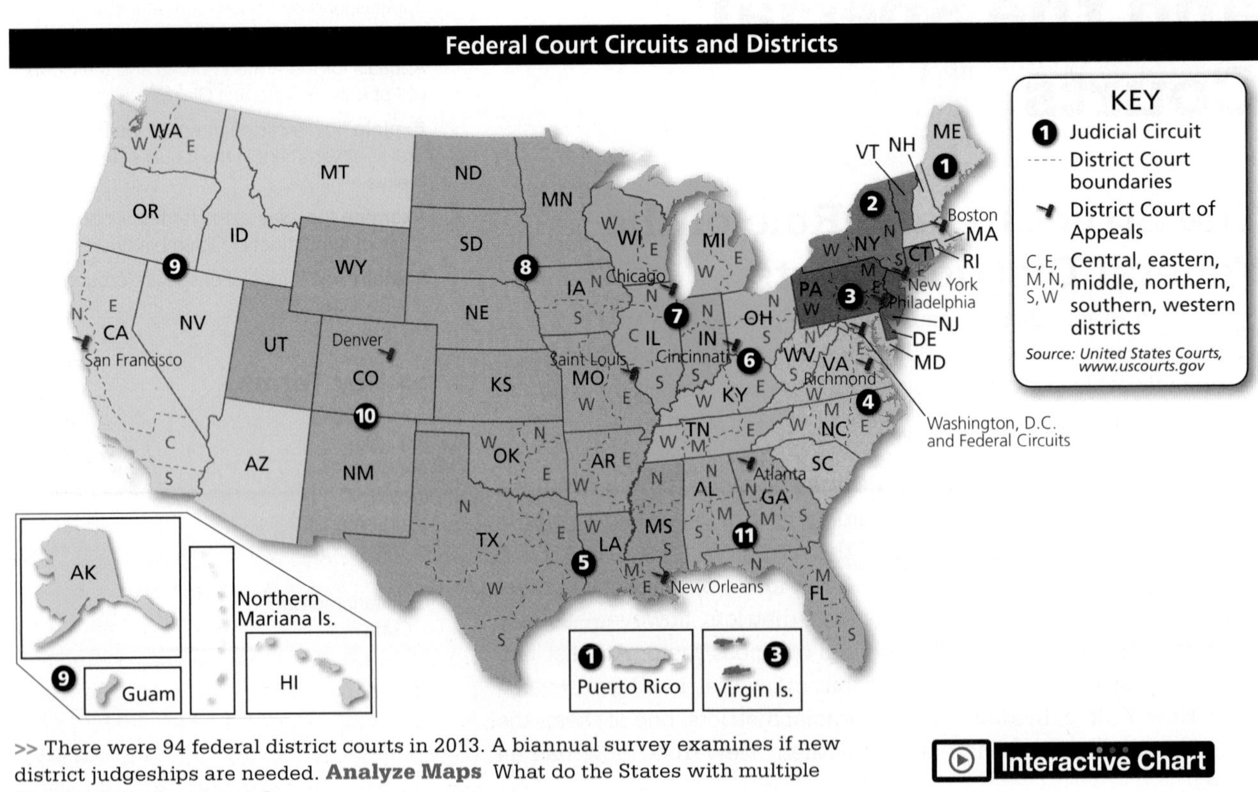

>> There were 94 federal district courts in 2013. A biannual survey examines if new district judgeships are needed. **Analyze Maps** What do the States with multiple districts have in common?

Interactive Chart

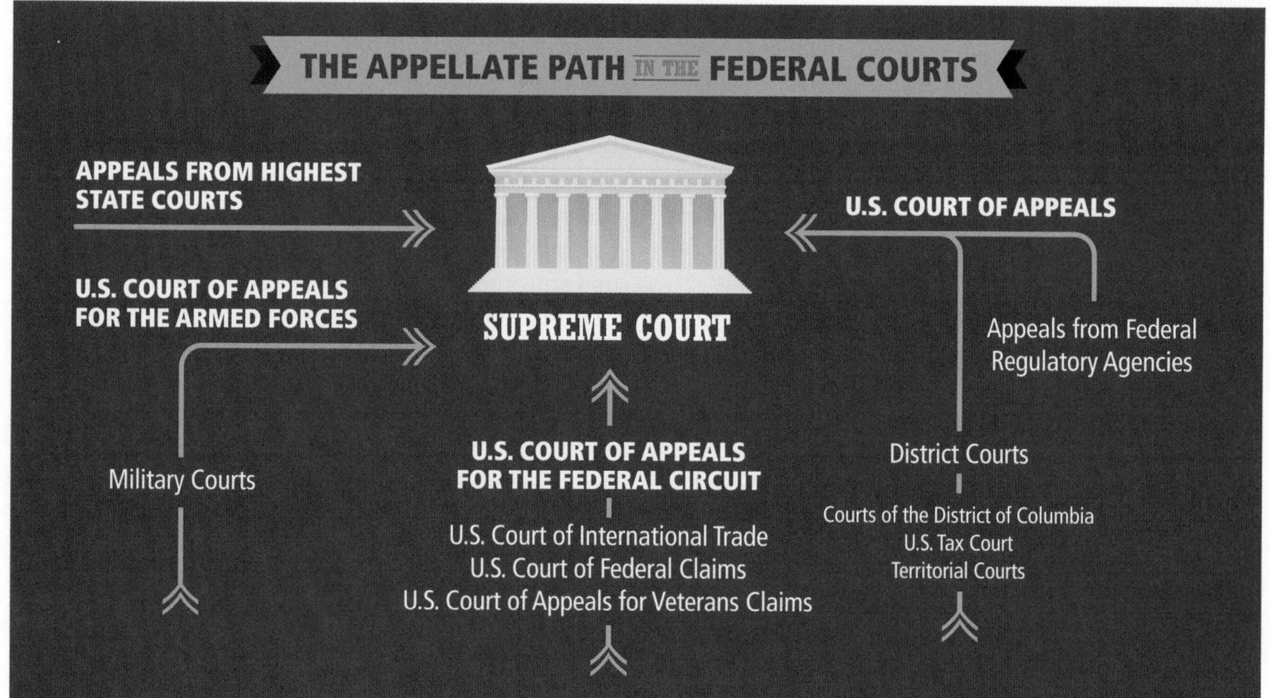

>> Cases originating in various courts can be appealed to the U.S. Supreme Court. **Analyze Charts** In which courts do you suppose the largest number of cases originate?

United States may be a litigant, as either the plaintiff or the defendant.

The district courts try criminal cases ranging from bank robbery, kidnapping, and mail fraud to counterfeiting, terrorism, and tax evasion. They hear civil cases arising under bankruptcy, postal, tax, public lands, civil rights, and other laws of the United States. These trial courts are the only federal courts that use grand juries to indict defendants, and petit juries to determine their guilt or innocence.

Final Decisions Most of the decisions made in the 94 federal district courts are final. That is, most federal cases not only begin in those courts, they end there as well. Losing parties do not often appeal a decision to a higher court. Still, a few cases are taken to the court of appeals in that judicial circuit or, in a few instances, directly to the Supreme Court.

? COMPARE AND CONTRAST How are the two constitutional courts devoted to combating terrorism different from other federal district courts? Do they compare in any way to the federal special courts? Explain.

The Structure and Role of the Federal Courts of Appeals

The courts of appeals were created by Congress in 1891. They were established as "gatekeepers" to relieve the Supreme Court of much of the burden of hearing appeals from the decisions of the district courts. Those appeals had become so numerous that the High Court was more than three years behind on its **docket**—its list of cases to be heard.

There are now 13 courts of appeals in the federal judiciary. These tribunals were originally called the circuit courts of appeals. Before 1891, each Supreme Court justice "rode circuit," hearing appeals from the district courts within that geographic area. Congress renamed these courts in 1948, but they still are often called the "circuit courts."

The country is divided into 12 judicial circuits, including the District of Columbia. There is one court of appeals for each of those circuits, and they hear cases on appeal from the various district courts within their circuit. The Court of Appeals for the Federal Circuit is the thirteenth of these appellate tribunals. It sits in the District of Columbia, but its jurisdiction is nationwide and it is mostly concerned with appeals of decisions in patent, copyright, and international trade cases.

Appellate Court Judges Each of these courts is composed of from 6 to 28 judges (179 in all). In addition, a justice of the Supreme Court is assigned to each. For example, the United States Court of Appeals for the Eleventh Circuit covers Alabama, Florida, and Georgia. The court is composed of 12 circuit judges and Associate Justice Clarence Thomas of the Supreme Court. The judges hold their sessions in a number of major cities within the circuit.

Each court of appeals usually sits in three-judge panels. Occasionally, however, and especially for an important case, a court will sit *en banc*—that is, with all of the judges on that court participating.

Circuit-Based Appellate Court Jurisdiction The 13 courts of appeals have only appellate jurisdiction. For the 12 circuit-based courts, most cases come to them from the district courts within their circuit, but some are appealed from the Tax Court and some from the territorial courts. Recall, they are also empowered to hear appeals from the decisions of several federal regulatory agencies—for example, the Federal Trade Commission and the National Labor Relations Board.

Court of Appeals for the Federal Circuit Jurisdiction Unlike the 12 circuit-based courts, the jurisdiction of the thirteenth, the Court of Appeals for the Federal Circuit, is nationwide in scope. Congress created this court in 1982, with the special purpose of centralizing and speeding up the handling of appeals in certain types of federal civil cases.

The Court of Appeals for the Federal Circuit hears appeals from the decisions rendered in several different courts. Many of its cases come from the other constitutional court, the Court of International Trade, and still others come from two of the special courts: the Court of Federal Claims and the Court of Appeals for Veterans Claims. It also hears the appeals taken in any patent, copyright, or trademark case decided in any of the 94 federal district courts.

An Important Role Again, these 13 tribunals are appellate courts. They do not conduct trials or accept new evidence in the cases they hear. Instead, they review the **record,** the transcript of proceedings made in the trial court, and they ponder the oral and written arguments (the briefs) submitted by attorneys representing parties to a case. The fact that less than one percent of their decisions are appealed to the Supreme Court underscores the importance of the place these tribunals occupy.

? DRAW CONCLUSIONS Why are two courts of appeals located in Washington, D.C.?

The Court of Appeals for the Federal Circuit

U.S. Court of Appeals for Veterans Claims

THE UNITED STATES COURT OF APPEALS FOR THE FEDERAL CIRCUIT

U.S. Court of International Trade

U.S. Court of Federal Claims

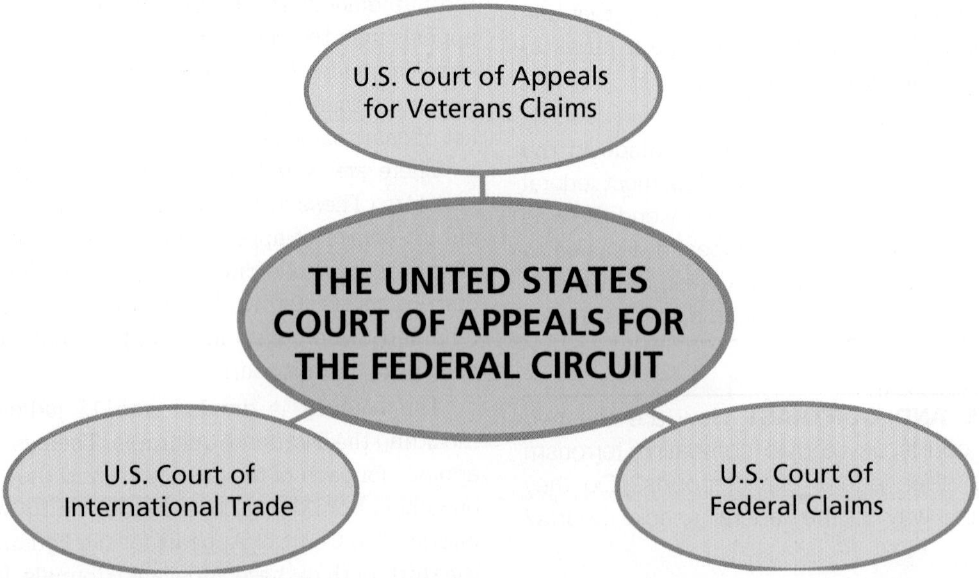

>> The court of appeals is authorized to hear a wide variety of cases outside of Washington, and has convened in many different cities. **Analyze Charts** When might this be necessary?

The Court of International Trade

Congress has established one other Article III court, the Court of International Trade. Often called the Trade Court, this body was originally created in 1890, and was restructured as a constitutional court in 1980.

The Trade Court now has nine judges, including its chief judge, appointed by the President and the Senate. Like the 94 district courts, it is a federal trial court, a court of first instance. It tries all civil (but not criminal) cases that arise out of the nation's customs and other trade-related laws. Its judges sit in panels of three and often hold jury trials in such major ports as New Orleans, San Francisco, Boston, and New York.

APPLY CONCEPTS Why wouldn't a case involving the piracy of a merchant vessel be tried in the Court of International Trade?

>> U.S. military courts, or courts-martial, employ lawyers and judges to try military personnel for crimes such as theft and assault, as well as for military offenses like desertion.

Military Justice—Special Courts and Commissions

Recall, the national court system is made up of two quite distinct types of federal courts. They are (1) the constitutional courts, sometimes called the regular or Article III courts, already discussed, and (2) the special courts, also known as the legislative or Article I courts.

Each of the special courts was established by Congress acting under the authority delegated to it in Article I, Section 8 of the Constitution—not under the power given to it in Article III to create courts to exercise the broad "judicial Power of the United States." That is to say, each of these courts has a very narrow jurisdiction; each hears only those cases that fall into a very limited class. The special courts differ from the constitutional courts in one other important regard. Although their judges are all appointed by the President and Senate, they serve for a fixed term—not for life "during good Behaviour."

The Purpose of Military Courts Beginning in 1789, Congress has created a system of military courts for each branch of the nation's armed forces, as an exercise of its expressed power to "make Rules for the Government and Regulation of the land and naval Forces." (Article I, Section 8, Clause 14.) These military courts—**courts-martial**—serve the special disciplinary needs of the armed forces and are *not* a part of the federal court system. Their judges, prosecutors, defense attorneys, court reporters, and other personnel are all members of the military; most of them are officers. They conduct trials of those members of the military who are accused of violating military law. Today, the proceedings in a court-martial are fairly similar to the trials held in civilian courts across the country. There are some important differences, however. For example, at a court-martial, only two thirds of the panel (the jury in the case) must agree on a guilty verdict, in contrast to the unanimous verdict usually required in cases tried in the civilian courts.

The Court of Appeals for the Armed Forces In 1950, Congress created the Court of Military Appeals, now titled the Court of Appeals for the Armed Forces, to review the more serious court-martial convictions of military personnel. This appellate court is a **civilian tribunal,** a part of the judicial branch, entirely separate from the military establishment. Appeals from the court's decisions can be taken to the Supreme Court. It is, then, the court of last resort in most cases that involve offenses against military law.

The Court of Appeals for Veterans Claims Acting under its power (Article I, Section 8, Clause 9) to "constitute Tribunals inferior to the supreme Court," Congress created the Court of Veterans Appeals in 1988 and changed its name in 1999 to the Court of Appeals for Veterans Claims.

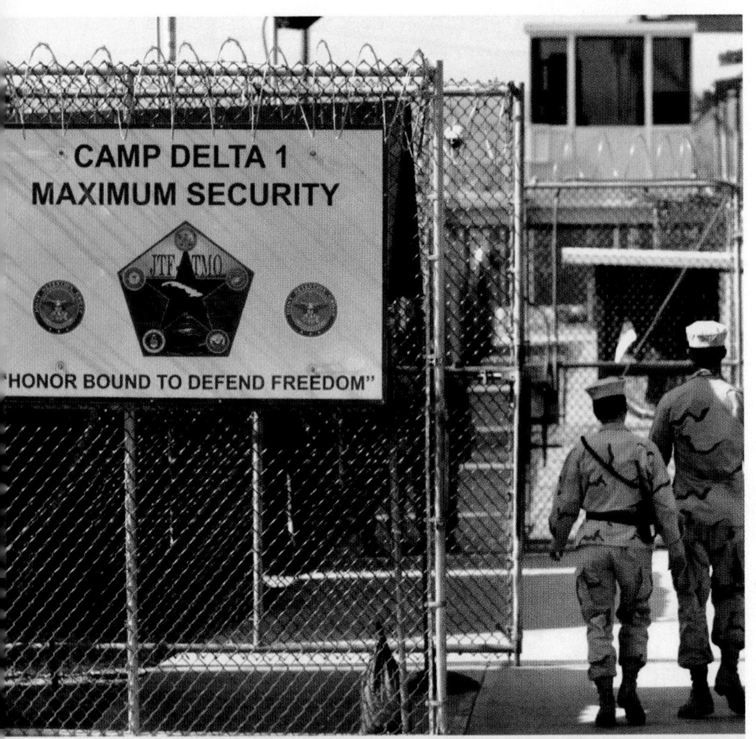

>> Since 2002, the U.S. Naval Station at Guantanamo Bay, Cuba, has housed Camp Delta, a military prison where suspected terrorists can be held indefinitely without a trial.

Interactive Gallery

>> In 2013, the Supreme Court ruled in favor of Maryland's DNA Collection Act. **Analyze Political Cartoons** What is the relationship between the long arm of the law and Lady Liberty?

This court has the power to hear appeals from the decisions of an administrative agency, the Board of Veterans' Appeals in the Department of Veterans Affairs (VA). Thus, this court hears cases in which individuals claim that the VA has denied or otherwise mishandled valid claims for veterans' benefits. Appeals from the decisions of the Court of Appeals for Veterans Claims can be taken to the Court of Appeals for the Federal Circuit.

Military Commissions In 2001, President Bush issued a controversial executive order creating several military commissions. These court-like bodies were set up, outside the regular courts-martial system, to try "unlawful enemy combatants"—suspected terrorists captured by American forces in Iraq and Afghanistan. Some 770 of those captives were held over a seven-year period in a military prison at the American naval base at **Guantanamo Bay, Cuba.**

Recall that in 2006, the Supreme Court found that those military commissions had been improperly established, in *Hamdan* v. *Rumsfeld.* The Court held that a chief executive could create such tribunals but only if authorized to do so by an act of Congress. Congress responded with the Military Commissions Act of 2006, but the commissions accomplished very little over the next three years.

Upon taking office, President Obama suspended the tribunals and ordered the closure of the Guantanamo Bay facility. Congressional resistance soon derailed those plans, however, and the daunting problem of the fate of some 170 detainees still held there remains.

? HYPOTHESIZE If a case settled in courts-martial is appealed, it is removed from the military system and placed into the federal judicial system. What is the rationale behind this approach?

Other Special Courts

The other special courts also have very narrow jurisdictions. They include the Court of Federal Claims, the territorial courts, the District of Columbia courts, and the U.S. Tax Court.

The Court of Federal Claims The United States government cannot be sued by anyone, in any court, for any reason, without its consent. The government is shielded from suit by the doctrine of sovereign immunity. The doctrine comes from an ancient principle of English public law: "The King can do no wrong." The rule is not intended to protect public officials from charges of wrongdoing; rather it is intended to prevent government from being hamstrung in its own courts. Congress has long since agreed to a long list of legitimate court actions against the government.

The government may be taken to court only in cases in which Congress has declared the United States to be open to suit. Originally, any person with a money claim against the United States could secure **redress**—satisfaction of a claim, payment—only by an act of Congress. In 1855, however, acting under its expressed power to pay the debts of the United States (Article I, Section 8, Clause 1), Congress set up the Court of Claims to hear such pleas. That body was renamed the United States Court of Federal Claims in 1992.

Methods of Compensation The Court of Federal Claims holds trials throughout the country, hearing claims for damages against the Federal Government. Those claims it upholds cannot in fact be paid until Congress appropriates the money, which it does almost as a matter of standard procedure. Appeals from the court's decisions may be carried to the Court of Appeals for the Federal Circuit.

Occasionally, those who lose in the Claims Court still manage to win some compensation. Some years ago, a Puget Sound mink rancher lost a case in which he claimed that low-flying Navy planes had frightened his animals and caused several of the females to become sterile. He asked $100 per mink. He lost, but then his congressman introduced a private bill that eventually paid him $10 for each animal.

The Territorial Courts Acting under its power (Article IV, Section 3, Clause 2) to "make all needful Rules and Regulations respecting the Territory . . . belonging to the United States," Congress has created courts for the nation's territories. These courts sit in the Virgin Islands, Guam, and the Northern Mariana Islands. They function much like the local courts in the 50 States.

The District of Columbia Courts Acting under its power to "exercise exclusive Legislation in all Cases whatsoever, over such District . . . as may . . . become the Seat of the Government of the United States" (Article I, Section 8, Clause 17), Congress has set up a judicial system for the nation's capital. Both the federal district court and the federal Court of Appeals for the District of Columbia hear cases as constitutional courts.

Congress has also established two local courts, much like the courts in the States: a superior court, which is the general trial court, and a court of appeals.

The United States Tax Court Acting under its power to tax (Article I, Section 8, Clause 1), Congress created the United States Tax Court in 1969 as "an independent judicial body" in the legislative branch. It is not, in fact, a part of the federal court system. The Tax Court hears civil but not criminal cases involving disputes over the application of the tax laws. Most of its cases, then, are generated by the Internal Revenue Service and other Treasury Department agencies. Its decisions may be appealed to the federal courts of appeals.

? **SUMMARIZE** Describe the factors that must fall into place for a U.S. citizen to successfully sue the federal government.

ASSESSMENT

1. **Integrate Information** Identify and describe the different roles of the legislative branch of the federal government with regard to the inferior constitutional courts and special courts of the judicial branch.
2. **Draw Conclusions** How does the large number of appellate courts support a democratic form of government?
3. **Interpret** Congress establishes special courts for particular reasons. These reasons often reflect what is happening in the country. Give an example of how understanding congressional decisions about special courts also reveals your knowledge of current events.
4. **Explain** Why is it necessary to have District of Columbia special courts?
5. **Compare and Contrast** How are the cases heard in the Court of Appeals for Veterans Claims and the Court of Federal Claims alike and different?

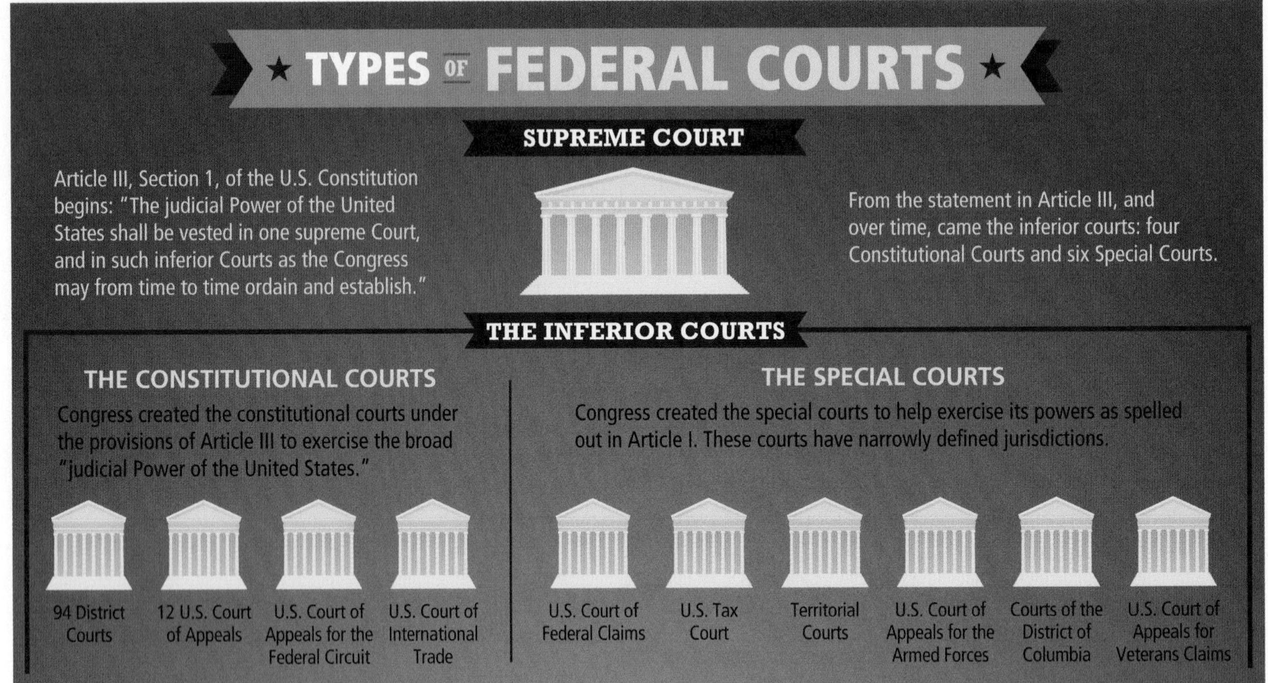
TYPES OF FEDERAL COURTS
SUPREME COURT
Article III, Section 1, of the U.S. Constitution begins: "The judicial Power of the United States shall be vested in one supreme Court, and in such inferior Courts as the Congress may from time to time ordain and establish."
From the statement in Article III, and over time, came the inferior courts: four Constitutional Courts and six Special Courts.
THE INFERIOR COURTS
THE CONSTITUTIONAL COURTS
Congress created the constitutional courts under the provisions of Article III to exercise the broad "judicial Power of the United States."
94 District Courts
12 U.S. Court of Appeals
U.S. Court of Appeals for the Federal Circuit
U.S. Court of International Trade
THE SPECIAL COURTS
Congress created the special courts to help exercise its powers as spelled out in Article I. These courts have narrowly defined jurisdictions.
U.S. Court of Federal Claims
U.S. Tax Court
Territorial Courts
U.S. Court of Appeals for the Armed Forces
Courts of the District of Columbia
U.S. Court of Appeals for Veterans Claims

1. **Compare Methods** Use the chart above and other sources to create a written or oral presentation about the process of selecting a federal judge for the constitutional courts and special courts. Consider such things as: Who nominates and appoints a federal judge? What are the requirements for federal judges? Compare constitutional judges vs. special court judges. Analyzing the chart, explain why and in what ways constitutional judges operate differently from special court judges?
2. **Understand the Role of Limited Government** Write a paragraph that describes the events in 1734 surrounding Governor William Cosby of New York and editor Peter Zenger of the *New York Weekly Journal* and how these events had an impact on the role of government in protecting individual rights. Consider such things as: colonists being upset with Governor William Cosby; the arrest of newspaper editor Peter Zenger; court rulings and implications on individual rights protection. Why were the events involving Governor William Cosby and editor Peter Zenger influential in enforcing protection of individual rights by governments and courts?
3. **Analyze functions and explain provisions** Write a paragraph that analyzes judicial review and the power of the Supreme Court. Consider the following: judicial review; the responsibilities of the Supreme Court; checks and balances among the executive, judicial, and legislative branches. Why is the Supreme Court the final authority on the meaning of the Constitution?
4. **Identify Contributions and Individuals** Write a paragraph that describes why the Supreme Court case of *Marbury v. Madison* was significant and identifies the key players in the case. Consider such things: Thomas Jefferson's election in 1800; John Adams's involvement; the case of *Marbury v. Madison*; John Marshall's ruling; how *Marbury v. Madison* strengthened the Supreme Court. Why was the *Marbury v. Madison* case and its players influential in the development of the U.S. government?

5. **Explain Provisions** Use the information from the chart below to write a paragraph that describes the responsibilities of the executive, legislative, and judicial branches. Then, complete the chart by visually presenting the checks and balances among the three branches of government.
6. **Analyze Issues** Create a written or oral presentation comparing and contrasting judicial activism and judicial restraint as practiced by federal judges. Consider these questions: What is judicial activism? What is judicial restraint? Which judicial philosophy is better for interpreting and applying provisions in the Constitution and acts of Congress? What are the difference between judicial activism and judicial restraint, and when should each judicial philosophy be used?
7. **Analyze Functions** Write a paragraph that analyzes the functions and powers of the Foreign Intelligence Surveillance Court, and the extent to which it may come in conflict with the Bill of Rights. Consider the following: the responsibilities of the Foreign Intelligence Surveillance Court; national security issues; the Foreign Intelligence Surveillance Court vs. the 4th Amendment.
8. **Analyze Structure and Functions** Create a visual presentation that analyzes the structure and function of the Federal Court of Appeals. Consider such things as: the purpose of the Federal Court of Appeals; how the judicial circuits are divided; the jurisdiction of the Court of Appeals for the Federal Circuit; Court of Appeals for the Armed Forces vs. the Court of Appeals for Veterans Claims. Why is the Federal Court of Appeals an important component of the federal judicial system?
9. **Analyze Functions** Use research materials to find out more about military courts and the debate surrounding military commissions in the aftermath of the terror attacks of 2001. Share your findings in the form of an oral presentation. Focus on a question about a contemporary government issue or a topic involving military courts you want to learn more about; plan the project by outlining goals and objectives; research information using valid primary and secondary sources; create the project; improve the project by editing and reevaluating your goals and objectives; present your project.

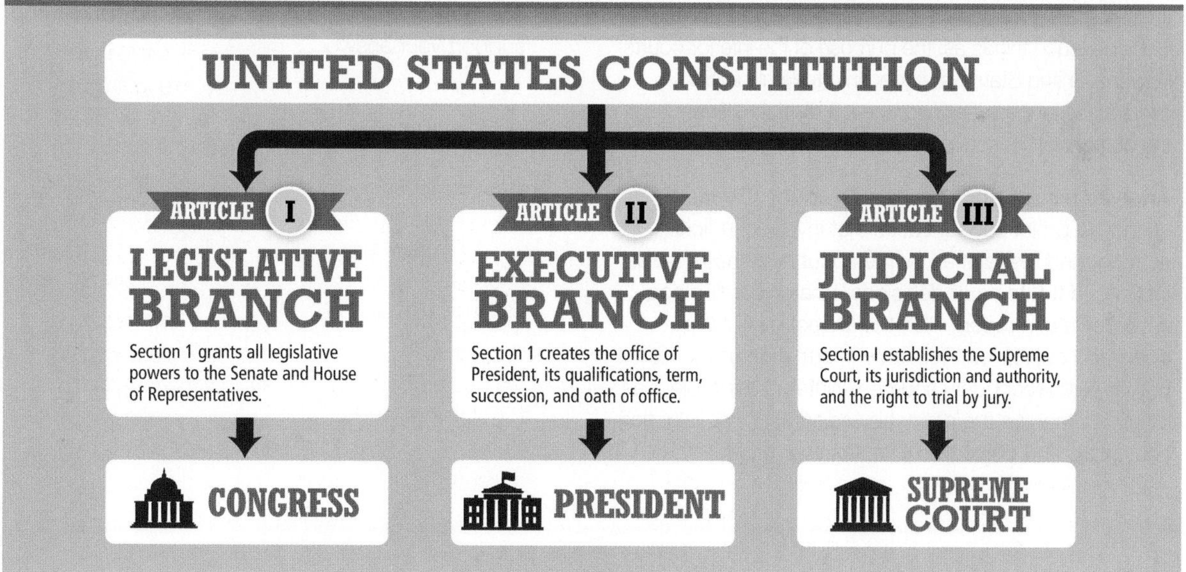
THE THREE BRANCHES OF GOVERNMENT
UNITED STATES CONSTITUTION
ARTICLE I
LEGISLATIVE BRANCH
Section 1 grants all legislative powers to the Senate and House of Representatives.
CONGRESS
ARTICLE II
EXECUTIVE BRANCH
Section 1 creates the office of President, its qualifications, term, succession, and oath of office.
PRESIDENT
ARTICLE III
JUDICIAL BRANCH
Section I establishes the Supreme Court, its jurisdiction and authority, and the right to trial by jury.
SUPREME COURT

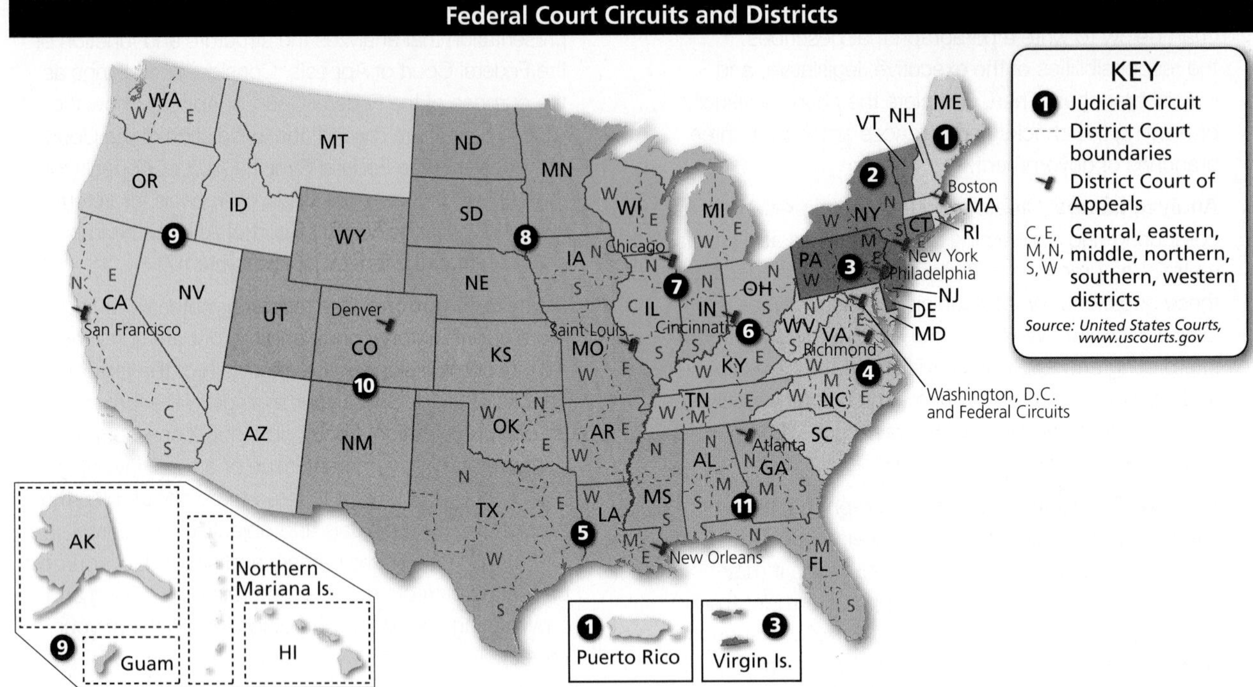

10. Analyze the Structure, Evaluate Data, and Interpret Information Use the map above to write a paragraph that analyzes the structure of the federal judicial districts. Consider such things as: the purpose of the inferior courts; how the United States is divided into federal judicial circuits; the judges assigned to each district; differences in the number of districts per U.S. state.

11. Analyze Issues and Create a Product Create an inquiry project about cases that involved judicial activism and restraint and write about how these cases influenced future court decisions. Share your findings in the form of a report. Plan the project by outlining goals and objectives. Research information using valid primary and secondary sources. Write up the project as a report. Improve the project by editing and reevaluating your goals and objectives. Present your project.

12. Write About the Essential Question Write an essay on the Essential Question: How should we handle conflict? Use evidence from your study of this Topic to support your answer.

Go online to PearsonRealize.com and use the texts, quizzes, interactivities, Interactive Reading Notepads, Flipped Videos, and other resources from this Topic to prepare for the Topic Test.

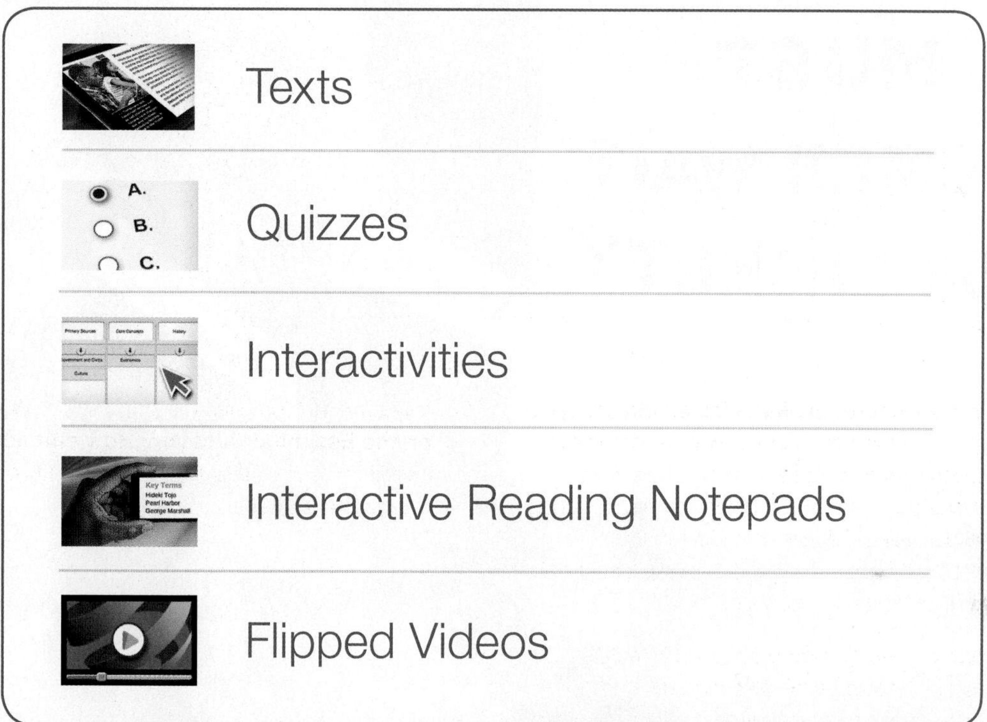

While online you can also check the progress you've made learning the topic and course content by viewing your grades, test scores, and assignment status.

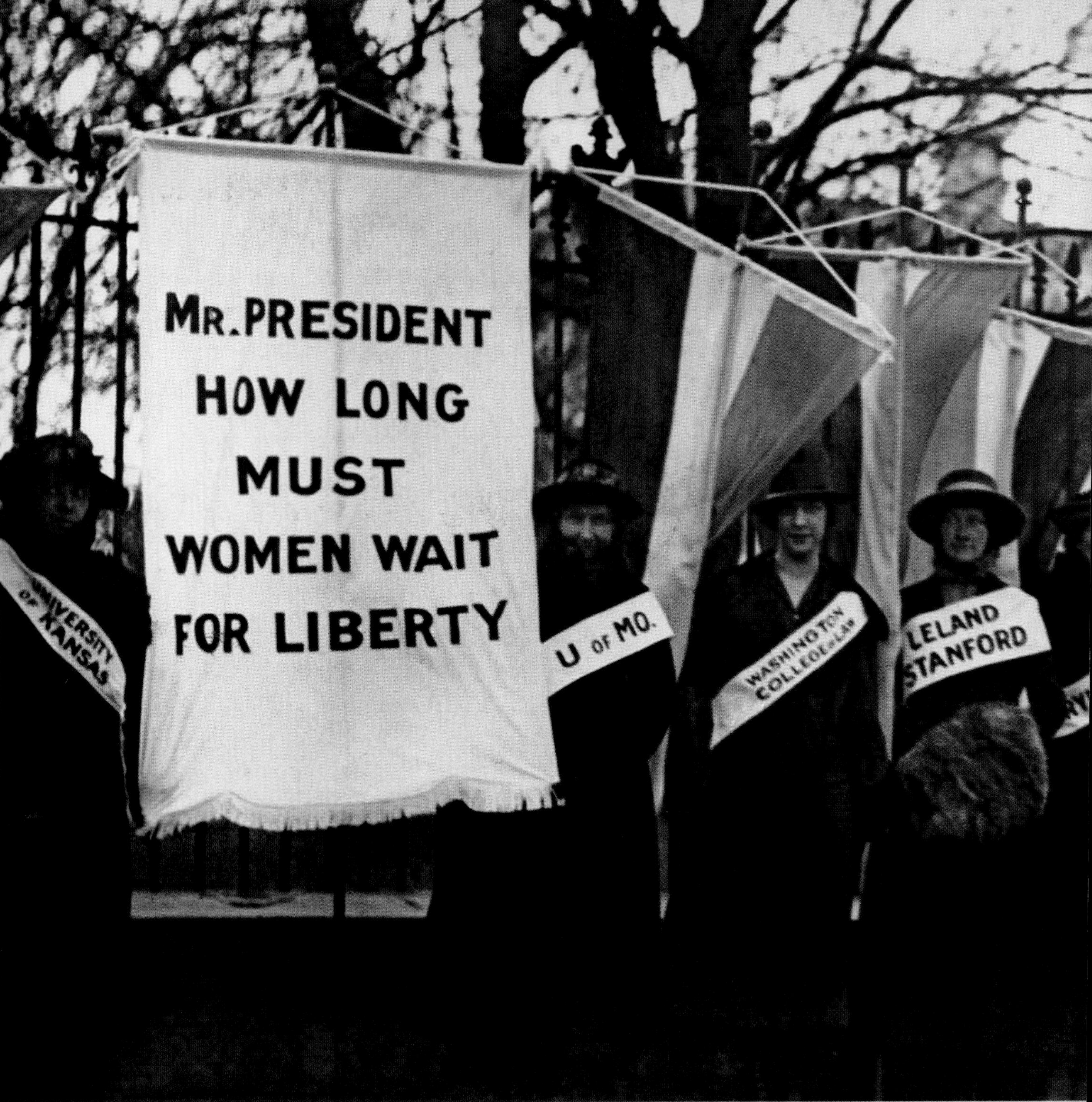

[ESSENTIAL QUESTION] How much power should the government have?

8 Protecting Civil Liberties

>> National Women's Party members demonstrate at the White House in 1918.

Enduring Understandings

- The Bill of Rights reflects the nation's commitment to personal freedom and limited government.
- The 1st Amendment guarantee of religious freedom creates a separation between church and state and protects the right to believe what one chooses in matters of religion.
- The 1st Amendment rights of free speech and press guarantee the freedom to express one's ideas.
- The 1st Amendment rights to assembly and petition guarantee the right to gather together and to bring one's views to the attention of public officials.
- Due process rights require the government to act fairly and in accord with established rules.

PEARSON realize NBC LEARN

Watch the My Story Video to learn how methods of surveillance can affect a person's privacy and security in the United States.

Access your digital lessons including:
Topic Inquiry • Interactive Reading Notepad • Interactivities • Assessments

>> Freedom Ride organizer James Farmer helped expand the civil rights of African Americans by contributing to the desegregation of interstate transportation in the United States.

Interactive Flipped Video

8.1 **Have you ever heard of Walter Barnette? How about Toyosaburo Korematsu? Dollree Mapp? Clarence Earl Gideon? Walter Barnette was a Jehovah's Witness in West Virginia who told his children not to salute the American flag or to recite the Pledge of Allegiance in school. Toyosaburo Korematsu was an American citizen interned by the Federal Government during World War II. Dollree Mapp was jailed for keeping "lewd and lascivious books" in her boarding house in Ohio. Clarence Earl Gideon went to prison for breaking into a poolroom in Florida.**

>> Objectives

Explain how Americans' commitment to freedom led to the creation of the Bill of Rights.

Understand that the obligation of citizenship requires that personal desires and interests be subordinated to the public good.

Describe efforts to extend some of the protections of the Bill of Rights to the States and analyze the impact of that process on the scope of fundamental rights and federalism.

Describe how the 9th Amendment helps protect individual rights.

>> Key Terms

Bill of Rights
civil liberties
civil rights
alien
Due Process Clause
process of incorporation
Robert H. Jackson
Oliver Wendell Holmes, Jr.
Pearl Harbor
James G. Blaine

The Unalienable Rights

A Commitment to Individual Rights

You will encounter these names again as you read about civil rights and liberties in the United States. Each of these people played an important part in building and protecting the rights of all Americans.

Constitutional Guarantees A commitment to personal freedom is deeply rooted in America's colonial past. For centuries, the people of England waged a continuing struggle for individual rights, and the early colonists brought a dedication to that cause with them to America.

Their commitment to freedom took root here, and it flourished. The Revolutionary War was fought to preserve and expand those very rights: the rights of the individual against government. In proclaiming the independence of the new United States, the founders of this country declared:

> We hold these truths to be self-evident, that all men are created equal, that they are

endowed by their Creator with certain unalienable Rights, that among these are Life, Liberty and the Pursuit of Happiness. That to secure these rights, Governments are instituted among Men. . . .

—Declaration of Independence

The Framers of the Constitution repeated the justification for the existence of government in the Preamble to the Constitution. That document, they said, was written to "secure the Blessings of Liberty to ourselves and our Posterity."

The Constitution, as it was written in Philadelphia, contained a number of important guarantees. The most notable of these can be found in Article I, Sections 9 and 10, and in Article III. Unlike many of the first State constitutions, however, the new national Constitution did not include a general listing of the rights of the people.

That omission raised an outcry. The objections were so strong that several States ratified the Constitution only with the understanding that a listing of rights would soon be added. The first session of the new Congress proposed a series of amendments. Ten of them, known as the **Bill of Rights,** were ratified by the States and became a part of the Constitution on December 15, 1791. Later amendments, especially the 13th and the 14th, have added to the Constitution's guarantees of personal freedom.

Civil Rights and Civil Liberties The Constitution guarantees both rights and liberties to the American people. The distinction between civil rights and civil liberties is murky at best. Legal scholars often disagree on the matter, and the two terms often are used interchangeably.

Think of the distinction this way: In general, **civil liberties** are protections *against government*. They are guarantees of the safety of persons, opinions, and property from arbitrary acts of government. Thus, freedom of religion, freedom of speech and press, and the guarantees of fair trial are prime examples of civil liberties.

In contrast, **civil rights** are often associated with *positive acts of government* that seek to make constitutional guarantees a reality for all people. Viewed from this perspective, laws against discrimination on the basis of race, sex, religious belief, or national origin set out in the Civil Rights Act of 1964 are leading examples of civil rights.

? COMPARE AND CONTRAST What is the difference between civil liberties and civil rights? Provide an example of each.

Limited Government

Remember, government in the United States is limited. The Constitution is filled with examples of this fact. Chief among them are its many guarantees of personal freedom. Each of those guarantees is either an outright prohibition or a restriction on the power of government to do something.

All governments have and use authority over individuals. The all-important difference between a democratic government and a dictatorial one lies in the extent of that authority.

In a dictatorial regime, the government's powers are practically unlimited. The government regularly suppresses dissent, often harshly. In the United States, however, governmental authority is strictly limited. As Justice **Robert H. Jackson** once put the point:

>> The Revolutionary War was fought to preserve and expand the rights of individuals against government, including that governments are established to protect every person's unalienable rights.

Interactive Gallery

If there is any fixed star in our constitutional constellation, it is that no official, high or petty, can prescribe what shall be orthodox in politics, nationalism, religion, or any other matters of opinion or force citizens to confess by word or act their faith therein.

—*West Virginia Board of Education v. Barnette*, 1943

Personal Interests and the Public Good The Constitution guarantees many rights to everyone in the United States. Still, no one has the right to do anything he or she pleases. Rather, all persons have the right to do as they please as long as they do not infringe on the rights of others. That is, each person's rights are *relative* to the rights of every other person. In other words, sometimes the public good takes precedence over the personal interests and desires of citizens.

To illustrate the point: Everyone in the United States has a right of free speech, but no one enjoys absolute freedom of speech. A person can be punished for using obscene language, or for using words in a way that causes someone to commit a crime—to riot or to desert from the military, for example. The Supreme Court dealt with this point most recently in *Federal Communications Commission* v. *Fox Television Stations,* 2009. In a 5–4 decision, the Court upheld the FCC's controversial policy of punishing broadcasters for even the one-time use of gross vulgarities on the air.

>> Justice Oliver Wendell Holmes, Jr.'s, opinion in *Schenck* v. *United States* set limits on free speech when it established the doctrine of "clear and present danger . . . which Congress has a right to prevent."

In this oft-quoted line, Justice **Oliver Wendell Holmes, Jr.,** put the relative nature of each person's rights in this way:

The most stringent protection of free speech would not protect a man in falsely shouting fire in a theatre and causing a panic.

—*Schenck* v. *United States,* 1919

Conflicting Rights On occasion, different guarantees of rights come into conflict with one another. For example, cases involving freedom of the press versus the right to a fair trial are not at all uncommon.

In one famous case, Dr. Samuel Sheppard of Cleveland, Ohio, had been convicted of murdering his wife. His lengthy trial was widely covered in the national media. On appeal, Sheppard claimed that the highly sensational coverage had denied him a fair trial. The Supreme Court agreed. In *Sheppard* v. *Maxwell,* 1966, the Court rejected the free press argument, overturned Sheppard's conviction, and ordered a new trial.

To Whom Are Rights Guaranteed? Most constitutional rights are extended to all persons. The Supreme Court has often held that "persons" includes **aliens**, people who are not citizens of the country in which they live. Not *all* rights are given to aliens, however. The right to travel freely throughout the country is guaranteed to all citizens, for example, but travel by aliens can be restricted. (See the two Privileges and Immunities clauses, in Article IV, Section 2, and the 14th Amendment.)

After the bombing of **Pearl Harbor** by Japan in 1941, all persons of Japanese descent living on the Pacific Coast were evacuated—forcibly moved—inland. Many suffered economic and other hardships. In 1944, the Supreme Court reluctantly upheld the forced evacuation as a reasonable wartime emergency measure (*Korematsu* v. *United States*, 1944). Still, the relocation was strongly criticized over the years. In 1988, the Federal Government admitted that the wartime relocation had been both unnecessary and unjust. Congress voted to pay $20,000 to each living internee. It also declared, "the Congress apologizes on behalf of the nation."

The current war on terrorism has created a political climate similar to that of the early days of World War II. Did the mistreatment of Japanese Americans then provide a lesson for today? Will the rights of Muslims and others of Middle Eastern descent continue to be respected by government as it fights terrorism here and abroad?

PARAPHRASE Explain the importance of having a limited government like the one found in the United States.

>> More than 100,000 persons of Japanese ancestry were sent to internment camps during World War II. **Draw Conclusions** Why did the government take that action?

The 14th Amendment, Fundamental Rights, and Federalism

The Framers crafted our Constitution on the principle of federalism—the division of power among a central government and several regional governments. Federalism is a complicated arrangement. It produces any number of problems—including a very complex pattern of guarantees of individual rights in the United States.

The Bill of Rights and the States Remember, the first ten amendments to the Constitution were originally intended as restrictions on the new National Government, not on the already existing States. The Supreme Court first held that the provisions of the Bill of Rights restrict only the National Government in *Barron* v. *Baltimore*, 1833. This was the first case in which the point was raised. The Supreme Court has followed that precedent ever since.

To illustrate this important point: The 5th Amendment says that no person can be charged with "a capital, or otherwise infamous crime" except by a grand jury. As a part of the Bill of Rights, this provision applies only to the National Government. The States may use the grand jury to bring accusations of serious crime—or, if they prefer, they can use some other process to do so. (The grand jury is a part of the criminal justice system in all but two States and the District of Columbia, however.)

>> When John Barron sued the city of Baltimore (shown here) because it had deposited sand in the waters near his wharf, the Court ruled that the 5th Amendment did not apply to the States.

Extending the Bill of Rights to the States Again, the provisions of the Bill of Rights apply against the National Government, not against the States. This does *not* mean, however, that the States can deny basic rights to the people.

In part, the States cannot do so because each of their own constitutions contains a bill of rights. In addition, they cannot deny these basic rights because of the 14th Amendment's **Due Process Clause**. It says

> No State shall . . . deprive any person of life, liberty, or property, without due process of law. . . .
>
> —14th Amendment, Section 1

The Supreme Court has often said that the 14th Amendment's Due Process Clause means that no State can deny to any person any right that is "basic or essential to the American concept of ordered liberty."

But what specific rights are "basic or essential"? The Supreme Court has answered that question in a long series of cases in which it has held that most (but not all) of the protections in the Bill of Rights are also covered by the 14th Amendment's Due Process Clause, and so apply against the States. In deciding those cases, the Court has engaged in what has come to be called the **process of incorporation**. It has incorporated—merged or combined—most of the guarantees in the Bill of Rights into the 14th Amendment's Due Process Clause.

Gitlow* v. *New York The Court began that historic incorporation in *Gitlow* v. *New York,* 1925. That landmark case involved Benjamin Gitlow, a founding member of the Communist Party USA, who had been convicted of criminal anarchy in the State courts. He had made several speeches and published a pamphlet calling for the violent overthrow of government in this country.

On appeal, the Court upheld Gitlow's conviction and the State law under which he had been tried. In deciding the case, however, the Court made this crucial point: Freedom of speech and press, which the 1st Amendment says cannot be denied by the National Government, are also "among the fundamental personal rights and liberties protected by the Due Process Clause of the 14th Amendment from impairment by the States."

Soon after *Gitlow,* the Court held each of the 1st Amendment's other guarantees to be covered by the 14th Amendment. It struck down State laws involving speech (*Fiske* v. *Kansas*, 1927; *Stromberg* v. *California*, 1931), the press (*Near* v. *Minnesota*, 1931), assembly and petition (*DeJonge* v. *Oregon*, 1937), and religion (*Cantwell* v. *Connecticut*, 1940). In each of those cases, the Court declared a State law unconstitutional as a violation of the 14th Amendment's Due Process Clause.

In the 1960s, the Court extended the scope of the 14th Amendment's Due Process Clause even further. In 2010, it added the 2nd Amendment to that coverage.

Provisions of the 14th Amendment's Due Process Clause

AMENDMENT	RIGHTS INCORPORATED	RIGHTS NOT INCORPORATED
1st Amendment	Freedoms of speech, press, assembly, petition; Free Exercise Clause; Establishment Clause	
2nd Amendment	Right to bear arms	
3rd Amendment		No quartering of troops
4th Amendment	No unreasonable searches or seizures	
5th Amendment	No self-incrimination; No double jeopardy	Grand jury
6th Amendment	Right to counsel; Right to confront and obtain witnesses; Speedy trial, Trial by jury in criminal cases	
7th Amendment		Trial by jury in civil cases
8th Amendment	No cruel and unusual punishment	

>> The Supreme Court has "nationalized" some rights into the 14th Amendment's Due Process Clause. **Analyze Charts** Why do you think only some of the rights have been incorporated?

A building with features of the Vatican is labeled Tammany Hall, a social organization with political influence in New York City.
Children trapped on the shore near a crumbling U.S. public school. A Bible represents a perceived Protestant influence in public schools.
Alligators representing Catholic bishops climb out of the Ganges, a river with spiritual significance.
THE AMERICAN RIVER GANGES.

>> This cartoon reflects the controversy in the 1800s over using public funds for parochial schools. **Analyze Political Cartoons** What do the elements represent? What is the cartoonist's viewpoint?

Blaine Amendment The Establishment Clause of the 1st Amendment says that the Federal Government cannot pass laws or spend money in ways that promote a religion. This might seem a simple matter, but in reality, it has posed many complex questions. One particularly vexing issue involves government aid to parochial (religious-based) schools. In the latter half of the nineteenth century, waves of immigrants arrived on American shores.

Many were Catholic, and in response to what was perceived as a strong Protestant influence in the public schools, many Catholic schools were created. In some instances, public monies were used to support those schools.

In 1875, the Speaker of the House of Representatives, **James G. Blaine** of Maine, proposed a constitutional amendment that would explicitly prohibit the use of State money for "sectarian" schools. Recall, the Establishment Clause had not yet been incorporated. The bill passed overwhelmingly in the House but was narrowly defeated in the Senate. In response, many States passed their own "Blaine amendments," making it clear that State funds could not be used for religious schools. Today, some 37 States have these restrictions.

Rather than fade into the history books, however, Blaine amendments have again become relevant as a growing number of States have started school voucher programs. These initiatives allow parents to use their public school allotment (voucher) to send their children to any public or private school to increase parents' choices and encourage competition among schools. Nevertheless, recent federal court rulings have said that States with explicit prohibitions—Blaine amendments—cannot allow vouchers to be used for parochial schools.

Impact on Fundamental Rights and Federalism

Over the years, the process of incorporation has increased the scope of fundamental rights by extending most of the rights guaranteed by the Bill of Rights to the States. In some respects, the application of the Bill of Rights to the States is noncontroversial. Most agree, for instance, that States should not be allowed to abridge an individual's freedom of speech or right to assemble. In fact, as you know, most State constitutions detail many of the same protections found in the United States Constitution.

In other ways, however, the incorporation process has had an impact on federalism. Take, for instance, the rights of those accused of committing a crime. Through a series of cases in the 1960s and 1970s, the Supreme Court applied federal-level protections to criminal defendants, thus altering the policies of many State and local law enforcement agencies.

The guarantee of the separation of church and state found in the 1st Amendment's Establishment Clause is another area in which the process of incorporation has had an impact on federalism. Prayer, or even a moment of silence, in public schools has been deemed a violation of the 1st Amendment. Thus, the Federal Government has outlawed a practice despite the fact that wide support for that practice can be found in many communities. Again, in some respects, the incorporation process has been a simple matter, but in other ways, it has broadened federal control in areas traditionally been left to the States.

The 9th Amendment The Constitution does *not* contain a complete catalog of all the rights held by Americans. The little-noted 9th Amendment says that there are, in fact, some guarantees beyond those set out in the Constitution:

> The enumeration in the Constitution, of certain rights, shall not be construed to deny or disparage others retained by the people.
>
> —9th Amendment

Over the years, the Supreme Court has found a number of other rights "retained by the people." They include, most notably, the guarantee that an accused person will not be tried on the basis of evidence unlawfully gained, and the right of a woman to choose to have an abortion without undue interference by government.

? SUMMARIZE What is the process of incorporation? Discuss its impact on federalism.

ASSESSMENT

1. **Identify Central Issues** How does the Constitution protect the rights of individuals against government?
2. **Generate Explanations** How are the Constitution's guarantees of personal freedom and the principle of limited government connected?
3. **Support Ideas with Examples** Why are individual rights not absolute? Cite two examples that support your thinking and explain how that right is not absolute.
4. **Compare and Contrast** Discuss the 14th Amendment and the 9th Amendment. How are they similar? How are they different?
5. **Identify Central Issues** How does federalism complicate guarantees of personal rights? How do the 14th Amendment and various Supreme Court rulings address this complication?

8.2 In the early 1830s, Frenchman Alexis de Tocqueville came to America to observe life in the young country. In his classic *Democracy in America,* he later noted that "the spirit of religion and the spirit of freedom" were "intimately united" in America. Wrote de Tocqueville: "I learned with surprise that [the clergy] filled no public appointments; not one of them is to be met with in the administration, and they are not even represented in the legislative assemblies. In several States the law excludes them from political life. . . ." de Tocqueville had discovered the American principle of the separation of church and state.

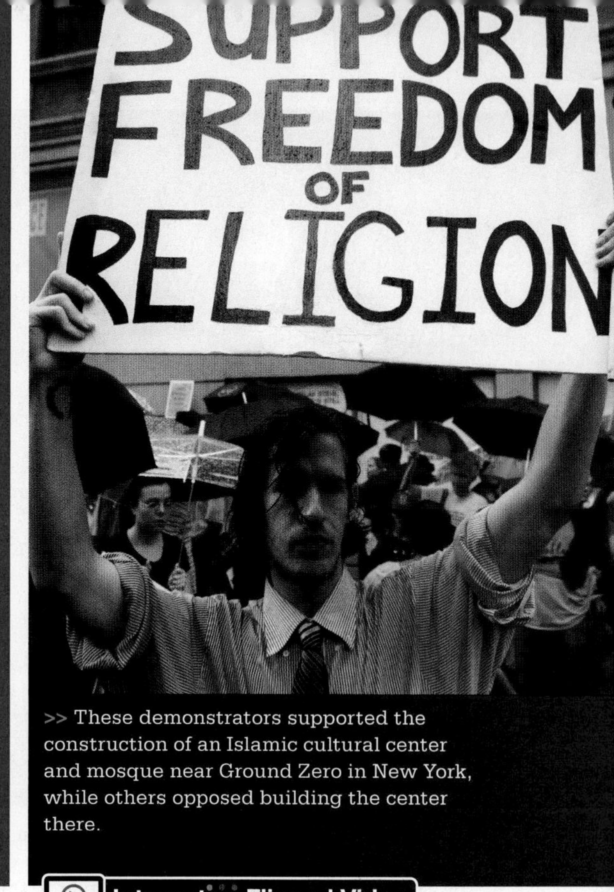

>> These demonstrators supported the construction of an Islamic cultural center and mosque near Ground Zero in New York, while others opposed building the center there.

Interactive Flipped Video

Freedom of Religion

Religious Liberty

Protecting Religious Freedom The Constitution declares that:

> Congress shall make no law respecting an establishment of religion, or prohibiting the free exercise thereof. . . .
>
> —1st Amendment

Notice that the 1st Amendment sets out *two* guarantees of religious freedom. It prohibits (1) "an establishment of religion" (in the **Establishment Clause**), and (2) any arbitrary interference by government with "the free exercise thereof" (in the **Free Exercise Clause**). Recall, the Supreme Court has incorporated both protections into the 14th Amendment's Due Process Clause, meaning that they apply against the States.

These constitutional guarantees were born out of centuries of opposition to government-established churches that had first been raised in the Reformation, and then were subsequently carried to America by early colonists. The Virginia Statute for Religious Freedom, adopted in 1786, was the immediate basis for the 1st Amendment. Drafted by Thomas Jefferson, that law provided for absolute religious

>> Objectives

Examine the reasons the Founding Fathers protected religious freedom and guaranteed its free exercise.

Understand the meaning of the phrase "separation of church and state."

Analyze Supreme Court interpretations of religious rights guaranteed by the Constitution in selected cases relating to education, including *Engel* v. *Vitale.*

Summarize Establishment Clause rulings in other areas, such as seasonal religious displays and public displays of the Ten Commandments.

Evaluate Supreme Court decisions that have affected a particular religious group, in particular those related to the Free Exercise Clause.

>> Key Terms

Establishment Clause
Free Exercise Clause
parochial
Alexis de Tocqueville

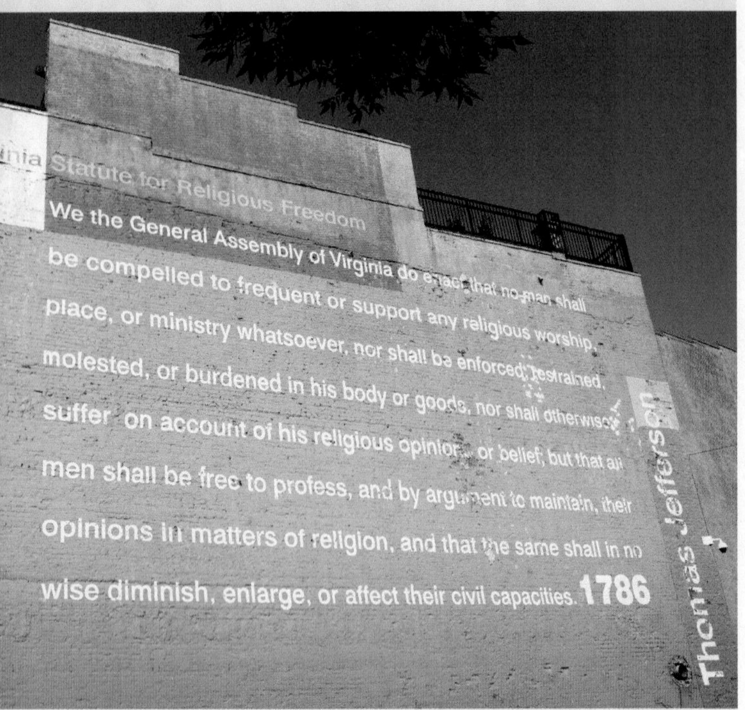

>> The Virginia Statute for Religious Freedom, shown painted on a wall in Richmond, Virginia, was written by Thomas Jefferson and was a precursor to the 1st Amendment's Establishment Clause.

>> The Establishment Clause does not prohibit members of Congress, such as Keith Ellison (D., Minnesota), from taking an oath of office. Ellison rested his hand on a Quran as he was sworn in.

freedom in Virginia by declaring that it could not require any person to profess any set of religious beliefs or support any religious institution.

Separation of Church and State The Establishment Clause sets up, in Thomas Jefferson's words, "a wall of separation between church and state." That wall is not infinitely high, however, and it is not impenetrable. The operation and formal institutions of Church and government are constitutionally separated in this country, but they are neither enemies nor even strangers to one another.

Government has done much to encourage churches and religion in the United States. Nearly all property of and contributions to religious sects are free from federal, State, and local taxation. Chaplains serve with each branch of the armed forces. Most public officials take an oath of office in the name of God. Sessions of Congress, most State legislatures, and many city councils open with prayer. The nation's anthem and its coins and currency make reference to God.

The limits imposed by the Establishment Clause remain a matter of continuing and often heated controversy. The Supreme Court did not hear its first Establishment Clause case until 1947. A few earlier cases did involve government and religion, but none of them involved a direct consideration of the "wall of separation."

The most important of those earlier cases that dealt with religion, but not the Establishment Clause, was *Pierce* v. *Society of Sisters,* 1925. There, the Court held an Oregon compulsory school attendance law to be unconstitutional. That law required parents to send their children to *public* schools. It was purposely intended to eliminate private and especially **parochial** (church-related) schools.

In striking down the law, the Court did not address the Establishment Clause question. Instead, it found the law to be an unreasonable interference with "the liberty of parents and guardians to direct the upbringing and education of children" and thus to be in conflict with the Due Process Clause of the 14th Amendment.

? IDENTIFY CENTRAL ISSUES Why did the Founding Fathers protect religious freedom and guarantee its free exercise?

Religion and Education

The foremost area of collision between religion and government has been issues pertaining to education. Can State and local governments give financial aid to parochial schools, for example? What about providing textbooks or assistance in busing students to these schools? Can public schools open their day or a high school commencement with a prayer, or even a moment of silence? Is it proper for religious student groups to hold meetings at public schools in the evenings?

The Court's first direct ruling on the Establishment Clause came in *Everson* v. *Board of Education,* a 1947 case often called the *New Jersey School Bus Case.* There, the Court upheld a State law that provided for the public, tax-supported busing of students attending any school in the State, including parochial schools.

Aid to Parochial Schools Many of the most recent Establishment Clause cases have centered on State aid to parochial schools. Those who support this kind of aid argue that parochial schools enroll large numbers of students who would otherwise have to be educated at public expense. Also, they maintain, the State should give some aid to parochial schools in order to relieve parents of some of the double burden they carry because they must pay taxes to support the public schools their children do not attend. Many advocates further insist that schools run by religious organizations pose no real church-state problems because they devote most of their time to secular (nonreligious) subjects.

Opponents of aid to parochial schools argue that parents who choose to send their children to religious-based schools should accept the financial consequences of that choice. Many of these critics also insist that it is impossible to draw clear lines between secular and sectarian courses in parochial schools. They say that religious beliefs are bound to have an effect on the teaching of nonreligious subjects.

The *Lemon* Test In a 1971 case, *Lemon* v. *Kurtzman,* the Supreme Court held that the Establishment Clause is designed to prevent three main evils: "sponsorship, financial support, and active involvement of the sovereign in religious activity." It struck down a Pennsylvania law that provided for reimbursements (money payments) to private schools to cover their costs for teachers' salaries, textbooks, and other teaching materials in nonreligious courses.

The Court introduced a three-pronged standard, now known as the *Lemon* test, to decide whether a State law amounts to an "establishment" of religion. That standard states: (1) a law must have a secular, not religious, purpose; (2) it must neither advance nor inhibit religion; and (3) it must not foster an "excessive entanglement" of government and religion.

More often than not, the Court has found laws that provide some form of public aid to church-related schools unconstitutional. Thus, it ruled in an Ohio

>> Private speech endorsing religion is protected by the Free Exercise Clause. However, a teacher endorsing religion in a public school would violate the Establishment Clause.

Interactive Chart

case that public funds cannot be used to pay for such things as field trips for parochial school students. Nor, as it ruled in a Michigan case, can tax monies be used to pay any part of the salaries of parochial school teachers, even those who teach only secular courses. The Court noted in that case that while the contents of, say, a textbook used in a course may be checked easily, the way a teacher handles that course cannot. The Court also invalidated a New York law that created a small school district purposely created to benefit handicapped school children in a tight-knit community of Hasidic Jews.

Some State laws have passed the *Lemon* test, however. For example, the Court has held that New York can pay church-related schools what it costs them to administer standardized tests, and that the use of public money in Arizona to provide an interpreter for a deaf student in a Catholic high school does not violate the Establishment Clause. The Constitution, said the Court, does not lay down an absolute barrier to the placing of a public employee in a religious school.

The High Court went much further in *Zelman* v. *Simmons-Harris* in 2002. There, it upheld Ohio's experimental "school choice" plan. Under that plan, parents in Cleveland can receive vouchers (grants for tuition payments) from the State and use them to send their children to private schools. Nearly all families who take the vouchers send their children to parochial schools. The Court found, 5–4, that the Ohio program is not intended to promote religion but, rather, to help children from low-income families.

Released Time and Student Groups Many other issues have arisen regarding religion and education. For example, should public schools be allowed to release students during school hours to attend religious classes? The Court said such "released time" programs are unconstitutional if held in public facilities, but not if the religious classes are held in private places off school grounds.

The Equal Access Act of 1984 declares that any public high school that receives federal funds (and nearly all do) must allow student religious groups to meet in the school on the same terms that it sets for other student organizations. The Supreme Court has ruled that the law does not violate the Establishment Clause. The Court has since gone much further than that ruling. In 2001, a school board had refused to allow the "Good News Club," a group of grade-school students, to meet after school to sing, pray, memorize scriptures, and hear Bible lessons. The school board based its action on the Establishment Clause. The Court, however, held that the board had violated Good News Club members' 1st and 14th amendment rights to free speech.

"When the teacher says 'heaven help me', is that praying in school?"

>> The Supreme Court has consistently ruled against prayer in public schools, but the issue continues to be debated. **Analyze Political Cartoons** Why might school prayer be so controversial?

Prayers and the Bible The Court has now decided several major cases involving the recitation of prayers and the reading of the Bible in public schools. In *Engel* v. *Vitale,* 1962, the Court outlawed the use, even on a voluntary basis, of a prayer written by the New York State Board of Regents. The prayer read: "Almighty God, we acknowledge our dependence upon Thee, and we beg Thy blessings upon us, our parents, our teachers, and our country."

In striking down the prayer, the Supreme Court held that

> [T]he constitutional prohibition against laws respecting an establishment of religion must at least mean that, in this country, it is no part of the business of government to compose official prayers for any group of the American people to recite as part of a religious program carried on by government.
>
> —Justice Hugo L. Black

The High Court extended that holding in two 1963 cases. In *Abington School District* v. *Schempp,* it struck down a Pennsylvania law requiring that each school day begin with readings from the Bible and a recitation of the Lord's Prayer. In *Murray* v. *Curlett*, the Court erased a similar rule in Baltimore.

Since then, the Supreme Court has found unconstitutional:

- a Kentucky law that ordered the posting of the Ten Commandments in all public school classrooms, *Stone* v. *Graham,* 1980;
- Alabama's "moment of silence" law, *Wallace* v. *Jaffree,* 1985, which provided for a one-minute period of silence for "meditation or voluntary prayer" at the beginning of each school day;
- the offering of prayer as part of a public school graduation ceremony, in a Rhode Island case, *Lee* v. *Weisman,*1992;
- a Texas school district's policy that permitted student-led prayer at high school football games, *Santa Fe Independent School District* v. *Doe,* 2000.

To sum up these rulings, the Court has held that public schools cannot sponsor religious exercises. It has *not* held that individuals cannot pray when and as they choose in schools or in any other place. Nor has it held that students cannot study the Bible in a literary or historical context in the schools.

These rulings have stirred a great deal of controversy. Many individuals and groups have long proposed that the Constitution be amended to allow voluntary prayer in the public schools. And, despite these decisions, both organized prayer and Bible readings are found in a great many public school classrooms today. On the other hand, supporters of these rulings maintain that they are necessary to uphold the separation of church and state guaranteed by the Establishment Clause.

Evolution One interesting set of religious liberty cases dealt with the teaching of evolution in public school biology classes. In 1968, the Court struck down a State law forbidding the teaching of the scientific theory of evolution. The Court held that the Constitution

> forbids alike the preference of a religious doctrine or the prohibition of theory which is deemed antagonistic to a particular dogma. . . . 'The State has no legitimate interest in protecting any or all religions from views distasteful to them.'
>
> —Justice Abe Fortas

The Court found a similar law to be unconstitutional in 1987. In *Edwards* v. *Aguilard*, it voided a 1981 Louisiana law that mandated that whenever the theory of evolution was taught, instruction in what the law termed "creation science" had to be offered as well.

SUMMARIZE Describe what the Supreme Court has ruled permissible in public schools and what is not permitted.

>> Lawyers Clarence Darrow (left) and William Jennings Bryan faced off in the 1925 trial of John Scopes, a Tennessee teacher accused of violating a State law against the teaching of evolution.

Other Establishment Clause Cases

Most church-state controversies have involved public education, as noted above. Some Establishment Clause cases have arisen in other policy areas, however.

Seasonal Displays Many public organizations sponsor celebrations of the holiday season with street decorations, programs in public schools, and the like. Can these publicly sponsored observances properly include expressions of religious belief?

In 1984, the Court held that the city of Pawtucket, Rhode Island, could include the Christian nativity scene in its holiday display, which also featured nonreligious objects such as candy canes and Santa's sleigh and reindeer. That ruling, however, left open this question: What about a public display made up *only* of a religious symbol?

The Court faced that question in 1989, when it ruled that if a seasonal display "endorsed Christian doctrine," it violated the 1st and 14th amendments. A county government had placed a large display celebrating the birth of Jesus on the grand stairway in the county courthouse, with a banner proclaiming "Glory to God in the Highest."

At the same time, however, the Court upheld another holiday display in *Pittsburgh* v. *ACLU*. The city's display consisted of a large Christmas tree, an 18-foot menorah, and a sign declaring the city's dedication to freedom.

The Ten Commandments In recent years, public displays of the Ten Commandments have ignited controversy in several places. In one 2005 case, the Court held that the Ten Commandments monument located on the grounds of the Texas State Capitol in Austin does not violate the 1st and 14th amendments.

The Court's 5–4 majority found that the monument (1) was erected in 1961 as part of a private group's campaign against juvenile delinquency, (2) is set among 37 other historical and cultural markers, and (3) had gone unchallenged for some 40 years. In short, the Court found the monument's overall message to be secular rather than religious and therefore acceptable.

In another case, a divided 5–4 majority ruled that the display of the Ten Commandments in Kentucky county courthouses was unacceptable. They were, said the Court, an impermissible endorsement of religion by government. Framed copies of the Commandments were first posted in county courthouses in 1991. Copies of other nonreligious documents, including the Bill of Rights, were added to the display some years later, but only after the original displays' content had been challenged. The Supreme Court found that the original displays had a clear religious purpose. The later additions were merely "a sham," an attempt to mask that unconstitutional religious purpose.

ANALYZE INFORMATION Analyze the rulings made by the Supreme Court regarding seasonal religious displays in public places and the public display of the Ten Commandments. What distinctions were made in terms of what was permissible under the Establishment Clause? What was not permitted?

>> A court ruling required the city of Duluth, Minnesota, to remove this monument of the Ten Commandments from outside city hall. **Hypothesize** Why was this ruling different from the Texas case?

The Free Exercise Clause

The second part of the constitutional guarantee of religious freedom is set out in the Constitution's Free Exercise Clause, which guarantees to each person the right to believe whatever he or she chooses to believe in matters of religion. No law and no other action by any government can violate that absolute constitutional right. It is protected by both the 1st and the 14th amendments.

No person has an absolute right to act as he or she chooses, however. The Free Exercise Clause does *not* give anyone the right to violate criminal laws, offend public morals, or threaten community safety simply because it might be done in the name of religion. The Supreme Court laid down the basic shape of the Free Exercise Clause in the first case it heard on the issue, *Reynolds* v. *United States,* 1879. Reynolds, a Mormon, had two wives. That practice, polygamy, was allowed by his church, but it was prohibited by federal law in any territory of the United States.

Reynolds was convicted under the law. The Supreme Court held that the 1st Amendment does not forbid Congress the power to punish those actions that are "violations of social duties or subversive of good order."

Limits on Free Exercise Over the years, the Court has approved many regulations of human conduct in the face of free exercise challenges, for the protection of the public good. For example, it has upheld laws that require the vaccination of schoolchildren, laws that forbid the use of poisonous snakes in religious rites, laws that require businesses to be closed on Sundays ("blue laws"), and a law requiring religious groups to have a permit to hold a parade on public streets. Further, the Court has ruled that the Federal Government can draft those who have religious objections to military service, *Welsh* v. *United States,* 1970.

Free Exercise Upheld Nevertheless, over time the Court has found many actions by governments to be incompatible with the free exercise guarantee. The Court did so for the first time in *Cantwell* v. *Connecticut,* 1940. There, the Court struck down a law requiring a person to obtain a license before soliciting money for a religious cause. The Court reaffirmed that holding in 2002.

The Supreme Court has decided a number of other cases in a similar way. Thus, Amish children cannot be forced to attend school beyond the 8th grade, because that sect's centuries-old "self-sufficient agrarian lifestyle is essential to their religious faith and is threatened by the exposure of their children to modern educational influences." On the other hand, the Amish, who provide support for their own elderly or disabled people, must pay Social Security taxes, as all other employers do.

The Jehovah's Witnesses have carried several important religious freedom cases to the High Court. Perhaps the stormiest controversy resulting from these cases arose out of the Witnesses' refusal to salute the flag because they see such conduct as a violation of the Bible's commandment against idolatry. In 1943, and after a series of back-and-forth decisions, the Supreme Court eventually held a compulsory flag-salute law unconstitutional. Justice Robert H. Jackson's words below are from the Court's powerful opinion in that case:

> To believe that patriotism will not flourish if patriotic ceremonies are voluntary and spontaneous, instead of a compulsory routine, is to make an unflattering estimate of the appeal of our institutions to free minds.
>
> —Justice Robert H. Jackson

>> In 1972, the Court ruled that the "requirement of compulsory formal education after the eighth grade would gravely endanger, if not destroy, the free exercise of [Amish] religious beliefs."

Interactive Chart

DRAW CONCLUSIONS Why have the courts upheld the law prohibiting poisonous snakes in religious rites?

ASSESSMENT

1. **Define** What is the meaning of the phrase "separation of church and state"? What part of the Constitution guarantees this separation?
2. **Check Understanding** The constitutional guarantee of religious freedom has two parts: the Establishment Clause and the Free Exercise Clause. What does each clause create or guarantee? What does each clause prohibit or NOT protect?
3. **Identify Central Issues** What does the *Lemon* test evaluate? How did the test originate?
4. **Compare and Contrast** Describe arguments for and against allowing State aid to parochial schools.
5. **Evaluate Arguments** Describe the Supreme Court decision related to the Jehovah's Witnesses objection to saluting the flag.

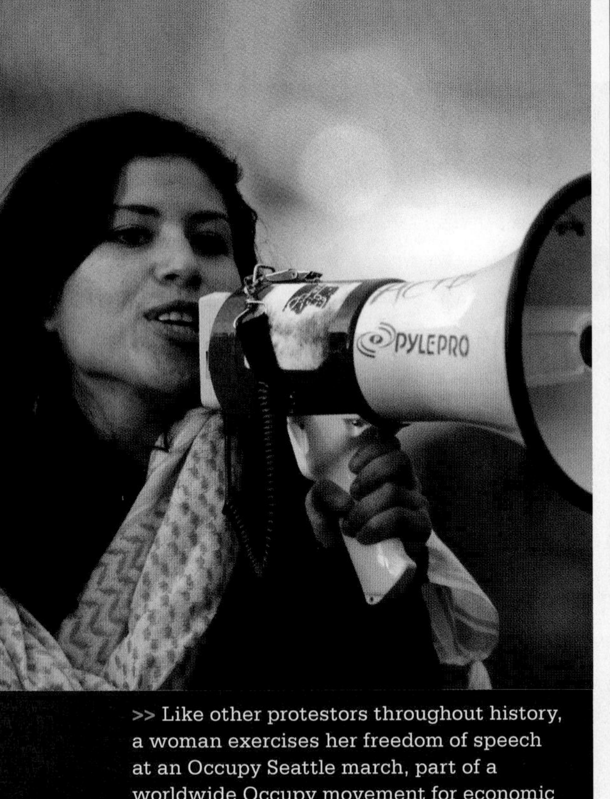

>> Like other protestors throughout history, a woman exercises her freedom of speech at an Occupy Seattle march, part of a worldwide Occupy movement for economic and social equality.

Interactive Flipped Video

8.3 **Think about this children's verse: "Sticks and stones may break my bones, but names will never hurt me." This rhyme says, in effect, that acts and words are separate things, and that acts can harm but words cannot.**

>> Objectives

Analyze the purpose and importance of the 1st Amendment rights of free speech and press.

Analyze Supreme Court interpretations of rights guaranteed by the Constitution in *Schenck* v. *U.S.*, and other rulings related to seditious and obscene speech.

Define symbolic and commercial speech and describe the limits on their exercise, including Supreme Court interpretations of rights guaranteed by the Constitution in *Texas* v. *Johnson*.

Examine the issues of prior restraint and press confidentiality, and describe the limits the Court has placed on the media.

>> Key Terms

libel
slander
sedition
seditious speech
symbolic speech
picketing
prior restraint
injunction
shield laws
John Roberts
Oliver Wendell Holmes, Jr.

Freedom of Speech and Press

The Right of Free Expression

Is that really true? Certainly not. You know that words can and do have consequences, sometimes powerful consequences. Words, spoken or written, can make you happy, sad, bored, informed, or entertained. They can also expose you to danger, deny you a job, or lead to other serious events.

The guarantees of free speech and press in the 1st and 14th amendments serve two fundamentally important purposes: (1) to guarantee to *each* person a right of free expression, in the spoken and the written word, and by all other means of communication; and (2) to guarantee to *all* persons a wide-ranging discussion of public affairs. That is, the 1st and 14th amendments give people the right to have their say *and* the right to hear what others have to say.

The American system of government depends on the ability of the people to make sound, reasoned judgments on matters of public concern. The people can best make such judgments when they know all the facts and can hear all the available interpretations of those facts.

Unpopular Views, Libel, and Slander Keep two other points in mind: First, the guarantees of free speech and press are intended

PEARSON realize™ www.PearsonRealize.com Access your Digital Lesson.

to protect the expression of unpopular views. The opinions of the majority need little or no constitutional protection. These guarantees ensure, as Justice Holmes put it, "freedom for the thought that we hate," (dissenting opinion, *Schwimmer* v. *United States,* 1929).

In 2011, for example, the Supreme Court issued a controversial 1st Amendment ruling relating to free speech. During the funeral of Matthew Snyder, a Marine killed in Iraq, members of a Baptist church picketed on public property near the church where the funeral was conducted. Finding the picketers' signs and statements insulting and offensive, Snyder's father sued.

In its 8–1 decision, the Court ruled in favor of the protestors, pointing out that they had properly notified authorities before their protest, that the protest took place on public property some distance away from the church, and that the views expressed related to matters of public concern. In the Court's opinion in *Snyder* v. *Phelps*, Chief Justice **John Roberts** wrote:

> "Speech is powerful. It can stir people to action, move them to tears of both joy and sorrow, and . . . inflict great pain. On the facts before us, we cannot react to that pain by punishing the speaker. As a nation, we have chosen a different course—to protect even hurtful speech on public issues to ensure that we do not stifle public debate."
>
> —Chief Justice John Roberts

Second, some forms of expression are not protected by the Constitution. No person has an unbridled right of free speech or free press. Reasonable restrictions can be placed on those rights. Think about Justice Holmes's comment about restricting the right to falsely shout "Fire!" in a crowded theater. Or consider this restriction: No person has the right to libel or slander another. **Libel** is the false and malicious use of printed words; **slander** is the false and malicious use of spoken words. Malicious means that the words are used to injure a person's character or reputation, or to expose that person to public contempt, ridicule, or hatred.

Public Figures and Slander Truth is generally an adequate defense against a claim of libel or slander. The law does not shield public officials nearly as completely as it protects private persons, however. In *New York Times* v. *Sullivan,* 1964, the Supreme Court held that public officials cannot recover damages for a published criticism, even if it is exaggerated or false, "unless that statement was made with actual malice—that is, knowledge that it was false or with a reckless disregard of whether it was false or not."

Several later decisions have extended that ruling to cover "public figures" and even private persons who simply happen to become involved in some newsworthy event.

Similarly, the law prohibits the use of obscene words, the printing and distributing of obscene materials, and false advertising. It also condemns the use of words to prompt others to commit a crime—for example, to riot or to attempt to overthrow the government by force.

? IDENTIFY CENTRAL ISSUES Why are "reasonable restrictions" allowed on freedom of expression?

Seditious Speech

Sedition is the crime of attempting to overthrow the government by force or to disrupt its lawful activities by violent acts. **Seditious speech** is the advocating, or urging, of such conduct. It is not protected by the 1st Amendment.

>> Answer Coalition members protest the war in Iraq. Other anti-war groups criticized Answer for its affiliations and tactics, but its members' right to be heard was guaranteed by the Constitution.

>> President John Adams used the Sedition Act to silence his opponents, even imprisoning a Vermont Congressman when he accused Adams of having "an unbounded thirst for ridiculous pomp."

The Alien and Sedition Acts Congress first acted to curb opposition to government in the Alien and Sedition Acts of 1798. Those acts gave the President the power to deport undesirable aliens and made "any false, scandalous, and malicious" criticism of the government a crime. The laws were meant to stifle the opponents of President John Adams.

The Alien and Sedition Acts were undoubtedly unconstitutional, but that point was never tested in the courts. Some 25 persons were arrested for violating them; of those, 10 were convicted. The Alien and Sedition Acts expired before Thomas Jefferson became President in 1801, and he soon pardoned those who had run afoul of them.

Sedition Law of 1917 Congress passed another sedition law during World War I, as part of the Espionage Act of 1917. That law made it a crime to encourage disloyalty, interfere with the draft, obstruct recruiting, incite insubordination in the armed forces, or hinder the sale of government bonds. The act also made it a crime to "willfully utter, print, write, or publish any disloyal, profane, scurrilous, or abusive language about the form of government of the United States."

More than 1,000 persons were convicted for violating the Espionage Act. The constitutionality of the law was upheld several times, most importantly in *Schenck* v. *United States,* 1919. Charles Schenck, an officer of the Socialist Party, had been found guilty of obstructing the war effort. He had sent fiery leaflets to some 15,000 draftees, urging them to resist the call to military service.

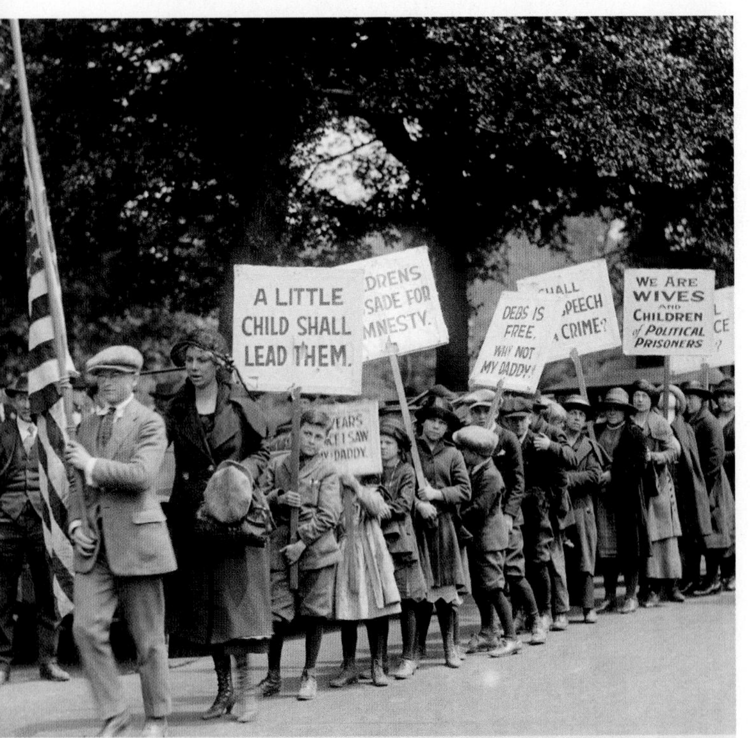

>> Women and children protest the imprisonment of relatives who had violated the Espionage Act of 1917.

> The question in every case is whether the words used are used in such circumstances and are of such nature as to create a clear and present danger that they will bring about the substantive evils that Congress has a right to prevent.
>
> —Justice Oliver Wendell Holmes

The Supreme Court upheld Schenck's conviction. The case is particularly noteworthy because the Court's opinion, written by Justice **Oliver Wendell Holmes, Jr.**, established the "clear and present danger" rule:

In short, the rule says that words can be outlawed. Those who utter them can be punished if there is an immediate danger that criminal acts will follow.

The Smith Act of 1940 Congress passed the Smith Act in 1940, just over a year before the United States entered World War II. That law is still on the books.

It makes it a crime for anyone to advocate the violent overthrow of the government of the United States, to distribute any material that teaches or advises violent overthrow, or to knowingly belong to any group with such an aim.

The Court upheld the Smith Act in *Dennis* v. *United States,* 1951. There, 11 Communist Party leaders had been convicted of advocating the overthrow of the Federal Government. On appeal, the Communist leaders argued that the Smith Act violated the 1st Amendment. They also claimed that no actions of theirs constituted a clear and present danger to this country. The Court disagreed.

Later, however, the Supreme Court modified the *Dennis* ruling in several cases. In *Yates* v. *United States,* 1957, for example, the Court overturned the Smith Act convictions of several Communist Party leaders. It held that merely to urge someone to *believe* something, in contrast to urging that person to *do* something, cannot be made illegal. In *Yates* and other Smith Act cases, the Court upheld the constitutionality of the law, but interpreted its provisions so that enforcing the Smith Act became practically impossible.

>> The U.S. Cavalry escorts a train through picketers during the 1894 Pullman Strike. Picketing became more common after 1932 when laws were passed to limit employers' right to stop strikes.

? ANALYZE INFORMATION The Supreme Court case *Schenck* v. *United States* established the "clear and present danger" rule. What is the impact of this ruling on 1st Amendment rights?

The 1st Amendment and Symbolic Speech

People also communicate ideas by their conduct, by the way they do a particular thing. Thus, a person can "say" something with a facial expression or a shrug of the shoulders, or by carrying a sign or wearing an armband. This expression by conduct is known as **symbolic speech**.

Clearly, not all conduct amounts to symbolic speech. If it did, murder or robbery or any other crime could be excused on grounds that the person who committed the act meant to say something by doing so.

Picketing Just as clearly, however, some conduct does express opinion. Take picketing in a labor dispute as an example. **Picketing** involves the patrolling of a business site by workers who are on strike. By their conduct, picketers attempt to inform the public of the controversy and to persuade others not to deal with the firm involved. Picketing is, then, a form of expression. If peaceful, it is protected by the 1st and 14th amendments.

The leading case on the point is *Thornhill* v. *Alabama,* 1940. There, the Court struck down a State law that made it a crime to loiter about or to picket a place of business in order to influence others not to trade or work there. Picketing that is "set in a background of violence," however, can be prevented. Even peaceful picketing can be restricted if it is conducted for an illegal purpose—for example, forcing someone to do something that is itself illegal.

Other Symbolic Speech Cases The Court has been sympathetic to the symbolic speech argument, but it has not given blanket 1st Amendment protection to that means of expression. Several key cases illustrate this point.

United States v. *O'Brien,* 1968, involved four young men who had burned their draft cards to protest the war in Vietnam. A court convicted them of violating a federal law that makes that act a crime. O'Brien appealed, arguing that the 1st Amendment protects "all modes of communication of ideas by conduct." The Court disagreed, saying: "We cannot accept the view that an apparently limitless variety of conduct can be labeled 'speech' whenever the person engaging in the conduct intends thereby to express an idea."

Acts of Dissent The Court also held that acts of dissent by conduct can be punished if: (1) the object of the protest is within the constitutional powers of the government; (2) whatever restriction is placed on expression is no greater than necessary; and (3) the government's real interest in the matter is not to squelch dissent.

Using that three-part test, the Court has sometimes denied claims of symbolic speech. Thus, in *Virginia* v. *Black*, 2003, it upheld a State law that prohibits the burning of a cross as an act of intimidation, a threat that can make a person fear for his safety. The Court also made this point: Those who burn crosses at rallies or parades as acts of political expression (acts not aimed at a particular person) cannot be prosecuted under the law.

Tinker v. *Des Moines School District*, 1969, on the other hand, is one of several cases in which the Court has come down on the side of symbolic speech. In *Tinker*, several students who had worn black armbands to school to dramatize their opposition to the war in Vietnam had been suspended by the district.

The Court found that school officials had overstepped their authority and violated the students' right to free expression. Arguing that the students' conduct did not cause a substantial disruption of normal school activities, the Court stated, "It can hardly be argued that either students or teachers shed their constitutional rights to freedom of speech or expression at the schoolhouse gate."

>> Mary Beth and John Tinker display the black armbands they wore to symbolize opposition to the Vietnam War. **Apply Concepts** Why did the Court rule in favor of the Tinkers?

Interactive Gallery

Campaign Contributions The Court first recognized campaign contributions as protected speech in *Buckley* v. *Valeo* in 1976. In this case, the Court found certain parts of the Federal Election Campaign Act of 1971 were unconstitutional, including limits on candidates' expenditures from their personal funds.

The Court upheld this ruling in *Citizens United* v. *FEC* in 2010. There, the Court ruled that the government ban on political spending by corporations or labor unions violated the 1st Amendment right to free speech.

Flag Burning A sharply divided Court has twice held that burning the American flag as an act of political protest is expressive conduct protected by the 1st and 14th amendments. In *Texas* v. *Johnson*, 1989, a 5–4 majority ruled that State authorities had violated a protester's rights by prosecuting him under a law that forbids the "desecration of a venerated object."

Johnson had set fire to an American flag during an anti-Reagan demonstration at the Republican National Convention in Dallas in 1984. Said the Court:

> If there is a bedrock principle underlying the 1st Amendment, it is that the government may not prohibit the expression of an idea simply because society finds the idea itself offensive. . . . We do not consecrate the flag by punishing its desecration, for in doing so we dilute the freedom that this cherished emblem represents.
>
> —Justice William J. Brennan, Jr.

The Supreme Court's decision in *Johnson* set off a firestorm of criticism around the country and prompted Congress to pass the Flag Protection Act of 1989. It, too, was struck down by the Court, 5–4, in *United States* v. *Eichman*, 1990. The Court based its decision on the same grounds as those set out a year earlier in *Johnson*. Since *Johnson* and *Eichman*, Congress has rejected several attempts to propose a constitutional amendment to outlaw flag burning.

? COMPARE AND CONTRAST Compare and contrast the Court's interpretation of symbolic speech in *Virginia* v. *Black*, involving the burning of a cross, with its interpretation in *Texas* v. *Johnson*, involving flag burning.

Prior Restraint on Expression

The Constitution allows government to punish some utterances after they are made—for example, in cases involving libel or slander, or obscenity. With almost no exceptions, however, government cannot curb ideas *before* they are expressed. That is, except in the most extreme situations, government cannot place any **prior restraint** on written or spoken expression.

Prior Restraint and Publications The concept of prior restraint is basic to the meaning of the 1st and 14th amendment protections of freedom of expression. *Near* v. *Minnesota,* 1931, is a leading case in point. There, the Supreme Court struck down a State law that allowed local public officials to prevent the publication of any "malicious, scandalous, and defamatory" periodical. Acting under that law, a local court had issued an order forbidding the publication of *The Saturday Press*. That Minneapolis newspaper had published a series of articles charging public corruption and attacking local officials as "grafters" and "Jewish gangsters."

The Court held that the guarantee of a free press does not allow a prior restraint on publication—*except* in such extreme situations as wartime, or when a publication is obscene or incites its readers to acts of violence. Even "miscreant purveyors of scandal" and anti-Semitism are entitled to constitutional protection, said the Court.

The Constitution does not forbid any and all forms of prior censorship, but "any prior restraint on expression comes to this Court with a 'heavy presumption' against its constitutional validity." The Court made this pronouncement in *Nebraska Press Association* v. *Stuart,* 1976, in which a State judge had ordered the media not to report certain details of a murder trial. The Court found the judge's gag order to be unconstitutional.

The Pentagon Papers Since that time, the Court has used this general rule on numerous occasions—for example, in the famous Pentagon Papers Case, *New York Times* v. *United States,* 1971. In that case, several newspapers had obtained copies of a set of classified documents, widely known as the Pentagon Papers. Officially titled *History of U.S. Decision Making Process on Viet Nam Policy*, those documents had been stolen from the Defense Department and then leaked to the press.

>> Daniel Ellsberg (right) and Anthony Russo speak to reporters outside the Federal Building in Los Angeles during their trial for the theft and release of the so-called "Pentagon Papers."

Interactive Chart

The Nixon administration sought an **injunction** to bar their publication, arguing that national security was at stake and the documents (government property) had been stolen. The newspaper argued the "public right to know," and it insisted that the 1st Amendment protected its right to publish the papers.

The Court found that the government had not shown that printing the documents would endanger the nation's security. The government, in effect, had not overcome the "heavy presumption" against prior censorship.

Court-Approved Prior Restraint The few prior restraints the Supreme Court has approved include:

- regulations prohibiting the distribution of political literature on military bases without the approval of military authorities, *Greer* v. *Spock*, 1976;
- a Central Intelligence Agency (CIA) rule that agents must never publish anything about the agency without the CIA's express permission, *Snepp* v. *United States,* 1980;
- a federal prison rule that blocks prisoners who are being punished for misbehavior from access to newspapers and magazines, *Beard* v. *Banks*, 2006.

The Court has also said that public school officials have a broad power to censor school newspapers, plays, and other "school-sponsored expressive activities." It did so in a case from Missouri, *Hazelwood School District* v. *Kuhlmeier,* 1988. There, the principal of a St. Louis high school had prohibited the publication of a series of articles written by student reporters for their school's paper. Those articles explored the impact that various events, among them pregnancy and parents' divorces, can have on teenagers.

Three students sued, but they finally lost their case when the High Court held that school administrators can exercise "editorial control over the style and content of student speech in school-sponsored expressive activities so long as their actions are reasonably related to legitimate pedagogical (educational) concerns."

? INFER What can you infer from the Court's decisions finding prior restraint unconstitutional in the case of the Pentagon Papers, but not in the case of CIA agents publishing of material without the agency's permission (*Snepp* v. *United States*)?

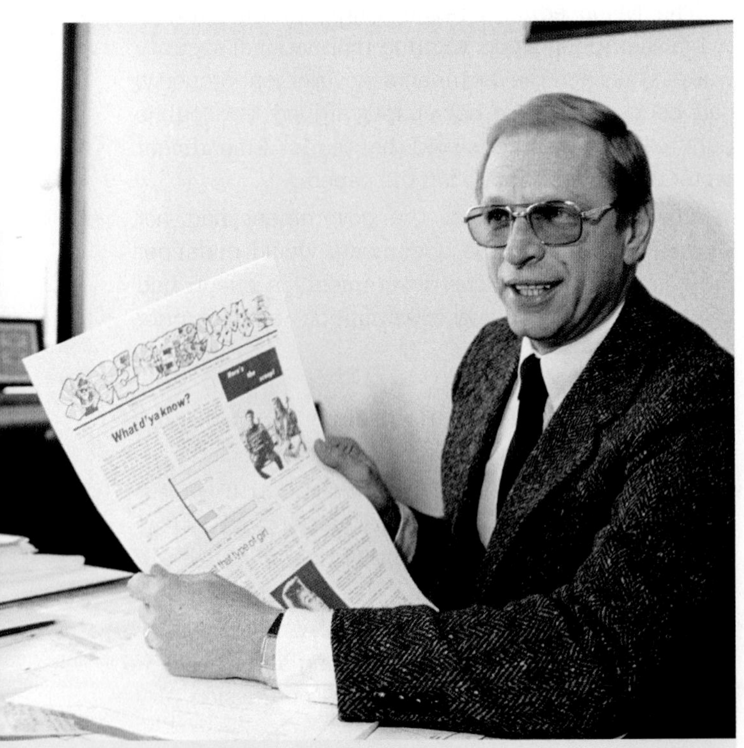

>> Principal Robert Reynolds holds a copy of his high school's newspaper. In *Hazelwood School District* v. *Kuhlmeier,* the Supreme Court ruled that his censorship of the paper was legal.

The Media in a Free Society

The 1st Amendment stands as a monument to the central importance of the media in a free society. That raises this question: To what extent can the media—whether print, radio, television, or the Internet—be regulated by government?

Confidentiality Can news reporters be forced to testify before a grand jury in court or before a legislative committee? Can those government bodies require journalists to name their sources and reveal other confidential information? Many reporters and news organizations insist that they must have the right to refuse to testify in order to protect their sources. They argue that without this right they cannot assure confidentiality, and therefore many sources will not reveal important, sensitive information.

Both State and federal courts have generally rejected the news media argument. In recent years, several reporters have refused to obey court orders directing them to give information, and they have gone to jail, thus testifying to the importance of these issues.

In the leading case, *Branzburg* v. *Hayes,* 1972, the Supreme Court held that reporters, "like other citizens, [must] respond to relevant questions put to them in the course of a valid grand jury investigation or criminal trial." If the media are to receive any special exemptions, said the Court, they must come from Congress and the State legislatures.

To date, Congress has not acted on the Court's suggestion, but every State except Wyoming has passed so-called **shield laws.** These laws give reporters some protection against having to disclose their sources or reveal other confidential information in legal proceedings in those States.

Motion Pictures The Supreme Court took its first look at motion pictures early in the history of the movie industry. In 1915, in *Mutual Film Corporation* v. *Ohio,* the Court upheld a State law that barred the showing of any film that was not of a "moral, educational, or amusing and harmless character." The Court declared that "the exhibition of moving pictures is a business, pure and simple," and "not . . . part of the press of the country." With that decision, nearly every State and thousands of communities set up movie review (really movie censorship) programs.

The Court reversed itself in 1952, however. In *Burstyn* v. *Wilson,* a New York censorship case, it found that "liberty of expression by means of motion pictures is guaranteed by the 1st and 14th amendments." Still, the Court has never held that the Constitution grants the film industry the same level of protection against prior restraint that it gives to newspapers. In fact, it has upheld a requirement that films be submitted to official censors so long as those censors are required to act reasonably and their decisions are subject to speedy court review, *Freedman* v. *Maryland,* 1965.

Very few of the once-common movie review boards still exist. Most people now rely on the film industry's own rating system and on the comments of movie critics to guide their viewing choices.

Radio and Television Both radio and television broadcasting are subject to extensive federal regulation. Most of this regulation is based on the often-amended Federal Communications Act of 1934, which is administered by the Federal Communications Commission (FCC). As the Supreme Court noted in *FCC* v. *Pacifica Foundation,* 1978: "Of all forms of communication, broadcasting has the most limited 1st Amendment protection."

The Court has several times upheld this wide-ranging federal regulation as a proper exercise of the commerce power. Unlike newspapers and other print media, radio and television use the public's property—the public airwaves—to distribute their materials. They have no right to use the limited broadcast frequencies without the public's permission in the form of a proper license, said the Court in *National Broadcasting Co.* v. *United States,* 1943.

>> In *FCC* v. *Fox*, the Court said that FCC rules against "fleeting expletives" uttered by performers like U2's Bono were "unconstitutionally vague" under the Due Process Clause.

The Court has regularly rejected the argument that the 1st Amendment prohibits such regulations. Instead, it has said that regulation of this industry implements the constitutional guarantee. In *Red Lion Broadcasting Co.* v. *FCC,* 1969, the Court held that there is no "unabridgeable 1st Amendment right to broadcast comparable to the right of every individual to speak, write, or publish." However, "this is not to say that the 1st Amendment is irrelevant to public broadcasting. . . . It is the right of the viewers and the listeners, not the right of the broadcasters. . . ."

The Federal Communications Act forbids prior censorship—and so the FCC cannot censor the content of programs before they are broadcast. However, the law does permit the FCC to ban the use of indecent language, and the Court has held that it can take violations of that ban into account when a station applies for the renewal of its operating license, *FCC* v. *Pacifica Foundation,* 1978.

In several recent decisions, the Supreme Court has given cable television somewhat broader 1st Amendment freedoms than those enjoyed by traditional network television. *United States* v. *Playboy Entertainment Group,* 2000, is fairly typical. There, the Court struck down an attempt by Congress to force many cable systems to limit sexually explicit channels to confine their programs to late night hours. The Court agreed that shielding children from such programming is a worthy goal; nevertheless, it found the 1996 law to be a violation of the 1st Amendment.

Commercial Speech Commercial speech is speech for business purposes; the term refers most often to advertising. Until the mid-1970s, it was thought that the 1st and 14th amendments did not protect such speech. In *Bigelow* v. *Virginia,* 1975, however, the Court held unconstitutional a State law that prohibited the newspaper advertising of abortion services. The following year, in *Virginia State Board of Pharmacy* v. *Virginia Citizens Consumer Council,* it struck down another Virginia law forbidding the advertisement of prescription drug prices.

Not all commercial speech is protected, however. Government can and does prohibit false and misleading advertisements, and the advertising of illegal goods or services. In fact, government can even forbid advertising that is neither false nor misleading. In 1970, Congress banned cigarette ads on radio and television. In 1986, it extended the ban to include chewing tobacco and snuff.

In most of its commercial speech cases, the Court has struck down arbitrary restrictions on advertising. In *44 Liquormart, Inc.* v. *Rhode Island,* 1996, the Court voided a State law that prohibited ads in which liquor prices were listed. In *Greater New Orleans Broadcasting Association* v. *United States,* 1999, it struck down a federal law that prohibited casino advertising on radio or television.

In 2001, the Court dealt with limits on smokeless tobacco and cigar advertising. Massachusetts had barred outdoor ads for these commodities within 1,000 feet of any school or playground. The Court held that the limit was a violation of the 1st and 14th amendments' guarantee of free speech, *P. Lorillard Co.* v. *Reilly.*

Obscene Material Both federal and State laws have made the dissemination of obscene material illegal, and the courts have generally agreed that obscenity is not protected by the 1st and 14th amendments. But what, exactly, is *obscenity*? Lawmakers and judges have wrestled with that question for decades. The Supreme Court's Justice Potter Stewart once famously said that, although he could not define the term, "I know it when I see it," *Jacobellis* v. *Ohio,* 1964.

A large part of the problem in defining *obscenity* lies in the fact that moral standards vary from time to time, place to place, and person to person. To illustrate that point: Much of what appears on television today would, in fact, have been banned as obscenity only a few decades ago.

>> President Clinton signs the Communications Decency Act of 1996, part of which was later declared unconstitutional by a unanimous decision of the Supreme Court.

Obscenity and the Mail In 1872, Congress passed the first in a series of laws that prevent the mailing of obscene matter. The current postal law, upheld in *Roth* v. *United States,* 1957, excludes "obscene, lewd, lascivious, or filthy" material from the mail. The Court found the law a proper exercise of the postal power (Article I, Section 8, Clause 7) and so not prohibited by the 1st Amendment. *Roth* marked the Court's first attempt to define obscenity.

Three-Part Test Today, the leading case is *Miller* v. *California,* 1973. There the Court laid down a three-part test to define obscenity. A book, film, recording, or other piece of material is legally obscene if (1) "the average person applying contemporary [local] community standards" finds that the work, taken as a whole, "appeals to the prurient interest"—that is, tends to excite lust; (2) "the work depicts or describes, in a patently offensive way," a form of sexual conduct specifically dealt with in an anti-obscenity law; and (3) "the work, taken as a whole, lacks serious literary, artistic, political, or scientific value."

In recent years, the Court has heard only a handful of cases involving questions of obscenity. Those cases have all involved the Internet.

The Internet and Free Speech The Internet has generated only a handful of Supreme Court cases—and many of them have involved attempts by Congress to regulate access to pornographic matter. Congress first attempted to protect minors from that material in the Communications Decency Act of 1996. That law made it a crime to "knowingly" transmit any "obscene or indecent" speech or image that is "patently offensive as measured by contemporary community standards" to any person under the age of 18.

The Court promptly declared that law unconstitutional in *Reno* v. *American Civil Liberties Union,* 1997. A majority of the justices found that the words "indecent" and "patently offensive" were too vague and that the overall effect of that law was to deny to adults materials that are protected by the 1st Amendment. "Regardless of the strength of the government's interest in protecting children," said the Court, "the level of discourse reaching a mailbox cannot be limited to that which would be suitable for a sandbox."

The Supreme Court did uphold an act of Congress dealing with pornography, the Internet, and public libraries in *United States* v. *American Library Association,* 2003. There, a majority could find no constitutional fault in the Children's Internet Protection Act (CIPA) of 2002. That law provides that those public libraries that receive federal money—nearly all of them do—must use filters to block their computers' access to pornographic sites on the Internet.

The Supreme Court first ventured into the realm of free speech and video games in 2011, when it heard the case *Brown* v. *Entertainment Merchants Association.* The case involved a California law prohibiting the sale of violent video games to minors. In its 7–2 ruling, the justices declared the law in violation of the 1st Amendment. The Court ruled that video games are a form of expression and noted that the State of California had failed to show a link between playing violent video games and violent behavior.

? IDENTIFY CENTRAL ISSUES What was the basis for the Court determination in *Red Lion Broadcasting Co.* v. *FCC*, 1969, that the regulation of the radio and television industries *implements* the constitutional guarantee of free speech?

ASSESSMENT

1. **Make Generalizations** How does the case of *Tinker* v. *Des Moines School District*, 1969, illustrate constitutional protection of symbolic speech?
2. **Apply Concepts** In the case *Burstyn, Inc.* v. *Wilson*, 1952, the Supreme Court voided a New York law that allowed censors to forbid the commercial showing of a motion picture that it had decided was "sacrilegious." The Court held that the law was a prior restraint on freedom of speech and of the press under the 1st Amendment. What is the meaning of the phrase "based on prior restraint on freedom of speech" in this case?
3. **Make Predictions** California is one State that is attempting to control cyber bullying by passing laws allowing school administrators to monitor student comments on social media sites. What 1st Amendment protections is the Court likely to review if asked to consider the constitutionality of these laws?
4. **Identify Central Issues** In the case *Bethel School District No. 403* v. *Fraser,* 1986, the court ruled that school officials had not violated the 1st Amendment rights of a student by suspending him for three days after he delivered a nominating speech before a student assembly whose content the administration found offensive. Why was the student's speech not protected under the 1st Amendment?
5. **Draw Conclusions** In the case *Brown* v. *Entertainment Merchants Association*, 2011, as well as other cases, the State's authority to pass laws restricting the sale or rental of violent video games to minors was challenged by the software industry. What aspects of the 1st Amendment could be argued in the software industry's favor?

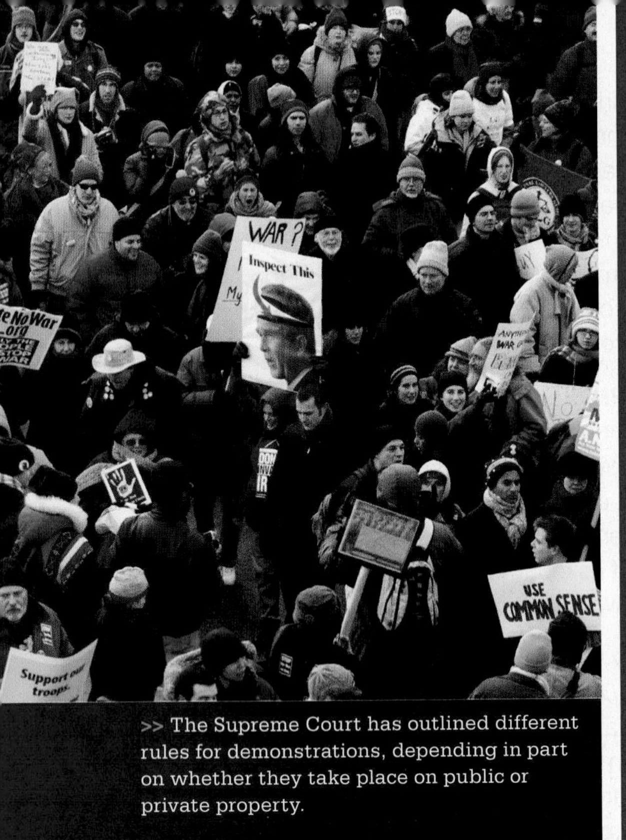

>> The Supreme Court has outlined different rules for demonstrations, depending in part on whether they take place on public or private property.

Interactive Flipped Video

8.4 A crowded street demonstration by opponents of a gas pipeline; a group of anti-Obama protestors at a campaign event; a candlelight vigil by opponents of the death penalty; a march opposing unmanned aerial drones outside an air force base. . . these are all contemporary examples of citizen movements to bring about political change or to maintain continuity—and they all involve the constitutional right to freedom of assembly and petition.

Freedom of Assembly and Petition

>> Objectives

Analyze the importance of the 1st Amendment rights of petition and assembly.

Analyze Supreme Court interpretations of rights guaranteed by the Constitution, including limits on the time, place, and manner of assembly.

Compare and contrast the freedom-of-assembly issues that arise on public versus private property.

Explore how the Supreme Court has interpreted freedom of association.

>> Key Terms

assemble
petition
civil disobedience
content neutral
right of association

Constitutional Provisions

Rights of Assembly and Petition The 1st Amendment guarantees "the right of the people peaceably to assemble, and to petition the Government for a redress of grievances." The 14th Amendment's Due Process Clause also protects those rights of assembly and petition against actions by the States or their local governments, *DeJonge* v. *Oregon,* 1937.

The Constitution protects the right of the people to **assemble** to express their views. It protects their right to organize to influence public policy, whether in political parties, interest groups, or other organizations. It also protects the people's right to **petition**—to bring their views to the attention of public officials by such varied means as written petitions, letters, or advertisements; lobbying; and parades or marches.

Notice, however, that the 1st and 14th amendments protect the rights of *peaceable* assembly and petition. The Constitution does not give to anyone the right to incite others to violence, block a public street, close a school, or otherwise endanger life, property, or public safety.

Civil Disobedience Note this important point as well: A significant part of the history of this country can be told in terms of **civil disobedience.** That is to say that much of our history has been built out of incidents in which people have purposely violated the law—nonviolently, but nonetheless deliberately, as a means of expressing their opposition to some particular law or public policy.

Do the 1st and 14th amendment guarantees of freedom of assembly and petition include a right of civil disobedience? That thorny question cannot be answered absolutely or without qualification because of the very nature of civil disobedience: those acts are expressions of opinion on some public matter.

Still, courts have consistently held that, as a general rule, civil disobedience is not a constitutionally protected right. Those who choose to take part in such activities are often aware of that fact, and they are usually willing to accept the consequences of their conduct.

? ANALYZE INFORMATION A group of U.S. military veterans are planning to gather at a memorial to read the names of fallen comrades and give speeches calling for an end to war. Under what circumstances would this assembly be protected by the 1st Amendment?

Time, Place, and Manner Rules

Government can make and enforce reasonable rules covering the time, place, and manner of assemblies. Thus, in *Grayned* v. *City of Rockford,* 1972, the Court upheld a city ordinance that prohibits making a noise or any other diversion near a school if that action has a disruptive effect on school activities. It has also upheld a State law that forbids parades near a courthouse when they are intended to influence court proceedings, *Cox* v.*Louisiana,* 1965.

Restrictions on Government Rules for keeping the public peace must be more than just reasonable, however. They must also be precisely drawn and fairly administered. In *Coates* v. *Cincinnati,* 1971, the Court struck down a city ordinance that made it a crime for "three or more persons to assemble" on a sidewalk or street corner "and there conduct themselves in a manner annoying to persons passing by, or occupants of adjacent buildings." The Court found the wording of the ordinance much too vague and therefore unconstitutional.

Government's rules must be **content neutral**. That is, although government can regulate assemblies on the basis of time, place, and manner, it cannot regulate gatherings on the basis of what might be said there. Thus, in *Forsyth County* v. *Nationalist Movement,* 1992, the Court threw out a Georgia county's ordinance that levied a fee of up to $1,000 for public demonstrations.

The law was contested by a white supremacist group seeking to protest the creation of a holiday to honor Martin Luther King, Jr. The Court found the ordinance not to be content neutral, particularly because county officials had unlimited power to set the exact fee to be paid by any group.

Free Speech Zones While the courts have said that governments cannot limit the *content* of political speech, under some circumstances it is reasonable for governments to limit the *place* and *time* of political speech by creating so-called "free speech zones." These zones are an attempt to balance the right of free speech with the right of the public to gather and move without interference from protesters.

Simply stated, free speech zones are designated areas—such as a particular section of a sidewalk—to

>> In an act of civil disobedience, immigrant rights activists, including business and community leaders, were arrested for blocking traffic during this demonstration near Capitol Hill.

Interactive Timeline

which protesters are confined. Free speech zones have stirred controversy over the years, with critics claiming that they violate the 1st Amendment guarantee of the right to free speech. Supporters maintain that the zones are necessary to protect both the public and the protesters.

IDENTIFY CENTRAL ISSUES A college student was prevented from obtaining signatures for a petition because he was outside the "free speech zone," a designated concrete slab big enough for two people. What might make these requirements unconstitutional?

Assemblies on Public and Private Property

Over the past several years, most of the Court's freedom of assembly cases have involved organized demonstrations. Demonstrations are, of course, assemblies. Most demonstrations take place in public places—on streets and sidewalks, in parks or public buildings, and so on. This is the case because it is the *public* the demonstrators want to reach.

Demonstrations almost always involve some degree of conflict. Most often, they are held to protest something, and so there is an inherent clash of ideas. Many times there is also a conflict with the normal use of streets or other public facilities. It is hardly surprising, then, that the tension can sometimes rise to a serious level.

Given all this, the Supreme Court has often upheld laws that require advance notice and permits for demonstrations in public places. In an early leading case, *Cox* v. *New Hampshire,* 1941, it unanimously approved a State law that required a license to hold a parade or procession on a public street.

Right-to-demonstrate cases raise many difficult questions. How and to what extent can government regulate demonstrators? Does the Constitution require that police officers allow an unpopular group to continue to demonstrate even when its activities have excited others to violence? When, in the name of public peace and safety, can police order demonstrators to disband?

Gregory* v. *Chicago A leading and illustrative case is *Gregory* v. *Chicago,* 1969. While under police protection, comedian Dick Gregory and others marched while singing, chanting, and carrying placards, from city hall to the mayor's home some five miles away. Marching in the streets around the mayor's house, they demanded the firing of the city's school superintendent and an end to de facto segregation in the city's schools.

A crowd of several hundred people, including many residents of the all-white neighborhood, quickly gathered. Soon, the bystanders began throwing insults and threats, as well as rocks, eggs, and other objects. The police tried to keep order, but after about an hour,

>> The Court has backed the government's right to place some limits on political speech. **Analyze Political Cartoons** What does this cartoon say about "free speech zones"?

they decided that serious violence was about to break out. At that point, they ordered the demonstrators to leave the area. When Gregory and others failed to do so, the police arrested them and charged them with disorderly conduct.

The convictions of the demonstrators were unanimously overturned by the Court. It noted that the marchers had exercised their constitutional rights of assembly and petition. The bystanders, not the demonstrators, had caused the disorder. As long as the demonstrators acted peacefully, they could not be punished for disorderly conduct.

Recent Cases Over recent years, many of the most controversial demonstrations have been those held by anti-abortion groups. For the most part, their efforts have been aimed at discouraging women from seeking the services of abortion clinics, and those efforts have generated many lawsuits.

There have been two particularly notable cases to date. In the first one, *Madsen* v. *Women's Health Services, Inc.,* 1994, the Supreme Court upheld a Florida judge's order directing protesters not to block access to an abortion clinic. The judge's order had drawn a 36-foot buffer zone around the clinic. The High Court found that to be a reasonable limit on the demonstrators' activities.

The other major case is *Hill* v. *Colorado,* 2000. There, the Court upheld, 5–4, a State law that limits "sidewalk counseling" at clinics where abortions are performed. That statute creates an eight-foot buffer zone around anyone who wants to enter. No one may make an "unwanted approach" to talk, hand out a leaflet, or wave a sign.

The Court found that the Colorado law does not deal with the content of abortion protestors' speech. It is aimed, instead, at *where, when,* and *how* their message is delivered.

Private Property What about demonstrations on private property—at shopping centers, for example? The Court has said that the 1st and 14th amendment rights of assembly and petition do not give people a right to trespass on private property, even to express political views.

Privately owned shopping centers are not "places of public assembly." Thus, no one has a constitutional right to do such things as hand out political leaflets or ask people to sign petitions in those places, according to the leading case on the subject, *Lloyd Corporation* v. *Tanner,* 1972.

DRAW CONCLUSIONS In 2013, a Eugene, Oregon, judge nullified twenty-one trespassing citations issued by police to a group that had staged a protest by pitching tents in a public plaza in Eugene. What constitutional safeguards most likely guided the judge's decision?

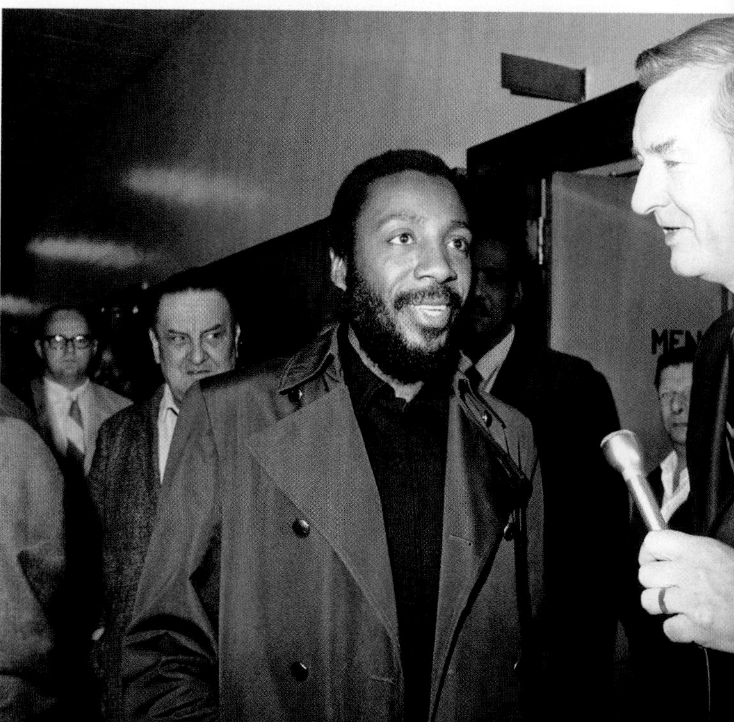

>> In *Gregory* v. *Chicago,* Justice Hugo Black said that arresting demonstrators due to bystanders' unruly behavior would be a "heckler's veto." Here, Gregory is interviewed during his 1966 trial.

Freedom of Association

The guarantees of freedom of assembly and petition include a **right of association**—the right to join with others to promote political, economic, and social causes. That right is not set out in so many words in the Constitution. However, in *National Association for the Advancement of Colored People* v. *Alabama,* 1958, the Supreme Court said, "it is beyond debate that freedom to engage in association for the advancement of beliefs and ideas is an inseparable aspect" of the Constitution's guarantees of free expression.

The case just cited is one of the early right-to-associate cases. There, a State law required the Alabama branch of the NAACP to disclose the names of all its members in that State. When the organization refused a court's order to do so, it was found in contempt of court and fined $100,000.

The Supreme Court overturned the contempt conviction. It said that it could find no legitimate reason

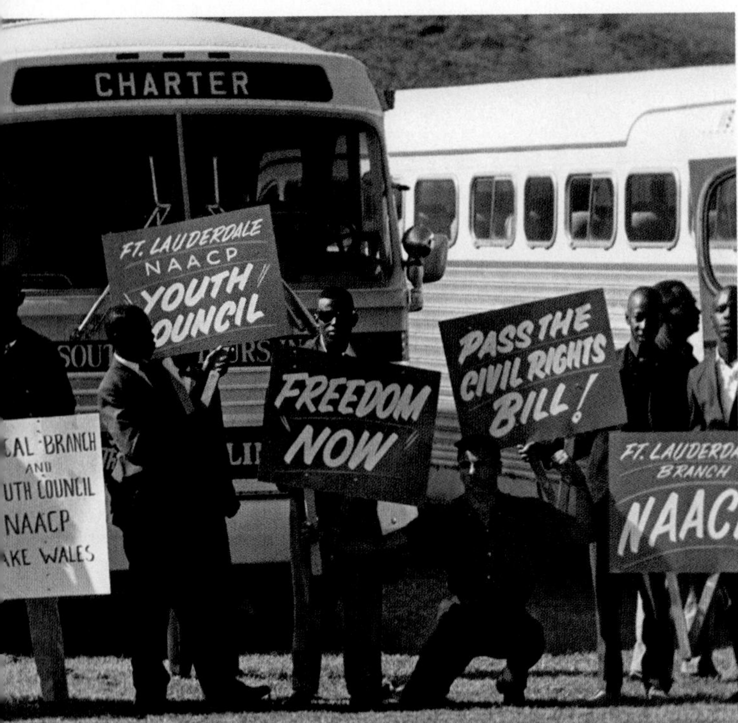

>> In 1958, the Supreme Court ruled that the NAACP did not have to disclose its membership list to the State of Alabama under the 1st Amendment's guarantee of freedom of association.

Interactive Gallery

why the State should have the NAACP's membership list.

A person cannot be fired from a job because of political associations—for example, membership in a political party, *Brown* v. *Socialist Workers '74 Campaign Committee*, 1982. And a person cannot be required to disclose his or her political associations in order to be licensed to practice law, *Gibson* v. *Florida*, 1966. On the other hand, the State of Washington's publication of the names of those registered voters who signed initiative petitions to put a measure on the general election ballot does not violate the Constitution's guarantee of a right of association, *Doe* v. *Reed*, 2010.

There is no absolute right of association, however. In *Boy Scouts of America* v. *Dale*, 2000, the Supreme Court held that the Boy Scouts have a constitutional right to exclude gays from their organization. The Court noted that opposition to homosexuality is a part of the Boy Scout organization's "expressive association"—that is, what they stand for.

In *Christian Legal Society* v. *Martinez*, 2010, however, the Court distinguished between independent groups and those that receive recognition and support from a larger organization. The Court held that the Christian Legal Society, a student group at the University of California Hastings Law School, could not require the signing of a "Statement of Faith" as a condition of membership, as long as it wished to remain a registered student organization at the law school.

? SUPPORT IDEAS WITH EXAMPLES In the case *Boy Scouts of America* v. *Dale*, 2000, what is the constitutional basis for the Supreme Court decision?

ASSESSMENT

1. **Apply Concepts** A sit-in was staged on the sidewalk in front of the State Department to protest a proposed pipeline from Alaska to the Gulf Coast. Was this event protected by the Constitution? Explain your answer.
2. **Identify Central Ideas** In what way do limits on the role of government protect 1st Amendment rights of petition and assembly?
3. **Apply Concepts** In *Collin* v. *Smith*, 1978, the Court allowed a group called "followers of Nazism" to publicly and peaceably assemble to express their views in Skokie, Illinois, overturning local ordinances prohibiting this group's assembly. What does the Court's ruling say about the 1st Amendment and the States?
4. **Make Generalizations** Given its significant role in our country's history, do you think the right of civil disobedience is constitutionally protected?
5. **Analyze Information** In the case *Rutan* v. *Republican Party of Illinois*, 1990, the Supreme Court ruled that state-employee Rutan's promotion could not be denied based on her nonsupport of the Republican party. What was the likely basis for the Court's decision?

8.5

Did you know that DNA evidence has led to the reversal of more than 200 wrongful convictions in recent years? That the use of evidence drawn from the scientific study of body tissues has proved that all those persons were convicted, and served time in prison, for crimes they did *not* commit? Did you know that there is a strong likelihood that an untold number of innocent persons remain in prison today? As you will soon see, this point alone illustrates the importance of due process of law.

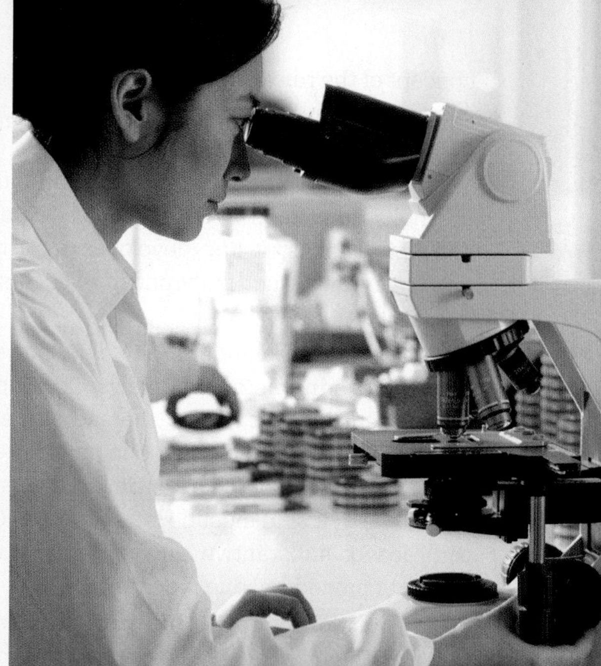

>> The use of scientific tests, such as DNA analysis, can help ensure due process for those accused of crime by evaluating evidence more accurately.

Interactive Flipped Video

Due Process of Law

>> Objectives

Explain the importance of due process rights to the protection of individual rights and in limiting the powers of government.

Define the police power and understand its relationship to the subordination of personal desires and interests to the public good.

>> Key Terms

due process
procedural due process
substantive due process
police power
search warrant
eminent domain

Understanding Due Process

The Constitution contains two due process clauses. The 5th Amendment declares that the Federal Government cannot deprive any person of "life, liberty, or property, without due process of law." The 14th Amendment places that same restriction on every one of the States—and, very importantly, on their local governments, as well. A thorough grasp of the meaning of these provisions is absolutely essential to an understanding of the American concept of civil rights and liberties.

It is impossible to define the two due process guarantees in exact and complete terms. The Supreme Court has consistently and purposely refused to do so. Instead, it has relied on finding the meaning of due process on a case-by-case basis. The Court first described that approach in *Davidson* v. *New Orleans,* 1878, as the "gradual process of inclusion and exclusion, as the cases presented for decision shall require."

Fundamentally, however, the Constitution's guarantee of **due process** means this: In whatever it does, government must act fairly and in accord with established rules. It may not act unfairly, arbitrarily, or unreasonably. The government can take private property for public use, for example, but it must fairly compensate the individual who loses the property—which means giving that person money equal to the fair market value of the land. Due process is a component of the

concept of the rule of law, which holds that government is never above the law. In the words of patriot Thomas Paine, "In America THE LAW IS KING."

The concept of due process began and developed in English and then in American law as a procedural concept. That is, it first developed as a requirement that government act fairly and use fair procedures to enforce law.

Fair procedures are of little value, however, if they are used to administer unfair laws. The Supreme Court recognized this fact toward the end of the nineteenth century. It began to hold that due process requires that both the ways in which government acts *and* the laws under which it acts must be fair. Thus, the Court added the idea of substantive due process to the original notion of procedural due process.

In short, **procedural due process** has to do with the *how* (the procedures, the methods) of governmental action. **Substantive due process** involves the *what* (the substance, the policies) of governmental action.

Classic Due Process Cases Any number of cases may be used to illustrate these two elements of due process. Take a classic case, *Rochin* v. *California,* 1952, to exemplify procedural due process.

Rochin was a suspected narcotics dealer. Acting on a tip, three Los Angeles County deputy sheriffs went to his rooming house. They forced their way into Rochin's room, found him sitting on a bed, and spotted two capsules on a nightstand. When one of the deputies asked, "Whose stuff is this?" Rochin popped the capsules into his mouth. Although all three officers jumped him, Rochin managed to swallow the pills.

The deputies took Rochin to a hospital, where his stomach was pumped. The capsules were recovered and found to contain morphine. The State then prosecuted and convicted Rochin for violating the State's narcotics laws.

The Supreme Court unanimously held that the deputies had violated the 14th Amendment's guarantee of procedural due process. Said the Court:

> This is conduct that shocks the conscience. Illegally breaking into the privacy of the petitioner, the struggle to open his mouth and remove what was there, the forcible extraction of his stomach's contents—this course of proceeding by agents of government to obtain evidence is bound to offend even hardened sensibilities. They are

"Government cannot deprive any person of life, liberty, or property without due process of law."

This limit is placed on the Federal Government in the **5th Amendment.**

This limit is placed on State and local governments in the **14th Amendment.**

Due process relates to both the **procedures** and the **laws** of government.

PROCEDURAL Due Process	**SUBSTANTIVE** Due Process
The procedures, the methods, the *how* of governmental action must be fair.	The substance, the meaning, the *what* of a law or action of government must be fair.

>> Both the procedures and the laws of government must be in accord with due process. **Analyze Charts** Why are procedural and substantive due process both necessary?

methods too close to the rack and the screw. . . .

—Justice Felix Frankfurter

The case *Pierce* v. *Society of Sisters,* 1925, illustrates substantive due process. In 1922, Oregon's voters had adopted a new compulsory school-attendance law that required all persons between the ages of 8 and 16 to attend *public* schools. The law was purposely written to destroy private, especially parochial, schools in the State.

A Roman Catholic order challenged the law's constitutionality, and the Supreme Court held that its provisions violated the 14th Amendment's Due Process Clause. The Court did not find that the State had enforced the law unfairly. Rather, it held that the law itself, in its contents, "unreasonably interferes with the liberty of parents and guardians to direct the upbringing and education of children under their control."

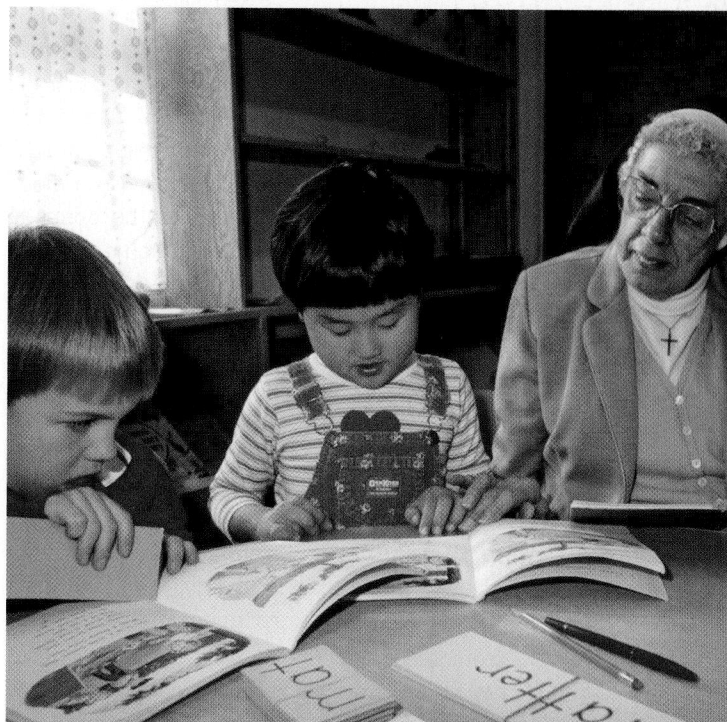

>> A nun reads to children at a parochial school. **Generate Explanations** Why is the Supreme Court ruling in *Pierce* v. *Society of Sisters* called the "Magna Carta of the parochial school system"?

The 14th Amendment and the Bill of Rights Recall these crucial points: The provisions of the Bill of Rights apply against the National Government *only.* However, the Supreme Court has held that the 14th Amendment's Due Process Clause includes within its meaning most of the protections set out in the Bill of Rights.

In a long series of decisions dating from 1925, the Court extended the protections of the Bill of Rights against the States through the 14th Amendment's Due Process Clause. Provisions of the Bill of Rights *incorporated* into the 14th Amendment's Due Process Clause include the 1st, 2nd, 4th, 5th, 6th, and 8th amendments. Provisions of the Bill of Rights *not incorporated* into the 14th Amendment's Due Process Clause include the 3rd, 5th, and 7th amendments.

APPLY CONCEPTS Think of an example of a violation of the 5th Amendment right to substantive due process. Explain how the right is being violated.

Individual Rights and the Public Good

In the federal system, the reserved powers of the States include the broad and important **police power.** The police power is the authority of each State to act to protect and promote the public health, safety, morals, and general welfare. In other words, it is the power of each State to safeguard the well-being of its people.

The Police Power and Civil Liberties The use of the police power often produces conflicts with civil liberty protections. When it does, courts must strike a balance between the needs of society, on the one hand, and of individual freedoms on the other. Any number of cases can be used to illustrate the conflict between police power and individual rights. Take as an example a matter often involved in drunk-driving cases.

Every State's laws allow the use of one or more tests to determine whether a person arrested and charged with drunk driving was in fact drunk at the time of the incident. Some of those tests are simple: walking a straight line or touching the tip of one's nose, for example. Some are more sophisticated, however, notably the breathalyzer test and the drawing of a blood sample.

Does the requirement that a person submit to such a test violate his or her rights under the 14th Amendment? Does the test involve an unconstitutional search for and seizure of evidence? Does it amount to forcing a person to testify against himself or herself (unconstitutional compulsory self-incrimination)? Or is that requirement a proper exercise of the police power?

Time after time, State and federal courts have come down on the side of the police power. They have supported the right of society to protect itself against drunk drivers and rejected the individual rights argument.

The leading case is *Schmerber* v. *California,* 1966. There, the Court found no objection to a situation in which a police officer had directed a doctor to draw blood from a drunk-driving suspect. The Court emphasized these points: The blood sample was drawn in accord with accepted medical practice. The officer had reasonable grounds to believe that the suspect was drunk. Further, had the officer taken the time necessary to secure a **search warrant**—a court order authorizing a search—whatever evidence was present could have disappeared from the suspect's system. In 2013, however, the Court clarified the *Schmerber* ruling, noting that, in certain instances urgent circumstances can justify a warrantless blood test of a suspected drunk driver, *Missouri* v. *McNeely.*

Protecting the Public Legislators and judges have often found the public's health, safety, morals, and/or welfare to be of overriding importance. For example:

1. To promote health, States can limit the sale of alcoholic beverages and tobacco, make laws to combat pollution, and require the vaccination of schoolchildren.

2. To promote safety, States can regulate the carrying of concealed weapons, require the use of seat belts, and punish drunk drivers.

3. To promote morals, States can regulate gambling and outlaw the sale of obscene materials and the practice of prostitution.

4. To promote the general welfare, States can enact compulsory education laws, provide help to the medically needy, and limit the profits of public utilities.

Clearly, governments cannot use the police power in an unreasonable or unfair way, however. In short, they cannot violate the 14th Amendment's Due Process Clause.

>> A California middle school student receives a free whooping cough booster shot. All 50 States require children to get certain vaccinations before entering public school.

Interactive Gallery

Just Compensation Another aspect of due process relates to the right of **eminent domain**, that is, the power of the government to take private property for public use. Contrary to what many believe, this right is real. It is described in the 5th Amendment to the Constitution, also sometimes called the "Takings Clause." The property must be used by the government, or be delegated to a third party for public use. The catch—and this is where due process come into play—is that the government must provide just compensation for any property it takes. This means that the property's owners must get fair market value for the property.

When the Interstate Highway System was built in the decades following World War II, tens of thousands of land owners lost portions of their property to the new roadways. These highways would become major arteries of the nation's economy, as well as make it much easier for people to travel long distances more quickly. For those who lost their homes, family farms, or the tranquility of their back yards, the Interstate Highway Act was a bitter pill to swallow. Under the 5th Amendment, however, they were all fairly compensated for their land.

Recently, the federal courts ruled that, in some cases, the "public use" might include economic development. In 2005, the city of New London, Connecticut, sought to create an economic development zone on the edge of the city. The idea was to set aside land for new businesses, which would lead to more jobs for city residents and more tax revenue. It made sense to find a way to bring as many as one thousand new jobs to an economically depressed area. The piece of land the city chose for the project however, was privately owned.

Can a government, this time a city, take private property for a public goal (economic development) but not necessarily public use? In *Kelo* v. *City of New London*, 2005, the Supreme Court ruled, in a controversial 5–4 decision, that the act was constitutional.

? IDENTIFY CENTRAL IDEAS Why do you think the Supreme Court held in *Kelo* v. *City of New London* that the taking of private property for the creation of an economic development zone was constitutional?

ASSESSMENT

1. **Explain** Explain the importance of due process rights to the protection of individual rights.
2. **Contrast** What is the difference between substantive due process and procedural due process?
3. **Connect** What is the relationship between the police power and the subordination of personal desires and interests to the public good?
4. **Infer** What did Thomas Paine mean when he said, "THE LAW IS KING"?
5. **Identify Main Ideas** Why is due process important in relation to the government's power of eminent domain?

>> *The Minuteman* statue was built to honor colonial militia. Militias consisted of ordinary citizens who acted to defend their nation. Colonists needed to be ready to serve "at a minute's notice."

8.6 The Constitution of the United States is, in very large part, a statement of limited government. Many of the restrictions it puts on governmental power are intended to protect the right of every American to be free. That is, those restrictions guard the right of individuals to be free from physical restraints, to be secure in their persons, and to be secure in their homes.

Interactive Flipped Video

Freedom and Security of the Person

>> Objectives

Evaluate how Supreme Court decisions regarding slavery and involuntary servitude have affected a particular racial group.

Analyze the importance of the 2nd Amendment's protection of the right to keep and bear arms.

Evaluate constitutional provisions for limiting the role of government, including those designed to guarantee the security of home and person.

Understand the Supreme Court's ongoing refinement of the exclusionary rule, including its ruling in *Mapp* v. *Ohio*.

Describe the right to privacy and its origins in constitutional law, and Supreme Court interpretations of rights guaranteed by the Constitution in selected cases, including *Roe* v. *Wade*.

>> Key Terms

involuntary servitude
discrimination
writs of assistance
probable cause
exclusionary rule

Slavery and Involuntary Servitude

The 13th Amendment was added to the Constitution in 1865, ending over 200 years of legalized slavery in America. Section 1 of the amendment declares: "Neither slavery nor involuntary servitude, . . . shall exist within the United States, or any place subject to their jurisdiction." Importantly, Section 2 of this amendment gives Congress the expressed power "to enforce this article by appropriate legislation."

Until 1865, each State could decide for itself whether to allow slavery within its borders. With the 13th Amendment, that power was denied to them, and to the National Government, as well.

The 13th Amendment: Section 1 As a widespread practice, slavery disappeared in the United States more than 140 years ago. There are still occasional cases of it, however. Most often, those cases have involved **involuntary servitude**—that is, forced labor. An 1867 federal law, the Anti-Peonage Act, makes it a crime to force someone to work for another in order to fulfill a contract or satisfy a debt. Several times, the Supreme Court has struck down State laws making it a crime for any person to fail to work after having received money or other benefits by promising to do so.

The 13th Amendment does not forbid all forms of involuntary servitude, however. Thus, in 1918, the Supreme Court drew a distinction between "involuntary servitude" and "duty" in upholding the constitutionality of the selective service system (the draft). Nor does imprisonment for crime violate the amendment, and those who are convicted of crime can be forced to work. Finally, note this important point: Unlike any other provision in the Constitution, the prohibitions in the 13th Amendment cover the conduct of private individuals as well as the behavior of government.

The 13th Amendment: Section 2 Shortly after the Civil War, Congress passed several civil rights laws based on the 13th Amendment. The Supreme Court, however, sharply narrowed the scope of federal authority in several cases, especially the *Civil Rights Cases,* 1883. In effect, the Court held that racial **discrimination** (prejudice, unfairness) against African Americans by *private individuals* was allowed. Private discrimination, ruled the Court, did not place the "badge of slavery" on African Americans nor keep them in servitude.

As a result, Congress soon repealed most of the civil rights laws based on the 13th Amendment. The enforcement of the few laws that remained was at best unimpressive. For years, it was generally thought that Congress did not have the power, under either the 13th or 14th amendment, to act against those who practiced race-based discrimination.

Nearly a century later, however, in *Jones* v. *Mayer,* 1968, the Supreme Court breathed new life into the 13th Amendment. The case centered on one of the post Civil War acts Congress had not repealed. Passed in 1866, that almost-forgotten law provided in part that:

> [All] citizens of the United States; . . . of every race and color, . . . shall have the same right, in every State and Territory of the United States, . . . to inherit, purchase, lease, sell, hold, and convey real and personal property, . . . as is enjoyed by white citizens, . . .
>
> —Civil Rights Act of 1866

Jones, an African American, had sued because Mayer had refused to sell him a home, solely because of his race. Mayer contended that the 1866 law was

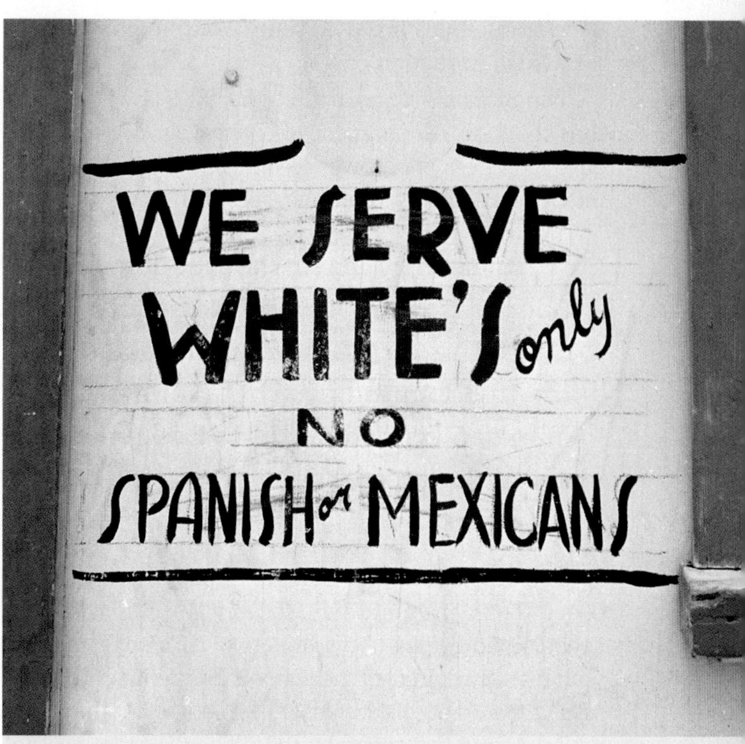

>> As this 1949 sign reveals, racial discrimination in the United States was not limited to African Americans, nor did it end with the banning of slavery in 1865.

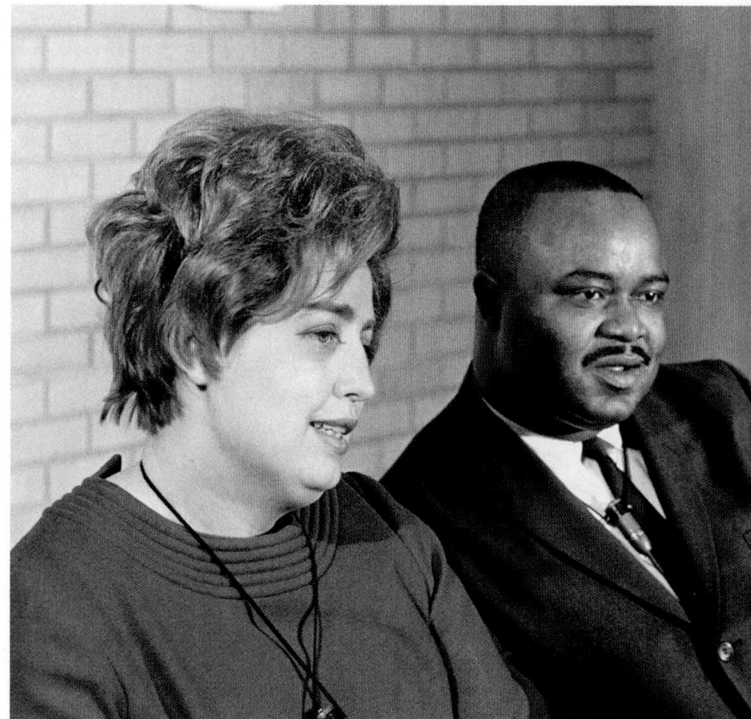

>> Discrimination prevented Joseph and Barbara Jones from buying property in a Missouri neighborhood. Their case brought attention to the long history of race-based housing discrimination.

unconstitutional, since it sought to prohibit private racial discrimination.

The Supreme Court upheld the 1866 law, declaring that the 13th Amendment abolished slavery and also gave Congress the power to abolish "the badges and incidents of slavery." Said the Court:

> At the very least, the freedom that Congress is empowered to secure under the 13th Amendment includes the freedom to buy whatever a white man can buy, the right to live wherever a white man can live.
>
> —Justice Potter Stewart

The Court affirmed that decision in several later cases. Thus, in *Runyon* v. *McCrary,* 1976, two private schools had refused to admit two African American students. By doing so, the schools had refused to enter into a contract of admission—a contract they had advertised to the general public. The Court found that the schools had violated another provision of the 1866 law, providing that: "[All] citizens of the United States, . . . of every race and color, . . . shall have the same right, . . . to make and enforce contracts . . . as is enjoyed by white citizens. . . ."

>> A sit-in at a department store in the 1960s involved a racially mixed group asking to be served at a segregated lunch counter. Actions such as this reinforced 13th Amendment rights.

The Court has also ruled that the Civil Rights Act of 1866 protects all "identifiable classes of persons who are subjected to intentional discrimination solely because of their ancestry or ethnic characteristics"—for example Jews, *Shaare Tefila Congregation* v. *Cobb,* 1987, and Arabs, *St. Francis College* v. *Al Khazraji,* 1987.

More recently, the Court has backed off a bit. In *Patterson* v. *McLean Credit Union,* 1989, it declared that although the 1866 law does prohibit racial discrimination in a contract of employment, any on-the-job discrimination should be handled in accord with the Civil Rights Act of 1964. Nevertheless, the Court has several times held that the 13th Amendment gives Congress significant power to attack "the badges and incidents of slavery," from whatever source they may come.

INFER How did Supreme Court rulings on racial discrimination cases in the 1800s impact civil rights laws?

Right to Keep and Bear Arms

The 2nd Amendment was added to the Constitution to protect the concept of the citizen-soldier. It reads:

> A well-regulated Militia, being necessary to the security of a free State, the right of the people to keep and bear Arms, shall not be infringed.
>
> —Constitution of the United States

What, exactly, do these words mean? Do they protect *only* the right of each State to keep a militia, especially against encroachments by the Federal Government? Or, does the 2nd Amendment do that *and also* give to individuals a right to keep and bear arms—just as, say, the 1st Amendment protects free speech?

For decades, the Supreme Court refused to accept the latter interpretation. In its one really important 2nd Amendment ruling, in *United States* v. *Miller,* 1939, the Court rejected the individual right argument. It upheld a section of the National Firearms Act of 1934 that made it a crime to ship sawed-off shotguns or sub-machine guns across State lines unless the shipper had a federal license to do so. The Court said that it could find no valid link between the shotgun involved in the case and "the preservation . . . of a well-regulated militia."

The High Court has substantially reshaped its interpretation of the 2nd Amendment in its most recent 5–4 decisions, however. In *District of Columbia* v. *Heller*, 2008, it struck down the District's very strict gun-control ordinance—finding that the right of law-abiding citizens to keep a handgun in their homes for self-defense is protected by the 2nd Amendment. And in *McDonald* v. *Chicago*, 2010, it went a step further, incorporating the 2nd Amendment into the 14th Amendment's Due Process Clause. Recall, the Court began that lengthy process of incorporation nearly 100 years ago, in 1925.

The Court also said in both *Heller* and *McDonald* that those cases do not overrule "long-standing prohibitions on the possession of firearms by felons or the mentally ill or laws forbidding the carrying of firearms in sensitive places such as schools and government buildings, or laws imposing conditions and qualifications on the commercial sale of arms."

Clearly, both federal and State courts will hear any number of cases challenging the many State and federal laws that limit an individual's right to keep and bear arms.

DRAW CONCLUSIONS Based on the Supreme Court's striking down the strict gun control ordinance of the District of Columbia in 2008, what is one important aspect of the 2nd Amendment?

>> The British Quartering Act of 1765 forced American colonists to provide food and housing to British soldiers at the colonists' own personal expense.

Security of Home and Person

The 3rd and 4th amendments say that government cannot violate the home or person of anyone in this country without just cause.

The 3rd and 4th Amendments The 3rd Amendment forbids the quartering (housing) of soldiers in private homes in peacetime without the owner's consent and not in wartime except "in a manner to be prescribed by law." The guarantee was added to prevent the British colonial practice of "quartering large bodies of troops among us" (Declaration of Independence). The 3rd Amendment has had little importance since 1791 and has never been the subject of a Supreme Court case.

The 4th Amendment also grew out of colonial practice. It was designed to prevent the use of **writs of assistance**—blanket search warrants with which British customs officials had invaded private homes to search for smuggled goods.

Each State constitution contains a similar provision. The guarantee also applies to the States through the 14th Amendment's Due Process Clause, *Mapp* v. *Ohio*, 1961. Unlike the 3rd Amendment, the 4th Amendment has proved a highly important guarantee.

The 4th Amendment and Probable Cause The basic rule laid down by the 4th Amendment is this: Police officers have no general right to search for evidence or to seize either evidence or persons. Except in special circumstances, they must have a proper warrant (a court order). That warrant must be obtained with **probable cause**—that is, a reasonable suspicion of crime.

Florida v. *J.L.*, 2000, illustrates the rule. There, Miami police received a tip that a teenager was carrying a concealed weapon. Two officers went to the bus stop where the tipster said the young man could be found. The police located him, searched him, pulled a gun from his pocket, and arrested him.

The Court held that the police acted illegally because they did not have a proper warrant. All they had was an anonymous tip, unsupported by any other evidence. Their conduct amounted to just the sort of thing the 4th Amendment was intended to prevent.

Police do not always need a warrant, however—for example, when evidence is "in plain view." Thus, the Court upheld a search and seizure involving two men who were bagging cocaine. A policeman spotted them through an open window, entered the apartment, seized

Stu's Views © Stu All Rights Reserved www.STUS.com

Of course I ate the fish. He was in "plain view". You, of all people, should understand how irresistible that is.

>> Under certain circumstances, the police can seize evidence even without a warrant. **Analyze Political Cartoons** What point is the cartoonist making about police attitudes toward such evidence?

>> Narcotics detection dogs are highly trained to work with police officers. When on duty, they are permitted to walk around a car at a traffic stop, as this takes place on public property.

the cocaine, and arrested them. The Court upheld their conviction, rejecting a claim to 4th Amendment protection, *Minnesota* v. *Carter,* 1998.

Many 4th Amendment cases are complicated. In *Lidster* v. *Illinois,* 2004, for example, the Court upheld the use of so-called "informational roadblocks." In 1997, police had set up barriers on a busy highway near Chicago, hoping to find witnesses to a recent hit-and-run accident. When Robert Lidster was stopped, an officer smelled alcohol on him. Lidster failed several sobriety tests and was arrested on a drunk-driving charge.

Lidster's attorney filed a motion to quash (set aside) that arrest. The lawyer argued that Lidster was forced to stop by officers who, before they stopped him, had no valid reason (no probable cause) to believe that he had committed any crime.

Lidster lost that argument. The Court upheld both his conviction and the use of informational roadblocks. Lidster had simply run afoul of the long arm of coincidence.

Finally, in *Florida* v. *Jardines*, 2013, the Court addressed circumstances in which a police officer is not in urgent pursuit of a suspect and does not have a warrant. In these cases, said the Court, the officer cannot bring a drug-sniffing dog onto the porch of home and then use the dog's indication of drugs in the house as a basis for probable cause to obtain a warrant, because the front porch of a home is protected by the 4th Amendment.

The 4th Amendment and Arrests An arrest is the seizure of a person. When officers make a lawful arrest, they do not need a warrant to search "the area from within which [the suspect] might gain possession of a weapon or destructible evidence," *Chimel* v. *California*, 1969. In fact, most arrests take place without a warrant. Police can arrest a person in a public place without one, provided they have probable cause to believe that person has committed or is about to commit a crime.

Illinois v. *Wardlow,* 2000, illustrates this point. There, four police cars were patrolling a high-crime area in Chicago. When Wardlow spotted them, he ran. An officer chased him down an alley, caught him, and found that Wardlow was carrying a loaded pistol. The Court later held, 5–4, that Wardlow's behavior—his flight—gave the police "common sense" grounds on which to believe that he was involved in some criminal activity. (Note, however, that the Court did not hold that police have a blanket power to stop anyone who flees at the sight of a police officer.)

When, exactly, does the 4th Amendment protection come into play? The Court has several times held that this point is reached "only when the officer, by means

Supreme Court at a Glance

TITLE OF CASE	ISSUE	DECISION
Mapp v. *Ohio,* 1961	States' use of illegally obtained evidence	Evidence seized illegally cannot be used in either federal or State courts.
Minnesota v. *Carter,* 1998	Seizure of evidence "in plain view"	Police do not need a warrant for a search and seizure when evidence is in plain view.
Illinois v. *Wardlow,* 2000	Arrest of an individual without a warrant	Flight can be an important factor in determining whether police have "reasonable suspicion" to stop a suspect.
California v. *Acevedo,* 1991	Warrantless search of a container in an automobile	Whenever police lawfully stop a car, they do not need a warrant to search anything in the vehicle that they have reason to believe holds evidence of a crime.

>> Several landmark Supreme Court cases have examined the 4th Amendment's protections of a citizen's home or person. **Analyze Graphs** How is *Mapp* v. *Ohio* different from the other three cases?

of physical force or show of authority, has in some way restrained the liberty of a citizen," *Terry* v. *Ohio,* 1968.

The 4th Amendment and Automobiles The Court has long had difficulty applying the 4th Amendment to automobiles. It has several times held that an officer needs no warrant to search an automobile, a boat, an airplane, or some other vehicle, when there is probable cause to believe that it is involved in illegal activities—because such a "movable scene of crime" could disappear while a warrant was being sought.

Carroll v. *United States,* 1925, is an early leading case on the point. There, the Court emphasized that "where the securing of a warrant is reasonably practicable, it must be used. . . . In cases where seizure is impossible except without a warrant, the seizing officer acts unlawfully and at his peril unless he can show the court probable cause."

The Court overturned a long string of automobile search cases in 1991. Before then, it had several times held that a warrant was usually needed to search a glove compartment, a paper bag, luggage, or other "closed containers" in an automobile. But, in *California* v. *Acevedo,* 1991, the Court set out what it called "one clear-cut rule to govern automobile searches." Whenever police lawfully stop a car, they do not need a warrant to search anything in that vehicle that they have reason to believe holds evidence of a crime. "Anything" includes a passenger's belongings, *Wyoming* v. *Houghton,* 1999.

Police, upon making a routine traffic stop, do not need to secure a warrant in order to use a trained dog to sniff around (search) the outside of a car for narcotics, *Illinois* v. *Caballes,* 2005. Unlike the front porch of a home, a vehicle sitting in a public place is not protected against a search by a drug dog's nose.

? CITE EVIDENCE Consider the following situation: A fugitive is fleeing from the authorities and is seen by the police entering an abandoned house. Upon entering the house, the police not only find the fugitive but also several individuals using illegal drugs. The individuals are arrested despite having nothing to do with the fugitive. Under the 4th Amendment, is this a lawful arrest? Cite evidence to support your answer.

The Exclusionary Rule

The heart of the guarantee against unreasonable searches and seizures lies in this question: If an unlawful search or seizure does occur, can that "tainted evidence" be used in court? If it can be used, the 4th Amendment offers no real protection to a person accused of crime.

To meet that problem, the Supreme Court has adopted, and is still refining, the **exclusionary rule.** Essentially, the rule is this: Evidence gained as the result of an illegal act by police cannot be used at the trial of the person from whom it was seized.

The rule was first laid down in *Weeks* v. *United States,* 1914. In that narcotics case, the Court held that evidence obtained illegally by federal officers could not be used in the federal courts. For decades, however, the Court left questions of the use of such evidence in State courts for each State to decide for itself.

>> Police officers follow strict protocols when conducting searches. Crime scene investigators must obtain each item legally; otherwise, the evidence could be challenged in court.

The Exclusionary Rule and the States The exclusionary rule was finally extended to the States in *Mapp* v. *Ohio,* 1961. There, the Court held that the 14th Amendment forbids unreasonable searches and seizures by State and local officers just as the 4th Amendment bars such actions by federal officers. It also held that the fruits of an unlawful search or seizure cannot be used in the State courts, just as they cannot be used in the federal courts.

In *Mapp,* Cleveland police had entered Dollree Mapp's home, forcibly and without a warrant. They claimed to be searching for both a fugitive in a bombing case and evidence of gambling. Their lengthy search found nothing on either count. But they did turn up some "dirty books." Mapp was then convicted of the possession of obscene materials and sentenced to jail. The Court overturned that conviction, holding that the evidence against her had been found illegally and so could not be used at her trial.

The exclusionary rule has always been controversial. It was intended to put teeth into the 4th Amendment, and it has. It says to police: As you enforce the law, obey the law. The rule seeks to prevent, or at least deter, police misconduct.

Critics of the rule say that it means that some persons who are clearly guilty nonetheless go free. Why, they ask, should criminals be able to "beat the rap" on "a technicality"? In response, the Court has gradually narrowed the scope of the rule over the years.

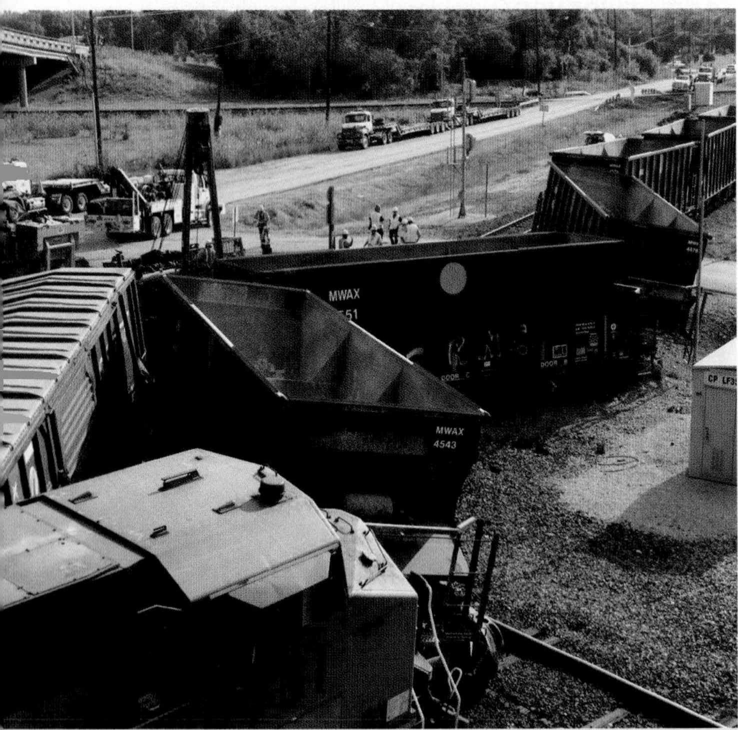

>> Operating a train while under the influence of drugs can have deadly consequences. For this reason, the Court allows the drug testing of railroad workers following a train accident.

Mandatory Drug Testing Federal drug testing programs involve searches of persons, and so are covered by the 4th Amendment. To date, however, the Court has held that those programs can be conducted without warrants or even any indication of drug use by those who must take the tests. It did so in two 1989 cases. One involved the mandatory testing of those drug enforcement officers of the U.S. Customs Service (now Immigration and Customs Enforcement) who carry firearms, *National Treasury Employees Union* v. *Von Raab.*

The other had to do with the testing of railroad workers after a train accident, *Skinner* v. *Railway Labor Executives' Association.* In effect, the Court said in both cases that the violations of privacy involved were outweighed by a legitimate governmental interest—for example, in *Skinner,* discovering the cause of a train accident.

The Court has also upheld two local school districts' drug-testing programs, both covered by the 14th Amendment's Due Process Clause. It sustained an Oregon school district's program that requires all students who take part in school sports to agree to be tested for drug use, *Vernonia School District* v. *Acton,* 1995.

That ruling was extended in a case from Oklahoma, *Board of Education of Independent School District No. 92 of Pottawatomie County* v. *Earls,* 2002. There, the Court upheld the random testing of students who want to participate in *any* competitive extracurricular activity. In both of these cases, the Court said that "a warrant and finding of probable cause are unnecessary in the public school context because [they] would unduly interfere with . . . swift and informal disciplinary procedures."

The USA Patriot Act The USA Patriot Act, commonly called the Patriot Act, is officially the Uniting and Strengthening America by Providing Appropriate Tools Required to Intercept and Obstruct Terrorism Act of 2001. It was passed by Congress and signed by President George W. Bush just six weeks after the terrorist attacks of 9/11. That 342-page statute was renewed, after some contentious debate and with some modifications, in 2006.

The law provides for greatly increased governmental powers to combat domestic and international terrorist activities. Its major provisions focus on three broad areas: surveillance and investigation, immigration, and the financing of terrorist groups. Several provisions raise significant civil liberties issues that, over time, will be tested in the courts.

Of particular 4th Amendment concern are the act's provisions that allow secret "sneak-and-peek searches." Under the statute, federal agents, acting with a warrant, may enter a person's home or office when no one is present and conduct a search—making notes, taking photos, and so on. The agents need not notify the person who is the subject of the search for weeks or even months—and so they are able to continue their investigation without that person's knowledge.

The 4th Amendment and Wiretapping Electronic eavesdropping, such as wiretapping, videotaping, and other more sophisticated means of "bugging," is now quite widely used in the United States. These various techniques of discovery present difficult search and seizure questions that the authors of the 4th Amendment could not possibly have foreseen.

The 4th Amendment has always applied to "searches" that involve a physical intrusion—for example, a police officer entering a building or reaching inside a car. The amendment has also always applied to "seizures" that produce some tangible object—for example, a gun or a packet of methamphetamines

>> Family members pay tribute to New York City firefighters who perished in the terrorist attacks of 9/11. Immediately after the attacks, citizens were more tolerant of government surveillance.

"Well, if you're going to wiretap your people you are going to hear things."

>> Electronic eavesdropping, or "bugging," may have wide-ranging effects on an individual's rights. **Analyze Political Cartoons** How might this king feel about 4th Amendment rights?

found inside a car. Listening in on a conversation electronically, from afar, is a quite different matter.

In fact, in its first eavesdropping case, *Olmstead* v. *United States*, 1928, the Court held that the wiretapping there did not constitute a "search." The case arose when federal agents tapped a Seattle bootlegger's telephone calls. Their bugs produced evidence that led to Olmstead's conviction under the National Prohibition Act. The Court upheld that conviction. It found that, although the agents had not secured a warrant, there had been no "actual physical invasion" of Olmstead's home or office, and so no violation of the 4th Amendment because the phone lines had been tapped *outside* those places.

Katz* v. *United States *Olmstead* stood for nearly forty years. It was finally overruled in what remains the leading case today, *Katz* v. *United States*, 1967. Katz had been convicted of transmitting gambling information across State lines. He had used a public phone booth in Los Angeles to call his contacts in Boston and Miami. Much of the evidence against him had come from an electronic tap placed on the roof—outside—of the phone booth.

The Court ruled that the bugging evidence could not be used against Katz. Despite the fact that he was in a public, glass-enclosed phone booth, he was entitled to make a *private* call, from a place where he had "a reasonable expectation of privacy." Said the Court: The 4th Amendment protects "persons, not just places." It noted, however, that the requirements of the amendment can be satisfied in such situations if police obtain a proper warrant before they install a listening device.

Congress responded to the Court's decision in *Katz* in a provision in the Omnibus Crime Control and Safe Street Act of 1968. There, Congress prohibited any wiretapping for domestic purposes except that authorized by a warrant issued by a federal judge.

Soon after September 11, President George W. Bush directed the National Security Agency (NSA), acting in secret and without court-approved warrants, to monitor the international telephone calls and e-mails of Americans with suspected ties to terrorists. The public did not become aware of that monitoring program until late 2005, and its disclosure brought a storm of protest. Many insisted that this NSA activity was illegal. Despite this, the Bush administration defended it as an appropriate exercise of the President's power as commander in chief and the practice was continued under the Obama administration.

Balancing Security and Liberty Balancing national security and American freedom remains a challenging

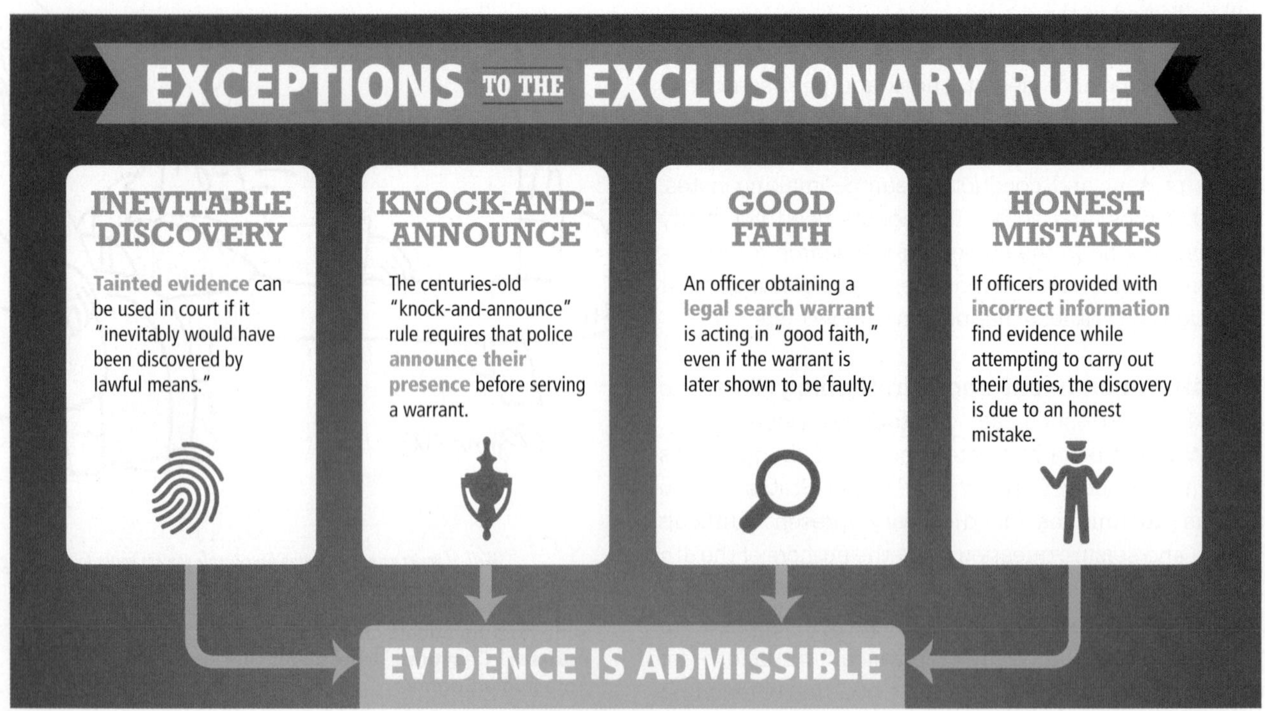

EXCEPTIONS TO THE EXCLUSIONARY RULE
INEVITABLE DISCOVERY
Tainted evidence can be used in court if it "inevitably would have been discovered by lawful means."
KNOCK-AND-ANNOUNCE
The centuries-old "knock-and-announce" rule requires that police announce their presence before serving a warrant.
GOOD FAITH
An officer obtaining a legal search warrant is acting in "good faith," even if the warrant is later shown to be faulty.
HONEST MISTAKES
If officers provided with incorrect information find evidence while attempting to carry out their duties, the discovery is due to an honest mistake.
EVIDENCE IS ADMISSIBLE

>> The Supreme Court has narrowed the scope of the exclusionary rule by allowing evidence to be admissible in cases that it previously had not. **Analyze Charts** What is the purpose of that rule?

task today and continues to be debated. Does it make sense for individual rights to be subordinated to the public good in the case of national security? Or is the Federal Government encroaching too far on Americans' constitutional rights? Caroline Fredrickson, director of the ACLU, has spoken against U.S. intelligence activities, saying, "Establishing new information collection and sharing authorities for the federal, state, and local law enforcement poses significant risks to our individual liberties, our democratic principles and, ironically, even our security."

Janet Napolitano, former Secretary of Homeland Security, voiced the opposing view: "We frequently hear about a simple inverse relationship between security and liberty. . . . If one is embraced, the other must be sacrificed. . . . The description doesn't do justice to the relationship between security and other values. . . . Security is interrelated with our core values, and among the aspects of the homeland that must be made secure are our fundamental rights and freedoms."

Public debate over the issue flared again in 2013 when a former National Security Agency (NSA) contractor and CIA employee, Edward Snowden, disclosed to several media outlets details about the agency's spying program. Many Americans, including public officials, were surprised to learn of the breadth of the program. To some, Snowden's leaks cast a necessary light on controversial government policies, but to others, including President Obama, the leak of classified documents was seen as damaging to national security, illegal, and traitorous.

INFER How did the Supreme Court interpret the 4th Amendment in *Mapp* v. *Ohio*, 1961?

The Right of Privacy

The constitutional guarantees of due process create a right of privacy—"the right to be free, except in very limited circumstances, from unwanted governmental intrusions into one's privacy," *Stanley* v. *Georgia,* 1969, and *Lawrence* v. *Texas*, 2003. It is, in the words of Justice Louis Brandeis, "the right to be let alone."

The Constitution makes no specific mention of the right of privacy, but the Supreme Court declared its existence in *Griswold* v. *Connecticut,* 1965. That case centered on a State law that outlawed birth control counseling and prohibited the use of all birth control devices. The Court held the law to be a violation of the 14th Amendment's Due Process Clause—and noted that the State had no business policing the marital bedroom.

>> In *Katz*, the Court ruled that calls from a public phone booth were considered private. **Analyze Political Cartoons** What does this cartoon say about this "reasonable expectation of privacy?"

Interactive Gallery

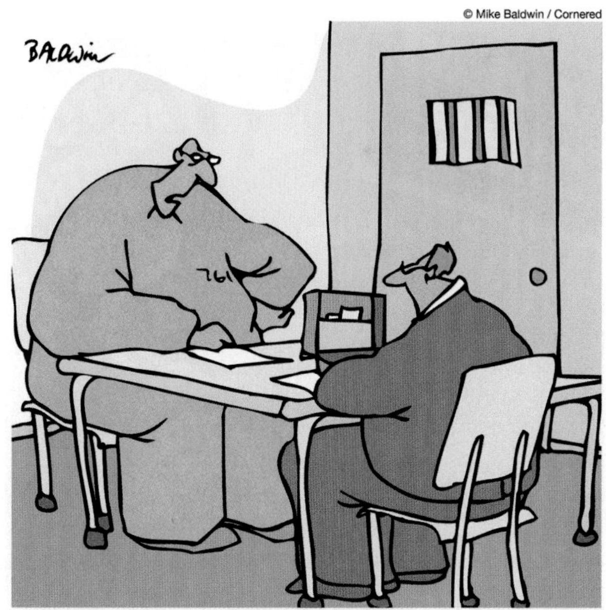

"Change it to, 'not guilty by reason of personal health issues.' Mentioning insanity violates my right to privacy."

>> This cartoon comments on the constitutional rights of every individual, including those accused of crimes. **Analyze Political Cartoons** What point is the cartoonist making?

The Supreme Court's Ruling in *Roe* v. *Wade* The most controversial applications of the right of privacy have come in cases that raise this question: To what extent can a State limit a woman's right to an abortion? The leading case is *Roe* v. *Wade,* 1973. There, the Supreme Court struck down a Texas law that made abortion a crime except when necessary to save the life of the mother.

In *Roe,* the Court held that the 14th Amendment's right of privacy "encompass[es] a woman's decision whether or not to terminate her pregnancy." More specifically, the Court ruled that:

1. In the first trimester of pregnancy (about three months), a State must recognize a woman's right to an abortion; it cannot interfere with medical judgments in that matter during that period.

2. In the second trimester, a State, acting in the interest of women who undergo abortions, can make reasonable regulations about how, when, and where abortions can be performed but cannot prohibit the procedure.

3. In the final trimester, a State, acting to protect the unborn child, can choose to prohibit all abortions except those necessary to preserve the life or health of the mother.

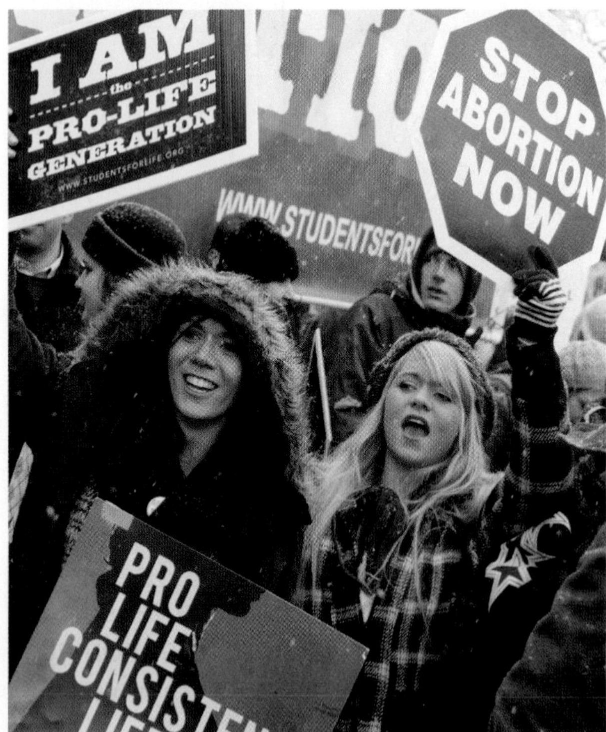

>> Students protest in Washington, D.C., in 2013. Founded in the 1970s, Students for Life of America provides resources for students interested in pro-life issues.

Challenges to *Roe* In several later cases, the Court rejected a number of challenges to its basic holding in *Roe.* As the composition of the Court has changed, however, so has the Court's position on abortion. That shift can be seen in the Court's decisions in later cases on the matter.

In *Webster* v. *Reproductive Health Services,* 1989, the Court upheld two key parts of a Missouri law. Those provisions prohibit abortions, except those that preserve the mother's life or health, (1) in any publicly operated hospital or clinic in that State, and (2) when the mother is 20 or more weeks pregnant and tests show that the fetus is viable (capable of sustaining life outside the mother's body).

Two cases in 1990 addressed the issue of minors and abortion. In those cases, the Court said that a State may require a minor (1) to inform at least one parent before she can obtain an abortion, *Ohio* v. *Akron Center for Reproductive Health*, and (2) to tell both parents of her plans, except in cases where a judge gives permission for an abortion without parental knowledge, *Hodgson* v. *Minnesota.*

The Court's most important decision on the issue since *Roe* v. *Wade* came in *Planned Parenthood of Southeastern Pennsylvania* v. *Casey* in 1992. There, the Court announced this rule: A State may place reasonable limits on a woman's right to have an abortion, but these restrictions cannot impose an "undue burden" on her choice of that procedure.

In *Casey,* the Court applied that new standard to Pennsylvania's Abortion Control Act. It upheld several sections of the law, finding that they did not place "a substantial obstacle in the path of a woman seeking an abortion of a non-viable fetus." Those provisions, it said, do not impose an "undue burden" on a woman's choice.

The Supreme Court did strike down another key part of the Pennsylvania law in *Casey,* however. That provision required that a married woman tell her husband of her plan to have an abortion. That requirement, said the Court, did indeed amount to an "undue burden."

Twenty-first Century Cases The High Court has decided only two abortion cases since 1992. Its 5–4 vote in the most recent one effectively overturned its 5–4 decision in the earlier case. Together, the two cases underscore the impact that changes in the composition of the Court can have on the outcome of cases that come before it.

In *Gonzales* v. *Carhart,* 2007, the justices applied *Casey's* "undue burden" rule to an act of Congress, the Partial Birth Abortion Ban Act of 2003, and found it constitutional. That statute prohibits a particular method of abortion, a medical procedure that opponents of abortion call "partial birth abortion." In fact, that operation had been performed in very few instances.

In the earlier case, *Stenberg* v. *Carhart,* 2000, the Court had applied *Casey* to strike down a Nebraska law that also banned partial birth abortions. The language in that opinion was very nearly identical to that used by Congress when it passed the federal law in 2003.

APPLY CONCEPTS How did the Supreme Court interpret the constitutional right to privacy in the case of *Roe* v. *Wade*?

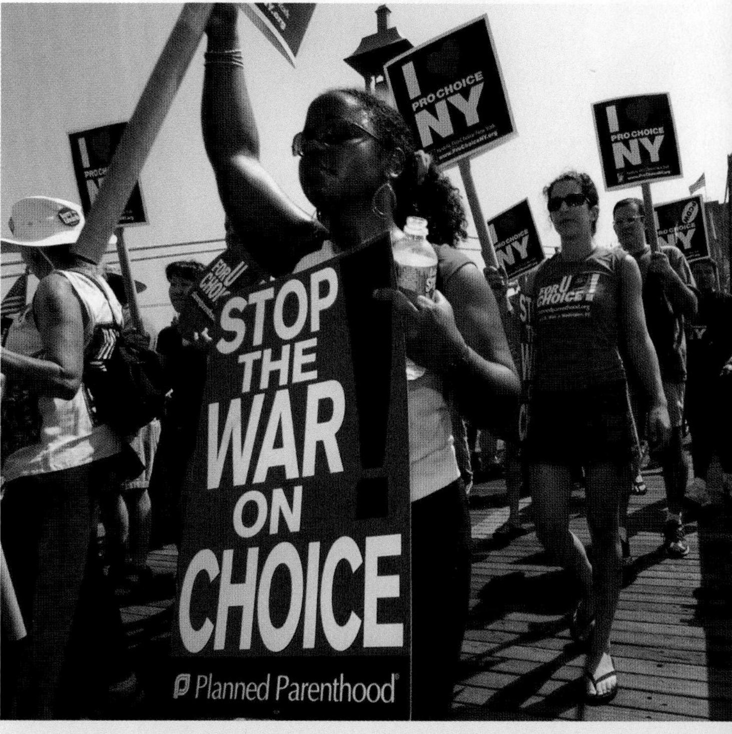

>> Planned Parenthood is a pro-choice nonprofit group that provides information on family planning and funds research on women's health issues.

ASSESSMENT

1. **Explain** How have Supreme Court decisions regarding slavery and involuntary servitude affected African Americans?
2. **Analyze Information** According to recent Supreme Court decisions, does the 2nd Amendment's protection of the right to keep and bear arms relate only to State militias, or also to the individual right to keep and bear arms? Give evidence to support your answer.
3. **Draw Conclusions** Which constitutional provisions limit the role of government in order to guarantee the security of home and person? Explain how the provisions limit the role of government.
4. **Infer** Why has the Supreme Court continued to refine the exclusionary rule?
5. **Interpret** How has the Supreme Court interpreted the Constitution in cases involving abortion?

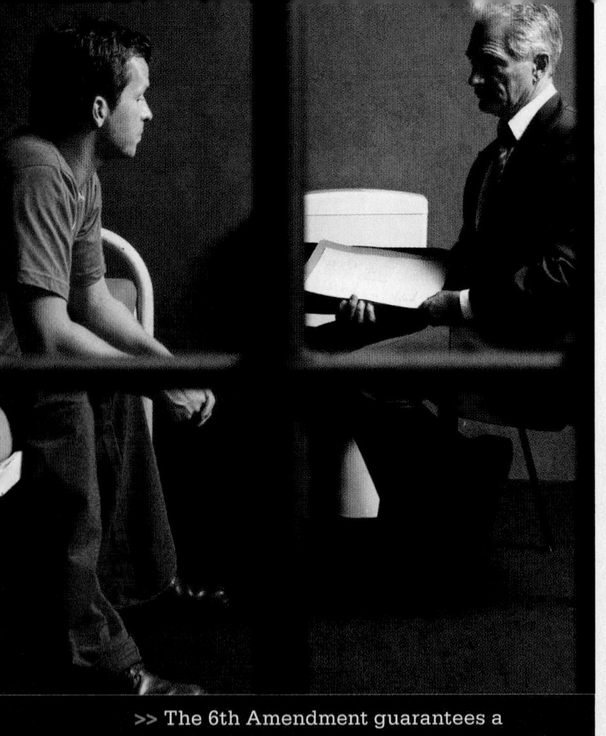

>> The 6th Amendment guarantees a defendant the right to an attorney regardless of his or her ability to pay for one. A defendant may also choose to represent him- or herself in court.

Interactive Flipped Video

8.7 **Think about this statement: "It is better that ten guilty persons go free than that one innocent person be punished." That maxim expresses one of the bedrock principles of the American legal system. Of course, society must punish criminals in order to preserve itself. However, the law intends that any person who is suspected or accused of a crime must be presumed innocent until proven guilty by fair and lawful means.**

>> Objectives

Understand the role of limited government in the protection of individual rights, including protections relating to the writ of habeas corpus, bills of attainder, and ex post facto laws

Outline how the right to a grand jury and the guarantee against double jeopardy help safeguard the rights of the accused.

Describe issues that arise from guarantees of speedy and public trials.

Identify the freedoms and rights guaranteed by the Bill of Rights, including the right to a fair trial by jury.

Examine Supreme Court interpretations in selected cases of the right to an adequate defense and the guarantee against self-incrimination, including *Gideon* v. *Wainwright* and *Miranda* v. *Arizona*.

>> Key Terms

grand jury
indictment
presentment
information
double jeopardy
bench trial
Miranda rule
bail
preventive detention
capital punishment
treason
Abraham Lincoln
Roger B. Taney
writ of habeas corpus
bill of attainder
ex post facto law

Rights of the Accused

Article I Protections

No Imprisonment Without Just Cause The **writ of habeas corpus,** sometimes called the writ of liberty, is intended to prevent unjust arrests and imprisonments. The phrase *habeas corpus* comes from the Latin, meaning "you should have the body," and those are the opening words of the writ. It is a court order directed to an officer holding a prisoner. It commands that the prisoner be brought before the court and that the officer show cause—explain, with good reason—why the prisoner should not be released.

The right to seek a writ of habeas corpus is protected against the National Government in Article I, Section 9 of the Constitution. That right is guaranteed against the States in each of their own constitutions.

The Constitution says that the right to the writ cannot be suspended, "unless when in Cases of Rebellion or Invasion the public Safety may require it." President **Abraham Lincoln** suspended the writ in 1861 during the Civil War. His order covered various parts of the country, including several areas in which war was not then being waged. Chief Justice **Roger B. Taney**, sitting as a circuit judge, held

Lincoln's action unconstitutional, *Ex parte Merryman,* 1861.

Taney ruled that the Constitution gives the power to suspend the writ to Congress alone. Congress then passed the Habeas Corpus Act of 1863. It gave the President the power to suspend the writ when and where, in his judgment, that action was necessary. In *Ex parte Milligan,* 1866, the Supreme Court ruled that neither Congress nor the President can suspend the writ in those locales where there is no actual fighting nor the likelihood of combat.

The right to the writ has been suspended only once since the Civil War and the Reconstruction Period that followed it. The territorial governor of Hawaii did so following the Japanese attack on Pearl Harbor in December 1941. The Supreme Court later ruled that the governor did not have the power to take that action, *Duncan* v. *Kahanamoku,* 1946.

>> Alexander Hamilton wrote in support of the writ of habeas corpus, stating that "arbitrary imprisonments have been in all ages the favourite and most formidable instruments of tyranny."

Guantanamo Bay In 2008, the Supreme Court held, for the first time, that foreign prisoners being held as enemy combatants at the U.S. naval base at Guantanamo Bay, Cuba, have a constitutional right to challenge their detention—that is, a right to seek writs of habeas corpus—in the federal courts, *Boumediene* v. *Bush* and *Al Odah* v. *United States.* The Bush administration had vigorously opposed that 5–4 ruling, but the Obama administration generally supports it.

Congress–Legislators, Not Judges A **bill of attainder** is a legislative act that provides for the punishment of a person without a court trial. The Constitution prohibits Congress from passing any such measure in Article I, Section 9, and it places the same prohibition on the States in Section 10.

The Framers wrote the ban on bills of attainder into the Constitution because Parliament and several of the colonial legislatures had passed many such bills. They have been quite rare in our national history, however.

The denial of the power to pass bills of attainder is both a protection of individual freedom and one of the Constitution's several provisions for separation of powers. In effect, the ban says to members of Congress and to the States' lawmakers: Be legislators, not judges. A legislative body can pass laws that define crime and set the penalties for violations of them. But it cannot pass a law that declares a person or identifiable group of persons guilty of a crime and provides for his or their punishment.

United States v. *Lovett,* 1946, is one of the few attainder cases ever decided by the Supreme Court. That case involved a provision in a law appropriating funds for the army that declared that none of the monies could be used to pay the salaries of three

>> After the attack on Pearl Harbor, the governor of Hawaii declared martial law, suspending the writ of habeas corpus and giving control of the government to the military.

named persons. Several members of the House thought that those three were "subversive," and they urged the President to discharge them. The Court found that provision to be a bill of attainder.

In another similar case, *United States* v. *Brown,* 1965, the Court overturned a provision in the Landrum-Griffin Act of 1959. That provision made it a federal crime for a member of the Communist Party to serve as an officer of a labor union.

No Retroactive Criminal Laws The Constitution, in Article I, Sections 9 and 10, prohibits Congress and the States from enacting ex post facto laws. An **ex post facto law** is a law applied to an act committed before the passage of that law. The phrase *ex post facto* is from the Latin, meaning "after the fact." An ex post facto law (1) is a criminal law—one defining a crime and/or providing for its punishment; (2) applies to an act committed before its passage; and (3) works to the disadvantage of the accused.

For example, a law making it a crime to sell marijuana cannot be applied to a sale that occurred before that law was passed. Or, a law that changes the penalty for murder from life in prison to death cannot be used to sentence a person who committed a murder before the punishment was made more severe.

>> Texas Congressman Martin Dies, Jr., (shown) led efforts to dismiss government employees, including Robert Lovett. Lovett sued, arguing that the action was an unconstitutional bill of attainder.

Retroactive civil laws are *not* forbidden. Thus, a law raising income tax rates could be passed in November and applied to income earned through the whole year.

? APPLY CONCEPTS How does the prohibition of ex post facto laws in criminal cases protect the rights of the accused?

Grand Jury and Double Jeopardy

A person suspected of a crime that could lead to death or imprisonment must be formally accused in order to be detained for prosecution. A grand jury made up of citizens holds a proceeding to decide if there is enough evidence to justify a trial. A prosecutor may also make a sworn statement that enough evidence is available for a trial.

The Right to a Grand Jury The 5th Amendment to the Constitution declares that

The **grand jury** is the formal device by which a person can be accused of a serious crime—that is, any offense for which the punishment is death or imprisonment. In federal cases, the grand jury is a body of from 16 to 23 persons drawn from the area of the district court that it serves. The votes of at least 12 of the grand jurors are needed to return an indictment or to make a presentment.

An **indictment** is a formal complaint that the prosecutor lays before a grand jury. It charges the accused with one or more crimes. If the grand jury finds that there is enough evidence to justify a trial, it returns a "true bill of indictment." The accused person is then held for prosecution. If the grand jury does not make such a finding, the charge is dropped and the accused is set free.

A **presentment** is a formal accusation brought by the grand jury on its own motion, rather than that of the prosecutor. It is rarely used in federal courts.

A grand jury's proceedings are not a trial. Since unfair harm could come if they were public, its sessions are secret. They are also one-sided—in the law, an *ex parte* judicial proceeding. That is, only the prosecution, not the defense, is present.

The right to grand jury is intended as a protection against overzealous prosecutors. Critics say that it is too time-consuming, too expensive, and too likely to follow the dictates of the prosecutor.

The 5th Amendment's grand jury provision is the only part of the Bill of Rights relating to criminal prosecution that the Supreme Court has not brought within the coverage of the 14th Amendment's Due Process Clause.

The Factors Lawyers Consider When Selecting a Jury

FACTORS	EXAMPLES
Demographics	What is their gender, race, age, etc.?
Personality	Are they stern, compassionate, resistant to social pressure, etc.?
Life experiences	Have they ever been the victim of a violent crime?
Value system	How do they feel about particular crimes, large corporations, etc.?
Leadership potential	Will they sway the other jurors to agree with their decision?
Nonverbal signals	Are they frowning, nodding, fidgeting, etc.?
Respect for court	Are they dressed neatly or sloppily?

>> The Constitution guarantees the right to a fair trial before an impartial jury.
Analyze Charts Why are these factors important for lawyers to consider when selecting a jury?

In the majority of States today, most criminal charges are not brought by grand jury indictment. They are brought, instead, by an **information,** an affidavit in which the prosecutor swears that there is enough evidence to justify a trial.

Guarantee Against Double Jeopardy The 5th Amendment's guarantee against double jeopardy is the first of several protections in the Bill of Rights especially intended to ensure fair trials in the federal courts. Fair trials are guaranteed in State courts by each State's constitution and, also, recall, by the 14th Amendment's Due Process Clause.

The 5th Amendment says in part that no person can be "twice put in jeopardy of life or limb." Today, this prohibition against **double jeopardy** means that once a person has been tried for a crime, he or she cannot be tried again for that same crime. The Constitution's ban of double jeopardy applies against the States through the 14th Amendment's Due Process Clause, *Benton* v. *Maryland,* 1969.

A person can violate both a federal *and* a State law in a single act, however—for example, by selling narcotics. That person can then be tried for the federal crime in a federal court and for the State crime in a State court. Thus, a single act can also result in several criminal charges. A person who breaks into a store, steals liquor, and sells it can be tried for illegal entry, theft, and selling liquor without a license.

In a trial in which a jury cannot agree on a verdict (a hung jury), there is no jeopardy. It is as though no trial had been held. Nor is double jeopardy involved when a case is appealed to a higher court.

Several States allow the continued confinement of violent sex predators after they have completed a prison term. The Court has twice held that that confinement is not punishment—and so does not involve double jeopardy. Rather, the practice is intended to protect the public from harm, *Kansas* v. *Hendrick,* 1987, and *Seling* v. *Young,* 2001.

? GENERATE EXPLANATIONS How does the 5th Amendment's ban on double jeopardy help to ensure a fair trial?

Going to Trial

The Constitution offers several other protections for a person accused of crime. These are found in both the 5th and 6th amendments. They cover such important areas as the right to a speedy and public trial, the right to trial by jury, the right to adequate defense, and a guarantee against self-incrimination.

Speedy Trial The 6th Amendment commands that:

> In all criminal prosecutions, the accused shall enjoy the right to a speedy and public trial, . . .
>
> —United States Constitution

The guarantee of a speedy trial is meant to ensure that the government will try a person accused of crime within a reasonable time and without undue delay. But how long a delay is too long? The Supreme Court has recognized that each case must be judged on its own merits.

In a leading case, *Barker* v. *Wingo,* 1972, the Court listed four criteria for determining if a delay has violated the constitutional protection. They are (1) the length of the delay, (2) the reasons for it, (3) whether the delay has in fact harmed the defendant, and (4) whether the defendant had asked for a prompt trial.

The Speedy Trial Act of 1974 says that the time between a person's arrest and the beginning of his or her federal criminal trial cannot be more than 100 days. The law does allow for some exceptions, however—for example, when the defendant must undergo extensive mental tests, or when the defendant or a key witness is ill.

The 6th Amendment guarantees a prompt trial in *federal* cases. The Supreme Court first applied this right against the States as part of the 14th Amendment's Due Process Clause in *Klopfer* v. *North Carolina,* 1967.

>> Billy Sol Estes (right) confers with attorneys. His pretrial hearing was broadcast live on television and radio and drew "[m]assive pretrial publicity totaling eleven volumes of press clippings."

>> During the high-profile murder and racketeering trial of James "Whitey" Bulger in 2013, photography was banned in the courtroom, and only a limited number of reporters were allowed inside.

Public Trial The 6th Amendment says that a trial must also be public. The right to be tried in public is also part of the 14th Amendment's guarantee of procedural due process, *In re Oliver,* 1948.

A trial must not be *too* speedy or *too* public, however. The Supreme Court threw out an Arkansas murder conviction in 1923 on just those grounds. The trial had taken only 45 minutes, and it had been held in a courtroom packed by a threatening mob.

Within reason, a judge can limit both the number and the kinds of spectators who may be present at a trial. Those who seek to disrupt a courtroom can be barred from it. A judge can order a courtroom cleared when the expected testimony may be embarrassing to a witness or to someone else who is not a party to the case.

Many questions about how public a trial should be involve the media—especially newspapers and television. The guarantees of fair trial and free press often collide in the courts. On the one hand, a courtroom is a public place where the media have a right to be present. On the other hand, media coverage can jeopardize a defendant's right to a fair trial. The Supreme Court has often held that the right to a public trial belongs to the defendant, not to the media.

What about televised trials? Television cameras are barred from all federal courtrooms. Yet most States do allow some form of in-court television reporting. Can televising a criminal trial violate a defendant's rights?

In an early major case, *Estes* v. *Texas,* 1965, the Supreme Court reversed the conviction of an oil man charged with swindling investors and others out of millions of dollars. The Court found that the media coverage of his trial had been so "circus-like" and

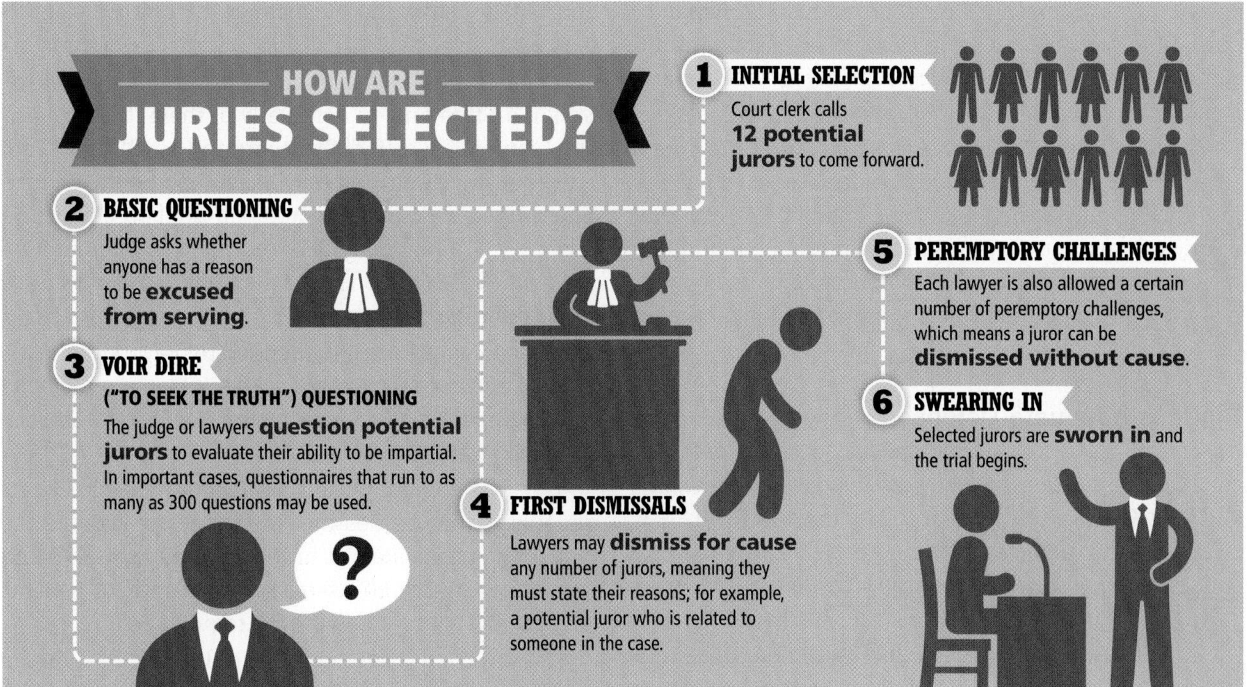

HOW ARE
JURIES SELECTED?
1 INITIAL SELECTION
Court clerk calls 12 potential jurors to come forward.
2 BASIC QUESTIONING
Judge asks whether anyone has a reason to be excused from serving.
3 VOIR DIRE
("TO SEEK THE TRUTH") QUESTIONING
The judge or lawyers question potential jurors to evaluate their ability to be impartial. In important cases, questionnaires that run to as many as 300 questions may be used.
4 FIRST DISMISSALS
Lawyers may dismiss for cause any number of jurors, meaning they must state their reasons; for example, a potential juror who is related to someone in the case.
5 PEREMPTORY CHALLENGES
Each lawyer is also allowed a certain number of peremptory challenges, which means a juror can be dismissed without cause.
6 SWEARING IN
Selected jurors are sworn in and the trial begins.

>> A defendant's right to a trial by jury has led courts to create a selection process for those who will serve on a jury. **Analyze Charts** How does this process help ensure an impartial jury?

disruptive that Estes had been denied his right to a fair trial.

Sixteen years later, the Court held in *Chandler* v. *Florida,* 1981, that nothing in the Constitution prevents a State from allowing the televising of a criminal trial. At least, televising is not prohibited as long as steps are taken to avoid too much publicity and to protect the defendant's rights.

Trial by Jury The 6th Amendment also says that a person accused of a federal crime must be tried "by an impartial jury." This guarantee reinforces an earlier one set out in the Constitution, Article III, Section 2. The right to trial by jury is also binding on the States, but only in cases involving "serious" crimes, meaning those for which imprisonment for more than six months is possible. The trial jury is often called the petit jury. *Petit* is the French word for "small."

The 6th Amendment adds that the members of a federal court jury must be drawn from "the State and district wherein the crime shall have been committed, which district shall have been previously ascertained by law." This stipulation gives the defendant any benefit there might be in having a jury familiar with the people and problems of the area.

A defendant may ask to be tried in another place—seek a "change of venue"—on grounds that the people of the locality are so prejudiced in the case that an impartial jury cannot be drawn. The judge must decide whether a change of venue is justified.

A defendant may also waive the right to a jury trial. However, he or she can do so only if the judge is satisfied that the defendant fully understands what that action means. In fact, a judge can order a jury trial even when a defendant does not want one. If a defendant waives the right, a **bench trial** is held, which means that a judge alone hears the case. (Of course, a defendant can plead guilty and so avoid any trial.)

In federal practice, the jury that hears a criminal case must have 12 members. However, some federal civil cases are tried before juries of as few as six members. Several States now provide for smaller juries, often of six members, in both criminal and civil cases. In the federal courts, the jury that hears a criminal case can convict the accused only by a unanimous vote. Most States follow the same rule.

Composition of the Jury In a long series of cases, dating from *Strauder* v. *West Virginia,* 1880, the Supreme Court has held that a jury must be "drawn from a fair cross section of the community." *Hernandez* v. *Texas,* 1954, tested the definition of "fair cross section" when it considered whether Pete Hernandez, a Mexican had received a fair trial in a murder case when no one on the jury was Mexican American or had a Hispanic surname. The court ruled in Hernandez' favor, stating that the exclusion of Hispanics from jury service denied him equal protection under the law.

In a later case, *Taylor* v. *Louisiana,* 1975, the court ruled that a person is denied the right to an impartial jury if he or she is tried by a jury from which members of any groups "playing major roles in the community" have been excluded. In short, no person can be kept off a jury on such grounds as race, color, religion, national origin, or gender.

Right to Adequate Defense Every person accused of a crime has the right to the best possible defense that circumstances will allow. In *Gideon* v. *Wainwright,* 1963, the Court held that an attorney must be furnished to a defendant who cannot afford one. In many places, a judge assigns a lawyer from the local community, or a private legal aid association provides counsel.

The 6th Amendment says that a defendant has the right (1) "to be informed of the nature and cause of the accusation," (2) "to be confronted with the witnesses against him" and question them in open court, (3) "to have compulsory process for obtaining witnesses in his favor" (that is, favorable witnesses can be subpoenaed), and (4) "to have the Assistance of Counsel for his defense."

>> After defending himself and being found guilty, Clarence Gideon wrote to the Supreme Court that he had been unconstitutionally denied counsel. The Court agreed and ordered a new trial.

These key safeguards apply in the federal courts. Still, if a State fails to honor any of them, the accused can appeal a conviction arguing that the 14th Amendment's Due Process Clause has been violated. The Supreme Court protected the right to counsel in *Gideon* v. *Wainwright,* 1963; the right of confrontation in *Pointer* v. *Texas,* 1965; and the right to call witnesses in *Washington* v. *Texas,* 1967.

These guarantees are intended to prevent the cards from being stacked in favor of the prosecution. One of the leading right-to-counsel cases, *Escobedo* v. *Illinois,* 1964, illustrates this point.

Chicago police picked up Danny Escobedo for questioning in the death of his brother-in-law. On the way to the police station, and then while he was being questioned there, he asked several times to see his lawyer. The police denied those requests.

They did so even though his lawyer was in the police station and was trying to see him, and the police knew the lawyer was there. Through a long night of questioning, Escobedo made several damaging statements. Prosecutors later used those statements in court as a major part of the evidence that led to his murder conviction.

The Supreme Court ordered Escobedo freed from prison four years later. It held that he had been improperly denied his 14th Amendment right to counsel.

GENERATE EXPLANATIONS Since the 6th Amendment requires that trials must be public, should all trials be televised? Why or why not?

Guarantee Against Self-Incrimination

The guarantee against self-incrimination is among the several protections set out in the 5th Amendment. That provision declares that no person can be "compelled in any criminal case to be a witness against himself." This protection must be honored in both the federal and State courts, *Malloy* v. *Hogan,* 1964.

In a criminal case, the burden of proof is always on the prosecution. The defendant does not have to prove his or her innocence. The ban on self-incrimination prevents the prosecution from shifting the burden of proof to the defendant.

Applying the Guarantee The language of the 5th Amendment suggests that the guarantee against self-incrimination applies only to criminal cases. In fact, it covers any governmental proceeding in which a person

MIRANDA WARNING
1. YOU HAVE THE RIGHT TO REMAIN SILENT.
2. ANYTHING YOU SAY CAN AND WILL BE USED AGAINST YOU IN A COURT OF LAW.
3. YOU HAVE THE RIGHT TO CONSULT AN ATTORNEY AND HAVE AN ATTORNEY PRESENT WHILE YOU ARE BEING QUESTIONED.
4. IF YOU CANNOT AFFORD TO HIRE A LAWYER, ONE WILL BE APPOINTED TO REPRESENT YOU BEFORE ANY QUESTIONING, IF YOU WISH.
5. YOU CAN DECIDE AT ANY TIME TO EXERCISE THESE RIGHTS AND NOT ANSWER ANY QUESTIONS OR MAKE ANY STATEMENTS.
WAIVER
DO YOU UNDERSTAND EACH OF THESE RIGHTS I HAVE EXPLAINED TO YOU?
HAVING THESE RIGHTS IN MIND, DO YOU WISH TO TALK TO US NOW?

>> Many police officers carry a Miranda warning card with them, although few need to read directly from the card, since they can recite the rule from memory.

is legally compelled to answer any question that could lead to a criminal charge. Thus, a person may claim the right ("take the Fifth") in a variety of situations: in a divorce proceeding (which is a civil matter), before a legislative committee, at a school board's disciplinary hearing, and so on.

The courts, not the individuals who claim it, decide when the right can be properly invoked. If the plea of self-incrimination is pushed too far, a person can be held in contempt of court.

The guarantee against self-incrimination is a personal right. One can claim it only for oneself. It cannot be invoked in someone else's behalf. Thus, a person can be forced to "rat" on another, with this major exception: A husband cannot be forced to testify against his wife, or a wife against her husband.

The privilege does not protect a person from being fingerprinted or photographed or required to submit a handwriting sample or appear in a police lineup. And it does not mean that a person does not have to submit to a blood test in a drunk-driving situation, *Schmerber* v. *California,* 1966.

A person cannot, however, be forced to confess to a crime under duress—that is, as a result of torture or other physical or psychological pressure. In *Ashcraft* v. *Tennessee,* 1944, for example, the Supreme Court threw out the conviction of a man accused of hiring another person to murder his wife. The confession on which his conviction rested had been secured only after some 36 hours of continuous, threatening interrogation. The questioning was conducted by officers who worked in shifts because, they said, they became so tired that they had to rest.

Miranda* v. *Arizona In a truly historic decision, the Court refined the Escobedo holding in *Miranda* v. *Arizona,* 1966. In this case, a mentally challenged man, Ernesto Miranda, had been convicted of kidnapping and rape. Ten days after the crime, the victim picked Miranda out of a police lineup. After two hours of questioning, during which the police did not tell him of his rights, Miranda confessed.

The Supreme Court struck down Miranda's conviction. More importantly, it said that it would no longer uphold convictions in cases in which suspects had not been told of their constitutional rights before police questioning. It thus laid down the **Miranda rule**—the requirement that police must read a suspect his or her rights before any questioning occurs.

The Supreme Court is still refining the rule on a case-by-case basis. Most often the rule is closely followed. But there are exceptions. Thus, the Court has held that once police have read a suspect his rights and questioning has begun, it is up to the person in custody to very clearly assert his right to remain silent, *Berghuis* v. *Thompkins,* 2010.

The Miranda rule has always been controversial. Critics say that it "puts criminals back on the streets." Others applaud the rule, arguing that criminal law enforcement is most effective when it relies on independently secured evidence, rather than on confessions gained by questionable tactics from defendants who do not have the help of a lawyer.

? ASSESS CREDIBILITY Why do some critics claim that the Miranda rule "puts criminals back on the streets"?

Bail and Preventive Detention

Again, think about this proposition: "It is better that ten guilty persons go free than that one innocent person be punished." How do you react to that comment now, after reading about the rights of persons accused of crime? Consider those persons who are found guilty, those who do not go free but are instead punished. How should they be treated? The Constitution gives its most specific answers to that question in the 8th Amendment.

The 8th Amendment says, in part:

>> A lawyer reviews her client's paperwork before a bail hearing. During the hearing, she will object if the bail set for her client is unreasonable.

Interactive Chart

> Excessive bail shall not be required, nor excessive fines imposed, . . .
>
> — United States Constitution

Each State constitution sets out similar restrictions. The general rule is that the bail or fine in a case must bear a reasonable relationship to the seriousness of the crime involved.

Limits on Bail The sum of money that the accused may be required to post (deposit with the court) as a guarantee that he or she will appear in court at the proper time is called **bail**. The use of bail is justified on two bases: First, that a person should not be jailed until his or her guilt has been established; and second, that a defendant is better able to prepare for trial outside of a jail.

Note that the Constitution does not say that all persons accused of a crime are automatically entitled to bail. Rather, it guarantees that, where bail is set, the amount will not be excessive.

The leading case on bail in the federal courts is *Stack* v. *Boyle,* 1951. There, the Court ruled that "bail set at a figure higher than an amount reasonably calculated" to assure a defendant's appearance at a trial "is 'excessive' under the 8th Amendment."

In *Stack,* 12 persons had been accused of violating the Smith Act of 1940, which, recall, made it a federal crime for any person to advocate the violent overthrow of government in the United States. A defendant can appeal the denial of release on bail or the amount of bail. Bail is usually set in accordance with the severity of the crime charged and with the reputation and financial resources of the accused. People with little or no income often have trouble raising bail. Therefore, the federal and most State courts release many defendants "on their own recognizance"—that is, on their honor. Failure to appear for trial, "jumping bail," is itself a punishable crime.

Preventive Detention In 1984, Congress provided for the **preventive detention** of some people accused of federal crimes. A federal judge can order that the accused be held, without bail, when there is good reason to believe that he or she will commit another serious crime before trial. Critics of the law claim that preventive detention amounts to punishment before trial. They say it undercuts the presumption of innocence to which all defendants are entitled.

The Supreme Court upheld the 1984 law, 6–3, in *United States* v. *Salerno,* 1987. The majority rejected the argument that preventive detention is punishment. Rather, it found the practice a legitimate response to a "pressing societal problem." And the Court has recently upheld a federal law that allows the government to keep those inmates who are deemed "sexually dangerous" behind bars even though they have served their sentenced time, *United States* v. *Comstock,* 2010.

CHECK UNDERSTANDING The 8th Amendment prohibits the setting of "excessive bail." What is considered "excessive"?

Cruel and Unusual Punishments

The 8th Amendment also forbids "cruel and unusual punishments." The 14th Amendment extends that prohibition against the States, *Robinson* v. *California,* 1962.

The Supreme Court decided its first cruel and unusual case in 1879 in *Wilkerson* v. *Utah.* There, a territorial court had sentenced a convicted murderer to death by a firing squad. The Court held that this punishment was not forbidden by the Constitution. The kinds of penalties the Constitution intended to prevent, said the Court, were such barbaric tortures as burning at the stake, crucifixion, drawing and quartering, "and all others in the same line of unnecessary cruelty." The Court took the same position a few years later when, for the first time, it upheld the electrocution of a convicted murderer in a case from New York, *In re Kemmler,* 1890.

Since then, the Court has heard only a handful of cruel and unusual cases, except for those relating to capital punishment. More often than not, it has rejected the cruel and unusual punishment argument. *Louisiana* v. *Resweber,* 1947, is fairly typical. There, the Court found that it was not unconstitutional to subject a convicted murderer to a second electrocution after the chair had failed to work properly on the first occasion. And in *Rhodes* v. *Chapman,* 1980, it held that putting two inmates in a cell that had been designed to hold only one did not violate the constitutional command.

The Court also denied the cruel and unusual claim in a 2003 8th Amendment case not involving the death penalty, centered on California's "three strikes" law, which says that any person convicted of three crimes must be sentenced to at least 25 years in prison. Leandro Andrade had received 50 years for stealing $153.54 worth of children's videos from two K-Mart stores. The K-Mart thefts were treated as separate offenses, and Andrade had an earlier burglary conviction on his record, as well.

8th Amendment Claims Upheld The Court has held some punishments to be cruel and unusual, but only a very few. It did so for the first time in *Weems* v. *United States* in 1910. There, the Court overturned the conviction of a Coast Guard official who had been found guilty of falsifying government pay records. He had been sentenced to 15 years at hard labor, constantly chained at wrist and ankle.

Incarcerated Persons in the U.S.*

YEAR	NUMBER
2000	1,938,500
2005	2,195,000
2010	2,270,100
2011	2,240,600
2012	2,228,400

*Includes local jail inmates and prisoners held in State or federal prisons or privately operated facilities.

SOURCE: Bureau of Justice Statistics, Correctional Populations in the United States, 2012

>> **Constitutional protections for the accused include a prohibition against "cruel and unusual punishment." Analyze Charts Are overcrowded prisons "cruel and unusual punishment"? Why or why not?**

In *Robinson* v. *California,* 1962, the Court ruled that a State law that defined narcotics addiction as a crime to be punished, rather than an illness, violated the 8th and 14th Amendments, and that mandatory sentences of life in prison without the possibility of parole cannot be imposed on juvenile offenders (*Jackson* v. *Hobbs; Miller* v. *Alabama,* 2012). The cruel and unusual prohibition was also violated, said the Court in 2011, by California's overcrowded prison system, *Brown* v. *Plata.* In its narrow 5–4 ruling, the Court ordered the State to reduce the size of its prison population by nearly 50,000 inmates.

GENERATE EXPLANATIONS Explain the role of the Supreme Court in applying the 8th Amendment's ban on "cruel and unusual punishments."

Capital Punishment and Treason

Laws providing for **capital punishment**—the death penalty—date back to at least the 18th century B.C. and the Code of Hammurabi, which set death as the penalty for more than 25 different offenses. The punishment has been a part of American law since the colonial period, and both the Federal Government and 32 States provide for it today.

Over time, the Supreme Court was reluctant to face this highly charged question: Is capital punishment cruel and unusual and therefore prohibited by the 8th Amendment?

State Laws Struck Down The Court did meet the issue, finally, and more or less directly, in *Furman* v. *Georgia,* 1972. There, it struck down all of the then-existing State laws providing for the death penalty—but not because that punishment is cruel and unusual.

Rather, the Court voided those laws because they gave too much discretion to judges or juries in deciding whether to impose the ultimate penalty. The Court found that of all the people convicted of capital crimes, only "a random few," most of them African American or poor, or both, were "capriciously selected" for execution.

Immediately, most States and Congress began to write new capital punishment laws. Those new statutes took one of two forms. Several States made a death sentence mandatory for certain crimes—for example, the killing of a police officer or a murder committed during a rape, kidnapping, or arson. Others provided, instead, for a two-stage process in capital cases: first, a trial to settle the question of guilt or innocence; then, for those convicted, a second proceeding to decide if the circumstances involved in the crime justify a sentence of death.

In considering scores of challenges to these new laws, the Supreme Court found mandatory death penalty statutes unconstitutional. In *Woodson* v. *North Carolina,* 1976, it ruled that those statutes were "unduly harsh and rigidly unworkable." They were, said the Court, simply attempts to "paper over" the decision in *Furman.*

Two-Stage Approach and Later Cases The two-stage approach was found to be constitutional in *Gregg* v. *Georgia,* 1976. There, the Court held for the first time that the "punishment of death does not invariably violate the Constitution." It declared that well-drawn two-stage laws could practically eliminate "the risk that it [the death penalty] would be inflicted in an arbitrary or capricious manner."

Opponents of the death penalty continue to appeal capital cases to the Supreme Court, but to no real avail. Most of their cases have centered on the application, not the constitutionality, of the punishment. The more important of those several cases have resulted in these rulings:

- The death penalty can be imposed only for "crimes resulting in the death of the victim," *Coker* v. *Georgia,* 1977.
- That penalty cannot be imposed on those who are mentally challenged, *Atkins* v. *Virginia,* 2002, or on those who were under the age of 18 when their crimes were committed, *Roper* v. *Simmons,* 2005.
- The question of whether the ultimate penalty is to be imposed must be decided by the jury that convicted the defendant, not the judge who presided at the trial, *Ring* v. *Arizona,* 2002.

And, most recently, these holdings: A delusional person who cannot understand why he has been

Capital Punishment Debate

48% PREFER DEATH PENALTY	50% PREFER LIFE WITHOUT PAROLE
"We may... assume safely that there are murderers, such as those who act in passion, for whom the threat of death has little or no deterrent effect. But for many others, the death penalty undoubtedly is a significant deterrent." —Justice Potter Stewart, *Gregg v. Georgia,* 1976	**"The barbaric death penalty violates our Constitution. Even the most vile murderer does not release the state from its obligation to respect dignity, for the state does not honor the victim by emulating his murderer. One day the Court will outlaw the death penalty. Permanently."** —William J. Brennan, former U.S. Supreme Court Justice, 1996

>> Capital punishment has had a lengthy history, and so has the controversy surrounding it. **Analyze Charts** How do these two opposing quotations summarize the debate on this issue?

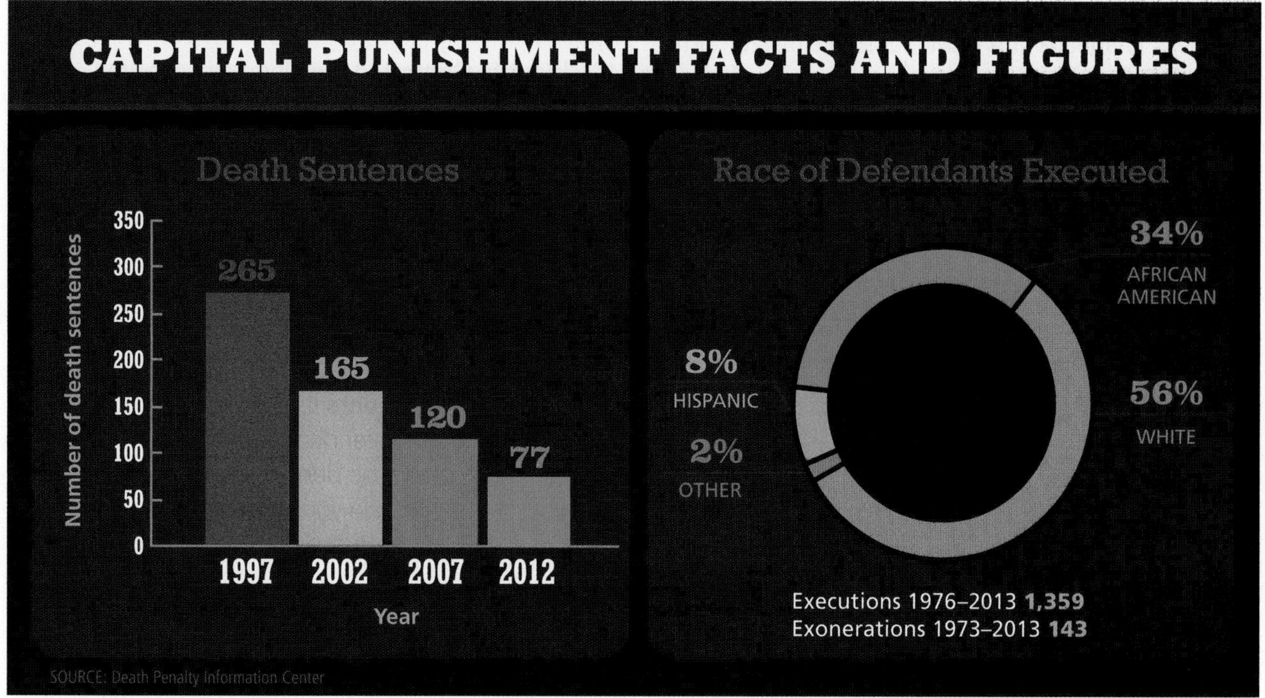

>> Capital punishment has been part of American law since colonial days. Nearly 3,100 persons sit on death row today. **Analyze Charts** What might explain the decrease in death sentences since 1997?

sentenced to death cannot be executed, *Panetti* v. *Quarterman,* 2007. Execution by lethal injection, the method most widely used today, does not violate the 8th Amendment, *Baze* v. *Rees,* 2008. The sum of the Court's many decisions over the past thirty years or so comes down to this: The death penalty, fairly applied, is constitutional.

Continuing Controversy Even so, the death penalty remains controversial. Even among supporters there are misgivings about the fairness with which this penalty is applied.

Clearly, the application of the death penalty must be closely monitored to protect the innocent and prevent wrongful convictions. The Death Penalty Information Center reports that over the past forty years, more than 140 persons who had been sentenced to death have been exonerated and released from prison. As retired Supreme Court Justice Sandra Day O'Connor once observed: "If statistics are any indication, the system may well be allowing some innocent defendants to be executed."

That fact has also prompted many who support capital punishment to insist that the remedies for issues in the administration of the penalty should not be to abolish it. Instead, they argue, those remedies should be found in the continuing improvement of the processes by which the ultimate penalty is imposed.

Treason Treason against the United States is the only crime defined in the Constitution. The Framers provided a specific definition of the crime because they knew that the charge of treason has long been a favorite weapon in the hands of tyrants.

Treason, says Article III, Section 3, can consist of only two things: either (1) levying war against the United States or (2) "adhering to their Enemies, giving them Aid and Comfort." The Constitution adds that no person can be convicted of the crime of treason "unless on the Testimony of two Witnesses to the same overt Act, or on Confession in open Court."

The law of treason covers all citizens of the United States, at home or abroad, and all permanent resident aliens. Congress has set death as the maximum sentence for someone convicted of the federal crime but no person has ever, in fact, been executed for that offense. Indeed, the death penalty was not imposed in a federal treason case until 1942. Then, four German-born American citizens were sentenced to be hanged for aiding a group of Nazi saboteurs who had been landed on the East Coast by a German submarine. But those sentences were never carried out.

Treason can only be committed in wartime. But Congress has made it a crime, during times of either peace or war, to commit either espionage or sabotage, to attempt to overthrow the government by force, or to conspire to do any of these things.

Most State constitutions also condemn treason. The fabled abolitionist John Brown was hanged as a traitor by Virginia after his raid on Harpers Ferry in 1859. He is believed to be the only person ever executed for treason against a State.

? EVALUATE ARGUMENTS What is the two-stage process and how has it affected the Supreme Court's view of the death penalty?

ASSESSMENT

1. **Identify Central Ideas** Name one way the justice system protects the rights of a person with little money who is accused of a crime.
2. **Compare and Contrast** What is the difference between a grand jury and a trial jury? How does each jury protect an individual's rights?
3. **Generate Explanations** Why is it important that a jury reflect the racial make-up of the community?
4. **Evaluate Arguments** If the right to a public trial belongs to the defendant and not the media, should reporters be denied access to the courtroom? Explain your answer.
5. **Interpret** How has the Court generally ruled when applying the 8th Amendment to the death penalty?

TOPIC 8 ASSESSMENT

1. **Define and Identify Unalienable Rights** Use the excerpt from the Declaration of Independence to write a paragraph that defines and identifies unalienable rights and explains why they are protected in the United States. Consider the following questions to support your response: What is the definition of *unalienable rights*? What are the unalienable rights, according to the Declaration of Independence? What are some examples of how unalienable rights are protected in society today?

   "We hold these truths to be self-evident, that all men are created equal, that they are endowed by their Creator with certain unalienable Rights, that among these are Life, Liberty and the Pursuit of Happiness. That to secure these rights, Governments are instituted among Men, deriving their powers from the consent of the governed. . . ."

   —Declaration of Independence

2. **Create a Presentation Analyzing Interpretations of Rights** Create a visual presentation analyzing U.S. Supreme Court interpretations of rights guaranteed by the U.S. Constitution in *Miranda* v. *Arizona*. Consider the following questions: What were the circumstances surrounding *Miranda* v. *Arizona*? How did the court rule? What is the Miranda rule? Why is the Miranda rule controversial?

3. **Create a Presentation Analyzing Interpretations of Rights** Create a written or oral presentation analyzing U.S. Supreme Court interpretations of rights in *Roe* v. *Wade*. Consider the following questions: What were the circumstances surrounding *Roe* v. *Wade*? How did the court rule? Why is the court's decision in *Roe* v. *Wade* controversial?

4. **Explain Due Process Rights** Write a paragraph that explains the importance of due process and how it protects individual rights. Consider the following questions to support your response: What is due process? How is due process addressed in the Constitution? How does due process protect individual rights?

5. **Describe Efforts to Extend the Bill of Rights to the States** Write a paragraph that describes how the rulings in *Gideon* v. *Wainwright, Pointer* v. *Texas,* and *Washington* v. *Texas* extended the rights guaranteed in the 6th Amendment to the states. Consider the following questions to support your response: What rights are guaranteed by the 6th Amendment? What were the major issues in each case? How did the Court rule in each case? How did the Court's decisions extend the Bill of Rights to the states?

6. **Create a Product That Identifies Freedoms and Rights** Create a product such as a website, poster, editorial, or blog that identifies the freedoms and rights guaranteed by each amendment in the Bill of Rights. Use the following process to complete the project: Identify a contemporary issue that involves one or more of the rights and freedoms guaranteed in the Bill of Rights. Make a list of questions you will need to answer in order to complete your project. Answer your questions as you go along, generating new questions and answers as you deepen your study. Conduct research needed for your project, using authoritative sources, keeping accurate notes as well as careful records of your sources. Create your project, being sure to explain how the issue you chose relates to the Bill of Rights. Be sure to proofread and revise.

7. **Analyze the Importance of the First Amendment** Write a paragraph that analyzes the importance of the right of free speech. Consider the following questions to support your response: What is the purpose of the right of free speech that is guaranteed in the First Amendment? Why are their restrictions on the right of free speech?

8. **Identify Significant Individuals** Write a paragraph about Abraham Lincoln in regard to the *writ of habeas corpus*. Consider the following questions to support your response: What is *habeas corpus?* Why did Abraham Lincoln suspend *habeas corpus?* How did the Court rule on Lincoln's action? Why is *habeas* corpus important?

9. **Examine the Reasons for the Protection of Religious Freedom** Use the excerpt below to write a paragraph that explains why the Founding Fathers included religious freedoms in the First Amendment. Consider the following questions to support your response: What two guarantees of religious freedom are protected by the First Amendment? How are the Establishment Clause and the Free Exercise Clause different? Why did the Founding Fathers include these religious freedoms in the Bill of Rights?

   "Congress shall make no law respecting an establishment of religion, or prohibiting the free exercise thereof . . ."

   —First Amendment

10. **Evaluate and Analyze Constitutional Provisions** Write a summary that evaluates constitutional provisions for limiting the role of the government in regard to civil liberties and civil rights. Consider the following: Bill of Rights; other constitutional provisions that protect individual rights.

11. **Analyze the Impact and Transfer Information** Write a paragraph that analyzes the scope of federalism and fundamental rights. Consider the following questions to support your response: What is federalism? How did the 14th Amendment expand the scope of federalism and fundamental rights? How do the Bill of Rights and 14th Amendment protect fundamental rights? When the paragraph is complete, transfer the information from the paragraph to a chart, graph, or graphic organizer using computer software.

12. **Evaluate a Court Decision** Write a paragraph that evaluates how the *Lemon* test affects parochial school funding. Consider the following questions to support your response: What policy did the court establish with the ruling in the case *Lemon* v. *Kurtzman*? What are the three standards outlined in the *Lemon* test? What is an example of how courts evaluate laws using the *Lemon* test?

13. **Identify Contributions and Significant Individuals** Write a paragraph that identifies Thomas Jefferson's influence on religious liberty in the United States. Consider the following questions to support your response: How does the First Amendment protect the freedom of religion? How did Thomas Jefferson influence the development of the U.S. government in regards to freedom of religion?

14. **Examine Reasons and Compare and Contrast** Write a paragraph that compares and contrasts the wording of the First Amendment with the phrase "separation of church and state." Consider the following questions to support your response: What is the meaning of the phrase "Congress shall make no law respecting an establishment of religion, or prohibiting the free exercise thereof"? How does the First Amendment compare with Thomas Jefferson's phrase "separation of church and state"?

15. **Evaluate Obligations of Citizenship** Write a paragraph that evaluates this issue of citizenship, and consider the following in your response: some specific obligations of citizenship and whether and/or when they require that personal desires and interests be subordinated to the public good; limits on civil liberties and whether and/or when they require that personal desires and interests be subordinated to the public good.

MIRANDA WARNING

1. YOU HAVE THE RIGHT TO REMAIN SILENT.
2. ANYTHING YOU SAY CAN AND WILL BE USED AGAINST YOU IN A COURT OF LAW.
3. YOU HAVE THE RIGHT TO CONSULT AN ATTORNEY AND HAVE AN ATTORNEY PRESENT WHILE YOU ARE BEING QUESTIONED.
4. IF YOU CANNOT AFFORD TO HIRE A LAWYER, ONE WILL BE APPOINTED TO REPRESENT YOU BEFORE ANY QUESTIONING, IF YOU WISH.
5. YOU CAN DECIDE AT ANY TIME TO EXERCISE THESE RIGHTS AND NOT ANSWER ANY QUESTIONS OR MAKE ANY STATEMENTS.

WAIVER

DO YOU UNDERSTAND EACH OF THESE RIGHTS I HAVE EXPLAINED TO YOU? HAVING THESE RIGHTS IN MIND, DO YOU WISH TO TALK TO US NOW?

16. **Give Examples and Analyze the Impact** Write a paragraph that provides examples of different Supreme Court cases that helped build and protect civil rights and liberties in the United States. Then choose one of the cases and write a paragraph that analyzes how it affected public policy and impacted political change. Consider the following questions: What was the case about? How did it affect public policy and impact political change?

17. **Understand the Role of Limited Government** Write a paragraph about the role of limited government in the protection of individual rights. Consider the following questions to support your response: What are individual rights? How does a limited government protect individual rights? Why aren't Americans allowed absolute freedom, such as absolute freedom of speech? Why do rights sometimes conflict with each other? What are some examples of when this has happened? What would happen to individual rights if the government had more authority? Provide an example.

18. **Analyze Interpretations of Rights** Use the chart above to write a paragraph that analyzes the rights guaranteed as a result of the decision in *Miranda* v. *Arizona*. Consider the following questions to support your response: What does the card show? Which Supreme Court case resulted in warnings such as this one? What were the circumstances surrounding this case? How did this case affect the criminal justice system?

19. **Write About the Essential Question Write an essay on the Essential Question: How much power should the government have?** Use evidence from your study of this Topic to support your answer.

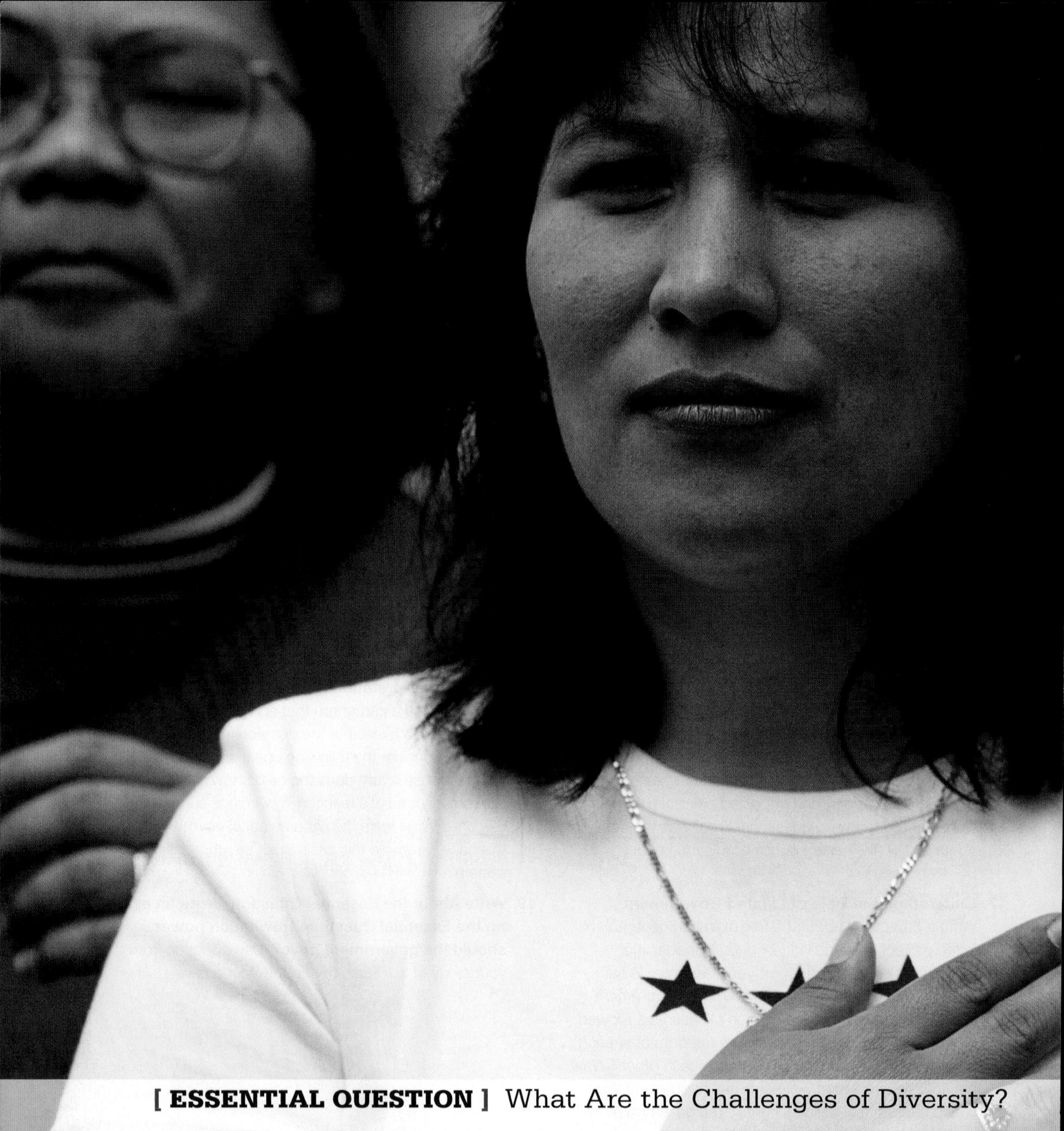

[**ESSENTIAL QUESTION**] What Are the Challenges of Diversity?

9 Citizenship and Civil Rights

>> New American citizens pledge allegiance at a nationalization ceremony.

Enduring Understandings

- The U.S. is a nation of immigrants, but current immigration policy is controversial.
- The Declaration of Independence declares that "all men are created equal," an ideal our nation still struggles to meet as race- and gender-based discrimination has declined but not disappeared.
- The nation has not yet achieved complete integration of educational systems, but legally enforced racial segregation in public life has been eliminated.
- Congress passed civil rights laws to carry out the Constitution's insistence on the equality of all before the law, although controversy still surrounds affirmative action today.

PEARSON realize™ NBC LEARN

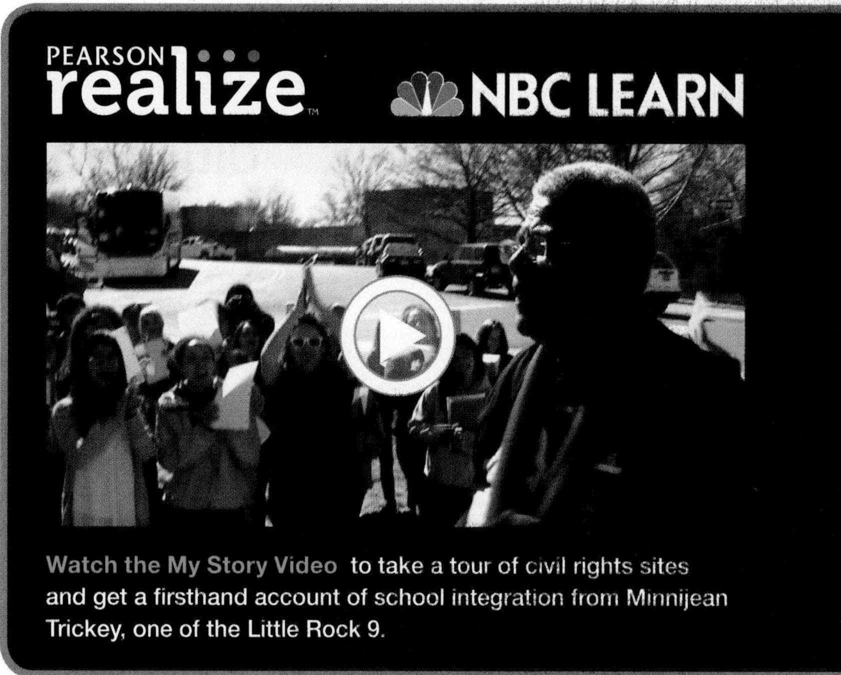

Watch the My Story Video to take a tour of civil rights sites and get a firsthand account of school integration from Minnijean Trickey, one of the Little Rock 9.

PEARSON realize™ www.PearsonRealize.com

Access your digital lessons including: Topic Inquiry • Interactive Reading Notepad • Interactivities • Assessments

>> These students recite the Pledge of Allegiance, a statement of loyalty to the United States, every morning before class. The Pledge was written in 1892 to promote American patriotism.

Interactive Flipped Video

9.1 **The concept of citizenship—of the free inhabitants of a city—was developed by the ancient Greeks and Romans. It replaced the earlier concept of kinship—of the blood relationships of the family and the tribe—as the basis for community. Today, citizenship is the badge of membership in a political society, and every state in the world has rules by which citizenship is determined. Much can be learned about the basic nature of a government by examining those rules. Who are and who may become citizens? Who are excluded from citizenship, and why?**

>> Objectives

Describe how people become American citizens by birth and by naturalization.

Explain how an American can lose his or her citizenship.

Illustrate how the United States is a nation of immigrants.

Compare and contrast the status of undocumented aliens and legal immigrants.

>> Key Terms

citizen
jus soli
jus sanguinis
naturalization
alien
expatriation
denaturalization
deportation

American Citizenship

Citizenship in the United States

An American **citizen** is one who owes allegiance to the United States and is entitled to both its protection and the privileges of its laws. As it was originally written, the Constitution referred to both "citizens of the United States" and "citizens of the States." Neither of those phrases were defined, however.

Throughout much of our earlier history, it was generally agreed that national citizenship followed that of the States. That is, a person who was a citizen of, say, Maryland, was also thought to be a citizen of the United States. Actually, the question was of little importance before the 1860s. Much of the population was the product of recent immigration, and little distinction was made between citizens and those who were not. The Civil War and the adoption of the 13th Amendment in 1865 raised the need for a constitutional definition, however. The 14th Amendment met that need in 1868.

All persons born or naturalized in the United States and subject to the jurisdiction thereof, are citizens of the United States and of the State wherein they reside.

—14th Amendment, Section 1

Thus, the Constitution declares that a person may become an American citizen in either of two ways: by birth or by naturalization.

SUMMARIZE What benefits are citizens of the United States entitled to in return for pledging their allegiance to the United States?

Natural-Born Citizens

Some 270 million Americans—nearly 90 percent—are citizens simply because they were born in this country. Another several million are also citizens by birth, although they were born outside the United States.

Two basic rules determine citizenship at birth: jus soli and jus sanguinis. According to **jus soli**—the law of the soil—citizenship is determined by place of birth, by *where* one is born.

A Leading Citizenship Case Notice that the 14th Amendment awards American citizenship according to the location of one's birth: "All persons born . . . in the United States. . . ." Congress has defined the United States to include, for purposes of citizenship, the 50 States, the District of Columbia, Puerto Rico, Guam, the Virgin Islands, and the Northern Mariana Islands. Native Americans were exceptions to the "All persons" covered by the amendment until 1924, when Congress granted citizenship to all Native Americans born in the United States.

Just how broad the 14th Amendment's statement of jus soli is can be seen from a leading case on citizenship, *United States* v. *Wong Kim Ark,* 1898.

Wong Kim Ark was born in San Francisco in 1873 to parents who were citizens of China. He made a brief trip to China in 1895. Upon Wong Kim Ark's return, he was refused entry to the United States by immigration officials at San Francisco. They insisted that the 14th Amendment should not be read so literally as to mean that he had become an American citizen at birth. They declared that he was an alien and so was denied entry by the Chinese Exclusion Act of 1882. The Supreme Court held, however, that under the clear wording of the 14th Amendment, he was indeed a native-born citizen of this country and so not subject to the terms of the Chinese Exclusion Act.

Complicated Citizenship Situations A very small number of persons who are born *physically* in the United States do not in fact become citizens at birth. They are those few who are born not "subject to the jurisdiction of the United States"—for example, children born to foreign diplomatic officials.

Acquiring Citizenship at Birth

JUS SOLI: LAW OF SOIL	JUS SANGUINIS: LAW OF BLOOD
A child becomes an American citizen if born: • in the United States, Puerto Rico, Guam, U.S. Virgin Islands, or Northern Mariana Islands	**A child born to an American citizen on foreign soil becomes a citizen if:** • both parents are American citizens, and at least one has lived in the United States or an American territory at some time. • one parent is an American citizen who has lived in the United States for at least five years, two of those years after age 14, and the child lived in the United States continuously for at least five years between the ages of 14 and 28.

>> Citizenship can be acquired at birth either through jus soli—law of soil—or jus sanguinis—law of blood.**Analyze Charts** What is the difference between jus soli and jus sanguinis?

According to **jus sanguinis,** the law of the blood, citizenship at birth may also be determined by parentage, to *whom* one is born. Thus, it is altogether possible for one to become a citizen at birth even when that birth occurs outside the United States. The 14th Amendment does not provide for jus sanguinis. However, Congress first recognized the doctrine in 1790 and its constitutionality has never been challenged.

? COMPARE Which is more far-reaching in terms of citizenship: jus soli or jus sanguinis?

Naturalized Citizens

Naturalization is the legal process by which a person can become a citizen of another country at some time after birth. Congress has the exclusive power to provide for naturalization (Article I, Section 8, Clause 4). No State may do so.

Individual Naturalization Naturalization is most often an individual process, conducted by a court. Generally, any person eligible to enter the United States as an immigrant may become a naturalized citizen. Hundreds of thousands of aliens are now naturalized each year. An **alien** is a citizen of a foreign state who lives in this country.

The U.S. Citizenship and Immigration Services in the Department of Homeland Security investigates each applicant, and then it reports its findings to the judge with whom a petition for naturalization has been filed. If the judge is satisfied, an oath or affirmation of citizenship is administered in open court.

Collective Naturalization At various times, entire groups have been naturalized *en masse.* This has most often happened when the United States has acquired new territory. Those living in the areas involved were naturalized by a treaty or by an act or a joint resolution passed by Congress.

The largest single instance of collective naturalization came with the ratification of the 14th Amendment. The most recent instance occurred in 1977, when Congress gave citizenship to the more than 16,000 native-born residents of the Northern Mariana Islands.

? CONTRAST What is the difference between individual naturalization and collective naturalization?

Losing One's Citizenship

Although it rarely happens, every American citizen, whether native-born or naturalized, has the right to renounce—voluntarily abandon—his or her citizenship. **Expatriation** is the legal process by which a loss of citizenship occurs.

The Supreme Court has several times held that the Constitution prohibits automatic expatriation. That is, Congress cannot take away a person's citizenship for something he or she has done. Thus, actions such as committing a crime, voting in a foreign election, or

Acquiring Citizenship Through Naturalization

INDIVIDUALLY	COLLECTIVELY
• Individual naturalization of both parents (or one parent if divorced or the other parent is deceased) automatically naturalizes children under the age of 16 who reside in the United States. • Adopted children born abroad are automatically naturalized if under age 18 when the adoption becomes final.	Collective naturalization—when entire groups are naturalized—usually occurs by: • treaty • by act or joint resolution of Congress.

>> Most Americans acquire citizenship at birth. **Analyze Charts** How else can people acquire American citizenship?

serving in the armed forces of another country are not grounds for automatic expatriation.

Naturalized citizens can lose their citizenship involuntarily. However, this **denaturalization** process can occur only by court order and only after it has been shown that the person became an American citizen by fraud or deception.

A person can neither gain nor lose American citizenship by marriage. The only significant effect that marriage has is to shorten the time required for the naturalization of an alien who marries an American citizen.

SUMMARIZE Under what circumstances can naturalized citizens of the United States be denaturalized?

>> In 2013, singer Tina Turner relinquished her U.S. citizenship and became a Swiss citizen. Born and raised in Tennessee, Turner has lived in Switzerland since 1994.

Government Immigration Policies

We are a nation of immigrants. Except for Native Americans—and even they may be the descendants of earlier immigrants—all of us have come here from abroad or are descended from those who did.

Early Immigration Congress has the exclusive power to regulate the crossing of this nation's borders, both inward (immigration) and outward (emigration). It alone has the power to decide who may be admitted to the country and under what conditions. In an early leading case on the point, the Court ruled that the power of the United States to "exclude aliens from its territory is . . . not open to controversy," *Chae Chan Ping* v. *United States,* 1889. The States have no power in the field, *The Passenger Cases,* 1849.

There were only some 2.5 million people in the United States when independence was declared in 1776. Since then, the population has grown more than a hundredfold, to well over 300 million today.

That extraordinary population growth has come from two sources: births and immigration. Some 70 million immigrants have come here since 1820, the year when such figures were first recorded.

Congress made no serious attempt to regulate immigration for more than a century after independence. As long as land was plentiful and expanding industry demanded more and still more workers, immigration was actively encouraged.

>> Between 1892 and 1954, twelve million immigrants entered the United States through Ellis Island, the country's busiest immigration inspection station.

Immigration Regulation Begins By 1890, however, the open frontier was a thing of the past, and labor was no longer in short supply. Then, too, the major source of immigration had shifted. Until the 1880s, most immigrants had come from the countries of northern and western Europe. The "new immigration" from the 1880s onward came mostly from southern and eastern Europe. All these factors combined to bring major changes in the traditional policy of encouraging immigration. Ultimately, the policy was reversed.

Congress placed the first major restrictions on immigration with the passage of the Chinese Exclusion Act in 1882. At the same time, it barred the entry of convicts, "lunatics," paupers, and others likely to become public charges. Over the next several years, a long list of "undesirables" was added to the law. Thus, contract laborers were excluded in 1885, immoral persons and anarchists in 1903, and illiterates in 1917. By 1920, more than 30 groups were denied admission on the basis of personal traits.

The tide of newcomers continued to mount, however. In the 10 years from 1905 through 1914, an average of more than a million persons, most of them from southern and eastern Europe, came to this country each year.

The Quota System Congress responded to pressure for tighter regulation by adding quantitative limits (numerical ceilings) to the qualitative restrictions (personal characteristics) already in place. The Immigration Acts of 1921 and 1924 and the National Origins Act of 1929 assigned each country in Europe a quota—a limit on the number of immigrants who could enter the United States from that country each year. Altogether, only 150,000 quota immigrants could be admitted in any one year.

The quotas were purposely drawn to favor northern and western Europe. The quota system was not applied to the Western Hemisphere, but immigration from Asia, Africa, and elsewhere was generally prohibited.

Quota System Changes In 1952, Congress passed yet another basic law, the Immigration and Nationality Act. That statute modified the quota system, extending it to include every country outside the Western Hemisphere.

Congress finally eliminated the country-based quota system in the Immigration and Nationality Act of 1965. That law allowed as many as 270,000 immigrants to enter the United States each year, without regard to race, nationality, or country of origin. The 1965 law gave special preference to immediate relatives of American citizens or of aliens legally residing in this country.

Current Immigration Policies Today, the admission of aliens to the United States is governed by the Immigration Act of 1990. Like its predecessors, it was adopted only after years of intense debate, and many of its provisions are the subject of continuing controversy.

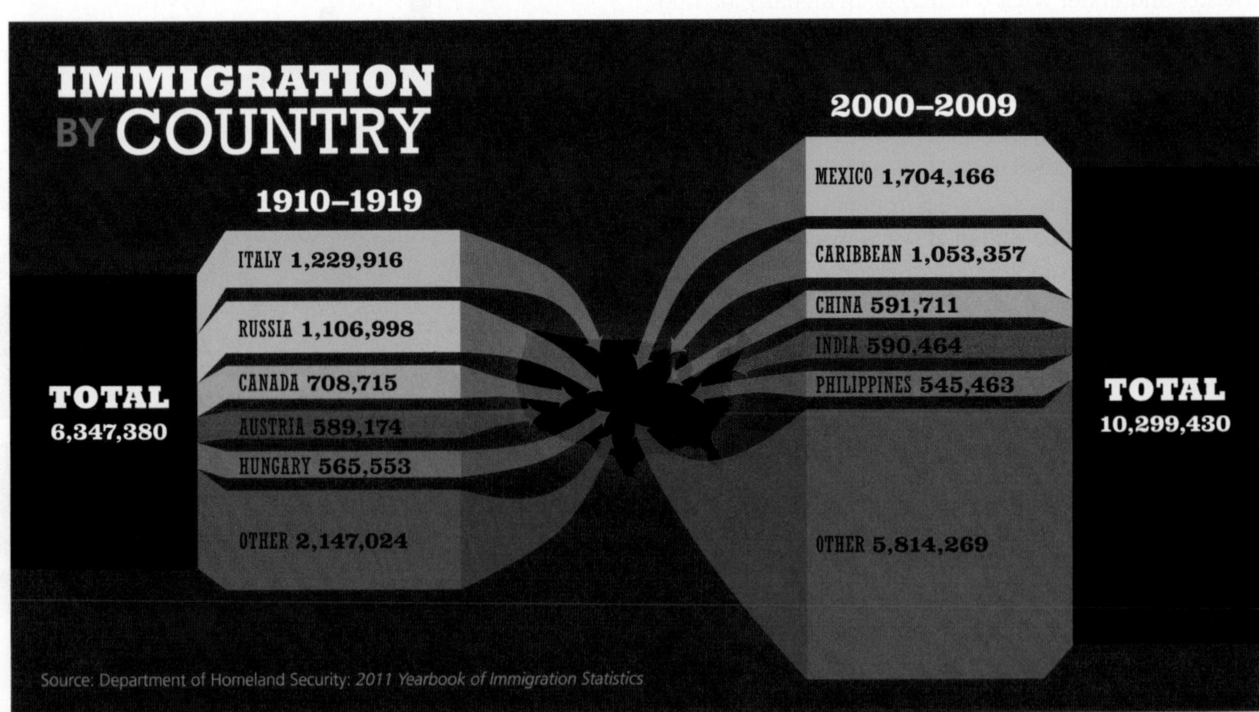

>> Immigration statistics have varied greatly over time. **Analyze Data** What does the chart say about countries of origin during the two decades?

The 1990 law provided for a substantial increase in the number of immigrants who may enter the United States each year. The annual ceiling is now set at 675,000. It also continues the family-preference policy first put in place in 1965; at least one third of those persons admitted under its terms must be the close relatives of either American citizens or resident aliens. Those immigrants who have occupational talents which are in short supply in the United States (notably, highly skilled researchers, engineers, and scientists) also receive special preference.

People Excluded from Immigrating Only those aliens who can qualify for citizenship can be admitted as immigrants. The law's list of "excludable aliens"—those barred because of some personal characteristic—is extensive. Among those excluded are: criminals (including suspected terrorists), persons with communicable diseases, drug abusers and addicts, illiterates, and mentally disturbed persons who might pose a threat to the safety of others.

Some 53 million persons—non-immigrants—come here each year for temporary stays. They are mostly tourists, students, and people traveling for business reasons.

>> This border checkpoint is one of many between the United States and Mexico. According to the Census Bureau, more than 11.6 million immigrants from Mexico live in the United States.

Deportation Most of the civil rights set out in the Constitution are guaranteed to "persons"—a term that covers aliens as well as citizens. In one important respect, however, the status of aliens is altogether unlike that of citizens: Aliens may be subject to **deportation,** a legal process by which aliens are legally required to leave the country.

The Supreme Court has long held that the United States has the same almost-unlimited power to deport aliens as it has to exclude them. In an early major case, the Court ruled that deportation is an inherent power, arising out of the sovereignty of the United States, and that deportation is not criminal punishment, and so does not require a criminal trial, *Fong Yue Ting* v. *United States,* 1893.

Reasons for Deportation An alien may be deported on any one of several grounds. The most common is illegal entry. Thousands of aliens who enter with false papers, sneak in by ship or plane, or slip across the border at night are caught each year and deported. Many of them are repeat offenders who will soon make yet another attempt to cross the border.

Conviction of any serious crime, federal or State, usually leads to a deportation order. In recent years, several thousand aliens have been expelled on the basis of their criminal records, especially narcotics violators. The war on terrorism has also quickened the pace of deportations. Because deportation is a civil, not a criminal, matter, several constitutional safeguards do not apply—for example, bail and the ban on ex post facto laws.

? DISTINGUISH How do the constitutional rights given to aliens differ from those granted to citizens?

Government Policies on Undocumented Aliens

No one knows just how many undocumented aliens reside in the United States today. Their numbers began rising in the 1980s, and best estimates by the Department of Homeland Security and other sources put their total today at about 11.5 million. Most enter the country by slipping across the Mexican or Canadian borders, usually at night. Some come with forged papers. Many others are aliens who enter legally, as non-immigrants, but then overstay their legal welcomes.

Well over half of all aliens who are here illegally have come from Mexico; most of the others come from other Latin American countries and from Asia. A majority of the Mexicans stay here only about four to six months a year, working on farms or in other seasonal jobs, and then they return home. Most others hope to remain here permanently.

Where Many Undocumented Aliens Live Once here, many of these aliens find it easy to become "invisible," especially in larger cities, and law-enforcement agencies find it very difficult to locate them. Even so, immigration officials have apprehended more than a million undocumented aliens in each of the last several years. Nearly all are sent home. Most go voluntarily, but some leave only as the result of formal deportation proceedings.

The presence of so many undocumented persons has caused a number of nagging problems. Those problems have grown worse over the past several years and, until recently, not much had been done to solve them.

Where Many Undocumented Aliens Work Consider this: Ever since 1987, it has been illegal for an employer to hire an undocumented alien to perform work anywhere in the United States. Even so, some eight million persons who now hold jobs in this country came here illegally. Some employers still hire aliens who are often willing to work for substandard wages and in substandard conditions.

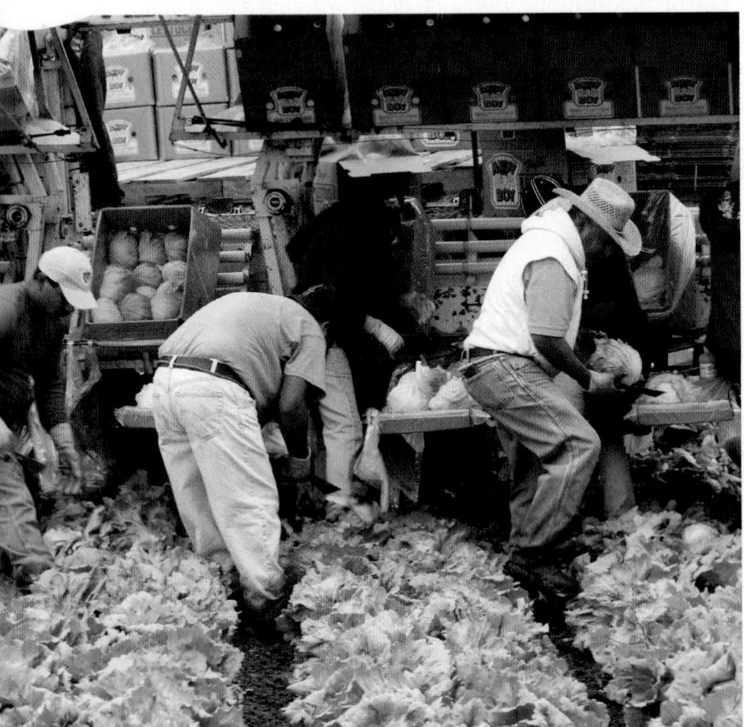

>> Migrant farmworkers are the support system behind the billion-dollar U.S. food industry. According to a 2009 survey, nearly half of the agricultural workers were undocumented aliens.

No one knows just how many undocumented aliens have taken jobs on farms or become day laborers. Or how many have become janitors or dishwashers, or seamstresses in sweatshops, or have found other menial work. However many they are, their presence has multiplied the burdens of already strained public school systems and welfare services of an increasing number of States, most notably California, Arizona, Texas, and Florida.

Current Law The problems posed by undocumented aliens trouble and divide many different interests in American politics—chief among them labor, farm, business, religious, ethnic, and civil rights organizations. After wrestling with the matter for years, Congress was finally able to pass the Immigration Reform and Control Act of 1986. Then, it enacted the Illegal Immigration Reform and Immigrant Responsibility Act of 1996.

The 1986 law did two major things. First, it established a one-year amnesty program under which many undocumented aliens could become legal residents. More than two million aliens used the process to legalize their status. Second, that law made it a crime to hire any person who is in this country illegally. Any employer who knowingly hires an undocumented alien can be fined from $250 to as much as $10,000. Repeat offenders can be jailed for up to six months.

The 1996 law made it easier to deport illegal aliens by streamlining the deportation process. It also toughened the penalties for smuggling aliens into this country and prevented undocumented aliens from claiming Social Security or public housing benefits. The statute also doubled the size of the Border Patrol—which is, today, the largest of the several federal law enforcement agencies.

Immigration Reform Stalls Congress has not been able to enact any meaningful immigration reform legislation for some two decades now, however. The principal reason for the impasse is a continuing dispute over how best to approach the matter.

Many insist that stemming the flow of illegal entries should be the nation's first concern. Others argue that the nation must confront the problems posed by the undocumented aliens already in this country. They want to make it possible for those undocumented aliens to become legal residents and, eventually, citizens of the United States. In 2012, President Obama, frustrated by the lack of congressional action, issued an executive order that suspended deportations of children of illegal immigrants for two years. Noting that "this is a temporary stopgap measure," the President urged

Congress to act to pass permanent immigration reform legislation.

When Congress still had not acted by late 2014, the President issued a second executive order, known as Deferred Action for Parents of Americans and Lawful Permanent Residents (DAPA). The order was intended to allow unauthorized immigrant parents of U.S. citizens to apply for work permits if they have lived in the country for five years and not committed any crimes.

DAPA was never implemented, however. Twenty-six States joined in a lawsuit against the President, charging that he had overstepped his authority. In *United States* v. *Texas*, 2016, the Supreme Court, hampered by the death of Justice Antonin Scalia, issued a split (4–4) decision. As a result, the lower courts' rulings were upheld.

It became clear during the 2016 presidential campaign that the American people remain deeply divided about these difficult issues. Republican Donald Trump, who won the election, tapped into these concerns with his pledge to build a wall between the United States and Mexico. President Trump also promised to confront the problems posed by the unauthorized persons currently living in the United States. In 2017, the Department of Homeland Security officially rescinded DAPA.

In the wake of DAPA's demise, Americans are still faced with these vexing questions: How can the flow of illegal entries be reduced? What should be done about the millions of unauthorized immigrants already in this country?

IMMIGRATION REFORM
"ANYBODY HOME?"

>> Immigration reform has been a contentious issue for years and an emotional issue for those directly affected. **Analyze Political Cartoons** What does the cartoon say about Congress's actions?

Interactive Cartoon

EXPRESS IDEAS CLEARLY What did the Illegal Immigration Reform and Immigrant Responsibility Act of 1996 provide? Do you think these provisions have been successful?

ASSESSMENT

1. **Evaluate Sources** Why does the definition of citizens in the 14th Amendment support jus solis rather than jus sanguinis?
2. **Analyze Information** Under what circumstances may a child born abroad become an American citizen at birth?
3. **Synthesize** What type of actions could result in an individual's involuntary expatriation?
4. **Determine Relevance** What was the significance of the Immigration and Nationality Act of 1965?
5. **Summarize** Why did the Immigration Reform and Control Act of 1986 come down so harshly on employers of illegal aliens?

>> A large gathering of people can reflect the ethnic and racial diversity of the United States today.

9.2 **Have you read George Orwell's classic, *Animal Farm*? Even if you have not, you may have heard its most oft-quoted line: "All animals are created equal, but some animals are more equal than others." You might keep Orwell's comment in mind as you read this material.**

Interactive Flipped Video

>> Objectives

Understand what it means to live in a heterogeneous society.

Summarize the history of race-based discrimination in the United States.

Examine discrimination against women in the past and present.

>> Key Terms

heterogeneous
immigrants
reservations
refugee
assimilation

Diversity and Discrimination

A Changing American Culture

A Heterogeneous Society The term **heterogeneous** is a compound of two Greek words: *hetero,* meaning "other or different," and *genos,* meaning "race, family, or kind." Something that is heterogeneous is composed of dissimilar parts, made up of elements that are unrelated to or unlike one another—in short, something composed of a mix of ingredients. "We the People of the United States" are a heterogeneous lot, and we are becoming more so, year to year.

The population of the United States is predominantly white. It is today and it has been historically. The first census in 1790 reported that there were 3,929,214 people living in this country. More than four out of five were white. African Americans made up the remaining 19 percent of the population counted in that census. As the nation's population grew over the decades, so, too, did the proportion of the American people who were white—until recently.

An Increasingly Diverse Society Today, the ethnic composition of the population is strikingly different from what it was only a generation ago. **Immigrants**—those aliens legally admitted as permanent residents—have arrived in near-record numbers every year since the mid-1960s. Over that period, the nation's African American, Hispanic American, and Asian American populations have grown at rates several times that of the white population. Indeed, the minority population now exceeds the white population in four States: California, Hawaii, New Mexico, and Texas. A look at gender balance in the population reveals that females are more numerous than males. This has been the case for more than half a century.

As a result of these changes in the American population, the United States is more heterogeneous today than ever before. That fact is certain to have a profound effect on the American social, political, and economic landscape on through the twenty-first century.

SYNTHESIZE This section ends with the statement that the nation's increasing heterogeneity will have social, political, and economic effects. Explain how increasing diversity might affect the nation's economy.

Discrimination in America

White Americans have been historically reluctant to yield to nonwhite Americans a full and equal place in the social, economic, and political life of this nation. Over time, the principal targets of that ethnic prejudice have been African Americans, Native Americans, Asian Americans, and Hispanic Americans. The white-male-dominated power structure has also been slow to recognize the claims of women to an equal place in American society.

Slavery and Discrimination Much of what you will read here focuses on discrimination against African Americans. There are three principal reasons for this focus. First, African Americans have been the victims of consistent and deliberate unjust treatment since colonial times. The ancestors of most African Americans came to this country in chains. Over a period of some two hundred years, tens of thousands of Africans were kidnapped, crammed aboard sailing ships, brought to America, and then sold in slave markets. As slaves, they were the legal property of other human beings. They could be bought and sold and forced to do their owners' bidding, however harsh the circumstances.

It took a civil war to end more than two centuries of slavery in this country. The 13th Amendment finally abolished slavery in 1865. Still, the Civil War and the ratification of that amendment did not end widespread racial discrimination in the United States.

Continued Discrimination Against African Americans We can look to the country's population figures for the second reason why discrimination

U.S. Population by Race

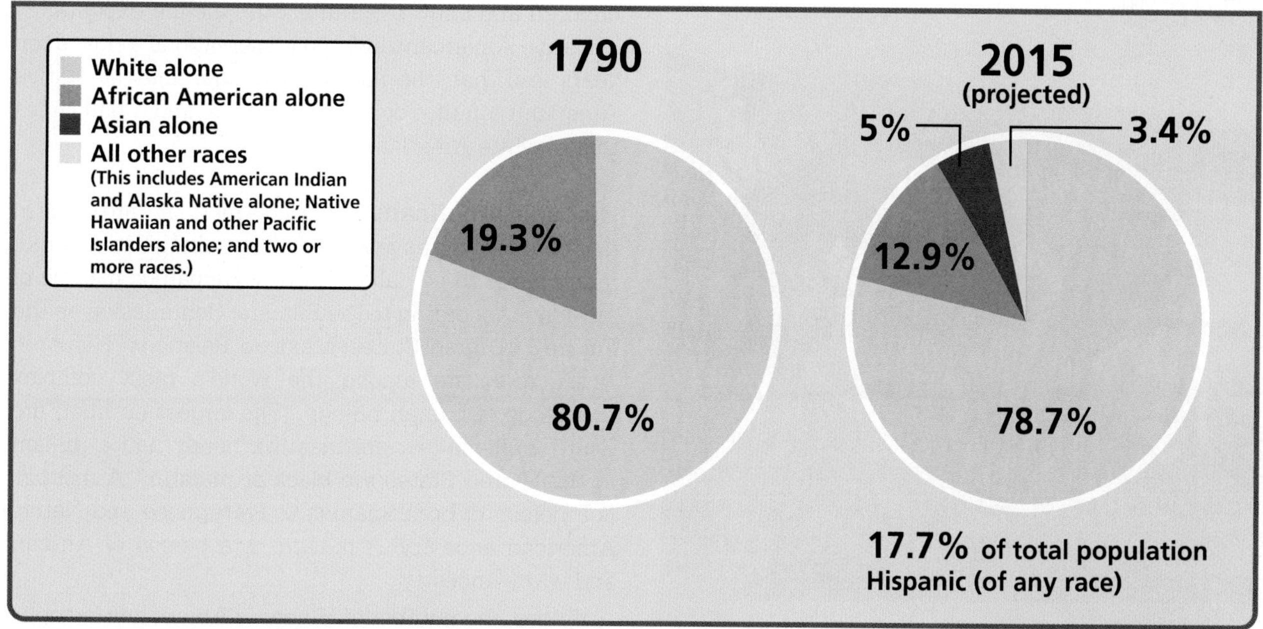

>> The separation of race and Hispanic origin acknowledges that persons of Hispanic origin may be of any race. **Analyze Graphs** How might legislation be linked to this type of Census Bureau data?

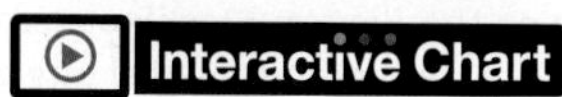

against African Americans receives so much focus. African Americans constitute a huge minority group in the United States. They number nearly 40 million today, around 13 percent of all of the American people.

Finally, most of the gains the nation has made in translating the Constitution's guarantees of equality into a reality for all persons have come out of efforts made by and on behalf of African Americans. Recall that, for example, the struggles of Martin Luther King, Jr., and others resulted in the Civil Rights Act of 1964 and then the Voting Rights Act of 1965.

America is now a thoroughly multiracial society. Still, unlike whites, African Americans live with the consequences of America's history of racial discrimination every day of their lives. Of course, this is not to say that other groups of Americans have not also suffered the effects of discrimination. Clearly, many have.

White Settlers Bring Discrimination White settlers first began to arrive in America in relatively large numbers in the mid-1600s. At the time, millions of Native Americans were living in territory that was to become the United States. By 1900, however, their number had fallen drastically.

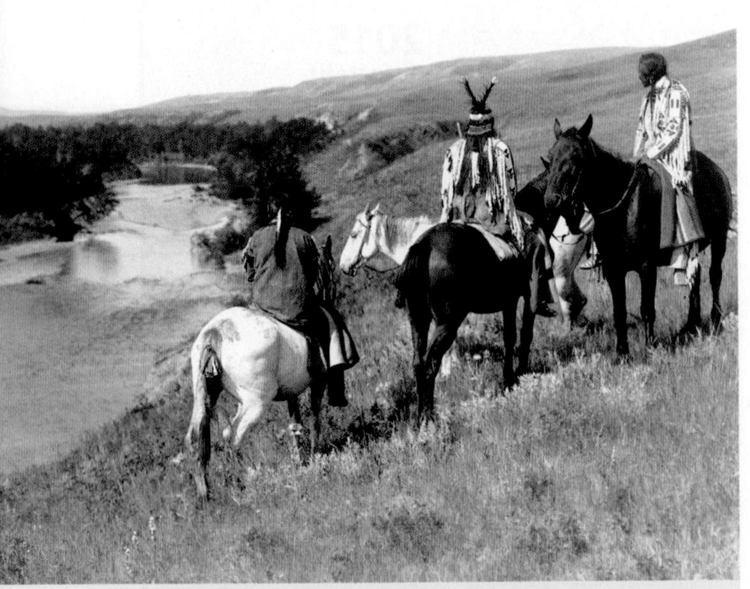

>> Cultural differences between Native Americans, such as the Piegan Blackfeet tribe, and white European immigrants created mutual mistrust, fear, and hatred, and often led to violence.

Diseases brought by white settlers decimated those first Americans. So, too, did the succession of military campaigns that accompanied the westward expansion of the United States. One leading commentator said the following about this expansion:

> 'The only good Indian is a dead Indian' is not simply a hackneyed expression from cowboy movies. It was part of the strategy of westward expansion, as settlers and U.S. troops mercilessly drove the eastern Indians from their ancestral lands to the Great Plains and then took those lands too.
>
> —Thomas E. Patterson, *The American Democracy*

Continued Discrimination Against Native Americans Today, about 5 million Native Americans live in this country (alone or in combination with other races). Nearly a quarter of them live on or near **reservations,** which are public lands set aside by the government for use by Native American tribes.

Like African Americans, Native Americans have been the victims of overwhelming discrimination. The consequences of that bias have been appalling, and they remain evident today. Poverty, joblessness, and alcoholism plague many reservations. The Indian Education Act of 1972 attempted to remedy the cycle of continual poverty by providing financial assistance to local educational agencies for Native American children and adult programs. Still, the life expectancy of Native Americans living on reservations today is ten years less than the national average, and the Native American infant mortality rate is one and a half times that of white Americans.

Hispanic Americans Hispanic Americans are those in this country who have a Spanish-speaking background; many prefer to be called *Latinos*. Hispanics may be of any race. According to the Bilateral Commission on the Future of United States–Mexican Relations, Hispanic Americans "are among the world's most complex groupings of human beings. [The largest number] are white, millions . . . are mestizo, nearly half a million in the United States are black or mulatto." A *mestizo* is a person of both Spanish or Portuguese and Native American ancestry. A *mulatto* is a person of African and white ancestry.

Today, the number of Hispanic Americans exceeds 50 million and they constitute the largest minority group in this country, having surpassed African Americans sometime around the year 2000. They are also the nation's fastest-growing population group.

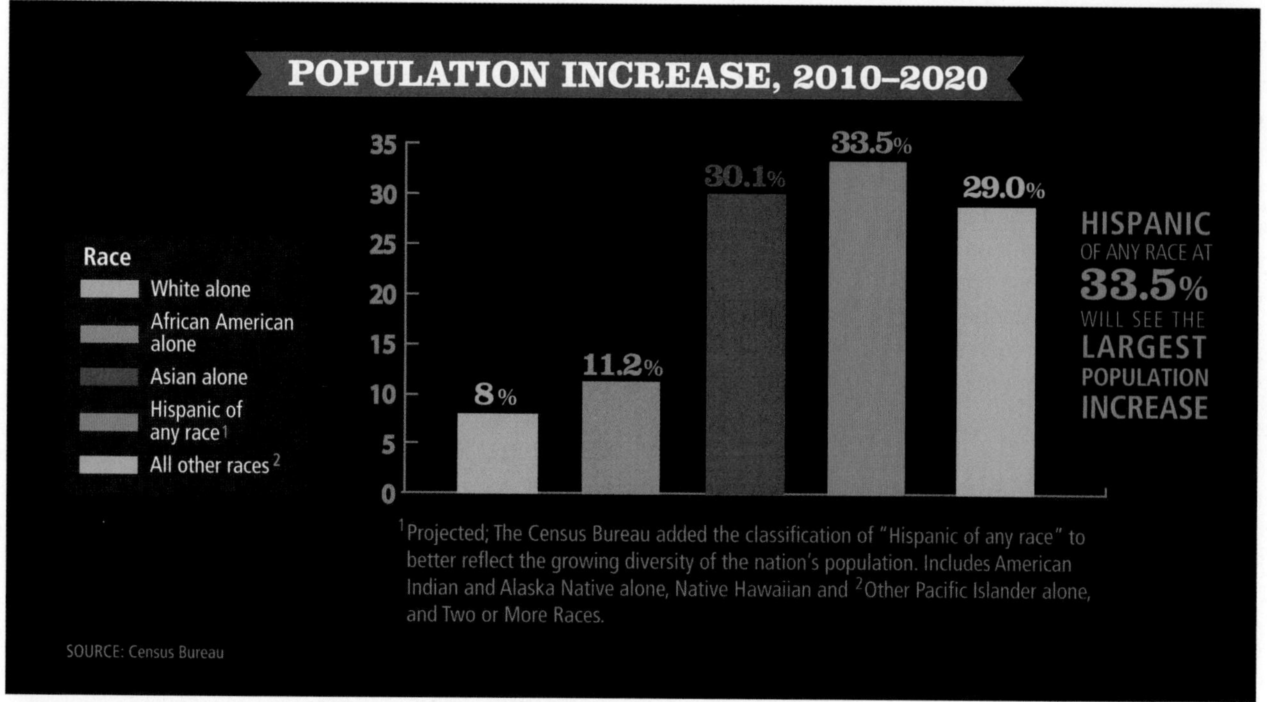

>> Minority populations have grown at a faster rate than the majority population.
Analyze Data What is the rate of growth for Asian Americans? What are the benefits of diversity in a community?

Mexican Americans Well over half of all Hispanics in the U.S., some 32 million persons, were either born in Mexico or trace their ancestry there. Those born in this country of Mexican parents are often called *Chicanos*.

Most of the Mexican American population lives in the States of California, Texas, Arizona, and Illinois, but that population is spreading throughout much of the country. A majority of the residents of such large cities as El Paso and San Antonio in Texas are Hispanic today, and such smaller border cities as Laredo and Brownsville in Texas are now over 90 percent Latino.

Hispanic Americans from Islands *Puerto Ricans* are another large group of Hispanics that have come to the mainland from the island of Puerto Rico. The Puerto Rican population of the United States now approaches five million. Most of them have settled in New York, Florida, and New Jersey.

The Hispanic population also includes some 1.8 million *Cuban Americans*. They are mostly people who fled the Castro dictatorship in Cuba, and their descendants. A majority of them have settled in Miami and elsewhere in South Florida, as well as in California and New Jersey.

Central and South Americans The fourth major subgroup of Hispanic Americans came here from Central and South America, many as refugees. A **refugee** is one who seeks protection (refuge) from war, persecution, or some other danger. Nearly 7 million persons have emigrated to the United States from Central and South American countries over the past 30 years or so; they have arrived in the largest numbers from El Salvador, Guatemala, Colombia, and Honduras. Many have also come from the Dominican Republic, an island nation in the Caribbean.

Discrimination Against Hispanic Americans Discrimination against Hispanic Americans began as soon as the United States began acquiring Mexican territory in the 1840s. Laws were passed that hampered voter participation and taxed Spanish-speaking workers as "foreign miners," even though they were United States citizens. Labor discrimination tactics continued in the form of deportations during tough economic times when white Americans needed jobs held by Hispanic Americans and the practice of hiring undocumented workers was used for the least desirable and most unsafe jobs.

Discrimination outside the workplace has most often resulted from the segregation of many Hispanic Americans from the rest of society and the resulting ignorance about the Latino culture. In the 1940s, for example, the Zoot Suit Riots occurred because white

Americans had no understanding of the fashionable dress for Hispanic Americans at the time. White Americans assumed that men dressed in "zoot suits" (high-waisted, wide-legged pants; long coats with padded shoulders; hats) were criminals, and violence broke out as a result of this mistaken assumption. In recent times, the immigration debates have also fueled discrimination and resulted in an increased number of hate crimes against Hispanic Americans. For many Mexican Americans in particular, the U.S./ Mexico border fence serves as a physical reminder of the anti-immigrant viewpoint that they feel leads to discrimination.

Discrimination Against Asian Americans The story of white America's mistreatment of Asians is a lengthy one, too. Asians have faced discrimination from the first day they arrived. As with all immigrant groups, assimilation into the white-dominated population has been difficult. **Assimilation** is the process by which people of one culture merge into and become part of another.

Chinese laborers were the first Asians to come to the United States in large numbers. They were brought here in the 1850s to 1860s as contract laborers to work in the mines and to build railroads in the West. Many white Americans, both native-born and immigrants, resented the competition of what they called "coolie labor." Their resentments were frequently expressed in acts of violence toward Asians.

>> Women participate in a Diwali festival in New York's Times Square. The "festival of lights" has been an important Hindu celebration of the victory of light over darkness.

Government Actions Against Asian Americans Congress brought Chinese immigration to a near halt with the Chinese Exclusion Act of 1882. Because of this and other governmental actions, only a very small number of Chinese, Japanese, and other Asians were permitted to enter the United States for more than 80 years.

Early in World War II, the Federal Government ordered the evacuation of all persons of Japanese descent from the Pacific Coast. Some 120,000 people, two thirds of them native-born American citizens, were forcibly removed to inland "war relocation camps." Years later, the government conceded that this action had been both unnecessary and unjust.

Diversity Among Asian Americans Congress made dramatic changes in American immigration policies in 1965. Since then, some 11 million Asian immigrants have come to this country, mostly from the Philippines, China, Korea, Vietnam, and India. The term "Asian American" encompasses an ever more diverse population. Asian Americans represent a tremendous variety of languages, religions, and cultures, and many recent immigrants from Asia have little in common with one another.

Today, Asian Americans number some 18 million. Asian Americans now live in every part of the United States. They constitute some 40 percent of the population in Hawaii and more than 10 percent of the population in California. New York City boasts the largest Chinese community outside Asia.

? SUPPORT IDEAS WITH EXAMPLES How has the United States government participated in acts of discrimination? Give examples from the text you have just read to support your answer.

Discrimination Against Women

Unlike the several ethnic groups described thus far, women are not a minority in the United States. They are, in fact, a majority group. Still, traditionally in American law and public policy, women have not enjoyed the same rights as men. Their status was even lower, in many instances, than men who were themselves the target of virulent discrimination. Women have been treated as less than equal in a great many matters—

including, for example, property rights, education, and employment opportunities.

Organized efforts to improve the place of women in American society date from July 19, 1848. On that day, a convention on women's rights met in Seneca Falls, New York, and adopted a set of resolutions that deliberately echoed the words of the Declaration of Independence.

> When, in the course of human events, it becomes necessary for one portion of the family of man to assume among the people of the earth a position different from that which they have hitherto occupied, . . We hold these truths to be self evident: that all men and women are created equal . . .
>
> —Declaration of Sentiments, 1848

Statistical Evidence of Discrimination Those who fought and won the long struggle for women's suffrage believed that, with the vote, women would soon achieve other basic rights. That assumption proved false.

Although almost 51 percent of the population is now female, women still hold only a minor fraction of the nation's top public offices. Even today, women hold less than 20 percent of the seats in Congress and less than 25 percent of the seats in the 50 State legislatures. Only 5 of the 50 State governors today are female. While women have made strides in the fields of medicine and law, they still comprise less than 40 percent of the nation's doctors and lawyers.

In the federal judiciary system, only around 30 percent of district court, or trial court, judges are female. Women are hugely underrepresented at the upper levels of corporate management and even more so in the engineering field, where they make up less than 10 percent of the workforce. At the same time, women are overrepresented in low-paying clerical and service occupations. The Bureau of Labor Statistics reports that 96 percent of all secretaries today are women; so too are 95 percent of childcare workers, 91 percent of registered nurses, 90 percent of bookkeepers and auditing clerks, and 91 percent of dieticians and nutritionists.

'Another day, another eighty cents.'

>> Studies have shown that women earn less than 80 cents for every dollar earned by men. **Analyze Political Cartoons** What does the 80 cents refer to? What factors may a person's pay be based on?

Unequal Pay It is illegal to pay women less than men for the same work. The Equal Pay Act of 1963 requires employers to pay men and women the same wages if they perform the same jobs in the same establishment under the same working conditions. The Civil Rights Act of 1964 also prohibits job discrimination based on sex. Yet, more than 45 years after

>> The Lily Ledbetter Fair Pay Act of 2009 was the first act signed by President Barack Obama. Once a supervisor at Goodyear, Ledbetter later became a women's equality activist.

Interactive Gallery

Congress passed those laws, working women earn, on the average, less than 80 cents for every dollar earned by working men.

Women earn less than men for a number of reasons—including the fact that the male workforce is, overall, better educated and has more job experience than the female workforce. (Note that these factors themselves can often be traced to discrimination.) In addition, some blame the so-called "Mommy track," in which women put their careers on hold to have children or work reduced hours to juggle child-care responsibilities. Others claim that a "glass ceiling" of discrimination in the corporate world and elsewhere, invisible but impenetrable, prevents women from rising to their full potential.

Movement Toward Fair Pay Efforts on behalf of equal rights for women have gained significant ground in recent years. In 2009, for example, Congress amended the Civil Rights Act of 1964, which outlawed pay discrimination on the basis of gender, with the Lilly Ledbetter Fair Pay Act. The original provision stipulated a 180-day "window" after the start of employment to file a discrimination law suit.

But what if a woman did not know she was being discriminated against for some time, maybe years? Perhaps, as was the case with Lilly Ledbetter, she simply did not immediately realize how much her male counterparts were being paid. The Lilly Ledbetter Act instructs that the statute of limitations for filing a suit be reset with each new pay period. In other words, women can now file a lawsuit whenever they learn of discrimination, rather than being restricted to the first 180 days of a new job.

? GENERATE EXPLANATIONS Those who fought for women's suffrage thought that by gaining the right to vote, women could then achieve other basic rights. Why did this assumption proved false?

ASSESSMENT

1. **Make Generalizations** What do the four States in which the minority population now exceeds the majority population have in common?
2. **Connect** Why might other minority groups look to African Americans for guidance in developing strategies for overcoming discrimination?
3. **Explain** What does it mean to live in a heterogeneous society?
4. **Compare** What do Hispanic Americans and Asian Americans have in common as minority groups in the United States?
5. **Explain** Explain why the Lilly Ledbetter Fair Pay Act was necessary and indicates an important shift toward equal pay for women.

9.3 The huge bronze statue of *Freedom* has stood atop the nation's Capitol in Washington, D.C., for about 150 years now. That bold figure is meant to symbolize the basic ideas upon which the United States exists—the concepts of individual liberty, of self-government, and of equal rights for all.

>> Although the statue of *Freedom* usually stands atop the Dome of the United States Capitol, it is periodically removed for restoration.

Interactive Flipped Video

Equality Before the Law

Equal Protection and Individual Rights

The irony is that records recently unearthed by the Architect of the Capitol show that at least 400 slaves worked on the construction of the Capitol from 1792 to its opening in 1800; and that those slaves cast the huge sculpture of *Freedom,* and even hoisted it atop the new building. Those old documents also record payments to several local slave owners—for example, "To Joseph Forest, for the hire of the Negro Charles." The owners were paid $5 a month for each slave who worked on the project.

The equality of all persons, proclaimed so boldly in the Declaration of Independence, is not set out in so many words in the Constitution. Still, that concept pervades the document.

The closest approach to a literal statement of equality is found in the 14th Amendment's **Equal Protection** Clause. It declares that "No State shall . . . deny to any person within its jurisdiction the equal protection of the laws."

Those words, added to the Constitution in 1868, were originally meant to benefit newly freed slaves. Over time, they have come to mean that the States (and their local governments) cannot draw

>> Objectives

Explain the importance of the Equal Protection Clause in safeguarding individual rights.

Describe the history of segregation in America.

Examine how classification by gender relates to discrimination.

>> Key Terms

equal protection
discriminate
rational basis test
strict scrutiny test
segregation
Jim Crow
separate-but-equal doctrine
integration
de jure
de facto
Earl Warren
Joseph P. Bradley
William J. Brennan

unreasonable distinctions between any classes of persons. The Supreme Court has often held that the 5th Amendment's Due Process Clause puts the same restrictions on the Federal Government.

Government Regulation of Individual Liberty Government must have the power to classify, to draw distinctions between persons and groups. Otherwise, it could not possibly regulate human behavior. That is to say, government must be able to **discriminate**—and it does. For example, those who rob banks fall into a special class, and they receive special treatment by government. Clearly, that sort of discrimination is reasonable.

Government may not discriminate *unreasonably,* however. Every State taxes the sale of cigarettes, and so taxes smokers but not nonsmokers. No State can tax only blonde smokers, however, or only male smokers.

Over time, the Supreme Court has rejected many equal protection challenges to a wide variety of actions by government. More often than not, however, the Supreme Court has found that what those governments have done is, in fact, constitutional.

The Reasoning Behind the Law The Supreme Court most often decides equal protection cases by applying a standard known as the **rational basis test.** This test asks: Does the classification in question bear a reasonable relationship to the achievement of some proper governmental purpose?

A California case, *Michael M.* v. *Superior Court,* 1981, illustrates that test. California law says that a man who has sexual relations with a girl under 18 to whom he is not married can be prosecuted for statutory rape. However, the girl cannot be charged with that crime, even if she is a willing partner. The Court found the law to bear a reasonable relationship to a proper public policy goal: preventing teenage pregnancies.

A Compelling Governmental Interest The Court imposes a higher standard in some equal protection cases, however. This is especially true when a case deals with (1) such "fundamental rights" as the right to vote, the right to travel between the States, or 1st Amendment rights; or (2) such "suspect classifications" as those based on race, sex, or national origin.

In these instances, the Court has said that a law must meet a higher standard than the rational basis test: the **strict scrutiny test.** A State must be able to show that some "compelling governmental interest" justifies the distinctions it has drawn between classes of people. Thus, in an alimony case, *Orr* v. *Orr,* 1979, an Alabama law that made women but not men eligible for alimony was held unconstitutional, as a denial of equal protection—because the law's distinction between men and women did not serve any compelling governmental interest.

>> The Federal Government has not banned smoking in all public buildings, but smoking is regulated in at least certain regions of 49 of the 50 States. Most courts have upheld these regulations.

CONTRAST How does the rational basis test for equal protection differ from the strict scrutiny test?

A History of Segregation

Beginning in the late 1800s, nearly half the States—including some outside the South—passed racial segregation laws. Used in this context, **segregation** refers to the separation of one group from another on the basis of race. Most of those statutes were **Jim Crow** laws—laws aimed at African Americans in particular. Some were also drawn to affect Mexican Americans, Asian Americans, and Native Americans. They regularly required segregation by race in the use of both public and private facilities: schools, parks and playgrounds, hotels and restaurants, streetcars and railroads, public drinking fountains, restrooms, and cemeteries. Many also prohibited interracial marriages.

Plessy* v. *Ferguson The Supreme Court provided a constitutional basis for Jim Crow laws by creating the **separate-but-equal doctrine** in 1896. In *Plessy*

v. *Ferguson,* the Court upheld a Louisiana law that required segregation in railroad coaches. It ruled that the law did not violate the Equal Protection Clause because the *separate* seating provided for African Americans was *equal* to the seating provided for whites.

The doctrine was soon extended to other fields. And it stood, largely unchallenged, for nearly 60 years.

Challenges to the Separate-but-Equal Doctrine The Supreme Court first began to chip away at the separate-but-equal doctrine in *Missouri ex rel. Gaines* v. *Canada* in 1938. Lloyd Gaines, an African American, was denied admission to the law school at the all-white University of Missouri. Gaines was fully qualified for admission—except for his race. The State did not have a separate law school for African Americans. However, it did offer to pay his tuition at a public law school in any of the four neighboring States, which did not discriminate by race. Gaines, however, insisted on a legal education in his home State.

The Court held that the separate-but-equal doctrine left Missouri with two choices: admit Gaines to the State's one law school or establish a separate-but-equal school for him. The State gave in. Gaines was admitted to the university's law school.

Over the next several years, the Court began to insist on equality of separate facilities. Thus, in 1950 the Court decided two major cases in line with its holding in *Gaines*: *Sweatt* v. *Painter* and *McLaurin* v. *Oklahoma.* Both cases involved African American university students for whom a State had provided separate educational facilities. The Court found that, in both instances, those separate facilities were, in fact, far from equal. Still, in neither of these cases did the Court re-examine the validity of the separate-but-equal doctrine.

Brown* v. *Board of Education Finally, in 1954, the Court reversed *Plessy* v. *Ferguson.* In *Brown* v. *Board of Education of Topeka,* it struck down the laws of Kansas, Delaware, South Carolina, and Virginia that allowed or required separate public schools for white and African American students. Unanimously, the Court held segregation by race in public education to be invalid.

> Does segregation of children in public schools solely on the basis of race, even though the physical facilities and other 'tangible' factors may be equal, deprive the children of the minority group of equal educational opportunities? We believe that it does. . . . To separate them from others of similar age and qualifications solely because of their race generates a feeling of inferiority as to their status in the community that may affect their hearts and minds in a way unlikely ever to be undone. . . . Separate educational facilities are inherently unequal.
>
> —Chief Justice Earl Warren

>> The Supreme Court ruling that segregation violated the 14th Amendment of the U.S. Constitution eventually, if painfully, led to integrated classrooms.

Interactive Timeline

In 1955 the Court directed the States to make "a prompt and reasonable start" to end segregation and to accomplish that goal "with all deliberate speed."

A "reasonable start" was made in Baltimore, Louisville, St. Louis, and elsewhere. In most of the Deep South, however, massive resistance soon developed. State legislatures passed laws, and school boards worked to block **integration**—the process of desegregation, of bringing a previously segregated group into the mainstream of society. Most of those efforts were clearly unconstitutional, but challenging them in court proved both costly and slow.

The pace of desegregation quickened after Congress passed the Civil Rights Act of 1964. That act forbids the use of federal funds to aid any State or local activity in which racial segregation is practiced. The statute also directed the Justice Department to file suits to spur desegregation efforts.

The Supreme Court hastened the process in 1969. In a case from Mississippi, *Alexander* v. *Holmes County Board of Education,* it ruled that, after 15 years, the time for "all deliberate speed" had ended. Said a unanimous Court: "[C]ontinued operation of segregated schools under a standard of allowing 'all deliberate speed' . . . is no longer constitutionally permissible."

Segregation by Neighborhood By the fall of 1970, school systems characterized by **de jure** segregation—segregation authorized by law—had been abolished. That is not to say that desegregation had been fully accomplished, however—far from it. Some States, several school districts, and many parents and private groups sought to avoid integrated schools through established, or, often, newly created private schools.

Many recent integration controversies have arisen in places where the schools have never been segregated by law. They have occurred, instead, in communities in which de facto segregation has long been present, and continues. **De facto** segregation is segregation that exists in fact, even if no law requires it. Housing patterns have most often been its major cause. The concentration of African Americans in certain sections of cities inevitably led to local school systems in which the student bodies of some schools are largely African American. That condition is quite apparent in many northern as well as southern communities today.

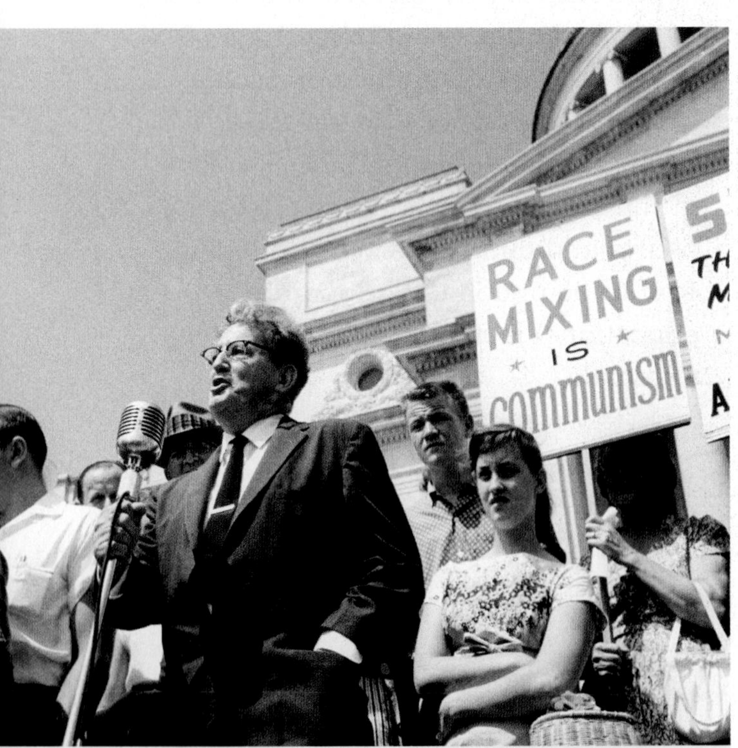

>> Some protestors in Little Rock, Arkansas, equated racial integration with class integration and warned that school integration would lead to a classless, or communist, society.

Efforts to desegregate those school systems have taken several forms over recent decades. Thus, for example, school district lines have been redrawn and the busing of students out of racially segregated neighborhoods has been tried. Those efforts have brought strong protests in many places and violence in some of them.

The Court first sanctioned busing in a North Carolina case, *Swann* v. *Charlotte-Mecklenburg Board of Education,* 1971. There it held that: "Desegregation plans cannot be limited to the walk-in school." Busing has been used since then to increase the racial mix in many school districts across the country—in some by court order, in others voluntarily.

In recent years, a growing number of school systems have turned to socioeconomic status—in particular, to income rather than race—in assigning students to schools within the district. That is, they have tried to promote schools with economically diverse student bodies. The results appear to be promising, both in terms of maintaining integrated schools and in improving the performance of disadvantaged students.

Other Types of Discrimination Public schools have not been fully integrated. But legally enforced racial segregation and discrimination against people based on race in all other areas of life has been eliminated. In the process, many State and local laws have either been repealed or been struck down by the courts.

The Supreme Court took a leading role in that process—holding in a number of cases that segregation by race is unconstitutional in other areas as well. Thus, it has held that the 14th Amendment's Equal Protection Clause forbids segregation in public swimming pools and all other public recreational facilities, *Baltimore* v. *Dawson,* 1955; local transportation, *Gayle* v. *Browder,* 1956, stemming from Dr. Martin Luther King, Jr.'s Montgomery, Alabama, bus boycott; and State prisons and local jails, *Lee* v. *Washington,* 1968. The High Court struck down all State miscegenation laws (statutes forbidding interracial marriages) in *Loving* v. *Virginia,* 1967.

While deciding cases that struck down segregation, the Court also considered the question of what constitutes a protected class. In *Hernandez* v. *Texas* (1954), the Court ruled that African Americans are not the only ethnic group to be protected by the 14th Amendment: Mexican Americans are protected, too, and must be allowed to serve on juries. This case paved the way for the Court to extend equal protection to other racial and ethnic groups that had historically been subjected to legal discrimination, such as Native Americans, Asian Americans, and members of religious groups.

IDENTIFY CENTRAL ISSUES Why did it become a problem when the Supreme Court ruled that school segregation must be ended "with all deliberate speed"?

>> Cadets celebrate graduation at the U.S. Military Academy at West Point. Established in 1802, the school first admitted women in 1976. In 2012, about 15 percent of entering freshmen were women.

Gender, Sexual Orientation, and Equality

The Constitution speaks of the civil rights of "the people," "persons," and "citizens." Nowhere does it make its guarantees only to "men" or separately to "women." Its only reference to gender is in the 19th Amendment, which forbids denial of the right to vote "on account of sex." Gender has long been used as a basis of classification in the law, however. That practice reflected society's long-held view of the "proper" role of women. Most often, laws that treated men and women differently were intended to protect "the weaker sex." Over the years, the Court read that view into the 14th Amendment.

Challenging Sex Discrimination In the first case to challenge sex discrimination, *Bradwell* v. *Illinois,* 1873, the Court upheld a State law barring women from the practice of law. In that case, Justice **Joseph P. Bradley** wrote the following as part of a concurring opinion:

> The civil law, as well as nature herself, has always recognized a wide difference in the respective spheres and destinies of man and woman. Man is, or should be, woman's protector and defender. The natural and proper timidity and delicacy which belongs to the female sex evidently unfits it for many of the occupations of civil life.
>
> —Concurring Opinion

Even as late as 1961, in *Hoyt* v. *Florida,* the Court could find no constitutional fault with a law that required men to serve on juries, but gave women the choice of serving or not.

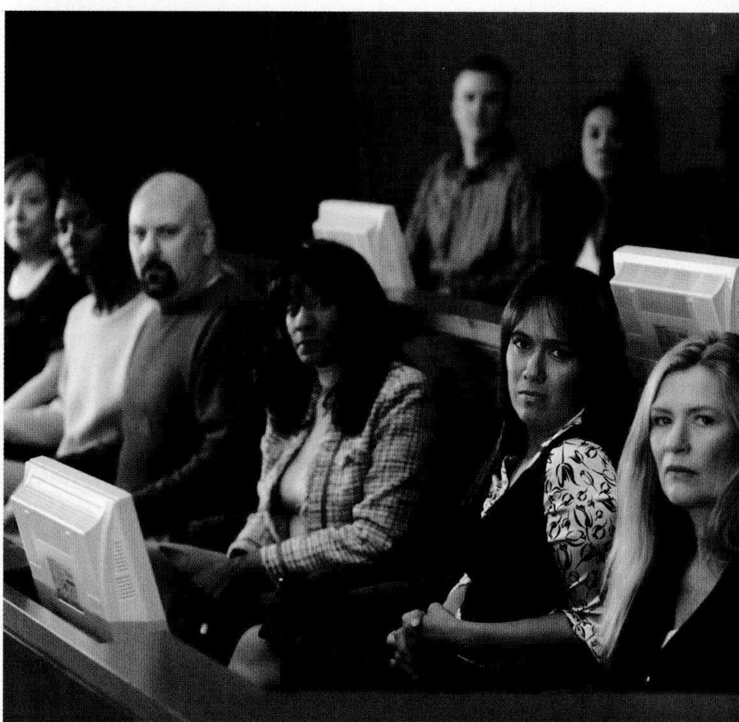

>> In 1975, the Supreme Court ruled that jury pools without women violated defendants' rights to be judged by a jury of their peers. Both men and women have served on juries since that ruling.

A Closer Look at Sex Discrimination Matters are far different today. The Court now takes a very close look at cases involving claims of sex discrimination. It first did so in *Reed* v. *Reed,* 1971; there, it struck down an Idaho law that gave fathers preference over mothers in the administration of their children's estates.

Since then, the Supreme Court has found a number of sex-based distinctions to be unconstitutional. In *Taylor* v. *Louisiana,* 1975, it held that the 14th Amendment's Equal Protection Clause forbids the States to exclude women from jury service. Among other examples of that line of cases, it struck down an Oklahoma law that prohibited the sale of beer to males under 21 and to females under 18, *Craig* v. *Boren,* 1976. And the Court found the practice of refusing to admit women to the rigorous citizen-soldier program offered by a public institution, the Virginia Military Institute, to be constitutionally unacceptable, *United States* v. *Virginia,* 1996.

The Court's changed attitude in cases involving sex-based discrimination was stated in the majority opinion in *Frontiero* v. *Richardson*, written by Justice **William Brennan** in 1973.

Not all sex-based distinctions are unconstitutional, however. The Court has upheld a Florida law that gives an extra property tax exemption to widows, but not to widowers, *Kahn* v. *Shevin,* 1974; an Alabama law forbidding women to serve as prison guards in all-male penitentiaries, *Dothard* v. *Rawlinson,* 1977; and the federal selective service law that requires only men to register for the draft and excludes women from any future draft, *Rostker* v. *Goldberg,* 1981.

In effect, these cases say this: Classification by gender is not in and of itself unconstitutional. However, laws that treat men and women differently will be overturned by the courts unless (1) they are intended to serve an "important governmental objective" and (2) they are "substantially related" to achieving that goal.

Discrimination Based on Sexual Orientation The 1970s brought change for the gay and lesbian rights movements in the United States. In 1971, a gay couple from Minnesota tried to get married. The State Supreme Court ruled that the Constitution does not protect "a fundamental right" for marriage between same-sex couples (a decision upheld by the Supreme Court), bringing the matter of gay marriage into sharper focus.

The issue continued to simmer, and by the 1990s, public policy seemed to be moving in contradictory directions. Many States passed laws and constitutional amendments defining marriage as the union of a man and a woman, and in 1996, the Federal Government implemented the Defense of Marriage Act. At the same time, a few States began making moves in the other direction. The Hawaii Supreme Court, for example, ruled that a ban on gay marriage violated the State's constitution.

Supreme Court Decisions on Gender Discrimination

CASE	YEAR	DECISION
Hoyt v. *Florida*	1961	States may make jury service optional for women.
Reed v. *Reed*	1971	States may not choose the executor of an estate based solely on gender.
Frontiero v. *Richardson*	1973	The Federal Government may not deny benefits to the husband of a female soldier.
Kahn v. *Shevin*	1974	States may grant a property tax exemption only to widows, and not to widowers, because women as a class earn less than men.
Dothard v. *Rawlinson*	1977	States may not discriminate against women who apply for jobs in law enforcement.
United States v. *Virginia*	1996	The Virginia Military Institute must admit women as well as men. An alternate, segregated school for women would not offer the same educational opportunities.

>> Since 1971, the Supreme Court has ruled many cases based on sex-based distinctions unconstitutional. **Analyze Charts** What additional issue did the Court rule on in *United States* v. *Virginia*?

During the late 1990s and early 2000s, the number of States that allowed gay marriage continued to grow. Then, in 2013, the Supreme Court struck down a key provision of the 1996 Defense of Marriage Act (*United States* v. *Windsor*). In its sharply divided 5–4 decision, the Court held that the section of the law that denied federal benefits to legally married gay and lesbian couples was invalid, stating that it "violates basic due process and equal protection principles."

Legal challenges to State laws continued to mount, and finally, in an historic 5–4 decision in 2015, the Court struck down all State bans on same-sex marriage, *Obergefell* v. *Hodges*. The decision means that States must allow same-sex couples to marry and also must recognize same-sex marriages from other States.

? INTERPRET How is the Supreme Court's decision regarding the Defense of Marriage Act an example of checks and balances between the legislative and judicial branches of government?

ASSESSMENT

1. **Check Understanding** Why did Congress add the Equal Protection Clause to the Constitution, as part of the 14th Amendment, after the Civil War? How does the Equal Protection Clause continue to affect Americans today and in the future?
2. **Interpret** In *Brown* v. *Board of Education*, why did the Court require desegregation to occur "with all deliberate speed"?
3. **Compare and Contrast** Compare and contrast *de jure* and *de facto* segregation.
4. **Apply Concepts** What type of segregation can result from differences in socioeconomic status?
5. **Make Generalizations** How might Justice Joseph Bradley's argument that a law barring women from practicing law could be upheld because of women's "timidity and delicacy" be regarded as an application of the rational basis test? How might it be regarded as unreasonable?

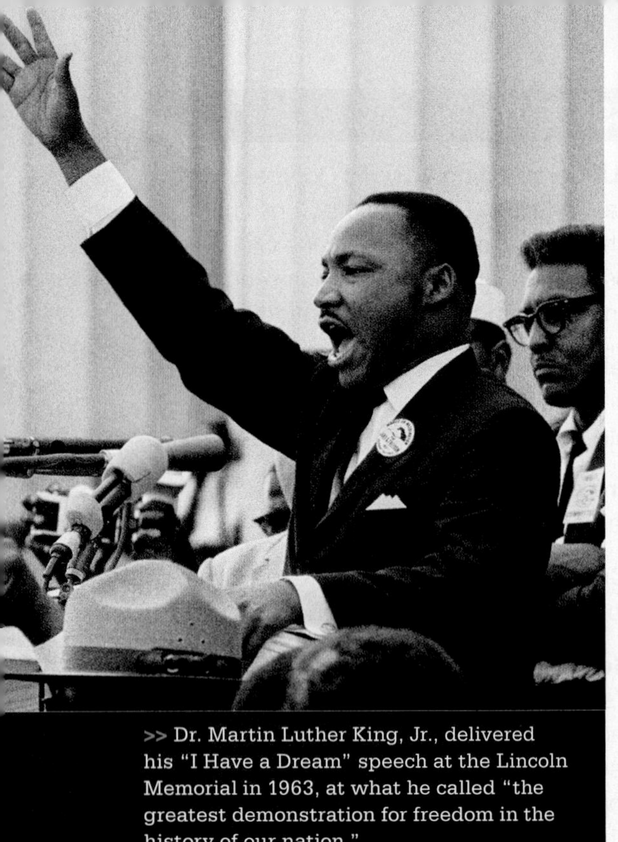

>> Dr. Martin Luther King, Jr., delivered his "I Have a Dream" speech at the Lincoln Memorial in 1963, at what he called "the greatest demonstration for freedom in the history of our nation."

9.4

Those who, for one reason or another, oppose the enactment of civil rights legislation often rely on this observation: "You can't legislate morality." That is, racism, sexism, and other forms of discrimination will not be eliminated by simply passing a law.

Interactive Flipped Video

>> Objectives

Outline the history of civil rights legislation from Reconstruction to today.

Explore the issues surrounding affirmative action.

>> Key Terms

affirmative action
Sandra Day O'Connor
Martin Luther King, Jr.
quota
reverse discrimination

Federal Civil Rights Laws

The History of Civil Rights Laws

The Reverend Dr. **Martin Luther King, Jr.**, responded to that contention this way: "Judicial decrees," he said, "may not change the heart, but they can restrain the heartless." Clearly, Congress has agreed with Dr. King—as it has enacted a number of civil rights laws over the past 40 years or so.

From the 1870s to the late 1950s, Congress did not pass a single piece of meaningful civil rights legislation. Several factors contributed to that fact. For example, through that period, the nation's predominantly white population was generally unaware of or little concerned with the plight of African Americans, Native Americans, or other nonwhites in this country. Also, southern white Democrats, bolstered by such devices as the seniority system and the filibuster, held many of the most strategic posts in Congress. In addition, during much of this period, Congress was focused on economic issues. For example, in 1944 Congress passed the Serviceman's Readjustment Act (commonly known as the GI Bill of Rights), which provided educational tuition, unemployment benefits, federal assistance with home loans, and job counseling for returning veterans.

Congress' civil rights logjam was finally broken in 1957, largely as a result of the pressures brought to bear by the civil rights movement led by Dr. King. Beginning in that year, Congress passed a number of civil rights laws—notably, the Civil Rights Acts of 1957, 1960, 1964, and 1968; the Voting Rights Acts of 1965, 1970, 1975, 1982, and 2006; and Title IX in the Education Amendments of 1972.

The Civil Rights Act of 1964 The 1964 law is the most far-reaching of those statutes. It was passed after the longest debate in Senate history (83 days), and only after the Senate invoked cloture (limited debate) to kill a filibuster. Beyond its voting rights provisions, the 1964 law outlaws discrimination in a number of areas. With its several later amendments, the law had three major sections. The law

- provides that no person may be denied access to or refused service in various "public accommodations"—hotels, motels, restaurants, theaters, and the like—because of race, color, religion, national origin, or physical disability (Title II);
- prohibits discrimination against any person on grounds of race, color, religion, national origin, sex, or physical disability in any program that receives any federal funding (Title VI);
- forbids both employers and labor unions to discriminate against any person on grounds of race, color, religion, sex, physical disability, or age in job-related matters (Title VII).

The Civil Rights Act of 1968 The Civil Rights Act of 1968 is often called the Open Housing Act. With minor exceptions, it forbids anyone to refuse to sell or rent a dwelling to any person on grounds of race, color, religion, national origin, sex, or disability. It also forbids refusal to sell or rent to a family with children.

At first, the burden of enforcing the law fell on those persons who claimed to be victims of housing discrimination; they could seek damages from alleged offenders. Congress finally strengthened the law in 1988, to allow the Justice Department to bring criminal charges against those who violate its terms. Still, housing remains among the most segregated areas of American life today.

Title IX In Title IX of the Education Amendments of 1972, Congress added a key gender-based guarantee to the provisions of the Civil Rights Act of 1964. Title IX forbids discrimination on the basis of gender "in any education program or activity receiving Federal financial assistance." The statute intends to ensure that women receive equal treatment in all aspects of education. Its provisions apply to all schools, public and private, that receive federal funds, and nearly all of them do.

Since its passage, Title IX has had its most telling effect on school athletics programs, especially at the college level, by requiring roughly equal funding and opportunities for women and men. The law has been in effect for nearly four decades now; still, it continues to generate controversy.

? COMPARE AND CONTRAST Compare and contrast the Civil Rights Acts of 1964 and 1968. Which act provided broader protection against discrimination? Why?

Government Policies on Affirmative Action

These civil rights statutes all come down to this: Discriminatory practices based on such factors as race, color, national origin, sex, or disability are illegal. But what about the effects of *past* discrimination? Consider an African American who, for no reason of his or her own making, did not get a decent education and so today cannot get a decent job. Of what real help to that

>> Civil rights activist Rosa Parks sits in the front of a Montgomery, Alabama, bus in 1956, after the Supreme Court ruled that segregation on city buses was illegal.

person are all of those laws that make illegal today what was done years ago?

So far, the Federal Government's chief answer to this troubling question has been a policy of **affirmative action.** That approach requires that most employers take positive steps (affirmative action) to remedy the effects of past discriminations. The policy applies to all agencies of the Federal Government, States and their local governments, and private employers who sell goods or services to any agency of the Federal Government. The Federal Government began to demand the adoption of affirmative action programs in 1965.

To illustrate the policy, take the case of a company that does business with the Federal Government. It must adopt an affirmative action plan designed to make its workforce reflect the general makeup of the population in its locale. The plan must include steps to correct or prevent inequalities in such matters as pay, promotions, and fringe benefits.

For many employers this has meant that they must hire and/or promote more workers with minority backgrounds and more females. The share of a group necessary to satisfy a particular affirmative action requirement—say, the number of females in a company's workforce or the number of African Americans in a school's student body—is often called a **quota.**

Is Affirmative Action Reverse Discrimination? Affirmative action policies remain highly controversial today. This is principally because those policies necessarily involve race-based and/or gender-based classifications. Critics argue that affirmative action programs amount to **reverse discrimination,** or discrimination against the majority group. Affirmative action demands that preference be given to females and/or nonwhites solely on the basis of sex or race. Critics say that the Constitution requires that all public policies be "color blind."

The opponents of affirmative action have attacked the policy at the State and local levels in several places in recent years. Most often, they have relied primarily on the reverse discrimination argument.

In 1996, California's voters gave overwhelming approval to a measure that eliminated nearly all affirmative action programs conducted by public agencies in that State. Since then, six other States have adopted constitutional amendments or passed statutes banning affirmative action programs, and Florida did so through executive action by the governor.

The First Major Affirmative Action Case The Supreme Court decided its first major affirmative action case, *Regents of the University of California* v. *Bakke,* in 1978. Allan Bakke, a white male, had been denied admission to the university's medical school at Davis. The school had set aside 16 of the 100 seats in each

States that Have Banned Affirmative Action

STATE	YEAR OF BAN	STATE ACTION
Oklahoma	2012	Voters: referendum affecting public education, state employment, state contracting.
New Hampshire	2011	Legislature: law affecting public education and state agencies.
Arizona	2010	Voters: proposition affecting public education, state jobs, state contracting.
Nebraska	2008	Voters: initiative affecting state colleges and universities.
Michigan	2006	Voters: initiative affecting state universities.
Florida	1999	Governor: executive order affecting public education, state jobs, state contracting.
Washington	1998	Legislature: law affecting public education, state jobs, state contracting.
California	1996	Legislature: law affecting public education, state jobs, state contracting.

>> Affirmative action programs have been banned in some States, but remain in place in some form in most. **Analyze Charts** In what institutions has affirmative action been banned?

year's entering class for nonwhite students. He sued the university, charging it with reverse discrimination and, so, a violation of the Equal Protection Clause. By a 5–4 majority, the Court held that Bakke had been denied equal protection and should be admitted to the medical school.

A differently composed 5–4 majority made the more far-reaching ruling in the case, however. Although the Constitution does not allow race to be used as the *only* factor in the making of affirmative action decisions, that majority of the justices held that both the Constitution and the 1964 Civil Rights Act do allow its use as one among several factors in such situations.

Affirmative Action Cases Begin to Receive Strict Scrutiny The Supreme Court has decided several affirmative action cases since *Bakke.* In some of them it has upheld quotas, especially in such industries as construction, where longstanding discrimination was involved. The High Court has also held, however, that quotas can be used in only the most extreme situations. Thus, the Court held in *Richmond* v. *Croson,* 1989, that the city of Richmond, Virginia, had not shown that its minority set-aside policy was justified by a record of past discrimination by the city.

This approach has become steadily more apparent in recent affirmative action decisions. In 1995, for example, the Court's decision in *Adarand Constructors* v. *Pena* marked a major departure from its previous rulings in such cases. *Adarand* arose when a white-owned Colorado company, Adarand Constructors, Inc., challenged a federal affirmative action policy. Under that policy, the government gave bonuses to highway contractors if ten percent or more of their construction work was subcontracted to "socially and economically disadvantaged" businesses, including those owned by racial minorities.

Until *Adarand,* the Court had regularly upheld affirmative action laws, regulations, and programs as mild but necessary restraints on behavior. In this case, however, the Court held that henceforth all affirmative action cases will be reviewed under strict scrutiny—that is, affirmative action programs will be upheld only if it can be shown that they serve some "compelling government interest." "The Constitution protects persons, not groups," wrote Justice Sandra Day O'Connor in the majority opinion. "Whenever the government treats any person unequally because of his or her race, that person has suffered an injury" covered by "the Constitution's guarantee of equal treatment." Affirmative action programs must be "narrowly tailored" to overcome specific cases of discrimination.

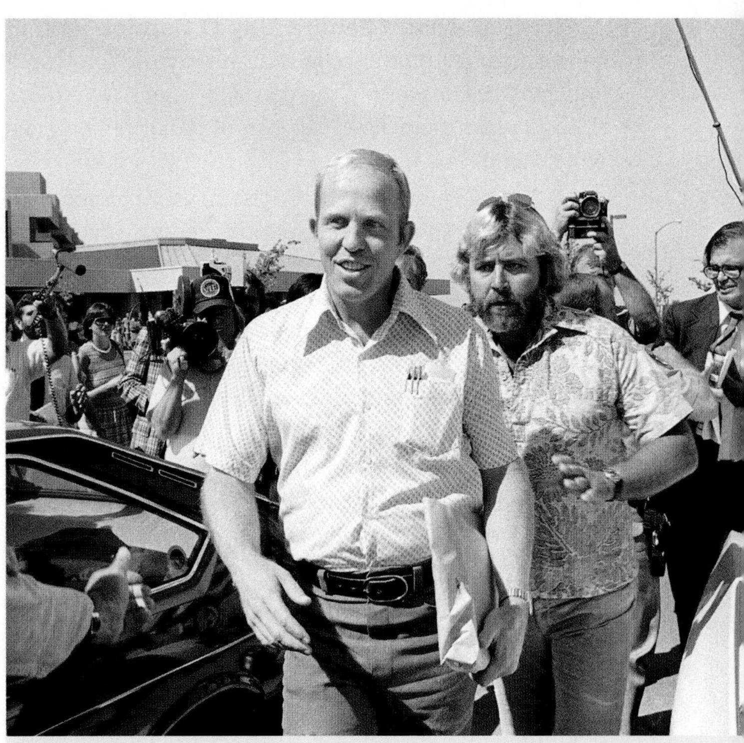

>> The Supreme Court ruling in favor of Allan Bakke (center) did not answer the question of how society can overcome the effects of discrimination and level the playing field for minorities.

Affirmative Action Regarded as a Temporary Measure As controversy continued to rage over the place of affirmative action in the twenty-first century, the Court's ruling in two Michigan cases signaled a continuation of the move away from this policy. The resolution of two cases, *Gratz* v. *Bollinger* and *Grutter* v. *Bollinger,* 2003, marked the High Court's most important statement on affirmative action since its decision in *Bakke* in 1978.

The cases involved the admissions policies of the University of Michigan. Jennifer Gratz applied for admission to the University as a freshman in 1997, and Barbara Grutter sought to enter the University's law school that same year. Both women are white, and both were rejected in favor of minority applicants with lower grade point averages and lower entry test scores. Both women sued the university. After losing in the lower courts, each appealed to the Supreme Court.

In deciding the cases, a majority of the Court found that the State of Michigan (and all the States) has a compelling interest in the diversity of the student bodies of its public educational institutions. That compelling interest justifies the narrowly tailored use of race as one factor in the student admissions policies of those institutions.

However, Justice **Sandra Day O'Connor**, writing for the majority, predicted that affirmative action would become unnecessary in the coming years. "We expect that 25 years from now, the use of racial preferences will no longer be necessary."

A 2007 Supreme Court decision underscored this trend away from affirmative action. *Parents Involved* v. *Seattle School District* and *Meredith* v. *Jefferson County Board of Education* both centered on this question: To what extent can public school officials use race as a factor in assigning students to particular schools as they seek to maintain racially integrated student bodies?

The Court split 5–4 in the two cases. The majority found that the student assignment policies in both districts relied too heavily on race and so ran afoul of the 14th Amendment's Equal Protection Clause. In fact, four of the five justices in the majority favored the total elimination of race as a factor in school admission decisions.

It seems clear that the days of affirmative action programs are drawing to a close. That point was made again in *Ricci* v. *DeStefano,* 2009. In this case, a group of white and Hispanic firefighters sued the city of New Haven, Connecticut. They claimed that they had been the victims of reverse discrimination when the results of an exam were discarded after few minority firefighters qualified for a promotion. The Court ruled, 5–4, in favor of the firefighters. It said, in effect, that race could not be used as the sole factor in promotions.

In *Fisher* v. *Texas*, 2013, the Court reaffirmed that affirmative action policies in college admissions must be "narrowly tailored" and pass strict scrutiny. In addition, the Court for the first time specified exactly how strict scrutiny should work. The courts must confirm in each case that no method other than the use of race will work to create a diverse student body. The Court's vote in *Fisher* was 7–1.

In 2014, the Court issued another affirmative action ruling, this time upholding, 6–2, a Michigan constitutional amendment that bans the use of affirmative action in the State university admissions process (*Schuette* v. *Coalition to Defend Affirmative Action*). The decision was based, at least in part, on the recognition that Michigan voters had approved the constitutional amendment. In the Court's opinion, Justice Anthony Kennedy noted "This case is not about how the debate about racial preferences should be resolved. It is about who may resolve it. There is no authority in the Constitution of the United States or in this court's precedents for the judiciary to set aside Michigan laws that commit this policy determination to the voters."

Controversy continues to rage over affirmative action in hiring and college admissions. Opponents maintain that affirmative action amounts to reverse discrimination. They also contend that affirmative action can do more harm than good if it reinforces stereotypes and leads to the perception that minorities have not achieved jobs or college admissions on merit, but only due to race- or gender-based preferences.

Supporters maintain that the need for such policies remains. They point to both historical and continued discrimination against minority groups and to facts such as this: Many of those States that have banned affirmative action in college admissions have seen a significant drop in the numbers of African Americans and Hispanic Americans who have enrolled at major public universities.

GENERATE EXPLANATIONS What is the role of the majority group in matters of discrimination and reverse discrimination?

>> Firefighters in New Haven won their case of reverse discrimination in *Ricci* v. *DeStefano*. Justice Anthony Kennedy wrote, "No individual should face workplace discrimination based on race."

Interactive Cartoon

ASSESSMENT

1. **Identify Patterns** What piece of federal legislation had the same effect on gender discrimination in education as the *Brown* v. *Board of Education* decision had on race discrimination in schools? Why?
2. **Identify Key Steps in a Process** Why was the Civil Rights Act of 1964 so effective in immediately taking away the de jure component of Jim Crow? How was the process of implementing this law different from the process of implementing the *Brown* v. *Board of Education* decision?
3. **Synthesize** How was a peaceful civil rights movement able to bring about broad changes in society, including changes in legislation passed by politicians who were elected by a majority of the voters? How did the civil rights movement manage to put pressure on politicians to change laws?
4. **Analyze Information** What is the relationship between affirmative action and quotas?
5. **Sequence Events** How, and why, are the Supreme Court's decisions about affirmative action changing over time?

"ANYBODY HOME?"

1. **Evaluate a U.S. Government Policy** Use the political cartoon above to write a paragraph evaluating U.S. government policy on immigration reform. Consider the following questions: What is the political cartoon's point of view on Congress and immigration reform? Do you agree with the political cartoon? Why or why not?
2. **Explain Changes in American Culture** Create a written or oral presentation explaining how the Immigration and Nationality Act of 1965 impacted immigration. Consider the following questions: What was the attitude toward immigration in the United States before the 1880s? What was the attitude toward immigration in the United States after the 1880s? What was the quota system? How did the Immigration and Nationality Act of 1965 impact the quota system? Do you think the Immigration and Nationality Act of 1965 was necessary? Explain.
3. **Explain Changes in American Culture** Create a written or oral presentation explaining changes in American culture brought about by the Immigration Reform and Control Act of 1986. In your written or oral presentation, consider the following questions: How did the Immigration Reform and Control Act of 1986 try to stem the tide of illegal immigrants? Why do you think employers hire illegal immigrants rather than United States citizens?
4. **Evaluate a Court Decision** Create a written or oral presentation evaluating the U.S. Supreme Court case *Grutter* v. *Bollinger*. In your presentation, consider the following questions: What is affirmative action? What were the circumstances surrounding *Grutter* v. *Bollinger*? Do you agree with the Supreme Court's decision? Why or why not?

5. **Evaluate a U.S. Government Policy** Create a visual presentation evaluating the Civil Rights Act of 1964 and how it outlawed discrimination in a number of different areas. Consider the following questions: In what ways did the Civil Rights Act of 1964 outlaw discrimination? How was society different before and after the Civil Rights Act of 1964?

6. **Explain Changes in American Culture** Create an inquiry project about racial integration. Research important cases such as the ruling of *Brown* v. *Board of Education* and the resistance that followed in the Deep South. In addition, research integration in schools and neighborhoods. Then share your findings in the form of a report. Use the following process: Ask a question about racial integration that you want to learn more about. Plan the project by outlining goals and objectives. Research information using primary and secondary sources. Create the project. Improve the project by editing and reevaluating your goals and objectives. Present your project.

7. **Explain Changes in American Culture** Use the quote below to write a paragraph explaining how the court case of *Brown* v. *Board of Education* changed American culture and helped end segregation. Consider the following questions: What was the ruling of *Brown* v. *Board of Education*? What argument did Chief Justice Earl Warren use to end segregation in public schools? How successful was *Brown* v. *Board of Education* in ending segregation? Explain.

   "Does segregation of children in public schools solely on the basis of race, even though the physical facilities and other 'tangible' factors may be equal, deprive the children of the minority group of equal educational opportunities? We believe that it does. . . . To separate them from others of similar age and qualifications solely because of their race generates a feeling of inferiority as to their status in the community that may affect their hearts and minds in a way unlikely ever to be undone. . . . Separate educational facilities are inherently unequal."

   —Chief Justice Earl Warren

8. **Analyze Contemporary Examples** Write a paragraph analyzing the Lilly Ledbetter Fair Pay Act of 2009. Consider the following questions: How did the Civil Rights Act of 1964 impact equal pay for women? What was the original provision for filing a lawsuit regarding discrimination based on gender? How did the Lilly Ledbetter Fair Pay Act of 2009 bring about change in fair pay for women?

9. **Give Examples of Processes** Write a paragraph analyzing Lloyd Gaines and the separate-but-equal doctrine. Consider the following questions: What is the separate-but-equal doctrine? When was the separate-but-equal doctrine upheld in court? What were the circumstances surrounding the case of *Missouri ex rel. Gaines* v. *Canada*? Why is this case significant regarding the separate-but-equal doctrine?

10. **Explain Changes in American Culture** Write a paragraph explaining government policies on affirmative action. Consider the following questions: How has American culture changed since the advent of affirmative action? Are affirmative action policies justified? Are there cases when the policies are not justified? Explain.

11. **Analyze Historical Examples** Write a paragraph analyzing how African Americans brought about political change from colonial times to the present. Consider the following: slavery; the Civil War; Civil Rights Act of 1964; *Brown* v. *Board of Education.*

12. **Evaluate Constitutional Provisions** Write a paragraph answering the following questions: Did the separate-but-equal doctrine and segregation protect individual rights? Why or why not? Why were they eventually overturned? Also, consider the following: 14th Amendment's Equal Protection Clause; rational basis test; strict scrutiny test; *Brown* v. *Board of Education of Topeka.*

13. **Explain Changes in American Culture** Use the information from the lessons in this topic and the political cartoon below to write a paragraph explaining changes brought about by affirmative action. Consider the following questions: What is affirmative action? Do you think this cartoonist would say that affirmative action programs have affected American culture in a positive or a negative way, or not at all? Explain your answer. Do you agree with the cartoonist's viewpoint? Why or why not?

THOSE PEOPLE GET ALL THE BREAKS.
©Darrin Bell.
Dist by WPWG, Inc.
cartoonistgroup.com

14. **Understand the Role of Limited Government** Explain the government's role in enforcing or overturning laws related to discrimination against certain groups' individual rights. Then write a paragraph answering the following questions: Why are some forms of discrimination reasonable? Why does the U.S. government only address certain equal protection cases? Should the government address more equal protection cases? Why? Also, consider the following: rational basis test; strict scrutiny test; race, gender, and sexual orientation equality.

15. **Understand the Role of the Rule of Law** Write a paragraph describing the role of the rule of law in the protection of individual rights, specifically in the case of *Michael M.* v. *Superior Court*, 1981. When writing the paragraph, focus on the *Michael M.* case and also answer the following questions: What were the circumstances surrounding *Swann* v. *Charlotte-Mecklenburg Board of Education*, 1971? How did the rule of law protect individual rights?

16. **Explain Changes in American Culture** Use the quote below to explain changes in culture for women since passage of the 19th Amendment guaranteed them the right to vote. Then write a paragraph answering the following questions: According to the quote, how were women's roles changing? How did the right to vote affect women's place in society? In your opinion, are women and men treated as equals? Why or why not? Also consider the following: female representation in American workforce; types of jobs held by women; pay and job compensation.

> *"When, in the course of human events, it becomes necessary for one portion of the family of man to assume among the people of the earth a position different from that which they have hitherto occupied, . . . We hold these truths to be self-evident: that all men and women are created equal . . ."*
>
> *—Declaration of Sentiments, 1848*

17. **Write about the Essential Question Write an essay on the Essential Question: What are the challenges of diversity?** Use evidence from your study of this Topic to support your answer.

PEARSON realize™ www.PearsonRealize.com
Access your Digital Lesson

Go online to PearsonRealize.com and use the texts, quizzes, interactivities, Interactive Reading Notepads, Flipped Videos, and other resources from this Topic to prepare for the Topic Test.

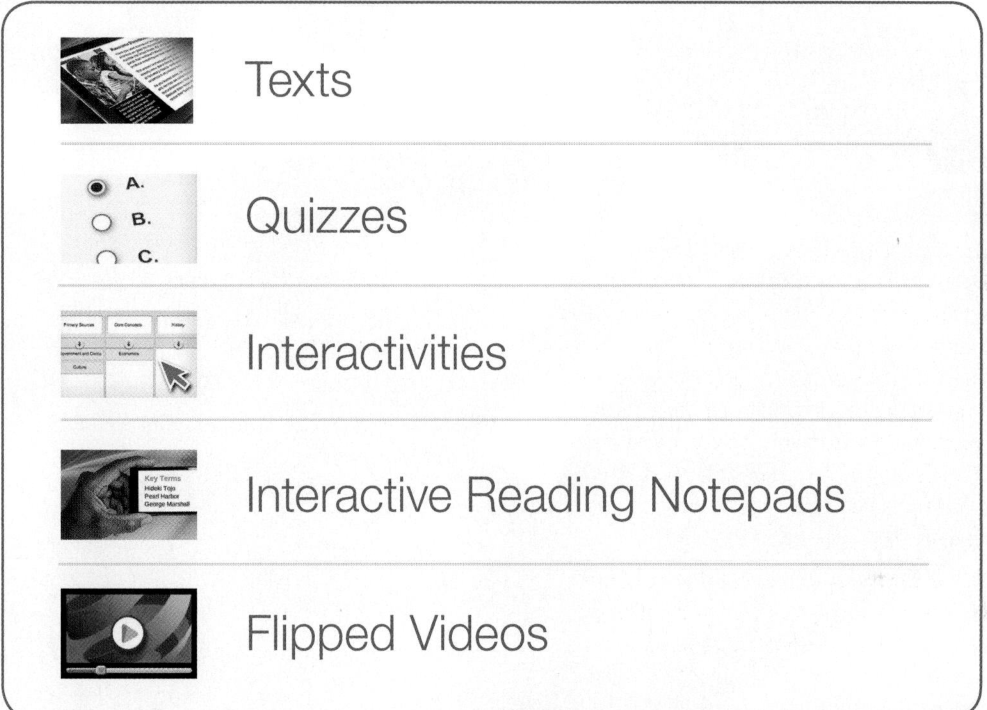

While online you can also check the progress you've made learning the topic and course content by viewing your grades, test scores, and assignment status.

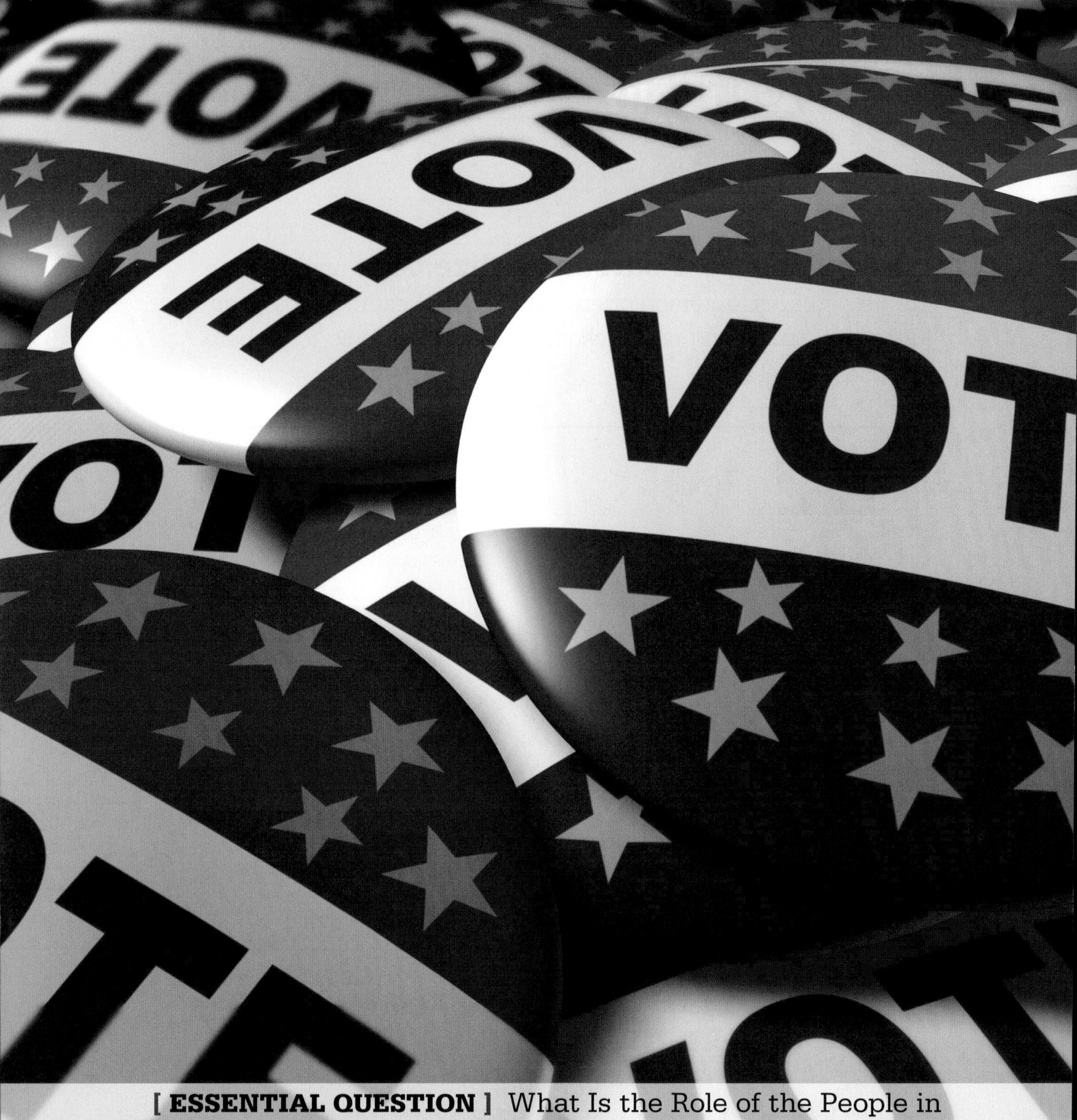

[ESSENTIAL QUESTION] What Is the Role of the People in Government?

10 Government by the People

>> A pile of "Vote" buttons

Enduring Understandings

- Political changes brought about by individuals and groups have led to the expansion of the electorate.
- Voting behavior results from a blend of psychological and sociological factors, and has a major impact on government.
- Voting procedures have been refined to increase participation, reduce fraud, and improve fairness and accuracy.
- Public opinion is a complex collection of the opinions of many different groups on public affairs issues.
- The mass media play a major role in the U.S. political system, but their influence is limited.
- Interest groups and lobbyists play a major role in the shaping of public policy.

PEARSON realize™ NBC LEARN

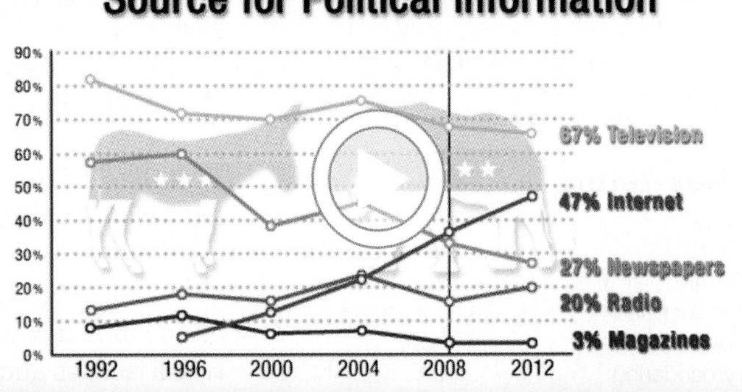

Watch the My Story Video to learn about the new ways that politicans are using social media to reach voters.

Access your digital lessons including:
Topic Inquiry • Interactive Reading Notepad • Interactivities • Assessments

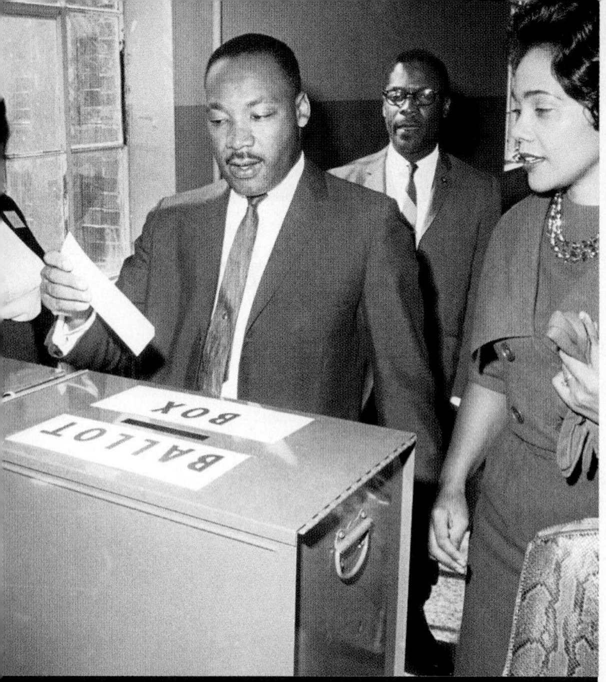

>> Dr. Martin Luther King, Jr., and Coretta Scott King vote in the presidential election of 1964, the same year the Civil Rights Act of 1964 outlawed discriminatory voting practices.

Interactive Flipped Video

10.1 **Soon, you will be eligible to vote—but will you exercise that right? The record suggests that while you may do so, many of your friends will not, at least not for some time. The record also suggests that some of your friends will never vote. Yet, clearly, the success of democratic government depends on popular participation and, in particular, on the regular and informed exercise of the right to vote.**

>> Objectives

Summarize the history of voting rights in the United States.

Identify the main intention of the 15th Amendment, and describe the results of its lack of enforcement.

Analyze the impact of political changes brought about by individuals with regard to the civil rights laws enacted in 1957, 1960, and 1964.

Analyze the provisions and effects of the Voting Rights Act of 1965.

>> Key Terms

suffrage
franchise
electorate
disenfranchised
poll tax
gerrymandering
injunction
preclearance
John Roberts
Martin Luther King, Jr.
Selma, Alabama
Lyndon B. Johnson

The History of Voting Rights

Voting Rights in the United States

The Framers of the Constitution purposely left the power to set suffrage qualifications to each State. **Suffrage** means the right to vote. **Franchise** is a synonym for the right to vote.

The Size of the American Electorate When the Constitution went into effect in 1789, the right to vote was generally restricted to white male property owners. In fact, probably not one in fifteen adult white males could vote in elections in the various States. Benjamin Franklin often made fun of this situation. He told of a man whose only property was a jackass and noted that the man would lose the right to vote if his jackass died. "Now," asked Franklin, "in whom is the right of suffrage? In the man or the jackass?"

Today, the size of the American **electorate**—the potential voting population—is truly impressive. More than 240 million people, nearly all citizens who are at least 18 years of age, qualify to vote. That huge number is a direct result of the legal definition of suffrage. In other words, it is the result of those laws that determine who can and cannot vote. It is also the result of more than 200 years of continuing, often bitter, and sometimes violent struggle over the right to vote.

PEARSON realize. www.PearsonRealize.com Access your Digital Lesson.

The history of American suffrage since 1789 has been marked by the gradual elimination of most restrictions on the right to vote, including religious belief, property ownership, tax payment, race, and gender. This expansion of voting rights has led to significant changes in American culture, not the least of which is the marked impact of the voices of minorities, women, and youth on American public policy. Others include a growth in the influence of the two major political parties as each has sought to win voters, an increase in the number of minority elected officials, and greater equality for women in the workplace.

The Struggle to Extend Voting Rights The growth of the American electorate has come in five identifiable stages:

1. The first stage of the struggle to extend voting rights came in the early 1800s. Religious qualifications, put in place in colonial days, quickly disappeared. No State has had a religious test for voting since 1810. Then, one by one, States began to eliminate property ownership and tax payment qualifications. By mid-century, almost all white adult males could vote in every State.

2. The second major effort to broaden the electorate followed the Civil War. The 15th Amendment, ratified in 1870, was intended to protect any citizen from being denied the right to vote because of race or color. Still, for nearly another century, African Americans were systematically barred from voting, and they remained the largest group of **disenfranchised** citizens, or citizens denied the right to vote, in the nation's population.

3. Wyoming, while still a territory, had given women the vote in 1869. By 1920, more than half of the States had followed that lead, but women were still denied the vote in federal elections. The long struggle of women to change that situation finally culminated with the ratification of the 19th Amendment in 1920. That amendment led to a host of cultural changes, including increasing attention to women's issues and growing numbers of women in public office.

4. A fourth major extension took place during the 1960s. During that time, federal legislation and court decisions focused on securing African Americans a full role in the electoral process in all States. With the passage and vigorous enforcement of a number of civil rights acts, especially the Voting Rights Act of 1965 and its later extensions, racial equality finally become fact in polling booths throughout the country.

The 23rd Amendment, passed in 1961, added the voters of the District of Columbia to the presidential electorate. The 24th Amendment, ratified in 1964, eliminated the poll tax (and any other tax) as a condition for voting in any federal election. A **poll tax** was a tax imposed by several States as a qualification for voting.

5. The fifth and latest expansion of the electorate came with the adoption of the 26th Amendment in 1971. It provides that no State can set the minimum age for voting at more than 18 years of age. In other words, those 18 and over were given the right to vote by this amendment.

? **CONNECT** What was the voting experience of African Americans after the war? What does this suggest about the legal expansion of voting rights?

The 15th Amendment

How important is the right to vote? For those who do not have it, that right can seem as important as life itself. Indeed, in the Deep South of the 1960s, civil rights workers suffered arrest, beatings, shocks with electric cattle prods, even death—all in the name of the right to vote. Their efforts inspired the nation and led to large-scale federal efforts to secure that right for African Americans and other minority groups in the United States.

>> George Caleb Bingham's *The County Election* depicts an 1850 Missouri election. At the time, voting was restricted to white males, but property and tax qualifications had been eliminated.

Interactive Timeline

The effort to extend the franchise to African Americans began with the 15th Amendment, which was ratified in 1870. It declares that the right to vote cannot be denied to any citizen of the United States because of "race, color, or previous condition of servitude." The amendment was plainly intended to ensure that African American men, nearly all of them former slaves and nearly all of them living in the South, could vote.

The 15th Amendment is not self-executing, however. In other words, simply stating a general principle without providing for a means of enforcement was not enough to carry out the intention of the amendment. To make it effective, Congress had to act. Yet for nearly 90 years the Federal Government paid little attention to the voting rights of African Americans.

Lack of Enforcement During that period, African Americans were generally and systematically kept from the polls in much of the South. White supremacists employed a number of tactics to that end. Their major weapon was violence. Other tactics included more subtle threats and social pressures—for example, firing an African American man who tried to register or vote, or denying his family credit at local stores.

More formal "legal" devices were used, as well. The most effective were literacy tests. White officials regularly manipulated those tests to disenfranchise African Americans. Registration laws served the same end. As written, they applied to all potential voters. In practice, however, they were often administered to keep African Americans from qualifying to vote. Poll taxes, "white primaries," gerrymandering, and several other devices were also used.

Gerrymandering is the practice of drawing electoral district lines (the boundaries of the geographic area from which a candidate is elected to a public office) in order to limit the voting strength of a particular group or party.

The white primary arose out of the decades-long Democratic domination of politics in the South. It was almost a given that the Democratic candidate for an office would be elected. Therefore, only the Democrats ordinarily nominated candidates, generally in primaries. In several southern States, political parties were defined by law as "private associations" that could exclude whomever they chose, and the Democrats regularly refused to admit African Americans. Because only party members could vote in the party's primary, African Americans were then excluded from a critical step in the public election process.

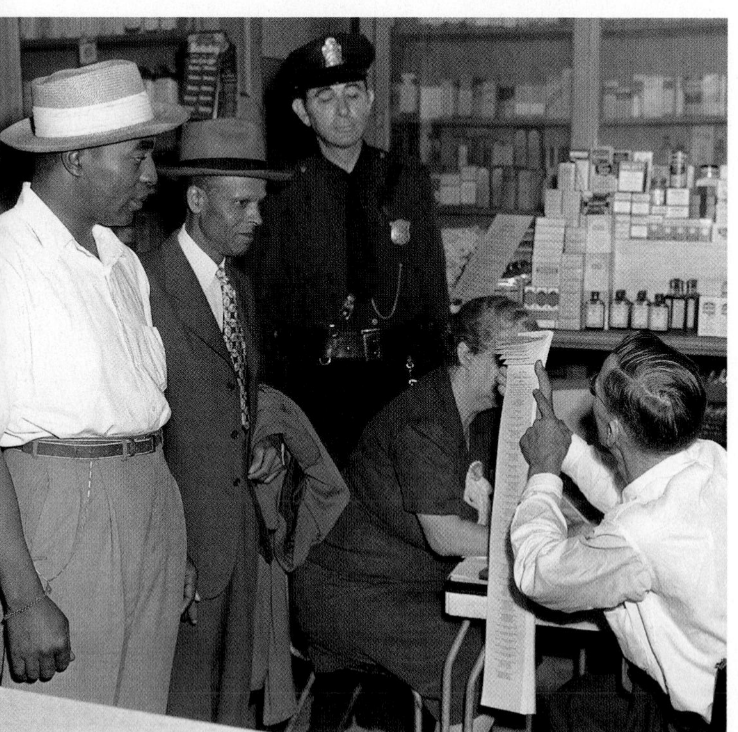

>> An Atlanta, Georgia, election official points out to World War II veteran Lewis McGuire and Dr. S. M. Lewis that the ballot states that only whites can vote in the 1945 Democratic primary.

Court Rulings Upholding Voting Rights The Supreme Court outlawed the white primary in a case from Texas, *Smith* v. *Allwright,* in 1944. The Court held that nominations are an integral part of the election process. So, when a political party holds a primary, it is performing a public function and is bound by the 15th Amendment.

The Supreme Court outlawed gerrymandering for racial discrimination in *Gomillion* v. *Lightfoot,* 1960. The Alabama legislature had redrawn the electoral districts of Tuskegee, effectively excluding blacks from the city limits. The Court ruled that the action violated the 15th Amendment, because the irregularly shaped district clearly was created to deprive blacks of political power.

Led by these decisions, the lower federal courts struck down many practices designed to deny the vote to African Americans in the 1940s and 1950s. Still, the courts could act only when individuals who claimed to be victims of discrimination sued in an effort to affect public policy. That case-by-case process was, at best, agonizingly slow.

? DRAW CONCLUSIONS How did white primaries and classifying political parties as private associations sidestep the 15th Amendment?

Civil Rights Acts of 1957, 1960, and 1964

Finally, largely in response to the civil rights movement led by Dr. **Martin Luther King, Jr.**, Congress was moved to act. In the late 1950s, it began to enact civil rights laws specifically intended to implement the 15th Amendment. These laws eventually led to many other changes in American culture, including better jobs and greater educational opportunities for African Americans.

1957 and 1960 The first of the laws Congress passed to enforce the 15th Amendment was the Civil Rights Act of 1957, which created the United States Commission on Civil Rights. One of the Commission's major duties is to inquire into claims of voter discrimination. The Commission reports its findings to Congress and the President and, through the media, to the public. The 1957 law also gave the attorney general the power to seek federal court orders to prevent interference with any person's right to vote in any federal election.

The Civil Rights Act of 1960 added an additional safeguard. It provided for the appointment of federal voting referees. Those officers were to serve anywhere a federal court found voter discrimination. They were given the power to help qualified persons to register and vote in federal elections.

The Civil Rights Act of 1964 The Civil Rights Act of 1964 is much broader and more effective than either of the two earlier measures. It outlaws discrimination in several areas, especially in job-related matters. With regard to voting rights, its most important section forbids the use of any voter registration or literacy requirement in an unfair or discriminatory manner.

The 1964 law continued a pattern set in the earlier laws. It relied on judicial action to overcome racial barriers and emphasized the use of federal court orders called injunctions. An **injunction** is a court order that either compels or restrains the performance of some act by a private individual or public official. The violation of an injunction amounts to contempt of court, a crime punishable by fine and/or imprisonment.

Dramatic events in **Selma, Alabama**, soon pointed out the shortcomings of this approach. Dr. King mounted a voter registration drive in that city in early 1965. He and his supporters managed to focus national attention on the issue of African American voting rights.

Their registration efforts were met with insults and violence by local white civilians, by city and county police, and then by State troopers. Three civil rights workers were murdered, and many were beaten when

>> African American students enter a school in Little Rock, Arkansas, where the governor blocked the integration of the schools in 1957, forcing President Eisenhower to intervene.

>> President Lyndon Johnson shakes hands with Martin Luther King, Jr., after signing the Civil Rights Act of 1964, which outlawed discrimination based on race, religion, or gender.

Interactive Gallery

they attempted a peaceful march to the State capitol. The nation saw much of the drama on television and was shocked. An outraged President **Lyndon B. Johnson** urged Congress to pass new and stronger legislation to ensure the voting rights of African Americans. Congress responded, and quickly.

IDENTIFY CENTRAL IDEAS How did the civil rights acts of 1957 and 1960 show that the Federal Government's approach to the 15th Amendment had changed?

Voting Rights Act of 1965—Then and Now

The Voting Rights Act of 1965 made the 15th Amendment, at long last, a truly effective part of the Constitution. Unlike its predecessors, this act applied to *all* elections held anywhere in this country—State and local, as well as federal.

Originally, the Voting Rights Act was to be in effect for a period of five years. Congress has extended its life on four occasions, in the Voting Rights Act Amendments of 1970, 1975, 1982, and, most recently, 2006. The present version of the law was made effective for 25 years; its provisions will not expire until 2031.

The 1965 law directed the attorney general to challenge the constitutionality of the remaining State poll-tax laws in the federal courts. That provision led directly to *Harper* v. *Virginia Board of Elections,* 1966.

The law also suspended the use of any literacy test or similar device in any State or county where less than half of the electorate had been registered or had voted in the 1964 presidential election. The law authorized the attorney general to appoint voting examiners to serve in any of those States or counties. It also gave these federal officers the power to register voters and otherwise oversee the conduct of elections in those areas.

Preclearance Provisions The Voting Rights Act of 1965 imposed another restriction on those States where a majority of the electorate had not voted in 1964. The act declared that no new election laws, and no changes in existing election laws, could go into effect in any of those States unless first approved—given **preclearance**—by the Department of Justice. Only those new or revised laws that do not dilute the voting rights of minority groups can survive the preclearance process and take effect.

The preclearance hurdle has produced a large number of court cases over the years. Those cases show that the laws most likely to run afoul of the preclearance requirement are those that make these kinds of changes: (1) the location of polling places; (2) the boundaries of election districts; (3) the deadlines in the election process; (4) a shift from ward or district election to at-large elections; or (5) the qualifications candidates must meet in order to run for office.

Any State or county subject to the voter examiner and preclearance provisions can be removed from the law's coverage through a "bail-out" process. That relief

African American Elected Officials in the U.S.

YEAR	MALE	FEMALE	TOTAL
1970	1,309	160	1,469
1975	2,973	530	3,503
1980	3,936	976	4,912
1985	4,697	1,359	6,056
1990	5,420	1,950	7,370
1995	5,782	2,637	8,419
2000	5,921	3,119	9,040

SOURCE: Joint Center for Political and Economic Studies

>> The Voting Rights Act sought to equalize access to voting. **Analyze Charts** What generalization can be made about the effect of this act on the number of elected black officials?

Why the Voting Rights Act Amendments Were Needed

DISCRIMINATORY TACTICS STILL IN USE, 1968	DISCRIMINATORY TACTICS STILL IN USE, 1975
• Extending the terms of incumbent white officials • Making certain offices appointive rather than elective • Changing the dates of elections suddenly • Changing the qualifications of office • Increasing the cost of filing fees candidates must pay to run for office • Use of gerrymandering and at-large elections to dilute the nonwhite vote	• Use of inadequate bilingual election materials • Threatening economic reprisals for voting • Locating polling places in areas where minorities are not welcomed • Use of gerrymandering and other tactics

>> The Voting Rights Act was amended in 1970, 1975, 1982, 1992, and 2006. **Analyze Charts** What was the goal of the tactics shown here? Why did the tactics change over time?

can come if the State shows the United States District Court in the District of Columbia that it has not applied any voting procedures in a discriminatory way for at least 10 years.

The voter-examiner and preclearance provisions of the 1965 Voting Rights Act originally applied to six entire States: Alabama, Georgia, Louisiana, Mississippi, South Carolina, and Virginia. In addition, these provisions applied to 40 counties in North Carolina.

The Supreme Court upheld the Voting Rights Act in 1966. In *South Carolina* v. *Katzenbach*, a unanimous Court rejected the claim that the law—and, most particularly, its preclearance provisions—violated the reserved power of each State to shape its own electoral system. Instead, the Court found the Voting Rights Act to be a proper exercise of the power granted to Congress in Section 2 of the 15th Amendment. That provision authorizes Congress to enact "appropriate legislation" to enforce the constitutional prohibition against racial discrimination in voting set out in Section 1 of the amendment.

The Voting Rights Act Extended The Voting Rights Act Amendments of 1970 extended the law for another five years. The 1968 elections were taken into account in determining jurisdictions with concerns; the result was that a number of counties in six more States (Alaska, Arizona, California, Idaho, New Mexico, and Oregon) were included in the law's coverage.

That 1970 law also provided that, for five years, no State could use literacy as the basis for any voting requirement. That temporary ban, as well as residence provisions outlined in the law, was upheld by the Supreme Court in *Oregon* v. *Mitchell* in 1970.

In 1975, the law was extended again, this time for seven years, and the five-year ban on literacy tests was made permanent. Since 1975, no State has been able to apply *any* sort of literacy qualification to *any* aspect of the election process. The law's voter-examiner and preclearance provisions were also broadened in 1975 to cover any State or county where more than 5 percent of the voting-age population belongs to certain "language minorities." These groups are defined to include all persons of Spanish heritage, Native Americans, Asian Americans, and Alaskan Natives.

This addition expanded the law's coverage to all of Alaska and Texas and to several counties in 24 other States, as well. In these areas, all ballots and other official election materials must be printed both in English and in the language of the minorities involved.

In 1982, further amendments extended the basic features of the act for another 25 years. In 1992, the law's language-minority provisions were revised: they now apply to any community that has a minority-language population of 10,000 or more. Finally, an amendment to the act passed in 2006 eliminated the voter-examiner requirement of the original 1965 law.

>> The controversial ruling in *Shelby County* v. *Holder* caused a storm of reaction across the country. **Analyze Political Cartoons** According to this cartoon, what might the ruling mean for voters?

>> Chief Justice John Roberts, shown shaking hands with President Barack Obama before the 2012 State of the Union speech, based his opinion in *Shelby County* partly on the concept of States' rights.

Preclearance Invalidated Over the years, the Supreme Court faced a number of challenges to the Voting Rights Act, but it consistently sidestepped the issue of the law's constitutionality. In 2013, however, in a monumental and controversial decision, the Supreme Court invalidated the preclearance provision of the Voting Rights Act. In a split 5–4 decision, the Court declared unconstitutional the formula used to determine which States and counties must gain permission from the Justice Department before changing any law affecting voting and elections.

In his majority opinion, Chief Justice **John Roberts** said the Voting Rights Act "employed extraordinary measures to address an extraordinary problem." He went on to note, however, that in the 40 years since the Voting Rights Act had been passed,

> voting tests were abolished, disparities in voter registration and turnout due to race were erased, and African Americans attained political office in record numbers. Yet the coverage formula that Congress reauthorized in 2006 ignores these developments, keeping the focus on decades-old problems, rather than current data reflecting current needs.

The Chief Justice also injected a note of caution, however, saying

> At the same time, voting discrimination still exists; no one doubts that. The question is whether the Act's extraordinary measures, including its disparate treatment of the States, continue to satisfy constitutional requirements. . . .
>
> —Chief Justice John Roberts, Opinion of the Court, *Shelby* v. *Holder*

The Court held that they did not. Although racial discrimination in voting is still illegal under the Voting Rights Act, "Congress must ensure that the legislation it passes to remedy the problem speaks to current conditions."

SUMMARIZE Give two ways that the extension of the Voting Rights Act has helped protect the right to vote.

ASSESSMENT

1. **Infer** Why might various groups throughout history—including women and African Americans—have fought for the right to vote?
2. **Infer** What does the fact that it took until 1920 to pass the 19th Amendment say about American society up until that time?
3. **Identify Central Issues** What were some of the biggest barriers to the success of the 15th Amendment?
4. **Interpret** What did Chief Justice Roberts mean when he stated that the Voting Rights Act "employed extraordinary measures to address an extraordinary problem"?
5. **Check Understanding** In invalidating preclearance provisions, what larger point was the Supreme Court making about voting rights?

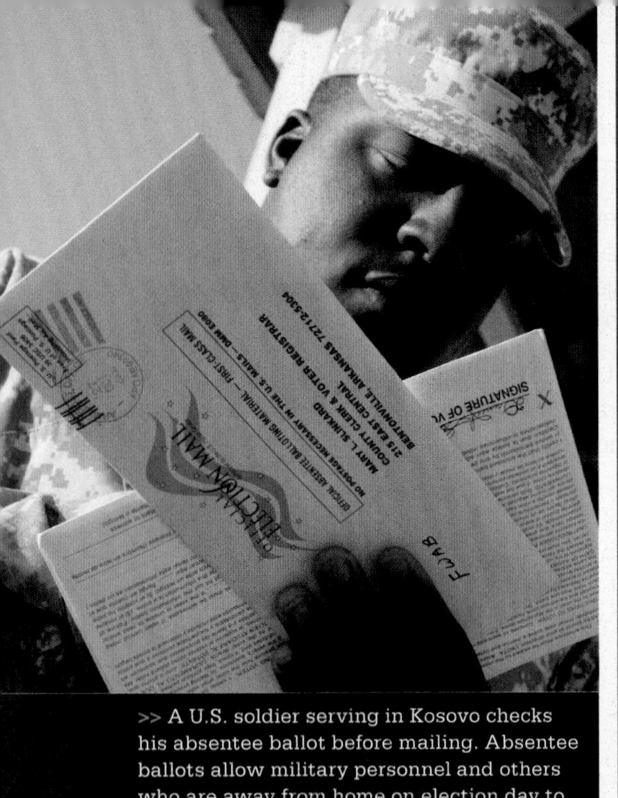

>> A U.S. soldier serving in Kosovo checks his absentee ballot before mailing. Absentee ballots allow military personnel and others who are away from home on election day to vote.

10.2 **The history of American suffrage has been marked by two long-term trends. You've already read about the first—the gradual expansion of the electorate. Second, a significant share of what was originally the States' power over the right to vote has been gradually assumed by the Federal Government. While the Constitution reserves the power to set suffrage qualifications to the States, several constitutional provisions do limit the role of State governments in this area.**

Interactive Flipped Video

>> Objectives

Identify and explain constitutional restrictions on the States' power to set voting qualifications.

Understand the criteria for voting in elections.

Understand the voter registration process and the controversies surrounding voter registration.

Explain the other requirements that States use or have used as voting qualifications.

>> Key Terms

transients
purging
poll books
registration
William O. Douglas
literacy
aliens

Your Right to Vote

Voting Qualifications and the Federal Government

Those constitutional provisions related to the right to vote include:

1. Any person whom a State allows to vote for members of the "most numerous Branch" of its own legislature must also be allowed to vote for representatives and senators in Congress (Article 1, Section 2, Clause 1 and the 17th Amendment). This restriction is of little real meaning today. With only minor exceptions, each of the States allows the same voters to vote in all elections within the State.
2. No State can deprive any person of the right to vote "on account of race, color, or previous condition of servitude" (15th Amendment).
3. No State can deprive any person of the right to vote on account of sex (19th Amendment).
4. No State can require payment of any tax as a condition for taking part in the nomination or election of any federal officeholder. That is, no State can levy any tax in connection with the selection of the President, the Vice President, or members of Congress (24th Amendment).
5. No State can deprive any person who is at least 18 years of age of the right to vote because of age (26th Amendment).

Beyond these five restrictions, remember that no State can violate any other provision in the Constitution in the setting of suffrage qualifications—or in anything else that it does. A case decided by the Supreme Court in 1975, *Hill* v. *Stone,* illustrates the point.

There, the Court struck down a section of the Texas constitution that declared that only those persons who owned taxable property could vote in city bond elections. The Court found the drawing of such a distinction for voting purposes—between those who do and those who do not own taxable property—to be an unreasonable classification prohibited by the 14th Amendment's Equal Protection Clause.

EXPLAIN Beyond the five restrictions listed in this reading, no State can violate any other provision in the Constitution when setting suffrage qualifications. Explain what this means in your own words.

>> This lithograph celebrates the passage of the 15th Amendment in 1870. **Analyze Images** What potential effects of the amendment does the lithograph portray?

Universal Criteria for Voting

Are you qualified to vote? Probably not—at least not yet. Do you know why? In this section, you will see how the States, including yours, determine who can vote. You will also see that the various qualifications they set are not very difficult to meet.

Today, every State requires that any person who wants to vote must be able to satisfy qualifications based on three factors: (1) citizenship, (2) residence, and (3) age. The States have some leeway in shaping the details of the first two of these factors; they have almost no discretion with regard to the third one.

Citizenship Criteria **Aliens**, foreign-born residents who have not become citizens, are generally denied the right to vote in this country. Still, nothing in the Constitution says that aliens cannot vote, and any State could allow them to do so if it chose. At one time, about a fourth of the States permitted those aliens who had applied for naturalization—that is, applied for citizenship—to vote. Typically, the western States did so to help attract settlers.

States may draw a distinction between native-born and naturalized citizens with regard to suffrage. The Pennsylvania constitution, for example, says that one must have become a citizen at least one month before an election in order to vote in that State.

>> In 1882 when this photograph was taken, the adults in this immigrant family could probably vote in State elections if they had applied for citizenship.

Residence Criteria To vote in this country today, one must be a legal resident of the State in which he or she wishes to cast a ballot. In many States, a person must have lived in the State for at least a certain period of time before he or she can vote.

The States adopted residence requirements for two reasons: (1) to keep a political machine from bringing in enough outsiders to affect the outcome of an election (a once common practice), and (2) to allow new voters at least some time in which to become familiar with the candidates and issues in an upcoming election.

For decades, every State imposed a fairly lengthy residence requirement—typically, a year in the State, 60 or 90 days in the county, and 30 days in the local precinct or ward. The requirement was longer in some southern States—for example, one year in the State, six months in the county, and three months in the precinct in Alabama, Louisiana, and South Carolina, and in Mississippi a year in the State, a year in the county, and six months in the precinct.

Residence requirements are not nearly so long today. In fact, most States now require that a voter be a legal resident but do not attach a time period to that qualification. About a third of them say that a voter must have lived in the State for at least 30 days. In a few, the period is somewhat shorter—for example, 29 days in Arizona, 20 in Minnesota, and 28 in Wisconsin.

Laws and Court Actions Today's much shorter requirements are a direct result of a 1970 federal law and a 1972 Supreme Court decision. In the Voting Rights Act Amendments of 1970, Congress banned any requirement of longer than 30 days for voting in presidential elections. And in *Dunn* v. *Blumstein,* 1972, the Court found Tennessee's requirement—at the time, a year in the State and 90 days in the county—unconstitutional. The Court found such a lengthy requirement to be an unsupportable discrimination against new residents and so in conflict with the 14th Amendment's Equal Protection Clause. The Supreme Court said that "30 days appears to be an ample period of time." Election law and practice among the States quickly accepted that standard.

Nearly every State does prohibit **transients**, persons who plan to live in a State for only a short time, from gaining legal residence status there. Thus, a traveling sales agent, a member of the armed services, or a college student usually cannot vote in a State where he or she has only a temporary physical presence. In several States, however, the courts have held that college students who claim the campus community as their legal residence must be allowed to vote there.

Age Criteria The 26th Amendment, added to the Constitution in 1971, declares,

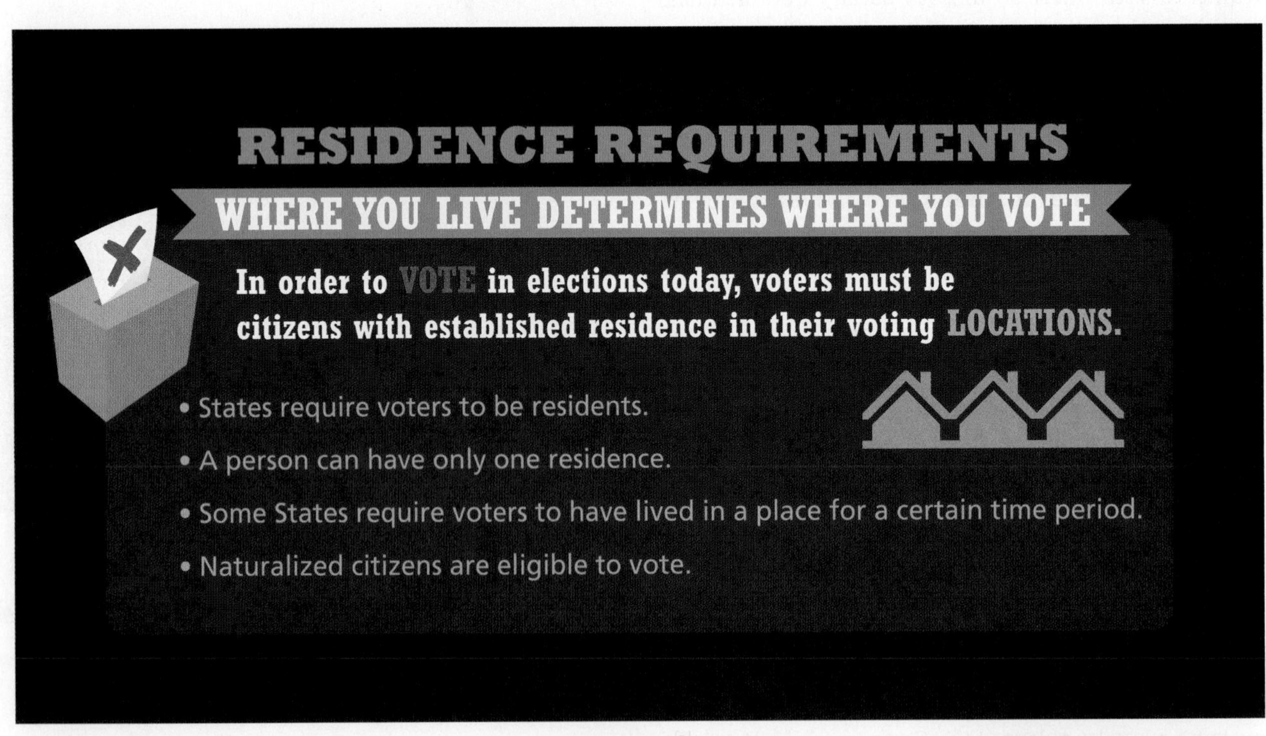

>> The Federal Government does not set any voting qualifications based on residence, but the States can and do set such requirements. **Analyze Charts** What is the purpose of residency requirements?

> The right of citizens of the United States, who are eighteen years of age or older, to vote shall not be denied or abridged by the United States or by any State on account of age.
>
> —26th Amendment

Thus, no State can set the minimum age for voting in any election at more than 18. In other words, the amendment extends suffrage to citizens who are at least 18 years of age. Notice, however, that any State can set the age at less than 18, if it chooses to do so.

Until the 26th Amendment was adopted, the generally accepted age requirement for voting was 21. In fact, until 1970, only four States had put the age at less than 21. Georgia was the first State to allow 18-year-olds to vote; it did so in 1943, in the midst of World War II. Kentucky followed suit in 1955. Alaska entered the Union in 1959 with the voting age set at 19, and Hawaii became a State later that same year with a voting age of 20.

Both Alaska and Hawaii set the age above 18 but below 21 to avoid potential problems caused by high school students voting in local school-district elections. Whatever the fears at the time, there have been no such problems in any State since the passage of the 26th Amendment.

Efforts to lower the voting age to 18 nationwide began in the 1940s, during World War II. They included lobbying members of Congress, State-by-State grassroots campaigns, and marches and demonstrations across the country. They were finally capped by the adoption of the 26th Amendment in 1971, during the war in Vietnam. That amendment was ratified more quickly than any other amendment to the Constitution. This fact is testament to the emotional weight of the principal argument in its favor: "Old enough to fight, old enough to vote."

The Youth Vote How have 18- to 20-year-olds responded to the 26th Amendment? Over time, young voters have been much less likely to vote than any other age group in the electorate. In 1972, 48 percent of the 18-to-20 age group voted, but by 2000 that figure had plummeted to 28 percent. It rose again, substantially, in 2004 and topped 37 percent in 2012. But contrast that figure with the turnout of Americans 65 and older. Despite the infirmities that may accompany their age, their voting rate regularly exceeds 60 percent, and it did so again in the presidential election of 2012.

In a growing number of States, some 17-year-olds can now cast ballots in primary elections. Those States allow anyone whose 18th birthday falls after the primary but before the general election to vote in the primary election.

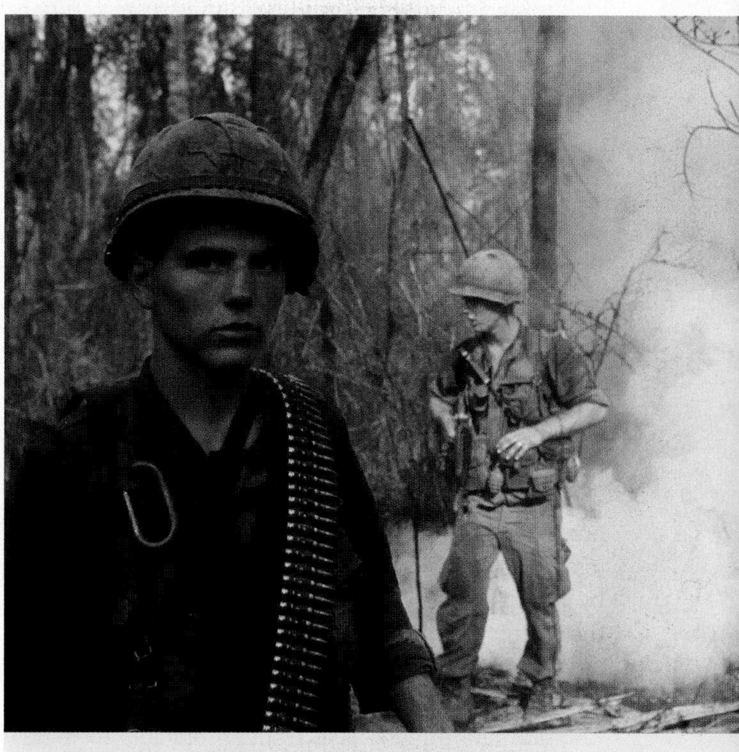

>> The service of young Americans in Vietnam helped spur passage of the 26th Amendment, which lowered the voting age to 18. Of the 58,000 soldiers killed in that war, 61 percent were 21 or under.

Several states have come very close to effectively lowering the voting age to 17 for *all* elections. In Nebraska, for example, any person who will be 18 by the Tuesday following the first Monday in November can qualify to vote in any election held during that calendar year.

INFER What factors led to a general decrease in the length of residence requirements among the States?

The Voter Registration Process

One other significant qualification, registration, is nearly universal among the States today. **Registration** is a procedure of voter identification intended to prevent fraudulent voting. It gives election officials a list of those persons who are qualified to vote in an election. Several States also use voter registration to identify voters in terms of their party preference and, thus, their eligibility to take part in closed primaries.

Registration Requirements Forty-nine States—all except North Dakota—require that most, and usually all, voters be registered in order to cast ballots. Voter registration became a common feature of State election law in the early 1900s. Today, most States require all voters to register in order to vote in any election held within the State. A few, however, do not impose the requirement for all elections.

Maine and Wisconsin allow voters to register at any time, up to and including election day. Elsewhere, a voter must be registered by a certain date, often 20 or 30 days before an election. That cutoff gives election officials time to prepare the poll books for an upcoming election.

Typically, a prospective voter must register his or her name, age, place of birth, present address, length of residence, and similar facts. The information is logged by a local official, usually a registrar of elections or the county clerk. A voter typically remains registered unless or until he or she moves, dies, is convicted of a serious crime, or is committed to a mental institution.

State law directs local election officials to review the lists of registered voters and to remove the names of those who are no longer eligible to vote. This process, known as **purging**, is usually done every two or four years. Unfortunately, the requirement is often ignored. When it is, the **poll books** (the official lists of qualified voters in each precinct) soon become clogged with the names of many people who, for one reason or another, are no longer eligible to vote.

>> Voter ID laws have mixed support and continue to be reviewed by the courts. **Analyze Political Cartoons** What is the cartoonist saying about the benefit of Voter ID laws?

Interactive Gallery

Controversies Surrounding Registration There are some who think that the registration requirement should be abolished everywhere. They see the qualification as a bar to voting, especially among the poor and less educated.

Those critics buttress their case by noting that voter turnout began to decline in the early 1900s, just after most States adopted a registration requirement. They also point to the fact that voter turnout is much higher in most European democracies than in the United States. In those countries, voter registration is not a matter of individual choice but is the law. Public officials must enter the names of all eligible citizens on registration lists. The United States is the only democratic country in which each person decides whether or not to register to vote.

Most people who have studied the problem favor keeping the registration requirement as a necessary defense against fraud. However, they also favor making the process a more convenient one. In short, they see the problem in these terms: Where is the line between making it so easy to vote that fraud is encouraged, and making it so difficult that legitimate voting is discouraged?

Most States have eased the registration process over the last several years. In 1993, Congress passed a law that required every State (but North Dakota) to do so. That law, dubbed the "Motor Voter Act," became effective in 1995. It directs the States to (1) allow all eligible citizens to register to vote when they apply for or renew a driver's license; (2) provide for voter registration by mail; and (3) make registration forms available at the local offices of State employment, welfare, and other social service agencies. The most striking change in American culture brought about by this government policy has been a huge number of new voters added to the poll books. The Federal Election Commission reported that by the year 2000, approximately 8 million persons had registered to vote as a direct result of the Motor Voter Law.

The law also requires every State to mail a questionnaire to each of its registered voters every four years, so that the poll books can be purged for deaths and changes of residence. It also forbids the States to purge for any other reason, including failure to vote.

Voter ID Laws Several States now have so-called voter ID laws that require people to prove their identity when they seek to register or vote, and nearly three quarters of the American people are in favor of those laws.

Some government-issued photo ID—a passport or a driver's license, for example—will usually satisfy the requirement to confirm their identity at the polls. Those who support these measures argue that they prevent people from voting under false identities and also bring greater integrity, accountability, and transparency to elections. Those opposed suggest the real intention of the laws is to limit the involvement of a particular type of voter—specifically, the elderly, disabled, poor, and minority groups.

State and federal courts have been charged with examining these contentious voter ID laws to determine whether they discriminate against any group and thus violate the Equal Protection Clause of the 14th Amendment. For the most part, the laws have been found to be constitutional, but the issue continues to generate legal challenges.

COMPARE AND CONTRAST Compare and contrast the arguments for and against voter registration.

>> A man studies a practice form for a voter registration test in 1962. Until the passage of the Voting Rights Act of 1965, many States used literacy tests to disenfranchise minority voters.

Historical Criteria for Voting

Suffrage qualifications based on two other factors—literacy and tax payment—were once fairly common among the States. They had a fairly long history but are no longer to be found anywhere.

Literacy Qualifications Today, no State has a suffrage qualification based on voter **literacy**—a person's ability to read and write. At one time, the literacy requirement could be, and in many places was, used to make sure that a qualified voter had the capacity to cast an informed ballot. Some States asked potential voters to prove that they could read; others asked for the ability to both read and write. And still others required those who registered to vote to show that they could read and write and also understand some piece of printed material—often, a passage from the State or Federal Constitution.

Connecticut adopted the first literacy qualifications in 1855. Massachusetts followed in 1857. Both States were trying to limit voting by Irish Catholic immigrants. Mississippi adopted a literacy requirement in 1890, and soon after, most of the other southern States followed suit. The literary qualification in most southern States included an "understanding" clause. Often, whites were asked to "understand" some short, plainly worded constitutional provision; but African Americans had to interpret a long, complex passage to the satisfaction of local election officials.

Grandfather Clauses While those qualifications had been aimed at disenfranchising African Americans, they sometimes had unintended effects. Several States soon found that they needed to adjust their voting requirements by adding so-called grandfather clauses to their constitutions. These grandfather clauses were designed to enfranchise those white males who were unintentionally disqualified by their failure to meet the literacy or taxpaying requirements.

A grandfather clause was added to the Louisiana constitution in 1898; Alabama, Georgia, Maryland, North Carolina, Oklahoma, and Virginia soon added them as well. These clauses stated that any man, or his male descendants, who had voted in the State before the adoption of the 15th Amendment (1870) could become a legal voter without regard to any literacy or taxpaying qualifications. The Supreme Court found the Oklahoma provision, the last to be adopted (in 1910), in conflict with the 15th Amendment in *Guinn* v. *United States* in 1915.

Literacy Tests Banned A number of States outside the South also adopted literacy qualifications, including Wyoming, California, Washington, New Hampshire, Arizona, New York, Oregon, and Alaska. Its unfair use finally led Congress to ban literacy qualifications in 1970. The Court agreed in *Oregon* v. *Mitchell,* 1970.

Some form of the literacy requirement was in place in 18 States when Congress finally banned its use.

Poll Taxes Property ownership, proved by the payment of property taxes, was once a very common suffrage qualification. For decades, several States also demanded the payment of a special tax, called the poll tax, as a condition for voting. Those requirements and others that called for the payment of a tax in order to vote have disappeared over the years.

The poll tax was once found throughout the South. Beginning with Florida in 1889, each of the 11 southern States adopted the poll tax as part of the effort to discourage voting by African Americans. The device proved to be of only limited effectiveness, however. That fact, and opposition to the use of the poll tax from within the South as well as elsewhere, led most of those States to abandon it. By 1966, the tax was still in use in only Alabama, Mississippi, Texas, and Virginia.

The 24th Amendment, ratified in 1964, outlawed the poll tax, or any other tax, as a condition for voting in any federal election. The Supreme Court finally eliminated the poll tax in 1966 as a qualification for voting in all elections. In *Harper* v. *Virginia Board of Elections,* the Court held the Virginia poll tax to be in conflict with the 14th Amendment's Equal Protection Clause. The Court could find no reasonable relationship between the act of voting on one hand and the payment of a tax on the other. Justice **William O. Douglas**, writing for the majority, put the point this way:

> Once the franchise is granted to the electorate, lines may not be drawn which are inconsistent with the Equal Protection Clause. . . . Voter qualifications have no relation to wealth nor to paying this or any other tax. . . . Wealth, like race, creed, or color, is not germane to one's ability to participate intelligently in the electoral process.
>
> —Justice William O. Douglas, Opinion of the Court

>> Associate Justice of the Supreme Court Hugo Black wrote the majority opinion in *Oregon* v. *Mitchell,* affirming the unconstitutionality of voter literacy tests.

Qualifications for Voting Clearly, democratic government can exist only where the right to vote is widely held, and the elimination of such practices as literacy tests and poll taxes has had profound effects on American culture as more and more Americans have been able to participate in government. Still, every State does purposely deny the vote to certain persons. For example, few of the 50 States allow people in mental institutions, or any other persons who have been legally found to be mentally incompetent, to vote.

Most States disqualify, at least temporarily, those persons who have been convicted of serious crimes. Until fairly recently, that disqualification was almost always a permanent one. Over recent years, however, most States have made it possible for the majority of convicted felons to regain the right to vote, although those guilty of such election-related offenses as bribery and ballot-box stuffing, however, are still regularly banned. A few States also do not allow anyone dishonorably discharged from the armed forces to cast a ballot.

INFER How do the basic principles of American government demand that voting rights not be restricted to those who own property?

ASSESSMENT

1. **Compare Points of View** Consider the views of those who think registration requirements should be abolished with those who favor keeping them. What are the pros and cons of each view? Explain.
2. **Infer** What was the idea behind citizens owning property in order to vote?
3. **Cause and Effect** What argument in favor of the 26th Amendment was considered crucial to its quick ratification?
4. **Infer** Why do most States, at least temporarily, bar those convicted of serious crimes from voting?
5. **Infer** Why did States with literacy requirements later create grandfather clauses? What does this say about those State's true intentions?

>> An enthusiastic delegate at the Democratic national convention shows support for her party. Citizens who identify with a political party are more likely to participate in the election process.

Interactive Flipped Video

10.3

"Your vote is your voice. Use it." That's the advice of Rock the Vote, an organization that encourages young voters ages 18 to 25 to participate in the election process. In the United States, and in other democratic countries, we believe all voices should be heard. That is, we believe in voting, because it is one of the processes that individuals can use to affect public policy.

>> Objectives

Examine the problem of nonvoting in the United States

Identify the reasons why some people do not vote and compare these attitudes to those of voters.

Recognize the sources of information about voter behavior.

Understand the factors that influence an individual's political attitudes and actions, including voting and voter behavior.

>> Key Terms

off-year elections
ballot fatigue
political efficacy
political socialization
gender gap
party identification
straight-ticket voting
split-ticket voting
independents
Barack Obama
Donald Trump
Ronald Reagan
George H.W. Bush
Bill Clinton

Voting Trends

Voter Turnout in the United States

Most elections in this country are built around two-candidate contests. How many choices does a voter have in a two-candidate race? More than most people think. Not just two but, in fact, *five* options. He or she can (1) vote FOR Candidate A, (2) vote AGAINST Candidate A, (3) vote FOR Candidate B, (4) vote AGAINST Candidate B, or (5) decide not to vote for either candidate. Throughout this lesson, you will look at voter behavior in this country—at who votes and who does not, and at why those people who do vote cast their ballots as they do.

Nonvoting The word *idiot* came to our language from the Greek. In ancient Athens, idiots *(idiotes)* were those citizens who did not vote or otherwise take part in public life.

Tens of millions of Americans vote in presidential and congressional elections; in State elections; and in city, county, and other public elections. By doing so, they fulfill one of the most important responsibilities of citizenship. Elected officials make decisions every day that affect your life and voting gives you a voice in what those decisions will be. Further, elected officials tend to pay more attention to groups and communities that turn out to vote, which further increases your ability to influence public policy. Despite these facts, millions of Americans do not vote.

On Election Day in 2012, there were an estimated 235 million persons of voting age in the United States. Yet only some 133 million of them—only some 56.5 percent—actually voted in the presidential election. Based on those figures, more than 102 million persons who might have voted did not.

Also in 2012, some 122 million votes were cast in the elections held across the country to fill the 435 seats in the House of Representatives. That is, roughly half of the electorate voted in those congressional contests. **Off-year elections**—that is, the congressional elections held in the even-numbered years between presidential elections—have even lower rates of turnout. Several facets of the nonvoter problem are not very widely known. Take, for example, this striking fact: There are millions of nonvoters *among those who vote*. Some 4 million persons who voted in the last presidential election could also have voted for a congressional candidate, but they did not choose to do so.

Ballot Fatigue "Nonvoting voters" are not limited to federal elections. In fact, they are much more common in State and local elections. As a general rule, the farther down the ballot an office is, the fewer the number of votes that will be cast for it. This phenomenon is sometimes called **ballot fatigue.** The expression suggests that many voters exhaust their patience and/or their knowledge as they work their way down the ballot. More votes are generally cast for the governorship than for other Statewide offices, such as lieutenant governor or secretary of state. More voters in a county usually vote in the races for Statewide offices than vote in the contests for such county offices as sheriff, county clerk, and so on.

There are other little-recognized facets of the nonvoter problem, too. Turnout in congressional elections is consistently higher in presidential years than it is in off-year elections. That same pattern holds among the States in terms of the types of elections; more people vote in general elections than in either primary or special elections.

? INFER Ballot fatigue is one reason voter turnout is far less for congressional elections for lower public offices compared to elections for President. What might be another reason?

Why People Do Not Vote

Why so many nonvoters? Why, even in a presidential election, do as many as half of those who could vote stay away from the polls?

Clearly, the time that it takes to vote should not be a significant part of the answer. For most people, it takes

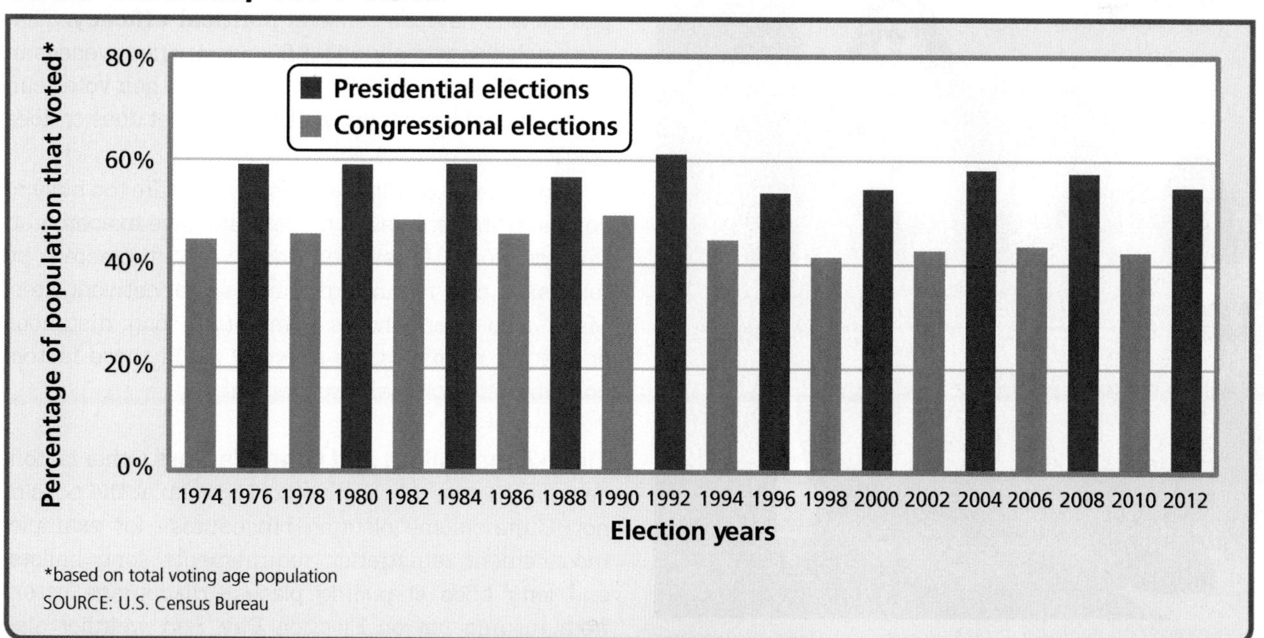

>> This graph is based on the U.S. population aged 18 and over. **Analyze Graphs** What can you conclude about voter turnout in presidential as opposed to off-year elections from this graph?

more time to choose a DVD to watch than it does to go to their neighborhood polling place and cast a ballot. So we must look elsewhere for answers.

"Cannot-Voters" To begin with, look at another of those little-recognized aspects of the nonvoter problem. Several million persons who are regularly identified as nonvoters can be much more accurately described as "cannot-voters." That is, although it is true that they do not vote, the fact is that they cannot do so.

The 2012 data support the point. Included in that figure of more than 102 million who did not vote in the last presidential election are at least 20 million who are resident aliens. Remember, they are barred from the polls in every State. Another 2 to 3 million citizens were so ill or otherwise physically disabled that they simply could not vote in an election. An additional 1 to 2 million persons were traveling suddenly and unexpectedly, and so could not vote.

Other groups of cannot-voters can be discovered in the nonvoting group. They include some 3 million adults who were ineligible to vote because they were in jail or prison, or were on parole or probation; and perhaps as many as a million who do not (cannot) vote because of their religious beliefs—for example, those who believe that acts such as voting amount to idolatry.

>> Turnout tends to be higher in places like Iran where the right to vote has been newly won. In some of those places, people turn out to vote despite the fact that doing so can be dangerous.

Racial, religious, and other biases still play a part here, too—despite the many laws, court decisions, and enforcement actions of the past several years aimed at eliminating such discrimination in the political process. An unknown number of people cannot vote today because of (1) the purposeful administration of election laws to keep them from doing so, and/or (2) various "informal" local pressures applied to that same end.

Actual Nonvoters Even so, there are millions of actual nonvoters in the United States. Thus, in 2012, some 74 million Americans who could have voted in the presidential election did not. There are any number of reasons for that behavior. As a leading example: Many who could go to the polls do not because they are convinced that it makes little real difference which candidate wins a particular election.

That fairly large group includes two quite different groups of nonvoters. On the one hand, there are many who generally approve of the way the public's business is being managed—that is, many who believe that no matter who wins an election, things will continue to go well for them and for the country.

On the other hand, that group also includes many people who feel alienated, cynical, or distrustful of political institutions and processes. These citizens deliberately refuse to vote because they don't trust political institutions and processes. They either fear or scorn "the system." To them, elections are meaningless, choiceless exercises.

Another large group of nonvoters is composed of people who have no sense of **political efficacy.** That is, they lack any feeling of influence or effectiveness in politics. They do not believe that they or their votes can have any real impact on what government does or does not do.

More than 3.5 million voters say they are too busy to vote, and the realities of modern life have exacerbated this problem. Americans today are distracted by television, new technologies, and social network sites. Many also spend hours commuting long distances or putting in extra time at work. All of these factors contribute to political disengagement.

Time-Zone Fallout and Other Factors Other factors can also dictate whether voters show up at the polls or not. Cumbersome election procedures—for example, inconvenient registration requirements, long ballots, and long lines at polling places—discourage voters from turning out on Election Day. Bad weather also tends to discourage voter turnout.

Another possible, though somewhat controversial, factor is the so-called "time-zone fallout" problem.

This expression refers to the fact that, in presidential elections, polls in States in the Eastern and Central time zones close an hour or more before polls in the Mountain and Pacific time zones do. Based on early returns from the East and Midwest, the news media often project the outcome of the presidential contest before all voters in the West have gone to the polls. Some people fear that such reports work to discourage western voters from casting their ballots.

The nature of campaigns and the media are also cited as reasons for voter alienation. Polls show that Americans dislike negative campaigning and may become disgusted with the entire process as a result. The news media contributes to voter burnout by seizing on every controversy, with the result that candidates can seem horribly tarnished by Election Day. Perhaps voting has declined in part because our enthusiasm for candidates has waned.

Of all the reasons for nonvoting that may be cited, however, the most simple is a lack of interest. Among nonvoters in 2012, nearly 20 percent reported that they did not vote because they were not interested or they forgot. Those who are indifferent, who just cannot be bothered, are usually woefully misinformed. Most often, they know little or nothing about the candidates and issues in an election. Many argue that the democratic process is well served by the fact that most of these people do not go to the polls.

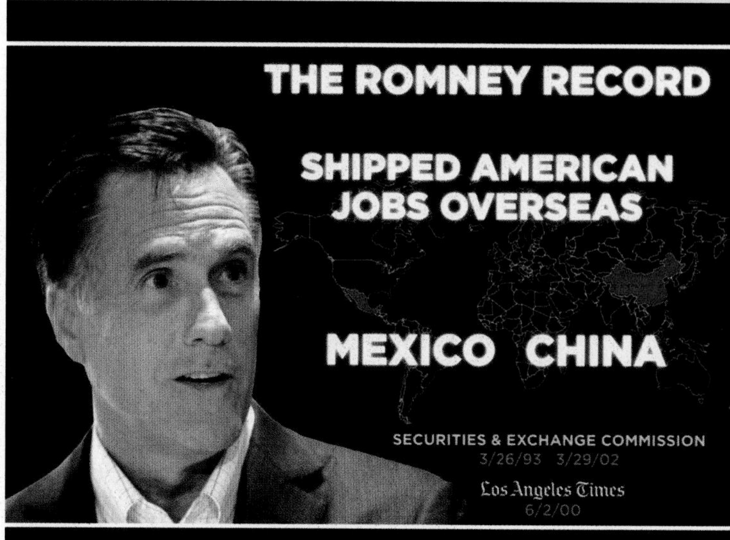

>> According to recent studies, this type of negative campaigning can cause voters to react unfavorably to both the target and the sponsor of the ad.

Comparing Voters and Nonvoters One useful way to get a handle on the problem of nonvoting is to contrast those persons who tend to go to the polls regularly with those who do not.

The people most likely to vote display such characteristics as higher levels of income, education, and occupational status. They are usually well integrated into community life. They tend to be long-time residents who are active in, or at least comfortable with, their surroundings. They are likely to have a strong sense of party identification, and to believe that voting is an important act. They are also likely to live in those areas where laws, customs, and competition between the parties all promote turnout.

The opposite characteristics produce a profile of those less likely to vote. Nonvoters are likely to be younger than age 35, unmarried, and unskilled. More nonvoters live in the South and in rural locales. Men are less likely to vote than women—a fact that first became apparent in the 1980s.

A few of the factors that help determine whether or not a person will vote are so important that they influence turnout even when they conflict with other factors. For example, those persons with a high sense of political efficacy are likely to vote—no matter what their income, education, age, race, and so on may be. The degree of two-party competition also has an extraordinary impact on participation. Thus, the greater the competition between candidates, the more likely people will be to go to the polls, regardless of other factors.

Despite the greater weight of some of these factors, however, note this point: It is the combined presence of several factors, not one of them alone, that tends to determine whether a person will or will not vote.

? CONNECT Many reasons have been cited as to why people choose not to vote. Can you think of another logical reason that eligible voters might decide not to go to the polls that is related to political parties?

Influences on Voters and Voting Behavior

As you have read, tens of millions of potential voters do not go to the polls in this country. But many millions more do. How do those who do vote behave? What prompts many to vote most often for Republicans and many others to support the Democratic Party? Research has produced a huge amount of information about why people tend to vote as they do.

Studying Voting Behavior Most of what is known about voter behavior comes from three sources.

1. *The results of particular elections.* How individuals vote in a given election is secret in the United States. However, careful study of the returns from areas populated largely by, say, African Americans or Catholics or high-income families will indicate how those groups voted in a given election.

2. *The field of survey research.* The polling of scientifically determined cross sections of the population is the method by which public opinion is most often identified and measured. The Gallup Organization and the Pew Research Center conduct perhaps the best known of these polls today.

3. *Studies of political socialization.* **Political socialization** is the process by which people gain their political attitudes and opinions. That complex process begins in early childhood and continues through each person's life. Political socialization involves all of the experiences and relationships that lead people to see the political world, and to act in it, as they do.

Factors That Influence Voters Observers still have much to learn about voter behavior, but many sociological and psychological factors clearly influence the way people cast their ballots. Sociology is the study of groups and how people behave within groups. The sociological factors affecting voter behavior are really the many pieces of a voter's social and economic life. Those pieces are of two broad kinds: (1) a voter's personal characteristics—age, race, income, occupation, education, religion, and so on; and (2) a voter's group affiliations—family, co-workers, friends, and the like.

Psychology is the study of the mind and individual behavior. The psychological factors that influence voter behavior are a voter's perceptions of politics—that is, how the voter sees the parties, the candidates, and the issues in an election.

The differences between these two kinds of influences are not nearly so great as they might seem. In fact, they are closely related and they constantly interact with one another. How voters look at parties, candidates, or issues is often shaped by their own social and economic backgrounds.

DRAW CONCLUSIONS Could the study of voter behavior help determine the outcome of upcoming elections? Why or why not?

" The tests show it's a boy . . we can't tell whether he'll vote Republican or not. "

>> While this cartoon pokes fun at the idea, it is nonetheless true that children often vote like their parents. **Analyze Images** Which influence on voter behavior does this cartoon portray?

Sociological Factors and Political Attitudes

Using data from past elections, you can draw a composite picture of the American voter in terms of a number of sociological factors. A word of caution here: Do not make too much of any one of these factors. Remember, each voter possesses not just one, but in fact *several* of the many characteristics involved here.

To illustrate the point: College graduates are more likely to vote Republican. So are persons over age 50. African Americans, on the other hand, are more likely to vote for Democrats. So are members of labor unions. How, then, would a 55-year-old, college-educated African American who belongs to the AFL-CIO decide to vote?

Income and Occupation For years, voters in lower income brackets were more likely to be Democrats, while voters with higher incomes tended to be Republicans. This pattern has shown signs of eroding somewhat at the higher income bracket over recent elections, however. Thus, in 2008, **Barack Obama** captured 52 percent of the votes of those with incomes over $200,000. In 2012, however, the pattern held true.

Voting by Income and Education, 2016

		TRUMP	CLINTON
INCOME	Less than $30,000*	41%	53%
	$50,000 to $99,999	50%	46%
	$100,000 to $199,999	48%	47%
EDUCATION	High school or less	51%	45%
	Some college	52%	43%
	College graduate	45%	49%
	Postgraduate	37%	58%

SOURCE: *New York Times* exit poll *annual income in U.S. dollars

>> This exit poll categorizes voters based on income and education. **Interpret Demographic Data** Did voters in the lowest income bracket support Donald Trump or Hillary Clinton? Did the same hold true for those with the least amount of education?

The majority of voters in the lowest income bracket favored Democrat Barack Obama. Those with higher incomes voted for Republican Mitt Romney. And in 2016, the majority of those with the lowest incomes chose Democrat Hillary Clinton, while those with incomes above $50,000 tended to vote for Republican **Donald Trump**.

Education Studies of voter behavior reveal that there is also a close relationship between the level of a voter's education and how he or she tends to vote. For many years, college graduates have tended to vote for Republicans in higher percentages than those with a high school education or less. This longstanding pattern was broken in the last three elections, however. In 2012, the vote among all educational levels was evenly split between Barack Obama and Mitt Romney, with one exception: 55 percent of voters who held postgraduate degrees favored President Obama.

In 2016, the pattern was turned on its head: 49 percent of college graduates voted for Hillary Clinton, while only 45 percent voted for Donald Trump. And among those with postgraduate degrees, the margin was even greater: 58 percent of those voters chose Hillary Clinton, while only 37 percent cast their ballots for Donald Trump.

Gender, Age There are often measurable differences between the partisan choices of men and women today. This phenomenon is known as the **gender gap**, and it first appeared in the 1980s. Women generally tend to favor the Democrats by a margin of five to ten percent, and men often give the GOP a similar edge. Thus, in 2016, Hillary Clinton won 54 percent of all votes cast by women, while 53 percent of men threw their support to Republican Donald Trump.

A number of studies show that men and women are most likely to vote differently when such issues as abortion, healthcare or other social welfare matters, or military involvements abroad are prominent in an election.

Traditionally, younger voters have been more likely to vote Democrat, while older voters are likely to find the GOP's candidates more attractive. This trend held true for every presidential election from 1960 through 1980. That long-standing pattern was broken by **Ronald Reagan**'s appeal to younger voters in 1984, and by **George H.W. Bush** in 1988. However, **Bill Clinton** restored the Democrats' claim to those voters in 1992 and 1996. In 2008, Barack Obama won a huge 66 percent of the under 30 vote, and in 2016, Hillary Clinton captured 55 percent of this group's vote.

Religion, Ethnic Background Historically, a majority of Protestants have preferred the GOP. Catholics and Jews have tended to be Democrats. The 2016 elections broke somewhat with this trend, however. While Donald Trump did win 58 percent of the votes cast by Protestants to Hillary Clinton's 39 percent, Catholics also threw their support to Mr. Trump. He captured 52 percent of their votes, to Clinton's 45 percent. Among Jewish voters, a huge 71 percent cast their ballots for Clinton, in line with that group's usual preference for Democratic candidates.

Church attendance has also emerged as a major indicator of partisan preference. For example, fifty-six percent of voters who go to church at least once a week marked their ballots for Mr. Trump in 2016. In fact, that group consistently voted for the Republican candidate in each of the last five presidential elections.

For decades now, African Americans have supported the Democratic Party consistently and massively. They are the only group that has given the Democratic candidate a clear majority in every presidential election since 1952. The nation's 43 million African Americans make up the country's second largest minority group.

In the North, African Americans generally voted Republican until the 1930s, but, with the coming of the New Deal, they moved away from the party of Abraham Lincoln. The civil rights movement of the 1960s led to much greater African American participation in the politics of the South. Today, African Americans vote overwhelmingly Democratic in that region, too.

The United States is now home to more than 56 million Latinos, people with Spanish-speaking backgrounds. Latinos generally favor Democratic candidates. Note, however, that the label "Latino" conceals differences among Cuban Americans, who most often vote Republican, and Mexican Americans and Puerto Ricans, who are strongly Democratic. Turnout among Latinos increased significantly in the historic election of 2008, and it has approached 50 percent in every election since.

Geography Geography—the part of the country, State, and/or locale in which a person lives—also has a measurable impact on voter behavior. After the Civil War, the States of the old Confederacy voted so consistently Democratic that the southeast quarter of the nation became known as the Solid South. For more than a century, most Southerners, regardless of any other factor, identified with the Democratic Party.

The Solid South is now a thing of the past. Republican candidates have been increasingly successful throughout the region over the past half-century. The GOP now carries at least most of the Southern States in the presidential contest every four years, and it is now widely successful at the State and local levels across the region, too.

Those States that have most consistently supported Republican candidates over time have been Idaho, Wyoming, and Utah in the West and Kansas, Nebraska, and the Dakotas in the Midwest. The Democrats have made significant inroads in former Republican strongholds in New England, over the past two decades or so.

Voting by Religion and Race, 2016

	2016	
Religious Preference	**TRUMP**	**CLINTON**
Protestant/Other Christian	58%	39%
Catholic	52%	45%
Jewish	24%	71%
Something else	29%	62%
None	26%	68%
Race/Ethnicity	**TRUMP**	**CLINTON**
White	58%	37%
African American	8%	88%
Hispanic/Latino American	29%	65%
Asian American	29%	65%
Other	37%	56%

SOURCE: *New York Times* exit poll

>> This chart looks at voter behavior based on religious affiliation and race. **Analyze Charts** How did religion and race influence voter choice in 2016?

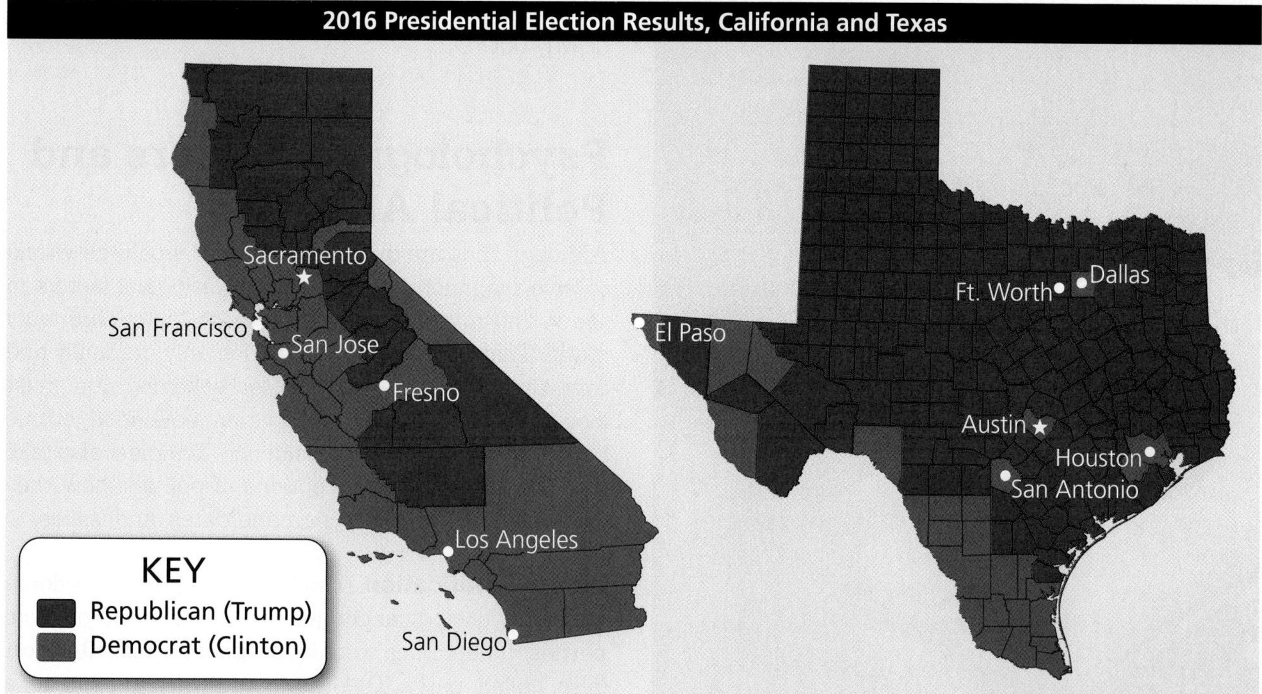

>> Voters in urban areas tend to vote Democratic, even in States like Texas that usually vote overwhelmingly Republican. **Analyze Maps** Did cities in California follow this pattern?

Voter attitudes also vary in terms of the size of the communities in which they live. Generally, the Democrats draw strength from the big cities of the North and East and on the Pacific Coast. Many white Democrats have moved from the central cities and taken their political preferences with them, but Republican voters still dominate much of suburban America. Voters in smaller cities and rural areas are also likely to be Republicans.

With the move of many older Americans to the "Sunbelt" States of Florida, Arizona, and Texas during the latter part of the 20th century, as well as a growing Latino population in that region, these States gained both voters and electoral college votes. In 2016, Republicans maintained a solid advantage in this region. In other Sunbelt States, however, such as California, the Democrats were the winners.

Population Shifts Population shifts from urban to rural areas, or vice versa, also affect voting patterns. Beginning with the New Deal era of the 1930s and 1940s, federal funds pouring into urban areas brought a migration from country to city, and with it, a move toward the Republican Party for the nation's cities. When the trend was reversed in the 1950s—from cities to suburbs—those voters took their Republican preference with them. Ronald Reagan, for example, captured the White House in 1980 without winning a single city. In recent years, however, Americans have been moving back into urban areas in large numbers. As immigrants, minorities, and young Americans swell city populations, they have contributed to the recent trend toward Democratic domination in urban areas—even in States that are seen as Republican-dominated overall.

Family and Other Groups To this point, you have seen the American voter sketched in terms of several broad social and economic characteristics. The picture can also be drawn on the basis of much smaller and more personal groupings, especially such primary groups as family, friends, and co-workers.

Typically, the members of a family vote in strikingly similar ways. Nine out of ten married couples share the same partisan leanings. As many as two out of every three voters follow the political attachments of their parents. Those who work together and circles of friends also tend to vote very much alike.

This like-mindedness is hardly surprising. People of similar social and economic backgrounds tend to associate with one another. In short, a person's group associations usually reinforce the opinions he or she already holds.

? MAKE PREDICTIONS In some democratic nations, voting is not only expected, it is required. Do you think

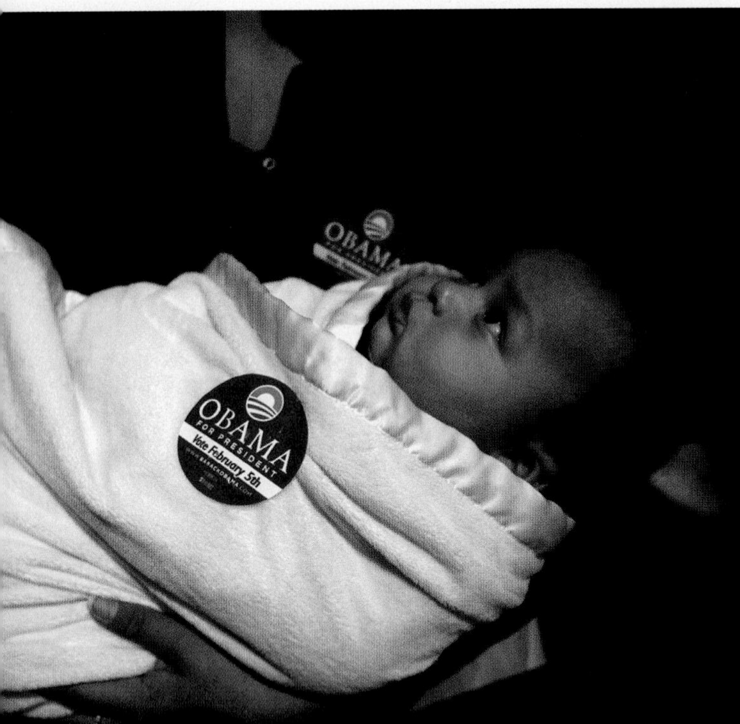

>> Family is a big factor in how a person tends to vote. Statistics show that this baby will likely vote Democratic upon turning 18.

Interactive Chart

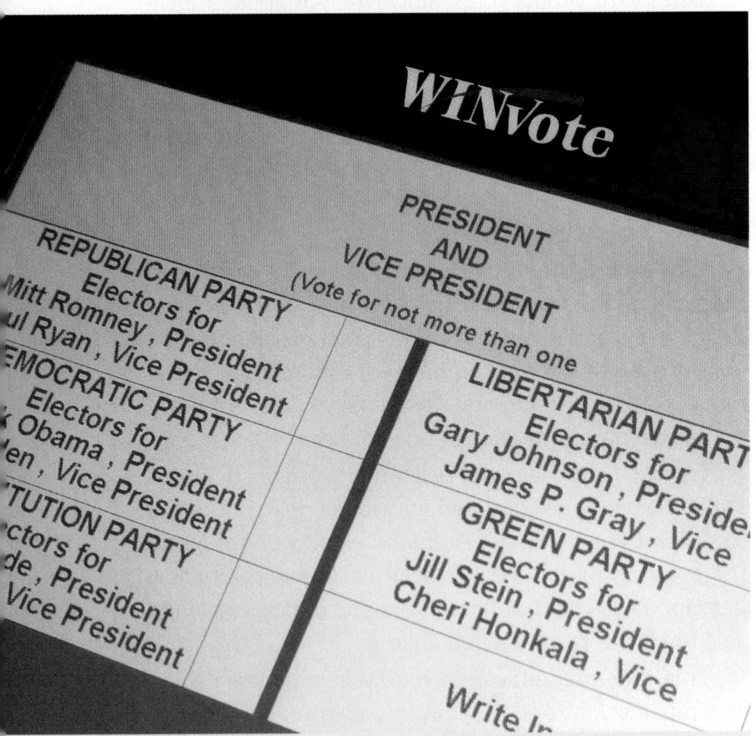

>> A voting machine lists presidential candidates. Over the last decade, the proportion of Americans who consider themselves independents has generally hovered between about 35 and 44 percent.

Interactive Chart

this approach would work in the United States? Why or why not?

Psychological Factors and Political Attitudes

Although they are quite important, it would be wrong to give too much weight to the sociological factors in the voting mix. For one thing, those factors are fairly static. That is, they tend to change only gradually and over time. To understand voter behavior, you must look beyond factors like occupation, education, ethnic background, and place of residence. You must also take into account voters' perceptions of politics: how they see and react to the parties, candidates, and issues.

Party Identification Many Americans have a deep-rooted psychological connection to one of the political parties. Indeed, one's so-called **party identification** (also called party ID)—the loyalty of a person to a particular political party—is the single best predictor of how a person will vote in any given election. A Democrat or a Republican will quite often vote for all or most of that party's candidates. The practice of voting for candidates of only one party in an election is called **straight-ticket voting.**

How a person establishes his or her party identification has been a topic of scholarly inquiry for decades. The social and economic factors described above can play a role, but the most important factor is political socialization. That is to say, most Americans form their party identification during their childhoods. Interestingly, that initial socialization often sticks with a person throughout his or her days.

The extent to which Americans identify with a political party has waxed and waned over the years. In the 1990s, for example, many indicators pointed to declining levels of partisanship. **Split-ticket voting**—the practice of voting for the candidates of more than one party in an election (the opposite of straight-ticket voting)—was quite common during this period. Also, the number of voters who called themselves **independents** rose. That term is used to identify those people who have no party affiliation.

In recent years, however, strong party identification has reemerged, with about two thirds of Americans considering themselves either Democrats or Republicans. A large portion of the others—those we might historically call independents—actually vote consistently for one party or the other. What is particularly unique about the recent period is the level of dislike and distrust of the "other" party. Democrats are increasingly hostile to Republicans, and vice versa.

Candidates and Issues Party identification is a long-term factor. While most voters identify with one or the other of the major parties and most often support its candidates, they do not always vote that way—even in the most recent period. One or more short-term factors can cause them to switch sides in a particular election, or at least vote a split ticket. In any given election, including in the recent period, roughly eight to ten percent of party identifiers will vote for a candidate of the other party.

The most important of these short-term factors are the candidates and the issues in an election. Clearly, the impression a candidate makes on the voters can have an impact on their choices in the voting booth. What image does a candidate project? How do the voters see that candidate in terms of personality, character, style, appearance, past record, abilities, and so on? And how do voters see the opposing candidate? This factor was certainly at play in the 2016 presidential election, with some Republicans finding it impossible to vote for Donald Trump and many Democrats unwilling to vote for Hillary Clinton.

Just as clearly, issues can sometimes have a large impact on voter behavior. The role of issues varies, however, depending on such things as the emotional content of the issues themselves, the voters' awareness of them, and the ways in which the contending candidates present them to the electorate. One of the most important short-term issues is the state of the economy—both the perception of the nation's economy and how well the voter feels he or she is doing. These types of concerns are sometimes referred to as "pocketbook issues."

Issues have become increasingly important to voters over the past 40 years or so. The tumultuous nature of politics over the period—highlighted by the civil rights movement, the Vietnam War, the feminist movement, the Watergate scandal, economic problems, and, over recent years, such critical matters as a severe economic recession, healthcare costs, and the climbing national debt—is most likely responsible for this heightened voter concern.

? IDENTIFY CENTRAL IDEAS Why could party identification be considered one of the more important factors to a political party in an election?

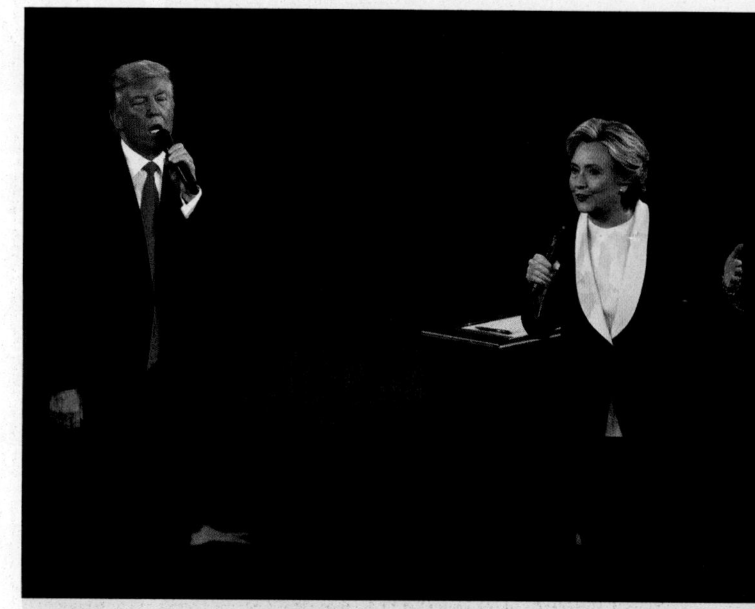

>> Donald Trump and Hillary Clinton debate during the 2016 presidential campaign. **Interpret** How might today's trend toward strong party identification affect the importance of presidential debates?

ASSESSMENT

1. **Draw Conclusions** Based on what you have learned about the meaning of the word *idiot,* what conclusion can you draw about Greek attitudes about participating in public life?
2. **Hypothesize** What is the importance of understanding the psychological factors of voting behavior?
3. **Analyze Information** What are some of the characteristics of a likely voter?
4. **Describe** What factors can produce split-ticket voting?
5. **Infer** How can the impression a candidate gives influence voters? How do the media help to portray a candidate's impression?

>> A voter in Madison County, Mississippi, casts her ballot on a direct response electronic voting machine (DRE). Since 2000, use of DREs has increased more than 300 percent.

10.4 **Most high school students are not old enough to vote. In some parts of the country, though, high school students can serve on local election boards. First in Hawaii and Oregon and now in several States, 16- and 17-year-olds can become full-fledged members of the panels that administer local elections.**

Interactive Flipped Video

>> Objectives

Analyze how the administration of elections in the United States helps make democracy work.

Compare different methods of filling public offices at the local, state, and national levels, including the role of local precincts and polling places in the election process.

Describe the various ways in which voters can cast their ballots.

Outline the role that voting devices play in the election process.

>> Key Terms

ballot
absentee voting
coattail effect
precinct
polling place

The Voting Process

Filling Elected Public Offices

We hold more elections in this country and we vote more often than most people realize. Indeed, elections are held somewhere in the United States nearly every month of the year. We also elect *far* more officeholders than most people realize—in fact, more than 500,000 of them, more than in any other country in the world.

Democratic government cannot possibly hope to succeed unless its elections are free, honest, and accurately reported. Many people see the details of the election process as much too complicated, too legalistic, too dry and boring to worry about. Those who do, really miss this vital point: voting is one of the most effective processes used by individuals to affect public policy. Thus, the methods of filling public elected offices—the administration of elections—is of primary importance.

Extent of Federal Control Nearly all elections in the United States are held to choose the more than 500,000 persons who hold elective office in the more than 90,000 units of government at the State and local levels. It is quite understandable, then, that most election law in the United States is *State*—not federal—law.

Even so, a body of federal election law does exist. The Constitution gives Congress the power to fix "[t]he Times, Places, and Manner of holding Elections" of members of Congress (Article I, Section 4, Clause

1; 17th Amendment). Congress also has the power to set the time for choosing presidential electors, to set the date for casting the electoral votes, and to regulate other aspects of the presidential election process (Article II, Section 1, Clause 4; 12 Amendment).

Congress has set the date for holding congressional elections as the first Tuesday following the first Monday in November of every even-numbered year. It has set the same date every fourth year for the presidential election. Thus, the next (off-year) congressional elections will be held on November 4, 2014, and the next presidential contest will be decided on November 8, 2016.

Congress has required the use of secret ballots and allowed the use of voting machines and similar devices in federal elections. It has also acted to protect the right to vote. Congress has also prohibited various corrupt practices and regulates the financing of campaigns for federal office, as you will see in the pages ahead.

Help America Vote Act Congress expanded the body of federal election law with the passage of the Help America Vote Act of 2002. That law came in response to the many ballot and voter registration problems that plagued several States in the presidential election in 2000. A **ballot** is the medium by which a voter registers a choice in an election. The word comes from the Italian *ballotta*, "little ball," and reflects the practice of dropping black or white balls into a box to indicate a choice. The term *blackball* also comes from that practice. It is believed that the ancient Romans used paper ballots as early as 139 B.C.

In its major provisions, the law requires that the States

1. replace all their lever-operated and punchcard voting devices by 2006—a deadline that, in fact, most States failed to meet;
2. upgrade their administration of elections, especially through the better training of local election officials and of those more than 2 million (mostly low-paid workers and volunteers) who work in precinct polling places on election day;
3. centralize and computerize their voter registration systems, to facilitate the identification of qualified voters on election day and so minimize fraudulent voting;
4. provide for provisional voting, so a person whose eligibility to vote has been challenged can nonetheless cast a ballot that will be counted if it is later found that he or she is, in fact, qualified to vote.

State law deals with all other matters relating to national elections—and with all of the details of State and local elections as well.

State Election Dates Most States hold their elections to fill State offices on the same date Congress has set for national elections: in November of every even-numbered year.

The "Tuesday-after-the-first-Monday" formula avoids holding election day on Sundays, a day of worship, and at the time it was passed in 1845, satisfied other Constitutional and practical requirements.

Some States do fix other dates for some offices, however. Louisiana, Mississippi, New Jersey, and Virginia elect the governor, other executive officers, and State legislators in November of odd-numbered years. In Kentucky, the governor and other executive officers are chosen in odd-numbered years, but legislators are elected in even-numbered years. City, county, and other local election dates vary from State to State. When those elections are not held in November, they generally take place in the spring.

An Increase in Early Voting Millions of Americans cast their ballots before election day. Indeed, more than 32 million did so in 2012.

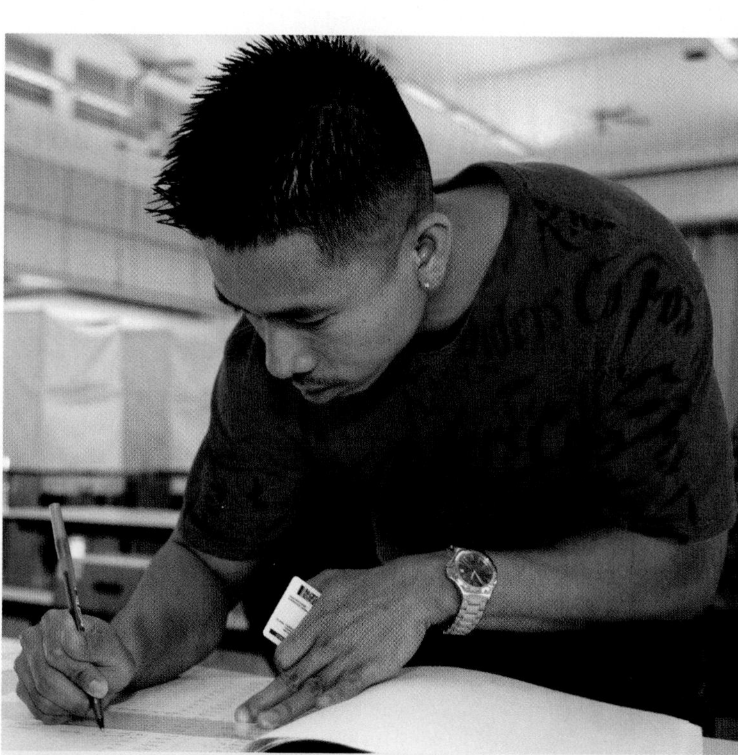

>> A young Hawaiian voter signs in at the polls. In Hawaii, teens can preregister to vote at age 16, but they must be 18 by election day to actually vote.

Interactive Gallery

Many of them did so by **absentee voting**—a process by which they could vote without going to their polling places on election day. Congress was responsible for the first instance of absentee voting. In the midst of the Civil War, it provided for the casting of absentee ballots by federal troops in the elections of 1864. Over the years, every State has made at least some provision for the process.

Today, many States allow "no excuse" absentee voting. In these States, voters can obtain an absentee ballot some weeks before an election, without offering an excuse. They mark those ballots and return them to the local election office, usually by mail, in a sealed envelope, and before election day.

State absentee voting was originally intended to serve a relatively small group of voters, especially the ill or disabled and those who expected to be away from home on election day. Most States have broadened their laws over recent years, however—to the point where, in most of them, any qualified voter can cast an absentee ballot simply because he or she wants to vote that way.

A majority of the States have now formalized early voting. They allow any voters who choose to do so to cast their ballots at any time over a period of several days before an election—not as an absentee ballot but as though they were voting on election day itself. Indeed, in many places, election day is now just the final day on which votes can be cast.

Election Dates and the Coattail Effect Some have long argued that all State and local elections should be held on dates other than those set for federal elections. This, they say, would help voters pay more attention to State and local candidates and issues and lessen the coattail effect a presidential candidate can have.

The **coattail effect** occurs when a strong candidate running for an office at the top of the ballot helps attract voters to other candidates on the party's ticket. In effect, the lesser-known office seeker "rides the coattails" of the more prestigious personality—for example, a Franklin D. Roosevelt, a Ronald Reagan, or a Barack Obama. The coattail effect is usually most apparent in presidential elections. However, a popular candidate for senator or governor can have the same kind of pulling power in State and local elections. In recent years, the coattail effect can occur off the ballot, simply by virtue of the media attention a particular candidate can generate.

A reverse coattail effect can occur, too. This happens when a candidate for some major office is less than popular with many voters—for example, Barry Goldwater as the Republican presidential nominee in 1964 and George McGovern for the Democrats in 1972. President Jimmy Carter's coattails were also of the reverse variety in 1980.

? APPLY CONCEPTS How might early voting lead to an expansion of the electorate?

Ways Americans Voted in the 2012 General Election

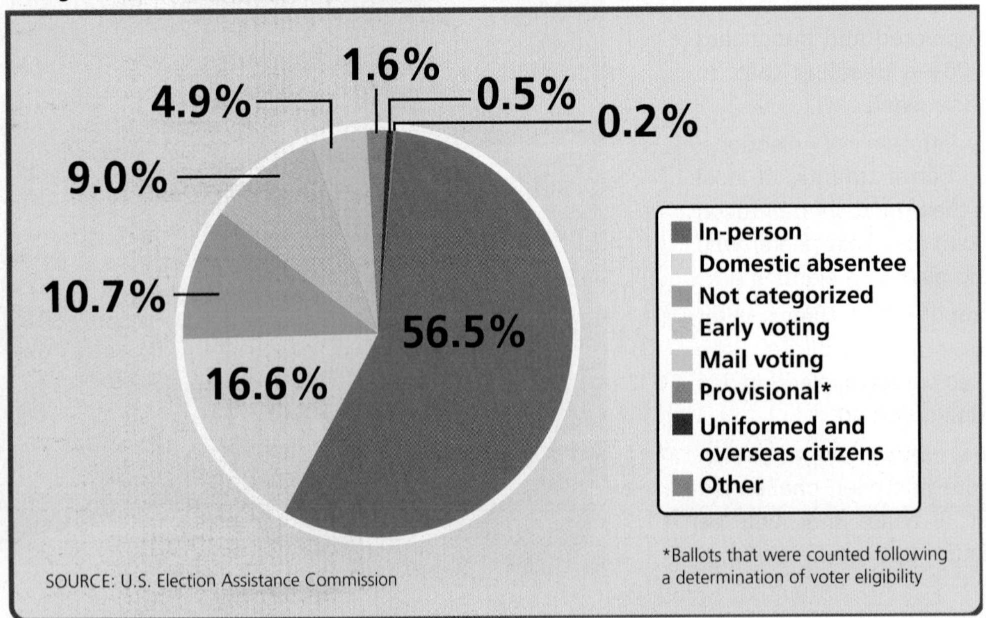

>> Americans used many different methods to cast their ballots in 2012. **Analyze Charts** What percentage of voters used methods other than in-person to vote?

Precincts, Polling Places, and Ballots

A **precinct** is a voting district. Precincts are the smallest geographic units for the conduct of elections. State law regularly restricts their size, generally to an area with no more than 500 to 1,000 or so qualified voters. A **polling place**—the place where the voters who live in a precinct actually vote—is located somewhere in or near each precinct.

A precinct election board supervises the polling place and the voting process in each precinct. Typically, the county clerk or county board of elections draws precinct lines, fixes the location of each polling place, and picks the members of the precinct boards.

The precinct board opens and closes the polls at the times set by State law. In most States, the polls are open from 7:00 or 8:00 A.M. to 7:00 or 8:00 P.M. The precinct election board must also see that the ballots and the ballot boxes or voting devices are available. It must make certain that only qualified voters cast ballots in the precinct. Often the board also counts the votes cast in the precinct and then sends the results to the proper place, usually to the county clerk or county board of elections.

Poll watchers, one from each party, are allowed at each polling place. They may challenge any person they believe is not qualified to vote, check to be sure that their own party's supporters do vote, and monitor the whole process, including the counting of the ballots.

>> Republican presidential candidate Barry Goldwater's landslide loss to President Lyndon B. Johnson also contributed to lost elections for dozens of Republicans running for Congress.

Types of Ballots A ballot can take a number of different forms, ranging from a piece of paper to optical scanners and touch screens. Whatever its form, however, it is clearly an important and sensitive part of the election process.

State law requires that ballots be cast in secret, but voting was a quite public process during the nation's earlier history. Paper ballots were used in some colonial elections, but voting was more commonly *viva voce*—by voice. Voters simply stated their choices, in public, to an election board. With suffrage limited to the privileged few, many people defended oral voting as the only "manly" way in which to participate. Whatever the merits of that view, the expansion of the electorate brought with it a marked increase in intimidation, vote buying, and other corruptions of the voting process.

Paper ballots were in general use by the mid-1800s. The first ones were unofficial—slips of paper that voters prepared themselves and dropped in the ballot box. Soon candidates and parties began to prepare ballots and hand them to voters to cast, sometimes paying them to do so. Those party ballots were often printed

>> A Maryland voter casts her ballot ten days before election day. By 2013, thirty-two States allowed early voting, some as much as six weeks early.

on distinctively colored paper, and anyone watching could tell for whom voters were voting.

Political machines—local party organizations capable of mobilizing or "manufacturing" large numbers of votes on behalf of candidates for political office—flourished in many places in the latter 1800s. Because these groups did not want to lose their ability to affect public policy, they fought all attempts to make voting a more dependably fair and honest process. The political corruption of the post–Civil War years brought widespread demand for ballot reforms.

The Australian Ballot A new voting arrangement was devised in Australia, where it was first used in an election in Victoria in 1856. Its successes there led to its use in other countries. By 1900, nearly all of the States were using it, and it remains the basic form of the ballot in this country today.

The Australian Ballot has four essential features: It (1) is provided at public expense; (2) lists the names of all candidates in an election; (3) is given out only at the polls, one to each qualified voter; and (4) can be marked in secret.

Two basic forms of the Australian ballot have been used in this country over the past century, the office-group ballot (all candidates for an office are grouped together under the title of that office) and the party-column ballot (lists all candidates under their party's name). Most States now use the office-group ballot; only a handful of them rely on the party-column ballot.

>> In the 1800s, political memorabilia, such as this advertisement for candidates Abraham Lincoln and Andrew Johnson, sometimes also served as the ballot.

Sample Ballots Sample ballots, clearly marked as such, are available in most States before an election. In some States they are mailed to all voters, and they appear in most newspapers and on the Internet. They cannot be cast, but they can help voters prepare for an election.

First in Oregon (1907), and now in several States, an official voter's pamphlet is mailed to voters before every election. It lists all candidates and measures that will appear on the ballot. In Oregon, each candidate is allowed space to present his or her qualifications and position on the issues. Supporters and opponents of ballot measures are allowed space to present their arguments as well.

Bed-sheet Ballots The ballot in a typical American election is lengthy, often and aptly called a "bed-sheet" ballot. It frequently lists so many offices, candidates, and ballot measures that even the most well-informed voters have a difficult time marking it intelligently.

The long ballot came to American politics in the era of Jacksonian Democracy in the 1830s. Many held the view at the time that the greater the number of elective offices, the more democratic the governmental system. That idea remains widely accepted today.

Generally, the longest ballots are found at the local level, especially among the nation's 3,000-odd counties. The list of elected offices is likely to include several commissioners, a clerk, a sheriff, one or more judges, a prosecutor, coroner, treasurer, assessor, surveyor, school superintendent, engineer, sanitarian, and even the proverbial dogcatcher.

Critics of the bed-sheet ballot reject the notion that the more people you elect, the more democratic the system. Instead, they say, the fewer the offices voters have to fill, the better they can know the candidates and their qualifications. Those critics often point to the factor of "ballot fatigue"—that is, to the drop-off in voting that can run as high as 20 to 30 percent at or near the bottom of the typical (lengthy) ballot.

There seems little, if any, good reason to elect such local officials as clerks, coroners, surveyors, and engineers. Their jobs do not carry basic policy-making responsibilities. Rather, they carry out policies made by others. Many believe that to shorten the ballot and promote good government, the rule should be: Elect those who make public policies; appoint those whose basic job it is to administer those policies.

COMPARE Compare the pro and con arguments for the "bed-sheet ballot."

Casting and Counting Ballots

Well over half the votes now cast in national elections are cast on some type of voting machine—and, increasingly, on some type of electronic voting device.

Thomas Edison received a patent for the first voting machine—the first mechanical device for the casting and counting of votes—in 1869, and the Myers Automatic Booth was first used in a public election in Lockport, New York, in 1892. The use of similar but much-improved devices soon spread to polling places across the country.

For the better part of a century, most voting machines were lever-operated, and quite cumbersome. Voters had to pull various levers in order to cast their ballots—one lever to open (unlock) the machine, others to indicate their choices of candidates, and yet another to close (lock) the machine and record their votes.

Those lever-operated machines did impact the political process by speeding up voting and reducing both fraud and counting errors. The machines were quite expensive, however, and they also posed major storage and transport problems from one election to the next.

Counting Votes Electronically Electronic data processing (EDP) techniques were first applied to the voting process in the 1960s. California and Oregon led the way and EDP is now a vital part of that process in most States.

For some years, the most widely used adaptations of EDP involved punch-card ballots, counted by computers. But punch-card ballots often produced problems—most frequently because voters failed to make clean punches. Their incomplete perforations left "hanging chads" that made the cards difficult or impossible for computers to read.

Punch-card ballots played a major role in the disputed presidential election vote count in Florida in 2000; and that fiasco led to the passage of the Help America Vote Act of 2002. As was noted earlier, that law required the elimination of all punch-card voting devices (and all lever-operated voting machines, as well).

Most States have turned to two other EDP-based voting systems. One of them involves the same optical-

>> Thomas Edison (shown here) invented a vote recorder in the late 1860s. When a colleague presented it to Congress, a committee chairman said, "if there is any invention on earth that we don't want down here, that is it."

Interactive Timeline

scanning technology used to grade the standardized tests students take in school. Voters mark their ballots by filling in circles, ovals, or rectangles or by completing arrows. A computer scans the marked ballots, counting and recording the votes cast.

The other system utilizes direct response electronic voting machines (DREs). Those machines are much like ATMs or cash machines. Voters make their choices on most models by touching a screen or, on some, by pushing buttons. Their votes are recorded electronically.

DREs have proved troublesome in many places. Some models have malfunctioned and some do not provide a paper record of voters' choices. Many computer scientists insist that DREs can be easily compromised by hackers. Several States abandoned them in recent elections. They turned, instead, to optical-scanning systems or even went back to hand-counted paper ballots.

Voting by Mail One method of casting a ballot—mail-in balloting—does not require any type of voting machine. Instead of going to the polls, voters fill out a ballot at home and mail it back to election officials. While most States allow "no excuse" absentee balloting, some have considered replacing all voting booths with mail-in balloting. As of 2014, however, only three States—Oregon, Washington, and Colorado—have actually done so.

The main reason for this is that voting by mail has stirred controversy. Critics fear that the process threatens the secret ballot principle. They worry about fraud, especially the possibility that some voters may be subjected to undue pressures when they mark their ballots at home or any place other than a secure voting booth.

In addition, scholars have found that vote-by-mail may not actually increase turnout. They note that vote-by-mail eliminates an important aspect of participatory government—that is, the ceremonial aspect of going to the polls, which generates energy, excitement, and a sense of community.

Supporters, on the other hand, say that more than ten years of voting by mail in Oregon indicates that that process can be as fraud-proof as any other method of voting. They also make this point: The mail-in process may increase voter participation in elections and most definitely reduces the costs of conducting them.

The Impact of the Internet Online voting—casting ballots via the Internet—has attracted considerable attention and some support in recent years. Will e-voting become widespread, even commonplace, as some predict? Obviously, only time will tell.

Online voting is not an entirely new phenomenon. The first e-vote was cast in November 1997. Election officials in Harris County, Texas, allowed astronaut David Wolf to vote in Houston's city election by e-mail from the space station *Mir*.

The first public election in which some votes were cast by computer was held in 2000, in Arizona's Democratic presidential primary. The Defense Department enabled 84 members of the military stationed abroad to vote electronically in the general election that year, but chose not to repeat the program because of worries about ballot security. In 2010, a minor party, the Independent Party of Oregon, became the first political party to nominate its candidates in a primary election that was held entirely online.

A number of public officials and private companies promote online voting. They claim that it will have an impact on the political process because it will make participation much more convenient, increase voter turnout, and reduce election costs.

Many skeptics believe that the electronic infrastructure is not ready for e-voting. Some fear digital disaster: jammed phone lines, blocked access, hackers, viruses, denial-of-service attacks, fraudulent vote counts, and violations of voter secrecy. Critics also

>> There are many reasons why a mail-in ballot may be considered invalid and not counted. **Analyze Charts** Does the data shown support or oppose the use of mail-in ballots?

point out that because not everyone can afford home computers, online voting could undermine the basic American principle of equality.

? IDENTIFY CENTRAL IDEAS What general concerns are voiced by critics of mail-in and online voting? On what do they base their concerns?

ASSESSMENT

1. **Cite Evidence** Cite evidence from the text to explain why punch-card voting is no longer legal.
2. **Check Understanding** America's first elections involved public voting by voice. With the many problems plaguing existing voting systems, is it possible that voice voting might make a comeback? Why or why not?
3. **Evaluate Arguments** How might online voting be made more democratic? What are the pros and cons of this solution?
4. **Apply Concepts** What might be an advantage of holding State elections separately from federal elections?
5. **Define** Define and give an example of ballot fatigue.

>> Many young people are used to being able to do many tasks using their smartphones or computers. **Analyze Political Cartoons** What point is the cartoonist making about technology and voting?

>> An interviewer's tone of voice and intonation can influence a respondant's replies, affecting poll results. Thus, telephone pollsters undergo extensive training.

Interactive Flipped Video

10.5 **Do you like broccoli? Blue fingernail polish? Tattoos? Hard rock music? What about sports? Old cars? You almost certainly have an opinion on each of those things. On some of them, you may hold strong opinions, and those opinions may be very important to you. Still, each of those opinions is your own view, your *private* opinion. None of them qualifies as *public* opinion.**

>> Objectives

Examine the term *public opinion* and understand why it is so difficult to define.

Understand the factors that influence an individual's political attitudes and actions.

Recognize how polls are used by individuals, political parties, interest groups, or the media to affect public policy and describe the challenges involved in measuring public opinion.

Identify the steps in the polling process, evaluate the role of the Internet and other electronic information on the polling process, and understand the challenges involved in evaluating polls.

Recognize the limits on the impact of public opinion in a democracy.

>> Key Terms

public affairs
public opinion
mass media
peer group
opinion leaders
mandate
interest groups
public opinion polls
straw vote
universe
sample
random sample
quota sample
pundit
George Gallup
Elmo Roper

Public Opinion and Polling

What Is Public Opinion?

Few terms in American politics are more widely used, and less well understood, than the term *public opinion*. It appears regularly in newspapers and magazines and on blogs, and you hear it frequently on radio and television.

Quite often, the phrase is used to suggest that all or most of the American people hold the same view on some public issues, such as global warming or deficit spending. Thus, time and again, politicians say that "the people" want such and such, television commentators tell us that "the public" favors this or opposes that, and so on.

In fact, there are very few matters about which all or nearly all of "the people" think alike. "The public" holds many different and often conflicting views on nearly every public issue.

To understand what public opinion is, you must recognize this important point: Public opinion refers to a complex collection of the opinions of many different people. It is the sum of all of their views. It is *not*the single and undivided view of some mass mind.

Who Is "the Public"? Many publics exist in the United States—in fact, too many to be counted. Each public is made up of all those individuals who hold the same view on some particular public issue. Each group of people with a differing point of view is a *separate* public with regard to that issue.

For example, the people who think that Congress should concentrate on paying down the national debt belong to the public that holds that view. People who believe that the President is doing an excellent job as chief executive, or that capital punishment should be abolished, or that prayer should be permitted in public school, are members of separate publics with those particular opinions. Clearly, many people can and do belong to more than one of those publics; but almost certainly only a very few belong to all four of them.

Notice this important point: Not many issues capture the attention of all—or even nearly all—Americans. In fact, those that do are few and far between. Instead, most public issues attract the interest of *some* people (and sometimes millions of them), but those same issues are of little or no interest to many (and sometimes millions of) other people.

>> Supporters and opponents of the Keystone XL pipeline, which would carry crude oil from Canada down the middle of the U.S. to Nebraska, face off at a demonstration in Lincoln, Nebraska.

Public Opinion Relates Only to Public Affairs This point is crucial, too: In its proper sense, public opinion includes only those views that relate to public affairs. **Public affairs** include politics, public issues, and the making of public policies—those events and issues that concern the people at large. To be a *public* opinion, a view must involve something of general concern and of interest to a significant portion of the people as a whole.

Of course, the American people as a whole are interested in many things—rock groups and symphony orchestras, the New York Yankees and the Dallas Cowboys, candy bars and green vegetables, and a great deal more. Many people have opinions on each of these things, views that are sometimes loosely called "public opinion." But, again, in its proper sense, public opinion involves only those views that people hold on such things as political parties and candidates, taxes, unemployment, welfare programs, national defense, foreign policy, and so on.

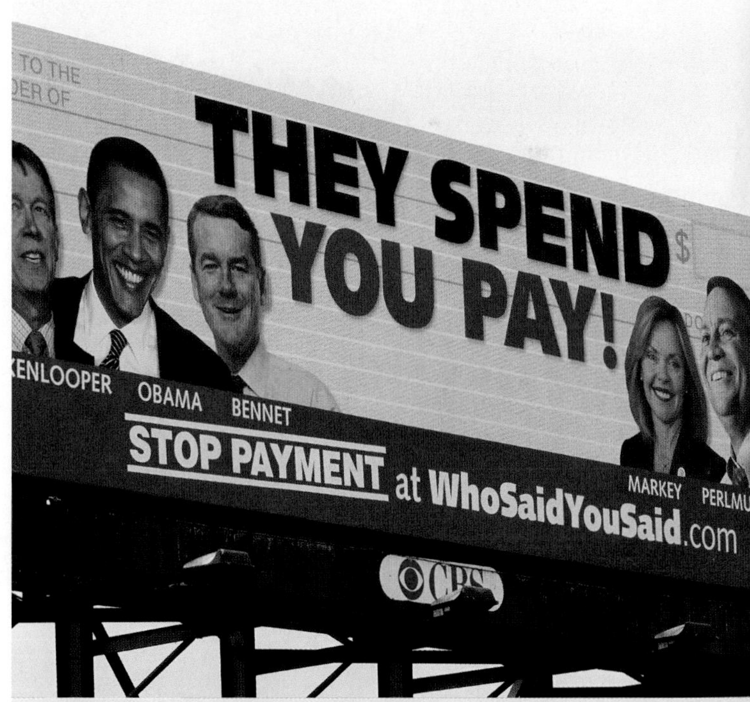

>> National and State politicians were featured on a Denver, Colorado, billboard during the 2012 election. **Analyze Images** Does the message on this sign qualify as public opinion? Why or why not?

Expressed Group Attitudes Clearly, public opinion is so complex that it cannot be readily defined. From what has been said about it to this point, however, **public opinion** can be described this way: those attitudes held by a significant number of people on matters of government and politics.

As we have suggested, you can better understand the term in the plural—that is, as public opinions, the opinions of different publics. Look at it this way: public opinion is made up of expressed group attitudes.

A view must be *expressed* in order to be an opinion in the public sense. Otherwise, it cannot be identified with any public. That expression need not be oral (spoken). It can take any number of other forms, as well: a protest demonstration, a film, a billboard, a vote for or against a candidate, and so on. The point is that a person's private thoughts on an issue enter the stream of public opinion only when those thoughts are expressed publicly.

? APPLY CONCEPTS Marcia tells her boyfriend that she believes their State should offer more financial aid to college students. According to the formal definition of the term, is this an example of public opinion? Why or why not?

Family, School, and Political Attitudes

No one is born with a set of attitudes about government and politics. Instead, each of us learns political opinions, and we do so in a lifelong "classroom" and from many different "teachers." In other words, public opinion is formed out of a very complex process. The factors involved in it are almost infinite.

You have already considered that point when examining why people vote as they do in a previous lesson. The reasons behind voter choices provide an extensive look at how public opinion is formed. The process by which each person acquires his or her political opinions is called *political socialization*. That complex process begins in early childhood, and it continues through one's lifetime. It involves all of the many experiences and relationships that lead each of us to see the political world and to act in it as we do.

There are many different agents of political socialization at work in the opinion-shaping process. Again, you looked at these agents in a previous lesson: age, race, income, occupation, residence, group affiliations, and many others. Here, look again at two of them, the family and school. They have so large an impact that they deserve another and slightly different discussion here.

>> A young girl waits for Barack Obama and Hillary Clinton to arrive at a campaign event. **Make Predictions** How is this girl likely to vote in the future?

The Influence of Family Most parents do not think of themselves as agents of political socialization, nor do other members of most families. Parents and other family members do nonetheless play an important part in this process.

Children first see the political world from within the family and through the family's eyes. They begin to learn about politics much as they begin to learn about most other things in life. They learn from what their parents have to say, from the stories that their older brothers and sisters bring home from school, from watching television with the family, and so on.

Most of what smaller children learn in the family setting cannot really be described as political opinions. Clearly, toddlers are not concerned with the wisdom of spending billions of dollars on an antimissile defense system, with the causes of global warming, or the pros and cons of the monetary policies of the Federal Reserve Board.

Early Attitudes Influence Later Political Views Young children do pick up some fundamental attitudes, however. With those attitudes, they acquire a basic slant toward such things as authority and rules of behavior, property, neighbors, people of other racial or religious backgrounds, and the like. In short, children lay some foundations on which they will later build their political opinions.

A large number of scholarly studies report what common sense also suggests. The strong influence the family has on the development of political opinions is largely a result of the near monopoly the family has on the child in his or her earliest, most impressionable years. Those studies also show that:

> Children raised in households in which the primary caregivers are

Democrats tend to become Democrats themselves, whereas children raised in homes where their caregivers are Republican tend to favor the GOP.

—Benjamin Ginsberg, Theodore Lowi, and Margaret Weir, *We the People*

The Influence of School The start of formal schooling marks the initial break in the influence of the family. For the first time, children become regularly involved in activities outside the home.

From the first day, schools teach children the values of the American political system. They work to indoctrinate the young, to instill in them loyalty to a particular cause or idea. In fact, preparing students to become good citizens is an important part of our educational system.

Students may salute the flag, recite the Pledge of Allegiance, and sing patriotic songs. They learn about George Washington, Abraham Lincoln, Susan B. Anthony, Martin Luther King, Jr., and other great Americans. From the early grades on, they pick up growing amounts of specific political knowledge, and they begin to form political opinions. In high school, they are often required to take a course in American government and even to read books such as this one.

Influences Outside the Classroom School involves much more than books and classes, of course. It is a complex bundle of experiences and a place where a good deal of informal learning occurs—about the similarities and differences among individuals and groups, about the various ways in which decisions can be made, and about the process of compromise that must often occur in order for ideas to move forward.

Once again, the family and school are *not* the only forces at work in the process by which opinions are formed. A number of other influences are part of the mix. These two factors are singled out here to highlight their leading roles in that process.

CONSTRUCT Describe a situation in which informal learning in a school setting might influence a person's political opinions.

>> Students say the Pledge of Allegiance at their high school graduation. Citizenship has been a major focus of American public education since the first school was founded in 1635.

Other Factors That Influence Political Attitudes and Actions

No factor, taken by itself, shapes a person's opinion on any single issue. Some factors do play a much larger role than others in that process, however. Thus, in addition to family and school, occupation and race are usually much more significant than, say, gender or place of residence.

For example, on the question of paying down the public debt, what a person does for a living and his or her level of income will almost certainly have a much greater impact on his or her views than will gender or where he or she happens to live.

On the other hand, the relative weight of each factor that influences public opinion also depends on the issue in question. If the issue involves, say, equal pay for women or the effects of a major oil spill in the Gulf of Mexico, then gender or where one lives will almost certainly loom larger in the opinion making mix.

Besides family, school, and such factors as occupation and race, four other factors have a major place in the opinion-making process. They are the mass media, peer groups, opinion leaders, and historic events.

The Influence of Mass Media The **mass media** include those means of communication that reach large, widely dispersed audiences (masses of people) simultaneously. No one needs to be told that the mass media, including newspapers, magazines, radio, and in particular, television and the Internet, have a huge effect on the formation of public opinion.

Take this as but one indication: The United States has 115.6 million homes with televisions, and 294 million people live in these homes. Nearly 120 million people in these homes own four or more TVs, and a growing number own tablets or smartphones. Viewers watch nearly 145 hours of television each month, and that doesn't include time they spend viewing videos on mobile devices. That's a mind-boggling number of person-hours spent focused on a screen. You will take a longer look at the influence of the mass media later in this lesson.

>> The mass media has a larger presence in people's homes today than at any time in history. **Analyze Images** To what extent might the mass media influence this family's opinions?

Influence of Peer Groups People with whom one regularly associates, including friends, classmates, neighbors, co-workers, and the like, make up one's **peer group.** When a child enters school, friends and classmates become important agents in shaping his or her attitudes and behavior. The influence of peer groups continues on through adulthood.

Belonging to a peer group usually reinforces what a person has already come to believe. One obvious reason for this is that most people trust the views of their friends. Another is that the members of a peer group have shared many of the same socializing experiences, and so tend to think along the same or similar lines.

To put this observation another way, contradictory or other unsettling opinions are not often heard within a peer group. Most people want to be liked by their friends and associates. As a result, they are usually reluctant to stray too far from what their peers think and how they behave.

>> George W. Bush chats with Oprah Winfrey during an appearance on her television show. TV personalities are opinion leaders whose ideas can greatly influence political attitudes.

Opinion Leaders and Pundits The views expressed by **opinion leaders** also bear heavily on the formation of public opinion. An opinion leader is any person who, for any reason, has an unusually strong influence on the views of others. These opinion shapers are a distinct minority in the total population, of course, but they are found everywhere.

Many opinion leaders hold public office. Some, often referred to as **pundits**, write for newspapers or magazines, or express their opinions on radio, television, or the Internet. Others are prominent in business, labor, agriculture, and civic organizations.

Many are professionals—doctors, lawyers, teachers, ministers, and rabbis—and have regular contact with large numbers of people. Many others are active members of their neighborhood or church or have leadership roles in their local communities.

Whoever they may be—the President of the United States, a network television commentator, the governor, the head of a local citizens committee, or even a local talk-show host—these opinion leaders are people to whom others listen and from whom others draw ideas and convictions. Whatever their political, economic, or social standing or outlook may be, opinion leaders play a significant role in the formation of public opinion.

Historic Events and Public Policy Historic events can have a major impact on the views of large numbers of people—and so have a major impact on the content and direction of public policy. The September 11, 2001, Islamist terrorist attacks and the onset of the global war on terror constitute a leading illustration of that point. American views on national security and foreign policy have undergone dramatic shifts as a result of those events. Our history affords many other examples, as well—not the least of them the Great Depression, which began in 1929 and lasted for the better part of a decade.

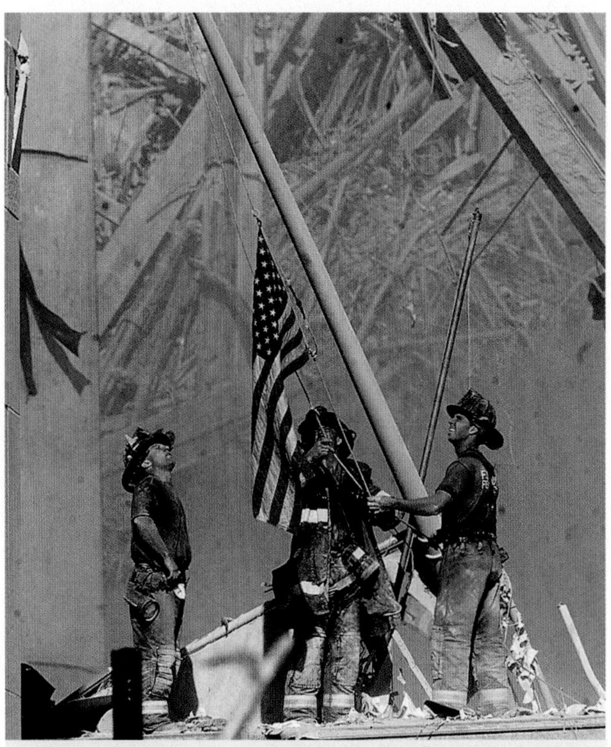

>> Firefighters raise the flag at New York's World Trade Center after the September 11, 2001, attacks by the Al Qaeda Islamist terrorist group. Events like this can affect political attitudes.

The Depression was a shattering national experience. Almost overnight, need and poverty became massive national problems. Hunger and despair stalked the land. In 1929, some two million people were unemployed in the United States. By just four years later, that number had climbed to 13.5 million. In 1935, some 18 million men, women, and children were wholly dependent on public emergency relief programs. Some 10 million workers had no employment other than that provided by temporary public projects.

The Depression's Effect on Government All of this changed the place of government in the United States. The Depression persuaded many Americans to support an expanded role for government—in particular, for the National Government—in the nation's economic and social life.

The Great Depression also prompted a majority of Americans to shift their loyalties from the Republicans to the Democrats. The Republicans had dominated the national political scene from Lincoln's election in 1860 to the onset of the Depression. That situation changed abruptly when Franklin D. Roosevelt's landslide victory in 1932 began nearly 40 years of Democratic domination.

Impact of the 1960s and 1970s on American Politics The turbulent politics of the 1960s and early 1970s furnish another example of the way in which significant occurrences can impact and shape opinions. The American people had emerged from World War II and the prosperity of the 1950s with a largely optimistic view of the future and of the United States' place in the world. That rose-colored outlook was reflected in a generally favorable, even respectful, attitude toward government in this country.

The 1960s and early 1970s changed all that. Those years were highlighted by a number of traumatic events. Of special note were the assassinations of President John Kennedy in 1963 and of the Reverend Martin Luther King, Jr., and Senator Robert Kennedy in 1968. This period also included the civil rights movement and the Vietnam War, with all of the protests, violence, and strong emotions that accompanied both of those chapters in this nation's life. The era ended with the Watergate scandal and the near-impeachment and subsequent resignation of President Richard Nixon in 1974.

Those years of turmoil and divisiveness produced a dramatic decline in the American people's estimate of their government—and most especially in their evaluation of its trustworthiness.

? EXPLAIN During a national crisis, a national television station features an interview with a well-known political correspondent. Identify the various influences on public opinion that this scenario illustrates.

Ways to Measure Public Opinion

How often have you heard this phrase: "According to a recent survey . . ."? Probably more than you can count, especially in the months leading up to an election. Polls are one of the most common means of gauging public opinion.

If public policy is to reflect public opinion, one needs to be able to find the answers to these questions: What are people's opinions on a particular issue? How many people share a given view on that issue? How firmly do they hold that view? In other words, there must be a way to "measure" public opinion.

The general shape of public opinion on an issue can be found through a number of key indicators. They include voting; lobbying; books; pamphlets; magazine and newspaper articles; editorial comments in the press and on radio, television, and the Internet; paid advertising; letters to editors and public officials; and so on.

"Get me some shares in public opinion."

>> The fortunes of business executives, politicians, and others can rise and fall based, in part, on public opinion. **Analyze Political Cartoons** How does the cartoonist make this point?

These and other means of expression are the devices through which the general direction of public opinion becomes known. Usually though, the means by which a view is expressed tells little—and often nothing reliable—about the size of the group that holds that opinion or how strongly it is held. In the American political system, this information is critically important. To find it, some effort must be made to measure public opinion. Elections, interest groups, the media, and personal contacts with the public all—at least to some degree—provide the means by which that measurement can be done.

Elections and Public Opinion In a democracy, the voice of the people is supposed to express itself through the ballot box. Election results are thus very often said to be indicators of public opinion. The votes cast for the various candidates are regularly taken as evidence of the people's approval or rejection of the stands taken by those candidates and their parties. As a result, a party and its victorious candidates regularly claim to have received a mandate to carry out their campaign promises. In American politics, a **mandate** refers to the instructions or commands a constituency gives to its elected officials.

In reality, however, election results are seldom an accurate measure of public opinion. Voters make choices in elections for any of several reasons, as you have seen. Very often, those choices have little or nothing to do with the candidates' stands on public questions. Then, too, candidates often disagree with some of the planks of their party's platform. And, as you know, candidates and parties often express their positions in broad, generalized terms.

In short, much of what you have read about voting behavior, and about the nature of parties, adds up to this: Elections are, at best, only useful indicators of public opinion. To call the typical election a mandate for much of anything other than a general direction in public policy is to be on very shaky ground.

How Accurately Do Interest Groups Reflect Public Opinion? Private organizations whose members share certain views and objectives, and who work to shape the making and the content of public policy are called **interest groups.** These organizations are also very aptly known as pressure groups and special interest groups.

Interest groups are a chief means by which public opinion is made known. They present their views (exert pressure) through their lobbyists, by letters, telephone calls, and e-mails, in political campaigns, and by other methods. In dealing with them, however, public officials often have difficulty determining two things: How many people does an interest group really represent? How strongly do those people hold the views that an organization says they hold?

The Media: Mirrors or Molders? Earlier, you read some impressive numbers about television that help describe the place of the media in the opinion process; you will read more of those numbers later. Here, recognize this point: The media are also a gauge for assessing public opinion.

The media are frequently said to be "mirrors" as well as "molders" of opinion. It is often claimed that the views expressed in newspaper editorials, syndicated columns, news magazines, television commentaries, and blogs are fairly good indicators of public opinion. In fact, however, the media are not very accurate mirrors of public opinion, often reflecting only the views of a vocal minority.

The Voice of the People Most public officials have frequent and wide-ranging contacts in many different forms with large numbers of people. In each of these contacts, they try to read the public's mind. Indeed, their jobs demand that they do so.

Members of Congress receive bags of mail and hundreds of phone calls and e-mails every day. Many of them make frequent trips "to keep in touch with the folks back home." Top administration figures are often on the road, too, selling the President's programs and gauging the people's reactions. Even the President does some of this, with speaking trips to different parts of the country.

Governors, State legislators, mayors, and other officials also have any number of contacts with the public. These officials encounter the public in their offices, in public meetings, at social gatherings, community events, and even at ball games.

Can public officials find "the voice of the people" in all of those contacts? Many can and do, and often with surprising accuracy. But some public officials cannot. They fall into an ever-present trap: They find only what they want to find, only those views that support and agree with their own.

EXPRESS IDEAS CLEARLY Why is it important in a democracy for elected leaders to have a mandate from the people?

>> Congressman Paul Ryan (R., Wisconsin) interacts with constituents in an effort to keep his finger on the pulse of public opinion.

Public Opinion Polls

Public opinion is best measured by **public opinion polls,** devices that attempt to collect information by asking people questions. The more accurate polls are based on scientific polling techniques.

Straw Votes Public opinion polls have existed in this country for more than a century. Until the 1930s, however, they were far from scientific. Most earlier polling efforts were of the **straw vote** variety. That is, they were polls that sought to read the public's mind simply by asking the same question of a large number of people. Straw votes are still fairly common. Many radio talk-show hosts pose questions that listeners can respond to by telephone, and television personalities regularly invite responses by e-mail.

The straw-vote technique is highly unreliable, however. It rests on the mistaken assumption that a relatively large number of responses will provide a fairly accurate picture of the public's views on a given question. The problem is this: The respondents are self-selected. Nothing in the process ensures that those who respond will represent a reasonably accurate cross section of the total population. The straw vote emphasizes the quantity rather than the quality of the sample to which its question is put.

>> Based on straw poll results, the *Literary Digest* predicted in 1936 that Alfred Landon (shown) would be the next President. The colossal failure of that poll led to more scientific methods.

>> While he gained fame in 1936 by accurately predicting the result of the presidential election, Dr. George Gallup wrongly predicted a win for Thomas Dewey over Harry Truman in 1948.

Interactive Gallery

Limitations of Straw Polls The most famous of all straw-polling mishaps took place in 1936. A widely read periodical, the *Literary Digest*, mailed postcard ballots to more than 10 million people and received answers from more than 2 million of them. Based on that huge return, the magazine confidently predicted the outcome of the presidential election that year. It said that Governor Alfred Landon, the Republican nominee, would easily defeat incumbent Franklin Roosevelt. Instead, Roosevelt won in a landslide. He captured more than 60 percent of the popular vote and carried every State but Maine and Vermont.

The *Digest* had drawn its sample on a faulty basis: from automobile registration lists and telephone directories. The *Digest* had failed to consider that in the mid-Depression year of 1936, millions of people could not afford to own cars or have private telephones.

The *Digest* poll failed to reach most of the vast pool of the poor and unemployed, millions of blue-collar workers, and most of the ethnic minorities in the country. Those were the very segments of the population from which Roosevelt and the Democrats drew their greatest support. The magazine had predicted the winner of each of the three previous presidential elections, but its failure to do so in 1936 was so colossal that it ceased publication not long thereafter.

Scientific Polling Serious efforts to take the public's pulse on a scientific basis date from the mid-1930s. They began with the work of such early pollsters as **George Gallup** and **Elmo Roper**. The techniques that they and others have developed over the decades since then have reached a highly sophisticated level.

Hundreds of national and regional polling organizations now operate in this country. Many of them do mostly commercial work. That is, they tap the public's preferences on everything from toothpastes and headache remedies to television shows and thousands of other things. A number of these polling organizations also poll the political preferences of the American people.

Among the best known of the national pollsters today are the Gallup Organization (the Gallup Poll) and the Pew Research Center for People and the Press.

The Work of National Pollsters A number of the leading national polls are joint efforts of major news-gathering and professional polling organizations. Their polls regularly report public attitudes on matters of current interest—including, for example, the level of public support of the President and/or Congress or, in election seasons, candidates running for such major offices as governor or member of the House or Senate. Those joint ventures that can most frequently be found

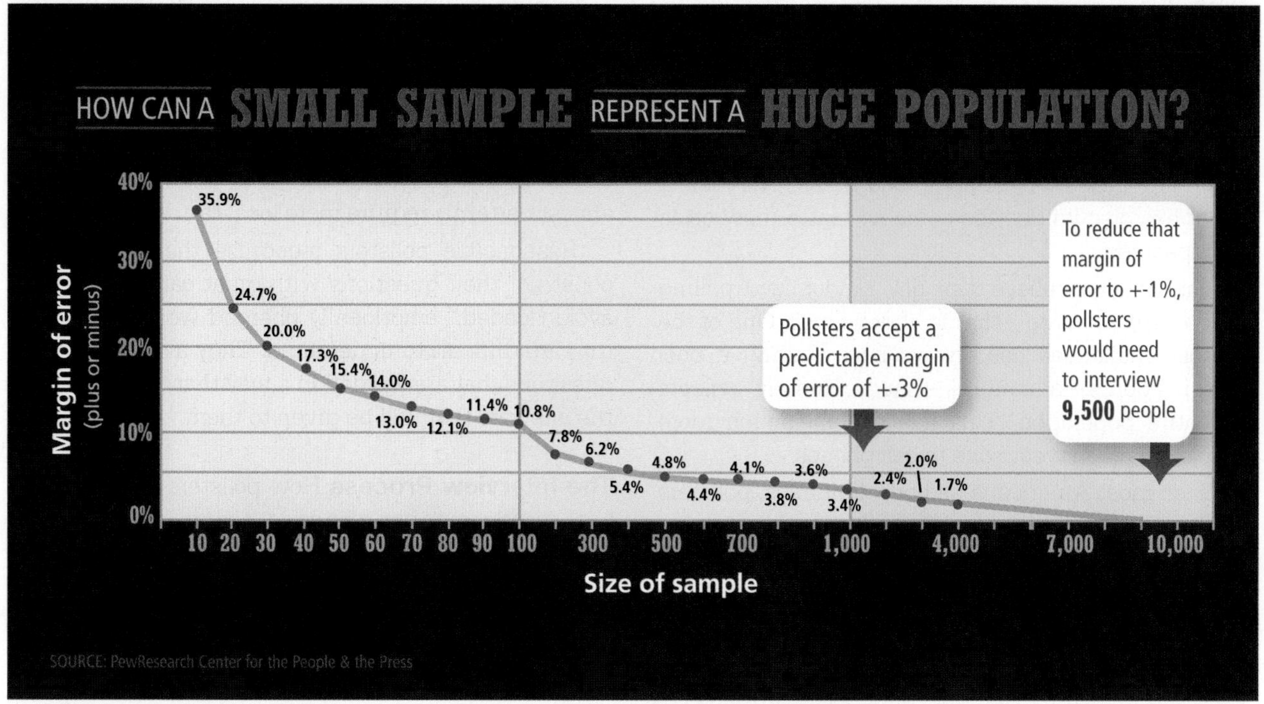

>> Due to the law of probability, 1,500 randomly selected adults accurately reflect the views of more than 200 million Americans. **Analyze Graphs** How is the margin of error related to sample size?

in print and on television and the Internet include the ABC News/*The Washington Post* poll, the CBS News/*The New York Times* poll, the NBC/*The Wall Street Journal* poll, and the CNN/*USA Today*/Gallup poll.

SUPPORT IDEAS WITH EXAMPLES What is the MAIN drawback of straw polls?

How Polls Are Designed and Administered

Scientific poll taking is an extremely complex process that can best be described in five basic steps. In their efforts to discover and report public opinion, pollsters must (1) define the universe to be surveyed; (2) construct a sample; (3) prepare valid questions; (4) select and control how the poll will be taken; and (5) analyze and report their findings to the public.

Defining the Universe The **universe** is a term that means the whole population that the poll aims to measure. It is the group whose opinions the poll will seek to discover. That universe can be all voters in Chicago, or every high school student in Texas, or all Republicans in New England, or all Democrats in Georgia, or all Catholic women over age 35 in the United States, and so on.

Constructing a Sample If the universe is very small—say, the 30 members of a high school class—the best way to discover what that entire universe thinks about some matter would be to question all of its members. Most polls involve much larger universes, however—for example, all of the people who live in a particular city or State or the United States. Clearly, each of those universes is so large that it would be impossible to interview all of its members. So pollsters construct a **sample**—a representative slice of the total universe.

Most pollsters draw random samples (often called probability samples). A **random sample** is composed of randomly selected people, and so it is one in which all the members of its universe stand an equal chance of being interviewed. Recall, the sample used for the infamous *Literary Digest* poll in 1936 was not picked at random and so did not accurately reflect the universe it sought to measure.

Sampling and the Law of Probability Most major national polls regularly use samples composed of some 1,500 or so people to represent the nation's adult population (of more than 200 million people) today. How can the views of so few people possibly represent the views of so many?

The answer to that question lies in the mathematical law of probability. Flip a coin a thousand times. The law of probability says that, given an honest coin and an honest flip, heads will come up 500 times. The results of that exercise will be the same no matter how often it is repeated.

Whether you believe it or not, randomized polling can be very accurate—that is, if done well. One of the greatest challenges has always been finding a pool of respondents—a sample—that accurately reflects the entire population. This has become much more complex in recent years due to cell phones.

When most Americans had only landlines, pollsters could randomly select numbers within a geographic area. But with cell phones, three things have changed. First, cell numbers are not listed; no directories are available from which to draw a sample. Second, even if there was a way to create a sample of cell numbers, they would not neatly represent people in one geographic area. When people move these days, they simply take their cells with them. Finally, most cell phones display the name of the caller, and many of us simply hang up on pollsters. Survey research is an important part of our political system, and it is here to stay. However, that does not mean that the job of pollsters will get easier in the years ahead.

Asking Well-Drawn Questions The way in which the questions are phrased is critically important to the reliability of any poll. To illustrate that point, most will probably say "yes" to a question put this way: "Should local taxes be reduced?" Many will also answer "yes" if asked this question: "Should the size of the city's police force be increased to fight the rising tide of crime in our community?" Yet, expanding the police force would almost certainly require more local tax dollars.

Responsible pollsters recognize the problem and construct their questions with great care. They try to avoid "loaded," emotionally charged words and terms that are difficult to understand. They also try to avoid questions that are worded in a way that tends to shape the answers that will be given to them.

The Interview Process How pollsters communicate with respondents can also affect accuracy. For decades, most polls were conducted door-to-door, face-to-face. That is, the interviewer questioned the respondent in person. Today, many pollsters do their work by telephone, with a sample selected by *random digit dialing.* Calls are placed to randomly chosen landline and, increasingly, cell phone, numbers within randomly chosen area codes around the country. Telephone surveys are less labor intensive and less expensive than door-to-door polling.

Still, most professional pollsters see advantages and drawbacks to each approach. However, they all agree that only one technique, not a combination of the two, should be used in any given poll. Most also agree that the effect of the Internet on the polling process has been mixed. Online polling, while having the potential

Questions to Ask About Polls

WHO?	WHAT?	HOW?	WHY?	WHEN?
Who conducted the poll?	**What is the poll's universe?**	**How was the sample chosen?**	**Why was the poll conducted?**	**When was the data collected?**
Polls sponsored by political campaigns may aim to mislead as much as inform.	The universe is the population the poll aims to measure. This allows you to judge whether the sample is truly representative.	Samples should be selected randomly. How were questions written and asked? The method of creating and asking questions can alter the results.	Polls meant to boost a candidate's approval ratings are not reliable.	Opinions change quickly during elections, so knowing when the data was collected is important.

>> You can ask several questions to help evaluate a poll's findings. **Analyze Charts** Why is it important to read poll results critically?

POLL RESULTS DEPEND UPON HOW YOU ASK THE QUESTION

HOW DO AMERICANS FEEL ABOUT THE JUSTICE DEPARTMENT REQUIRING THE ASSOCIATED PRESS TO TURN OVER THEIR TELEPHONE RECORDS?

"Do you approve or disapprove of the Justice Department's decision to subpoena the phone records of AP journalists as part of an investigation into the disclosure of classified information?"

APPROVE	36%
DISAPPROVE	44%
NO OPINION	20%

"The AP reported classified information about U.S. anti-terrorism efforts and prosecutors have obtained AP's phone records through a court order. Do you think this action by federal prosecutors is or is not justified?"

JUSTIFIED	52%
NOT JUSTIFIED	33%
NO OPINION	15%

"As you may know, after the AP ran news stories that included classified information about U.S. anti-terrorism efforts, the Justice Department secretly collected phone records for reporters and editors who work there....Do you think that the actions of the Justice Department were acceptable or unacceptable?"

ACCEPTABLE	43%
UNACCEPTABLE	52%
NO OPINION	5%

SOURCE: Pew Research Center

>> This chart gives an example of the way the wording of a question can affect the results of a poll. **Analyze Charts** In the example shown, how did the language used influence the responses?

to reach more respondents, also has serious drawbacks. Results from online polls must be approached with caution, largely because their samples frequently are not random.

The interview itself is a very sensitive point in the process. An interviewer's tone of voice or the emphasis he or she gives to certain words can influence a respondent's replies and so affect the validity of a poll. If the questions are not carefully worded, some of the respondent's replies may be snap judgments or emotional reactions. Others may be answers that the person being interviewed thinks "ought" to be given. Thus, polling organizations try to hire and train their interviewing staff very carefully.

Analyzing Findings Polls, whether scientific or not, try to measure people's attitudes. To be of any real value, however, someone must analyze and report the results. Scientific polling organizations today collect huge amounts of raw data. In order to handle these data, computers and other electronic hardware have become routine parts of the process. Pollsters use these technologies to tabulate and interpret their data, draw their conclusions, and then publish their findings.

? EXPLAIN How is it possible for a random sampling of just 1,500 people to accurately represent the opinions of all Americans?

Poll Reliability

How good are polls? On balance, the major national polls are fairly reliable. So, too, are most of the regional surveys around the country. Still, they are far from perfect. Fortunately, most responsible pollsters readily acknowledge the limits of their polls. Many of them are involved in continuing efforts to refine every aspect of the polling process.

Pollsters know that they have difficulty measuring the intensity, stability, and relevance of the opinions they report. *Intensity* is the strength of feeling with which an opinion is held. *Stability* (or fluidity) is the relative permanence or changeableness of an opinion. *Relevance* (or pertinence) is how important a particular opinion is to the person who holds it.

Polls and pollsters are sometimes said to shape the opinions they are supposed to measure. Some critics say that in an election, for example, pollsters often create a "bandwagon effect." That is, some voters, wanting to be with the winner, jump on the bandwagon of the candidate who is ahead in the polls.

In spite of these criticisms, it is clear that scientific polls are the most useful tools there are for the difficult task of measuring public opinion. Although they may not always be precisely accurate, they do offer reasonably reliable guides to public thought. Moreover, they help to focus attention on public questions and to stimulate the discussion of them.

? APPLY CONCEPTS How might the difficulty of measuring the stability of an opinion affect the number and frequency of polls that are conducted?

ASSESSMENT

1. **Analyze Information** If a candidate wishes to receive a mandate for his or her policies in an upcoming election, what steps might be taken before the election to formulate stands on issues that best reflect public opinion?
2. **Compare and Contrast** Compare and contrast the kind of information about public opinion that can be gathered through a poll versus the kind of information about public opinion that can be gathered through reading newspaper editorials, watching television, listening to the radio, or reading blogs on the Internet.
3. **Check Understanding** Explain why peer groups have a significant impact on individuals' political opinions.
4. **Evaluate Arguments** A national, scientifically run poll finds that 66 percent of Americans are in favor of increasing national investments in green energy. To what degree would it be fair to say that "the American public agrees that green energy is important?"
5. **Express Ideas Clearly** Name several types of factors that are MOST likely to influence an individual's political attitudes about a particular issue, such as whether or not the Social Security program should be eliminated. Explain your answer.

10.6

Did you go online today using your cell phone, computer, or tablet? If so, you joined the 95 percent of teens who say they use the Internet at least occasionally. According to the Pew Research Center, a growing number of teenagers are "cell mostly" Internet users, who go online using mostly their cell phones. And if you visited a social media site today, you joined 84 percent of teens who also use social networking sites. The Internet is a form of mass media, and its use continues to grow. Other forms, however, such as television and radio, are also part of American culture.

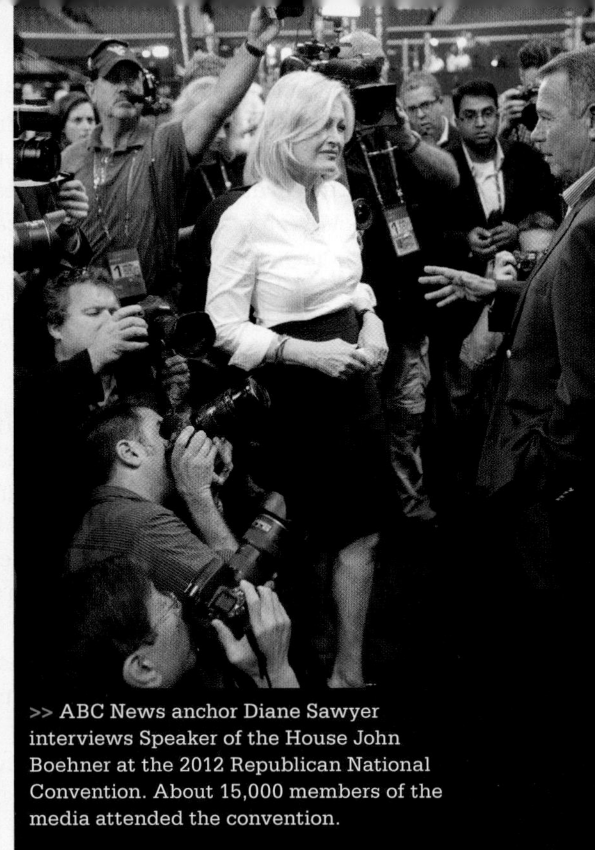
>> ABC News anchor Diane Sawyer interviews Speaker of the House John Boehner at the 2012 Republican National Convention. About 15,000 members of the media attended the convention.

Interactive Flipped Video

Influencing Public Opinion: The Mass Media

The Role of Mass Media

A **medium** is a means of communication; it transmits some kind of information. *Media* is the plural of medium. The *mass media* include those means of communication that can reach large, widely dispersed audiences simultaneously.

Five major elements of the mass media are especially significant in American politics today: television, the Internet, newspapers, radio, and magazines. Other forms of media, including books, films, and satellite radio, play a lesser but still relevant role in the political process.

Importantly, the mass media do not function as an arm of government in the United States. They are, instead, almost entirely privately owned and operated. Unlike political parties and interest groups, their prime goal is *not* that of influencing the course of public affairs. They are, nonetheless, an extremely potent force in American politics.

Along with entertainment, the media provide political information. They do so directly when they report the news, in an online newspaper

>> Objectives

Examine the role of the mass media in providing the public with political information.

Understand the role played by the mass media in the U.S. political system and give examples of the processes used by the media to affect public policy.

Analyze the impact of political changes brought about by the media, including the Internet and other electronic information, and understand the factors that limit the influence of the media on the political process.

>> Key Terms

medium
public agenda
sound bite
Thomas Jefferson
Theodore Roosevelt

or a television newscast, for example. The media also provide a large amount of political information less directly—for example, in radio and television programs, magazine articles, and blogs. These venues often deal with such public topics as crime, healthcare, climate change, or some aspect of American foreign policy. Either way, people acquire most of what they know about government and politics from the various forms of media.

Television Politics and television have gone hand in hand since the technology first appeared. The first public demonstration of television occurred at the New York World's Fair in 1939. President Franklin D. Roosevelt opened the fair on camera, and a comparative handful of local viewers watched him do so on tiny five- and seven-inch screens.

Today, television is all-pervasive. As you read earlier, there is at least one television set in 98 percent of the nation's 115 million households. Television replaced newspapers as the principal source of political information for a majority of Americans in the early 1960s, and it is still the principal source of news for an estimated 55 percent of the population.

Three major national networks have dominated television from its infancy: the Columbia Broadcasting System (CBS), the American Broadcasting Company (ABC), and the National Broadcasting Company (NBC). Those three giants furnish most of the programming for more than 500 local stations, and that programming accounts for nearly half of all television viewing time today. The major networks' audience share has declined over recent years, however. Their main challenges have come from the 24/7 programming of cable broadcasters—notably, Turner Broadcasting's Cable News Network (CNN) and the Fox Network—and the Internet.

N. E. Numb. 1.

The Boston News-Letter.

Published by Authority.

From Monday April 17. to Monday April 24. 1704.

>> This is one of the first issues ever published of the *Boston News-Letter.* This early paper was able to avoid the censorship problems that had plagued earlier newspapers.

Newspapers, the Oldest Mass Media The world's first newspaper was almost certainly the *Acta Diurna*, a daily gazette in Rome dating from 59 B.C. Another very early forerunner of today's newspapers was *Tipao*, a court journal in Beijing first published during the Han dynasty (202 B.C.to A.D. 221).

The first regularly published newspaper in America, the *Boston News-Letter,* appeared in 1704. Other papers soon followed, in Boston and then in Philadelphia, New York, Annapolis, and elsewhere. Those first papers regularly carried political news. Several spurred the colonists to revolution, carrying the news of independence and the text of the Declaration of Independence to people throughout the colonies. **Thomas Jefferson** marked the vital role of the press in the earliest years of the nation when, in 1787, he wrote to a friend:

> . . . were it left to me to decide whether we should have a government without newspapers or newspapers without a government, I should not hesitate a moment to prefer the latter.
>
> —Thomas Jefferson, Letter to Colonel Edward Carrington, January 16, 1787

Today, some 1,300 daily newspapers are published in the United States, down from about 1,480 in 2000. That number has been declining for decades, in fact, and the Internet and television have been major factors in that downward trend. Nevertheless, newspapers are still an important source of information about government and politics. Most papers cover stories in greater depth than television does, and many are local papers that focus on events closer to home than most Internet news sources.

Radio Then and Now Radio as it exists today began in 1920. On November 2 of that year, station KDKA in Pittsburgh went on the air with presidential election returns. The new medium soon became immensely popular.

By the 1930s, radio had assumed much of the role in American society that television has today. It was a major entertainment medium, and millions of people planned their daily schedules around their favorite programs. President Franklin Roosevelt was the first major public figure to use radio effectively. The late author David Halberstam described the impact of FDR's famous fireside chats:

> He was the first great American radio voice. For most Americans of [that] generation, their first memory of politics would be of sitting by a radio and hearing that voice, strong, confident, totally at ease. . . . Most Americans in the previous 160 years had never even seen a President; now almost all of them were hearing him, in their own homes. It was literally and figuratively electrifying.
>
> —David Halberstam, *The Powers That Be*

>> A family gathers around the radio in the mid 1920s. Radio shows of the era included "Grand Ole Opry," "Great Moments in History," "The Happiness Boys," and "The National Farm and Home Hour."

Many thought that the arrival of television would bring the end of radio as a major medium. Radio has survived, however, in large part because it is so conveniently available. People can hear music, news, sports, and other radio programs in a great many places where they cannot watch television—in their cars, at work, in remote areas, and in any number of other places and situations. The arrival of satellite and Internet radio has added to radio's popularity.

Most radio stations spend little time on public affairs today. Many do devote a few minutes every hour to "the news"—really, to a series of headlines. Over recent years, talk radio has become an important source of political comment. The opinions and analyses offered by a number of talk show hosts can be found on hundreds of stations across the United States. Among the most prominent talk broadcasters today are conservatives Rush Limbaugh and Sean Hannity, and liberals Thom Hartmann and Rachel Maddow. Their programs air nationally and attract millions of listeners every weekday.

A NAUSEATING JOB, BUT IT MUST BE DONE

>> In this early 1900s image, President Roosevelt rakes through the "muck" to expose wrongdoing in the meat industry. **Analyze Political Cartoons** Who in the media might be considered muckrakers today?

Magazines, a Changing Media Several magazines were published in colonial America. Benjamin Franklin began one of the very first, his *General Magazine,* in Philadelphia in 1741. The progressive reform period in the early 1900s spawned several journals of opinion, including a number that featured articles by the day's leading muckrakers. The *muckrakers* were journalists who exposed wrongdoing in politics, business, and industry. The term was coined by **Theodore Roosevelt** in 1906 and is derived from the raking of muck—that is, manure and other barnyard debris. The muckrakers set the pattern for what is now called investigative reporting. Their work contributed to changes in the nation's laws, which had a positive impact on the lives of many Americans. For decades before radio and television, magazines constituted the only national medium.

Today's magazines include trade publications, such as *Interior Design,* and periodicals that target some special personal interest, such as *Golf Digest, Seventeen,* and *American Rifleman.* One newsmagazine, *Time,* ranks in the top 25 periodicals in terms of circulation.

Like all other forms of media, magazine publishers have seen their circulations decline as the Internet's popularity has risen. Many now offer online versions of their publications to cater to the changing trends in media use in the United States.

The Rise of the Internet The Internet is a leading, and growing, source of political news and information for the American people. Its roots can be traced to a Defense Department research project of the Cold War era. In 1969, the DoD's Advanced Research Projects Agency established a four-computer network in the Pentagon designed to protect military secrets from hostile actions. Two years later, that grid (ARPANET) had grown to include some two dozen computers at 15 widely scattered locations across the country.

>> While computer connectivity has increased dramatically with the development of the Internet, the size of computers has decreased from room-size to pocket-size.

Interactive Gallery

From those beginnings, the Internet has grown phenomenally, and it continues to do so. Ongoing advances in computer technologies allow ever faster access to information, and an ever-growing number of people are availing themselves of that technology. Today, some 85 percent of the American people report that they have access to a computer at home or elsewhere, and over 50 percent of adults have a smartphone they use to go online. The percentage who get news by means of online sources has doubled in the last few years.

Television remains the most widely used source for political news and information, but the Internet is now in second place, ahead of newspapers, radio, and magazines. Three of every four people say they go online to "get the news." Younger people are especially inclined to do so. In addition, many people are adding their voices to an ongoing dialogue about public affairs, thereby increasing popular participation in government.

In addition to newspapers, magazines, and television stations, virtually all government agencies, interest groups, political parties, elected officials, and candidates' campaign organizations maintain Web sites. Also popular are blogs devoted to some specific subject. There were some 12,000 active blogs in 2000 and more than 180 million by 2012. Those devoted to public affairs typically feature links to a variety of sources. Podcasts, digital recordings that are posted and can be downloaded from the Internet, have also grown spectacularly over recent years. Other electronic information, such as e-mail and instant messaging, have also impacted the political process by revolutionizing communications between political leaders and voters, among government officials, and among voters. Electronic voting-counting has resulted in much faster election results than hand-counting of ballots.

A Social Media Phenomenon The Internet has dramatically altered the way Americans acquire and share information, and that transformation has been taken a step further by social networking sites. Beginning in the late 1990s, a variety of social media sites were launched, some of which charged a fee. Myspace was launched in 2003, and Facebook in 2004. By 2005, about 8 percent of Americans were using social networking sites. Twitter joined the top sites in 2007, while Facebook became the largest social media network in the world, with approximately one billion members and 500 million daily users in 2012.

Today, roughly 70 percent of Americans use social networking sites, and that figure is much higher for younger Americans. Some 30 percent of Americans report that they get their news from Facebook, and 8 percent get news on Twitter. Nearly one half of those who get their news on Twitter are under 29 years old.

Social media networks have had a major impact on politics and government. They have become important tools for fundraising, mobilizing supporters, and uniting political activists worldwide. Humanitarian efforts have been greatly aided by these sites, as well. When a major earthquake and tsunami struck Japan in 2011, for example, aid workers used social media for activities such as locating displaced victims, raising disaster relief funds, and disseminating information, to name just a few.

IDENTIFY CAUSE AND EFFECT How have modern changes in media changed politics?

>> This cartoon comments on the power of the media in American politics. **Analyze Political Cartoons** If the media simply reports the news objectively, how might it still affect politics?

How the Media Affects Politics

Clearly, the media play a significant role in American politics. Just how significant that role is, and just how much influence the media have, is the subject of a long, still unsettled debate.

Whatever its weight, the media's influence can be seen in any number of situations. It is most visible in two particular areas: (1) public policy and (2) the field of electoral politics.

The Media and Public Policy The media play a very large role in shaping the **public agenda,** the societal problems that the nation's political leaders and the general public agree need government attention. As they report and comment on events, issues, policies, and personalities, the media determine to a very large extent what public matters the people will think and talk about—and, so, those matters about which public-policy makers will be most concerned.

Put another way, the media have the power to focus the public's attention on a specific issue. They do so by emphasizing some things and downplaying others. For example, they feature certain items on the front page or at the top of the newscast and bury others in the latter pages or segments of the program.

It is not correct to say that the media tell the people *what* to think; but it is clear that they tell the people what to think *about.* A look at any issue of a daily newspaper or a quick review of the content of any

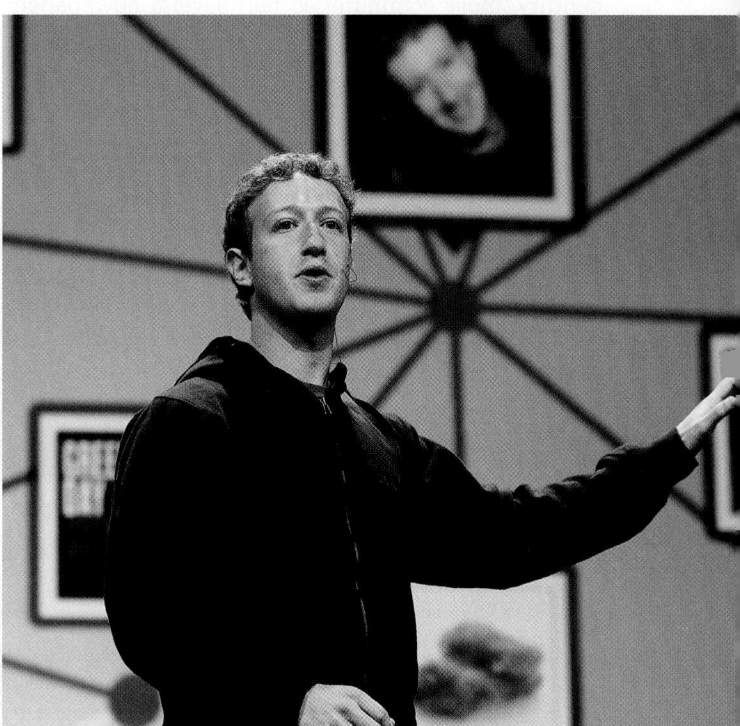

>> Mark Zuckerberg, an entrepreneur and computer programmer, co-founded the highly successful social-networking Web site Facebook while a student at Harvard.

Interactive Illustration

television or Internet news story will demonstrate that point. Remember, people rely on the media for most of the information they receive on public issues.

The mass media also have a direct impact on the nation's leaders. Some years ago, Stephen Hess, a widely respected authority on the media, identified several news organizations that form the "inner ring" of influence in Washington, D.C. He cited the three major television networks, CBS, ABC, and NBC; three newspapers, *The New York Times, The Washington Post,* and *The Wall Street Journal;* the leading news wire service, the Associated Press (AP); and the three major news weeklies, *Time, Newsweek,* and *U.S. News & World Report.* CNN, MSNBC, Fox News, Reuters, and *USA Today* have since joined that select group, as have the Web sites of these top media outlets.

Leading political figures in and out of government pay close and continuing attention to these sources. In fact, the President receives a daily digest of the news reports, analyses, and editorial comments that these and other sources broadcast and publish. At the same time, public leaders use new media—that is, the Internet and, especially, social media—to shape public opinion on issues.

Reemergence of the Partisan Press In the 19th century, most communities had several newspapers, each representing a different partisan perspective. This so-called "partisan press" was based on the loyalty of large numbers of engaged citizens to their political parties—and to their papers. But as news became more nationalized in the early part of the 20th century, and as local party organizations began to wane after the New Deal, the partisan press faded into the history books. The standard for good news reporting became fairness and objectivity.

In the last decade or so, however, many scholars have pointed out the reemergence of the partisan press, including conservative talk radio, partisan Internet news sites, and nontraditional cable television news channels, such as Fox and MSNBC. The model for their success appears similar to that of the partisan press in the 19th century: loyal audiences.

So has the partisan press returned? It is fair to note that many do not see these news outlets as particularly partisan, but rather as simply offering information that is different from mainstream sources. And a vast majority of news outlets still work hard to offer objective information.

Probably more important than the development of partisan news programs has been a perceived change in consumers' habits. With so many options available, people tend to seek out a wide range of information. Yet, it seems that most find outlets that match their

WHAT IS YELLOW JOURNALISM?
TYPE OF JOURNALISM
FIRST USED IN THE LATE
1800s
BY COMPETING
NEWSPAPER OWNERS
WILLIAM RANDOLPH HEARST
& JOSEPH PULITZER
CONTRIBUTED
TO THE U.S. DECISION TO
DECLARE WAR
ON SPAIN IN 1898
USED DRAMATIC
NEWS
HEADLINES
INFLAMMATORY
PHOTOS
FIERY
EDITORIALS
EXAGGERATED
STORIES
AND FEW REAL FACTS
TO INFLUENCE PUBLIC OPINION
& SELL NEWSPAPERS
"YOU FURNISH THE PICTURES... I'LL FURNISH THE WAR."
—Comment made by William Randolph Hearst in 1897, referring to his newspaper's role in stirring up public opinion in favor of war with Spain

>> Throughout history, the press has had tremendous power to influence the public. **Analyze Charts** What characteristics of "yellow journalism" can still be seen in some publications today?

Where Do Americans Get Their Campaign News?

	2000	2004	2008	2012
Local TV news	48%	42%	40%	32%
Nightly network news	45%	35%	32%	26%
Daily newspapers	40%	31%	31%	20%
Cable news networks	34%	38%	38%	36%
Internet	9%	13%	24%	25%

SOURCE: The Pew Research Center for the People & the Press, February 2012

>> The Internet, and social media sites in particular, are a growing source of political information for Americans. **Analyze Charts** How do you predict this chart might look in 2020?

preexisting ideas. This has been called the "echo chamber" phenomenon. Many worry that if citizens never listen to other perspectives, the nation will grow less tolerant and find it more difficult to reach compromise solutions to tough policy questions.

Electoral Politics You have seen several illustrations of the media's importance in electoral politics. Recall, for example, the fact that the media, and in particular television, have contributed to a decline in the place of political parties in American politics.

Television has made candidates far less dependent on party organizations than they once were. Before television, the major parties generally dominated the election process. They recruited most candidates who ran for office, and they ran those candidates' campaigns. The candidates depended on party organizations in order to reach the voters.

Now, both television and the Internet allow candidates to appeal directly to the people, without the help of a party organization. Candidates for office need not be experienced politicians who have worked their way up a party's political ladder over the course of several elections. It is not unusual for candidates to assemble their own campaign organizations and operate with only loose connections to their political parties.

Remember, too, that how voters see a candidate—the impressions they have of that candidate's personality, character, abilities, and so on—is one of the major factors that influence voting behavior. Candidates and professional campaign managers are quite aware of this fact. They know that the kind of "image" a candidate projects in the media can have a telling effect on the outcome of an election.

Candidates regularly try to manipulate media coverage to their advantage. Campaign strategists understand that, even with the Internet, most people learn almost everything they know about a candidate from television. They therefore plan campaigns that emphasize television exposure. Such technical considerations as timing, location, lighting, and camera angles loom large, often at the expense of such substantive matters as the issues involved in an election or a candidate's qualifications for public office.

Good campaign managers also know that most television news programs are built out of stories that (1) take no more than a minute or two of air time, and (2) show people doing something interesting or exciting. Newscasts seldom feature "talking heads," speakers who drone on and on about some complex issue.

Instead, newscasts featuring candidates are usually short, sharply focused **sound bites**—snappy reports that can be aired in 30 or 45 seconds or so. Staged and carefully orchestrated visits to historic sites, factory gates, toxic-waste dumps, football games, and the like, have become a standard part of the electoral scene.

The Internet has added yet another type of media to electoral politics and the impact of the political changes it has brought about is dramatic. Not only are candidates no longer dependent upon their political party—they are also no longer dependent on television to get their message to the people. In addition, the Internet allows candidates to fundraise, campaign, and mobilize supporters much more easily—and more cheaply—than in earlier times.

? HYPOTHESIZE What might happen to the nature of the media if the 1st Amendment guarantee of freedom of the press were to be repealed?

The Media's Limited Influence

Having said all this, it is all too easy to overstate the media's role in American politics. A number of built-in factors work to limit the media's impact on the behavior of the American voting public.

In the past, it has been commonplace for relatively few people to follow international, national, or even local political events very closely. However, this trend is changing. Due in part to the rise of social media, as many as 43 percent of people pay very close attention to national politics, especially during election years. In sum, a small but increasing portion of the public takes in and understands much of what the media have to say about public affairs.

Among those people who do pay attention to politics, however, most are likely to be selective about it. That is, they most often watch, listen to, and read those sources that generally agree with their own viewpoints. They regularly ignore those sources with which they disagree. Thus, for example, many Democrats do not watch the televised campaign appearances or visit the Web sites of Republican candidates. Nor do many Republicans read newspaper stories about the campaign efforts of Democratic candidates.

The Media and Public Affairs Another important limit on the media's impact is the content the media carries. This is especially true of radio and television. Most television programs, for example, have little or nothing to do with public affairs, at least not directly. (A number of popular programs do relate to public affairs in an indirect way, however. Thus, many are "crime shows," and crime is certainly a matter of public concern. Many also carry a political message—for example, that the police are hard-working public servants.) Advertisers who pay the high costs of television air time want to reach the largest possible audiences. Because most people are more interested in being entertained than in being informed about public issues, few public-affairs programs air in prime time.

Americans and the Media

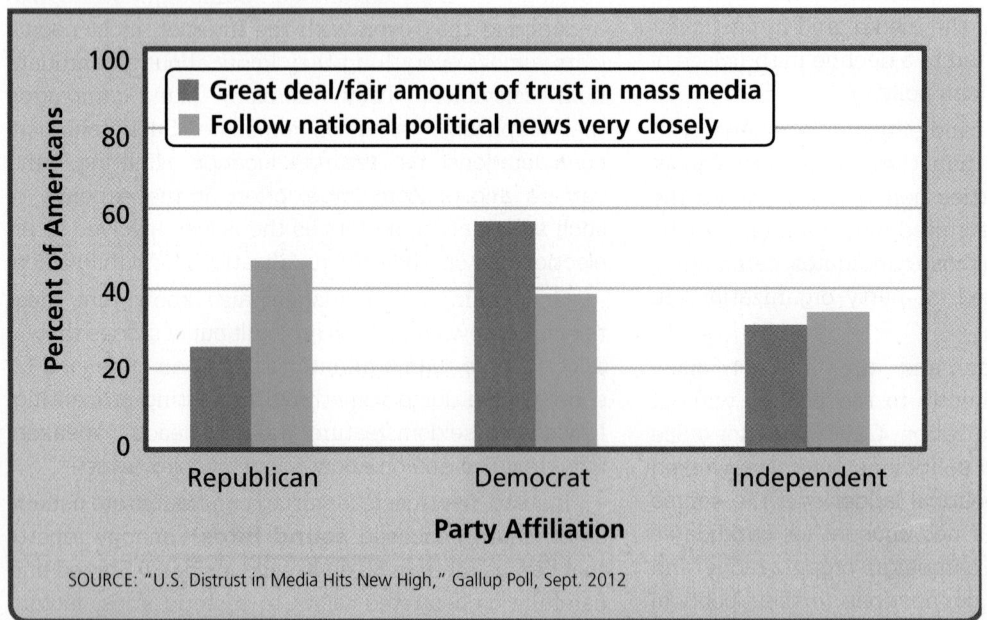

>> The media's role in U.S. politics is affected by the behaviors and beliefs of Americans. **Analyze Graphs** What does this Gallup Poll indicate about Americans' attention to national political news?

Readership Percentage of Daily Newspaper Sections

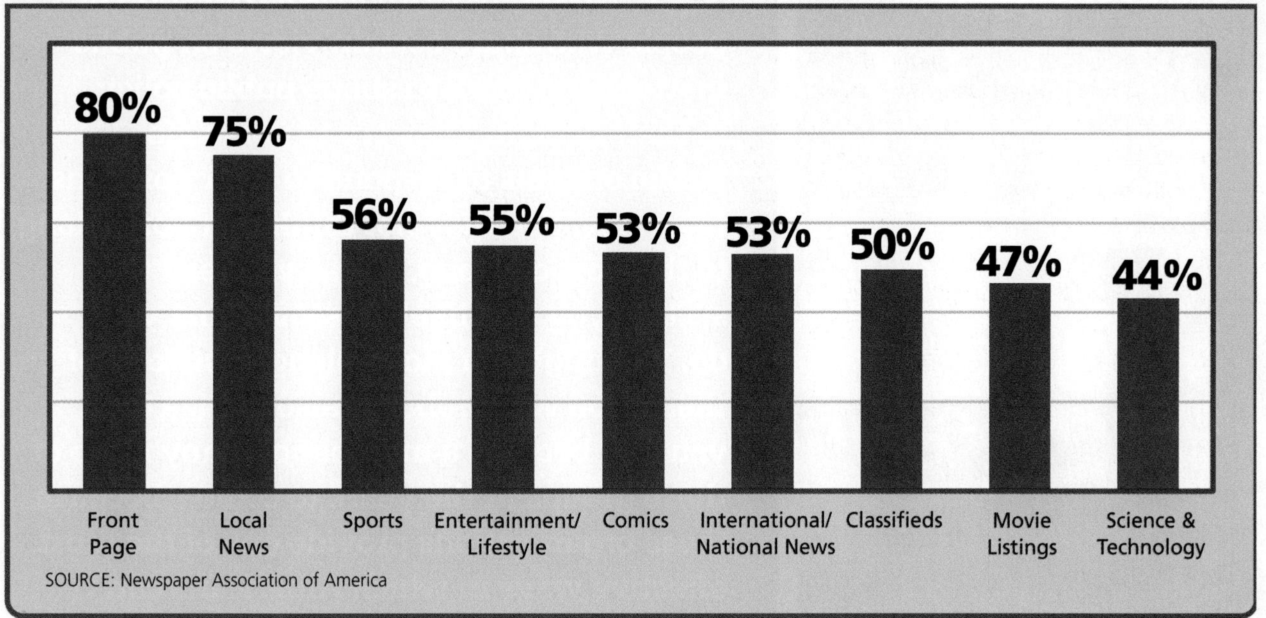

>> Any political news that does not make the front page or the local news would appear in the international/national section. **Analyze Graphs** How does relevance influence readership?

Radio and television mostly "skim" the news. They report only what their news editors determine to be the most important or the most interesting stories of the day. Even on widely watched evening news programs, most reports are presented in 60- to 90-second time slots. In short, the broadcast media seldom give the kind of in-depth coverage that a good newspaper can supply.

Newspapers are not as hampered as many other media in their ability to cover public affairs. Still, much of the content of most newspapers is nonpolitical. Like nearly all of television and radio, newspapers depend on their advertising revenues, which in turn depend on producing a product with the widest possible appeal. Newspaper readers are often more interested in the sports pages and the social, travel, advertising, and entertainment sections of a newspaper than they are in its news and editorial pages.

In-Depth News In-depth coverage of public affairs is available in the media to those who want it and will seek it out. There are a number of good newspapers around the country. In-depth coverage can also be found on the Internet, in several magazines, and on a number of radio and television stations, including public broadcast outlets. Remember, however, that there is nothing about democracy that guarantees an alert and informed public. Like voting and other forms of political participation, being an informed citizen requires some effort.

? DRAW CONCLUSIONS What does the popularity of sound bites across different media, including political ads, suggest?

ASSESSMENT

1. **Make Predictions** How might the increasing popularity of social media, such as Facebook and Twitter, affect the popularity of radio in the future?
2. **Contrast** Contrast the level of importance of a candidate's party affiliation today and 50 years ago. What has changed?
3. **Generate Explanations** What is one way in which the media influences public policy?
4. **Apply Concepts** If a man chooses to listen to his favorite candidate's podcast on immigration but skips the opposing candidate's Web meeting on the same issue, what concept does this illustrate and why?
5. **Hypothesize** If a candidate noticed too few "Likes" on her Facebook page, what might she be likely to do and why?

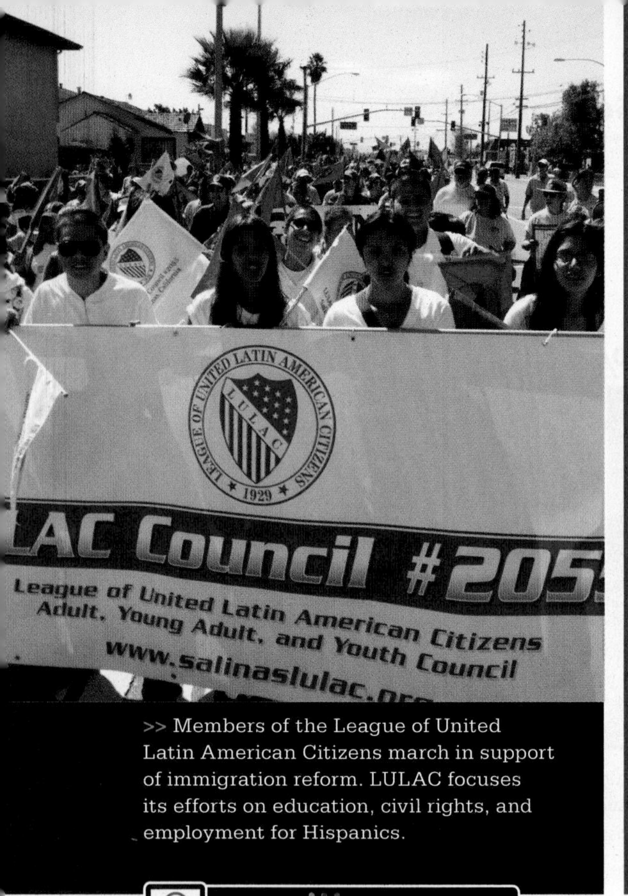

>> Members of the League of United Latin American Citizens march in support of immigration reform. LULAC focuses its efforts on education, civil rights, and employment for Hispanics.

10.7 **An interest group is a collection of people who share certain views on public matters and work to shape public policy to their benefit. They try to persuade public officials to respond to their positions favorably. You may not think that you belong to this sort of group, but as you read this section you will likely discover that you do. You might, in fact, belong to several of them. You will probably also realize that you will become a member of many more of these groups in the years to come—because these organizations provide one of the most effective ways in which Americans can get government to react to their needs and wants.**

Interactive Flipped Video

Understanding Interest Groups

>> Objectives

Understand the role played by interest groups in the U.S. political system.

Analyze the impact of political changes brought about by interest groups and examine the viewpoints of those who see interest groups as both good and bad for American politics, including that of James Madison in the *Federalist Papers* Number 10.

Describe the various types of interest groups in the United States.

Give examples of the direct approach used by interest groups to affect public policy by influencing the legislative, executive, and judicial branches of government.

Examine the indirect lobbying approach and its use of grass-roots pressure, media, propaganda, and political campaigns to influence public opinion and policy.

>> Key Terms

interest group
public policy
public affairs
lobbying
lobbyist
amicus curiae brief
grass-roots pressures
trade association
labor union
Capitol Hill
James Madison
Alexis de Tocqueville

What Are Interest Groups?

Where do you stand on the question of gun control? What about global warming? Campaign finance reform? Abortion? Prayer in public schools? What can you do to promote your views on these and other public questions? How can you increase the chance that your positions will carry the day?

Joining with others who share your opinions is both practical and democratic. Organization can provide the route to power, and organized efforts to further group interests are a fundamental part of the democratic process. Moreover, the right to do so is protected by the Constitution. Remember, the 1st Amendment guarantees "the right of the people peaceably to assemble, and to petition the Government for a redress of grievances."

Interest Groups Shape Public Policy Interest groups are sometimes called "pressure groups" and often "organized interests" or "special interests." They try to influence what government does in some specific area of special interest to them. They give themselves a variety of labels: leagues, associations, clubs, federations, unions, committees, and so on. But whatever they call themselves, every interest group seeks to influence the making and content of **public policy.**

Used in this general sense, public policy includes all of the goals that a government pursues in the many areas of human affairs in which it is involved—everything from seat belts, speed limits, zoning to flood control, old-age pensions, and the use of military force in international affairs.

Because interest groups exist to shape public policy, they can be found wherever those policies are made or can be influenced. They operate at every level of government—on **Capitol Hill** and elsewhere in Washington, D.C., in every one of the 50 State capitals, in thousands of city halls and county courthouses, and in many other places at the local level all across the country. In short, as diplomat and historian Lord Bryce put it somewhat indelicately more than a century ago: "Where the body is, there will the vultures be gathered."

Remember, our society is pluralistic. It is not dominated by any one elite. It is, instead, composed of several distinct cultures and groups. Increasingly, the members of various ethnic, racial, religious, and other groups compete for and share in the exercise of political power in the United States.

Comparing and Contrasting Political Parties and Interest Groups Interest groups are made up of people who join together for some political purpose, much like political parties. The major parties and interest groups overlap in a number of ways. They differ from each other in three significant ways, however: (1) with respect to the making of nominations, (2) in their basic focus, and (3) in the scope of their interests.

First, parties nominate candidates for public office; interest groups do not. Recall, the making of nominations is a prime function of political parties. If an interest group were to nominate candidates, it would, in effect, become a political party.

Interest groups do attempt to affect the outcome of primaries and other nominating contests. They do not pick candidates who then run for office under their labels, however. It may be widely known that a particular interest group supports this or that candidate, but the candidate seeks votes as a Republican or a Democrat.

Second, parties are chiefly interested in winning elections and thereby controlling government. Interest groups are chiefly concerned with controlling or influencing the policies of government. Unlike parties, those groups do not face the problems involved in trying to appeal to the largest possible number of people. In short, political parties are mostly interested in the *who*, and interest groups are mostly concerned with the *what*, of government. To put it another way, parties focus mostly on the candidate; interest groups focus mostly on policy questions.

Interest Groups v. Political Parties

INTEREST GROUPS	Both	POLITICAL PARTIES
• support specific candidates • are interested in influencing government policies • concentrate on those issues important to their members • are private organizations	• are concerned with public policy • unite people for a political purpose	• nominate candidates for public office • are interested in winning elections • concentrate on all public affairs issues • are accountable to the public

>> Political parties and interest groups have more differences than similarities.
Analyze Charts Based on the information shown, why do you think interest groups are sometimes criticized?

Third, political parties are necessarily concerned with the whole range of public affairs, with everything of concern to voters. Interest groups almost always concentrate only on those issues that most directly affect the interests of their members.

Finally, interest groups are private organizations. Unlike political parties, they are not accountable to the public. Their members, not the voters, pass judgment on their performance.

? EXPRESS IDEAS CLEARLY In what way do interest groups raise awareness of public affairs and help shape public policy?

Different Views of Interest Groups

Do interest groups pose a threat to the well-being of the American political system? Or are they, instead, a valuable part of that system? The argument over the merit of interest groups goes back to the beginnings of the Republic.

Madison and de Tocqueville Many have long viewed interest groups with suspicion and foreboding. They have feared that some would become so powerful that they would be able to shape public policies to their own narrow and selfish ends. **James Madison** gave voice to that view in 1787. In *The Federalist* No. 10, he argued that, inevitably, people join together to pursue common interests. They form "factions," Madison's term for what we now call interest groups. He warned that those factions, left unchecked, could dominate public decision making because of size, resources, and/or leadership.

Madison believed that a society could eliminate factions only by eliminating the people's fundamental freedoms. He argued that "the mischiefs of factions" could best be controlled by a political system in which the powers of government, or the ability to make public policies, are fragmented. That is a major reason why, he said, the Constitution provides for a separation of powers and checks and balances, and for a federal system of government—to make it unlikely that one group can override the interests of other (competing) groups.

Nearly 50 years later, **Alexis de Tocqueville** was deeply impressed by the vast number of organizations he found in this country. Tocqueville, a Frenchman, toured much of what was the United States in the 1830s. In his work, *Democracy in America,* he wrote that

> In no country in the world has the principle of association been more successfully used, or more unsparingly applied to a multitude of different objects, than in America.
>
> —Alexis de Tocqueville

And, in a similar vein, he also observed that

Early Interest Groups

Frederick Douglass 1818–1895 formerly enslaved, American Anti-Slavery Society	**Mary Church Terrell** 1863–1954 founder, National Association of Colored Women	**Lewis Hine** 1874–1940 photographer, National Child Labor Committee	**Oliver Hudson Kelly** 1826–1913 farmer, founder of the National Grange

>> These early interest group founders sought a wide range of goals: equality, labor, and economic reforms. **Analyze Charts** What tactics might these leaders have used to accomplish their goals?

> Americans of all ages, all conditions, and all dispositions, constantly form associations . . . not only commercial and manufacturing . . . but . . . of a thousand other kinds—religious, moral, serious, futile, extensive or restricted, enormous or diminutive.
>
> —Alexis de Tocqueville

Are those "associations," or interest groups, good or bad? To answer that question you must weigh, on the one hand, the functions those groups perform in American politics and, on the other, the various criticisms often leveled at them.

>> Habitat for Humanity volunteers build an affordable house in Austin, Texas. **Describe** How has your local area benefited from the work of special interest groups?

Positive Aspects of Interest Groups *First,* among their several commendable functions, organized interests help to stimulate awareness of and interest in **public affairs.** Public affairs are those issues and events that concern the people at large. Interest groups raise awareness of public affairs mostly by developing and publicizing those policy positions they favor and by opposing those they see as threats to the interests of their members.

Second, interest groups represent their members on the basis of shared attitudes rather than on the basis of geography—by what their members think as opposed to where they happen to live. Public officials are elected from districts drawn on maps. But many of the issues that concern and unite people today have less to do with where they live than with, say, how they make a living. A labor union member who lives in Chicago may have much more in common with someone who does the same kind of work in Seattle than he or she does with someone who owns a business in Chicago or runs a farm in another part of Illinois.

Third, organized interests often provide useful, specialized, and detailed information to government—for example, on employment, price levels, or the sales of new and existing homes. These data are important to the making of public policy, and government officials often cannot obtain them from any other source. This flow of information works both ways: interest groups frequently get useful information from public agencies and pass it along to their members.

Fourth, interest groups are vehicles for political participation. Most people are not inclined to run for and hold public office, or even to volunteer for a campaign. For many Americans, then, interest groups are a convenient and less time-consuming way to help shape public policy. They are a means through which like-minded citizens can pool their resources and channel their energies into collective political action.

>> The interest group Mothers Against Drunk Driving seeks to focus attention on the dangers of drinking and driving. **Draw Conclusions** How might such interest groups benefit the public?

One mother concerned about drunk driving cannot accomplish very much acting alone. Thousands of people united in an organization like MADD (Mothers Against Drunk Driving) certainly can and do.

Fifth, interest groups add another element to the checks-and-balances feature of the political process. Many of them keep close tabs on the work of various public agencies and officials and thus help to make sure that they perform their tasks in responsible and effective ways.

Finally, interest groups regularly compete with one another in the public arena. That competition places a very real limit on the lengths to which some groups might otherwise go as they seek to advance their own interests. For example, the automotive industry may work to weaken or postpone auto emission standards imposed under the Clean Air Act. Their efforts may be opposed—and to some extent counterbalanced—by environmental and health-related organizations.

Negative Aspects of Interest Groups All of what has just been said is not meant to suggest that interest groups are above reproach. On the contrary, they can be, and often are, criticized on several counts.

The potentially negative side of interest groups is sometimes all too apparent. Many groups push their own special interests which, despite their claims to the contrary, are not always in the best interests of other Americans. Their critics often make several more specific charges.

First, some interest groups have an influence far out of proportion to their size, or, for that matter, to their importance or contribution to the public good. Thus, the contest over "who gets what, when, and how" is not always a fair fight. The more highly organized and better-financed groups often have a decided advantage in that struggle.

Second, it is sometimes hard to tell just who or how many people a group really represents. Many groups have titles that suggest that they have thousands—even millions—of dedicated members. Some organizations that call themselves such things as "The American Citizens Committee for . . ." or "People United Against . . ." are, in fact, only "fronts" for a very few people with very narrow interests.

Third, many groups do not in fact represent the views of all of the people for whom they claim to speak. Very often, both in and out of politics, an organization is dominated by an active minority who conduct the group's affairs and make its policy decisions.

Finally, some groups use tactics that, if they were to become widespread, would undermine the whole political system. These practices include bribery and other heavy-handed uses of money, overt threats of revenge, and so on. Instances of that sort of behavior are not at all common; they are not altogether unknown, however.

>> College students sign petitions supporting affirmative action. **Hypothesize** Why might interest groups seek support for their causes on college campuses?

The Abramoff Scandal The illegal behavior of a number of representatives of special interests was exposed in Washington during the Abramoff scandal. Jack Abramoff, several of his associates, and a member of Congress were sent to federal prison, convicted of bribery and other offenses. Abramoff and the other special interest representatives funneled hundreds of thousands of dollars into congressional campaigns, provided all-expense-paid trips to resorts, and doled out such things as skybox tickets to professional football games, free dinners, and even jobs for some congressional spouses—all in exchange for legislative favors. Those favors included the introduction of bills written to benefit Abramoff's clients and other attempts to shape lawmaking to that same end.

? DETERMINE POINT OF VIEW In *The Federalist* No. 10, James Madison refers to interest groups as "factions" in the following statement: "There are two methods of curing the mischiefs of faction: the one, by removing its causes; the other, by controlling its effects." To what effects might Madison be referring?

Evaluating Interest Groups

PROS	CONS
• Raise awareness of public affairs • Represent people based on shared attitudes rather than geography • Provide useful data to government • Act as vehicles for political participation • Act as watchdogs over public officials • Compete with one another in the public arena	• Can push their own interests to the detriment of others • Can have influence exceeding their size • Can misrepresent their own size • Do not always represent the views of everyone in the group • Can use unethical tactics and exert undue influence on policy makers

>> The involvement of interest groups in politics has pros and cons. **Analyze Charts** Why might tactics such as donating money to political campaigns be considered a drawback?

Why Do Individuals Join Interest Groups?

"Everything from A to Z." That expression can certainly be applied to the many interest groups in this country. They include, among thousands of others, AAA (the American Automobile Association), ACLU (the American Civil Liberties Union), Amnesty International, the Zionist Organization of America, the NRA (National Rifle Association), the NAACP (National Association for the Advancement of Colored People), and the Zoological Association of America. All of those thousands of organizations can be more or less readily classified and, so, usefully described as interest groups.

An American Tradition The United States has often been called "a nation of joiners." Recall Alexis de Tocqueville's observations cited in the previous section. His comments, true when he made them, have become even more accurate over time.

No one really knows how many associations exist in the United States today. There are thousands upon thousands of them, however, and at every level in society. Each one becomes an interest group whenever it tries to influence the actions of government in order to promote its own goals.

Interest groups come in all shapes and sizes. They may have thousands or even millions of long-established members or only a handful of new or temporary members. They may be well or little known, highly structured or quite loose and informal, wealthy or with few resources. No matter what their characteristics, they are found in every field of human activity in this country.

Based on Interests and Ideas The largest number of these groups has been founded on the basis of an economic interest, and especially on the basis of business, labor, agricultural, and professional interests. Some groups are grounded in a geographic area.

Others have been born out of a cause or an idea, such as prohibition of alcohol, environmental protection, or gun control. Many groups seek to influence some aspect of the nation's foreign policy. Still others exist to promote the welfare of certain groups of people—veterans, senior citizens, a racial minority, the homeless, women, people with disabilities, and so on.

Many people belong to a number of local, regional, or national interest groups—often without realizing they do. A car dealer, for example, may belong to the local Chamber of Commerce, a car dealers' association, the American Legion, a local taxpayers' league, a garden club, a church, and the American Cancer Society. All of these are, to one degree or another, interest groups—including the church and the garden club, even though the car dealer may never think of these groups in that light.

Churches often take stands on such public issues as drinking, curfew ordinances, and legalized gambling, and they often try to influence public policy on those matters. Garden clubs frequently try to persuade cities to do such things as improve public parks and beautify downtown areas. Not every group to which people belong can properly be called an interest group, of course. However, the point is that many groups that are not considered to be interest groups are, in fact, just that.

Many people belong to groups that take conflicting stands on political issues. For example, the taxpayers' league may endorse a plan to eliminate plantings in traffic islands while the garden club wants to keep and even enlarge them.

Types of Interest Groups Most interest groups are formed on the basis of economic interests. Among those groups, the most active are those representing business, labor, agriculture, and certain professions.

Most segments of the business community also have their own interest groups, often called **trade associations**. Those that represent the pharmaceutical, oil, and natural gas industries are generally regarded as the most powerful and effective interest groups today.

A **labor union** is an organization of workers who share the same type of job or who work in the same industry. The AFL-CIO (American Federation of Labor and Congress of Industrial Organizations) is by far the largest.

Issue-oriented groups and religious organizations are other types of interest groups. Still others focus on the welfare of certain segments of the population, such as veterans, or, at the other end of the spectrum, on the common good of the overall community.

Two popular interest groups that seek to promote the interests of particular parts of the population are the National Association for the Advancement of Colored People (NAACP) and the League of United Latin American Citizens (LULAC). Founded in 1909, the NAACP is the oldest and largest civil rights interest group in the United States and is committed to the "elimination of all barriers to political, educational, social, and economic equality" of African Americans and other minority groups. The NAACP works to put public policies into place that support its point of view on important contemporary issues, including civic engagement, education, health, legal issues, and media diversity. On the issue of participation in government, for example, the NAACP works to register minority voters and end voter suppression.

Similarly, LULAC was founded in 1929 and is the oldest civil rights organization for Hispanics in the United States. Like the NAACP, LULAC focuses on many important contemporary issues, such as civil rights, economic empowerment, housing, immigration, and technology. LULAC urges Congress to monitor the enforcement of hate-crime laws, for example, and supports comprehensive immigration reform.

The Changing State of Labor

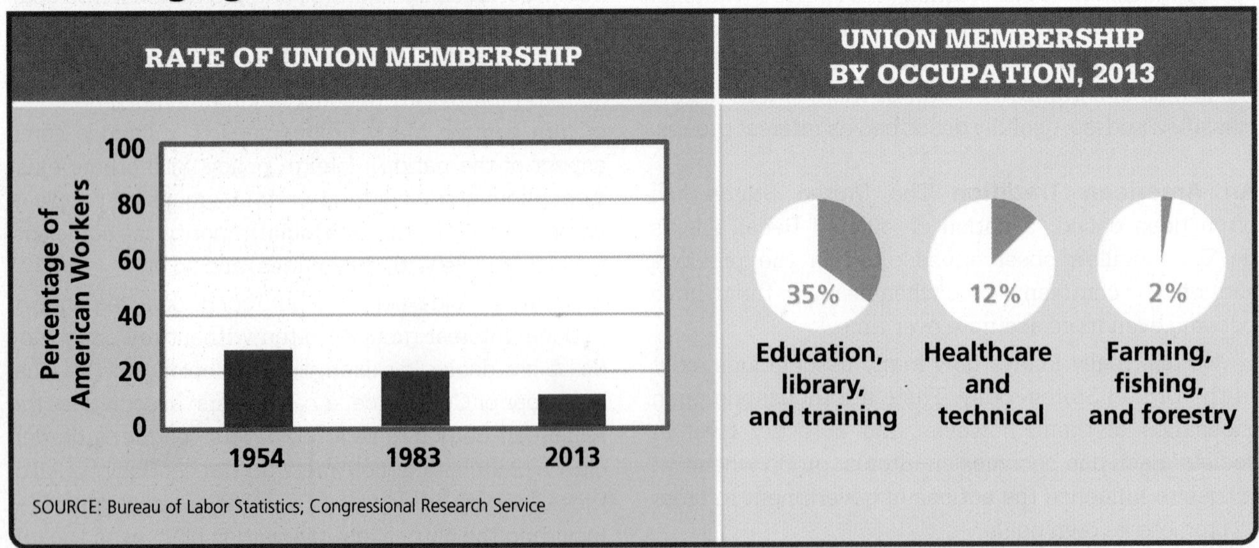

>> Union membership has declined as the economy has shifted from manufacturing to service industries. **Analyze Charts** How might the interests of labor unions have shifted with the changing economy?

The Interest Group Explosion The number of interest groups vying for political power exploded in the late 1960s. The growth was dramatic, and it occurred for several reasons.

First, many Americans began looking for different ways to shape public policy during the "counter-culture revolution." To many, political parties no longer seemed the best way to bring about change because they were "part of the problem." Interest groups, on the other hand, seemed unencumbered by the old rules and "establishment" leaders.

Second, following World War II, a host of new issues caught the public's attention, including civil rights, women's rights, the environment, and the Vietnam War. Many Americans did not have faith that traditional avenues could address these new issues. They sought different pathways for change, including interest groups.

Third, the explosion occurred because the new groups were effective, which led to the formation of opposing groups. Finally, many astute leaders, dubbed by scholars as "public interest entrepreneurs," understood the potential of group mobilization, and they employed a host of techniques to grow their organizations. Direct mail, for example, used to enlist supporters and raise money, became common in the 1970s. This led to higher membership, more powerful organizations, and ever more interest groups vying for power.

GENERATE EXPLANATIONS The interest group Common Cause was formed in 1970, and one of the first issues its members tackled was an attempt to bring an end to the Vietnam War. How does its formation and mission relate to the interest group explosion of the late 1960s?

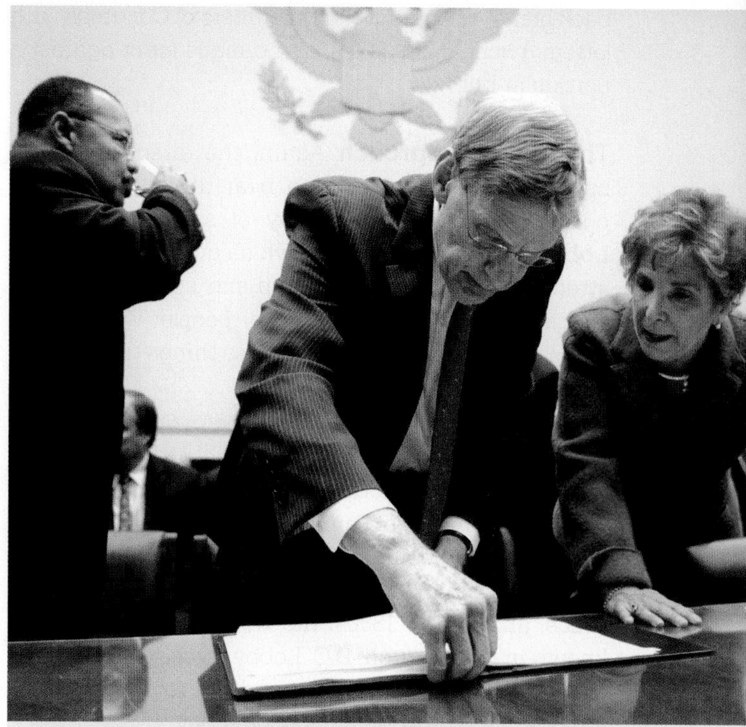

>> Major league baseball lobbyist Lucy Calaitti speaks with Bud Selig, major league baseball commissioner, as he prepares to testify before a House committee on steroid use in professional baseball.

>> An Environmental Defense Fund (EDF) employee collects data. The EDF grew out of a groundbreaking case in the mid-1960s in which scientists and lawyers went to court on behalf of the environment.

Processes Used By Interest Groups—The Direct Approach

Interest groups exist to influence the making and the content of public policy, and they do so in a great many ways and in a great many places. They are, in effect, an excellent illustration of political scientist Harold D. Lasswell's notion that politics is all about "who gets what, when and how."

Interest groups approach government both directly and indirectly in their attempts to influence policy. Their *direct* efforts involve immediate, face-to-face contacts with policymakers. Their *indirect* efforts entail more subtle tactics—for example, mobilizing "the folks back home" to contact their members of Congress with letters, phone calls, faxes, and e-mails for or against a particular bill.

The Direct Approach Again, the direct approach, bringing group pressures to bear directly on public policymakers, is another way of saying "lobbying." **Lobbying** is the process by which organized interests attempt to affect the decisions and actions of public officials. **Lobbyists** are those people who try to persuade public officials to do those things that interest groups want them to do.

The term *lobbying* was first used in Great Britain in the 17th century, referring to members of the public who waited in the public lobbies of the House of Commons to talk with members of Parliament. The term *lobby-agent* was reportedly being used to identify favor-seekers at sessions of New York's legislature in Albany by the late 1820s, and by the 1830s, the word *lobbyist* was well-known in Washington, D.C. Lobbying is still frequently defined in terms of legislators and legislation. However, it has a much broader application today.

Lobbying occurs wherever public policy is made, including Washington, D.C., every State capital, and all of the county courthouses and city halls across the country. It is a big business today. Every important interest and many lesser ones—business groups, labor unions, farm organizations, the professions, churches, veterans, environmental groups, and many more—maintain lobbyists in Washington. In 2016, the Center for Responsive Politics put the total number of registered lobbyists at more than 11,000 and lobbyist spending at some $3.1 billion.

Most lobbyists are professionals. Some are freelancers, "hired guns" who will use their contacts and talents for anyone willing to pay what they charge. Most larger companies and labor unions have their own full-time lobbyists. Many work for the hundreds of Washington law firms and public relations agencies, concentrated along K Street, that specialize in that kind of work.

Regulations The Abramoff scandal prompted Congress to tighten the statutes regulating lobbyists' behavior in 2007. As the law now stands, all persons and organizations that seek to influence members of Congress, their staffers, or any policy-making officer in the executive branch must register with the clerk of the House and the secretary of the Senate. They are required to supply such basic information as name, address, and principal place of business, plus a general description of their activities. Every lobbyist must describe his or her ongoing work in detail and account for the income from it in quarterly reports.

Former senators and top-level executive branch officials must now wait two years, but ex-House members wait only one year, before they can become lobbyists. And, since 2007, no member of Congress can receive *any* gift from lobbyists or their clients.

Lobbying Congress The benefits of maintaining close relationships with members of Congress are fairly obvious, for Congress is the prime place for the making of public policy in the Federal Government. Some lobbying efforts target individual lawmakers and their staffs, but most are aimed at the standing committees of the House and Senate. More than a century ago, Woodrow Wilson described "Congress in its committee rooms" as "Congress at work," and that remains the case today.

Lobbyists testify before congressional committees and regularly submit prepared statements that set out their organization's views on proposed legislation. What happens in a legislative body often excites the interest of several different and competing groups. For example, if the House Committee on the Judiciary is considering a bill to regulate the sale of firearms, those companies that make guns, those that sell them, and those that produce or sell ammunition and a host of other related products all have a clear stake in the bill's contents and

©Wiley Ink, inc./Distributed by Universal Uclick via Cartoonstock

>> **Analyze Political Cartoons** What is being suggested about the ways people can bring concerns to the government? Which is more successful according to this cartoon? Do you agree or disagree?

LOBBYING IN ACTION

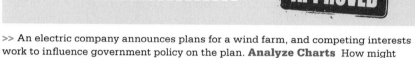

- electric company announce plans for **wind farm**
- area is **upscale vacation homes**
- promoted as **non-polluting** form of energy

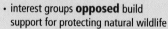

- interest groups **in favor** build support for clean energy
- interest groups **opposed** build support for protecting natural wildlife

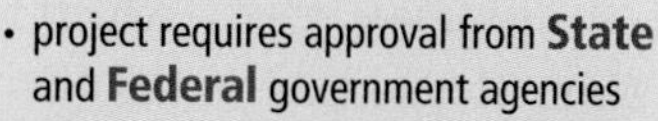

- project requires approval from **State** and **Federal** government agencies
- **government agencies** consider all impacts, such as to the electric power industry and the environment
- **interest groups** try to influence agencies

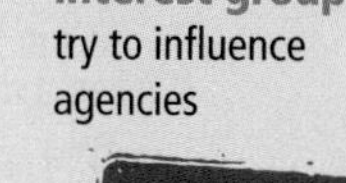

- agencies issue **rulings** on project
- rulings may require **legislative action**

>> An electric company announces plans for a wind farm, and competing interests work to influence government policy on the plan. **Analyze Charts** How might interest groups exert their influence?

its fate. So, too, do law enforcement agencies, hunters, wildlife conservationists, such groups as the National Rifle Association and the American Civil Liberties Union, and several others. Representatives of all of these groups are certain to be invited, or to ask for the opportunity, to present their views to the committee.

Lobbyists often provide useful information to Congress. To the point, John F. Kennedy, who served three terms in the House and was in his second term in the Senate when he won the presidency, observed:

> Competent lobbyists can present the most persuasive arguments in support of their positions. Indeed, there is no more effective manner of learning all important arguments and facts on a controversial issue than to have the opposing lobbyists present their case.
>
> —John F. Kennedy

Lobbyists are ready to do such things as make campaign contributions, provide information, write speeches, and even draft legislation. The contributions are welcome, the information is usually quite accurate, the speeches are forceful, and the bills are well drawn. Most lobbyists know that if they behaved otherwise (gave false or misleading information, for example), they would damage, if not destroy, their credibility and so their overall effectiveness.

Lobbyists work hard to influence committee action, floor debate, and then the final vote in a legislative body. If they fail in one house, they carry their fight to the other. If they lose there, too, they may turn to the executive branch, and perhaps to the courts, as well.

Lobbying and the Executive Branch A vast amount of public policy is made by those who administer the law—that is, by the executive branch. Many of the laws that Congress enacts are written in fairly broad terms. More specific details, such as the day-to-day enforcement of the measure, are left to be worked out in the executive branch. As a practical matter, Congress cannot do such things as prescribe the design specifications for military aircraft, or dictate the advice that federal extension agents are to give to farmers, or determine which of several vaccines will be most effective in the next flu season.

Because meetings with the President and Cabinet officers are difficult to arrange, most executive-branch lobbying focuses, instead, on senior aides in the White House and on the various agencies in the President's administration. The primary job of one of those White House aides, the Director of Public Engagement, is to nurture good relations with major interest groups, especially those that support the President's policies.

Organized interests regularly try to influence the President's appointment of the top officials in various agencies. If an industry group is successful in such efforts, it can improve its chances for favorable treatment by, for example, the Federal Communications Commission or the Bureau of Reclamation in the Department of the Interior.

The most successful lobbyists rely on their networks of contacts as they deal with federal agencies. Ed Rollins, sometime lobbyist and major White House aide in recent Republican administrations, puts that point this way:

> I've got many friends all through the agencies and equally important, I don't have many enemies. . . . I tell my clients I can get your case moved to the top of the pile.
>
> —Ed Rollins

Lobbying and the Courts Organized interests have only recently recognized the fact that they can use the courts to realize their policy goals. You almost certainly know that in 1954, in *Brown* v. *Topeka Board of Education,* the United States Supreme Court held that segregation by race in public schools is unconstitutional. But do you know that *Brown* was taken to the Supreme Court by an interest group, the National Association for the Advancement of Colored People? The massive impact that that case has had made the special-interest community realize just how useful the courts can be.

Lawsuits brought by interest groups are not at all uncommon today. For some, like the American Civil Liberties Union, legal action is the primary means by which they seek to influence public policy. The ACLU regularly takes on unpopular causes—for example, those involving the free speech rights of fringe groups. Those causes usually have little chance of success in legislative bodies, but they may prevail in a courtroom.

An interest group may also file an ***amicus curiae*** ("friend of the court") **brief** in a case to which it is not itself a party but in which it does have a stake. An *amicus* brief consists of written arguments presented to a court in support of one side in a dispute. More than 100 different organizations submitted *amicus* briefs to the Supreme Court in 2003, arguing for or against the University of Michigan's affirmative action policies in *Gratz* v. *Bollinger* and *Grutter* v. *Bollinger.*

Organized interests often try to influence the selection of federal judges. Thus, over recent years, both pro-life and pro-choice organizations have urged Republican and Democratic administrations to make

Top Spenders

RANK	LOBBYIST	RANK	LOBBYIST
20	Amazon.com ($11.3 million)	10	Business Roundtable ($15.7 million)
19	Exxon Mobil ($11.8 million)	9	AT&T Inc. ($16.4 million)
18	Northrop Grumman ($12 million)	8	National Assn. of Broadcasters ($16.4 million)
17	FedEx Corp. ($12.5 million)	7	Boeing Co. ($17 million)
16	NCTA The Internet & Television Assn. ($13.4 million)	6	American Medical Association ($19.4 million)
15	Lockheed Martin ($13.6 million)	5	Pharmaceutical Research & Manufacturers ($19.7 million)
14	Dow Chemical ($13.6 million)	4	American Hospital Assn. ($22.1 million)
13	Southern Co. ($13.9 million)	3	Blue Cross/Blue Shield ($25 million)
12	Comcast Corp. ($14.3 million)	2	National Assn. of Realtors ($64.8 million)
11	Alphabet Inc. ($15.4 million)	1	U.S. Chamber of Commerce ($103.9 million)

SOURCE: Center for Responsive Politics, 2016

>> Watchdog organizations track contributions and top recipients in order to keep the public informed. **Analyze Charts** What can you infer about issues Congress is working on based on this chart?

nominees' stances on abortion a major condition for appointment to the federal bench.

GENERATE EXPLANATIONS Why is it important for the government to monitor lobbyists and their behavior?

Processes Used By Interest Groups—The Indirect Approach

Organized interests also approach government in a number of indirect ways. No matter the particular tactic used, however, the goal is exactly the same as it is when they approach public officials directly—that is, to shape policies to their liking. Not infrequently, interest groups try to mask their involvement in some indirect approach, hoping to make the effort appear to be spontaneous. Their indirect approaches include what is often called "grass-roots lobbying," the molding of public opinion, and various election-related activities.

Grass-roots Lobbying Most lobbyists know how to bring **grass-roots pressures**—pressures from members of an interest group or from the people at large, often beginning at a very basic level—to bear on public officials. Many of the groups that the lobbyists speak for can mount campaigns using letters, postcards, phone calls, faxes, and e-mails from their supporters, often on very short notice.

Some members of Congress downplay the effectiveness of such efforts, and all of them know that groups orchestrate outpourings of letters, phone calls, e-mails, and the like. Still, every congressional office monitors those communications as a way of tracking constituents' opinions.

No organization uses grass-roots lobbying more effectively than AARP, a group originally known as the American Association of Retired Persons. Founded in 1958, it now has more than 40 million members. Whenever legislation or some administrative action that affects retirees is pending, AARP swings into action. Members of Congress receive more letters, phone calls, and e-mails from members of AARP than they do from any other group.

The Internet and Interest Groups The Internet has been a real boon to interest groups, and to cause-related organizations in particular. Nearly every organized interest has a Web site, an expanding e-mail list, and a growing presence on social media. Blogging and Twitter are used by many groups and have proved

HAGEN © 2013
Apparently, the antelopes are lobbying for an anti-stalking law to be passed...

>> **Analyze Political Cartoons** What grass-roots lobbying tactic does this cartoon highlight?

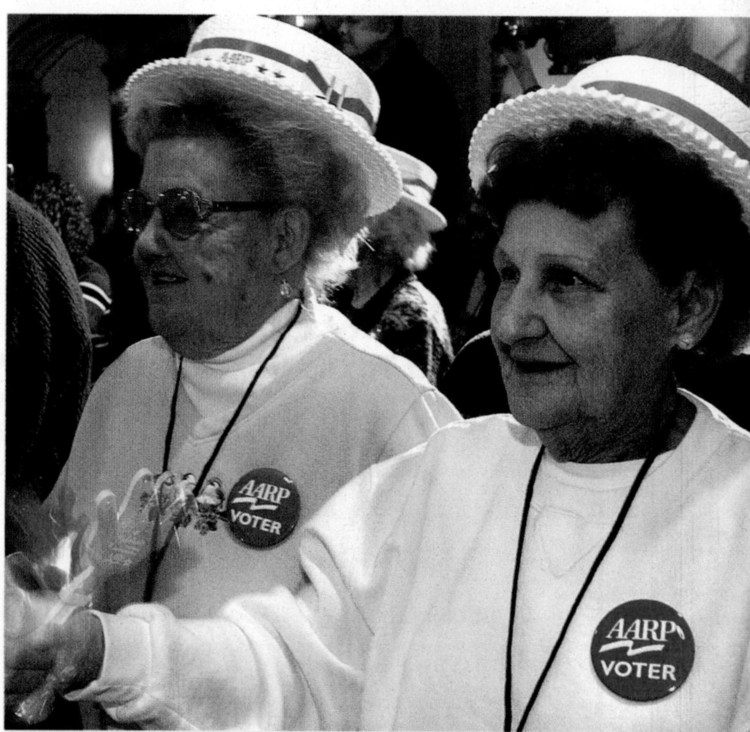

>> AARP members honor lawmakers who passed legislation benefiting seniors. The AARP, an interest group for people age 50 and older, is one of the most powerful lobbying groups in the United States.

quite effective in reaching people in younger age groups.

The Internet has been especially useful to those who want to organize a group but can do so only on a low budget. Left-leaning MoveOn.org is a prime example of the Internet's capacity to organize. It was started by a pair of Silicon Valley entrepreneurs in Berkeley, California, in 1998. Eventually, they formed an Internet network linking hundreds of thousands of citizens who could be mobilized to support liberal candidates and causes. MoveOn.org raised more than $21 million for Democratic candidates in 2012, and it also conducted a massive get-out-the-vote effort.

Demonstrations and protest marches are another form of grass-roots lobbying. Most are efforts to show public officials that some group's cause does have broad public support. Some involve an element of political theater or an eye-catching gimmick to attract media (especially television) coverage. Thus, for example, peace groups often stage "die-ins" to protest war, and farmers might drive their tractors to Washington in "tractorcades" to dramatize their opposition to some agricultural policy.

Several groups now publish ratings of members of Congress. These rankings are based on the votes cast on measures these groups regard as crucial to their interests. Among the more prominent organizations that do so are such liberal groups as Americans for Democratic Action (ADA) and the American Civil Liberties Union (ACLU) and such conservative ones as the American Conservative Union (ACU) and the Chamber of Commerce of the United States.

Each of these groups sees to it that the mass media publicize their ratings. They also distribute them to the group's membership. Their ultimate objective is either to persuade less-than-friendly legislators to change their voting behavior or to help bring about their defeat in future elections.

Interest Groups and Public Opinion Many organized interests spend much of their time and energy on attempts to mold public opinion. Groups that can make enough people regard them and their cause in the best possible way, and can persuade enough people to convey that feeling to public officials, have taken a major step toward achieving their policy goals.

Television screens, newspapers, and magazines are filled with costly advertisements by oil, cell phone, drug, insurance companies, and many others—all seeking to cast the sponsor of the ad in a favorable light. Most of those ads go well beyond promoting some particular product and try also to suggest that the organizations behave as good citizens or defend family values or protect the environment, and so on.

A group's own membership can be used to shape opinions. Thus, in its decades-long opposition (since abandoned) to national health insurance proposals, the American Medical Association persuaded many doctors to put literature condemning those proposals as "socialized medicine" in their waiting rooms and to talk with patients about the issue. Using those tactics, the AMA capitalized on the tendency of most patients to respect their own physicians and regard them as experts.

U.S. Chamber of Commerce Rating of Selected Texas Representatives*

NAME	PARTY	DISTRICT	% "FOR" VOTES 2012	% LIFETIME "FOR" VOTES
Sam Johnson	R	3	89	92
Ruben Hinojosa	D	15	22	54
Sheila Jackson Lee	D	18	11	38
Charles A. Gonzalez	D	20	22	48
John R. Carter	R	31	100	93

*Based on votes cast on top Chamber issues.
"For" votes are those supporting the chamber's position.

SOURCE: U.S. Chamber of Commerce, 2012

>> The Chamber of Commerce ranks members of Congress based on how often they supported top Chamber issues. **Analyze Charts** What does this data show about party support for the Chamber?

Many groups, such as the National Rifle Association (NRA), use well-regarded personalities or trusted public figures to persuade people to support the group's cause. The National Rifle Association, formed in 1871 and the longest standing civil rights organization in the United States, provides a good example of this strategy.

The NRA is a major political force today, with millions of active members who write letters, contact their members of Congress, and raise awareness regarding important contemporary issues related to 2nd Amendment rights. The group also supports firearms education and lobbies vigorously to influence proposed gun control legislation across the nation. The NRA helps get its viewpoint out to the public through such famous personalities as the late Charlton Heston. Mr. Heston served two terms as president of the NRA and had a long record of support for the 2nd Amendment. He was much better known, however, for his long career as an actor. The wide recognition of his name and the moral authority associated with many of the characters he played in movies were extremely helpful to the NRA in its efforts to protect and expand the rights of Americans to keep and bear arms.

>> Former boxing champion Muhammad Ali and actor Michael J. Fox lend their names to raising awareness and funds for Parkinson's Disease.

The Mass Media and Interest Groups Almost certainly, though, the most effective vehicle for the molding of opinions and attitudes is the mass media. Interest groups know that people are more likely to regard their positions favorably if their activities are covered by the media as news rather than presented to the public in paid advertisements. With that in mind, interest groups produce a veritable flood of press releases, interviews, studies, and other materials, hoping to attract media coverage.

Propaganda Techniques Interest groups try to create the public attitudes they want by using propaganda. Propaganda is a technique of persuasion aimed at influencing individual or group behaviors. Its goal is to create a particular belief among the audience. That belief may be completely true or false, or it may lie somewhere between those extremes. Today, people tend to think of propaganda as a form of lying and deception. As a technique, however, propaganda is neither moral nor immoral; it is, instead, amoral.

Propaganda does not use objective logic. Rather, it begins with a conclusion. Then it brings together any evidence that will support that conclusion and disregards information that will not. Propagandists are advertisers, persuaders—and occasionally even brain washers—who are interested in influencing others to agree with their point of view.

The development of the mass media in this country encouraged the use of propaganda, first in the field of

>> PACs and SuperPACs are two groups that lobby the government. **Analyze Political Cartoons** What is this cartoonist saying about the influence of interest groups on elections?

commercial advertising, and then in politics. To be successful, propaganda must be presented in simple, interesting, and credible terms. Talented propagandists almost never attack the logic of a policy they oppose. Instead, they often attack it with name-calling. That is, they attach such labels as "communist" or "fascist." Other labels include "ultra-liberal," "ultraconservative," "pie-in-the-sky," or "greedy." Or, they try to discredit a policy or person by card stacking—that is, presenting only one side of the issue.

Policies that propagandists support receive labels that will produce favorable reactions. They use such glittering generalities as "American," "sound," "fair," and "just." Symbols are often used to elicit those positive reactions from people, too: Uncle Sam and the American flag are favorites. So, too, are testimonials—endorsements, or supporting statements, from such well-known personalities as television stars or professional athletes. The bandwagon approach, which urges people to follow the crowd, is another favorite technique. The plain-folks approach, in which the propagandist pretends to be one of the common people, gets heavy use, too.

Propaganda is spread through newspapers, radio, television, the Internet, movies, billboards, books, magazines, pamphlets, posters, speeches—in fact, through every form of mass communication. The more controversial or less popular a group's position, the more necessary the propaganda campaign becomes.

Interest Groups and Electioneering The most useful and the most appreciated thing that an interest group can do for a public official is to help that person win office. From the group's perspective, electing officeholders like members of Congress, State legislators, governors, and other State and local policymakers sympathetic to their interests is among the most effective things it can do. Once elected, these individuals can shape legislation and allocate money to meet the needs of the interest groups.

Groups can and do help those who run for office, and they do so in a variety of ways. Many do so through their political action committees. Recall that PACs are political arms of interest groups. They make financial contributions and hold fundraisers for candidates. They conduct voter registration and get-out-the-vote drives, supply professional campaign consultants, and provide information to be used in campaign speeches. Occasionally they even provide audiences to hear those speeches. And PACs do such other things as help staff local campaign offices, distribute campaign literature,

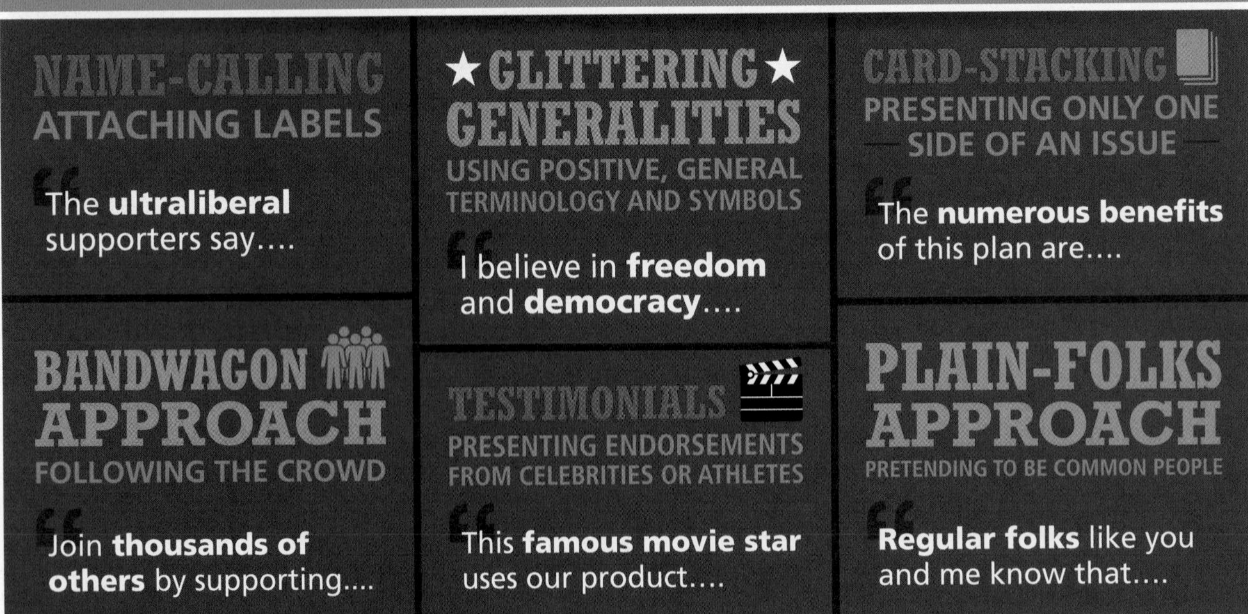

MAJOR PROPAGANDA TECHNIQUES
NAME-CALLING
ATTACHING LABELS
"The ultraliberal supporters say....
GLITTERING GENERALITIES
USING POSITIVE, GENERAL TERMINOLOGY AND SYMBOLS
"I believe in freedom and democracy....
CARD-STACKING
PRESENTING ONLY ONE SIDE OF AN ISSUE
"The numerous benefits of this plan are....
BANDWAGON APPROACH
FOLLOWING THE CROWD
"Join thousands of others by supporting....
TESTIMONIALS
PRESENTING ENDORSEMENTS FROM CELEBRITIES OR ATHLETES
"This famous movie star uses our product....
PLAIN-FOLKS APPROACH
PRETENDING TO BE COMMON PEOPLE
"Regular folks like you and me know that....

>> Using a variety of persuasive techniques, propaganda seeks to create a desired belief. **Analyze Charts** How do these techniques encourage the public to "join the crowd"?

work phone banks, and take voters to the polls on election day.

? INFER Why do interest groups continue to utilize propaganda, and why is it particularly effective?

ASSESSMENT

1. **Connect** Explain the relationship between interest groups and legislation.
2. **Compare** How are political parties and interest groups similar?
3. **Draw Conclusions** How do the American people benefit MOST from public-interest groups?
4. **Classify** If a lobbyist were to organize a large-scale protest march, would this be an example of effective direct lobbying? Why or why not?
5. **Explain** Imagine that the Lone Star Chapter of the Sierra Club sends e-mails on behalf of its members to government leaders regarding water conservation issues in their State. Explain the type of lobbying the Sierra Club is employing and why it can be effective.

TOPIC 10 ASSESSMENT

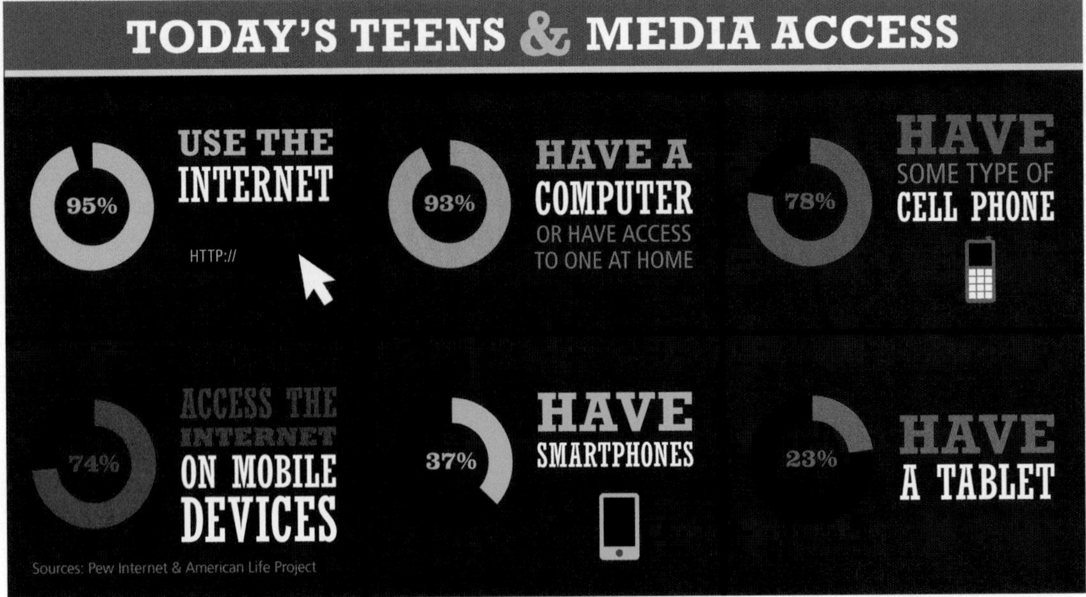

1. **Evaluate the Impact of Electronic** Use the graphic above to write a paragraph from the point of view of a person running for Congress. What method should you use to reach younger voters? In your paragraph, evaluate the impact of electronic information on the political process. Identify at least two options, predict the consequences of each, and describe the action you would take to implement your decision. Consider the following questions: What does the graphic tell you about how information is accessed by younger people and the number of people who use it? What impact does this fact have on the political process? If you were a candidate trying to reach younger voters, how would you do so?

2. **Evaluate Policies and Decisions that Affect Particular Groups** Write a paragraph evaluating how the Civil Rights Act of 1964 affected African Americans. Consider the following questions: What new government policies resulted from the Civil Rights Act of 1964? How did the act affect African Americans? Did the act accomplish all that civil rights leaders and others hoped? Why or why not?

3. **Analyze the Federalist Papers** Use the quotation below to write a paragraph analyzing which principle of the American constitutional system of government is reflected in this excerpt from *Federalist* Number 10. Consider the following questions: Madison was concerned about the "mischief of factions." Did he believe that factions should or could be eliminated under the American constitutional system? What basic principle of the American constitutional system of government is reflected in this excerpt? What was Madison's frame of reference when he wrote this document in 1787? How did this frame of reference influence the opinion he expresses in this excerpt?

"There are again two methods of removing the causes of faction: the one, by destroying the liberty which is essential to its existence; the other, by giving to every citizen the same opinions, the same passions, and the same interests.

It could never be more truly said than of the first remedy, that it was worse than the disease. Liberty is to faction what air is to fire, an aliment [food; nourishment] without which it instantly expires.

—James Madison, Federalist Number 10

4. **Identify Significant Individuals** Write a paragraph identifying Franklin D. Roosevelt and why his use of mass media was significant. Consider the following questions: Who was Franklin D. Roosevelt? What role did he play in the development of the mass media? Why was his use of the media so important?

5. **Understand Voter Registration** Write a paragraph describing each step in the voter registration process. Consider the following questions: Where can a citizen register to vote? What information must prospective voters provide when registering to vote? How far in advance of an election can prospective voters register to vote?

6. **Understand the Criteria for Voting** Write a paragraph summarizing the criteria for voting and analyzing why each is necessary. Consider the following questions to support your response: What are the three universal criteria for voting in elections? Why did States establish each criteria?

7. **Understand the Responsibilities of Citizenship** Write a paragraph explaining why voting is an important responsibility of citizenship. Consider the following questions: What percentage of the eligible population votes? Why is it important to vote?

8. **Understand Voting Patterns** Write a paragraph that answers the following questions: How did urban and rural population shifts affect voting patterns during the New Deal era? How have urban and rural population shifts affected voting patterns in recent years?

9. **Evaluate the Impact of the Internet** Write a paragraph evaluating the impact of online voting. Consider the following questions: How often has online voting been used? What are the benefits and drawbacks of online voting?

10. **Compare Methods of Filling Public Offices** Write a paragraph focusing on election law at the federal, state, and local levels. Consider the following questions: Who sets the date for federal elections? For state and local elections? When are Texas elections held? When are your local elections held? At what levels of government is early voting allowed?

11. **Examine Points of View of Interest Groups** Use the excerpt below from a secondary source to write a paragraph examining the point of view of the League of United Latin American Citizens (LULAC) on immigration reform. Consider the following questions: What is LULAC's point of view on immigration reform? What reasons does LULAC give for this viewpoint?

> *According to its Web site, the League of United Latin American Citizens supports comprehensive immigration reform. The group is making a strong effort to educate Americans on this topic, as well as to push members of Congress to pass legislation that will benefit immigrants, as well as American citizens. LULAC believes that reforming the visa system will benefit the United States by encouraging highly skilled workers from other countries to start businesses in the U.S. This will create jobs and help the U.S. succeed in the global economy. In addition, LULAC urges Congress to pass legislation that will help immigrants become legal citizens by streamlining the application process and allowing undocumented workers to become citizens. This will help to put a stop to the low wages and poor working conditions that affect not only these workers, but all American workers.*
>
> *—Based on information from the League of Latin American Citizens Web site*

12. **Understand the Responsibilities of Citizenship** Write a paragraph explaining why voting is an important responsibility of citizenship. Consider the following questions: How have voting rights changed since the founding of the United States? Why is it important to vote?

13. **Explain Changes in American Culture** Use the image above to write a paragraph explaining the changes in American culture brought about by the 15th Amendment, according to the artist of this lithograph. Consider the following questions: What changes does the image imply the 15th Amendment made in American culture? What was the reality of the changes brought about by the 15th Amendment in the late 1800s? What biases may have influenced this illustration?

14. **Analyze the Impact of Political Changes** Write a paragraph analyzing the impact of political changes brought about by the television and the Internet. Consider the following questions: What political changes were brought about the advent of television? What was the impact of these changes? What political changes have been brought about by the Internet? What is the impact of these changes?

15. **Understand Influences on Political Attitudes** Write a paragraph about political attitudes that answers the following questions: What is political socialization? What factors influence political socialization? Choose one factor and explain how it influences political attitude?

16. **Examine Points of View of Interest Groups** Choose one of the public affairs topics listed below or another of your own choosing. Then conduct research to find (1) an interest group that concerns itself with public policy related to this topic and (2) an interest group that takes the opposing side on the topic. Then create a written summary of the different points of view of these two groups. From your summary, design a chart, graph, or graphic organizer that shows the information visually. Finally, present your interest groups and visual summary to the class in an oral presentation. Choose from the following public affairs topics: the environment; civil rights for a particular racial group; energy; foreign affairs; immigration; national security; technology and communication.

17. Identify Examples of Research Write a paragraph that answers the following question: What mass media-related computer and communication technologies were developed through government research that was shared with the private sector? Describe how that technology was developed.

18. Analyze Citizen Movements Analyze the efforts by the members of the American Medical Association (AMA) to help defeat proposals for national health insurance. Consider the following questions: Why are the efforts of the American Medical Association considered a "citizen movement"? How did AMA members act to maintain continuity with regard to public policies on national health insurance?

19. Give Examples of Processes to Affect Public Policy Write a paragraph giving examples of how public opinion is used to affect public policy. Consider the following questions: Why is it important to be able to measure public opinion? How is public opinion measured? How can the results be used to affect public policy?

20. Evaluate Constitutional Provisions Write a paragraph evaluating constitutional provisions for limiting the role of government with regard to voting rights. Consider the following questions: How does the Constitution limit the Federal Government's role in setting suffrage qualifications? How does the Constitution limit State governments' role in setting suffrage qualifications?

21. Evaluate Arguments for Point of View and Frame of Reference The quotation below is from a speech given by lawyer and U.S. representative Abraham Lincoln during the famous Lincoln-Douglas debates of 1858. The debates were held to help voters choose which man they would elect to the U.S. Senate from Illinois. Use the quotation to write a paragraph identifying which process used to affect public policy Lincoln is describing in his comment, as well as how important he finds this particular process. Consider the following questions to support your response: What process used to affect public policy is Lincoln describing in this quotation? How important does Lincoln find this process? Based on Lincoln's point of view and frame of reference, how valid is his argument?

"In this age, in this country, public sentiment is everything. With it, nothing can fail; against it, nothing can succeed. Whoever molds public sentiment goes deeper than he who enacts statutes, or pronounces judicial decisions."

—Abraham Lincoln, Lincoln-Douglas debates, 1858

22. Write About the Essential Question Write an essay on the Essential Question: What is the role of the people in government? Use evidence from your study of this Topic to support your answer.

[ESSENTIAL QUESTION] Who Gets Elected?

11 Elections

>> Election campaign signs of political candidates in Boise, Idaho

Enduring Understandings

- Political parties work to get their candidates elected in order to influence governmental policies and programs.
- Minor parties rarely win elections but can have a significant impact on election outcomes.
- The nominating process determines which candidates appear on the ballot in local, State, and national elections.
- Although the popular vote represents the people's choice, the electoral college actually elects the President, so a candidate may win the popular vote but fail to win the presidency.
- Money plays a critical role in political campaigns but raises the danger of abuses of campaign finance regulations.

PEARSON realize™ NBC LEARN

Watch the My Story Video for an introduction to the methods that political operatives use to influence public opinion.

PEARSON realize™ www.PearsonRealize.com

Access your digital lessons including: Topic Inquiry • Interactive Reading Notepad • Interactivities • Assessments

>> This aerial view of the 2012 Republican National Convention shows the festivity and crowd reaction as nominee Mitt Romney accepted the Republican presidential nomination.

11.1 "Winning isn't everything; it's the only thing." So said legendary football coach Vince Lombardi. Lombardi was talking about teams in the National Football League. He might just as well have had the Republican and Democratic parties in mind. They, too, are in the business of competing and winning.

Interactive Flipped Video

>> Objectives

Understand the origins of political parties in the United States and analyze their major functions.

Understand multiparty and one-party systems and how they affect the functioning of a political system, and explain the two-party system of the United States.

Evaluate the role of minor parties that have been active in American politics, and understand why they are important despite the fact that none has ever won the presidency.

Understand why the major parties have a decentralized structure.

Describe the national party machinery and party organization at the State and local levels.

>> Key Terms

political party
political spectrum
partisanship
single-member districts
plurality
bipartisan
consensus
coalition
ideological
single-issue parties
economic protest parties
splinter parties
ward
precinct
George Washington
Theodore Roosevelt
Thomas Jefferson

Political Parties and What They Do

What Is a Political Party?

A **political party** is a group of persons who seek to control government through the winning of elections and the holding of public office. This definition of a political party is broad enough to cover any party, including the two major parties in American politics, the Republicans and the Democrats. Another, more specific definition can be used to describe most political parties, both here and abroad: a group of persons, joined together on the basis of certain common principles, who seek to control government in order to secure the adoption of certain public policies and programs.

This latter definition, with its emphasis on principles and policy positions, will not fit the two major parties in the United States, however. The Republican and Democratic parties are not primarily principle- or issue-oriented. They are, instead, *election*-oriented.

You can better understand our two major parties if you recognize that each of them is an organization made up of three separate but closely related elements, three separate groups of party loyalists:

1. *The party organization.* This element of the party includes its leaders, its other activists, and its many "hangers-on"—all those who give their time, money, and skills to the party. In short, these are the

party "professionals," those who run the party at the national, State, and local levels.

2. *The party in government.* This component includes the party's candidates and officeholders, those thousands of persons who run for or hold elective or appointive offices in the executive, legislative, and judicial branches at the federal, State, and local levels of government.

3. *The party in the electorate.* These are the millions of people who call themselves Republicans or Democrats, and who support the party and its candidates through thick and thin. Many of them cast their votes on the basis of the party label, without regard to candidates or issues in an election. Observers sometimes criticize this kind of voting behavior as thoughtless. Yet knowing that a candidate is a Republican or Democrat often provides useful clues about where a candidate stands on key issues.

DRAW CONCLUSIONS Why would voters cast their votes based solely on a candidate's party affiliation?

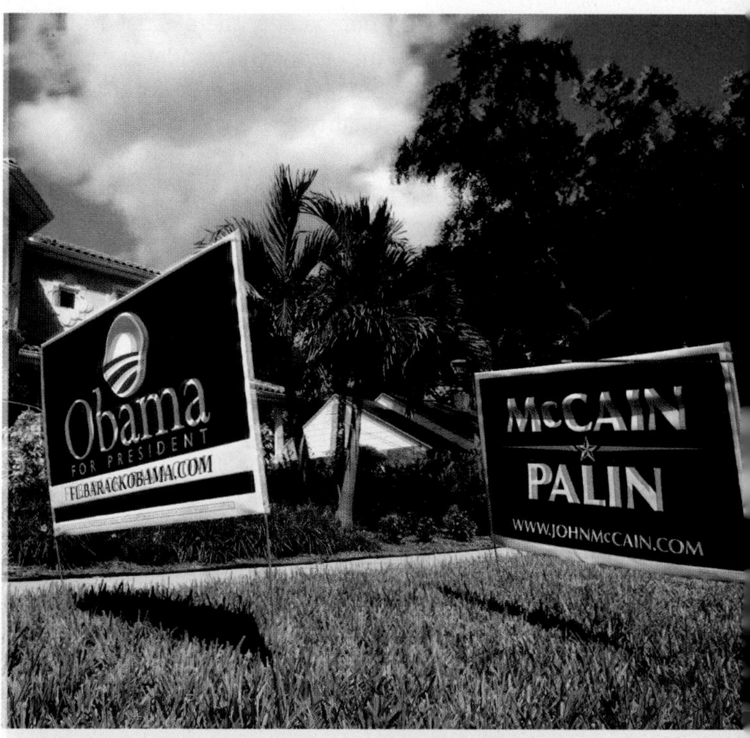

>> The two campaign signs in the yard of this home demonstrate that even members of the same family can have different opinions about which political candidate should be elected.

The Role of Political Parties

It is clear from our history, and from the histories of other peoples as well, that political parties are absolutely essential to democratic government. They are a vital link between the people and their government, between the governed and those who govern. Indeed, many observers argue that political parties are the principal means by which the will of the people is made known to government and by which government is held accountable to the people.

Parties serve the democratic ideal in another significant way: They work to blunt conflict; they are "power brokers." Political parties seek to modify the contending views of various interests and groups, encourage compromise, and so help to unify, rather than divide, the American people. They are very often successful in their attempts to soften the impact of extremists at both ends of the **political spectrum**, the range of political views.

Again, parties are indispensable to democratic government and, so, to American government. That fact is underscored by the several significant functions they perform.

>> The grassroots Tea Party movement, which gained national attention during the 2010 election campaign, advocated lower taxes, less government, and reduction of the national debt.

Nominating Candidates The major function of a political party is to nominate—name—candidates for public office. That is, parties select candidates and present them to the voters. Then the parties work to help those nominees win elections.

In a functioning democracy, there must be some way to find (choose and recruit) candidates for office. There must also be some mechanism to gather support for those candidates. Parties are the best device yet found to do these jobs.

The nominating function is almost exclusively a party function in the United States. It is the one activity that most clearly sets political parties apart from all of the other groups that operate in the political process.

Informing and Activating Supporters Parties inform the people and inspire and activate their interest and their participation in public affairs, including encouraging changes on political issues. Other groups also perform this function—in particular, the news media and interest groups.

Parties try to inform and inspire voters in several ways. Mostly, they do so by campaigning for their candidates, taking stands on current issues, and criticizing opposing candidates and the positions they adopt.

How Political Parties Inform People Each party tries to inform the people as it thinks they should be informed—that is, to its own advantage. It conducts its "educational" efforts through pamphlets, signs, buttons, and stickers; advertisements in newspapers and magazines and via radio, television, the Internet, and text messaging; at speeches, rallies, and conventions; and in a variety of other ways.

Remember, both parties want to win elections, and that consideration has much to do with the stands they take on most issues. Both Republicans and Democrats try to shape positions that will attract as many voters as possible—and at the same time, offend as few as possible.

The Bonding Agent Function In the business world, a bond is an agreement that protects a person or a company against loss caused by a third party. In politics, a political party acts as a "bonding agent," to ensure the good performance of its candidates and elected officeholders.

In choosing its candidates, the party tries to make sure that they are men and women who are both qualified and of good character—or, at the least, that they are not unqualified for the public offices they seek.

The party also prompts its successful candidates to perform well in office. The democratic process imposes this bonding agent function on a party, whether the party really wants to perform it or not. If it fails to assume the responsibility, both the party and its candidates may suffer the consequences of that failure in future elections.

>> The stage for the 2012 Democratic National Convention, with the theme Americans Coming Together, exemplified the goal of such events: to create enthusiasm for the party's candidates.

Governing In several respects, government in the United States is government by party. For example, public officeholders—those who govern—are regularly chosen on the basis of party. Congress and the State legislatures are organized on party lines, and they conduct much of their business on the basis of **partisanship**—the strong support of their party and its policy stands. Most appointments to executive offices, at both the federal and State levels, are made with an eye to party.

Political Parties Help the Government Run More Smoothly In yet another sense, parties provide a basis for the conduct of government. In the complicated separation of powers arrangement, the executive and legislative branches must cooperate with one another if government is to accomplish anything. It is political parties that regularly provide the channels through which these two branches are able to work together. Political parties have also played a role in the process of constitutional change.

Consider this important example: The Constitution's cumbersome system for choosing a President works principally because political parties reshaped it in its earliest years, and they have made it work ever since.

The Watchdog Function Parties act as watchdogs over the public's business. This is particularly true of the party out of power, which criticizes the policies of the party in power. In American politics, the party in power has traditionally been the party that controls the executive branch of government.

This definition is useful under a unified government. Since the late 1960s, however, government in the United States has been more often divided, with one party controlling the White House and the other controlling one or both houses of Congress. In this situation, the term party in power loses some of its meaning, because it is no longer as obvious which party that is.

During President Obama's first two years in office, the government was unified under the Democrats while the Republicans attempted to convince the voters to "throw the rascals out." This scrutiny by the "out" party tends to make the "rascals" more careful of their public charge and more responsive to the people. The party out of power plays the important role of "the loyal opposition"—opposed to the party in power but loyal to the people and the nation.

During the last six years of Barack Obama's presidency, however, the Republicans controlled at least one house of Congress. While the Democrats were theoretically the party in power, their agenda was checked at every turn. So which party had more control over the direction of public policy for those six years—and which was the watchdog?

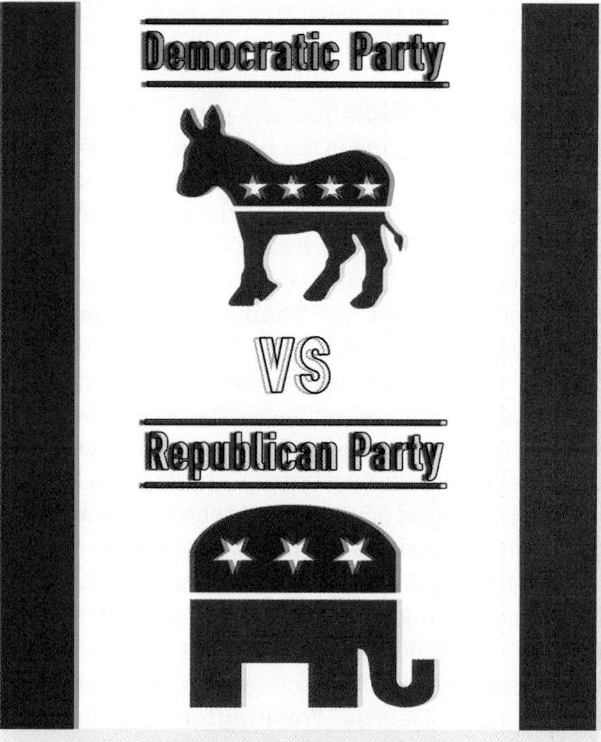

>> A political party logo is a symbol that represents the entire party. The Republicans and Democrats have adopted the elephant and the donkey respectively to represent their parties.

Interactive Timeline

Political Parties Help Make Democracy Work Again, these functions performed by political parties and, particularly, the two major parties, testify to the important role they play in making democracy work in this country. You might well remember that point the next time a comedian on late-night television ridicules some candidate, party, or officeholder.

There was a time when the parties played an even larger role in the nation's affairs than they do today. For example, in what has been called "the golden age of parties," from roughly the late nineteenth to the mid-twentieth century, party organizations operated as major welfare organizations in many places in the United States. They regularly helped newly arrived immigrants and many others among the poor to obtain food, housing, and jobs. Often they did this to win the support of these people at the polls. That once-important welfare function has long since been taken over by a number of government programs put in place in the twentieth century.

IDENTIFY CENTRAL ISSUES How do political parties help to unify the American people?

The Two-Party System

Two major parties, the Republicans and the Democrats, dominate American politics. That is to say, this country has a two-party system. In a typical election in the United States, only the Republican or the Democratic Party's candidates have a reasonable chance of winning public office.

It is true that in some States, and in many local communities, one of the two major parties may be overwhelmingly dominant, winning election after election. And it may do so for a long time—as, for example, the Democratic Party dominated the politics of the South from the years after the Civil War into the 1960s. But, on the whole, and through most of our history, the United States has been a two-party nation.

Several factors explain why America has had and continues to have a two-party system. No one of these factors, alone, offers a wholly satisfactory explanation for the phenomenon. Taken together, however, they are quite persuasive.

The Historical Basis The two-party system in the United States is rooted in the beginnings of the nation itself. The Framers of the Constitution were opposed to political parties. As you know, the ratification of the Constitution gave rise to America's first two parties: the Federalists, led by Alexander Hamilton, and the Anti-Federalists, led by **Thomas Jefferson**. The Federalists were, by and large, the party of "the rich and well-born" and had supported the Constitution and a stronger national government. The Anti-Federalists were more concerned for the "common man" than were the Federalists, and they favored a much more limited role for the national government. In short, the American party system *began* as a two-party system.

The Framers hoped to create a unified country; they sought to bring order out of the chaos of the Critical Period of the 1780s. To most of the Framers, parties were "factions," and therefore agents of divisiveness and disunity. **George Washington** reflected this view when, in his Farewell Address in 1796, he warned the new nation against "the baneful effects of the spirit of party."

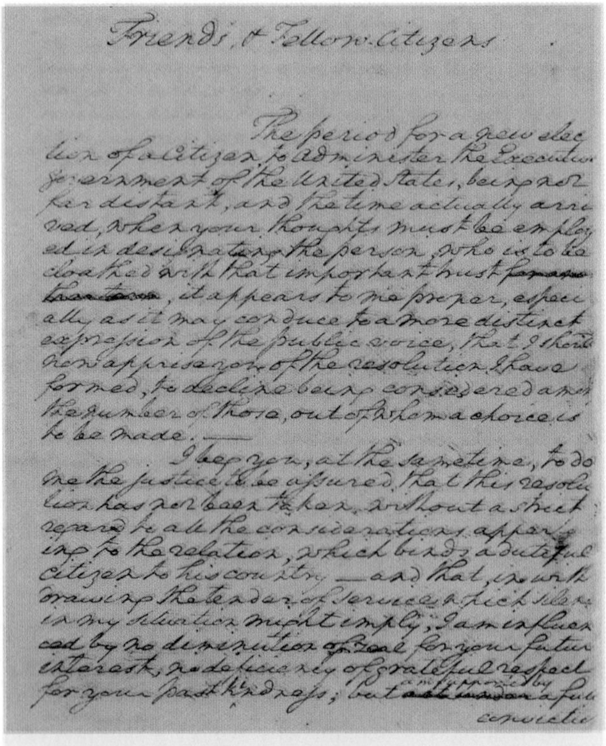
Friends, & Fellow-Citizens.

The period for a new election of a Citizen to administer the Executive government of the United States, being not far distant, and the time actually arrived, when your thoughts must be employed in designating the person, who is to be cloathed with that important trust, it appears to me proper, especially as it may conduce to a more distinct expression of the public voice, that I should now apprise you of the resolution I have formed, to decline being considered among the number of those, out of whom a choice is to be made.

I beg you, at the same time, to do me the justice to be assured that this resolution has not been taken, without a strict regard to all the considerations appertaining to the relation, which binds a dutiful citizen to his country — and that, in withdrawing the tender of service which silence in my situation might imply, I am influenced by no diminution of zeal for your future interest, no deficiency of grateful respect for your past kindness; but supported by a full conviction

>> In his Farewell Address, Washington said, "The common and continual mischiefs of the spirit of party are sufficient to make it the interest and duty of a wise people to discourage and restrain it."

In this light, it is hardly surprising that the Constitution made no provision for political parties. The Framers could not foresee the ways in which the governmental system they created would develop.

The Federalist and Anti-Federalist parties first clashed in the election of 1796 when John Adams defeated Jefferson, but in the election of 1800 Jefferson and his party, now named the Democratic-Republican Party, defeated the Federalist President Adams. The Federalists never returned to power.

Unexpected Effects The history of the American party system since 1800 can be divided into four major periods. Through the first three of these periods, one or the other of the two major parties was dominant, regularly holding the presidency and usually both houses of Congress. The nation is now in a fourth period, much of it marked by divided government.

The Framers could not have possibly known that two major parties would emerge as prime instruments of government in the United States. Nor could they know that those two parties would tend to be moderate, most often choose "middle-of-the-road" positions, and so help to unify rather than divide the nation.

The Force of Tradition Once established, human institutions are likely to become self-perpetuating. So it has been with the two-party system. The very fact that the nation began with a two-party system has been a leading reason for the retention of a two-party system in this country. Over time, it has become an increasingly important, self-reinforcing reason as well.

The point can be made this way: Most Americans accept the idea of a two-party system simply because there has always been one. This inbred support for the arrangement is a principal reason why challenges to the system—by minor parties, for example—have made so little headway. In other words, America has a two-party system because America has a two-party system.

The Electoral System Several features of the American electoral system tend to promote the existence of but two major parties. The basic shape, and many of the details, of the election process work in that direction and to discourage minor parties.

The prevalence of **single-member districts** is one of the most important of these features. Nearly all of the elections held in this country—from the presidential contest to those at the local levels—are single-member district elections.

That is, they are contests in which only one candidate is elected to each office on the ballot. They are winner-take-all elections. The winning candidate is the one who receives a **plurality**, or the largest number of votes cast for the office. Note that a plurality need not be a majority, or more than half of all votes cast in any given election.

The single-member district pattern works to discourage third and minor parties. Because only one winner can come out of each contest, voters usually face only two viable choices: They can vote for the candidate of the party holding the office, or they can vote for the candidate of the party with the best chance of replacing the current officeholder. In short, the single-member district arrangement has led many voters to think of a vote for a minor party candidate as a "wasted vote."

Election Law Discourages Non-Major-Party Candidates Another important aspect of the electoral system works to the same end. Much of American election law is purposely written to discourage non-major-party candidates.

In fact, almost all of the nearly 7,400 State legislators—nearly all of those persons who make State law—are either Democrats or Republicans. Only a handful of minor party members or independents now sit, or have ever sat, in State legislatures. The GOP (The Republican Party) and the Democrats regularly act in a **bipartisan** way in this matter. That is, the two major parties find common ground here. They work together to shape election laws in such a way that minor party or independent candidates have a much harder time winning elective office.

Every four years, the presidential contest offers a striking illustration of this situation. In 2016, Democrat Hillary Clinton and Republican Donald Trump were listed on the ballots of all 50 States and the District of Columbia. However, only one of the other non-major party candidates— Libertarian Gary Johnson—made it to the ballot in every State.

Green Party candidate Jill Stein came close to reaching that goal. She was on the ballots of 45 States in 2016. The Constitution Party's Darrell Castle was listed in 24 States, Reform Party candidate Roque De La Fuente in 20, and independent Evan McMullin in 11. All of the other minor party candidates fell far short of those totals, however. Indeed, most suffered their usual fate: 13 managed to make the ballots of only one State and nine were listed in two or three States.

The American Ideological Consensus Americans are, on the whole, an ideologically homogeneous people. That is, over time, the American people have shared many of the same ideals, the same basic principles, and the same patterns of belief.

This is not to say that Americans are all alike. Clearly, this is not the case. The United States is a

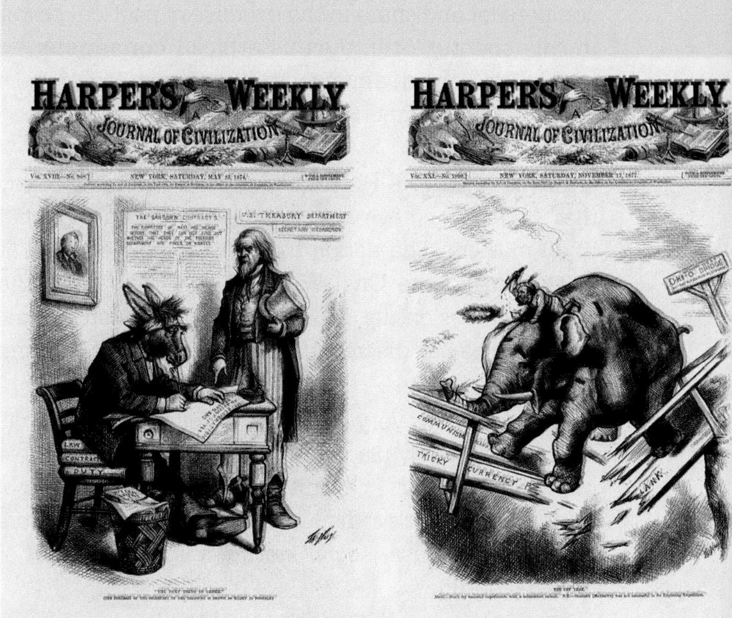

>> Cartoonist Thomas Nast is credited with popularizing the donkey and elephant symbols. **Analyze Political Cartoons** What characteristics of each animal might appeal to its respective party?

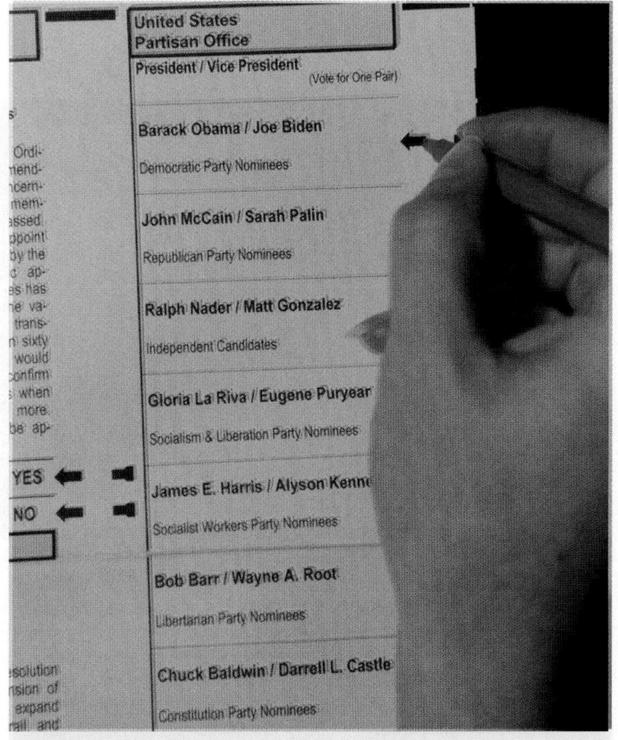

>> This absentee ballot from the 2008 presidential election lists all the candidates from the major parties and the minor parties.

pluralistic society—one consisting of several distinct cultures and groups. Increasingly, the members of various ethnic, racial, religious, and other social groups compete for and share in the exercise of political power in this country. Still, there is a broad **consensus**—a general agreement among various groups—on matters of fundamental importance.

No Unbridgeable Political Divisions Nor is it to say that Americans have always agreed with one another in all matters. The nation has been deeply divided at times: during the Civil War and in the years of the Great Depression, for example, and over such critical issues as racial discrimination, the war in Vietnam, and abortion.

Still, note this very important point: This nation has not been regularly plagued by sharp and unbridgeable political divisions. The United States has been free of longstanding, bitter disputes based on such factors as economic class, social status, religious beliefs, or national origin.

Those conditions that could produce several strong rival parties simply do not exist in this country. In this way, the United States differs from most other democracies. In short, the realities of American society and politics simply do not permit more than two major parties.

How This Ideological Consensus Affects Political Parties This ideological consensus has had another very important impact on American parties. It has given the nation two major parties that often look very much alike. Both tend to be moderate. Both are built on compromise and usually try to occupy "the middle of the road." Both parties seek the same prize: the votes of a majority of the electorate. To do so, they must win over essentially the same people. Each party usually takes policy positions that do not differ a great deal from those of the other major party.

This is not to say that there are no significant differences between the two major parties today. There are many. For example, the Democratic Party, and those who usually vote for its candidates, are more likely to support such things as social welfare programs, government regulation of business practices, and efforts to improve the status of minorities. On the other hand, the Republican Party and its supporters are much more likely to favor the play of private market forces in the economy and to argue that the Federal Government should be less extensively involved in social welfare programs.

? SUMMARIZE Describe how single-member districts discourage minor parties.

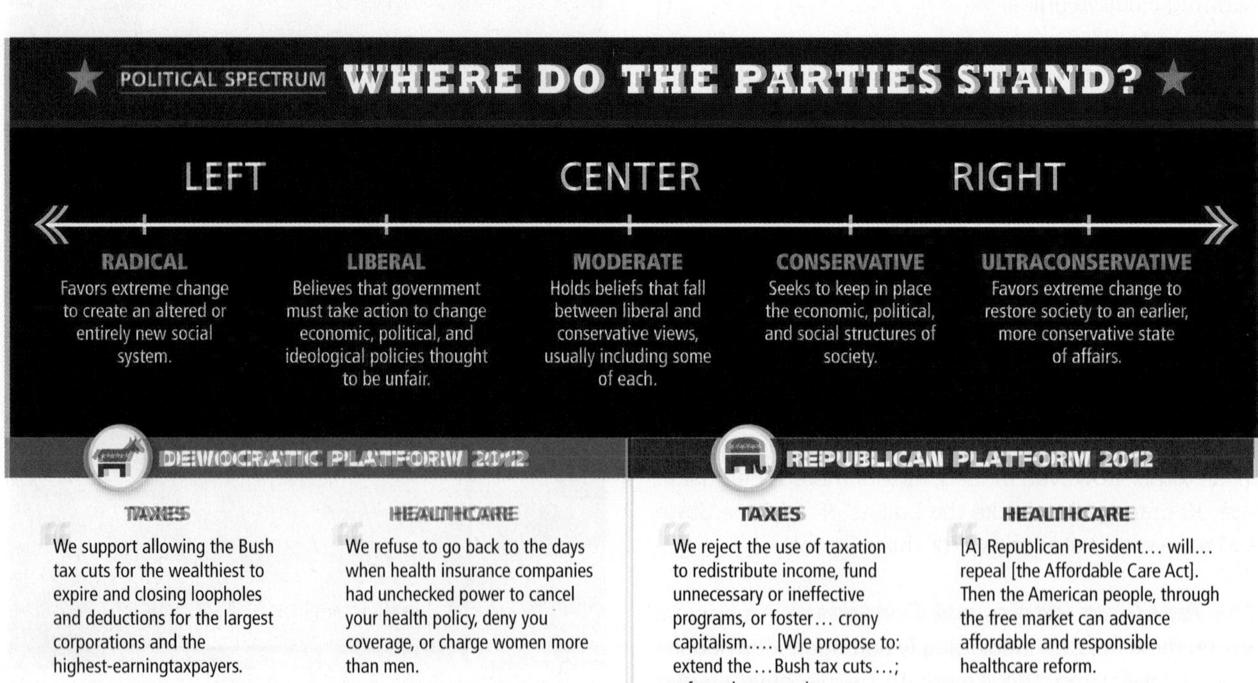

POLITICAL SPECTRUM
WHERE DO THE PARTIES STAND?
LEFT
CENTER
RIGHT
RADICAL
Favors extreme change to create an altered or entirely new social system.
LIBERAL
Believes that government must take action to change economic, political, and ideological policies thought to be unfair.
MODERATE
Holds beliefs that fall between liberal and conservative views, usually including some of each.
CONSERVATIVE
Seeks to keep in place the economic, political, and social structures of society.
ULTRACONSERVATIVE
Favors extreme change to restore society to an earlier, more conservative state of affairs.
DEMOCRATIC PLATFORM 2012
TAXES
We support allowing the Bush tax cuts for the wealthiest to expire and closing loopholes and deductions for the largest corporations and the highest-earningtaxpayers.
HEALTHCARE
We refuse to go back to the days when health insurance companies had unchecked power to cancel your health policy, deny you coverage, or charge women more than men.
REPUBLICAN PLATFORM 2012
TAXES
We reject the use of taxation to redistribute income, fund unnecessary or ineffective programs, or foster… crony capitalism…. [W]e propose to: extend the…Bush tax cuts…; reform the tax code…
HEALTHCARE
[A] Republican President… will… repeal [the Affordable Care Act]. Then the American people, through the free market can advance affordable and responsible healthcare reform.

>> The Democratic and Republican parties had different platforms for taxes and healthcare in the 2012 election. **Analyze Charts** How do the party platforms reflect the political spectrum?

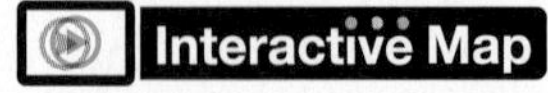

Multiparty Versus Two-Party Systems

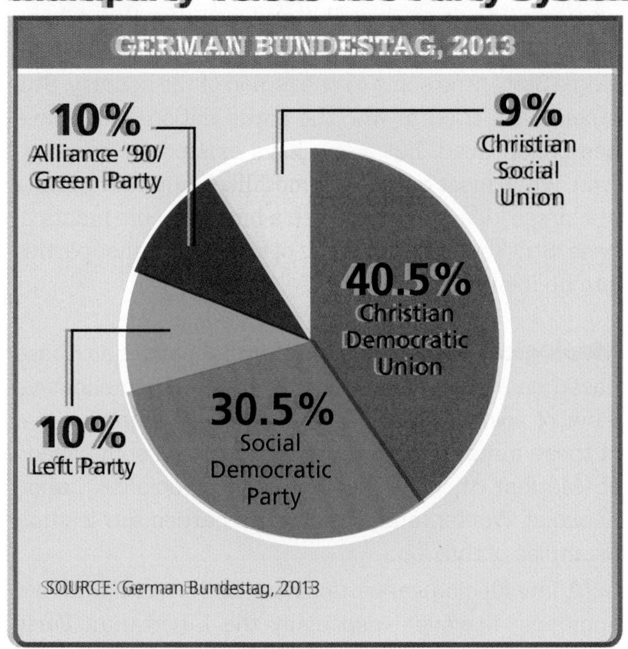

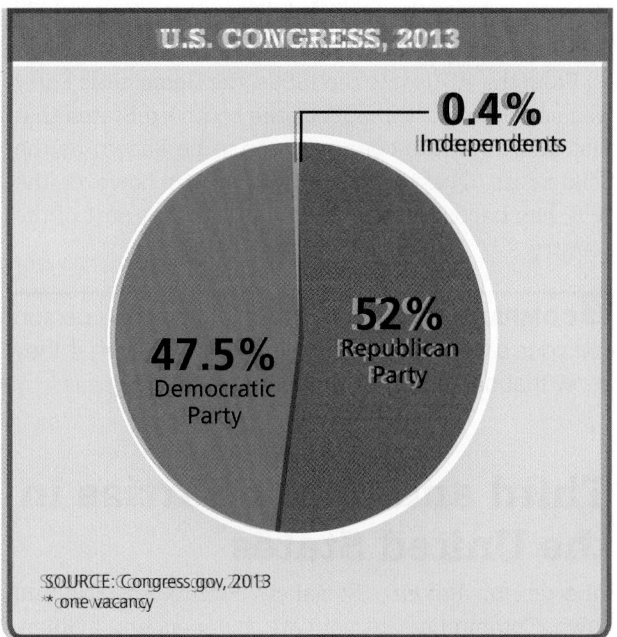

>> In Germany's multiparty system, power is shared by several parties. In America, two parties have a monopoly on power. **Analyze Charts** How are majorities built in the German Bundestag?

Multiparty and One-Party Politics

Some critics argue that the American two-party system should be scrapped. They would replace it with a multiparty arrangement, a system in which several major and many lesser parties exist, seriously compete for, and actually win public offices. Multiparty systems have long been a feature of most European democracies, and they are now found in many other democratic societies elsewhere in the world.

In the typical multiparty system, the various parties are each based on a particular interest, for example on economic class, religious belief, sectional attachment, or political ideology. Those who favor such an arrangement for this country say that it would provide for a broader representation of the electorate and be more responsive to the will of the people. They claim that a multiparty system would give voters a much more meaningful choice among candidates and policy alternatives than the present two-party system does.

Multiparty Politics Strengths and Weaknesses Multiparty systems do tend to produce a broader, more diverse representation of the electorate. That strength, however, is also a major weakness of a multiparty system. It often leads to instability in government. One party is often unable to win the support of a majority of the voters. As a result, the power to govern must be shared by a number of parties in a **coalition**. A coalition is a temporary alliance of several groups who come together to form a working majority and so to control a government. Several of the multiparty nations of Western Europe have experienced frequent changes in party control as coalitions shift and dissolve.

Historically, the American people have shunned a multiparty approach to politics. They have refused to give substantial support to any but the two major parties and their candidates. Two of the factors mentioned here—single-member districts and the American ideological consensus—seem to make the multiparty approach impossible in the United States.

One-Party Politics In the typical dictatorship, only one political party, the party of the ruling clique, is allowed to exist. For all practical purposes, the resulting one-party system really amounts to a "no-party" system.

Many Americans are quite familiar with one-party systems of a quite different sort. What are often called "modified one-party systems" are found in roughly a fourth of the States today. That is, in those States one of the two major parties—either the Republicans or the Democrats—consistently wins most of the elections held there. Although in the remaining States there is more or less vigorous two-party competition at the

Statewide level, there are also many locales in most of them where the political landscape is regularly dominated by a single party.

From the 1870s into the 1960s, the Democratic Party was so dominant throughout the southern States that that quarter of the country came to be known as the Solid South. Over the past 40 years or so, however, the GOP has become the leading party in that part of the country.

COMPARE POINTS OF VIEW Why might a person consider a vote for a minority candidate, even if they know that candidate is not likely to win?

Third and Minor Parties in the United States

Libertarian, Reform, Socialist, Prohibition, Natural Law, Communist, American Independent, Green, Constitution—these are only some of the many parties that have fielded presidential candidates in recent years and continue to do so. You know that none of these parties or their candidates has any real chance of winning the presidency. But this is not to say that third and minor parties are unimportant. The bright light created by the two major parties too often blinds us to the vital role several minor parties have played in American politics.

Their number and variety make third and minor parties difficult to describe and classify. Some have limited their efforts to a particular locale, others to a single State, and some to one region of the country. Still others have tried to woo the entire nation. Most have been short-lived, but a few have existed for decades. And, while most have lived, mothlike, around the flame of a single idea, some have had a broader, more practical base. Still, four distinct types of third and minor parties can be identified.

Ideological Parties The **ideological** parties are those based on a particular set of beliefs—a comprehensive view of social, economic, and political matters. Most of these minor parties have been built on some shade of Marxist thought; the Socialist, Socialist Labor, Socialist Worker, and Communist parties are leading examples of that fact.

A few ideological parties have had a quite different approach, however—especially the Libertarian Party of today, which emphasizes individualism and calls for doing away with most of government's present functions and programs. The ideological parties have seldom been able to win many votes. As a rule, however, they have been long-lived.

Single-Issue Parties The **single-issue parties** focus on a single public question. Their names have usually indicated their primary concern. Thus, the Free

Minor Parties in the 2012 Presidential Election*

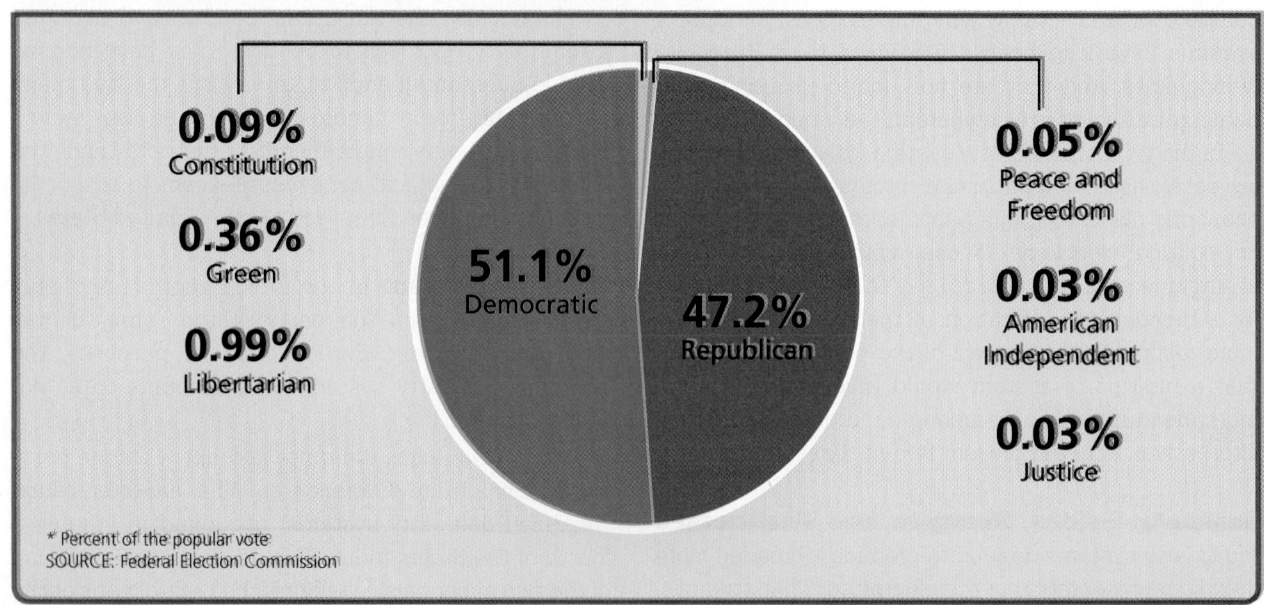

>> The pie chart shows the percentage of the popular vote each party garnered in the 2012 presidential election. **Analyze Charts** Did the minor parties affect the election results? Explain.

Soil Party opposed the spread of slavery in the 1840s and 1850s; the American Party, also called the "Know Nothings," opposed Irish-Catholic immigration in the 1850s; and the Right to Life Party opposes abortion today.

Most of the single-issue parties have faded into history. They died away as events have passed them by, as their themes have failed to attract voters, or as one or both of the major parties have taken their key issues as their own.

>> Libertarian Party presidential candidate Gary Johnson serves up lunch for supporters in 2012. Johnson went on to get more votes that year than all the other minor party candidates combined.

Economic Protest Parties The **economic protest parties** have been rooted in periods of economic discontent. Unlike the socialist parties, these groups have not had any clear-cut ideological base. Rather, they have proclaimed their disgust with the major parties and demanded better times, and have focused their anger on such real or imagined enemies as the monetary system, "Wall Street bankers," the railroads, or foreign imports.

Often, they have been sectional parties, drawing their strength from the agricultural South and West. The Greenback Party tried to take advantage of agrarian discontent from 1876 through 1884. It appealed to struggling farmers by calling for the free coinage of silver, federal regulation of the railroads, an income tax, and labor legislation. A descendant of the Greenbacks, the Populist Party of the 1890s also demanded public ownership of railroads, telephone and telegraph companies, lower tariffs, and the adoption of the initiative and referendum.

Each of these economic protest parties has disappeared as the nation has climbed out of the difficult economic period in which that party arose.

>> The Free Soil Party, whose 1848 presidential candidate was Martin Van Buren, was a single-issue party that campaigned against the spread of slavery into the western States and territories.

Splinter Parties Those that have split away from one of the major parties are known as **splinter parties**. Most of the more important third and minor parties in our politics have been splinter parties. Among the leading groups that have split away from the Republicans are **Theodore Roosevelt's** "Bull Moose" Progressive Party of 1912 and Robert La Follette's Progressive Party of 1924. From the Democrats have come Henry Wallace's Progressive Party and the States' Rights (Dixiecrat) Party, both of 1948, and George Wallace's American Independent Party of 1968.

Most splinter parties have formed around a strong personality—most often someone who has failed to win his or her major party's presidential nomination. These parties have faded or collapsed when that leader has stepped aside.

Thus, the Bull Moose Progressive Party passed away when Theodore Roosevelt returned to the Republican fold after the election of 1912. Similarly, the

American Independent Party lost nearly all of its brief strength when Governor George Wallace rejoined the Democrats after his strong showing in the presidential race in 1968.

The Green Party Like many third and minor parties in American politics, the Green Party, founded in 1996, is difficult to classify. The Green Party began as a classic single-issue party but, as the party has evolved, it simply will not fit into any of the categories set out here. The Green Party came to prominence in 2000, with Ralph Nader as its presidential nominee. His campaign was built around a smorgasbord of issues—environmental protection, of course, but also universal healthcare, campaign finance reform, restraints on corporate power, and much more.

The Greens refused to nominate Ralph Nader in either 2004 or 2008. In 2004, they instead chose attorney and political activist David Cobb—who built his presidential campaign around most of the positions the Greens had supported in 2000.

In 2008, the Green Party nominated Cynthia McKinney, a former Democratic congresswoman from Georgia. Among the positions supported by McKinney were an end to the war in Iraq, universal healthcare, and repeal of the Patriot Act.

Why Third and Minor Parties Are Important Even though most Americans do not support them, third and minor parties have still had a considerable impact on American politics and on the major parties. For example, it was a minor party, the Anti-Masons, that first used a national convention to nominate a presidential candidate in 1831. The National Republicans and then the Democrats followed suit in 1832. Ever since, national conventions have been used by both the Democrats and the Republicans to pick their presidential tickets.

Third and minor parties can have a telling effect in other ways. Thus, a strong third-party candidacy can play a decisive role—often a "spoiler role"—in an election. In a presidential contest, even if a minor party ticket fails to win any electoral votes, it can still pull enough support away from one of the major parties to affect the outcome of the election. Many analysts think that Ralph Nader and the Green Party did exactly that to Al Gore and the Democratic Party in 2000. The spoiler effect can occur in any national, State, or local election.

In 1912, a split in the Republican Party resulted in Theodore Roosevelt's third-party candidacy. Almost certainly, if Roosevelt had not quit the Republican Party, William Howard Taft would have fared much better, and Woodrow Wilson would not have become President.

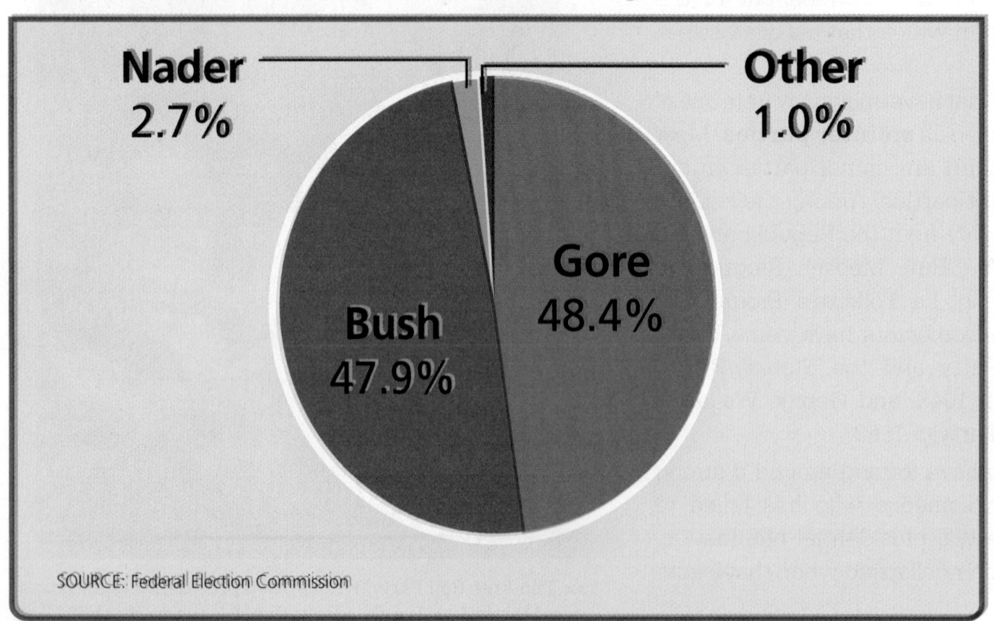

>> Third-party votes in the 2000 presidential election may have affected the outcome. **Analyze Charts** If all third party votes had gone to Al Gore, how would these percentages been different?

Strong Minor Party Efforts*

YEAR	PARTY	% POPULAR VOTE	ELECTORAL VOTES
1920	Socialist	3.45	---
1924	Progressive	16.61	13
1932	Socialist	2.22	---
1948	States' Rights (Dixiecrat)	2.41	39
	Progressive	2.37	---
1968	American Independent	13.53	46
1996	Reform	8.40	---
2000	Green	2.74	---

* Includes all minor parties that polled at least 2% of the popular vote.

SOURCE: U.S. Census Bureau; *Historical Statistics of the United States, Colonial Times to 1970*

>> Minor parties have sometimes had a significant impact on presidential elections. **Analyze Charts** Using the data in the chart, which of these minor parties may have changed election results?

The Innovator Role Played by Minor Parties Historically, however, minor parties have been most important in their roles of critic and innovator. Unlike the major parties, they have been ready, willing, and able to take quite clear-cut stands on controversial issues.

Many of the more important issues of American politics were first brought to the public's attention by a minor party—among them, the progressive income tax, women's suffrage, and railroad and banking regulation. Oddly enough, this very important innovator role of the minor parties has also been a major source of their frustration. When their proposals have gained any real degree of popular support, one and sometimes both of the major parties have taken over those ideas. The late Norman Thomas, who was six times the Socialist Party's candidate for President, often complained that "the major parties are stealing from my platform."

Altogether, 27 minor-party and independent presidential candidates, some of them nominated by more than one party, appeared on the ballots of at least one State in 2012. The most visible minor-party presidential campaigns in the most recent election were those of the Libertarian, Green, Constitution, Justice, Peace and Freedom, and American Independent parties. More than a thousand minor-party and independent candidates also sought seats in Congress and ran for various State and local offices around the country.

? DETERMINE POINT OF VIEW Why do you think a leader or a group might seek to create a minor party even though their chances of winning are less than those of a major party?

The Decentralized Nature of the Parties

How strong, how active, and how well organized are the Republican and Democratic parties in your community? Contact the county chairperson or another official in one or both of the major parties. They are usually not very difficult to find. For starters, try the telephone directory or the Internet.

The two major parties are often described as though they were highly organized, close-knit, well-disciplined groups. However, neither party is anything of the kind. They are, instead, highly decentralized, fragmented, and often plagued by factions and internal squabbling.

Neither party has a chain of command running from the national through the State to the local level. Each of the State party organizations is only loosely tied to the party's national structure. By the same token, local party organizations are often quite independent of their parent State organizations. These various party units usually cooperate with one another, of course—but that is not always the case.

The Role of the Presidency The President's party is almost always more solidly united and better organized than the other major party. The President is automatically the party's leader, and asserts that leadership with such tools as ready access to the media, personal popularity, the power to make appointments to federal office, and the ability to dispense other favors.

The other party has no one in an even faintly comparable position. Indeed, in the American party system, there is seldom any one person who can truly be called the leader of the party out of power. Rather, a number of personalities, frequently in competition with one another, form a loosely identifiable leadership group in that party.

The Impact of Federalism Federalism is a major reason for the decentralized nature of the two major political parties. Remember, the basic goal of the major parties is to gain control of government by winning elective offices.

Today there are more than *half a million* elective offices in the United States. We elect more people to public office in this country than do the voters of any other country on the planet. In the American federal system, those offices are widely distributed over the national, State, and local levels. In short, because the governmental system is highly decentralized, so too are the major parties that serve it.

The Nominating Process The nominating process is also a major cause of party decentralization. Recall that the nominating process has a central role in the life of political parties. Consider two related aspects of the process of candidate selection.

First, candidate selection is an intraparty process. That is, nominations are made *within* the party. Second, the nominating process can be, and often is, a divisive one. Where there is a fight over a nomination, that contest pits members of the same party against one another: Republicans fight Republicans; Democrats battle Democrats. In short, the prime function of the major parties—the making of nominations—is also a prime cause of their highly fragmented character.

EXPRESS PROBLEMS CLEARLY Why do you think the process of nominating candidates from within the party creates more conflict within parties than the other forms of the nominating process?

>> Valarie Wilson was elected president of the Georgia School Boards Association in 2012. She was one of the many local officials elected in this country.

National Party Functions

At the national level, both major parties are composed of five basic elements. They are structured around a national convention, a national committee, a national chairperson, and two congressional campaign committees.

The National Convention The national convention, often described as the party's national voice, meets in the late summer of every presidential election year to pick the party's presidential and vice-presidential candidates. It also performs a few other functions, including the adoption of the party's rules and the writing of its platform.

Beyond that, however, the convention has little authority. It has no control over the party's selection of candidates for any other offices nor over the policy stands those nominees take. Often, a national convention does play a role in making peace among various factions in the party, helping them to accept a party platform that will appeal to a wide range of voters in the general election.

The National Committee Between conventions, the party's affairs are handled, at least in theory, by the national committee and by the national chairperson. For years, each party's national committee was composed of a committeeman and a committeewoman from each State and several of the territories. They were chosen by the State's party organization. Over the past several years, however, both parties have expanded the committee's membership.

Make Up of the RNC and DNC Today, the Republican National Committee (RNC) also seats the party chairperson from each State and members from the District of Columbia, Guam, American Samoa, Puerto Rico, and the Virgin Islands. Representatives of such GOP-related groups as the National Federation of Republican Women also serve on the RNC.

The Democratic National Committee (DNC) is an even larger body. In addition to the committeeman and -woman from each State, it now includes the party's chairperson and vice-chairperson from every State and the territories. Moreover, its ranks now include a few dozen members from the party organizations of the larger States, and up to 75 at-large members chosen by the DNC itself. Several members of Congress, as well as governors, mayors, and members of the Young Democrats, also have seats on the DNC.

On paper, the national committee appears to be a powerful organization loaded with many of the party's leading figures. In fact, it does not have a great deal of clout. Most of its work centers on the staging of the party's national convention every four years.

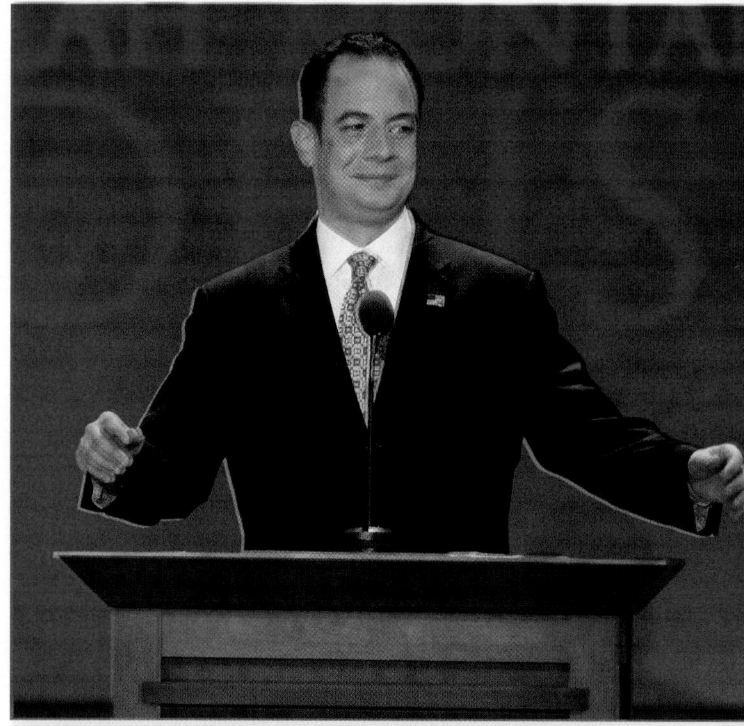

>> Reince Priebus opened the 2012 Republican National Convention in his second term as chairperson of the RNC. Only seven people have served four years or more as Republican Party chairperson.

The National Chairperson In each party, the national chairperson is the leader of the national committee. He or she is chosen to a four-year term by the national committee, at a meeting held right after the national convention. The choice is made by the just-nominated presidential candidate and is then ratified by the national committee.

Only three women have ever held that top party post. Jean Westwood of Utah chaired the DNC from her party's 1972 convention until late 1972; Mary Louise Smith of Iowa headed the RNC from 1974 until early 1977; and Debbie Wasserman Schultz of Florida, chosen in 2011, currently leads the DNC. To this point, only two African Americans have served as major party chairmen: Ron Brown (DNC, 1989–1993) and Michael Steele (RNC, 2009–2011).

>> Florida Congresswoman Debbie Wasserman Schultz served as the Democratic Party's national chairperson during the 2012 elections.

Duties of the National Committee The national chairperson directs the work of the party's headquarters and its professional staff in Washington. In presidential election years, the committee's attention is focused on the national convention and then the campaign.

In between presidential elections, the chairperson and the committee work to strengthen the party and its fortunes. They do so by promoting party unity, raising money, recruiting new voters, and otherwise preparing for the next presidential season. Of course, it is only with the help nationally of many citizen volunteers that they are able to complete all of these tasks. Both parties have lately established state-of-the-art technical facilities to help their candidates and officeholders better communicate with voters. Those sophisticated facilities include such things as television studios, satellite uplinks, constantly updated Web sites, and computerized voter registration lists.

Congressional Campaign Committees Each party also has a campaign committee in each house of Congress. These committees work to reelect incumbents and to make sure that "open seats," seats given up by retiring members, remain in the party. The committees also take a hand in carefully selected campaigns to unseat incumbents in the other party, in those races where the chances for success seem to justify those efforts.

In both parties and in both houses, the members of these congressional campaign committees are chosen by their colleagues. They serve for two-year terms—that is, for a term of Congress.

SUMMARIZE Describe the role of the congressional campaign committees for each party.

State and Local Party Functions

National party organization is largely the product of custom and of rules adopted by the party's national conventions over time. At the State and local levels, on the other hand, party structure is largely determined by State law.

State Organization In most States, party structure is decentralized, much as it is at the national level. It is usually built around a State central committee, headed by a State chairperson. The chairperson, chosen by the committee, may be an important political figure in his or her own right. More often than not, however, he or she fronts for the governor, a U.S. senator, or some other powerful figure or group in the politics of the State.

The party's State central committee is almost everywhere composed of members who represent major geographic subdivisions, usually counties. They are chosen in primary elections, by local caucuses, or at State conventions. Because most of these committees meet only infrequently, the chairperson has great independence in conducting the party's affairs.

Together, the chairperson and the central committee work to further the party's interests in the State. Most of the time, they attempt to do this by

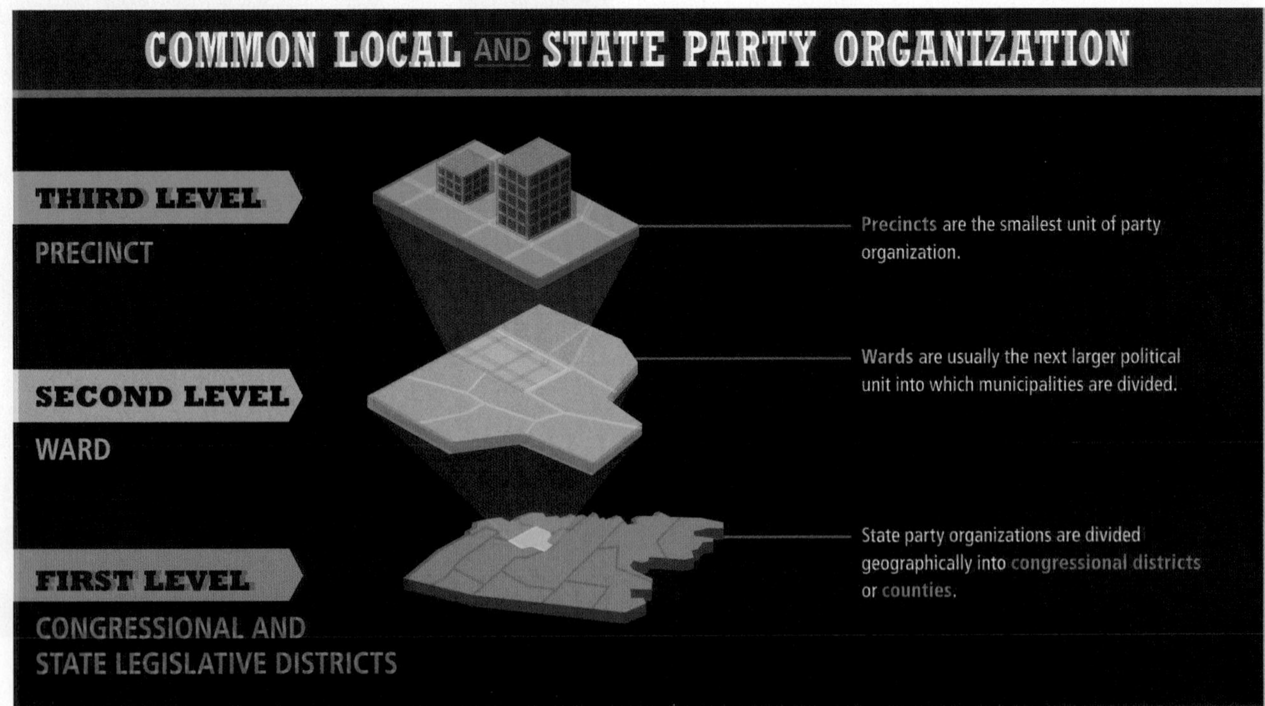
COMMON LOCAL AND STATE PARTY ORGANIZATION
THIRD LEVEL
PRECINCT
Precincts are the smallest unit of party organization.
SECOND LEVEL
WARD
Wards are usually the next larger political unit into which municipalities are divided.
FIRST LEVEL
CONGRESSIONAL AND STATE LEGISLATIVE DISTRICTS
State party organizations are divided geographically into congressional districts or counties.

>> Local party organization can vary from State to State, but this chart shows a common example. **Analyze Charts** What is the difference between a ward and a precinct?

building an effective organization and promoting party unity, finding candidates and campaign funds, and so on. Again, much of this work is done by volunteers from the State. Remember, however, both major parties are highly decentralized, fragmented, and sometimes torn by struggles for power. This can really complicate the chairperson's and the committee's job.

Local Organization Local party structures vary so widely that they nearly defy even a brief description. Generally, they follow the electoral map of the State, with a party unit for each district in which elective offices are to be filled: congressional and legislative districts, counties, cities and towns, wards, and precincts. A **ward** is a unit into which cities are often divided for the election of city council members. A **precinct** is the smallest unit of election administration; the voters in each precinct cast their ballots at one polling place located within the precinct.

In most larger cities, a party's organization is further broken down by residential blocks and sometimes even by apartment buildings. In some places, local party organizations are active year-round, but most often they are inactive except for those few hectic months before an election. It is especially at those times when the local party organization makes use of local citizen volunteers to help them accomplish all that needs to be done.

>> Bruce Clark, the Precinct 2 chairperson for Jackson County, Iowa, counts participants at the start of a Democratic caucus in 2012.

CHECK UNDERSTANDING Explain the differences between party organization at the national level compared to the State and local level.

ASSESSMENT

1. **Infer** How is the ideological consensus of the American electorate reflected in the membership of the major parties?
2. **Express Problems Clearly** Explain the meaning of this statement: "A minor party is likely to be a victim of its own success."
3. **Categorize** Describe the place of the President in national party organization.
4. **Identify Cause and Effect** Why is party unity harder to achieve for the party out of power than it is for the party in power?
5. **Draw Conclusions** Explain the roles played by the Federalists, led by Alexander Hamilton, and the Anti-Federalists, led by Thomas Jefferson, in the formation of the two-party system in America.

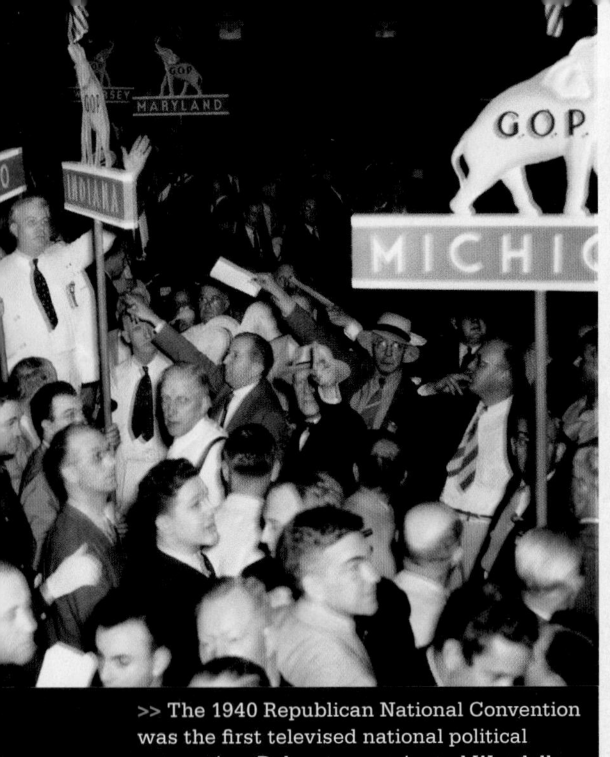

>> The 1940 Republican National Convention was the first televised national political convention. Delegates nominated Wendell Willkie for President and Charles McNary for Vice President.

11.2 Suppose your teacher stood in front of the class and said: "Here's a $100 bill. Who'd like to have it?" You, and everyone else in the room, would promptly say, or at least think: "Me!" Suppose the teacher then said: "Okay, we'll hold an election. The person who wins the most votes gets the money."

Interactive Flipped Video

>> Objectives

Explain why the nominating process is a critical first step in the process for filling public offices.

Describe self-announcement, the caucus, and the convention as nominating methods.

Discuss the direct primary as the principle nominating method used in the United States today, and understand why some candidates use the petition as a nominating device.

>> Key Terms

nomination
general elections
direct primary
closed primary
open primary
blanket primary
runoff primary
nonpartisan elections
Ross Perot
Andrew Jackson
caucus
platform

Nominations

Nominations: A Critical First Step

What would happen? If the election were held immediately, it is likely that each member of the class would vote for himself or herself. A few might vote for a friend. Almost certainly, however, the election would end in a tie. No one would win the money.

But suppose the teacher said: "We'll hold the election tomorrow." What do you suppose would happen then? As you think about the answer to that question, you begin to get a sense of the practical importance of the nominating process—the first step in the process of electing or appointing candidates for filling public office.

The nominating process is the process of candidate selection. **Nomination**—the naming of those who will seek office—is a critically important step in the election and appointment process at the national, State, and local levels.

Impact of the Nominating Process You have already seen two major illustrations of the significance of the nominating process. You have read about the making of nominations (1) as a prime function of political parties in American politics, and (2) as a leading reason for the decentralized character of the two major parties in the United States.

The nominating process for filling offices also has a very real impact on the right to vote. In the typical election in this country, voters can choose between only two candidates for each office on the ballot. They can vote for the Republican or they can vote for the Democratic candidate. Other choices are sometimes listed, but they are not often meaningful alternatives. Most voters conclude that candidates who are not members of one of the two major parties are not likely to win, so they opt not to vote for them. This is another way of saying that we have a two-party system in the United States. It is also another way to say that the nominating stage is a critically important step in the electoral process. Those who make nominations place real, very practical limits on the choices that voters can make in the general election. For filling appointed offices there may be more limited choice on nominees.

>> Lifelong Democrat Michael Bloomberg switched parties in a delayed primary in 2001 to become the Republican mayoral nominee.

Methods of Nomination In one-party constituencies (those areas where one party regularly wins elections), the nominating process is usually the only point at which there is any real contest for public office. Once the dominant party has made its nomination, the general election is little more than a formality.

Dictatorial regimes point up the importance of the nominating process. Many of them hold **general elections**—regularly scheduled elections at which voters make the final selection of officeholders—much as democracies do. But, typically, the ballots used in those elections list only one candidate for each office—the candidate of the ruling clique; and those candidates regularly win with majorities approaching 100 percent. In a dictatorial regime, appointed offices may be filled by the leader by naming someone to the office.

Nominations to fill elective office are made in five different ways in this country. Candidates are named to the ballot by (1) self-announcement, (2) caucus, (3) convention, (4) direct primary, and (5) petition.

>> Many dictatorships hold general elections, but there is often only one candidate on the ballot, such as when Saddam Hussein of Iraq was unanimously reelected in 2002.

Self-Announcement Self-announcement is the oldest form of the nominating process in American politics. First used in colonial times, it is still often found at the small-town and rural levels in many parts of the country.

The method is quite simple. A person who wants to run for office or who wishes to be appointed to an office simply announces that fact. Modesty or local custom may dictate that someone else actually makes the candidate's announcement, but, still, the process amounts to the same thing.

Historical Examples Self-announcement is sometimes used by someone who failed to win a regular party nomination or by someone unhappy with the party's choice. Note that whenever a write-in

"This day learned that the Caucus Club meets, at certain times, in the garret of Tom Dawes, the Adjutant of the Boston Regiment. He has a large house, and he has a moveable partition in his garret which he takes down, and the whole club meets in one room. There they smoke tobacco till you cannot see from one end of the garret to the other. There they drink flip, I suppose, and they choose a moderator, who puts questions to the vote regularly; and selectmen, assessors, collectors, wardens, fire-wards, and representatives, are regularly chosen before they are chosen in the town.

—Charles Francis Adams (ed.) *The Works of John Adams* (1856)

>> In 1763, John Adams expressed his disapproval for Boston's Caucus Club, where influential community members met privately to decide who they would support in upcoming elections.

candidate appears in an election, the self-announcement process has been used.

In recent history, four prominent presidential contenders have made use of the process: George Wallace, who declared himself to be the American Independent Party's nominee in 1968; and independent candidates Eugene McCarthy in 1976; John Anderson in 1980; and **Ross Perot** in 1992. And all of the 135 candidates who sought to replace Governor Gray Davis of California in that State's recall election in 2003—including the winner, Arnold Schwarzenegger—were self-starters.

? HYPOTHESIZE What impact does the nominating process have on the right to vote?

The Caucus

As a nominating device, a **caucus** is a group of like-minded people who meet to select the candidates they will support in an upcoming election. The first caucus nominations were made during the later colonial period, probably in Boston in the 1720s. John Adams described the caucus this way in 1763:

> This day learned that the Caucus Club meets, at certain times, in the garret of Tom Dawes, the Adjutant of the Boston Regiment. He has a large house, and he has a moveable partition in his garret which he takes down, and the whole club meets in one room. There they smoke tobacco till you cannot see from one end of the garret to the other. There they drink flip, I suppose, and they choose a moderator, who puts questions to the vote regularly; and selectmen, assessors, collectors, wardens, fire-wards, and representatives, are regularly chosen before they are chosen in the town.
>
> —Charles Francis Adams (ed.) *The Works of John Adams* (1856)

The Original Caucus Originally the caucus was a private meeting of a few influential figures in the community. As political parties began to appear in the late 1700s, they took over the device and soon broadened the membership of the caucus considerably.

The coming of independence brought the need to nominate candidates for State offices: governor, lieutenant governor, and others above the local level. The legislative caucus—a meeting of a party's members in the State legislature—took on the job. At the national level, both the Federalists and the Democratic-Republicans in Congress were, by 1800, choosing their presidential and vice presidential candidates through the congressional caucus.

The legislative and congressional caucuses were quite practical in their day. Transportation and communication were difficult at best. Since legislators were already gathered regularly in a central place, it made sense for them to take on the nominating responsibility. The spread of democracy, especially in the newer States on the frontier, spurred opposition to the use of caucuses, however. They were widely condemned for their closed, unrepresentative character.

>> Residents of Harpswell, Maine, vote during a Republican town caucus. Typically, a caucus is a small representative group whose members share a specific, usually political, affiliation.

Criticisms of the Caucus Criticism of the caucus reached its peak in the early 1820s. The supporters of three of the leading contenders for the presidency in 1824—**Andrew Jackson**, Henry Clay, and John Quincy Adams—boycotted the Democratic-Republicans' congressional caucus that year. In fact, Jackson and his supporters made "King Caucus" a leading campaign issue. The other major contender, William H. Crawford of Georgia, became the caucus nominee at a meeting attended by fewer than one third of the Democratic-Republican Party's members in Congress.

Crawford ran a poor third in the electoral college balloting in 1824, and the reign of King Caucus at the national level was ended. With its death in presidential politics, the caucus system soon withered at the State and local levels, as well.

The caucus is still used to make local nominations in some places, especially in New England. There, a caucus is open to all members of a party, and it only faintly resembles the original closed and private process.

GENERATE EXPLANATIONS During the 1800s, why were people opposed to the use of the caucus?

The Convention

As the caucus method collapsed, the convention system took its place. The first national convention to nominate a presidential candidate was held by a minor party, the Anti-Masons, in Baltimore in 1831. The newly formed National Republican (soon to become Whig) Party also held a convention later that same year. The Democrats picked up the practice in 1832. All major-party presidential nominees have been chosen by conventions ever since. By the 1840s, conventions had become the principal means for making nominations at every level in American politics.

On paper, the convention process seems perfectly suited to representative government. A party's members meet in a local caucus to pick candidates for local offices and, at the same time, to select delegates to represent them at a county convention. (The meeting at which delegates to local conventions are chosen are still often called caucuses.)

At the county convention, the delegates nominate candidates for county offices and select delegates to the next rung on the convention ladder, usually the State convention. There, the delegates from the county conventions pick the party's nominees for governor and other Statewide offices. State conventions also send delegates to the party's national convention, where the party selects its presidential and vice-presidential candidates.

Problems with the Convention In theory, the will of the party's rank and file membership is passed up through each of its representative levels. Practice soon pointed up the weaknesses of the theory, however, as party bosses found ways to manipulate the process. By playing with the selection of delegates, usually at the local levels, they soon dominated the entire system.

As a result, the caliber of most conventions declined at all levels, especially during the late 1800s. How low some of them fell can be seen in this description of a Cook County (Chicago), Illinois, convention in 1896:

> Of [723] delegates, those who had been on trial for murder numbered 17; sentenced to the penitentiary for murder or manslaughter and served sentence, 7; served terms in the penitentiary for burglary, 36; served terms in the penitentiary for picking pockets, 2; served terms in the penitentiary for arson, 1; . . . jailbirds identified by detectives, 84; keepers of gambling houses, 7; keepers of houses of ill-fame, 2; convicted of mayhem, 3; ex-prize fighters, 11; poolroom proprietors, 2; saloon keepers, 265; . . . political employees, 148; no occupation, 71; . . .
>
> —R.M. Easley "The Sine qua Non of Caucus Reform" Review of Reviews (Sept. 1897)

Replacing the Convention Many people had hailed the change from caucus to convention as a major change for the better in American politics. The abuses of the new device soon dashed their hopes. By the 1870s, the convention system was itself under attack as a major source of evil in the nation's politics. By the 1910s, the direct primary had replaced the convention in most States as the principal nominating method in American politics.

Conventions still play a major role in the nominating process in some States—notably, Connecticut, Michigan, South Dakota, Utah, and Virginia. And, as you will see, no adequate substitute for the device has yet been found at the presidential level.

COMPARE AND CONTRAST What are some similarities and differences between the caucus and the convention as nominating methods?

>> During the 1876 presidential election, charges of voter fraud were widespread and many arrests were made. **Infer** How might unscrupulous party leaders have manipulated the political system?

The Direct Primary

A **direct primary** is an *intra*party election. It is held within a party to pick that party's candidates for the general election. Wisconsin adopted the first Statewide direct primary law in 1903; several other States soon followed its lead. Every State now makes at least some provision for its use.

In most States, State law requires that the major parties use the primary to choose their candidates for the United States Senate and House of Representatives, for the governorship and all other Statewide offices, and for most local offices as well. In a few States, however, different combinations of convention and primary are used to pick candidates for the top offices.

Using the Direct Primary In Michigan, for example, the major parties choose their candidates for the United States Senate and House, the governorship, and the State legislature in primaries. Nominees for lieutenant governor, secretary of state, and attorney general are picked by conventions. (In most States, minor parties are required to make their nominations by other, more difficult processes, usually in conventions or by petition. This is another of the several ways in which

State election laws often, purposely, make life difficult for minor parties.)

Although the primaries are party-nominating elections, they are closely regulated by law in most States. The State usually sets the dates on which primaries are held, and it regularly conducts them, too. The State, not the parties, provides polling places and election officials, registration lists and ballots, and otherwise polices the process.

Forms of the Direct Primary Caucuses are also found in the presidential selection process. They are used to select national convention delegates in a handful of States.

Two basic forms of the direct primary are in use today: (1) the closed primary and (2) the open primary. The major difference between the two lies in the answer to this question: Who can vote in a party's primary—*only* those qualified voters who are party members, or *any* qualified voter?

The Closed Primary Today, more than half the States provide for the **closed primary**—a nominating election in which only declared party members can vote. The primary is closed to all but those party members. (The Supreme Court has held that a State's closed primary law cannot forbid a party to allow independent voters to participate in its primary if the party itself chooses to allow them to do so.)

In most of the closed primary States, party membership is established by registration. When voters appear at their polling places on primary election day, their names are checked against the poll books and each voter is handed the primary ballot of the party in which he or she is registered. The voter can mark only that party's ballot; he or she can vote only in that party's primary.

In some of the closed primary States, however, a voter can change his or her party registration on election day. In those States, then, the primary is not as completely "closed" as it is elsewhere.

The Open Primary The **open primary**—or crossover primary—is a party's nominating election in which *any* qualified voter can cast a ballot. Although it is the form in which the direct primary first appeared, it is now found in fewer than half the States.

When voters go to the polls in some open primary States, they are handed a ballot of each party holding a primary. Usually, they receive only two ballots, those of the Republican and the Democratic parties.

Then, in the privacy of the voting booth, each voter marks the ballot of the party in whose primary he or she chooses to vote. In other open primary States, a voter must ask for the ballot of the party in whose primary he or she wants to vote. That is, each voter must make a *public* choice of party in order to vote in the primary.

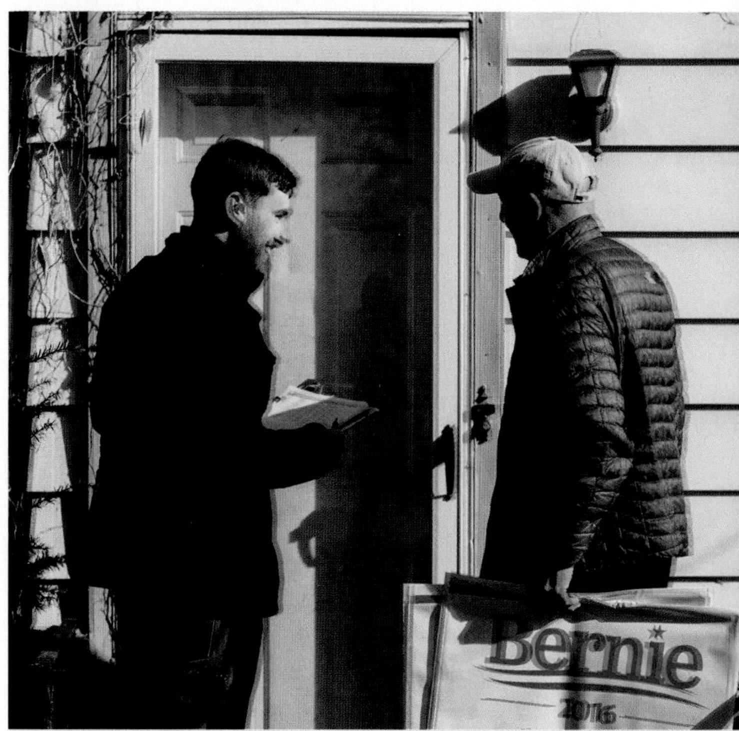

>> Volunteers canvass in support of Democratic presidential candidate Bernie Sanders. Before an election, volunteers interact with voters to win supporters, distribute information, increase candidate name recognition, and raise funds.

The Blanket Primary Through 2000, three States used a different version of the open primary—the **blanket primary**, sometimes called the "wide-open primary." Washington adopted the first blanket primary law in 1935. Alaska followed suit in 1970, and California did so in 1996. In a blanket primary, every voter received the same ballot— a long one that listed *every* candidate, regardless of party, for every nomination to be made at the primary. Voters could participate however they chose. They could confine themselves to one party's primary; or they could switch back and forth between the parties' primaries, voting to nominate a Democrat for one office, a Republican for another, and so on down the ballot.

The Supreme Court found California's version of the blanket primary unconstitutional in 2000, however. In *California Democratic Party* v. *Jones*, the High Court held that that process violated the 1st and 14th amendments' guarantees of the right of association. It ruled that a State cannot force a political party to associate with outsiders—that is, with members of other parties or with independents—when it picks its candidates for public office.

Versions of the Open Primary The Court's decision in *Jones* made the blanket primary a thing of the past. Alaska responded by adopting a more traditional version of the open primary. But California and Washington have gone quite another way.

Those two States now provide for the "top two" form of the open primary. In both States, the names of *all* those who seek nomination are listed, by office, on a single primary ballot. Then the top two vote-getters for each office, regardless of party, face one another in the general election. Thus, two Republicans, or two Democrats, may battle one another in November.

Louisiana uses yet another version of the open primary, under what is sometimes called its "open-election law." There, as in Washington, all candidates for nomination are listed on a single ballot, and the top two vote-getters, regardless of party, face off in the general election. But if a candidate wins a majority of the votes in the primary, he or she is declared the winner of the office involved—so, the primary becomes, in effect, the election. (Louisiana's "open-election" primary law applies to its State and local elections, which are held in November of the *odd*-numbered years. Since 1872, federal law has directed that congressional elections be held in November of the *even*-numbered years, and Louisiana abides by that law. It holds traditional closed primaries in the *even*-numbered years to choose candidates for seats in the United States House and Senate.)

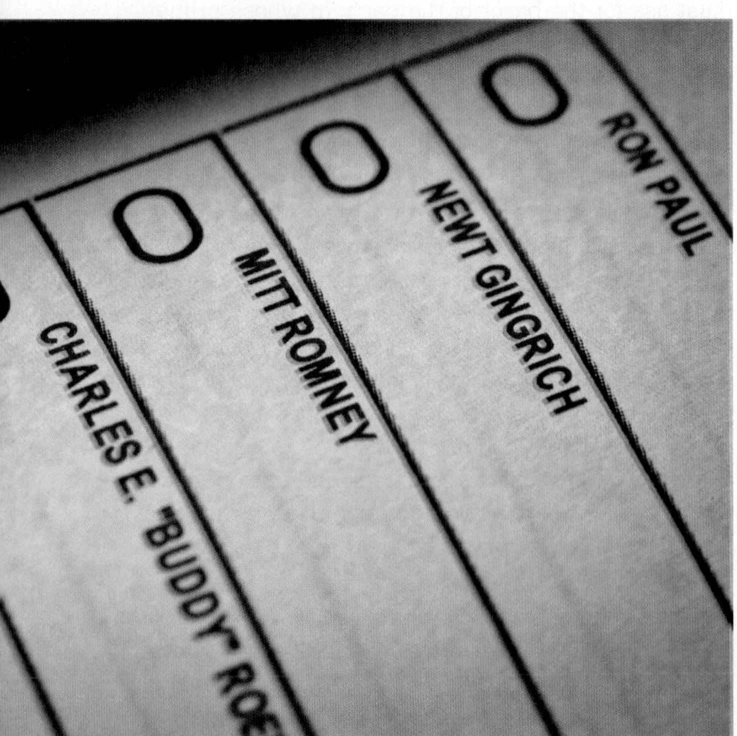

>> A California primary ballot lists the names of all candidates for an office. The top vote-getters from each party run against the other for office.

Interactive Map

Closed vs. Open Primaries The merits of the two basic forms of the direct primary have been argued for decades. Those who support the closed primary rely on three major arguments. They regularly claim that:

1. The closed primary prevents one party from "raiding" the other's primary in the hope of nominating weaker candidates in the opposition party.
2. It helps to make candidates more responsive to the party, its **platform**, and its members.
3. It helps make voters more thoughtful, because they must choose between the parties in order to vote in the primaries.

Those who criticize the closed primary usually contend that:

1. It compromises the secrecy of the ballot, because it forces voters to make their party preferences known in order to participate.
2. It tends to exclude independent voters from the nominating process.

The advocates of the open primary believe that that nominating arrangement addresses both of those objections to the closed primary. They say that in the typical open primary (1) voters are not forced to make their party preferences a matter of public record, and (2) independent voters are not excluded from the nominating process.

The Runoff Primary In most States, candidates need to win only a plurality of the votes cast in the primary to win their party's nomination. (Remember, a *plurality* is the greatest number of votes won by any candidate, whether a *majority* or not.) In eight States, however, an absolute majority is needed to carry a primary: Alabama, Arkansas, Georgia, Mississippi, Oklahoma, South Carolina, Texas—and Louisiana under its unique "open-election law." If no one wins a majority in a race, a **runoff primary** is held a few weeks later. In that runoff contest, the two top vote-getters in the first primary face one another to determine the party's nomination, and the winner of that vote becomes the party's nominee.

The Nonpartisan Primary In most States all or nearly all of the elected school and municipal offices are filled in **nonpartisan elections**. These are elections in which candidates are not identified by party labels.

About half of all State judges are chosen on nonpartisan ballots, as well. The nomination of candidates for these offices takes place on a nonpartisan basis, too, and most often in nonpartisan primaries.

Typically, a contender who wins a clear majority in a nonpartisan primary then runs unopposed in the general election, subject only to write-in opposition. In many States, however, a candidate who wins a majority in the primary is declared elected at that point. If there is no majority winner, the names of the two top contenders are placed on the general election ballot.

The primary first appeared as a partisan nominating device. Many have long argued that it is not well suited for use in nonpartisan elections. Instead, they favor the petition method, as you will see in a moment.

>> Sheila Abdus-Salaam being sworn in as a New York State Court of Appeals judge. In many states, judges are chosen in nonpartisan elections, in which they are not identified by party.

The Presidential Primary The presidential primary developed as an offshoot of the direct primary. It is *not* a nominating device, however. Rather, the presidential primary is an election that is held as one part of the process by which presidential candidates are chosen.

The presidential primary is a very complex process that was in place in a large majority of States in the most recent presidential election. It is one or both of two things, depending on the State involved. It is a process in which a party's voters elect some or all of a State party organization's delegates to that party's national convention; and/or it is a preference election in which voters can choose (vote their preference) among various contenders for the grand prize, the party's presidential nomination.

Much of what happens in presidential politics in the early months of every fourth year centers on this very complicated process.

>> Businessman Donald Trump greets supporters in South Carolina. He campaigned to win the Republican presidential nomination in 2016.

? CONTRAST What is the major difference between the closed and the open primary?

Evaluation of the Primary

The direct primary, whether open or closed, is an *intra*party nominating election. It came to American politics as a reform of the boss-dominated convention system. It was intended to take the nominating function away from the party organization and put it in the hands of the party's rank-and-file membership.

The basic facts about the primary have never been very well understood by most voters, however. So, in closed primary States, many voters resent having to declare their party preference in order to vote in the primary. And, in both open and closed primary States, many are upset because they cannot express their support for candidates in more than one party.

Many are also annoyed by the "bed-sheet ballots" they regularly see in primary elections—not realizing that the use of the direct primary almost automatically means a long ballot. And some are concerned because the primary (and, in particular, its closed form) tends to exclude independents from the nominating process.

Problems with the Primary All of these factors, combined with a lack of appreciation of the important role that primaries play in the election process, result in this unfortunate and significant fact: Nearly everywhere, voter turnout in primary elections is usually less than half what it is in the general elections in November.

Primary contests can be quite costly. The fact that successful contenders must then wage—and finance—a general election campaign adds to the money problems that bedevil American politics. Unfortunately, the financial facts of political life in the United States mean that some well-qualified people refuse to seek public office simply because they cannot muster the funding absolutely necessary to finance a campaign.

Other Problems with the Primary The nominating process, whatever its form, can have a very divisive effect on a party. Remember, the process takes place *within* the party—so, when there is a contest for a nomination, that is where the contest occurs: Republicans fight with Republicans, Democrats do battle with Democrats. A bitter fight in the primaries can so wound and divide a party that it cannot recover in time to present a united front for the general election. Many a primary fight has cost a party an election.

Finally, because many voters are not very well informed, the primary places a premium on name familiarity. That is, it often gives an edge to a contender who has a well-known name or a name that sounds like that of some well-known person. But, notice, name familiarity in and of itself usually has little or nothing to do with a candidate's qualifications for public office.

Obviously, the primary is not without its problems, nor is any other nominating device. Still, the primary does give a party's members the opportunity to participate at the very core of the political process.

? SUMMARIZE What are some of the issues voters have with the open and closed primary as a nominating method?

Petition

One other nominating method is used fairly widely at the local level in American politics today—nomination by petition. Where this process is used, candidates for public office are nominated by means of petitions

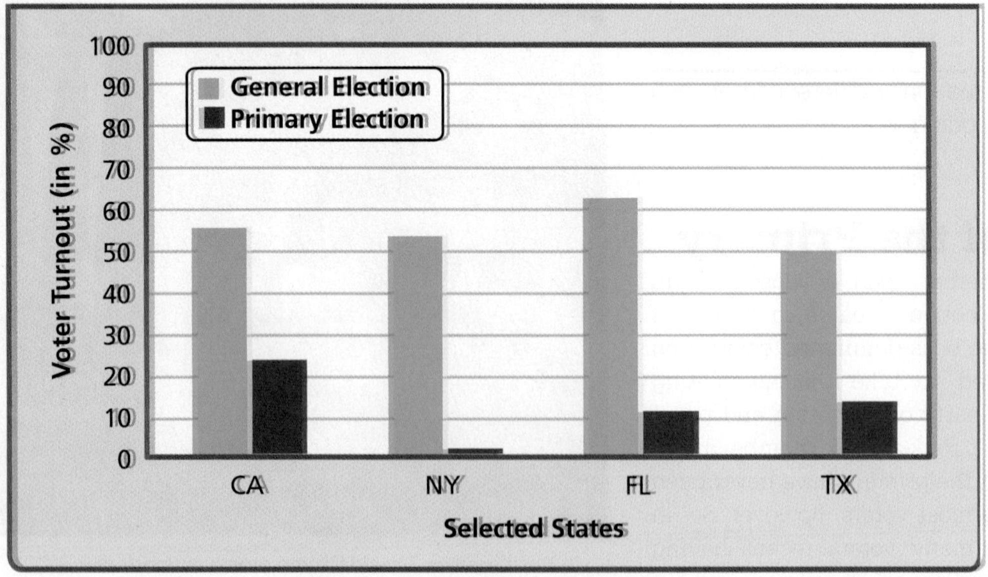

SOURCE: United States Elections Project, George Mason University

>> Voter turnout for primary and general elections for selected States in a presidential election year is compared. **Analyze Graphs** What information can you learn from studying the chart?

signed by a certain number of qualified voters in the election district.

Nomination by petition is found most widely at the local level, chiefly for nonpartisan school posts and municipal offices in medium-sized and smaller communities and, increasingly, for judgeships. It is also the process usually required by State law for nominating minor-party and independent candidates in many of the States. (Remember, the States often purposely make the process of getting on the ballot difficult for those candidates.) The details of the petition process vary widely from State to State, and even from one city or county to the next. Usually, however, the higher the office and/or the larger the constituency represented by the office, the greater the number of signatures needed for nomination by petition.

Filling Appointed Offices Filling appointed offices can be done with similar methods used for filling elective office. A person can be nominated for office by a local, State, or national political entity or person, such as a mayor, a State legislator, or the President. On the national level, many nominations, such as those for cabinet secretaries, ambassadors, and judges, come from the executive branch. Such nominations are subject to approval by vote of the legislative branch. On a State and local level, the process can be very similar for offices such as local advisory committees or State boards of various kinds.

INFER Why is nomination by petition most widely found at the local level of government?

>> Winning nomination by petition can be a time-consuming process. Candidates may even need to go door-to-door to gather support.

Interactive Gallery

ASSESSMENT

1. **Draw Conclusions** Why is the nominating process a critical first step in the process for filling elected or appointed public offices?
2. **Describe** Describe self-announcement as a nominating method and when it is used.
3. **Compare** Compare the caucus and the convention as nominating methods.
4. **Draw Conclusions** Why is the direct primary used as the principle nominating method in the United States today?
5. **Infer** Why do some candidates use the petition as a nominating device?

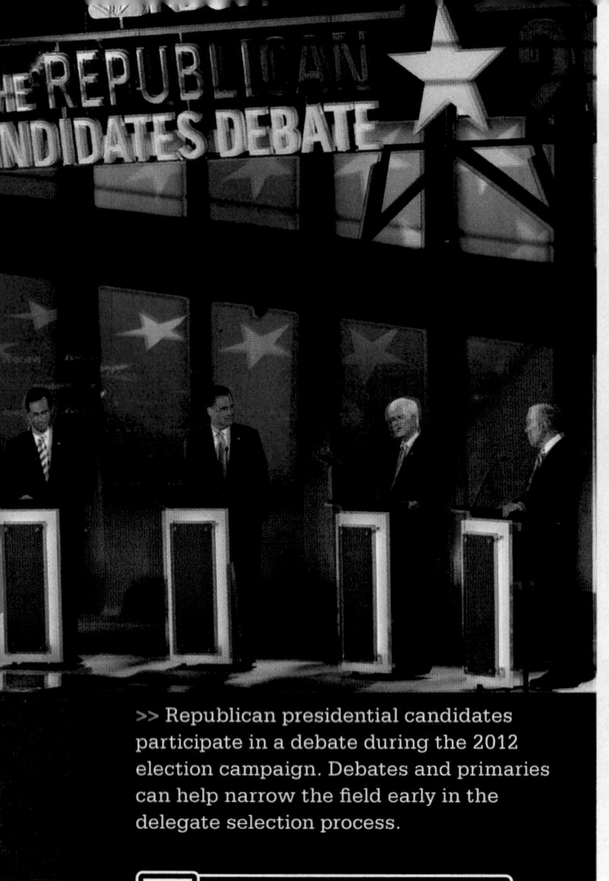

>> Republican presidential candidates participate in a debate during the 2012 election campaign. Debates and primaries can help narrow the field early in the delegate selection process.

Interactive Flipped Video

11.3 **Recall, the congressional caucus was the first method the parties developed to pick their presidential candidates. The closed, unrepresentative character of that arrangement led to its downfall in the mid-1820s. For the election of 1832, both major parties turned to the national convention as their presidential nominating device, and it has continued to serve them ever since.**

>> Objectives

Describe the role of conventions in the presidential nominating process, understand the caucus-convention process, and outline the events that take place during a national convention.

Evaluate the importance of presidential primaries.

Examine the characteristics that determine who is nominated as a presidential candidate.

Describe the features of the presidential campaign.

Analyze how the electoral college provides for the election of the President.

Identify several flaws in the electoral college system and outline the advantages and disadvantages of proposed reforms of the electoral college.

>> Key Terms

presidential primary
winner-take-all
proportional representation
Ronald Reagan
keynote address
swing voters
battleground States
Richard M. Johnson
district plan
proportional plan
national popular vote plan

Electing the President

Presidential Primaries

More than three fourths of all the delegates to both parties' conventions come from States that hold presidential primaries. Many of those primaries are major media events. Serious contenders in both the Democratic and Republican parties must make the best possible showing in at least most of them.

Depending on the State, a **presidential primary** is an election in which a party's voters (1) choose some or all of a State party organization's delegates to their party's national convention, and/or (2) express a preference among various contenders for their party's presidential nomination.

History of the Presidential Primary The presidential primary first appeared in the early 1900s as part of the reform movement aimed at the party boss-dominated convention system. Wisconsin passed the first presidential primary law in 1905, providing for the popular election of national convention delegates. Several States soon followed that lead, and Oregon added the preference feature in 1910. By 1916 half the States had adopted presidential primary laws.

For a time, the primary system fell into disfavor so that by 1968, primaries were found in only 16 States and the District of Columbia. Efforts to reform the national convention process, especially in the Democratic Party, reversed that downward trend in the 1970s, however. Some form of the presidential primary can now be found in most States. For 2012, the system was in place in 38 States, and in the District of Columbia and Puerto Rico, as well.

A System with Many Variables Recall, a presidential primary is either or both of two things: a delegate-selection process and/or a candidate preference election. Once that much has been said, however, the system becomes very hard to describe, except on a State-by-State basis.

The difficulty comes largely from two sources: (1) the fact that in each State the details of the delegate-selection process are set by State law—and those details vary from State to State, and (2) the ongoing reform efforts in the Democratic Party.

Ever since 1968, when the Democratic Party was shattered by disputes over Vietnam and civil rights policies, the Democratic National Committee has written and rewritten the party's rules in an effort to promote greater grass-roots participation. Most States treat the two parties alike in their election laws; so, as States have responded to Democratic Party reforms, the Republicans have had to revise some of their procedures, as well.

Significance of Primary Timing Even a matter that seems as simple as the date for the primary illustrates the crazy-quilt pattern of State laws. Since 1920, New Hampshire has held the first of the presidential primaries. The State guards its first-in-the-nation title with a law that provides that its primary is to be held at least a week before the date any other State picks for its contest.

Most States grew to prefer an early date, so the primary schedule became heavily "front-loaded" over recent years. In 2008, the scramble for an early date meant that 16 States held their primaries on the same day—"Super Tuesday"—and three fourths of the contests had been held by mid-March.

That was not the case in 2012, however. That year, rule changes within the Republican Party, along with other factors, resulted in a long, drawn-out primary election season. Only seven States held primaries on Super Tuesday in 2012, and by mid-March, more than two thirds of the contests had yet to be held.

Name recognition and money have always been important factors in the primary process, and front-loading multiplied their importance. In 2012, however, candidates could hope to build a following over several weeks—similar to the momentum gained by Bill

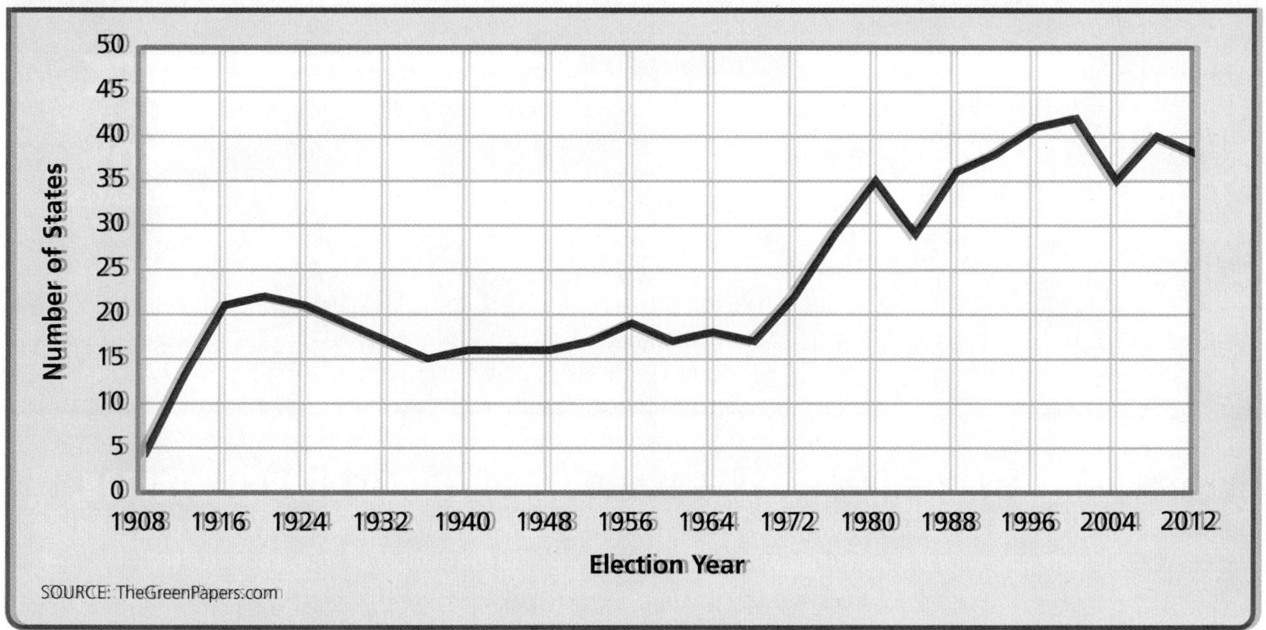

>> The popularity of the primary method of nominating presidential candidates has gone up and down through the years. **Analyze Graphs** When did the popularity of primaries peak?

Clinton in 1992. In addition, voters had more time to learn about the candidates and their stands on the issues. The front-loaded process left little or no time for that strategy. Instead, contenders had to mount (and pay for) campaigns in a number of geographically separated States that held their primaries early and often within a few days of one another.

Shifting Primary Styles For decades, most presidential primaries were both delegate-selection and preference exercises. Several were also **winner-take-all** contests: The candidate who won the preference vote automatically won the support of all of the delegates chosen at that primary.

Winner-take-all primaries have now all but disappeared, however. The Democratic Party's rules actually prohibit them. Instead, the Democrats now have a complex **proportional representation** rule. Any candidate who seeks the party's presidential nomination who wins at least 15 percent of the votes cast in a primary gets the number of that State's Democratic convention delegates that corresponds to his or her share of that primary vote. Take, for example, a State that has 40 convention delegates. If a candidate wins 45 percent of the primary vote, he or she automatically gains the support of at least 18 of the delegates.

Following Republican rule changes in 2012, any State that held its primary before April 1 was prohibited from using a winner-take-all system, with the hope of discouraging the pile-up of early primaries. Still, a few States do permit winner-take-all primaries, and the Republicans continue to hold them in some States—California, for example.

Preference Primary The proportional representation rule had another major impact on the shape of presidential primaries. It led several States to give up the popular selection of delegates. More than half of the presidential primary States now hold only a preference primary. The delegates themselves are actually chosen later, at party conventions. In most of these States, the delegates must be picked in line with the results of the preference primary—for example, for the Republicans in 2012, so many delegates for Mitt Romney, so many for Ron Paul, so many for Michele Bachmann, and so on. In a few States, the preference vote does not govern the choice of the delegates. In those States—Nebraska, for example—the preference primary is often called a "beauty contest."

Most of the preference contests are also "all-candidate" primaries. These are contests in which all generally recognized contenders for a party's

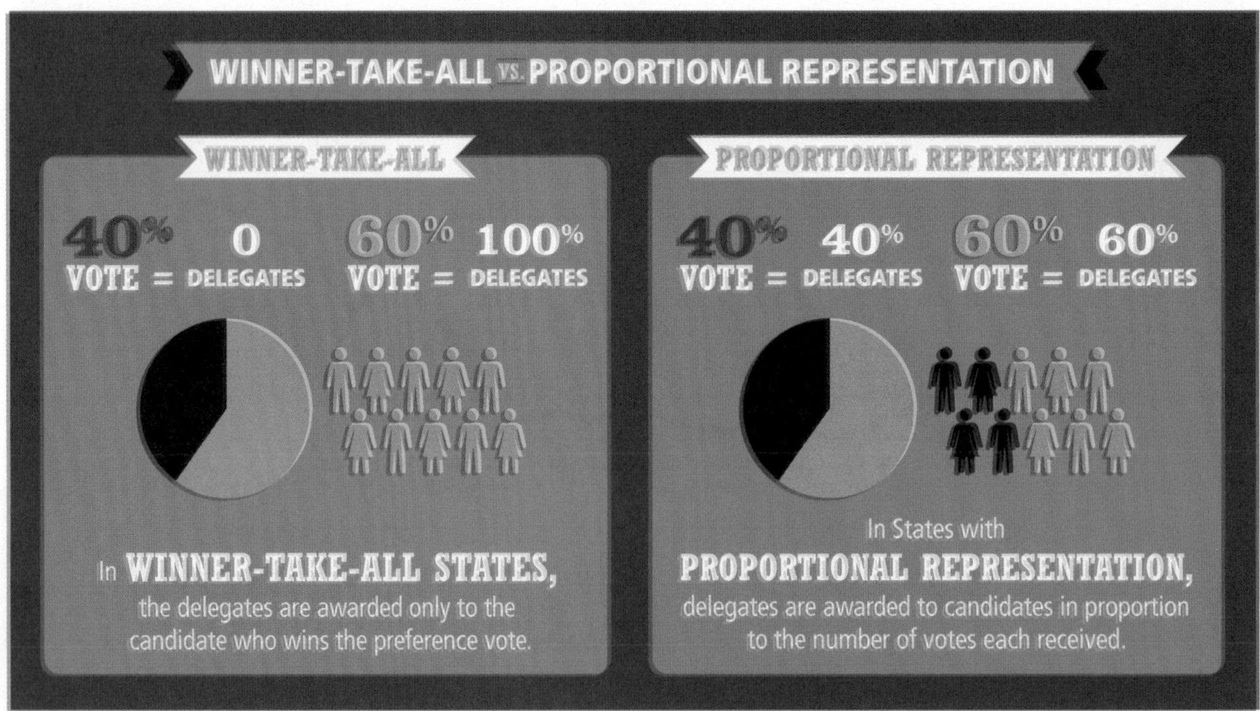

>> Political party rule changes often lead to changes in how primaries are conducted. **Analyze Data** Why do you think candidates who receive less than 15% of the vote are not assigned delegates?

presidential nomination must be listed on that party's preference ballot.

MAKE GENERALIZATIONS Based on what you have learned about the changes that were made in most State primaries by 2012, how do you think presidential candidates would feel about the effect on their candidacies?

>> Voters participate in a lively debate at the start of the 2012 Iowa caucus. At caucuses, party members discuss candidates, debate the party platform, and choose convention delegates.

Evaluation of the Presidential Primary

No one who has surveyed the presidential primary system needs to be told that it is complicated, or that it is filled with confusing variations. Still, these primaries are vital. For half a century now, they have played *the* major part in deciding the presidential nominating contests in both parties—and particularly in the party out of power.

Out of Power vs. In Power Presidential primaries tend to democratize the delegate-selection process. And, importantly, they force would-be nominees to test their candidacies in actual political combat.

For the party out of power, the primaries are often "knock-down, drag-out" affairs. Without the unifying force of the President as party leader, top personalities and factions in the party vie with one another, vigorously, for the presidential nomination. Here, a key function of the presidential primary can be seen: the screening out of the lesser possibilities to the point where only one or a few contenders for the nomination remain in the contest.

Such hard-fought contests do occur, but are not common, in the party in power. This tends to be true either because the President (1) is seeking reelection, or (2) is backing a personal favorite for the nomination. In either case the President regularly prevails.

A sitting President is seldom challenged for renomination, but that situation does sometimes happen. Thus, for example, **Ronald Reagan** made a stiff run at President Gerald Ford in 1976, and Senator Edward Kennedy gave President Carter a real fight in 1980.

Reform Proposals The fact that so many States now hold presidential primaries places large demands on contenders in terms of time, effort, money, scheduling, and, not least, fatigue. The lengthy primary season tests the public's endurance, as well.

Some think that each of the major parties should hold a single, nationwide primary, and have both parties choose their presidential candidates in those contests. National conventions would be done away with—except perhaps to pick their vice-presidential nominees and/or write party platforms.

Most often, however, critics of the present arrangement favor one version or another of a regional primary plan. A series of primaries would be held at two- or three-week intervals across the country.

The prospects for reform are uncertain at best. Major changes would require joint action by Congress, the several States, and both major parties. Neither major party has ever expressed any interest in abandoning its national convention. Both parties see the conventions as a device to promote compromise and, out of it, party unity.

Presidential Caucuses In those States that do not hold presidential primaries, delegates to the national conventions are selected in a system of local caucuses and district and/or State conventions. A caucus is a closed meeting of members of a political party who gather to select delegates to the national convention. The process works basically as it is described here, but the details do differ from State to State.

A party's voters meet in local caucuses, most often at the precinct level. There they often express a preference among the contenders for the party's presidential nomination and select delegates to a local or district convention, where delegates to a State convention are elected. At the State level, and sometimes in the district conventions as well, delegates to the national convention are chosen.

Decline in Popularity The caucus-convention process dates back to the 1840s and is the oldest method for choosing national convention delegates. Its use has declined significantly over the years, however. In 2012, less than a fourth of all delegates to either party's national convention came from States that still use this method of delegate choice.

The Iowa caucuses generally get the most attention, largely because they are now the first delegate-selection event held in every presidential election season. Iowa schedules the start of its caucus process early, and has purposely done so ever since 1972. In 2012, the event took place on January 3, one week before New Hampshire held its first-in-the-nation presidential primary.

HYPOTHESIZE What benefits might Iowa experience from holding the nation's first caucus?

The National Convention

Once all the primaries and caucuses have been held and all of the delegates have been chosen, another event looms large. The two major parties hold their national conventions, the quadrennial meetings at which the delegates select their presidential and vice-presidential candidates.

Convention Arrangements Not only does the Constitution say nothing about presidential nominations, but there is, as well, almost no federal or State statutory law on the matter. The convention process has been built over the years almost entirely by the two major parties.

In both parties, the national committee makes the arrangements for the party's convention. The committee picks the place and also sets the date for that meeting. Several of the nation's larger cities regularly bid for the honor (and the financial boost to local business) of hosting the quadrennial gatherings. For their 2012 conventions, the Democrats picked Charlotte, North Carolina, and the GOP opted for Tampa Bay, Florida.

Apportioning Delegates With the date and the location set, the national committee issues its "call" for the convention. That formal announcement names the time and place. It also tells the party's State organizations how many delegates the States may send to the national gathering.

By tradition, both parties give each State party a certain number of delegates based on that State's

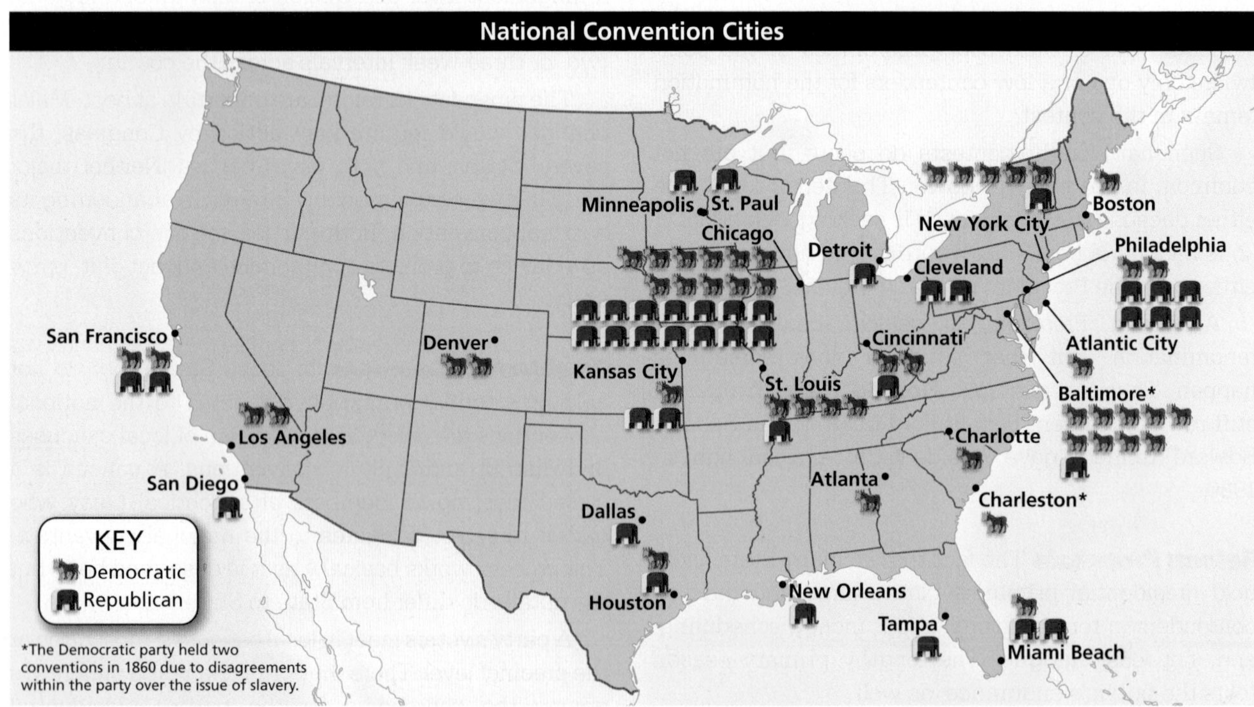

>> Democratic and Republican national conventions have been held in cities across the country. **Analyze Maps** Why might certain cities be chosen for conventions more frequently than others?

electoral vote. Over the past several conventions, both parties have developed complicated formulas that also award bonus delegates to those States that have supported the party's candidates in recent elections.

For 2012, the GOP's formula produced a convention of 2,286 delegates. The Democrats' more complicated plan called for 5,552 delegates. Given those large numbers, it should be fairly clear that neither party's national convention can be called "a deliberative body," an assembly able to give each of its decisions thoughtful consideration.

Both parties allot delegates to the District of Columbia, Puerto Rico, the Virgin Islands, Guam, and American Samoa. The Democratic convention also includes a large number of "superdelegates"—mostly party officers and Democrats who hold major elective public offices and other party activists. More than 720 superdelegates were seated at the 2012 Democratic convention.

Convention Goals For over a century, national conventions were highly dramatic, often chaotic, and even stormy affairs at which, after days of heated bargaining, the party would finally nominate its presidential and vice-presidential candidates. Both parties' meetings have become much tamer in recent years—largely because there is now little doubt about who will win the party's grand prize. Regularly, the leading contender has won enough delegates in the primaries and caucuses to lock up the nomination long before the convention meets.

Each party's convention remains a major event, nonetheless. The conventions have three major goals: (1) naming the party's presidential and vice-presidential candidates, (2) bringing the various factions and the leading personalities in the party together in one place for a common purpose, and (3) adopting the party's platform—its formal statement of basic principles, stands on major policy matters, and objectives for the campaign and beyond.

Both parties hope that their convention will do a number of other things, as well. They want the meeting to promote party unity, capture the interest and attention of the country at large, and generate support for the party's ticket in the upcoming campaign.

Opening the Convention Each party's convention now meets in one or two sessions per day over three or four days. Each of those sessions is tightly scheduled and closely scripted. In short, they are now made for media coverage.

The first day is dedicated to welcoming the delegates and organizing the convention, and to dozens of short speeches by an array of party figures.

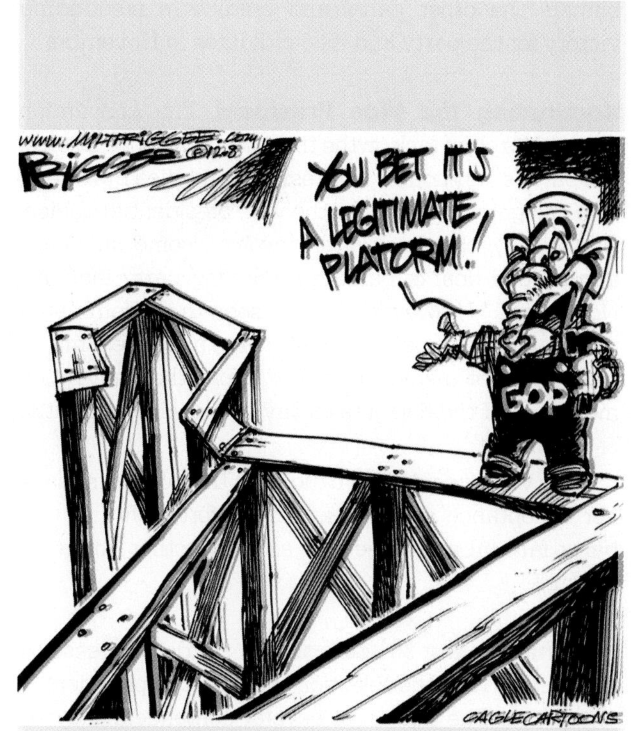

>> A representative of the Republican Party defends the party's political platform. **Analyze Political Cartoons** What do you think are the characteristics of a "legitimate" party platform?

The second day sees a continuing parade of speakers but is highlighted by two major events: the adoption of the party's platform and the delivery of the keynote address.

Showcasing the Platform and the Party The platform comes to the convention floor as a report by the committee on platform and resolutions. In fact, it has been drawn up by the party's leadership beforehand.

Platform-writing is a fine art. Recall, the platform is a statement of party principles and stands on policy matters. But it is also an important campaign document aimed at appealing to as many people and as many groups as possible. So both parties tend to produce somewhat generalized comments on some of the hard questions facing the nation at the time. Platforms are regularly criticized for blandness. Still, the platforms are important. They do set out a number of hard-and-fast stands in many policy areas. They also reflect the compromising nature of American politics and of the two major parties.

The **keynote address** is usually a barn-burner, delivered by one of the party's most accomplished orators. The address, like nearly all the speeches the delegates hear, follows a predictable pattern. It glorifies the party, its history, its leaders, and its programs, blisters the other party, and predicts a resounding victory for the party and its candidates in November.

Nominating the Vice President The convention turns to its chief task on the third day: the nomination of the party's candidates for President and Vice President. The delegates turn first to the vice-presidential choice. Historically, that task often involved some suspense and a good deal of bargaining among party factions. Nowadays, however, the soon-to-be-nominated presidential candidate sometimes announces his or her choice of a running mate before the convention meets—and the delegates ratify that choice with little or no dissent.

The vice-presidential candidate then delivers his or her acceptance speech—another effort to fire up the party faithful and appeal to as many other voters as possible.

Nominating the President The third day's session culminates with the selection of the party's presidential candidate. The names of several contenders may be offered, especially in the party out of power. Once the nominating (and several seconding) speeches are made, the delegates vote. The convention secretary calls the States in alphabetical order, and the chair of each State delegation announces how that delegation's votes are cast. Each complete roll call is known as a ballot, and the balloting continues until one of the contenders wins a majority of the delegates' votes.

Most often, the first ballot produces a winner. Over the 30 conventions held by each party since 1900, the Republicans have made a first-ballot choice 26 times and the Democrats 25 times. Indeed, the GOP has not had to take a second ballot since 1948, and the Democrats since 1952.

With its candidates named, the convention comes to the final major item on its agenda: the presidential candidate's acceptance speech. That speech caps the convention and launches the party's general election campaign.

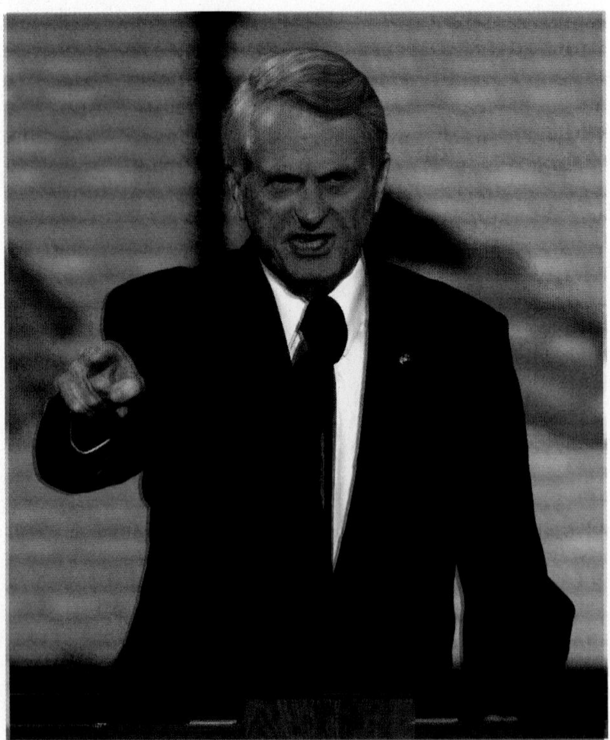

>> Georgia Democratic Senator Zell Miller crossed party lines at the 2004 Republican National Convention and delivered the keynote address in support of President George W. Bush.

? INFER At what time of day are most major events in the national conventions held? Why?

Who Is Nominated?

If an incumbent President wants another term, and the 22nd Amendment is not in play, the convention's choice is easily made. The sitting President is virtually certain to gain the nomination, and usually with no real opposition from within the party. The President's advantages are immense: the majesty and publicity of the office and close control of the party's machinery.

When the President is not in the field, up to a dozen or more contenders may surface in the pre-convention period. At most, two or three of them may survive to contest the prize at the national convention. Who will win the nomination?

The historical record suggests that this will be the usual answer: the contender who is the most electable. Both parties want to pick candidates who can win, those with the broadest possible appeal, within the party and in the electorate.

Political Experience Most presidential candidates come to their nominations with substantial, well-known records in public office. This pattern has not held true in recent elections, however. In 2012, the Republicans picked Mitt Romney, who had served just one term as governor of Massachusetts. His Democratic opponent also lacked a lengthy public service record. Barack Obama had served only four years in the Senate before being elected to the presidency in 2008.

In 2016, Donald Trump, a wealthy businessman with no prior experience in government, became another exception to this trend when he won the Republican nomination. The only other major party nominee to have no experience in either government or the military was Republican candidate Wendell Wilkie in 1940.

Prominence at Home Historically, governorships have produced the largest number of presidential candidacies. Of the 41 men and 1 woman nominated by the two major parties (some were nominated more than once) from 1900 to 2016, 17 were either serving or had once served as governor. Put another way, the Democrats and Republicans nominated governors or former governors 27 times out of the 60 presidential nominations made during that time period.

For a time, the Senate was a prime source of presidential candidates. In the four elections from 1960 through 1972, every major party nominee had served in the Senate. Viewed through a wider lens, however, senators are not as likely to be chosen to run for the presidency as are governors. From 1900 to 2016, the major parties nominated present or former senators 18 times out of the 60 nominations made.

Other Characteristics Most leading contenders for the nomination have been Protestants. The most notable exceptions to that statement are Democrats Alfred E. Smith (1928), John F. Kennedy (1960), and John Kerry (2004), all Catholics; and Republican Mitt Romney (2012), a Mormon.

Nominees usually have a pleasant and healthy appearance, seem to be happily married, and have an attractive (and exploitable) family. Only six have ever been divorced. One (Donald Trump) was divorced twice.

A well-developed speaking ability has always been a plus in American politics. The ability to project well over television, pioneered by John F. Kennedy in 1960, has long since become a must, as well.

Shattering Barriers In the last twenty years, several longstanding barriers to the nation's highest office have been overcome. Over time, most major party first-time presidential candidates have been in their 50s or 60s when nominated. None has ever been as old as Bob Dole, who turned 73 a few weeks before he became the GOP's candidate in 1996. Indeed, the age spread between the two major party candidates in that election (23 years) was greater than it had been in any presidential election in history.

Until 2008, neither major party had ever nominated a member of any minority group as its presidential candidate. In that year, however, Senator Barack Obama, the child of a white mother from Kansas and a black father from Kenya, made history by winning the Democratic Party nomination. His groundbreaking election ended the racial barrier to the nation's highest office and moved the nation forward one huge step in its quest for racial equality.

>> Dwight D. Eisenhower was a soldier and war hero with no background in politics when he ran for President in 1952, but a platform of peace and prosperity won him the election by a landslide.

In that same election, former secretary of state Hillary Clinton tried to become the first woman presidential candidate in the nation's history. She lost that bid to Barack Obama, but in 2016, Mrs. Clinton finally shattered what she called "that highest and hardest glass ceiling." In that year, she became the first woman presidential candidate in the country's history by winning the Democratic nomination.

? GENERATE EXPLANATIONS The text states that the ability to project well over television is a must for any presidential candidate. Why do you think this is the case?

The Presidential Campaign

As you know, the Constitution calls for a presidential election to be held every four years. The first one was held in 1789, and, like clockwork, 57 of those contests have followed along, right on schedule. That remarkable fact is unmatched in the history of any other nation in the world. Even during a civil war, two world wars, several economic depressions, and various other crises, the Constitution's command has been met.

Saturating the Country The presidential campaign is an all-out effort to win the votes of the American people. For decades, that slugfest began soon after the two parties' conventions had adjourned. But, over recent decades, it has been quite apparent some weeks, or even a month or more, before the conventions who the delegates would nominate. So those campaigns have in fact begun at some point before the candidates were formally nominated.

The campaign itself is organized chaos, and it dominates the national news scene up to election day. The candidates' campaign organizations work to show their standard bearers in the best possible light and, with negative jabs, to undercut the claims of the opposition. The voters are bombarded with radio and television interviews, speeches and advertisements, direct mail, Internet messages, "whistle-stop" tours, press conferences and press releases, rallies and party dinners, stickers and buttons, pamphlets, balloons, and billboards. The candidates pose for hundreds of photographs and shake thousands of hands as each of them tries to convince the voters that he or she is the best bet for the country.

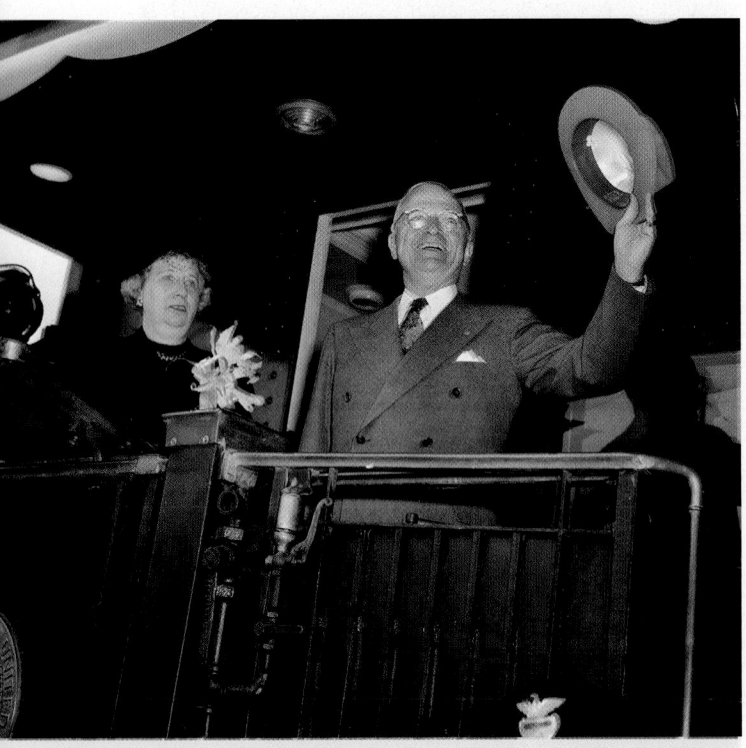

>> Harry Truman and his wife, Bess, arrive in Philadelphia during his 1948 "whistle stop" campaign tour. *Ferdinand Magellan,* the railroad car they rode, was custom built for U.S. Presidents.

Targeting Key Voters Both campaigns focus much of their efforts on **swing voters**—the roughly one third of the electorate who have not made up their minds at the start of the campaign and are open to persuasion by either side. Campaign strategy is also driven by the electoral college, as you will see in a moment. The would-be Presidents target the **battleground States**—those States in which the outcome is "too close to call" and either candidate could win. Both campaigns tend to concentrate their organizational efforts, campaign funds, and candidate appearances in those States.

Debates A series of presidential debates now highlights the campaign. An incumbent President, or a candidate ahead in the polls, may not really want to debate, but both major party contenders now regularly agree to do so.

The debates are now sponsored by a nonpartisan body created by Congress in 1987, called the Commission on Presidential Debates. The participants must be party-nominated candidates who are (1) supported by at least 15 percent of the respondents in five national polls and (2) listed on the ballot of States which, taken together, will cast at least a majority (270) of the electoral votes in the upcoming election. In effect, the Commission's rules all but exclude minor party and independent candidates from the debates.

The first presidential debates, in 1960, featured then-Vice President Richard Nixon and his Democratic opponent, Senator John F. Kennedy. Their four televised debates, which were really little more than joint appearances, generated a great deal of interest, and many analysts credit John Kennedy's strong performance in them as one of the keys to his very narrow victory in the election that year.

The next set of debates came in 1976, between President Gerald Ford and his Democratic opponent, Jimmy Carter; with another involving their vice-presidential running mates, Bob Dole and Walter Mondale. That general pattern has been followed in every campaign since then. Thus, in 2016, there were three debates between Donald Trump and Hillary Clinton, and one that pitted Mike Pence against Tim Kaine.

Who's Watching? The 2016 presidential debates included two traditional debates and one with a "town hall" format. The first debate broke the viewership record set by the 1980 debate between President Jimmy Carter and Ronald Reagan (81 million viewers). Some 84 million people tuned in to watch businessman Donald Trump and former secretary of state, senator, and First Lady Hillary Clinton face off. The second debate drew 66.5 million viewers and the third, 72 million. Some 37 million viewers watched the single vice-presidential debate between Governor Mike Pence of Indiana and Senator Tim Kaine of Virginia.

Election Day The presidential campaign finally comes to an end on election day. Millions of voters go to the polls in all 50 States and the District of Columbia. But the President, whoever that is to be, is not formally elected until the presidential electors' votes are cast and counted, several weeks later.

IDENTIFY CENTRAL IDEAS Whether voters are watching debates or receiving media messages from the candidates, describe the two general approaches—and the tone of each—that campaigns take to convince voters to choose their candidates on Election Day.

>> Bill Clinton, Ross Perot, and George H.W. Bush participate in the first town hall-style debate in 1992. The format allows selected voters to pose their own questions to the candidates.

Interactive Timeline

The Electoral College

You have arrived at one of the least understood points in the American political process. As the people vote in the presidential election, they do not cast a vote directly for one of the presidential candidates. They vote, instead, for presidential electors.

Recall, the Constitution provides for the election of the President by the electoral college, in which each State has as many electors as it has members of Congress. The Framers expected the electors to use their own judgment in selecting a President. Today the electors, once chosen, are, in fact, just "rubber stamps." They are expected to vote automatically for their party's candidates for President and Vice President. In short, the electors go through the form set out in the Constitution in order to meet the letter of the Constitution, but their behavior is far from the original intent of that document.

>> In 1787, George Mason said the size of the country made it impossible for all Americans to evaluate candidates. **Make Predictions** How has modern media changed the way presidents are elected?

Choosing Electors The electors are chosen by popular vote in every State on the same day: the Tuesday after the first Monday in November of every fourth year. So the 2020 presidential election is set for November 3, 2020. In every State except Maine and Nebraska, the electors are chosen at large. That is, they are chosen on a winner-take-all basis. The presidential candidate—technically, the slate of elector-candidates nominated by the party—who receives the largest number of popular votes in a State regularly wins all of that State's electoral votes.

Today, the names of the individual elector-candidates appear on the ballot in only a handful of States. In most States, only the names of the presidential and vice-presidential candidates are listed. They stand as "shorthand" for the elector slates.

Counting the Electoral Votes The Constitution provides that the date Congress sets for the electors to meet "shall be the same throughout the United States." (Article II, Section 1, Clause 4) The 12th Amendment provides that "the Electors shall meet in their respective States." The electors therefore meet at their State capital on the date set by Congress, now the Monday after the second Wednesday in December. There they each cast their electoral votes, one for President and one for Vice President. The electors' ballots, signed and sealed, are sent by registered mail to the president of the Senate.

Who has won a majority of the electoral votes, and who then will be the next President of the United States, is usually known by midnight of election day, more than a month before the electors cast their ballots. But the *formal* election of the President and Vice President takes place in early January.

On that date, the president of the Senate opens the electoral votes from each State and counts them before a joint session of Congress. The candidate who receives a majority of the electors' votes for President is declared elected, as is the candidate with a majority of the votes for Vice President.

Special Cases If no candidate has won a majority—today, at least 270 of 538 electoral votes—the election is put to the House of Representatives. This happened in 1800 and in 1824. The House chooses a President from among the top three candidates voted for by the electoral college. Each State delegation has one vote, and at least 26 votes are needed. If the House fails to choose a President by January 20, the 20th Amendment provides that the newly elected Vice President shall act as President until a choice is made.

The 20th Amendment also says that "the Congress may by law provide for the case wherein neither a President elect nor a Vice President elect shall have qualified" by Inauguration Day. Congress has done so, in the Presidential Succession Act of 1947. The Speaker of the House would "act as President . . . until a President or Vice President shall have qualified."

If no one receives a majority of the electoral votes for Vice President, the Senate decides between the top two candidates. It takes a majority of the whole Senate

Electoral Votes by State

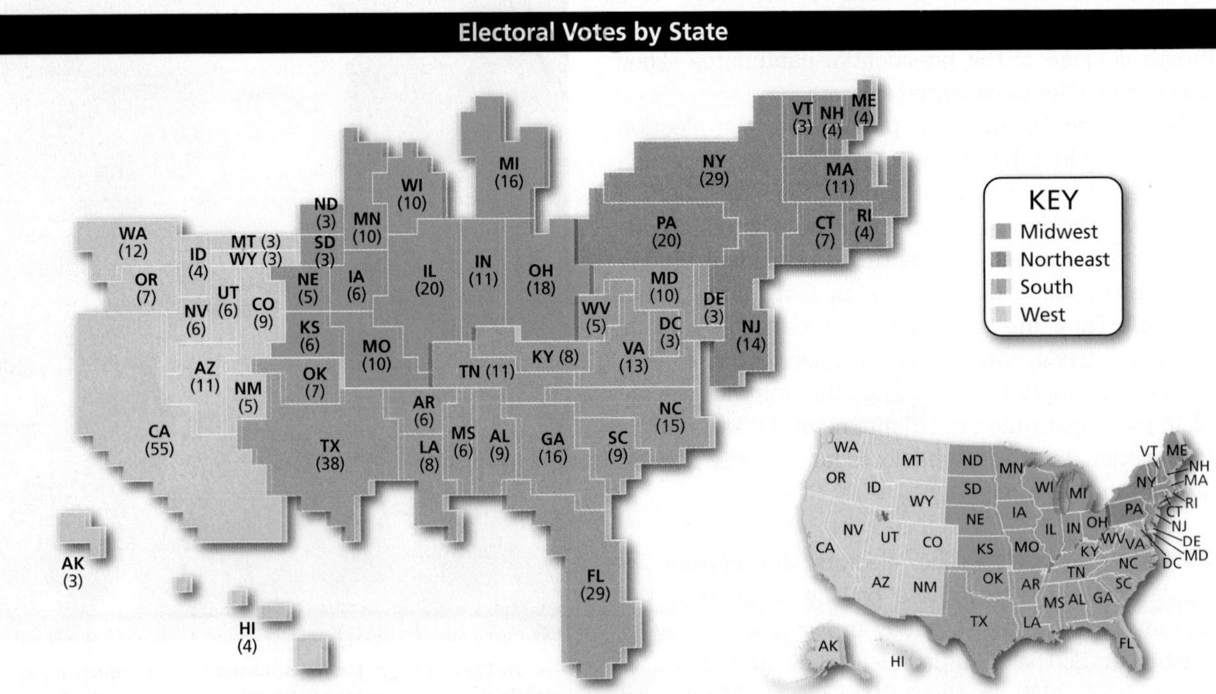

>> The large map shows each State sized in proportion to its number of electoral votes. **Analyze Maps** What do these maps suggest about the electoral vote strength of the Northeast?

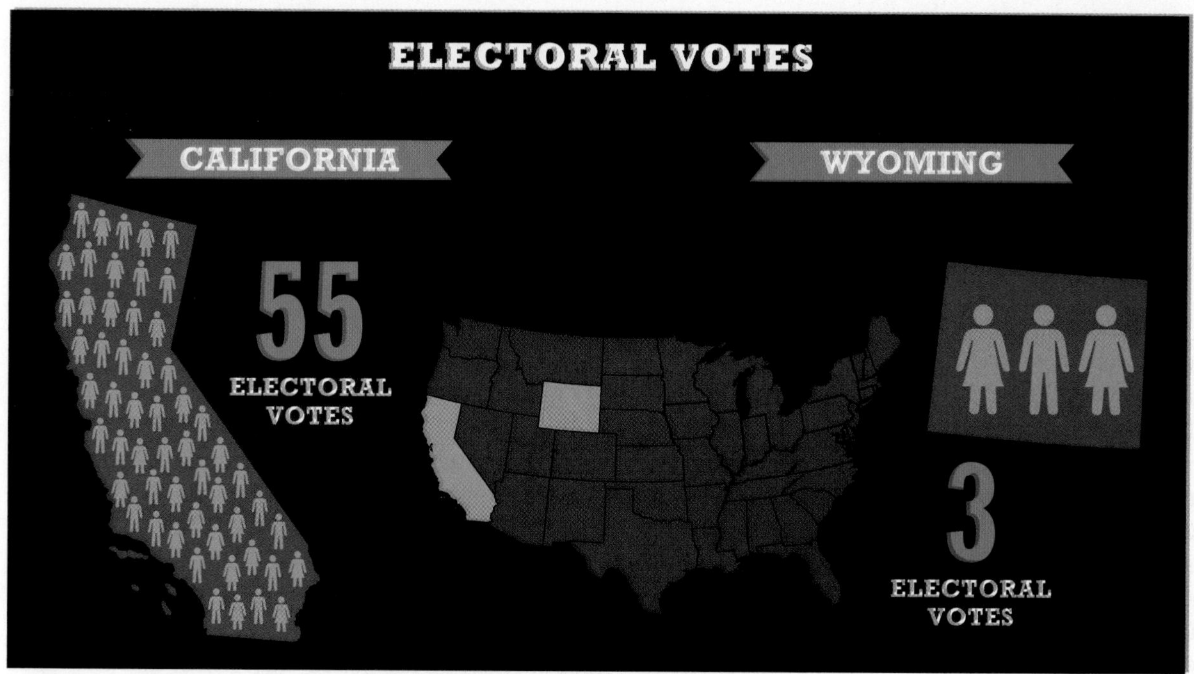

>> In 2016, California's 55 electoral votes went to Democrat Hillary Clinton, while Republican Donald Trump got Wyoming's 3. **Analyze Charts** Why are the figure icons in Wyoming so much larger than those in California?

to elect. The Senate has chosen a Vice President only once: **Richard M. Johnson** in 1837.

GENERATE EXPLANATIONS Explain why the Framers of the Constitution put the House of Representatives, rather than the Senate, in charge of choosing a President when the election process does not yield a majority winner.

Flaws in the Electoral College

The electoral college system is plagued by three major defects: (1) the winner of the popular vote is not guaranteed the presidency; (2) electors are not required to vote in accord with the popular vote; and (3) any election might have to be decided in the House of Representatives.

The First Major Defect There is the ever-present threat that the winner of the popular vote will not win the presidency. This danger is largely the result of two factors. The most important is the winner-take-all feature of the electoral college system. That is, the winning candidate receives all of a State's electoral votes. Thus, in 2016, President Trump won just 48 percent of the popular vote in Pennsylvania, to Hillary Clinton's 47.5 percent. Still, he won all of that State's 20 electoral votes—despite the fact that nearly 3 million Pennsylvanians voted for Secretary Clinton.

The other major culprit here is the way the electoral votes are distributed among the States. Remember, two of the electors in each State are allotted because of a State's two Senate seats, regardless of population. So the distribution of electoral votes among the States does not match the facts of population and voter distribution.

Consider an extreme case: California has 55 electoral votes, one for each 677,345 persons in the State, based on its 2010 population of 37,253,956 residents. Wyoming has 3 electoral votes, one for each 187,875 persons, based on its 2010 population of 563,626 residents.

When the Defect Becomes Reality The popular vote winner has, in fact, failed to win the presidency five times: in 1824, 1876, 1888, 2000, and 2016. In 2000, the Democratic candidate, Vice President Al Gore, won 50,999,897 popular votes—543,895 more votes than his Republican opponent, the then-governor of Texas, George W. Bush. However, Mr. Bush received 271 electoral votes—one more than the bare majority in the electoral college, and so he became the nation's 43rd President.

Florida's then 25 electoral votes were decisive in this election. The popular vote results in several Florida counties were challenged after the polls closed there. The next five weeks were filled with partisan infighting, several recounts, and a number of court disputes.

The United States Supreme Court brought an end to the bitter contest on December 12. It ruled, in *Bush* v. *Gore,* that the differing ways in which various counties were recounting votes violated the 14th Amendment's Equal Protection Clause. The Court's controversial 5–4 decision ended those recounts. It also preserved Mr. Bush's 537 vote lead in the Statewide count, giving him Florida's 25 electoral votes.

A Consistent Problem To this point, 19 Presidents have won the White House with less than a majority (that is, less than 50 percent) of the popular votes cast in their elections. The most recent of these "minority Presidents" were Bill Clinton in both 1992 and 1996, George W. Bush in 2000, and Donald J. Trump in 2016.

By now, you see the point: The winner-take-all factor produces an electoral vote that is, at best, only a distorted reflection of the popular vote.

The Second Major Defect Nothing in the Constitution, nor in any federal statute, requires the electors to vote for the candidate favored by the popular vote in their States. Several States do have such laws, but they are of doubtful constitutionality, and none has ever been enforced.

>> Members of Congress, in a joint session, count the electoral votes to certify that Barack Obama has won the 2008 presidential election.

To this point, however, electors have "broken their pledges," refused to vote for their party's presidential nominee, on only a handful of occasions—most recently in 2016. That year, an astonishing seven electors, two Republicans and five Democrats, did not cast their ballots for their party's presidential candidate. Their defections underscored the contention and bitterness that had characterized that election. To that point, no election in modern times had had more than one "faithless elector" in a single election.

In no case has the vote of a "faithless elector" had a bearing on the outcome of a presidential election. But the potential is most certainly there.

The Third Major Defect In any presidential election, it is possible that the contest will be decided in the House. This has happened only twice, and not since 1824. In several other elections, however—most recently, 1968—a strong third-party bid has threatened to make it impossible for either major party candidate to win a majority in the electoral college, and so throw the election into the House of Representatives.

Objections to Election by the House of Representatives Three serious objections can be raised regarding election by the House. First, the voting in such cases is by States, not by individual members. A State with a small population, such as Alaska, Wyoming, or Vermont, would have as much weight as the most populous State. Second, if the representatives from a State were so divided that no candidate was favored by a majority, that State would lose its vote. Third, the Constitution requires a majority of the States for election in the House—today, 26 States. If a strong third-party candidate were involved, there is a real possibility that the House could not make a decision by Inauguration Day.

In such a case, the 20th Amendment states that "the Vice President elect shall act as President until a President shall have qualified." If no Vice President elect is available, the Presidential Succession Act would come into play. Note that it is even mathematically possible for the minority party in the House to have control of a majority of the individual State delegations. That party could then elect its candidate, even though he or she may have run second or even third in both the popular and the electoral vote contests.

? DRAW CONCLUSIONS If, in the future, third parties become more powerful, how would the electoral college system be affected?

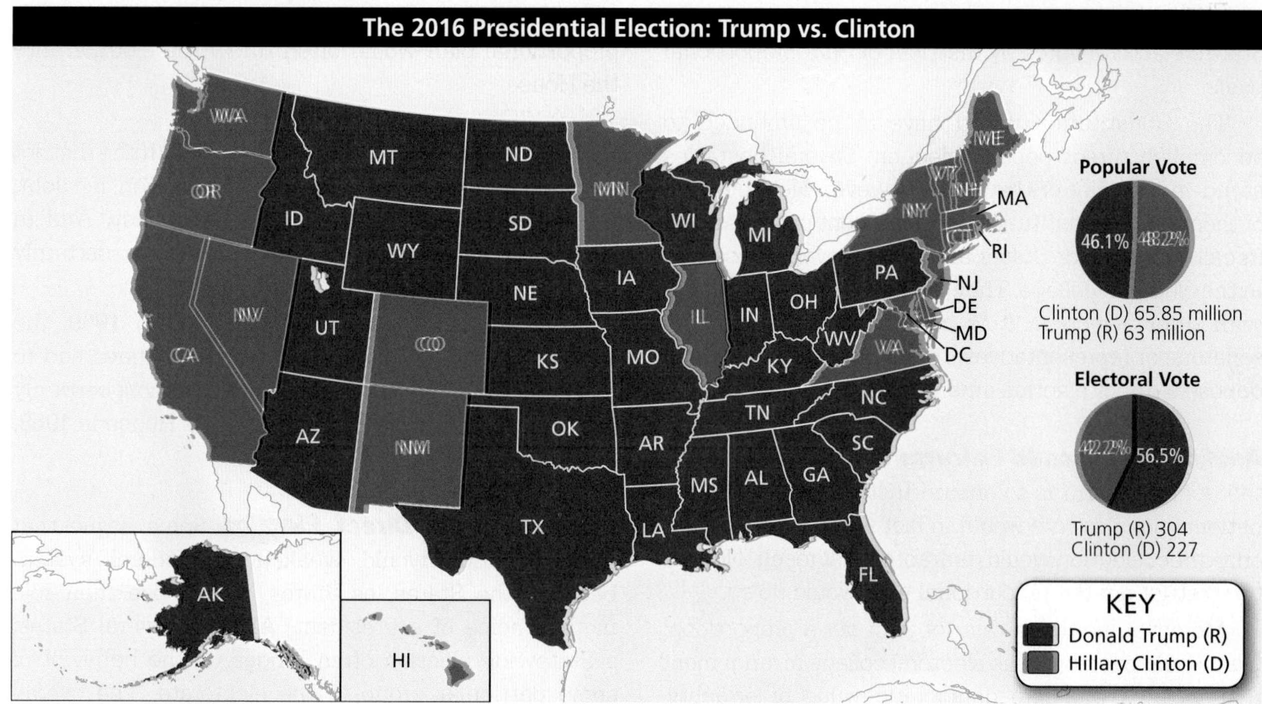

>> Donald Trump lost the popular vote in 2016, but won in the electoral college. **Analyze Maps** How do these results show the significance of the winner-take-all factor in State contests?

Proposed Reforms and a Defense

The several shortcomings of the electoral college have long been recognized. To that point, Thomas Jefferson once called its original version "the most dangerous blot" on the Constitution. Amendments to revise or eliminate the electoral college have been introduced in every term of Congress since 1789. Most of the proposals fall under four headings: the district plan, the proportional plan, direct popular election, and the national popular vote plan. Over recent years, most advocates of change have supported proposals for the direct election of the President.

District and Proportional Plans Under the **district plan**, each State would choose its electors much as it chooses its members of Congress. That is, two electors would be chosen from the State at large, and they would be required to cast their electoral votes in line with the popular vote in their State. The State's other electors would be chosen, separately, in each of that State's congressional districts. The votes of these electors would be cast in accord with the popular vote in their districts. Remember, two States—Maine and Nebraska—already choose their electors on a district plan basis.

Under the **proportional plan**, each presidential candidate would receive a share of each State's electoral vote equal to his or her share of that State's popular vote. So a candidate who won, say, 62 percent of the votes cast in a State with 20 electors would receive 12.4 of that State's electoral votes.

Direct Popular Election Proposals for direct popular election would not reform but, instead, abolish the electoral college system. The voters in all 50 States and the District of Columbia would be given the power to actually choose the President and the Vice President. Each vote, cast anywhere in the country, would count equally in the national result. The winner would, therefore, always be the choice of a majority or at least a plurality of the nation's voters.

A majority of the American people have consistently supported direct popular election for several decades now. The fact that the loser of the popular vote nevertheless won the presidency in 2000 has given added weight to the case for direct election.

What About the Constitution? In their basic forms, neither the district nor the proportional plan would require a constitutional amendment to become effective. Remember, the Constitution leaves the manner of selecting the electors up to the State legislatures. Any of them could decide to allocate the State's electoral votes by districts or on a proportional basis.

The Constitution would have to be amended to accomplish direct popular election. Several obstacles stand in the way of that plan, however. Not the least of them is the constitutional amendment process itself. Recall, the smaller States are heavily overrepresented in the electoral college. They would lose that advantage with direct election. It is highly likely that enough senators, or representatives, from smaller States would oppose a direct election amendment to kill it.

Analyzing Proposed Reforms in Light of Goals If the goal of reform is to ensure that the winner of the national popular vote would in fact win the presidency, only direct election would guarantee that result. Neither the district nor the proportional plan would do so.

Moreover, neither a district plan nor a proportional plan would overcome the electoral college arrangement that violates the core democratic value of equality. The district scheme prevents the weighing of all votes equally. It does, in major part, because, recall, every State has two electoral votes because it has two seats in the Senate, no matter what its population.

The proportional plan does do a better job of weighing popular votes equally. Still, because each of the smaller States is overrepresented by its two Senate-based electors, that arrangement would make it possible for the loser of the popular vote to win the White House in the electoral vote. And, again, the proportional plan would often throw the election into the House.

Applying the Plans to Real Scenarios If the district plan had been in place in 1960, Richard Nixon, not John F. Kennedy, would have won the presidency. And in 1976 the presidential election would almost certainly have had to be decided by the House.

Were a proportional plan in effect, in 1960, the Kennedy-Nixon election would very likely have had to go to the House. And, the House would almost certainly have had to decide who won the White House in 1968, 1976, 1992, 1996, and 2000.

States Against Direct Election Some argue that direct election would weaken the federal system because the States, as States, would lose their role in the choice of a President. Also, in several States, a Statewide election often hinges on the behavior of some particular group in the electorate. The overall result in the State depends in large part on how that group of voters cast their ballots or, often more importantly, on how heavily they do or do not turn out to vote. As but one of many examples of the point, the African American vote in Cook County (Chicago) is regularly decisive in a presidential election in Illinois. With direct election, those key groups would not have the critical power they now enjoy, and so many of them oppose direct election of the President.

Different Possible Outcomes: 1960 Presidential Election

PLANS	OUTCOME		
Electoral College (actual)	☑ John F. Kennedy	☐ Richard Nixon	
District Plan	☐ John F. Kennedy	☑ Richard Nixon	
Proportional Plan	☐ John F. Kennedy	☐ Richard Nixon	☑ Undecided, election is thrown into the House of Representatives
Direct Popular Election	☑ John F. Kennedy	☐ Richard Nixon	
National Popular Vote Plan	☑ John F. Kennedy	☐ Richard Nixon	

SOURCE: Dave Leip's Atlas of U.S. Presidential Elections, uselectionatlas.org

>> Seeing how past elections might have turned out is one way to illustrate the impact of the different plans. **Analyze Charts** Based on this information, did Kennedy win the majority of votes?

Other Arguments Against Direct Election Some believe that direct election would put too great a load on the election process. They believe this because every vote, no matter where it was cast, would count in the national result. And so candidates would have to campaign strenuously everywhere. The impact that would have on campaign time, effort, and finances would be huge and, opponents argue, probably unmanageable.

Others claim that, inevitably, direct election would spur various forms of voter fraud. That, they predict, would lead to lengthy, bitter, and highly explosive post-election challenges.

Given all of this, there seems little chance that the electoral college will be abolished and direct election put in its place any time in the near future.

The National Popular Vote Plan A quite different approach to electoral college reform has recently surfaced: the **national popular vote plan**—in effect, a proposal to bring about the direct popular election of the President—and to do so without making any change in the words of the Constitution.

This new plan looks to the State legislatures to take the lead in electoral college reform. It calls upon each State's lawmaking body to (1) amend State election laws to provide that all of a State's electoral votes are to be awarded to the presidential candidate who wins the national popular vote and (2) enter into an interstate compact, the Agreement Among the States to Elect the President by National Popular Vote. That compact, and with it each State's election law changes, would come into force only if and when the compact has been agreed to by enough States to account for a majority (at least 270) of the 538 electoral votes.

Could This Be the Answer? The national popular vote plan is the only proposal to reform the electoral college that attracts any significant amount of public attention today. By 2017, it had been approved by ten States—California, Hawaii, Illinois, Maryland, Massachusetts, New Jersey, Vermont, Washington, Rhode Island, and New York—as well as the District of Columbia. It is under serious consideration in several others.

This innovative plan is sponsored by a number of prominent Republicans, Democrats, and independents. It has attracted the support of several nonpartisan groups as well as major newspapers around the country. The plan's popularity stems, in large part, from two main facts: (1) it appears to satisfy the major objections that have been raised to the electoral college as it currently operates, and (2) it does so without the need for an amendment to the Constitution.

>> Thomas Jefferson opposed the electoral college, calling it "the most dangerous blot in our Constitution, and one which some unlucky chance will someday hit and give us a pope and anti-pope."

Defending the Electoral College Although their case is not often heard, the present electoral college system does have its defenders. They react to the several proposed reforms by raising the various objections to them you have just read. Beyond that, most of these supporters argue that critics regularly exaggerate the "dangers" they see in the present system. Thus, they note that only two presidential elections have ever gone to the House of Representatives and that none has gone there in more than 180 years.

Those who support the present electoral college system do grant the point that the candidate who loses the popular vote has in fact won the presidency five times—and as recently as 2016. But, they note, that circumstance has happened only five times over the course of 58 presidential elections, and they add that it has happened only twice in more than a century.

Stating the Electoral College's Strengths Supporters also say that the present arrangement, whatever its warts, has three major strengths:

1. It is a *known* process. Each of the proposed, but untried, reforms may very well have defects that can't be known until they appear in practice.

2. In nearly every instance, the present system identifies the President-to-be quickly and certainly. Rarely does the nation have to wait very long to know the outcome of the presidential election.

3. Although it does present an enormous obstacle to minor party candidates, the present arrangement does help promote the nation's two-party system.

? COMPARE AND CONTRAST Explain the similarities and differences between direct election and the national popular vote plan.

ASSESSMENT

1. **Identify Cause and Effect** Explain how reforms in the Democratic Party led to changes in how presidential national primaries are conducted.
2. **Sequence Events** Comment on the rationale behind the ordering of events during a typical national convention.
3. **List** One general characteristic that political party leaders consider when putting forth presidential candidates is the candidates' religious beliefs. List three other characteristics, and explain why they are important.
4. **Check Understanding** Explain the biggest potential danger to democracy in the electoral college system and why it is not addressed by either the district or proportional plans.
5. **Evaluate Arguments** Which argument in favor of maintaining the electoral party system do you find most compelling? Why?

11.4 **Running for public office costs money—and often quite a lot of it. That fact creates some very real problems. It presents the possibility that candidates will try to buy their way into office. It also makes it possible for special interests to try to buy favors from those who hold office.**

>> Elections are expensive. According to government data, Donald Trump and Hillary Clinton's spending for the 2016 presidential election topped $900 million dollars.

Interactive Flipped Video

Money and Elections

>> Objectives

Analyze the impact of campaign spending on the media.

Explain how campaign contributions by individuals and organizations affect the political process.

Explain how public funding of candidates affects the political process.

Explain how campaign finance laws have changed over time.

Distinguish hard money from soft money.

>> Key Terms

political action committees (PACs)
subsidy
FECA
BCRA
soft money
Federal Election Commission (FEC)
Super PAC
Presidential Election Campaign Fund
hard money
527 organizations
John McCain
Russ Feingold

The Price of an Election

Clearly, government by the people must be protected from those dangers. But how? Parties and candidates must have money. Without it, they cannot campaign or do any of the many other things they must do to win elections.

In short, dollars are absolutely necessary campaign resources. Yet, the getting and spending of campaign funds can corrupt the entire political process.

How Much Gets Spent? No one really knows how much money is spent on political campaigns in the United States. Remember, there are more than 500,000 elective offices in this country—most of them at the State and local levels.

The presidential election consumes by far the largest share of campaign dollars. For 2016, total spending for all of the major- and minor-party presidential efforts—for primaries and caucuses, conventions, general election campaigns, for everything—exceeded a mind-boggling $1.5 billion. That's not including outside spending by PACs, super PACS, and other groups, which you will read about in this lesson.

The vast sums spent on congressional campaigns also continue to climb, election after election. In 2016, an average winning Senate candidate spent more than $10 million, while a House seat cost an average of $1.5 million. The most expensive Senate race, in Pennsylvania, cost a whopping $27.8 million. All told, some $1.6 billion was spent just by the candidates—not by their parties or PACS—on congressional races in 2016.

What Does Campaign Money Pay For? Radio and television time, professional campaign managers and consultants, newspaper advertisements, pamphlets, buttons, posters and bumper stickers, office rent, polls, data processing, mass mailings, Web sites, travel—these and a host of other items make up the huge sums spent in campaigns. Television ads are far and away the largest item in most campaign budgets today, even at the local level. As humorist Will Rogers put it years ago, "You have to be loaded just to get beat."

The total amount spent in particular races varies widely, of course. How much depends on several things: the office involved, the candidate and whether he or she is the incumbent or the challenger, the nature of the opposition, and much more— including, not least, the availability of campaign funds.

IDENTIFY What are some of the reasons campaign expenses have risen over the years?

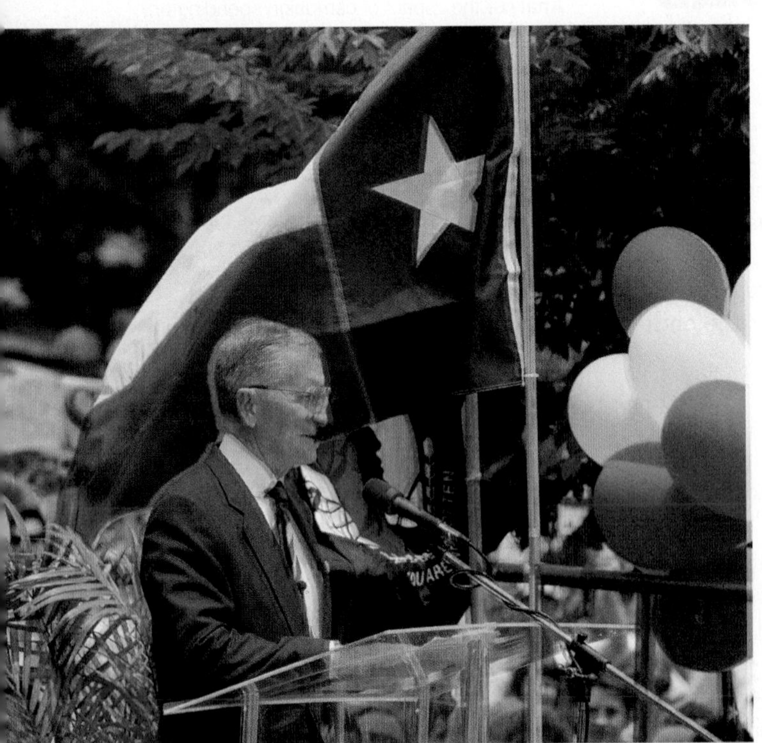

>> Born in Texas in 1930, H. Ross Perot became one of America's wealthiest executives. He is best known for being one of the most successful third-party candidates in American history.

Where the Money Comes From

Parties and candidates draw money from two main sources: private contributors and the public treasury.

Individual Contributors Private givers have always been the major source of campaign funds in American politics. They come in various shapes and sizes:

1. Small contributors—those who give $20 or $30 or so, and only occasionally. Even in today's age of Internet fundraising, less than 10 percent of people of voting age ever make a campaign contribution, so parties and candidates must look to other places for much of their funding.

2. Wealthy individuals and families—the "fat cats," who can make large donations and find it in their best interest to do so.

3. Candidates—both incumbents and challengers, their families, and, importantly, people who hold and want to keep appointive public offices. Independent Ross Perot, who ran for President in 1992, and Republican Donald Trump, who won the office in 2016, are tied for the all-time record in this category. Both men spent some $65 million of their own money on their bids for the presidency.

4. Nonparty groups—especially **political action committees (PACs)** and **Super PACs**. Political action committees are the political arms of special-interest groups and other organizations with a stake in elections. Super PACs are independent political action committees, unaffiliated with any political party.

5. Temporary organizations—groups formed mainly to raise campaign funds. Hundreds of these short-lived units spring up every two years at every level in American politics.

Fundraising Parties and their candidates often hold fundraisers of various sorts. The most common are $100-, $500-, and $1,000-a-plate luncheons, dinners, picnics, and similar gatherings. Some of these events now reach the $100,000-or-more level in presidential campaigns. Direct-mail requests, telethons, and Internet solicitations are also among fundraisers' oft-used tools.

Over recent years, the Internet has become, by far, the most productive of those tools. Often, donations spike immediately after an important speech or primary election victory or when the candidate challenges donors to give. Web sites identify and profile congressional candidates for their readers to support. Social media has greatly increased political engagement with younger voters, which could have a huge impact on elections in the future.

Government Money Public funds—subsidies from the federal and some State treasuries—are now another prime source of campaign money. A **subsidy** is a grant of money, usually from a government. Subsidies have so far been most important at the presidential level, as you will see shortly. Several States also provide some form of public funding of parties and/or candidacies.

Reasons for Contributing Campaign donations are a form of political participation. Those who donate do so for a number of reasons. Many small donors give simply because they believe in a party or in a candidate. Many of those who give, however, want something in return. They want access to government, and hope to get it by helping their "friends" win elections. And, notice, some contributors give to both sides in a contest: Heads they win and tails they still win.

APPLY CONCEPTS Why do you think a candidate might prefer to have many small contributions rather than a few large ones?

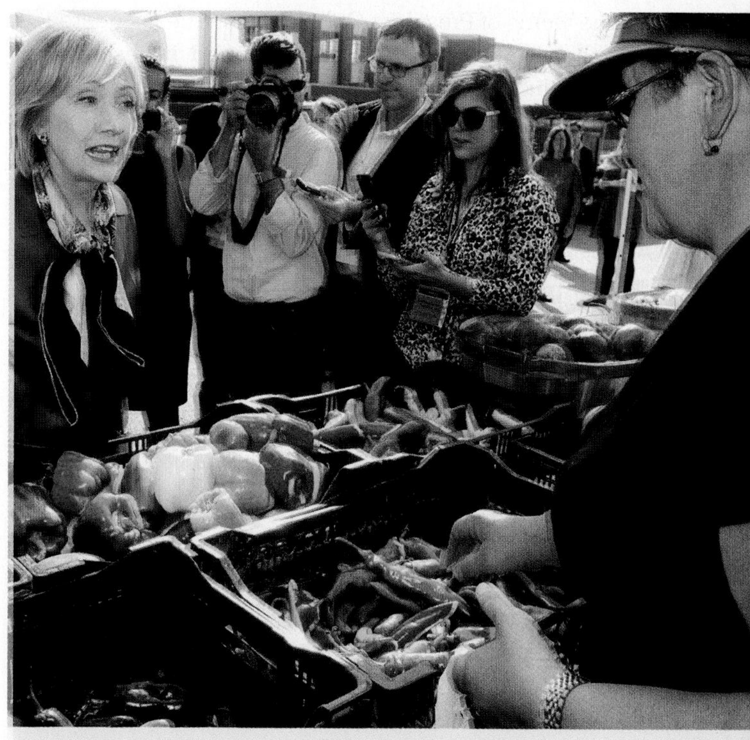

>> Democratic presidential candidate Hillary Clinton (left) talks with an Iowa voter after a campaign event. Interactions such as these are one way candidates raise their visibility, which is critical to winning campaign contributions.

Federal Finance Laws

Congress first began to regulate the use of money in federal elections in 1907. In that year, it became unlawful for any corporation or national bank to make "a money contribution in any election" to candidates for federal office. Since then, Congress has passed several laws to regulate the use of money in presidential and congressional campaigns. Today, these regulations are found in four detailed laws: **FECA,** the Federal Election Campaign Act of 1971, the FECA Amendments of 1974 and of 1976, and **BCRA,** the Bipartisan Campaign Reform Act of 2002.

The History of Campaign Finance Regulation The earliest federal laws were loosely drawn, not often obeyed, and almost never enforced. The 1971 law replaced them. The 1974 law was the major legislative response to the Watergate scandal of the Nixon years. The 1976 law was passed in response to a landmark Supreme Court decision, *Buckley* v. *Valeo*, in 1976. The 2002 law attempted to close the **"soft money"** loophole in the 1974 and 1976 statutes; it was upheld by the High Court in *McConnell* v. *FEC* in 2003.

In 2010, the Supreme Court issued a stunning and controversial ruling that struck down part of the BCRA and called into question portions of the 1907 and 1971 laws. In *Citizens United* v. *Federal Election Commission*, a divided Court ruled, 5–4, that the government ban on political spending by corporations or labor unions violated the 1st Amendment right to free speech. Some supported the ruling. Others feared that it would, in

>> Arizona Republican Senator John McCain and Wisconsin Democratic Senator Russ Feingold coauthored the Bipartisan Campaign Reform Act of 2002.

the words of President Obama, "open the floodgates for special interests." Legislation crafted in response to the ruling has yet to make it through Congress.

Congress cannot regulate the use of money in State and local elections. Every State now regulates at least some aspects of campaign finance, however—some of them do so more effectively than others.

? IDENTIFY CAUSE AND EFFECT Why can't Congress limit the amount of money spent on State and local elections?

FEC Requirements

The **Federal Election Commission** (FEC) administers all federal law dealing with campaign finance. Set up by Congress in 1974, the FEC is an independent agency in the executive branch. Its six members are appointed by the President, with Senate confirmation.

Federal campaign finance laws are both strongly worded and closely detailed. But they are not very well enforced. In large part this is because the FEC is both underfunded and understaffed. That is to say, members of Congress—who, remember, raise and spend campaign money—have made it practically impossible for the FEC to do an effective job. In short, the FEC finds itself in a situation much like that of the chickens who must guard the hen house.

The laws that the FEC is supposed to enforce cover four broad areas. They (1) require the timely disclosure of campaign finance data, (2) place limits on campaign contributions, (3) place limits on campaign expenditures, and (4) provide public financing for several parts of the presidential election process.

Disclosure Requirements Congress first required the reporting of certain campaign finance information in 1910. Today, the disclosure requirements are intended to spotlight the place of money in federal campaigns, and they were not affected by the Court's ruling in *Citizens United* in 2010. Those requirements are so detailed that most candidates for federal office must now include at least one certified public accountant in their campaign organization.

Disclosing Campaign Finances to the Public No individual or group can make a contribution in the name of another. Cash gifts of more than $100 are prohibited, as are contributions and spending from foreign sources.

Once a candidate has raised $5,000, he or she must register with the FEC and begin filing reports. Those reports are available to the public. All contributions to a candidate for federal office must be made through a single campaign committee. All contributions and spending must be closely accounted for by that one committee. Any contribution or loan of more than $200 must be identified by source and by date. Spending in any amount must be identified by the name of the person or firm to whom payment was made, by date, and by purpose. Any contribution of more than $1,000 received in the last 20 days of a campaign must be reported to the FEC no later than 48 hours after it is received.

Limits on Individual Donations Congress first began to regulate campaign contributions in 1907, when it outlawed donations by corporations and national banks. A similar ban was first applied to labor unions in 1943. Individual contributions have been regulated since 1939.

Today, no person can give more than $2,500 per election to any federal candidate. Also, no person can contribute more than $5,000 in any year to a political action committee (PAC), or $30,800 to a national party committee. The total of any person's contributions to federal candidates, political parties, and committees must be limited to no more than $117,000 in an election

>> The Supreme Court's *Citizens United* ruling prompted cartoons depicting its effects. **Analyze Political Cartoons** What point does this cartoon make about the ruling?

Top Six PAC Spenders in 2012

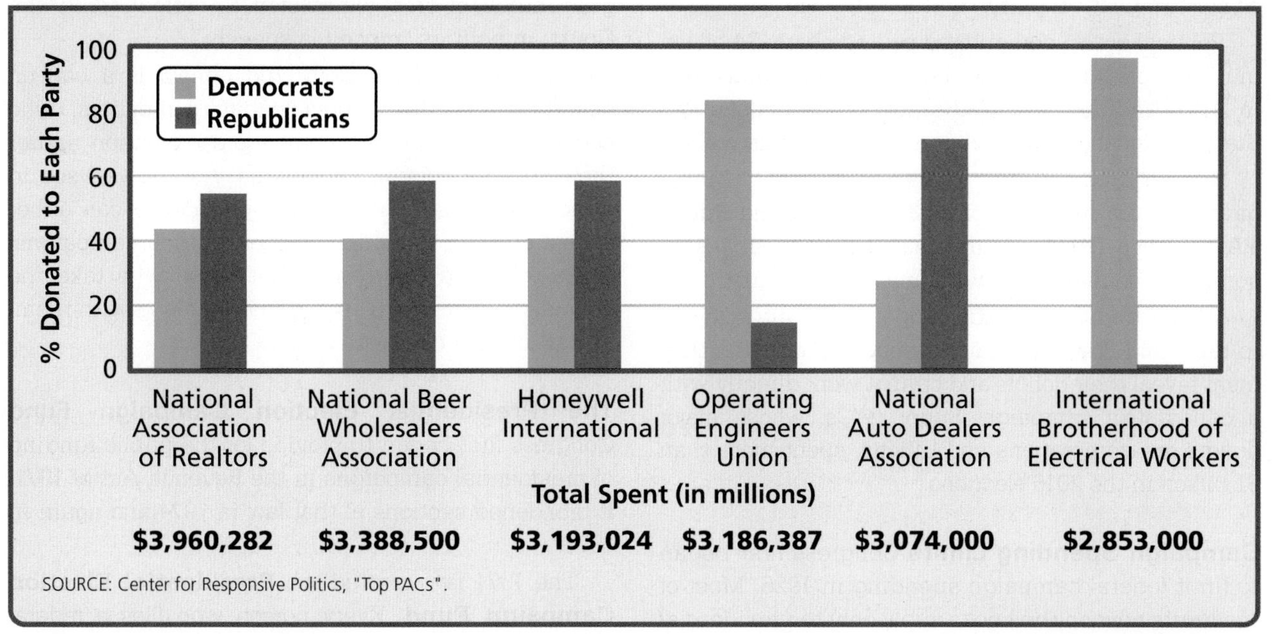

>> Each of these PACs supported both Democrats and Republicans in the 2012 campaign. **Analyze Graphs** What do the two PACs giving the most to Democrats have in common?

cycle (the two years from one general election to the next). The FEC adjusts these figures, to account for inflation, every two years.

Those limits may seem generous; in fact, they are very tight. Before limits were imposed in 1974, many wealthy individuals gave far larger amounts. In 1972, for example, W. Clement Stone, a Chicago insurance executive, contributed more than $2 million (equal to more than $20 million in today's money) to President Richard Nixon's reelection campaign.

Contributions from Political Action Committees (PACs) Neither corporations nor labor unions can contribute directly to any candidate for federal office. Their political action committees, however, can and do.

Political action committees (PACs) seek to affect the making of public policy, and so they are very interested in the outcome of elections in the United States. Some 5,500 PACs are active today, and those organizations are of two distinct types:

1. Most PACs are the political arms of special interest groups—and especially of business associations, labor unions, and professional organizations. These groups are known in the law as "segregated fund committees." They can raise funds *only* from their members—from the executives, the employees, and the stockholders of a corporation, from the members of a labor union, and so on. They *cannot* seek contributions from the general public. Each of these PACs is a part of its parent organization. BIPAC (the Business-Industry Political Action Committee) and COPE (the AFLCIO's Committee on Political Education) are among the most active of these groups.

2. Some 2,000 PACs are known as "non-connected committees." Each of them was established as an independent entity, not as a unit in some larger organization. Many are ideologically based. These PACs can raise money from the public at large. One major example is EMILY's List, which actively recruits and funds pro-choice women as Democratic candidates. (The group takes its name from this political maxim: Early Money Is Like Yeast, it makes the dough rise.)

PACs fill their war chests with contributions from the members of the PAC's parent organization or with the dollars they raise from the public. They "bundle" the money they gather—that is, each PAC pools its many contributions into a single large fund. Then they distribute that money to those candidates who (1) are sympathetic to the PAC's policy goals, and (2) have a reasonable chance of winning their races.

Limits on PAC Contributions No PAC can give more than $5,000 to any one federal candidate in an election. However, there is no overall limit on PAC giving to candidates. Each political action committee can give up to $5,000 per election to each of as many candidates as it chooses. A PAC may also contribute up to $15,000 a year to a political party.

Political action committees poured nearly $4 billion into the presidential and congressional campaigns in 2016. And they funneled untold other millions into State and local contests around the country, as well.

3. The Court's 2010 ruling in *Citizens United* gave rise to a new type of PAC, known as the **Super PAC**. Super PACs are independent political action committees, unaffiliated with any political party.

Unlike traditional PACs, Super PACs are allowed to raise and spend unlimited amounts, although they must reveal their donors and cannot work directly with a candidate's campaign. Super PACs, whose major donors are corporations and unions, spent more than $1 billion in the 2016 elections.

Campaign Spending Limits Congress first began to limit federal campaign spending in 1925. Most of the limits now on the books apply only to presidential (not congressional) elections. This fact is due mostly to the Supreme Court's decision in *Buckley* v. *Valeo*, 1976. In *Buckley*, the High Court struck down all but one of the spending limits set by the FECA Amendments of 1974. It held each of the other restrictions to be contrary to the 1st Amendment's guarantees of free expression. In effect, said the Court, in politics "money is speech."

The one limit the Court did uphold is a cap on spending by those presidential contenders who accept FEC subsidies for their preconvention and/or their general election campaigns. As you will see in a moment, those who seek the presidency can either accept or reject that public money for their campaigns. In *Buckley*, the Court said that those who take the subsidies must take a spending limit along with them, as part of their deal with the FEC.

>> Public funding is also available for candidates in presidential elections. Every federal income tax return allows taxpayers to easily donate to the Presidential Election Campaign Fund.

The Presidential Election Campaign Fund Congress first began to provide for the public funding of presidential campaigns in the Revenue Act of 1971. It broadened sections of that law in 1974 and again in 1976.

The 1971 law created the **Presidential Election Campaign Fund**. Every person who files a federal income tax return can "check off" (assign) three dollars of his or her tax bill (six dollars on a joint return) to the fund. The money is used to subsidize preconvention campaigns, national conventions, and presidential election campaigns. The FEC administers the various subsidies involved.

Preconvention Campaigns To be eligible for the public funds, a presidential contender must raise at least $100,000 in contributions from individuals (not organizations).

That amount must be gathered in $5,000 lots in each of at least 20 States, with each lot built from individual donations of no more than $250. That convoluted requirement is meant to discourage frivolous candidacies.

For each presidential hopeful who passes that test and applies for the subsidy, the FEC will match the first $250 of each individual contribution to the candidate, up to a total of half of the overall limit on preconvention spending. So, in 2012, the FEC could give a contender about $22.8 million, because the preconvention ceiling was $45.6 million. The FEC does not match contributions from PACs or from any other political organizations.

In both 2012 and 2016, the Democratic and Republican presidential candidates all refused the public money. President Trump went on to raise some $134 million in private contributions in his campaign for the Republican nomination, while Hillary Clinton raised more than $405 million.

Presidential Election Campaigns Each major-party nominee automatically qualifies for a public subsidy to pay for the general election campaign. For 2012, that subsidy was $91.2 million. A candidate can refuse that funding, of course, and, in that event, be free to raise however much he or she can from private sources.

Until 2008, the nominees of both major parties took the public money each time. Because they did, each (1) could spend no more than the amount of the subsidy in the general election campaign and (2) could not accept campaign funds from any other source.

For 2008, Republican John McCain ran with the FEC money. The Republican National Committee, other party organizations, and independent groups also backed the McCain effort—to the tune of some $210 million. Barack Obama, on the other hand, became the first presidential nominee in the 32-year history of the program to reject the public money. He raised and spent more than $500 million on his successful postconvention campaign.

>> Political campaigns require candidates to raise a great deal of money. **Analyze Political Cartoons** How does the need for substantial funds exclude many Americans from the election process?

The 2012 and 2016 Presidential Races In 2012, both President Obama and Republican Mitt Romney refused the public money. Republican Donald Trump and Democrat Hillary Clinton followed suit in 2016. This fact led many to pronounce the public funding system dead, a casualty of the ever-accelerating rise in the costs of campaigning. In the words of Democratic presidential hopeful Bernie Sanders, "Nobody can become President based on that system."

The massive effect of soaring costs on the whole matter of campaign finance and its regulation can be seen in this stunning fact: For 2016, just one item (direct mail), for just one candidate (Hillary Clinton), amounted to $14 million in spending.

>> By donating their time, campaign volunteers can help reduce campaign costs for their party and its candidates.

Minor Party Candidates A minor party's candidate can also qualify for the FEC funding, but none does so automatically. For a minor party nominee to be eligible, his or her party must either (1) have won at least five percent of the popular vote in the last presidential election, or (2) win at least that much of the total vote in the current election. Since 1972, only Ross Perot in 1992 and 1996 has come even close to qualifying.

In the latter case, the public money is received *after* the election and so could not possibly help the candidate win votes in that election. (Remember, many provisions in both federal and State election law are purposely drawn to discourage the efforts of minor party and independent candidacies.)

ANALYZE INFORMATION Why do you think that campaign finance reformers wanted to place limits on political contributions?

"Some of it is soft and some of it is hard, but the main thing is that all of it is money."

>> Fundraising happens even in the shadow of the Capitol. **Analyze Political Cartoons** How can fundraising be maximized while minimizing the potential for fraud by contributors?

Loopholes in Finance Laws

More than 40 years ago, President Lyndon Johnson described the then-current body of federal campaign finance law as "more loophole than law." Over recent years, we have come dangerously close to the point where LBJ's description can be applied to the federal election money statutes.

Hard Money and Soft Money Since the 1970s, federal law has placed limits on **hard money**—that is, those contributions that are given directly to candidates for their campaigns for Congress or the White House, are limited in amount, and must be reported. That kind of campaign money is usually more difficult to raise than soft money—funds given to parties or to other political organizations, in unlimited amounts, to be used for such "party-building activities" as voter registration or get-out-the-vote drives or for campaigns for or against particular public policies.

Both major parties began to exploit the soft-money loophole in the 1980s. Officially, those funds were to be used for party-building purposes, but both parties found it easy to filter them into their presidential and congressional campaigns.

>> On the McCain-Feingold law, President Bush said, "Taken as a whole, this bill improves the current system of financing for federal campaigns, and therefore I have signed it into law."

Campaign Finance Reform The torrent of money rushing through the soft-money loophole rose from about $19 million in 1980 to almost $500 million in 2000. Those huge numbers convinced many people that the nation's campaign finance laws were in serious need of reform. With much effort from Republican Senator **John McCain** of Arizona and Democratic Senator **Russ Feingold** of Wisconsin, the Bipartisan Campaign Reform Act (BCRA) was passed and signed into law by President George W. Bush in 2002, after years of debate and delay.

The aim of this bill, also known as the McCain-Feingold Bill, was to reduce the amount of unregulated soft money in the system. In many key respects, that outcome has been achieved. The BCRA bans soft-money contributions to political parties, but the law does not say that other political organizations cannot raise and spend those dollars.

Spending by Super PACs

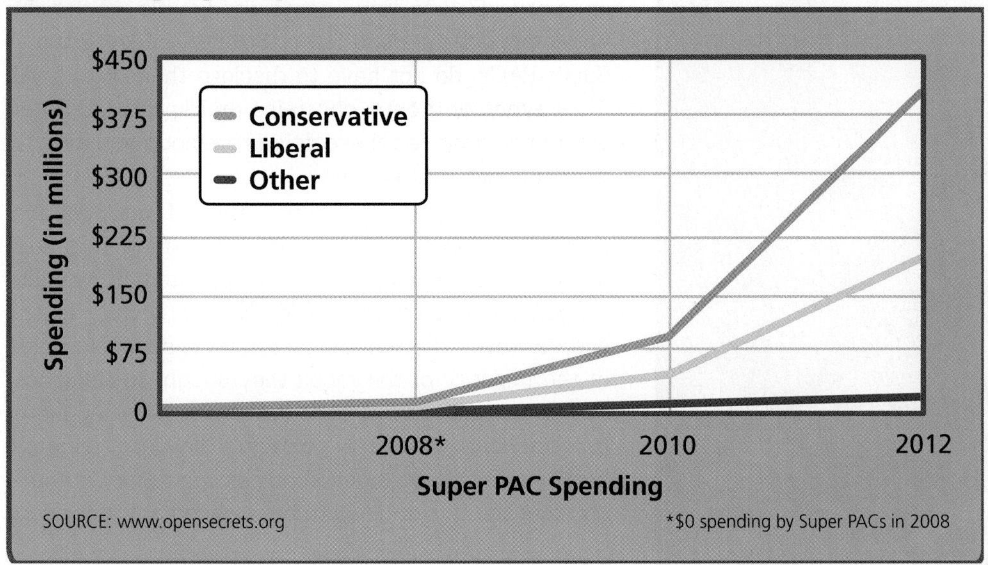

>> Interest groups spent large amounts of money in the 2012 election. **Analyze Charts** Approximately by what factor did conservative groups outspend other groups in the 2012 election?

Almost immediately, creative minds in both parties found ways to skirt the ban. An important by-product of this reform has been the growing number of groups not aligned with a political party but quite interested in certain candidates and policies. These groups have been named **527 organizations** (after Section 527 of the Internal Revenue Code, which regulates their practices). They are allowed to raise unlimited sums of money. Most 527s are advocacy groups that try to influence the outcome of elections through voter mobilization efforts and television advertisements that praise or criticize a candidate's record. A great deal of the funds now flowing to 527s had previously gone to the parties in the form of soft money.

Two prominent examples of 527s in the 2004 election were the Swift Boat Veterans and POWs for Truth and MoveOn.org. The Swift Boat Veterans organization was set up to portray Democratic candidate John Kerry's past military service in a negative light. MoveOn.org, by contrast, was run by a group of Americans who were dissatisfied with President George W. Bush. These groups were able to raise massive sums of money. Indeed, one estimate is that 527 groups spent some $519 million on television ads alone in 2004.

Citizens United* v. *FEC The most recent chapter in the story of money in American elections was a decision handed down by the Supreme Court on January 21, 2010. The case was *Citizens United* v. *Federal Election Commission*, and it dealt with a provision of BCRA that outlawed explicit campaigning by nonpartisan groups within 30 days of a general election and 60 days prior to a primary election.

When the case was originally heard by the Supreme Court, the issue seemed to center on the prohibitions stipulated in BCRA. But when the justices heard arguments a second time, the topic appeared to be much broader: whether prohibitions on corporations and unions from directly spending in campaigns, established a half century before and upheld in several prior cases, were constitutional. In a 5–4 decision, the Court ruled that unions and corporations were entitled to spend money from their general treasuries (without the use of PACs) on federal elections. They could not give directly to candidates, but they were free to spend lavishly on their behalf.

The decision sent shock waves across the political system. Some suggested the ruling represented a tremendous victory for free speech; a straightforward application of basic 1st Amendment principles. However, others feared that the decision would set loose a flood of money and lead to greater corruption. One thing is for certain, the amount of "outside money" (that is, money coming from sources independent of a candidate's campaign) skyrocketed in the 2010 and 2012 elections.

Groups were quickly formed to collect massive contributions and to distribute them strategically. The most prominent of these groups was American Crossroads, a conservative group headed by a former

>> Campaign spending is not always successful. In 2012, the Super PAC co-founded by Karl Rove, American Crossroads, spent $105 million dollars but influenced few election outcomes.

Bush administration official, Karl Rove. This single organization, for example, spent over $5 million in a 2010 effort to defeat the Democratic Senate candidate in Colorado. For better or worse, the amount of money in the election process has certainly not declined, and the number of groups spending this money has skyrocketed.

The Court's 2010 *Citizens United* ruling did not radically affect spending by 527s. Other independent groups, however, including Super PACs and 501(c) organizations, began spending unprecedented amounts. 501(c)s are nonprofit groups registered under the IRS tax code 501(c). 501(c)s, unlike 527s and Super PACs, do not have to disclose their donors. All three types of groups can raise and spend unlimited amounts, as long as those dollars are not given directly to a candidate or campaign.

In 2012, some $1.3 billion poured into political campaigns from these sources. This staggering sum dwarfed previous records and appeared to validate concerns about the effect of *Citizens United*. In the end, however, the two biggest outside spenders failed in the majority of the races they sought to influence, suggesting that money may not be the deciding factor in American electoral politics. The fact remains, however, that both sides spent extraordinary sums—and that trend is unlikely to be reversed anytime soon.

? **COMPARE AND CONTRAST** What are the similarities and differences between hard money and soft money?

ASSESSMENT

1. **Apply Concepts** In your own words, explain why some people are opposed to "outside money" coming into State and local campaigns.
2. **Interpret** Explain why a PAC would donate to a political campaign.
3. **Determine Relevance** In a democracy, why is it important for candidates to disclose where they get their campaign funds?
4. **Identify Central Issues** How did the *Citizens United* case affect campaign finance options?
5. **Apply Concepts** Give an example of hard money and an example of soft money.

TOPIC 11 ASSESSMENT

COMMON LOCAL AND STATE PARTY ORGANIZATION

THIRD LEVEL
PRECINCT

Precincts are the smallest unit of party organization.

SECOND LEVEL
WARD

Wards are usually the next larger political unit into which municipalities are divided.

FIRST LEVEL
CONGRESSIONAL AND STATE LEGISLATIVE DISTRICTS

State party organizations are divided geographically into congressional districts or counties.

1. **Identify the Contributions** Write a paragraph identifying the contributions of Alexander Hamilton, and consider the following questions: Who were the Federalists and Anti-Federalists? Who led each group? What did the Federalists and Anti-Federalists support? Why did the Anti-Federalists support a Bill of Rights?

2. **Compare Methods** Write a paragraph comparing how elected public officials have been nominated in caucuses over the years. Consider the following questions: What is a caucus? How were candidates selected in the original caucus? Why were some people against caucuses? How has the caucus changed over the years on the national, state, and local levels? Why does a caucus work better on a local level rather than on a national level?

3. **Examine Political Boundaries** Use the graph above to examine the distribution of political power on the local and state levels of party organization. Then write a paragraph that answers the following questions: What can you infer about the types of policies that precincts will enforce and how they will affect you? For example, will policies set by precincts affect you more or less than state policies? Explain.

4. **Identify Significant Individuals** Use the quotation below to write a paragraph that answers the following questions: What is George Washington referring to when he describes the "common and continual mischiefs of the spirits of the party?" According to Washington, who is responsible for the actions of the government and why?

> *"The common and continual mischiefs of the spirit of party are sufficient to make it the interest and duty of a wise people to discourage and restrain it."*
>
> *—George Washington*

5. **Evaluate the Role and Analyze Historical Examples** Write a paragraph evaluating how The Free Soil Party brought about political change. Consider the following questions: What is a single-issue party? What did The Free Soil party stand for? Do single-issue parties such as The Free Soil party have a large or a small impact in American politics? Explain.
6. **Explain the Two-Party System** Write a paragraph that explains the two-party system in American politics. Consider the following: the Federalists and the Anti-Federalists; tradition; the electoral system; election laws.
7. **Evaluate the Impact** Write a paragraph evaluating the impact of the Internet on the political process, such as elections. Consider the following questions: How is the Internet used by presidential candidates? Why is the Internet such a productive fundraising tool? What would be the potential impact on society and on the political process if the Internet did not exist?
8. **Give Examples of the Processes** Write a paragraph giving examples of the processes used by political groups to affect public policy. Consider the following questions: What are 527 organizations? What was the Swift Boat Veterans? What is MoveOn.org? How do 527 organizations affect public policy?
9. **Analyze the Impact** Write a paragraph analyzing the impact of the case *Citizen's United* v. *Federal Elections Commission (FEC).* Consider the following questions: What were the circumstances surrounding *Citizen's United* v. *FEC*? How did the ruling affect campaigns? Do you agree with the ruling? Why or why not?
10. **Examine Different Points of View** Use the graph below to write a paragraph examining the Republican and Democratic points of view on healthcare and taxes. Consider the following questions: What was the Democratic platform on taxes and healthcare in 2012? What was the Republican platform on taxes and healthcare in 2012? Based on the chart below, what can you conclude about the point of view of moderate Republicans and moderate Democrats on taxes and healthcare?

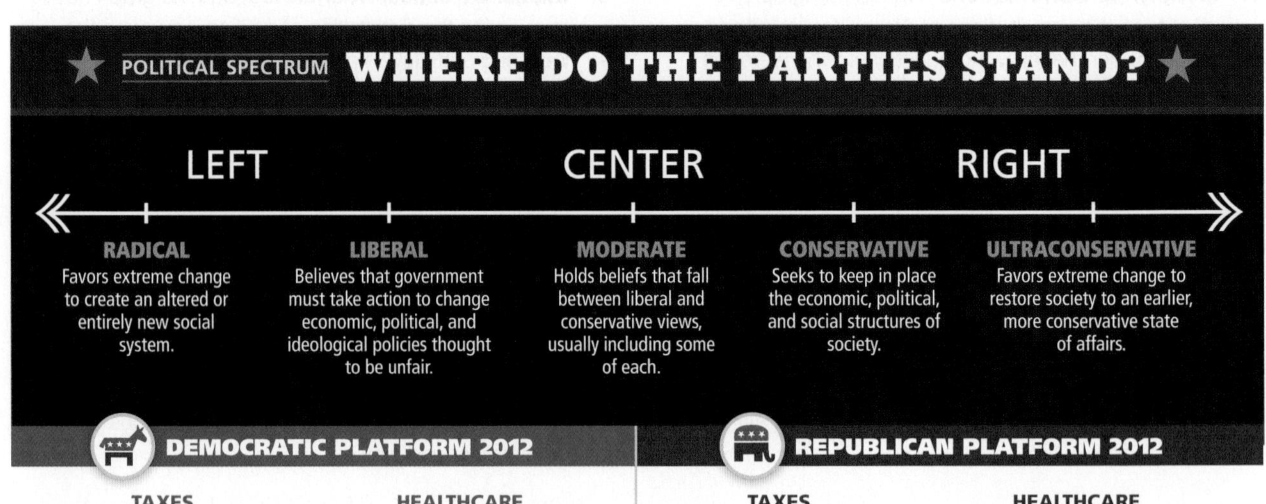
POLITICAL SPECTRUM
WHERE DO THE PARTIES STAND?
LEFT
CENTER
RIGHT
RADICAL
Favors extreme change to create an altered or entirely new social system.
LIBERAL
Believes that government must take action to change economic, political, and ideological policies thought to be unfair.
MODERATE
Holds beliefs that fall between liberal and conservative views, usually including some of each.
CONSERVATIVE
Seeks to keep in place the economic, political, and social structures of society.
ULTRACONSERVATIVE
Favors extreme change to restore society to an earlier, more conservative state of affairs.
DEMOCRATIC PLATFORM 2012
REPUBLICAN PLATFORM 2012
TAXES
We support allowing the Bush tax cuts for the wealthiest to expire and closing loopholes and deductions for the largest corporations and the highest-earningtaxpayers.
HEALTHCARE
We refuse to go back to the days when health insurance companies had unchecked power to cancel your health policy, deny you coverage, or charge women more than men.
TAXES
We reject the use of taxation to redistribute income, fund unnecessary or ineffective programs, or foster… crony capitalism…. [W]e propose to: extend the… Bush tax cuts…; reform the tax code…
HEALTHCARE
[A] Republican President… will… repeal [the Affordable Care Act]. Then the American people, through the free market can advance affordable and responsible healthcare reform.

Electoral Votes by State

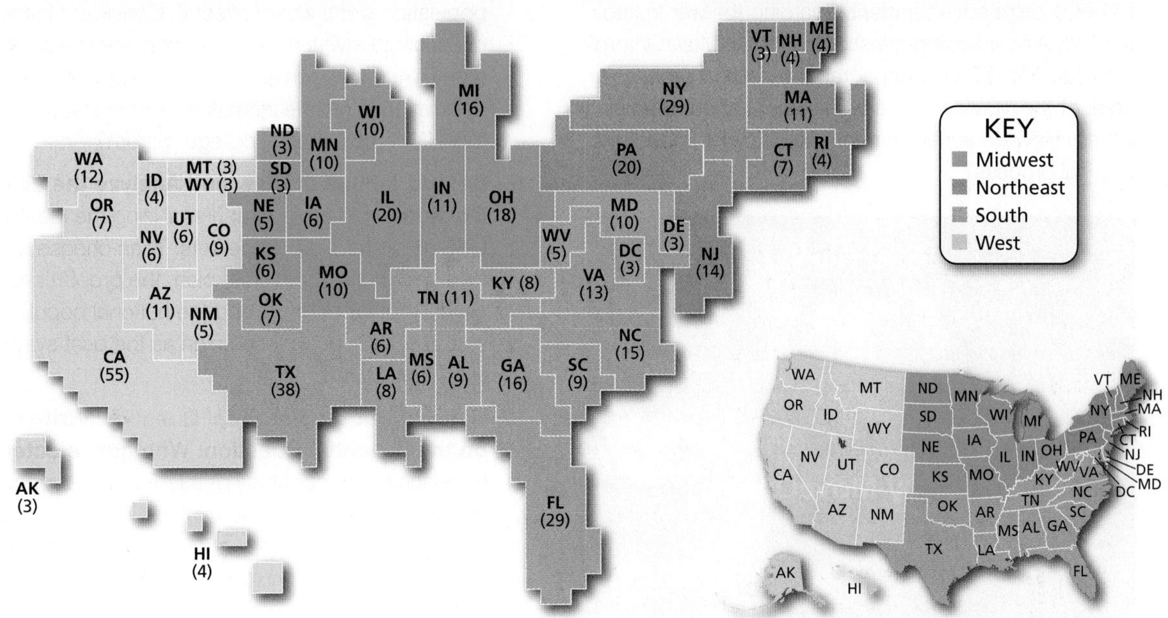

11. Analyze the Electoral College and Evaluate Government Data Use the map above to write a paragraph that answers the following questions: A presidential candidate needs 270 electoral votes to win the election. What is the lowest number of states it would take to reach the target of 270 electoral votes? In your opinion, is it a problem that states with a small number of electoral votes do not factor heavily in the presidential election? Why or why not?

12. Analyze Electoral College and Interpret Information Use the map above to write a paragraph that answers the following questions about the electoral college: Which area of the United States has the most electoral votes? What percentage of the total number of electoral votes are in the Midwest and South regions?

13. Explain the Process of Electing the President of the United States Write a paragraph explaining the process of the presidential primaries. Consider the following questions: What is a presidential primary? How are presidential primaries different from caucuses? Why is a presidential primary better than a party caucus for selecting candidates?

14. Identify Opportunities Identify opportunities for citizens to participate in political party activities at [the] local, state, and national level. Then write a paragraph answering the following questions: How can citizens become involved in political activities at the local, state, and national level? Why do citizens participate in political activities? Consider the following in your paragraph: private contributors; fundraising; volunteering.

15. Analyze the Function of Political Parties Write a paragraph answering the following question: What do political parties do that make them important to the political system?

16. **Evaluate the Impact** Use the advertisement below to evaluate the impact of electronic information, such as MoveOn.org's advertisement regarding the war in Iraq. Consider the following questions: What is MoveOn.org? How has MoveOn.org impacted the political process? Look at the MoveOn.org advertisement about the war in Iraq. How do advertisements like this one impact the political process?

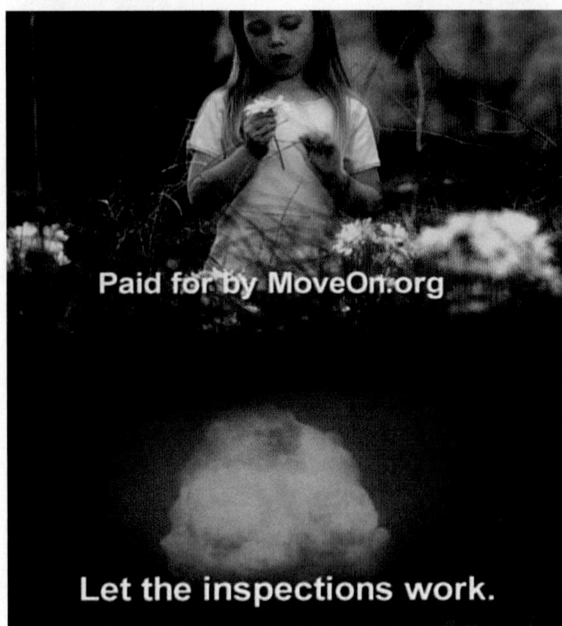

17. **Understand Population Shifts** Write a paragraph examining the Electoral College and describing how population shifts would affect it. Consider the following questions: How is the number of electoral votes determined for each state? What happens when the population in a state increases or decreases? How does this affect the electoral college system?

18. **Defend a Point of View and Analyze the Electoral College** Write a paragraph analyzing the Electoral College system and its defects. Then choose one of the following plans: the district plan, the proportional plan, direct popular election, and the national popular vote plan. Defend your chosen plan as the best system to elect a president.

19. **Write About the Essential Question Write an essay on the Essential Question: Who gets elected?** Use evidence from your study of this Topic to support your answer.

Go online to PearsonRealize.com and use the texts, quizzes, interactivities, Interactive Reading Notepads, Flipped Videos, and other resources from this Topic to prepare for the Topic Test.

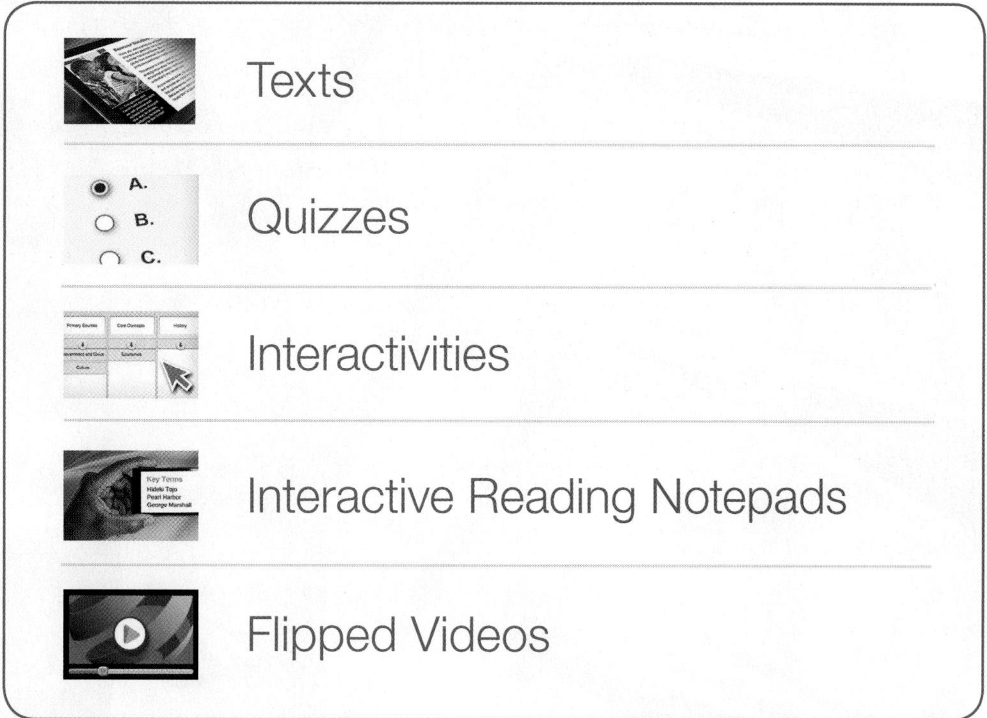

While online you can also check the progress you've made learning the topic and course content by viewing your grades, test scores, and assignment status.

[ESSENTIAL QUESTION] What is the proper role of government in the economy?

12 Government and the Economy

>> Newly printed $100 bills at the Bureau of Engraving and Printing

Topic 12 Government and the Economy

Enduring Understandings

- The main types of economic systems are differentiated by the role played by government in the economy. Capitalism is based on freedom of choice and minimal government involvement, socialism features greater involvement, and communism is marked by strict government control.
- The U.S. government uses fiscal and monetary policies to influence the economy at the local, State, and national levels.
- The power to tax has a major impact on the U.S. economy.
- The federal budget is a major political statement of U.S. public policies.
- The executive and legislative branches both work to set international trade and fiscal policies.

PEARSON realize™ NBC LEARN

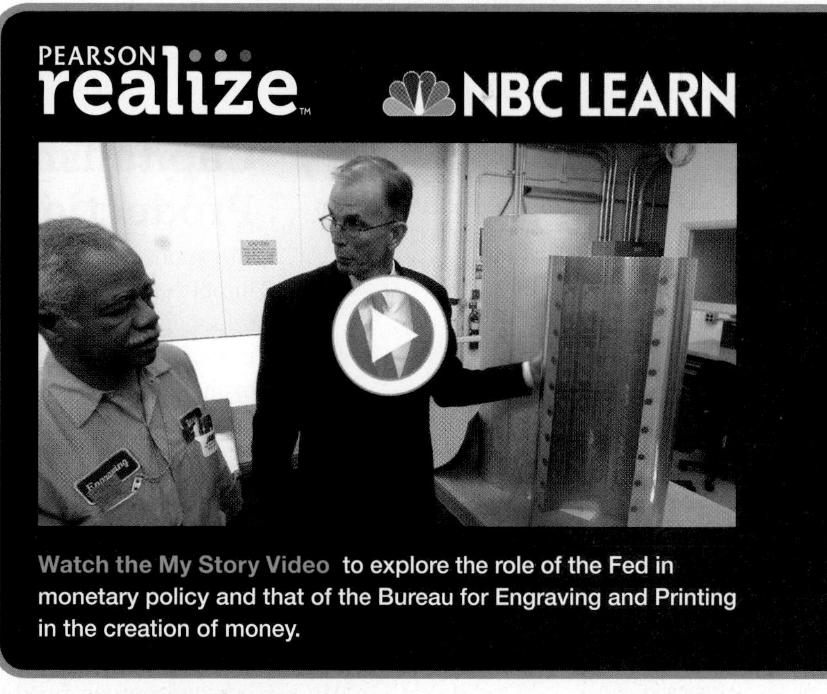

Watch the My Story Video to explore the role of the Fed in monetary policy and that of the Bureau for Engraving and Printing in the creation of money.

Access your digital lessons including:
Topic Inquiry • Interactive Reading Notepad • Interactivities • Assessments

>> Freedom of choice and competition mean that a vast variety of goods are available in a capitalist economy. Here, shoppers peruse wares at historic Charleston City Market in South Carolina.

Interactive Flipped Video

12.1 You have confronted these questions several times already: What functions should a government undertake? What should it have the power to do? What should it not be allowed to do? These questions are particularly significant in the realm of economic affairs.

>> Objectives

Identify the factors of production.

Understand the role played by the National Government in both the public and private sectors of the U.S. free enterprise system.

Understand the relationship between U.S. government policies and the economy in a mixed economy.

Describe the four fundamental factors in a free enterprise system and understand how the Federal Government fosters competition and entrepreneurship, as well as how government regulation can serve as a restriction to private enterprise.

>> Key Terms

capitalism
factors of production
capital
entrepreneur
free enterprise system
free market
monopoly
Great Leap Forward
law of supply and demand
laissez-faire theory
Karl Marx
socialism
communism
collectivization
privatization
command economies
Adam Smith
Hugo Chávez
Josef Stalin
Mikhail Gorbachev
Fidel Castro
Mao Zedong
Deng Xiaoping

Types of Economic Systems

Capitalism and the Factors of Production

Questions of politics and economics are inseparable. The most important economic questions faced by a nation are also political questions. For example: Who should decide what goods will be produced? How should goods and services be distributed and exchanged? What types of income or property ought to be taxed? What social services should a government provide?

Capitalism provides one response to these questions. **Capitalism** is an economic system in which individuals are free to own the means of production and maximize profits. Many aspects of capitalism will be familiar to you because the United States and most other nations in the world today have adopted this economic system.

Certain resources are necessary to any nation's economy, no matter what economic system is in place. Economists call these basic resources, used to make all goods and services, the **factors of production.**

Land Land, which in economic terms includes all natural resources, is an important factor of production. Land has a variety of economic uses, such as agriculture, mining, and forestry. Along with farms and other property, economists categorize the water in rivers and lakes and the coal, iron, and petroleum found beneath the ground as part of the land itself.

Capital A second factor of production is **capital**—all the human-made resources that are used to produce goods and services. Physical capital (also called "capital goods") includes the buildings, machines, computers, and other materials workers need to turn land and another factor, labor, into goods and services. Note that capital is a product of the economy that is then put back into the economy.

Labor Yet another factor of production is a human resource—labor. Men and women who work in mines, factories, offices, hospitals, and other places all provide labor that is an essential part of a nation's economy. In a capitalist, or free market, economy, individuals "own" their labor and can sell it to any employer. Human capital includes the knowledge and skills that workers gain from their work experiences—an investment in themselves.

One who owns capital and puts it to productive use is called a *capitalist*. That term is applied to people who own large businesses or factories as well as investors and the owners of small businesses. The American economy is called *capitalistic* because its growth depends very largely on the energy and drive of thousands of individual capitalists, not the government.

Entrepreneurs To actually produce goods and services, someone must bring together and organize the factors of production. An **entrepreneur**—literally, an "enterpriser"—is an individual with the drive and ambition to combine land, labor, and capital resources to produce goods or offer services, and is willing to risk losses and failure. Entrepreneurs start businesses and make them grow, creating jobs and goods and services that contribute to a high standard of living.

? DISTINGUISH Are all capitalists entrepreneurs? Explain.

The American Free Enterprise System

Capitalism is often referred to as a **free enterprise system,** which is an economic system characterized by private ownership of capital and by investments that are determined by private decision, not by public authorities. This system needs a **free market,** a

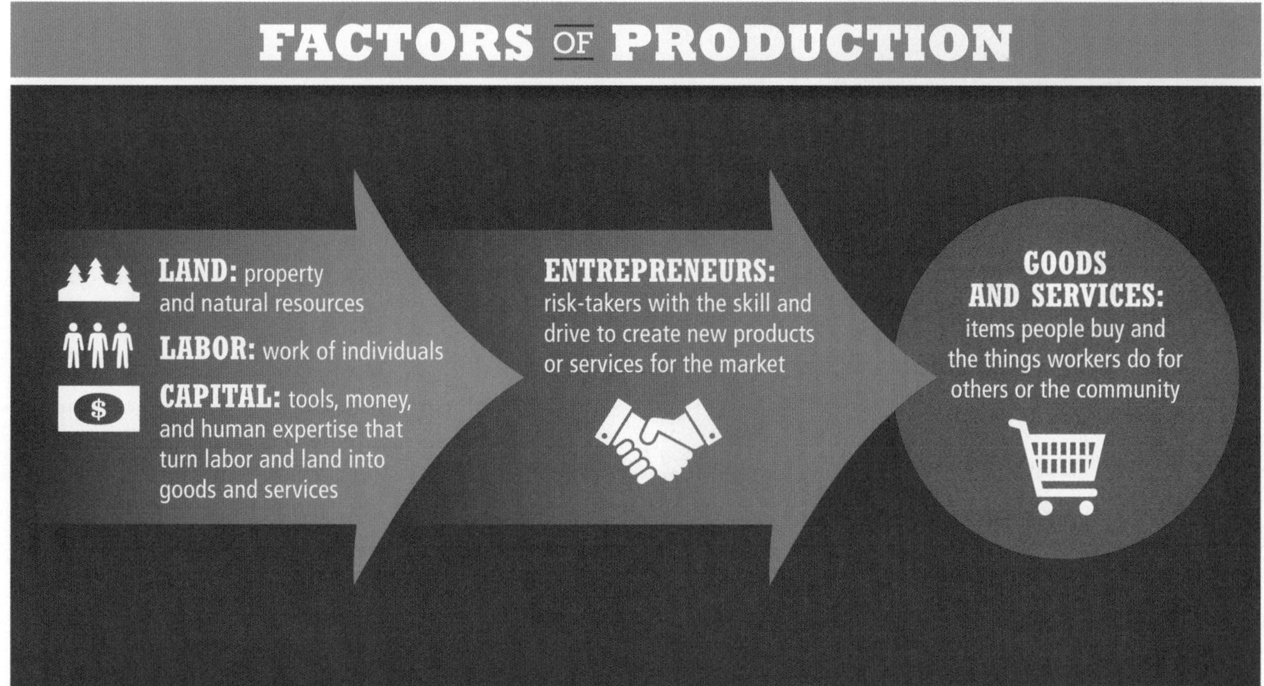

FACTORS OF PRODUCTION
LAND: property and natural resources
LABOR: work of individuals
CAPITAL: tools, money, and human expertise that turn labor and land into goods and services
ENTREPRENEURS: risk-takers with the skill and drive to create new products or services for the market
GOODS AND SERVICES: items people buy and the things workers do for others or the community

>> Land, labor, and capital are the building blocks of the economy known as the factors of production. **Analyze Information** What role do entrepreneurs play in a capitalist economy?

market in which buyers and sellers are free to buy and sell as they wish. A free market is most likely to exist in a democratic nation, such as the United States, where security and the rule of law are protected by the government.

A free enterprise system lets consumers, entrepreneurs, and workers enjoy freedom of choice. Consumers can choose from a variety of products and services. Entrepreneurs can switch from one business to another. Workers can quit their jobs and seek new ones, and they can choose to organize labor unions as a way to bargain for better working conditions or benefits.

A capitalistic system—a free enterprise system—is based on four fundamental factors: private ownership, individual initiative, profit, and competition.

Private Ownership In a capitalistic system, private individuals and companies own most of the factors of production—the basic resources used to produce goods and services. They decide how this productive property will be used—for example, to build a business or invest in technology. What the property produces is theirs, as well. The owners of productive property are sometimes individuals, but more often they are groups of people who share ownership of a company.

>> A small business owner cuts the ribbon at the grand opening of her bakery. The 23 million small businesses in the United States account for 54 percent of national sales and 55 percent of jobs.

In a free enterprise system, individuals own the right to their own labor. They sell that labor by taking a job, and the pay they receive represents the price paid for their work. In other economic systems, workers may have little choice as to the kinds of work they will do and little opportunity to change jobs or pay.

The protection of the rights of private ownership is also important, particularly in the United States. The 5th and 14th amendments declare that no person may be deprived "of life, liberty, or property, without due process of law." The 5th Amendment also says that "just compensation" must be paid to owners when their private property is taken for some public use.

Individual Initiative In our economy, entrepreneurs are an essential factor in the production of goods and services. Under a free enterprise system, all individuals are free to start and run their own businesses (their own enterprises). They are also free to dissolve those businesses. Importantly, the atmosphere of a free market, as well as a free society that encourages the exchange of ideas, can and often does lead to innovation and scientific and technological discoveries. All these conditions promote growth in the economy and often improve the quality of everyday life.

That is not necessarily true in other economic systems. In some countries, government planners decide what will be produced and how it will be made. There, centralized decision making, not individual initiative, controls the production and distribution of goods and services.

The Profit Motive Just as individuals are free to choose how they will spend or invest their capital in a free enterprise system, they are also entitled to benefit from whatever their investment or enterprise earns or gains in value. The "profit motive" is the desire to gain from business dealings. It drives entrepreneurs to create goods and services people will want to buy, and is a major reason why entrepreneurs are willing to take risks.

The Role of Competition The freedom to enter or start a new business at any time leads to competition. Competition is a situation in which a number of companies offer similar products or services. They must compete against one another for customers. In a free enterprise system, competition often helps to hold down prices and keep quality high. This is usually the case because customers are likely to buy from the company with the best product at the lowest price. Competition promotes efficiency; the producer has the incentive (more sales) to keep costs low.

Supply and Demand

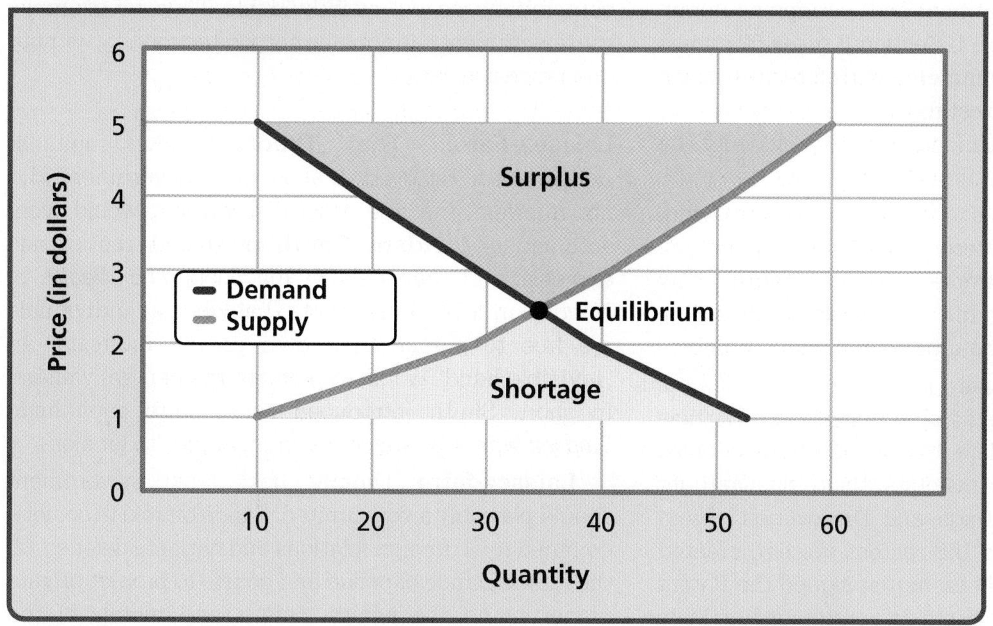

>> A surplus occurs when supply is high and demand is low. Equilibrium occurs when supply and demand are in balance. **Analyze Graphs** What conditions are necessary for a shortage to occur?

Under these competitive conditions, the **law of supply and demand** determines the market price for goods or services. Supply is the quantity of goods or services available for sale at a range of prices. As the price increases, more of a product will be offered for sale. Demand is buyers' desire and ability to purchase a good or service.

As the price falls, more of a product will be demanded by buyers. If supply increases and demand remains the same, prices will fall. If demand decreases and supply stays the same, prices will also fall. On the other hand, if demand increases and supply remains the same, prices will rise.

Monopolies and Trusts Competition does not always work smoothly. Sometimes a single business becomes so successful that all its rivals go out of business. A firm that is the only source of a product or service is called a **monopoly.** Monopolies can be very powerful in the marketplace.

Practically speaking, they can charge as much as they want for a product. Since there is no other supplier of that good or service, the consumer must pay the monopoly's price or do without.

In the late nineteenth century, political leaders in the United States gradually became convinced that certain monopolies were stifling competition and interfering with the free market. They were especially concerned about a type of monopoly called a *trust.* A trust exists when several corporations in the same line of business work together to eliminate competition from the market and regulate prices. By the latter part of the nineteenth century, trusts had gained tight-fisted control over the markets for petroleum, steel, coal, beef, sugar, and other commodities.

Constitutional Protections and Government Regulation In response, Congress acted under its commerce power to pass the Sherman Anti-Trust Act in 1890, which remains the basic law to curb monopolies—and thus, foster entrepreneurship—today. The Sherman Anti-Trust Act prohibits "every contract, combination in the form of a trust or otherwise, or conspiracy in restraint of trade or commerce among the several States, or with foreign nations."

Again acting under its commerce power, Congress established the Anti-Trust Division in the Department of Justice in 1933, to further promote entrepreneurship and foster competition. The Anti-Trust Division monitors business activities to determine whether competition within an industry is threatened. It can, for example, stop the sale or merger of a company if that move threatens competition in a particular market. On rare occasions, the Justice Department has acted to break up a monopoly to restore competition.

The Constitution offers several other protections that foster both competition and entrepreneurship. Thus, for example, Article I, Section 8 gives Congress the power to regulate commerce with foreign nations and among the States, to establish bankruptcy laws, to regulate the value of U.S. money, and to provide for the punishment of counterfeiting.

All of these protections together create a framework within which the free enterprise system can function. This means that entrepreneurs can start new businesses and compete in the marketplace knowing, for example, that there is a uniform national currency.

Another constitutional protection that fosters competition and entrepreneurship is also found in Article I, Section 8 (Clause 8). Here, the Constitution specifies that Congress can grant inventors "the exclusive Right to their respective Writings and Discoveries." From these words evolved the U.S. patent system, created in 1790 when President Washington signed the Patent Act. Since that time, inventors and entrepreneurs have invested money and effort on innovations, secure in the knowledge that others cannot copy their ideas for a given period of time—today, generally twenty years.

Finally, the 5th and 14th amendments forbid both the Federal Government and the States (and their local governments) from acting in any unfair or arbitrary way. These amendments apply to businesses and corporations, as well as individuals. Thus, for example, the government cannot take corporate property without due process of law.

>> This engraving shows economist Adam Smith, who believed that government regulations on commerce are ill-founded and counterproductive.

Laissez-Faire: The Theory Early capitalist philosophers believed that if only government did not interfere, the free enterprise system would work automatically. **Adam Smith** presented the classic expression of that view in his book, *The Wealth of Nations,* in 1776. Smith wrote that when all individuals are free to pursue their own private interests, an "invisible hand" works to promote the general welfare. In short, Smith introduced laissez-faire capitalism. *Laissez-faire* is a French idiom meaning "to let alone."

Laissez-faire theory holds that government should play only a very limited, hands off role in society, confined to: (1) foreign relations and national defense, (2) the maintenance of police and courts to protect private property and the health, safety, and morals of the people, and (3) those few other functions that cannot be performed by private enterprise at a profit. The proper role of government in economic affairs should be restricted to functions intended to promote and protect the free play of competition and the operation of the laws of supply and demand.

True laissez-faire capitalism has never in fact operated in this country, yet it has a profound effect on the structure of the nation's economic system, which can be described as laissez-faire capitalism with limited government involvement.

? ANALYZE INFORMATION Choose one of the four factors of a free enterprise system and explain why it is essential to the success of the system.

What Is a Mixed Economy?

Although the American economic system is essentially private in character, government has always played a part in it. Economists usually describe an economy in which private enterprise and governmental participation coexist as a mixed economy.

Government Regulations and the Economy Government at every level regulates the various features of American economic life. At the national level, the government prohibits trusts, protects the environment, and ensures the quality of the food we eat, among its many other functions.

At the State level, examples of economic regulations are found in the insurance industry and in State-chartered financial institutions. Locally, regulations

GOVERNMENT REGULATION AND PRIVATE ENTERPRISE

AREA OF REGULATION	ADVERTISING AND PRODUCT LABELING	EMPLOYMENT AND LABOR	ENVIRONMENT	PRIVACY	SAFETY AND HEALTH
HANDLED BY	Federal Trade Commission	• Labor Department • Occupational Safety and Health Administration, and others	Environmental Protection Agency	Federal Trade Commission	• Consumer Product Safety Commission • Food and Drug Administration
REGULATORY FOCUSES	Advertisements and labels must: • be truthful, not misleading • make only provable claims • be fair to competitors, customers	Ensure: • minimum wages, benefits, equal opportunity • workplace safety • citizenship or work visas for all workers	Regulate: • hazardous waste • emissions • pollution	Protect sensitive information of: • employees • customers • children	Establish standards for: • product safety • food purity • drug, cosmetic safety

>> Federal regulations can affect many areas of a business. **Analyze Information** Which government agency would a company that produces gasoline interact with regularly?

impacting the economy include those controlling rents, zoning, and the sale of fireworks, to name just a few.

Opponents of government regulation argue that it restricts free enterprise. For example, the high costs of obtaining licenses, keeping extensive amounts of paperwork updated, and putting products through rigorous safety testing are all viewed as discouraging for entrepreneurs. Opponents also say that costly regulations decrease profits to the point that people are not willing to invest in starting new businesses—and that regulatory costs also drive existing companies out of business or raise prices for consumers. Those supporting government regulations, on the other hand, cite the generally accepted roles of government in areas such as ensuring the safety of citizens, protecting resources, and keeping competition healthy. Supporters believe that regulations are necessary to achieve these goals.

Government Involvement in the Economy Government also promotes some aspects of American economic life. It constructs roads and highways, provides such services as public health programs, the census, and weather reports, and operates Social Security and other insurance programs. It also offers a number of subsidies and various loan programs to help entrepreneurs and businesses prosper.

Federal, State, and local governments conduct some enterprises that might well be operated privately—for example, public education, the postal system, and municipal water and power systems. It has also assumed some functions that have proved unprofitable to private enterprise—for example, many local transit systems and waste disposal and recycling projects. These sorts of public efforts are sometimes called "ash-can socialism."

Mixed Economies Around the World In Europe and in most former communist countries, the concept of a mixed economy is slightly different than in the United States because the government is involved more extensively in social and economic matters. In the United Kingdom, for example, the government provides free medical care to all. The government of the People's Republic of China owns steel mills and factories. Germany's federal government requires large companies to give workers representation on managing boards. France once banned most companies from asking employees to work more than 35 hours per week. In each of these mixed economies, government intervention coexists with independent companies and market forces.

? GENERATE EXPLANATIONS Why is regulation sometimes viewed as intrusive? Write an argument against government regulation, including examples of how it might interrupt the free enterprise system.

Socialism, Communism, and Karl Marx

In the United States all people are entitled to equal protection under the law. Political equality, of course, is not the same as economic equality. The capitalist system of the United States enables some to achieve greater financial rewards than others. However, other economic systems—socialism and communism—do seek to distribute wealth more evenly across the society.

Karl Marx The father of modern socialism and communism, **Karl Marx** (1818–1883) was the most significant critic of capitalism as it developed during the early Industrial Revolution. He envisioned a society where social classes would vanish and the people would own all property in common. Exploitation of labor and unemployment would disappear.

>> German philosopher and political economist Karl Marx called capitalism the "dictatorship of the proletariat" and believed it would eventually self-destruct and be replaced by communism.

Abundant goods would be available to all according to their needs, not necessarily how much work they contributed. Marx also expected that workers in different countries—for example, France and Germany—would share a bond far stronger than national loyalties. Thus, he theorized that communism would also end nationalism, a major cause of European wars.

Branching Out from Marxism Many European workers and thinkers of the middle and late nineteenth century accepted Marx's criticism of capitalism. His followers were deeply divided, however, by the question of how best to achieve a more equitable economy. Some argued that economic equality could be attained by peaceful, democratic means. Today, the terms **socialism** and *socialist* are usually used to identify those evolutionary ideals and the people who support them. Others argued that a fair society could come only out of a violent revolution, born out of class struggle. Over time, those who took that more strictly Marxist view came to be called communists, the advocates of **communism**.

Socialism Today Socialist governments around the world are in some ways similar to one another, but in other respects a good bit different. In most, the government places certain key industries under its control—particularly, utilities, transportation, and steel production. Many smaller companies remain in private hands, however.

These governments also aim to guarantee the public welfare by providing for the equal distribution of such necessities and services as retirement pensions, universal healthcare, free university education, and housing. Any country that provides extensive social services at little or no direct cost to consumers is a welfare state. Because social welfare services are quite expensive, taxes in socialist countries tend to be relatively high compared to capitalist countries.

The High Price Tag of Socialism At various times in recent history, elected socialist parties have controlled governments and instituted socialist programs through democratic means. Gradually, however, most socialist parties in Europe have given up such traditional goals as nationalizing industries. And many socialist parties in Britain, France, and Germany have lost power or have abandoned some of their socialist objectives that have become too expensive and unpopular to maintain.

Marxist Economies

SOCIALISM	COMMUNISM
Goal: Change capitalism through peaceful means to bring about economic equality	**Goal:** Destroy capitalism through revolution to bring about economic equality
Some central planning	Centrally planned economy
Most property privately owned	All land and housing state owned
Large industries nationalized	No privately owned businesses
High taxes to fund healthcare, child care, education	State-provided healthcare, child care, education
Free elections	Controlled elections
Strong unions and worker protections	State-controlled unions

>> The writings of Karl Marx inspired two competing movements. **Analyze Charts** How well do socialism and communism respect the rights of people as defined in a free market economy?

Socialism in Developing Countries Socialism has won a large following in developing countries in Africa and more recently in Latin America. One reason for its appeal in these nations is that large existing industries have often been owned by foreign companies. By nationalizing a foreign-owned industry and placing local people in charge, a political leader can win broad public support. He or she can also gain power by promising to provide socialist-style "cradle-to-grave" services and to redistribute land from large land owners to the poor.

After he came to power in 1999, for example, Venezuelan President **Hugo Chávez** and his nationalist-socialist party, Movement for the Fifth Republic (MVR), nationalized the oil industry, and used the profits to fund free education, healthcare, and low-cost housing. Chávez also nationalized the telecommunications and electricity industries. These moves brought Chávez enormous support, especially among the urban poor, and helped him retain power, despite broad resistance to many of his socialist, or even communist, goals.

? INTERPRET Why did Karl Marx believe that communism would end nationalism?

Communism

Marx believed that the revolution against capitalism would come first in industrialized countries with large working-class populations—in particular, France, Germany, Great Britain, and then the United States. Ironically, the revolution occurred first in Russia, then a backward, mainly agricultural nation, in 1917. A few years later, and as several neighboring nations were pulled under its control, the Soviet Union was born. Its new leader, **Josef Stalin**, tightened that control and built a totalitarian dictatorship.

Stalin's Communism Stalin demanded **collectivization** of agriculture and a heightened production of chemicals, petroleum, and steel. He also emphasized heavy industry, and the Soviet Union achieved rapid, if uneven, industrialization. Unfortunately, those advances came at great a cost in the form of scarce consumer goods, housing, and urban services.

The Soviet Union did provide its citizens with free education, medical care, and even youth summer camps. It was far from a classless society, however. An elite class owed its privileged status to the Communist Party. In addition, many free government services were either unavailable or of poor quality.

The Decline of Communism By the late 1980s, Soviet leader **Mikhail Gorbachev** introduced a policy of *glasnost* (openness) and *perestroika* (restructuring), and the Soviet Union began to dismantle the political and economic structures of communism. In 1991, the Soviet Union dissolved into 15 independent countries. The largest and most populous of them was Russia.

Many state-owned companies in Russia were privatized. **Privatization** is the process of returning nationalized enterprises to private ownership. Today, Russia is a country with some features of free enterprise, but also extensive state intervention in the economy.

In fact, very few communist economies exist today. Most communist nations, like China and Russia, have incorporated elements of free enterprise into their economic systems.

Cuba, led by **Fidel Castro** from 1959 to 2008, developed a communist economy heavily dependent on Soviet economic aid during the Cold War. As a result, the fall of the Soviet Union caused an economic crisis in Cuba. Despite modest reforms, most Cubans still live and work within the state-controlled economy.

? IDENTIFY CAUSE AND EFFECT What factors account for the general failure of communism?

The Special Case of China

Mao Zedong, the founder of the People's Republic of China, was a Marxist. However, he believed the peasantry, not industrial workers, were the key to a successful communist revolution in agricultural China.

After Mao took control of the country in 1949, China developed its own version of a planned economy. Despite its huge population, the country lacked skilled workers. The government improved technical and scientific education and then assigned workers to jobs in the state sector. The government regulated the labor market, giving people little choice about where and for whom they worked.

The Great Leap Forward The **Great Leap Forward** of 1958 to 1960 was a drastic attempt to modernize China quickly. All elements of free enterprise were eliminated. Collective farms were brought together into a larger unit, the commune. Communes grew into self-sufficient bodies run by Communist Party officials.

Communist Party officials oversaw farms, industries, and government in a region, and they also managed social policy. Workers received the same rewards no matter how much they produced, so there were few incentives to work hard. The Great Leap Forward was a disastrous failure and it was followed by a severe famine.

Dissolving the Soviet Union

>> A number of countries were formed when the Soviet Union was dissolved. **Analyze Maps** What is one major reason that Russia was originally able to seize control of these areas?

U.S. Free Enterprise System and Other Economic Systems

CAPITALISM/FREE ENTERPRISE	SOCIALISM	COMMUNISM
Definition: Individuals, not government, are in charge of production and can profit from their labor. **Laissez-Faire** very limited government role **Mixed Economy** some government regulation	**Definition:** The state makes many economic decisions. Some central planning	**Definition:** The state makes all economic decisions. Centrally planned economy
Characteristics: • individual initiative essential in the production of goods and services • profit driven • competition holds down prices and keeps quality high • private ownership • supply and demand determine price	**Characteristics:** • state owns large industries • state provides social services and collects high taxes	**Characteristics:** • five-year plans by state establish economic goals • state owns and controls all aspects of economy

>> The role of the government varies in different types of economic systems. **Analyze Charts** How would capitalist, socialist, and communist governments interact with businesses?

Deng Xiaoping and China Today A new leader, **Deng Xiaoping**, came to power in 1977 and made great changes in the economy. Deng's program of the "Four Modernizations" aimed at improving agriculture, industry, science and technology, and defense. He began to move China toward a market economy and opened the country to foreign investment.

Today, China's economic system is a maze of different levels of government bodies and economic units. Although the Communist Party remains in power and directs economic growth, the state-owned sector has shrunk. The government encourages private enterprise and investment and China has enjoyed many years of strong economic growth.

COMPARE POINTS OF VIEW How are Stalin's and Mao's approaches to communism alike and different?

Comparing the Free Enterprise System with Other Economic Systems

Free market and **command economies**, in which government bureaucrats plan and direct most economic activity, differ in a number of significant ways. The most obvious is the level of government involvement in the economy. This main difference leads to other, less obvious distinctions.

Advantages of the Free Enterprise System Critics argue that large bureaucracies in socialist countries sometimes complicate decision making and have a depressing effect on individual initiative. As a result, these systems, unlike free enterprise models such as that of the United States, are slow to take advantage of new technologies.

Too many unpredictable events are involved, and too many clashing interests are at stake. They argue that the invisible hand of the free market economy works more efficiently than the ever-present hand of central planning.

Command economies are also criticized because they deprive people of basic freedoms, such as whether to start a new business or how to use the bulk of their income. Since workers get to keep only a part of their earnings after taxes, they have little incentive to work harder and earn more and no incentive to innovate or create new products. Why work hard when your basic needs will be taken care of anyway? In a free enterprise system, on the other hand, individual initiative is not only rewarded, it actually underpins the entire economic system.

Comparison with Command Economies Theorists who defend the ideas behind socialism and

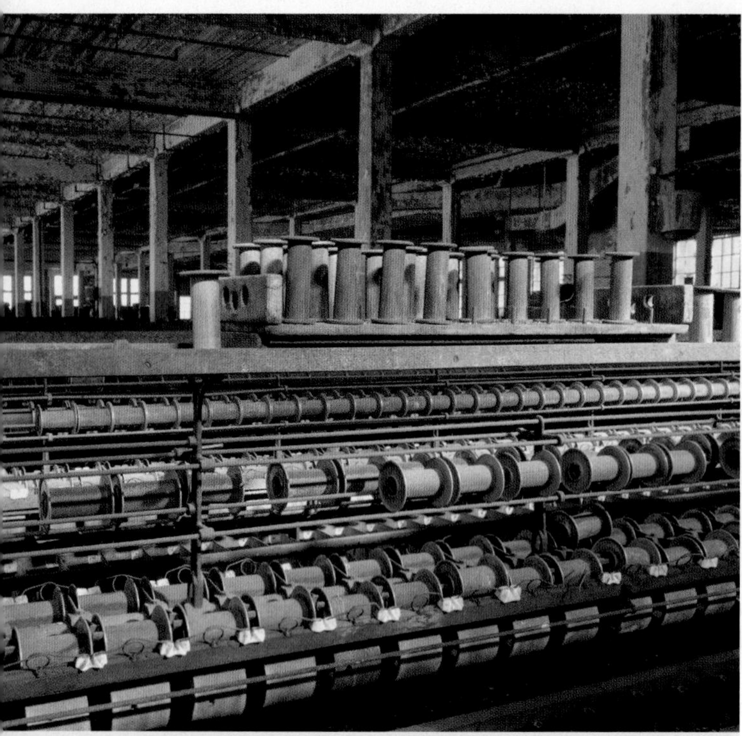

>> Although capitalism is not perfect, as evidenced by this abandoned textile mill, many countries have incorporated elements of the free enterprise system into their economies.

Interactive Gallery

communism—in their purest forms—reply that these systems aim to supply everyone with such basic needs as medical care, housing, and education. They point to the inequalities of wealth and power that exist under capitalism. In their view, socialism makes political democracy work more smoothly, in theory, by meshing it with economic democracy.

Defenders of socialism and communism also say that in these systems, workers theoretically have more say in the running of a company. Rather than a company's management abruptly deciding to close an unprofitable factory, for example, even though such a decision can throw thousands out of work and disrupt an entire community, workers on the company's board would help decide what is best for the entire work force and community.

Despite these criticisms, perhaps the best evaluation of free enterprise versus command economies can be found in this fact: Both China and Russia, once strictly communist, are gradually incorporating elements of the free enterprise system into their economies. So, too, are countries in Asia, Africa, and Eastern Europe, such as Mongolia, Albania, and the Czech Republic.

? EVALUATE ARGUMENTS Using China during Mao Zedong's reign as an example, how could you debunk the argument that command economies give people more control over their daily lives than a free enterprise system allows?

ASSESSMENT

1. **Identify Central Ideas** Explain how a country with little land and few natural resources could make up for such deficits—without depending on other countries—and have a healthy economy.
2. **Identify Cause and Effect** What impact does a monopoly have on consumers?
3. **Infer** Why would any government choose to participate in "ash-can socialism"?
4. **Contrast** How does government participation in the economy differ between socialist and communist countries?
5. **Identify** In a mixed economy, where can bureaucracies be found?

12.2

For the first 120 years or so of its existence, the Federal Government played only a very limited role in the economy—whether at the local, State, or national level—and in the economic well-being of the American people. However, beginning in the early twentieth century, there were repeated economic panics and recessions. These panics and recessions culminated in the Great Depression of the 1930s, when the amount of governmental involvement began to change.

>> Crowds gather at New York City's American Union Bank during a 1931 run on the bank. The Great Depression led to New Deal legislation that greatly increased the government's role in banking.

Interactive Flipped Video

Fiscal and Monetary Policy

>> **Objectives**

Explain the major responsibilities of the Federal Government for domestic economic policy.

Describe the overall goals of the Federal Government's actions in the economy.

Explain how government fiscal policy influences the economy at the national level.

Explain how government monetary policy influences the economy at the national level.

>> **Key Terms**

panic
gross domestic product
inflation
deflation
recession
fiscal policy
monetary policy
open market operations
reserve requirement
discount rate
interest
Bill Clinton
George H.W. Bush
John Maynard Keynes
George W. Bush
Barack Obama

The Federal Government and the Domestic Economy

The American free enterprise system fosters competition and entrepreneurship. The Federal Government tries to support this system by attempting to ensure fairness in the market place, and, with it, the health and well-being of both consumers and workers. Because the economy functions at three levels in the United States—national, State, and local—that means that the Federal Government's fiscal, monetary, and regulatory policies necessarily influence the economy at not only the national level, but at the State and local levels, as well.

In addition to fostering competition and entrepreneurship, both the executive and legislative branches help set fiscal and monetary policy. To this end, a number of independent agencies within the executive branch of the government have been created. Many of them have an important role in the regulation of economic activities within the United States. Among the most important of them are the Federal Reserve System, the Securities and Exchange Commission (SEC), and such organizations as the Occupational Safety & Health Administration (OSHA) in the Department of Labor. Despite the prominence of some of these agencies, it is important to note that the government must continually balance the call for regulation with the equally critical demand for limited government involvement in the nation's economic life.

The Federal Reserve System Known as "the Fed," the Federal Reserve System is one of the most important tools the Federal Government uses to attempt to regulate the nation's economy. The Fed was established by Congress in 1913 as the central banking system for the United States. It is part of the executive branch and consists of a Board of Governors appointed by the President (one of whom is appointed to act as the chairperson), 12 regional banks, and many other member banks. The main responsibility of the Fed is to use the tools of monetary policy to promote price stability, full employment, economic growth, and other national economic goals.

Mainly, this means adjusting the federal funds rate—an interest rate at which banks lend money to other banks on a daily basis. The Fed does this to either contract or expand the amount of money in the economy in response to changes in inflation or unemployment. Raising interest rates makes money more expensive to borrow, and so, in theory, contracts the economy.

Lowering interest rates makes money less expensive to borrow, and so tends to expand the economy. The rate adjustments that the Fed makes can influence other lending rates, foreign exchange rates, and the levels of money and credit available in the economy, as well as employment and prices.

A Key Regulatory Agency The Securities and Exchange Commission (SEC) is a federal regulatory agency in the executive branch. It consists of five commissioners appointed by the President, who also selects the SEC's chairperson from among those five commissioners. Congress created the SEC in 1934 in the aftermath of the stock market crash that contributed to the Great Depression.

The commission's central responsibility is to oversee the nation's stock markets and ensure that corporations do not engage in such abuses as insider trading, which is the practice of buying or selling stock based on company information not known to other investors. The SEC also ensures that publicly traded companies truthfully disclose their finances. It brings court actions against those who violate securities laws—for example, through insider trading, fraudulent accounting practices, or providing false information to investors.

The Role of the Department of Labor The Federal Government provides protections for the basic rights of workers and oversees issues of fairness and safety

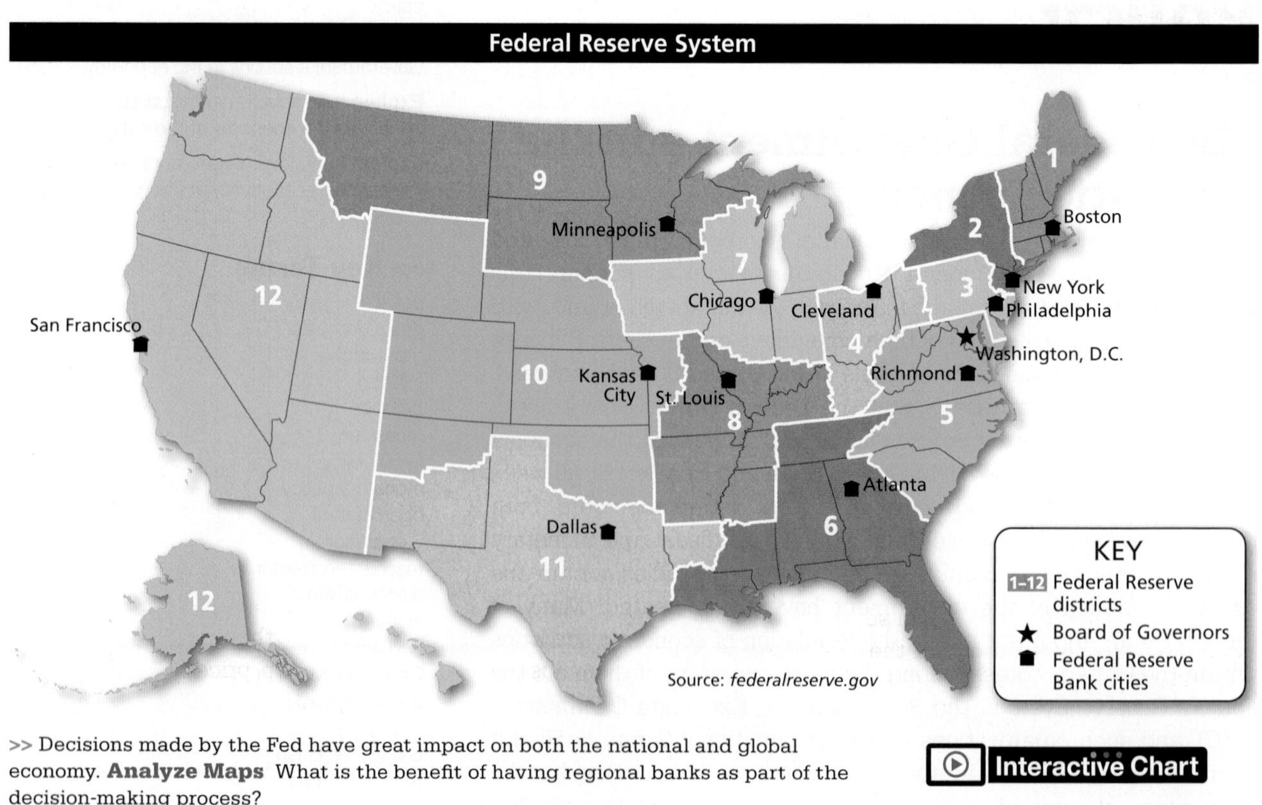

>> Decisions made by the Fed have great impact on both the national and global economy. **Analyze Maps** What is the benefit of having regional banks as part of the decision-making process?

Interactive Chart

in the workplace. Much of this is accomplished by the Department of Labor, part of the executive branch of the government.

To meet these aims, the department works through its various agencies. For example, since the Occupational Safety & Health Administration (OSHA) was established in 1971, its inspectors have worked with employers and employees to decrease deaths in the workplace. The Employment Standards Administration (ESA) monitors fairness in contracts, benefits, and wages. The Bureau of Labor Statistics tracks major economic statistics, such as the unemployment rate and the Consumer Price Index (CPI). These data are used to evaluate the health of the nation's economy.

These various regulatory agencies have both supporters and detractors. Some feel that the rules and regulations they establish are important to the protection of American workers. Others believe that they are overly burdensome to business owners and that their influence and reach should be scaled back to better allow the free enterprise system to operate.

EXPLAIN What is the Security and Exchange Commission's main role?

>> James Carville was the lead strategist for Bill Clinton's 1992 presidential campaign. Carville's strategy recognized that voters were most concerned with the economy in that election year.

Key Goals for the Economy

"It's the economy, stupid." That slogan has become a watchword in electoral politics. It first appeared during the presidential campaign of 1992, on a sign that hung on the wall of political advisor James Carville's office in **Bill Clinton's** campaign headquarters. Mr. Clinton, the Democratic Party's nominee, faced a daunting challenge in that election: How could he possibly convince the voters that he, not incumbent **George H.W. Bush**, should sit in the White House?

Mr. Bush, the 41st President of the United States, brought a substantial record to the contest—a record highlighted by the end, at long last, of the cold war and a stunning victory in the Persian Gulf War. Mr. Clinton, and Carville and Paul Begala, his chief campaign advisor, were convinced that the key to success in November lay in the domestic, not the foreign policy realm. The nation's economy was in shambles and, to their minds, the incumbent President was vulnerable on that score, and events proved them right.

The successful management of the economy is vital not only to a President's political survival. It has a very direct and immediate effect on the well-being of every man, woman, and child in this country. We will now explore the Federal Government's key economic goals and the principal mechanisms with which it attempts to achieve those ends.

Overall Economic Goals The American economy is enormously complex. The nation's **gross domestic product** (GDP)—the total value of all final goods and services produced in the country each year—now exceeds $15 trillion. While private corporations and individuals have the most substantial impact on the economy's performance, the Federal Government also plays a part. In general, it seeks to achieve three key goals in the economic realm: full employment, price stability, and economic growth.

Full Employment Full employment, as you might guess, means that there are enough jobs available to employ all those who are able and willing to work. The Bureau of Labor Statistics, in the Department of Labor, compiles employment and unemployment data. Its reports are a major indicator of the nation's economic health.

Price Stability Price stability refers to the absence of significant ups and downs in the prices of goods and services. A general increase in prices throughout the economy is called **inflation.** A general decrease in prices is known as **deflation.** The Consumer Price Index, also reported by the Bureau of Labor Statistics, tracks trends in the prices of consumer goods.

Both inflation and deflation have harmful effects on the economy. Higher prices due to inflation rob consumers of purchasing power because their dollars buy less than they once did. Deflation makes it difficult for people and businesses to borrow money because the assets they use to borrow against decline in value.

Deflation also hurts farmers and other producers, who receive less for their products. This makes it difficult for them to pay off their loans, which in turns hurts banks and investors.

Economic Growth A growing economy is one in which the GDP constantly increases. That growth helps produce a higher standard of living. When there is an absence of growth and the economy shrinks, a **recession** occurs.

? COMPARE AND CONTRAST Compare and contrast the effects of inflation and deflation on the economy.

INFLATION SLOWS
"Great news! The rate of our descent into poverty has reduced by 0.2%"

>> Inflation can affect a family's economic decisions and style of living. **Analyze Political Cartoons** What message does this cartoon convey about economic conditions?

How Fiscal Policy Influences the Economy

Fiscal policy is a major tool with which both the executive and legislative branches of the Federal Government seek to achieve broad economic goals. Fiscal policy consists of the government's powers to tax and spend to influence the economy. The President, aided by agenices such as the Council of Economic Advisors, often makes specific recommendations with regard to the economy, while the legislative branch enacts laws to put fiscal policies into action. The executive branch then carries out those laws through its various executive departments and independent agencies.

In addition to deciding how to raise money through taxation and how to spend money, policymakers in both the executive and legislative branches must consider what effects their taxing and spending decisions will have on the overall economy. Federal spending represents about 20 percent of the nation's GDP. How money is taxed and spent can have a real effect throughout the domestic economy—on private enterprise, on employment, on prices, and on growth. In fact, the effects of taxing and spending may be felt well beyond the economy.

For example, the Servicemen's Readjustment Act of 1944 (GI Bill of Rights) allowed veterans to attend college, receive training, and buy houses. This increase in government spending helped lead to the prosperity and cultural changes of the late 1940s and 1950s. In particular, the GI Bill helped change the notion that a college education was only for the elite. Instead, regular Americans began to see college as a path to upward mobility. In addition, the bill began an era of government involvement in higher education and also led to an unprecedented housing boom as veterans took advantage of government-backed loans. Some scholars believe that these changes helped create a new American middle class and also contributed to the high birth rates of the time.

As a general matter, an increase in government expenditures means heightened economic activity; spending cuts tend to dampen that activity. Tax increases take money out of people's pockets and can slow economic growth. Tax cuts can boost economic activity.

Historical Use of Fiscal Policy For the better part of 150 years, Congress and the executive branch did not make vigorous use of fiscal policy. Federal income and outgo represented just a bare fraction of GDP. As recently as 1930, that fraction amounted to just over 3 percent of GDP. The ups and downs of the economy were seen by most economists as an inevitable and healthy feature of a free enterprise system.

The Great Depression of the 1930s was a particularly severe downturn. In the midst of that crisis, British economist **John Maynard Keynes** advocated an increase in governmental spending and a decrease in taxes to help end the economic misery. Over time, Keynes's ideas gained acceptance. Now, during a downturn, policymakers in Congress and the executive branch usually seek to expand the economy with greater spending and/or lower taxes. This is precisely what happened in 2008 and 2009. At that time, Congress, pressed by President **George W. Bush** and then by President **Barack Obama**, enacted a number of economic stimulus measures. One of those measures, the 2008 Troubled Asset Relief Program (TARP), was controversial. Some questioned its effectiveness and the way it was administered, while others expressed doubts about the large levels of government spending it authorized. Supporters argued that the spending was necessary to prevent the collapse of the nation's financial sector.

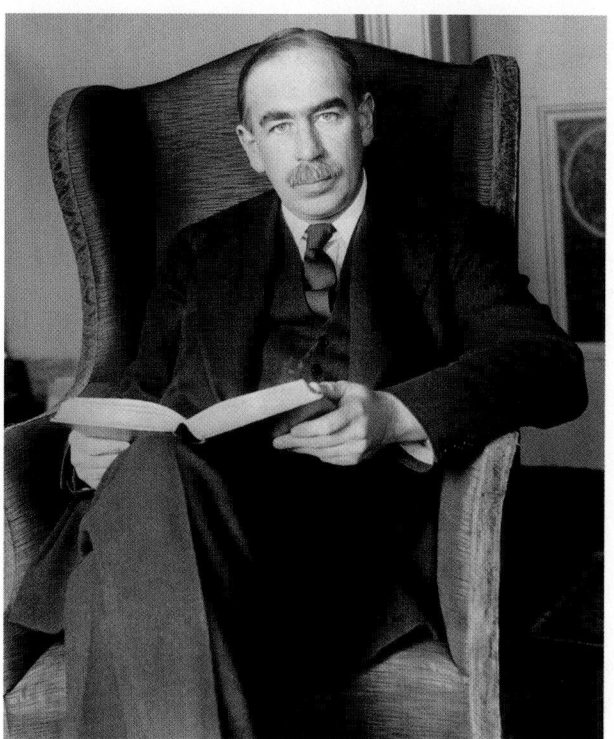

>> British economist John Maynard Keynes advocated government intervention to ease the adverse effects of the inevitable expansion and contraction of the economy.

Another Use for Fiscal Policy Fiscal policy can also be used to slow inflation. In theory, cuts in government spending and/or tax increases can tamp down inflation across the entire economy.

Fiscal policy does have its limits, however. For one thing, it takes time for policy changes—for example, an increase or reduction in expenditures—to have a measurable effect on the economy. Timing the delivery of hikes or cuts is a very tricky matter. Further, some types of tax cuts often have a relatively small effect on the overall economy. In addition, some Americans would prefer to allow the nation's economy to correct itself through the natural ebb and flow of the economic cycle, rather than through government involvement. So policymakers often resort to other means to influence economic activity.

? DRAW CONCLUSIONS Should the Federal Government have the authority to take actions that can alter the nation's economy? Why or why not?

How Monetary Policy Influences the Economy

Monetary policy is another means by which the legislative and executive branches of the Federal Government can influence the nation's economy. **Monetary policy** involves the money supply (the amount of currency in circulation) and the availability of credit in the economy.

The Federal Reserve Board (the Fed) is responsible for the regulation of the government's monetary policy. Its Board of Governors directs the work of the Federal Reserve System as an independent agency created by Congress. It was established to function as the nation's central bank.

Congress intended the Fed to impose some order on a patchwork banking system that had become increasingly prone to panics. In banking, panics occur when depositors lose confidence in banks and rush to recover their funds. If enough customers do so, a bank can be overrun and driven out of business. A panic can spread to infect other banks and, conceivably, an entire banking system. The Fed was designed to avert such a calamity. It serves as a source of emergency funding to prevent panics.

The Key Function of the Fed Again, the key function of the Fed is to regulate monetary policy. By taking steps to increase the money supply, it can theoretically provide a short-term boost to the economy, leading to economic growth and an increase in employment. In theory, the Fed can produce the opposite effect by decreasing the supply of money and consequently slowing inflationary pressures.

The Fed can alter the money supply through three major mechanisms. Its tools for that purpose are open market operations, reserve requirements, and the discount rate.

Open Market Operations When the Fed seeks to alter the money supply, it does not simply send out trucks that carry bundles of cash to or from member banks. Its operations are far more sophisticated. It operates through what are called **open market operations**—a process that involves the buying or selling of government securities, such as bonds, from and to the nation's banks. By buying these government securities back from the banks, the Fed provides money to banks, which can then make loans to individuals and to businesses. If its aim is to decrease the money supply, the Fed sells government bonds through its open market operations. As it receives money from the banks that buy those securities, money is removed from circulation. Subsequently, the banks have less money to loan or invest, and so business activity slows.

Reserve Requirements The Fed can also influence or alter the amount of money in circulation by changing the reserve requirements that all banks and similar financial institutions must meet. The **reserve requirement** is the amount of money that the Federal Reserve Board determines banks must keep "in reserve" in their vaults or on deposit with one of the 12 Federal Reserve Banks. Those funds cannot be used to make loans or for any other purpose. They remain, instead, out of circulation, available for use in the event of sudden, unexpected demand.

If the Fed seeks to lower the money supply, on the other hand, it can require that banks increase the amount they have in reserve. Or the reserve requirement can be relaxed by the Fed to increase the amount of money in circulation.

Discount Rate The third mechanism available to the Fed involves the discount rate. The **discount rate** is the rate of interest a bank must pay when it borrows money from a Federal Reserve Bank.

Interest is the cost borrowers incur and must repay in order to borrow money. If the Fed raises the discount rate, banks find it more difficult to obtain money. Banks must then charge higher interest rates to their customers; borrowing decreases and less money flows into the economy. Cutting the discount rate has the opposite effect.

Fiscal and Monetary Policies at the State and Local Levels While the use of fiscal policy is important at the national level, it is also critical at the State and local levels, as well. One approach sometimes used by the States during a recession, for example, is to spend more money than the government takes in through taxes. The idea behind this type of expansionary spending is to use government funds to help citizens who are struggling, to ease the tax burden, and to pump money into local economies in order to stimulate growth. At other times, States might take the opposite approach

Main Tools Used by the Federal Government to Influence the Economy

FISCAL POLICY	MONETARY POLICY
Taxes • Decrease taxes to heighten economic activity • Increase taxes to reduce economic activity and slow inflation **Spending** • Reduce government spending to slow inflation • Increase spending to increase employment and tax revenues	**Decrease money supply** • Sell securities • Increase reserve requirement • Raise interest rates **Increase money supply** • Purchase securities • Decrease reserve requirement • Lower interest rates

>> The Fed has a variety of tools at its disposal to influence the nation's economy.
Analyze Charts Which of these strategies might produce the quickest results?

by spending less than what is collected through taxes. This use of fiscal policy is often employed to pay off government debt.

For example, a local government might impose a hotel occupancy and restaurant consumption tax to help pay for the construction of a new sports arena. Or, a State might bump up local property tax rates in order to pay for improvements in their college and university system.

The balance between taxes and spending is always a contentious matter—particularly when trying to predict long-term benefits. Will heavy State and local government investment in, for example, sports stadiums pay off because of broader economic development? Most people support the idea of good schools, but how high should local property taxes be raised in order to reach that goal? Will people move away if taxes are too high, or will they move in because the schools are excellent? Every State wants new businesses, but how far should they lower their taxes in order to attract that business?

In the fall of 2013, Boeing Aerospace, one of the world's largest builders of aircraft, announced that it was looking for a location for a new facility. Plans for the new plant called for a massive 4.2 million-square-foot, $10 billion facility. Up for grabs were thousands of new jobs. One State after another offered tremendous tax incentives to lure the new facility.

In the end, Washington State's $9 billion in incentives was enough to keep the company in that State. Many in Washington were relieved, but others thought the legislature had gone too far. Again, fiscal policy is always controversial.

Monetary policy, on the other hand, refers to the regulation of the supply of money in an economy, springing from the manipulation of interest rates by the Federal Reserve System. One of the most serious problems with the Articles of Confederation was that each State was able to regulate its own currency—in essence, shape its own monetary policy. Because the Framers of the Constitution were adamant that the nation have a unified currency, State and local governments do not regulate monetary policy today. However, their leaders do voice their opinions regarding federal monetary policy. And why not? Even the slightest change in interest rates can have an enormous impact on the economic well-being of their governments and their citizens.

? **EXPLAIN** How can open market operations theoretically help to boost the economy?

ASSESSMENT

1. **Identify Cause and Effect** What main event prompted the Federal Government to take a stronger role in the nation's economy?
2. **Explain** What are the three key economic goals the government aims to achieve, and why are these goals critical to a healthy economy?
3. **Generate Explanations** Why might policymakers hesitate to use fiscal policy to influence the nation's economy?
4. **Connect** How can the use of fiscal and monetary policy influence the overall domestic economy?
5. **Classify** Name three agencies within the executive branch that have important roles in the regulation of American economic activities.

>> An engraver works on a model of a 2014 "America the Beautiful" quarter. The Federal Government is financed largely through revenue from various types of taxes.

Interactive Flipped Video

12.3 **This text is mostly about fiscal policy—a subject that has a tendency to make most people's eyes glaze over. It is, nonetheless, a matter of very considerable importance to everyone in the United States.**

>> Objectives

Explain how the Constitution gives Congress the power to tax and at the same time places limits on that power, as well as, how government taxation and regulation can serve as restrictions to private enterprise.

Identify the sources of revenue of the U.S. government today, including both tax and non-tax revenues.

>> Key Terms

fiscal policy
progressive tax
payroll tax
regressive tax
excise tax
estate tax
gift tax
interest
Benjamin Franklin
Oliver Wendell Holmes, Jr.
George W. Bush
Barack Obama
inheritance tax
customs duty

Financing Government

The Power to Tax

The word *fiscal* comes from the Latin word *fiscus,* meaning originally a reed basket and later a purse or treasury. In ancient Rome, the *fiscus* was the public treasury, the emperor's purse. A government's **fiscal policy** consists of the various means it uses to raise and spend money and thereby influence the nation's economy. The rate at which government takes in money and the level at which it spends that income have a very substantial impact on economic conditions. In simplest terms, it comes to this: A cut in taxes means more money in the hands of consumers, and their increased spending power means more jobs. An increase in taxes takes money away from consumers and so can tend to slow the economy and reduce inflation.

The Treasury Department was among the first executive departments established by Congress. Since its creation in 1789, it has been the agency responsible for issuing the currency of the United States, collecting taxes and other revenues, and paying the bills of the Federal Government.

No one really likes taxes—except, perhaps, late-night television personalities who often find fodder for their monologues in that subject. They are far from the first to joke about taxes, however. More than two centuries ago, **Benjamin Franklin** famously said that "in this world nothing can be said to be certain, except death and taxes."

The Constitution underscores the central importance of the power to tax by listing it first among all of the many powers granted to Congress. The Constitution gives Congress the power

> To lay and collect Taxes, Duties, Imposts and Excises, to pay the Debts and provide for the common Defence and general Welfare of the United States. . . .
>
> —Article I, Section 8, Clause 1

First and foremost, Congress exercises its power to tax in order to raise the money needed to operate the Federal Government. However, Congress does sometimes exercise that power for purposes other than raising revenue. Usually, that other purpose is to regulate, even discourage, some activity that the government believes to be harmful to the general public.

Thus, much of the Federal Government's regulation of narcotics and other dangerous drugs is based on the power to tax. Federal law provides that only those who hold a valid license can legally manufacture, sell, or otherwise deal in those drugs—and licensing is a form of taxation. The government also regulates a number of other things by licensing—including, for example, the sale of certain firearms, prospecting on public lands, and the hunting of migratory birds.

In 1912, Congress used its taxing power to destroy a part of the domestic match industry. It did so by levying a tax of two cents per one hundred matches on those matches made with white or yellow phosphorus. Those highly poisonous substances were harmful to workers who produced the matches. Matches made from other substances sold for a penny a hundred at the time. As a result, the tax drove phosphorus matches from the market.

The Supreme Court first upheld the use of the power to tax for nonrevenue purposes in *Veazie Bank* v. *Fenno,* 1869. The Court said that Congress was acting within its powers when it levied a 10 percent tax on private bank notes. Congress had imposed that tax in 1865 to eliminate private bank notes from the economy and establish a single national currency. In 2012, the Court upheld another nonrevenue use of the power to tax. The Patient Protection and Affordable Care Act of 2010 requires citizens to buy health insurance or pay a fine. The Court ruled that this provision was unconstitutional under the Commerce Clause, but allowable under Congress's power to tax.

Limits on the Power to Tax The power to tax is not unlimited. As with all of its other powers, Congress must exercise its power to tax in accord with every provision in the Constitution. Thus, for example, Congress cannot levy a tax on church services—clearly, such a tax would violate the 1st Amendment. In more specific terms, the Constitution puts four expressed limits—and one very significant implied limit—on the power to tax.

First, it declares that Congress is given the power to tax in order to "pay the Debts and provide for the common Defence and general Welfare of the United States." That is, taxes can be levied *only* for public purposes, not for the benefit of some private interest.

The second expressed limit is the prohibition of export taxes. Article I, Section 9, Clause 5 declares that "No Tax or Duty shall be laid on Articles exported from any State." Thus, customs duties (tariffs) can be applied only to imports—goods brought into the United States.

They may not be applied to exports, goods sent out of the country. Recall, this restriction was a part

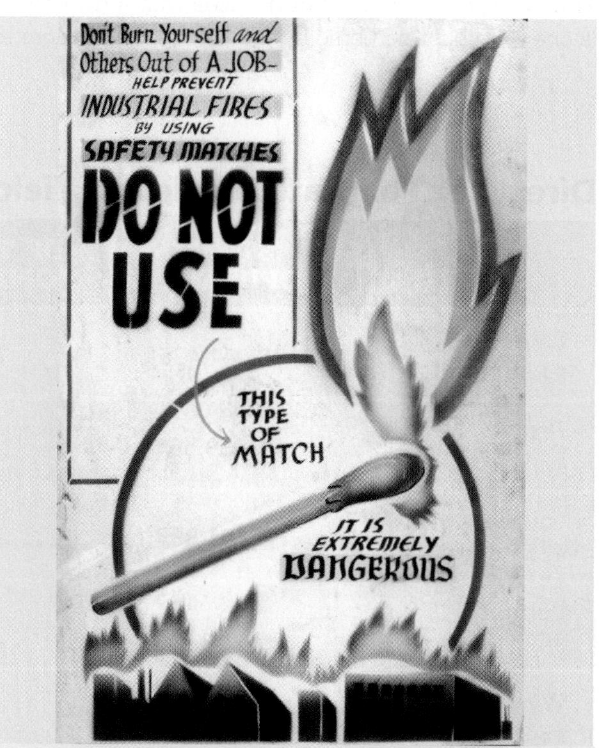

>> When the Diamond Match Company patented the first nonpoisonous match in 1910, the U.S. government distributed promotional literature to discourage the use of phosporous matches.

of the Commerce Compromise made by the Framers at Philadelphia in 1787.

While Congress cannot tax exports, it can and does *prohibit* the export of certain items. It does so under its expressed power to regulate foreign commerce, usually for the reason of national security. For example, Congress has banned the export of computer software that allows people to encrypt files in a code no government can crack.

Third, direct taxes must be equally apportioned—that is, evenly distributed—among the States according to their populations. The Constitution originally provided that

> No Capitation, or other direct, Tax shall be laid, unless in Proportion to the Census or Enumeration herein before directed to be taken.
>
> —Article I, Section 9, Clause 4

This restriction was a part of the Three-Fifths Compromise at the Philadelphia Convention. In effect, delegates from the northern States insisted that if enslaved people were to be counted in the populations of the southern States, those States would have to pay for them.

The Direct Tax Restriction Recall that a direct tax is one that must be borne by the person upon whom it is levied. Examples include a tax on land or buildings, which must be paid by the owner of the property; or a capitation tax—a head or poll tax—laid on each person. Other taxes are indirect taxes, levies that may be shifted to another for payment—as, for example, the federal tax on liquor. That tax, placed initially on the distiller, is ultimately paid by the person who buys the liquor.

The direct tax restriction means, in effect, that any direct tax that Congress levies (except for the income tax) must be apportioned among the States according to their populations. Thus, a direct tax that raised, say, $1 billion would have to produce just about $120 million in California and close to $10 million in Mississippi because California has about 12 percent of the nation's population, while Mississippi has less than one percent.

Wealth is not evenly distributed among the States, of course. Therefore, a direct tax laid in proportion to population would be grossly unfair; the tax would fall more heavily on the residents of some States than it would on others. As a result, Congress has not imposed a direct tax—except for the income tax—outside the District of Columbia since 1861.

Income taxes affect businesses as well as individuals. But the effect of taxes on a business depends on how the business is structured. The most common form of business organization is a sole proprietorship—a business owned and run by one person, who pays taxes on the business income as part of his or her own income tax. Owners of an LLC—a

Direct Tax Per State Needed to Yield $1 Billion in Revenue

STATE	STATE POPULATION	% OF TOTAL U.S. POPULATION*	DIRECT TAX PER STATE
California #1 in population	38,041,430	12.10	121,000,000
Texas #2 in Population	26,059,561	8.30	8,300,000
Louisiana #25 in population	4,601,893	1.50	1,500,000
Vermont #49 in population	626,011	0.20	200,000
Wyoming #50 in population	576,412	0.18	180,000

SOURCE: www.census.gov

* Based on total U.S. Population of 313,914,040

>> Under a direct tax, more populous States would contribute more revenue. **Analyze Charts** What is the only type of direct tax imposed by the Federal Government?

Top 10 Corporations in Tax Payments

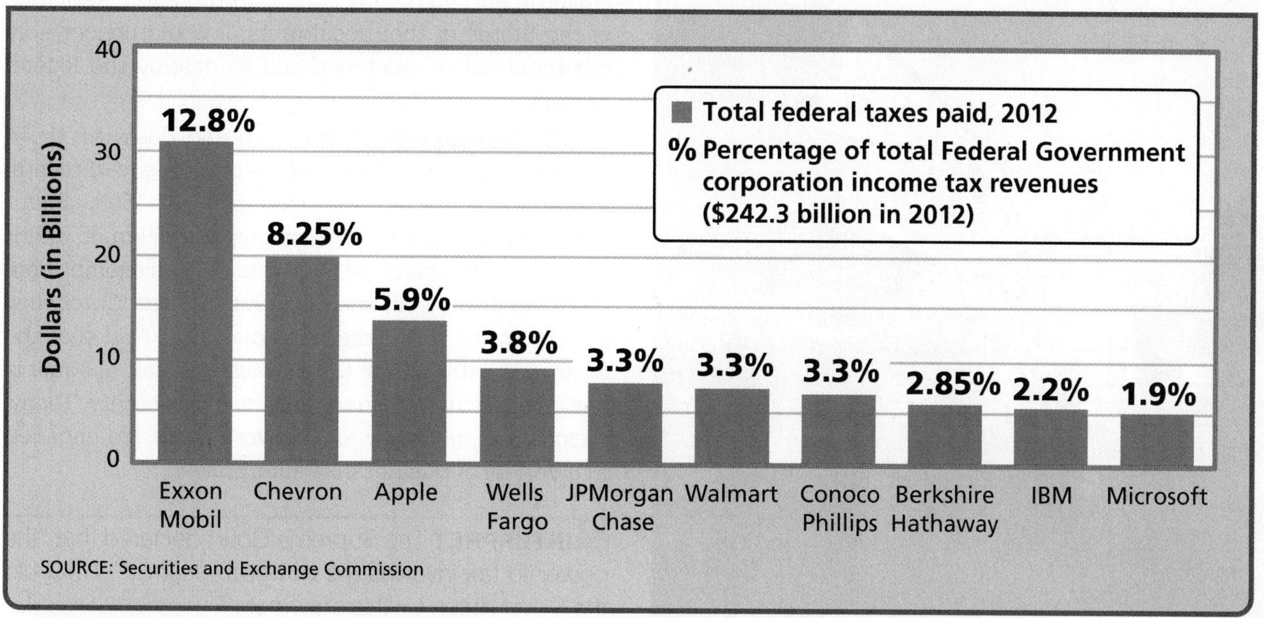

>> At 35 percent, the United States has the highest corporate tax rate in the world. **Analyze Charts** How much income tax did Chevron pay to the Federal Government in 2012?

limited liability company—also include business income on their own personal income taxes.

Corporate tax structure, however, is much more complicated. Corporations are classified as separate tax-paying entities. Payments that corporations distribute to shareholders and employees are reported by the shareholders and employees on their personal income tax returns. This means that some corporate profits can be taxed twice, once when the company earns its profits and once when each individual who has been paid by the company pays personal income tax. However, corporations can also count payroll as a tax deduction, because it is a business expense.

An income tax—whether it is for an individual or a business—is a direct tax, but it may be laid without regard to population.

> The Congress shall have power to lay and collect taxes on incomes, from whatever source derived, without apportionment among the several States, and without regard to any census or enumeration.
>
> —16th Amendment

Congress first levied an income tax in 1861, to help finance the Civil War. That tax, which expired in 1872, was later upheld by the Supreme Court in *Springer* v. *United States*, 1881. A unanimous Court found that that income tax was an indirect rather than a direct tax.

However, a later income tax law, enacted in 1894, was declared unconstitutional in *Pollock* v. *Farmers' Loan and Trust Co.*, 1895. There, the Court held that the 1894 law imposed a direct tax that Congress should have apportioned among the several States. The impossibility of taxing incomes fairly in accord with any plan of apportionment led to the adoption of the 16th Amendment, in 1913.

The fourth and final limit, in Article I, Section 8, Clause 1, declares that "all Duties, Imposts and Excises shall be uniform throughout the United States." That is, all of the indirect taxes levied by the Federal Government must be set at the same rate in all parts of the country.

Additional Limits on the Power to Tax The Federal Government cannot tax the States or any of their local governments in the exercise of their proper governmental functions. That is, federal taxes cannot be imposed on those governments when they are performing such tasks as providing public education, protecting the public health, providing police protection, or building streets and highways.

The Supreme Court laid down that rule in *McCulloch* v. *Maryland* in 1819, when it declared that "the power

>> Because the State of Texas is performing a "proper governmental function" with the construction of this bridge in Fort Worth, the project cannot be taxed by the Federal Government.

>> A pay stub shows the amount of money in federal taxes withheld from one individual's paycheck. They include personal income tax, Medicare tax, and Social Security tax.

Interactive Illustration

to tax involves the power to destroy." If the Federal Government could tax the governmental activities of the States or their local units, it could conceivably tax them out of existence and so destroy the federal system.

The Federal Government can and does tax those State and local activities that are of a nongovernmental character, however. For example, in 1893, South Carolina created a State monopoly to sell liquor, and it claimed that each of its liquor stores was exempt from the federal saloon license tax. But in *South Carolina* v. *United States*, 1905, the Supreme Court held that the State was liable for the tax, because the sale of liquor is not a necessary or usual governmental activity. Today, most State and many local governments are engaged in a variety of businesslike enterprises.

INTERPRET The Supreme Court declared that "the power to tax involves the power to destroy." What did the Court mean by this statement?

Federal Taxes Today

Paying taxes is a responsibility of citizenship. Without citizens' tax dollars, the Federal Government could not execute the nation's public policies or conduct the business of government. In the words of **Oliver Wendell Holmes, Jr.**, taxes are "what we pay for civilized society." This comment represents one viewpoint on taxes—the notion that tax-funded government services and programs, such as police, fire, public schools, and Social Security, have led to increased safety, reduced crime and poverty, increased levels of education, and other tangible benefits. Others, however, argue that taxes represent undue government interference with the economy and have a negative effect on both individuals and businesses. These differing viewpoints fuel the ongoing debates over which types of taxes we should have and how high or low they should be set.

Taxes on Income You will recall that the income tax was authorized by the 16th Amendment, in 1913. It is the largest source of federal revenue today. It first became the major source in 1917 and 1918. And, except for a few years in the midst of the Depression of the 1930s, it has remained so.

Several features of the income tax fit its dominant role. It is a flexible tax, because its rates can be adjusted to produce whatever amount of money Congress thinks is necessary. The income tax is also easily adapted to the principle of ability to pay. It is a **progressive tax**—that is, the higher one's income, the higher the tax rate.

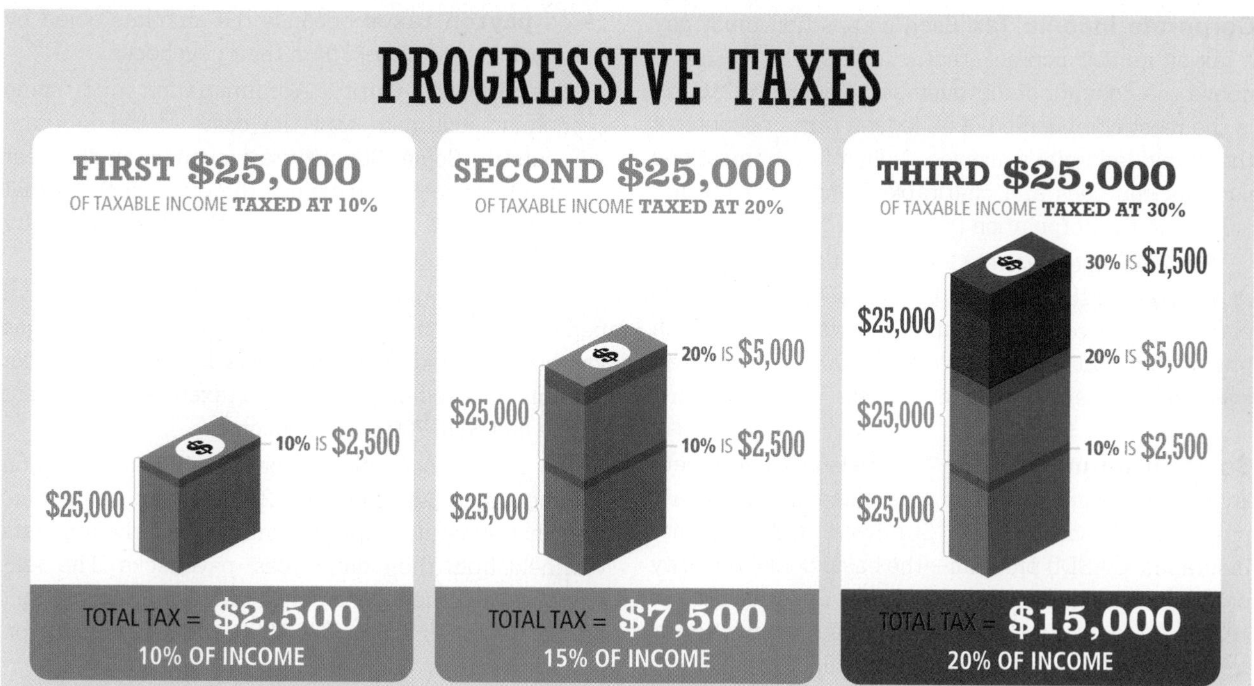

>> With a progressive tax, as one's income increases, so does the amount of one's income taxes. **Analyze Data** What percentage of total income would be paid on salaries of $30,000 and $95,000?

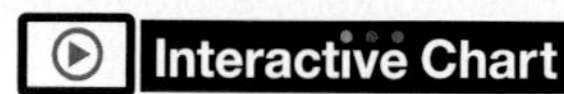

The tax is levied on the earnings of both individuals and corporations.

Individual Income Tax The tax on individuals' incomes regularly produces the largest amount of federal revenue. For fiscal year 2014, the individual income tax was expected to provide nearly $1.4 trillion.

The tax is levied on each person's taxable income—that is, one's total income in the previous year less certain exemptions and deductions. On returns filed in 2013, covering income received in 2012, most taxpayers had a personal exemption of $3,800, and another of the same amount for each dependent. The personal exemption is adjusted to account for inflation each year. Deductions are allowed for a number of things, including the cost of some medical care, most State and local taxes (except sales taxes), interest paid on home mortgages, and charitable contributions. For some people, after these exemptions and deductions, their taxable income is zero, therefore they pay no federal income tax.

By April 15 of any given year, everyone who earned taxable income in the preceding calendar year must file a tax return—a declaration of that income and of the exemptions and deductions he or she claims. The returns are filed, by mail or online, with the Internal Revenue Service. The IRS now receives more than 239 million tax returns each year; more than three fourths of those are e-filed.

At President **George W. Bush**'s urging, Congress passed major tax-cut legislation in 2001 and 2003. Those tax cuts were set to expire at the end of 2010, but a stubbornly sluggish economy prompted President **Barack Obama** to push for, and Congress to pass, legislation extending the cuts through 2012. As a result, all taxable income earned in 2013 was taxed (in 2014) at one of seven rates (brackets). Those rates ranged from 10 percent in the lowest bracket (those taxpayers earning upto $8,925 for individuals; $17,850 for married couples) and up to 39.6 percent on the highest incomes (over $400,000 for individuals; $450,000 for married couples).

Most people who pay income taxes do so through withholding, a pay-as-you-go plan. Employers are required to withhold a certain amount from each employee's paycheck and send that money to the IRS. When the employee files a tax return, he or she receives a refund if the employer withheld more money than the employee owed in taxes, or must pay an additional amount if too little was withheld. Those who earn income from sources not subject to withholding (for example, rent or royalties) must estimate the tax they will owe and make quarterly payments on that amount through the year.

Corporate Income Tax Each corporation must pay a tax on its net income—that is, on all of its earnings above the costs of doing business. The corporate tax is the most complicated of all federal taxes because of the many deductions allowed. Nonprofit organizations such as churches and charitable foundations are not subject to the corporation income tax.

For 2013, the Federal Government's corporate tax rates began at 15 percent for the first $50,000 of taxable earnings. Above that amount, the rate varied, with businesses that made more than $100,000 paying an average of 36 percent in federal taxes.

Social Insurance Taxes The Federal Government levies other taxes to finance three major social welfare programs: (1) the Old-Age, Survivors, and Disability Insurance (OASDI) program—the basic Social Security program, established by the Social Security Act of 1935; (2) Medicare—healthcare for the elderly, added to the Social Security program in 1965; and (3) the unemployment compensation program—benefits paid to jobless workers, a program also established by the Social Security Act in 1935.

OASDI and Medicare are supported by taxes imposed on nearly all employers and their employees, and on self-employed persons. These levies are often called **payroll taxes** because the amounts owed by employees are withheld from their paychecks.

The Social Security Administration and some economists estimate that the costs of the program will outstrip Social Security tax revenues in the near future. Other economic experts, however, contend that concerns about the solvency of the Social Security program are exaggerated.

For 2013, employees paid an OASDI tax of 6.2 percent on the first $113,700 of their salary or wages for the year, and their employers had to match that amount. The self-employed were taxed at 12.4 percent on the first $113,700 of their income.

For Medicare, employees pay a 1.45 percent tax on income up to $200,000 and 2.35 percent on income over that amount. Employers must match the amounts withheld from their employees' paychecks. The self-employed pay the full 2.9 percent Medicare tax on their annual incomes up to $200,000 and 3.8 percent on income over that amount.

The unemployment insurance program is a joint federal–State operation that makes payments to workers who lose their jobs for reasons beyond their control. The program now covers most workers in this country. Each State and the District of Columbia, Puerto Rico, and the Virgin Islands have their own unemployment compensation laws. The amount of a worker's weekly

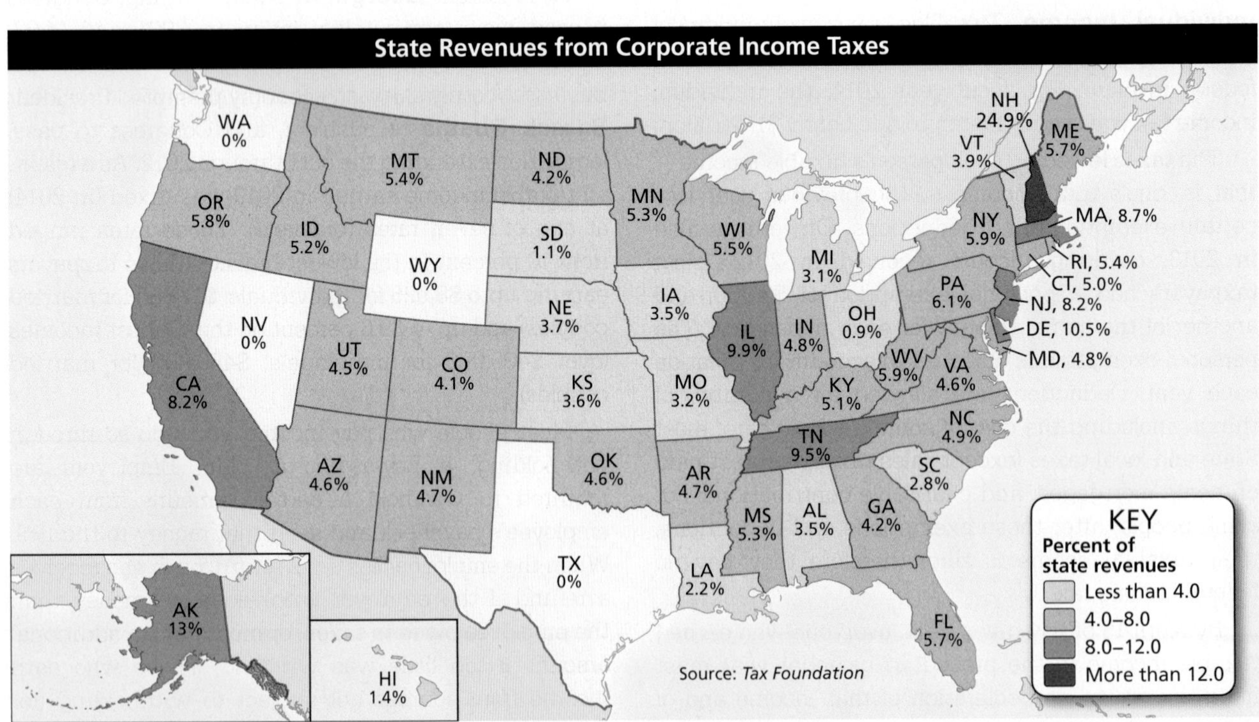

>> The portion of tax revenue from corporate income tax varies from State to State. **Analyze Maps** Which States do not levy a corporate income tax? Which State levies the highest?

How Taxes Affect the Cost of Gasoline

COST OF ONE GALLON OF REGULAR GASOLINE*	CALIFORNIA	FLORIDA	OHIO	TEXAS
COST BEFORE TAXES	$3.86	$3.33	$3.44	$3.24
+ STATE TAX	$0.3905	$0.04	$0.28	$0.2
+ SALES TAX	$0.14	$0.314	$0.0	$0.0
+ FEDERAL EXCISE TAX	$0.184	$0.184	$0.184	$0.184
TOTAL CONSUMER COST	$4.5745	$3.868	$3.904	$3.624

*September 2013 SOURCE: Internal Revenue Service

>> Residents of different States can pay vastly different prices for gas. **Analyze Charts** Given that the federal excise tax is consistent, what contributes to the varying prices consumers pay?

benefits, and how many weeks these benefits last, are determined by State law.

The federal unemployment tax is 6 percent of the first $7,000 an employer pays to each employee in a year. Each employer is given a credit of up to 5.4 percent against that tax for unemployment taxes that the employer pays to the State. So, the federal tax amounts to 0.6 percent on taxable wages.

Notice that these social insurance taxes for OASDI, Medicare, and unemployment compensation are not progressive taxes. They are, instead, **regressive taxes**—taxes levied at a fixed rate, without regard to the level of a taxpayer's income or his or her ability to pay them. In fact, the regressive OASDI and Medicare taxes now take more money out of the paychecks of many low and middle income workers than does the progressive federal income tax.

The IRS collects these social insurance taxes. The money is then credited to trust accounts maintained by the Treasury, and Congress appropriates funds for the social insurance programs as they are needed.

Excise Taxes An **excise tax** is a tax laid on the manufacture, sale, or consumption of goods and/or the performance of services. The Federal Government has imposed and collected excise taxes since Congress acquired its taxing power in 1789.

Today, federal excise taxes are imposed on a long list of items, including gasoline, oil, tires, tobacco, alcohol, firearms, telephone services, airline tickets, and more. Many excise taxes are called "hidden taxes" because they are collected from producers who then figure them into the price that the retail customer finally pays. Some are called "luxury taxes" because they are imposed on goods not usually considered necessities. And some excise taxes are known as "sin taxes," particularly those laid on tobacco, alcohol, and gambling.

Estate and Gift Taxes An **estate tax** is a levy imposed on the assets (the estate) of someone who dies. An **inheritance tax** is another form of the so-called death tax. It is not levied on the entire net estate but, instead, on the portion inherited by each heir. Most States impose inheritance, not estate, taxes; most States also levy gift taxes. A **gift tax** is one imposed on a gift from one living person to another. Congress first provided for the estate tax in 1916. It added the gift tax in 1932 to plug a loophole in the estate tax that allowed people to avoid the estate tax by giving away money or other property before death.

Most estates are not subject to the federal tax, however, because those valued below a certain threshold are exempt. For 2013, that threshold was set at $5.25 million. In addition, deductions are allowed for such things as State estate taxes and bequests to religious and charitable groups. Anything a husband or wife leaves to the other is taxed, if at all, only when the surviving spouse dies.

Any person may now make up to $14,000 in tax-free gifts to any other person in any one year. Gifts that spouses make to each other are not taxed, regardless of value. The estate and gift taxes are separate taxes, but they are levied at the same rate. For 2013, the top rate was 40 percent.

Customs Duties **Customs duties** are taxes laid on goods brought into the United States from abroad. Customs duties are also known as tariffs, import duties,

>> Container shipping is used to transport large quantities of items across the world. Each country has its own regulations regarding customs duties for items brought into that country.

or imposts. Congress decides which imports will be dutied and at what rates. Most imports are duties, but some are not—for example, Bibles, coffee, bananas, and up to $800 of a tourist's purchases abroad. Once the major source of income for the Federal Government, customs duties now produce just over one percent of government revenue taken in each year.

Nontax Revenues Large sums of money reach the federal treasury from a multitude of nontax sources. These miscellaneous receipts now total more than $100 billion a year and come from dozens of places. A large portion comes from the earnings of the Federal Reserve System, mostly in interest charges. **Interest** is a charge for borrowed money, generally a percentage of the amount borrowed. The interest on other loans, canal tolls, and fees for such items as passports, copyrights, patents, and trademarks also generate large sums. So do the sale or lease of public lands and such other items as the fines imposed by the federal courts.

The Treasury Department maintains a "conscience fund" for the money that people pay to ease their minds over past taxpaying mistakes. Another little-known source of nontax money is *seigniorage*—the profit the United States Mint makes on the production of coins. The U.S. Postal Service sells more than $210 million in mint-condition stamps to collectors each year, and collectors spend untold millions more at local post offices.

? DRAW CONCLUSIONS How might the economy be affected when income taxes go up?

ASSESSMENT

1. **Summarize** Where does the Federal Government get its revenue?
2. **Compare and Contrast** How does the way Congress regulates exports differ from the way it regulates imports?
3. **Categorize** List the different types of taxes that are paid in the United States, and explain who pays which tax.
4. **Compare and Contrast** Explain the difference between progressive taxes and regressive taxes.
5. **Draw Conclusions** How do taxes affect the economy?

12.4 The Federal Government is projected to spend some $3.8 trillion in fiscal year 2014. If you were to place 3.8 trillion $1 bills end to end, they would stretch out nearly 360 million miles. Compare that to the distance between Earth and the planet Jupiter—some 366 million miles at its closest point. In this lesson, you will see how the Federal Government spends that vast amount of money and how it plans for that spending through the budget process.

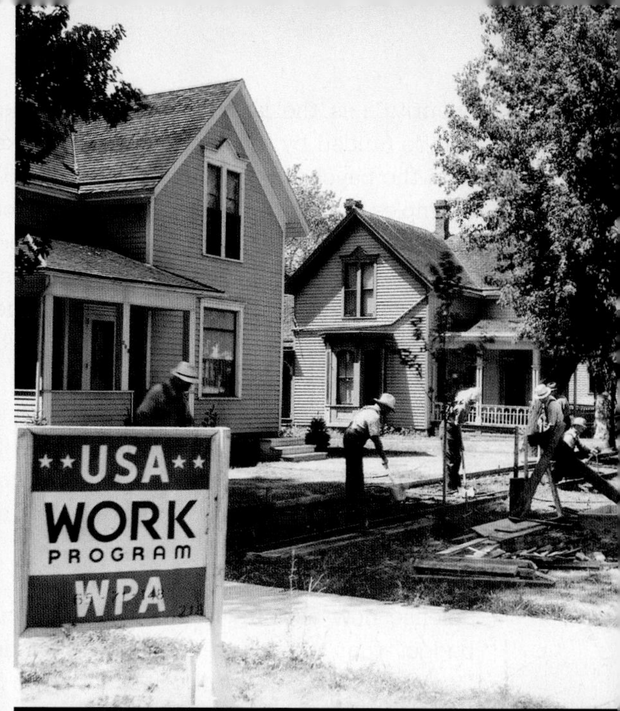

>> The Works Progress Administration (WPA) was part of President Roosevelt's New Deal program, which ushered in a new era of government intervention in the economy.

Interactive Flipped Video

Spending and Borrowing

>> **Objectives**

Identify the sources of expenditures of the U.S. government and define controllable and uncontrollable spending.

Analyze the executive branch function of creating the federal budget, in conjunction with Congress.

Understand the relationship between U.S. government policies as set out in the yearly federal budget and the economy.

Analyze the impact of Federal Government sources of revenue and expenditures on the U.S. economy.

Analyze the causes and effects of the public debt.

>> **Key Terms**

entitlements
controllable spending
uncontrollable spending
continuing resolution
deficit
surplus
demand-side economics
supply-side economics
public debt
Panama Canal
Herbert Hoover
Franklin D. Roosevelt
Ronald Reagan
George Washington

Federal Expenditures

For more than half of our national history—from independence in 1776 to the mid-1930s—the government's income and spending were so comparatively small that they had little real impact on the nation's economy. That situation changed, dramatically, with the coming of the Great Depression of the 1930s and then World War II in the early 1940s.

Today, the Federal Government takes nearly $3 trillion from some segments of the national economy. It then pumps those trillions back into other segments of the economy—all with huge effects on the economy as a whole, of course.

Spending Priorities The Department of Health and Human Services now spends more money than any other federal agency—over $886 billion a year, in fact. Most of this department's spending goes for Medicare, Medicaid, and other entitlement programs.

Entitlements are benefits that federal law says *must* be paid to all those who meet the eligibility requirements—for example, being above a certain age or below a certain income level. OASDI (the Old Age, Survivors, and Disability Insurance program)—often called "Social

Security"—is the largest entitlement program today, and, is funded by the social insurance taxes withheld from the paychecks of American workers. Other major examples include Medicare, Medicaid, food stamps, unemployment insurance, and veterans' pensions and other benefits. The government guarantees assistance for all who qualify for those benefits. In effect, the law says that the people who receive those benefits are *entitled* (that is, have a right) to them.

OASDI is administered by an independent agency, the Social Security Administration (SSA). The department's outlays for OASDI—$867 billion in 2013—make SSA the second-largest government spender.

Defense and the Public Debt Outlays for national defense now account for a much larger share of the budget than they have over the past decade. The Department of Defense (DoD) spent some $608 billion in 2013.

As large as this number is, it does not include the defense-related expenditures of several other federal agencies, notably the nuclear weapons development work of the Department of Energy and many of the functions of the Department of Homeland Security.

Interest on the public debt is now the fourth-largest category of federal spending. Stoked by years of deficit financing, it has consumed a larger and still larger part of the federal budget over the last several years. Interest on the debt is included in the Treasury Department's spending. For fiscal year 2013, the net interest on the debt came to some $416 billion.

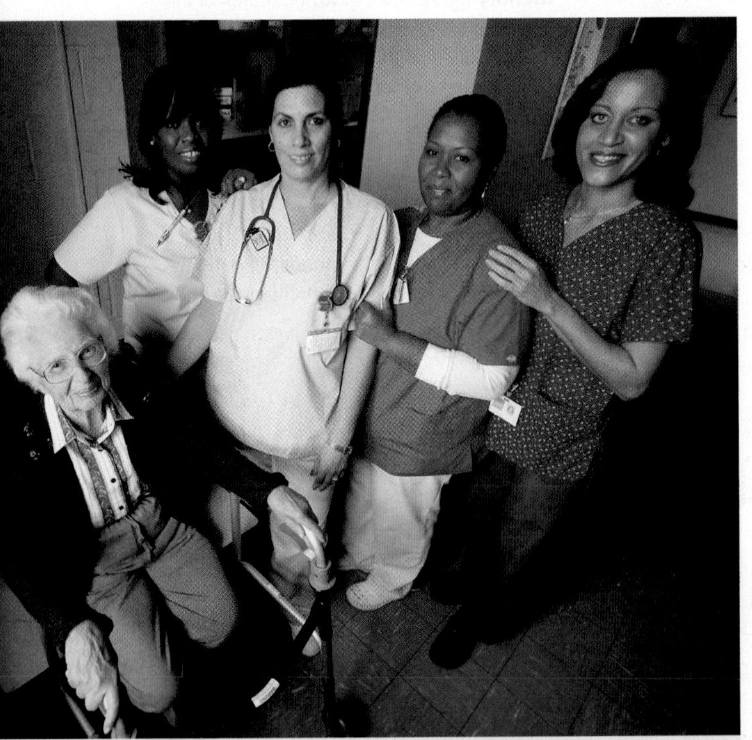

>> An elderly patient receives medical care financed by Medicare, which provides health coverage to people over 65; in 2013, $590 billion of the federal budget went to Medicare.

Types of Spending What the Federal Government spends can be described in terms of **controllable spending** and **uncontrollable spending.** Most specific items in the federal budget are controllable. That is, Congress and the President can decide each year just how much will be spent on many of the things that the Federal Government does—for example, on national parks, highway projects, aid to education, civil service pay, and so on. Defense spending is by far the largest controllable item in the federal budget today. Economists often use the term "discretionary spending" to describe spending on those budget items about which Congress and the President can make choices.

Much federal spending is uncontrollable, however. It is because "mandatory spending" was built into many public programs when Congress created them. That level of spending cannot be changed unless Congress changes the law(s) that set the funding for those programs.

Take the interest on the public debt as a leading example of uncontrollable spending. That interest amounts to a fixed charge; once the Federal Government borrows the money, the interest on that loan must be paid when it comes due—and at the rate the government promised to pay.

Social Security benefits, food stamps, and most other entitlements are also largely uncontrollable. Once Congress has set the standards of eligibility for those programs, it really has no control over just how many people will meet those standards. Thus, Congress does not—really cannot—determine how many people covered by Social Security will become eligible for retirement benefits each year.

"Controlling" Uncontrollable Spending Those expenditures are not completely uncontrollable, however. Congress could redefine eligibility standards, or it could reduce the amount of money each beneficiary is to receive. But, clearly, those actions would be politically difficult.

In general, the percentage of federal spending that is uncontrollable has grown in recent years, while the percentage of controllable spending has decreased. In fact, the Office of Management and Budget estimates that over 60 percent of all federal spending today falls into the uncontrollable category. These trends cause

THE EXECUTIVE BRANCH AND THE BUDGET

On the first Monday in February, the President proposes a budget outlining the administration's policies and funding priorities and estimating spending, income, and borrowing for the coming fiscal year.

- Each federal agency prepares an estimate of its spending needs for the next year.
- Those spending plans are submitted to the Office of Management and Budget (OMB).
- The OMB reviews the agency proposals, often in budget hearings.
- After the OMB's review, revised spending plans for all of the agencies become part of the budget document.
- The President submits the budget document to Congress.

>> The President, Congress, and many federal agencies are involved in creating the budget. **Analyze Charts** What is the President's role in creating the budget?

concern to those officials who are responsible for maintaining control of the budget.

DRAW CONCLUSIONS Are entitlement programs examples of controllable or uncontrollable spending? Why do you think so?

Creating the Budget

The Constitution gives to Congress the fabled "power of the purse"—the very significant power to control the financing of the Federal Government and all of its operations.

> No Money shall be drawn from the Treasury, but in Consequence of Appropriations made by Law. . . .
>
> —Article I, Section 9, Clause 7

Congress—and only Congress—has the power to provide the enormous sums that the government consumes each year. In short, it is Congress that decides *how much* the government can spend and, just as importantly, for exactly *what* it can spend that money.

Still, despite the fact that Congress holds the power of the purse, it is the President who initiates the process by which the Federal Government spends its money. The chief executive does so by submitting (proposing) a budget to Congress soon after that body begins each of its yearly sessions. The word *budget* comes from the French *bougette*, meaning a small pouch or bag with its contents. In the eighteenth century, the budget was the bag in which the British chancellor of the exchequer (the treasurer) carried the financial documents.

The Importance of the Budget Remember, the federal budget is a hugely important document. It is, of course, a financial statement—a lengthy and detailed estimate of federal income and proposed outgo for the upcoming fiscal year. But it is also much more than that, much more than a dry listing of so many dollars from this and so many dollars for that. The budget is a major political statement, a declaration of the public policies of the United States. Put another way, the federal budget is the President's work plan for the conduct of the government and the execution of its public policies in the next fiscal year.

The annual budget-making process is a joint effort of the President and both houses of Congress. The President prepares the budget and submits it to Congress. Congress then reacts to the President's budget proposals, over a period of several months. It usually enacts most of those proposals, many of them in some altered form, in a number of appropriations measures.

The Executive Branch and the Budget The process of building the budget is a lengthy one. In fact, it begins at least 18 months before the start of the fiscal year for which the budget is intended. First, each federal agency prepares detailed estimates of its spending needs for that 12-month period. Each agency then submits its spending plans to the President's budget-making agency, the Office of Management and Budget (OMB). The OMB reviews all of the many agency proposals, often in budget hearings at which agency officials must defend their dollar requests.

Following the OMB's review, revised and usually lowered spending plans for all of the agencies in the executive branch are fitted into the President's overall program. They become a part of the budget document—a part of the political statement—the President sends to Capitol Hill.

Congress enacts a separate budget to cover its own expenses. The federal courts' spending requests are prepared by the Administrative Office of the United States Courts and sent directly to Congress.

Congress and the Budget Remember, Congress depends upon and works through its standing committees. The President's budget proposals, therefore, are referred to the Budget Committee in each chamber. There, in both the House and Senate committees, those money requests are studied and dissected with the help of the Congressional Budget Office (CBO).

The CBO is a staff agency created by Congress in 1974. It provides both houses of Congress and their committees with basic budget and economic data and analyses. The information that the CBO supplies is independent of the information provided by the OMB, the President's budget agency.

All tax proposals included in the President's budget are referred to the House Ways and Means Committee and, separately, to the Senate's Finance Committee. The President's budget is also sent to both the House and the Senate Appropriations Committees. Their subcommittees hold extensive hearings in which they examine agency requests, quiz agency officials, and take testimony from a wide range of interested parties.

Lobbyists for many interest groups are actively involved in those hearings. They testify, bring grass-roots pressures to bear on committee members, and otherwise work to promote the interests of the organizations they represent. (And campaign contributions from these groups often find their way

CONGRESS AND THE BUDGET

Using the President's budget as a guide, the House and Senate work individually and then together to determine the size of the budget, estimate revenue, and set discretionary spending levels.

- House and Senate Budget committees conduct hearings on the President's budget.

- House and Senate debate and vote on their respective committee's budget resolution.
- Conference committee blends both resolutions into one final resolution.
- Each house votes on final version of the budget resolution.

>> The House and Senate spend eight months or so determining the final allocation of federal funds. **Analyze Charts** Why do you think Budget Committee hearings are usually open to the public?

FINAL STEPS TO PASSING THE BUDGET

Guided by the budget resolution, Congress sets the budget for each federal agency in detail and provides the legal authority to spend funds. As each appropriations bill is approved by Congress, it is sent to the President to veto or sign into law.

- House and Senate Appropriations committees each develop 13 separate massive spending bills.
- Conference committee settles on one bill for each of the 13 appropriations measures.

- Each house votes on final version of each appropriations bill.
- President signs or vetoes the bills. If not approved by October 1st, Congress must pass a continuing resolution for unfunded agencies to ensure their continued operation.

>> Both the President and Congress are involved in the final steps of passing the budget. **Analyze Charts** Why are both the legislative and executive branches involved in the budget process?

to members of those subcommittees—in particular, to their chairmen and ranking members.)

The two Appropriations Committees shape measures that later are reported to the floor of each house. Those measures are the bills that actually appropriate the funds on which the government will operate.

Final Steps to Passing the Budget The two Budget Committees propose a concurrent resolution on the budget to their respective chambers. That measure, which must be passed by both houses by May 15, sets overall targets for federal receipts and spending in the upcoming fiscal year. The estimates are intended to guide the committees in both houses as they continue to work on the budget.

The two Budget Committees propose a second budget resolution in early September. Congress must pass that resolution by September 15, just two weeks before the beginning of the next fiscal year. That second budget resolution sets binding expenditure limits for all federal agencies in that upcoming year. No appropriations measure can provide for any spending that exceeds those limits.

Congress passes 13 major appropriations bills each year. Recall, each of these measures must go to the White House for the President's action. Every year, Congress hopes to pass all 13 of the appropriations measures by October 1—that is, by the beginning of the Federal Government's fiscal year.

It seldom does so, however. This means that Congress must then pass emergency spending legislation to avoid a shutdown of those agencies for which appropriations have not yet been signed into law. That legislation takes the form of a **continuing resolution.** When signed by the President, the measure allows the affected agencies to continue to function on the basis of the previous year's appropriations. Should Congress and the President fail to act, many agencies of the Federal Government would, in fact, have to suspend their operations. This has, in fact, happened at various times in the nation's history, most recently in 2013.

? IDENTIFY CENTRAL ISSUES What programs do you think are considered high priorities by most Americans? How are these priorities taken into account during the creation of the federal budget?

Borrowing and the Deficit

In *Hamlet*, Shakespeare wrote, "Neither a borrower nor a lender be." That advice may make good sense in many situations. However, it most certainly has *not* been followed by the government of the United States, which has been both a borrower and a lender for more than 200 years now.

The Constitution gives Congress the power "[t]o borrow Money on the credit of the United States" in Article I, Section 8, Clause 2. Congress first exercised that power in 1790, and it has done so hundreds of times since then. For the better part of 150 years, the power to borrow was seen as a way for the government to (1) meet the costs of crisis situations, most notably wars, and/or (2) pay for large-scale projects that could not be financed out of current income— for example, the construction of the **Panama Canal** in the early 1900s.

Beginning with the Depression years of the 1930s, the Federal Government has borrowed, regularly and heavily, for yet another purpose: to finance budget deficits. In nearly every one of the last 80 years, it has spent more than it has collected from taxpayers. That is, the government has run up a **deficit** (the shortfall between income and outgo) in each of those years—and it has borrowed to make up the difference.

Indeed, the government's financial books did not show a **surplus** (more income than outgo) in any fiscal year from 1970 to 1998. In fact, from 1930 to 2013, the Federal Government ended only 13 fiscal years "in the black"—that is, with a budget surplus. For fiscal year 2014, which extends from October 1, 2013, to September 30, 2014, the government expects to spend some $3.8 trillion—and it will take in some $744 billion less than that stupendous sum. It will have to borrow to cover that shortfall.

The Depression and Deficit Spending The collapse of the stock market in October 1929 triggered the Great Depression of the 1930s. To meet that catastrophe, deficit financing became a constant element of federal fiscal policy.

A few statistics begin to suggest the depths of that economic calamity and the miseries that accompanied it. Two million Americans were unemployed in 1929. By 1933, that number had climbed to 13.5 million. One fifth of the nation's labor force was out of work—and millions more were working for, literally, pennies a day. By 1935, 18 million people, including children and the aged, were completely dependent on emergency public relief programs.

Between 1929 and 1932, more than 5,000 banks—one of every five in the country—had failed, and their customers' deposits had vanished. By 1932, net farm income had plunged to 33 percent of its level in 1929.

Few States had made any provision for such a crisis, and those that had were overwhelmed. So, too, were churches and other private charities. Poverty and need had become national problems overnight.

In the elections of 1932, the voters overwhelmingly rejected the tentative efforts of President **Herbert Hoover** and a Republican-controlled Congress to solve the nation's economic woes. Mr. Hoover and his advisors were committed to the traditional view of the place of government in the economy. They held that government had only a very limited power to deal with what they believed was a private economic crisis. Government, they thought, should ensure a stable

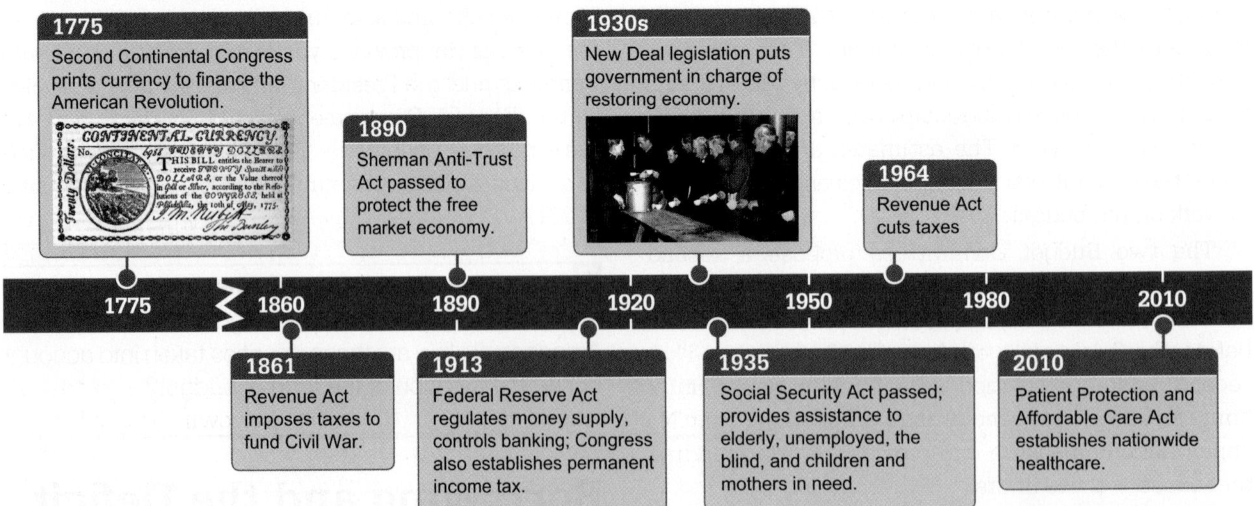
Government Economic Actions
1775
Second Continental Congress prints currency to finance the American Revolution.
CONTINENTAL CURRENCY
1890
Sherman Anti-Trust Act passed to protect the free market economy.
1930s
New Deal legislation puts government in charge of restoring economy.
1964
Revenue Act cuts taxes
1775
1860
1890
1920
1950
1980
2010
1861
Revenue Act imposes taxes to fund Civil War.
1913
Federal Reserve Act regulates money supply, controls banking; Congress also establishes permanent income tax.
1935
Social Security Act passed; provides assistance to elderly, unemployed, the blind, and children and mothers in need.
2010
Patient Protection and Affordable Care Act establishes nationwide healthcare.

>> Since 1775, the government has taken action on many occasions to regulate the economy. **Analyze Images** Which government programs addressed the problems of the Great Depression?

UNDERSTANDING THE ECONOMIC CRISIS OF 2007–2008

CAUSES	EFFECTS	TARP
• Easy availability of mortgages created an unsustainable housing boom • Households and businesses had too much excess debt • U.S. financial system grew too fast • Regulatory framework was outdated • Too many investors were insensitive to risk	• **September 15, 2008:** Lehman Brothers filed for bankruptcy • **September 16, 2008:** Stock market fell 500 points; financial sector panic ensued • U.S. financial system at risk of collapse • Millions of jobs lost • Congress passed Emergency Economic Stabilization Act; the **Troubled Asset Relief Program (TARP)** was created under the act	• Initial authorization of **$700 billion**; later lowered to **$475 billion**, most of which was repaid by 2013 • Estimated total cost of the bailout at end of 2013: **$40.3 billion**

Source: Treasury Department

>> A combination of factors caused the economic crisis that led to the creation of TARP. **Analyze Charts** Which effect likely had the largest impact on the average American?

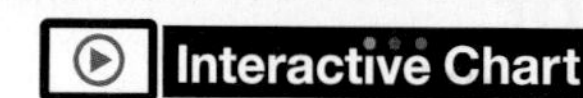

money supply; beyond that, the success or failure of businesses was a matter best left to the workings of the free market.

The voters turned, instead, to the Democrats. **Franklin D. Roosevelt** won the presidency in a landslide, and his party captured huge majorities in both houses of Congress.

Keynesian Economics Almost immediately, the President and Congress launched the New Deal—a series of government spending and jobs programs designed to stimulate the economy and put Americans back to work. That response to the Depression was built largely on the theories advanced by British economist John Maynard Keynes (1883–1946), most fully developed in his work *The General Theory of Employment, Interest, and Money,* published in 1936. In particular, it was based on the Keynesian view that government should influence the economy by large increases in public spending in times of high unemployment.

Keynesians argue that even if government must borrow to support that increased spending, the higher employment that results will soon produce higher tax revenues. This element of Keynesian economics is sometimes called **demand-side economics.**

Keynesian economic thinking continues to influence federal fiscal policy. However, President **Ronald Reagan** (1981–1989) and more recently George W. Bush (2001–2009) insisted that lower taxes, not greater spending, provide the best route to a stronger economy. This view, which is sometimes called **supply-side economics** or "Reaganomics," is based on the assumption that tax cuts increase the supply of money in private hands and so stimulate the economy.

A steep downturn in the nation's economy that began in 2007 and continued into 2009 led President Bush and then President Obama to persuade Congress to enact a series of "economic stimulus" plans—pump-priming measures that could very well have been written by John Maynard Keynes himself. Those laws were variously designed to inject more than $1.5 *trillion* into the nation's ailing economy in order to (1) shore up the loan-making capacities of the nation's banks and other financial institutions, (2) overcome a marked decline in consumer spending, and (3) combat a rising tide of unemployment.

The Borrowing Process Congress must authorize all federal borrowing. The actual borrowing is done by the Treasury Department, which issues various kinds of securities to investors. These investors are principally individuals, banks, and other financial institutions, and, of late, the government of China. The securities usually take the form of Treasury notes or bills, often referred to as T-bills, for short-term borrowing, and bonds for long-term purposes. They are, in effect, IOUs—promissory notes in which the government agrees to repay a certain sum, plus interest, on a certain date.

The Federal Government is regularly able to borrow money at lower rates of interest than the rates charged to private borrowers. This is true largely because investors can find no safer securities than those issued by the United States. If this country could not pay its debts, no one else would be able to do so, either. Federal securities are also attractive because the interest they earn cannot be taxed by any of the States or their local governments.

SUPPORT A POINT OF VIEW WITH EVIDENCE Do you think deficit financing is an acceptable method to fund the Federal Government? Explain why or why not.

Understanding the Public Debt

Borrowing produces a debt, of course. The public debt is the result of the Federal Government's borrowing over time. More precisely, the **public debt** is the total outstanding indebtedness of the Federal Government. It includes all of the money the government has borrowed and not yet repaid, plus the accrued interest on that borrowing. The Treasury Department's Bureau of the Public Debt acts as the Federal Government's borrowing agent. It issues Treasury bills, notes, and bonds and manages the U.S. Savings Bond Program.

The Federal Government has built up a huge debt over the years. Recall, the Federal Government first went into debt during **George Washington's** administration. Still, it took 193 years—from 1789 to 1982—for the public debt to reach $1 trillion. The public debt exploded over the past three decades, and by 2014, had reached nearly $18 trillion.

The amounts involved here are absolutely mind-boggling. In 1981, as the debt approached $1 trillion, President Reagan said that he found "such a figure—a trillion dollars—incomprehensible." He then drew this verbal picture: "[I]f you had a stack of $1,000 bills in your hand only four inches high, you'd be a millionaire. A trillion dollars would be a stack 67 miles high." Mr. Reagan's stack would have to be more than 1,000 miles high to equal the national debt today!

There is no constitutional limit on the amount that may be borrowed, and so there is no constitutional limit on the public debt. Congress has put a statutory ceiling on the debt, but simply raises that ceiling whenever fiscal realities seem to call for it.

The debt has always been controversial, and its rapid rise in recent years has fueled the fire. The annual interest on the debt is the amount that must be paid each year to those from whom the government has borrowed. That interest came to some $416 billion in fiscal year 2013.

Whom Does the Federal Government Owe?

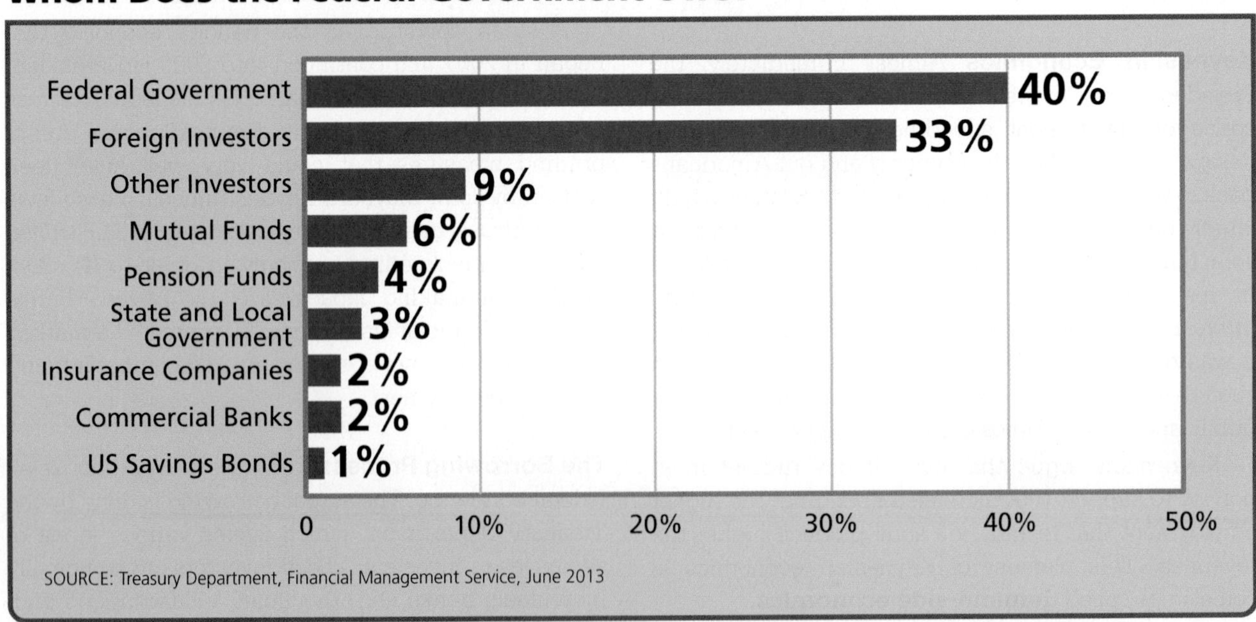

>> Today's debt of trillions of dollars is owed to several sources. **Analyze Graphs** To which creditor does the Federal Government owe the most money?

Most of those who are concerned about the size of the debt are worried about its impact on future generations of Americans. They say that years of shortsightedness and failure to operate government on a pay-as-you-go basis has produced monumental debt and interest obligations that will have to be met by tomorrow's taxpayers.

? COMPARE AND CONTRAST What is the difference between an annual deficit and the public debt?

ASSESSMENT

1. **Generate Explanations** For over 150 years, the revenue and expenditures of the Federal Government had very little impact on the economy of the United States. What were some major events that caused this situation to change?
2. **Predict Consequences** What might occur if the OMB accepted all agency funding requests without holding budget hearings? What would be the advantages and disadvantages if this were to occur?
3. **Identify Steps in a Process** Describe the basic steps involved in creating the federal budget.
4. **Analyze Information** Why do you think that for many years Congress and the President have chosen to borrow money rather than balance the federal budget?
5. **Support a Point of View with Evidence** Do you think the concern about the size of the public debt is justified? Why or why not?

>> As vast as the world appears, even from 22,000 miles away, globalization has brought nations closer together and greatly impacted markets and economies.

12.5 **There is a growing economic interdependence among nations of the world. This interdependence, often called globalization, has been both driven and enabled by many remarkable advancements in communication and transportation technologies. Everything from the enormous increase in computing power, the Internet, communications satellites, and even the building of larger ships has increased the flow of goods, and, as well, the flow of information that connects world markets. Globalization has also developed out of the drive for increased international trade promoted by the United States in the years since the Great Depression.**

Interactive Flipped Video

>> Objectives

Explain the causes of globalization, including recent scientific discoveries and technological innovations, and its effects on the American economy, including why certain places or regions are important to the United States.

Understand the roles of the executive and legislative branches in setting international trade and fiscal policies.

Identify international trade organizations and alliances to which the United States belongs.

Recognize the benefits and drawbacks of the global economy, including the significance to the United States of the location and key natural resources of selected global places or regions.

Understand world economic trends today.

>> Key Terms

globalization
protectionism
tariff
import quota
trade embargo
North American Free Trade Agreement (NAFTA)
International Monetary Fund (IMF)
World Bank
World Trade Organization
Group of 8 (G8)

The U.S. in a Global Economy

A Global Economy

All nations engage in trade. Trade is one of the hallmarks of civilization, and has been for thousands of years. However, improvements in transportation and communication technologies and the pressure to find new markets have spurred the growth of worldwide markets.

The United States produces a great many different goods, but it does not produce everything this country needs. No country does because of the unequal distribution of natural resources and other factors of production, such as skilled workers, among countries. The unequal distribution of factors of production means that one nation can more effectively specialize in producing certain goods—for example, petroleum or computer chips. That nation will then export petroleum or computer chips and use the profits to purchase, or import, goods from other nations who have an advantage in the production of, for example, food stuffs or automobiles.

Consider this example: the United States produces petroleum, but not enough to meet the nation's energy needs. So the United States imports crude oil from other countries, especially Canada, Saudi Arabia, Mexico, and Venezuela, and American companies have long been banned from exporting crude oil. At the same time, the United

States is able to grow many crops that are in demand in other countries. The United States is the world's leading exporter of wheat and corn, for example.

In some cases, countries import and export the same products, providing greater variety to consumers in each country, as well as creating jobs in the manufacturing and transportation industries. The United States, for example, exports automobiles, computers, and telecommunications equipment, but also imports these items.

The Benefits of Trade Trade allows Americans to acquire the goods they want, which this nation cannot produce as cost-effectively or efficiently as it does other goods. Equally importantly, trade provides Americans with a market for goods and services produced in the United States—and by doing so, it provides Americans with jobs.

According to the Peterson Institute for International Economics, American incomes are approximately 9 percent higher than they otherwise would be as the result of free trade with other countries since the end of World War II. Trade accounts for 25 percent of the U.S. gross domestic product (GDP).

It is the role of the Federal Government to support trade and other economic opportunities around the world, while at the same time, protecting American producers and consumers. To accomplish this, the President negotiates free trade agreements with other countries, while Congress has the authority to approve or reject these agreements.

U.S. Imports and Exports Today, as it has been for several decades, Canada is the United States' chief trade partner, although regionally, the United States conducts the greater part of its trade with the European Union. Canada and the United States import vehicles, machinery, oil, and plastics from each other, while Canada also relies on the United States as a source of fruits and vegetables.

After the North American Free Trade Agreement (NAFTA) became effective in 1994, Mexico moved up in rank to second among the United States' main trade partners. Mexico also trades in machinery, vehicles, and oil with the United States. At the same time, Mexico and the United States rely on each other for food: the United States imports fresh fruit and vegetables from Mexico, while Mexico imports grains, meat, soybeans, and dairy products from the United States.

By the end of 2005, China had surpassed Mexico to become the United States' second leading trading partner. This remains true today. The United States imports machinery, toys and sports equipment, furniture, and footwear from China, as well as processed fruits and vegetables, juices, snacks, and

Top 10 U.S. Trade Partners, 2012

RANK	COUNTRY	EXPORTS	IMPORTS	TOTAL U.S. TRADE
1	Canada	292.4	324.2	16.1%
2	China	110.6	425.6	14.0%
3	Mexico	216.3	277.7	12.9%
4	Japan	70.0	146.4	5.7%
5	Germany	48.8	108.5	4.1%
6	United Kingdom	54.8	54.9	2.9%
7	South Korea	42.3	58.9	2.6%
8	Brazil	43.7	32.1	2.0%
9	Saudi Arabia	18.1	55.7	1.9%
10	France	30.8	41.6	1.9%

SOURCE: www.census.gov

>> The chart shows trade in billions of dollars between the United States and other countries. **Analyze Charts** From which country does the United States import the largest dollar amount of goods?

spices. China buys machinery, grain, seeds, soybeans, cars, and aircraft from the United States

The United States is a world leader in foreign trade. This nation is second only to China in the export of goods, and it is the world's largest exporter of services, a sizeable and quickly growing sector of world trade. Major American exports include telecommunications, aerospace, medical, and military equipment.

This country also exports soybeans, corn, fruit, automobiles, and a great many other products. United States service exports include business, professional, and technical services, insurance services, financial services, and travel.

The United States is the world's number one importer of both goods and services. More than $2.3 trillion in goods and services enter this country each year—about 13 percent of all the world's imports. Consumer goods as clothing, toys, and electronics, as well as capital goods, which include computers, electronic parts, and industrial machinery, are among this nation's major imports. Another import category is food and beverages, including animal feed. Automobiles and auto parts constitute a fourth import category.

Industrial Supplies The largest category of imported goods is industrial supplies and materials, including crude oil. The United States imports about 16 percent of its energy supply, and was the largest importer of crude oil in the world until it was overtaken by China in 2013. Most of that oil comes from the countries of Canada, Saudi Arabia, Mexico, Venezuela, and Nigeria.

>> An oil tanker enters a Texas port. In 2012, the United States imported about 57 percent of its crude oil. Canada was by far the country's top crude oil supplier, at about 2.5 million barrels a day.

Interactive Gallery

The location of U.S. trade partners matters tremendously. The United States trades with some countries, such as Canada and Mexico, because they are geographically close. It makes sense to transport goods over a shorter distance rather than a longer one. It is also easier to trade with Pacific Rim countries because the Pacific Ocean can act as a shipping route. For other trade partners, such as Saudi Arabia and China, proximity to natural resources like oil and rare earth metals is more important.

DRAW CONCLUSIONS How might economic dependence on another country affect the political relationship of the United States with that country?

U.S. Trade Policies

One goal of the Federal Government has often been to protect American producers and workers by keeping prices, and therefore profits, high, while minimizing competition from imports. The executive branch of government must do this (with congressional approval) through such agencies as the Department of Commerce and the International Trade Commission without jeopardizing relationships with its trade partners. It has employed several tools for this tricky task.

Economic Resources and Foreign Policy Most national governments try to control imports to protect native industries from foreign competition. The goals of this practice, known as **protectionism,** include safeguarding of jobs, protecting emerging or weakened industries, and enhancing national security. Governments often pursue these goals with trade barriers that hinder free trade and raise the prices consumers must pay for imported goods. These trade barriers are generally of three types: tariffs, import quotas, and trade embargoes. In the United States, the decision to set up such trade barriers must ultimately be made by Congress.

A **tariff** is a tax on imported goods. A tariff increases the cost of an imported item and makes American-made products more attractive to the domestic customer. The government regularly places high tariffs on goods that are produced by important American industries. For example, the tariff on steel is relatively high because Americans produce a great deal of it and the steel industry is considered vital to national security, so the government does not wish

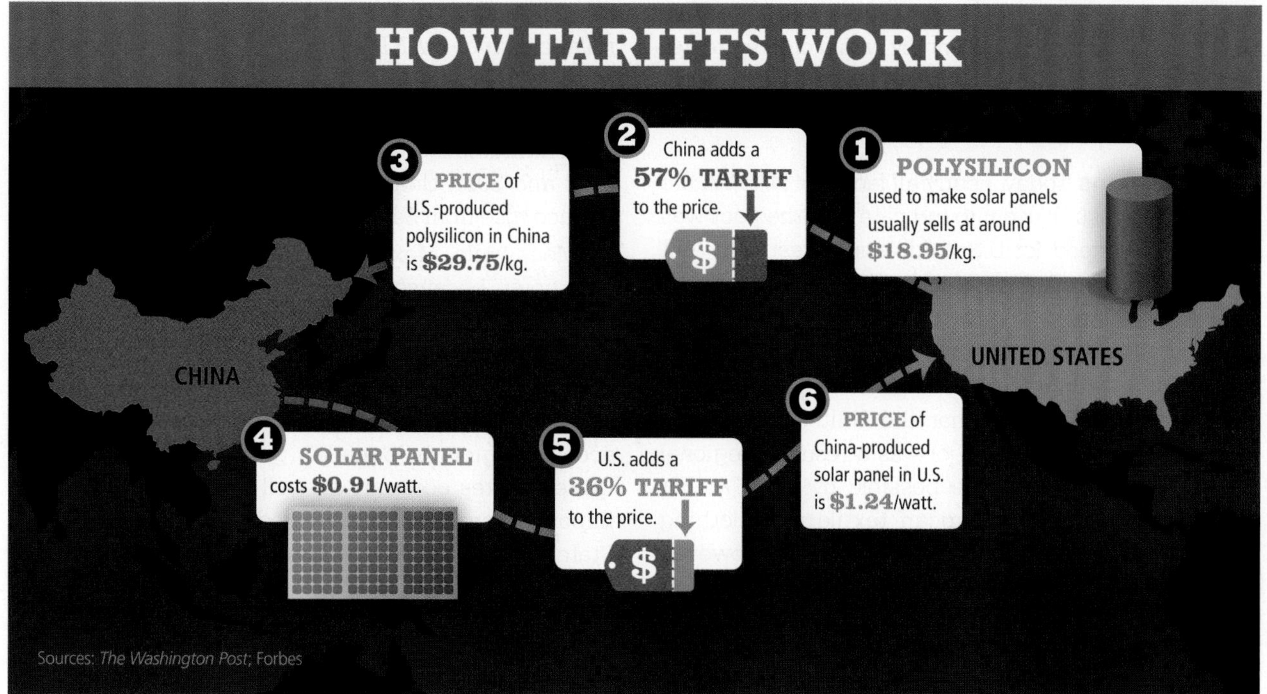
HOW TARIFFS WORK
1 POLYSILICON used to make solar panels usually sells at around $18.95/kg.
2 China adds a 57% TARIFF to the price.
3 PRICE of U.S.-produced polysilicon in China is $29.75/kg.
4 SOLAR PANEL costs $0.91/watt.
5 U.S. adds a 36% TARIFF to the price.
6 PRICE of China-produced solar panel in U.S. is $1.24/watt.
CHINA
UNITED STATES
Sources: The Washington Post; Forbes

>> Tariffs protect industries from foreign competition. **Analyze Charts** How would the cost of a China-produced solar panel be affected by a decrease in the tariff on U.S.-produced polysilicon?

cheaper imports to put domestic steel mills out of business.

An **import quota** is a limit on the amount of a commodity that can be imported into a country. While recently limited by international agreements, import quotas are still in place in the United States on such items as cotton, sugar, and milk. Many European nations have put a quota on American films and television shows to encourage the production of their own features and to protect national cultures.

Trade Embargoes and Sanctions Trade embargoes and sanctions are more significant trade barriers—and are more often used to apply diplomatic pressure or as a punishment rather than as an economic tool. A **trade embargo** is a ban on trade with a particular country. Sanctions are similar to embargoes. An embargo might be placed on all goods or only specific items. It can be placed on exports or, separately, on imports. The United States has used trade embargoes largely to promote its foreign policy positions. For example, the United States has maintained a complete economic embargo on communist Cuba since the early 1960s. Despite the reopening of formal diplomatic ties between the U.S. and Cuba in 2014, the trade embargo remains in place. In fact, President Trump broadened the embargo in 2017.

Embargoes can be effective, but notice that they may also hurt the domestic economy of the nation imposing them. The U.S. embargo on Cuba has not yet changed Cuba's political regime but does close off Cuba to American businesses.

Free Trade in North America The North American Free Trade Agreement, known as **NAFTA,** became effective in 1994. NAFTA established free trade among the United States, Canada, and Mexico, and intended to eliminate, in steps, all tariffs and other barriers to trade by 2009. It created what amounts to the world's largest free trade zone.

NAFTA was approved only after a great deal of controversy and resistance, especially in the United States. Advocates of NAFTA argued that the United States should be able to trade freely with its nearest neighbors, and that improving the economy of the entire region could not help but be good for the U.S. economy as well.

Opponents of the agreement were concerned that American manufacturing operations would be moved to Mexico, where wages are lower and regulations are fewer, and lead to huge job losses. Others worried that imports without tariffs would put American businesses at a huge disadvantage. Supporters insisted that the expected increase in exports to Canada and Mexico would mean an increase in American jobs. They also argued that an improved economy would create greater prosperity and stability in Mexico, and so reduce illegal immigration from that country.

Pros and Cons Today, nearly all facets of NAFTA are in place; the results seem to indicate that the pact was on the whole good for U.S. trade and investment, but not positive for all American workers. Although the long-term results are hard to distinguish from other trends, it appears that NAFTA accelerated the loss of high-paying manufacturing jobs.

Economists estimate that the United States has lost approximately 600,000 jobs as a result of regional competition for work made possible by NAFTA. For example, jobs in the American textile and clothing sectors, already in decline, decreased steeply. However, many manufacturing jobs that have left the United States have moved to countries other than Mexico or Canada. Meanwhile, Mexico has lost agricultural jobs, and some of its agricultural workers have illegally immigrated to the United States.

In addition to its effects on the total number of manufacturing jobs in the U.S., NAFTA has affected the amount that industrial workers overall are paid. Wages paid for factory jobs within the United States have dropped, or in some cases have not risen to meet inflation, since NAFTA was passed.

On the positive side, trade—in agricultural products especially—has increased dramatically with the elimination of nearly all trade barriers. Between 1993 and 2011, United States merchandise exports to Mexico rose from $41 billion to more than $198 billion.

Meanwhile, Mexico's own manufacturing industry has grown because the United States imposes tariffs on high-tech goods coming from countries that are not part of NAFTA, so goods produced in Mexico cost less for American consumers. Of the three countries that agreed to NAFTA, Canada has experienced the highest economic growth. Canada's growth has affected the United States economy as well because Canada now imports more agricultural products from the United States than it did before signing NAFTA.

>> Mining equipment is one example of exports from the United States to Australia. Trade between the two countries rose 23 percent in 2005, the year after a free trade agreement (AUSFTA) was signed.

Other Trade Agreements While NAFTA affects only trade with Canada and Mexico, it provides a model for freer trade with other countries. The United States has signed similar treaties, although involving much smaller trade flows, with Australia and countries in Latin America, the Middle East, Africa, and Asia. For example, in 2012 Congress ratified a free trade agreement reducing tariffs on goods imported from South Korea and making the Korean market more accessible to U.S. auto manufacturers, U.S. law firms, and U.S. suppliers of financial services.

The United States International Trade Commission estimated that the agreement with South Korea would result in an increase of between $10 billion and $12 billion to the United States GDP each year, mostly in merchandise exports to Korea.

As of 2014, President Barack Obama was also negotiating a free trade agreement with the European Union—an agreement that he hopes will increase the GDP by another $122 billion. This agreement, called the Transatlantic Trade and Investment Partnership (TTIP), could rival NAFTA in its size and scope if approved by Congress.

? COMPARE What is the difference between a trade embargo and a tariff?

Trade Alliances and Organizations

The United States employs the tools of protectionism to support industries and workers at home. It also uses them to enlarge economic opportunities, strengthen international ties, and open new markets abroad. It often

Top 10 Countries in the International Monetary Fund by Votes

COUNTRY	PERCENTAGE OF IMF VOTES
United States	16.75%
Japan	6.23%
Germany	5.81%
United Kingdom	4.29%
France	4.29%
China	3.81%
Italy	3.16%
Saudi Arabia	2.80%
Canada	2.56%
Russian Federation	2.39%

>> Voting power in the International Monetary Fund is connected to a country's contribution to the fund. **Analyze Charts** What percentage of the IMF's votes is comprised by the top ten countries?

does this through membership in free trade agreements and international alliances and organizations.

As you can imagine, no single actor or institution can do a lot to shape the world's economy. However, it is also fair to say that the United States probably plays a greater role in influencing international fiscal policy than any other nation. It does so mainly through its leadership in two important organizations: the International Monetary Fund (IMF) and the World Bank. The World Trade Organization (WTO) and the Group of 8 (G8) are also international economic organizations to which the United States belongs.

The International Monetary Fund Headquartered in Washington, D.C., the **International Monetary Fund** was created after World War II by 29 nations. Since then it has grown to nearly 200 countries. Some of the the goals of this organization are to structure international trade, create fiscal stability, promote cross-border investment, reduce world poverty, and provide loans to developing nations.

The United States has three times the voting power in the IMF of any other nation, based on its contribution to the fund. Both the executive and legislative branches of the Federal Government play a role in U.S. involvement in the IMF. The President, with the advice and consent of the Senate, is in charge of appointing U.S. representatives to the IMF, while Congress is responsible for authorizing and appropriating U.S. financial commitments.

The World Bank The **World Bank** is a similar institution, and it was created at the same time as the IMF. Its mission is a bit narrower, however, centering on strategies to reduce world poverty, promote global literacy, and raise the standard of living around the world. These strategies include making loans to developing nations to build bridges, dams, and to make other tangible improvements and provide advice and training.

The United States is the largest shareholder in the World Bank, which, like the IMF, is headquartered in Washington, D.C. As a result, the leader of the World Bank has traditionally been an American citizen nominated by the President. Here, too, Congress is responsible for authorizing and appropriating U.S. funds for the World Bank. Because of the various strategies used by these organizations to promote stable economic policies and reduce poverty across the globe, the IMF and the World Bank have been a source of controversy, both abroad and in the United States.

The World Trade Organization and the G8 The **World Trade Organization** was created in 1995 to help carry out and extend the goals of a 1947 treaty, the General Agreement on Tariffs and Trade (GATT), which intended to increase trade. With 157 members, the WTO provides a set of rules for international commerce, a forum for the creation of new trade agreements, and an arena in which to resolve trade issues.

Another important group to which the United States belongs is the **Group of 8**, or the "G8," an annual meeting of the leaders of eight wealthy and industrialized nations: the United States, Canada, France, Germany, Italy, Japan, Russia, and the United Kingdom. The group has no rigid structure, and leaders meet as representatives of their governments to discuss world affairs and crises.

Regional Trade Alliances The European Union (EU) is the most successful of the world's free trade organizations. It also formulates policies in other areas, such as the environment and security. The evolution of the EU began in 1957, when six European nations established the European Common Market to coordinate economic policies and trade. Over time, most Western European nations joined the group. In 1986, they created the European Economic Community (EEC) and, in an historic step, eliminated all tariffs on trade between EU members.

In 1993, the organization went even further to blur international boundaries by forming the European Union. The EU operates much like a weak Federal Government, with its own parliament, its own flag, and even an anthem. Citizens of most member nations can now travel as tourists or workers across national borders freely, without a passport. By 2011, seventeen of the member nations had given up their individual currencies and replaced them with the EU's currency, the euro. The EU is now comprised of 28 nations, including many of the former Soviet republics.

Inspired by the success of the EU, other nations have formed trade alliances. One of the largest is the Asian-Pacific Economic Cooperation (APEC). Its 21 members include nations bordering the Pacific Rim, such as the United States, Japan, Canada, Chile, and China. The Southern Common Market, or MERCOSUR, is a regional trade bloc that today includes Brazil, Argentina, Paraguay, Uruguay, and Venezuela.

? COMPARE Explain the difference between the World Trade Organization and the International Monetary Fund.

The Consequences of the Global Economy

For the most part, a global economy seems to be a positive development. It means that more goods are available to more consumers, and that there are more markets in which producers can sell goods. Globalization and international partnerships also help developing nations expand their economies and raise

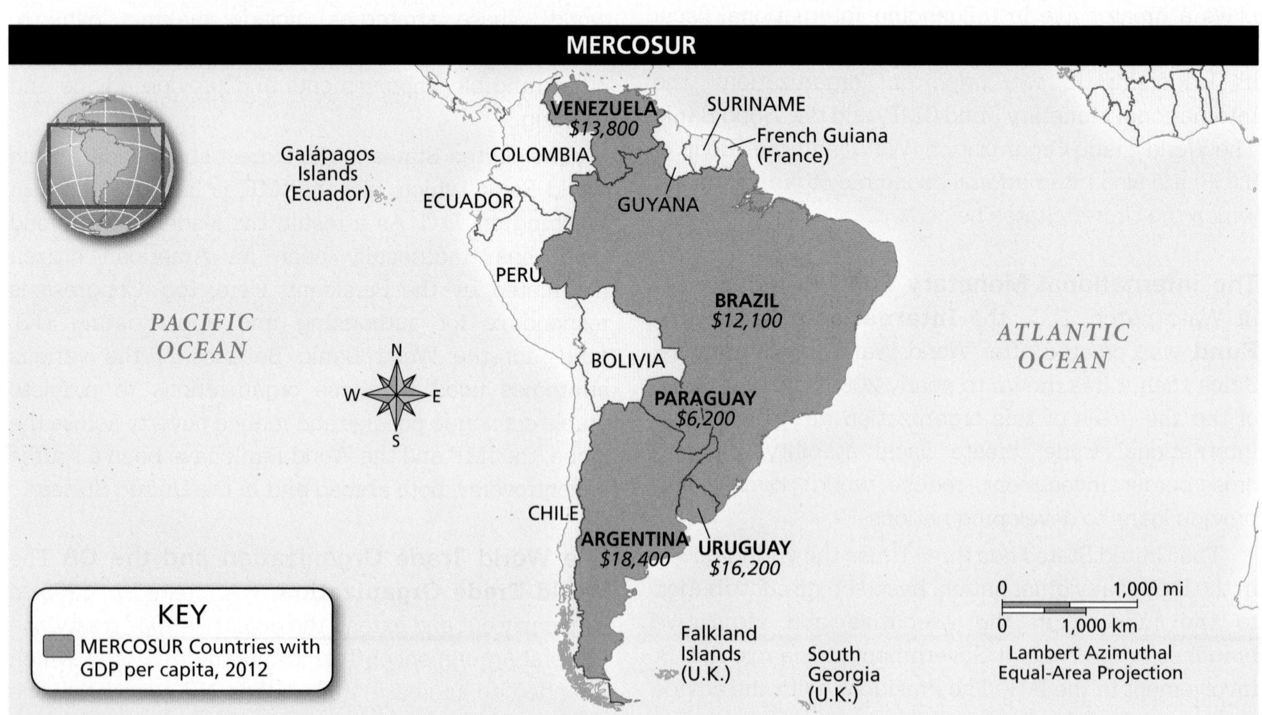

>> MERCOSUR is one of the world's major trade alliances. **Analyze Maps** U.S. gross domestic product in 2013 was $52,800. How does that compare with the GDPs of these MERCOSUR countries?

Manufacturing v. Services in the U.S. Economy

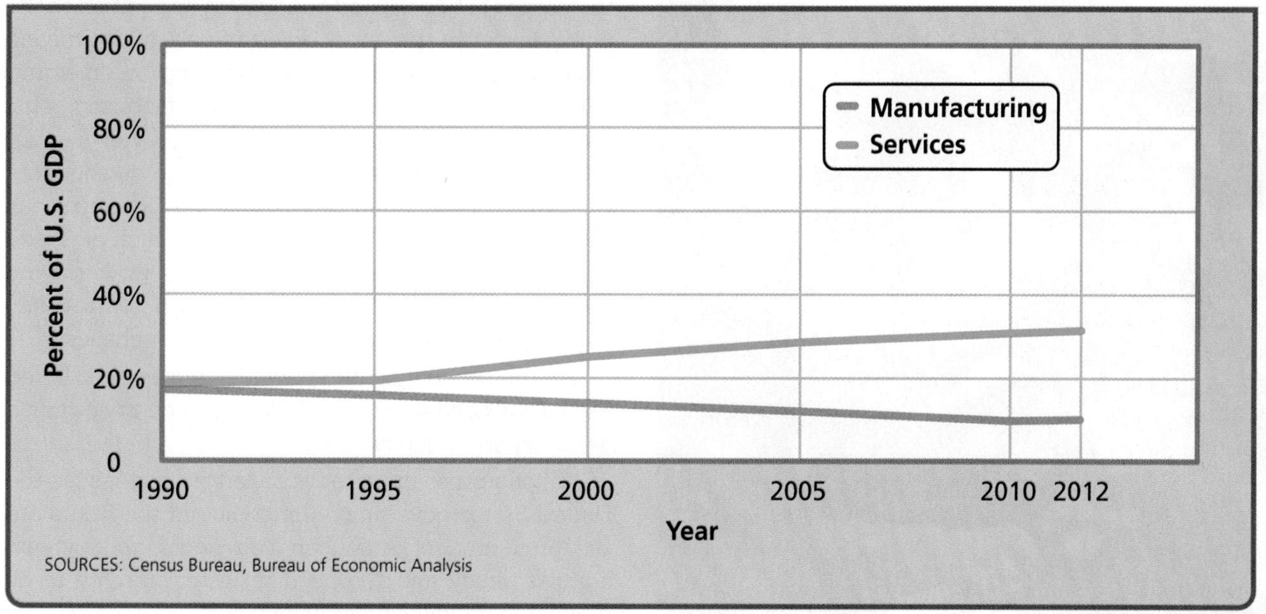

>> In the last two decades, the United States has transitioned from a manufacturing to a service economy. **Analyze Charts** How does this trend affect workers in both areas?

their standards of living by enabling them to sell goods to more affluent countries.

And, clearly, competition in a global market lowers the price of goods. Goods made overseas, unblocked by tariffs, are less expensive and become more affordable for Americans. Increases in jobs and higher wages, in turn, allow consumers in developing nations to buy American goods and services, and this helps to increase or at least maintain American jobs.

Additionally, new, creative approaches to outsourcing may actually create new American jobs by lowering costs so that corporations are able to use the savings to grow and develop innovative products and services. Importantly, increased economic interdependence may lead to more political cooperation and so to fewer conflicts.

Risks However, with interdependence comes risk. A crisis in another nation on which Americans depend for an important commodity can have quick, profound, and direct economic effects. Thus, in recent years, war in Iraq and instability in Nigeria—both major oil-producing nations—contributed to higher oil and gas prices in the United States.

Some people worry that international trade agreements may affect a nation's sovereignty if they have to get "permission" from partner nations to make decisions about such matters as civil rights, defense, or the environment. With instantaneous communications, economic downturns or market fluctuations in one part of the world now cause instability in other markets within hours.

Globalization has led to the exploitation of workers in some less developed countries. Some multinational corporations have been criticized—and some have been sued in U.S. courts—for allowing unhealthy working conditions, paying workers wages that are below poverty level, and employing children to work in factories and elsewhere.

The United States is also adversely affected by trade deficits. For example, the United States buys much more from China than China buys from the United States, and so an enormous trade deficit has developed. China has financed the deficit by lending the United States government money and by buying American assets. This means that China, along with Japan and many oil-exporting countries, owns a portion of the American economy, with possible implications for the economic health and future of this nation.

The United States is also moving from a manufacturing economy to a service economy, in large part because American workers cannot compete with workers in other nations who are paid much less. According to the Office of the U.S. Trade Representative, service industries now compose 68 percent of the gross domestic product. In the ten years between 2000 and 2010, the United States lost nearly one third of its manufacturing jobs.

>> Production line workers at a factory in Gimpo, South Korea, assemble mobile phones. A free trade agreement between the United States and the Republic of Korea (KORUS FTA) went into effect in 2012.

Tomorrow's Marketplace The trend today in the world economy is toward greater interdependence among nations—increased globalization. Along with the United States, most nations are joining multiple trade alliances, such as NAFTA and the EU, to open new markets and promote free trade. Developing nations are working to diversify their economies and open their markets. The United States continues to build partnerships by establishing new trade agreements with nations such as Peru, South Korea, Singapore, and Colombia and working with China to lower the U.S. trade deficit with that nation.

The good news for Americans is that the huge increase in the demand for services worldwide means that the United States will probably continue to see an increase in service exports and retain its position as the global leader in that area. Unfortunately, it also means increase in free trade and outsourcing to emerging nations means further loss of manufacturing jobs. Although economic analysts have mixed views about the overall cost in American jobs due to outsourcing, thousands or even millions of jobs could move overseas in the coming years. Federal programs such as Trade Adjustment Assistance, which retrains workers who are laid off due to outsourcing or foreign competition, will help American workers deal with this challenge.

As the economy shifts toward services, the United States will need to rely on intellectual property as much as on exported goods.

Among other important challenges and issues the United States government must face in the future are the protection of American copyrights and patents against piracy and the need to foster stability in oil producing nations and regions.

? INFER How do trade alliances affect the United States economy as a whole?

ASSESSMENT

1. **Identify Supporting Details** What are the advantages of NAFTA for the United States?
2. **Categorize** Is NAFTA a protectionist agreement? Why or why not?
3. **Identify Supporting Details** Give an example of a way in which U.S. foreign policy is driven by the nation's economic needs.
4. **Compare and Contrast** Distinguish between the role of the President and the role of Congress in determining U.S. economic policies.
5. **Draw Conclusions** How can economic policies affect national security?

TOPIC 12 ASSESSMENT

Marxist Economies

SOCIALISM	COMMUNISM
Goal: Change capitalism within rules of democracy.	**Goal:** Destroy capitalism with revolutions followed by communist dictatorships.
Some central planning	Centrally planned economy
Most property privately owned	All land and housing state owned
Large industries nationalized	No privately owned businesses
High taxes to fund healthcare, child care, education	State-provided healthcare, child care, education
Free elections	Controlled elections
Strong unions and worker protections	State-controlled unions

1. **Compare the Role of Government in Economic Systems** Use the chart above to write a paragraph comparing the role of government in the U.S. free enterprise system with the role of government in socialist and communist systems. Consider the following questions: What are the key characteristics of a free enterprise system? What are the key characteristics of socialism? What are the key characteristics of communism? How do communism and socialism differ? How do Marxist systems differ from the U.S. system?

2. **Compare the U.S. to Historical Forms of Government** Compare the U.S. constitutional republic to a socialist form of government. Consider the following questions: What is a mixed economy? How is the U.S. a mixed economy? How are modern socialist states mixed economies? What are some differences between government involvement in the U.S. economy versus government involvement in socialist economies?

3. **Explain Fiscal and Monetary Policies** Write a paragraph that answers the following questions: What is the difference between fiscal and monetary policy? How do fiscal policies influence the economy at the State and local levels? At the federal level? How do monetary policies influence the economy at the State and local levels? At the federal level?

4. **Explain Government Regulatory Policies** Use visual aids as appropriate to create an oral presentation explaining how government regulatory policies influence the economy at the local, State, and federal levels. Consider the following questions: Why does the Federal Government regulate the economy? What are some key government regulatory agencies in place today? How do government regulatory polices influence the economy at the local, State, and federal levels?

TOPIC 12 ASSESSMENT

5. **Understand Constitutional Protections** Use the quotation below to write a paragraph that answers the following questions: What is the Sherman Anti-Trust Act and on what constitutional basis does it rest? How does the Sherman Anti-Trust Act foster competition in the United States? What other constitutional protections foster competition?

   "Every contract, combination in the form of a trust or otherwise, or conspiracy, in restraint of trade or commerce among the several States, or with foreign nations, is hereby declared to be illegal."

   —*Sherman Anti-Trust Act*

6. **Understand Government Regulation** Write a paragraph explaining how government regulation can limit private enterprise.

7. **Explain Cultural Changes** Write a paragraph about the GI Bill that answers the following questions: What was the Servicemen's Readjustment Act (GI Bill of Rights) of 1944? How did it effect the U.S. economy and change American culture?

8. **Identify Revenue Sources** Identify the sources of revenue of the U.S. government. Write a paragraph that answers the following questions: What is the major source of government revenue? What are the specific types of taxes? What other sources of revenue does the Federal Government have?

9. **Understand How Taxation Restricts Enterprise** Use the map below to complete the following: If the State of New Hampshire's total revenues for 2013 were $1.24 billion, how much revenue did corporate taxes contribute to that total? Choose five states and show the data on the map for those five States in bar graph form. How can government taxation serve as a restriction to private enterprise?

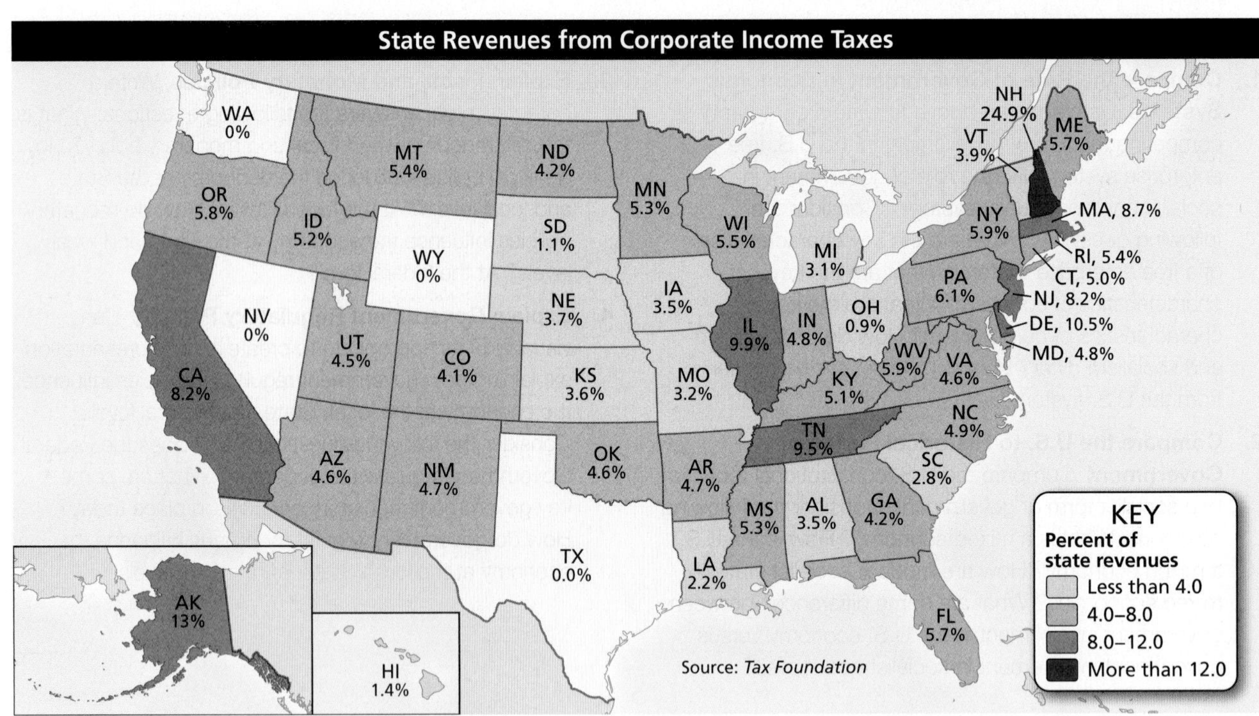

10. **Identify Individuals in Government and Politics** Use the quotation below to write a paragraph identifying Franklin Roosevelt and explaining his significance in terms of economic theories. Consider the following questions: Who was Franklin Roosevelt? What was the New Deal? According to the quotation, why did Roosevelt support the New Deal? What is the significance of Franklin Roosevelt and the New Deal to federal fiscal policy today?

    "Not only our future economic soundness but the very soundness of our democratic institutions depends on the determination of our government to give employment to idle men."

    —Franklin Roosevelt, Fireside Chat, April 14, 1938

11. **Analyze Functions of the Legislative Branch** Write a paragraph about the role of congressional committees in the federal budget process. Consider the following questions: Which congressional committees are most directly involved in creating the budget? What is the role of these committees in the budget process?

12. **Explain Domestic Policy Responsibilities** Write a paragraph that answers the following questions: What is fiscal policy? How are fiscal policy and domestic policy related? Why are taxes an important part of federal government?

13. **Understand the Responsibilities of Citizenship** Write a paragraph that answers the following questions: What is the main purpose of taxes? Why is paying taxes a responsibility of citizenship? How do citizens benefit from taxes?

14. **Identify the Significance of Places** Write a paragraph explaining the significance of the location of trade partners to the United States. Consider the following questions: In what way does the location of Canada and Mexico contribute to their importance as U.S. trade partners? What other factors in addition to location influence the importance of U.S. trade partnerships?

15. **Identify and Analyze Expenditures** Create an informational poster identifying the expenditures of the U.S. government and analyzing their impact on the U.S. economy. Using a combination of graphs, charts, statements, and other appropriate devices, your poster should first identify the expenditures of the U.S. government in terms of spending priorities and the two major categories of spending, with examples. Then the poster should illustrate the impact of federal spending on the economy. Use the following process: Consult several sources on the impact of federal spending on the economy. Analyze those sources for point of view, frame of reference, and any potential bias to make sure they are reliable. Use the information in the sources as the basis for the part of your poster focusing on the impact of government spending on the economy.

16. **Examine Economic Resources in Foreign Policy** Write a paragraph examining how the U.S. government uses trade embargoes in foreign policy. Consider the following questions: What are trade embargoes and why are they used? What is one example of the use of trade embargoes as part of U.S. foreign policy?

17. **Analyze U.S. Foreign Policy** Create a written presentation analyzing how the decision to approve the North American Free Trade Agreement affects selected places. Consider the following questions: What is the North American Free Trade Agreement (NAFTA)? How does NAFTA affect Canada and Mexico?

18. **Analyze Functions of the Executive Branch** Write a paragraph explaining the constitutional role of the president in trade agreements and organizations. Consider the following questions to support your response: What does the Constitution name as the president's role in trade agreements and organizations? How does the president accomplish this today? Has this role changed?

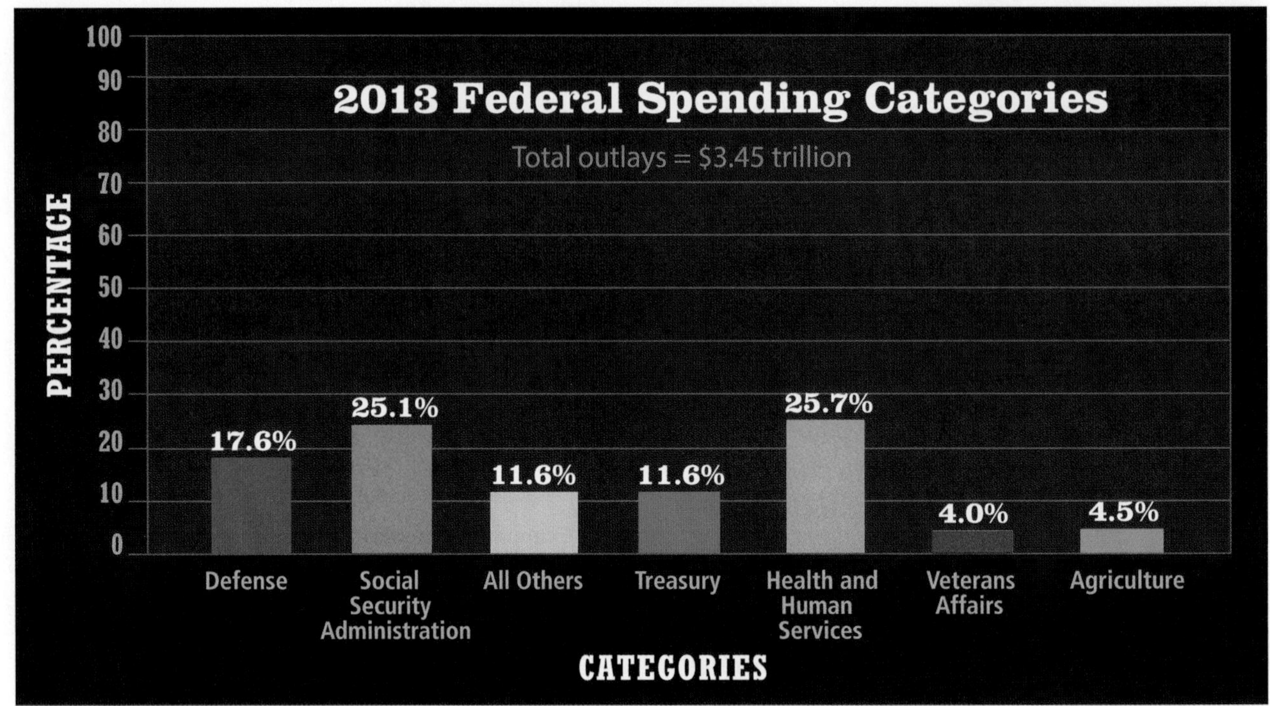

19. **Explain Domestic Policy Responsibilities** Use the graph above showing major categories of federal spending in 2013 to write a response to the following question: The federal budget is more than a financial statement. It is also a declaration of the public policies of the United States. Given that fact, what does the spending shown in the graph reveal about the Federal Government's responsibilities for domestic policy? Also consider the following questions: According to the graph, how much larger is spending related to domestic affairs than spending related to foreign affairs? (Note: Do not include the "All Others" category in your calculations, since some of that figure includes foreign affairs spending.) What dollar amount of the budget was earmarked for Agriculture in 2013? For Health and Human Services? The "All Others" category includes the following departments: State, Justice, Interior, Commerce, Labor, Housing and Urban Development, Transportation, Energy, Education, and Homeland Security. What does the inclusion of so many departments in one category tell you about national priorities for these areas?

20. **Understand the Role of the Executive Branch in Trade Policy** Create a graphic organizer that summarizes and explains the executive branch's role in setting international trade policy.

21. **Understand the Executive Role in National Fiscal Policy** Write a paragraph that answers the following questions: How does fiscal policy influence the economy? How can fiscal policy slow inflation or boost the economy? What is the role of the executive branch in setting fiscal policy?

22. **Write About the Essential Question** **Write an essay on the Essential Question: What is the proper role of the government in the economy?** Use evidence from your study of this Topic to support your answer.

Go online to PearsonRealize.com and use the texts, quizzes, interactivities, Interactive Reading Notepads, Flipped Videos, and other resources from this Topic to prepare for the Topic Test.

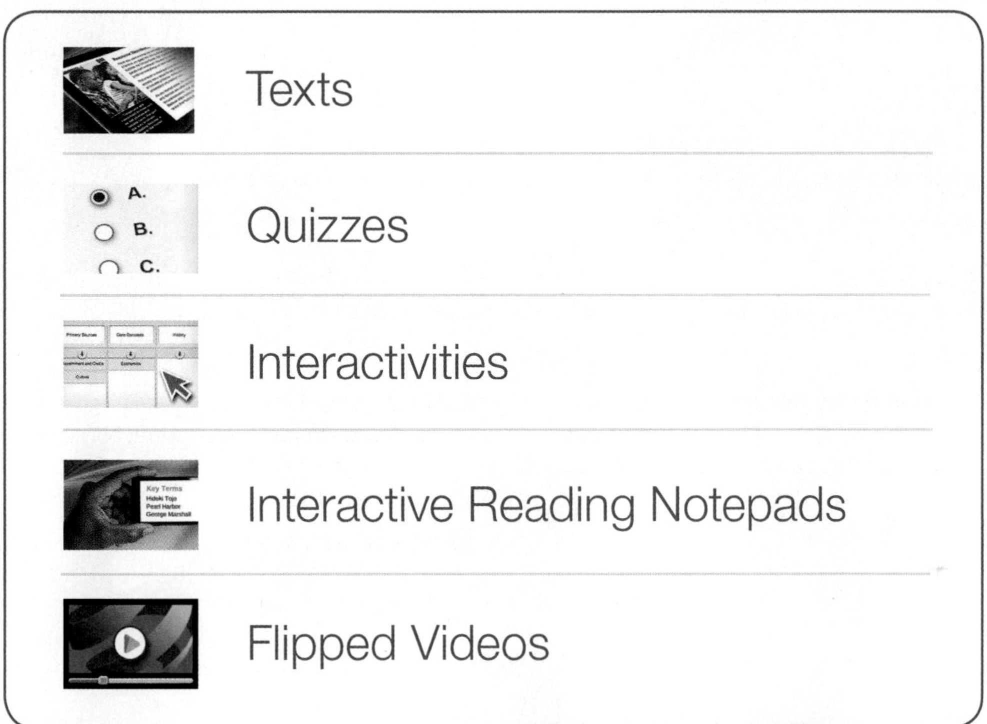

While online you can also check the progress you've made learning the topic and course content by viewing your grades, test scores, and assignment status.

[**ESSENTIAL QUESTION**] What Should Governments Do?

13 State and Local Governments

Topic 13 State and Local Governments

>> Oklahoma Governor Mary Fallin, second from right, tours a tornado-damaged neighborhood.

Enduring Understandings

- Every State has a unique written constitution that defines the State's government and values according to its citizens' views.
- Governors possess some legislative and judicial powers, and most share executive power with other elected officials.
- Local courts deal with a wide range of cases, and those involving difficult points of law rise to appellate courts or the State supreme court on appeal.
- County, town, and township governments both supply basic services of daily life and provide a wide range of public services to residents.
- The U.S. Constitution reserves to the States all powers not delegated to the Federal Government or not denied to the States.
- The State budget is the plan for the control and use of public money; sources of funding include taxes, federal grants, and borrowing.

Watch the My Story Video, Governorship, A Stepping Stone to the Presidency.

Access your digital lessons including: Topic Inquiry • Interactive Reading Notepad • Interactivities • Assessments

>> A mural hanging in the Massachusetts State House depicts the drafting of that State's constitution. Massachusetts was the first State to submit its constitution to the voters for approval.

Interactive Flipped Video

13.1 Not very many people have ever seen a State constitution, let alone read one. Join a rather exclusive club and look at your State's document. This step should prove useful as you read this Lesson.

>> **Objectives**

Examine the history, content, and significance of the first State constitutions.

Describe the basic principles common to all State constitutions today.

Explain the procedures used to change State constitutions.

Analyze why State constitutions are in need of reform.

>> **Key Terms**

popular sovereignty
fundamental laws
statutory law
initiative
limited government

State Constitutions

The First State Constitutions

A State constitution is that State's supreme law. It sets out the ways in which the government of the State is organized, and it distributes powers among the various branches of that government. It authorizes the exercise of power by government and, at the same time, puts limits on the exercise of power by government. Every State's constitution is superior to any and all other forms of State and local law within that State.

Recall, however: Each State's constitution is subordinate to the Constitution of the United States. No provision in any State's constitution may conflict with any form of federal law.

Each of the 50 States has a *written* constitution. From the beginning, government in this country has been based on written constitutions.

Our experience with such documents dates from 1606, when King James I granted a charter to the Virginia Company. That act led to the settlement at Jamestown in the following year and, with it, the first government in what would become British North America. Later, each of the other English colonies was also established and governed on the basis of a written charter.

Independence When the 13 colonies became independent, each faced the problem of establishing a new government. On May 15,

1776, the Second Continental Congress, meeting in Philadelphia, advised each of the new States to adopt

> such governments as shall, in the opinion of the representatives of the people, best conduce to the happiness and safety of their constituents in particular, and America in general.
>
> —Second Continental Congress

Most of the colonial charters served as models for the first State constitutions. Indeed, in Connecticut and Rhode Island, the charters seemed so well suited to the needs of the day that they were carried over into statehood as constitutions almost without change.

The earliest State constitutions were adopted in a variety of ways. However, the people played no direct part in the process in any State.

Six of the revolutionary legislatures drew up new documents and proclaimed them in force in 1776. In none of those States—Maryland, New Jersey, North Carolina, Pennsylvania, South Carolina, and Virginia—was the new constitution offered to the people for their judgment.

In Delaware and New Hampshire in 1776, and in Georgia and New York in 1777, the constitutions were prepared by conventions called by the legislature. In each case, the new document had to be approved by the legislature in order to become effective, but in none was popular approval required.

In 1780, a popularly elected convention prepared a new constitution for Massachusetts. It was then ratified by a vote of the people. Thus, Massachusetts set the pattern of popular participation in the constitution-making process, a pattern generally followed among the States ever since.

Assemblies representing the people drafted all of the present State constitutions; most of them became effective only after a popular vote. Only the present-day documents of Delaware (1897), Mississippi (1890), South Carolina (1895), and Vermont (1793) came into force without popular ratification.

Principles of State Constitutions Because the first State constitutions came out of the same revolutionary ferment, they shared many basic features. Each proclaimed the principles of **popular sovereignty** and **limited government.** That is, in each of them the people were recognized as the sole source of authority for government, and the powers given to the new government were closely limited. Seven documents began with a lengthy bill of rights. All of them made it clear that the sovereign people held "certain unalienable rights" that government must respect.

The doctrines of separation of powers and checks and balances were also built into each of the new constitutions. In practice, however, the memory of the hated royal governors was still fresh. Thus, most of the authority that each State government had was given to the legislature. For example, only New York, Massachusetts, and South Carolina allowed the governor to veto acts of the legislature. In all the States except Georgia (until 1789) and Pennsylvania (until 1790), the legislature was bicameral. Vermont, which became the 14th State in 1791, had a unicameral legislature until 1836. Only Nebraska has a one-house legislative body today, and it has had one since 1937.

For their time, the early State constitutions were fairly democratic. Each however, contained several provisions (and some important omissions) that were quite undemocratic by today's standards. Thus, none of them provided for full religious freedom. Each one set rigid qualifications for voting and for officeholding, and all gave property owners a highly favored standing.

? APPLY CONCEPTS Describe the elements of the first State constitutions that were influenced by the Revolutionary period.

"Look — if I'd had any idea what a constitution was, I never would have signed the darn thing, okay?"

>> Early State constitutions reflected the struggle for independence. **Analyze Political Cartoons** What is the cartoonist saying about the emphasis many constitutions place on popular sovereignty?

State Constitutions Today

The present-day State constitutions are the direct descendants of those earlier documents. Only 17 of the current State constitutions were written after 1900, and nearly all have been amended dozens of times.

Subject only to the broad limitations set out in the Federal Constitution, the people of each State can create whatever kind of "Republican Form of Government" they choose. Unique provisions can be found in each of the 50 present-day State constitutions. Still, all of them are quite similar in general outline.

Basic Principles Every State's constitution is built on the principles of popular sovereignty and limited government. Each of them recognizes that government exists only with the consent of the people, and that it must operate within certain, often closely defined, bounds. In every State, the powers of government are divided among executive, legislative, and judicial branches. Each branch has powers with which it can restrain the actions of the other two. That is, each of the 50 documents proclaims separation of powers and, with it, checks and balances. Each also provides, either expressly or by implication, for the power of judicial review.

Protections of Civil Rights Each document features a bill of rights, a listing of the rights that individuals hold against the State and its officers and agencies. Most constitutions set out guarantees much like those in the first ten amendments to the national Constitution. Several of them include a number of other guarantees as well—for example, the right to self-government, to be safe from imprisonment for debt, and to organize labor unions and bargain collectively.

Governmental Structure Every State constitution deals with the structure of government at both the State and the local levels, including all three branches of State government and the organization of counties and local governments. A few follow the national pattern, providing only a broad outline. Most, however, cover the subject in considerable and often quite specific detail.

Governmental Powers and Processes Each document lists, in detail, the powers vested in the executive branch (the governor and other executive officers), the legislature, the courts, and the units of local government. The powers to tax, spend, borrow, and provide for education are very prominent. So, too, are such processes as elections, judicial procedures, legislation, and intergovernmental (State-local) relations.

Constitutional Change Constitutions are the product of human effort. None are perfect. Sooner or

Elements of State Constitutions

PRINCIPLES	CIVIL RIGHTS	STRUCTURE	POWERS	CHANGE	OTHER
VOTE					
• Popular sovereignty and limited government	• Similar to U.S. Bill of Rights • May also restrict State government or enhance individual liberty	• Outline of State and local government • Separation of powers • Checks and balances	• Lists powers held by State officials to govern and provide services • Empowers State to tax, spend, and borrow	• Processes for amendment	• Preambles without legal force • "Dead letter" material—provisions that no longer apply

>> State constitutions establish in detail the organization and powers of the State government. **Analyze Charts** How are State constitutions similar to the U.S. Constitution?

later, changes become necessary, or at least desirable. So, each State constitution sets out the means by which it may be revised or amended. Constitutions are **fundamental laws**—laws of such basic and lasting importance they cannot be changed as ordinary law can be. Constitutional changes are more difficult to bring about, as you shall see.

Miscellaneous Provisions Every State constitution contains several sections of a miscellaneous character. Thus, most begin with a preamble, which has no legal force but does set out the purposes of those who drafted and adopted the document. Most also contain a schedule, a series of provisions for putting a new document into effect and for avoiding conflicts with its predecessor. And most include a number of "dead letter" provisions, items that have no current force or effect but nonetheless remain a part of the constitution.

COMPARE How are the State constitutions of today similar to the U.S. Constitution?

>> The State of Florida has more methods by which to amend its constitution than any other State. One method involves the passage of a joint resolution by the Florida legislature.

Interactive Gallery

Constitutional Change

Like the national Constitution, the State constitutions have been altered over time by formal amendment and by such other processes as court decisions and custom. However, those other processes have not been nearly so important at the State level as at the national level.

State constitutions are much less flexible, and much more detailed, than the national document. Constitutional change and development at the State level has come about mostly through formal amendment rather than by other means.

Two kinds of formal changes have been used: amendments, which usually deal with one or a few provisions in a constitution; and revisions, the term usually used to refer to changes of a broader scope. Revisions might include, for example, an entirely new document. Most of the formal changes made in State constitutions are made by amendment.

Procedures for Change The process of formal change involves two basic steps: proposal and then ratification. Proposals for change can be made by a constitutional convention, the legislature, or (in several States) by the voters themselves. Ratification is by popular vote in every State except Delaware.

The constitutional convention is the usual device by which new constitutions have been written and older ones revised. More than 200 such conventions have been held. In every State, the legislature has the power to call a convention, and that call is generally subject to voter approval. In 14 States, the question of calling a convention must be submitted to the voters at regular intervals. Conventions can also propose amendments. However, because they are both costly and time-consuming, conventions are most often used for the broader purpose of revision.

Most amendments are proposed by the legislature. The process is comparatively simple in some States, while it is quite difficult in others. In Massachusetts, an amendment must be approved by the legislature at two successive annual sessions before it goes to the voters for approval or rejection. In California, a proposal must be approved by the legislature at a single session before being sent on to the voters. Not surprisingly, more amendments are proposed (and adopted) in those States with simpler processes, such as California, than in States such as Massachusetts.

In 18 States, the voters themselves can propose constitutional amendments through the **initiative,** a process by which a certain number of qualified voters sign petitions in favor of a proposal. The proposal then goes either to the State legislature or directly to the ballot, for approval or rejection by the people.

Ratification of Amendments In every State except Delaware, an amendment must be approved by vote of the people in order to become part of the constitution.

The ratification process, like the proposal process, varies among the States.

Typically, the approval of a majority of those voting on an amendment adds it to the State constitution, though some States require a majority of all who vote in an election. On many occasions, in several States, amendments have been defeated though they received more *yes* votes than *no* votes. Most often, this happens because many voters fail to vote on all or at least some ballot measures.

COMPARE AND CONTRAST Explain how the process of amending a State constitution differs from amending the U.S. Constitution.

The Need for Reform

Almost without exception, State constitutions are in urgent need of reform. The typical document is cluttered with unnecessary details, burdensome restrictions, and obsolete sections. It also carries much repetitious, even contradictory, material. Moreover, it fails to deal with many of the pressing problems that the States and their local governments currently face.

>> The average State constitution is four times as long as the U.S. Constitution. **Analyze Political Cartoons** What else does the cartoon imply about comprehensive State constitutions?

Even the newest and most recently rewritten constitutions tend to carry over a great deal of material from earlier documents and suffer from these same faults. The need for reform can be demonstrated in several ways. Looking at the documents from two standpoints, their lengths and their ages, can produce some useful insights.

The Problem of Length Length was not a problem for the first State constitutions. They were quite short, ranging from New Jersey's 1776 document (2,500 words) to the 1780 Massachusetts constitution (12,000 words). Those early constitutions were meant simply to be statements of basic principle and organization. Purposely, they left to the legislature—and to time and practice—the task of filling in the details as they became necessary.

Through the years, however, State constitutions have grown and grown. Most today are between 15,000 and 50,000 words. The shortest are those of Vermont (1793), with some 8,500 words, and Iowa (1857), with just over 11,000 words. At the other extreme, Alabama's 1901 constitution now runs to more than 376,000 words. A leading cause of this expansion is popular distrust of government, a historical and continuing fact of American political life. That distrust has often led to the insertion into State constitutions of detailed provisions aimed at preventing the misuse of government power.

Many restrictions on that power, which could be set out in ordinary law, have been purposely written into the State constitution, where they cannot be easily ignored or readily, and quietly, changed. Special interest groups learned long ago that public policies of particular benefit to them are much more secure in the State constitution than in a mere statute.

There has been a marked failure in every State to distinguish *fundamental law*, that which is basic and of lasting importance and should be in the constitution, from **statutory law**, that which should be enacted as ordinary law by the legislature. The line separating fundamental and statutory law may be blurry in some cases. But who can seriously argue that fundamental law includes the regulation of the length of wrestling matches, as in California's constitution, or the problem of off-street parking in the city of Baltimore, as in Maryland's document?

Two other factors have contributed to the growth of State constitutions. First, the functions performed by the States, and by most of their local governments, have multiplied over recent decades. That development has prompted many new constitutional provisions. Second, the "people" have not been stingy in the use of the initiative in those States where it is available.

The Problem of Age Most State constitutions are severely outdated. They were written for another time and are in urgent need of revision. All too often, their many amendments have aggravated the problem, adding to the clutter of the document.

The Oregon constitution provides a typical example of the situation. It was written by delegates to a territorial convention in 1857 and became effective when Oregon entered the Union in 1859. It has been amended more than 240 times; it now contains more than 55,000 words and includes *two* Articles VII and *seventeen* Articles XI!

Like most of the other State charters, the Oregon document is overloaded with statutory material. One of those Article XIs devotes nearly 2,000 words to a closely detailed treatment of veterans' farm and home loans. The document also contains a number of obsolete provisions, including one that bars any person who has ever engaged in a duel from holding any public office in the State.

Some States' charters have proved to be more stable than others. The oldest of all the constitutions are those in Massachusetts (1780), New Hampshire (1784), and Vermont (1793). Nineteen States still have the constitutions with which they entered the Union and, all told, 35 have documents that are now more than 100 years old.

A number of States have had several constitutions. Louisiana holds the record, with eleven. Georgia's current charter, its tenth, is the most recently rewritten document; it was adopted in 1982 and became effective the following year.

? SUMMARIZE Describe the reasons why most State constitutions are in need of reform.

ASSESSMENT

1. **Identify Central Ideas** List the basic principles on which all State constitutions are based.
2. **Draw Conclusions** How might the two basic methods for changing State constitutions contribute to the need for reform?
3. **Compare and Contrast** Explain the differences between *fundamental law* and *statutory law*. Describe the role these two categories of law play in constitutional change and reform.
4. **Identify Central Issues** Describe the governmental structure that is established in each State constitution.
5. **Summarize** List and explain the ways changes to State constitutions may be proposed.

>> The Maryland State House in Annapolis, the only State capitol that has also served as the nation's Capitol, is the oldest such building still in use.

13.2 **In every State, the legislature, whatever it is called, is the lawmaking branch of State government. So, its basic function goes to the very heart of democratic government: It is charged with translating the public will into the public policy of the State.**

Interactive Flipped Video

>> Objectives

Describe State legislatures.

Explain the election, terms, and compensation of legislators.

Examine the powers and organization of State legislatures.

Describe how voters may write and pass laws through direct legislation.

>> Key Terms

police power
constituent power
referendum

State Legislatures

The Legislature

Several features of their lawmaking bodies vary among the 50 States. This is notably true with regard to both name and size.

State Legislature Structure Just over half the States call their lawmaking body, officially, the "legislature." In 19 States it is known as the "General Assembly," in two States it is called the "Legislative Assembly," and in two others, the "General Court."

All but one of the 50 State legislatures are bicameral, having two chambers. The upper house is known everywhere as "the Senate." The lower house is most commonly titled "the House of Representatives," but may also be "the Assembly," "the General Assembly," or "the House of Delegates." Nebraska, the only State with a one-house legislature, calls it "the Legislature."

As with Congress, bicameralism came to the States' legislative bodies out of the colonial experience. Unicameralism is regularly cited as one of the most significant steps that could be taken to improve State legislatures. Despite its apparent successes in Nebraska, efforts to accomplish it elsewhere have been notably unsuccessful. Those who defend bicameralism usually claim that one house can and does act as a check on the other, and so prevents the passage of unwise legislation. Whether that widely held view is justified or not, it has proved a major barrier to the spread of one-chamber lawmaking bodies.

State Legislature Size There may be no ideal size for a legislative body, but two basic considerations are important. First, a legislature, and each of its houses, should not be so large as to hamper the orderly conduct of the people's business. Second, it should not be so small that the many views and interests within the State cannot be adequately represented.

The upper house in most States has from 30 to 50 members, with as few as 20 senators in Alaska and as many as 67 in Minnesota. The lower house usually ranges between 100 and 150 members. However, there have been at times only 40 seats in Alaska's lower chamber, and New Hampshire's has had as many as a whopping 400!

? EXPLAIN How can the size of a State's legislature ensure fair representation of all citizens?

State Legislators

In 2013, there were 7,383 State legislators—5,411 representatives and 1,972 senators—among the 50 States. Nearly all of them are Republicans or Democrats; fewer than 30 belong to a minor party or are independents.

To really understand your own State's legislature and its members, you have to know a good deal about that institution and those people that you will not find in a textbook. As one widely respected authority on State government and politics tells us,

> [Y]ou need to know about all sorts of things . . . which party is in control and by how much . . . who the governor is, and how he gets along with the legislators . . . what sorts of people those legislators are: not just what they say but how long they have been there, where they come from, what they did before they ran for office and how they got elected. . . .
>
> —Alan Ehrenhalt, "Clueless in Boise," *Governing* magazine

State Legislator Qualifications Every State's constitution sets out formal requirements of age, citizenship, and residence for legislators. Most everywhere, a representative must be at least 18 or 21 years old and, in over half the States, senators must be at least 25. The realities of the politics of the State add informal qualifications far more difficult to meet. They have to do with a candidate's vote-getting abilities, and are based on such things as occupation, name recognition, party, race, religion, national origin, and the like.

Election of Legislators Everywhere, legislators are chosen by popular vote and, almost everywhere, candidates for the legislature are nominated at party primaries. Nominees are picked by conventions in only a few States. In Nebraska, the unicameral legislature is organized on a nonpartisan basis. Candidates are nominated at nonpartisan primaries, and they are not identified by party in the general election.

In most States, the lawmakers are elected in November of even-numbered years. In four States, however—Mississippi, New Jersey, Virginia, and Louisiana—they are chosen in the odd-numbered years, in the hope of separating State and local issues from those in national politics.

Legislative Districts Every State's constitution requires that legislators be chosen from districts within

>> State legislators, such as California's Nancy Skinner, preside over the annual budget and make suggestions regarding expenditures. Ms. Skinner chairs the Assembly Budget Committee in her State.

the State, and nearly all are now elected from single-member districts. Those districts are drawn by the legislature itself in most States, and they are redrawn (reapportioned) every ten years, in line with the federal census. Gerrymandering is quite common.

Most State legislatures were long dominated by the rural, less-populated areas of the State. In *Baker* v. *Carr,* 1962, however, the United States Supreme Court held the unfair, unequal distribution of State legislative seats to be a violation of the Equal Protection Clause of the 14th Amendment. That historic decision was soon followed by *Reynolds* v. *Sims* in 1964. There, the Court held that the Equal Protection Clause requires every State to draw its legislative districts on the basis of population equality.

Legislator Terms Legislators are elected to either two-year or four-year terms. Representatives serve two-year terms in 44 States and four-year terms in Alabama, Louisiana, Maryland, Mississippi, and North Dakota. Senators win four-year terms in 37 States (including Nebraska), two-year stints in 12, and a combination of two- and four-year terms in Illinois.

Fifteen States now limit the number of terms any person can serve. In most, the limit is placed on service in each chamber, separately. In a few, the restriction is applied to total legislative service in either house.

The rate of turnover in legislative seats is fairly high, although it tends to vary from State to State and time to time. In a given year, some 20 percent of all lawmakers around the country are serving their first term in office. The major reasons for that turnover appear to be low pay, political instability, and term limits. Lawmakers tend to remain in office longer in those States that pay higher salaries and where one party regularly wins elections.

Legislator Compensation Far too often, capable men and women refuse to run for seats in the legislature because of the financial sacrifices that service usually entails. Legislative pay varies considerably and so the situation is more trying in some States than others. As of 2013, California paid lawmakers $95,291 per year, plus expenses and benefits. Oregon provided a more typical example of the compensation package. There, each member was paid some $22,000 per year, plus expenses and benefits.

Clearly, decent salaries in line with the responsibilities of the job will not automatically bring the most able men and women into State legislatures. Better pay would no doubt make public service much more appealing to qualified people, however.

Legislative Sessions Little more than a generation ago, only a handful of State legislatures met in regular sessions each year, and then usually for only a few months or so. Most met only every other year. It has long since become apparent that the legislature's workload cannot be properly handled on so limited a basis.

Today, 46 State legislatures meet for at least a short time every year; most of those sessions run for three

Supreme Court Decisions

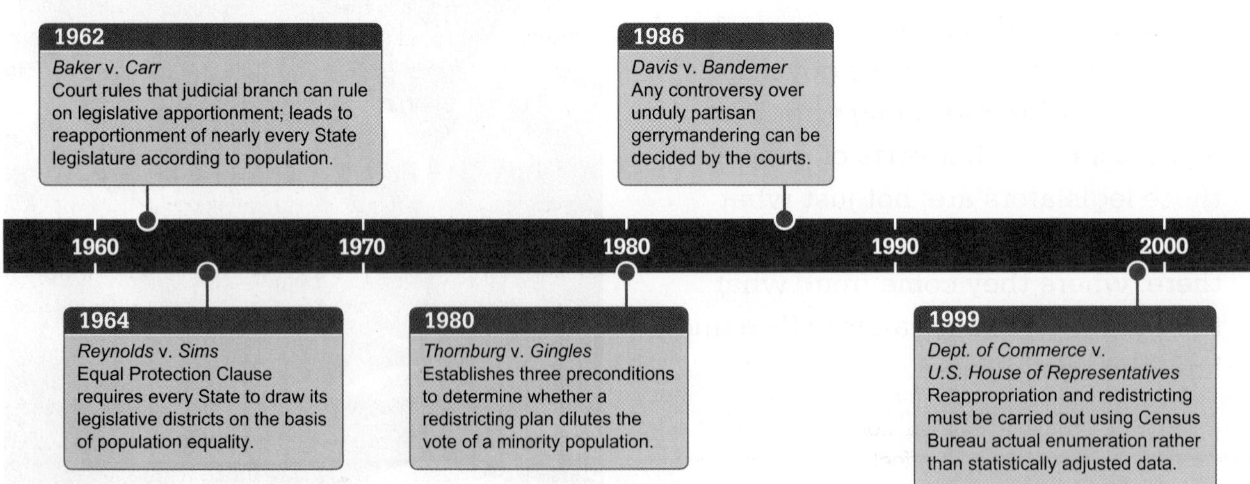

1962
Baker v. *Carr*
Court rules that judicial branch can rule on legislative apportionment; leads to reapportionment of nearly every State legislature according to population.
1986
Davis v. *Bandemer*
Any controversy over unduly partisan gerrymandering can be decided by the courts.
1960
1970
1980
1990
2000
1964
Reynolds v. *Sims*
Equal Protection Clause requires every State to draw its legislative districts on the basis of population equality.
1980
Thornburg v. *Gingles*
Establishes three preconditions to determine whether a redistricting plan dilutes the vote of a minority population.
1999
Dept. of Commerce v. *U.S. House of Representatives*
Reappropriation and redistricting must be carried out using Census Bureau actual enumeration rather than statistically adjusted data.

SOURCE: Cornell Law School Legal Information Institute; Senate.gov

>> Supreme Court decisions have affected the way congressional districts are drawn, at both the national and the State level. **Analyze Information** What trend can you see in the decisions shown?

State Legislatures: Workload and Compensation

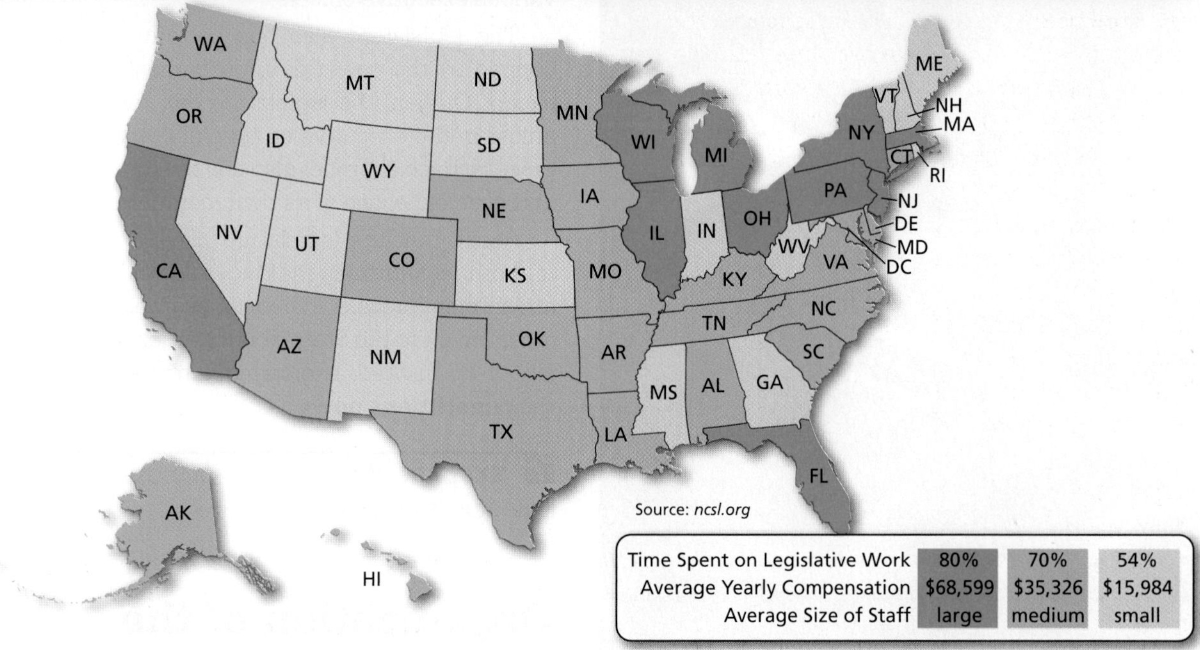

>> The country's State lawmakers serve in either full- or part-time legislatures, but in general, the length of sessions is increasing. **Analyze Maps** How does the compensation of part- and full-time legislators compare?

to five months or more. Several legislatures are now in session nearly year-round.

In every State, the governor, and in three fourths of them the legislature itself, can call the body into special session. Those meetings, most common in States where legislators meet infrequently, allow the consideration of urgent matters between their regularly scheduled sessions.

PREDICT CONSEQUENCES What would be the likely result if legislatures were not reapportioned using accurate census data?

Powers of the Legislature

No State's constitution lists all of the powers vested in the legislature—nor could it. In each State, the legislature has all of those powers that (1) the State constitution does not grant exclusively to the executive or judicial branches or to local governments, and (2) neither the State constitution nor the United States Constitution denies to it. In effect, most of the powers held by a State are vested in its legislature.

Legislative Powers The fact that the legislature can enact any law that does not conflict with any provision in federal law or in the State constitution means that there can be no all-inclusive list of the legislature's powers. Its more important powers are usually set out in the State constitution, however. Those most often mentioned include the powers to tax, spend, borrow, establish courts and fix their jurisdiction, define crimes and provide for their punishment, regulate commercial activities, and maintain public schools.

Every State's legislature possesses the **police power**—the State's hugely important power to protect and promote the public health, public safety, public morals, and the general welfare. Recall, most of what government does in this country today is done by the States (and their local governments), and most of what they do is done through the exercise of the police power. In short, that extraordinarily broad authority is the power to safeguard the welfare of the people of the State, and it is the basis for much of what State legislatures do.

Nonlegislative Powers All 50 State legislatures possess certain nonlegislative powers, in addition to those they exercise when they make a law.

In the separation of powers and checks and balances scheme, the legislature exercises some *executive* powers—for example, it has the power to approve or reject the governor's appointment of a number of

>> Each State legislature possesses the police power to protect the public's safety, health, and general welfare. One aspect of this is authorizing State inspectors to check food deliveries for safety.

Interactive Chart

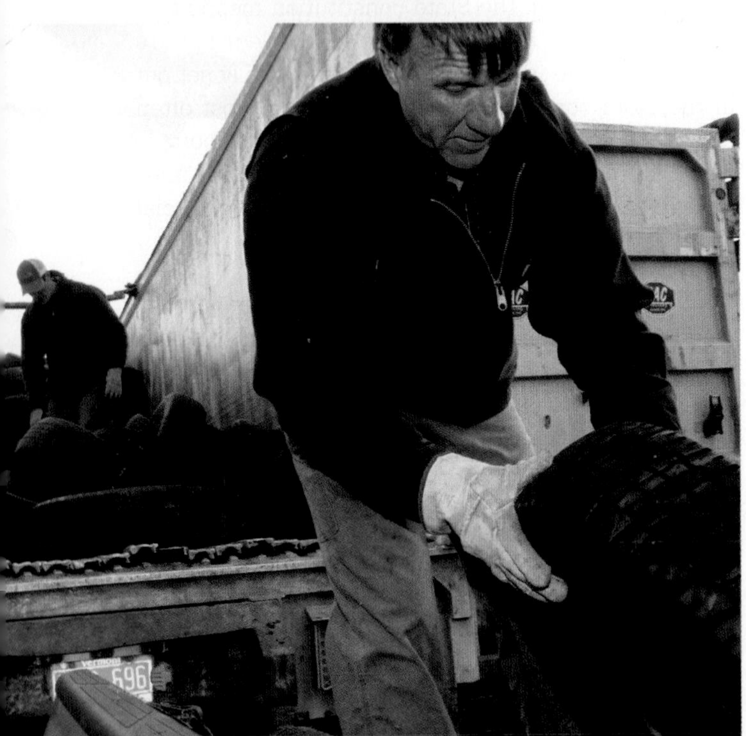

>> Vermont Lieutenant Governor Phil Scott assumes many responsibilities, including the promotion of community initiatives like Wheels for Warmth, which helps people recycle tires.

officials. In some States, the legislature itself appoints various executive officers.

The legislature also has certain *judicial* powers, capped by the power of impeachment. In every State except Oregon, the legislature can remove any State officer in the executive or judicial branch through that process. Each chamber also has the power to discipline and even expel one of its own members.

Recall that the legislature plays a significant role in both constitution-making and the constitutional amendment process. When, for example, it proposes an amendment to the State's constitution, it is not making law. It is, instead, exercising a nonlegislative power: the **constituent power**.

EXPLAIN What is the purpose of the State legislature's police power?

Organization of the Legislature

Both the organization and procedures of State legislatures are similar to those found in Congress. Much of their work centers around presiding officers and a committee system.

Presiding Officers Those who preside over the sessions of the States' lawmaking chambers are almost always powerful political figures, not only in the legislature itself but elsewhere in State politics.

The lower house in each of the 49 bicameral bodies elects its own presiding officer, known everywhere as the speaker. The senate chooses its own presiding officer in 23 States; in the other 27, including Nebraska, the lieutenant governor has the authority to serve as president of the senate in various capacities. Where the lieutenant governor does preside, the senate selects a president *pro tempore* to serve in the lieutenant governor's absence.

Except for the lieutenant governors, each of these presiding officers is chosen by a vote on the floor of his or her chamber. In fact, the majority party's caucus usually picks those who fill the leadership posts, just before the legislature begins a new term.

The chief duties of these presiding officers revolve around the conduct of the legislature's floor business. They refer bills to committee, recognize members who seek the floor, and interpret and apply the rules of their chamber to its proceedings.

Unlike the Speaker of the House in Congress, the speaker in nearly every State appoints the chair and other members of each house committee. The senate's president or president *pro tem* has that same power in just over half the States. The presiding officers regularly use this power much as they do their other powers: to reward their friends, punish their enemies, and otherwise work their influence on the legislature and its product.

Legislative Committee System Several hundred or, in many larger States, several thousand measures are introduced at each session of the legislature. That flood of bills makes the committee system as practical and necessary at the State level as it is in Congress. Much of the work of the legislature is done in committee, where members sift through that pile of proposed legislation, deciding which bills will go on to floor consideration and which will fall by the wayside.

The standing committees of each house are regularly organized on a subject-matter basis—as committees on finance, education, highways, and so on. A bill referred to one of these committees may be amended or even largely rewritten there. Or, as frequently happens, it may be ignored altogether.

"Pigeonholing" occurs in the States as in Congress. In fact, in most States one of the standing committees in each house is usually the "graveyard committee." Bills are sent there to be buried. The judiciary committee, to which bills may be referred "on grounds of doubtful constitutionality," often fills this role. A striking illustration of a graveyard committee existed for several years in landlocked Oklahoma: the Committee on Deep Sea Navigation.

Sources of Bills Legally, only a member may introduce a bill in either house in any State's legislature. So, in the strictest sense, legislators themselves are the source of all measures the legislature considers. In broader terms, however, the lawmakers are the authors of only a handful of bills.

A large number of measures come from public sources, from officers and agencies in the State executive branch, and from local governments. Every State governor has a legislative program, often extensive and bold.

Many bills come from the private sector. Indeed, interest groups appear to be the largest single source of proposed legislation. Remember, those groups and the lobbyists who represent them exist for one overriding purpose: to influence public policy to the benefit of their own interests. Of course, some measures do originate with private individuals—business owners, farmers, union members, and other citizens—who, for one reason or another, think, "There ought to be a law. . . ."

"We realize it is an unnecessary department, but the acronym was just too cool to shut it down."

>> Similar to the Federal Government, State and local governments have many layers of departments, agencies, and committees. **Analyze Political Cartoons** What comment does this cartoon make on the usefulness of some government agencies?

DRAW CONCLUSIONS Who are the legislative presiding officers, and why are they considered to be powerful political figures?

Direct Legislation

In several States, voters themselves can take a direct part in the lawmaking process. The main vehicles for that participation are the initiative and the referendum.

Initiative Process Through the initiative process, voters can propose amendments to the State's constitution. In some States, they can also use that process to propose ordinary statutes. The initiative takes two quite different forms: the more common direct initiative and the little-used indirect initiative.

In both forms, a certain number of qualified voters (which varies from State to State) must sign petitions to initiate a law. Where the direct initiative is in place, a measure with sufficient signatures goes directly to the ballot, usually in the next general election. If voters approve the measure, it becomes law. If not, it dies. Where the indirect form is found, a proposed measure

Direct Legislation in the States

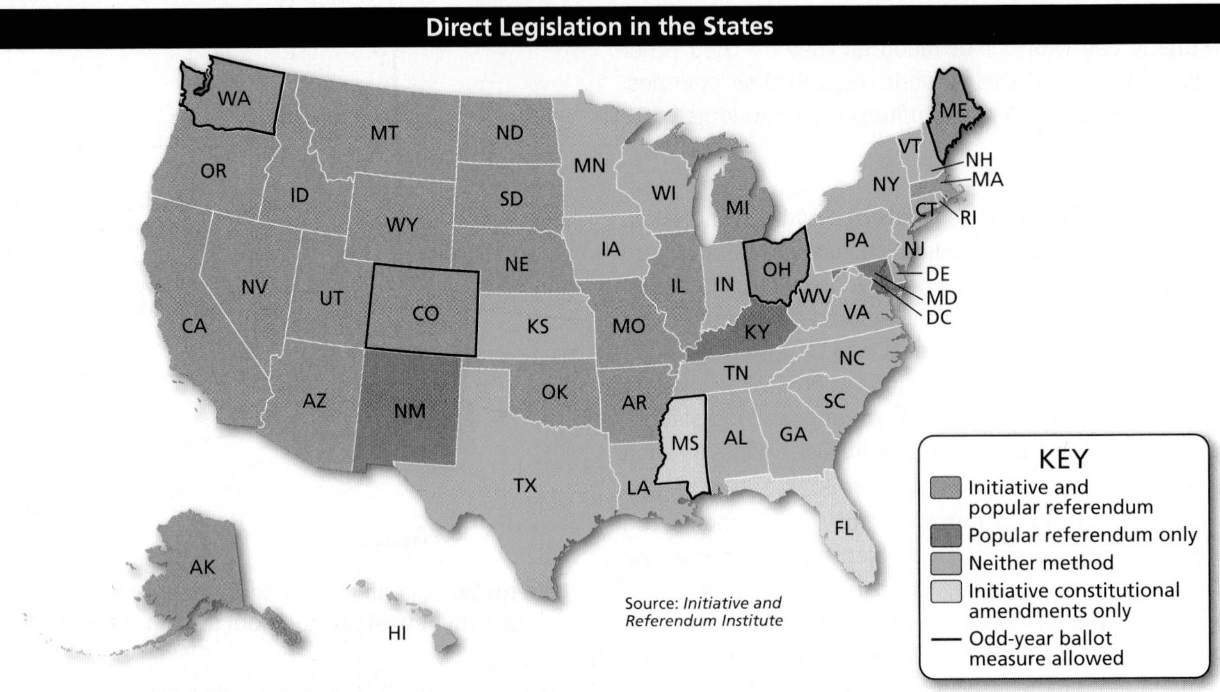

>> Ballot initiatives and referendums take a variety of forms in those States that allow their use. **Analyze Maps** What pattern can you see nationwide?

goes first to the legislature for its consideration. If the lawmakers approve the measure, it becomes law. If the legislature fails to pass it, the measure then goes to the voters.

Referendum Process A **referendum** is a process in which the legislature refers a measure to the voters for final approval or rejection. The referendum takes three different forms: mandatory, optional, and popular.

A *mandatory referendum* occurs in those situations in which the legislature must send a measure to the voters. Recall, in every State except Delaware, a proposed constitutional amendment must be submitted to the electorate. In several States some other measures, such as those providing for the borrowing of funds, must also go to the voters.

An *optional referendum* involves a measure that the legislature has referred to the voters voluntarily. Such measures are rare. They usually involve "hot potato" issues: issues that lawmakers would prefer not to take direct responsibility for deciding themselves.

Under the *popular referendum*, a group of citizens may demand by petition that a measure passed by the legislature be referred to the voters for final action. Most attempts to use this form of the referendum fail. Most often, the opponents of a particular measure simply cannot gather the required number of signatures to force a popular vote on the target of their ire.

? IDENTIFY STEPS IN A PROCESS In some States, voters can actually take part in the lawmaking process. What are the steps that must occur in order for a proposal to become law using the direct initiative? ?

ASSESSMENT

1. **Identify Central Issues** How is the initiative process a reflection of the principle of representative government?
2. **Compare and Contrast** How are the powers of a State legislature different from the powers of Congress?
3. **Generate Explanations** Explain the effect of the Supreme Court's decision in *Baker* v. *Carr.*
4. **Analyze Information** What would be the advantage for voters of having a nonpartisan primary compared to a partisan primary?
5. **Interpret** In what way do the nonlegislative powers of the State legislature serve as checks on the other branches of State government?

13.3 The governor is the principal executive officer in each of the 50 States. He or she is always a central figure in State politics and is often a well-known national personality as well. Governors today occupy an office that is the direct descendant of the earliest public office in American politics, the colonial governorship, first established in Virginia in 1607.

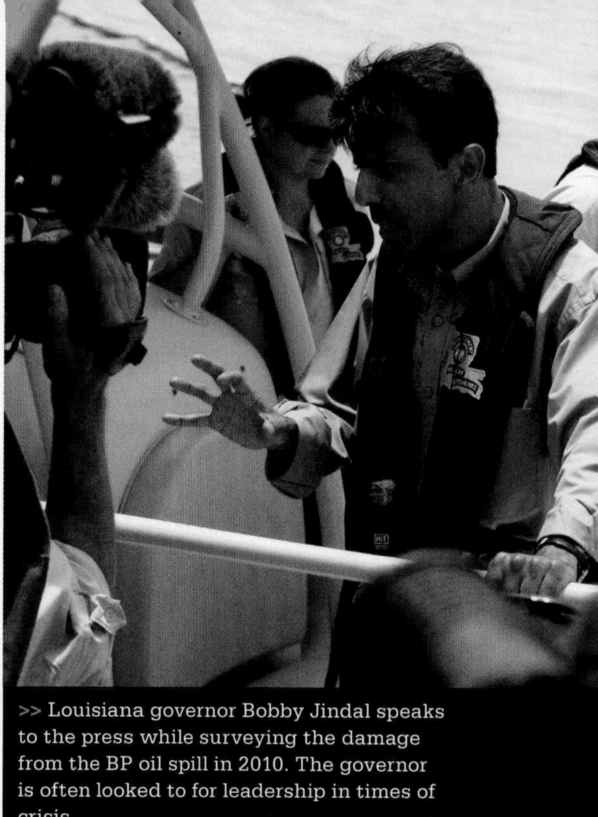

>> Louisiana governor Bobby Jindal speaks to the press while surveying the damage from the BP oil spill in 2010. The governor is often looked to for leadership in times of crisis.

Interactive Flipped Video

The Governor and State Administration

>> Objectives

Describe the main features of the office of governor.

Summarize a governor's roles, powers, duties, and the limitations of the office.

List and describe the other executive offices at the State level.

>> Key Terms

recall
item veto
clemency
pardon
commutation
reprieve
parole

The Governorship

In colonial America, the actions of the royal governors inspired much of the resentment that fueled the Revolution. That attitude was carried over into the first State constitutions. Most of the powers of government were given to the legislatures; the new State governors, for the most part, had little real authority. In every State except Massachusetts and New York, the governor was chosen by the legislature, and in most of them only for a one-year term. And only in three States did the governor have a veto power.

That original separation of powers soon proved unsatisfactory. Many of the State legislatures abused their powers. Several fell prey to special interests, and the governors were unable to respond. So, as new constitutions were written, and the older ones revised, the powers of the legislatures were curbed and the powers of the governors generally increased.

Beginning with Illinois in 1917, most States have redesigned and strengthened the executive branch to make the governor the State's chief executive in more than name. Some States have gone further than others in this direction, but, overall, governors are much more powerful figures today than in decades past.

Qualifications Anyone who wants to become the governor of a State must be able to satisfy a set of formal qualifications. Typically, he or she must be an American citizen, of at least a certain age (usually 25 or 30), have lived in the State for a given period of time (most often for at least five years), and be a qualified voter.

Clearly, these formal qualifications for office are not very difficult to meet. It is the informal qualifications that have real meaning. To become a governor, a person must have those characteristics that will first attract a party's nomination, and then attract the voters in the general election. Those characteristics vary from State to State, and even from election to election within a State. Race, sex, religion, name recognition, personality, party identification, experience, ideology, the ability to use television effectively—these and several other factors are all part of the mix.

Today, most governors are attorneys in their 50s and 60s. Nearly all of them were State legislators or held another elective office in the State, such as lieutenant governor, attorney general, or mayor of a large city. California's former governor, Arnold Schwarzenegger, however, is a leading illustration of the fact that someone who has never held public office does sometimes win a governorship.

>> Arnold Schwarzenegger became California's second actor-turned-governor in 2003. Other candidates in that race included a comedian, a golfer, a retired meat packer, and a sumo wrestler.

The first gubernatorial elections occurred in 1775 and more than 2,500 persons have now served as governors of the various States. To this point (2013), only 35 of those governors have been women.

Two women succeeded their husbands as governor in 1924: Nellie Taylor Ross in Wyoming and Miriam "Ma" Ferguson in Texas. Over the past 30 years or so, a growing number of women have won the office. Five currently serve: Jan Brewer (R., Arizona), Susana Martinez (R., New Mexico), Mary Fallin (R., Oklahoma), Nikki Haley (R., South Carolina), and Maggie Hassan (D., New Hampshire). Governor Haley, who captured the office in 2010, is the nation's first female Indian American governor.

Only three African Americans have ever held the office: Douglas Wilder (D., Virginia, 1989); Deval Patrick (D., Massachusetts), chosen in 2006 and again in 2010; and David Patterson (D., New York), who succeeded to the post in 2008. Bobby Jindal (R., Louisiana; 2007 and 2011) is the nation's first Indian American governor.

Selection The governor is chosen by popular vote in every State. In all but four, only a plurality is needed for election. If no candidate wins a clear majority in Georgia or Louisiana, the two top vote-getters meet in a runoff election. If no one wins a majority in Mississippi, the lower house of the legislature picks the new governor. In Vermont, both houses make the choice.

The major parties' gubernatorial candidates are usually picked in primaries. In a few States, however, conventions choose the nominees. Just over half the States now provide for the joint election of the governor and lieutenant governor. In those States, each party's candidates for those offices run as a team, and the voter casts one vote to fill both posts.

Term The one-year gubernatorial term has long since disappeared. Governors are now chosen to four-year terms nearly everywhere. Thirty-six States limit the number of terms a chief executive may serve, most often to two terms. Those governors who seek reelection usually do so successfully.

Succession Governors are mortal. Occasionally, one of them dies in office. Many of them are also politically ambitious. Every so often, one resigns in midterm—to become a United States senator or accept an appointment to the President's Cabinet, for example.

When a vacancy does occur, it sets off a game of political musical chairs. The political plans and timetables of ambition of a number of public personalities are affected by the event. No matter what causes a vacancy, every State's constitution provides for a successor. In 44 States the lieutenant governor is first in line. In Maine, New Hampshire, and West Virginia, the president of the senate succeeds. In Arizona, Oregon, and Wyoming, the office passes to the secretary of state.

Removal The governor may be removed from office by impeachment in every State except Oregon. Only six governors have been impeached and removed since the turbulent Reconstruction years after the Civil War. The most recent to suffer that fate: Rod Blagojevich (D., Illinois) in 2009.

In 19 States, the governor may be recalled by the voters. The **recall** is a petition procedure by which voters may remove an elected official from office before the completion of his or her regular term.

The process generally works this way: If a certain number of qualified voters—usually 25 percent of the number who voted in the last election held for the office—sign recall petitions, a special election must be held in which the voters decide whether to remove or instead, retain, the officeholder.

To this point, only two governors have ever been recalled: Governor Lynn J. Frazier of North Dakota, a Republican, in 1921, and Governor Gray Davis of California, a Democrat, in 2003.

>> Former Illinois Governor Rod Blagojevich departs a federal courthouse after being found guilty of corruption in 2011, two years after being impeached by the State legislature.

Compensation In many respects, a governor's job is not unlike that of the chief executive officer of one of the nation's larger corporations. Both administer hugely complex organizations, manage the work of thousands of employees, and oversee the spending of incredible amounts of money. Governors are not paid nearly so well as the CEOs of large companies, however. The latter make tens of millions of dollars per year in salary and benefits. The average salary for governors is some $130,000 per year. Most States provide their chief executive with an official residence, often called a governor's mansion, and money for travel and other expenses.

To the governor's salary and other material compensations must be added the intangibles of honor and prestige that go with the office. It is this factor, and a sense of public duty, that often persuades many of our better citizens to seek the post. Several Presidents were governors before reaching the White House—most recently, Bill Clinton and George W. Bush.

>> In 2003, 135 candidates sought to replace California governor Gray Davis in a recall referendum. **Analyze Political Cartoons** Why did the cartoonist include a clown among the candidates?

COMPARE How do the selection of a governor and the succession of a governor reflect popular sovereignty? How does this process vary in some states?

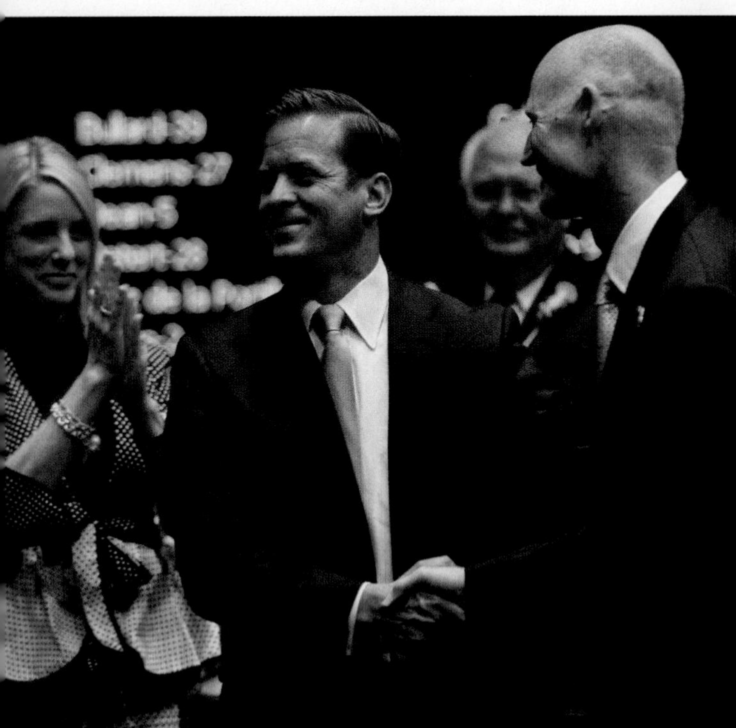

>> Governors must be adept at working with State officers. Here, Florida Governor Rick Scott (right) congratulates Lt. Governor Carlos Lopez-Cantera on his election to the Florida legislature.

>> Susana Martinez, New Mexico's first female governor and the first Hispanic female elected governor in the United States, promotes fire prevention in Albuquerque, New Mexico.

The Governor's Powers

Much like the President, a governor plays a number of different roles. He or she is, simultaneously, an executive, an administrator, a legislator, a party leader, an opinion leader, and a ceremonial figure. What the office amounts to depends, in no small part, on how well the governor plays each—and all—of these roles. And that must depend, in turn, on his or her personality, political muscle, and overall abilities.

Many of a governor's formal powers are hedged with constitutional and other legal restrictions. Nonetheless, the powers a governor does have, together with the prestige of the office, make it quite possible for a capable, dynamic person to be a "strong" governor, one who can accomplish much for the State and for the public good.

Executive The presidency and the governorships are similar in several ways, but the comparison can be pushed too far. Remember, the Constitution of the United States makes the President *the* executive in the National Government. State constitutions, on the other hand, regularly describe the governor as the *chief* executive in the State's government. The distinction here, between *the* executive and the *chief* executive, is a critical one. The executive authority is fragmented in most States, but it is not at the national level.

In nearly every State, the executive authority is shared by a number of "executive officers"—a secretary of state, an attorney general, a treasurer, and so on. Most of these executive officers are, like the governor, popularly elected, and for that reason, very largely beyond the governor's direct control.

In short, most State constitutions so divide the executive authority that the governor can best be described as a "first among equals." Yet, whatever the realities of the distribution of power, the people look to the governor for leadership in State affairs. It is also the governor whom they hold responsible for the conduct of those affairs and for the overall condition of the State.

The governor's basic legal responsibility is regularly found in a constitutional provision that directs the chief executive to "take care that the laws be faithfully executed." Though the executive power may be divided, the governor is given a number of specific powers with which to accomplish that task.

Appointment and Removal The governor can best execute the law with subordinates of his or her own choosing. Hence, the powers of appointment and removal are, or should be, among the most important.

A leading test of any administrator is his or her ability to select loyal and able assistants. Two major factors work against the governor's effectiveness here, however. First is the existence of those other elected executives; the people choose them and the governor cannot remove them. Second, the State's constitution and statutes place restrictions on the governor's power to hire and fire. Most State constitutions require that the majority of the governor's major appointees be confirmed by the State senate.

Moreover, the legislature often sets qualifications that must be met by the governor's appointees. In a vigorous two-party State, for example, the law often requires that not more than a certain number of the members of each board or commission be from the same political party. Thus, a governor must appoint some members of the opposing party to posts.

Administering the Executive Branch The governor is the State's chief administrator. Alone and unaided, he or she could not possibly "take care that the laws be faithfully executed." The day-to-day work of enforcing the State's laws, of performing its many functions, and of delivering its many services is done by the thousands of men and women in all of the agencies that make up the executive branch. The governor must supervise that work.

Here again, the constitution and statutes of the State often limit a governor's authority. Many agencies are subject to his or her direct control, but many are not. That situation puts a premium on the governor's powers of persuasion and on his or her ability to operate through such informal channels as party leadership and appeals to the public.

The Budget Always remember: A government's budget is much more than a mere bookkeeping exercise. It is a political document, a statement of public policy. Its numbers, its dollar figures, reflect the struggle over "who gets what" and who doesn't.

In most States the governor prepares the budget that goes to the legislature. The lawmakers can and do make changes in the governor's financial plan. Still, the governor's recommendations carry a great deal of weight.

The governor's budget-making power can be a highly effective tool with which to control State administration. Although unable to appoint or remove the head of a particular agency, for example, the governor can use the budget-making power to affect that agency's programs and have a real impact on those who work in that agency.

Military Powers Every State's constitution makes the governor the commander in chief of the State militia—in effect, of the State's units of the National Guard.

>> The governors of New York and New Jersey each appoint six board members to the Port Authority of New York and New Jersey, an interstate compact for managing harbor facilities.

Interactive Chart

The National Guard is the organized part of the State militia. In a national emergency, the National Guard may be "called up," ordered into federal service by the President.

All of the States' National Guard units were federalized in 1940 and served as part of the nation's armed forces in World War II. Many units also saw combat duty in Korea, Vietnam, and the Persian Gulf War. Today, National Guard units are on duty in such farflung places as Bosnia, Kosovo, Afghanistan, and Iraq. Indeed, the Defense Department has relied very heavily on the Guard in the prosecution of recent wars.

When the State's Guard units are not in federal service (which is most of the time), they are commanded by the governor. On occasion, governors find it necessary to call out the Guard to deal with such emergencies as prison riots, to help fight a dangerous forest fire, to aid in relief and evacuation after a flood, to prevent looting during and after some other natural disaster, and so on.

Legislative The State's principal executive officer exercises three significant legislative powers. Those powers, together with the chief executive's personality, popularity, and political muscle, can make the governor, in fact, the State's chief legislator.

The Message Power Essentially, the message power is the power to recommend legislation. Remember, much of what lawmakers do is prompted by what the governor has urged them to do. The most effective governors push their wish lists by combining their use of the formal message power with such informal tactics as close contacts with key legislators and appeals to the public.

Special Sessions The governor in every State has the power to call the legislature into special session. As you know, that power is meant to permit the State to meet extraordinary situations. It can also be an important part of the governor's legislative arsenal. On many occasions, governors have persuaded reluctant lawmakers to pass a particular bill by threatening to call them back in a special session if they adjourn their regular meeting without having approved that measure.

The Veto Power Every governor can veto measures enacted by the legislature. The veto power—including the timely use of threats to invoke the power—can be very useful to the governor as he or she tries to influence what the legislature does or doesn't do.

In most States, the governor has only a very few days in which to sign or veto a bill—most often, five. If no action is taken within the prescribed period, the measure becomes law without his or her signature.

Only 11 States give the governor a pocket veto. So, in most States, those bills a governor neither signs nor vetoes become law. Forty-four States give the governor the **item veto**—the power to eliminate one or more items from a bill without rejecting the entire measure. It is used most often on spending measures.

As in the Federal Government, the legislature may attempt to override a veto. In most States, a veto requires a two-thirds majority in both houses.

Judicial In every State the chief executive has some authority of a judicial nature. Principally, the governor has various powers of executive **clemency**: powers of mercy that may be shown to persons convicted of crime.

With the power of **pardon**, the governor may relieve someone of the legal consequences of a crime. In most States, a pardon may be full or conditional, and usually it can be granted only after conviction. The power of **commutation** may be used to commute a sentence imposed by a court. Thus, a death sentence might be commuted to life in prison, or a sentence might be commuted to "time served," which leads to the release of a prisoner from custody.

The power to **reprieve** can be used to postpone the execution of a sentence. Reprieves are normally granted for very brief periods—for example, to allow time for an appeal or because of the late discovery of new evidence in a case. The power of **parole** permits the release of a prisoner short of the completion of a sentence.

The governor may have some or all of these powers of executive clemency. They are often shared, however. For example, the governor may share the power to pardon with an appointed board of pardons.

Special Sessions Called by Governors

DATE	GOVERNOR	STATE	SAMPLE AGENDA ITEM
2014	Phil Bryant (R)	Mississippi	Approval of disaster aid funding after a series of tornadoes
2013	Jay Nixon (D)	Missouri	Approval of $150 million annual economic incentive package to attract Boeing jobs to the State
2012	John Kitzhaber (D)	Oregon	Tax protections for Nike, the sportswear company based in Oregon
2011	Scott Walker (R)	Wisconsin	Discussion of jobs creation under his "Back to Work Wisconsin" plan
2010	Steve Beshear (D)	Kentucky	Push to end legislative stalemate and approve State budget

>> The governor's power to call special sessions can be a persuasive tool in getting policies enacted into law. **Analyze Charts** What are the most common issues addressed in special sessions?

★ CHOOSING EXECUTIVE OFFICERS ★

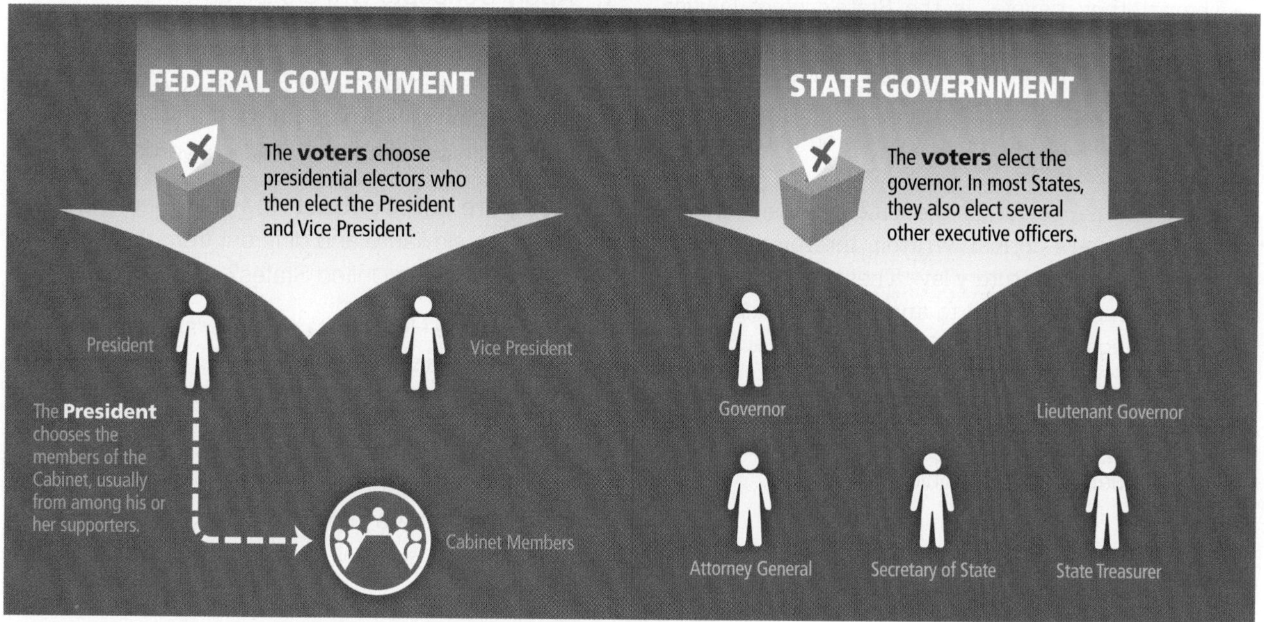

>> Many jobs filled by presidential appointment in the Federal Government are decided by elections at the State level. **Analyze Charts** How does the election of executive officers empower voters?

Governors have not often abused their clemency powers, but in her first term (1925–1927), Governor Miriam "Ma" Ferguson of Texas pardoned 3,737 convicted felons, an average of more than five per day. The pardons came so thick and fast that several Texas newspapers ran daily "pardon columns" rather than separate news stories.

Miscellaneous Duties In addition to the exercise of executive, legislative, and judicial powers, every chief executive must perform several other, often time-consuming duties. These duties are only hinted at by a listing of the powers of the office.

Among many other things, the governor receives official visitors and welcomes other distinguished personalities to the State, dedicates parks and public and private buildings, opens the State fair, and addresses countless organizations and public gatherings. Beyond those chores, he or she is often called upon to settle labor disputes, travel elsewhere in the country and sometimes abroad to promote the State and its trade interests, endorse any number of worthy causes, and on and on.

COMPARE Describe how the division of power between the executive and legislative branches of State government reflects the concept of checks and balances in the U.S. Constitution.

Other Executive Officers

In nearly every State, the governor must share control of the administration with a number of other executive officers. Most of those other officials are, like the governor, chosen by voters. The following four positions are found in most, but not all, State governments today.

The lieutenant governor must be ready to succeed to the governorship should a vacancy occur, and, in half the States, presides over the senate. The office can be a stepping-stone to the governorship by succession or by future elections. It remains, in many places, not much more than a part-time job.

The secretary of state serves as the State's chief clerk and records-keeper. He or she has charge of a great variety of public documents, records the official acts of the governor and the legislature, and usually administers the election laws.

The treasurer is the custodian of State funds, often the State's chief tax collector, and regularly the State's paymaster. Other names for this position include chief financial officer, director of finance, the commissioner of finance, and the comptroller of public accounts. The treasurer's major job is to make payments out of the

State treasury to pay salaries and bills associated with State government.

The attorney general is the State's chief lawyer. He or she acts as the legal advisor to State officers and agencies as they perform their official functions, represents the State in court, and oversees the work of local prosecutors as they try cases on behalf of the State.

Much of the power of the office centers on the attorney general's formal written interpretations of constitutional and statutory law. These interpretations, called opinions, are issued to answer questions raised by officials regarding the lawfulness of their actions or proposed actions.

? CONTRAST Describe how State executive officers vary from federal executive officers.

ASSESSMENT

1. **Apply Concepts** Why are the governor's budgetary powers so important?
2. **Compare and Contrast** Explain how the U.S. Constitution gives more power to the President than State constitutions give to governors.
3. **Compare and Contrast** How is the lieutenant governor similar to and different from the vice president of the United States?
4. **Summarize** How can a governor's legislative powers impact legislation?
5. **Summarize** Describe the governor's power to appoint and remove subordinates, and explain why it is important. Describe any checks and balances that are in place.

13.4 **The principal function of the State courts is to decide disputes between private parties and between private parties and government. In addition, because nearly all of these courts have the power of judicial review, they act as checks on the conduct of all other agencies of both State and local government.**

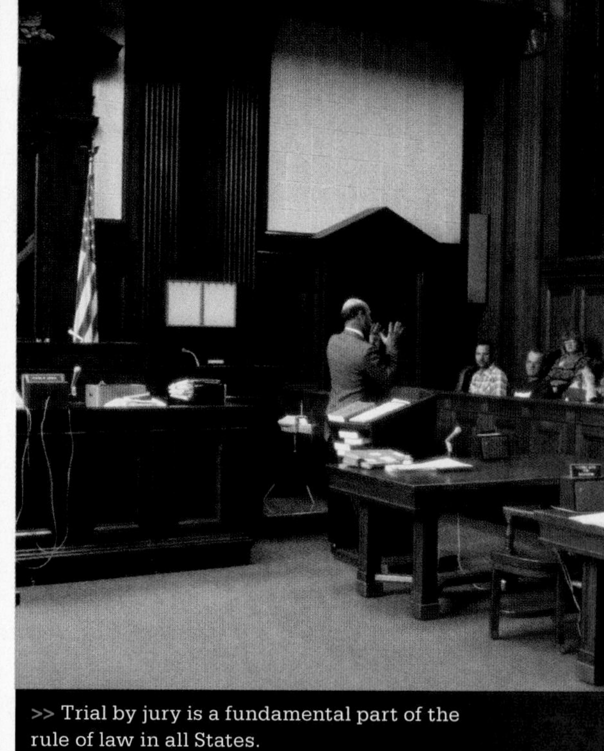

>> Trial by jury is a fundamental part of the rule of law in all States.

Interactive Flipped Video

State Courts

State Courts and the Law

The law is the code of conduct by which society is governed. It is made up of several different forms, including constitutional law, statutory law, administrative law, common law, and equity.

The highest form of law in this country is **constitutional law.** It is based on the United States Constitution, the State constitutions, and judicial interpretations of those documents. **Statutory law** consists of the statutes (laws) enacted by legislative bodies, including the United States Congress, the State legislature, the people, and local governments. **Administrative law** is composed of the rules, orders, and regulations issued by federal, State, or local executive officers, acting under proper constitutional and/or statutory authority.

Common Law The common law makes up a large part of the law of each State except Louisiana. Because of an early French influence, Louisiana's legal system is largely based on French legal concepts, derived from Roman law. Nevertheless, the common law has worked its way into some aspects of Louisiana law, as well.

Common law is unwritten, judge-made law that has developed over centuries from those generally accepted ideas of right and wrong that have gained judicial recognition. It covers nearly all aspects of human conduct. State courts apply common law except when it is in conflict with written law.

>> Objectives

Identify and define the kinds of law applied in State courts.

Compare and contrast criminal law and civil law.

Describe the types and purposes of juries and juror selection.

Explain how State courts are organized and describe the work that each type of court does.

Examine and evaluate the different methods by which judges are selected among the States.

>> Key Terms

common law
precedent
criminal law
felony
misdemeanor
civil law
tort
contract
jury
information
bench trial
justice of the peace
warrant
preliminary hearing
magistrate
appellate jurisdiction
equity
petit jury
Missouri Plan
constitutional law
statutory law
administrative law

www.PearsonRealize.com
Access your Digital Lesson.

The common law originated in England. It grew out of the decisions made by the king's judges on the basis of local customs. It developed as judges, coming upon situations similar to those found in earlier cases, applied and reapplied the rulings from those earlier cases. Thus, little by little, the law of those cases became *common* throughout England and, in time, throughout the English-speaking world.

American courts generally follow that same rule. A decision, once made, becomes a **precedent**, a guide to be followed in all later, similar cases, unless compelling reasons call for either an exception or its abandonment and the setting of a new precedent.

The common law is extremely important. Statutory law does override common law, but many statutes are based on the common law. A great many statutes are, in effect, common law translated into written law.

Equity The **equity** branch of the law supplements common law. It developed in England to provide equity—"fairness, justice, and right"—when remedies under the common law fell short of that goal.

The common law is mostly remedial, while equity is preventative. Thus, the common law applies to or provides a remedy for matters *after* they have happened; equity seeks to stop wrongs *before* they occur.

Suppose your neighbors plan to add a room to their house. You think that a part of the planned addition will be on your land and will destroy your rose garden. You can prevent the construction by getting an injunction, a court order prohibiting a specified action by the party named in the order.

A court is likely to grant the injunction for two reasons: (1) the immediacy of the threat to your property, and (2) the fact that the law can offer no fully satisfactory remedy once your garden has been destroyed. No money award can give back the pride or the pleasure your roses now give you.

At first, different courts administered equity and common law. In time, most States provided for the administration of both forms by the same courts, and the procedural differences between the two are disappearing.

Criminal Law The law as it is applied by courts in this country can also be described as either criminal or civil law. **Criminal law** is that branch of the law that regulates human conduct. It identifies and defines those actions that are crimes and provides for their punishment. A crime is a public wrong considered so damaging to society at large that it has been prohibited by law. The government (State or federal) is always a party to a criminal case, as prosecutor.

Crimes are of two kinds. A **felony** is the greater offense, punishable by a heavy fine, imprisonment, or even death—for example, murder, robbery, assault, or kidnapping. A **misdemeanor** is a lesser wrong and may be punished by a lighter fine and/or a shorter

The Use of Precedent

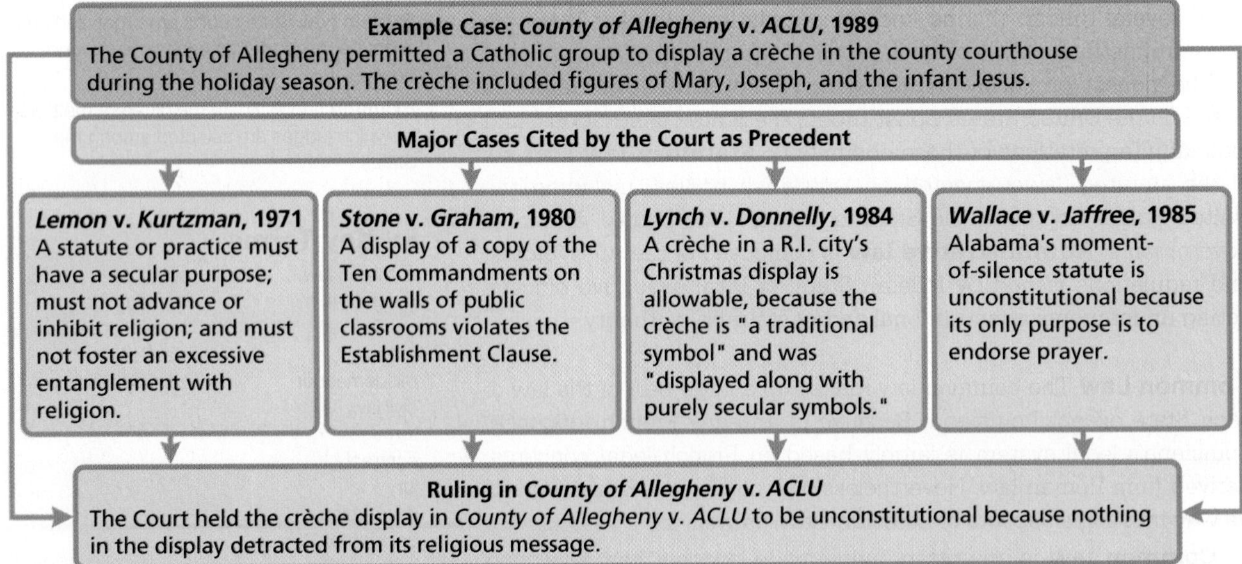

Example Case: County of Allegheny v. ACLU, 1989
The County of Allegheny permitted a Catholic group to display a crèche in the county courthouse during the holiday season. The crèche included figures of Mary, Joseph, and the infant Jesus.
Major Cases Cited by the Court as Precedent
Lemon v. Kurtzman, 1971
A statute or practice must have a secular purpose; must not advance or inhibit religion; and must not foster an excessive entanglement with religion.
Stone v. Graham, 1980
A display of a copy of the Ten Commandments on the walls of public classrooms violates the Establishment Clause.
Lynch v. Donnelly, 1984
A crèche in a R.I. city's Christmas display is allowable, because the crèche is "a traditional symbol" and was "displayed along with purely secular symbols."
Wallace v. Jaffree, 1985
Alabama's moment-of-silence statute is unconstitutional because its only purpose is to endorse prayer.
Ruling in County of Allegheny v. ACLU
The Court held the crèche display in County of Allegheny v. ACLU to be unconstitutional because nothing in the display detracted from its religious message.

SOURCE: *County of Allegheny et al. v. ACLU*, 1989, Opinion of the Court

>> Previous court rulings often serve as the starting point during a judge's deliberations on a case. **Analyze Charts** How did previous cases inform the *Allegheny* v. *ACLU* ruling?

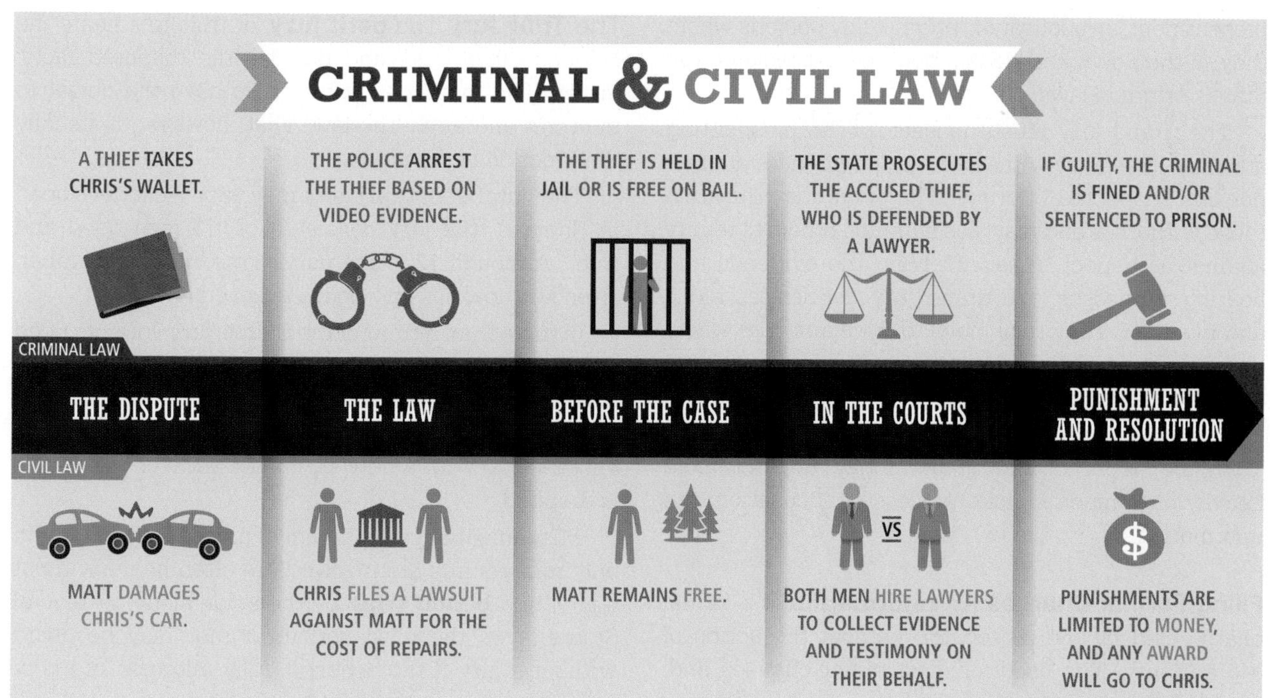

CRIMINAL & CIVIL LAW
A THIEF TAKES CHRIS'S WALLET.
THE POLICE ARREST THE THIEF BASED ON VIDEO EVIDENCE.
THE THIEF IS HELD IN JAIL OR IS FREE ON BAIL.
THE STATE PROSECUTES THE ACCUSED THIEF, WHO IS DEFENDED BY A LAWYER.
IF GUILTY, THE CRIMINAL IS FINED AND/OR SENTENCED TO PRISON.
CRIMINAL LAW
THE DISPUTE
THE LAW
BEFORE THE CASE
IN THE COURTS
PUNISHMENT AND RESOLUTION
CIVIL LAW
VS
$
MATT DAMAGES CHRIS'S CAR.
CHRIS FILES A LAWSUIT AGAINST MATT FOR THE COST OF REPAIRS.
MATT REMAINS FREE.
BOTH MEN HIRE LAWYERS TO COLLECT EVIDENCE AND TESTIMONY ON THEIR BEHALF.
PUNISHMENTS ARE LIMITED TO MONEY, AND ANY AWARD WILL GO TO CHRIS.

>> A criminal defendant can be arrested and detained in jail even before trial, but a civil defendant is never imprisoned. **Analyze Charts** Why don't those convicted of civil crimes serve prison time?

jail term—for example, a traffic violation, underage drinking, or disorderly conduct.

Civil Law The area of law related to human conduct that is not criminal in nature is known as **civil law**. Civil law relates to those disputes between private persons and between private persons and government that are not covered by criminal law. Civil law involves a wide range of issues, including divorce and custody disputes, torts, and contracts.

Both tort law and contract law are major and often-used branches of civil law. A **tort** is a wrongful act that involves injury to one's person, property, or reputation in a situation not covered by the terms of a contract—for example, an automobile accident, product liability, or libel. A **contract** is a legally binding agreement in which one party agrees to do something with or for another party—for example, an agreement covering the sale of property or the terms of employment.

COMPARE AND CONTRAST What is the difference between common law and equity?

Understanding the Jury System

A **jury** is a body of persons selected according to law to hear evidence and decide questions of fact in a court case. There are two basic types of juries in the American legal system: (1) the grand jury and (2) the petit jury.

The major function of the grand jury is to determine whether the evidence against a person charged with a crime is sufficient to justify a trial. The grand jury is used only in criminal proceedings. The petit jury is the trial jury, and it is used in both civil and criminal matters.

The Grand Jury The grand jury has from 6 to 23 persons, depending on the State. Where larger juries are used, generally at least 12 jurors must agree that an accused person is probably guilty before a formal accusation is made. Similarly, with smaller juries, an extraordinary majority is needed to indict, which means to bring the formal charge.

When a grand jury is impaneled, the judge instructs the jurors to find a true bill of indictment against any and all persons whom the prosecuting attorney brings to their attention and whom they think are probably guilty. The judge also instructs them to bring a presentment, an accusation, against any persons whom they, of their own knowledge, believe have violated the State's criminal laws.

The grand jury meets in secret. The prosecuting attorney presents witnesses and evidence against persons suspected of crime. The jurors may question those witnesses and may also summon others to testify against a suspect. After receiving the evidence and hearing witnesses, the grand jury deliberates alone and in secret. They then move to the courtroom where their report, including any indictments they may have returned, is read in their presence.

The grand jury is expensive and time-consuming. Therefore, most of the States today depend more heavily on a much simpler process of accusation: the information.

Filing Formal Charges An **information** is a formal charge filed by the prosecutor, without the action of a grand jury. It is used for most minor offenses and, in many States, for some serious cases. It is far less costly and time-consuming than a grand jury. Also, since grand juries most often follow the prosecutor's recommendations, many argue that a grand jury is really unnecessary. Others feel that the grand jury prevents prosecutors from abusing their powers.

>> All-male juries, such as this 1925 Tennessee jury, were the norm for many years, even after Utah in 1898 became the first State to allow women to serve.

The Trial Jury The **petit jury**, or trial jury, hears the evidence in a case and decides the disputed facts. In very few instances, it may also have the power to interpret and apply the law. That, however, is usually the function of the judge.

The number of trial jurors may vary. As it developed in England, the jury consisted of "12 men good and true." Although 12 is the usual total, a lesser number, often six, now fills jury boxes in several States.

In more than a third of the States, jury verdicts need not be unanimous in civil and minor criminal cases. Rather, some extraordinary majority is needed. If a jury cannot agree on a verdict (a so-called hung jury), either another trial with a new jury takes place or the matter is dropped.

Misdemeanor cases and civil proceedings in which only minor sums are involved are often heard without a jury, in a **bench trial**, by the judge alone. In several States, even the most serious crimes may be heard without a jury if the accused, fully informed of his or her rights, waives the right to trial by jury.

Selecting Jurors Jurors are picked in more or less the same way in most States. Periodically, a county official or special jury commissioners prepare a list of persons eligible for jury service, with names drawn from poll books, tax rolls, driver's license records, or other sources. The sheriff serves each person with a court order to appear. After eliminating those who, for good reason, cannot serve, the judge prepares a list of those who can. Persons under 18 and over 70 years of age, those who cannot read and write, the ill, and criminals are commonly excluded. Those in occupations vital to the public interest or for whom jury service would mean real hardship are often excused, too.

As with the grand jury, the States are moving away from the use of the trial jury. Leading reasons are the greater time and cost of jury trials. The competence of the average jury and the impulses that may lead it to a verdict are often questioned, as well. Much criticism of the jury system is directed not so much at the system itself as at its operation.

Several things should be said in favor of the jury system, however. It has a long and honorable place in the development of Anglo-American law. Its high purpose is to promote a fair trial, by providing an impartial body to hear the charges brought against the accused. A jury tends to bring the common sense of the community to bear on the law and its application. Finally, the jury system gives citizens a chance to take part in the administration of justice, and it fosters a greater confidence in the judicial system.

APPLY CONCEPTS What happens if a grand jury does not return an indictment?

How the State Courts Are Organized

They deal with everything from traffic tickets to murder, from disputes over nickels and dimes to settlements involving millions. They are the State and local courts and the judges who sit in them. Here, you will look at the way these courts are organized and how they conduct their business.

Each of the State constitutions creates a court system for that State. Some of the documents deal with the courts at great length, but most of them leave much of the detail of judicial organization and procedure to the legislature.

Local Trial Courts **Justices of the peace**—JPs—stand on the lowest rung of the State judicial ladder. They preside over what are commonly called justice courts.

JPs were once found nearly everywhere in the country. In their day, they seemed well-suited to their purpose. In justice courts, people could obtain a hearing for minor offenses quickly. JPs and their justice courts have been done away with in several States. However, they can still be found in many smaller towns and rural areas.

JPs are usually popularly elected. For the most part, they try misdemeanors—that is, cases involving such petty offenses as traffic violations, disturbing the peace, public drunkenness, and the like. JPs can almost never settle civil disputes involving more than a few hundred dollars. They do issue certain kinds of warrants, hold preliminary hearings, and often perform marriages.

A **warrant** is a court order authorizing, or making legal, some official action. Search warrants and arrest warrants are the most common of these documents. A **preliminary hearing** is generally the first step in a major criminal prosecution. There, the judge decides if the evidence is, in fact, enough to hold that person—bind that person over—for action by the grand jury or the prosecutor.

In some places, JPs are still paid out of the fines they take in. The more fines they impose, the higher their incomes. This "fee system" can lead to any number of abuses and raises serious questions about the fairness of the treatment a defendant can expect.

"He's big, all right, and he's definitely a wolf, but it'll be up to a jury to decide whether or not he's bad."

>> Suspects are innocent until proven guilty, which leaves jurors with a critical duty. **Analyze Political Cartoons** What does this cartoon suggest about the task of a jury? How can its effectiveness be evaluated?

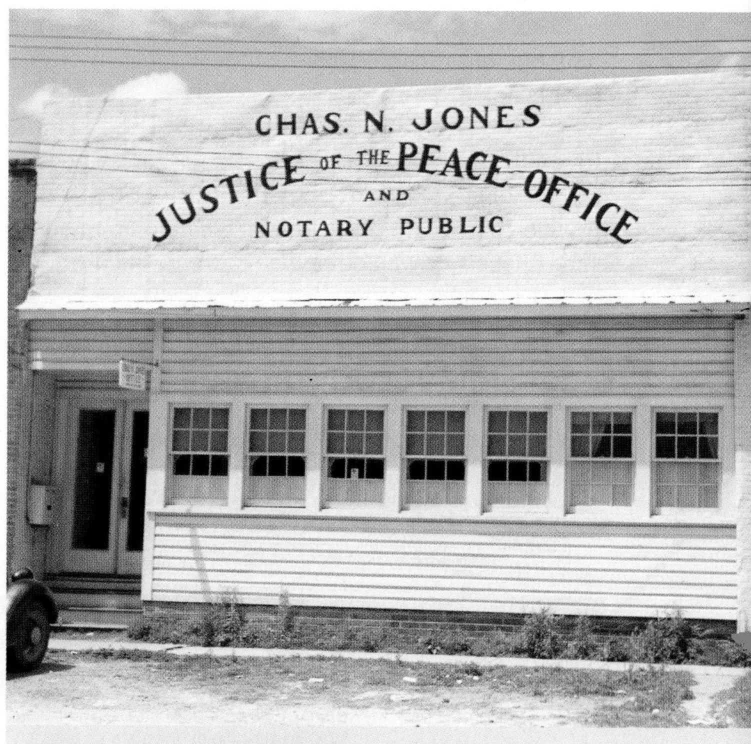

>> The origin of the justice of the peace dates back to 1195. The term itself was first used in an English law passed in 1361. Justice of the peace courts were later established across the U.S.

Magistrates are the city cousins of JPs. For the most part, magistrates handle those minor civil complaints and misdemeanor cases that arise in an urban setting. They preside over what often are called magistrates' courts or police courts. Magistrates, like JPs, are usually popularly elected for fairly short terms.

Municipal Courts Municipal courts were first established in Chicago in 1906. They are now found in most large cities and many smaller ones.

The jurisdiction of municipal courts is citywide. They can often hear civil cases involving several thousands of dollars as well as the usual run of misdemeanors. Many municipal courts are organized into divisions, which hear cases of a given kind—for example, civil, criminal, small claims, traffic, and probate divisions.

Consider the small claims division, often called the small claims court. Many people cannot afford the costs of suing for the collection of a small debt. A newspaper carrier, for example, can hardly afford a lawyer to collect a month's subscription from a customer. The owner of a two-family house may have the same problem with a tenant's back rent, and many merchants are forced to forget an overdue bill or sell it to a collection agency.

Small claims courts are designed for just such situations. There, a person can bring a claim for little or no cost. The proceedings are usually informal, and the judge often handles the matter without attorneys for either side.

Juvenile Courts Individuals under 18 years of age are generally not subject to the jurisdiction of the courts in which adults are tried. Minors who are arrested for some offense, or who otherwise come to the attention of the police or other authorities, may appear in juvenile courts.

The juvenile justice system is designed to address the special needs and problems of young people. This system generally emphasizes rehabilitation more than punishment. However, under some circumstances, juvenile courts do refer certain offenders to a regular criminal court for trial.

In the 1980s and 1990s, most States responded to juvenile crime with tougher criminal laws. Often these statutes make it easier to try juveniles as adults when they are charged with serious crimes. In 46 States, juvenile court judges may assign certain cases involving juveniles to adult courts. In several States, cases that meet certain standards *must* be tried in adult courts.

General Trial Courts Most of the more important civil and criminal cases are heard in the States' general trial courts. Every State is divided into a number of judicial districts, or circuits, each generally covering one or more counties. For each district, there is a general trial court, which may be known as a district, circuit, chancery, county, or superior court, or as a court of common pleas.

These general trial courts are courts of "first instance." That is, they exercise original jurisdiction over most of the cases they hear. Most legal actions brought under State law begin in these courts. When cases do come to them on appeal from some lower court, a new trial (a trial *de novo*) is usually held.

The cases heard in trial courts are tried before a single judge. Most often a petit jury (the trial jury) hears and decides the facts at issue in a case, and the judge interprets and applies the law involved. Criminal cases

Juvenile Justice Timeline

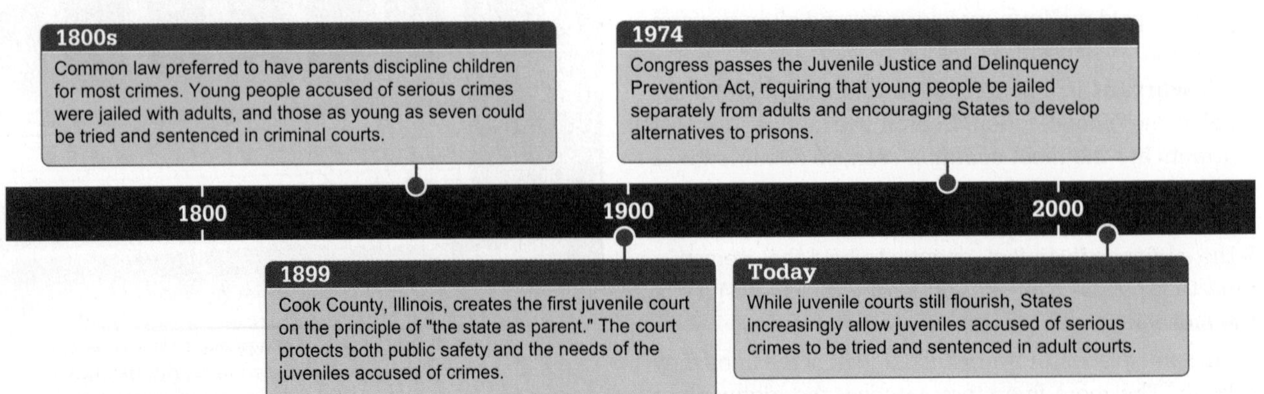

1800s
Common law preferred to have parents discipline children for most crimes. Young people accused of serious crimes were jailed with adults, and those as young as seven could be tried and sentenced in criminal courts.
1974
Congress passes the Juvenile Justice and Delinquency Prevention Act, requiring that young people be jailed separately from adults and encouraging States to develop alternatives to prisons.
1800
1900
2000
1899
Cook County, Illinois, creates the first juvenile court on the principle of "the state as parent." The court protects both public safety and the needs of the juveniles accused of crimes.
Today
While juvenile courts still flourish, States increasingly allow juveniles accused of serious crimes to be tried and sentenced in adult courts.

>> Juvenile courts arose from decades of struggle at the State level. **Analyze Timelines** Why do you think reformers sought separate jails and prisons for young people?

are presented for trial either by a grand jury or, most often, on motion of the prosecuting attorney.

The trial court is seldom limited as to the kinds of cases it may hear. Although this court's decision on the facts in a case is usually final, disputes over questions of law may be carried to a higher court.

Courts of Appeal Most States now have one or more intermediate appellate courts. They are courts of appeal that stand between the trial courts and the State's supreme court. These appellate courts act as "gatekeepers" to ease the burden of the State's highest court.

The appellate courts have different names among the States, but they are most often called the court of appeals. Most of their work involves the review of cases decided in the trial courts. That is, these appeals courts exercise mostly **appellate jurisdiction**. Their original jurisdiction, where it exists, is limited to a few specific kinds of cases—election disputes, for example.

In exercising their appellate jurisdiction, these courts do not hold trials. Rather, they hear oral arguments from attorneys, study the briefs (written arguments) that attorneys submit, and review the record of the case in the lower court.

Ordinarily, an intermediate appellate court does not concern itself with the facts in a case. Rather, its decision turns on whether the law was correctly interpreted and applied in the court below. Its decision may be reviewed by the State's high court; its disposition of a case is usually final, however.

State Supreme Courts The State's supreme court is the highest court in its judicial system. Its major function is to review the decisions of lower courts in those cases that are appealed to it.

The size of each State supreme court is fixed by that State's constitution, usually at five or seven justices. A chief justice presides over the sessions of each State's top court.

The governor appoints the justices in just over half of the States. The voters elect them elsewhere, except in two States where the legislature chooses.

The State supreme court is the court of last resort in the State's judicial system. It has the final say in all matters of State law. The United States Supreme Court *may* review some State supreme court decisions touching on federal law. But not very many State decisions actually go to the federal Supreme Court. Recall that an appeal from a State's highest court will be heard in the federal Supreme Court only if (1) a "federal question"—some matter of federal law—is involved in the case and (2) the Supreme Court agrees

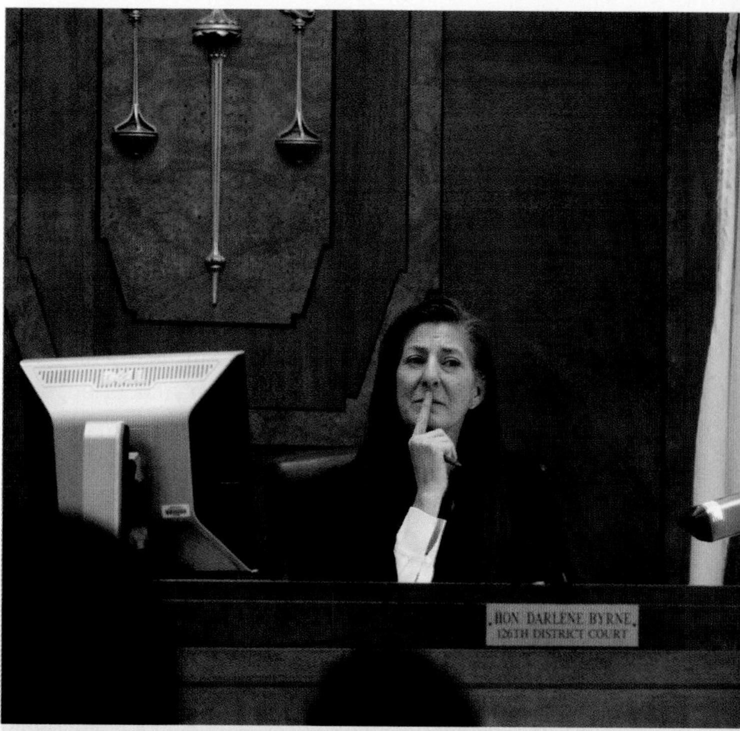

>> Family court justice Darlene Byrne presides over family matters, including adoption, divorce, child support, and visitation.

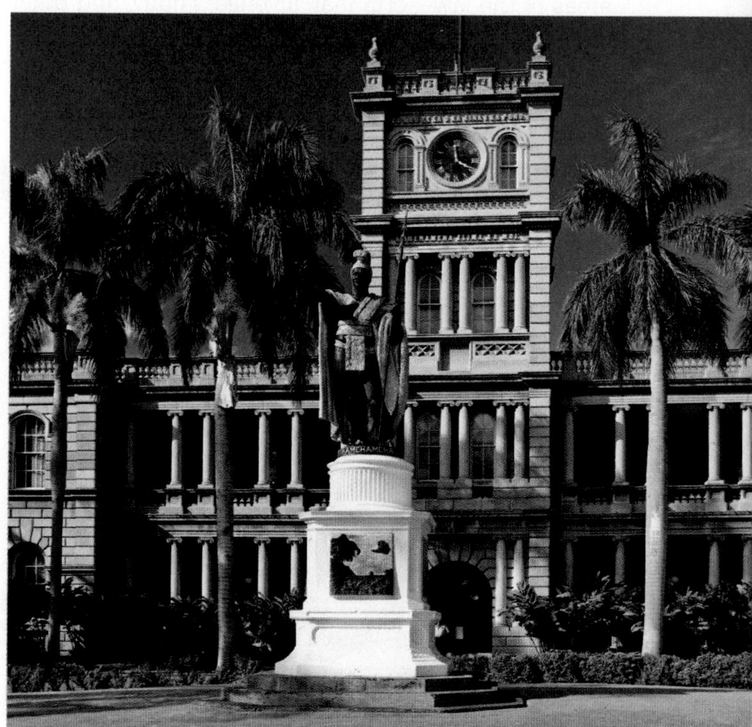
>> Hawaii's court system consists of the Supreme Court, intermediate court of appeals, circuit courts, family courts, and district courts. The State supreme court is located in Honolulu.

to hear that appeal. In short, most State supreme court decisions are final.

Unified Court Systems The typical State court system is organized geographically rather than by type of cases. Thus, the general trial courts are most often set up so that each hears those cases arising within its own district, circuit, or county, no matter what the subject matter may be.

In these map-based, or geographically based, court systems, a judge must hear cases in nearly all areas of the law. A backlog of cases can and often does build up in some courts, while judges sit with little to do in others. Moreover, uneven interpretations and application of the law sometimes occurs from one part of the State to another. To overcome these difficulties, a number of States have turned to a unified court system—one that is organized on a functional, or case-type, basis.

In a completely unified court system, there is technically only one court for the entire State. It is presided over (administered) by a chief judge or judicial council. The single court has a number of levels, such as supreme, intermediate, appellate, and general trial sections. Within each section, divisions are established to hear cases in certain specialized or heavy caseload areas of the law—criminal, juvenile, family, and other areas that need special attention.

In such an arrangement, a judge can be assigned to that section or division to which his or her talents and interest seem best suited. To relieve overcrowded dockets, judges may be moved from one section or division to another. In short, the unified court system is a modern response to the old common law adage: "Justice delayed is justice denied."

COMPARE AND CONTRAST What are the pros and cons of map-based court systems versus unified court systems?

How Judges Are Selected

Clearly, the quality of any court system—indeed, the quality of justice itself—depends in large measure on the selection of competent, well-trained judges. More than 22,000 judges and another 9,000 judicial officers (magistrates, JPs, associate judges, and so on) now sit in the States' various trial and appellate courts. Nearly all of them came to office in one of three ways: (1) by popular election, (2) by appointment by the governor, or (3) by appointment by the legislature.

Popular election is by far the most widely used method of judicial selection. In fact, the only way to become a judge in about half of the States is by popular election. Midterm vacancies, caused by death or resignation, provide the only exception to that blanket

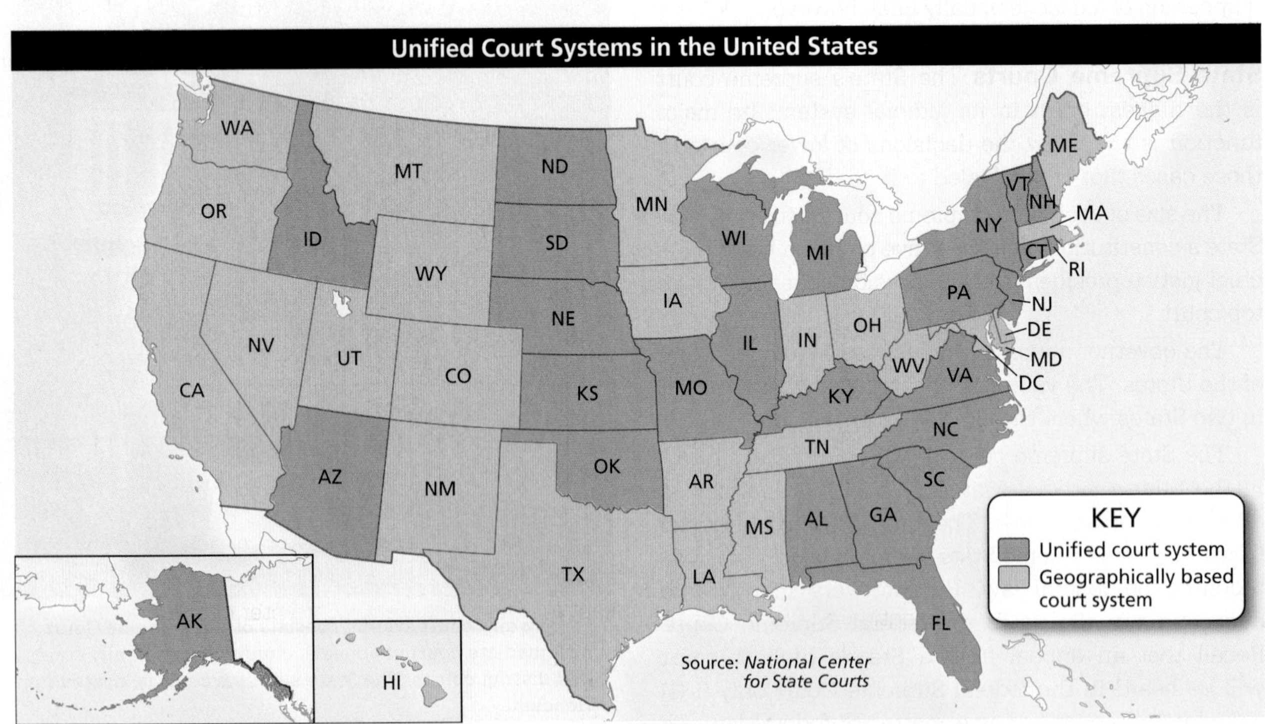

>> States rely on either unified or geographically based court systems. **Analyze Maps** What overall patterns does the map show about State court systems?

★ VOICES OF GOVERNMENT ★

New Hampshire Supreme Court Justice Joe Nadeau served nearly four decades as a judge in New Hampshire's State court system. Nadeau now dedicates his time to training new judges. During a conference in Jordan in 2006, Nadeau addressed what it means to be a judge.

"A black robe does not cloak a judge in wisdom, understanding or compassion. Those characteristics each person must bring to the bench and continuously work to strengthen. With the robe, however, comes the responsibility to make difficult choices without fear or favor, along with the responsibility to treat everyone fairly and impartially, and to seek justice and do justice."

— Retired New Hampshire Supreme Court Justice Joe Nadeau

>> Justice Nadeau believes that judges require personal attributes in addition to professional skills. **Analyze Information** What other characteristics do you think a judge needs?

rule; those vacancies are usually filled by gubernatorial appointment. Almost half of all judicial elections are nonpartisan contests today.

Selection by the legislature is the method least often used. The lawmakers now choose all or at least most judges in only two States: South Carolina and Virginia.

In half the States, governors now select most judges. In some cases, those selections must be approved by the legislature. In others, the governor must choose from a list compiled by a nominating commission, a method known as the Missouri Plan.

Election or Appointment? Most people believe that judges should be independent, that they should "stay out of politics." Whatever method of selection is used should be designed with that goal in mind.

Nearly all authorities agree that selection by the legislature is the most political of all the methods of choice. Few favor it. So, the question really becomes: Which is better, the popular election of judges or their appointment by the governor?

Those who favor popular election generally make the democratic argument. Because judges "say the law" (interpret and apply it), they should be chosen by and answer directly to the people. Some also argue that the separation of powers is undercut if the executive names the members of the judicial branch.

Those who favor appointment by the governor argue that the judicial function should be carried out only by those who are well qualified. The fact that a person has the support of a political party or is a good vote-getter does not mean that person has the capacity to be a good judge. Proponents of executive appointment insist that it is the best way to ensure that those persons who preside in courts will have the qualities most needed in that role: absolute honesty and integrity, fairness, and the necessary training and ability in the law.

Deciding between these two positions is difficult at best. The people have often made excellent choices, and governors have not always made wise and nonpolitical ones. Still, most authorities come down on the side of gubernatorial appointment—largely because those characteristics that make a good judge and those that make a good candidate are not too often found in the same person.

Popular election is both widely used and widely supported by citizens and party organizations. So, most moves to revise methods of judicial selection have kept at least some element of voter choice.

The Missouri Plan—A Mixed Approach For most of the past century, the American Bar Association (ABA) has sponsored an approach that combines election and appointment. The method is often called "the **Missouri**

Plan," and some form is now in place in just over half the States.

In Missouri's version of this method, the governor appoints the seven justices of the State supreme court, the 32 judges of the court of appeals, and all judges who sit in the trial courts in the most heavily populated parts of the State. The governor must make each appointment from a panel, or list, of three candidates recommended by a judicial nominating commission. The commission is made up of a sitting judge, several members of the bar, and private citizens.

Each judge named by the governor serves until the first general election after he or she has been in office for at least a year. The judge's name then appears on the ballot without opposition. The voters decide, in a retain-reject election, whether or not that judge should be kept in office. Should the voters reject a sitting judge, the process begins again.

? INTERPRET What does it mean when people say that they believe judges should "stay out of politics"?

ASSESSMENT

1. **Classify** Describe the different kinds of law applied in State courts.
2. **Compare and Contrast** What are the differences between civil law and criminal law?
3. **Draw Conclusions** What does the trend away from jury trials say about overall trends in the American justice system?
4. **Check Understanding** What is appellate jurisdiction and which State courts have this jurisdiction?
5. **Explain** How are judges selected?

13.5 **You know that the Census Bureau is in the people-counting business. Do you know that it also counts a great many other things—including units of government? In 2012, the Bureau's Census of Governments found an astounding 90,107 governments in the United States, including the Federal Government, the 50 States, and 90,056 local governments across the country.**

>> Services such as fire protection may be provided by a special unit of local government or by the city or county government.

Interactive Flipped Video

Local Governments

>> Objectives

Describe the typical county, its governmental structure and functions, and the need for reform in county government.

Identify the responsibilities of tribal governments.

Examine the governments of towns, townships, and special districts.

Explain the process of incorporation and compare and contrast the major forms of city government.

Evaluate the need for city planning and list some major municipal functions.

Outline the challenges that face suburbs and metropolitan areas.

>> Key Terms

county
township
municipality
special district
incorporation
charter
mayor-council government
strong-mayor government
weak-mayor government
commission government
council-manager government
zoning
metropolitan area

Counties Across the United States

Those local units come in many different shapes and sizes. Some have only a handful of employees and operate with only meager budgets. Others have tens of thousands of employees and budgets of a billion dollars or more. Many perform only a single public function, such as providing fire protection or water service. Others, including nearly all cities and most urban counties, deliver a long list of services, limited only by budgetary and legal restraints.

The Constitution of the United States says nothing about local governments. So, cities, towns, counties, school districts, and all other local governments, unlike the Federal Government and the 50 States, have no independent constitutional standing. They are, instead, creatures of the States.

Counties: Some Key Facts Recall that each of the 50 States is a *unitary* government. Each one of them has the reserved power to create local governments and structure them in whatever ways it chooses—and also to abolish them, if it chooses to do so. Whether they are providing services, regulating activities, collecting taxes, or doing anything else, local governments can only act because the State that established them has given them the power to do so.

A **county** is a major unit of local government in most States. Like all local governments, it is created by the State. There are 3,031 county

governments in the United States today. No close relationship exists between the size of any given State and the number of counties in that State. The number of county governments per State ranges from none in Connecticut and Rhode Island and three in Delaware to as many as 254 in Texas.

In Louisiana, units of government known elsewhere as counties are called *parishes*. In Alaska, they are known as *boroughs*. In addition to the entire States of Connecticut and Rhode Island, several other places across the country have no organized county government. About 10 percent of the nation's population lives in those areas today.

The functions of counties vary, often widely, from region to region. They serve almost solely as judicial districts in some of the New England States. There, towns carry out most of the functions undertaken by counties elsewhere in the country. In many Mid-Atlantic and Midwestern States, counties are divided into subdivisions called **townships**. In those States, counties and townships share the functions of rural local government. In the South and the West, counties are the major governing unit in rural areas.

In terms of area, San Bernardino County in California is the largest in the continental United States; it spreads across 20,057 square miles. Kalawao County in Hawaii is the smallest; it covers just 12 square miles. Counties within each State often vary widely in area.

Counties also differ greatly in terms of population. Some 10 million people now live in Los Angeles County in Southern California, but census takers could find only 82 residents of Loving County, Texas, in 2010. Almost three quarters of all counties serve populations of fewer than 50,000 today.

How County Governments Are Structured The structures of county governments differ, too, and often considerably. Even so, a county typically has four major elements: a governing body, a number of boards or commissions, appointed bureaucrats, and a variety of elected officials.

The county's governing body is frequently called the county board. It is also known as the board of commissioners, board of supervisors, police jury, assembly, legislature, and board of chosen freeholders, among other names.

The members of this governing body are almost always popularly elected. Terms of office run from two to six years, but four-year terms are the most common. Board members are usually chosen from districts within the county rather than on an at-large basis.

Generally, county boards can be grouped into two types: boards of commissioners and boards of

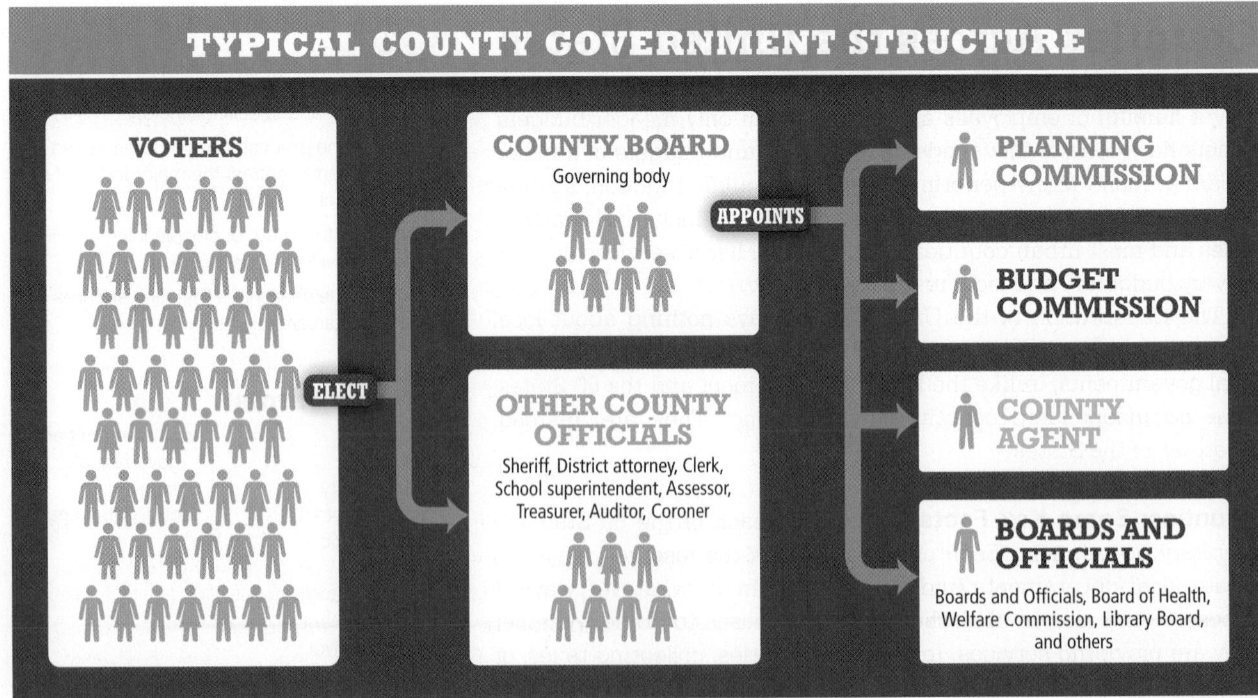

>> A county government has a governing body, commissions, and various officials.
Analyze Charts Why might confusion result from the county board sharing powers with other elected officials?

Duties of County Officials

County Board	• Levies taxes and sets spending • Administers roads, county buildings and programs • Appoints boards and officials	**Clerk**	• Registers and records documents for property, birth, and death • Runs county elections
Assessor	• Sets the value of taxable property • Collects property taxes	**Sheriff**	• Runs county jail • Provides rural police protection • Carries out court orders • May collect taxes
Auditor	• Keeps financial records	**Treasurer**	• Keeps county funds
School Superintendent	• Administers public schools	**District Attorney**	• Conducts criminal investigations • Prosecutes criminal cases
Coroner	• Investigates violent deaths • Certifies causes of death		

>> Each county official has specialized duties for which he or she is responsible.
Analyze Charts Which officials are most likely to be responsible for county financial matters?

supervisors. The board of commissioners is the smaller, more common type. It is found everywhere in the South and West, and it is also well known elsewhere. A board of commissioners most often has three or five members, but some have seven or more.

The board of supervisors is typically a much larger body. It averages about 15 members but can run to 80 or more. The supervisors are elected from single-member districts in the county. Each supervisor may be an officer of his or her township, as well as a member of the countywide governing body.

County Government Powers The State constitution and acts of the State legislature spell out the powers held by county governing bodies. Those powers are usually both executive and legislative, despite the American tradition of separation of powers.

County governments' most important legislative powers deal with finance. Everywhere, county boards levy taxes, appropriate funds, and can incur limited debts. They also have a number of other legislative powers—for example, in the fields of public health and corrections.

Most boards also carry out a number of administrative functions. They supervise the county road program and manage county property, including the courthouse, jails, hospitals, and parks. They are often responsible for the administration of welfare (cash assistance) programs and the conduct of elections. They are also responsible for the hiring of most county employees—from a few dozen or so in many rural places to several thousand in most metropolitan areas. And, importantly, they determine the pay of nearly all of the people who work for the county.

Other Elected Officials In addition to its governing body, the typical county's government regularly includes a number of other elected officials.

Then, too, county governments usually feature several boards and commissions, whose members are also sometimes elected. Those agencies frequently include a fair board, a planning commission, a board of health, a library board, and a board of road viewers. Altogether, the nation's 3,031 counties now employ some three million men and women who do the day-to-day work of those units of local government.

County Functions Because counties are creations of the State, they are responsible for the administration of State laws. They also administer such county laws as the State's constitution and legislature allow their governing bodies to make.

Historically, nearly all counties have been institutions of rural government. Most remain rurally oriented today. Although there are some differences from State to State, the major functions of counties still reflect their rural character.

Their most common functions are to keep the peace and maintain jails and other correctional facilities; assess property for tax purposes; collect taxes and spend county funds; build and repair roads, bridges, drains, and other public works; and maintain schools. Counties record deeds, mortgages, marriage licenses, and other documents; issue licenses for such things as hunting, fishing, and marriage; administer elections; care for the poor; and work to safeguard the health of the people who live in the county.

Many counties have taken on other functions as they have become more urban. Several of these more

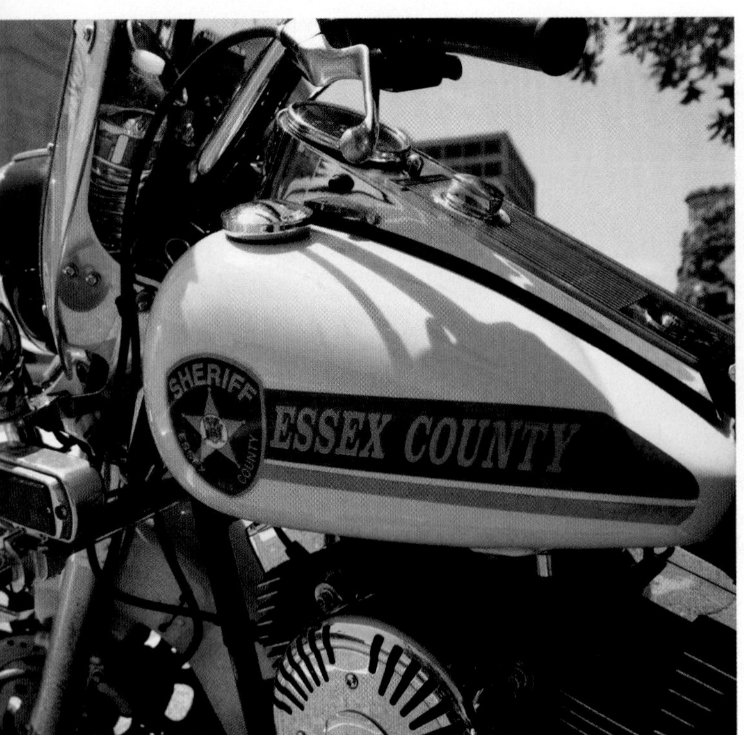

>> Counties often provide policing services through a sheriff's office. County police provide security for local courthouses and county-owned facilities and parks. Some also provide road patrol.

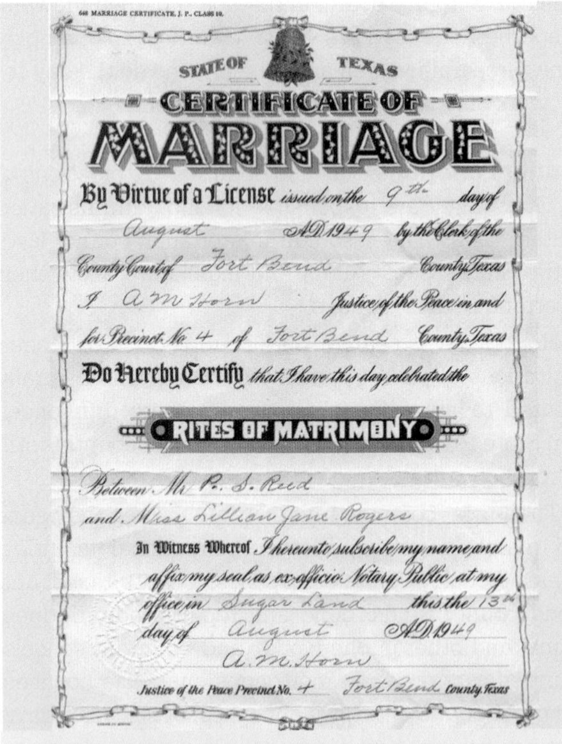

STATE OF TEXAS

CERTIFICATE OF MARRIAGE

By Virtue of a License issued on the 9th day of August A.D. 1949 by the Clerk of the County Court of Fort Bend County, Texas I A. M. Horn Justice of the Peace in and for Precinct No. 4 of Fort Bend County, Texas

Do Hereby Certify that I have this day celebrated the

RITES OF MATRIMONY

Between Mr. P. S. Reed
and Miss Lillian Jane Rogers

In Witness Whereof I hereunto subscribe my name and affix my seal as ex officio Notary Public at my office in Sugar Land this the 13th day of August A.D. 1949

A. M. Horn

Justice of the Peace Precinct No. 4 Fort Bend County, Texas

>> Issuing marriage licenses and certificates is one of the duties a county government performs.

heavily populated counties now offer many of the public services and facilities that are usually found in cities. They provide water and sewer service; have professionally trained police, fire, and medical units; and operate airports and mass transit systems. Some also enforce zoning and other land-use regulations. Many have built and now operate auditoriums, stadiums, golf courses, and other recreational facilities.

Challenges Faced by County Governments County organization is often chaotic. In the typical county, no single official can really be called the *chief* administrator. Rather, authority is divided among a number of elected boards and officials, each largely independent of the others. Too often, it is impossible to identify who is responsible for inefficiency or inaction (or worse) in the conduct of county affairs.

The large number of popularly elected officials adds to the chaos. Faced with the typical county's long ballot, voters are often hard-pressed to make informed choices. Also, many of those elected officials have no basic public policy-making responsibilities. Many people are convinced that popular election is not the best way to fill those offices.

The size and the number of counties in most States are another source of weakness. Nearly every county now in existence was laid out in the days of the horse and the stagecoach. Then, it made good sense to draw county lines so that no one lived more than a dozen miles or so from the county seat. Today, however, most counties are geographically ill-suited to the realities of the modern world.

One way in which many States have attempted to reform county government is through county home rule. That is, those 37 States allow some or all of their counties, subject to approval by the local voters, to decide the details of their own governmental structure.

Another approach to reform seeks to deal with the fragmented authority of counties. It does so by creating the position of county manager, modeled along the lines of the council-manager form of city government. Still another approach is county-city consolidation—where a major city and the county around it join into a single unit of government. San Francisco, California, and Nashville, Tennessee, are leading examples.

? **EXPLAIN** Why is there a need to reform the organization of many county governments?

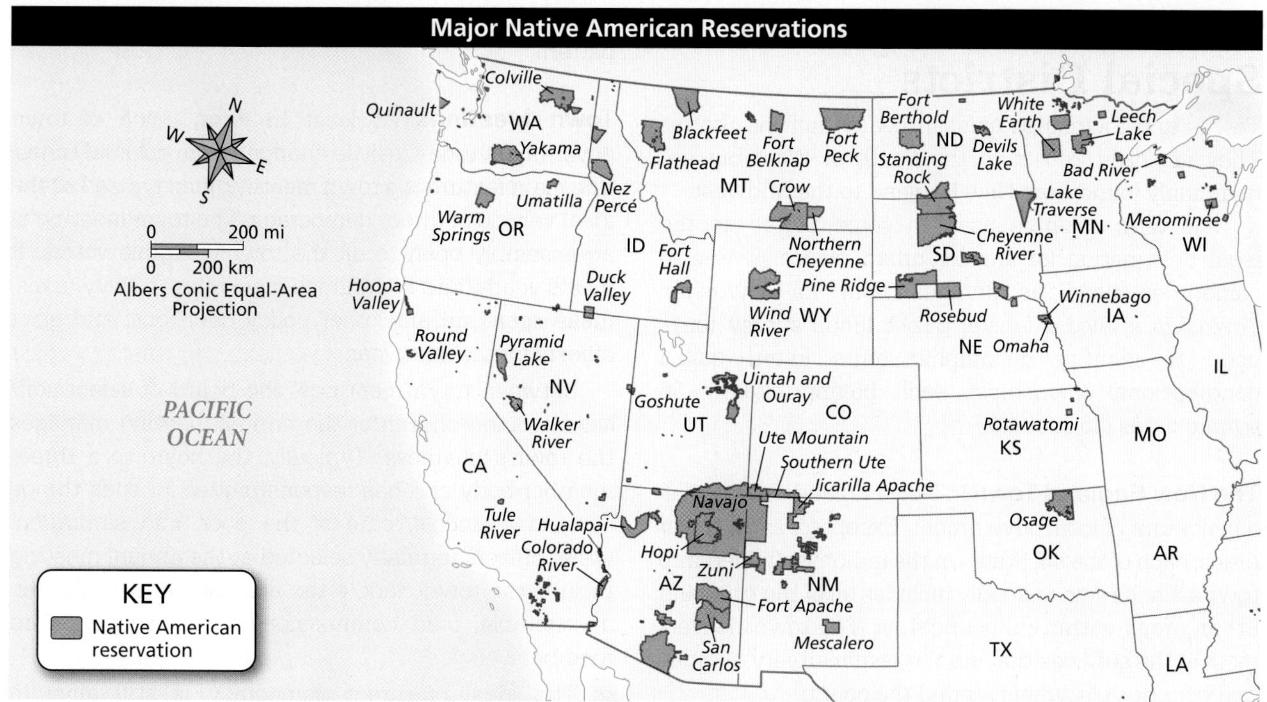

>> Sovereign Native American governments have a special relationship to Federal and State governments. **Analyze Maps** Why do you think most reservations are in the Midwest and West?

Tribal Governments

Tribal governments exist as a distinct form of government. Unlike State, county, or city governments, however, the governments of Native American nations have a unique "government-to-government" relationship with the United States. These Native American tribes are considered sovereign nations, with the right to govern their own people on their own territories unless otherwise specified by treaty or acts of Congress.

Sovereignty of Tribal Governments Official recognition by the Federal Government is crucial for tribal governments because it establishes their sovereignty and exempts them from State or local control. For example, some tribes have established gambling casinos on their reservations, even though the territory lies within States that do not allow that type of gambling. Because the officially recognized tribes are sovereign, they are not subject to State laws and regulations. Also, recognized tribes are eligible to receive federal funds that can be used to provide local services. Today, there are some 566 federally recognized tribal governments in this country, with authority over the lives of approximately 2 million people.

Typically, a tribal government has an elected leader called a chief or chairman. Most tribes also have a council, which can vary in size from only two or three to almost 100 members. Other than these common features, tribal governments vary widely in size and structure. Some, such as the Cherokee and Navajo tribes, have a written code or constitution that provides for a State-like government with executive, legislative, and judicial branches. Others are small and loosely organized.

Structure and Services of Tribal Governments Like State and county governments, tribal governments use federal funds and tax revenue to provide services. These services depend on the size, history, and needs of the tribe. Many tribes have executive officers or departments that oversee policy and manage funds to provide healthcare, education, and welfare to tribe members. They also oversee cultural events and sites, as well as distribute information about the tribe. Even smaller tribal governments provide some services, especially housing and health and education information and support.

? EXPLAIN Explain the main responsibilities of tribal governments.

Towns, Townships, and Special Districts

Towns and townships exist in nearly half the States. They are little known in the South or West but are commonly found from New England to the Midwest.

The term *town* is used in some States as the legal designation for smaller urban places. It is also sometimes used as another word for *township*. *Township* is also a federal public lands survey term, used to identify geographic units (often called congressional townships), each having exactly 36 square miles (36 sections).

The New England Town In New England, the town is a major unit of local government. Except for a few major cities, each of the six States in the region is divided into towns. Each town generally includes all of the rural and urban areas within its boundaries. The town delivers most of the services that are the responsibility of cities and counties elsewhere around the country.

The roots of the New England town reach back to the early colonial period. The Pilgrims landed at Plymouth Rock in 1620 as an organized congregation. They quickly set up a close-knit community in which their church and their government were almost one. Other Puritan congregations followed the Pilgrims' pattern.

>> In early New England towns, all male property owners were allowed to vote in town meetings.

Town Meetings At least in form, much of town government today is little changed from colonial times. The main feature is a town meeting, long praised as the ideal vehicle of direct democracy. The town meeting is an assembly open to all the town's eligible voters. It meets yearly, and sometimes more often, to levy taxes, make spending and other policy decisions, and elect officers for the next year.

Between town meetings, the board of selectmen/selectwomen chosen at the annual meeting manages the town's business. Typically, the board is a three-member body and has responsibilities for such things as roads, schools, care of the poor, and sanitation. Other officers regularly selected at the annual meeting include the town clerk, a tax assessor, a tax collector, a constable, road commissioners, and school board members.

The ideal of direct democracy is still alive in many smaller New England towns. It has given way, however, to the pressures of time, population, and the complexities of public problems in many of the larger towns. There, representative government has largely replaced it. Town officers are often elected before the yearly gathering. Many of the decisions once made by the assembled voters are now made by the selectmen and selectwomen. In recent years, several towns have gone to a town manager system for the day-to-day administration of local affairs.

Townships Townships are units of local government found principally in the Northeast and the Midwest. Nowhere do townships blanket an entire State, however.

In New York, New Jersey, and Pennsylvania, townships were formed as areas were settled and the people needed the services of local government. Consequently, the township maps of those States often resemble crazy quilts. From Ohio westward, they mostly follow the regular lines drawn in federal public land surveys. Many are perfect squares.

About half of these States provide for annual township meetings, like those held in New England towns. Otherwise, the governing body is usually a three- or five-member board, generally called the board of trustees or board of supervisors. Its members are elected for fixed terms or serve because they hold other elected township offices. Township offices often include a supervisor, a clerk, a treasurer, an assessor, a constable, a justice of the peace, and a body of road commissioners.

A **municipality** is an urban political unit within a township that usually exists as a separate governmental entity. As a result, township functions tend to be rural. They regularly involve such matters as roads, cemeteries, drainage, and minor law enforcement. In some States, however, the township is also the basic unit of public school administration.

Many people believe that townships have outlived their usefulness. More than half the States get along without them. Many rural townships have been abolished as a result of declining populations, improvements in transportation, and other factors.

Some of the more densely populated townships appear to have brighter futures than their country cousins, however. This seems especially true in the suburban areas around some larger cities. Some States, such as Pennsylvania, now allow townships to exercise many of the powers and furnish many of the services once reserved for cities.

Special Districts There are now tens of thousands of special districts across the country. A **special district** is an independent unit created to perform one or more related governmental functions at the local level. These districts are found in mind-boggling variety and in every State. School districts—some 14,000 of them—are by far the most common example. More than 37,000 other special districts also blanket the country, and their numbers are growing.

Special districts are found most often, but not always, in rural and suburban areas. Many have been created to provide water, sewage, or electrical service; to furnish fire or police protection; and to build and maintain bridges, airports, swimming pools, libraries, or parks. Others have been created for such purposes as soil conservation, housing, public transportation, irrigation, or reforestation. There are even, in many places, special districts for dog or mosquito control purposes.

A leading reason for the creation of special districts has been the need to provide a particular service in a wider or a smaller area than that covered by a county or a city. For example, a special district might be needed to handle pollution in the several counties through which a river flows. On the other hand, a special district might be set up to provide fire or police protection in some out-of-the-way locale.

In many cases, special districts have been formed because other local governments could not, or would not, provide the services desired. Others have been created to sidestep constitutional limits on the size of a city's or a county's debt; to finance a public service out of users' fees instead of general tax revenue; and to take advantage of some federal grant program.

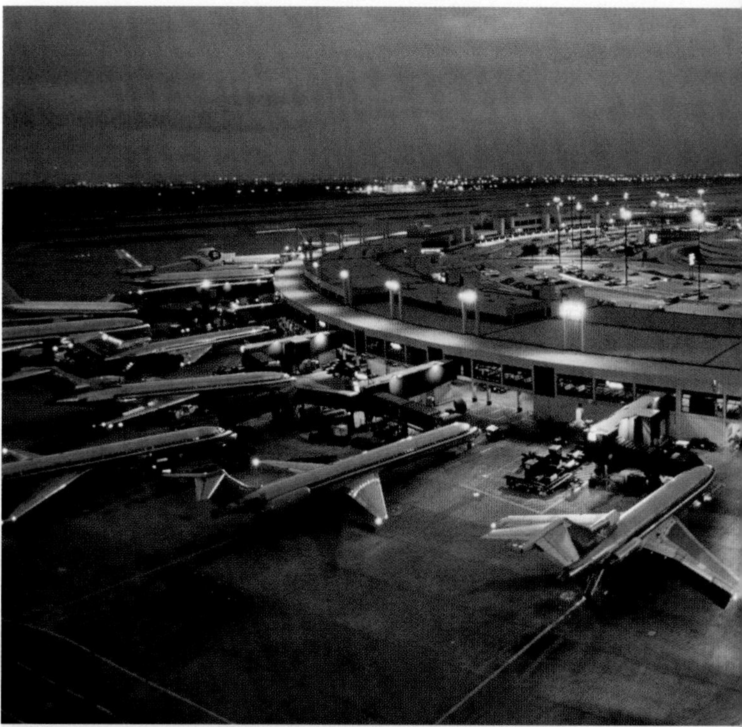

>> Special districts, such as the Dallas/Fort Worth International Airport, are formed for a wide variety of reasons, and they often provide cross-county services.

Interactive Gallery

The governing body for a special district is almost always an elected board. It has the power to lay taxes (usually on property) or charge fees, as well as the power to spend and to carry out the function(s) for which it was created.

COMPARE AND CONTRAST What are the similarities and differences between the town meeting and the township forms of local government?

City Government

We are fast becoming a nation of city dwellers. Where once our population was small, mostly rural, and agricultural, it is now large, mostly urban, and dominated by technology, manufacturing, and service industries. In 1790, a mere 5 percent of the population lived in the nation's few cities. Today, some 260 million people—more than 80 percent of the population—live in the nation's cities and their surrounding suburbs. For local governments, that change has had dramatic consequences.

Urbanization The larger the number of people living in close contact with one another, the greater the strains on local governments. The larger the population, the greater the problems in providing water, police and fire protection, sewers, waste removal, streets and traffic regulation, public health services, schools, recreational facilities, and more. The larger the population, the more extensive—and expensive—all of this becomes.

Remember, each of the 50 States is a unitary government. That means that each State has complete control over all of the units of local government within its borders. All those units, including cities, were created by the State, received their powers from the State, and are subject to a variety of limitations imposed by the State.

Depending on local custom and State law, municipalities may be known as cities, towns, boroughs, or villages. The use and meaning of these terms vary among the States. The larger municipalities are known everywhere as cities, and the usual practice is to use that title only for those communities with significant populations.

Incorporation The procedure by which a State establishes a city as a legal body is called **incorporation**. Each State sets out in its constitution, or by statute, the conditions and the procedures under which a community may become an incorporated municipality. Typically, a State requires that a minimum number of persons live within a given area before incorporation can take place.

The fact that cities are incorporated highlights an important difference between city and county government. Cities are created largely at the request of their residents, because residents want certain public services. Counties, on the other hand, exist largely to serve the administrative needs of the State. Cities do act as agents of the State, of course—for example, in law enforcement and public health. But the principal reason for the existence of a city is for the convenience of those who live there.

>> The Gateway Arch in St. Louis, Missouri, commemorates the city's role in westward expansion. At the time of the 1850 census, St. Louis was the most populous city west of the Mississippi River.

City Charters A **charter** is a city's basic law, its constitution. Its contents may vary from city to city, but commonly the charter names the city, describes its boundaries, and declares it to be a municipal corporation. As a municipal corporation, a city has the right to sue and be sued in the courts; to have a corporate seal; to make contracts; and to acquire, own, manage, and dispose of property.

Generally, the charter sets out the other powers vested in the city and outlines its form of government. It also provides how and for what terms its officers are to be chosen, outlines their duties, and deals with finances and other matters.

? EXPLAIN How do States control the process of incorporation?

Forms of City Government

Although variations can and do exist, each city has one of three basic forms of government. A city has (1) a mayor-council, (2) a commission, or (3) a council-manager form of government.

The Mayor-Council Form The **mayor-council government** is the oldest and still the most widely used type of city government. It features an elected mayor as the chief executive and an elected council as its legislative body.

The council is almost always unicameral and typically has five, seven, or nine members. Some larger cities have more. New York City has the largest council, with 51 members. Members of the council are popularly elected, almost always from districts (wards) within the city. Terms of office vary from one to six years. Four-year terms are the most common.

A move to nonpartisan city government began in the early 1900s. Its champions believed that (1) political parties were a major source of corruption in city government, and (2) partisan contests at the State and

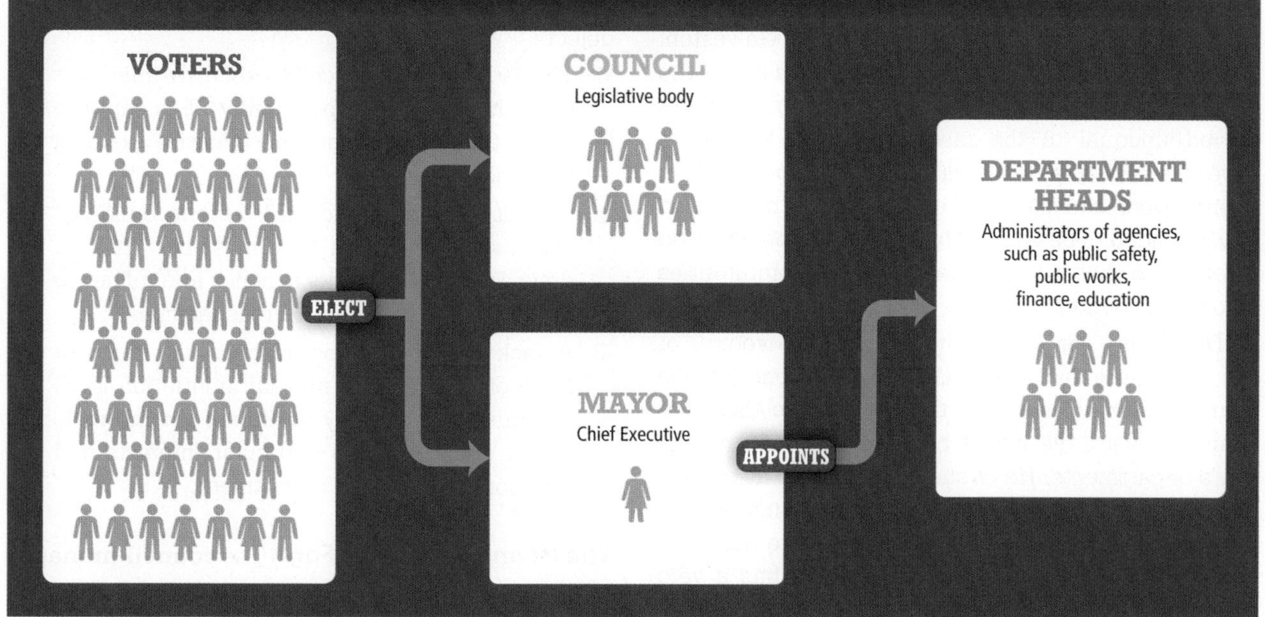

>> Use of the strong-mayor form of city government often eliminates questions about who is in charge. **Analyze Charts** What can you conclude about this as a model for large cities?

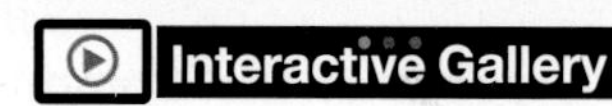

national levels have little to do with municipal problems and local issues. Today, less than one third of all cities still run their elections on a partisan basis.

Strong and Weak Mayors Generally, the voters elect the mayor. In some places, however, the council chooses one of its members to serve as mayor. The mayor presides at council meetings, usually may vote only to break a tie, and may recommend—and often veto—ordinances. In most cities, the council can override the veto.

Mayor-council governments are often described as either the strong-mayor or the weak-mayor type, depending on the powers given to the mayor. This classification is useful for purposes of description. It blurs the importance of informal power in city politics, however.

In a **strong-mayor government,** the mayor heads the city's administration, usually has the veto power, can hire and fire employees, and prepares the budget. Typically, the mayor is able to exercise strong leadership in making city policy and running the city's affairs.

In a **weak-mayor government,** the mayor has much less formal power. Executive duties are shared with other elected officials—for example, a clerk, treasurer, city engineer, police chief, and even council members.

Powers of appointment, removal, and budget are shared with the council or exercised by that body alone. The mayor seldom has a veto power.

Most mayor-council cities operate under the weak-mayor rather than the strong-mayor plan. The strong-mayor form is most often found in larger cities.

The success of the mayor-council form depends in very large measure on the power, ability, and influence of the mayor. In weak-mayor cities, responsibility for action or inaction is hard to assign. The strong-mayor plan helps to solve the problems of leadership and responsibility. Still, the mayor-council form has three large defects:

1. It depends quite heavily on the capabilities of the mayor.
2. An ongoing dispute between the mayor and the council can stall the workings of a city's government.
3. It is quite complicated and, so, is often little understood by the average citizen.

The Commission Form The **commission government** is simple in structure. Three to nine, but usually five, commissioners are popularly elected. Together, they form the city council, pass ordinances, and control the purse strings. Individually, they head the different departments of city government: police, fire, public works, finance, parks, and so on. Thus, both legislative and executive powers are centered in one body.

The commission form was born in Galveston, Texas, in 1901, after a tidal surge had devastated the city. When the existing mayor-council government proved unequal to the task, the Texas legislature gave Galveston a new charter, providing for five commissioners to make and enforce law in the stricken city. Intended to be temporary, the arrangement proved so effective that it soon spread to other communities across the country.

Depending on the city, either the voters or the commissioners themselves choose one of the commissioners to serve as the mayor. Like the other commissioners, the mayor heads one or more of the city's departments. He or she also presides at council meetings and represents the city for ceremonial purposes. The mayor generally has no more authority than the other commissioners and rarely has a veto power.

Weaknesses of the Commission Form Although many reformers supported the commission form at first, experience pointed up serious defects in the system, and its popularity fell off rapidly. Only a very few American cities have a commission form of government today.

The commission form suffers from three chief defects:

1. The lack of a single chief executive makes it difficult to assign responsibility. This can also mean that the city has no effective political leadership.
2. A built-in tendency toward "empire building" often surfaces. Each commissioner tries to draw as much of the city's money and influence as possible to his or her own department.
3. A lack of coordination plagues the topmost levels of policymaking and administration. Each commissioner is likely to equate the citywide public good with the particular interests and functions of his or her department.

The Council-Manager Form The **council-manager government** is a modification of the mayor-council form. Its main features are (1) a strong council of usually five or seven members elected at-large on a nonpartisan ballot; (2) a weak mayor chosen by the voters; and (3) a manager, the city's chief administrative officer, named by the council.

The form first appeared in Ukiah, California. In 1904, that city's council appointed an "executive officer" to

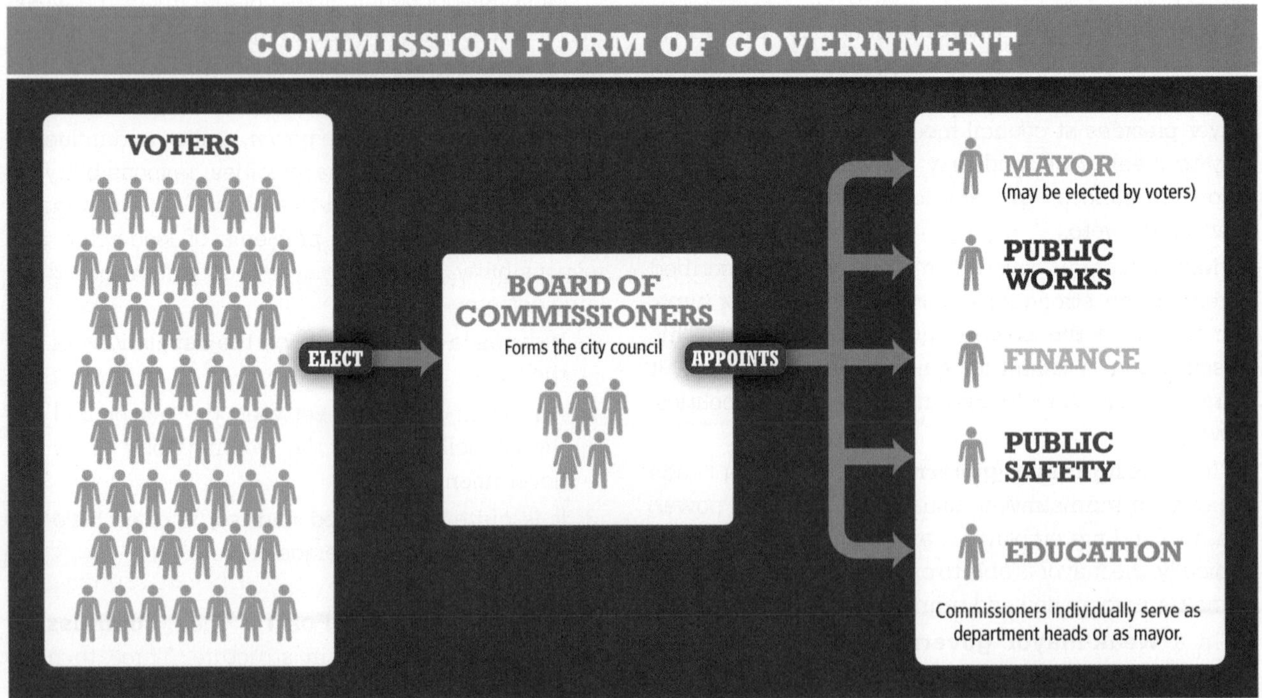

>> The commission form of government is one of the simplest governing systems for a city. **Analyze Charts** Does a system of checks and balances exist in this form of government?

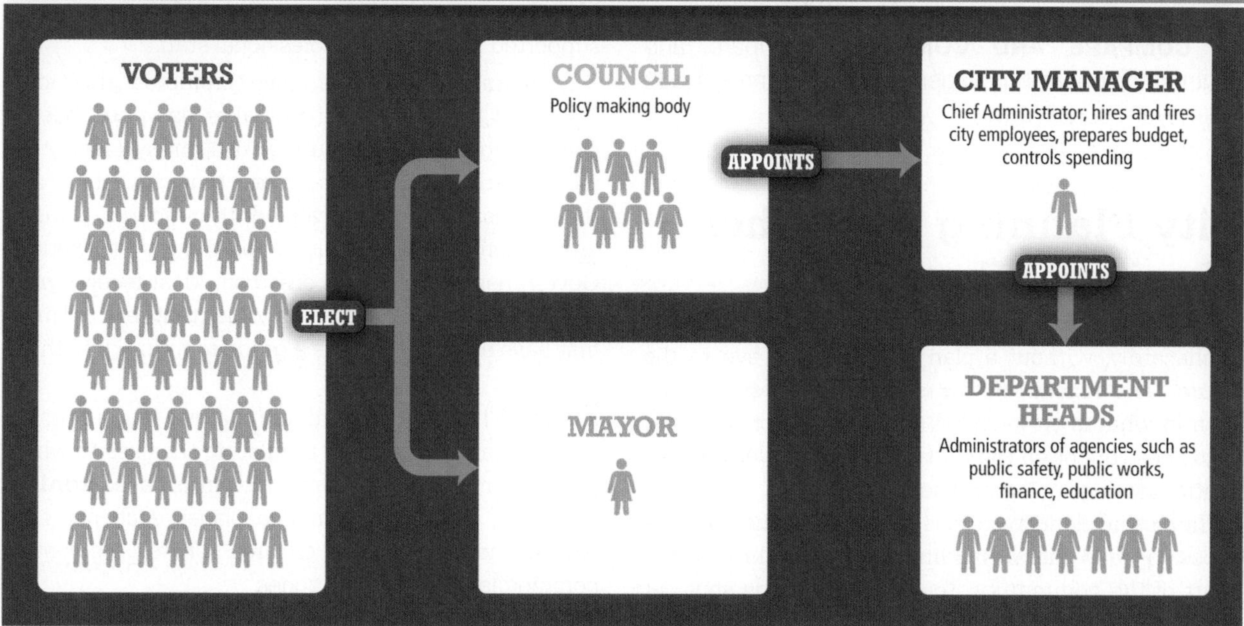

>> In the council-manager form of government, a professional manager oversees necessary services for city residents. **Analyze Charts** What are the advantages of this type of government?

direct the work of city government. The first charter expressly providing for the council-manager form was granted to the city of Sumter, South Carolina, in 1912.

City Managers The council is the city's policymaking body. The manager carries out the policies the council makes. He or she is directly responsible to that body for the efficient administration of the city. The manager serves at the council's pleasure and may be dismissed at any time and for any reason.

Today, most city managers are professionally trained career administrators. As chief administrator, the manager directs the work of all city departments and has the power to hire and fire all city employees. The manager also prepares the budget for council consideration and controls the spending of the funds the council appropriates.

The council-manager plan is backed by most experts on municipal affairs, and its use has spread widely. It is now found in more than 3,600 cities with populations of 2,500 or more. In fact, some 92 million people live under this form of government today.

Pros and Cons of the Council-Manager Form The council-manager plan has three major advantages over other forms of city government:

1. It is simple in form.
2. It is fairly clear who is responsible for policy, on the one hand, and for its application, on the other.
3. It relies on highly trained experts who are skilled in modern techniques of budgeting, planning, computerization, and other administrative tools.

In theory, the nonpolitical manager carries out the policies enacted by the council. Yet, in practice, sharp distinctions between policymaking and policy-application seldom exist. The manager is very often the chief source for new ideas and fresh approaches to the city's problems. On the other hand, the city council often finds it politically useful to share the responsibility for controversial decisions with the "expendable" city manager.

Some critics of the council-manager form hold that it is undemocratic because its chief executive is not popularly elected. Others say that it lacks strong political leadership. This is a particular shortcoming, they argue, in larger cities, where the population is often quite diverse and there can be many competing interests. Support for this view can be seen in the fact that only a handful of cities with more than a half a million residents have a council-manager government in place today.

? COMPARE AND CONTRAST Compare and contrast the council-manager form of government with the mayor-council form.

City Planning and Other Municipal Functions

With few exceptions, most American cities developed haphazardly, without a plan, and with no eye to the future. The results of this shortsightedness can be seen in what is often called the core area or the inner city. These are often the older and usually overcrowded central sections of larger cities.

Industrial plants were placed anywhere their owners chose to build them. Rail lines were run through the heart of the community. Towering buildings shut out the sunlight from the narrow streets below. Main roads were laid out too close together and sometimes too far apart. Schools, police and fire stations, and other public buildings were squeezed onto cheap land or put where the political organization could make a profit. The many examples of this shortsightedness are nearly endless.

>> The 59-mile San Bernardino freeway in southern California is one of the busiest and most congested freeways in the United States. As a result, it is also one of the most dangerous.

Guiding Growth Fortunately, many cities have seen the need to create order out of their random growth. Most have established some sort of planning agency, supported by a trained professional staff.

A number of factors have prompted this step. The need to correct past mistakes has often been a compelling reason, of course. Also, many cities have recognized both the advantages that can result, and the pitfalls that can be avoided, through well-planned and orderly development. Importantly, the Federal Government has spurred cities on. Most federal grant and loan programs require that cities that seek aid must first have a master plan as a guide to future growth.

Zoning The practice of dividing a city into a number of districts, or zones, and regulating the uses to which property in each of them may be put is called **zoning**. Generally, a zoning ordinance places each parcel of land in the city into one of three spheres: residential, commercial, or industrial zones.

Each of these zones is then divided into subzones. For example, each of several residential zones may be broken down into several areas. One may be reserved for single-family residences, another may allow one-family and two-family dwellings, and a third, large apartment buildings.

Most zoning ordinances also prescribe limits on the height and area of buildings, determine how much of a lot may be occupied by a structure, and set out several other such restrictions on land use. They often have "setback" requirements, providing that structures must be placed at least a certain distance from the street and from other property lines.

Pros and Cons of Zoning Zoning still meets opposition from many who object to this interference with their right to use their property as they choose. Even so, nearly every city of any size in the United States is zoned today. The city of Houston, where zoning was turned down three times by popular vote, remains the only major exception.

Zoning ordinances must be reasonable. Remember that the 14th Amendment prohibits any State, and thus its cities, from depriving any person of life, liberty, or property without due process of law. Each of the 50 State constitutions contains a similar provision.

Clearly, zoning does deprive a person of the right to use his or her property for certain purposes. Thus, if an area is zoned for single-family dwellings only, one cannot build an apartment house or a service station on property in that zone. Zoning can also reduce the value of a particular piece of property. A choice corner lot, for example, may be much more valuable with a drive-through restaurant or gas station on the property rather than a house.

Noncomforming uses in existence before a zoning ordinance is passed are almost always allowed to continue. Most ordinances give the city council the right to grant exceptions, called variances, in those cases where property owners might suffer undue hardships.

While zoning may at times deprive a person of liberty or property, the key question is always this: Does it do so without due process? That is, does it do so unreasonably?

The question of reasonableness is one for the courts to decide. The Supreme Court first upheld zoning as a proper use of the police power in *Euclid* v. *Amber Realty Co.*, 1926, a case involving an ordinance enacted by the city council of Euclid, Ohio.

City Services The services a city provides day in and day out are so extensive that it is almost impossible to catalog them. Most larger cities, and many smaller ones, issue annual reports on the city's condition. These are often booklength publications.

Consider just a few of the many things that most or all cities do. They provide police and fire protection. They build and maintain streets, sidewalks, bridges, street lights, parks and playgrounds, swimming pools, golf courses, libraries, hospitals, schools, correctional institutions, day-care centers, airports, public markets, parking facilities, auditoriums, and sports arenas. They furnish public health and sanitation services, including sewers and wastewater treatment, garbage collection and disposal, and disease prevention programs.

Cities operate water, gas, electrical, and transportation systems. They regulate traffic, building codes, pollution, and public utilities. Many cities also build and manage public housing projects, provide summer youth camps, build and operate docks and other harbor facilities, and maintain tourist attractions.

? EXPLAIN Explain how the U.S. Constitution relates to the implementation of zoning laws.

Suburbs and Metropolitan Areas

The growth of urban areas has raised many problems for city dwellers. Urban growth also affects residents of nearby suburbs.

The Suburban Boom About half of all Americans now live in suburbs. The nation's suburbs first began to grow rapidly in the years after World War II, and that

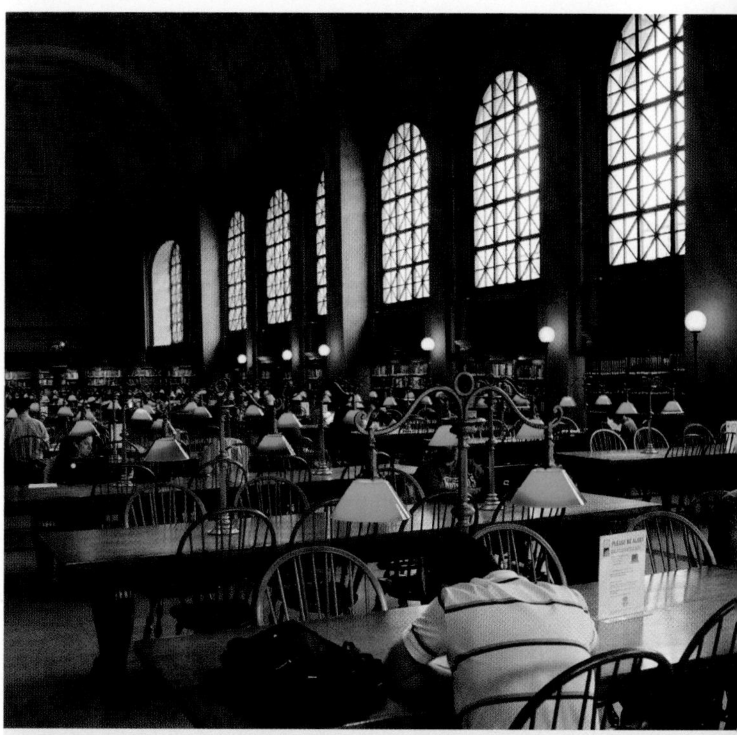

>> The Boston public library is known as a "palace for the people." Public libraries are funded by cities. They loan books and other media and offer meeting space, classes, and Internet access.

>> In the economic boom after World War II, inexpensive new housing like this development in Levittown, Pennsylvania, and cheap government mortgages helped fuel a shift from urban to suburban living.

growth has continued. As suburban populations have mushroomed, many of the nation's larger cities have actually lost residents.

These dramatic population shifts stemmed, in large part, from peoples' desire for more room, cheaper land, greater privacy, and less smoke, dirt, noise, and congestion. Many have also sought less crime, newer and better schools, safer streets and playing conditions, lower taxes, and higher social status. The car and the freeway turned millions of rooted city dwellers into mobile suburbanites.

Businesses followed customers to the suburbs, often clustering in shopping centers or malls instead of traditional downtowns. Many industries moved from the central city in search of cheaper land, lower taxes, and a more stable labor supply. Industries also sought an escape from city building codes, health inspectors, and other regulations.

This "suburbanitis" has added to city dwellers' woes. As high-income families have moved out, they have taken their civic, financial, and social resources with them. They have left behind center cities with high percentages of older people, low-income families, and minorities. Both the need for, and the stress on, city services have multiplied.

>> A cartoonist depicts the possible future of urban sprawl. **Analyze Political Cartoons** What does the view suggest about urban sprawl and its impact?

The Challenges of Metropolitan Areas Suburbanites face their share of problems, too, including the need for water supplies, sewage disposal, police and fire protection, transportation, and traffic control. Duplication of such functions by city and suburb or by city and county can be wasteful, even dangerous. More than one fire has raged while neighboring fire departments quibbled over the responsibility for fighting it.

Attempts to meet the needs of the nation's **metropolitan areas**—cities and the areas around them—have taken several forms. Over the years, annexation has been the standard means. Outlying areas have simply been brought within a city's boundaries. Many suburbanites resist annexation, however, and many cities have been hesitant to take on the burdens involved.

Urban Special Districts Another approach has been to create special districts designed to meet the problems of heavily populated urban areas. Their boundaries frequently cut across county and city lines to include an entire metropolitan area. They often are called metropolitan districts and can serve one purpose (for example, maintaining parks) or many.

In Oregon, a regional agency known as Metro manages several activities in an area that includes Portland, the State's largest city, and 25 other municipalities. Within this region, Metro is responsible for land-use and transportation planning, solid-waste disposal programs, and the operation of the Oregon Convention Center, the Oregon Zoo, and other facilities.

Yet another approach to the challenges facing metropolitan areas is increasing the authority of counties. Among local governments around the country, counties are generally the largest in area and are most likely to include those places demanding new and increased services. In Miami-Dade County, Florida, a countywide metropolitan government took responsibility for areawide functions following a 1957 charter. Responsibilities include fire and police protection; an integrated water, sewer, and drainage system; zoning; and expressway construction. Miami and the county's other 34 municipalities continue to perform strictly local functions and services.

? EXPLAIN How has the suburban boom that followed World War II affected city governments?

ASSESSMENT

1. **Check Understanding** Describe one major flaw of county government.
2. **Express Ideas Clearly** Describe the various means through which metropolitan areas can gain access to basic services.
3. **Interpret** Why might zoning be used to exclude certain businesses from residential neighborhoods?
4. **Summarize** Summarize the basic organization of the most common form of city government.
5. **Identify Central Issues** What are some pros and cons of having a professional manager as part of a city government?

>> Through bicycle police units, such as this one in Arkansas, officers can be more accessible to citizens, providing opportunities for positive interactions with the community.

13.6 The 50 State governments and their tens of thousands of local governments are principally responsible for many of the public services with which most Americans are familiar. The many differences among States means that there can be variations in both the quantity and the quality of those public services, but they include, especially, those in the areas of education, public safety, welfare, streets and highways, and public health. The several States deliver services to their residents in two ways: (1) directly, through State agencies conducting State-operated programs, and (2) through the many local governments the States have created.

Interactive Flipped Video

>> Objectives

Explain why State and local governments have a major role in providing important services.

Identify State and local services in the fields of education, public welfare, public safety, and highways.

Describe the major federal and State limits on raising revenue.

List the four principles of sound taxation.

Identify major tax and nontax sources of State and local revenues.

Explain the State budget process.

>> Key Terms

Medicaid
welfare
entitlement
sales tax
regressive tax
income tax
progressive tax
property tax
assessment
inheritance tax
estate tax
budget

State and Local Spending and Revenue

Education, Public Health, and Welfare

Public Education Funding Public education is among the oldest of all State responsibilities. Boston Latin School, in Massachusetts, is the oldest public school in continuous existence in the United States; it opened its doors in 1635. The State of New York created the first school districts in 1812. Today, public education is also among the most important of all State responsibilities. This is reflected in the fact that education is the most expensive item in every State's budget, accounting for nearly 30 percent of all State spending.

Funding for public education has risen sharply over recent decades. In fact, the amount of money spent per pupil in public schools has nearly doubled over the past 25 years.

Primary and secondary public education is largely the responsibility of local governments. Local taxes, especially property taxes, provide much of the funding for schools.

Of course, the States do provide some financial assistance to their local governments for education. The level of that aid varies, however. Some States contribute well over half the cost of primary and secondary education. Others provide only a minor fraction of the cost.

In addition, States set guidelines in order to promote quality in the schools. For example, State laws establish teacher qualifications, curricula, quality standards for educational materials, and the length of the school year.

State interest and involvement in these matters have intensified in recent years. Most States have established "curriculum frameworks" or "content standards" outlining the material that must be covered in core subjects. In addition, many States have adopted the national Common Core State Standards, a State-led effort to develop criteria for mathematics and English curriculums. Every State now also has an extensive Statewide testing program, fueled by the No Child Left Behind Act signed by President Bush in 2002.

College and University Support At the college and university levels, the States also play a major role. States understand that, in order for businesses to succeed in the State, a ready supply of highly trained college graduates is key. Every State has a public higher education system, which may include universities, technical schools, and community colleges. Education at State universities and colleges is generally much less expensive than at private institutions. On average, tuition at four-year public colleges and universities is about one fourth that of private four-year schools. Nevertheless, many public institutions—for example, the University of California at Berkeley—are ranked among the world's finest schools.

Public Health States take an active role in promoting the health and welfare of their residents. They pursue that goal through a variety of means. Most States fund ambitious public health programs. States operate public hospitals and offer direct care to millions of citizens. They immunize children against dangerous childhood diseases, such as measles and mumps. With the Federal Government, they administer such programs as **Medicaid**, which provides medical care and some other health services to low-income families. Recent soaring costs in the healthcare industry have placed a great strain on many States' budgets.

Cash Assistance Another major area in which States contribute to the well-being of their citizens is cash assistance to the poor, commonly called **welfare**. States now take a leading role in this area.

Between 1936 and 1996, the Federal Government provided cash assistance to needy families through the Aid to Families with Dependent Children (AFDC) program. AFDC was an **entitlement** program, which

State and Local Spending

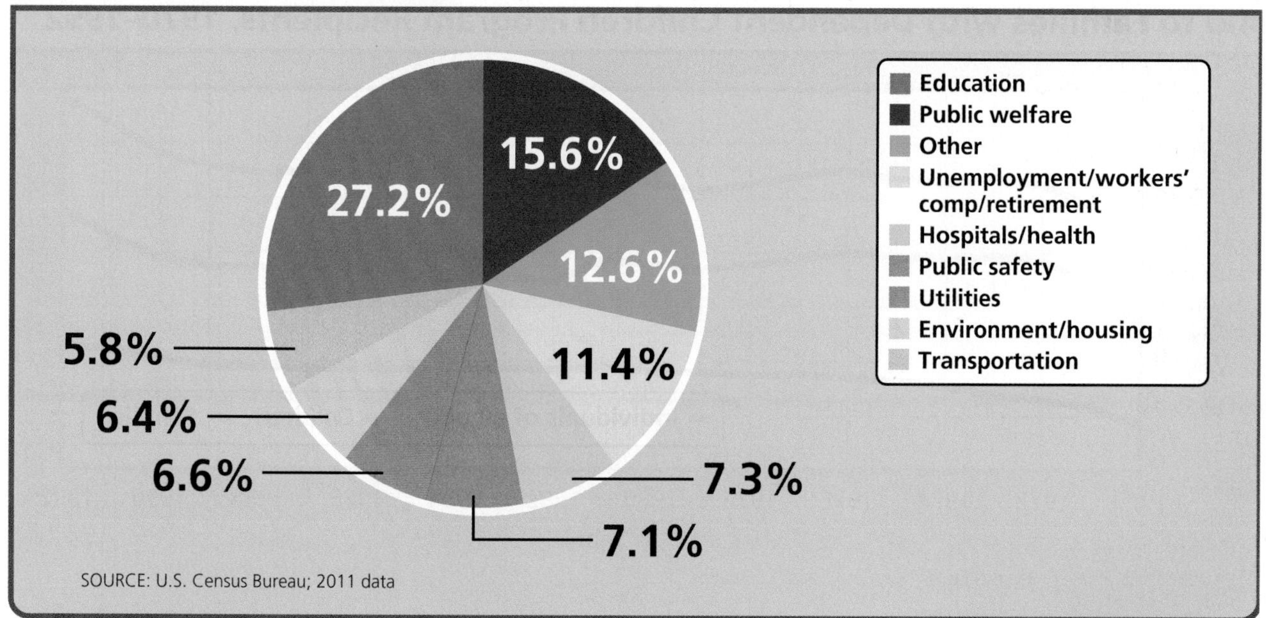

>> Education accounts for over a quarter of State and local government spending. **Analyze Graphs** According to the graph, on which category do State and local governments spend the least?

means that anyone who met the eligibility requirements was entitled to receive benefits under the program. The Federal Government and the States shared the costs of providing AFDC benefits.

Critics of AFDC pointed to soaring costs, expanding caseloads, and the absence of time limits on benefits as serious problems with the program. Because of these issues, critics argued that the program encouraged people to depend on government assistance rather than become self-supporting.

Temporary Assistance to Needy Families (TANF) In 1996, AFDC was replaced with a new and strikingly different program, Temporary Assistance to Needy Families (TANF). Unlike AFDC, TANF is a block grant program: The Federal Government gives States a fixed amount of money each year, regardless of whether the number of TANF recipients rises or falls. The States are then free to use the federal grant, plus the State funds they are obliged to contribute, to design and implement their own welfare programs. TANF limits recipients to a total of five years of assistance during the course of their lifetimes, and recipients must work or participate in some form of vocational training or community service.

The number of families on welfare has plunged since the mid-1990s. Many who remain on welfare must overcome a number of barriers, such as physical or mental disabilities or substance abuse, in order to obtain and hold jobs. Now that States have the primary responsibility for welfare, it is their task to find ways to help these families.

Other Efforts States do much more to promote their citizens' health and welfare. They make and enforce antipollution laws to protect the environment, they inspect factories and other workplaces to protect worker safety, they license healthcare practitioners to ensure quality care, and the list goes on and on.

? IDENTIFY CAUSE AND EFFECT How might variations in local governments' revenue sources be expected to affect public education?

Public Safety, Highways, and Other Services

One of the oldest law-enforcement groups, the legendary Texas Rangers, was established in 1835. Today, a variety of police forces, from the local sheriff to academy-trained State police, operate in every State to preserve law and order.

The State police are perhaps the most visible group, since they patrol the State's roads and highways. State law-enforcement forces perform other vital services, as well. They may function as the primary police force in rural communities, investigate crimes, provide centralized files for fingerprints and other information,

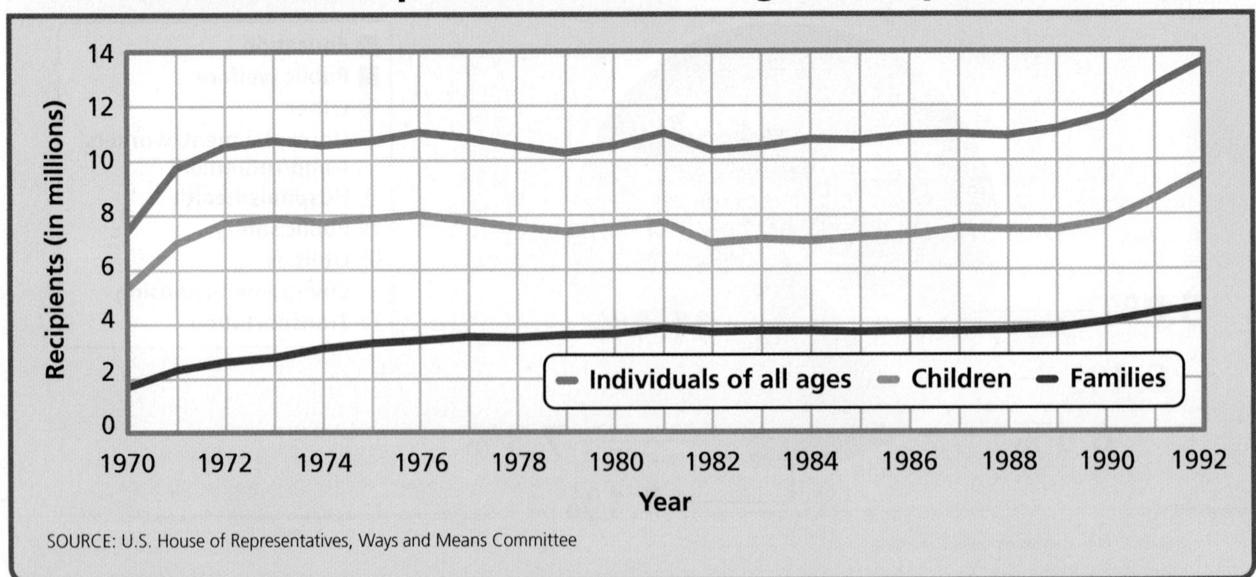

>> The number of AFDC recipients rose dramatically from 1970 to 1992, leading to the block grant program, TANF. **Analyze Graphs** What time periods reflect the most significant growth in recipients?

and provide training and many other services to support local law enforcement agencies.

Corrections System Each State has its own corrections system for dealing with those convicted of State crimes. States operate prisons, penitentiaries, and other correctional facilities, including those for juvenile offenders.

Operating these disciplinary systems is a growing burden for States. Today, more than 2.3 million people are incarcerated, more than half of them in State prisons.

Two leading causes of booming prison populations are (1) increases in the number of people sentenced for violent crimes and (2) the increasing length of the average prison sentence. One result is prison overcrowding. Another result is rising State corrections spending, which has more than doubled over the past 20 years. The States now spend more than $40 billion each year to build, staff, and maintain prisons and to house prisoners.

In an effort to expand their prison capacity more affordably, many States have hired private contractors to operate some of their prisons. More than 5 percent of all State prisoners are now held in private facilities.

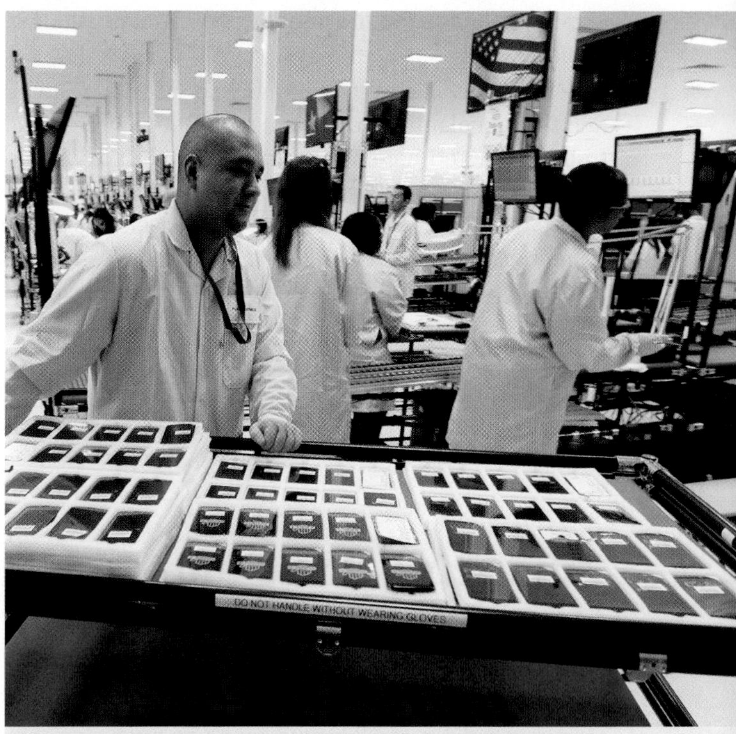

>> States inspect workplaces such as this cell phone factory in order to ensure the safety of workers.

Interstate Highway System Building and maintaining roads and highways is an enormous job. It regularly ranks among the most expensive of all the many items in State budgets. Again, the Federal Government is a partner with the States in funding highways. The most impressive example is the Interstate Highway System, a network of high-speed roadways that spans the length and breadth of the continental United States. Construction of the system began with the 1956 Federal-Aid Highway Act and continues to this day.

The Interstate Highway System, now officially known as the Dwight D. Eisenhower System of Interstate and Defense Highways, is 99 percent finished. When finally complete, it will total some 45,000 miles. The Federal Government has paid roughly 90 percent of its total cost.

While the interstate system is a magnificent achievement, it constitutes only a tiny fraction of the nation's more than 4 million miles of roads. Many roadways are built with State, not federal, funds; and the States maintain those roads, as well.

>> In 1919, a young Dwight D. Eisenhower participated in a 3,251-mile army transcontinental motor convoy. This expedition later inspired him to push Congress to fund an interstate highway system.

Driver Safety State and local governments must also look after the physical safety of drivers on thousands of miles of roads and highways. Besides patrolling the roads, State and local governments set speed limits. The States license drivers to ensure their competence, and many States require periodic safety inspections of vehicles.

As indicated earlier, the many services the States and their local units provide are really far too numerous to be recounted here. This fact does not discount the importance of such functions as the setting aside of public lands for purposes such as conservation and recreation, the regulation of business practices, and the protection of consumers from a variety of dangers and inconveniences.

CONNECT Why might the construction of highways and roads be considered an example of federalism at work?

Financing State and Local Government

Altogether, despite the recent recession, the 50 States and their thousands of local governments take in and spend well over $3 *trillion* per year. Such huge sums are difficult to comprehend. Where do those governments get all that money, and what do they do with it?

The States now take in well over $750 billion in taxes a year. And their local governments collect nearly 580 billion tax dollars every year. Those two basic levels of government also receive more than $2 trillion from several nontax sources, too—much of it from the Federal Government.

The power to tax is one of the major powers of the States in the federal system. In a strictly legal sense, then, their taxing power is limited only by the restrictions imposed by the federal Constitution and those imposed by a State's own fundamental law. Of course, the power to tax is also limited by any number of practical considerations—including, especially, economic and political factors.

Federal Tax Limitations The federal Constitution does place some restrictions on the taxing abilities of State and local governments. Although few in number, those limits do have a major impact.

The Constitution prohibits the States from taxing interstate and foreign trade. Remember, the Supreme Court's decision in *McCulloch* v. *Maryland,* in 1819, bars States from taxing the Federal Government or any of its agencies or functions.

The 14th Amendment's Due Process and Equal Protection clauses place important limits on the power to tax at the State and local levels. Essentially, the Due Process Clause requires that taxes be (1) imposed and administered *fairly,* (2) not so heavy as to actually confiscate property, and (3) imposed only for *public* purposes.

The Equal Protection Clause forbids the making of unreasonable classifications for the purpose of taxation.

State and Local Revenues

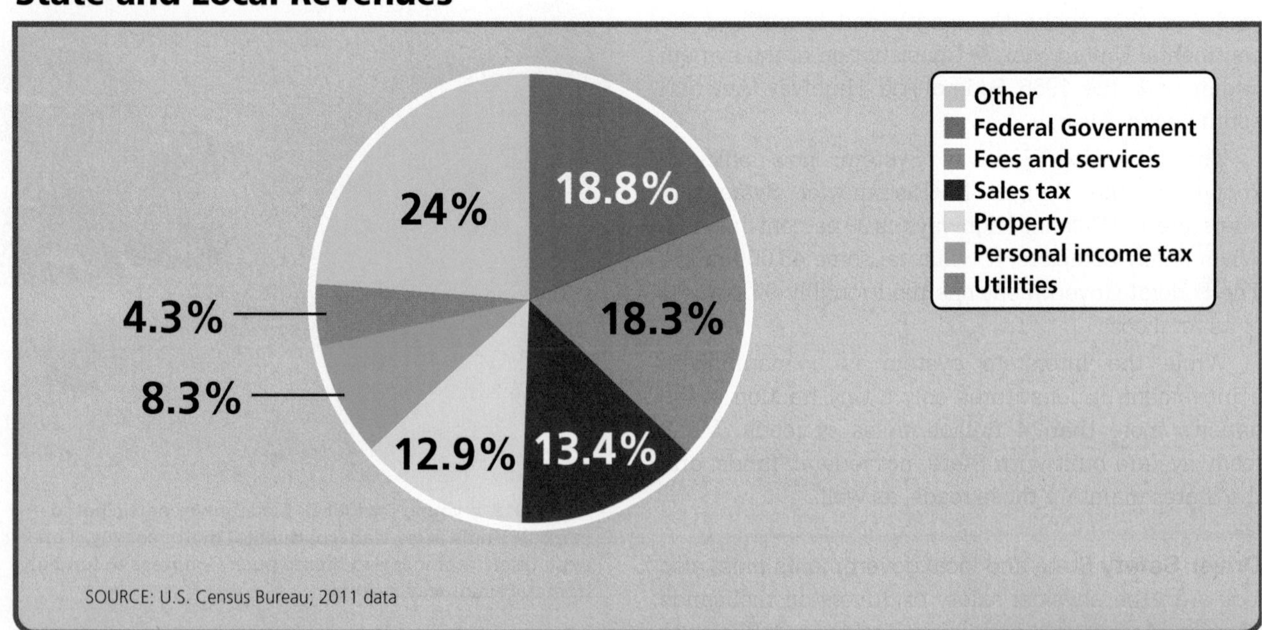

>> State and local governments do not rely solely on taxes for revenue. **Analyze Graphs** Which sources of revenue draw most heavily from young people?

Interactive Illustration

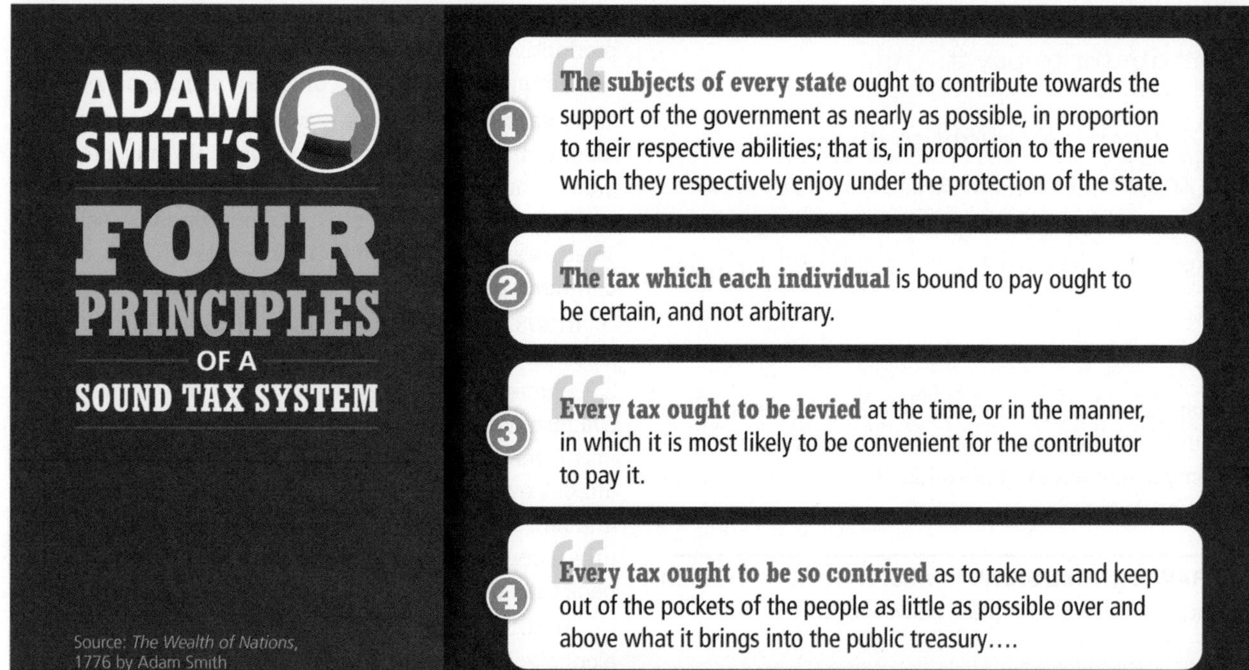
ADAM SMITH'S
FOUR PRINCIPLES
OF A
SOUND TAX SYSTEM
1
The subjects of every state ought to contribute towards the support of the government as nearly as possible, in proportion to their respective abilities; that is, in proportion to the revenue which they respectively enjoy under the protection of the state.
2
The tax which each individual is bound to pay ought to be certain, and not arbitrary.
3
Every tax ought to be levied at the time, or in the manner, in which it is most likely to be convenient for the contributor to pay it.
4
Every tax ought to be so contrived as to take out and keep out of the pockets of the people as little as possible over and above what it brings into the public treasury....
Source: The Wealth of Nations, 1776 by Adam Smith

>> The 18th-century economist Adam Smith attempted to establish uniform rules that would govern a sound system of taxation. **Analyze Information** Which principles ensure fairness to taxpayers?

The clause thus forbids tax classifications based on race, religion, nationality, political party membership, or any other factors beyond what is reasonable.

Most tax laws do involve some form of classification, however. Thus, a cigarette tax is collected only from those who buy cigarettes, a classification many people agree is a reasonable one.

State Tax Limitations Each State's constitution limits a State's taxing powers. State constitutions also limit the taxing powers of their local governments, often in great detail.

Most State constitutions create tax exemptions for religious and other nonprofit groups. State codes often set maximum rates for levies such as sales taxes or local property taxes. Some States prohibit certain taxes—for example, a general sales tax or a personal income tax.

Since local governments have no independent powers, the only taxes they can impose are those that the State allows them to levy. States have been restrictive in the matter. Even local units with home-rule charters are closely limited as to what and how they can tax.

Principles of Sound Taxation Any tax, if taken by itself, can be shown to be unfair. If a government's total revenues were to come from one tax—say, a sales, an income, or a property tax—its tax system would be very unfair. Some people would bear a much greater burden than others, and some would bear little or none. Each tax should thus be defensible as part of a tax system.

In his classic 1776 work, *The Wealth of Nations,* Scottish economist Adam Smith laid out four principles of a sound tax system:

> 1. The subjects of every state ought to contribute towards the support of the government as nearly as possible, in proportion to their respective abilities; that is, in proportion to the revenue which they respectively enjoy under the protection of the state.
>
> 2. The tax which each individual is bound to pay ought to be certain, and not arbitrary.
>
> 3. Every tax ought to be levied at the time, or in the manner, in which it

is most likely to be convenient for the contributor to pay it.

4. Every tax ought to be so contrived as to both take out and to keep out of the pockets of the people as little as possible over and above what it brings into the public treasury. . . .

—*The Wealth of Nations*

Shaping a tax system that unfailingly meets those standards of equality, certainty, convenience, and economy is just about impossible. Still, that goal should always be pursued.

DRAW CONCLUSIONS In what ways does the 14th Amendment limit the States' power to tax?

Sources of State Revenue

Beyond the limits noted, a State can levy taxes as it chooses. The legislature decides what taxes the State will impose, and at what rates. It decides, too, what taxes localities can levy.

Sales Tax Revenue The sales tax is the most productive source of State-levied income today. It accounts for about a third of all tax monies collected.

A **sales tax** is a tax placed on the sale of various commodities; the purchaser pays it. It may be either *general* or *selective* in form. A general sales tax is one applied to the sale of most commodities. A selective sales tax is one placed on the sale of only certain commodities.

In 1932, Mississippi became the first State to levy a sales tax. Today, 45 States do so. The rates range from 2.9 percent in Colorado to as much as 7.5 percent in California; most States now peg the rate at between 5 and 7 percent. Some things are exempted from the tax almost everywhere—most commonly, food, medicine, and newspapers. A growing number of cities, and some urban counties, also levy sales taxes today—a "piggy-back tax," added on to and collected with the State tax.

All 50 States impose a selective sales tax on gasoline, alcoholic beverages, cigarettes, and insurance policies. Many of them also place selective sales taxes on such things as hotel and motel accommodations, restaurant meals, and theater and other amusement admissions.

Sales taxes are widely used for two major reasons: They are easy to collect, and they are dependable revenue producers. Yet a sales tax is a **regressive tax**—that is, it is not levied according to a person's ability to pay. The tax falls most heavily on those least able to pay it.

State Tax Revenue

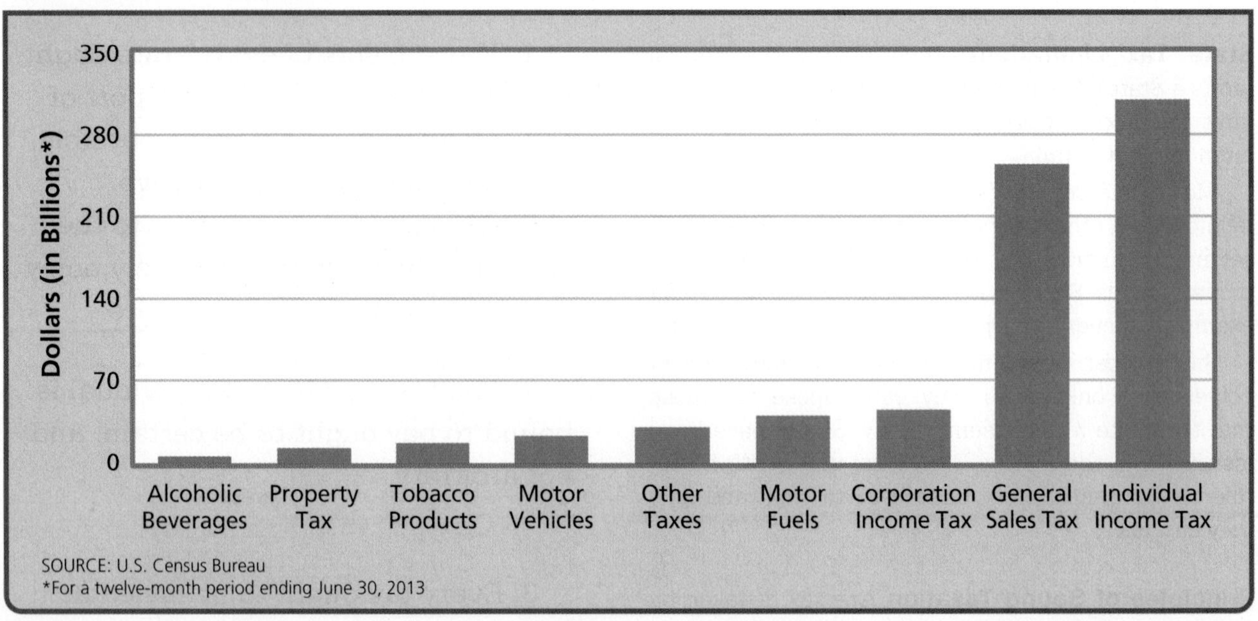

>> Taxes, a large source of State revenue, include sales tax and taxes on vehicles and houses. **Analyze Graphs** What factors might affect this source of income?

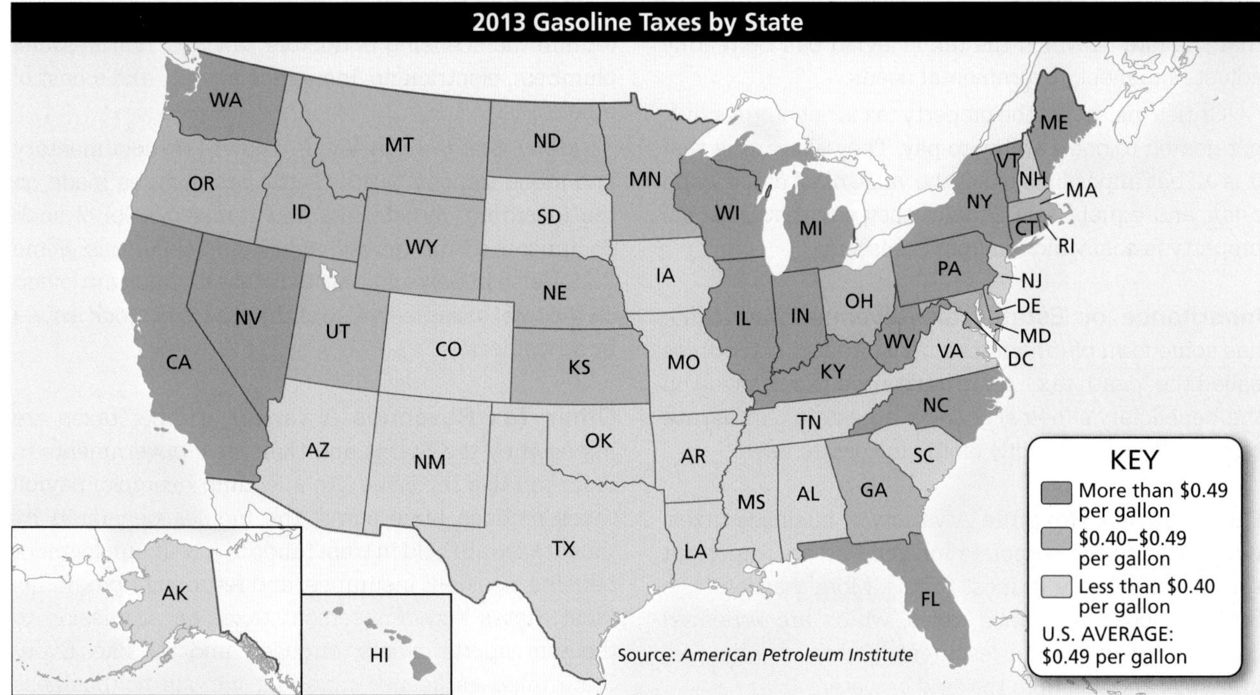

>> Gasoline taxes are an example of a State tax with a "reasonable" classification. **Analyze Maps** What generalization can you make about the States with the highest gasoline taxes?

States are prohibited from collecting the sales taxes on most Internet purchases. That is because products made in one State are sold online to customers across the country. As more and more people shop via the Internet, the States complain that the drain on their sales tax receipts could very well lead to a reduction of public services and/or an increase in their sales tax and other tax rates. In 2007, Congress, acting under its commerce power, put a seven-year moratorium on State taxation of e-commerce.

Income Tax Revenue The **income tax**, which is levied on the income of individuals and/or corporations, yields a quarter of State and local tax revenues today. Wisconsin enacted the first State income tax in 1911. Today, 43 States levy an individual income tax; 46 have some form of corporate income tax.

The individual income tax is usually a **progressive tax**—that is, the higher your income, the more tax you pay. Income tax rates vary among the States, from 1 or 2 percent on lower incomes in most States to 9 percent or more on the highest incomes in a few States. Those who pay the tax receive various exemptions and deductions in calculating their taxable income.

Corporate income tax rates are usually a uniform (fixed) percentage of income. Only a few States set the rates on a graduated basis.

The progressive income tax is held by many to be the fairest—or the least unfair—form of taxation, because it can be geared to a person's ability to pay. If the rates are too high, however, the tax can discourage individual enterprise.

Property Tax Revenue Property taxes have been a major source of governmental revenue since the early colonial period. Once the major source of State revenue, they are now levied almost exclusively at the local level. They provide roughly three fourths of all local government tax income today.

A **property tax** is a levy on (1) real property, such as land, buildings, and improvements that go with the property if sold; or (2) personal property, either tangible or intangible. Tangible personal property is movable wealth that is visible and the value of which can be easily assessed—for example, computers, cars, and books. Intangible personal property includes such things as stocks, bonds, mortgages, and bank accounts.

The process of determining the value of the property to be taxed is known as **assessment**. An elected county, township, or city assessor usually carries out the task.

Supporters of the property tax argue that, because government protects property and often enhances its value, property owners can logically be required to contribute to the support of government. They note that the rate at which the tax is levied can be readily adjusted to meet governmental needs.

Critics insist that the property tax is not progressive, not geared to one's ability to pay. They also argue that it is all but impossible to set the value of all property on a fair and equal basis. Finally, they say that personal property is easily hidden from assessors.

Inheritance or Estate Tax Revenue Every State has some form of inheritance or estate tax, sometimes called the "death tax." An **inheritance tax** is levied on the beneficiary's (heir's) share of an estate. An **estate tax** is one levied directly on the full estate itself.

Business Tax Revenue A variety of business taxes, in addition to the corporate income tax, are important sources of revenue in most States. More than half the States impose severance taxes, which are levies on the removal of natural resources such as timber, oil, minerals, and fish from the land or water.

Every State has various license taxes that permit people to engage in certain businesses, occupations, or activities. For example, all States require that corporations be licensed to do business in the State. Certain kinds of businesses—chain stores, amusement parks, taverns, and transportation lines—must have an additional operating license. Most States also require the licensing of doctors, lawyers, hairdressers, plumbers, electricians, insurance agents, and a host of others.

Many States have levies known as documentary and stock transfer taxes. These are charges made on the recording, registering, and transfer (sale) of such documents as mortgages, deeds, and securities. Some States also impose capital stock taxes, which are levied on the total assessed value of the shares of stock issued by a business.

Other Tax Revenues A variety of other taxes are imposed by the States and their local governments in order to raise revenues. As a leading example, payroll taxes produce huge sums; the monies generated by those taxes are held in trust funds to pay unemployment benefits, accident insurance, and retirement programs. Most States levy amusement taxes for admission to theaters, sports events, circuses, and the like. Every State imposes license taxes for various nonbusiness purposes—notably, on motor vehicles and drivers, and for such things as hunting, fishing, and marriage.

Nontax Revenues Taxes have never been very popular, and so State and local officials have long looked for nontax revenue sources. Today, the States and their

Average Property Tax*

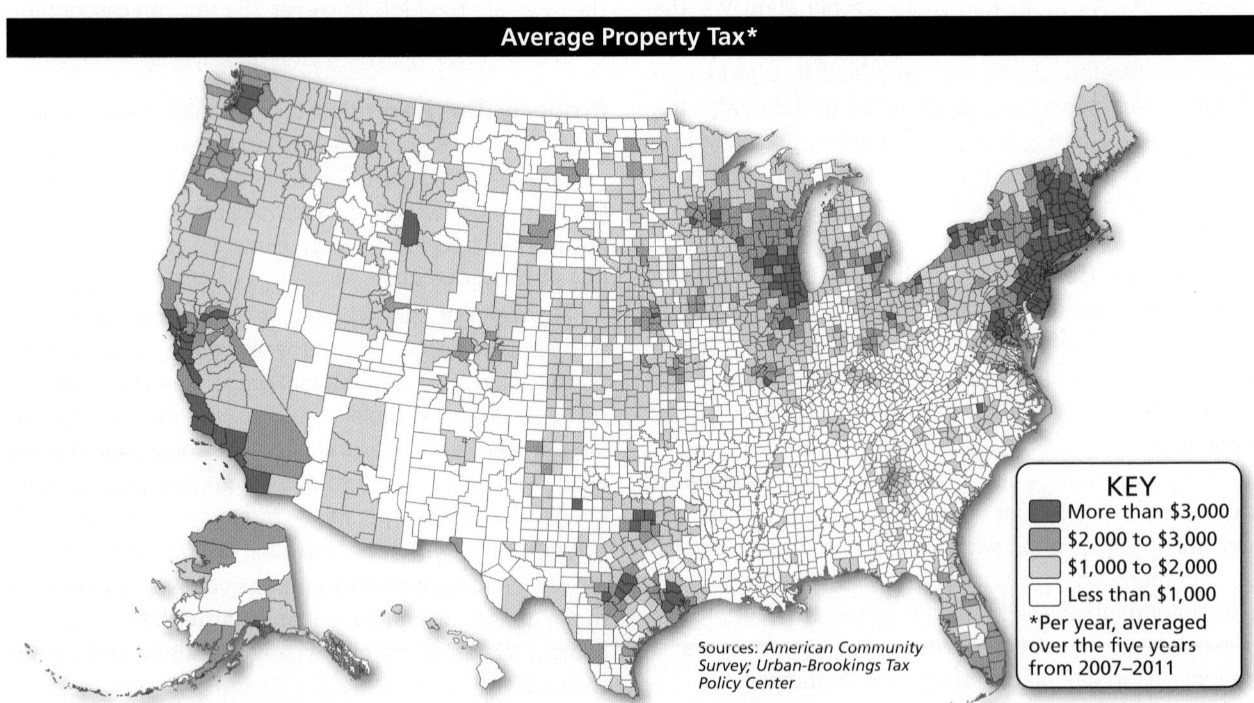

>> Property taxes are usually levied by local governments and so vary across each State. **Analyze Maps** What generalization can be made about the areas with the highest property taxes?

many local governments take in more than $2 trillion a year from these sources. Much of that huge amount comes as grants from the Federal Government.

Business enterprises and user fees. State and local governments also make money from a variety of publicly operated business enterprises. Toll roads and bridges are especially popular in the East. Several States, notably Washington, are in the ferry business. North Dakota markets a baking flour, sold under the brand name "Dakota Maid," and is also in the commercial banking business. Eighteen States are in the liquor business, selling alcohol in State-operated stores.

Many cities own and operate their water, electric power, and bus transportation systems. Some cities run farmers' markets; rent space in their office buildings, warehouses, and housing projects; and operate dams and wharves. Receipts from such businesses support the local governments that own them. Other nontax sources include court fines, sales and lease of public lands, and interest from loans, investments, and late tax payments. Among the many public services for which those who use them must now pay a fee are hospitals, airports, parks, water, sewers, and garbage disposal.

Lotteries. For many years, nearly all forms of gambling were outlawed in every State except Nevada. Most States have relaxed their anti-gambling laws, hoping to attract dollars, jobs, and tourists. Today, only Hawaii and Utah do not permit any kind of gambling.

State-run lotteries net some $19 billion per year for 43 States, the District of Columbia, Puerto Rico, and the U.S. Virgin Islands. Lotteries provide revenue without raising taxes. Supporters note that they are popular, voluntary, and offer an alternative to illegal gambling. Opponents say that lotteries prey on the poor and encourage compulsive gambling.

Lottery proceeds are used for a number of purposes among the States. About half of the States with lotteries earmark all or most of their revenue for education. Some channel the money directly to the State's general fund, while others dedicate most of it to economic development or a wide range of other uses.

Borrowing Funds The States and many of their local governments regularly borrow money to pay for such large undertakings as the construction of schools, highways, hospitals, sports facilities, and college dormitories. Much of that borrowing is done by issuing bonds, much as the Federal Government does. Generally, State and local bonds are fairly easy to market because the interest paid on them is not subject to State or federal income taxes.

At various times in the past, many State and local governments defaulted on their debts. Thus, most State constitutions now place quite detailed limits on the power to borrow. Altogether, the 50 States' debts now total about $5.1 trillion and local governments owe more than $1.8 trillion.

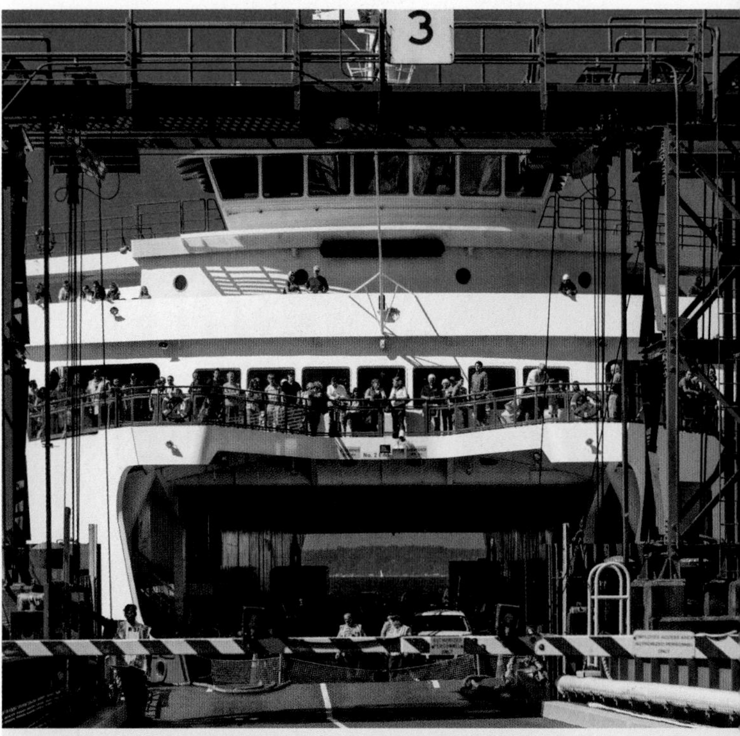

>> State-run businesses, such as the Washington State ferry system, are another source of revenue for State governments.

? HYPOTHESIZE Why do you think it is advantageous for States to generate revenue from a wide variety of sources?

State Budgets

A public **budget** is much more than bookkeeping entries and dollar signs. It is a financial plan, a plan for the control and use of public money, public personnel, and public property. It is also a political document, a highly significant statement of public policy. In the State budget, the State's leaders establish their State's priorities and decide who gets what, and who doesn't.

The Budget Process in the Past For more than 150 years, State budgets were the product of haphazard and uncoordinated steps centered in the legislature. Various State agencies appeared before legislative committees, each seeking its own funding, often in fierce competition with one another. Their chances of success depended far less on need or merit than on whatever political muscle they could bring to bear.

>> Jerry Brown, governor of California, introduces his 2014–2015 budget proposal, one of the largest in State history, at the State capitol in Sacramento, California.

When the legislature adjourned, no one had any real idea of how much had been appropriated or for what. Inevitably, extravagance and waste, unresolved problems, debt, favoritism, and graft were all part of the process.

State budgets are strikingly different things today. They remain highly charged political documents, but they are the end products of what is, by and large, an orderly and systematic process.

The Budget Process Today Forty-seven States have adopted the executive budget, which gives the governor two vital powers: (1) to prepare the State's budget, and, after the legislature has acted upon his or her recommendations, (2) to manage the spending of the monies set aside by the legislature. In Mississippi, South Carolina, and Texas, the process is somewhat different. There, the initial responsibility for preparing the budget is shared by the governor and the legislature.

Under the executive budget, the basic steps in the budget process are much the same at the State, local, and federal levels:

1. Each agency prepares estimates of its needs and proposed expenditures in the upcoming fiscal period.

2. Those estimates are reviewed by an executive budget agency.

3. Revised estimates, with supporting information, are brought together in a consolidated financial plan, the budget, which the governor then presents to the legislature for its consideration.

4. The legislature reacts to the proposed budget, part by part, appropriates the funds it deems necessary to pay for governmental activities, and enacts whatever revenue measures may be needed.

5. The governor supervises the execution of the budget—the actual spending of the funds provided by the legislature.

6. The execution of the budget is subject to an independent check—a post audit.

? HYPOTHESIZE Why is it important that a State's legislature shares budget-making responsibility with the governor?

ASSESSMENT

1. **Determine Relevance** What makes Adam Smith's four principles of sound taxation important at all levels of government?
2. **Check Understanding** Why did the Constitution place limits on the power of State and local government to tax?
3. **Identify Central Issues** What is the central conflict in the relationship between taxation and government services?
4. **Identify Cause and Effect** What likely effect would the replacement of AFDC with the TANF block grant program have had on the federal budget? Explain your answer.
5. **Generate Explanations** How is a State's budget both a financial and a political statement?

TOPIC 13 ASSESSMENT

1. **Explain the Importance and Understand the Role** Create a written or oral presentation explaining the importance of a written constitution and the role of limited government in the protection of individual rights. The presentation should also consider the following question: How are States' written constitutions important in the protection of basic principles and civil rights?
2. **Identify Major Traditions** Use the information from the lessons in this topic to create a written or oral presentation identifying English common law and how it influenced State laws. When creating the presentation, answer the following questions: What is English common law? How is English common law different from statutory law?
3. **Compare Different Methods of Filling Public Offices** Use the information from the lessons in this topic to create a visual presentation comparing different methods of selecting State and local judges. In your presentation, answer the following questions: Describe the different ways judges are selected today. In your opinion, is one method of selecting judges better than the others? Explain your answer.
4. **Evaluate Constitutional Provisions** Write a paragraph evaluating checks and balances in a typical State constitution. Consider the following questions: How are the basic powers of government separated in the State constitution? Why are checks and balances incorporated into both the federal and State constitutions?
5. **Compare the Functions** Write a paragraph answering the following question: A woman sues a grocery store for price gouging after a recent flood. She claims that the grocery store intentionally raised prices inconsistent with the competitive fair market price. Which executive department would handle this issue, and why?
6. **Examine Different Methods of Filling Public Offices** Use the information from lessons in this topic and the chart below to write a paragraph examining the methods of filling public offices in a weak mayor government. When writing the paragraph, answer the following questions: According to the chart, how do the council and the heads of other departments get into office in a weak mayor government? How does the chart illustrate the weakness of the mayor under this form of government?

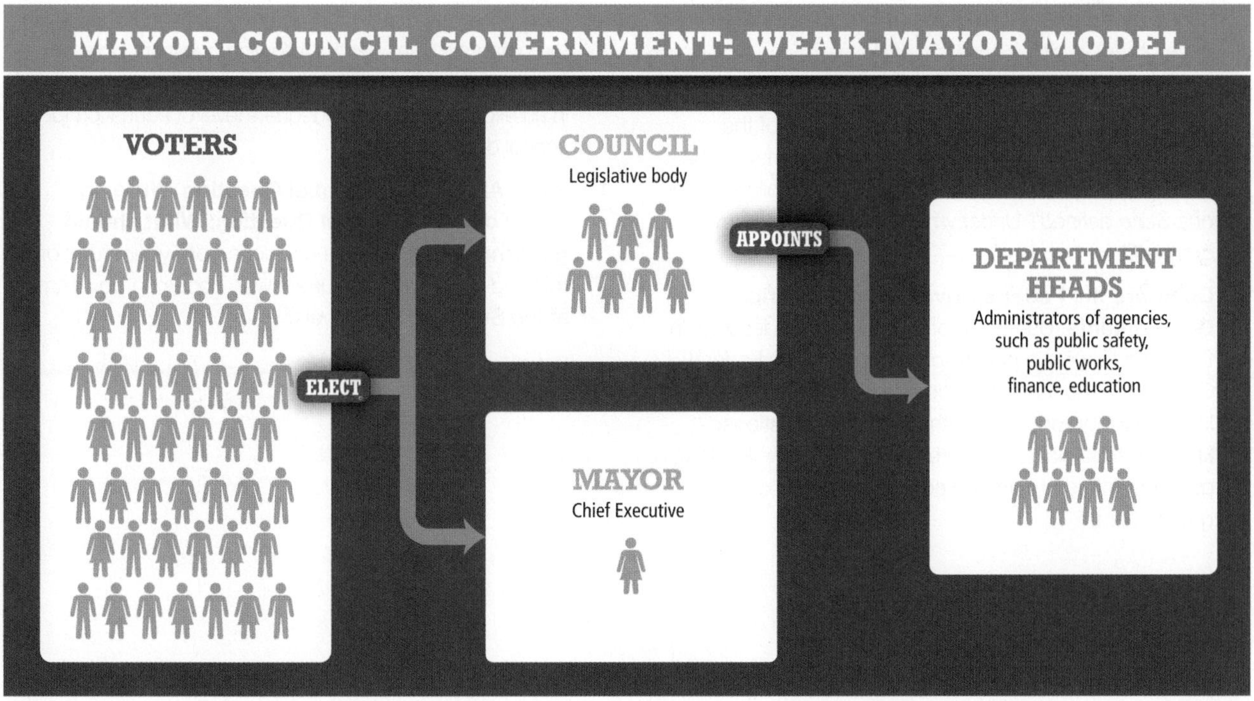

MAYOR-COUNCIL GOVERNMENT: WEAK-MAYOR MODEL

VOTERS

ELECT

COUNCIL
Legislative body

APPOINTS

MAYOR
Chief Executive

DEPARTMENT HEADS
Administrators of agencies, such as public safety, public works, finance, education

7. **Explain the Importance** Write a paragraph evaluating the advantages and disadvantages of longer State constitutions.

8. **Explain How Political Divisions Are Crafted and Affected** *"Most State legislatures were long dominated by the rural, less-populated areas of the State. In Baker v. Carr, 1962, however, the United States Supreme Court held the unfair, unequal distribution of State legislative seats to be a violation of the Equal Protection Clause of the 14th Amendment."*

   Use the information from the lessons in this topic, and the quotation above, to create a written or oral presentation explaining how the Supreme Court decision *Baker* v. *Carr* impacted reapportionment. When creating the presentation, answer the following questions: How are the number of State districts and representatives determined? Why was *Baker* v. *Carr* significant in redistricting? Do urban areas or rural areas have more political power after *Baker* v. *Carr*?

9. **Explain Government Fiscal Policies** Use the information from lessons in this topic to write a paragraph explaining the tax limitations placed on State governments. When writing the paragraph, answer the following questions: What limits the power of State and local governments to tax individuals and businesses? How does the 14th Amendment limit the power to tax at the State and local levels?

10. **Compare State and Local Governments** Use the information from the lessons in this topic to compare and contrast the organization and powers of the typical county government with those of the typical State government.

11. **Understand State Powers** Use the information from lessons in this topic to explain the purposes of the police power. When writing the paragraph, answer the following questions: How and where is the police power of a State defined? Under what authority is this power granted?

12. **Compare the Federal Government and Tribal Governments** Use the information from the lessons in this topic to write a paragraph comparing the Federal Government to tribal governments in the United States. In your paragraph, answer the following questions: How are tribal nations sovereign states? How do tribal governments compare to Federal, State and county governments?

13. **Explain Different Methods of Filling Public Offices** Use the information from the lessons in this topic to create a visual presentation that explains the Missouri Plan. In your presentation, answer the following questions: What is the Missouri Plan? How does the Missouri Plan use a mixed approach to selecting judges? Is the Missouri Plan a fair method for selecting judges? Why or why not?

14. **Identify the Effects of Population Shifts** *"About half of all Americans now live in suburbs. The nation's suburbs first began to grow rapidly in the years after World War II, and that growth has continued. As suburban populations have mushroomed, many of the nation's larger cities have actually lost residents."*

    Use the information from the lessons in this topic and the quotation above to write a paragraph identifying the ways that the phenomenon described in the quotation has affected the United States. In your paragraph, answer the following questions: What phenomenon is being described in this quotation? How has this event affected the nation's cities? How has this event affected the nation's suburbs?

15. **Compare the Functions** Use the information from the lessons in this topic to write a paragraph comparing and contrasting criminal and civil law. In your paragraph, answer the following question: Should people charged with violent crimes be allowed to raise bail? Explain.

16. **Explain Government Fiscal Policies** Use the information from lessons in this topic to write a paragraph explaining the relationship between State government fiscal policy and the economics of education. When writing the paragraph, answer the following question: How do local school boards and State governments use tax rates in an effort to ensure an adequate level of education for all school districts?

17. **Write About the Essential Question Write an essay on the Essential Question: What should governments do?** Use evidence from your study of this Topic to support your answer. Focus on government at the State and local levels.

Go online to PearsonRealize.com and use the texts, quizzes, interactivities, Interactive Reading Notepads, Flipped Videos, and other resources from this Topic to prepare for the Topic Test.

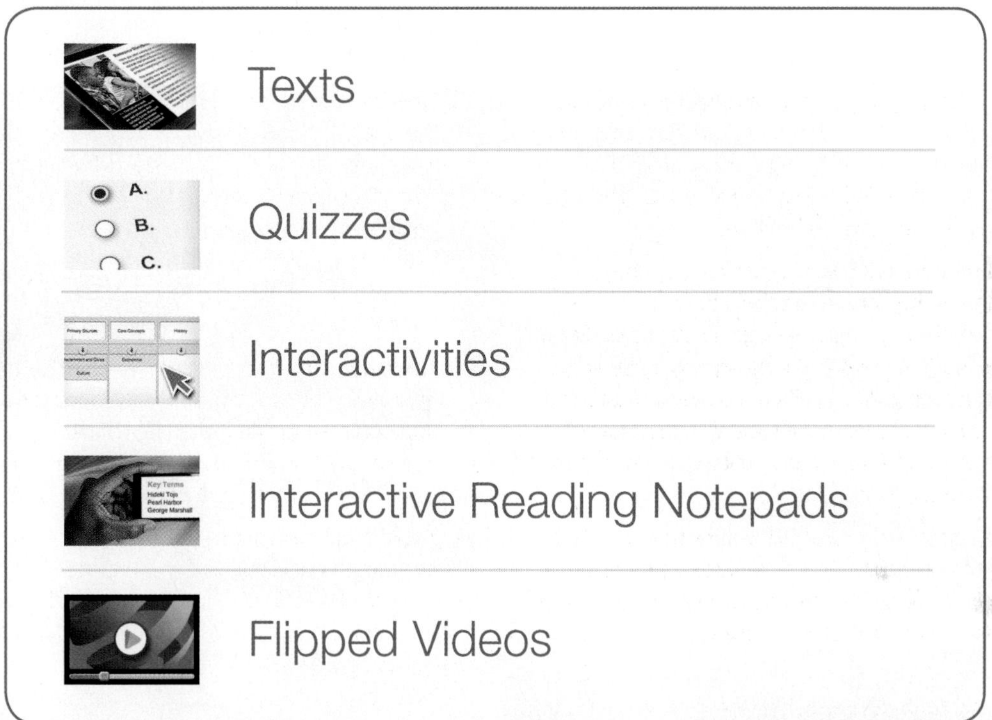

While online you can also check the progress you've made learning the topic and course content by viewing your grades, test scores, and assignment status.

[ESSENTIAL QUESTION] What Makes a Government Successful?

14 Comparative Political Systems

>> Great Hall of the People, Beijing, China

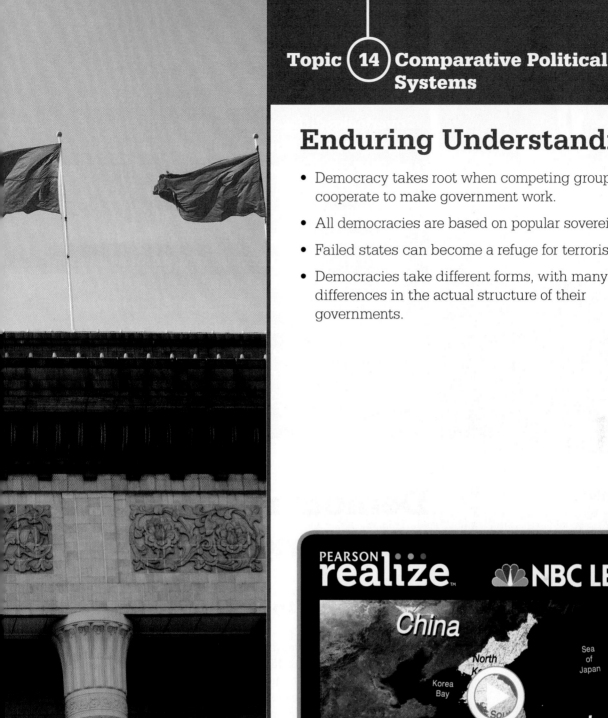

Topic 14 Comparative Political Systems

Enduring Understandings

- Democracy takes root when competing groups cooperate to make government work.
- All democracies are based on popular sovereignty.
- Failed states can become a refuge for terrorists.
- Democracies take different forms, with many differences in the actual structure of their governments.

Watch the My Story Video to explore economic development in North and South Korea.

Access your digital lessons including: Topic Inquiry • Interactive Reading Notepad • Interactivities • Assessments

>> Germans celebrate the fall of the Berlin Wall in 1989. The wall stood for 28 years, dividing communist and democratic states; its fall was a symbol of Germany's transition to democracy.

14.1 **We tend to categorize countries as complete opposites: democratic or undemocratic. But such a clear distinction overlooks differences among countries, such as Myanmar (Burma), that are transitioning to democracy from established democracies. The late political scientist Robert Dahl suggested that countries become more democratic as they allow opposing sides to be heard and as democratic institutions develop that lead to greater public participation and more equal citizen influence. Democratizing countries may have achieved some competition among opposing leadership, but they often have not cultivated the institutions that lead to sufficient public participation and influence.**

Interactive Flipped Video

>> Objectives

Examine how regimes can make transitions to democracy.

Analyze why some countries experience setbacks or failed transitions to democracy.

Explain the factors necessary for democratic consolidation to take place.

Describe democratic change and continuity in selected countries today.

>> Key Terms

democratization
hard-liners
reformers
Lech Walesa
Nelson Mandela
Aung San Suu Kyi
Mikhail Gorbachev
Boris Yeltsin
democratic consolidation
failed states
state-building

Democracy and the Changing World

Transitions to Democracy

Democratization refers to the change from dictatorship to democracy and is marked by the holding of free and fair elections. Democratization may be difficult, but dictatorships are largely frowned upon in the world today. The digital age has allowed pro-democracy advocates to bring international pressure in support of domestic critics of dictatorships. This internal and external pressure may pit ruling **hard-liners**, who often blame foreign enemies or internal critics for undermining the state, against ruling **reformers**, who may recognize the need to relinquish some power even if not to fully give up power or to democratize.

This is why the small step of recognizing an opposition leader or party is actually a significant step toward democracy. This may pressure governing institutions to reform without fundamentally undermining the social order. Some of the most notable transitions to democracy in recent times have followed this model. This also provides opposition figures with the ability to modify their movement into electoral and governing institutions like political parties. In fact, some of the biggest democratizing figures such as **Lech Walesa** in Poland in the 1980s, **Nelson Mandela** in South Africa in the 1990s, and **Aung San Suu Kyi** in Burma in the 2000s have bargained with ruling reformers even though they had earlier been punished or imprisoned by the government. Each later won election to lead their country.

? INFER How has the Internet and globalization contributed to other countries' transition to democracy?

Examples of Transitions to Democracy

We often forget that even the American democratization process required time, reconsideration, and institutional tinkering. The Framers of the Constitution reworked our democracy after the Articles of Confederation faltered, and we have subsequently become more democratic by expanding the vote to African Americans, women, and eighteen-year-olds. Remember that the U.S. ultimately became a constitutional republic. Governments in transition may choose, instead, to strive for direct democracy enabling citizens to decide government policy directly. This differs from the representative democracy in the U.S. where citizens elect representatives who create government policy. There is a lack of direct democracy at a national level anywhere in the modern world; direct democracy is a form of government that becomes unwieldy once a country and its population become very large. Democratization is not a one-off event.

As political scientist Samuel Huntington argued, democratization has often come in waves. The first wave involved North American and many northern European democracies and began in the 1800s. Many democracies succeeded, but some like fascist Italy and Nazi Germany failed. The second wave came after World War II. This time Italy, Japan, Germany, and others became strong democracies, but some postcolonial democracies failed.

The final wave began in the 1970s with southern European countries like Portugal, Spain, and Greece successfully democratizing. Democracies developed in Central and South America, in Africa and Asia, and in eastern and central Europe. The fall of the Soviet Union and its many allies in eastern and central Europe affected dozens of countries; the fall of the Soviet Union exemplifies the challenges, successes, and failures of democratic transitions.

Post-Soviet Democratic Transitions The Russian Revolution in 1917 created a Communist government in Russia, which expanded into the Soviet Union with more countries becoming Soviet Republics. Fearing another invasion from the West, the Soviets pressured countries it freed from Nazi control to become part of the communist Soviet bloc following World War II. The Soviets and these so-called Soviet bloc countries squared off against the U.S. and western European countries during the Cold War period from the late 1940s through the late 1980s. These communist countries squashed internal dissent, directed pro-communist education and media, and controlled the movement and actions of their people.

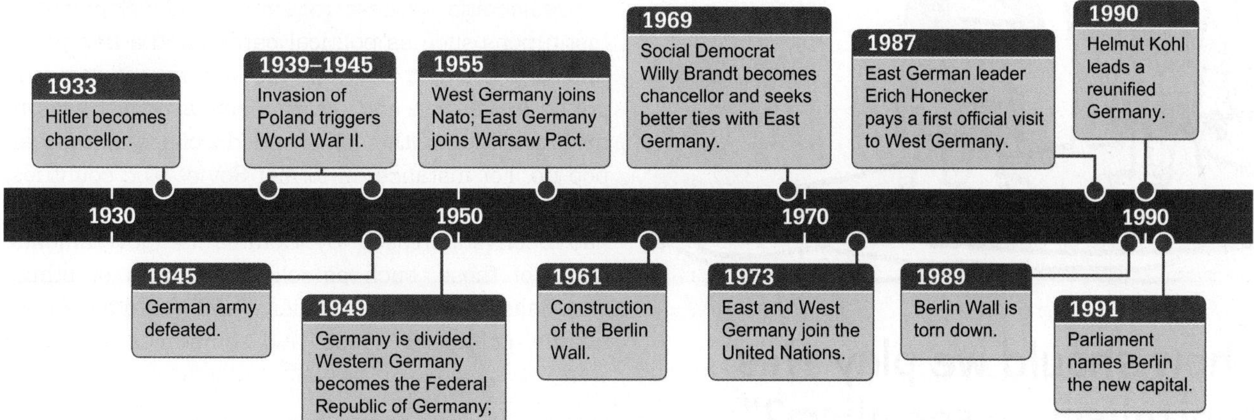

>> It took time for Germany to consolidate under one new form of government.
Analyze Charts What factors might have been most challenging for citizens during this time?

In other words, the Soviet bloc attempted to socialize people to be free of democratic values. Even though these countries had high levels of education, the Soviet bloc became a superpower. Pro-freedom movements had been stopped by force in Hungary in 1956, Czechoslovakia in 1968, and by martial law in Poland in 1981.

Economic stagnation, external pressure from the West, and internal dissent eroded the Soviet bloc. In the 1980s, the reformist Soviet leader **Mikhail Gorbachev** pushed both *perestroika*, a wide-ranging restructuring of political and economic life, and *glasnost*, a policy of openness where the Soviet government increased its tolerance of dissent and freedom of expression. The hunger for openness spread to the central European Soviet bloc countries. In 1989, the Polish reform party Solidarity competed in parliamentary elections, Hungarians enjoyed the freedom to visit Austria, and pro-democratic protests in East Germany led Communist governments to fold throughout the region.

The Soviet Union itself disintegrated in 1991. Changes occurred rapidly after **Boris Yeltsin** was elected president of Russia in 1991. Russia was then still a republic within the Soviet Union. Although Russia was not independent, Yeltsin used his position to confront Gorbachev and resigned from the Communist Party. That summer, when hard-liners moved to re-exert Soviet government power by placing Soviet leader Gorbachev under house arrest, Russian president Yeltsin led massive protests against the coup, and within days the hard-liners gave up. Each of the Soviet Republics declared their independence from the Soviet Union that autumn, and by 1992 the Soviet Union failed to exist.

"So, how should we play this — capitalism or socialism?"

>> Transitions in government can result in many new choices for citizens. **Analyze Political Cartoons** What is the cartoonist saying about the public's perception of options for government?

Discontinuity in Democratic Transitions The dramatic fall of a superpower to the democratic demands of citizens is instructive of how the process of democratic transition is not automatic. Democracy requires that established governing institutions, such as the military and police force, give up power, which can disrupt the social order people may be conditioned to expect government to provide. Other economic and cultural strains that come with democratic change also upset the democratization of Soviet bloc countries.

Economic downturns can spell doom for the political fortunes of politicians and Presidents in the United States, one of the world's richest nations and a democracy for over two centuries. Significant structural economic problems in a new and fragile democratic state can devastate the public's view of democracy itself beyond just the fortunes of a particular leader. Soviet bloc countries had to shift from a centrally planned communist economy to more capitalist economies. These countries had strictly limited private property rights and now had to figure out how to recognize and provide private property rights. Communism provided citizens with a baseline of economic security, even if economic growth was stunted. Opening up people's livelihoods to market forces led to great economic success for some but new economic struggles for many, which further undermined the sense of social order.

Democratic success requires the development of institutions such as political parties and a free press. Should these not develop, the disconnect between public expression and government response leads to dissatisfaction. Other unintended consequences can pop up. For instance, in former Soviet bloc countries, new freedoms encouraged the expression of ideas that had been suppressed by Communist governments. Some of these, such as religious beliefs or ethnic nationalism, were quite divisive and led to governing strains, political violence, and sometimes even civil war.

? APPLY CONCEPTS Provide an example of how a free press is an essential component of a democracy.

WHAT MAKES DEMOCRACY SUCCEED?
FACTORS
WHY THEY MATTER
A FREE PRESS
The media reports on the government's actions and regularly communicates ideas for change
MULTIPLE PARTIES
Competition forces the government to listen to voters
CIVILIAN CONTROL OF THE MILITARY
Clear control prevents the military from taking power
ECONOMIC OPPORTUNITY FOR ALL
Education and hard work reward people for working within the law
PROFESSIONAL CIVIL SERVICE
Bureaucrats are less likely to be corrupt and keep government functioning when changes in leadership occur
COMMON TRUST AMONG CITIZENS
Everyone shares a wish for the government to thrive and settle disputes peacefully

>> Several factors must be in place in order for a democratic system of government to take root and flourish. **Analyze Charts** Which of these factors do you think is most important?

Outcomes of Transitions to Democracy

As the challenges of the post-Soviet era transitions to democracy demonstrate, ending authoritarian governance does not automatically lead to democracy. Some countries end up democratic because they develop the necessary factors for democracy. Other nations do not and either experience a chronically underperforming government or slide back into dictatorship. Still others fail to develop any democratic political culture, and the governments lose authority over society and become failed states.

Democratic Consolidation As the ultimate positive outcome of democratization, **democratic consolidation** occurs when a country firmly establishes the necessary factors for vibrant democracy and social order. These factors include the following: a free press, a competitive group of political parties, a civilian-controlled military and security force, and a number of engaged interest groups. Additionally, an economic system that rewards innovation and hard work and a professional civil service implementing governing decisions are needed.

Some of these elements may not be present in the early stages of transition, but as Germany and Japan demonstrated after World War II, and many former Soviet bloc nations have shown, these key factors develop and become firmly established over time as people become socialized into democratic political culture.

Most of all, democratic consolidation occurs when a society establishes a sense of common trust among its citizens. Because many transitions take place following a civil war or a dictatorship that pits one group against another, mutual trust can be difficult to establish. Trust is vital because democracy requires that losers of elections accept the outcomes instead of trying to undermine the opponents' newly won democratic institutions. The British have long referred to this as "the loyal opposition." Losers oppose the other party, but they remain loyal to British democracy. When such interpersonal trust is achieved, democracy stands on a solid footing.

These factors may not emerge sufficiently even if countries hold elections. Democratically elected rulers may limit competition in elections, control media content, disallow interest groups, or rely on pro-ruling party officials to decide election outcomes. Elections themselves do not equate to consolidated democracy, and frustration with weak democracy may lead to broader internal strife that weakens the social order.

Observers of Iraqi politics worry that Iraq's young democracy is failing to develop the needed factors for democratic success. Iraqis have held elections, and there has not been the government-sponsored violence against opposition seen during the Dictator of Iraq Saddam Hussein's era. Nevertheless, with ethnic and religious differences concentrated in particular regions of the country, the lack of trust among Sunni Arab Iraqis, Shi'ite Arab Iraqis, and Kurdish Iraqis has left continued sectarian violence and little traction toward developing the factors needed for a consolidated democracy. The success of Iraqi democracy depends on the three competing ethnic groups to move beyond current, deep, and sometimes violent divisions to work together to build democratic institutions acceptable to all.

Failed States Other countries remain similarly troubled. Their inability to find stability has even raised security concerns for other states. Countries such as Sudan and the Democratic Republic of Congo include large regions that remain outside the control of their own governments. Somalia, in East Africa, does not have a functioning government, and most of the country is ruled by warlords. These countries are known as **failed states.** In most of these areas, security is nonexistent, the economy has collapsed, the healthcare and school systems are in shambles, and corruption flourishes.

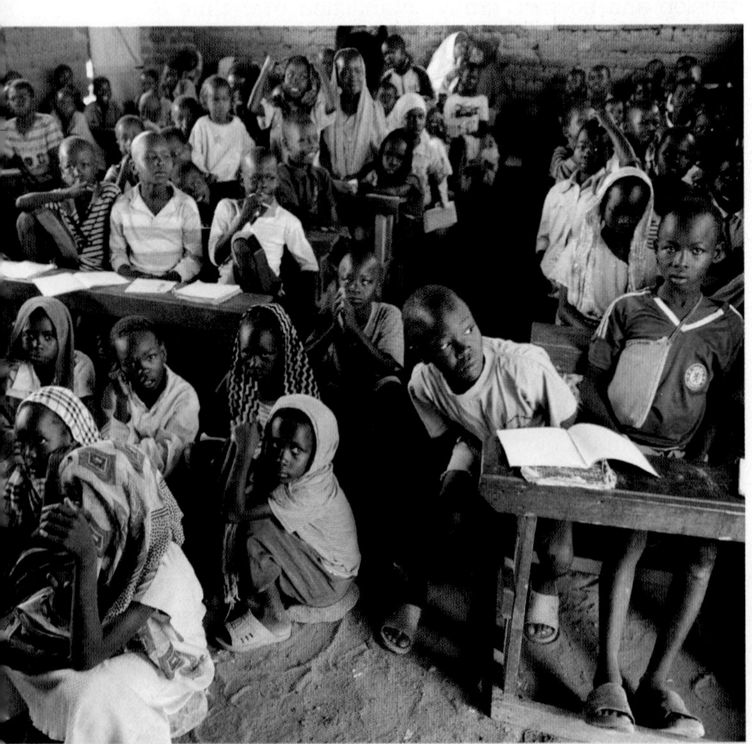

>> The Kakuma Refugee Camp in the Turkana region of Kenya serves tens of thousands of refugees from surrounding failed states.

International terrorist groups have found refuge in these lawless lands and have used them as bases to plan and train for acts of violence. A deadly attack on a Kenyan mall in 2013 by Somali terrorists came in response to Kenya's military intervention into Somalia to establish order in key cities. Americans are more familiar with Afghanistan.

The Soviet Union occupied Afghanistan in the 1980s. When it withdrew in 1989, it left the country utterly devastated. Groups of Afghans who had fought against the Soviets now turned their arms against one another. The anarchy provided a haven for Osama bin Laden and his al Qaeda terrorists to plan their September 11, 2001, attacks on the United States. In response to those attacks, a coalition of troops led by the United States moved into Afghanistan with the hope of rooting out the Taliban and creating a democratic nation.

After years of fighting, President Obama increased American troop levels in 2009. The surge was successful in many respects. By 2011, bin Laden and other al Qaeda leaders had been killed or captured, and the President announced that American troops would leave Afghanistan by the end of 2014. The decision raised concerns around the world that the **state-building** efforts might fail if the Afghan government was not yet able to protect its people against a still defiant Taliban. These state-building efforts involve outside countries attempting to strengthen the governing institutions of a country. Afghanistan's future as a stable or a failed state is uncertain.

? EXPRESS IDEAS CLEARLY Why have Iraq and Russia experienced different outcomes in their respective transitions to democracy?

Democratic Change and Continuity Today

Many nations are struggling toward democracy today. One of the most undemocratic areas of the world has been the Middle East, where ruling parties, leaders, or families have maintained power by squashing political opposition. Nevertheless, in December 2011, a fruit merchant in Tunisia protested police bullying and the government's indifference by setting himself on fire. This sparked the Arab Spring, in which mass protests across North Africa and the Middle East unleashed civil unrest in some countries and civil war or the overthrow of governments in others.

In Egypt, protests ousted President Hosni Mubarak. The Muslim Brotherhood, which had been illegal for decades, transformed into a political party that won both parliamentary and presidential elections.

What looked at first to be a clear sign of democratization slid backward when the Muslim Brotherhood reneged on some press freedoms, changed the constitution for its own benefit, and ignored other parties' concerns. In turn, the military arrested the elected Muslim Brotherhood President Mohammed Morsi in July of 2013 and cracked down violently on Muslim Brotherhood protestors. Egypt, like its neighbors Libya and Syria, has demonstrated a democratic impulse by standing up to authoritarianism; however, Egypt thus far lacks the factors necessary for democratic consolidation.

? GENERATE EXPLANATIONS How might a country that is transitioning to democracy move farther away from democracy instead of closer to it?

>> Thousands gather for a mass protest in central Cairo on January 25, 2011. Protesters demanded the removal of President Hosni Mubarak.

ASSESSMENT

1. **Identify Central Issues** For what reasons might a dictatorship change to a democracy?
2. **Hypothesize** What are some significant governmental changes that a country would experience when moving from communism to democracy?
3. **Express Ideas Clearly** Why are democratization and democratic consolidation both important when establishing a new democracy?
4. **Categorize** Was Mikhail Gorbachev a hard-liner or a reformer? Explain your reasoning.
5. **Explain** What factors make the process of forming democratic governments difficult in some Middle Eastern countries, as well as other Asian and African countries?

>> Queen Elizabeth II visits the maternity ward of a hospital. As the longest-reigning British monarch since Queen Victoria, she has been a steadfast figure in the United Kingdom since 1952.

14.2 No other country has rivaled the democratic durability of the United Kingdom. The United Kingdom is a monarchy, but the royalty lacks any governing power. British democracy seats considerable power in the prime minister, gives political parties substantial power over public policy, and makes elections particularly influential on public policy. Like the United States, the United Kingdom is a prime example of constitutionalism, government in which power is distributed and limited by a system of laws that must be obeyed by its rulers.

Interactive Flipped Video

>> Objectives

Explain the United Kingdom's legacy of constitutionalism.

Outline the structure of government in the United Kingdom.

Examine public policy and elections in the United Kingdom.

Compare government in the United Kingdom with that of the United States.

>> Key Terms

constitutionalism
parliamentary system
coalition
ministers
shadow cabinet
common law
devolution
backbenchers
party government

The United Kingdom

A Legacy of Constitutionalism

Americans celebrate Independence day, and the French celebrate Bastille Day. However, in the United Kingdom, instead of one democratizing moment, British democracy has risen slowly like an incoming tide. In 1215, the king signed the Magna Carta, which assured nobles that the king could not imprison them nor take their land without the support of the noble's peers. This established the idea of limited governance; Parliament would create laws that the monarchy would execute.

The United Kingdom is composed of England, Scotland, Wales, and Northern Ireland. As a set of islands geographically removed from the land wars that plagued the European continent, Britain was able to establish a global empire. Its location also allowed for internal political institutions to develop without the disruption of invasion and war. Consequently, the governing institutions have been set since the 1600s, competitive political parties have been steady since the 1800s, and full voting rights expanded to all Britons by the early 1900s.

APPLY CONCEPTS The United States and the United Kingdom are both prime examples of constitutionalism. Explain how constitutionalism is portrayed in the United States.

Government in the United Kingdom

Political observers refer to the United Kingdom as a **parliamentary system**, where the chief executive—the prime minister—is chosen by the Parliament rather than being directly elected. The United Kingdom is a unitary system with governing sovereignty held at the national government level with the Parliament.

Parliament Britain's storied Parliament is the core institution of government. It holds both the legislative and the executive powers of the nation—powers that in the United States are divided between separate branches of the government. It is a bicameral body, made up of the House of Lords and the House of Commons, though only the House of Commons holds true legislative power.

The House of Commons The House of Commons possesses genuine legislative power. It has 650 members who are elected from single-member districts called constituencies. There are now 533 constituencies in England, 59 in Scotland, 40 in Wales, and 18 in Northern Ireland.

The party that controls the most constituencies dominates the House of Commons. On paper, the House of Commons shares similar functions with the United States Congress. It has committees that work on legislation and send it to the entire House of Commons to be voted up or down. However, the work of these committees is mostly limited to providing advice rather than actually writing legislation. Most new laws originate with the government (executive branch) but the House of Commons must debate and vote on those bills. The greatest power the majority party holds is the selection of the prime minister and his or her cabinet.

The House of Lords Until the 1800s, the House of Lords held greater governing power than the House of Commons. Its membership was based on lordships being passed down through heredity. Today, the House of Lords is largely powerless. In fact, the House of Commons eliminated the majority of the House of Lords' hereditary members in 1999. Most of its 800 or so members are appointed by the Queen, on the advice of the prime minister; members are often appointed after lifetime accomplishments in the sciences, literature, arts, politics, or business. The fact that the House of Commons could redefine membership of the House of Lords demonstrates the strengths of each chamber.

The Lords have meager lawmaking power; any measure passed by the Commons but then rejected by

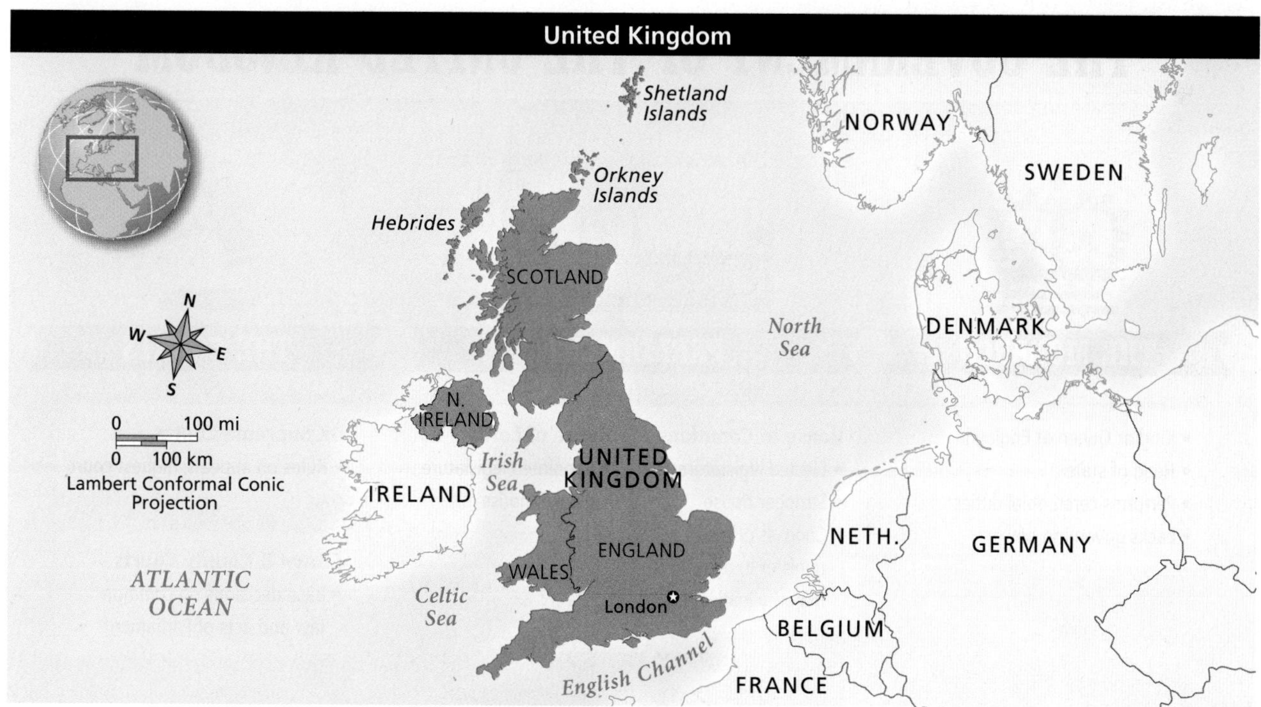

>> Despite its size, England established the British Empire as a powerful monarchy and colonial network. **Analyze Maps** How did geographic location and a strong navy aid this expansion?

the Lords has only to be approved a second time by the Commons in order to become law.

The Prime Minister The prime minister's party legislates and carries out its policy agenda in ways completely foreign to Americans; in the United States, legislative and executive powers are sharply separated. The source of the prime ministers' powers are party loyalty, merged legislative and executive power, and a clear policy mandate from election results.

Most often, one party wins a majority of the House of Commons. If no single party holds a majority, then two or more parties form a **coalition**, a temporary alliance of parties for the purpose of forming a government. Coalition government, however, has been rare. Prior to the exceptional situation following the 2010 British general election when no single party received a majority, Winston Churchill during World War II had been the last prime minister of a coalition government. Following the 2010 election, the Conservative Party had to form a coalition with the Liberal Democrats.

There are no term limits on the post of prime minister. Further, prime ministers can call elections at any time within a five-year window from the previous election, which means they can time elections to maximize their party's popularity.

As party leader, chief executive, and a member of the House of Commons, prime ministers dominate Parliament. The only real check that the House of Commons has over the prime minister comes from a vote of no confidence, where the government is defeated on a critical vote.

This occurs rarely because a vote of no confidence dissolves Parliament as well, so members of the unpopular prime minister's party are unlikely to want to cross the prime minister to face the electorate themselves. This means that a prime minister can stay in office unless he or she becomes extremely unpopular. The last vote of no confidence occured in 1979; the previous one occured in 1924.

The Cabinet The prime minister selects the members of the cabinet, or **ministers,** from the House of Commons, although a few may sit in the House of Lords. Collectively, the prime minister and the cabinet make and carry out policy. Cabinet ministers head the various executive departments, such as the Department of Defence, the HM Treasury, or the Department of Health.

The opposition parties appoint their own teams of potential cabinet members. Each opposition member of Parliament (MP) watches, or shadows, one particular member of the cabinet. If an opposition party should win the next election, its so-called **shadow cabinet** would run the government.

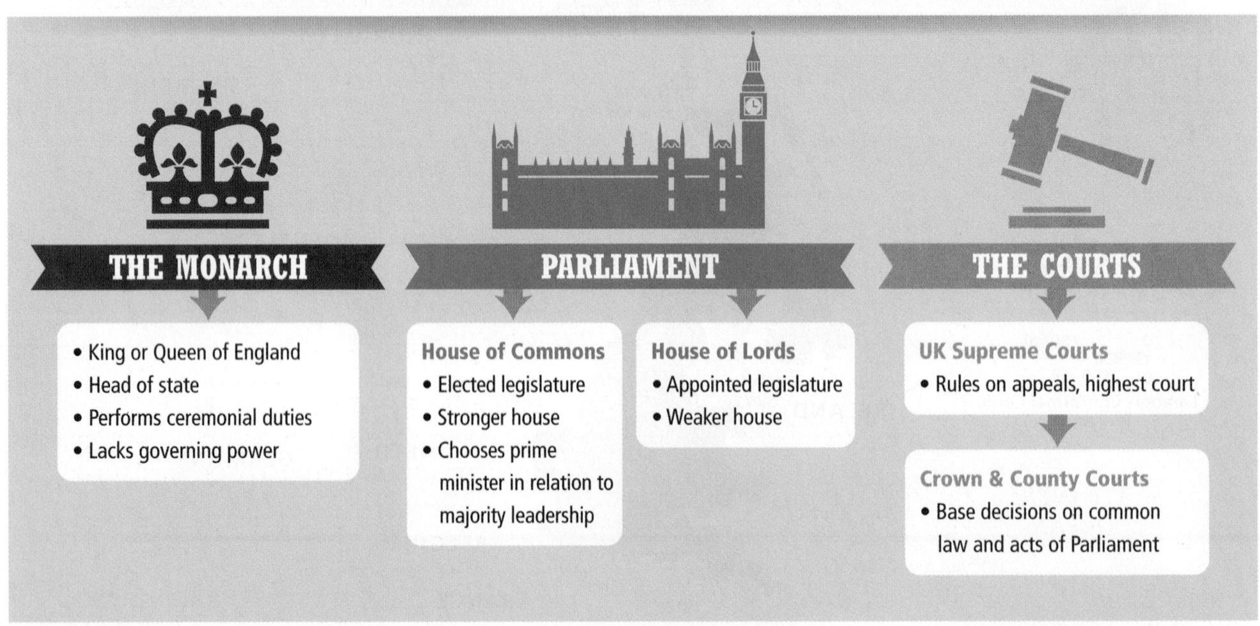

>> The government of the United Kingdom is made up of Parliament, the monarchy, the courts, and the regional and local governments. **Analyze Charts** What are the primary responsibilities of Parliament?

The Monarchy Many formal but strictly ceremonial duties are given to the monarchy. For example, the current Queen of England, Queen Elizabeth II, "appoints" the prime minister, but in reality she simply recognizes the election outcome. The Queen opens Parliament with a speech on a yearly basis, but the speech is largely a set of policy goals written by the prime minister. However, as head of state, the Queen provides a significant point of pride. She receives foreign ambassadors, entertains visiting heads of state, and makes state visits overseas. The monarchy is considered to be a point of stability during political or social change, and it supports those who serve others both in the public and volunteer sectors.

The Courts Because there is no established constitution, no court in the United Kingdom has the power of judicial review—the power to deem legislation or the execution of legislation unconstitutional, as the Supreme Court does in the United States. There is a United Kingdom Supreme Court that acquired the House of Lords' power of judicial oversight over legislation in 2009, but the House of Commons retains supreme governing power.

The United States court system grew from the system used in the United Kingdom, which decides cases based on **common law**, where laws are adjudicated on judicial precedent. Because there is no singular constitution, weighing decisions based on previous court decisions is vital for British democratic consistency.

For criminal cases and civil suits, the United Kingdom has three separate court systems: one for England and Wales, one in Northern Ireland, and one in Scotland. In England and Wales, most civil cases are tried in county courts. Judges and juries try the more serious criminal cases and civil disputes in the Crown Court. Less serious criminal cases are tried in the magistrates' courts. The court system in Northern Ireland is similar to the system in England and Wales, but the Scottish system is simpler, with fewer hierarchical layers.

Regional and Local Government As a unitary government, ultimate sovereignty belongs to the United Kingdom Parliament. To whatever extent local governments do govern, they can do so only because the central government has created them, given them powers, and financed them.

Because of the historical and cultural distinctions England has with Scotland, Wales, and Northern Ireland, the United Kingdom Parliament recognized the distinctive governmental needs of these nations in the late 1990s and began a process of **devolution**—the delegation of authority from the central government back to regional governments. Consequently, the National Assembly for Wales, Northern Ireland Assembly, and Scottish Parliament create education, health, and other social service policies for themselves. The British Parliament has reserved for itself the exclusive power to legislate on defense, foreign policy, and macroeconomic policy that affect the whole United Kingdom, as well as broadly governing England.

>> Justices from the highest court in the United Kingdom, the Supreme Court, head to Westminster Abbey for an annual service marking the beginning of the legal year.

There are some 470 local governing authorities of varying types in the United Kingdom. Much as in the United States, local governments in the United Kingdom perform a broad range of functions, from running local schools and libraries to collecting trash and maintaining roads.

? COMPARE POINTS OF VIEW In the United Kingdom, what are some of the pros and cons of having no term limit for the post of prime minister?

Public Policy and Elections

The seating in the House of Commons suggests how policy is made. The prime minister and cabinet ministers sit in the front bench on one side of the House of Commons across from the shadow cabinet of the main opposition party. Fellow party members sit on benches behind the cabinet ministers or shadow cabinet and are thus referred to as **backbenchers**, who have little or no influence over policy. Government in the United Kingdom is referred to as a **party government**, where a winning party creates and carries out policy based on the party's platform with overwhelming party loyalty. Parties command loyalty because they control nominations and will only select loyal partisans. Also, advancement from the back benches to a ministerial post requires loyal party voting.

Crafting Legislation The prime minister and cabinet craft legislation. The only real influence the opposing party or the ruling party's backbenchers have is during *Prime Minister's Questions*.

These tend to be raucous weekly events with sharply worded questions for the prime minister and government, punctuated by shouts of "here-here" or "boo" as the ministers provide their answers. When policies come to a vote, party loyalty is nearly universal.

Policy gets carried out by a professional civil service. The number of government workers is large compared to the United States because of the relatively large military, significant foreign service from its past empire, and extensive social services—especially since health care is provided by the government.

>> Prime Minister David Cameron answers questions from Parliament in the House of Commons. *Prime Minister's Questions,* held every Wednesday at noon, is broadcast live on television.

The Election Process In 2011, the Fixed Term Parliament Act established that a general election—an election in which all the seats in the Commons are at stake—be held the first Thursday in May every five years. Election campaigns last about one month.

Customarily, the prime minister calls an election when the political climate favors the majority party. Only in the most extreme occasions have votes of no confidence triggered an election.

In the United States, elections tend to be candidate-centered elections, but elections in the United Kingdom are all about parties. People vote and candidates win or lose based on party fortune. Once the results of the general election become official, the head of the winning party is appointed prime minister by the Queen and immediately moves into his or her 10 Downing Street office/home.

Two parties have dominated British politics: the Conservative Party (historically known as the Tories) and the Labour Party. The Conservatives have long drawn support from middle and upper-class Britons. They tend to favor free market initiatives over government regulation, though British Conservatives support social welfare programs more than American parties. The working class has regularly supported the Labour Party, which favors government regulation and more social equality policies.

The Liberal Democratic Party has emerged as an alternative that blends left-wing and moderate views. They have increased their share of the vote and joined the Conservatives in a coalition government after the 2010 general elections.

British parties are more highly organized and centrally directed than American political parties. High levels of party loyalty and discipline characterize the British party system. Voters regularly select candidates for the House of Commons on the basis of the candidates' party membership, not their individual qualifications. Therefore, political party fortunes drive United Kingdom general election results and determine public policy.

? **COMPARE AND CONTRAST** Describe the differences between government elections in the United States and those in the United Kingdom.

UK Political Parties

PARTY	SEATS	DESCRIPTION
Conservative	303	• promotion of private property and enterprise • strong military • preservation of traditional cultural values and institutions
Labour	256	• economic prosperity • social services
Liberal Democrat	56	• middle ground between Conservative and Labour Parties
Democratic Unionist	8	• represents Northern Ireland • regularly adopts conservative position on most social issues
Scottish National	6	• wants Scottish independence
Independent	5	• wants UK to withdraw from the European Union
Sinn Fein	5	• wants to end the British presence in Northern Ireland
Other	11 (1 vacant; 1 Speaker)	• Plaid Cymru, Social Democratic and Labour, Alliance, Green, and Respect Parties

>> There are many political parties currently represented in the United Kingdom's House of Commons, each with their own ideas and agendas. **Analyze Charts** Which party's ideas are dominantly represented?

Comparison to the United States

Given its British origins, it is no wonder that the United States has many similarities to the government of the United Kingdom. Although the United States is the world's only superpower, both countries have a large international presence. Both have similar common law judicial systems that rely on precedent from earlier decisions to guide a judge's decisions. Constitutionalism, the rule of law, and recognition of citizen rights play a large part of both democracies.

The two countries differ greatly in regard to many factors, however. First, the United States is a federal system with some areas of policy reserved to States, while the United Kingdom is a unitary system with Parliament having sovereignty over the whole country, even with recent devolution. The United Kingdom is a parliamentary system where Parliament chooses the prime minister, rather than the executive being publicly elected like the American President.

This provides the prime minister with considerable legislative and executive power. The prime minister dominates the United Kingdom Parliament. Consequently, British general elections provide the winning party with absolute policy control. American Presidents are elected separately from Congress, cannot directly write legislation, and are closely checked by Congress. Further, the President is both head of state and head of government. He must act presidential and represent the American public like the British Queen, which means the President cannot be as aggressive politically as is the United Kingdom prime minister, whose only role is head of government.

Britain's government is a party government. Parties dominate by selecting House of Commons candidates and persuading them to always vote for their party's position. The U.S. Congress is not nearly as party oriented. Recently, there has been polarization among American parties; additionally, American party nomination is left up to the public, and at times, one singular party does not have control over the governing agenda.

? COMPARE AND CONTRAST What are the pros and cons to having a separate head of government and head of state as in the United Kingdom, compared to having a single head of both government and state like the United States?

ASSESSMENT

1. **Explain** Describe the United Kingdom's legacy of constitutionalism.
2. **Describe** Describe the structure of the United Kingdom's Parliament.
3. **Explain** How are elections held and positions filled in the United Kingdom's Parliament?
4. **Compare** What are some of the similarities between the governments of the United States and the United Kingdom?
5. **Explain** Why did the United Kingdom decide to allow for regional governments in Scotland, Wales, and Northern Ireland?

(14.3) **The Russian Federation is an enormous country that straddles Europe and Asia. The country is only two decades old, but its history affects its contemporary form and practice. The government is considered a semi-presidential system. The president is elected separately from the legislature, the Federal Assembly. The president also appoints a prime minister to lead government. The president holds considerable power over government.**

>> Prime Minister Vladimir Putin (right) of Russia reversed many democratic reforms of the 1990s and effectively chose his own replacement as president, Dmitry Medvedev.

Interactive Flipped Video

The Russian Federation

>> Objectives

Examine Russia and its history since the Bolshevik Revolution.

Outline the structure of Russia's government.

Examine how public policy is created in Russia.

Compare government in Russia with that of the United States.

>> Key Terms

Vladimir Lenin
Josef Stalin
purge
Vladimir Putin

Russia and Its History

As its name suggests, Russia is a federal system with many regional governments of differing types. Russia remains an international power whose democratic development, especially the rule of law and constitutional rights, has not matched that of consolidated democracies according to critics.

The Bolshevik Revolution The Russian empire was formally established by Peter the Great in 1721. A succession of tyrannical czars ruled the empire until its collapse after heavy losses in the Russo-Japanese War (1904–1905) and World War I (1914–1918).

In the wake of World War I, a revolution in March 1917 forced the abdication of Czar Nicholas II, and the fluid situation ultimately led to the Bolshevik Revolution led by **Vladimir Lenin** on November 7, 1917. Lenin was the architect of the Communist Party and its control over what became the Soviet Union, which transformed Russia from an underdeveloped, tradition-bound country into the world's first communist state.

Stalin **Josef Stalin** became the Soviet leader after Lenin's death in 1924 and consolidated his power in a series of **purges**, purifying governing power by removing rivals. Through an intensive and brutal program of industrialization and forced collectivization of agriculture, he built the Soviet Union into a major industrial and military power.

The Soviets suffered staggering losses in World War II. Nevertheless, at war's end, they controlled all of Eastern Europe and emerged as one of the world's two superpowers. Rivalry with the United States and an aggressive foreign policy brought on the Cold War, which lasted from the late 1940s until the early 1990s.

Soviet Government The Soviet Union—officially, the Union of Soviet Socialist Republics (USSR)—comprised 15 republics, each inhabited by a major nationality group, such as Georgians or Tajiks. The largest and most important of the republics was Russia, which comprised over 70 percent of Soviet land area and more than half of its population. Soviet government had many layers, but the real power of Soviet government stemmed from the top Communist Party leadership.

From the revolution of 1917 until 1990, the Communist Party of the Soviet Union (CPSU) was the only political party in the Soviet Union. The CPSU was an elite hierarchical party. At the top of the party was the general secretary, who held the top post in government and headed the Politburo (political bureau), whose experienced and powerful party leaders held key government posts.

The Central Committee involved broader Communist Party officials and elected the Politburo. The Supreme Soviet served as the legislative body, but it met infrequently to simply rubber-stamp the decrees of the Politburo and general secretary.

Reform Led by Gorbachev When Mikhail Gorbachev became general secretary of the party in 1985, he undertook a reform program that rested on the principles of *perestroika,* the restructuring of political and economic life, and *glasnost*, the policy of openness under which the government increased its tolerance of dissent and freedom of expression.

Gorbachev created a new legislative body, the Congress of People's Deputies, two-thirds of whom were elected by competitive elections. Gorbachev also took over the new office of president of the Soviet Union, which replaced the general secretary as governing leader. These reforms eroded the Communist Party's power, perhaps emphasized by the Soviet critic Boris Yeltsin winning the presidency of the Russian Republic as a non-Communist Party candidate.

Districts of the Russian Federation

>> The Russian Federation has a land area of 6,592,735 square miles and covers one-eighth of the world's land surface. **Analyze Maps** What bodies of water border the Russian Federation?

Throughout this time, a wave of democratization flowed across the Soviet bloc, beginning with the fall of East Germany's communist government in November 1989. By 1992, each Soviet republic claimed its independence, and the USSR ceased to exist, leaving the Russian Republic's government sovereign over Russia.

The transition to a democratic Russian Federation was not easy. President Yeltsin's market reforms were controversial and unpopular with many leaders of the Russian Parliament. Yeltsin dissolved the Parliament in 1993, despite dissolution not being a presidential power. In turn, parliamentarians impeached Yeltsin and selected their own president. The situation deteriorated; ultimately, the military intervened to attack the parliamentary building and arrest the parliamentarians in October 1993. Subsequently, the Russian Federation ratified a new constitution in December 1993.

SUMMARIZE Describe how Russia changed between the Bolshevik Revolution and the 1980s under the leadership of Vladimir Lenin and Josef Stalin.

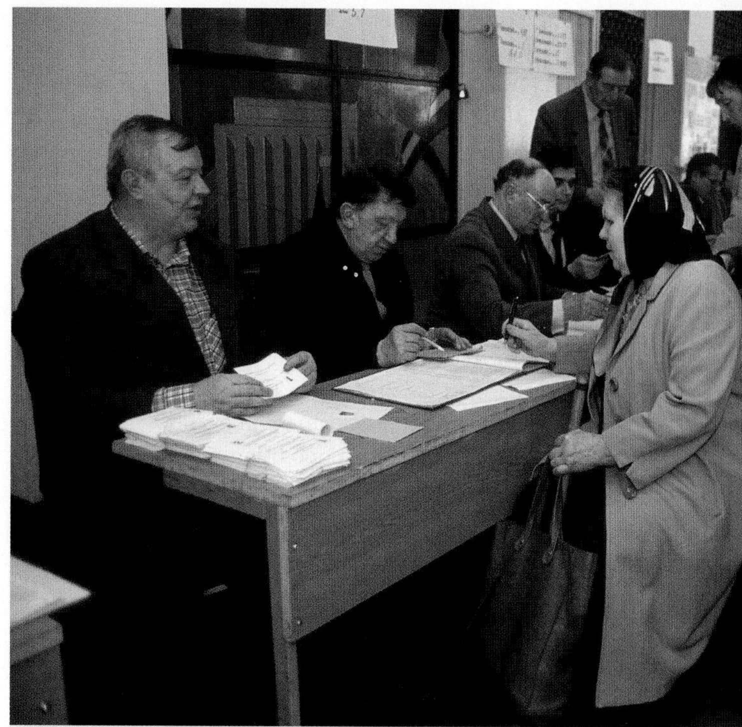

>> A woman votes on a referendum in Moscow on April 26, 1993. Later the same year, Russians voted in favor of a new constitution.

Interactive Gallery

Government in the Russian Federation

A new constitution was approved in a national referendum in late 1993. It proclaims the Russian Federation to be "a democratic federal legally-based state with a republican form of government." As constitutions do, it ensures an extensive list of individual rights, including guarantees of freedom of speech, press, association, and religious belief. The constitution also assures every citizen a right to freedom of movement within the federation, housing, and free medical care and education. Critics have questioned whether many of these liberties have been sufficiently protected from the state. The 1993 constitution also sets out a new government structure that provided significant power to the Russian presidency,which has grown based on the governing practices of Boris Yeltsin and **Vladimir Putin.**

The Executive Branch The Russian executive branch is similar to the French system. A presidential election determines the head of state. The executive is semi-presidential because a second key executive position is the prime minister. It is the prime minister who heads the government, the group of key executive ministers and advisors who create and execute policies passed by the Russian Parliament.

The exact power divide between the president and prime minister is not entirely clear for two reasons. First, presidents appoint prime ministers, but there are few constitutionally detailed policy powers specified for each office. Second, the practice of presidential control over the prime minister has been inconsistent. President Yeltsin named and fired prime ministers frequently. Vladimir Putin then ascended to the presidency from prime minister and has held tight power over the prime minister.

Complicating things further, Putin became prime minister when his two-term limit as president expired in 2008. He supported Prime Minister Dmitry Medvedev's presidential candidacy and then became prime minister. Most observers felt that Putin retained real governing power. He again won the presidency in 2012, with Medvedev returning to the prime minister post.

The Presidency The 1993 constitution created a government built on a separation of powers between executive and legislative branches, but in reality the constitution gives the president the most crucial governing role. The president has strong powers as commander in chief and is supposed to define "the basic directions of domestic and foreign policy" according to the constitution.

The president is elected by direct popular vote and may not serve more than two consecutive terms. The presidential term was changed from four to six years in 2008, under Dmitry Medvedev. He or she must be a Russian citizen, at least thirty-five years old, and a resident of Russia for 10 years.

Boris Yeltsin kept his Russian presidency under the new constitution in 1993 and surprised many by winning the 1996 presidential election. His health problems and accusations of his inner circle's corruption led him to resign, leaving Prime Minister Vladimir Putin as president. Putin won the office on his own in elections held in March 2000, and he was reelected without much opposition in 2004 and 2012.

Some argue that the ordered society that centralized leadership brought Tsarist and Soviet-era Russia means strong presidents will be favored in Russian governance. Such observers worry that Putin is not a dedicated democrat and is bent instead on what has come to be called "Putinism"—the creation of a one-party state fueled by impressive economic growth.

The Prime Minister The prime minister leads the government and carries the administration's programs to Parliament. He or she is second-in-command of the executive branch and first in line of succession. The prime minister often is the administrator of the president's policy goals; he or she does not create or implement policy alone, however. Because of the president's power, the prime minister tends to have considerable influence over the Russian legislature.

The Legislature: Federal Assembly Russia's legislature, the Federal Assembly, is a bicameral body. Its upper house, the Federation Council, is composed of 166 members, two members from each of Russia's eighty-three constituent regions. The lower house, the State Duma, has 450 members. Parties compete nationwide for Duma seats, while the Federation Council members are selected by each region.

The Duma is the more powerful chamber. Any measure passed by the Duma but rejected by the Federation Council may nonetheless become law if it is passed again by the Duma by at least a two-thirds majority. The Duma also must approve the president's choice of a prime minister. Presidential vetoes can be overridden by a two-thirds vote in each house.

Constitutional Court A nineteen-member Constitutional Court can rule on the constitutionality of federal laws, regional laws, and situations of civilian liberties. The Constitutional Court is the body to interpret the constitution, but it tends not to challenge the power of the presidency.

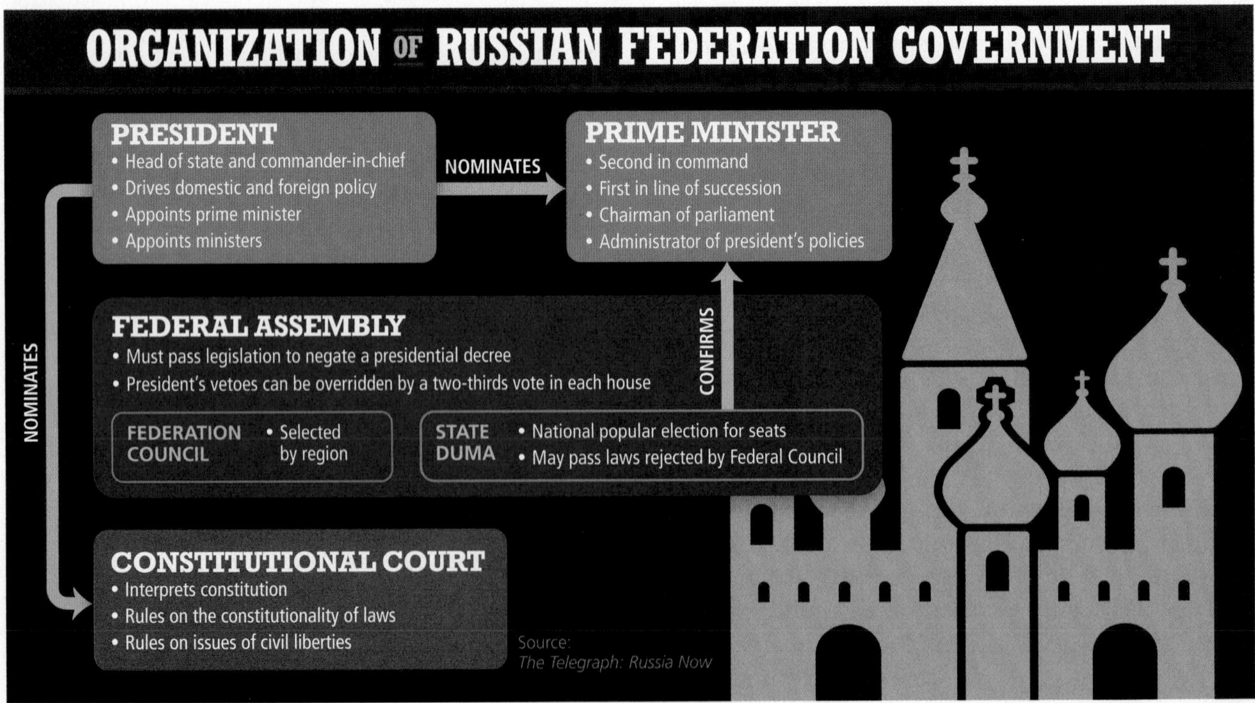

ORGANIZATION OF RUSSIAN FEDERATION GOVERNMENT
PRESIDENT
• Head of state and commander-in-chief
• Drives domestic and foreign policy
• Appoints prime minister
• Appoints ministers
NOMINATES
PRIME MINISTER
• Second in command
• First in line of succession
• Chairman of parliament
• Administrator of president's policies
CONFIRMS
FEDERAL ASSEMBLY
• Must pass legislation to negate a presidential decree
• President's vetoes can be overridden by a two-thirds vote in each house
FEDERATION COUNCIL
• Selected by region
STATE DUMA
• National popular election for seats
• May pass laws rejected by Federal Council
NOMINATES
CONSTITUTIONAL COURT
• Interprets constitution
• Rules on the constitutionality of laws
• Rules on issues of civil liberties
Source: The Telegraph: Russia Now

>> Both the Russian Federation and the U.S. governments have three independent branches and a bicameral legislature. **Analyze Charts** How do the Presidents' interactions with their assemblies differ?

The criminal and commercial courts do not hold much power. Most judicial power comes from procuracy, the government bureau charged with ensuring legality, which holds considerable power over criminal investigations and ultimately controls the business before the courts.

Regional and Local Governments Regional governments in Russia are a patchwork of different organizational structures. The Russian Federation is made up of forty-six *oblasts* (provinces) and nine large, thinly populated territories, all of which are headed by elected governors. The governors of these regions have traditionally exercised great power.

The federation also includes twenty-one republics, which are home to ethnic, non-Russian minorities, and eight autonomous areas. Each republic elects a president. Independence is a burning issue in some republics. In particular, the Republic of Chechnya attempted to break away from the Russian Federation in 1994, and the Russian military invaded and occupied the region. It has since battled Chechen rebels, who have launched numerous terrorist attacks.

Political Parties The one-party system of the Soviet era has given way to a multiparty system. In the 1990s, the Communist Party did rather well, as did the right-wing nationalist Liberal Democratic Party. With the emergence and popularity of Vladimir Putin, the United Russia party has become the dominant party in both elections for the Duma and presidency.

SUMMARIZE What is the structure of the Russian executive branch, and what powers does it exert?

Public Policy Creation

The Russian presidency drives much of the Russian Federation's public policy. Further, the president holds considerable foreign policy powers and powers as commander in chief.

The constitutional powers and practice of presidents have given Russia's presidents considerable power to set policy by decree. In other words, unlike in the United States, Russian presidents can order the government to carry out a policy of the president's choice, and the legislature must pass legislation should they want to negate the decree. Further, presidents can offer amendments to legislation coming from the Federal Assembly that can become law with a simple majority of the Duma and Federation Council.

Vladimir Putin has increased presidential power based on his own popularity and his party's electoral success. Putin returned some stability to Russian life.

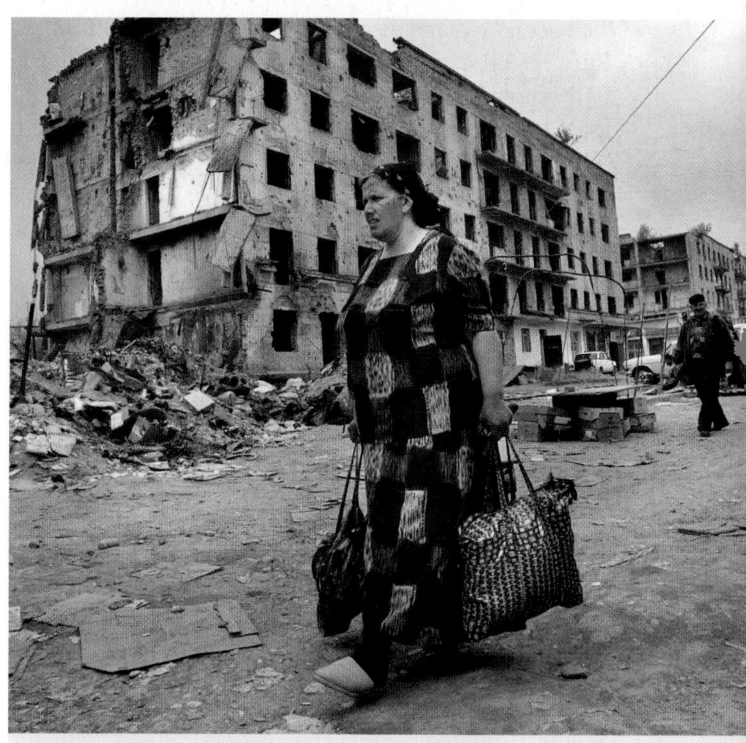

>> Residents walk through Grozny, the capital of Chechnya. While democratic principles are strong throughout the Federation, some areas, like Chechnya, continue to struggle with rebellion.

>> The Udmurtneft oil field is Russia's largest venture with China. Putin has gained support for his presidency by improving Russia's economy and, as a result, the daily lives of its people.

The economy was also bolstered by rising profits from Russian oil and gas exports. Putin's United Russia party provides his policy agenda with great support in the Federal Assembly.

APPLY CONCEPTS Describe how public policy is created in the Russian Federation. What role does the president play? The legislature?

Comparison to the United States

The United States and Russia share some distinct similarities. As a former superpower in Soviet times, Russia retains an enormous international role and has a powerful military.

Both countries are also federal democracies with far-flung and diverse regional governments. Both have separately elected presidents, though the Russian system includes a prime minister. Both the United States Congress and the Federal Assembly are bicameral institutions with the United States Senate and the Federation Council built to represent regions—or States—with equal representation, rather than being composed by population.

The similarities between the presidencies and the legislatures are offset by key differences in these institutions. Russian presidents have far more policy control than American Presidents based on institutional powers and in practice. The Russian president's control over the prime minister and government help to control the legislative agenda to a much greater extent. Also, Russian presidential decrees go further and have fewer checks than executive orders from American Presidents.

American political culture guards against centralization of power, as witnessed by America's Federal Government having considerable checks and balances. Russian political culture appreciates strong centralized leadership. This does not mean that Tsarist Russian or Soviet Russian authoritarianism is likely; rather, Russians prefer strong leaders and will vote them in with a mandate to government. Consequently, other actors like interest groups and the media that affect American politics significantly lack major influence in Russia.

COMPARE AND CONTRAST Compare and contrast the president of the Russian Federation and the President of the United States. Which president has more power? Explain.

Comparing United States and Russian Legislatures

UNITED STATES		RUSSIA	
Senate Upper House	**House of Representatives**	**Federation Council**	**State Duma**
• 100 members: 2 senators from each State • 6-year terms • Popularly elected	• 435 members • Seats are distributed among the States based on their populations • 2-year terms • Popularly elected • Speaker of the House elected by the representatives • Elections held to fill vacancies	• 166 members: 2 members from each of Russia's 83 constituent regions • Selected by region • Not directly elected	• 450 members • Parties compete nationwide for seats • Popularly elected • More powerful chamber • Any measure rejected by Federal Council can become law if passed again by Duma by 2/3 majority • Duma approves president's choice of prime minister

SOURCE: The United States Senate; the United States House of Representatives; the Federal Assembly of the Russian Federation

>> While both countries' legislatures appear organizationally similar, there are notable differences. **Analyze Charts** How is popular representation different for the two legislatures?

ASSESSMENT

1. **Generate Explanations** Who was Mikhail Gorbachev, and what was his contribution toward the development of the Russian Federation?
2. **Summarize** Describe Russia's transition to democracy, including the changes in Russian leadership from the 1980s to today.
3. **Apply Concepts** Describe the government in the Russian Federation, as set forth in the constitution of 1993 and in practice. Where is most of the power found?
4. **Explain** Describe the State Duma. How is it formed? What power does it have?
5. **Generate Explanations** Describe the impact Vladimir Putin has had on the Russian Federation. What does "Putinism" refer to?

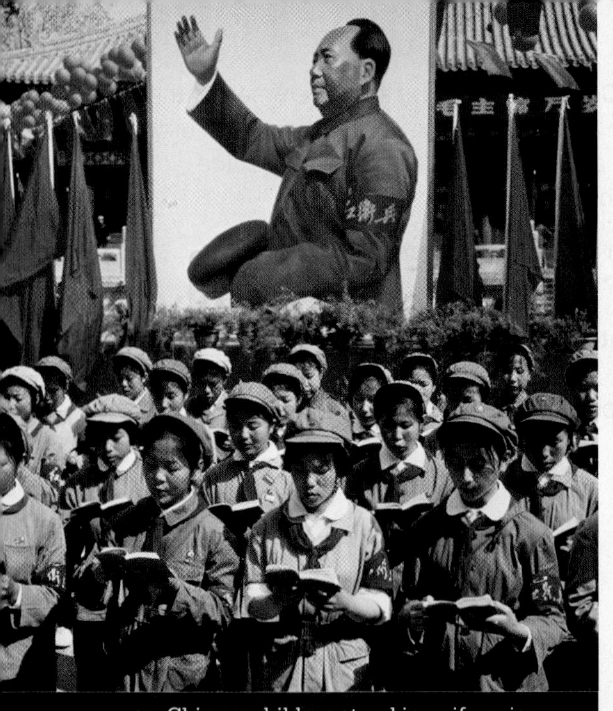

>> Chinese children stand in uniform in front of a picture of Mao Zedong while reading from Mao's "Little Red Book," which included quotations and writings by Mao Zedong.

Interactive Flipped Video

14.4 China's government system is unlike the other countries profiled. China is a communist country with the world's largest population. Despite its geographic size and numerous ethnic groups, China's government is a unitary system with sovereignty held nationally. Regional governments exist but are administration units of the Chinese government rather than autonomous bodies.

>> Objectives

Examine China and its history starting with the birth of the People's Republic.

Outline the structure of China's government.

Examine how public policy is created in China.

Compare government in China with that of the United States.

>> Key Terms

Mao Zedong
Cultural Revolution
Chiang Kai-shek
Deng Xiaoping

China

China and Its History

Chinese political history is very long and its recent economic and social transformations have been massive. Nevertheless, it remains an undemocratic, single-party system that tightly controls political thought, yet permits major economic freedoms. China's socialist market economy has led to enormous economic, educational, and infrastructure development with economic autonomy, but little citizen influence on governance.

Although the political history of what is today China can be traced back some 5,000 years, China's present-day government has existed for just over 65 years. The People's Republic of China was born in 1949 after decades of civil war. Those years of bitter strife pitted China's Nationalist government, led by **Chiang Kai-shek**, against rebel communists led by **Mao Zedong**. The United States supported Chiang's Nationalist government.

At the same time, Mao organized a patriotic movement that appealed to the Chinese peasantry, whom the Nationalist elite had long ignored. In 1949, Mao's Red Army defeated the Nationalists, who fled to Taiwan, and renamed mainland China as the People's Republic of China.

China Under Mao Mao was determined to increase agricultural and industrial production. He turned to central planning and instituted a series of Five-Year Plans. Frequent and often drastic changes in policy produced chaos and regularly thwarted economic development.

By the mid-1960s, Mao pursued a **Cultural Revolution,** where young dedicated Red Guards attacked and bullied teachers, intellectuals, and anyone else who seemed to lack revolutionary fervor. Artists and scholars were sent to farms to be "re-educated"; ancient books and art were destroyed. By 1968, however, the havoc created by the Cultural Revolution persuaded Mao to abandon that effort.

Reform and Repression **Deng Xiaoping** came into power after Mao's death in 1976. As the new leader of the Chinese Communist Party, Deng embarked on what is known as the Four Modernizations to strengthen agriculture, industry, technology, and defense. He reversed the trend of state centralization and lessened the party's focus on class struggle to allow for looser government control of the economy and to encourage some forms of private enterprise.

Although the Chinese government relaxed economic controls under Deng, it tolerated no political dissent. In May 1989, some 100,000 students and workers occupied Beijing's Tiananmen Square, demanding democratic reforms. Their demonstrations were soon crushed, however. Chinese troops and tanks moved into the square, killing hundreds of protestors and maiming thousands more. Democratic governments continue to raise concerns over China's record of human rights.

The economic growth in the quarter-century since Tiananmen Square has overshadowed the lack of democratic freedoms for Chinese citizens in the eyes of many international actors. China has grown to the world's second largest economy. As the government has permitted migration from rural to urban areas, Chinese cities have boomed while agricultural land is limited and rural poverty remains high.

Additionally, the successful reforms that Deng Xiaoping undertook became a lesson for subsequent Chinese Communist Party leaders. Each successive generation has chosen new avenues for economic reform, even if the economic freedoms that they produce have not translated into political freedoms.

? IDENTIFY CAUSE AND EFFECT Explain one reason why Mao Zedong and his rebel communists were able to defeat Chiang Kai-Shek and the Nationalist government.

Government in China

When the communists gained power, the People's Political Consultative Conference adopted a provisional constitution. That document became the basis for a new constitution adopted by the first session of the National People's Congress in 1954.

Unlike the Constitution of the United States and those of most other nations, China's constitution is not intended to be fundamental law. Instead, it is supposed to reflect current governmental policies. China has had four constitutions since its founding—in 1954, 1975, 1978, and 1982.

China's Communist Party China remains a communist state. The role of the Communist Party is not to mobilize people to vote; even though the Chinese Communist Party is the world's largest party with 82 million members, that translates to about six percent of the Chinese public. Rather, the role of the Communist Party is to govern. The top-ranking members of the party hold the highest positions in the government and the military. In short, the Communist Party *is* the government of China.

The Chinese constitution frequently discusses the "people's democratic dictatorship," which the

>> The Forbidden City, located in Beijing, was home to twenty-four emperors over a period of 500 years, beginning with the Ming Dynasty in the early thirteenth century.

Communist Party leads. It is a very hierarchical party. Chinese governing institutions and the Communist Party share the same structure, which allows party leadership over those institutions. The Chinese government's main units are the National Party Congress, the Central Committee, the Politburo, and the Secretariat.

The National Party Congress has some 2,200 members chosen by party members throughout China. It meets approximately every five years to elect a Central Committee of about 200 members, which meets about once a year. The Central Committee in turn elects the Politburo, which has about 25 members. It is the Politburo that makes party policy. The Secretariat, including the General Secretary, makes the party's day-to-day decisions.

The National Government The national government of China is composed of two main bodies, the National People's Congress and the State Council.

The National People's Congress. The nearly 3,000 deputies of the National People's Congress are elected for five-year terms by local people's congresses throughout China. According to the Chinese constitution, the National People's Congress is the highest governmental authority. In reality, however, the Congress has little power. It performs its major function when it passes the policy decisions of the State Council and the Communist Party to the lower levels of government.

The National People's Congress has a Standing Committee of around 150 members who work on legislative issues year-round. The Standing Committee has become more influential in recent decades by regularly studying issues and even drafting legislation.

The State Council. The State Council is the main body in the executive branch of Chinese government. It is headed by the premier, who is chosen by the Central Committee of the Communist Party. The premier, several vice-premiers, several members of the state council, and the secretary-general meet regularly as a standing committee. This Standing Committee of the State Council possesses major decision-making authority, and its decisions have the force of law. As is the case with the National People's Congress, the Communist Party directly leads the actions of the State Council.

The Judicial System A nationwide system of "people's courts" deals with both criminal and civil cases. Those courts are supervised by the Supreme People's Court—in effect, the nation's Supreme Court.

Capital punishment may be imposed for conviction of any of a long list of crimes: murder, treason, bribery, embezzlement, smuggling, drug-dealing, and many others. Most of the guarantees to a fair trial known

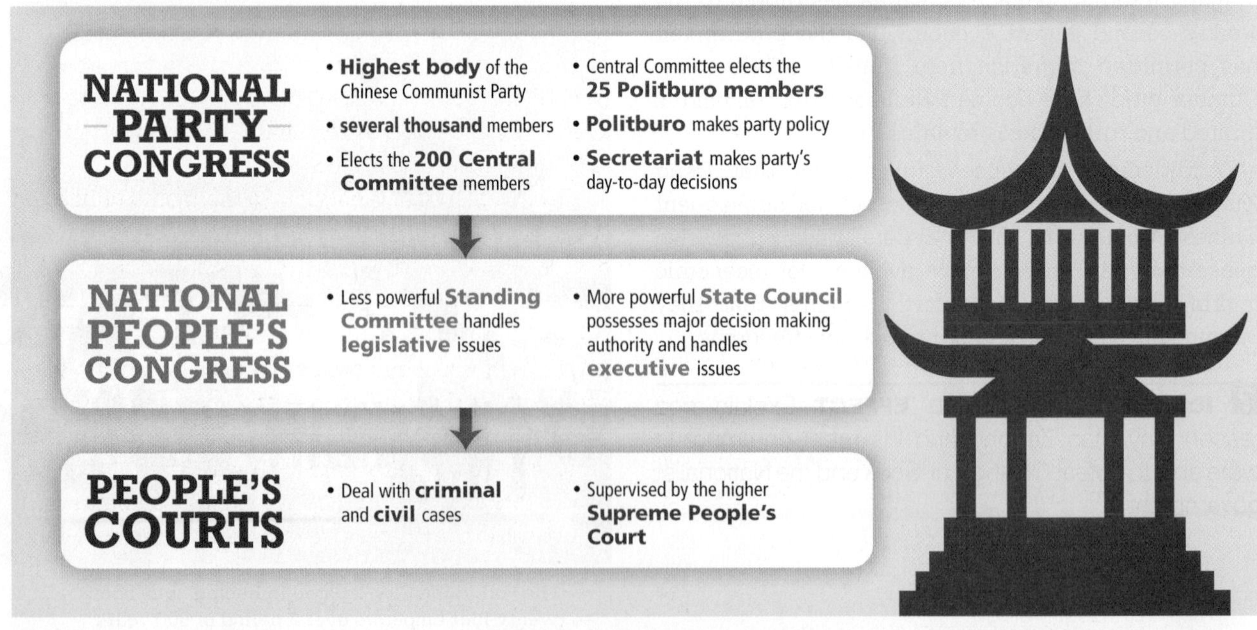

GOVERNMENT IN THE PEOPLE'S REPUBLIC OF CHINA
NATIONAL PARTY CONGRESS
• Highest body of the Chinese Communist Party
• several thousand members
• Elects the 200 Central Committee members
• Central Committee elects the 25 Politburo members
• Politburo makes party policy
• Secretariat makes party's day-to-day decisions
NATIONAL PEOPLE'S CONGRESS
• Less powerful Standing Committee handles legislative issues
• More powerful State Council possesses major decision making authority and handles executive issues
PEOPLE'S COURTS
• Deal with criminal and civil cases
• Supervised by the higher Supreme People's Court

>> China's main governing body is the National People's Congress led by the Chinese Communist Party. **Analyze Charts** How is power divided to reflect a hierarchy?

Interactive Gallery

>> China is a vast country in Asia, encompassing various groups of people and cultures. **Analyze Maps** What are the two largest groups of administrative divisions in China?

to Western democracies are completely absent from Chinese law.

Local Political Divisions China has a unitary government, with the central government exerting direct control over local subdivisions. Local administrative regions include twenty-two provinces (not including Taiwan) and five autonomous (independent) regions whose people are mostly ethnic minorities. Hong Kong, which the British returned to China's control in 1997, is a special administrative region of China with its own governor and provisional legislature.

Taiwan When Mao's forces took over the mainland in 1949, Chiang Kai-shek and the Nationalists fled to the island of Formosa (Taiwan), establishing the Republic of China. Today the People's Republic of China considers Taiwan one of its provinces. In turn, the Republic of China (Taiwan) takes the position that its National Assembly rules all of China. This conflict has left the United States in an awkward position of being officially pro-Taiwan, but also recognizing the global power status of the People's Republic of China.

EXPLAIN Describe how legislation is created and passed in the Chinese government.

Comparison to the United States

The Communist Party dominates the policy process. Any policy coming from the National People's Congress or the State Council really reflects the policy leadership of the Communist Party. In fact, the Communist Party reviews legislation and can reject it before it can be voted upon. The Communist Party has officials throughout the country. The party holds authority over regional governments, controls their policies, and determines personnel decisions.

Other political actors, such as the media or interest groups seen in constitutional republics like the United States, do not influence governing decisions. In fact, the media is controlled and regulated by the government, which also imposes tight restrictions over the Internet.

Chinese economic policy has opened up in recent years and privatization has led to great personal wealth for many Chinese. However, individuals cannot translate this wealth into political power. Further, people lack property rights that exist in constitutional republics, so the Chinese government can seize land for economic development without substantial payment. Such seizures of land have been a controversial issue, as rural Chinese have increasingly resisted land redevelopment.

>> Chinese President Xi Jinping meets with President Barack Obama in 2013. Despite political differences, China and the United States maintain relations and rely on each other for trade and commerce.

There are very few comparisons to draw between American politics and Chinese politics. American politics tends to be decentralized, full of checks and balances, and influenced by multiple actors such as interest groups, the media, and public opinion. Further, Americans tend to distrust political parties and public opinion polls show that they dislike having their political choices limited, even to two parties.

China, on the other hand, is completely governed by a single party, and more specifically by the top level of that party. There are no formal mechanisms for citizens to affect governance or policy, such as elections, and other forms of influence such as protests usually bring strong security responses.

Ironically, both countries govern themselves differently but have become increasingly linked internationally. Many of our foreign policy interests conflict with Chinese policy and American criticism of China's human rights record is consistent. Yet both countries' business and trade interests drive them toward closer interactions, even if their relations remain difficult.

? DRAW CONCLUSIONS What is the purpose of the Chinese government controlling and regulating the media?

ASSESSMENT

1. **Describe** Explain how China's current government was created.
2. **Infer** Why did the United States support Chiang Kai-Shek and the Nationalist Government during the war between the Red Army and the Nationalists?
3. **Explain** Describe the basic structure of China's government.
4. **Apply Concepts** Explain how public policy is created in China's government.
5. **Identify Central Issues** Clearly the governments of both the United States and China are quite different. However, what is one way in which they are linked?

TOPIC 14 ASSESSMENT

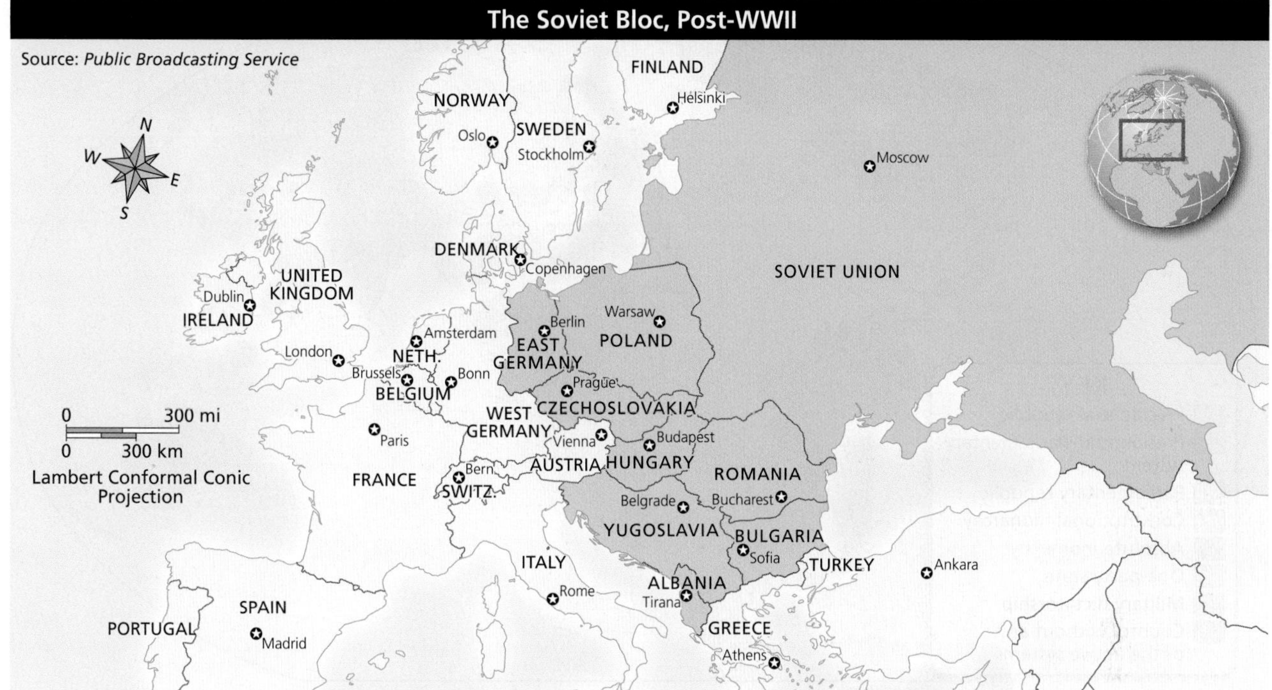

1. **Identify the Significance to the United States** Use information from the map above to write a paragraph about the Soviet bloc. When writing the paragraph, answer the following questions: How many European nations had communist governments in 1955? Study the countries' locations on the map. Why did the Soviet regime try to squash internal dissent and democratic values in Soviet bloc countries such as East Germany, Czechoslovakia, Hungary, and Yugoslavia?

2. **Identify the Significance to the United States** Create a written or oral presentation identifying the significance of the Soviet Union to the United States, and summarizing the Soviet Union's transition to democracy. When creating the presentation, consider the following information: the Soviet Union's significance to the United States; the United States and the Soviet Union during the Cold War; Mikhail Gorbachev; *Perestroika*; *Glasnost*; Boris Yeltsin.

3. **Compare the U.S. Constitutional Republic to Contemporary Forms of Government** Use the quote below to write a paragraph comparing and contrasting the freedom to speak out against the government in the United States and China. When writing the paragraph, answer the following question: Why do you think the United States continues to work with authoritarian governments such as China?

   "Each succeeding generation [of Chinese Communist Party leaders] has chosen new avenues for economic reform, even if the individual economic freedoms that it produces have not translated into political freedoms."

4. **Compare the U.S. Constitutional Republic to Historical Forms of Government** Create a written or oral presentation comparing how the Magna Carta influenced the U.S. constitutional republic and the British monarchy. When writing the paragraph, answer the following questions: How did the Magna Carta democratize the British government? How did the Magna Carta influence the U.S. constitutional republic? Why is the Magna Carta an important document?

Types of Governments By Country Around the World

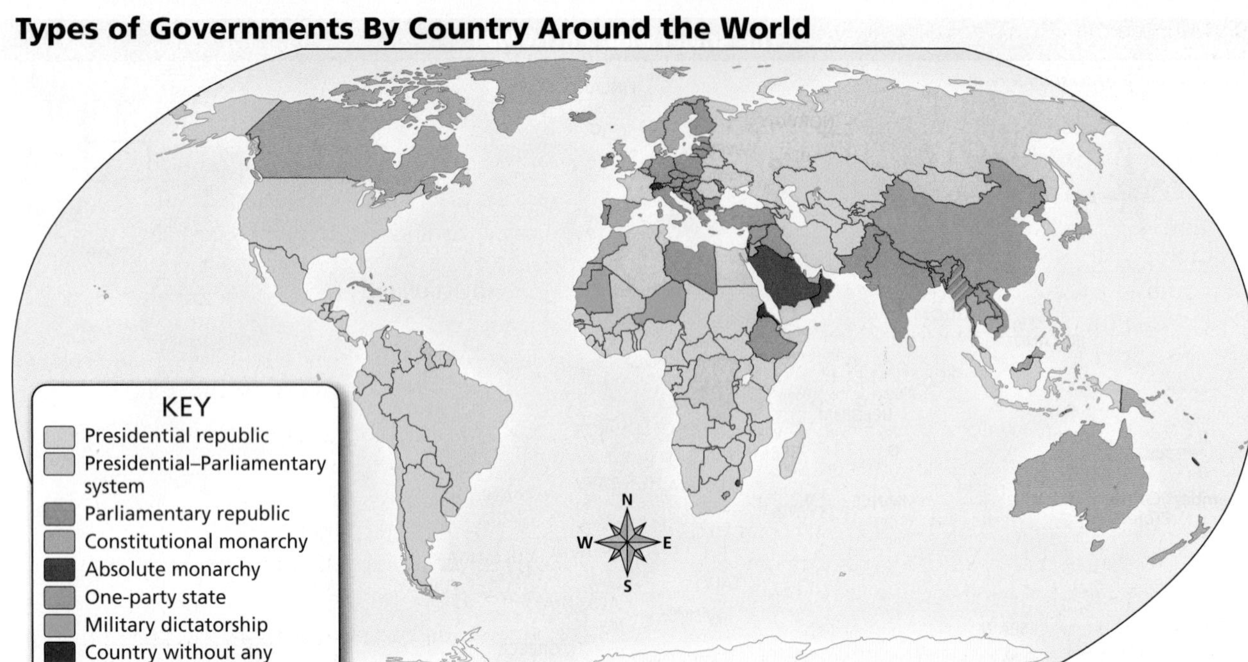

5. **Identify the Significance and Evaluate Government Data** Use the information from the map above to write a paragraph evaluating and identifying the different governments around the world. When writing the paragraph, answer the following questions: How many military dictatorship governments are there in the world? Comparatively speaking, why do you think there are so few military dictatorships in the world?

6. **Compare the U.S. Constitutional Republic to Contemporary Forms of Government** Compare the U.S. constitutional republic to Egypt under the Muslim Brotherhood. When writing the paragraph, answer the following questions: What was the Arab Spring? How did it start? What was the Muslim Brotherhood? How was Egypt under Muslim Brotherhood rule different from democracy in the United States?

7. **Compare the U.S. Constitutional Republic to Historical and Contemporary Forms of Government** Compare the structure of the U.S. constitutional republic to that of the Soviet Union. When writing the paragraph, consider the following: Communist Party of the Soviet Union; general secretary; Politburo; Supreme Soviet.

8. **Compare the U.S. Constitutional Republic to Historical and Contemporary Forms of Government** Create an inquiry project that compares the U.S. constitutional republic to Afghanistan, including the struggle for Afghanistan and other countries to stabilize the region and promote democracy. Then share your findings in the form of a report. When creating your project, use the following process: Ask a question about Afghanistan that you want to learn more about. Plan the project by outlining goals and objectives. Research information using valid primary and secondary sources. Create the project. Improve the project by editing and reevaluating your goals and objectives. Present your project.

9. **Identify Major Traditions** Review and identify the impact of English common law and constitutionalism in the founding of the United States. Then write a paragraph that answers the following: Describe how the United States' court system was influenced by common law and the judicial system in the United Kingdom, and how common law in the United States addressed issues of liberty, rights, and responsibilities of individuals.

10. **Compare the U.S. Constitutional Republic to Contemporary Forms of Government** Create a visual presentation comparing the structure of the U.S. constitutional republic to that of the contemporary government in the United Kingdom. When creating the presentation, consider the following: prime minister; Parliament.

11. **Compare the U.S. Constitutional Republic to Historical Forms of Government** Write a paragraph comparing the U.S. constitutional republic to the authoritarian government in China. When writing the paragraph, consider the following: Communist Party; single-party vs. two-party system; elections.

12. **Compare the U.S. Constitutional Republic to Historical Forms of Government** Write a paragraph that answers the following: Compare and contrast the use of media or interest groups to influence governing decisions in the United States and China. Which method do you agree with more and why?

13. **Compare the U.S. Constitutional Republic to Contemporary Forms of Government** Use the following quote to write a paragraph comparing the rule of the British monarch with the President of the United States. When writing the paragraph, answer the following questions: What does "The British monarch reigns but does not rule" mean? How does the British monarch compare with the President of the United States?

"The British monarch reigns but does not rule."

14. **Analyze Advantages and Disadvantages** Write a paragraph that analyzes the advantages and disadvantages of the presidential system of government in Russia. When writing the paragraph, consider the following: checks and balances; policy control; head of state and government; centralized leadership.

15. **Analyze Advantages and Disadvantages** Write a paragraph that analyzes the advantages and disadvantages of the parliamentary system of government in the United Kingdom. When writing the paragraph, consider the following: sovereignty; elections; prime minister.

16. **Write About the Essential Question Write an essay on the Essential Question: What makes a government successful?** Use evidence from your study of this Topic to support your answer.

Stock Connection Blue/Alamy

Constitution Quick Study Guide

Preamble

Articles

Article I. Legislative Department

Section 1.	Legislative Power, the Congress
Section 2.	House of Representatives
Section 3.	Senate
Section 4.	Elections and Meetings
Section 5.	Legislative Proceedings
Section 6.	Compensation, Immunities, and Disabilities of Members
Section 7.	Revenue Bills; President's Veto
Section 8.	Powers of Congress
Section 9.	Powers Denied to Congress
Section 10.	Powers Denied to the States

Article II. Executive Department

Section 1.	Executive Power; The President; Term; Election; Qualifications; Compensation; Oath of Office
Section 2.	President's Powers and Duties
Section 3.	President's Powers and Duties
Section 4.	Impeachment

Article III. Judicial Department

Section 1.	Judicial Power; Courts; Terms of Office
Section 2.	Jurisdiction
Section 3.	Treason

Article IV. Relations Among the States

Section 1.	Full Faith and Credit
Section 2.	Privileges and Immunities of Citizens
Section 3.	New States, Territories
Section 4.	Protection Afforded to States by the Nation

Article V. Provisions for Amendment

Article VI. Public Debts; Supremacy of National Law; Oath

Section 1.	Validity of Debts
Section 2.	Supremacy of National Law
Section 3.	Oaths of Office

Article VII. Ratification of Constitution

Amendments

1st Amendment:	**Freedom of Religion, Speech, Press, Assembly, and Petition**
2nd Amendment:	**Right to Keep, Bear Arms**
3rd Amendment:	**Lodging Troops in Private Homes**
4th Amendment:	**Search, Seizures, Proper Warrants**
5th Amendment:	**Criminal Proceedings, Due Process, Eminent Domain**
6th Amendment:	**Criminal Proceedings**
7th Amendment:	**Jury Trials in Civil Cases**
8th Amendment:	**Bail; Cruel, Unusual Punishment**
9th Amendment:	**Unenumerated Rights**
10th Amendment:	**Powers Reserved to the States**
11th Amendment:	**Suits Against the States**
12th Amendment:	**Election of President and Vice President**
13th Amendment:	**Slavery and Involuntary Servitude**
Section 1.	Slavery and Involuntary Servitude Prohibited
Section 2.	Power of Congress
14th Amendment:	**Rights of Citizens**
Section 1.	Citizenship; Privileges and Immunities; Due Process; Equal Protection
Section 2.	Apportionment of Representation
Section 3.	Disqualification of Officers
Section 4.	Public Debt
Section 5.	Powers of Congress
15th Amendment:	**Right to Vote—Race, Color, Servitude**
Section 1.	Suffrage Not to Be Abridged
Section 2.	Power of Congress
16th Amendment:	**Income Tax**
17th Amendment:	**Popular Election of Senators**
Section 1.	Popular Election of Senators
Section 2.	Senate Vacancies
Section 3.	Inapplicable to Senators Previously Chosen
18th Amendment:	**Prohibition of Intoxicating Liquors**
Section 1.	Intoxicating Liquors Prohibited
Section 2.	Concurrent Power to Enforce
Section 3.	Time Limit on Ratification
19th Amendment:	**Equal Suffrage—Sex**
Section 1.	Suffrage Not to Be Abridged
Section 2.	Power of Congress
20th Amendment:	**Commencement of Terms; Sessions of Congress; Death or Disqualification of President-Elect**
Section 1.	Terms of President, Vice President, members of Congress
Section 2.	Sessions of Congress
Section 3.	Death or Disqualification of President-Elect
Section 4.	Congress to Provide for Certain Successors
Section 5.	Effective Date
Section 6.	Time Limit on Ratification
21st Amendment:	**Repeal of 18th Amendment**
Section 1.	Repeal of Prohibition
Section 2.	Transportation, Importation of Intoxicating Liquors
Section 3.	Time Limit on Ratification
22nd Amendment:	**Presidential Tenure**
Section 1.	Restriction on Number of Terms
Section 2.	Time Limit on Ratification
23rd Amendment:	**Inclusion of District of Columbia in Presidential Election Systems**
Section 1.	Presidential Electors for District
Section 2.	Power of Congress
24th Amendment:	**Right to Vote in Federal Elections—Tax Payment**
Section 1.	Suffrage Not to Be Abridged
Section 2.	Power of Congress
25th Amendment:	**Presidential Succession; Vice Presidential Vacancy; Presidential Inability**
Section 1.	Presidential Succession
Section 2.	Vice Presidential Vacancy
Section 3.	Presidential Inability
26th Amendment:	**Right to Vote—Age**
Section 1.	Suffrage Not to Be Abridged
Section 2.	Power of Congress
27th Amendment:	**Congressional Pay**

The Preamble states the broad purposes the Constitution is intended to serve—to establish a government that provides for greater cooperation among the States, ensures justice and peace, provides for defense against foreign enemies, promotes the general well-being of the people, and secures liberty now and in the future. The phrase We the People emphasizes the twin concepts of popular sovereignty and of representative government.

PREAMBLE

We the People of the United States, in Order to form a more perfect Union, establish Justice, insure domestic Tranquility, provide for the common defence, promote the general Welfare, and secure the Blessings of Liberty to ourselves and our Posterity, do ordain and establish this Constitution for the United States of America.

Legislative Department

Section 1. Legislative power; Congress

Congress, the nation's lawmaking body, is bicameral in form; that is, it is composed of two houses: the Senate and the House of Representatives. The Framers of the Constitution purposely separated the lawmaking power from the power to enforce the laws (Article II, the Executive Branch) and the power to interpret them (Article III, the Judicial Branch). This system of separation of powers is supplemented by a system of checks and balances; that is, in several provisions the Constitution gives to each of the three branches various powers with which it may restrain the actions of the other two branches.

Article I.

Section 1.

All legislative Powers herein granted shall be vested in a Congress of the United States, which shall consist of a Senate and House of Representatives.

Section 2. House of Representatives

▶ **Clause 1. Election** Electors means voters. Members of the House of Representatives are elected every two years. Each State must permit the same persons to vote for United States representatives as it permits to vote for the members of the larger house of its own legislature. The 17th Amendment (1913) extends this requirement to the qualification of voters for United States senators.

▶ **Clause 2. Qualifications** A member of the House of Representatives must be at least 25 years old, an American citizen for seven years, and a resident of the State he or she represents. In addition, political custom requires that a representative also reside in the district from which he or she is elected.

▶ **Clause 3. Apportionment** The number of representatives each State is entitled to is based on its population, which is counted every 10 years in the census. Congress reapportions the seats among the States after each census. In the Reapportionment Act of 1929, Congress fixed the permanent size of the House at 435 members with each State having at least one representative. Today there is one House seat for approximately every 700,000 persons in the population.

The words "three-fifths of all other persons" referred to slaves and reflected the Three-Fifths Compromise reached by the Framers at Philadelphia in 1787; the phrase was made obsolete, was in effect repealed, by the 13th Amendment in 1865.

* The gray words indicate portions of the Constitution altered by subsequent amendments to the document.

Section 2.

▶1. The House of Representatives shall be composed of Members chosen every second Year by the People of the several States, and the Electors in each State shall have the Qualifications requisite for Electors of the most numerous Branch of the State Legislature.

▶ 2. No Person shall be a Representative who shall not have attained to the age of twenty-five Years, and been seven Years a Citizen of the United States, and who shall not, when elected, be an Inhabitant of that State in which he shall be chosen.

▶ 3. Representatives and direct Taxes* shall be apportioned among the several States which may be included within this Union, according to their respective Numbers, which shall be determined by adding to the whole Number of free Persons, including those bound to Service for a Term of Years and excluding Indians not taxed, three fifths of all other Persons. The actual Enumeration shall be made within three Years after the first Meeting of the Congress of the United States, and within every subsequent term of ten Years, in such Manner as they shall by Law direct. The Number of Representatives shall not exceed one for every thirty Thousand, but each State shall have at Least one Representative; and, until such enumeration shall be made, the State of New Hampshire shall be entitled to choose three, Massachusetts eight, Rhode Island and Providence Plantations one, Connecticut five, New York six, New Jersey four, Pennsylvania eight, Delaware one, Maryland six, Virginia ten, North Carolina five, South Carolina five, and Georgia three.

▶ **Clause 4. Vacancies** The executive authority refers to the governor of a State. If a member leaves office or dies before the expiration of his or her term, the governor is to call a special election to fill the vacancy.

▶4. When vacancies happen in the Representation from any State, the Executive Authority thereof shall issue Writs of Election to fill such Vacancies.

▶5. The House of Representatives shall choose their Speaker and other Officers; and shall have the sole Power of Impeachment.

▶ **Clause 5. Officers; impeachment** The House elects a Speaker, customarily chosen from the majority party in the House. Impeachment means accusation. The House has the exclusive power to impeach, or accuse, civil officers; the Senate (Article I, Section 3, Clause 6) has the exclusive power to try those impeached by the House.

Section 3.

▶1. The Senate of the United States shall be composed of two Senators from each State chosen by the Legislature thereof for six Years; and each Senator shall have one Vote.

▶2. Immediately after they shall be assembled in Consequences of the first Election, they shall be divided, as equally as may be, into three Classes. The Seats of the Senators of the first Class shall be vacated at the Expiration of the second Year; of the second Class, at the Expiration of the fourth Year; and of the third Class, at the Expiration of the sixth Year; so that one-third may be chosen every second Year; and if Vacancies happen by Resignation, or otherwise, during the Recess of the Legislature of any State, the Executive thereof may make temporary Appointments until the next Meeting of the Legislature, which shall then fill such Vacancies.

▶3. No Person shall be a Senator who shall not have attained to the Age of thirty Years, and been nine Years a Citizen of the United States, and who shall not, when elected, be an Inhabitant of that State for which he shall be chosen.

▶4. The Vice President of the United States shall be President of the Senate but shall have no Vote, unless they be equally divided.

▶5. The Senate shall choose their other Officers, and also a President pro tempore, in the Absence of the Vice President, or when he shall exercise the Office of President of the United States.

▶6. The Senate shall have the sole Power to try all Impeachments. When sitting for that Purpose, they shall be on Oath or Affirmation. When the President of the United States is tried, the Chief Justice shall preside: And no Person shall be convicted without the Concurrence of two thirds of the Members present.

▶7. Judgment in Cases of Impeachment shall not extend further than to removal from Office, and disqualification to hold and enjoy any Office of honor, Trust, or Profit under the United States: but the Party convicted shall nevertheless be liable and subject to Indictment, Trial, Judgment and Punishment, according to Law.

Section 3. Senate

▶ **Clause 1. Composition, election, term** Each State has two senators. Each serves for six years and has one vote. Originally, senators were not elected directly by the people, but by each State's legislature. The 17th Amendment, added in 1913, provides for the popular election of senators.

▶ **Clause 2. Classification** The senators elected in 1788 were divided into three groups so that the Senate could become a "continuing body." One-third of the Senate's seats are up for election every two years.

The 17th Amendment provides that a Senate vacancy is to be filled at a special election called by the governor; State law may also permit the governor to appoint a successor to serve until that election is held.

▶ **Clause 3. Qualifications** A senator must be at least 30 years old, a citizen for at least nine years, and must live in the State from which elected.

▶ **Clause 4. Presiding officer** The Vice President presides over the Senate, but may vote only to break a tie.

▶ **Clause 5. Other officers** The Senate chooses its own officers, including a president pro tempore to preside when the Vice President is not there.

▶ **Clause 6. Impeachment trials** The Senate conducts the trials of those officials impeached by the House. The Vice President presides unless the President is on trial, in which case the Chief Justice of the United States does so. A conviction requires the votes of two-thirds of the senators present.

No President has ever been convicted. In 1868 the House voted eleven articles of impeachment against President Andrew Johnson, but the Senate fell one vote short of convicting him. In 1974 President Richard M. Nixon resigned the presidency in the face of almost certain impeachment by the House. The House brought two articles of impeachment against President Bill Clinton in late 1998. Neither charge was supported by even a simple majority vote in the Senate, on February 12, 1999.

▶ **Clause 7. Penalty on conviction** The punishment of an official convicted in an impeachment case has always been removal from office. The Senate can also bar a convicted person from ever holding any federal office, but it is not required to do so. A convicted person can also be tried and punished in a regular court for any crime involved in the impeachment case.

Section 4. Elections and Meetings

▶ **Clause 1. Election In 1842** Congress required that representatives be elected from districts within each State with more than one seat in the House. The districts in each State are drawn by that State's legislature. Seven States now have only one seat in the House: Alaska, Delaware, Montana, North Dakota, South Dakota, Vermont, and Wyoming. The 1842 law also directed that representatives be elected in each State on the same day: the Tuesday after the first Monday in November of every even-numbered year. In 1914 Congress also set that same date for the election of senators.

▶ **Clause 2. Sessions Congress** must meet at least once a year. The 20th Amendment (1933) changed the opening date to January 3.

Section 4.

▶1. The Times, Places and Manner of holding Elections for Senators and Representatives, shall be prescribed in each State by the Legislature thereof; but the Congress may at any time by law make or alter such Regulations, except as to the Places of choosing Senators.

▶2. The Congress shall assemble at least once in every Year, and such Meeting shall be on the first Monday in December, unless they shall by Law appoint a different Day.

Section 5. Legislative Proceedings

▶ **Clause 1. Admission of members; quorum** In 1969 the Supreme Court held that the House cannot exclude any member-elect who satisfies the qualifications set out in Article I, Section 2, Clause 2.

A majority in the House (218 members) or Senate (51) constitutes a quorum. In practice, both houses often proceed with less than a quorum present. However, any member may raise a point of order (demand a "quorum call"). If a roll call then reveals less than a majority of the members present, that chamber must either adjourn or the sergeant at arms must be ordered to round up absent members.

▶ **Clause 2. Rules** Each house has adopted detailed rules to guide its proceedings. Each house may discipline members for unacceptable conduct; expulsion requires a two-thirds vote.

▶ **Clause 3. Record** Each house must keep and publish a record of its meetings. The Congressional Record is published for every day that either house of Congress is in session, and provides a written record of all that is said and done on the floor of each house each session.

▶ **Clause 4. Adjournment** Once in session, neither house may suspend (recess) its work for more than three days without the approval of the other house. Both houses must always meet in the same location.

Section 5.

▶1. Each House shall be the Judge of the Elections, Returns and Qualifications of its own Members, and a Majority of each shall constitute a Quorum to do Business; but a smaller Number may adjourn from day to day, and may be authorized to compel the Attendance of absent Members, in such Manner, and under such Penalties, as each House may provide.

▶2. Each House may determine the Rules of its Proceedings, punish its Members for disorderly Behavior, and, with the Concurrence of two thirds, expel a Member.

▶3. Each House shall keep a Journal of its Proceedings, and from time to time publish the same, excepting such Parts as may in their Judgment require Secrecy; and the Yeas and Nays of the Members of either House on any question shall, at the Desire of one fifth of those Present, be entered on the Journal.

▶4. Neither House, during the Session of Congress, shall, without the Consent of the other, adjourn for more than three days, nor to any other Place than that in which the two Houses shall be sitting.

Section 6.

▶1. The Senators and Representatives shall receive a Compensation for their Services, to be ascertained by Law, and paid out of the Treasury of the United States. They shall in all Cases, except Treason, Felony, and Breach of the Peace, be privileged from Arrest during their Attendance at the Session of their respective Houses, and in going to and returning from the same; and for any Speech or Debate in either House, they shall not be questioned in any other Place.

Section 6. Compensation, Immunities, and Disabilities of Members

▶ **Clause 1. Salaries; immunities** Each house sets its members' salaries, paid by the United States; the 27th Amendment (1992) modified this pay-setting power. This provision establishes "legislative immunity." The purpose of this immunity is to allow members to speak and debate freely in Congress itself. Treason is strictly defined in Article III, Section 3. A felony is any serious crime. A breach of the peace is any indictable offense less than treason or a felony; this exemption from arrest is of little real importance today.

▶2. No Senator or Representative shall, during the Time for which he was elected, be appointed to any civil Office under the Authority of the United States, which shall have been created, or the Emoluments whereof shall have been increased during such time; and no Person holding any Office under the United States, shall be a Member of either House during his Continuance in Office.

▶ **Clause 2. Restrictions on office holding** No sitting member of either house may be appointed to an office in the executive or in the judicial branch if that position was created or its salary was increased during that member's current elected term. The second part of this clause—forbidding any person serving in either the executive or the judicial branch from also serving in Congress—reinforces the principle of separation of powers.

Section 7.

▶1. All Bills for raising Revenue shall originate in the House of Representatives; but the Senate may propose or concur with amendments as on other Bills.

Section 7. Revenue Bills, President's Veto

▶ **Clause 1. Revenue bills** All bills that raise money must originate in the House. However, the Senate has the power to amend any revenue bill sent to it from the lower house.

▶2. Every Bill which shall have passed the House of Representatives and the Senate, shall, before it become a law, be presented to the President of the United States: If he approve, he shall sign it, but if not he shall return it, with his Objections to that House in which it shall have originated, who shall enter the Objections at large on their Journal, and proceed to reconsider it. If after such Reconsideration two thirds of the House shall agree to pass the Bill, it shall be sent, together with the Objections, to the other House, by which it shall likewise be reconsidered, and if approved by two thirds of that House, it shall become a Law. But in all such Cases the Votes of both Houses shall be determined by Yeas and Nays, and the Names of the Persons voting for and against the Bill shall be entered on the Journal of each House respectively. If any Bill shall not be returned by the President within ten Days (Sunday excepted) after it shall have been presented to him, the Same shall be a law, in like Manner as if he had signed it, unless the Congress by their Adjournment, prevent its Return, in which Case it shall not be a Law.

▶ **Clause 2. Enactment of laws; veto** Once both houses have passed a bill, it must be sent to the President. The President may (1) sign the bill, thus making it law; (2) veto the bill, whereupon it must be returned to the house in which it originated; or (3) allow the bill to become law without signature, by not acting upon it within 10 days of its receipt from Congress, not counting Sundays. The President has a fourth option at the end of a congressional session: If he does not act on a measure within 10 days, and Congress adjourns during that period, the bill dies; the "pocket veto" has been applied to it. A presidential veto may be overridden by a two-thirds vote in each house.

▶3. Every Order, Resolution, or Vote to which the Concurrence of the Senate and House of Representatives may be necessary (except on a question of adjournment) shall be presented to the President of the United States; and before the Same shall take Effect, shall be approved by him, or, being disapproved by him, shall be repassed by two thirds of the Senate and House of Representatives, according to the Rules and Limitations prescribed in the Case of a Bill.

▶ **Clause 3. Other measures** This clause refers to joint resolutions, measures Congress often passes to deal with unusual, temporary, or ceremonial matters. A joint resolution passed by Congress and signed by the President has the force of law, just as a bill does. As a matter of custom, a joint resolution proposing an amendment to the Constitution is not submitted to the President for signature or veto. Concurrent and simple resolutions do not have the force of law and, therefore, are not submitted to the President.

Section 8. Powers of Congress

▶ **Clause 1.** The 18 separate clauses in this section set out 27 of the many expressed powers the Constitution grants to Congress. In this clause Congress is given the power to levy and provide for the collection of various kinds of taxes, in order to finance the operations of the government. All federal taxes must be levied at the same rates throughout the country.

▶ **Clause 2.** Congress has power to borrow money to help finance the government. Federal borrowing is most often done through the sale of bonds on which interest is paid. The Constitution does not limit the amount the government may borrow.

▶ **Clause 3.** This clause, the Commerce Clause, gives Congress the power to regulate both foreign and interstate trade. Much of what Congress does, it does on the basis of its commerce power.

▶ **Clause 4.** Congress has the exclusive power to determine how aliens may become citizens of the United States. Congress may also pass laws relating to bankruptcy.

▶ **Clause 5.** has the power to establish and require the use of uniform gauges of time, distance, weight, volume, area, and the like.

▶ **Clause 6.** Congress has the power to make it a federal crime to falsify the coins, paper money, bonds, stamps, and the like of the United States.

▶ **Clause 7.** Congress has the power to provide for and regulate the transportation and delivery of mail; "post offices" are those buildings and other places where mail is deposited for dispatch; "post roads" include all routes over or upon which mail is carried.

▶ **Clause 8.** Congress has the power to provide for copyrights and patents. A copyright gives an author or composer the exclusive right to control the reproduction, publication, and sale of literary, musical, or other creative work. A patent gives a person the exclusive right to control the manufacture or sale of his or her invention.

▶ **Clause 9.** Congress has the power to create the lower federal courts, all of the several federal courts that function beneath the Supreme Court.

▶ **Clause 10.** Congress has the power to prohibit, as a federal crime: (1) certain acts committed outside the territorial jurisdiction of the United States, and (2) the commission within the United States of any wrong against any nation with which we are at peace.

Section 8.

The Congress shall have Power

▶1. To lay and collect Taxes, Duties, Imposts and Excises to pay the Debts and provide for the common Defence and general Welfare of the United States; but all Duties, Imposts and Excises, shall be uniform throughout the United States;

▶2. To borrow Money on the credit of the United States;

▶3. To regulate Commerce with foreign Nations, and among the several States, and with the Indian Tribes;

▶4. To establish an uniform Rule of Naturalization, and uniform Laws on the subject of Bankruptcies throughout the United States;

▶5. To coin Money, regulate the Value thereof, and of foreign Coin, and fix the Standard of Weights and Measures;

▶6. To provide for the Punishment of counterfeiting the Securities and current Coin of the United States;

▶7. To establish Post Offices and post Roads;

▶8. To promote the Progress of Science and useful Arts, by securing, for limited Times to Authors and Inventors the exclusive Right to their respective Writings and Discoveries;

▶9. To constitute Tribunals inferior to the supreme Court;

▶10. To define and punish Piracies and Felonies committed on the high Seas, and Offences against the Law of nations;

▶ 11. To declare War, grant Letters of Marque and Reprisal, and make Rules concerning Captures on Land and Water;

▶ **Clause 11.** Only Congress can declare war. However, the President, as commander in chief of the armed forces (Article II, Section 2, Clause 1), can make war without such a formal declaration. Letters of marque and reprisal are commissions authorizing private persons to outfit vessels (privateers) to capture and destroy enemy ships in time of war; they were forbidden in international law by the Declaration of Paris of 1856, and the United States has honored the ban since the Civil War.

▶ 12. To raise and support Armies; but no Appropriation of Money to that Use shall be for a longer Term than two Years;

▶ 13. To provide and maintain a Navy;

▶ **Clauses 12 and 13.** Congress has the power to provide for and maintain the nation's armed forces. It established the air force as an independent element of the armed forces in 1947, an exercise of its inherent powers in foreign relations and national defense. The two-year limit on spending for the army insures civilian control of the military.

▶ 14. To make Rules for the Government and Regulation of the land and naval Forces;

▶ **Clause 14.** Today these rules are set out in three principle statutes: the Uniform Code of Military Justice, passed by Congress in 1950, and the Military Justice Acts of 1958 and 1983.

▶ 15. To provide for calling forth the Militia to execute the Laws of the Union, suppress Insurrections and repel Invasions;

▶ 16. To provide for organizing, arming, and disciplining the Militia, and for governing such Part of them as may be employed in the Service of the United States, reserving to the States respectively the Appointment of the Officers, and the Authority of training the Militia according to the discipline prescribed by Congress;

▶ **Clauses 15 and 16.** In the National Defense Act of 1916, Congress made each State's militia (volunteer army) a part of the National Guard. Today, Congress and the States cooperate in its maintenance. Ordinarily, each State's National Guard is under the command of that State's governor; but Congress has given the President the power to call any or all of those units into federal service when necessary.

▶ 17. To exercise exclusive Legislation in all Cases whatsoever, over such District (not exceeding ten Miles square) as may, by Cession of Particular States, and the Acceptance of Congress, become the Seat of the Government of the United States, and to exercise like Authority over all Places purchased by the Consent of the Legislature of the State in which the Same shall be, for the Erection of Forts, Magazines, Arsenals, Dockyards and other needful Buildings;—And

▶ **Clause 17.** In 1791 Congress accepted land grants from Maryland and Virginia and established the District of Columbia for the nation's capital. Assuming Virginia's grant would never be needed, Congress returned it in 1846. Today, the elected government of the District's 69 square miles operates under the authority of Congress. Congress also has the power to acquire other lands from the States for various federal purposes.

▶ 18. To make all Laws which shall be necessary and proper for carrying into Execution the foregoing Powers and all other Powers vested by this Constitution in the Government of the United States, or in any Department or Officer thereof.

▶ **Clause 18.** This is the Necessary and Proper Clause, also often called the Elastic Clause. It is the constitutional basis for the many and far-reaching implied powers of the Federal Government.

Section 9.

▶ 1. The Migration or Importation of such Persons as any of the States now existing shall think proper to admit, shall not be prohibited by the Congress prior to the Year one thousand eight hundred and eight, but a Tax or duty may be imposed on such Importation, not exceeding ten dollars for each Person.

Section 9. Powers Denied to Congress

▶ **Clause 1.** The phrase "such persons" referred to slaves. This provision was part of the Commerce Compromise, one of the bargains struck in the writing of the Constitution. Congress outlawed the slave trade in 1808.

▶ **Clause 2.** A writ of habeas corpus, the "great writ of liberty," is a court order directing a sheriff, warden, or other public officer, or a private person, who is detaining another to "produce the body" of the one being held in order that the legality of the detention may be determined by the court.

▶ **Clause 3.** A bill of attainder is a legislative act that inflicts punishment without a judicial trial. See Article I, Section 10, and Article III, Section 3, Clause 2. An ex post facto law is any criminal law that operates retroactively to the disadvantage of the accused. See Article I, Section 10.

▶ **Clause 4.** A capitation tax is literally a "head tax," a tax levied on each person in the population. A direct tax is one paid directly to the government by the taxpayer—for example, an income or a property tax; an indirect tax is one paid to another private party who then pays it to the government—for example, a sales tax. This provision was modified by the 16th Amendment (1913), giving Congress the power to levy "taxes on incomes, from whatever source derived."

▶ **Clause 5.** This provision was a part of the Commerce Compromise made by the Framers in 1787. Congress has the power to tax imported goods, however.

▶ **Clause 6.** All ports within the United States must be treated alike by Congress as it exercises its taxing and commerce powers. Congress cannot tax goods sent by water from one State to another, nor may it give the ports of one State any legal advantage over those of another.

▶ **Clause 7.** This clause gives Congress its vastly important "power of the purse," a major check on presidential power. Federal money can be spent only in those amounts and for those purposes expressly authorized by an act of Congress. All federal income and spending must be accounted for, regularly and publicly.

▶ **Clause 8.** This provision, preventing the establishment of a nobility, reflects the principle that "all men are created equal." It was also intended to discourage foreign attempts to bribe or otherwise corrupt officers of the government.

Section 10. Powers Denied to the States

▶ **Clause 1.** The States are not sovereign governments and so cannot make agreements or otherwise negotiate with foreign states; the power to conduct foreign relations is an exclusive power of the National Government. The power to coin money is also an exclusive power of the National Government. Several powers forbidden to the National Government are here also forbidden to the States.

▶ **Clause 2.** This provision relates to foreign, not interstate, commerce. Only Congress, not the States, can tax imports; and the States are, like Congress, forbidden the power to tax exports.

▶2. The Privilege of the Writ of Habeas Corpus shall not be suspended, unless when in Cases of Rebellion or Invasion the public safety may require it.

▶3. No Bill of Attainder or ex post facto Law shall be passed.

▶4. No Capitation, or other direct, Tax shall be laid, unless in Proportion to the Census of Enumeration hereinbefore directed to be taken.

▶5. No Tax or Duty shall be laid on Articles exported from any State.

▶6. No Preference shall be given by any Regulation of Commerce or Revenue to the Ports of one State over those of another: nor shall Vessels bound to, or from, one State, be obliged to enter, clear or pay Duties in another.

▶7. No Money shall be drawn from the Treasury, but in Consequence of Appropriations made by Law; and a regular Statement and Account of the Receipts and Expenditures of all public Money shall be published from time to time.

▶8. No Title of Nobility shall be granted by the United States: And no Person holding any Office of Profit or Trust under them, shall, without the Consent of the Congress, accept of any present, Emolument, Office, or Title, of any kind whatever, from any King, Prince, or foreign State.

Section 10.

▶1. No State shall enter into any Treaty, Alliance, or Confederation; grant Letters of Marque and Reprisal; coin Money; emit Bills of Credit; make any Thing but gold and silver Coin a Tender in Payment of Debts; pass any Bill of Attainder, ex post facto Law, or Law impairing the Obligation of Contracts, or grant any Title of Nobility.

▶2. No State shall, without the Consent of the Congress, lay any Imposts or Duties on Imports or Exports, except what may be absolutely necessary for executing its inspection Laws; and the net Produce of all Duties and Imposts, laid by any State on Imports or Exports, shall be for the Use of the Treasury of the United States; and all such Laws shall be subject to the Revision and Control of the Congress.

▶3. No State shall, without the Consent of Congress, lay any Duty of Tonnage, keep Troops, or Ships of War in time of Peace, enter into any Agreement or Compact with another State, or with a foreign Power, or engage in War, unless actually invaded, or in such imminent Danger as will not admit of delay.

▶ **Clause 3.** A duty of tonnage is a tax laid on ships according to their cargo capacity. Each State has a constitutional right to provide for and maintain a militia; but no State may keep a standing army or navy. The several restrictions here prevent the States from assuming powers that the Constitution elsewhere grants to the National Government.

Article II

Section 1.

Executive Department

Section 1. President and Vice President

▶1. The executive Power shall be vested in a President of the United States of America. He shall hold his Office during the Term of four Years, and, together with the Vice President, chosen for the same Term, be elected as follows:

▶ **Clause 1. Executive power, term** This clause gives to the President the very broad "executive power," the power to enforce the laws and otherwise administer the public policies of the United States. It also sets the length of the presidential (and vice-presidential) term of office; see the 22nd Amendment (1951), which places a limit on presidential (but not vice-presidential) tenure.

▶2. Each State shall appoint, in such Manner as the Legislature thereof may direct, a Number of Electors, equal to the whole Number of Senators and Representatives to which the State may be entitled in the Congress: but no Senator or Representative, or Person holding an Office of Trust or Profit, under the United States, shall be appointed an Elector.

▶ **Clause 2. Electoral college** This clause establishes the "electoral college," although the Constitution does not use that term. It is a body of presidential electors chosen in each State, and it selects the President and Vice President every four years. The number of electors chosen in each State equals the number of senators and representatives that State has in Congress.

▶3. The Electors shall meet in their respective States, and vote by Ballot for two Persons, of whom one at least shall not be an Inhabitant of the same State with themselves. And they shall make a List of all the Persons voted for, and of the Number of Votes for each; which List they shall sign and certify, and transmit sealed to the Seat of the Government of the United States, directed to the President of the Senate. The President of the Senate shall, in the Presence of the Senate and House of Representatives, open all the Certificates, and the Votes shall then be counted. The Person having the greatest Number of Votes shall be the President, if such Number be a majority of the whole Number of Electors appointed; and if there be more than one who have such Majority, and have an equal Number of Votes, then, the House of Representatives shall immediately choose by Ballot one of them for President; and if no Person have a Majority, then from the five highest on the List the said House shall in like Manner choose the President. But in choosing the President, the Votes shall be taken by States, the Representatives from each State having one Vote; a quorum for this Purpose shall consist of a Member or Members from two thirds of the States, and a Majority of all the States shall be necessary to a Choice. In every Case, after the Choice of the President, the Person having the greatest Number of Votes of the Electors shall be the Vice President. But if there should remain two or more who have equal Votes, the Senate shall choose from them by Ballot the Vice President.

▶ **Clause 3. Election of President and Vice President** This clause was replaced by the 12th Amendment in 1804.

▶ **Clause 4. Date** Congress has set the date for the choosing of electors as the Tuesday after the first Monday in November every fourth year, and for the casting of electoral votes as the Monday after the second Wednesday in December of that year.

▶4. The Congress may determine the Time of choosing the Electors, and the Day on which they shall give their Votes; which Day shall be the same throughout the United States.

▶ **Clause 5. Qualifications** The President must have been born a citizen of the United States, be at least 35 years old, and have been a resident of the United States for at least 14 years.

▶5. No Person except a natural born Citizen, or a Citizen of the United States, at the time of the Adoption of this Constitution, shall be eligible to the Office of President; neither shall any person be eligible to that Office who shall not have attained to the Age of thirty-five Years, and been fourteen Years a Resident within the United States.

▶ **Clause 6. Vacancy** This clause was modified by the 25th Amendment (1967), which provides expressly for the succession of the Vice President, for the filling of a vacancy in the Vice Presidency, and for the determination of presidential inability.

▶6. In Case of the Removal of the President from Office, or of his Death, Resignation, or Inability to discharge the Powers and Duties of the said Office, the Same shall devolve on the Vice President, and the Congress may by Law provide for the Case of Removal, Death, Resignation or Inability, both of the President and Vice President, declaring what Officer shall then act as President, and such Officer shall act accordingly, until the Disability be removed, or a President shall be elected.

▶ **Clause 7. Compensation** The President now receives a salary of $400,000 and a taxable expense account of $50,000 a year. Those amounts cannot be changed during a presidential term; thus, Congress cannot use the President's compensation as a bargaining tool to influence executive decisions. The phrase "any other emolument" means, in effect, any valuable gift; it does not mean that the President cannot be provided with such benefits of office as the White House, extensive staff assistance, and much else.

▶7. The President shall, at stated Times, receive for his Services, a Compensation, which shall neither be increased nor diminished during the Period for which he shall have been elected, and he shall not receive within that Period any other Emolument from the United States, or any of them.

▶ **Clause 8. Oath of office** The Chief Justice of the United States regularly administers this oath or affirmation, but any judicial officer may do so. Thus, Calvin Coolidge was sworn into office in 1923 by his father, a justice of the peace in Vermont.

▶8. Before he enter on the Execution of his Office, he shall take the following Oath or Affirmation:
"I do solemnly swear (or affirm) that I will faithfully execute the Office of President of the United States, and will to the best of my Ability, preserve, protect and defend the Constitution of the United States."

Section 2. President's Powers and Duties

▶ **Clause 1. Military, civil powers** The President, a civilian, heads the nation's armed forces, a key element in the Constitution's insistence on civilian control of the military. The President's power to "require the opinion, in writing" provides the constitutional basis for the Cabinet. The President's power to grant reprieves and pardons, the power of clemency, extends only to federal cases.

Section 2.

▶1. The President shall be Commander in Chief of the Army and Navy of the United States, and of the Militia of the several States, when called into the actual Service of the United States; he may require the Opinion, in writing, of the principal Officer in each of the executive Departments, upon any Subject relating to the Duties of their respective Offices, and he shall have Power to Grant Reprieves and Pardons for Offences against the United States, except in Cases of Impeachment.

2. He shall have Power, by and with the Advice and Consent of the Senate, to make Treaties, provided two thirds of the Senators present concur; and he shall nominate, and by and with the Advice and Consent of the Senate, shall appoint Ambassadors, other public Ministers and Consuls, Judges of the supreme Court, and all other Officers of the United States, whose Appointments are not herein otherwise provided for, and which shall be established by Law: but the Congress may by Law vest the Appointment of such inferior Officers, as they think proper, in the President alone, in the Courts of Law, or in the Heads of Departments.

▶ **Clause 2. Treaties, appointments** The President has the sole power to make treaties; to become effective, a treaty must be approved by a two-thirds vote in the Senate. In practice, the President can also make executive agreements with foreign governments; these pacts, which are frequently made and usually deal with routine matters, do not require Senate consent. The President appoints the principal officers of the executive branch and all federal judges; the "inferior officers" are those who hold lesser posts.

3. The President shall have Power to fill up all Vacancies that may happen during the Recess of the Senate, by granting Commissions which shall expire at the End of their next Session.

▶ **Clause 3. Recess appointments** When the Senate is not in session, appointments that require Senate consent can be made by the President on a temporary basis, as "recess appointments." Recess appointments are valid only to the end of the congressional term in which they are made.

Section 3.

He shall from time to time give to the Congress Information of the State of the Union, and recommend to their Consideration such Measures as he shall judge necessary and expedient; he may, on extraordinary Occasions, convene both Houses, or either of them, and in Case of Disagreement between them, with Respect to the Time of Adjournment, he may adjourn them to such Time as he shall think proper; he shall receive Ambassadors and other public Ministers; he shall take Care that the Laws be faithfully executed, and shall Commission all the Officers of the United States.

Section 3. President's Powers and Duties

The President delivers a State of the Union Message to Congress soon after that body convenes each year. That message is delivered to the nation's lawmakers and, importantly, to the American people, as well. It is shortly followed by the proposed federal budget and an economic report; and the President may send special messages to Congress at any time. In all of these communications, Congress is urged to take those actions the Chief Executive finds to be in the national interest. The President also has the power: to call special sessions of Congress; to adjourn Congress if its two houses cannot agree for that purpose; to receive the diplomatic representatives of other governments; to insure the proper execution of all federal laws; and to empower federal officers to hold their posts and perform their duties.

Section 4.

The President, Vice President and all Civil Officers of the United States, shall be removed from Office on Impeachment for and Conviction of, Treason, Bribery, or other high Crimes and Misdemeanors.

Section 4. Impeachment

The Constitution outlines the impeachment process in Article I, Section 2, Clause 5 and in Section 3, Clauses 6 and 7.

Article III

Section 1.

The judicial Power of the United States, shall be vested in one supreme Court, and in such inferior Courts as the Congress may from time to time ordain and establish. The Judges, both of the supreme and inferior Courts, shall hold their Offices during good Behaviour, and shall, at stated Times, receive for their Services, a Compensation, which shall not be diminished during their Continuance in Office.

Judicial Department

Section 1. Judicial Power, Courts, Terms of Office

The judicial power conferred here is the power of federal courts to hear and decide cases, disputes between the government and individuals and between private persons (parties). The Constitution creates only the Supreme Court of the United States; it gives to Congress the power to establish other, lower federal courts (Article I, Section 8, Clause 9) and to fix the size of the Supreme Court. The words "during good Behaviour" mean, in effect, for life.

Section 2. Jurisdiction

▶ **Clause 1. Cases to be heard** This clause sets out the jurisdiction of the federal courts; that is, it identifies those cases that may be tried in those courts. The federal courts can hear and decide—have jurisdiction over—a case depending on either the subject matter or the parties involved in that case. The jurisdiction of the federal courts in cases involving States was substantially restricted by the 11th Amendment in 1795.

▶ **Clause 2. Supreme Court jurisdiction** Original jurisdiction refers to the power of a court to hear a case in the first instance, not on appeal from a lower court. Appellate jurisdiction refers to a court's power to hear a case on appeal from a lower court, from the court in which the case was originally tried. This clause gives the Supreme Court both original and appellate jurisdiction. However, nearly all of the cases the High Court hears are brought to it on appeal from the lower federal courts and the highest State courts.

▶ **Clause 3. Jury trial in criminal cases** A person accused of a federal crime is guaranteed the right to trial by jury in a federal court in the State where the crime was committed; see the 5th and 6th amendments. The right to trial by jury in serious criminal cases in the State courts is guaranteed by the 6th and 14th amendments.

Section 2.

▶1. The judicial Power shall extend to all Cases, in Law and Equity, arising under this Constitution, the Laws of the United States, and Treaties made, or which shall be made, under their Authority;— to all Cases affecting Ambassadors, other public ministers, and Consuls;— to all Cases of Admiralty and maritime Jurisdiction;— to Controversies to which the United States shall be a Party;— to Controversies between two or more States;— between a State and Citizens of another State;— between Citizens of different States;— between Citizens of the same State claiming Lands under Grants of different States, and between a State, or the Citizens thereof, and foreign States, Citizens, or Subjects.

▶2. In all Cases affecting Ambassadors, other public Ministers and Consuls, and those in which a State shall be a Party, the supreme Court shall have original Jurisdiction. In all the other Cases before mentioned, the supreme Court shall have appellate Jurisdiction, both as to Law and Fact, with such Exceptions, and under such Regulations as the Congress shall make.

▶3. The trial of all Crimes, except in Cases of Impeachment, shall be by Jury; and such Trial shall be held in the State where the said Crimes shall have been committed; but when not committed within any State, the Trial shall be at such Place or Places as the Congress may by Law have directed.

Section 3. Treason

▶ **Clause 1. Definition** Treason is the only crime defined in the Constitution. The Framers intended the very specific definition here to prevent the loose use of the charge of treason—for example, against persons who criticize the government. Treason can be committed only in time of war and only by a citizen or a resident alien.

▶ **Clause 2. Punishment** Congress has provided that the punishment that a federal court may impose on a convicted traitor may range from a minimum of five years in prison and/or a $10,000 fine to a maximum of death; no person convicted of treason has ever been executed by the United States. No legal punishment can be imposed on the family or descendants of a convicted traitor. Congress has also made it a crime for any person (in either peace or wartime) to commit espionage or sabotage, to attempt to overthrow the government by force, or to conspire to do any of these things.

Section 3.

▶1. Treason against the United States shall consist only in levying War against them, or in adhering to their Enemies, giving them Aid and Comfort. No Person shall be convicted of Treason unless on the Testimony of two Witnesses to the same overt Act, or on Confession in open Court.

▶2. The Congress shall have Power to declare the Punishment of Treason, but no Attainder of Treason shall work Corruption of Blood, or Forfeiture except during the Life of the Person attainted.

Article IV

Section 1.

Full Faith and Credit shall be given in each State to the public Acts, Records, and judicial Proceedings of every other State. And the Congress may by general Laws prescribe the Manner in which such Acts, Records and Proceedings shall be proved, and the Effect thereof.

Section 2.

▶1. The Citizens of each State shall be entitled to all Privileges and Immunities of Citizens in the several States.

▶2. A Person charged in any State with Treason, Felony, or other Crime, who shall flee from justice, and be found in another State, shall on Demand of the executive Authority of the State from which he fled, be delivered up, to be removed to the State having Jurisdiction of the Crime.

▶3. No Person held to Service or Labor in one State, under the Laws thereof, escaping into another, shall, in Consequence of any Law or Regulation therein, be discharged from Service or Labor, but shall be delivered up on Claim of the Party to whom such Service or Labor may be due.

Section 3.

▶1. New States may be admitted by the Congress into this Union; but no new State shall be formed or erected within the Jurisdiction of any other State; nor any State be formed by the Junction of two or more States, or Parts of States, without the Consent of the Legislatures of the States concerned as well as of the Congress.

▶2. The Congress shall have Power to dispose of and make all needful Rules and Regulations respecting the Territory or other Property belonging to the United States; and nothing in this Constitution shall be so construed as to Prejudice any Claims of the United States, or of any particular State.

Section 4.

The United States shall guarantee to every State in this Union a Republican Form of Government, and shall protect each of them against Invasion; and on Application of the Legislature, or of the Executive (when the Legislature cannot be convened) against domestic Violence.

Relations Among States

Section 1. Full Faith and Credit

Each State must recognize the validity of the laws, public records, and court decisions of every other State.

Section 2. Privileges and Immunities of Citizens

▶ **Clause 1. Residents of other States** In effect, this clause means that no State may discriminate against the residents of other States; that is, a State's laws cannot draw unreasonable distinctions between its own residents and those of any of the other States. See Section 1 of the 14th Amendment.

▶ **Clause 2. Extradition** The process of returning a fugitive to another State is known as "interstate rendition" or, more commonly, "extradition." Usually, that process works routinely; some extradition requests are contested however—especially in cases with racial or political overtones. A governor may refuse to extradite a fugitive; but the federal courts can compel an unwilling governor to obey this constitutional command.

▶ **Clause 3. Fugitive slaves** This clause was nullified by the 13th Amendment, which abolished slavery in 1865.

Section 3. New States; Territories

▶ **Clause 1. New States** Only Congress can admit new States to the Union. A new State may not be created by taking territory from an existing State without the consent of that State's legislature. Congress has admitted 37 States since the original 13 formed the Union. Five States—Vermont, Kentucky, Tennessee, Maine, and West Virginia—were created from parts of existing States. Texas was an independent republic before admission. California was admitted after being ceded to the United States by Mexico. Each of the other 30 States entered the Union only after a period of time as an organized territory of the United States.

▶ **Clause 2. Territory, property** Congress has the power to make laws concerning the territories, other public lands, and all other property of the United States.

Section 4. Protection Afforded to States by the Nation

The Constitution does not define "a republican form of government," but the phrase is generally understood to mean a representative government. The Federal Government must also defend each State against attacks from outside its border and, at the request of a State's legislature or its governor, aid its efforts to put down internal disorders.

Provisions for Amendment

This section provides for the methods by which formal changes can be made in the Constitution. An amendment may be proposed in one of two ways: by a two-thirds vote in each house of Congress, or by a national convention called by Congress at the request of two-thirds of the State legislatures. A proposed amendment may be ratified in one of two ways: by three-fourths of the State legislatures, or by three-fourths of the States in conventions called for that purpose. Congress has the power to determine the method by which a proposed amendment may be ratified. The amendment process cannot be used to deny any State its equal representation in the United States Senate. To this point, 27 amendments have been adopted. To date, all of the amendments except the 21st Amendment were proposed by Congress and ratified by the State legislatures. Only the 21st Amendment was ratified by the convention method.

National Debts, Supremacy of National Law, Oath

Section 1. Validity of Debts

Congress had borrowed large sums of money during the Revolution and later during the Critical Period of the 1780s. This provision, a pledge that the new government would honor those debts, did much to create confidence in that government.

Section 2. Supremacy of National Law

This section sets out the Supremacy Clause, a specific declaration of the supremacy of federal law over any and all forms of State law. No State, including its local governments, may make or enforce any law that conflicts with any provision in the Constitution, an act of Congress, a treaty, or an order, rule, or regulation properly issued by the President or his subordinates in the executive branch.

Section 3. Oaths of Office

This provision reinforces the Supremacy Clause; all public officers, at every level in the United States, owe their first allegiance to the Constitution of the United States. No religious qualification can be imposed as a condition for holding any public office.

Ratification of Constitution

The proposed Constitution was signed by George Washington and 37 of his fellow Framers on September 17, 1787. (George Read of Delaware signed for himself and also for his absent colleague, John Dickinson.)

Article V

The Congress, whenever two thirds of both Houses shall deem it necessary, shall propose Amendments to this Constitution, or, on the Application of the Legislatures of two thirds of the several States, shall call a Convention for proposing Amendments, which, in either Case, shall be valid to all Intents and Purposes, as Part of this Constitution, when ratified by the Legislatures of three fourths of the several States, or by Conventions in three fourths thereof, as the one or the other Mode of Ratification may be proposed by the Congress; Provided that no Amendment which may be made prior to the Year One thousand eight hundred and eight shall in any Manner affect the first and fourth Clauses in the Ninth section of the first Article; and that no State, without its Consent, shall be deprived of its equal Suffrage in the Senate.

Article VI

Section 1.

All Debts contracted and Engagements entered into, before the Adoption of this Constitution, shall be as valid against the United States under this Constitution, as under the Confederation.

Section 2.

This Constitution, and the Laws of the United States which shall be made in Pursuance thereof; and all Treaties made, or which shall be made, under the Authority of the United States, shall be the supreme Law of the Land; and the Judges in every State shall be bound thereby, anything in the constitution or Laws of any State to the Contrary notwithstanding.

Section 3.

The Senators and Representatives before mentioned, and the Members of the several State legislatures, and all executive and judicial Officers, both of the United States and of the several States, shall be bound by Oath or Affirmation, to support this Constitution; but no religious Test shall ever be required as a Qualification to any Office or public Trust under the United States.

Article VII

The ratification of the Conventions of nine States, shall be sufficient for the Establishment of this Constitution between the States so ratifying the same.

Done in Convention by the Unanimous Consent of the States present the Seventeenth Day of September in the Year of our Lord one thousand seven hundred and Eighty-seven and of the Independence of the United States of America the twelfth. In witness whereof We have hereunto subscribed our Names.

Attest:
William Jackson,
Secretary
George Washington,
President and Deputy from Virginia

New Hampshire
John Langdon
Nicholas Gilman

Massachusetts
Nathaniel Gorham
Rufus King

Connecticut
William Samuel Johnson
Roger Sherman

New York
Alexander Hamilton

New Jersey
William Livingston
David Brearley
William Paterson
Jonathan Dayton

Pennsylvania
Benjamin Franklin
Thomas Mifflin
Robert Morris
George Clymer
Thomas Fitzsimons
Jared Ingersoll
James Wilson
Gouverneur Morris

Delaware
George Read
Gunning Bedford, Jr.
John Dickinson
Richard Bassett
Jacob Broom

Maryland
James McHenry
Daniel of St. Thomas Jenifer
Daniel Carroll

Virginia
John Blair
James Madison, Jr.

North Carolina
William Blount
Richard Dobbs Spaight
Hugh Williamson

South Carolina
John Rutledge
Charles Cotesworth Pinckney
Charles Pinckney
Pierce Butler

Georgia
William Few
Abraham Baldwin

Amendments

The first 10 amendments, the Bill of Rights, were each proposed by Congress on September 25, 1789, and ratified by the necessary three-fourths of the States on December 15, 1791. These amendments were originally intended to restrict the National Government—not the States. However, the Supreme Court has several times held that most of their provisions also apply to the States, through the 14th Amendment's Due Process Clause.

1st Amendment. **Freedom of Religion, Speech, Press, Assembly, and Petition**

The 1st Amendment sets out five basic liberties: The guarantee of freedom of religion is both a protection of religious thought and practice and a command of separation of church and state. The guarantees of freedom of speech and press assure to all persons a right to speak, publish, and otherwise express their views. The guarantees of the rights of assembly and petition protect the right to join with others in public meetings, political parties, interest groups, and other associations to discuss public affairs and influence public policy. None of these rights is guaranteed in absolute terms, however; like all other civil rights guarantees, each of them may be exercised only with regard to the rights of all other persons.

2nd Amendment. **Bearing Arms**

The right of the people to keep and bear arms was insured by the 2nd Amendment.

3rd Amendment. **Quartering of Troops**

This amendment was intended to prevent what had been common British practice in the colonial period; see the Declaration of Independence. This provision is of virtually no importance today.

4th Amendment. **Searches and Seizures**

The basic rule laid down by the 4th Amendment is this: Police officers have no general right to search for or seize evidence or seize (arrest) persons. Except in particular circumstances, they must have a proper warrant (a court order) obtained with probable cause (on reasonable grounds). This guarantee is reinforced by the exclusionary rule, developed by the Supreme Court: Evidence gained as the result of an unlawful search or seizure cannot be used at the court trial of the person from whom it was seized.

5th Amendment. **Criminal Proceedings; Due Process; Eminent Domain**

A person can be tried for a serious federal crime only if he or she has been indicted (charged, accused of that crime) by a grand jury. No one may be subjected to double jeopardy—that is, tried twice for the same crime. All persons are protected against self-incrimination; no person can be legally compelled to answer any question in any governmental proceeding if that answer could lead to that person's prosecution. The 5th Amendment's Due Process Clause prohibits unfair, arbitrary actions by the Federal Government; a like prohibition is set out against the States in the 14th Amendment. Government may take private property for a legitimate public purpose; but when it exercises that power of eminent domain, it must pay a fair price for the property seized.

1st Amendment

Congress shall make no law respecting an establishment of religion, or prohibiting the free exercise thereof, or abridging the freedom of speech, or of the press; or the right of the people peaceably to assemble, and to petition the Government for a redress of grievances.

2nd Amendment

A well-regulated Militia being necessary to the security of a free State, the right of the people to keep and bear Arms, shall not be infringed.

3rd Amendment.

No Soldier shall, in time of peace be quartered in any house, without the consent of the Owner, nor, in time of war, but in a manner to be prescribed by law.

4th Amendment.

The right of the people to be secure in their persons, houses, papers, and effects, against unreasonable searches and seizures, shall not be violated, and no Warrants shall issue, but upon probable cause, supported by Oath or affirmation, and particularly describing the place to be searched, and the persons or things to be seized.

5th Amendment.

No person shall be held to answer for a capital, or otherwise infamous crime, unless on a presentment or indictment of a Grand Jury, except in cases arising in the land or naval forces, or in the Militia, when in actual service in time of War, or public danger; nor shall any person be subject for the same offence to be twice put in jeopardy of life or limb; nor shall be compelled in any criminal case to be a witness against himself, nor be deprived of life, liberty, or property, without due process of law; nor shall private property be taken for public use, without just compensation.

6th Amendment

In all criminal prosecutions, the accused shall enjoy the right to a speedy and public trial, by an impartial jury of the State and district wherein the crime shall have been committed, which district shall have been previously ascertained by law, and to be informed of the nature and cause of the accusation; to be confronted with the witnesses against him; to have compulsory process for obtaining witnesses in his favor, and to have the Assistance of Counsel for his defence.

6th Amendment. Criminal Proceedings

A person accused of crime has the right to be tried in court without undue delay and by an impartial jury; see Article III, Section 2, Clause 3. The defendant must be informed of the charge upon which he or she is to be tried, has the right to cross-examine hostile witnesses, and has the right to require the testimony of favorable witnesses. The defendant also has the right to be represented by an attorney at every stage in the criminal process.

7th Amendment

In Suits at common law, where the value in controversy shall exceed twenty dollars, the right of trial by jury shall be preserved, and no fact tried by a jury, shall be otherwise re-examined in any Court of the United States, than according to the rules of the common law.

7th Amendment. Civil Trials

This amendment applies only to civil cases heard in federal courts. A civil case does not involve criminal matters; it is a dispute between private parties or between the government and a private party. The right to trial by jury is guaranteed in any civil case in a federal court if the amount of money involved in that case exceeds $20 (most cases today involve a much larger sum); that right may be waived (relinquished, put aside) if both parties agree to a bench trial (a trial by a judge, without a jury).

8th Amendment

Excessive bail shall not be required, nor excessive fines imposed, nor cruel and unusual punishment inflicted.

8th Amendment. Punishment for Crimes

Bail is the sum of money that a person accused of crime may be required to post (deposit with the court) as a guarantee that he or she will appear in court at the proper time. The amount of bail required and/or a fine imposed as punishment must bear a reasonable relationship to the seriousness of the crime involved in the case. The prohibition of cruel and unusual punishment forbids any punishment judged to be too harsh, too severe for the crime for which it is imposed.

9th Amendment

The enumeration in the Constitution, of certain rights, shall not be construed to deny or disparage others retained by the people.

9th Amendment. Unenumerated Rights

The fact that the Constitution sets out many civil rights guarantees, expressly provides for many protections against government, does not mean that there are not other rights also held by the people.

10th Amendment

The powers not delegated to the United States by the Constitution, nor prohibited by it to the States, are reserved to the States respectively, or to the people.

10th Amendment. Powers Reserved to the States

This amendment identifies the area of power that may be exercised by the States. All of those powers the Constitution does not grant to the National Government, and at the same time does not forbid to the States, belong to each of the States, or to the people of each State.

11th Amendment. Suits Against States

Proposed by Congress March 4, 1794; ratified February 7, 1795, but official announcement of the ratification was delayed until January 8, 1798. This amendment repealed part of Article III, Section 2, Clause 1. No State may be sued in a federal court by a resident of another State or of a foreign country; the Supreme Court has long held that this provision also means that a State cannot be sued in a federal court by a foreign country or, more importantly, even by one of its own residents.

11th Amendment

The Judicial power of the United States shall not be construed to extend to any suit in law or equity, commenced or prosecuted against one of the United States by Citizens of another State, or by Citizens or Subjects of any Foreign State.

12th Amendment. Election of President and Vice President

Proposed by Congress December 9, 1803; ratified June 15, 1804. This amendment replaced Article II, Section 1, Clause 3. Originally, each elector cast two ballots, each for a different person for President. The person with the largest number of electoral votes, provided that number was a majority of the electors, was to become President; the person with the second highest number was to become Vice President. This arrangement produced an electoral vote tie between Thomas Jefferson and Aaron Burr in 1800; the House finally chose Jefferson as President in 1801. The 12th Amendment separated the balloting for President and Vice President; each elector now casts one ballot for someone as President and a second ballot for another person as Vice President. Note that the 20th Amendment changed the date set here (March 4) to January 20, and that the 23rd Amendment (1961) provides for electors from the District of Columbia. This amendment also provides that the Vice President must meet the same qualifications as those set out for the President in Article II, Section 1, Clause 5.

12th Amendment

The Electors shall meet in their respective States and vote by ballot for President and Vice President, one of whom, at least, shall not be an inhabitant of the same State with themselves; they shall name in their ballots the person voted for as President, and in distinct ballots the person voted for as Vice President, and they shall make distinct lists of all persons voted for as President, and of all persons voted for as Vice President, and of the number of votes for each, which lists they shall sign and certify, and transmit sealed to the seat of the government of the United States, directed to the President of the Senate;— The President of the Senate shall, in the presence of the Senate and the House of Representatives, open all the certificates and the votes shall then be counted;— the person having the greatest Number of votes for President shall be the President, if such number be a majority of the whole number of Electors appointed; and if no person have such a majority, then, from the persons having the highest numbers not exceeding three on the list of those voted for as President, the House of Representatives shall choose immediately, by ballot, the President. But in choosing the President, the votes shall be taken by States, the representation from each State having one vote; a quorum for this purpose shall consist of a member or members from two thirds of the States, and a majority of all the States shall be necessary to a choice. And if the House of Representatives shall not choose a President whenever the right of choice shall devolve upon them, before the fourth day of March next following, then the Vice President shall act as President, as in case of death or other constitutional disability of the President. The person having the greatest number of votes as Vice President, shall be the Vice President, if such number be a majority of the whole number of Electors appointed, and if no person have a majority, then from the two highest numbers on the list, the Senate shall choose the Vice President; a quorum for the purpose shall consist of two thirds of the whole number of Senators, a majority of the whole number shall be necessary to a choice. But no person constitutionally ineligible to the office of President shall be eligible to that of Vice-President of the United States.

13th Amendment. Slavery and Involuntary Servitude

Proposed by Congress January 31, 1865; ratified December 6, 1865. This amendment forbids slavery in the United States and in any area under its control. It also forbids other forms of forced labor, except punishments for crime; but some forms of compulsory service are not prohibited—for example, service on juries or in the armed forces. Section 2 gives to Congress the power to carry out the provisions of Section 1 of this amendment.

13th Amendment

Section 1. Neither slavery nor involuntary servitude, except as a punishment for crime whereof the party shall have been duly convicted, shall exist within the United States, or any place subject to their jurisdiction.

Section 2. Congress shall have power to enforce this article by appropriate legislation.

14th Amendment

Section 1. All persons born or naturalized in the United States and subject to the jurisdiction thereof, are citizens of the United States and of the State wherein they reside. No State shall make or enforce any law which shall abridge the privileges or immunities of citizens of the United States; nor shall any State deprive any person of life, liberty, or property, without due process of law; nor deny to any person within its jurisdiction the equal protection of the laws.

Section 2. Representatives shall be apportioned among the several States according to their respective numbers, counting the whole number of persons in each State, excluding Indians not taxed. But when the right to vote at any election for the choice of electors for President and Vice President of the United States, Representatives in Congress, the Executive and Judicial officers of a State, or the members of the Legislature thereof, is denied to any of the male inhabitants of such State, being twenty-one years of age and citizens of the United States, or in any way abridged, except for participation in rebellion, or other crime, the basis of representation therein shall be reduced in the proportion which the number of such male citizens shall bear to the whole number of male citizens twenty-one years of age in such State.

Section 3. No person shall be a Senator or Representative in Congress, or elector of President and Vice President, or hold any office, civil or military, under the United States, or under any State, who, having previously taken an oath, as a member of Congress, or as an officer of the United States, or as a member of any State legislature, or as an executive or judicial officer of any State, to support the Constitution of the United States, shall have engaged in insurrection or rebellion against the same, or given aid or comfort to the enemies thereof. But Congress may, by a vote of two thirds of each House, remove such disability.

Section 4. The validity of the public debt of the United States, authorized by law, including debts incurred for payment of pensions and bounties for services in suppressing insurrection or rebellion, shall not be questioned. But neither the United States nor any State shall assume or pay any debt or obligation incurred in aid of insurrection or rebellion against the United States, or any claim for the loss or emancipation of any slave; but all such debts, obligations and claims shall be held illegal and void.

Section 5. The Congress shall have power to enforce, by appropriate legislation, the provisions of this article.

14th Amendment. Rights of Citizens

Proposed by Congress June 13, 1866; ratified July 9, 1868. Section 1 defines citizenship. It provides for the acquisition of United States citizenship by birth or by naturalization. Citizenship at birth is determined according to the principle of jus soli—"the law of the soil," where born; naturalization is the legal process by which one acquires a new citizenship at some time after birth. Under certain circumstances, citizenship can also be gained at birth abroad, according to the principle of jus sanguinis—"the law of the blood," to whom born. This section also contains two major civil rights provisions: the Due Process Clause forbids a State (and its local governments) to act in any unfair or arbitrary way; the Equal Protection Clause forbids a State (and its local governments) to discriminate against, draw unreasonable distinctions between, persons.

Most of the rights set out against the National Government in the first eight amendments have been extended against the States (and their local governments) through Supreme Court decisions involving the 14th Amendment's Due Process Clause.

The first sentence here replaced Article I, Section 2, Clause 3, the Three-Fifths Compromise provision. Essentially, all persons in the United States are counted in each decennial census, the basis for the distribution of House seats. The balance of this section has never been enforced and is generally thought to be obsolete.

This section limited the President's power to pardon those persons who had led the Confederacy during the Civil War. Congress finally removed this disability in 1898.

Section 4 also dealt with matters directly related to the Civil War. It reaffirmed the public debt of the United States; but it invalidated, prohibited payment of, any debt contracted by the Confederate States and also prohibited any compensation of former slave owners.

15th Amendment. Right to Vote—Race, Color, Servitude

Proposed by Congress February 26, 1869; ratified February 3, 1870. The phrase "previous condition of servitude" refers to slavery. Note that this amendment does not guarantee the right to vote to African Americans, or to anyone else. Instead, it forbids the States from discriminating against any person on the grounds of his "race, color, or previous condition of servitude" in the setting of suffrage qualifications.

15th Amendment

Section 1. The right of citizens of the United States to vote shall not be denied or abridged by the United States or by any State on account of race, color, or previous condition of servitude.

Section 2. The Congress shall have power to enforce this article by appropriate legislation.

16th Amendment. Income Tax

Proposed by Congress July 12, 1909; ratified February 3, 1913. This amendment modified two provisions in Article I, Section 2, Clause 3, and Section 9, Clause 4. It gives to Congress the power to levy an income tax, a direct tax, without regard to the populations of any of the States.

16th Amendment

The Congress shall have power to lay and collect taxes on incomes, from whatever source derived, without apportionment among the several States, and without regard to any census or enumeration.

17th Amendment. Popular Election of Senators

Proposed by Congress May 13, 1912; ratified April 8, 1913. This amendment repealed those portions of Article I, Section 3, Clauses 1 and 2 relating to the election of senators. Senators are now elected by the voters in each State. If a vacancy occurs, the governor of the State involved must call an election to fill the seat; the governor may appoint a senator to serve until the next election, if the State's legislature has authorized that step.

17th Amendment

The Senate of the United States shall be composed of two Senators from each State, elected by the people thereof, for six years; and each Senator shall have one vote. The electors in each State shall have the qualifications requisite for electors of the most numerous branch of the State legislatures.

When vacancies happen in the representation of any State in the Senate, the executive authority of such State shall issue writs of election to fill such vacancies: Provided, That the legislature of any State may empower the executive thereof to make temporary appointments until the people fill the vacancies by election as the legislature may direct.

This amendment shall not be so construed as to affect the election or term of any Senator chosen before it becomes valid as part of the Constitution.

18th Amendment. Prohibition of Intoxicating Liquors

Proposed by Congress December 18, 1917; ratified January 16, 1919. This amendment outlawed the making, selling, transporting, importing, or exporting of alcoholic beverages in the United States. It was repealed in its entirety by the 21st Amendment in 1933.

18th Amendment.

Section 1. After one year from the ratification of this article the manufacture, sale, or transportation of intoxicating liquors within, the importation thereof into, or the exportation thereof from the United States and all territory subject to the jurisdiction thereof for beverage purposes is hereby prohibited.

Section 2. The Congress and the several States shall have concurrent power to enforce this article by appropriate legislation.

Section 3. This article shall be inoperative unless it shall have been ratified as an amendment to the Constitution by the legislatures of the several States, as provided in the Constitution, within seven years of the date of the submission hereof to the States by Congress.

19th Amendment. Equal Suffrage—Sex

Proposed by Congress June 4, 1919; ratified August 18, 1920. No person can be denied the right to vote in any election in the United States on account of his or her sex.

19th Amendment

The right of citizens of the United States to vote shall not be denied or abridged by the United States or by any State on account of sex.

Congress shall have power to enforce this article by appropriate legislation.

20th Amendment

Section 1. The terms of the President and Vice President shall end at noon on the 20th day of January, and the terms of Senators and Representatives at noon on the 3d day of January, of the years in which such terms would have ended if this article had not been ratified; and the terms of their successors shall then begin.

Section 2. The Congress shall assemble at least once in every year, and such meeting shall begin at noon on the 3d day of January, unless they shall by law appoint a different day.

Section 3. If, at the time fixed for the beginning of the term of the President, the President elect shall have died, the Vice President elect shall become President. If a President shall not have been chosen before the time fixed for the beginning of his term, or if the President-elect shall have failed to qualify, then the Vice President elect shall act as President until a President shall have qualified; and the Congress may by law provide for the case wherein neither a President elect nor a Vice President elect shall have qualified, declaring who shall then act as President, or the manner in which one who is to act shall be selected, and such person shall act accordingly until a President or Vice President shall have qualified.

Section 4. The Congress may by law provide for the case of the death of any of the persons from whom the House of Representatives may choose a President whenever the right of choice shall have devolved upon them, and for the case of the death of any of the persons from whom the Senate may choose a Vice President whenever the right of choice shall have devolved upon them.

Section 5. Sections 1 and 2 shall take effect on the 15th day of October following the ratification of this article.

Section 6. This article shall be inoperative unless it shall have been ratified as an amendment to the Constitution by the legislatures of three fourths of the several States within seven years from the date of its submission.

20th Amendment. Commencement of Terms; Sessions of Congress; Death or Disqualification of President-Elect

Proposed by Congress March 2, 1932; ratified January 23, 1933. The provisions of Sections 1 and 2 relating to Congress modified Article I, Section 4, Clause 2, and those provisions relating to the President, the 12th Amendment. The date on which the President and Vice President now take office was moved from March 4 to January 20. Similarly, the members of Congress now begin their terms on January 3. The 20th Amendment is sometimes called the "Lame Duck Amendment" because it shortened the period of time a member of Congress who was defeated for reelection (a "lame duck") remains in office.

This section deals with certain possibilities that were not covered by the presidential selection provisions of either Article II or the 12th Amendment. To this point, none of these situations has occurred. Note that there is neither a President-elect nor a Vice President-elect until the electoral votes have been counted by Congress, or, if the electoral college cannot decide the matter, the House has chosen a President or the Senate has chosen a Vice President.

Congress has not in fact ever passed such a law. See Section 2 of the 25th Amendment, regarding a vacancy in the vice presidency; that provision could some day have an impact here.

Section 5 set the date on which this amendment came into force.

Section 6 placed a time limit on the ratification process; note that a similar provision was written into the 18th, 21st, and 22nd amendments.

21st Amendment

Section 1. The eighteenth article of amendment to the Constitution of the United States is hereby repealed.

Section 2. The transportation or importation into any State, Territory, or possession of the United States for delivery or use therein of intoxicating liquors, in violation of the laws thereof, is hereby prohibited.

Section 3. This article shall be inoperative unless it shall have been ratified as an amendment to the Constitution by conventions in the several States, as provided in the Constitution, within seven years from the date of the submission hereof to the States by the Congress.

21st Amendment. Repeal of 18th Amendment

Proposed by Congress February 20, 1933; ratified December 5, 1933. This amendment repealed all of the 18th Amendment. Section 2 modifies the scope of the Federal Government's commerce power set out in Article I, Section 8, Clause 3; it gives to each State the power to regulate the transportation or importation and the distribution or use of intoxicating liquors in ways that would be unconstitutional in the case of any other commodity. The 21st Amendment is the only amendment Congress has thus far submitted to the States for ratification by conventions.

22nd Amendment. Presidential Tenure

Proposed by Congress March 21, 1947; ratified February 27, 1951. This amendment modified Article II, Section I, Clause 1. It stipulates that no President may serve more than two elected terms. But a President who has succeeded to the office beyond the midpoint in a term to which another President was originally elected may serve for more than eight years. In any case, however, a President may not serve more than 10 years. Prior to Franklin Roosevelt, who was elected to four terms, no President had served more than two full terms in office.

22nd Amendment

Section 1. No person shall be elected to the office of the President more than twice, and no person who has held the office of President, or acted as President, for more than two years of a term to which some other person was elected President shall be elected to the office of the President more than once. But this Article shall not apply to any person holding the office of President, when this Article was proposed by the Congress, and shall not prevent any person who may be holding the office of President, or acting as President, during the term within which this Article becomes operative from holding the office of President or acting as President during the remainder of such term.

Section 2. This article shall be inoperative unless it shall have been ratified as an amendment to the Constitution by the legislatures of three fourths of the several states within seven years from the date of its submission to the States by the Congress.

23rd Amendment. Presidential Electors for the District of Columbia

Proposed by Congress June 16, 1960; ratified March 29, 1961. This amendment modified Article II, Section I, Clause 2 and the 12th Amendment. It included the voters of the District of Columbia in the presidential electorate; and provides that the District is to have the same number of electors as the least populous State—three electors—but no more than that number.

23rd Amendment.

Section 1. The District constituting the seat of Government of the United States shall appoint in such manner as the Congress may direct:

A number of electors of President and Vice President equal to the whole number of Senators and Representatives in Congress to which the District would be entitled if it were a State, but in no event more than the least populous State; they shall be in addition to those appointed by the States, they shall be considered, for the purposes of the election of President and Vice President, to be electors appointed by a State; and they shall meet in the District and perform such duties as provided by the twelfth article of amendment.

24th Amendment. Right to Vote in Federal Elections—Tax Payment

Proposed by Congress August 27, 1962; ratified January 23, 1964. This amendment outlawed the payment of any tax as a condition for taking part in the nomination or election of any federal officeholder.

24th Amendment.

Section 1. The right of citizens of the United States to vote in any primary or other election for President or Vice President, for electors for President or Vice President, or for Senator or Representative in Congress, shall not be denied or abridged by the United States or any State by reason of failure to pay any poll tax or other tax.

Section 2. The Congress shall have power to enforce this article by appropriate legislation.

25th Amendment. Presidential Succession, Vice Presidential Vacancy, Presidential Inability

Proposed by Congress July 6, 1965; ratified February 10, 1967. Section 1 revised the imprecise provision on presidential succession in Article II, Section 1, Clause 6. It affirmed the precedent set by Vice President John Tyler, who became President on the death of William Henry Harrison in 1841. Section 2 provides for the filling of a vacancy in the office of Vice President. The office had been vacant on 16 occasions and remained unfilled for the rest of each term involved. When Spiro Agnew resigned the office in 1973, President Nixon selected Gerald Ford per this provision; and, when President Nixon resigned in 1974, Gerald Ford became President and chose Nelson Rockefeller as Vice President.

25th Amendment.

Section 1. In case of the removal of the President from office or of his death or resignation, the Vice President shall become President.

Section 2. Whenever there is a vacancy in the office of the Vice President, the President shall nominate a Vice President who shall take office upon confirmation by a majority vote of both Houses of Congress.

Section 3. Whenever the President transmits to the President pro tempore of the Senate and the Speaker of the House of Representatives his written declaration that he is unable to discharge the powers and duties of his office, and until he transmits to them a written declaration to the contrary, such powers and duties shall be discharged by the Vice President as Acting President.

This section created a procedure for determining if a President is so incapacitated that he cannot perform the powers and duties of his office.

Section 4. Whenever the Vice President and a majority of either the principal officers of the executive departments or of such other body as Congress may by law provide, transmit to the President pro tempore of the Senate and the Speaker of the House of Representatives their written declaration that the President is unable to discharge the powers and duties of his office, the Vice President shall immediately assume the powers and duties of the office as Acting President.

Thereafter, when the President transmits to the President pro tempore of the Senate and the Speaker of the House of Representatives his written declaration that no inability exists, he shall resume the powers and duties of his office unless the Vice President and a majority of either the principal officers of the executive department or of such other body as Congress may by law provide, transmit within four days to the President pro tempore of the Senate and the Speaker of the House of Representatives their written declaration that the President is unable to discharge the powers and duties of his office. Thereupon Congress shall decide the issue, assembling within forty-eight hours for that purpose if not in session. If the Congress, within twenty-one days after receipt of the latter written declaration, or, if Congress is not in session, within twenty-one days after Congress is required to assemble, determines by two-thirds vote of both Houses that the President is unable to discharge the powers and duties of his office, the Vice President shall continue to discharge the same as Acting President; otherwise, the President shall resume the powers and duties of his office.

Section 4 deals with the circumstance in which a President will not be able to determine the fact of incapacity. To this point, Congress has not established the "such other body" referred to here. This section contains the only typographical error in the Constitution; in its second paragraph, the word "department" should in fact read "departments."

26th Amendment.

Section 1. The right of citizens of the United States, who are eighteen years of age or older, to vote shall not be denied or abridged by the United States or by any State on account of age.

Section 2. The Congress shall have the power to enforce this article by appropriate legislation.

26th Amendment. Right to Vote—Age

Proposed by Congress March 23, 1971; ratified July 1, 1971. This amendment provides that the minimum age for voting in any election in the United States cannot be more than 18 years. (A State may set a minimum voting age of less than 18, however.)

27th Amendment.

No law varying the compensation for the services of the Senators and Representatives, shall take effect, until an election of Representatives shall have intervened.

27th Amendment. Congressional Pay

Proposed by Congress September 25, 1789; ratified May 7, 1992. This amendment modified Article I, Section 6, Clause 1. It limits Congress's power to fix the salaries of its members—by delaying the effectiveness of any increase in that pay until after the next regular congressional election.

Name	Party	State [a]	Entered Office	Age On Taking Office	Vice President(s)
George Washington (1732–1799)	Federalist	Virginia	1789	57	John Adams
John Adams (1735–1826)	Federalist	Massachusetts	1797	61	Thomas Jefferson
Thomas Jefferson (1743–1826)	Dem-Rep[b]	Virginia	1801	57	Aaron Burr/George Clinton
James Madison (1751–1836)	Dem-Rep	Virginia	1809	57	George Clinton/Elbridge Gerry
James Monroe (1758–1831)	Dem-Rep	Virginia	1817	58	Daniel D. Tompkins
John Q. Adams (1767–1848)	Dem-Rep	Massachusetts	1825	57	John C. Calhoun
Andrew Jackson (1767–1845)	Democrat	Tennessee (SC)	1829	61	John C. Calhoun/Martin Van Buren
Martin Van Buren (1782–1862)	Democrat	New York	1837	54	Richard M. Johnson
William H. Harrison (1773–1841)	Whig	Ohio (VA)	1841	68	John Tyler
John Tyler (1790–1862)	Democrat	Virginia	1841	51	none
James K. Polk (1795–1849)	Democrat	Tennessee (NC)	1845	49	George M. Dallas
Zachary Taylor (1784–1850)	Whig	Louisiana (VA)	1849	64	Millard Fillmore
Millard Fillmore (1800–1874)	Whig	New York	1850	50	none
Franklin Pierce (1804–1869)	Democrat	New Hampshire	1853	48	William R. King
James Buchanan (1791–1868)	Democrat	Pennsylvania	1857	65	John C. Breckinridge
Abraham Lincoln (1809–1865)	Republican	Illinois (KY)	1861	52	Hannibal Hamlin/Andrew Johnson[c]
Andrew Johnson (1808–1875)	Democrat	Tennessee (NC)	1865	56	none
Ulysses S. Grant (1822–1885)	Republican	Illinois (OH)	1869	46	Schuyler Colfax/Henry Wilson
Rutherford B. Hayes (1822–1893)	Republican	Ohio	1877	54	William A. Wheeler
James A. Garfield (1831–1881)	Republican	Ohio	1881	49	Chester A. Arthur
Chester A. Arthur (1829–1896)	Republican	New York (VT)	1881	51	none
Grover Cleveland (1837–1908)	Democrat	New York (NJ)	1885	47	Thomas A. Hendricks
Benjamin Harrison (1833–1901)	Republican	Indiana (OH)	1889	55	Levi P. Morton
Grover Cleveland (1837–1908)	Democrat	New York (NJ)	1893	55	Adlai E. Stevenson

Name	Party	State [a]	Entered Office	Age On Taking Office	Vice President(s)
William McKinley (1843–1901)	Republican	Ohio	1897	54	Garret A. Hobart/ Theodore Roosevelt
Theodore Roosevelt (1858–1919)	Republican	New York	1901	42	Charles W. Fairbanks
William H. Taft (1857–1930)	Republican	Ohio	1909	51	James S. Sherman
Woodrow Wilson (1856–1924)	Democrat	New Jersey (VA)	1913	56	Thomas R. Marshall
Warren G. Harding (1865–1923)	Republican	Ohio	1921	55	Calvin Coolidge
Calvin Coolidge (1872–1933)	Republican	Massachusetts (VT)	1923	51	Charles G. Dawes
Herbert Hoover (1874–1964)	Republican	California (IA)	1929	54	Charles Curtis
Franklin Roosevelt (1882–1945)	Democrat	New York	1933	51	John N. Garner/ Henry A. Wallace/Harry S Truman
Harry S Truman (1884–1972)	Democrat	Missouri	1945	60	Alben W. Barkley
Dwight D. Eisenhower (1890–1969)	Republican	New York (TX)	1953	62	Richard M. Nixon
John F. Kennedy (1917–1963)	Democrat	Massachusetts	1961	43	Lyndon B. Johnson
Lyndon B. Johnson (1908–1973)	Democrat	Texas	1963	55	Hubert H. Humphrey
Richard M. Nixon (1913–1994)	Republican	New York (CA)	1969	56	Spiro T. Agnew [d]/Gerald R. Ford [e]
Gerald R. Ford (1913–2006)	Republican	Michigan (NE)	1974	61	Nelson A. Rockefeller [f]
James E. Carter (1924–)	Democrat	Georgia	1977	52	Walter F. Mondale
Ronald W. Reagan (1911–2004)	Republican	California (IL)	1981	69	George H. W. Bush
George H.W. Bush (1924–)	Republican	Texas (MA)	1989	64	J. Danforth Quayle
William J. Clinton (1946–)	Democrat	Arkansas	1993	46	Albert Gore, Jr.
George W. Bush (1946–)	Republican	Texas	2001	54	Richard B. Cheney
Barack Obama (1961–)	Democrat	Illinois (HI)	2009	47	Joseph R. Biden
Donald J. Trump (1946–)	Republican	New York	2017	70	Michael R. Pence

[a] State of residence when elected; if born in another State, that State in parentheses.
[b] Democratic-Republican
[c] Johnson, a War Democrat, was elected Vice President on the coalition Union Party ticket.
[d] Resigned October 10, 1973.
[e] Nominated by Nixon, confirmed by Congress on December 6, 1973.
[f] Nominated by Ford, confirmed by Congress on December 19, 1974.

[Declaration of Independence]

Introduction

By signing the Declaration of Independence, members of the Continental Congress sent a clear message to Britain that the American colonies were free and independent states. Starting with its preamble, the document spells out all the reasons the people of the United States have the right to break away from Britain.

Primary Source

The Unanimous Declaration of the Thirteen United States of America

When in the Course of human events, it becomes necessary for one people to dissolve the political bands which have connected them with another, and to assume among the powers of the earth, the separate and equal station to which the Laws of Nature and of Nature's God entitle them, a decent respect to the opinions of mankind requires that they should declare the causes which impel [force] them to the separation. We hold these truths to be self-evident, that all men are created equal, that they are endowed [gifted] by their Creator with certain unalienable [cannot be taken away] Rights, that among these are Life, Liberty and the pursuit of Happiness. That to secure these rights, Governments are instituted among Men, deriving their just powers from the consent of the governed. That whenever any Form of Government becomes destructive of these ends, it is the Right of the People to alter or to abolish it, and to institute new Government, laying its foundation on such principles and organizing its powers in such form, as to them shall seem most likely to effect their Safety and Happiness. Prudence [cautiousness], indeed, will dictate that Governments long established should not be changed for light and transient causes; and accordingly all experience hath shown that mankind are more disposed to suffer, while evils are sufferable, than to right themselves by abolishing the forms to which they are accustomed. But when a long train of abuses and usurpations [unjust uses of power], pursuing invariably the same Object evinces a design to reduce them under absolute Despotism [rule of absolute power], it is their right, it is their duty, to throw off such Government, and to provide new Guards for their future security.

Such has been the patient sufferance of these Colonies; and such is now the necessity which constrains them to alter their former Systems of Government. The history of the present King of Great Britain is a history of repeated injuries and usurpations, all having in direct object the establishment of an absolute Tyranny over these States. To prove this, let Facts be submitted to a candid world.

He has refused his Assent to Laws, the most wholesome and necessary for the public good.

He has forbidden his Governors to pass Laws of immediate and pressing importance, unless suspended in their operation till his Assent should be obtained; and when so suspended, he has utterly neglected to attend to them.

He has refused to pass other Laws for the accommodation of large districts of people, unless those people would relinquish [give up] the right of Representation in the Legislature, a right inestimable [priceless] to them and formidable to tyrants only.

He has called together legislative bodies at places unusual, uncomfortable, and distant from the depository of their public Records, for the sole purpose of fatiguing them into compliance with his measures.

He has dissolved Representative Houses repeatedly, for opposing with manly firmness his invasions on the rights of the people.

He has refused for a long time, after such dissolutions [closing down], to cause others to be elected; whereby the Legislative powers, incapable of Annihilation, have returned to the People at large for their exercise; the State remaining in the mean time exposed to all the dangers of invasion from without, and convulsions [riots] within.

He has endeavoured to prevent the population of these States; for that purpose obstructing the Laws for Naturalization of Foreigners; refusing to pass others to encourage their migrations hither, and raising the conditions of new Appropriations of Lands.

He has obstructed the Administration of Justice by refusing his Assent to Laws for establishing Judiciary powers.

He has made Judges dependent on his Will alone, for the tenure [term] of their offices, and the amount and payment of their salaries.

He has erected a multitude of New Offices, and sent hither swarms of Officers to harass our people, and eat out their substance.

He has kept among us, in times of peace, Standing Armies without the Consent of our legislatures.

He has affected to render the Military independent of and superior to the Civil power.

He has combined with others to subject us to a jurisdiction foreign to our constitution, and unacknowledged by our laws; giving his Assent to their Acts of pretended Legislation:

For quartering [lodging] large bodies of armed troops among us:

For protecting them, by a mock Trial, from punishment for any Murders which they should commit on the Inhabitants of these States:

For cutting off our Trade with all parts of the world:

For imposing Taxes on us without our Consent:

For depriving us in many cases, of the benefits of Trial by Jury: For transporting us beyond Seas to be tried for pretended offences:

For abolishing the free System of English Laws in a neighbouring Province, establishing therein an Arbitrary government, and enlarging its Boundaries so as to render it at once an example and fit instrument for introducing the same absolute rule into these Colonies:

For taking away our Charters, abolishing our most valuable Laws, and altering fundamentally the Forms of our Governments:

For suspending our own Legislatures, and declaring themselves invested with power to legislate for us in all cases whatsoever.

He has abdicated Government here, by declaring us out of his Protection and waging War against us.

He has plundered our seas, ravaged our Coasts, burnt our towns, and destroyed the lives of our people.

He is at this time transporting large Armies of foreign Mercenaries [soldiers] to complete the works of death, desolation, and tyranny, already begun with circumstances of Cruelty and perfidy [dishonesty] scarcely paralleled in the most barbarous ages, and totally unworthy the Head of a civilized nation.

He has constrained our fellow Citizens taken Captive on the high Seas to bear Arms against their Country, to become the executioners of their friends and Brethren, or to fall themselves by their Hands.

He has excited domestic insurrections amongst us, and has endeavoured to bring on the inhabitants of our frontiers, the merciless Indian Savages whose known rule of warfare, is an undistinguished destruction of all ages, sexes and conditions.

In every stage of these Oppressions We have Petitioned for Redress [correction of wrongs] in the most humble terms: Our repeated Petitions have been answered only by repeated injury. A Prince, whose character is thus marked by every act which may define a Tyrant, is unfit to be the ruler of a free people.

Nor have We been wanting in attentions to our British brethren. We have warned them from time to time of attempts by their legislature to extend an unwarrantable jurisdiction over us. We have reminded them of the circumstances of our emigration and settlement here. We have appealed to their native justice and magnanimity [generosity], and we have conjured [begged] them by the ties of our common kindred, to disavow these usurpations, which would inevitably interrupt our connections and correspondence. They too have been deaf to the voice of justice and of consanguinity [relation by blood]. We must, therefore, acquiesce in the necessity, which denounces our Separation, and hold them, as we hold the rest of mankind, Enemies in War, in Peace Friends.

We, therefore, the Representatives of the United States of America, in General Congress, Assembled, appealing to the Supreme Judge of the world for the rectitude [justness] of our intentions, do, in the Name, and by Authority of the good People of these Colonies, solemnly publish and declare, That these United Colonies are, and of Right ought to be Free and Independent States; that they are Absolved from all Allegiance to the British Crown, and that all political connection between them and the State of Great Britain, is and ought to be totally dissolved; and that as Free and Independent States, they have full Power to levy War, conclude Peace, contract Alliances, establish Commerce, and to do all other Acts and Things which Independent States may of right do. And for the support of this Declaration, with a firm reliance on the protection of Divine Providence, we mutually pledge to each other our Lives, our Fortunes and our sacred Honor.

ASSESSMENT

1. **Identify Cause and Effect** How might the ideas about equality expressed in the Declaration of Independence have influenced later historical movements, such as the abolitionist movement and the women's suffrage movement?
2. **Identify Key Steps in a Process** Why was the Declaration of Independence a necessary document for the founding of the new nation?
3. **Draw Inferences** English philosopher John Locke wrote that government should protect "life, liberty, and estate." How do you think Locke's writing influenced ideas about government put forth in the Declaration of Independence?
4. **Analyze Structure** How does the Declaration organize its key points from beginning to end?

[The Magna Carta]

Introduction

King John ruled England from 1199 to 1216. During his troubled reign, he found himself in conflict with England's feudal barons. The nobles especially resented John's attempts to tax them heavily. In 1215, the barons forced John to sign the Magna Carta, or Great Charter. Most of this document was intended to protect the rights of the barons. However, over time, the document came to guarantee some basic rights of English citizens. When English colonists came to North America, they brought these ideas with them. Eight of the 63 clauses of the Magna Carta are printed here.

Primary Source

12. No [tax] nor aid shall be imposed on our kingdom, unless by common counsel [consent] of our kingdom, except for ransoming our person, for making our eldest son a knight, and for once marrying our eldest daughter; and for these there shall not be levied more than a reasonable aid. . . .

30. No sheriff or bailiff [tax collector] of ours, or other person, shall take the horses or carts of any freeman for transport duty, against the will of the said freeman.

31. Neither we nor our bailiffs shall take, for our castles or for any other work of ours, wood which is not ours, against the will of the owner of that wood. . . .

38. No bailiff for the future shall, upon his own unsupported complaint, put any one to his "law," without credible [believable] witnesses brought for this purpose.

39. No freeman shall be taken or imprisoned . . . or exiled or in any way destroyed, nor will we go upon him nor send upon him, except by the lawful judgment of his peers [people of equal rank] or by the law of the land.

40. To no one will we sell, to no one will we refuse or delay, right or justice. . . .

45. We will appoint as justices, constables, sheriffs, or bailiffs only such as know the law of the realm [kingdom] and mean to observe it well. . . .

63. Wherefore it is our will, and we firmly enjoin [order], that the English Church be free, and that the men in our kingdom have and hold all the aforesaid liberties, rights, and concessions, well and peaceably, freely and quietly, fully and wholly, for themselves and their heirs, of us and our heirs, in all respects and in all places for ever, as is aforesaid.

ASSESSMENT

1. **Determine Author's Purpose** Why did the barons write the Magna Carta, and how did it affect the power of the king?
2. **Determine Central Ideas** What do you think is the most important right that this excerpt from the Magna Carta protects? Explain your answer.
3. **Identify Steps in a Process** How was the Magna Carta an important first step in the development of constitutional democracy?

[Mayflower Compact]

Introduction

The Pilgrims arrived at Massachusetts in 1620. Before disembarking, they signed a covenant that established a basis for self-government derived from the consent of the governed. Forty-one men signed the compact, agreeing to abide by the laws of the government. Women, who did not enjoy equal rights, were not asked to sign.

Primary Source

In the name of God, Amen. We, whose names are underwritten, the loyal subjects of our dread Sovereign Lord King James, by the grace of God, of Great Britain, France and Ireland king, defender of the faith, etc. Having undertaken, for the glory of God, and advancement of the Christian faith, and honor of our king and country, a voyage to plant the first colony in the Northern parts of Virginia, do by these presents solemnly and mutually in the presence of God and one of another, covenant [agree] and combine ourselves together into a civil body politick, for our better ordering and preservation, and furtherance [advancement] of the ends aforesaid; and by virtue hereof to enacte, constitute [establish], and frame such just and equal laws, ordinances, acts, constitutions and offices, from time to time, as shall be thought most meet [suitable] and convenient for the general good of the Colony unto which we promise all due submission and obedience. In witness whereof we have hereunder subscribed our names at Cape Cod the eleventh of November, in the year of the reign of our Sovereign Lord, King James, of England, France and Ireland, the eighteenth, and of Scotland the fifty-fourth. Anno Dom. 1620.

ASSESSMENT

1. **Identify Cause and Effect** How do you think that having this compact might have affected the Pilgrims once they arrived in North America?
2. **Analyze Interactions** What does the Mayflower Compact say about equality, and how might this view have influenced the system of government in the United States?
3. **Analyze Interactions** How do you think the organization of the Pilgrims "together into a civil body politick" influenced later ideas about government in the United States?

[English Bill of Rights]

Introduction

When the Catholic king, James II, was forced from the English throne in 1688, Parliament offered the crown to his Protestant daughter Mary and her husband, William of Orange. Parliament, however, insisted that William and Mary submit to a bill of rights. This document sums up the powers that Parliament had been seeking since the Petition of Right in 1628.

Primary Source

Whereas, the late King James II . . . did endeavor to subvert and exirpate [eliminate] the Protestant religion and the laws and liberties of this kingdom . . . and whereas the said late king James II having abdicated the government, and the throne being vacant. . . . The said Lords [Parliament] . . . being now assembled in a full and free representative [body] of this nation . . . do in the first place . . . declare

- That the pretended [untruthfully claimed] power of suspending the laws or the execution of laws by regal authority without consent of Parliament is illegal;
- That the pretended power of dispensing with laws or the execution of laws by regal authority, as it hath been assumed and exercised of late, is illegal; . . .
- That levying [collecting] money for or to the use of the Crown by pretence of prerogative [a right exclusive to a king or queen], without grant of Parliament, for longer time, or in other manner than the same is or shall be granted, is illegal;
- That it is the right of the subjects to petition [make a request of] the king, and all commitments and prosecutions for such petitioning are illegal;
- That the raising or keeping a standing army within the kingdom in time of peace, unless it be with consent of Parliament, is against law;
- That the subjects which are Protestants may have arms for their defence suitable to their conditions and as allowed by law;
- That election of members of Parliament ought to be free;
- That the freedom of speech and debates or proceedings in Parliament ought not to be impeached [discredited] or questioned in any court or place out of Parliament;
- That excessive bail ought not to be required, nor excessive fines imposed, nor cruel and unusual punishments inflicted;
- That jurors ought to be duly [done at a proper time] impaneled [registered on a panel of jurors] and returned [released from service], and jurors which pass upon men in trials for high treason ought to be freeholders [property owners with unconditional rights];
- That all grants and promises of fines and forfeitures of particular persons before conviction are illegal and void;
- And that for redress [correction] of all grievances, and for the amending, strengthening and preserving of the laws, Parliaments ought to be held frequently.

ASSESSMENT

1. **Analyze Interactions** Review the American Declaration of Independence. What similarities do you notice between the two documents?
2. **Determine Central Ideas** Which ideas in the English Bill of Rights influenced the formation of the United States government?

3. **Cite Evidence** How did the English Bill of Rights expand the rights of common Englishmen? Cite specific examples from the text to support your answer.
4. **Determine Central Ideas** How did the English Bill of Rights make Parliament more powerful? Provide specific examples from the text in your response.

[*Two Treatises of Government:* John Locke]

Introduction

English philosopher John Locke (1632–1704) published *Two Treatises of Government* in 1690. Locke believed that all people had the same natural rights of life, liberty, and property. In this essay, Locke states that the primary purpose of government is to protect these natural rights. He also states that governments hold their power only with the consent of the people. Locke's ideas greatly influenced revolutions in America and France.

Primary Source

But though men, when they enter into society give up the equality, liberty, and executive power they had in the state of Nature into the hands of society . . . the power of the society or legislative constituted by them can never be supposed to extend farther than the common good. . . . Whoever has the legislative or supreme power of any commonwealth, is bound to govern by established standing laws, promulgated [published or made known] and known to the people, and not by extemporary [without any preparation] decrees, by indifferent and upright judges, who are to decide controversies by those laws; and to employ the force of the community at home only in the execution of such laws, or abroad to prevent or redress foreign injuries and secure the community from inroads [advances at the expense of someone] and invasion. And all this to be directed to no other end but the peace, safety, and public good of the people. . . .

The reason why men enter into society is the preservation of their property; and the end while they choose and authorize a legislative is that there may be laws made, and rules set, as guards and fences to the properties of all the society, . . .

Whensoever, therefore, the legislative [power] shall transgress [go beyond; break] this fundamental rule of society, and either by ambition, fear, folly, or corruption, endeavor to grasp themselves, or put into the hands of any other, an absolute power over the lives, liberties, and estates of the people, by this breach of trust they forfeit the power the people had put into their hands for quite contrary ends, and it devolves [passes] to the people; who have a right to resume their original liberty, and by the establishment of a new legislative (such as they shall think fit), provide for their own safety and security. . .

ASSESSMENT

1. **Summarize** What does Locke say is the duty of government?
2. **Cite Evidence** What evidence is there in the text to support Locke's belief that a land should only be governed with the consent of the governed?
3. **Identify Cause and Effect** Based on what you already know, what aspects of Locke's *Treatises* likely affected the events leading to the founding of America? Cite evidence from the text to support your response.

[*The Spirit of Laws*: Baron de Montesquieu]

Introduction

In 1748, the French aristocrat Baron de Montesquieu (1689–1755) wrote *The Spirit of Laws*, in which he concluded that the separation of the executive, legislative, and judicial powers was in the best interests of the people. Both the French revolutionary thinkers and the Framers of the United States Constitution were influenced by Montesquieu's ideas.

Primary Source

The principle of democracy is corrupted not only when the spirit of equality is extinct, but likewise when they fall into a spirit of extreme equality, and when each citizen would fain be [be satisfied] upon a level with those whom he has chosen to command him. Then the people, incapable of bearing the very power they have delegated, want to manage everything themselves, to debate for the senate, to execute for the magistrate [judicial officer of limited authority], and to decide for the judges.

When this is the case, virtue can no longer subsist [survive] in the republic. The people are desirous of exercising the functions of the magistrates, who cease to be revered. . . .

Democracy has, therefore, two excesses to avoid—the spirit of inequality, which leads to aristocracy or monarchy, and the spirit of extreme equality, which leads to despotic [authoritarian; tyrannical] power, as the latter is completed by conquest. . . .

In the state of nature, indeed, all men are born equal, but they cannot continue in this equality. Society makes them lose it, and they recover it only by the protection of the laws.

Such is the difference between a well-regulated democracy and one that is not so, that in the former men are equal only as citizens, but in the latter they are equal also as magistrates, as senators, as judges, as fathers, as husbands, or as masters.

The natural place of virtue is near to liberty; but it is not nearer to excessive liberty than to servitude. . . .

Democratic and aristocratic states are not in their own nature free. Political liberty is to be found only in moderate governments; and even in these it is not always found. It is there only when there is no abuse of power. . . .

To prevent this abuse, it is necessary from the very nature of things that power should be a check to power. A government may be so constituted, as no man shall be compelled to do things to which the law does not oblige him, nor forced to abstain from things which the law permits. . . .

When the legislative and executive powers are united in the same person, or in the same body of magistrates, there can be no liberty; because apprehensions may arise, lest the same monarch or senate should enact tyrannical laws, to execute them in a tyrannical manner. . . .

Again, there is no liberty, if the judiciary power be not separated from the legislative and executive. Were it joined with the legislative, the life and liberty of the subject would be exposed to arbitrary control; for the judge would be then the legislator. Were it joined to the executive power, the judge might behave with violence and oppression.

There would be an end of everything, were the same man or the same body, whether of the nobles or of the people, to exercise those three powers, that of enacting laws, that of executing the public resolutions, and of trying the causes of individuals.

ASSESSMENT

1. **Determine Author's Purpose** For what reasons does Montesquieu promote the separation of powers?
2. **Analyze Interactions** How is the influence of Montesquieu's ideas revealed in the United States Constitution?
3. **Determine Meaning** Explain the distinction Montesquieu makes between democracy and liberty (or equality).

[*The Social Contract:* Jean-Jacques Rousseau]

Introduction

Jean-Jacques Rousseau (1712–1778) was one of the leaders of the intellectual movement known as the Enlightenment. Enlightenment philosophers, inspired by the scientific advances made by Isaac Newton and others, tried to explain various aspects of human existence based on logic and reason.

In *The Social Contract* (1762), Rousseau states that early people living in a state of nature were free, in the sense that they could do whatever they wanted. Of course, they were also at the mercy of other people who were doing whatever they wanted.

In forming or joining a society, Rousseau says, each person enters into an implicit contract. A social contract exists between each person and the group of all people. The individual gives up some of his or her freedom in exchange for the protection and benefits offered by the group.

Rousseau referred to this group of people, acting as one for the benefit of all, as the "body politic," or the "Sovereign." It is this Sovereign that establishes the government.

Primary Source

What we have just said confirms . . . that the depositaries of [people who are entrusted with] the executive power are not the people's masters, but its officers; that it can set them up and pull them down when it likes; that for them there is no question of contract, but of obedience and that in taking charge of the functions the State imposes on them they are doing no more than fulfilling their duty as citizens, without having the remotest right to argue about the conditions. . . .

It is true that … the established government should never be touched except when it comes to be incompatible with the public good; but the circumspection [careful thought and judgment] this involves is a maxim [general truth or rule of conduct] of policy and not a rule of right, and the State is no more bound to leave civil authority in the hands of its rulers than military authority in the hands of its generals. . . .

The periodical assemblies of which I have already spoken are designed to prevent or postpone this calamity, above all when they need no formal summoning; for in that case, the prince cannot stop them without openly declaring himself a law-breaker and an enemy of the State.

The opening of these assemblies, whose sole object is the maintenance of the social treaty, should always take the form of putting two propositions that may not be suppressed, which should be voted on separately.

The first is: "Does it please the Sovereign to preserve the present form of government?"

The second is: "Does it please the people to leave its administration in the hands of those who are actually [currently] in charge of it?"

ASSESSMENT

1. **Determine Meaning** What does the underlined pronoun refer to in this excerpt, and what effect does this usage have on Rousseau's message? "What we have just said confirms . . . that the depositaries of [people who are entrusted with] the executive power are not the people's masters, but its officers; that <u>it</u> can set them up and pull them down when it likes . . . ."
2. **Determine Author's Purpose** In Paragraph 3 of the excerpt, what does the phrase "this calamity" refer to, and how does it affect Rousseau's overall purpose?
3. **Compare and Contrast** According to Rousseau, how is the government like the military?
4. **Assess an Argument** The assemblies Rousseau mentions are periodic meetings of all the citizens of a State in which various matters are voted upon. Do you think this is a good idea? Explain your reasoning.

["Give Me Liberty or Give Me Death": Patrick Henry]

Introduction

Patrick Henry was born in Virginia in 1735. Trained as an attorney while a young man, he became known for his speaking skills. Henry was elected to the Virginia House of Burgesses in 1765 and strongly opposed the Stamp Act. In a speech related to the crisis, he spoke against Parliament and the king, declaring, "If this be treason, make the most of it." Bitter criticism from delegates forced him to apologize for the statement and affirm his loyalty to the king.

In March 1775, Henry made the following speech, which became his best known. Some credit this speech with being the deciding act in gaining Virginia's troops for the Revolutionary cause. At the end of the speech, members of the assembly jumped from their seats and shouted, "To Arm! To Arms!"

Primary Source

They tell us, sir, that we are weak; unable to cope with so formidable an adversary [enemy; opponent]. But when shall we be stronger? Will it be the next week, or the next year? Will it be when we are totally disarmed, and when a British guard shall be stationed in every house? Shall we gather strength by irresolution [uncertainty on how to act] and inaction? Shall we acquire the means of effectual resistance by lying supinely [reclined on one's back] on our backs and hugging the delusive [unreal; misleading] phantom of hope, until our enemies shall have bound us hand and foot?

Sir, we are not weak if we make a proper use of those means which the God of nature hath placed in our power. Three millions of people armed in the holy cause of liberty, and in such a country as that which we possess, are invincible by any force which our enemy can send against us. . . . The battle, sir, is not to the strong alone; it is to the vigilant [on the alert for danger], the active, the brave.

Besides, sir, we have no election. If we were base enough to desire it, it is now too late to retire from the contest. There is no retreat but in submission and slavery! Our chains are forged! Their clanking may be heard on the plains of Boston! The war is inevitable—and let it come! I repeat, sir, let it come!

It is vain, sir, to extenuate [to excuse; to make light of] the matter. The gentlemen may cry, Peace, peace! But there is no peace. The war has actually begun! The next gale that sweeps from the north will bring to our ears the clash of resounding arms! Our brethren are already in the field! Why stand we here idle? What is it that gentlemen wish? What would they have? Is life so dear or peace so sweet as to be purchased at the price of chains and slavery? Forbid it, almighty God. I know not what course others may take, but as for me, give me liberty or give me death!

ASSESSMENT

1. **Analyze Word Choices** What militaristic words does Henry use when making his argument? How do they impact the effectiveness of his speech?
2. **Assess an Argument** Do you think Henry's argument is effective? Refer to a specific part of the speech in your response.
3. **Explain an Argument** Suppose someone was unconvinced by Henry's argument. What would be the counter-argument to his speech?

[*Common Sense*: Thomas Paine]

Introduction

In 1776, after the battles at Lexington and Concord, Thomas Paine published a fiery fifty-page pamphlet that challenged the authority of the British government and the royal monarchy. Paine appealed to the people of America to seek independence from Great Britain.

Primary Source

. . . As to the government matters, it is not in the power of Britain to do this continent justice: The business of it will soon be too weighty, and intricate, to be managed with any tolerable degree of convenience, by a power, so distant from us, and so very ignorant of us. . . .

[L]et a day be solemnly set apart for proclaiming the charter; . . . let a crown be placed thereon, by which the world may know, that so far as we approve of monarchy, that in America the law is king. For as in absolute governments the King is law, so in free countries the law ought to be King; and there ought to be no other. But lest any ill use should afterwards arise, let the crown at the conclusion of the ceremony be demolished, and scattered among the people whose right it is.

A government of our own is our natural right: And when a man seriously reflects on the precariousness of human affairs, he will become convinced, that it is infinitely wiser and safer, to form a constitution of our own in a cool deliberate manner, while we have it in our power, than to trust such an interesting event to time and chance.

ASSESSMENT

1. **Summarize** What are the main points Paine makes in this excerpt?
2. **Distinguish Among Fact, Opinion, and Reasoned Judgment** Reread the first and third passages excerpted here. Determine whether each one is fact, opinion, or reasoned judgment. Explain your reasoning.

[Virginia Declaration of Rights]

Introduction

The Virginia Declaration of Rights was largely the work of George Mason (1725–1792), one of Virginia's wealthiest planters and a neighbor and friend of George Washington. The Declaration was adopted unanimously by the Virginia Convention of Delegates on June 12, 1776, and was later incorporated within the Virginia state constitution. It influenced a number of later documents, including the Declaration of Independence and the Bill of Rights.

Primary Source

A declaration of rights made by the representatives of the good people of Virginia, assembled in full and free convention; which rights do pertain to them and their posterity, as the basis and foundation of government.

I That all men are by nature equally free and independent, and have certain inherent rights, of which, when they enter into a state of society, they cannot, by any compact, deprive or divest their posterity [descendants]; namely, the enjoyment of life and liberty, with the means of acquiring and possessing property, and pursuing and obtaining happiness and safety.

II That all power is vested in [placed in possession of], and consequently [therefore] derived from, the people; that magistrates [government officials] are their trustees and servants, and at all times amenable to them.

III That government is, or ought to be, instituted for the common benefit, protection, and security of the people, nation or community; of all the various modes and forms of government that is best, which is capable of producing the greatest degree of happiness and safety and is most effectually secured against the danger of maladministration; and that, whenever any government shall be found inadequate or contrary [opposed; opposite] to these purposes, a majority of the community hath an indubitable [unquestionable], unalienable [incapable of being transferred], and indefeasible [incapable of being declared invalid] right to reform, alter or abolish it, in such manner as shall be judged most conducive to the public weal [well-being].

IV That no man, or set of men, are entitled to exclusive or separate emoluments [payment] or privileges from the community, but [except] in consideration of public services; which, not being descendible [capable of being inherited], neither ought the offices of magistrate, legislator, or judge be hereditary.

V That the legislative and executive powers of the state should be separate and distinct from the judicative; and, [in order] that the members of the two first may be restrained [shielded] from oppression by feeling and participating the burthens [burdens] of the people, they should, at fixed periods, be reduced to a private station, return into that body from which they were originally taken, and the vacancies be supplied by frequent, certain, and regular elections in which all, or any part of the former members, to be again eligible, or ineligible, as the laws shall direct.

VI That elections of members to serve as representatives of the people in assembly ought to be free; and that all men, having sufficient evidence of permanent common interest with, and attachment to, the community have the right of suffrage [voting] and cannot be taxed or deprived of their property for public uses without their own consent or that of their representatives so elected, nor bound by any law to which they have not, in like manner, assented, for the public good.

VII That all power of suspending laws, or the execution of laws, by any authority without consent of the representatives of the people is injurious to their rights and ought not to be exercised.

VIII That in all capital or criminal prosecutions a man hath a right to demand the cause and nature of his accusation to be confronted with the accusers and witnesses, to call for evidence in his favor, and to a speedy trial by an impartial jury of his vicinage [neighbors], without whose unanimous consent he cannot be found guilty, nor can he be compelled [forced] to give evidence against himself; that no man be deprived of his liberty except by the law of the land or the judgement of his peers.

IX That excessive bail ought not to be required, nor excessive fines imposed; nor cruel and unusual punishments inflicted.

X That general warrants, whereby any officer or messenger may be commanded to search suspected places without evidence of a fact committed, or to seize any person or persons not named, or whose offense is not particularly [specifically] described and supported by evidence, are grievous and oppressive and ought not to be granted.

XI That in controversies respecting property and in suits between man and man, the ancient trial by jury is preferable to any other and ought to be held sacred.

XII That the freedom of the press is one of the greatest bulwarks of liberty and can never be restrained but [except] by despotic governments.

XIII That a well regulated militia, composed of the body of the people, trained to arms, is the proper, natural, and safe defense of a free state; that standing [permanent] armies, in time of peace, should be avoided as dangerous to liberty; and that, in all cases, the military should be under strict subordination to, and be governed by, the civil power.

XIV That the people have a right to uniform government; and therefore, that no government separate from, or independent of, the government of Virginia, ought to be erected or established within the limits thereof.

XV That no free government, or the blessings of liberty, can be preserved to any people but by a firm adherence to justice, moderation, temperance, frugality, and virtue and by frequent recurrence to fundamental principles.

XVI That religion, or the duty which we owe to our Creator and the manner of discharging it, can be directed by reason and conviction, not by force or violence; and therefore, all men are equally entitled to the free exercise of religion, according to the dictates of conscience; and that it is the mutual duty of all to practice Christian forbearance, love, and charity towards each other.

ASSESSMENT

1. **Determine Author's Point of View** What do you think was Mason's attitude toward government? Cite specific articles to support your analysis.
2. **Integrate Information from Diverse Sources** How might Mason's words in Article I have influenced Thomas Jefferson when he wrote the preamble to the Declaration of Independence? Cite specific examples from one or both documents in your answer.

[Virginia Statute for Religious Freedom: Thomas Jefferson]

Introduction

In 1786, the Virginia legislature adopted the Statute for Religious Freedom, written by Thomas Jefferson. The law is still part of the Virginia state constitution.

Other states followed Virginia's lead. The Statute for Religious Freedom later became the basis for the First Amendment to the United States Constitution, which guarantees freedom of religion.

Primary Source

I. *Whereas* Almighty God hath created the mind free … that to compel a man to furnish contributions of money for the propagation [spreading] of opinions which he disbelieves and abhors [hates], is sinful and tyrannical … that our civil rights have no dependence on our religious opinions, any more than our opinions in physics or geometry….

II. *Be it … enacted by the General Assembly*, that no man shall be compelled to frequent or support any religious worship, place, or ministry whatsoever, nor shall be enforced, restrained, molested, or burdened in his body or goods, nor shall otherwise suffer, on account of his religious opinions or belief; but that all men shall be free to profess, and by argument to maintain, their opinions in matters of religion, and that the same shall in no wise diminish, enlarge, or affect their civil capacities.

III. And although we well know that this Assembly, elected by the people for the ordinary purpose of legislation only, have no power to restrain the acts of succeeding assemblies, constituted with powers equal to our own, and that therefore to declare this act to be irrevocable [impossible to invalidate or take back] would be of no effect in law; yet we are free to declare, and do declare, that the rights hereby asserted are of the natural rights of mankind, and that if any act shall hereafter be passed to repeal the present, or to narrow its operation, such an act will be infringement of natural right.

ASSESSMENT

1. **Cite Evidence** What part of this excerpt could be cited as support for the idea that government funds, which come from sources such as taxes, should not be given to religious institutions?
2. **Analyze Structure** What is the purpose of each of the three articles in the Statute?

[Articles of Confederation]

Introduction

The Articles of Confederation were approved on November 15, 1777, and were in effect from March 1, 1781, when they were finally ratified by all 13 states, until March 4, 1789. They established a weak central government, which led to conflicts among the states. Demand soon grew for a stronger central government, leading to the creation of the United States Constitution.

Primary Source

To all to whom these Presents shall come, we the undersigned Delegates of the States affixed to our Names send greeting. Whereas the Delegates of the United States of America in Congress assembled did on the fifteenth day of November in the Year of our Lord One Thousand Seven Hundred and Seventy seven, and in the Second Year of the Independence of America agree to certain articles of Confederation [an alliance of states, usually for the purpose of defense] and perpetual [continuing forever] Union between the States of New Hampshire, Massachusetts Bay, Rhode Island and Providence Plantations, Connecticut, New York, New Jersey, Pennsylvania, Delaware, Maryland, Virginia, North Carolina, South Carolina and Georgia in the Words following, viz. [namely] "Articles of Confederation and perpetual Union between the states of New Hampshire, Massachusetts Bay, Rhode Island and Providence Plantations, Connecticut, New York, New Jersey, Pennsylvania, Delaware, Maryland, Virginia, North Carolina, South Carolina and Georgia."

[ART. I.] The Stile [style; name] of this confederacy shall be "The United States of America."

[ART. II.] Each state retains its sovereignty [the ability to make one's own laws and govern oneself], freedom and independence, and every Power, Jurisdiction and right, which is not by this confederation expressly delegated to the United States, in Congress assembled.

[ART. III.] The said states hereby severally enter into a firm league of friendship with each other, for their common defence, the security of their Liberties, and their mutual and general welfare, binding themselves to assist each other, against all force offered to, or attacks made upon them, or any of them, on account of religion, sovereignty, trade, or any other pretence whatever.

[ART. IV.] The better to secure and perpetuate mutual friendship and intercourse [communication and actions] among the people of the different states in this union, the free inhabitants of each of these states, paupers, vagabonds and fugitives from Justice excepted, shall be entitled to all privileges and immunities of free citizens in the several states; and the people of each state shall have free ingress [entrance] and regress [return] to and from any other state, and shall enjoy therein all the privileges of trade and commerce, subject to the same duties [taxes on imports or exports], impositions [taxes] and restrictions as the inhabitants thereof respectively, provided that such restriction shall not extend so far as to prevent the removal of property imported into any state, to any other state of which the Owner is an inhabitant; provided also that no imposition, duties or restriction shall be laid by any state, on the property of the united states, or either of them.

If any Person guilty of, or charged with treason, felony, or other high misdemeanor in any state, shall flee from Justice, and be found in any of the united states, he shall upon demand of the Governor or executive power, of the state from which he fled, be delivered up and removed to the state having jurisdiction of his offence.

Full faith and credit shall be given in each of these states to the records, acts and judicial proceedings of the courts and magistrates of every other state.

[ART. V.] For the more convenient management of the general interests of the united states, delegates shall be annually appointed in such manner as the legislature of each state shall direct, to meet in Congress on the first Monday in November, in every year, with a power reserved to each state, to recall its delegates, or any of them, at any time within the year, and to send others in their stead, for the remainder of the Year.

No state shall be represented in Congress by less than two, nor by more than seven Members; and no person shall be capable of being a delegate for more than three years in any term of six years; nor shall any person, being a delegate, be capable of holding any office under the united states, for which he, or another for his benefit receives any salary, fees or emolument [payment] of any kind.

Each state shall maintain its own delegates in a meeting of the states, and while they act as members of the committee of the states.

In determining questions in the united states, in Congress assembled, each state shall have one vote.

Freedom of speech and debate in Congress shall not be impeached or questioned in any Court, or place out of Congress, and the members of congress shall be protected in their persons from arrests and imprisonments, during the time of their going to and from, and attendance on congress, except for treason, felony, or breach of the peace.

[ART. VI.] No state without the Consent of the united states in congress assembled, shall send any embassy to, or receive any embassy from, or enter into any conference, agreement, or alliance or treaty with any King, prince or state; nor shall any person holding any office of profit or trust under the united states, or any of them, accept of any present, emolument, office or title of any kind whatever from any king, prince or foreign state; nor shall the united states in congress assembled, or any of them, grant any title of nobility.

No two or more states shall enter into any treaty, confederation or alliance whatever between them, without the consent of the united states in congress assembled, specifying accurately the purposes for which the same is to be entered into, and how long it shall continue.

No state shall lay any imposts [taxes] or duties, which may interfere with any stipulations [conditions] in treaties, entered into by the united states in congress assembled, with any king, prince or state, in pursuance of any treaties already proposed by congress, to the courts of France and Spain.

No vessels of war shall be kept up in time of peace by any state, except such number only, as shall be deemed necessary by the united states in congress assembled, for the defence of such state, or its trade; nor shall any body of forces be kept up by any state, in time of peace, except such number only, as in the judgment of the united states, in congress assembled, shall be deemed requisite to garrison [assign troops to] the forts necessary for the defence of such state; but every state shall always keep up a well regulated and disciplined militia, sufficiently armed and accounted, and shall provide and constantly have ready for use, in public stores, a due number of field pieces and tents, and a proper quantity of arms, ammunition and camp equipage.

No state shall engage in any war without the consent of the united states in congress assembled, unless such state be actually invaded by enemies, or shall have received certain advice of a resolution being formed by some nation of Indians to invade such state and the danger is so imminent as not to admit of a delay, till the united states in congress assembled can be consulted: nor shall any state grant commissions to any ships or vessels of war, nor letters of marque [written permissions to cross a border] or reprisal, except it be after a declaration of war by the united states in congress assembled, and then only against the kingdom or state and the subjects thereof, against which war has been so declared, and under such regulations as shall be established by the united states in congress assembled, unless such state be infested by pirates, in which case vessels of war may be fitted out for that occasion, and kept so long as the danger shall continue, or until the united states in congress assembled shall determine otherwise.

[ART. VII.] When land-forces are raised by any state for the common defence, all officers of or under the rank of colonel, shall be appointed by the legislature of each state respectively by whom such forces shall be raised, or in such manner as such state shall direct, and all vacancies shall be filled up by the state which first made the appointment.

[ART. VIII.] All charges of war, and all other expences that shall be incurred for the common defence or general welfare, and allowed by the united states in congress assembled, shall be defrayed out of a common treasury, which shall be supplied by the several states, in proportion to the value of all land within each state, granted to or surveyed for any Person, as such land and the buildings and improvements thereon shall be estimated according to such mode as the united states in congress assembled, shall from time to time direct and appoint. The taxes for paying that proportion shall be laid and levied by the authority and direction of the legislatures of the several states within the time agreed upon by the united states in congress assembled.

[ART. IX.] The united states in congress assembled, shall have the sole and exclusive right and power of determining on peace and war, except in the cases mentioned in the sixth article—of sending and receiving ambassadors—entering into treaties and alliances, provided that no treaty of commerce shall be made whereby the legislative power of the respective states shall be restrained from imposing such imposts and duties on foreigners, as their own people are subjected to, or from prohibiting the exportation or importation of any species of goods or commodities whatsoever—of establishing rules for deciding in all cases, what captures on land or water shall be legal, and in what manner prizes taken by land or naval forces in the service of the united states shall be divided or appropriated—of granting letters of marque and reprisal in times of peace—appointing courts for the trial of piracies and felonies committed on the high seas and establishing courts for receiving and determining finally appeals in all cases of captures, provided that no member of congress shall be appointed a judge of any of the said courts.

The united states in congress assembled shall also be the last resort on appeal in all disputes and differences now subsisting [existing] or that hereafter may arise between two or more states concerning boundary, jurisdiction or any other cause whatever; which authority shall always be exercised in the manner following. Whenever the legislative or executive authority or lawful agent [of any] state in controversy with another shall present a petition to congress stating the matter in question and praying for a hearing, notice thereof shall be given by order of congress to the legislative or executive authority of the other state in controversy, and a day assigned for the appearance of the parties by their lawful agents, who shall then be directed to appoint by joint consent, commissioners or judges to constitute a court for hearing and determining the matter in question; but if they cannot agree, congress shall name three persons out of each of the united states, and from the list of such persons each party shall alternately strike out one, the petitioners beginning, until the number shall be reduced to thirteen; and from that number not less than seven, nor more than nine names as congress shall direct, shall in the presence of congress be drawn out by lot, and the persons whose names shall be so drawn or any five of them, shall be commissioners or judges, to hear and finally determine the controversy, so always as a major part of the judges who shall hear the cause shall agree in the determination: and if either party shall neglect to attend at the day appointed, without shewing [showing] reasons, which congress shall judge sufficient, or being present shall refuse to strike, the congress shall proceed to nominate three persons out of each state, and the secretary of congress shall strike in behalf of such party absent or refusing; and the judgment and sentence of the court to be appointed, in the manner before prescribed, shall be final and conclusive; and if any of the parties shall refuse to submit to the authority of such court, or to appear to defend their claim or cause, the court shall nevertheless proceed to pronounce sentence, or judgment, which shall in like manner be final and decisive, the judgment or sentence and other proceedings being in either case transmitted to congress, and lodged among the acts of congress for the security of the parties concerned: provided that every commissioner, before he sits in judgment, shall take an oath to be administered by one of the judges of the supreme or superior court of the state, where the cause shall be tried, "well and truly to hear and determine the matter in question, according to the best of his judgment, without favour, affection or hope of reward;" provided also that no state shall be deprived of territory for the benefit of the united states.

All controversies concerning the private right of soil claimed under different grants of two or more states, whose jurisdictions as they may respect such lands, and the states which passed such grants are adjusted, the said grants or either of them being at the same time claimed to have originated antecedent to such settlement of jurisdiction, shall on the petition of either party to the congress of the united states, be finally determined as near as may be in the same manner as is before prescribed for deciding disputes respecting territorial jurisdiction between different states.

The united states in congress assembled shall also have the sole and exclusive right and power of regulating the alloy and value of coin struck by their own authority, or by that of the respective states—fixing the standard of weights and measures throughout the united states—regulating the trade and managing all affairs with the Indians, not members of any of the states, provided that the legislative right of any state within its own limits be not infringed or violated— establishing and regulating post-offices from one state to another, throughout all the united states, and exacting such postage on the papers passing thro' [through] the same as may be requisite to defray [pay] the expences of the said office—appointing all officers of the land forces, in the service of the united states, excepting regimental officers—appointing all the officers of the naval forces, and commissioning all officers whatever in the service of the united states—making rules for the government and regulation of the said land and naval forces, and directing their operations.

The united states in congress assembled shall have authority to appoint a committee, to sit in the recess of congress, to be denominated "A Committee of the States," and to consist of one delegate from each state; and to appoint such other committees and civil officers as may be necessary for managing the general affairs of the united states under their direction—to appoint one of their number to preside, provided that no person be allowed to serve in the office of president more than one year in any term of three years; to ascertain the necessary sums of Money to be raised for the service of the united states, and to appropriate and apply the same for defraying the public expences—to borrow money, or emit bills on the credit of the united states, transmitting every half year to the respective states an account of the sums of money so borrowed or emitted— to build and equip a navy—to agree upon the number of land forces, and to make requisitions from each state for its quota, in proportion to the number of white inhabitants in such state; which requisition shall be binding, and thereupon the legislature of each state shall appoint the regimental officers, raise the men and clothe, arm and equip them in a soldier like manner, at the expence of the united states, and the officers and men so clothed, armed and equipped shall march to the place appointed, and within the time agreed on by the united states in congress assembled. But if the united states in congress assembled shall, on consideration of circumstances judge proper that any state should not raise men, or should raise a smaller number than its quota, and that any other state should raise a greater number of men than the quota thereof, such extra number shall be raised, officered, clothed, armed and equipped in the same manner as the quota of such state, unless the legislature of such state shall judge that such extra number cannot be safely spared out of the same, in which case they shall raise, officer, clothe, arm and equip as many of such extra number as they judge can be safely spared. And the officers and men so clothed, armed and equipped, shall march to the place appointed, and within the time agreed on by the united states in congress assembled.

The united states in congress assembled shall never engage in a war, nor grant letters of marque and reprisal in time of peace, nor enter into any treaties or alliances, nor coin money, nor regulate the value thereof, nor ascertain the sums and expences necessary for the defence and welfare of the united states, or any of them, nor emit bills, nor borrow money on the credit of the united states, nor appropriate money, nor agree upon the number of vessels of war, to be built or purchased, or the number of land or sea forces to be raised, nor appoint a commander in chief of the army or navy, unless nine states assent to the same: nor shall a question on any other point, except for adjourning from day to day be determined, unless by the votes of a majority of the united states in congress assembled.

The congress of the united states shall have power to adjourn to any time within the year, and to any place within the united states, so that no period of adjournment be for a longer duration than the space of six Months, and shall publish the Journal of their proceedings monthly, except such parts thereof relating to treaties, alliances or military operations as in their judgment require secrecy; and the yeas and nays of the delegates of each state on any question shall be entered on the Journal, when it is desired by any delegate; and the delegates of a state, or any of them, at his or their request shall be furnished with a transcript of the said Journal, except such parts as are above excepted, to lay before the legislatures of the several states.

[ART. X.] The committee of the states, or any nine of them, shall be authorised to execute, in the recess of congress, such of the powers of congress as the united states in congress assembled, by the consent of nine states, shall from time to time think expedient to vest them with; provided that no power be delegated to the said committee, for the exercise of which, by the articles of confederation, the voice of nine states in the congress of the united states assembled is requisite.

[ART. XI.] Canada acceding to this confederation, and joining in the measures of the united states, shall be admitted into, and entitled to all the advantages of this union: but no other colony shall be admitted into the same, unless such admission be agreed to by nine states.

[ART. XII.] All bills of credit emitted, monies borrowed and debts contracted by, or under the authority of congress, before the assembling of the united states, in pursuance of the present confederation, shall be deemed and considered as a charge against the united states, for payment and satisfaction whereof the said united states, and the public faith are hereby solemnly pledged.

[ART. XIII.] Every state shall abide by [conform to; agree to] the determinations of the united states in congress assembled, on all questions which by this confederation are submitted to them. And the Articles of this confederation shall be inviolably observed by every state, and the union shall be perpetual; nor shall any alteration at any time hereafter be made in any of them; unless such alteration be agreed to in a congress of the united states, and be afterwards confirmed by the legislatures of every state.

And whereas it hath pleased the Great Governor of the World to incline [bend something in a certain direction] the hearts of the legislatures we respectively represent in congress, to approve of, and to authorize us to ratify the said articles of confederation and perpetual union. Know ye that we the undersigned delegates, by virtue of the power and authority to us given for that purpose, do by these presents, in the name and in behalf of our respective constituents, fully and entirely ratify and confirm each and every of the said articles of confederation and perpetual union, and all and singular the matters and things therein contained: And we do further solemnly plight [pledge] and engage the faith of our respective constituents, that they shall abide by the determinations of the united states in congress assembled, on all questions, which by the said confederation are submitted to them. And that the articles thereof shall be inviolably [without failure] observed by the states we respectively represent, and that the union shall be perpetual. In Witness whereof we have hereunto set our hands in Congress. Done at Philadelphia in the state of Pennsylvania the ninth Day of July in the Year of our Lord one Thousand seven Hundred and Seventy-eight, and in the third year of the independence of America.

Josiah Bartlett
John Wentworth Junr
August 8th 1778
On The Part & Behalf Of The State Of New Hampshire

John Hancock
Samuel Adams
Elbridge Gerry
Francis Dana
James Lovell
Samuel Holten
On The Part And Behalf Of
The State Of Massachusetts Bay

William Ellery
Henry Marchant
John Collins
On The Part And Behalf
Of The State Of Rhode Island
And Providence Plantations

Roger Sherman
Samuel Huntington
Oliver Wolcott
Titus Hosmer
Andrew Adams
On The Part And Behalf Of
The State Of Connecticut

Jas Duane
Fras Lewis
Wm Duer.
Gouv Morris
On The Part And Behalf Of
The State Of New York

Jno Witherspoon
Nathl Scudder
On The Part And In Behalf Of
The State Of New Jersey.
Novr 26, 1778.—

Robt Morris
Daniel Roberdeau
Jona Bayard Smith.
William Clingan
Joseph Reed
22d July 1778
On The Part And Behalf Of
The State Of Pennsylvania

Tho Mckean
Feby 12 1779
John Dickinson
May 5th 1779
Nicholas Van Dyke,
On The Part & Behalf Of
The State Of Delaware

John Hanson
March 1 1781
Daniel Carroll Do
On The Part And Behalf
Of The State Of Maryland

Richard Henry Lee
John Banister
Thomas Adams
Jno Harvie
Francis Lightfoot Lee
On The Part And Behalf Of
The State Of Virginia

John Penn
July 21st 1778
Corns Harnett
Jno Williams
On The Part And Behalf
Of The State Of No Carolina

Henry Laurens
William Henry Drayton
Jno Mathews
Richd Hutson.
Thos Heyward Junr
On The Part & Behalf Of
The State Of South Carolina

Jno Walton
24th July 1778
Edwd Telfair.
Edwd Langworthy
On The Part And Behalf Of
The State Of Georgia

ASSESSMENT

1. **Draw Conclusions** As you have learned, a *confederation* is an alliance of states that typically forms for the purpose of defense. Why do you think the idea of a confederation was favored by the Framers at this point in American history? How would the idea continue to influence the Framers in subsequent years?
2. **Determine Central Ideas** Historians commonly criticize the Articles of Confederation for setting up only a "loose" confederation of states. In what way was the confederation of states "loose"? Explain your answer with evidence from the text.
3. **Explain an Argument** Explain the argument that one weakness of the Articles of Confederation was that Congress was not granted the power to levy taxes.
4. **Draw Conclusions** Taken as a whole, the Articles of Confederation did not establish a strong national government, despite rules, such as those in Article VI, denying states certain powers. Give an example of a power granted to Congress that could have been strengthened, thereby creating a stronger national government.

[Anti-Federalist Papers]

Introduction

When the Constitutional Convention of 1787 produced the new constitution, many opposed its adoption. There were numerous men who made strong arguments on behalf of the opponents, known as the Anti-Federalists. The following excerpts provide a sampling of Anti- Federalist arguments. Richard Henry Lee, a Virginian, wrote the best-known Anti-Federalist essays of the time, "Letters from the Federal Farmer to the Republican." The first selection below is from letters Lee wrote in October 1787. Luther Martin, the leading Anti-Federalist from Maryland, attended the Constitutional Convention as a delegate. The second selection is from a speech Martin gave on November 29, 1787. In it, he defends his decision to leave the Convention before its work was finished. Findley, Whitehill, and Smilie believed that they were prevented from expressing their views because of the political maneuverings of the Federalists. The third selection below is from "The Address and Reasons of Dissent of the Minority of the Convention of the State of Pennsylvania to their Constituents," which the three men published in the *Pennsylvania Packet and Daily Advertiser* on December 18, 1787.

Primary Source

"Letters from the Federal Farmer to the Republican," by Richard Henry Lee

The present moment discovers a new face in our affairs. Our object has been all along to reform our federal system and to strengthen our governments to establish peace, order, and justice in the community—but a new object now presents. The plan of government now proposed is evidently calculated totally to change, in time, our condition as a people. Instead of being thirteen republics under a federal head, it is clearly designed to make us one consolidated government. . . . This consolidation of the states has been the object of several men in this country for some time past. Whether such a change can ever be effected, in any manner; whether it can be effected without convulsions and civil wars; whether such a change will not totally destroy the liberties of this country, time only can determine. . . .

The Confederation was formed when great confidence was placed in the voluntary exertions of individuals and of the respective states; and the framers of it, to guard against usurpation [an illegal grab of power, authority, or sovereignty], so limited and checked the powers that, in many respects, they are inadequate to the exigencies [requirements; demands] of the Union. We find, therefore, members of Congress urging alterations in the federal system almost as soon as it was adopted. . . .

We expected too much from the return of peace, and, of course, we have been disappointed. Our governments have been new and unsettled; and several legislature, [by their actions] . . . have given just cause of uneasiness. . . .

The conduct of several legislatures touching paper-money and tender [method of payment] laws has prepared many honest men for changes in government, which otherwise they would not have thought of—when by the evils, on the one hand, and by the secret instigations of artful men, on the other, the minds of men were become sufficiently uneasy, a bold step was taken, which is usually followed by a revolution or a civil war. A general convention for mere commercial purposes was moved for—the authors of this measure saw that the people's attention was turned solely to the amendment of the federal system; and that, had the idea of a total change been started, probably no state would have appointed members to the Convention. The idea of destroying, ultimately, the state government and forming one consolidated system could not have been admitted. A convention, therefore, merely for vesting in Congress power to regulate trade was proposed. . . .

The plan proposed appears to be partly federal, but principally, however, calculated ultimately to make the states one consolidated government.

The first interesting question therefore suggested is how far the states can be consolidated into one entire government on free principles. In considering this question, extensive objects are to be taken into view, and important changes in the forms of government to be carefully attended to in all their consequences. The happiness of the people at large must be the great object with every honest statesman, and he will direct every movement to this point. If we are so situated as a people as not to be able to enjoy equal happiness and advantages under one government, the consolidation of the states cannot be admitted.

There are certain unalienable and fundamental rights, which in forming the social compact ought to be explicitly ascertained and fixed. A free and enlightened people, in forming this compact, will not resign all their rights to those who govern, and they will fix limits [a bill of rights] to their legislators and rulers, which will soon be plainly seen by those who are governed, as well as by those who govern; and the latter will know they cannot be passed unperceived by the former and without giving a general alarm. These rights should be made the basis of every constitution; and if a people be so situated, or have such different opinions, that they cannot agree in ascertaining and fixing them, it is a very strong argument against their attempting to form one entire society, to live under one system of laws only.

It may also be worthy our examination how far the provision for amending this plan, when it shall be adopted, is of any importance. No measures can be taken toward amendments unless two-thirds of the Congress, or two-thirds of the legislature of the several states, shall agree. While power is in the hands of the people, or democratic part of the community, more especially as at present, it is easy, according to the general course of human affairs, for the few influential men in the community to obtain conventions, alterations in government, and to persuade the common people that they may change for the better, and to get from them a part of the power. But when power is once transferred from the many to the few, all changes become extremely difficult; the government in this case being beneficial to the few, they will be exceedingly artful and adroit [skillful] in preventing any measures which may lead to a change; and nothing will produce it but great exertions and severe struggles on the part of the common people. Every man of reflection must see that the change now proposed is a transfer of power from the many to the few, and the probability is the artful and ever active aristocracy will prevent all peaceful measures for changes, unless when they shall discover some favorable moment to increase their own influence.

It is true there may be danger in delay; but there is danger in adopting the system in its present form. And I see the danger in either case will arise principally from the conduct and views of two very unprincipled parties in the United States—two fires, between which the honest and substantial people have long found themselves situated. One party is composed of little insurgents [people rising in opposition to a government], men in debt, who want no law and who want a share of the property of others—these are called levelers,

Shaysites [opponents of the new Constitution], etc. The other party is composed of a few but more dangerous men, with their servile [submissive] dependents; these avariciously [greedily] grasp at all power and property. You may discover in all the actions of these men an evident dislike to free and equal government, and they will go systematically to work to change, essentially, the forms of government in this country— these are called aristocrats . . . . . .

The fact is, these aristocrats support and hasten the adoption of the proposed Constitution merely because they think it is a stepping-stone to their favorite object. I think I am well-founded in this idea; I think the general politics of these men support it, as well as the common observation among them that the proffered plan is the best that can be got at present; it will do for a few years, and lead to something better. . . .

A speech given before the Maryland State legislature, November 29, 1787, by Luther Martin

It was the states as states, by their representatives in Congress, that formed the Articles of Confederation; it was the states as states, by their legislatures, who ratified those Articles; and it was there established and provided that the states as states (that is, by their legislatures) should agree to any alterations that should hereafter be proposed in the federal government, before they should be binding; and any alterations agreed to in any other manner cannot release the states from the obligation they are under to each other by virtue of the original Articles of Confederation. The people of the different states never made any objection to the manner in which the Articles of Confederation were formed or ratified, or to the mode by which alterations were to be made in that government—with the rights of their respective states they wished not to interfere. Nor do I believe the people, in their individual capacity, would ever have expected or desired to have been appealed to on the present occasion, in violation of the rights of their respective states, if the favorers of the proposed Constitution, imagining they had a better chance of forcing it to be adopted by a hasty appeal to the people at large (who could not be so good judges of the dangerous consequence), had not insisted upon this mode . . . .

It was also my opinion that, upon principles of sound policy, the agreement or disagreement to the proposed system ought to have been by the state legislatures; in which case, let the event have been what it would, there would have been but little prospect of the public peace being disturbed thereby; whereas the attempt to force down this system, although Congress and the respective state legislatures should disapprove, by appealing to the people and to procure [acquire] its establishment in a manner totally unconstitutional, has a tendency to set the state governments and their subjects at variance with each other, to lessen the obligations of government, to weaken the bands of society, to introduce anarchy and confusion, and to light the torch of discord and civil war throughout this continent. All these considerations weighed with me most forcibly against giving my assent to the mode by which it is resolved that this system is to be ratified, and were urged by me in opposition to the measure.

. . . [A] great portion of that time which ought to have been devoted calmly and impartially to consider what alterations in our federal government would be most likely to procure and preserve the happiness of the Union was employed in a violent struggle on the one side to obtain all power and dominion in their own hands, and on the other to prevent it; and that the aggrandizement of particular states, and particular individuals, appears to have been much more the subject sought after than the welfare of our country . . . .

When I took my seat in the Convention, I found them attempting to bring forward a system which, I was sure, never had entered into the contemplation of those I had the honor to represent, and which, upon the fullest consideration, I considered not only injurious to the interest and rights of this state but also incompatible with the political happiness and freedom of the states in general. From that time until my business compelled me to leave the Convention, I gave it every possible opposition, in every stage of its progression. I opposed the system there with the same explicit frankness with which I have here given you a history of our proceedings, an account of my own conduct, which in a particular manner I consider you as having a right to know. While there, I endeavored to act as became a free man and the delegate of a free state. Should my conduct obtain the approbation [act of approval] of those who appointed me, I will not deny it would afford me satisfaction; but to me that approbation was at most no more than a secondary consideration—my first was to deserve it. Left to myself to act according to the best of my discretion, my conduct should have been the same had I been even sure your censure would have been my only reward, since I hold it sacredly my duty to dash the cup of poison, if possible, from the hand of a state or an individual, however anxious the one or the other might be to swallow it . . . .

"The Address and Reasons of Dissent of the Minority of the Convention of the State of Pennsylvania to their Constituents," by William Findley, Robert Whitehill, and John Smilie

Our objections are comprised under three general heads of dissent, viz. [namely]:

We dissent, first, because it is the opinion of the most celebrated writers on government, and confirmed by uniform experience, that a very extensive territory cannot be governed on the principles of freedom otherwise than by a confederation of republics, possessing all the powers of internal government but united in the management of their general and foreign concerns. . . .

We dissent, secondly, because the powers vested in Congress by this Constitution must necessarily annihilate and absorb the legislative, executive, and judicial powers of the several states, and produce from their ruins one consolidated government, which from the nature of things will be an iron-handed despotism, as nothing short of the supremacy of despotic sway could connect and govern these United States under one government.

As the truth of this position is of such decisive importance, it ought to be fully investigated, and if it is founded, to be clearly ascertained; for, should it be demonstrated that the powers vested by this Constitution in Congress will have such an effect as necessarily to produce one consolidated government, the question then will be reduced to this short issue, viz.: whether satiated [satisfied] with the blessings of liberty, whether repenting [regretting] of the folly of so recently asserting their unalienable rights against foreign despots at the expense of so much blood and treasure, and such painful and arduous struggles, the people of America are now willing to resign every privilege of freemen, and submit to the dominion of an absolute government that will embrace all America in one chain of despotism; or whether they will, with virtuous indignation, spurn at the shackles prepared for them, and confirm their liberties by a conduct becoming freemen. . . .

We dissent, thirdly, because if it were practicable to govern so extensive a territory as these United States include, on the plan of a consolidated government, consistent with the principles of liberty and the happiness of the people, yet the construction of this Constitution is not calculated to attain the object; for independent of the nature of the case, it would of itself necessarily produce a despotism, and that not by the usual gradations [small steps or changes] but with the celerity [speed] that has hitherto only attended revolutions effected by the sword.

To establish the truth of this position, a cursory [hasty] investigation of the principles and form of this Constitution will suffice.

The first consideration that this review suggests is the omission of a Bill of Rights ascertaining and fundamentally establishing those unalienable and personal rights of men, without the full, free, and secure enjoyment of which there can be no liberty, and over which it is not necessary for a good government to have the control—the principal of which are the rights of conscience, personal liberty by the clear and unequivocal establishment of the writ of habeas corpus, jury trial in criminal and civil cases, by an impartial jury of the vicinage [neighborhood] or county, with the common law proceedings for the safety of the accused in criminal prosecutions; and the liberty of the press, that scourge of tyrants, and the grand bulwark [safeguard] of every other liberty and privilege. The stipulations [conditions of agreement] heretofore made in favor of them in the state constitutions are entirely superseded by this Constitution. . . .

ASSESSMENT

1. **Compare and Contrast** How are the arguments of the Anti-Federalists represented in these excerpts similar and different?
2. **Assess an Argument** What do you think are the strongest and weakest parts of the Anti-Federalists' overall argument? Cite specific examples in the text.
3. **Analyze Interactions** How have Anti-Federalist viewpoints such as those expressed in the excerpts influenced the system of government of the United States? Consider the Bill of Rights and the final version of the U.S. Constitution as part of your answer.

[*Federalist* No. 10: James Madison]

Introduction

Of the 85 *Federalist Papers*, it is believed that 29 of them were written by James Madison. Among them was *Federalist* No. 10, which presents Madison's observations on dealing with the "mischiefs of faction" and the advantages of a republican (representative) form of government over that of a pure democracy. It was first published on November 23, 1787.

Primary Source

Among the numerous advantages promised by a well constructed Union, none deserves to be more accurately developed than its tendency to break and control the violence of faction [a group within a larger political group]. The friend of popular governments never finds himself so much alarmed for their character and fate, as when he contemplates their propensity [tendency] to this dangerous vice. He will not fail, therefore, to set a due value on any plan which, without violating the principles to which he is attached, provides a proper cure for it. The instability, injustice, and confusion introduced into the public councils, have, in truth, been the mortal diseases under which popular governments have everywhere perished; as they continue to be the favorite and fruitful topics from which the adversaries to liberty derive their most specious [seemingly true, but actually false] declamations.

The valuable improvements made by the American constitutions on the popular models, both ancient and modern, cannot certainly be too much admired; but it would be an unwarrantable partiality, to contend that they have as effectually obviated [made unnecessary] the danger on this side, as was wished and expected. Complaints are everywhere heard from our most considerate and virtuous citizens, equally the friends of public and private faith, and of public and personal liberty, that our governments are too unstable, that the public good is disregarded in the conflicts of rival parties, and that measures are too often decided, not according to the rules of justice and the rights of the minor party, but by the superior force of an interested and overbearing majority. However anxiously we may wish that these complaints had no foundation, the evidence, of known facts will not permit us to deny that they are in some degree true.

It will be found, indeed, on a candid review of our situation, that some of the distresses under which we labor have been erroneously charged on the operation of our governments; but it will be found, at the same time, that other causes will not alone account for many of our heaviest misfortunes; and, particularly, for that prevailing and increasing distrust of public engagements, and alarm for private rights, which are echoed from one end of the continent to the other. These must be chiefly, if not wholly, effects of the unsteadiness and injustice with which a factious spirit has tainted our public administrations.

By a faction, I understand a number of citizens, whether amounting to a majority or a minority of the whole, who are united and actuated [caused to do something] by some common impulse of passion, or of interest, adversed to the rights of other citizens, or to the permanent and aggregate interests of the community.

There are two methods of curing the mischiefs of faction: the one, by removing its causes; the other, by controlling its effects.

There are again two methods of removing the causes of faction: the one, by destroying the liberty which is essential to its existence; the other, by giving to every citizen the same opinions, the same passions, and the same interests.

It could never be more truly said than of the first remedy, that it was worse than the disease. Liberty is to faction what air is to fire, an aliment without which it instantly expires. But it could not be less folly to abolish liberty, which is essential to political life, because it nourishes faction, than it would be to wish the annihilation of air, which is essential to animal life, because it imparts to fire its destructive agency.

The second expedient [a way of achieving a result] is as impracticable as the first would be unwise. As long as the reason of man continues fallible [capable of being wrong], and he is at liberty to exercise it, different opinions will be formed. As long as the connection subsists [exists] between his reason and his self- love, his opinions and his passions will have a reciprocal influence on each other; and the former will be objects to which the latter will attach themselves. The diversity in the faculties of men, from which the rights of property originate, is not less an insuperable [uncontrollable] obstacle to a uniformity of interests. The protection of these faculties is the first object of government. From the protection of different and unequal faculties of acquiring property, the possession of different degrees and kinds of property immediately results; and from the influence of these on the sentiments and views of the respective proprietors, ensues a division of the society into different interests and parties.

The latent causes of faction are thus sown in the nature of man; and we see them everywhere brought into different degrees of activity, according to the different circumstances of civil society. A zeal for different opinions concerning religion, concerning government, and many other points, as well of speculation as of practice; an attachment to different leaders ambitiously contending for pre-eminence and power; or to persons of other descriptions whose fortunes have been interesting to the human passions, have, in turn, divided mankind into parties, inflamed them with mutual animosity, and rendered them much more disposed to vex and oppress each other than to co-operate for their common good. So strong is this propensity of mankind to fall into mutual animosities, that where no substantial occasion presents itself, the most frivolous and fanciful distinctions have been sufficient to kindle their unfriendly passions and excite their most violent conflicts. But the most common and durable source of factions has been the various and unequal distribution of property. Those who hold and those who are without property have ever formed distinct interests in society. Those who are creditors, and those who are debtors, fall under a like discrimination. A landed interest, a manufacturing interest, a mercantile interest, a moneyed interest, with many lesser interests, grow up of necessity in civilized nations, and divide them into different classes, actuated by different sentiments and views. The regulation of these various and interfering interests forms the principal task of modern legislation, and involves the spirit of party and faction in the necessary and ordinary operations of the government.

No man is allowed to be a judge in his own cause, because his interest would certainly bias his judgment, and, not improbably, corrupt his integrity. With equal, nay with greater reason, a body of men are unfit to be both judges and parties at the same time; yet what are many of the most important acts of legislation, but so many judicial determinations, not indeed concerning the rights of single persons, but concerning the rights of large bodies of citizens? And what are the different classes of legislators but advocates and parties to the causes which they determine? Is a law proposed concerning private debts? It is a question to which the creditors are parties on one side and the debtors on the other. Justice ought to hold the balance between them. Yet the parties are, and must be, themselves the judges; and the most numerous party, or, in other words, the most powerful faction must be expected to prevail.

Shall domestic manufactures be encouraged, and in what degree, by restrictions on foreign manufactures? These are questions which would be differently decided by the landed and the manufacturing classes, and probably by neither with a sole regard to justice and the public good. The apportionment of taxes on the various descriptions of property is an act which seems to require the most exact impartiality; yet there is, perhaps, no legislative act in which greater opportunity and temptation are given to a predominant party to trample on the rules of justice. Every shilling with which they overburden the inferior number, is a shilling saved to their own pockets.

It is in vain to say that enlightened statesmen will be able to adjust these clashing interests, and render them all subservient to the public good. Enlightened statesmen will not always be at the helm. Nor, in many cases, can such an adjustment be made at all without taking into view indirect and remote considerations, which will rarely prevail over the immediate interest which one party may find in disregarding the rights of another or the good of the whole.

The inference to which we are brought is, that the CAUSES of faction cannot be removed, and that relief is only to be sought in the means of controlling its EFFECTS.

If a faction consists of less than a majority, relief is supplied by the republican principle, which enables the majority to defeat its sinister views by regular vote. It may clog the administration, it may convulse the society; but it will be unable to execute and mask its violence under the forms of the Constitution. When a majority is included in a faction, the form of popular government, on the other hand, enables it to sacrifice to its ruling passion or interest both the public good and the rights of other citizens. To secure the public good and private rights against the danger of such a faction, and at the same time to preserve the spirit and the form of popular government, is then the great object to which our inquiries are directed. Let me add that it is the great desideratum [something wanted or needed] by which this form of government can be rescued from the opprobrium [disgrace; strong disapproval] under which it has so long labored, and be recommended to the esteem and adoption of mankind.

By what means is this object attainable? Evidently by one of two only. Either the existence of the same passion or interest in a majority at the same time must be prevented, or the majority, having such coexistent passion or interest, must be rendered, by their number and local situation, unable to concert and carry into effect schemes of oppression. If the impulse and the opportunity be suffered to coincide, we well know that neither moral nor religious motives can be relied on as an adequate control. They are not found to be such on the injustice and violence of individuals, and lose their efficacy in proportion to the number combined together, that is, in proportion as their efficacy becomes needful.

From this view of the subject it may be concluded that a pure democracy, by which I mean a society consisting of a small number of citizens, who assemble and administer the government in person, can admit of no cure for the mischiefs of faction. A common passion or interest will, in almost every case, be felt by a majority of the whole; a communication and concert result from the form of government itself; and there is nothing to check the inducements to sacrifice the weaker party or an obnoxious individual. Hence it is that such democracies have ever been spectacles of turbulence and contention; have ever been found incompatible with personal security or the rights of property; and have in general been as short in their lives as they have been violent in their deaths. Theoretic politicians, who have patronized this species of government, have erroneously supposed that by reducing mankind to a perfect equality in their political rights, they would, at the same time, be perfectly equalized and assimilated in their possessions, their opinions, and their passions.

A republic, by which I mean a government in which the scheme of representation takes place, opens a different prospect, and promises the cure for which we are seeking. Let us examine the points in which it varies from pure democracy, and we shall comprehend both the nature of the cure and the efficacy which it must derive from the Union.

The two great points of difference between a democracy and a republic are: first, the delegation of the government, in the latter, to a small number of citizens elected by the rest; secondly, the greater number of citizens, and greater sphere of country, over which the latter may be extended.

The effect of the first difference is, on the one hand, to refine and enlarge the public views, by passing them through the medium of a chosen body of citizens, whose wisdom may best discern the true interest of their country, and whose patriotism and love of justice will be least likely to sacrifice it to temporary or partial considerations. Under such a regulation, it may well happen that the public voice, pronounced by the representatives of the people, will be more consonant to the public good than if pronounced by the people themselves, convened for the purpose. On the other hand, the effect may be inverted. Men of factious [divisive] tempers, of local prejudices, or of sinister designs, may, by intrigue, by corruption, or by other means, first obtain the suffrages, and then betray the interests, of the people. The question resulting is, whether small or extensive republics are more favorable to the election of proper guardians of the public weal; and it is clearly decided in favor of the latter by two obvious considerations:

In the first place, it is to be remarked that, however small the republic may be, the representatives must be raised to a certain number, in order to guard against the cabals of a few; and that, however large it may be, they must be limited to a certain number, in order to guard against the confusion of a multitude. Hence, the number of representatives in the two cases not being in proportion to that of the two constituents, and being proportionally greater in the small republic, it follows that, if the proportion of fit characters be not less in the large than in the small republic, the former will present a greater option, and consequently a greater probability of a fit choice.

In the next place, as each representative will be chosen by a greater number of citizens in the large than in the small republic, it will be more difficult for unworthy candidates to practice with success the vicious arts by which elections are too often carried; and the suffrages of the people being more free, will be more likely to centre in men who possess the most attractive merit and the most diffusive and established character.

It must be confessed that in this, as in most other cases, there is a mean, on both sides of which inconveniences will be found to lie. By enlarging too much the number of electors, you render the representatives too little acquainted with all their local circumstances and lesser interests; as by reducing it too much, you render him unduly attached to these, and too little fit to comprehend and pursue great and national objects. The federal Constitution forms a happy combination in this respect; the great and aggregate interests being referred to the national, the local and particular to the State legislatures.

The other point of difference is, the greater number of citizens and extent of territory which may be brought within the compass of republican than of democratic government; and it is this circumstance principally which renders factious combinations less to be dreaded in the former than in the latter. The smaller the society, the fewer probably will be the distinct parties and interests composing it; the fewer the distinct parties and interests, the more frequently will a majority be found of the same party; and the smaller the number of individuals composing a majority, and the smaller the compass within which they are placed, the more easily will they concert and execute their plans of oppression. Extend the sphere, and you take in a greater variety of parties and interests; you make it less probable that a majority of the whole will have a common motive to invade the rights of other citizens; or if such a common motive exists, it will be more difficult for all who feel it to discover their own strength, and to act in unison with each other. Besides other impediments, it may be remarked that, where there is a consciousness of unjust or dishonorable purposes, communication is always checked by distrust in proportion to the number whose concurrence is necessary.

Hence, it clearly appears, that the same advantage which a republic has over a democracy, in controlling the effects of faction, is enjoyed by a large over a small republic,—is enjoyed by the Union over the States composing it. Does the advantage consist in the substitution of representatives whose enlightened views and virtuous sentiments render them superior to local prejudices and schemes of injustice? It will not be denied that the representation of the Union will be most likely to possess these requisite endowments. Does it consist in the greater security afforded by a greater variety of parties, against the event of any one party being able to outnumber and oppress the rest? In an equal degree does the increased variety of parties comprised within the Union, increase this security. Does it, in fine, consist in the greater obstacles opposed to the concert and accomplishment of the secret wishes of an unjust and interested majority? Here, again, the extent of the Union gives it the most palpable advantage.

The influence of factious leaders may kindle a flame within their particular States, but will be unable to spread a general conflagration [a large conflict] through the other States. A religious sect may degenerate into a political faction in a part of the Confederacy; but the variety of sects dispersed over the entire face of it must secure the national councils against any danger from that source. A rage for paper money, for an abolition of debts, for an equal division of property, or for any other improper or wicked project, will be less apt to pervade the whole body of the Union than a particular member of it; in the same proportion as such a malady is more likely to taint a particular county or district, than an entire State.

In the extent and proper structure of the Union, therefore, we behold a republican remedy for the diseases most incident to republican government. And according to the degree of pleasure and pride we feel in being republicans, ought to be our zeal in cherishing the spirit and supporting the character of Federalists.

ASSESSMENT

1. **Explain an Argument** Why does Madison say a republican form of government best suits the United States as it forms a new constitution?
2. **Assess an Argument** Do you agree with Madison's contention that a democratic republic is preferable to a pure democracy? Explain your position.
3. **Analyze Interactions** What do you think was the impact of *Federalist* No. 10 on the U.S. Constitution?

[*Federalist* No. 39: James Madison]

Introduction

In *Federalist* No. 39, James Madison takes on critics of the republican form of government favored by Madison and his allies. Those who opposed this form felt that the new government stripped individual states of their powers. They feared a federal government with too much power. Madison rebuts this argument by saying that a republic is precisely the right form of government for the young nation and that the proposed constitution will establish a strong national government and preserve some powers of the states.

Primary Source

THE last paper having concluded the observations which were meant to introduce a candid survey of the plan of government reported by the convention, we now proceed to the execution of that part of our undertaking.

The first question that offers itself is, whether the general form and aspect of the government be strictly republican. It is evident that no other form would be reconcilable with the genius of the people of America;

with the fundamental principles of the Revolution; or with that honorable determination which animates every votary [devotee] of freedom, to rest all our political experiments on the capacity of mankind for self-government. If the plan of the convention, therefore, be found to depart from the republican character, its advocates must abandon it as no longer defensible.

What, then, are the distinctive characters of the republican form? Were an answer to this question to be sought, not by recurring [referring back] to principles, but in the application of the term by political writers, to the constitution of different States, no satisfactory one would ever be found. Holland, in which no particle of the supreme authority is derived from the people, has passed almost universally under the denomination of a republic. The same title has been bestowed on Venice, where absolute power over the great body of the people is exercised, in the most absolute manner, by a small body of hereditary nobles. Poland, which is a mixture of aristocracy and of monarchy in their worst forms, has been dignified with the same appellation [designation]. The government of England, which has one republican branch only, combined with an hereditary aristocracy and monarchy, has, with equal impropriety, been frequently placed on the list of republics. These examples, which are nearly as dissimilar to each other as to a genuine republic, show the extreme inaccuracy with which the term has been used in political disquisitions.

If we resort for a criterion to the different principles on which different forms of government are established, we may define a republic to be, or at least may bestow that name on, a government which derives all its powers directly or indirectly from the great body of the people, and is administered by persons holding their offices during pleasure, for a limited period, or during good behavior. It is ESSENTIAL to such a government that it be derived from the great body of the society, not from an inconsiderable proportion, or a favored class of it; otherwise a handful of tyrannical nobles, exercising their oppressions by a delegation of their powers, might aspire to the rank of republicans, and claim for their government the honorable title of republic. It is SUFFICIENT for such a government that the persons administering it be appointed, either directly or indirectly, by the people; and that they hold their appointments by either of the tenures just specified; otherwise every government in the United States, as well as every other popular government that has been or can be well organized or well executed, would be degraded from the republican character. According to the constitution of every State in the Union, some or other of the officers of government are appointed indirectly only by the people. According to most of them, the chief magistrate himself is so appointed. And according to one, this mode of appointment is extended to one of the coordinate branches of the legislature. According to all the constitutions, also, the tenure of the highest offices is extended to a definite period, and in many instances, both within the legislative and executive departments, to a period of years. According to the provisions of most of the constitutions, again, as well as according to the most respectable and received opinions on the subject, the members of the judiciary department are to retain their offices by the firm tenure of good behavior.

On comparing the Constitution planned by the convention with the standard here fixed, we perceive at once that it is, in the most rigid sense, conformable to it. The House of Representatives, like that of one branch at least of all the State legislatures, is elected immediately by the great body of the people. The Senate, like the present Congress, and the Senate of Maryland, derives its appointment indirectly from the people. The President is indirectly derived from the choice of the people, according to the example in most of the States. Even the judges, with all other officers of the Union, will, as in the several States, be the choice, though a remote choice, of the people themselves, the duration of the appointments is equally conformable to the republican standard, and to the model of State constitutions The House of Representatives is periodically elective, as in all the States; and for the period of two years, as in the State of South Carolina. The Senate is elective, for the period of six years; which is but one year more than the period of the Senate of Maryland, and but two more than that of the Senates of New York and Virginia. The President is to continue in office for the period of four years; as in New York and Delaware, the chief magistrate is elected for three years, and in South Carolina for two years. In the other States the election is annual. In several of the States, however, no constitutional provision is made for the impeachment of the chief magistrate. And in Delaware and Virginia he is not impeachable till out of office. The President of the United States is impeachable at any time during his continuance in office. The tenure by which the judges are to hold their places, is, as it unquestionably ought to be, that of good behavior. The tenure of the ministerial offices generally, will be a subject of legal regulation, conformably to the reason of the case and the example of the State constitutions.

Could any further proof be required of the republican complexion of this system, the most decisive one might be found in its absolute prohibition of titles of nobility, both under the federal and the State governments; and in its express guaranty of the republican form to each of the latter.

"But it was not sufficient," say the adversaries of the proposed Constitution, "for the convention to adhere to the republican form. They ought, with equal care, to have preserved the FEDERAL form, which regards the Union as a CONFEDERACY of sovereign states; instead of which, they have framed a NATIONAL government, which regards the Union as a CONSOLIDATION of the States." And it is asked by what authority this bold and radical innovation was undertaken? The handle which has been made of this objection requires that it should be examined with some precision.

Without inquiring into the accuracy of the distinction on which the objection is founded, it will be necessary to a just estimate of its force, first, to ascertain the real character of the government in question; secondly, to inquire how far the convention were authorized to propose such a government; and thirdly, how far the duty they owed to their country could supply any defect of regular authority.

First. In order to ascertain the real character of the government, it may be considered in relation to the foundation on which it is to be established; to the sources from which its ordinary powers are to be drawn; to the operation of those powers; to the extent of them; and to the authority by which future changes in the government are to be introduced.

On examining the first relation, it appears, on one hand, that the Constitution is to be founded on the assent and ratification of the people of America, given by deputies elected for the special purpose; but, on the other, that this assent and ratification is to be given by the people, not as individuals composing one entire nation, but as composing the distinct and independent States to which they respectively belong. It is to be the assent and ratification of the several States, derived from the supreme authority in each State, the authority of the people themselves. The act, therefore, establishing the Constitution, will not be a NATIONAL, but a FEDERAL act.

That it will be a federal and not a national act, as these terms are understood by the objectors; the act of the people, as forming so many independent States, not as forming one aggregate nation, is obvious from this single consideration, that it is to result neither from the decision of a MAJORITY of the people of the Union, nor from that of a MAJORITY of the States. It must result from the UNANIMOUS assent of the several States that are parties to it, differing no otherwise from their ordinary assent than in its being expressed, not by the legislative authority, but by that of the people themselves. Were the people regarded in this transaction as forming one nation, the will of the majority of the whole people of the United States would bind the minority, in the same manner as the majority in each State must bind the minority; and the will of the majority must be determined either by a comparison of the individual votes, or by considering the will of the majority of the States as evidence of the will of a majority of the people of the United States. Neither of these rules have been adopted. Each State, in ratifying the Constitution, is considered as a sovereign body, independent of all others, and only to be bound by its own voluntary act. In this relation, then, the new Constitution will, if established, be a FEDERAL, and not a NATIONAL constitution.

The next relation is, to the sources from which the ordinary powers of government are to be derived. The House of Representatives will derive its powers from the people of America; and the people will be represented in the same proportion, and on the same principle, as they are in the legislature of a particular State. So far the government is NATIONAL, not FEDERAL. The Senate, on the other hand, will derive its powers from the States, as political and coequal societies; and these will be represented on the principle of equality in the Senate, as they now are in the existing Congress. So far the government is FEDERAL, not NATIONAL. The executive power will be derived from a very compound source. The immediate election of the President is to be made by the States in their political characters. The votes allotted to them are in a compound ratio, which considers them partly as distinct and coequal societies, partly as unequal members of the same society. The eventual election, again, is to be made by that branch of the legislature which consists of the national representatives; but in this particular act they are to be thrown into the form of individual delegations, from so many distinct and coequal bodies politic. From this aspect of the government it appears to be of a mixed character, presenting at least as many FEDERAL as NATIONAL features.

The difference between a federal and national government, as it relates to the OPERATION OF THE GOVERNMENT, is supposed to consist in this, that in the former the powers operate on the political bodies composing the Confederacy, in their political capacities; in the latter, on the individual citizens composing the nation, in their individual capacities. On trying the Constitution by this criterion, it falls under the NATIONAL, not the FEDERAL character; though perhaps not so completely as has been understood. In several cases, and particularly in the trial of controversies to which States may be parties, they must be viewed and proceeded against in their collective and political capacities only. So far the national countenance of the government on this side seems to be disfigured by a few federal features. But this blemish is perhaps unavoidable in any plan; and the operation of the government on the people, in their individual capacities, in its ordinary and most essential proceedings, may, on the whole, designate it, in this relation, a NATIONAL government.

But if the government be national with regard to the OPERATION of its powers, it changes its aspect again when we contemplate it in relation to the EXTENT of its powers. The idea of a national government involves in it, not only an authority over the individual citizens, but an indefinite supremacy over all persons and things, so far as they are objects of lawful government. Among a people consolidated into one nation, this supremacy is completely vested in the national legislature. Among communities united for particular purposes, it is vested partly in the general and partly in the municipal legislatures. In the former case, all local authorities are subordinate to the supreme; and may be controlled, directed, or abolished by it at pleasure. In the latter, the local or municipal authorities form distinct and independent portions of the supremacy, no more subject, within their respective spheres, to the general authority, than the general authority is subject to them, within its own sphere. In this relation, then, the proposed government cannot be deemed a NATIONAL one; since its jurisdiction extends to certain enumerated objects only, and leaves to the several States a residuary [residual; left over] and inviolable sovereignty over all other objects. It is true that in controversies relating to the boundary between the two jurisdictions, the tribunal which is ultimately to decide, is to be established under the general government. But this does not change the principle of the case. The decision is to be impartially made, according to the rules of the Constitution; and all the usual and most effectual precautions are taken to secure this impartiality. Some such tribunal is clearly essential to prevent an appeal to the sword and a dissolution of the compact; and that it ought to be established under the general rather than under the local governments, or, to speak more properly, that it could be safely established under the first alone, is a position not likely to be combated.

If we try the Constitution by its last relation to the authority by which amendments are to be made, we find it neither wholly NATIONAL nor wholly FEDERAL. Were it wholly national, the supreme and ultimate authority would reside in the MAJORITY of the people of the Union; and this authority would be competent at all times, like that of a majority of every national society, to alter or abolish its established government. Were it wholly federal, on the other hand, the concurrence of each State in the Union would be essential to every alteration that would be binding on all. The mode provided by the plan of the convention is not founded on either of these principles. In requiring more than a majority, and principles. In requiring more than a majority, and particularly in computing the proportion by STATES, not by CITIZENS, it departs from the NATIONAL and advances towards the FEDERAL character; in rendering the concurrence of less than the whole number of States sufficient, it loses again the FEDERAL and partakes of the NATIONAL character.

The proposed Constitution, therefore, is, in strictness, neither a national nor a federal Constitution, but a composition of both. In its foundation it is federal, not national; in the sources from which the ordinary powers of the government are drawn, it is partly federal and partly national; in the operation of these powers, it is national, not federal; in the extent of them, again, it is federal, not national; and, finally, in the authoritative mode of introducing amendments, it is neither wholly federal nor wholly national.

ASSESSMENT

1. **Summarize** How does Madison define a republic?
2. **Cite Evidence** What evidence does Madison offer to support his claim that the new government will be "neither wholly federal nor wholly national"?
3. **Analyze Interactions** How did *Federalist* No. 39 influence the U.S. Constitution?

[*Federalist* No. 51: James Madison]

Introduction

Federalist No. 51 was first published on February 8, 1788, and was probably written by James Madison. It argues that the federal system and the separation of powers proposed in the Constitution provide a system of checks and balances that will protect the rights of the people.

Primary Source

TO WHAT expedient [resource], then, shall we finally resort, for maintaining in practice the necessary partition of power among the several departments, as laid down in the Constitution? The only answer that can be given is, that as all these exterior provisions are found to be inadequate, the defect must be supplied, by so contriving the interior structure of the government as that its several constituent parts may, by their mutual relations, be the means of keeping each other in their proper places. Without presuming to undertake a full development of this important idea, I will hazard a few general observations, which may perhaps place it in a clearer light, and enable us to form a more correct judgment of the principles and structure of the government planned by the convention.

In order to lay a due foundation for that separate and distinct exercise of the different powers of government, which to a certain extent is admitted on all hands to be essential to the preservation of liberty, it is evident that each department should have a will of its own; and consequently should be so constituted that the members of each should have as little agency as possible in the appointment of the members of the others. Were this principle rigorously adhered to, it would require that all the appointments for the supreme executive, legislative, and judiciary magistracies should be drawn from the same fountain of authority, the people, through channels having no communication whatever with one another. Perhaps such a plan of constructing the several departments would be less difficult in practice than it may in contemplation appear. Some difficulties, however, and some additional expense would attend the execution of it. Some deviations, therefore, from the principle must be admitted. In the constitution of the judiciary department in particular, it might be inexpedient to insist rigorously on the principle: first, because peculiar qualifications being essential in the members, the primary consideration ought to be to select that mode of choice which best secures these qualifications; secondly, because the permanent tenure by which the appointments are held in that department, must soon destroy all sense of dependence on the authority conferring them.

It is equally evident, that the members of each department should be as little dependent as possible on those of the others, for the emoluments [monetary payments] annexed to their offices. Were the executive magistrate, or the judges, not independent of the legislature in this particular, their independence in every other would be merely nominal.

But the great security against a gradual concentration of the several powers in the same department, consists in giving to those who administer each department the necessary constitutional means and personal motives to resist encroachments [intrusions; unwanted advances] of the others. The provision for defense must in this, as in all other cases, be made commensurate to the danger of attack. Ambition must be made to counteract ambition. The interest of the man must be connected with the constitutional rights of the place. It may be a reflection on human nature, that such devices should be necessary to control the abuses of government. But what is government itself, but the greatest of all reflections on human nature? If men were angels, no government would be necessary. If angels were to govern men, neither external nor internal controls on government would be necessary. In framing a government which is to be administered by men over men, the great difficulty lies in this: you must first enable the government to control the governed; and in the next place oblige it to control itself. A dependence on the people is, no doubt, the primary control on the government; but experience has taught mankind the necessity of auxiliary precautions.

This policy of supplying, by opposite and rival interests, the defect of better motives, might be traced through the whole system of human affairs, private as well as public. We see it particularly displayed in all the subordinate distributions of power, where the constant aim is to divide and arrange the several offices in such a manner as that each may be a check on the other—that the private interest of every individual may be a sentinel over the public rights. These inventions of prudence cannot be less requisite in the distribution of the supreme powers of the State.

But it is not possible to give to each department an equal power of self-defense. In republican government, the legislative authority necessarily predominates. The remedy for this inconveniency is to divide the legislature into different branches; and to render them, by different modes of election and different principles of action, as little connected with each other as the nature of their common functions and their common dependence on the society will admit. It may even be necessary to guard against dangerous encroachments by still further precautions. As the weight of the legislative authority requires that it should be thus divided, the weakness of the executive may require, on the other hand, that it should be fortified. An absolute negative on the legislature appears, at first view, to be the natural defense with which the executive magistrate should be armed. But perhaps it would be neither altogether safe nor alone sufficient. On ordinary occasions it might not be exerted with the requisite firmness, and on extraordinary occasions it might be perfidiously [traitorously; treachorously] abused. May not this defect of an absolute negative be supplied by some qualified connection between this weaker department and the weaker branch of the stronger department, by which the latter may be led to support the constitutional rights of the former, without being too much detached from the rights of its own department?

If the principles on which these observations are founded be just, as I persuade myself they are, and they be applied as a criterion to the several State constitutions, and to the federal Constitution it will be found that if the latter does not perfectly correspond with them, the former are infinitely less able to bear such a test.

There are, moreover, two considerations particularly applicable to the federal system of America, which place that system in a very interesting point of view.

First. In a single republic, all the power surrendered by the people is submitted to the administration of a single government; and the usurpations [illegal seizures of power] are guarded against by a division of the government into distinct and separate departments. In the compound republic of America, the power surrendered by the people is first divided between two distinct governments, and then the portion allotted to each subdivided among distinct and separate departments. Hence a double security arises to the rights of the people. The different governments will control each other, at the same time that each will be controlled by itself.

Second. It is of great importance in a republic not only to guard the society against the oppression of its rulers, but to guard one part of the society against the injustice of the other part. Different interests necessarily exist in different classes of citizens. If a majority be united by a common interest, the rights of the minority will be insecure. There are but two methods of providing against this evil: the one by creating a will in the community independent of the majority—that is, of the society itself; the other, by comprehending in the society so many separate descriptions of citizens as will render an unjust combination of a majority of the whole very improbable, if not impracticable. The first method prevails in all governments possessing an hereditary or self-appointed authority. This, at best, is but a precarious security; because a power independent of the society may as well espouse the unjust views of the major, as the rightful interests of the minor party, and may possibly be turned against both parties. The second method will be exemplified in the federal republic of the United States. Whilst all authority in it will be derived from and dependent on the society, the society itself will be broken into so many parts, interests, and classes of citizens, that the rights of individuals, or of the minority, will be in little danger from interested combinations of the majority.

In a free government the security for civil rights must be the same as that for religious rights. It consists in the one case in the multiplicity of interests, and in the other in the multiplicity of sects. The degree of security in both cases will depend on the number of interests and sects; and this may be presumed to depend on the extent of country and number of people comprehended under the same government. This view of the subject must particularly recommend a proper federal system to all the sincere and considerate friends of republican government, since it shows that in exact proportion as the territory of the Union may be formed into more circumscribed Confederacies, or States oppressive combinations of a majority will be facilitated: the best security, under the republican forms, for the rights of every class of citizens, will be diminished: and consequently the stability and independence of some member of the government, the only other security, must be proportionately increased. Justice is the end of government. It is the end of civil society. It ever has been and ever will be pursued until it be obtained, or until liberty be lost in the pursuit. In a society under the forms of which the stronger faction can readily unite and oppress the weaker, anarchy may as truly be said to reign as in a state of nature, where the weaker individual is not secured against the violence of the stronger; and as, in the latter state, even the stronger individuals are prompted, by the uncertainty of their condition, to submit to a government which may protect the weak as well as themselves; so, in the former state, will the more powerful factions or parties be gradually induced, by a like motive, to wish for a government which will protect all parties, the weaker as well as the more powerful. It can be little doubted that if the State of Rhode Island was separated from the Confederacy and left to itself, the insecurity of rights under the popular form of government within such narrow limits would be displayed by such reiterated oppressions of factious majorities that some power altogether independent of the people would soon be called for by the voice of the very factions whose misrule had proved the necessity of it.

In the extended republic of the United States, and among the great variety of interests, parties, and sects which it embraces, a coalition of a majority of the whole society could seldom take place on any other principles than those of justice and the general good; whilst there being thus less danger to a minor from the will of a major party, there must be less pretext, also, to provide for the security of the former, by introducing into the government a will not dependent on the latter, or, in other words, a will independent of the society itself. It is no less certain than it is important, notwithstanding the contrary opinions which have been entertained, that the larger the society, provided it lie within a practical sphere, the more duly capable it will be of self-government. And happily for the REPUBLICAN CAUSE, the practicable sphere may be carried to a very great extent, by a judicious modification and mixture of the FEDERAL PRINCIPLE.

ASSESSMENT

1. **Assess an Argument** Do you agree with Madison that, "In a free government the security for civil rights must be the same as that for religious rights"? Considering the history of the United States on the issue of civil rights for both women and racial minorities, in what way is Madison's remark ironic?
2. **Analyze Interactions** What effect did *Federalist* No. 51 have on the final U.S. Constitution?
3. **Explain an Argument** Why does Madison think it is important that the new government exercise a separation of powers?

[*Federalist* No. 78: Alexander Hamilton]

Introduction

The *Federalist Papers* were the brainchild of Alexander Hamilton, who conceived them and recruited James Madison and John Jay to the project. Hamilton is usually credited as the author of 51 of the 85 essays in the collection. Here, he discusses the national judiciary to be established by Article III in the proposed constitution. He emphasizes the vital need for an independent judiciary and its role in the interpretation of laws and the determination of their constitutionality. It was first published April 11, 1788.

Primary Source

WE PROCEED now to an examination of the judiciary department of the proposed government.

In unfolding the defects of the existing Confederation, the utility and necessity of a federal judicature [system of courts] have been clearly pointed out. It is the less necessary to recapitulate the considerations there urged, as the propriety of the institution in the abstract is not disputed; the only questions which have been raised being relative to the manner of constituting it, and to its extent. To these points, therefore, our observations shall be confined.

The manner of constituting it seems to embrace these several objects: 1st. The mode of appointing the judges. 2d. The tenure by which they are to hold their places. 3d. The partition of the judiciary authority between different courts, and their relations to each other.

First. As to the mode of appointing the judges; this is the same with that of appointing the officers of the Union in general, and has been so fully discussed in the two last numbers, that nothing can be said here which would not be useless repetition.

Second. As to the tenure by which the judges are to hold their places; this chiefly concerns their duration in office; the provisions for their support; the precautions for their responsibility.

According to the plan of the convention, all judges who may be appointed by the United States are to hold their offices during good behavior; which is conformable to the most approved of the State constitutions and among the rest, to that of this State. Its propriety having been drawn into question by the adversaries of that plan, is no light symptom of the rage for objection, which disorders their imaginations and judgments. The standard of good behavior for the continuance in office of the judicial magistracy, is certainly one of the most valuable of the modern improvements in the practice of government. In a monarchy it is an excellent barrier to the despotism of the prince; in a republic it is a no less excellent barrier to the encroachments and oppressions of the representative body. And it is the best expedient which can be devised in any government, to secure a steady, upright, and impartial administration of the laws.

Whoever attentively considers the different departments of power must perceive, that, in a government in which they are separated from each other, the judiciary, from the nature of its functions, will always be the least dangerous to the political rights of the Constitution; because it will be least in a capacity to annoy or injure them. The Executive not only dispenses the honors, but holds the sword of the community. The legislature not only commands the purse, but prescribes the rules by which the duties and rights of every citizen are to be regulated. The judiciary, on the contrary, has no influence over either the sword or the purse; no direction either of the strength or of the wealth of the society; and can take no active resolution whatever. It may truly be said to have neither FORCE nor WILL, but merely judgment; and must ultimately depend upon the aid of the executive arm even for the efficacy of its judgments.

This simple view of the matter suggests several important consequences. It proves incontestably, that the judiciary is beyond comparison the weakest of the three departments of power; that it can never attack with success either of the other two; and that all possible care is requisite to enable it to defend itself against their attacks. It equally proves, that though individual oppression may now and then proceed from the courts of justice, the general liberty of the people can never be endangered from that quarter; I mean so long as the judiciary remains truly distinct from both the legislature and the Executive. For I agree, that "there is no liberty, if the power of judging be not separated from the legislative and executive powers." And it proves, in the last place, that as liberty can have nothing to fear from the judiciary alone, but would have every thing to fear from its union with either of the other departments; that as all the effects of such a union must ensue from a dependence of the former on the latter, notwithstanding a nominal and apparent separation; that as, from the natural feebleness of the judiciary, it is in continual jeopardy of being overpowered, awed, or influenced by its co-ordinate branches; and that as nothing can contribute so much to its firmness and independence as permanency in office, this quality may therefore be justly regarded as an indispensable ingredient in its constitution, and, in a great measure, as the citadel of the public justice and the public security.

The complete independence of the courts of justice is peculiarly essential in a limited Constitution. By a limited Constitution, I understand one which contains certain specified exceptions to the legislative authority; such, for instance, as that it shall pass no bills of attainder, no ex post facto laws, and the like. Limitations of this kind can be preserved in practice no other way than through the medium of courts of justice, whose duty it must be to declare all acts contrary to the manifest tenor of the Constitution void. Without this, all the reservations of particular rights or privileges would amount to nothing.

Some perplexity respecting the rights of the courts to pronounce legislative acts void, because contrary to the Constitution, has arisen from an imagination that the doctrine would imply a superiority of the judiciary to the legislative power. It is urged that the authority which can declare the acts of another void, must necessarily be superior to the one whose acts may be declared void. As this doctrine is of great importance in all the American constitutions, a brief discussion of the ground on which it rests cannot be unacceptable.

There is no position which depends on clearer principles, than that every act of a delegated authority, contrary to the tenor of the commission under which it is exercised, is void. No legislative act, therefore, contrary to the Constitution, can be valid. To deny this, would be to affirm, that the deputy is greater than his principal; that the servant is above his master; that the representatives of the people are superior to the people themselves; that men acting by virtue of powers, may do not only what their powers do not authorize, but what they forbid.

If it be said that the legislative body are themselves the constitutional judges of their own powers, and that the construction they put upon them is conclusive upon the other departments, it may be answered, that this cannot be the natural presumption, where it is not to be collected from any particular provisions in the Constitution. It is not otherwise to be supposed, that the Constitution could intend to enable the representatives of the people to substitute their will to that of their constituents. It is far more rational to suppose, that the courts were designed to be an intermediate body between the people and the legislature, in order, among other things, to keep the latter within the limits assigned to their authority.

The interpretation of the laws is the proper and peculiar [particular] province of the courts. A constitution is, in fact, and must be regarded by the judges, as a fundamental law. It therefore belongs to them to ascertain its meaning, as well as the meaning of any particular act proceeding from the legislative body. If there should happen to be an irreconcilable variance between the two, that which has the superior obligation and validity ought, of course, to be preferred; or, in other words, the Constitution ought to be preferred to the statute, the intention of the people to the intention of their agents.

Nor does this conclusion by any means suppose a superiority of the judicial to the legislative power. It only supposes that the power of the people is superior to both; and that where the will of the legislature, declared in its statutes, stands in opposition to that of the people, declared in the Constitution, the judges ought to be governed by the latter rather than the former. They ought to regulate their decisions by the fundamental laws, rather than by those which are not fundamental.

This exercise of judicial discretion, in determining between two contradictory laws, is exemplified in a familiar instance. It not uncommonly happens, that there are two statutes existing at one time, clashing in whole or in part with each other, and neither of them containing any repealing clause or expression. In such a case, it is the province of the courts to liquidate and fix their meaning and operation. So far as they can, by any fair construction, be reconciled to each other, reason and law conspire to dictate that this should be done; where this is impracticable, it becomes a matter of necessity to give effect to one, in exclusion of the other. The rule which has obtained in the courts for determining their relative validity is, that the last in order of time shall be preferred to the first. But this is a mere rule of construction, not derived from any positive law, but from the nature and reason of the thing. It is a rule not enjoined upon the courts by legislative provision, but adopted by themselves, as consonant to truth and propriety, for the direction of their conduct as interpreters of the law. They thought it reasonable, that between the interfering acts of an EQUAL authority, that which was the last indication of its will should have the preference.

But in regard to the interfering acts of a superior and subordinate authority, of an original and derivative power, the nature and reason of the thing indicate the converse of that rule as proper to be followed. They teach us that the prior act of a superior ought to be preferred to the subsequent act of an inferior and subordinate authority; and that accordingly, whenever a particular statute contravenes the Constitution, it will be the duty of the judicial tribunals to adhere to the latter and disregard the former.

It can be of no weight to say that the courts, on the pretense of a repugnancy [something that is offensive], may substitute their own pleasure to the constitutional intentions of the legislature. This might as well happen in the case of two contradictory statutes; or it might as well happen in every adjudication [judgment] upon any single statute. The courts must declare the sense of the law; and if they should be disposed to exercise WILL instead of JUDGMENT, the consequence would equally be the substitution of their pleasure to that of the legislative body. The observation, if it prove any thing, would prove that there ought to be no judges distinct from that body.

If, then, the courts of justice are to be considered as the bulwarks [defenders] of a limited Constitution against legislative encroachments, this consideration will afford a strong argument for the permanent tenure of judicial offices, since nothing will contribute so much as this to that independent spirit in the judges which must be essential to the faithful performance of so arduous a duty.

This independence of the judges is equally requisite to guard the Constitution and the rights of individuals from the effects of those ill humors, which the arts of designing men, or the influence of particular conjunctures, sometimes disseminate among the people themselves, and which, though they speedily give place to better information, and more deliberate reflection, have a tendency, in the meantime, to occasion dangerous innovations in the government, and serious oppressions of the minor party in the community. Though I trust the friends of the proposed Constitution will never concur with its enemies, in questioning that fundamental principle of republican government, which admits the right of the people to alter or abolish the established Constitution, whenever they find it inconsistent with their happiness, yet it is not to be inferred from this principle, that the representatives of the people, whenever a momentary inclination happens to lay hold of a majority of their constituents, incompatible with the provisions in the existing Constitution, would, on that account, be justifiable in a violation of those provisions; or that the courts would be under a greater obligation to connive [secretly work to injure] at infractions in this shape, than when they had proceeded wholly from the cabals [secret political groups] of the representative body. Until the people have, by some solemn and authoritative act, annulled or changed the established form, it is binding upon themselves collectively, as well as individually; and no presumption, or even knowledge, of their sentiments, can warrant their representatives in a departure from it, prior to such an act. But it is easy to see, that it would require an uncommon portion of fortitude in the judges to do their duty as faithful guardians of the Constitution, where legislative invasions of it had been instigated by the major voice of the community.

But it is not with a view to infractions of the Constitution only, that the independence of the judges may be an essential safeguard against the effects of occasional ill humors in the society. These sometimes extend no farther than to the injury of the private rights of particular classes of citizens, by unjust and partial laws. Here also the firmness of the judicial magistracy is of vast importance in mitigating the severity and confining the operation of such laws. It not only serves to moderate the immediate mischiefs of those which may have been passed, but it operates as a check upon the legislative body in passing them; who, perceiving that obstacles to the success of iniquitous [wicked] intention are to be expected from the scruples [hesitations; doubts] of the courts, are in a manner compelled, by the very motives of the injustice they meditate, to qualify their attempts. This is a circumstance calculated to have more influence upon the character of our governments, than but few may be aware of. The benefits of the integrity and moderation of the judiciary have already been felt in more States than one; and though they may have displeased those whose sinister expectations they may have disappointed, they must have commanded the esteem and applause of all the virtuous and disinterested. Considerate men, of every description, ought to prize whatever will tend to beget or fortify that temper in the courts: as no man can be sure that he may not be to-morrow the victim of a spirit of injustice, by which he may be a gainer to-day. And every man must now feel, that the inevitable tendency of such a spirit is to sap the foundations of public and private confidence, and to introduce in its stead universal distrust and distress.

That inflexible and uniform adherence to the rights of the Constitution, and of individuals, which we perceive to be indispensable in the courts of justice, can certainly not be expected from judges who hold their offices by a temporary commission. Periodical appointments, however regulated, or by whomsoever made, would, in some way or other, be fatal to their necessary independence. If the power of making them was committed either to the Executive or legislature, there would be danger of an improper complaisance [willingness to please] to the branch which possessed it; if to both, there would be an unwillingness to hazard the displeasure of either; if to the people, or to persons chosen by them for the special purpose, there would be too great a disposition to consult popularity, to justify a reliance that nothing would be consulted but the Constitution and the laws.

There is yet a further and a weightier reason for the permanency of the judicial offices, which is deducible from the nature of the qualifications they require. It has been frequently remarked, with great propriety, that a voluminous code of laws is one of the inconveniences necessarily connected with the advantages of a free government. To avoid an arbitrary discretion in the courts, it is indispensable that they should be bound down by strict rules and precedents, which serve to define and point out their duty in every particular case that comes before them; and it will readily be conceived from the variety of controversies which grow out of the folly and wickedness of mankind, that the records of those precedents must unavoidably swell to a very considerable bulk, and must demand long and laborious study to acquire a competent knowledge of them. Hence it is, that there can be but few men in the society who will have sufficient skill in the laws to qualify them for the stations of judges. And making the proper deductions for the ordinary depravity [moral corruption] of human nature, the number must be still smaller of those who unite the requisite integrity with the requisite knowledge. These considerations apprise us, that the government can have no great option between fit character; and that a temporary duration in office, which would naturally discourage such characters from quitting a lucrative line of practice to accept a seat on the bench, would have a tendency to throw the administration of justice into hands less able, and less well qualified, to conduct it with utility and dignity. In the present circumstances of this country, and in those in which it is likely to be for a long time to come, the disadvantages on this score would be greater than they may at first sight appear; but it must be confessed, that they are far inferior to those which present themselves under the other aspects of the subject.

Upon the whole, there can be no room to doubt that the convention acted wisely in copying from the models of those constitutions which have established good behavior as the tenure of their judicial offices, in point of duration; and that so far from being blamable on this account, their plan would have been inexcusably defective, if it had wanted this important feature of good government. The experience of Great Britain affords an illustrious comment on the excellence of the institution.

ASSESSMENT

1. **Summarize** What does Hamilton say is the role of judges?
2. **Analyze Interactions** How has *Federalist* No. 78 influenced the U.S. government?

[Northwest Ordinance]

Introduction

Adopted in 1787 by the Second Continental Congress, the Northwest Ordinance created a method for admitting new states to the Union. While the Articles of Confederation lacked a bill of rights, the Ordinance provided one that included many of the basic liberties that would later be included in the Constitution's Bill of Rights.

Primary Source

. . . ART. 1. No person, demeaning himself in a peaceable and orderly manner, shall ever be molested on account of his mode of worship or religious sentiments, in the said territory.

ART. 2. The inhabitants of the said territory shall always be entitled to the benefits of the writ of habeas corpus [a legal action that says an arrested person must be presented in court], and of the trial by jury. . . .

ART. 3. Religion, morality, and knowledge, being necessary to good government and the happiness of mankind, schools and the means of education shall forever be encouraged. . . .

ART. 6. There shall be neither slavery nor involuntary servitude in the said territory, otherwise than in the punishment of crimes whereof the party shall have been duly convicted: Provided, always, That any person escaping into the same, from whom labor or service is lawfully claimed in any one of the original States, such fugitive may be lawfully reclaimed and conveyed to the person claiming his or her labor or service as aforesaid.

ASSESSMENT

1. **Compare and Contrast** Which ideals expressed in this excerpt from the Northwest Ordinance became influential in other founding documents of the United States? Use specific examples in your response.
2. **Analyze Interactions** How do these excerpts from the Northwest Ordinance connect to the phrase "life, liberty, and the pursuit of happiness" from the Declaration of Independence?

[Farewell Address: George Washington]

Introduction

As he prepared to leave office in 1796, President George Washington made a speech describing his vision of the nation's future. The speech became known as Washington's Farewell Address. The speech deals with a wide range of topics, from the need to keep down the nation's debt to the importance of education. The two most enduring ideas from Washington's address were his caution against the dangers of forming political parties, and the issue of neutrality. Washington's ideas about foreign relations influenced American foreign policy for generations.

Primary Source

Let me now take a more comprehensive view, and warn you in the most solemn manner against the baneful [harmful, destructive] effects of the spirit of party generally.

This spirit, unfortunately, is inseparable from our nature, having its root in the strongest passions of the human mind. It exists under different shapes in all governments, more or less stifled, controlled, or repressed; but, in those of the popular form, it is seen in its greatest rankness [state of being excessive and unpleasant], and is truly their worst enemy. . . .

It agitates the community with ill-founded jealousies and false alarms, kindles the animosity of one part against another, foments [stirs up] occasionally riot and insurrection. It opens the door to foreign influence and corruption, which finds a facilitated [made easier] access to the government itself through the channels of party passions. Thus the policy and the will of one country are subjected to the policy and will of another. . . .

So likewise, a passionate attachment of one nation for another produces a variety of evils. Sympathy for the favorite nation, facilitating the illusion of an imaginary common interest in cases where no real common interest exists, and infusing into one the enmities [feelings of hostility] of the other, betrays the former into a participation in the quarrels and wars of the latter without adequate inducement or justification. It leads also to concessions to the favorite nation of privileges denied to others which is apt doubly to injure the nation making the concessions. . . .

The jealousy of a free people ought to be constantly awake, since history and experience prove that foreign influence is one of the most baneful foes of republican government. But that jealousy to be useful must be impartial [not favoring one side]. . . .

The great rule of conduct for us in regard to foreign nations is, in extending our commercial [relating to trade] relations, to have with them as little political connection as possible. So far as we have already formed engagements, let them be fulfilled with perfect good faith. Here let us stop. Europe has a set of primary interests which to us have none; or a very remote relation. Hence she must be engaged in frequent controversies, the causes of which are essentially foreign to our concerns. . . . Why, by interweaving our destiny with that of any part of Europe, entangle our peace and prosperity in the toils of European ambition, rivalship, interest, humor or caprice [sudden change]?

It is our true policy to steer clear of permanent alliances with any portion of the foreign world; so far, I mean, as we are now at liberty to do it; for let me not be understood as capable of patronizing [supporting] infidelity [disloyalty; unfaithfulness] to existing engagements. I hold the maxim [wise saying] no less applicable to public than to private affairs, that honesty is always the best policy. I repeat, therefore, let those engagements be observed in their genuine sense. But, in my opinion, it is unnecessary and would be unwise to extend them.

ASSESSMENT

1. **Determine Author's Purpose** What was Washington's purpose for writing this speech?
2. **Analyze Interactions** In his speech, Washington highlighted the problems with maintaining foreign alliances, but what are some ways that alliances can be constructive and useful?
3. **Assess an Argument** Washington cautions future generations against the nature of political parties and permanent foreign alliances. With the benefit of hindsight, which of these two warnings shows more foresight? Explain your answer.
4. **Draw Conclusions** In what way did Washington demonstrate presidential leadership by issuing his address?

[*Democracy in America:* Alexis de Tocqueville]

Introduction

Alexis de Tocqueville, a young French writer, visited the United States in 1831. During his travels, he observed firsthand the impact of Jacksonian democracy. After returning to France, Tocqueville began writing *Democracy in America*, a detailed look at American politics, society, economics, religion, and law. The first volume was published in 1835. The book is still studied and quoted by historians and politicians today. In these excerpts from *Democracy in America*, Tocqueville discusses the role of the American people in their government and gives his view of the American character.

Primary Source

The general principles which are the groundwork of modern constitutions–principles which were imperfectly known in Europe, and not completely triumphant even in Great Britain, in the seventeenth century–were all recognized and determined by the laws of New England: the intervention of the people in public affairs, the free voting of taxes, the responsibility of authorities, personal liberty, and trial by jury, were all positively established without discussion. From these fruitful principles consequences have been derived and applications have been made such as no nation in Europe has yet ventured to attempt.

. . . it is at least true that in the United States the county and the township are always based upon the same principle, namely, that everyone is the best judge of what concerns himself alone, and the most proper person to supply his private wants.

In America the people name those who make the law and those who execute it; they themselves form the jury that punishes infractions [violations] of the law. Not only are the institutions democratic in their principle, but also in all their developments; thus the people name their representatives directly and generally choose them every year in order to keep them more completely under their dependence. It is therefore really the people who direct. . . . This majority is composed principally of peaceful citizens who, either by taste or by interest, sincerely desire the good of the country. Around them parties constantly agitate. . . .

The American taken randomly [chosen without a plan] will therefore be a man ardent [intense] in his desires, enterprising [full of energy; willing to take on new projects], adventurous—above all, an innovator [a person who creates a new way of doing something]. This spirit is in fact found in all his works; he introduces it into his political laws, his religious doctrines, his theories of social economy, his private industry; he brings it with him everywhere, into the depths of the woods as into the heart of towns.

To evade the bondage of system and habit, of family maxims, class-opinions, and in some degree, of national prejudices; to accept tradition only as a means of information, and existing facts only as a lesson used in doing otherwise and doing better; to seek the reason of things for oneself, and in oneself alone; to tend to results without being bound to means, and to aim at the substance through the form;—such are the principle characteristics of what I shall call the philosophical method of the Americans. But if I go further, and if I seek among those characteristics the principle one which includes almost all the rest, I discover that, in most operations of the mind, each American appeals only to the individual effort of his own understanding.

ASSESSMENT

1. **Determine Central Ideas** In what way do the people "direct" the American democracy, according to Tocqueville?
2. **Summarize** What impressed Tocqueville during his time in America? Cite examples to support your answer.
3. **Draw Conclusions** In what way could Tocqueville's book be relevant today?

[Emancipation Proclamation: Abraham Lincoln]

Introduction

Five days after the Union victory at Antietam, Abraham Lincoln issued the Emancipation Proclamation. The presidential decree freed all enslaved persons in states under Confederate control as of January 1, 1863. One of the most important documents in American history, it changed the nature of the Union cause and paved the way for the eventual abolition of slavery by the Thirteenth Amendment in 1865.

Primary Source

Whereas on the twenty-second day of September, in the year of our Lord one thousand eight hundred and sixty-two, a proclamation was issued by the President of the United States, containing, among other things, the following, to wit [namely]:

That on the first day of January, in the year of our Lord one thousand eight hundred and sixty-three, all persons held as slaves within any State or designated part of a State, the people whereof shall then be in rebellion against the United States, shall be then, thenceforward [from then on], and forever free; and the Executive Government of the United States, including the military and naval authority thereof, will recognize and maintain the freedom of such persons, and will do no act or acts to repress such persons, or any of them, in any efforts they may make for their actual freedom. . . .

And by virtue of the power, and for the purpose aforesaid, I do order and declare that all persons held as slaves within said designated States, and parts of States, are, and henceforward shall be free; and that the Executive government of the United States, including the military and naval authorities thereof, will recognize and maintain the freedom of said persons.

And I hereby enjoin [direct; order] upon the people so declared to be free to abstain from all violence, unless in necessary self- defence; and I recommend to them that, in all cases when allowed, they labor faithfully for reasonable wages.

And I further declare and make known, that such persons of suitable condition, will be received into the armed services of the United States to garrison [occupy with troops] forts, positions, stations, and other places, and to man vessels of all sorts in said service.

And upon this act, sincerely believed to be an act of justice, warranted [authorized; justified] by the Constitution, upon military necessity, I invoke the considerate judgment of mankind, and the gracious favor of Almighty God. . . .

ASSESSMENT

1. **Draw Conclusions** The number of enslaved people who were freed because of the Emancipation Proclamation increased gradually over time. Why do you think that was?
2. **Determine Author's Purpose** Why do you think President Lincoln issued the proclamation? Explain your answer.
3. **Explain an Argument** What justification does Lincoln give for issuing the proclamation?
4. **Assess an Argument** Do you agree with the justifications you cited in the previous answer? Why or why not?

[Charter of the United Nations]

Introduction

After World War I, more than 50 countries joined together to form the League of Nations. The League was supposed to prevent future wars by providing a forum for the peaceful settlement of international disputes. The United States never joined the League.

The idea of an international peacekeeping organization was revisited after World War II. In 1944, representatives from the United States, the Soviet Union, China, and the United Kingdom met for several months to work out the framework for the United Nations.

In 1945, representatives of 50 countries met in San Francisco to sign the United Nations charter, bringing the organization into being.

Here are the preamble and first two articles of that charter.

Primary Source

WE THE PEOPLES OF THE UNITED NATIONS DETERMINED

- to save succeeding [later] generations from the scourge of war, which twice in our lifetime has brought untold sorrow to mankind, and
- to reaffirm faith in fundamental human rights, in the dignity and worth of the human person, in the equal rights of men and women and of nations large and small, and
- to establish conditions under which justice and respect for the obligations arising from treaties and other sources of international law can be maintained, and
- to promote social progress and better standards of life in larger freedom,

AND FOR THESE ENDS

- to practice tolerance and live together in peace with one another as good neighbours, and

- to unite our strength to maintain international peace and security, and
- to ensure, by the acceptance of principles and the institution of methods, that armed force shall not be used, save in the common interest, and
- to employ international machinery for the promotion of the economic and social advancement of all peoples,

HAVE RESOLVED TO COMBINE OUR EFFORTS TO ACCOMPLISH THESE AIMS

Accordingly, our respective Governments, through representatives assembled in the city of San Francisco, who have exhibited their full powers found to be in good and due form, have agreed to the present Charter of the United Nations and do hereby establish an international organization to be known as the United Nations.

CHAPTER I: PURPOSES AND PRINCIPLES

Article 1

The Purposes of the United Nations are:

1. To maintain international peace and security, and to that end: to take effective collective measures for the prevention and removal of threats to the peace, and for the suppression of acts of aggression or other breaches of the peace, and to bring about by peaceful means, and in conformity with the principles of justice and international law, adjustment or settlement of international disputes or situations which might lead to a breach of the peace;

2. To develop friendly relations among nations based on respect for the principle of equal rights and self-determination of peoples, and to take other appropriate measures to strengthen universal peace;

3. To achieve international co-operation in solving international problems of an economic, social, cultural, or humanitarian character, and in promoting and encouraging respect for human rights and for fundamental freedoms for all without distinction as to race, sex, language, or religion; and

4. To be a centre for harmonizing the actions of nations in the attainment of these common ends.

Article 2

The Organization and its Members, in pursuit of the Purposes stated in Article 1, shall act in accordance with the following Principles.

1. The Organization is based on the principle of the sovereign equality of all its Members.

2. All Members, in order to ensure to all of them the rights and benefits resulting from membership, shall fulfill in good faith the obligations assumed by them in accordance with the present Charter.

3. All Members shall settle their international disputes by peaceful means in such a manner that international peace and security, and justice, are not endangered.

4. All Members shall refrain in their international relations from the threat or use of force against the territorial integrity or political independence of any state, or in any other manner inconsistent with the Purposes of the United Nations.

5. All Members shall give the United Nations every assistance in any action it takes in accordance with the present Charter, and shall refrain from giving assistance to any state against which the United Nations is taking preventive or enforcement action.

6. The Organization shall ensure that states which are not Members of the United Nations act in accordance with these Principles so far as may be necessary for the maintenance of international peace and security.

7. Nothing contained in the present Charter shall authorize the United Nations to intervene in matters which are essentially within the domestic jurisdiction of any state or shall require the Members to submit such matters to settlement under the present Charter; but this principle shall not prejudice the application of enforcement measures under Chapter Vll.

ASSESSMENT

1. **Cite Evidence** The government of a country is inflicting terrible human rights abuses on members of the opposition party. Based on the excerpt, can the United Nations intervene? Cite the part(s) of the charter that support your opinion.
2. **Explain an Argument** Several years of drought in western Asia have led to widespread famine. The UN arranges to bring convoys of food to starving people. One country, a member of the UN, does not want to let relief workers come inside its borders. Does any part of the charter cited here support or rebut the country's position? Explain your answer.

3. **Draw Conclusions** Has the United Nations been successful in its mission "to save succeeding generations from the scourge of war"? Explain your answer.

[*Silent Spring*: Rachel Carson]

Introduction

Rachel Carson was a marine biologist and conservationist who wrote extensively about ocean life. *Silent Spring*, published in 1962, examined how synthetic pesticides used by farmers and landowners were poisoning people and wildlife alike. The book issued a pointed critique against the ways human activities harmed the natural world. *Silent Spring* help launched a movement of concerned consumers, which led to the creation of the Environmental Protection Agency and a ban on a number of pollutants.

Primary Source

There once was a town in the heart of America where all life seemed to live in harmony with its surroundings. . . . Then a strange blight [plant disease] crept over the area and everything began to change. Mysterious maladies [illnesses] swept across the flocks of chickens; the cattle and sheep sickened and died. . . . There was a strange stillness. The birds, for example—where had they gone? . . . On the mornings that had once throbbed with the dawn chorus of robins, catbirds, doves, jays, wrens, and scores of other bird voices there was now no sound; only silence lay over the fields and woods and marsh. . . . No witchcraft, no enemy action had silenced the rebirth of new life in this stricken [distressed] world. The people had done it to themselves.

. . . Only within the moment of time represented by the present century has one species—man—acquired significant power to alter the nature of his world.

During the past quarter century this power has not only increased to one of disturbing magnitude [great size] but it has changed in character. The most alarming of all man's assaults upon the environment is the contamination of air, earth, rivers, and sea with dangerous and even lethal [enough to cause death] materials. This pollution is for the most part irrecoverable [unable to be recovered]; the chain of evil it initiates not only in the world that must support life but in living tissues is for the most part irreversible. In this now universal contamination of the environment, chemicals . . . [are] changing the very nature of the world—the very nature of its life.

ASSESSMENT

1. **Draw Inferences** Why do you think Carson chose to write this book? What changes do you think she hoped to instigate?
2. **Analyze Style and Rhetoric** How would you describe Carson's writing style in this passage, and how do you think this style advances her argument?
3. **Assess an Argument** Why do you think *Silent Spring* was controversial when it was first published? Why do you think some readers might have objected to Carson's argument?

Sequence

Sequence means "order," and placing things in the correct order is very important. What would happen if you tried to put toppings on a pizza before you put down the dough for the crust? When studying history and government, you need to analyze the information by sequencing significant events, individuals, and time periods in order to understand them. Practice this skill by using this reading.

> Richard Nixon was elected to the House of Representatives in 1946 and then to the Senate four years later. In 1952, with Dwight Eisenhower's election as President, Nixon became Vice President. However, Nixon lost to John F. Kennedy in the 1960 presidential election, and two years later lost an election for governor of California. However, in 1968, Nixon defeated Hubert Humphrey to win the presidency.

[1.] Identify the topic and the main events that relate to the topic. Quickly skim titles and headings to determine the topic of the passage. As you read the passage, write a list of significant events, individuals, or time periods related to the topic.

[2.] Note any dates and time words such as "before" and "after" that indicate the chronological order of events. Look through your list of events, individuals, or time periods and write down the date for each. This will give you information to apply absolute chronology by sequencing the events, individuals, or time periods. Remember that some events may have taken place over a number of months or years. Is your date the time when the event started or ended? Make sure to note enough details that you can remember the importance of the information. If no date is given, look for words such as "before" or "after" that can tell you where to place this event, time period, or individual compared to others on your list. This will allow you to apply relative chronology by sequencing the events, individuals, or time periods.

[3.] Determine the time range of the events. Place the events in chronological order on a timeline. Look for the earliest and latest events, individuals, or time periods on your list. The span of time between the first and last entries gives you the time range. To apply absolute chronology, sequence the entries by writing the date of the first event on the left side of a piece of paper and the date of the last event on the right side. Draw a line connecting the two events. This will be your timeline. Once you have drawn your timeline, put the events in order by date along the line. Label their dates. To apply relative chronology, sequence the significant individuals, events, or time periods on an undated timeline, in the order that they happened. You now have a clear image of the important events related to this topic. You can organize and interpret information from visuals by analyzing the information and applying absolute or relative chronology to the events. This will help you understand the topic better when you can see how events caused or led to other events. You will also be able to analyze information by developing connections between historical events over time.

www.PearsonRealize.com
View Video Tutorials and other 21st Century Skills

Categorize

When you analyze information by categorizing, you create a system that helps you sort items into categories, or groups with shared characteristics, so that you can understand the information. Categorizing helps you see what groups of items have in common. Practice this skill as you study the map on this page.

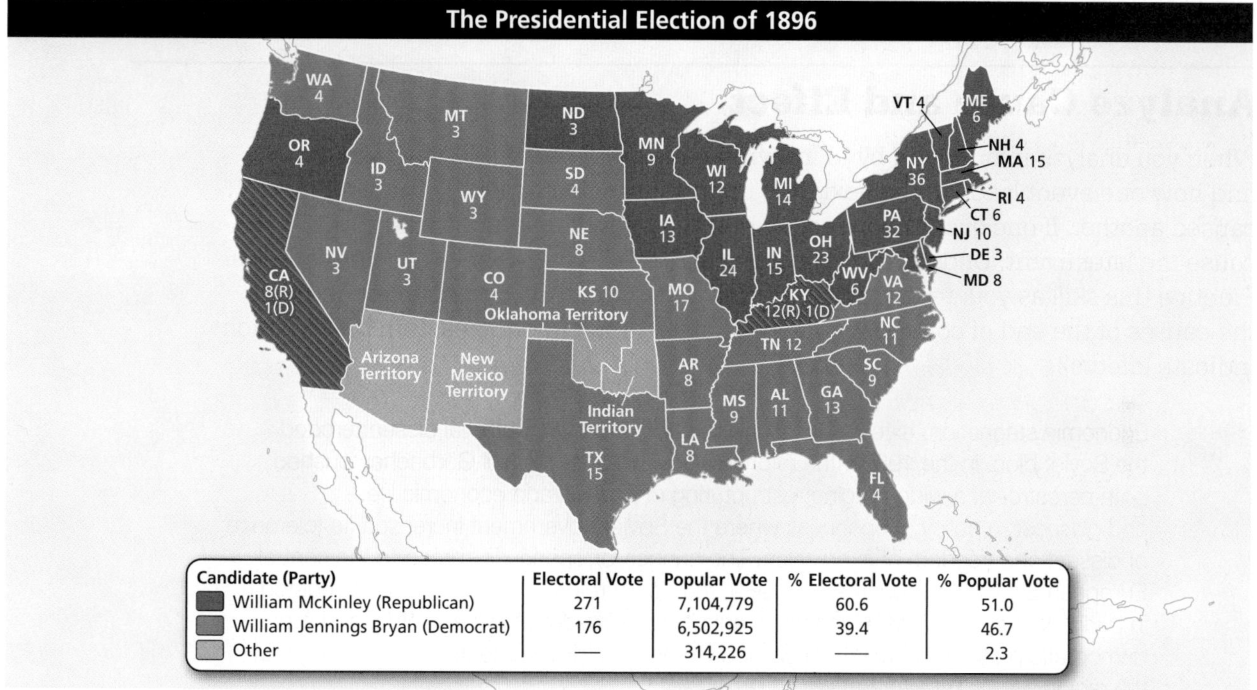

Candidate (Party)	Electoral Vote	Popular Vote	% Electoral Vote	% Popular Vote
William McKinley (Republican)	271	7,104,779	60.6	51.0
William Jennings Bryan (Democrat)	176	6,502,925	39.4	46.7
Other	—	314,226	—	2.3

[1.] Identify similarities and differences among items you need to understand. You need to pay careful attention and sometimes do research to find the similarities and differences among the facts, topics, or objects that you need to understand. Scientists find groups, or categories, of related animals by analyzing the details of the animals' bodies. For example, insects with similar wings, legs, and mouth-parts probably belong in the same category. Gather similar information about all the things you need to understand. For example, if you know the location of one thing, try to find the locations of all the things you are studying. If you have different types of information about your topics, you will not be able to group them easily.

[2.] Create a system to group items with common characteristics. Once you have gathered similar kinds of information on the items you need to understand, look for items that share characteristics or features. Create categories based on a feature shared by all of the facts, topics, or objects you need to understand. For example, if you have gathered information on the population and political systems of several countries, you could categorize them by the size of their population or their type of political system.

[3.] Form the groupings. Put each of the items that you are studying into one of the categories that you have created. If some items do not fit, you may need to make a new category or modify your categories. Label each category for the characteristic shared by its members. Examples of labels for categories might include "Countries with more than 100 million people," "Countries with fewer than 1 million people," "Democracies," or "Dictatorships."

Analyze Cause and Effect

When you analyze information by identifying cause-and-effect relationships, you find how one event leads to the next. It is important to find evidence that one event caused another. If one event happened earlier than another, it did not necessarily cause the later event. Understanding causes and effects can help you solve problems. Practice this skill as you read the text on this page. What words in the text indicate the causes of the end of communism in the Soviet Union and the eastern bloc? Which indicate effects?

> Economic stagnation, external pressure from the West, and internal dissent eroded the Soviet bloc. In the 1980s, the reformist Soviet leader Mikhail Gorbachev pushed both *perestroika*, a wide-ranging restructuring of political and economic life, and *glasnost*, a policy of openness where the Soviet government increased its tolerance of dissent and freedom of expression. The hunger for openness spread to the central European Soviet bloc countries. In 1989, the Polish reform party Solidarity competed in parliamentary elections, Hungarians enjoyed the freedom to visit Austria, and pro-democratic protests in East Germany led Communist governments to fold throughout the region.

[1.] Choose a starting point of observation. When trying to understand a historical event, choose the time of that event. If you are trying to understand a current event, you can work backward from a starting point in the present.

[2.] Consider earlier events to try to find connections to your starting point, including any language that signals causes. Put the evidence together to identify true causes. When reading, look for events that come before your starting point. Analyze whether these earlier events caused later events. Identify words that signal cause, such as "reason," "because," and "led to." Analyze the information by developing connections between historical events. Make sure that there is evidence showing that the earlier events caused the later events and did not just happen earlier.

[3.] Consider later events to try to find connections to your starting point, including any language that signals effects. Put the evidence together to determine true effects. Look for events that come after your starting point. Analyze the information in order to determine whether these later events are effects of earlier events. Identify words that signal effect, such as "led to," "so," and "therefore." Make sure that there is evidence showing that these later events were caused by earlier events and did not just happen later.

[4.] Summarize the cause-and-effect relationship and draw conclusions. Once you have identified the cause-and-effect relationships between different events, describe these relationships. Draw a diagram that develops the connections between the two historical events. Draw conclusions about any relationships that you see.

Compare and Contrast

When you analyze information by comparing and contrasting two or more things, you look for similarities and differences between them. This skill helps you understand the things that you are comparing and contrasting. It is also a skill that you can use in making choices. Practice this skill as you read the text excerpt on this page. Compare and contrast the critics of the New Deal.

> While Roosevelt had little difficulty gaining support from Congress for his proposals, a minority of Americans expressed their opposition to the New Deal. Critics on the political right thought the changes the New Deal brought were too radical. Critics on the left thought that they were not radical enough. Several of FDR's critics attracted mass followings and made plans to challenge him for the presidency in 1936.

[1.] Look for related topics and characteristics that describe them. When you are looking for similarities and differences between two things, it can help to start by identifying relationships between them. What do the two things have in common? If two things have nothing in common, such as a dog and a piece of pie, it will be difficult to find similarities or differences. On the other hand, you can compare and contrast two countries or political systems. Look through the information you have on the things or topics you want to compare and contrast, and identify the characteristics, or features, that describe those things or topics.

[2.] Look for words that signal comparison ("both," "similar to," "also") or contrast ("unlike," "different," "instead"). Look for words that show comparison, or similarity, and those that show contrast, or difference. Take notes on these similarities and differences. This will make it possible to analyze information more quickly.

[3.] Identify similarities and differences in the topics, and draw conclusions about them. Look through your notes and analyze the ways in which your topics are similar and different. Usually, topics have both similarities and differences. Try to find patterns in these similarities and differences. For example, all the similarities between two countries might be related to climate, and all the differences might be related to economics. Draw conclusions based on these patterns. In this example, you might conclude that a country's economy does not depend on its climate. Identifying similarities and differences by comparing and contrasting two topics lets you draw conclusions that help you analyze both topics as well as other topics like them.

Identify Main Ideas and Details

You can analyze information in a selection by finding the main idea. A main idea is the most important point in a selection. Identifying the main idea will help you remember details, such as names, dates, and events, which should support the main idea. Practice this skill by reading the paragraph on this page. Find the main idea of this paragraph and the supporting details.

> During his first hundred days in office, which became known as the Hundred Days, Roosevelt proposed and Congress passed 15 major bills. These measures had three goals: relief, recovery, and reform. Roosevelt wanted to provide relief from the immediate hardships of the depression and achieve a long-term economic recovery. He also instituted reforms to prevent future depressions.

[1.] Scan titles, headings, and visuals before reading to see what the selection is about. Often, important ideas are included in titles, headings, and other special text. Special text may be primary sources, words that are highlighted, or ideas listed with bullet points. Also, take a look at visuals and captions. By analyzing these parts of the text, you should quickly get a sense of the main idea of the article.

[2.] Read the selection and then identify the main point of the selection, the point that the rest of the selection supports: this is the main idea. Read through the selection to identify the main idea. Sometimes, the main idea will be the first or second sentence of one of the first few paragraphs. Sometimes, it will be the last sentence of the first paragraph. Other times, no single sentence will tell you the main idea. You will have to come up with your own sentence answering the question, "What is the main point of this selection?"

[3.] Find details or statements within the selection that support or build on the main idea. Once you have identified the main idea, look for details that support the main idea. Many or most of the details should be related to the main idea. If you find that many of the details are not related to what you think is the main idea, you may not have identified the main idea correctly. Identify the main idea that the details in the selection support. Analyze the information in the text by finding the main idea and supporting details.

Summarize

When you analyze information by summarizing, you restate the main points of a passage in your own words. Using your own words helps you understand the information. Summarizing will help you understand a text and prepare for tests or assignments based on the text. Practice this skill by following the steps to summarize this excerpt.

> The Texas legislature carries out that responsibility as a bicameral body modeled after the Congress of the United States. Texas' upper house is called the Senate, and the lower house is called the House of Representatives. In fact, all State legislatures but one are bicameral. The exception is Nebraska, which calls its single chamber the Legislature.

Although there is no ideal size for a legislative body, two basic considerations are important. First, a legislature, and each of its houses, should not be so large as to hamper the orderly conduct of the people's business. Second, it should not be so small that the many views and interests within the State cannot be represented adequately. The Texas Senate has 31 members, representing 31 districts that are about equal in population. The Texas House of Representatives has 150 members, elected from 150 districts that are all about equal in population.

[1.] Identify and write down the main point of each paragraph in your own words. You may identify the main idea right at the beginning of each paragraph. In other cases, you will have to figure out the main idea. As you read each paragraph, ask yourself, "What is the point this paragraph makes?" The point the paragraph makes is the main idea. Write this idea down in your own words.

[2.] Use these main points to write a general statement of the overall main idea of the passage in your own words. Once you have written down the main idea for each paragraph, write down the main idea of the passage. Write the main idea in your own words. If you have trouble identifying the main idea of the passage, review the titles and headings in the passage. Often, titles and headings relate to the main idea. Also, the writer may state the main idea in the first paragraph of the passage. The main idea of a passage should answer the question, "What is the point this passage makes?"

[3.] Use this general statement as a topic sentence for your summary. Then, write a paragraph tying together the main points of the passage. Leave out unimportant details. Analyze the information in the passage by summarizing. Use the main idea of the passage as a topic sentence for your summary paragraph. Use the main ideas that you identified for each paragraph of the passage to write sentences supporting the main idea of the passage. Leave out details that are not needed to understand the main idea of the passage. Your summary should be in your own words, and it should be much shorter than the original passage. Once your summary is written, review it to make sure that it contains all the main points of the passage. If any are missing, revise your summary to include them. If the summary includes unimportant details, remove them.

Generalize

One good way to analyze materials about a particular subject is to make generalizations and predictions. What are the patterns and connections that link the different materials? What can you say about the different materials that is true of all them? Practice this skill by analyzing the chart, Strong Minor Party Efforts. What generalization can you make about minor political parties in the United States?

Strong Minor Party Efforts*

YEAR	PARTY	% POPULAR VOTE	ELECTORAL VOTES
1920	Socialist	3.45	---
1924	Progressive	16.61	13
1932	Socialist	2.22	---
1948	States' Rights (Dixiecrat)	2.41	39
	Progressive	2.37	---
1968	American Independent	13.53	46
1996	Reform	8.40	---
2000	Green	2.74	---

* Includes all minor parties that polled at least 2% of the popular vote.
SOURCE: U.S. Census Bureau; *Historical Statistics of the United States, Colonial Times to 1970*

[1.] Make a list. Listing all of the specific details and facts about a subject will help you find patterns and connections.

[2.] Generate a statement. From your list of facts and specific details, decide what most of the items listed have in common. Analyze your information by making generalizations and predictions.

[3.] Ensure your generalization is logical and well supported by facts. Generalizations can be valid or invalid. A generalization that is not logical or supported by facts is invalid.

Make Predictions

You can analyze information by making generalizations and predictions. Predictions are educated guesses about the future, based on clues you find in written material and information you already have. When you analyze information by making generalizations and predictions, you are thinking critically about the material you read. Practice this skill by analyzing this graph and predicting the effect an economic downturn, with lower corporate and individual earnings, would have on government receipts.

Federal Receipts, 2014 (Estimated)

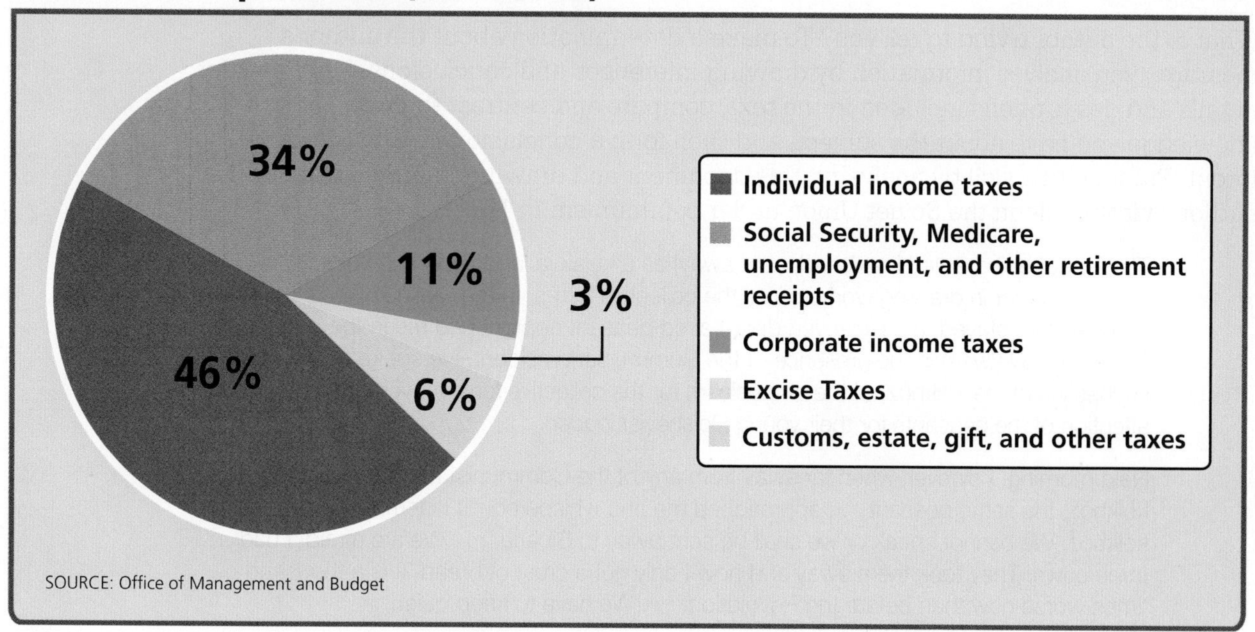

[1.] Review the content. Read your material carefully and research any terms or concepts that are new to you. It's important to understand the material before analyzing the information to make a prediction.

[2.] Look for clues. Gathering evidence is an important part of making predictions. Look for important words, statements, and evidence that seem to support the writer's point of view. Ask questions about what you are reading, including who, what, where, when, why, and how. Look for and analyze clues to help you generalize and predict.

[3.] Consider what you already know. Use related prior knowledge and/or connect to your own experiences to help you make an informed prediction. If you have experience with the subject matter, you have a much better chance of making an accurate prediction.

[4.] Generate a list of predictions. After studying the content, list the clues you've found. Then use these clues, plus your prior knowledge, to form your predictions. List as many possible outcomes as you can based on clues in the material and the questions you have considered.

Draw Inferences

What is the author trying to tell you? To make a determination about the author's message, you analyze information by drawing inferences and conclusions. You consider details and descriptions included in the text, compare and contrast the text to prior knowledge you have about the subject, and then form a conclusion about the author's intent. Practice this skill by analyzing this document and drawing inferences about the author's view of life in the Soviet Union under communism in 1931.

> The fear of being exiled [banished, sent away] as a kulak [a landowner] has been a powerful factor in drawing workers into the collective farms. In the Stalin kolkhoz [collective farm] where I stayed, a sharp-eyed dark-haired peasant approached me in the Village Soviet hut. We were in the presence of the Communist president. He spoke to me of the successes of the kolkhoz, of the enthusiasm for the collective farm movement, and of the affection of the peasants for their young Bolshevist leader.
>
> Next morning, however, when far away from any of the Communist members of the kolkhoz, the same peasant . . . approached me and whispered, "It is terrible here in the kolkhoz. We cannot speak or we shall be sent away to Siberia. . . . We are afraid. I had three cows. They took them away and now I only get a crust of bread. It is a thousand times worse now than before the Revolution. . . . We have to keep quiet.
>
> "The Real Russia: The Peasant on the Farm," Gareth Jones, *The Times*, October 14, 1931

[1.] Study the image or text. Consider all of the details and descriptions included. What is the author trying to tell you? Look for context clues that hint at the topic and subject matter.

[2.] Make a connection. Use related prior knowledge to connect to the text or image. Analyze information by asking questions such as who, what, where, when, and how. Look for cause-and-effect relationships; compare and contrast. This strategy will help you think beyond the available surface details to understand what the author is suggesting or implying.

[3.] Form a conclusion. When you draw an inference, you combine your own ideas with evidence and details you found within the text or image to form a new conclusion. This action leads you to a new understanding of the material.

Draw Conclusions

When you analyze information by drawing inferences and conclusions, you connect the ideas in a text with what you already know in order to understand a topic better. Using this skill, you can "fill in the blanks" to see the implications or larger meaning of the information in a text. Practice this skill by reading the excerpt on this page. What conclusions can you draw based on the information in the paragraph?

Challenging Economic Times

From the Oval Office, Hoover worked hard to end the depression. But to many out-of-work Americans, the President became a symbol of failure. Some people blamed capitalism, while others questioned the responsiveness of democracy. Many believed the American system was due for an overhaul. Although some questioned the ability of America's capitalistic and democratic institutions to overcome the crisis, most Americans never lost faith in their country.

[1.] Identify the topic, main idea, and supporting details. Before reading, look at the titles and headings within a reading. This should give you a good idea of the topic, or the general subject, of a text. After reading, identify the main idea. The main idea falls within the topic and answers the question, "What is the main point of this text?" Find the details that the author presents to support the main idea.

[2.] Use what you know to make a judgment about the information. Think about what you know about this topic or a similar topic. For example, you may read that the English settlers of Jamestown suffered from starvation because many of them were not farmers and did not know how to grow food. Analyzing the information about their situation and what you know about people, you could draw the conclusion that these settlers must have had little idea, or the wrong idea, about the conditions that they would find in America.

[3.] Check and adjust your judgment until you can draw a well-supported conclusion. Look for details within the reading that support your judgment. Reading a little further, you find that these settlers thought that they would become rich after discovering gold or silver, or through trading with Native Americans for furs. You can use this information to support your conclusion that the settlers were mistaken about the conditions that they would find in America. By analyzing the information further, you might infer that the settlers had inaccurate information about America. To support your conclusions, you could look for reliable sources on what these settlers knew before they left England.

Interpret Sources

Outlines and reports are good sources of information. In order to interpret these sources, though, you'll need to identify the type of document you're reading, identify the main idea, organize the details of information, and evaluate the source for point of view and bias. Practice this skill by finding a newspaper or online report on a bill recently passed by Congress or a decision recently decided by the Supreme Court. What steps will you take to interpret this report?

[1.] Identify the type of document. Is the document a primary or secondary source? Determine when, where, and why it was written.

[2.] Examine the source to identify the main idea. After identifying the main idea, identify details or sections of text that support the main idea. If the source is an outline or report, identify the topic and subtopics; review the supporting details under each subtopic. Organize the information from the outline or report and think about how it connects back to the overall topic listed at the top of the outline or report.

[3.] Evaluate the source for point of view and bias. Primary sources often have a strong point of view or bias; it is important to analyze primary sources critically to determine their validity. Evaluating each source will help you interpret the information they contain.

Create Databases

Databases are organized collections of information which can be analyzed and interpreted. You decide on a topic, organize data, use a spreadsheet, and then pose questions which will help you to analyze and interpret your data. Practice this skill as you create a database of key facts about five counties in your state. You can find many kinds of county data in the U.S. Census. (census.gov)

[1.] Decide on a topic. Identify the information that you will convert into a table. This information may come from various sources, including textbooks, reference works, and Internet sites.

[2.] Organize the data. Study the information and decide what to include in your table. Only include data that is pertinent and available. Based on the data you choose, organize your information. Identify how many columns there will be and what the column headings will be. Decide the order in which you are going to list the data in the rows.

[3.] Use a spreadsheet. A spreadsheet is a computer software tool that allows you to organize data so that it can be analyzed. Spreadsheets allow you to make calculations as well as input data. Use a spreadsheet to help you create summaries of your data. For instance, you can compute the sum, average, minimum, and maximum values of the data. Use the graphing features of your spreadsheet program to show the data visually.

[4.] Analyze the data. Once all of your data is entered and you have made any calculations you need, you are ready to pose questions to analyze and interpret your data. Organize the information from the database and use it to form conclusions. Be sure to draw conclusions that can be supported by the data available.

www.PearsonRealize.com
View Video Tutorials and other 21st Century Skills

Analyze Data and Models

Data and models can provide useful information about geographic distributions and patterns. To make sense of that information, though, you need to pose and answer questions about data and models. What does the data say? What does it mean? What patterns can you find? Practice this skill as you study the data in the map. What might explain the differences among states shown here?

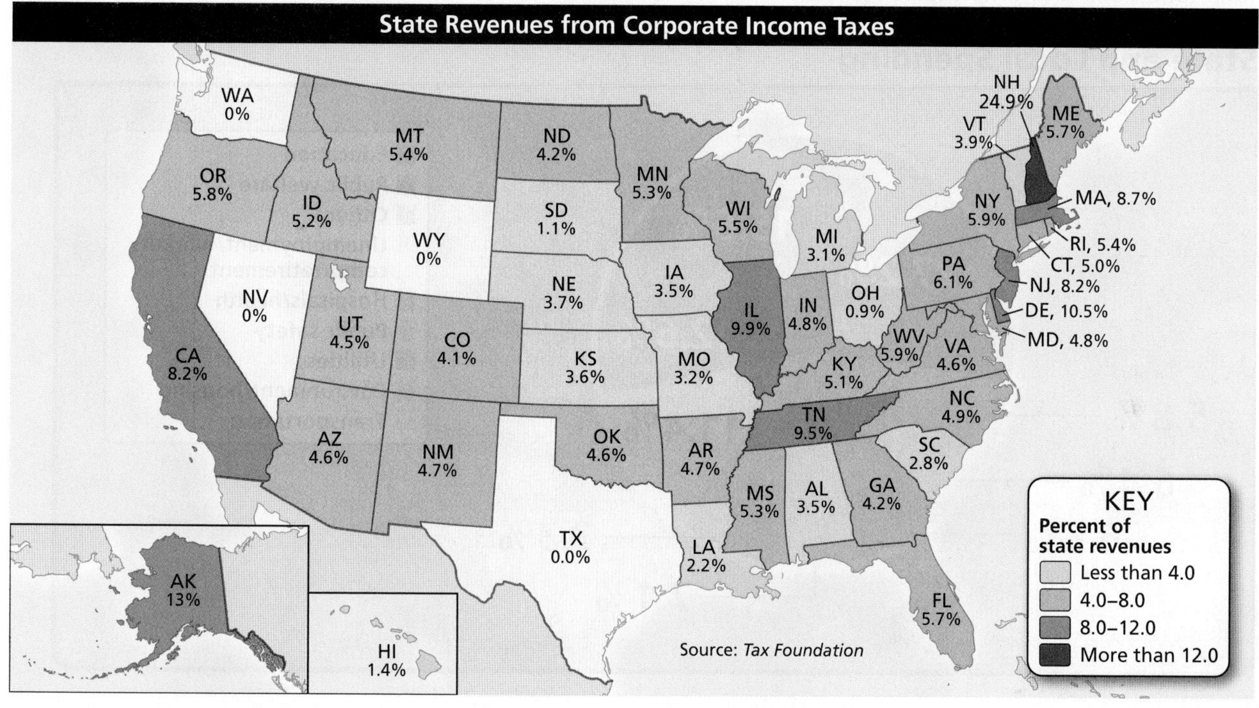

[1.] Read the title to learn the geographic distributions represented by the data set, graph, or model.

[2.] Read the data given. When reviewing a graph, read the labels and the key to help you comprehend the data provided. Pose and answer questions to further understand the material. For example, you might ask "Who could use this data?" or "How could this data be used?" or even "Why is this data presented in this particular format?" Thinking critically about the data presented will help you make predictions and comprehend the data.

[3.] Study the numbers, lines, and/or colors to find out what the graphs or data represent. Next, find similarities and differences between multiple models of the same data. Do any additional research to find out more about why the information in the models differs.

[4.] Interpret the graph, data set, or model. Look for interesting geographic distributions and patterns in the data. Look at changes over time or compare information from different categories. Draw conclusions.

Read Charts, Graphs, and Tables

If you pose and answer questions about charts, graphs, or tables you find in books or online, you can find out all sorts of information, such as how many calories are in your favorite foods or what the value of a used car is. Analyzing and interpreting the information you find in thematic charts, graphs, and tables can help you make decisions in your life. Practice this skill as you study the circle graph below. What questions does this graph raise for the future?

State and Local Spending

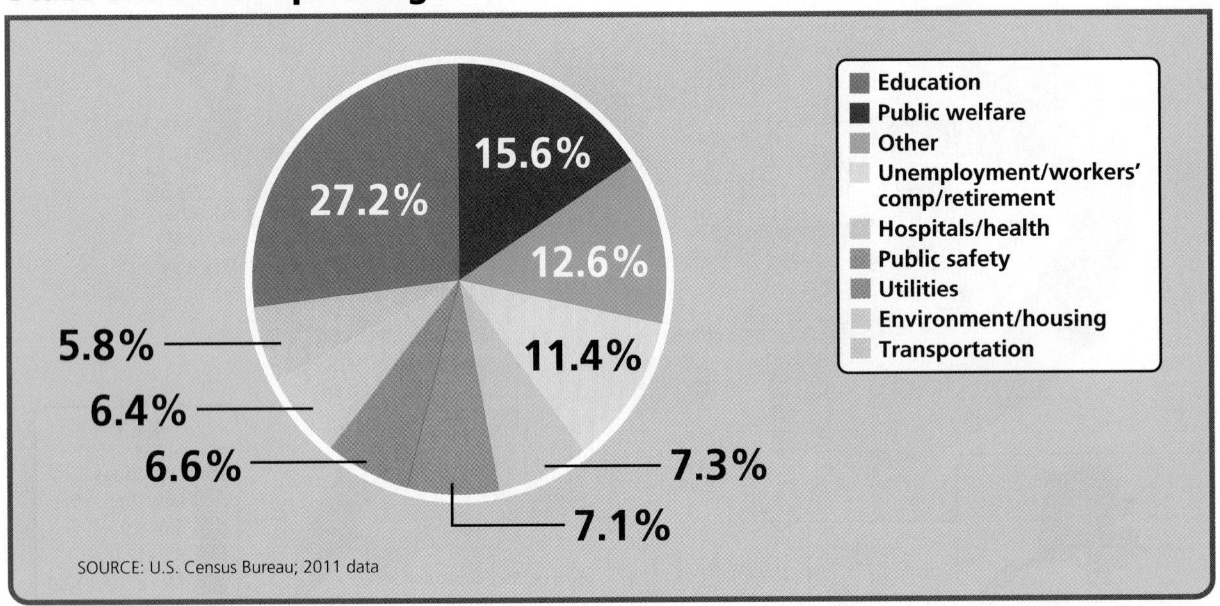

[1.] Identify the title and labels of a chart, graph, or table, and read the key, if there is one, to understand the information presented. The title often tells you the topic of the chart, graph, or table, or the type of information you will find. Make sure you understand how the graph shows information. A key or legend often appears in a small box near the edge of the graph or chart. The key will tell you the meaning of lines, colors, or symbols used on the chart or graph. Notice also the column and row headings, and use your reading skills to figure out the meanings of any words you don't know.

[2.] Determine consistencies and inconsistencies, to see whether there is a trend in a graph, chart, or table. Organize information from visuals such as charts and graphs and decide whether or not there is a trend or pattern in the information that you see. Evaluate the data and determine whether the trend is consistent, or steady. Remember that there could be some inconsistencies, or exceptions to the pattern. Try not to miss the overall pattern because of a couple of exceptions.

[3.] Draw conclusions about the data in a chart, graph, or table. Once you understand the information, try to analyze and interpret the information and draw conclusions. If you see a pattern, does the pattern help you to understand the topic or predict future events?

[4.] Create a chart or graph to make the data more understandable or to view the data in a different way. Does the data in the chart or graph help you answer questions you have about the topic or see any causes or effects? For example, you could use your mathematical skills to create circle graphs or bar graphs that visually organize the data in a different way that allows you to interpret the data differently.

[5.] Use the data or information in charts and graphs to understand an issue or make decisions. Use your social studies skills to make inferences, draw conclusions, and take a stand on the issue.

Create Charts and Maps

Thematic charts, graphs, and maps are visual tools for representing information. When you create a thematic chart, graph, or map you will start by selecting the type of data you want to represent. Then you will find appropriate data to include, organize your data, and then create symbols and a key to help others understand your chart, graph, or map. Practice this skill by creating a map showing how your state's counties voted in the most recent presidential election. Research the data, then use computer software to generate the map. What patterns do you see? How might you explain them?

[1.] To create a chart or map, first select a region or set of data. Use a map to represent data pertaining to a specific region or location; use a chart to represent trends reflected in a set of data.

[2.] Research and find the data you would like to present in the chart or map. Your choice of data will be based on the theme you wish to explore. For example, a chart or map that explores the theme of changing demographics in Texas might include data about the location of different ethnic groups in Texas in the nineteenth, twentieth, and twenty-first centuries.

[3.] Organize the data according to the specific format of your chart or map.

[4.] Create symbols, a key (as needed), and a title. Create symbols to represent each piece of data you would like to highlight. Keep each symbol simple and easy to understand. After you have created the symbols, place them in a key. Add a title to your map or chart that summarizes the information presented. Your symbols and key will make it easier for others to interpret your charts and maps.

Analyze Political Cartoons

Political cartoons are visual commentaries about events or people. As you learn to analyze political cartoons, you will learn to identify bias in cartoons and interpret their meaning. You can start by carefully examining the cartoon and considering its possible meanings. Then you can draw conclusions based on your analysis. Practice this skill as you study this political cartoon.

[1.] Fully examine the cartoon. Identify any symbols in the cartoon, read the text and title, and identify the main character or characters. Analyze the cartoon to identify bias and determine what each image or symbol represents. Conduct research if you need more information to decipher the cartoon.

[2.] Consider the meaning. Think about how the cartoonist uses the images and symbols in the cartoon to express his or her opinion about a subject. Try to interpret the artist's purpose in creating the image.

[3.] Draw conclusions. Use what you have gleaned from the image itself, plus any prior knowledge or research, to analyze, interpret, and form a conclusion about the artist's intentions.

Read Physical Maps

What mountain range is closest to where you live? What major rivers are closest to you? To find out, you would look at a physical map. You can use appropriate reading skills to interpret social studies information such as that found on different kinds of maps. Physical maps show physical features, such as elevation, mountains, valleys, oceans, rivers, deserts, and plains. Practice this skill as you study this map. Remember the location of your state capital. What advantages can you see to locating the state capital there? What disadvantages?

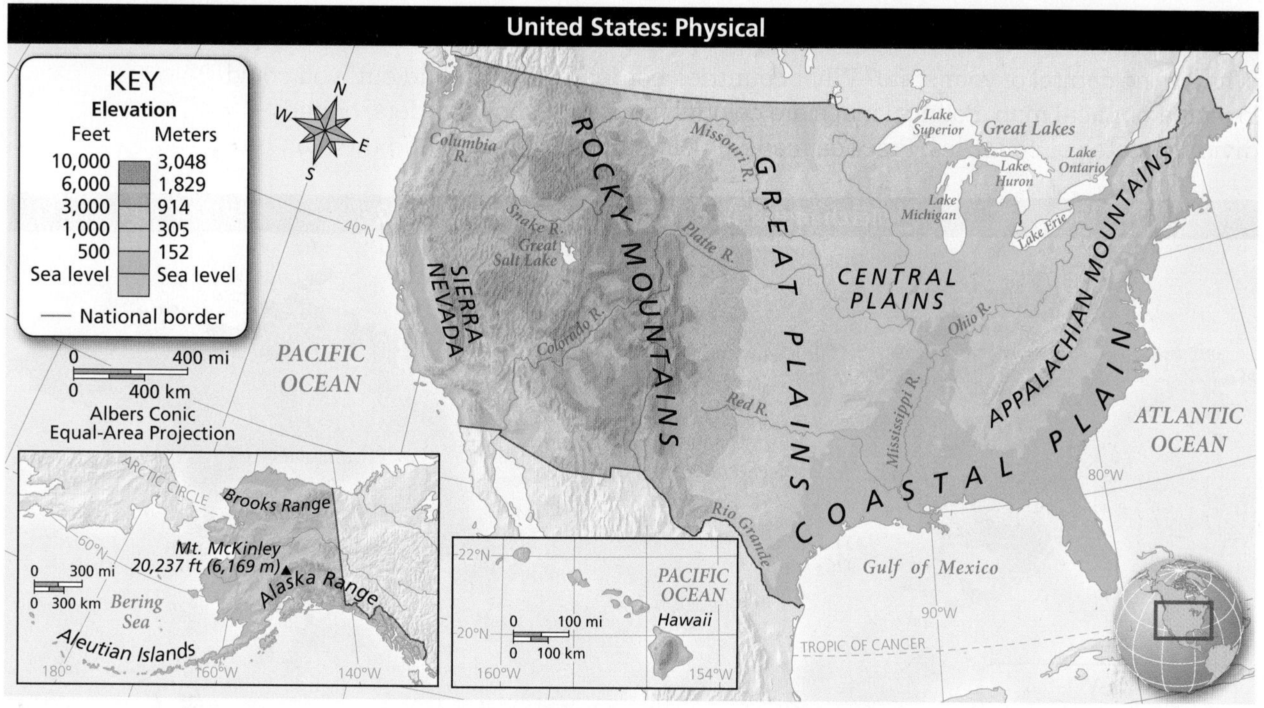

[1.] Identify the title and region shown on a map. A map's title can help you to identify the region covered by the map. The title may also tell you the type of information you will find on the map. If the map has no title, you can identify the region by reading the labels on the map.

[2.] Use the map key to interpret symbols and colors on a map. A key or legend often appears in a small box near the edge of the map. The legend will tell you the meaning of colors, symbols, or other patterns on the map. On a physical map, colors from the key often show elevation, or height above sea level, on the map.

[3.] Identify physical features, such as mountains, valleys, oceans, and rivers. Using labels on the map and colors and symbols from the key, identify the physical features on the map. The information in the key allows you to interpret the information from visuals such as a map. Rivers, oceans, lakes, and other bodies of water are usually colored blue. Colors from the key may indicate higher and lower elevation, or there may be shading on the map that shows mountains.

[4.] Draw conclusions about the region based on natural resources and physical features. Once you understand all the symbols and colors on the map, try to interpret the information from the map. Is it very mountainous or mostly flat? Does it have a coastline? Does the region have lots of lakes and rivers that suggest a good water supply? Pose and answer questions about geographic distributions and patterns shown on the map. Physical maps can give you an idea of lifestyle and economic activities of people in the region.

Read Political Maps

What is the capital of your state? What countries border China? To find out, you could look at a political map. Political maps are colorful maps that show borders, or lines dividing states or countries. Practice reading political maps by studying the map below.

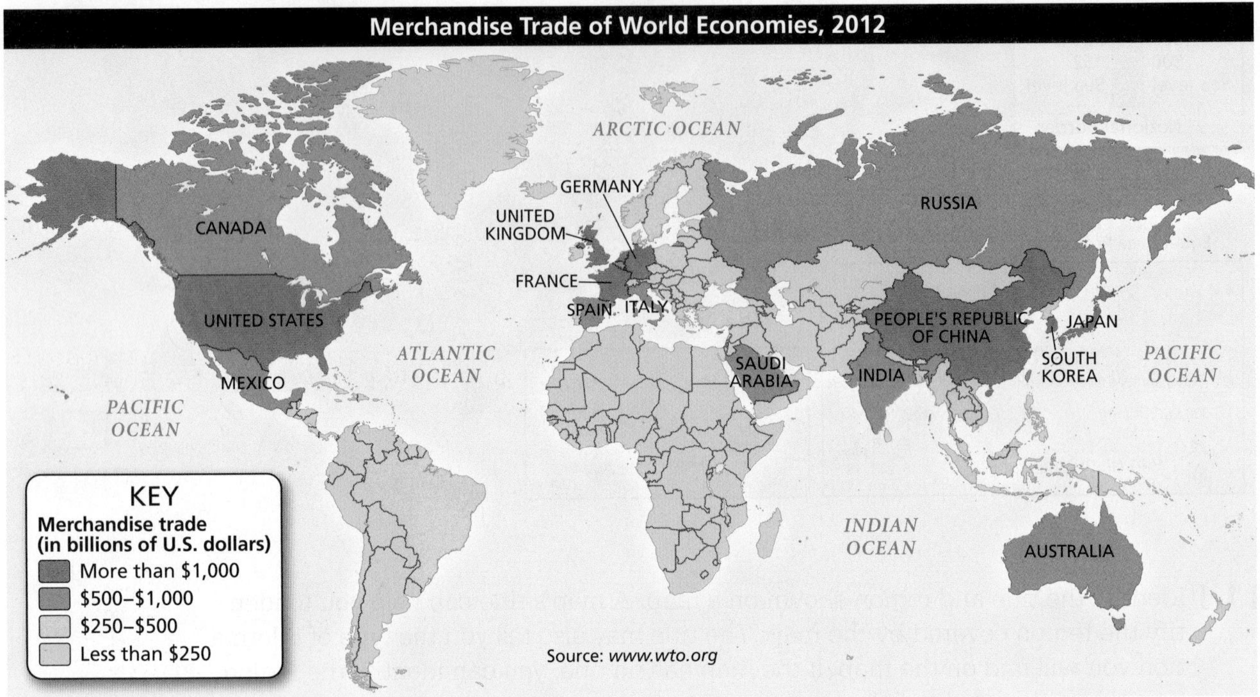

[1.] Identify the title of the political map and the region shown. A map's title can help you identify the region covered by the map. The title may also tell you the type of information you will find on the map. If the map has no title, you can identify the region by reading the labels on the map.

[2.] Use the map key to interpret symbols and colors on the map. A key or legend often appears in a small box near the edge of the map. The key will help you interpret information from visuals, including maps, by telling you the meaning of colors, symbols, or other patterns on the visual.

[3.] Identify boundaries between nations or states. Evaluate government data, such as borders, using the map. It is often easy to see borders, because each state or country will be a different color. If you cannot find the borders, check the key to find the lines used to mark borders on the map.

[4.] Locate capital cities. Look at the key to see whether capital cities are shown on the map. They are often marked with a special symbol, such as a star.

[5.] Draw conclusions about the region based on the map. Once you understand all the symbols and colors on the map, use appropriate reading and mathematical skills to interpret social studies information, such as that shown on the map, in order to draw conclusions about the region. For example, are some countries very large with many cities? These countries are likely to be powerful and influential.

Read Special-Purpose Maps

Some maps show specific kinds of information. These special-purpose maps may show features such as climate zones, ancient trade routes, economic and government data, geographic patterns, or population. Locating and interpreting information from visuals, including special-purpose maps, is an important research skill. Practice this skill as you study the map on this page.

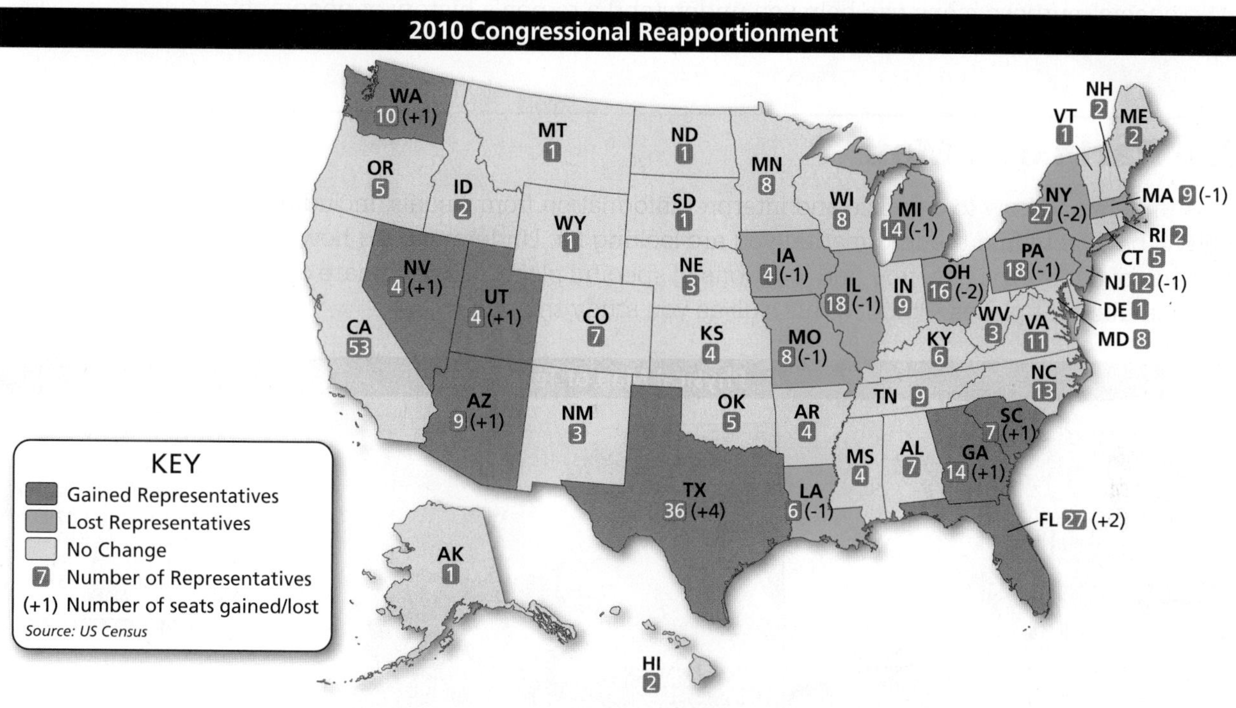

[1.] Identify the title and determine the purpose of a map. A map's title can help you identify the region covered by the map. The title may also tell you the purpose of the map. If the map has no title, see what information the map shows to determine its purpose.

[2.] Use the map key to make sense of symbols and colors on a map. A key or legend often appears in a small box near the edge of the map. The key will tell you the meaning of colors, symbols, or other patterns on the map. Special-purpose maps use these colors and symbols to present information.

[3.] Draw conclusions about the region shown on a map. Once you understand all the symbols and colors on the map, you can use appropriate skills, including reading and mathematical skills, to analyze and interpret social studies information such as maps. You can pose and answer questions about geographic patterns and distributions that are shown on maps. For example, a precipitation or climate map will show you which areas get lots of rainfall and which are very dry. You can evaluate government and economic data using maps. For example, a population map will show you which regions have lots of people and which have small, scattered populations. A historical map will show you the locations of ancient empires or trade routes. Thematic maps focus on a single theme or topic about a region. For example, you can interpret information from a thematic map representing various aspects of Texas during the nineteenth or twentieth century by studying the Great Military Map, which shows forts established in Texas during the nineteenth century, or by studying a map covering Texas during the Great Depression and World War II. By mapping this kind of detailed information, special-purpose maps can help you understand a region's history or geography.

Use Parts of a Map

If you understand how to organize and interpret information from visuals, including maps, you will be able to find the information you are looking for. Understanding how to use the parts of a map will help you find locations of specific places and estimate distances between different places. Practice this skill as you study this map.

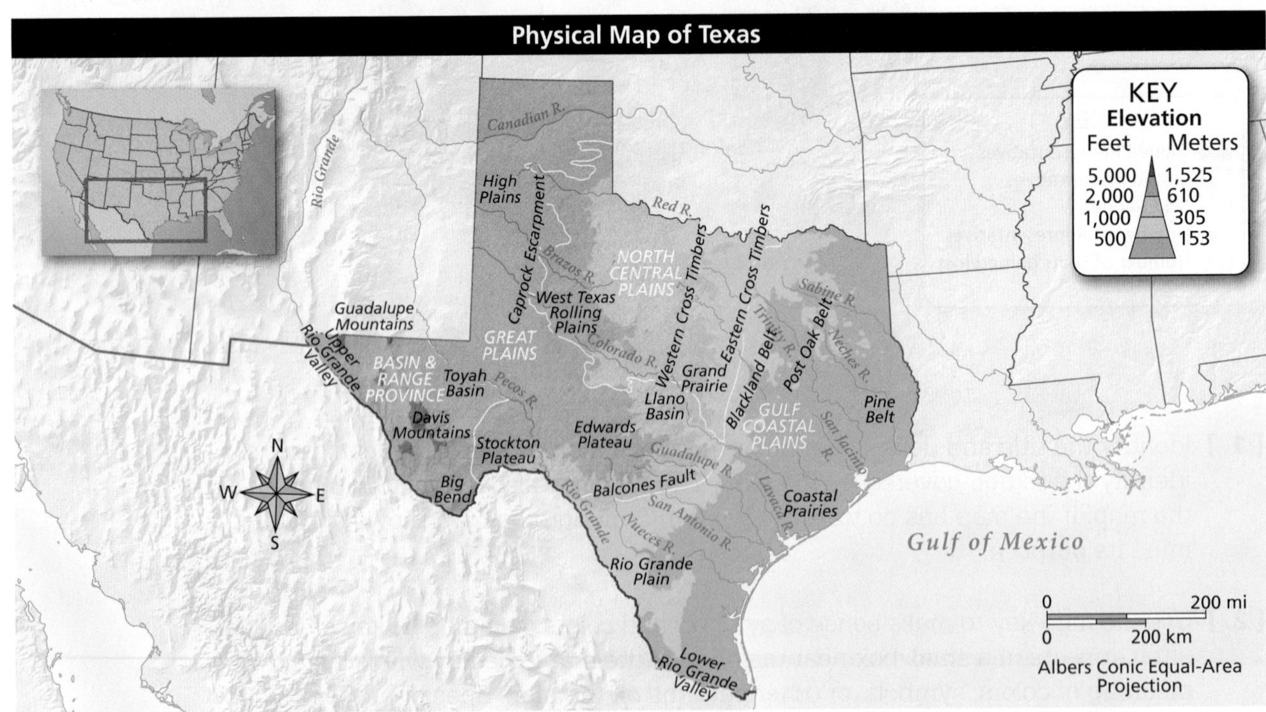

[1.] Identify the title and region of a map. Use appropriate reading skills to interpret social studies information such as map labels. A map's title can help you to identify the region covered by the map. The title may also tell you the type of information you will find on the map. If the map has no title, you can identify the region by reading the labels on the map.

[2.] Use the compass rose to determine direction. Although on most maps north is at the top of the map, you should always double check the compass rose. Often, on the compass rose, the first letter of each direction represents that direction. For example, "N" represents the direction "north." Some compass roses are as simple as an arrow pointing north.

[3.] Use the scale to estimate the distance between places. Use appropriate mathematical skills to interpret social studies information such as a map scale. The scale on a map shows how a measurement on the map compares to the distance on the ground. For example, if one inch on the map represents a mile, the number of inches between two places on the map is the distance in miles.

[4.] Use the key or legend on a map to find information about colors or symbols on a map. A key or legend often appears in a small box near the edge of the map. The legend will tell you the meaning of colors, symbols, or other patterns on the map.

[5.] Use the latitude and longitude grid to determine absolute locations. An absolute location is an exact description of a location on Earth's surface based on latitude and longitude. You can use the latitude and longitude lines on a map to find the absolute location of a place.

Analyze Primary and Secondary Sources

Primary sources are firsthand accounts of events. By contrast, secondary sources are secondhand accounts of events. Both sources are useful, but it is important to differentiate between valid primary and secondary sources. In this lesson, you'll learn how to locate and use primary and secondary sources to acquire information about the United States. Practice this skill by analyzing two selections below arguing whether or not to ratify the Constitution and distinguishing between the primary and secondary source.

> "...[T]he great powers of the President, connected with his duration in office would lead to oppression and ruin. That he would be governed by favorites and flatterers, or that a dangerous council would be collected from the great officers of state, ...that the president possessed of the power, given him by this frame of government differs but very immaterially from the establishment of monarchy in Great Britain, ...that no attention has been paid to either the numbers or property in each state in forming the senate; that the mode in which they are appointed and their duration, will lead to the establishment of an aristocracy, that the senate and president are improperly connected...these are some of the many evils that will attend the adoption of this government."
>
> —Letter V by "Cato," *The New York Journal,* November 22, 1787

Antifederalists appealed to Tom Paine's sentiment, "That government is best which governs least." They viewed with alarm the omission of annual elections and rotation in office.... Elderly radicals such as General James Warren and his gifted wife Mercy, who believed that the states were the true guardians of "Republican Virtue," predicted that the new Constitution would encourage vice and speculation, and that under it America would soon go the way of imperial Rome.

—Samuel Eliot Morison, *The Oxford History of the American People,* 1965

[1.] Determine who created the source as well as when and why it was created. Determine whether it is a primary or secondary source. Identify the author of the document. Next, look for the date the document was written or the date when the document was first published. Most primary sources are written close to the date of the events described. Secondary sources are often written well after the events described. Firsthand observers or participants in an event create primary sources. People who did not witness an event create secondary sources. Primary sources record an event. Secondary sources analyze or draw conclusions about events. Secondary sources rely on both primary and secondary sources. Good research requires you to analyze and evaluate the validity of information, arguments, and counterarguments from a primary or secondary source for frame of reference.

[2.] Identify the main idea and supporting details, and determine whether they are facts or opinions. Read the text carefully and ask yourself, "What point is this text making?" This point is the main idea. Then reread the text and list details that support this main idea. Decide whether these details are facts or opinions. If the details are facts, it should be possible to confirm them in other sources. If the author uses emotional language that shows feelings, the supporting details are probably opinions. Carefully analyze and evaluate the validity of information, arguments, and counterarguments from primary and secondary sources for point of view.

[3.] Decide whether the source's information is biased or if it is accurate and credible. Check statements in the text against reliable sources, such as encyclopedias or books written by experts on the topic. If reliable sources agree with the text, it is probably fairly accurate. If most of the text seems to be opinions rather than facts, it is not an accurate source of information. Still, these opinions can teach you about the author's world. A writer who observed an exciting or scary event may use emotional language to describe the event, but the source may still be a reliable account. An important part of research is analyzing and evaluating the validity of the information, arguments, and counterarguments from primary and secondary sources for bias or propaganda.

Compare Viewpoints

When people disagree about a topic, they have different viewpoints. Knowing how to analyze and evaluate the validity of information, arguments, and counterarguments from both primary and secondary sources for point of view can help you to learn more about a topic. Practice this skill by reading these quotes and comparing the viewpoints.

"Dictatorship…involves costs which the American people will never pay: The cost of having our children brought up, not as free and dignified human beings, but as pawns…

–Franklin Roosevelt, State of the Union Address, January 4, 1939

"The [Nazi Party] has laid down the directive…we must insist that all organs of education… have to [fulfill] their duty towards the community…

–Adolf Hitler, Speech delivered in German Reichstag on January 30, 1937

[1.] Identify the authors of texts presenting different points of view and identify each author's frame of reference. Frame of reference is a term that describes the experiences, values, and ideas that influence a person's opinions and actions. It can also be referred to as *point of view*. First, identify the group or individual that wrote each text. Determine if the source is primary or secondary. As you read, take note of any information about the author's experiences or background. Also, look for any signs of what the author thinks is important. These types of statements can help you analyze and evaluate the validity of information, arguments, and counterarguments from both primary and secondary sources for point of view.

[2.] Recognize any similarities and differences between the authors' frames of reference and identify the opinion of each author. Pay attention to any similarities and differences between the two authors' experiences, values, and ideas. Read carefully to identify the opinion of each author. In an article about a rock band, an author who played guitar in a band for ten years argues that Band A is the best band today because of its great guitarist. In a second article, another author who sang for many years argues that Band B is the best because of its lead singer. Notice how authors' arguments and counterarguments are shaped by their frame of reference, or point of view.

[3.] Draw conclusions about similarities and differences between authors' points of view. With some information about the point of view of each author, you can understand why they have different opinions. This helps you to analyze and evaluate the validity of the information, arguments, and counterarguments. In the example of the two authors writing about rock bands, each author stresses his or her own areas of expertise. You might decide to listen to the band recommended by the singer if you share an interest in vocals. If you are more interested in instrumentals, you might choose the band recommended by the guitarist.

Identify Bias

Being able to analyze and evaluate the validity of information, arguments, and counterarguments for bias helps you to determine whether primary or secondary sources you find online, in books, or in the media are reliable. When you are able to identify bias in written, oral, and visual material, you can see when someone is presenting only one side of an issue or basing an argument on emotion instead of facts. Practice this skill by applying the steps below whenever you read an editorial or an op-ed piece in the news media.

[1.] Identify the author of a source and the author's purpose. First, identify the author of the source. The author may be a group or an organization rather than a single person. The author may state his or her purpose very clearly in the source. If not, the type of source may give you an idea of the purpose. For example, the writer of an encyclopedia aims to summarize information about a subject. The author of a political Web site may want you to vote for a candidate.

[2.] Identify the main idea, and check whether the main idea is supported with facts or opinions. Read the document carefully and ask yourself, "What is the main point of this selection?" Your answer to this question is the main idea. Reread the document and list details that support this main idea. Decide whether these details are facts or opinions. To find out whether they are facts, check whether other reliable sources include the same information. If your source uses statements that shows feelings, those statements are probably opinions.

[3.] Look for the use of emotional language or one-sided opinions. Look for words that can show opinions such as "good" and "bad." Be aware of statements that make you feel angry, scared, or excited. Also, watch out for statements that only express one side of an issue. These are all signs of bias.

[4.] Draw conclusions about the author's bias, if any. Is the author using mostly emotional language with few facts to support his or her ideas? Are there insults or other very negative language in the source? If so, the source is probably biased. Similarly, if you notice that the author is presenting only one side of an issue, the source is probably not reliable. It is important to analyze and evaluate the information, arguments, and counterarguments in both primary and secondary sources for bias.

Evaluate Existing Arguments

When you evaluate existing arguments, you must evaluate and analyze the point of view and biases of your sources and their authors. Who is the author and what is he or she trying to accomplish? How valid are the arguments in your primary and secondary sources? If you master these skills, you will be able to analyze and interpret social studies information such as speeches. Practice this skill as you read and evaluate the excerpt on this page.

> We hold these truths to be self-evident: that all men and women are created equal; that they are endowed by their Creator with certain inalienable rights; that among these are life, liberty, and the pursuit of happiness. . . .
>
> The history of mankind is a history of repeated injuries and usurpations [seizures] on the part of man toward woman, having in direct object the establishment of an absolute tyranny over her. To prove this, let facts be submitted to a candid [fair] world.
>
> He has never permitted her to exercise her inalienable right to the elective franchise.
>
> He has compelled her to submit to law in the formation of which she had no voice. . . .

> He has made her, if married, in the eye of the law, civilly dead. He has taken from her all right in property, even to the wages she earns. . . .
>
> Now, in view of this entire disfranchisement of one-half the people of this country, their social and religious degradation, in view of the unjust laws above mentioned, and because women do feel themselves aggrieved, oppressed, and fraudulently deprived of their most sacred rights, we insist that they have immediate admission to all the rights and privileges which belong to them as citizens of the United States.
>
> —*Declaration of Sentiments and Resolutions,* 1848

[1.] Identify the claim or thesis. What is the author or source claiming? The claim or thesis is usually found in the introduction and/or conclusion of a written or spoken argument.

[2.] Identify the reasons (claims to truth or facts) the author offers in support of his or her claim. What evidence does the author or source provide to support their claims? Make a list of the evidence provided to support each claim.

[3.] Evaluate the argument. Analyze and evaluate the validity of the evidence presented to support each claim. Use the appropriate skills to analyze and interpret social studies information, such as speeches. Research each claim to be sure that the author's statements are accurate. Carefully check for evidence of bias or propaganda. Be sure you understand the author's point of view and his or her frame of reference. Finally, check to be sure that the author's conclusions follow logically from the evidence presented. If the evidence is accurate, the author is free from bias, and conclusions follow logically from the evidence, the claims are probably valid.

Consider and Counter Opposing Arguments

Before you can effectively counter opposing arguments, you'll need to analyze possible counterarguments for frame of reference, bias, point of view, and propaganda. You'll plan your response ahead of time, collecting research and data. Then, you'll make a point of acknowledging the opposing view before presenting your counterarguments. To practice this skill, suppose you are preparing for a debate about raising the minimum wage in your state. Choose a side of the debate to support. What arguments will you use to support your side of the debate? What counterarguments will you anticipate the other side using? Why is it useful to anticipate the other side's arguments?

[1.] Fully understand your argument and the potential counter points. Do research as needed to find out more about other opposing views. Analyze and evaluate the validity of possible counterarguments from primary and secondary sources for frame of reference, bias, point of view, and propaganda.

[2.] Make predictions and outline a response to several of the opposing views. Continue researching as needed. Researching, analyzing, and evaluating the validity of opposing arguments will help you support and strengthen your own. Opposing arguments can consist of any reasons, conclusions, or claims that oppose yours. Outline your response to each opposing reason, conclusion, or claim.

[3.] To counter an opposing argument, first acknowledge the opposing view. This strategy shows that you have heard the opposing argument and are responding accordingly. Consider using statements such as "I understand your point, but you should also consider the following..." You can also respond by refuting facts, logic, etc. Be sure to respond to each opposing argument. Ignoring or dismissing a counterargument shows that your response is weak and unsupported.

Participate in a Discussion or Debate

When you participate in a discussion or debate, your goal is to explain, analyze, and defend a point of view–often related to a current political or economic issue. To be a successful debater, you'll do your research, present your position, and defend your point of view in a courteous manner. Use the steps below to prepare for a discussion on this question: Do you think the United States should act as a "global policeman?" Why or why not?

[1.] Research. Before participating in a discussion or debate, do research to gain knowledge of your subject so that you may be an informed and prepared participant. Take notes as needed to help you prepare. Jot down main points and any questions you may have. As you research, decide where you might stand on the issue. Be sure to gather research and sources that will allow you to explain, analyze, and defend your point of view.

[2.] Present your position. After you have organized your thoughts and decided where you stand, explain and defend your point of view. Be sure to stay focused on the topic and your line of argument. Ask questions that challenge the accuracy, logic, or relevance of opposing views.

[3.] During the discussion or debate, be patient and courteous. Listen attentively, be respectful and supportive of peers, and speak only when instructed to do so by the moderator. Be sure to allow others to express their views; do not monopolize the debate or discussion. Speak clearly and slowly.

Give an Effective Presentation

When you create a written, visual, and oral presentation, you teach, convince, or share information with an audience. Effective presentations use both words and visuals to engage audiences. Delivery is also important. For example, you can use the way you move, speak, and look at the audience to keep people interested. Use the steps below to prepare and deliver a presentation on the history of the White House building.

[**1.**] Identify the purpose of your presentation and your audience. Think about the purpose of your written, visual, and oral presentation. If this is a research report, you will need facts and data to support your points. If you are trying to persuade your audience, look for powerful photos. Keep your audience in mind. Consider their interests and present your topic in a way that will engage them.

[**2.**] Write the text and find visual aids for your presentation. Look online and in books and magazines for information and images for your presentation. Organize the information and write it up carefully so that it is easy for your audience to understand. Diagrams can show complicated information in a clear way. Visuals also get people interested in the presentation. So choose large, colorful images that people in the back of the audience will be able to see.

[**3.**] Practice and work to improve your presentation. Keep practicing your oral presentation until you know the material well. Then, practice some more, focusing on improving your delivery.

[**4.**] Use body language, tone of voice, and eye contact to deliver an effective presentation. Answer questions if the audience has them. At the beginning of your oral presentation, take a breath, smile, and stand up tall. Speak more loudly and more clearly than you would in normal conversation. Also, try not to rush through the presentation. Glance at your notes but speak naturally, rather than reading. Look at people in the audience. If people are confused, pause to clarify. Finally, leave time for people in the audience to ask questions.

Write an Essay

There are four steps to writing an essay. You'll start by selecting a topic and research sources, then you'll write an outline and develop a thesis or point of view. After drafting your essay, you'll carefully proofread it to be sure you've used standard grammar, spelling, sentence structure, and punctuation. Finally, you'll revise and polish your work. To practice this skill, select a topic that interests you about the U.S. presidency and develop a thesis. Then explain to a partner the steps you will take to write your essay.

[**1.**] Choose your topic and research sources. Check which types of sources you will need. Gather different types of reliable sources that support the argument you will be making.

[**2.**] Write an outline and generate a thesis. First write your topic at the top of the page then list all the points or arguments you want to make about the topic; also list the facts and examples that support these points. Your thesis statement will inform the reader of the point you are making and what question you will be answering about the topic. When writing your thesis, be as specific as possible and address one main idea.

[3.] Draft your essay. After finishing your research and outline, begin writing the body of your essay; start with the introduction then write a paragraph for each of your supporting points, followed by a conclusion. As you write, do your best to use standard grammar, spelling, sentence structure, and punctuation. Be sure any terminology is used correctly.

[4.] Revise. An important part of the writing process involves checking for areas in which information should be added, removed, or rewritten. Try to imagine that this paper belongs to someone else. Does the paper have a clear thesis? Do all of the ideas relate back to the thesis? Read your paper out loud and listen for awkward pauses and unclear ideas. Lastly, check for mistakes in standard grammar, spelling, sentence structure, punctuation, and usage.

Avoid Plagiarism

When you don't attribute ideas and information to source materials and authors, you are plagiarizing. Plagiarizing–claiming others' ideas and information as your own–is considered unethical. You can avoid plagiarizing by carefully noting down which authors and sources you'll be using, citing those authors and sources in your paper, and listing them in a bibliography. To practice this skill, suppose you have been assigned to write a research paper on the impact of the Internet on the political process. Name three types of sources you might use to help you gather information. Explain how you will avoid plagiarism when you use these sources.

[1.] Keep a careful log of your notes. As you read sources to gain background information on your topic, keep track of ideas and information and the sources and authors they come from. Write down the name of each source next to your notes from that particular source so you can remember to cite it later on. Create a separate section in your notes where you keep your own thoughts and ideas so you know which ideas are your own. Using someone else's words or paraphrasing their ideas does not make them yours.

[2.] Cite sources in your paper. You must identify the source materials and authors you use to support your ideas. Whenever you use statistics, facts, direct quotations, or paraphrases of others' views, you need to attribute them to your source. Cite your sources within the body of your paper. Check your assignment to find out how they should be formatted.

[3.] List your sources in a bibliography at the end of your paper. List your source materials and authors cited in alphabetical order by author, using accepted formats. As you work, be sure to check your list of sources from your notes so that none are left out of the bibliography.

www.PearsonRealize.com
View Video Tutorials and other 21st Century Skills

Solve Problems

Problem solving is a skill that you use every day. It is a process that requires an open mind, clear thinking, and action. Practice this skill by considering the lack of volunteers for a local project such as a food bank or park clean up and using these steps to solve the problem.

[1.] Understand the problem. Before trying to solve a problem, make sure that you gather as much information as possible in order to identify the problem. What are the causes and effects of the problem? Who is involved? You will want to make sure that you understand different perspectives on the problem. Try not to jump to conclusions or make assumptions. You might end up misunderstanding the problem.

[2.] Consider possible solutions and choose the best one. Once you have identified the problem and gathered some information, list and consider a number of possible options. Right away, one solution might seem like the right one, but try to think of other solutions. Be sure to consider carefully the advantages and disadvantages of each option. It can help to take notes listing benefits and drawbacks. Look for the solution whose benefits outweigh its drawbacks. After considering each option, choose the solution you think is best.

[3.] Make and implement a plan. Choose and implement a solution. Make a detailed, step-by-step plan to implement the solution that you choose. Write your plan down and assign yourself a deadline for each step. That will help you to stay on track toward completing your plan. Try to think of any problems that might come up and what you will do to address those problems. Of course, there are many things that you cannot predict. Stay flexible. Evaluate the effectiveness of the solution and adjust your plan as necessary.

Make Decisions

Everyone makes decisions. The trick is to learn how to make good decisions. How can you make good decisions? First, identify a situation that requires a decision and gather information. Then, identify possible options and predict the consequences of each option. Finally, choose the best option and take action to implement a decision. Practice this skill by considering the steps you should take when making a decision about which candidate you should vote for in a local, state, or national election.

[1.] Determine the options between which you must decide. In some cases, like ordering from a menu at a restaurant, your options may be clear. In other cases, you will need to identify a situation that requires a decision, gather information, and identify the options that are available to you. Spend some time thinking about the situation and brainstorm a number of options. If necessary, do a little research to find more options. Make a list of options that you might choose.

[**2.**] Review the costs and benefits of each option. Carefully predict the consequences of each option. You may want to make a cost-benefit list for each option. To do this, write down the option and then draw two columns underneath it. One column will be the "pro" or benefit list. The other column will be the "con" or cost list. Note the pros and cons for each of your options. Try not to rush through this process. For a very important decision, you may even want to show your list to someone you trust. This person can help you think of costs and benefits that you had not considered.

[**3.**] Determine the best option and act on it. Look through your cost-benefit lists. Note any especially serious costs. If an option has the possibility of an extremely negative consequence, you might want to cross it off your list right away. Look closely at the options with the most benefits and the fewest costs, and choose the one that you think is best. Once you have made a choice, take action to implement a decision. If necessary, make a detailed plan with clear steps. Set a deadline to complete the steps to keep yourself moving toward your goal.

Being an Informed Citizen

Informed citizens understand the responsibilities, duties, and obligations of citizenship. They are well informed about civic affairs, involved with their communities, and politically active. When it comes to issues they personally care about, they take a stand and reach out to others.

[**1.**] Learn the issues. A great way to begin to understand the responsibilities of citizenship is to first find topics of interest to you. Next, become well informed about civic affairs in your town, city, or country. Read newspapers, magazines, and articles you find online about events happening in your area or around the world. Analyze the information you read to come to your own conclusions. Radio programs, podcasts, and social media are also great ways to keep up with current events and interact with others about issues.

[**2.**] Get involved. Attend community events to speak with others who know the issues. Become well informed about how policies are made and changed. Find out who to speak to if you would like to take part in civic affairs and policy creation. There are government websites that can help direct you to the right person. These websites will also provide his or her contact details.

[**3.**] Take a stand and reach out. Write, call, or meet with your elected officials to become a better informed, more responsible citizen. Do research about candidates who are running for office to be an informed voter. Start your own blog or website to explore issues, interact with others, and be part of the community or national dialogue.

Political Participation

Political participation starts with an understanding of the responsibilities, duties and obligations of citizenship, such as serving the public good. When you understand your role as a political participant, you can get involved through volunteering for a political campaign, running for office, or interacting with others in person or online.

[1.] Volunteer for a political campaign. Political campaigns offer a wide variety of opportunities to help you become involved in the political process and become a responsible citizen by serving the public good. As a political campaign volunteer you may have the opportunity to attend events, make calls to voters, and explore your community while getting to know how other voters think about the responsibilities, duties, and obligations of citizenship.

[2.] Run for office in your school or community. A good way to become involved in your school or community is to run for office. Student council or community positions offer a great opportunity for you to become familiar with the campaign and election process.

[3.] Reach out to others. Start or join an interest group. Interest groups enable people to work together on common goals related to the political process. Write a letter or email to a public official. By contacting an elected official from your area, you can either support or oppose laws or policies. You can also ask for help or support regarding certain issues.

[4.] Interact online. Social networking sites and blogs offer a great way for people of all ages to interact and write about political issues. As you connect with others, you'll become more confident in your role as a citizen working for the public good.

Voting

Voting is not only a right. It is also one of the primary responsibilities, duties, and obligations of citizenship. Before you can legally vote, however, you must understand the voter registration process and the criteria for voting in elections. You should also understand the issues and know where different candidates stand on those issues.

[1.] Check eligibility and residency requirements. In order to vote in the United States, you must be a United States citizen who is 18 years or older, and you must be a resident of the place where you plan to vote.

[2.] Register to vote. You cannot vote until you understand the voter registration process. You can register at city or town election offices, or when you get a driver's license. You can also register by mail or online. You may also have the option of registering at the polls on Election Day, but this does not apply in all states. Make sure to find out what you need to do to register in your state, as well as the deadline for registering. You may have the option of declaring a political party when registering.

[3.] Learn the issues. As the election approaches, research the candidates and issues in order to be an informed voter. Watch televised debates, if there are any. You can also review the candidates' websites. By doing these things and thinking critically about what you learn, you will be prepared to exercise your responsibility, duty and obligation as a United States citizen.

[4.] Vote. Make sure to arrive at the correct polling place on Election Day to cast your ballot. Research to find out when the polls will be open. Advance voting, absentee voting, and voting by mail are also options in certain states for those who qualify.

Serving on a Jury

As an American, you need to understand the duties, obligations and responsibilities of citizenship; among these is the expectation that you may be required to serve on a jury. You will receive a written notice when you are summoned to jury duty and you'll receive instruction on the special duties and obligations of a juror. You'll follow the American code of justice which assumes that a person is innocent until proven guilty, and you'll follow instructions about keeping trial information confidential.

[1.] Wait to receive notification. If you are summoned to serve as a juror, you will be first notified by mail. If you are chosen to move on to the jury selection phase, lawyers from both sides will ask you questions as they select the final jury members. It is an honor to serve as a juror, as it is a responsibility offered only to American citizens.

[2.] Follow the law and remain impartial. Your job is to determine whether or not someone broke the law. You may also be asked to sit on the jury for civil cases (as opposed to criminal cases); these cases involve lawsuits filed against individuals or businesses for any perceived wrong doing (such as broken contracts, trespassing, discrimination, etc.). Be sure to follow the law as it is explained to you, regardless of whether you approve of the law or not. Your decision about the trial should not be influenced by any personal bias or views you may have.

[3.] Remember that the defendant is presumed innocent. In a criminal trial, the defendant must be proven guilty "beyond a reasonable doubt" for the verdict to be guilty. If the trial team fails to prove the defendant to be guilty beyond a reasonable doubt, the jury verdict must be "not guilty."

[4.] During the trial, respect the court's right to privacy. As a juror, you have specific duties, obligations, and responsibilities under the law. Do not permit anyone to talk about the case with you or in your presence, except with the court's permission. Avoid media coverage once the trial has begun so as to prevent bias. Keep an open mind and do not form or state any opinions about the case until you have heard all of the evidence, the closing arguments from the lawyers, and the judge's instructions on the applicable law.

Paying Taxes

Paying taxes is one of the responsibilities of citizenship. How do you go about figuring out how much you've already paid in taxes and how much you still owe? It's your duty and obligation to find out, by determining how much has been deducted from your pay and filing your tax return.

[1.] Find out how taxes are deducted from your pay. In the United States, payroll taxes are imposed on employers and employees, and they are collected and paid by the employers. Check your pay stub to find out how much money was deducted for taxes. Be sure to also save the W-2 tax form your employer sends to you. You will need this form later on when filing your tax paperwork. Also save any interest income statements. All this information will help you fulfill your obligation as an American taxpayer.

[2.] Check the sales taxes in your state. All but five states impose sales and use taxes on retail sale, lease, and rental of many goods, as well as some services. Sales tax is calculated as the purchase price times the appropriate tax rate. Tax rates vary widely from less than one percent to over ten percent. Sales tax is collected by the seller at the time of sale.

[3.] File your tax return. Filing your tax return is more than an obligation: it's also a duty and responsibility of citizenship. You may receive tax forms in the mail, or pick them up at the local Post Office or library. Fill the forms in and then mail or electronically send completed tax forms and any necessary payments to the Internal Revenue Service (IRS) and your state's department of revenue. The IRS provides free resources to help people prepare and electronically file their tax returns; go to IRS.gov to learn more. Note: certain things such as charitable donations and business expenses are tax deductible.

The United States: Political

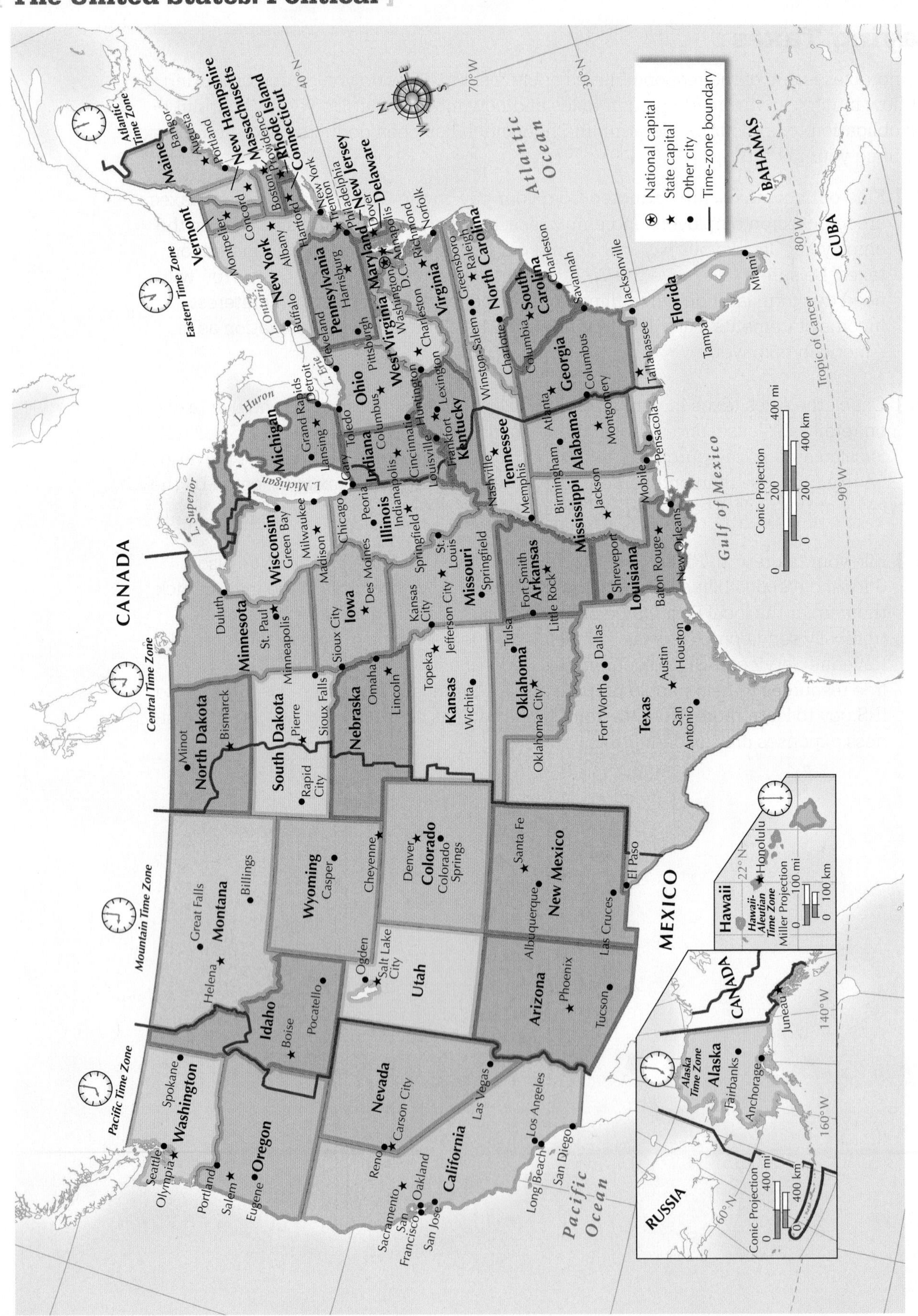

The United States: Physical

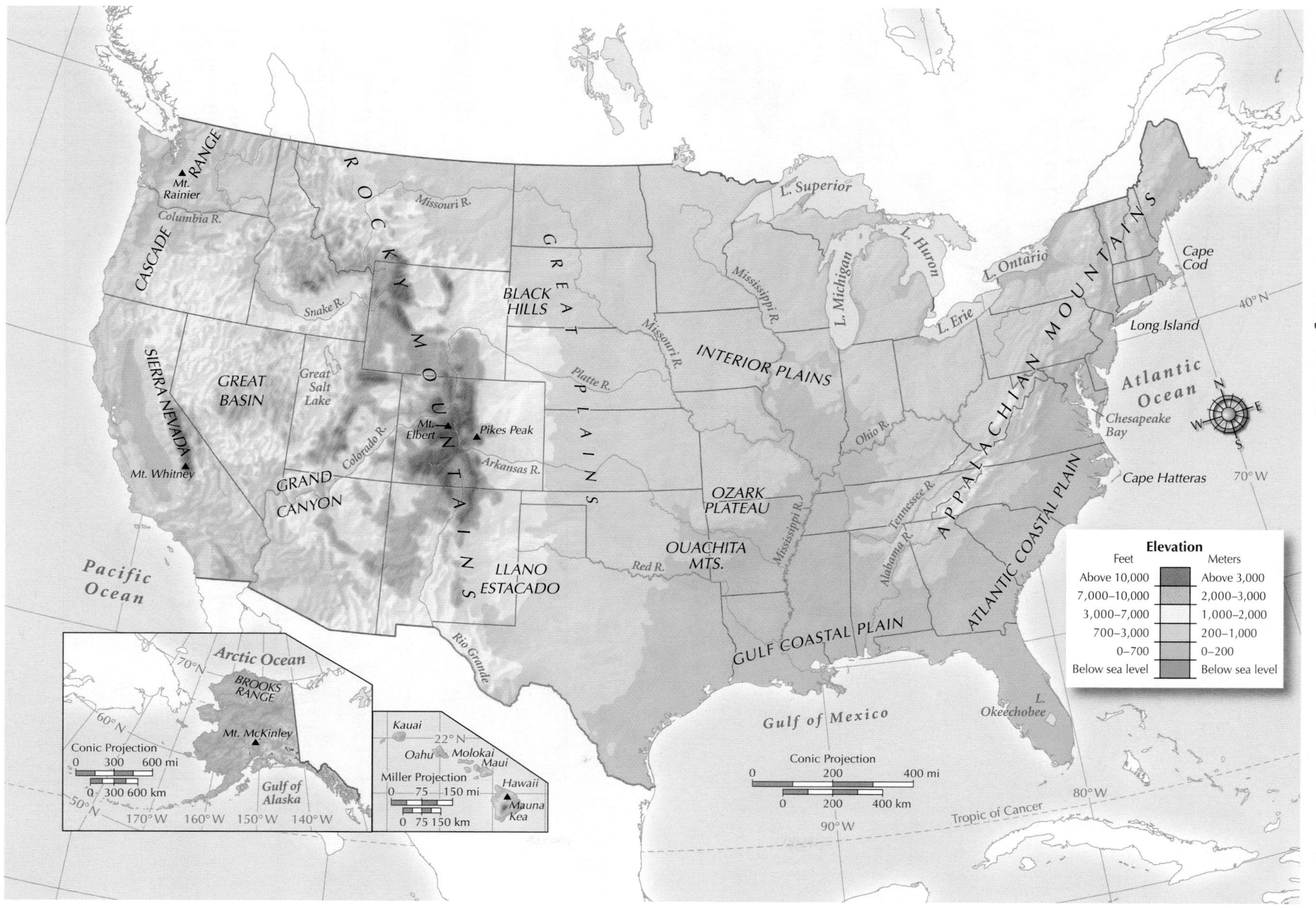

Elevation
Feet
Meters
Above 10,000
Above 3,000
7,000–10,000
2,000–3,000
3,000–7,000
1,000–2,000
700–3,000
200–1,000
0–700
0–200
Below sea level
Below sea level
Atlantic Ocean
Pacific Ocean
Gulf of Mexico
Cape Cod
Long Island
Chesapeake Bay
Cape Hatteras
APPALACHIAN MOUNTAINS
ATLANTIC COASTAL PLAIN
GULF COASTAL PLAIN
L. Okeechobee
Tropic of Cancer
L. Ontario
L. Erie
L. Huron
L. Michigan
L. Superior
Ohio R.
Tennessee R.
Alabama R.
Mississippi R.
INTERIOR PLAINS
OZARK PLATEAU
OUACHITA MTS.
Missouri R.
Red R.
Platte R.
GREAT PLAINS
BLACK HILLS
Arkansas R.
Pikes Peak
Mt. Elbert
LLANO ESTACADO
Rio Grande
ROCKY MOUNTAINS
Colorado R.
Snake R.
Great Salt Lake
GRAND CANYON
GREAT BASIN
SIERRA NEVADA
Mt. Whitney
CASCADE RANGE
Mt. Rainier
Columbia R.
Conic Projection
0 200 400 mi
0 200 400 km
40° N
70° W
80° W
90° W
Kauai
Oahu
Molokai
Maui
Hawaii
Mauna Kea
22° N
Miller Projection
0 75 150 mi
0 75 150 km
Arctic Ocean
BROOKS RANGE
Mt. McKinley
Gulf of Alaska
70° N
60° N
50° N
140° W
150° W
160° W
170° W
Conic Projection
0 300 600 mi
0 300 600 km

The World: Political

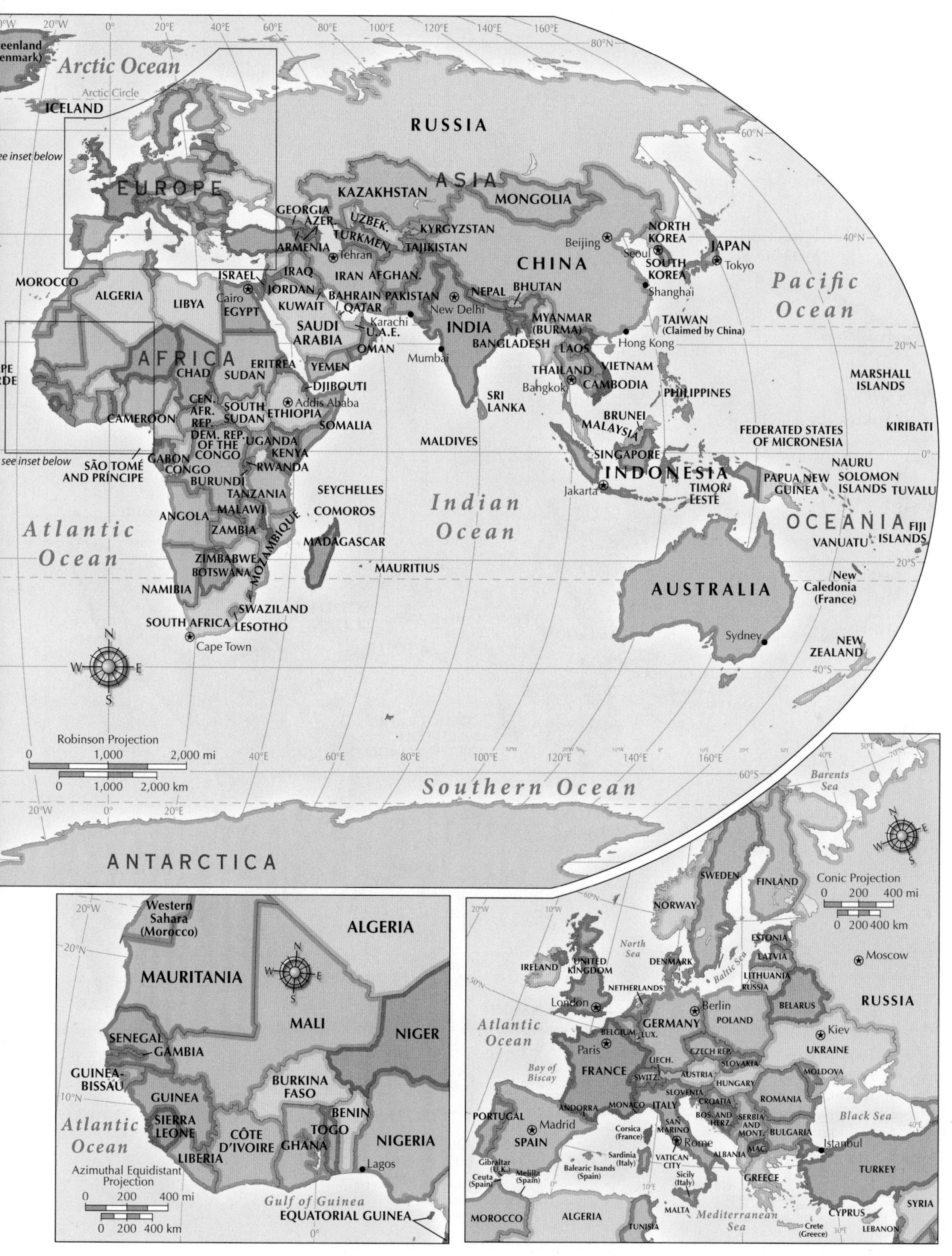
Arctic Ocean
Arctic Circle
ICELAND
see inset below
EUROPE
RUSSIA
ASIA
KAZAKHSTAN
MONGOLIA
GEORGIA
AZER.
ARMENIA
UZBEK.
TURKMEN.
KYRGYZSTAN
TAJIKISTAN
Tehran
Beijing
NORTH KOREA
SOUTH KOREA
Seoul
JAPAN
Tokyo
CHINA
Shanghai
MOROCCO
ALGERIA
LIBYA
ISRAEL
Cairo
EGYPT
IRAQ
JORDAN
KUWAIT
IRAN
AFGHAN.
BAHRAIN
QATAR
PAKISTAN
New Delhi
NEPAL
BHUTAN
Karachi
SAUDI ARABIA
U.A.E.
OMAN
INDIA
Mumbai
BANGLADESH
MYANMAR (BURMA)
LAOS
TAIWAN (Claimed by China)
Hong Kong
Pacific Ocean
AFRICA
CHAD
SUDAN
ERITREA
YEMEN
DJIBOUTI
THAILAND
Bangkok
VIETNAM
CAMBODIA
PHILIPPINES
MARSHALL ISLANDS
CEN. AFR. REP.
SOUTH SUDAN
Addis Ababa
ETHIOPIA
SOMALIA
SRI LANKA
BRUNEI
MALAYSIA
FEDERATED STATES OF MICRONESIA
KIRIBATI
CAMEROON
DEM. REP. OF THE CONGO
UGANDA
KENYA
RWANDA
MALDIVES
SINGAPORE
INDONESIA
Jakarta
NAURU
PAPUA NEW GUINEA
SOLOMON ISLANDS
TUVALU
TIMOR-LESTE
see inset below
SÃO TOMÉ AND PRÍNCIPE
GABON
CONGO
BURUNDI
TANZANIA
SEYCHELLES
Indian Ocean
ANGOLA
MALAWI
COMOROS
OCEANIA
FIJI ISLANDS
VANUATU
Atlantic Ocean
ZAMBIA
MOZAMBIQUE
MADAGASCAR
ZIMBABWE
BOTSWANA
MAURITIUS
NAMIBIA
AUSTRALIA
New Caledonia (France)
SWAZILAND
SOUTH AFRICA
LESOTHO
Cape Town
Sydney
NEW ZEALAND
Robinson Projection
0 1,000 2,000 mi
0 1,000 2,000 km
Southern Ocean
ANTARCTICA
Western Sahara (Morocco)
ALGERIA
MAURITANIA
MALI
NIGER
SENEGAL
GAMBIA
GUINEA-BISSAU
GUINEA
BURKINA FASO
BENIN
SIERRA LEONE
TOGO
CÔTE D'IVOIRE
GHANA
NIGERIA
Atlantic Ocean
LIBERIA
Lagos
Azimuthal Equidistant Projection
0 200 400 mi
0 200 400 km
Gulf of Guinea
EQUATORIAL GUINEA
Barents Sea
SWEDEN
FINLAND
Conic Projection
0 200 400 mi
0 200 400 km
NORWAY
North Sea
ESTONIA
LATVIA
Moscow
IRELAND
UNITED KINGDOM
DENMARK
Baltic Sea
LITHUANIA
RUSSIA
NETHERLANDS
London
Berlin
BELARUS
RUSSIA
POLAND
Atlantic Ocean
BELGIUM
LUX.
GERMANY
Kiev
Paris
CZECH REP.
UKRAINE
SLOVAKIA
FRANCE
LIECH.
AUSTRIA
MOLDOVA
Bay of Biscay
SWITZ.
HUNGARY
SLOVENIA
CROATIA
ROMANIA
ANDORRA
MONACO
ITALY
PORTUGAL
Madrid
SPAIN
Corsica (France)
SAN MARINO
BOS. AND HERZ.
SERBIA
MONT.
Black Sea
BULGARIA
Rome
Sardinia (Italy)
VATICAN CITY
ALBANIA
MAC.
Istanbul
Gibraltar (U.K.)
Ceuta (Spain)
Melilla (Spain)
Balearic Islands (Spain)
Sicily (Italy)
GREECE
TURKEY
MOROCCO
ALGERIA
TUNISIA
MALTA
Mediterranean Sea
CYPRUS
Crete (Greece)
LEBANON
SYRIA

Africa: Political

Africa: Physical

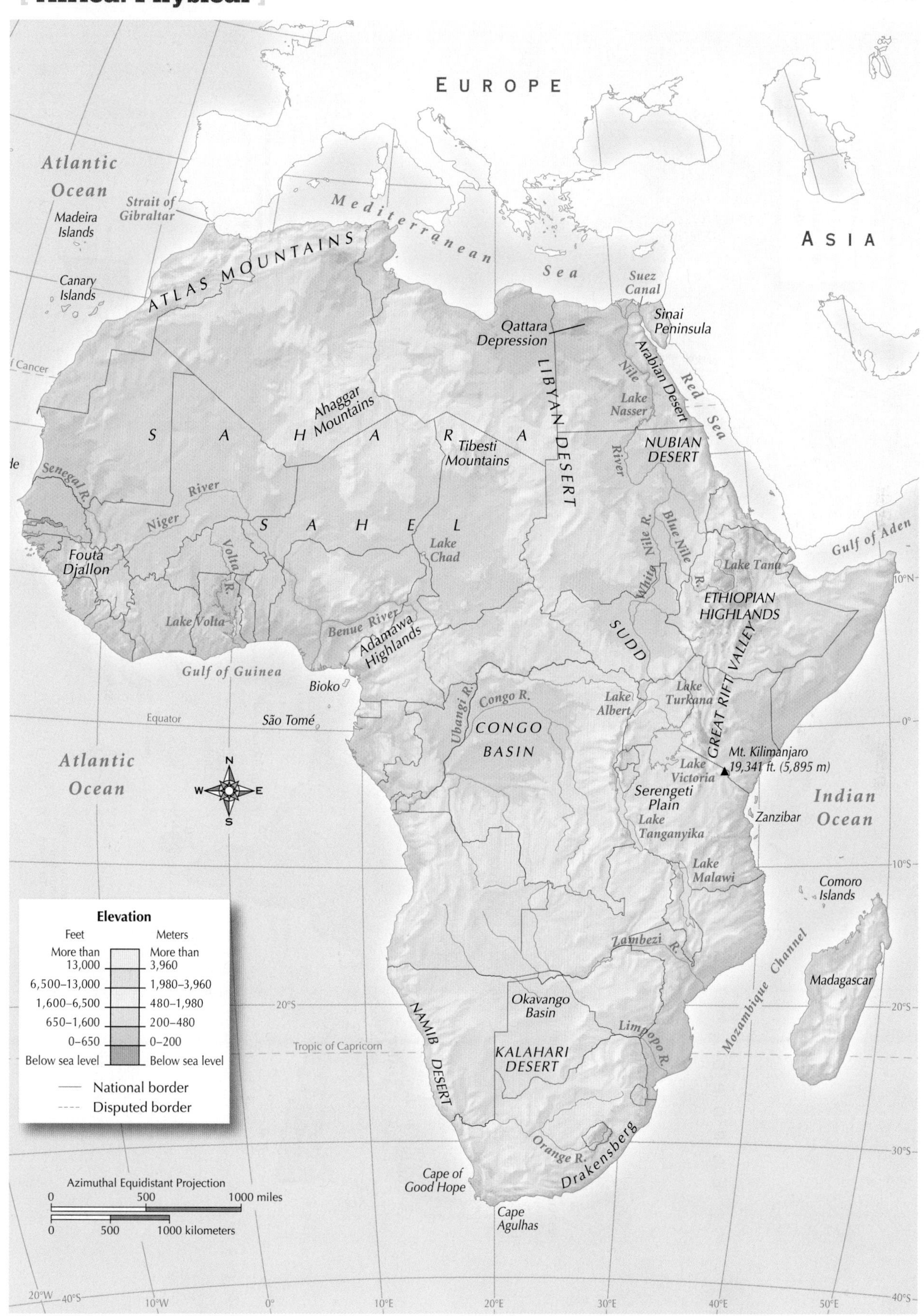

EUROPE
ASIA
Atlantic Ocean
Madeira Islands
Strait of Gibraltar
Canary Islands
Mediterranean Sea
ATLAS MOUNTAINS
Suez Canal
Sinai Peninsula
Qattara Depression
LIBYAN DESERT
Arabian Desert
Nile
Lake Nasser
Red Sea
Ahaggar Mountains
SAHARA
Tibesti Mountains
NUBIAN DESERT
River
Senegal R.
Niger River
SAHEL
Lake Chad
White Nile R.
Blue Nile R.
Gulf of Aden
Lake Tana
Fouta Djallon
Volta R.
Lake Volta
Benue River
Adamawa Highlands
ETHIOPIAN HIGHLANDS
SUDD
GREAT RIFT VALLEY
Gulf of Guinea
Bioko
Lake Turkana
Lake Albert
Ubangi R.
Congo R.
CONGO BASIN
São Tomé
Equator
Atlantic Ocean
Lake Victoria
Mt. Kilimanjaro 19,341 ft. (5,895 m)
Serengeti Plain
Lake Tanganyika
Zanzibar
Indian Ocean
Lake Malawi
Comoro Islands
Zambezi R.
Mozambique Channel
Madagascar
Okavango Basin
Limpopo R.
KALAHARI DESERT
NAMIB DESERT
Tropic of Capricorn
Orange R.
Drakensberg
Cape of Good Hope
Cape Agulhas
Elevation
Feet
Meters
More than 13,000
More than 3,960
6,500–13,000
1,980–3,960
1,600–6,500
480–1,980
650–1,600
200–480
0–650
0–200
Below sea level
Below sea level
National border
Disputed border
Azimuthal Equidistant Projection
0 500 1000 miles
0 500 1000 kilometers
N
S
E
W
10°N
0°
10°S
20°S
30°S
40°S
20°W
10°W
0°
10°E
20°E
30°E
40°E
50°E

Asia: Political

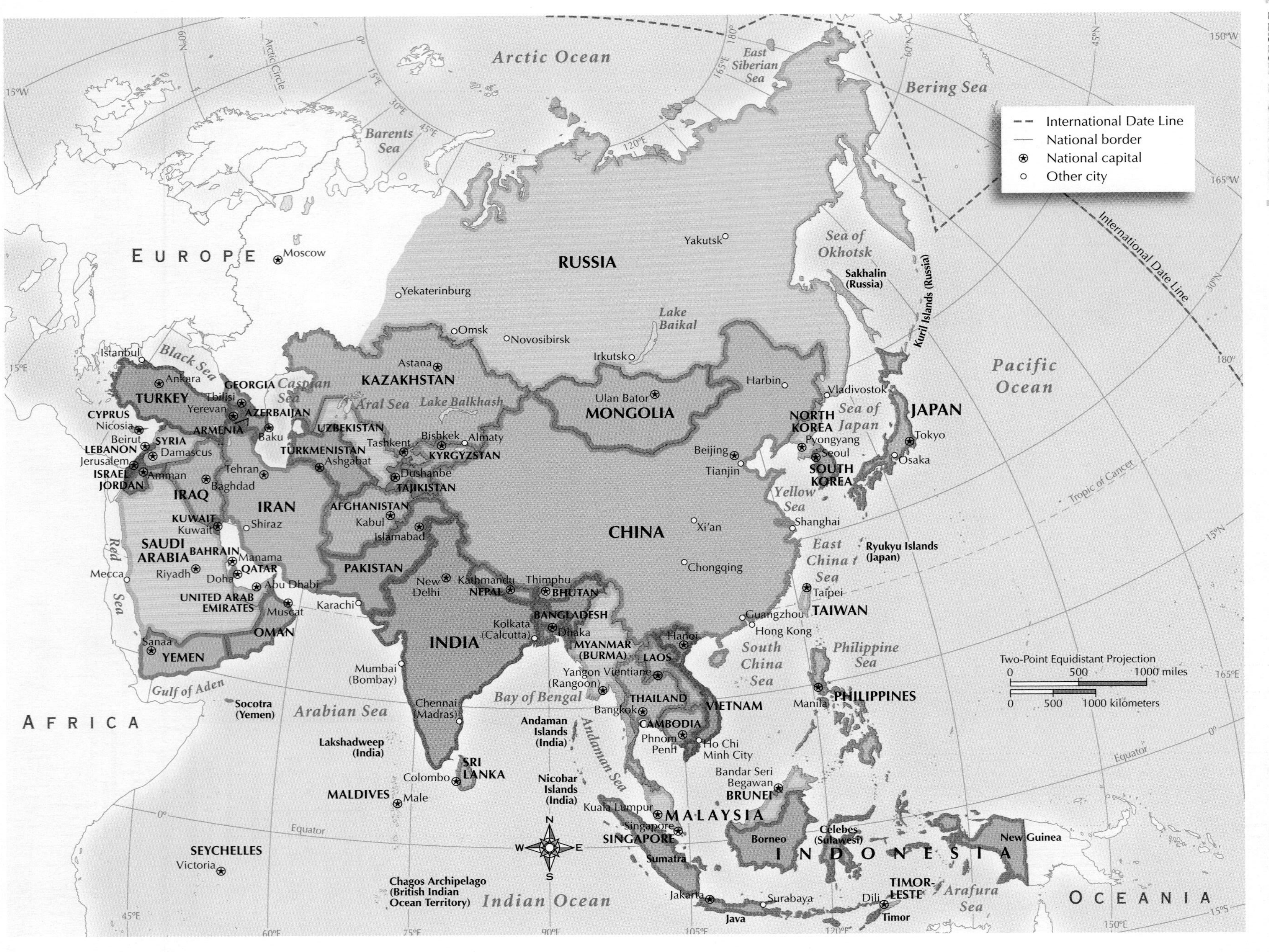

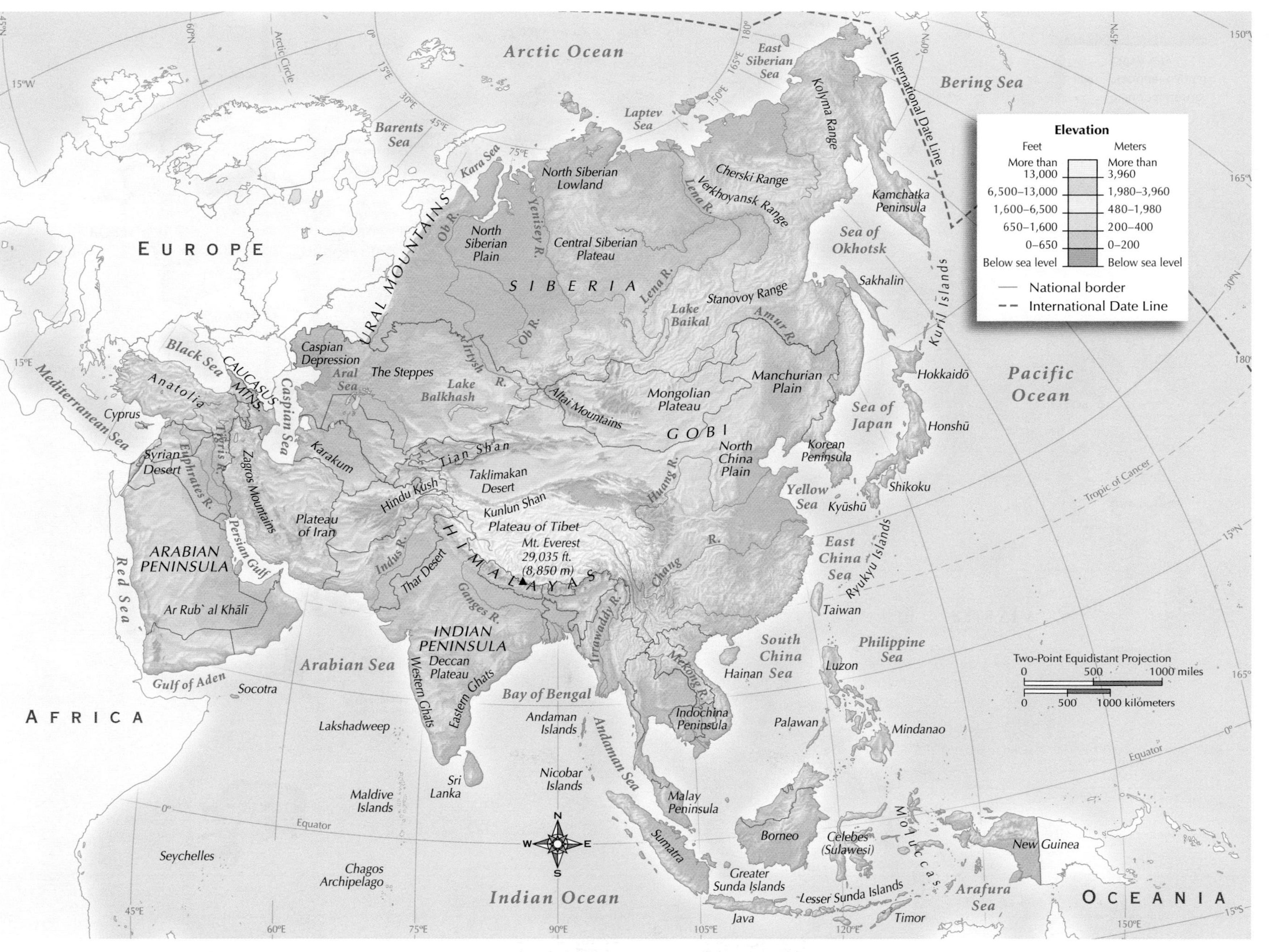
Elevation
Feet
Meters
More than 13,000
More than 3,960
6,500–13,000
1,980–3,960
1,600–6,500
480–1,980
650–1,600
200–400
0–650
0–200
Below sea level
Below sea level
National border
International Date Line
Two-Point Equidistant Projection
0
500
1000 miles
0
500
1000 kilometers
Arctic Ocean
Pacific Ocean
Indian Ocean
Bering Sea
Sea of Okhotsk
Sea of Japan
Yellow Sea
East China Sea
South China Sea
Philippine Sea
Laptev Sea
East Siberian Sea
Kara Sea
Barents Sea
Arafura Sea
Andaman Sea
Bay of Bengal
Arabian Sea
Red Sea
Persian Gulf
Gulf of Aden
Black Sea
Mediterranean Sea
Caspian Sea
Aral Sea
Lake Balkhash
Lake Baikal
EUROPE
AFRICA
OCEANIA
SIBERIA
GOBI
HIMALAYAS
URAL MOUNTAINS
CAUCASUS MTNS.
International Date Line
Kolyma Range
Cherski Range
Verkhoyansk Range
Stanovoy Range
Kamchatka Peninsula
Kuril Islands
Sakhalin
Hokkaidō
Honshū
Shikoku
Kyūshū
Ryukyu Islands
Taiwan
Luzon
Mindanao
Palawan
Borneo
Celebes (Sulawesi)
Moluccas
New Guinea
Timor
Lesser Sunda Islands
Greater Sunda Islands
Java
Sumatra
Malay Peninsula
Indochina Peninsula
Hainan
Korean Peninsula
Manchurian Plain
North China Plain
Mongolian Plateau
Amur R.
Lena R.
Huang R.
Chang R.
Mekong R.
Irrawaddy R.
Yenisey R.
Ob R.
Irtysh R.
Ganges R.
Indus R.
Tigris R.
Euphrates R.
North Siberian Lowland
Central Siberian Plateau
North Siberian Plain
Altai Mountains
Tian Shan
Taklimakan Desert
Kunlun Shan
Plateau of Tibet
Mt. Everest 29,035 ft. (8,850 m)
Hindu Kush
The Steppes
Caspian Depression
Karakum
Plateau of Iran
Zagros Mountains
Anatolia
Cyprus
Syrian Desert
ARABIAN PENINSULA
Ar Rub` al Khālī
Socotra
INDIAN PENINSULA
Deccan Plateau
Thar Desert
Western Ghats
Eastern Ghats
Sri Lanka
Andaman Islands
Nicobar Islands
Lakshadweep
Maldive Islands
Chagos Archipelago
Seychelles
Arctic Circle
Tropic of Cancer
Equator
N
S
E
W

Europe: Political

Europe: Physical

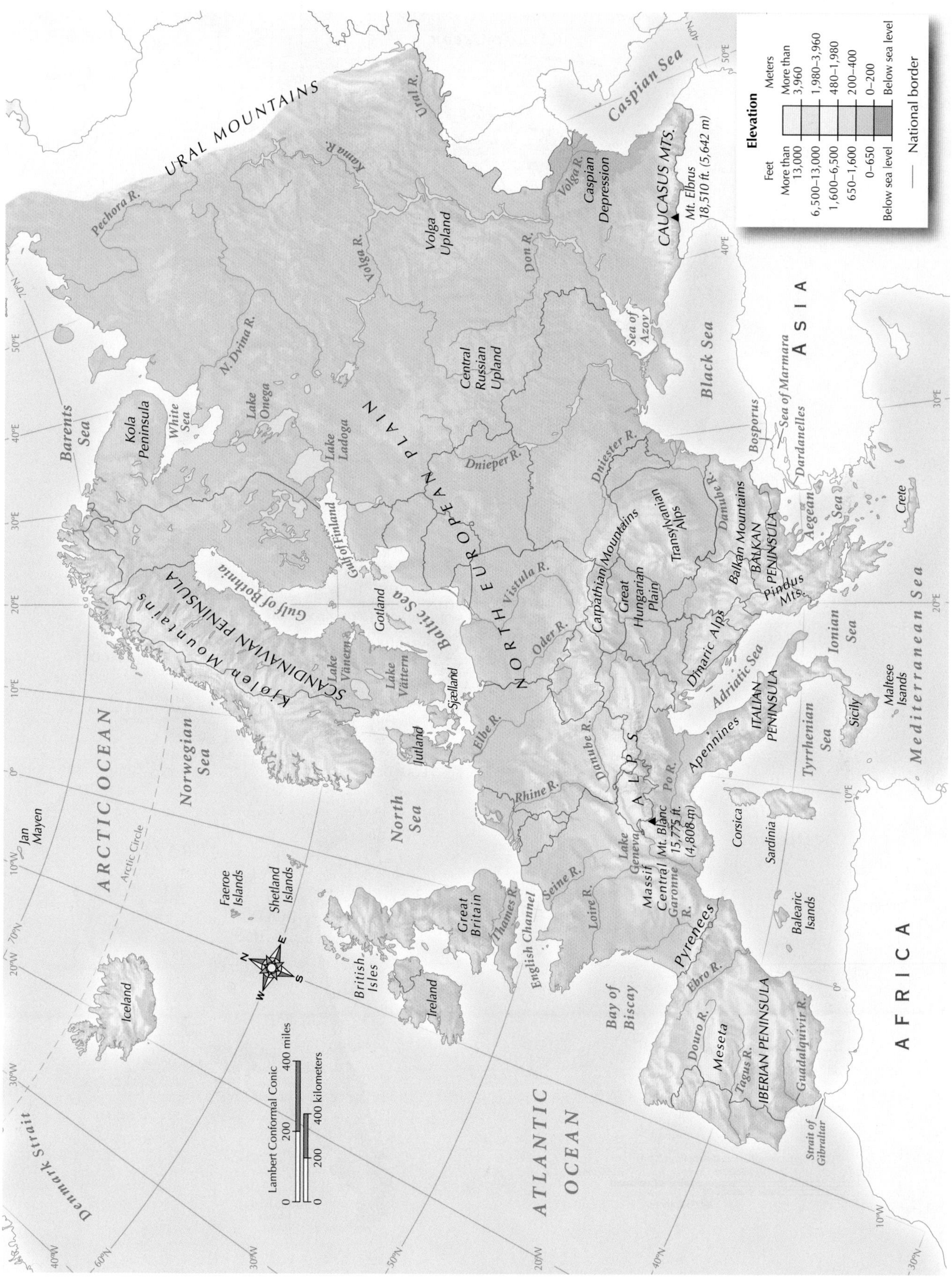

ARCTIC OCEAN
Arctic Circle
Jan Mayen
Denmark Strait
Iceland
Faeroe Islands
Shetland Islands
Norwegian Sea
Barents Sea
Kola Peninsula
White Sea
North Sea
British Isles
Great Britain
Ireland
Thames R.
English Channel
ATLANTIC OCEAN
Bay of Biscay
Kjølen Mountains
SCANDINAVIAN PENINSULA
Gulf of Bothnia
Gulf of Finland
Baltic Sea
Gotland
Lake Vänern
Lake Vättern
Sjælland
Jutland
Lake Ladoga
Lake Onega
N. Dvina R.
Pechora R.
URAL MOUNTAINS
Ural R.
Kama R.
Volga R.
Volga Upland
Don R.
Central Russian Upland
NORTH EUROPEAN PLAIN
Dnieper R.
Dniester R.
Vistula R.
Oder R.
Elbe R.
Rhine R.
Seine R.
Loire R.
Garonne R.
Massif Central
Lake Geneva
Mt. Blanc 15,775 ft. (4,808 m)
ALPS
Danube R.
Po R.
Apennines
Carpathian Mountains
Transylvanian Alps
Great Hungarian Plain
Dinaric Alps
Balkan Mountains
BALKAN PENINSULA
Pindus Mts.
Adriatic Sea
ITALIAN PENINSULA
Tyrrhenian Sea
Ionian Sea
Aegean Sea
Crete
Sicily
Maltese Isands
Corsica
Sardinia
Balearic Isands
Pyrenees
Ebro R.
Douro R.
Meseta
Tagus R.
Guadalquivir R.
IBERIAN PENINSULA
Strait of Gibraltar
Mediterranean Sea
AFRICA
ASIA
Black Sea
Sea of Azov
Bosporus
Sea of Marmara
Dardanelles
Caspian Sea
Caspian Depression
CAUCASUS MTS.
Mt. Elbrus 18,510 ft. (5,642 m)

Lambert Conformal Conic
0 200 400 miles
0 200 400 kilometers

Elevation

Feet	Meters
More than 13,000	More than 3,960
6,500–13,000	1,980–3,960
1,600–6,500	480–1,980
650–1,600	200–480
0–650	0–200
Below sea level	Below sea level

National border

North and South America: Political

Arctic Ocean
ASIA
EUROPE
Bering Strait
International Date Line
Beaufort Sea
Alaska (United States)
Bering Sea
Greenland (Denmark)
Baffin Bay
Davis Strait
Arctic Circle
Nuuk
Great Bear Lake
Great Slave Lake
Gulf of Alaska
Hudson Bay
Labrador Sea
CANADA
Lake Winnipeg
Vancouver
Great Lakes
Ottawa
Toronto
Chicago
New York
Washington, D.C.
UNITED STATES
Los Angeles
Atlantic Ocean
Houston
Tropic of Cancer
Gulf of Mexico
Nassau
MEXICO
Havana
BAHAMAS
DOMINICAN REPUBLIC
CUBA
HAITI
Puerto Rico (United States)
Mexico City
JAMAICA
U.S. Virgin Islands (United States)
Belmopan
BELIZE
Kingston
Port-au-Prince
Santo Domingo
Guadeloupe (France)
Guatemala City
HONDURAS
Martinique (France)
Tegucigalpa
Caribbean Sea
GUATEMALA
San Salvador
NICARAGUA
DOMINICA
BARBADOS
EL SALVADOR
Managua
Caracas
TRINIDAD AND TOBAGO
San José
Panama
GUYANA
COSTA RICA
VENEZUELA
Georgetown
Paramaribo
PANAMA
French Guiana (France)
Cayenne
Bogotá
COLOMBIA
SURINAME
Equator
Quito
Galápagos Islands (Ecuador)
ECUADOR
N
W
E
S
Pacific Ocean
PERU
BRAZIL
Lima
Lake Titicaca
La Paz
Brasília
BOLIVIA
Sucre
Tropic of Capricorn
PARAGUAY
Rio de Janeiro
Asunción
São Paulo
CHILE
ARGENTINA
Santiago
URUGUAY
Buenos Aires
Montevideo
Río de la Plata
Atlantic Ocean
National border
International Date Line
National capital
Other city
Lambert Azimuthal Equal-Area Projection
0
1000
2000 miles
0
1000
2000 kilometers
Falkland Islands (U.K.)
180°
0°
60°N
45°N
30°N
15°N
0°
15°S
30°S
45°S
165°W
150°W
135°W
120°W
105°W
90°W
75°W
60°W
45°W
30°W
15°W

North and South America: Physical

Arctic Ocean
ASIA
EUROPE
Bering Strait
Ellesmere Island
Beaufort Sea
International Date Line
Mt. McKinley (Denali) 20,320 ft. (6,194 m)
Alaska Range
Bering Sea
Aleutian Islands
Gulf of Alaska
Victoria Island
Greenland
Baffin Bay
Baffin Island
Davis Strait
Arctic Circle
Mackenzie R.
Yukon R.
Great Bear Lake
Great Slave Lake
Hudson Bay
Labrador Sea
ROCKY MOUNTAINS
CANADIAN SHIELD
Lake Winnipeg
Great Lakes
St. Lawrence R.
Island of Newfoundland
Cascades
Missouri R.
GREAT PLAINS
Great Salt Lake
Sierra Nevada
Colorado R.
APPALACHIAN MTS.
Ohio R.
Mississippi R.
Atlantic Ocean
Rio Grande
Gulf of California
Sierra Madre Occidental
Sierra Madre Oriental
Baja California
Tropic of Cancer
Gulf of Mexico
Yucatán Peninsula
Cuba
Jamaica
Hispaniola
Greater Antilles
Lesser Antilles
Caribbean Sea
Isthmus of Panama
Pacific Ocean
Llanos
Orinoco R.
Guiana Highlands
Galápagos Islands
Equator
Amazon R.
AMAZON BASIN
ANDES MOUNTAINS
Lake Titicaca
Paraguay R.
Paraná R.
São Francisco R.
Brazilian Highlands
Gran Chaco
Tropic of Capricorn
Aconcagua 22,834 ft. (6,960 m)
Pampas
Río de la Plata
Atlantic Ocean
Patagonia
Falkland Islands
Tierra del Fuego
Cape Horn
Elevation
Feet
Meters
More than 13,000
More than 3,960
6,500–13,000
1,980–3,960
1,600–6,500
480–1,980
650–1,600
200–400
0–650
0–200
Below sea level
Below sea level
National border
International Date Line
Lambert Azimuthal Equal-Area Projection
0
1000
2000 miles
0
1000
2000 kilometers
180°
0°
60°N
45°N
30°N
15°N
0°
15°S
30°S
45°S
165°W
150°W
135°W
120°W
105°W
90°W
75°W
60°W
45°W
30°W
15°W

Australia, New Zealand, and Oceania: Political-Physical

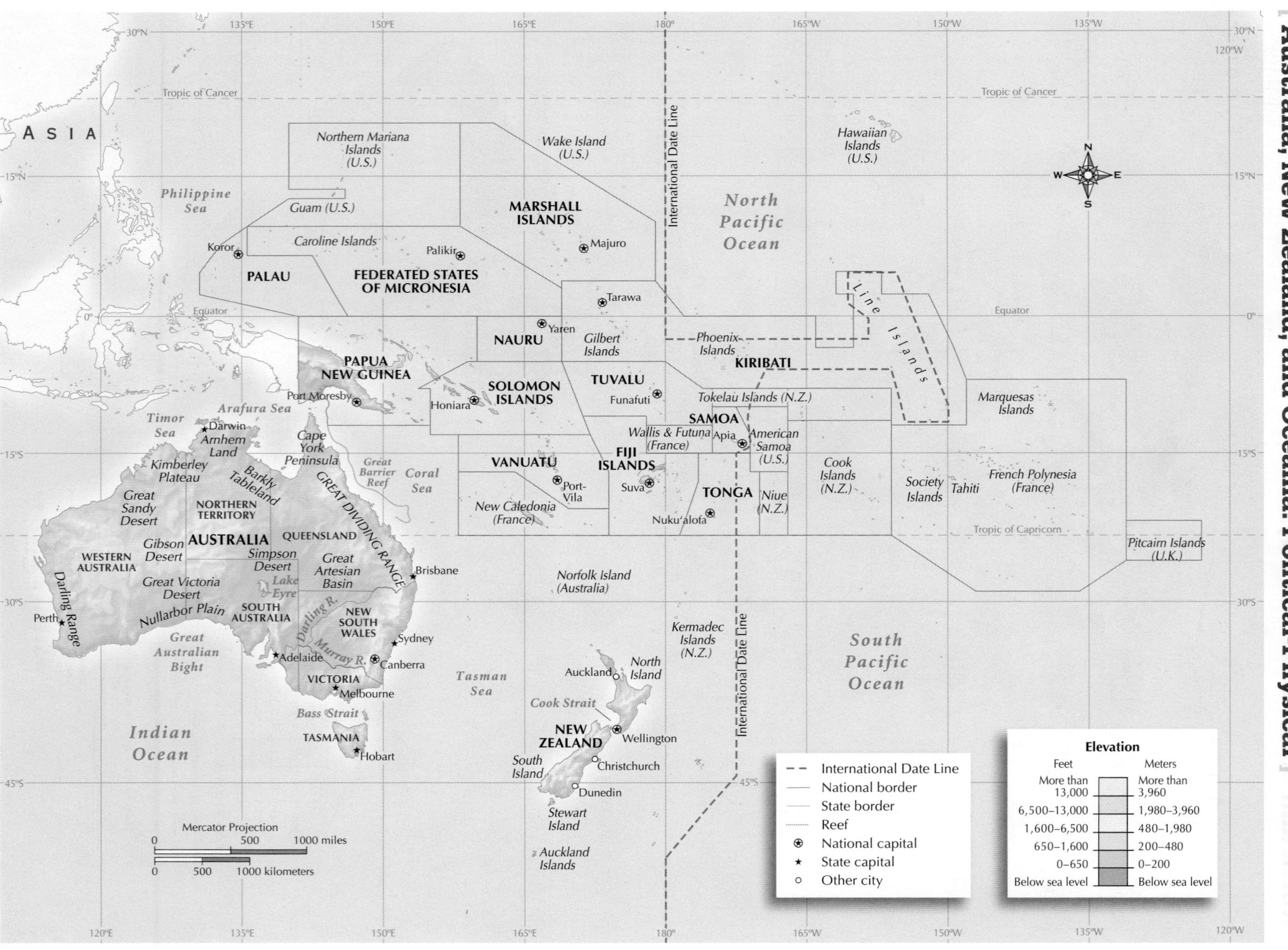

ASIA
Tropic of Cancer
Equator
Tropic of Capricorn
International Date Line
Northern Mariana Islands (U.S.)
Wake Island (U.S.)
Hawaiian Islands (U.S.)
Philippine Sea
Guam (U.S.)
MARSHALL ISLANDS
North Pacific Ocean
Caroline Islands
Koror
Palikir
Majuro
PALAU
FEDERATED STATES OF MICRONESIA
Tarawa
Line Islands
Yaren
NAURU
Gilbert Islands
Phoenix Islands
KIRIBATI
PAPUA NEW GUINEA
SOLOMON ISLANDS
TUVALU
Port Moresby
Honiara
Funafuti
Tokelau Islands (N.Z.)
Marquesas Islands
Arafura Sea
Timor Sea
Darwin
Arnhem Land
Cape York Peninsula
SAMOA
Wallis & Futuna (France)
Apia
American Samoa (U.S.)
FIJI ISLANDS
VANUATU
Kimberley Plateau
Barkly Tableland
Great Barrier Reef
Coral Sea
Cook Islands (N.Z.)
Society Islands
Tahiti
French Polynesia (France)
Great Sandy Desert
NORTHERN TERRITORY
GREAT DIVIDING RANGE
Port-Vila
Suva
TONGA
Niue (N.Z.)
New Caledonia (France)
Nuku'alofa
AUSTRALIA
QUEENSLAND
Gibson Desert
WESTERN AUSTRALIA
Simpson Desert
Great Artesian Basin
Lake Eyre
Brisbane
Norfolk Island (Australia)
Pitcairn Islands (U.K.)
Darling Range
Great Victoria Desert
Perth
Nullarbor Plain
SOUTH AUSTRALIA
Darling R.
NEW SOUTH WALES
Sydney
Kermadec Islands (N.Z.)
South Pacific Ocean
Great Australian Bight
Adelaide
Murray R.
Canberra
VICTORIA
Melbourne
Tasman Sea
Auckland
North Island
Cook Strait
Bass Strait
Indian Ocean
TASMANIA
Hobart
NEW ZEALAND
Wellington
South Island
Christchurch
Dunedin
Stewart Island
Auckland Islands
Mercator Projection
0 500 1000 miles
0 500 1000 kilometers
International Date Line
National border
State border
Reef
National capital
State capital
Other city
Elevation
Feet
Meters
More than 13,000
More than 3,960
6,500–13,000
1,980–3,960
1,600–6,500
480–1,980
650–1,600
200–480
0–650
0–200
Below sea level
Below sea level

The Arctic: Physical

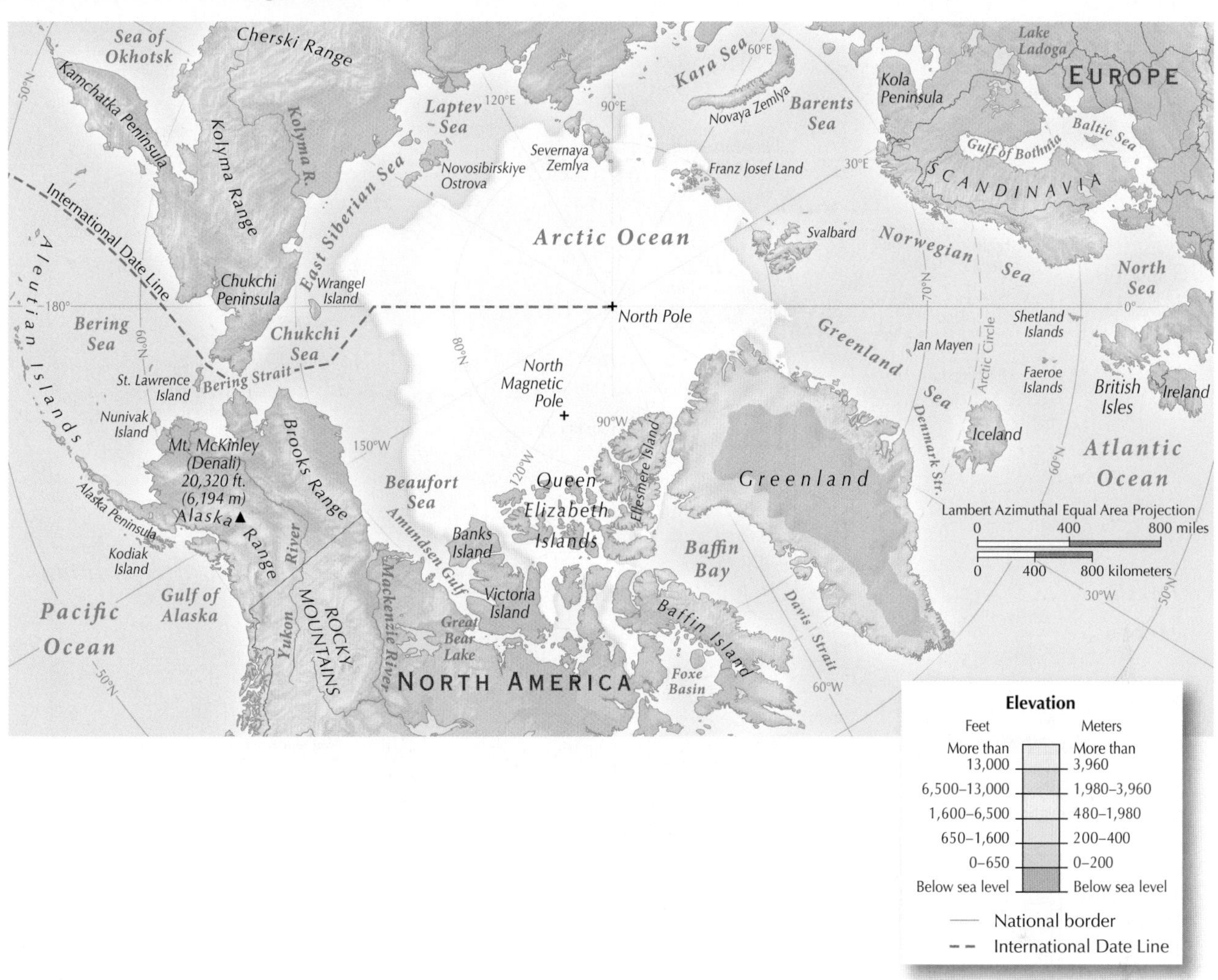

Sea of Okhotsk
Cherski Range
Kamchatka Peninsula
Kolyma Range
Kolyma R.
Laptev Sea
Kara Sea
Novaya Zemlya
Barents Sea
Kola Peninsula
Lake Ladoga
EUROPE
Baltic Sea
Gulf of Bothnia
SCANDINAVIA
East Siberian Sea
Novosibirskiye Ostrova
Severnaya Zemlya
Franz Josef Land
International Date Line
Arctic Ocean
Svalbard
Norwegian Sea
North Sea
Aleutian Islands
Chukchi Peninsula
Wrangel Island
North Pole
Bering Sea
Chukchi Sea
Greenland Sea
Jan Mayen
Shetland Islands
Faeroe Islands
British Isles
Ireland
St. Lawrence Island
Bering Strait
North Magnetic Pole
Arctic Circle
Denmark Str.
Iceland
Nunivak Island
Brooks Range
Mt. McKinley (Denali) 20,320 ft. (6,194 m)
Alaska Range
Alaska Peninsula
Beaufort Sea
Queen Elizabeth Islands
Ellesmere Island
Greenland
Atlantic Ocean
Lambert Azimuthal Equal Area Projection
0 400 800 miles
0 400 800 kilometers
Kodiak Island
Yukon River
Amundsen Gulf
Banks Island
Baffin Bay
Gulf of Alaska
Pacific Ocean
ROCKY MOUNTAINS
Mackenzie River
Victoria Island
Great Bear Lake
Baffin Island
Davis Strait
NORTH AMERICA
Foxe Basin
180°
150°W
120°W
90°W
60°W
30°W
0°
30°E
60°E
90°E
120°E
50°N
60°N
70°N
80°N
Elevation
Feet
Meters
More than 13,000
More than 3,960
6,500–13,000
1,980–3,960
1,600–6,500
480–1,980
650–1,600
200–400
0–650
0–200
Below sea level
Below sea level
National border
International Date Line

Antarctica: Physical

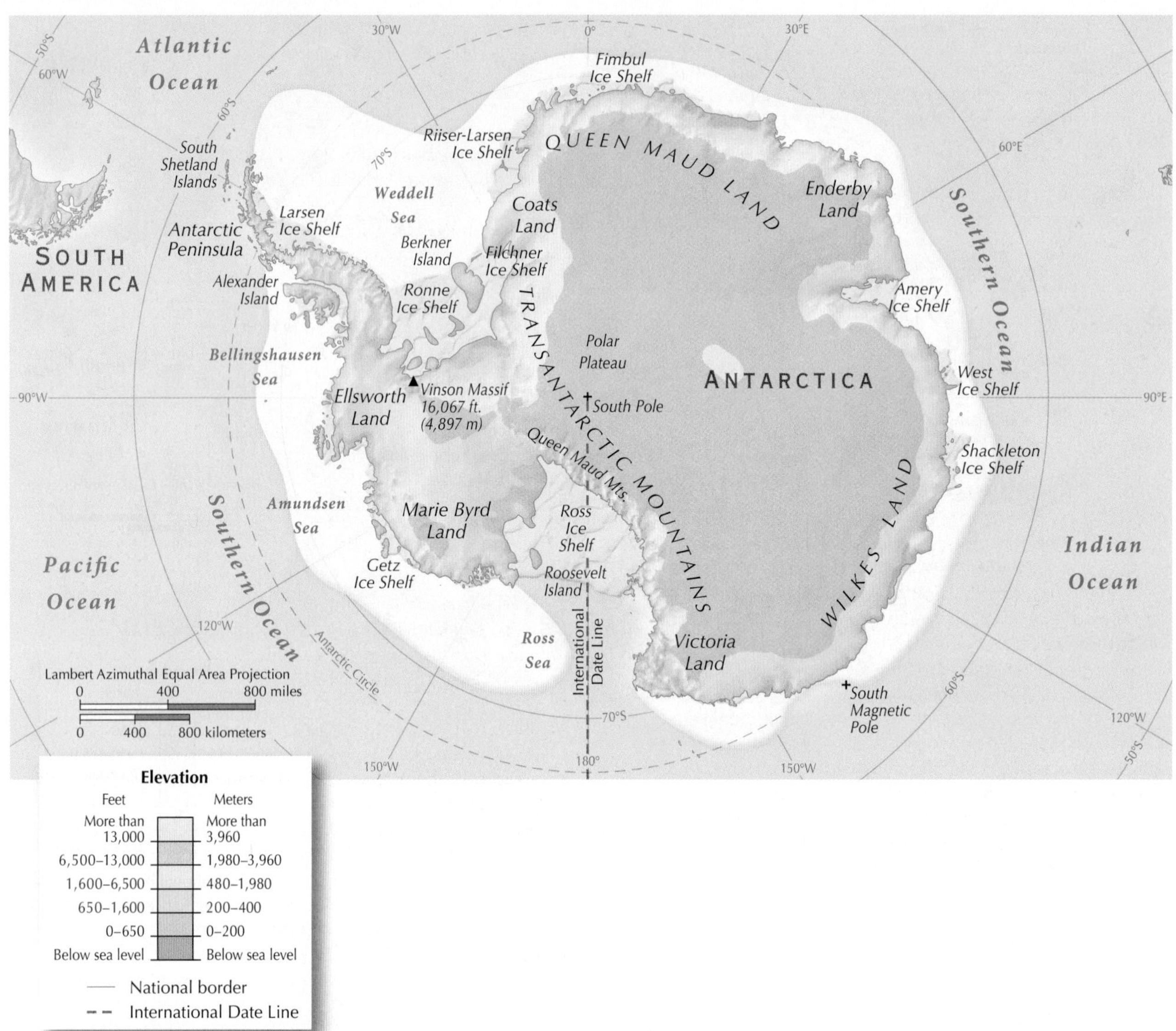

A

absentee voting provisions made for those unable to go to their regular polling places on election day

acquit to find not guilty of a charge

act of admission congressional act admitting a new State to the Union

Adams, John Adams (1735–1826) was a lawyer in Massachusetts, legislator, diplomat, and second U.S. President. He defended British military officers in the Boston Massacre out of a sense of fairness but became a leading advocate of American independence at the First and Second Continental Congresses. He was the principal author of the Massachusetts State constitution. Adams helped negotiate a peace treaty with Great Britain after the Revolutionary War, attained diplomatic recognition of the new United States, and structured free trade with all nations.

Adams, John Quincy (1767–1848) the 6th President of the United States from 1825 to 1829 and author of the Monroe Doctrine. John Quincy was the son of President John Adams (1797–1801). Prior to being elected President, Adams was Secretary of State. Adams served as a congressman after his presidency, from 1831 to 1848, and fought against slavery. In 1848, Adams suffered a stroke and collapsed on the floor of the House and died two days later.

Adams, Samuel A Founding Father, Adams (1722–1803) became a leader in Boston politics through his writing. He was a delegate to the First and Second Continental congresses and helped draft the Declaration of Rights.

adjourn suspend, as in a session of Congress

administration the officials in the executive branch of a government and their policies and principles

administrative law composed of the rules, orders, and regulations issued by federal, State, or local executive officers, acting under proper constitutional and/or statutory authority

affirmative action a policy of taking active steps to remedy past discrimination

Albany Plan of Union a plan proposed by Benjamin Franklin in 1754 for cooperation among the thirteen colonies but was never adopted

Albright, Madeleine Albright (1937–) served as U.S. ambassador to the United Nations from 1993 to 1997. Later, President Bill Clinton nominated her to became the first woman to hold the Cabinet post of U.S. secretary of state. She held that position from 1997 to 2001; thereafter she became a speaker, consultant, and author.

alien foreign-born resident, or noncitizen

aliens foreign-born residents, or non-citizens

Alito, Samuel (1950–) received a law degree from Yale University in 1975, where he was editor of the Yale Law Journal. Alito served in several judicial positions during the presidencies of Ronald Reagan and George H.W. Bush. In 2005, Alito was nominated by President George W. Bush and took his seat as a justice on the Supreme Court on January 31, 2006.

ambassador an official representative of the United States appointed by the President to represent the nation in matters of diplomacy

amendment a change in, or addition to a constitution or law

amicus curiae brief legal Latin term meaning "friend of the court"; a document that consists of written arguments presented to a court in support of one side in a dispute

amnesty a blanket pardon offered to a group of law violators

Anti-Federalists those persons who opposed the ratification of the Constitution in 1787–1788

appellate jurisdiction the authority of a court to review decisions of inferior (lower) courts

apportioned distributed, as in seats in a legislative body

appropriate to assign to a particular use

Aristotle (384–322 B.C.) Greek philosopher who viewed the lives of individual humans as linked in a social context. He wrote about various types of government and the obligations of the individual citizen.

Arouet, François-Marie Also known as Voltaire, Arouet (1694–1778) was an important Enlightenment thinker and writer. Voltaire's beliefs in reason, science, and religious freedom were echoed in his plays, poems, novels, essays, and historical and scientific works. Voltaire spent much of his life in exile from his home country of France, writing and speaking about his philosophy.

Arthur, Chester The 21st President of the United States, serving from 1881 to 1885, Arthur (1829–1886) took office after the assassination of President James Garfield. Arthur signed the Pendleton Act, which eliminated the spoils system and established merit as the basis for jobs in the federal workforce.

Articles of Confederation plan of government adopted by the Continental Congress after the American Revolution; established "a firm league of friendship" among the States but allowed few important powers to the Federal Government

assemble to gather with one another in order to express views on public matters

assessment the process of determining the value of property to be taxed

assimilation the process by which people of one culture merge into, and become part of, another culture

at-large election of an officeholder by the voters of an entire governmental unit (e.g. a State or country) rather than by the voters of a district or subdivision

attorney general the head of the Department of Justice

autocracy a form of government in which a single person holds unlimited power

B

backbenchers a member of the House of Commons who is not a party leader

bail sum of money that the accused may be required to post (deposit with the court) as a guarantee that he or she will appear in court at the proper time

balance the ticket when a presidential candidate chooses a running mate who can strengthen his chance of being elected by virtue of certain ideological, geographical, racial, ethnic, gender, or other characteristics

Balkans The Balkans, sometimes called Balkan Peninsula, is a geographic area in Central Europe that usually includes Slovenia, Croatia, Bosnia and Herzegovina, Serbia, Kosovo, Montenegro, Macedonia, Albania, Bulgaria, Romania, and Moldova. The term may have different interpretations of the geography, culture, and history.

ballot device that voters use to register a choice in an election

ballot fatigue phenomenon by which voters cast fewer votes for offices listed toward the bottom of the ballot

bankruptcy the legal proceeding by which a bankrupt person's assets are distributed among those to whom he or she owes debts
battleground States States in which the outcome of an election is too close to call and either candidate could win
BCRA The 2002 Bipartisan Campaign Reform Act attempted to close the soft-money loophole in earlier campaign finance laws.
bench trial trial in which the judge alone hears the case
bicameral an adjective describing a legislative body composed of two chambers
Biden, Joe (1942–) Democratic senator from Delaware; first elected in 1972. Served as the 47th Vice President of the United States from 2009 under President Barack Obama.
bill a proposed law presented to a legislative body for consideration
bill of attainder legislative act that inflicts punishment without a court trial
Bill of Rights the first ten amendments to the Constitution
bills proposed laws presented to a legislative body for consideration
bipartisan supported by two parties
Blackstone, William Blackstone (1723–1780) was an English judge who wrote the *Commentaries on the Laws of England,* a series of four books that had a profound influence on the writers of America's Declaration of Independence and Constitution. Blackstone, an important Enlightenment figure, believed in protecting the rights of the innocent, and in basing judgments on common law, that is, on previous decisions about similar issues.
Blaine, James G. Blaine (1830–1893), a congressman from Maine and Speaker of the House from 1869 to 1875, was an unsuccessful candidate for President in 1876 and 1880. He served as Secretary of State in 1881 and again from 1889 to 1892.
blanket primary a voting process in which voters receive a long ballot containing the names of all contenders, regardless of party, and can vote however they choose
block grants one type of federal grants-in-aid for some particular but broadly define area of public policy
Boehner, John (1949–) Republican Congressman from Cincinnati, Ohio, elected to the United States House of Representatives in 1990. He served as a majority leader in 2006 and a minority leader from 2007 to 2011. He became Speaker of the House in 2011.
Boston the capital and largest city of the Commonwealth of Massachusetts
Bradley, Joseph P. An Associate Justice of the Supreme Court from 1870 to 1892, Joseph P. Bradley (1813–1892) was appointed by President Ulysses S. Grant. Bradley was one of several justices to narrow the protections that the then-newly-passed Fourteenth Amendment offered to African Americans.
Brennan, William J. Like Earl Warren, William J. Brennan, Jr., (1906–1997) was appointed to the Supreme Court by President Dwight D. Eisenhower, and like Warren, Brennan later proved to be one of the most liberal judges ever appointed to the Court, voting on many important equal protection cases. He served on the Court from 1956 to 1990.
brief written statement that spells out the party's legal position and cites relevant facts and legal precedents
Bryce, James Bryce (1838–1922) was a British politician who served as an ambassador to the United States from 1907 to 1913. He became especially popular upon writing *The American Commonwealth,* which is a favorable study of the U.S. government.
budget a financial plan for the use of money, personnel, and property
bureaucracy a large, complex administrative structure that handles the everyday business of an organization
bureaucrat a person who works for a bureaucratic organization
Bush, George H.W. After graduating from Yale University, Bush (born 1924) began a career in the oil industry of Texas. He served two terms as a representative to Congress from Texas, and was later appointed ambassador to the United Nations and Director of the CIA. Bush was Vice President under Ronald Reagan and was elected the 41st President, serving from 1989 to 1993.
Bush, George W. (1946–) graduated from Yale University and Harvard Business School before returning to Texas to work in the oil industry. Serving first as Governor of Texas, he was elected the 43rd President, holding office from 2001 to 2009. His election marked only the second time in American history that the son of a President (George H.W. Bush) went on to become President.
Byrd, Robert C. Byrd (1917–2010) was the U.S. representative from West Virginia from 1953 to 1959 and a senator from 1959 until 2010, serving longer than any other member in U.S. history. He considered himself a "child of the Appalachian coalfields" and spent his political career battling persistent poverty in West Virginia.

C

Cabinet an advisory body to the President
Calvert, George (Lord Baltimore) A member of Parliament who founded Maryland as a haven for Catholics, Calvert (1578 or 1579–1632) came to North America in 1628 but was not accepted due to his religion. He returned to England and requested a royal charter to establish a colony where he could practice his religion. The charter was granted in 1632, shortly after his death.
capital all the human-made resources that are used to produce goods and services
capital punishment death penalty
capitalism economic system in which individuals are free to own the means of production and maximize profits
Capitol Hill The U.S. Capitol is located inside the historic residential district called Capitol Hill in Washington, D.C. Other buildings on Capitol Hill include the U.S. Supreme Court and Library of Congress. Capitol Hill is also a figure of speech that simply means Congress.
Carter, Jimmy Carter (1924–) was the 39th President of the United States, serving from 1977 to 1981. A former naval officer and governor of Georgia, Carter was awarded the Nobel Peace prize in 2002 and is the author of twenty-seven books. During his presidency, Carter created the Department of Education, expanded the national park system, and established a relationship with the People's Republic of China.
Castro, Fidel Castro (born 1926) was the dictatorial political leader of Cuba from 1959 to 2008. Through revolutionary tactics, he turned the island nation into the first communist state in the Western hemisphere.

categorical grants one type of federal grants-in-aid; made for some specific, closely defined purpose
caucus as a nominating device, a group of like-minded people who meet to select the candidates they will support in an upcoming election
censure to issue a formal condemnation
certificate the result of a process in which a lower court asks the Court to certify the answer to a specific question, such as a procedure or rule of law
Charles I, King Charles I (1600–1649) was king of England, Scotland, and Ireland from 1625 to 1649. He ruled with strict authority, and his quarrels with Parliament triggered a civil war. In 1649, Charles was found guilty of treason and executed.
charter a city's basic law, its constitution; a written grant of authority from the king
Chávez, Hugo Chávez (1954–2013) became president of Venezuela in 1999, sailing into office via public outrage against the traditional political elite in that country. Known as outspoken and controversial, Chávez insisted throughout his presidency that his socialist revolution would benefit everyone in Venezuela, but especially the poor.
checks and balances system of overlapping the powers of the legislative, executive, and judicial branches to permit each branch to check the actions of the others
Chiang Kai-shek (1887–1975) was a Chinese soldier and statesman. He was the head of the Nationalist government from 1928 until 1949.
chief administrator term for the President as head of the administration of the Federal Government
chief citizen term for the President as the representative of the people, working for the public interest
chief diplomat term for the President as the main architect of foreign policy and spokesperson to other countries
chief economist term for the President as monitor of the nation's economic condition
chief executive term for the President as vested with the executive power of the United States
chief legislator term for the President as architect of public policy and the one who sets the agenda for Congress
chief of party term for the President as the leader of his or her political party
chief of state term for the President as the ceremonial head of the United States, the symbol of all the people of the nation
Churchill, Winston Churchill (1874–1965) was a British statesman who served as prime minister of the United Kingdom from 1940 to 1945 during most of World War II and from 1951 to 1955. He was the first honorary U.S. citizen and was granted the Nobel Prize in Literature.
citizen a member of a state or nation who owes allegiance to it by birth or naturalization and is entitled to full civil rights
civil case a case involving a noncriminal matter such as a contract dispute or a claim of patent infringement
civil disobedience a form of protest in which people deliberately but non-violently violate the law as a means of expressing their opposition to some particular law or public policy
civil law the portion of the law relating to human conduct, to disputes between private parties, and to disputes between private parties and government not covered by criminal law
civil liberties guarantees of the safety of persons, opinions, and property from the arbitrary acts of government, including freedom of speech and freedom of religion
civil rights term used for positive acts of government that seek to make constitutional guarantees a reality for all people, e.g., prohibitions of discrimination
civil service those civilian employees who perform the administrative work of government
civilian nonmilitary
civilian tribunal a court operating as part of the judicial branch, entirely separate from the military establishment
clemency mercy or leniency granted to an offender by a chief executive
Clinton, Bill (1946–) William J. Clinton was elected Governor of Arkansas in 1978, and was elected to be the 42nd President, serving from 1993–2001. During his administration, the United States largely enjoyed a period of peace and economic growth. In 1998, he was the 2nd president to be impeached by the House of Representatives, but was found not guilty of the charges by the Senate and remained in office.
Clinton, Hillary Rodham Clinton (1947–) became First Lady of the United States when her husband Bill Clinton was elected to the presidency in 1993. In 2001, Clinton became a senator from New York State, during which time she made an unsuccessful bid for the presidency. In 2009, Clinton was tapped to become secretary of state in the administration of President Barack Obama, a position she held until her resignation in 2013.
closed primary a party nominating election in which only declared party members can vote
cloture a procedure to limit or end floor debate, especially during a filibuster
coalition a temporary alliance of several groups who come together to form a working majority and so to control a government
coattail effect effect of a strong candidate running for an office at the top of a ballot, helping to attract voters to other candidates on the party's ticket
cold war a period of more than 40 years during which relations between the two superpowers (United States and Soviet Union) were at least tense, and often hostile; a time of threats and military build-up
collective security the keeping of international peace and order
collectivization collective or state ownership of the means of production
colonialism the control of one nation over foreign lands
command economies systems in which government bureaucrats plan and direct most economic activity
commander in chief term for the President as commander of the nation's armed forces
Commerce and Slave Trade Compromise an agreement reached at the Constitutional Convention to protect slaveholders; it denied Congress the power to tax the export of goods from any State and, for twenty years, denied Congress the power to act on the slave trade
commerce power exclusive power of Congress to regulate interstate and foreign trade
commission government type of city government which has three to nine popularly elected commissioners who form the city council and combine both legislative and executive powers in one body
committee chair member who heads a standing committee in a legislative body

common law an unwritten law made by a judge that has developed over centuries from those generally accepted ideas of right and wrong that have gained judicial recognition

communism ideology which calls for the collective, or state, ownership of land and other productive property

commutation the power to reduce (commute) the length of a sentence or fine for a crime

compromise an adjustment of opposing principles or systems by modifying some aspect of each in order to find the position most acceptable to the majority

concurrent jurisdiction power shared by federal and State courts to hear certain cases

concurrent powers those powers that both the National Government and the States possess and exercise

concurrent resolution a statement of position on an issue used by the House and Senate acting jointly; does not have the force of law and does not require the President's signature

concurring opinion an opinion which is basically in agreement with the decision that the Court has made, but which bases that opinion on different reasons

confederation a joining of several groups for a common purpose

conference committee temporary joint committee created to reconcile any differences between the two houses' versions of a bill

Connecticut Compromise an agreement reached during the Constitutional Convention that Congress should be composed of a Senate, in which each State would be represented equally, and a House, in which each State would be represented based on the State's population

consensus general agreement among various groups on fundamental matters; broad agreement on public questions

constituencies the people and interests that an elected official represents

constituent power the non-legislative power of Constitution-making and the constitutional amendment process

constitutional law based on the United States Constitution, the State constitutions, and judicial interpretations of those documents

constitutionalism basic principle that government and those who govern must obey the law; the rule of law

containment a policy based in the belief that if communism could be kept within its existing boundaries, it would collapse under the weight of its internal weaknesses

content neutral the government may not regulate assemblies on the basis of what might be said

continuing resolution measure that allows agencies to continue working based on the previous year's appropriations

continuous body governing unit (e.g. the United States Senate) whose seats are never all up for election at the same time

contract a legally binding agreement in which one party agrees to do something with or for another party

controllable spending amount decided upon by Congress and the President to determine how much will be spent each year on many individual government expenditures, including environment protection programs, aid to education, and so on

convene to begin a new session of Congress

copyright the exclusive, legal right of a person to reproduce, publish, and sell his or her own literary, musical, or artistic creations

council-manager government a modification of the mayor-council form of government, consisting of a strong elected council, a weak elected mayor, and a manager named by the council

county a major unit of local government in most States

courts-martial courts composed of military personnel, for the trial of those accused of violating military law

criminal case a case in which a defendant is tried for committing a crime as defined by the law

criminal law the portion of the law that defines public wrongs and provides for their punishment

Cultural Revolution launched by Chinese Communist Party chairman Mao Zedong during his last decade in power (1966–1976) to renew the spirit of the Chinese Revolution. Young and dedicated Red Guards attacked and bullied intellectuals, and those that lacked revolutionary fervor. Some were sent to work farms to be re-educated.

Cunningham, Randy "Duke" Cunningham (1941–) was a U.S. Navy flying ace during the Vietnam War, followed by a career as a Republican member of the U.S. House of Representatives from 1991 to 2005. He was convicted of accepting $2.4 million in bribes from defense contractors, and sentenced to more than eight years in prison in 2006.

customs duty tax laid on goods brought into the United States from abroad, also known as tariffs, import duties, or imposts

D

de facto the situation as it exists in fact

de jure in accordance with the law

defendant in a civil suit, the person against whom a court action is brought by the plaintiff; in a criminal case, the person charged with the crime

deficit yearly shortfall between revenue and spending

deficit financing the practice of funding government by borrowing to make up the difference between government spending and revenue

deflation general decrease in prices throughout the economy

delegated powers those powers, expressed, implied, or inherent, granted to the National Government by the Constitution

delegates people with authority to represent others at a conference or convention

demand-side economics theory that the higher employment that results from government borrowing will produce higher tax revenues

democracy form of government where supreme authority rests with the people

democratic consolidation the process of establishing the factors considered necessary for a democracy to succeed

democratization the change from dictatorship to democracy, marked by the holding of free and fair elections

denaturalization the process through which naturalized citizens may involuntarily lose their citizenship

Deng Xiaoping Deng Xiaoping (1904–1997) ascended to power in China in 1977, on the heels of the unpopular Cultural Revolution begun by Mao Zedong in 1966. Deng continued the authoritarian style of his predecessor, but he opened China to a market economy that lifted millions of peasants out of poverty.

deportation a legal process in which aliens are legally required to leave the United States

détente French term meaning "a relaxation of tensions"
deterrence the policy of making America and its allies so militarily strong that their very strength will discourage, or prevent, any attack
devolution the delegation of authority from the central government to regional governments
dictatorship form of government where those who rule cannot be held responsible to the will of the people
diplomatic immunity when ambassadors are not subject to the laws of the state to which they are accredited
direct primary an election held within a party to pick that party's candidates for the general election
discharge petition enables members to force a bill that has remained in committee 30 days (7 for the Rules Committee) onto the floor for consideration
discount rate rate of interest a bank must pay when it borrows money from a Federal Reserve Bank
discriminate treat certain categories of people differently than people falling into other categories
discrimination bias, unfairness
disenfranchised denied the right to vote
dissenting opinions an opinion written by a justice who does not agree with the Court's decision, explaining the reasons why not.
District of Columbia the capital of the United States
district plan proposal for choosing presidential electors by which two electors would be selected in each State according to the Statewide popular vote and the other electors would be selected separately in each of the State's congressional districts
divine right of kings the belief that God grants authority to a government
division of powers basic principle of federalism; the constitutional provisions by which governmental powers are divided on a geographic basis (in the United States, between the National Government and the States)
docket a court's list of cases to be heard
domestic affairs all matters not directly connected to the realm of foreign affairs
double jeopardy part of the 5th Amendment stating that no person can be put in jeopardy of life or limb twice; once a person has been tried for a crime, he or she cannot be tried again for the same crime
Douglas, William O. Douglas (1898–1980) was the longest serving justice on the United States Supreme Court. Appointed to the Court as an associate justice by President Franklin D. Roosevelt in April 1939, he served for over 36 years, until his retirement in November 1975.
draft conscription, or compulsory military service
due process doctrine that holds that the government must act fairly and in accord with established rules in all that it does
Due Process Clause part of the 14th Amendment which guarantees that no State deny basic rights to its people
duty a tax on imports

E

economic protest parties parties rooted in poor economic times, lacking a clear ideological base, dissatisfied with current economic conditions and demanding better times
Eisenhower, Dwight Elected to the presidency in 1953, Eisenhower (1890–1969) brought with him the prestige of having been commanding officer of the Allied forces in Europe during World War II, a culmination of a long military career. As the 34th President, serving from 1953 to 1961, he advocated peace and supported desegregation in schools and the military.
electoral college group of persons chosen in each State and the District of Columbia every four years who make a formal selection of the President and Vice President
electorate all of the people entitled to vote in a given election
eminent domain the power of a government to take private property for public use
enabling act a congressional act directing the people of a United States territory to frame a proposed State constitution as a step toward admission to the Union
English Bill of Rights document written by Parliament and agreed to by William and Mary of England in 1689, designed to prevent abuse of power by English monarchs; forms the basis for much in American government and politics today
engrossed a bill printed in its final form
entitlement a benefit that federal law says must be paid to all those who meet the eligibility requirements, e.g., Medicare, food stamps, and veterans' pensions
entitlements benefit that federal law says must be paid to all those who meet the eligibility requirements, e.g., Medicare, food stamps, and veterans' pension
entrepreneur individual with the drive and ambition to combine land, labor, and capital resources to produce goods or offer services
equal protection idea that the laws of a State, or of the nation, must treat any given individual in the same way as it would treat other individuals who are in similar conditions and circumstances
equity a branch of the law that supplements common law by taking a preventative approach
espionage spying
Establishment Clause part of the 1st Amendment of the Constitution that guarantees the separation of church and State
estate tax levy imposed on the assets of one who dies
ex post facto law law applied to an act committed before its passage
excise tax tax laid on the manufacture, sale, or consumption of goods and/or the performance of services
exclusionary rule ruling stating that evidence gained as the result of an illegal act by police cannot be used against the person from whom it was seized
exclusive powers those powers which can be exercised by the National Government alone
executive agreement a pact made by the President directly with the head of a foreign state; a binding international agreement with the force of law but which (unlike a treaty) does not require Senate consent
Executive Article Article II of the Constitution. Establishes the presidency and gives the executive power of the Federal Government to the President
executive departments often called the Cabinet departments, they are the traditional units of federal administration
Executive Office of the President an organization of several agencies staffed by the President's closest advisors
executive order directive, rule, or regulation issued by a chief executive or subordinates, based upon constitutional or statutory authority and having the force of law

executive power the power to execute, enforce, and administer laws

executive privilege the President's power to refuse to disclose information

expatriation the legal process by which a loss of citizenship occurs

expressed powers those delegated powers of the National Government that are spelled out, expressly, in the Constitution; also called the "enumerated powers"

extradition the legal process by which a fugitive from justice in one State is returned to that State

F

factors of production basic resources that are used to make all goods and services

failed states nations in which security is nonexistent, the economy has collapsed, healthcare and school systems are in shambles, and corruption is flourishing

FECA The Federal Election Campaign Act of 1971 was the first federal law regulating the use of money in presidential and congressional campaigns.

federal budget a detailed financial document containing estimates of federal income and spending during the coming fiscal year

Federal Election Commission (FEC) an independent agency in the executive branch that administers all federal law dealing with campaign finance

federal government a form of government in which powers are divided between a central government and several local governments

federalism a system of government in which a written constitution divides power between a central, or national, government and several regional governments like States.

Federalists those persons who supported the ratification of the Constitution in 1787–1788

Feingold, Russ A former Democratic senator from Wisconsin, Feingold (1993–2010) was co-sponsor of the Bipartisan Campaign Reform Act of 2002.

felony a serious crime which may be punished by a heavy fine and/or imprisonment or even death

feudalism a loosely organized system in which powerful lords divided their land among other, lesser lords

filibuster a stalling tactic in which senators monopolize the Senate floor with talk and other delays so a bill cannot be brought to a vote

First Lady the President's wife

fiscal policy various means the government uses to raise and spend money

fiscal year the 12-month period used by a government and the business world for its record-keeping, budgeting, revenue-collecting, and other financial management purposes

527 organizations political advocacy groups filed in accordance with Section 527 of the Internal Revenue Code, which are not aligned with a political party but try to influence political policies, and are allowed to raise unlimited sums of money

floor consideration the process by which proposed laws are considered and acted upon by the full membership of the House or Senate

floor leaders members of the House and Senate picked by their parties to carry out party decisions and steer legislative action to meet party goals

Ford, Gerald Ford (1913–2006) was President of the United States from 1974 to 1977. After the Watergate scandal forced President Nixon from office in 1974, Vice President Ford became President and served the remainder of the second Nixon term. Ford acted vigorously to maintain United States power abroad and worked to prevent a new war in the Middle East. Ford lost the presidency in 1976 due to economic problems, the effects of Watergate, and his pardon of former President Nixon.

foreign affairs a nation's relationships with other countries

foreign aid economic and military aid to other countries

foreign policy a group of policies made up of all the stands and actions that a nation takes in every aspect of its relationships with other countries; everything a nation's government says and does in world affairs

formal amendment change or addition that becomes part of the written language of the Constitution itself through one of four methods set forth in the Constitution

Framers group of delegates who drafted the United States Constitution at the Philadelphia Convention in 1787

franchise right to vote

franking privilege benefit allowing members of Congress to mail letters and other materials postage-free

Franklin, Benjamin An American author, inventor, diplomat, and legislator, Franklin (1706–1790) proposed the Albany Plan of Union that foresaw the benefits of colonial unity. He later signed the Declaration of Independence and helped frame the Constitution, urging delegates to cooperate and sign the final draft.

free enterprise system an economic system characterized by private or corporate ownership of capital goods; investments that are determined by private decision rather than by state control and determined in a free market

Free Exercise Clause the second part of the constitutional guarantee of religious freedom; guarantees to each person the right to believe whatever he or she chooses to believe in matters of religion

free market market in which buyers and sellers are free to buy and sell as they wish

full faith and credit clause requiring that each State accept the public acts, records, and judicial proceedings of every other State

Full Faith and Credit Clause Constitution's requirement that each State accept the public acts, records, and judicial proceedings of every other State

fundamental laws laws of basic and lasting importance which may not easily be changed

G

Gallup, George Gallup (1901–1984) was a pollster and statistician who founded the famous Gallup Poll. In addition to conducting polls and developing new methods to ensure polling accuracy, Gallup was a professor and an author. He also founded the American Institute of Public Opinion, the British Institute of Public Opinion, and the Audience Research Institute, Inc.

Garfield, James Garfield (1831–1881) was the 20th President of the United States, serving from March to September of 1881. He holds the record for the second-shortest time in office. A former major general in the Civil War and a member of the House Representatives from Ohio for nine consecutive terms, President Garfield was shot by Charles J. Guiteau in 1881 after refusing to appoint Guiteau to a diplomatic post.

gender gap measurable differences between the partisan choices of men and women today

general elections the regularly scheduled election at which voters make a final selection of officeholders

George II, King George II (1683–1760) was king of Great Britain from 1727 to 1760. The colony of Georgia was named in his honor after he signed a charter granting the colony to its twenty trustees in 1732. King George thought the colony would be an important buffer between the Spanish-controlled lands to the south and the other English colonies to the north.

gerrymandering the drawing of electoral district lines to the advantage of a party or group

gift tax tax on a gift by a living person

Ginsburg, Ruth Bader Ruth Bader Ginsburg (born 1933) was the second woman appointed to the Supreme Court. President Clinton nominated her to serve as an associate justice of the Supreme Court in 1993, and she continues to serve.

globalization economic interdependence among nations of the world

Glorious Revolution events that led to Parliament in 1688 inviting William and Mary of Orange to peacefully replace King James II on condition that they recognize the authority of Parliament and the rights of individuals; with the signing of the Bill of Rights, the Glorious Revolution helped calm the centuries-long struggle for supremacy between the monarchy and Parliament in England.

Gorbachev, Mikhail General Secretary of the Communist Party of the Soviet Union from 1985 to 1991, Gorbachev (born 1931) became president of the Soviet Union in 1990. Within a year, his focus on democratizing the political system and decentralizing the economy led to the collapse of the Soviet Union. Gorbachev resigned from the presidency in 1991. He received the Nobel Prize for Peace in 1990.

government the institution through which a society makes and enforces its public policies

government corporations corporations within the executive branch subject to the President's direction and control, set up by Congress to carry out certain business-like activities

grand jury formal device by which a person can be accused of a serious crime

Grant, Ulysses S. Grant (1822–1885) was President of the United States from 1869 to 1877. Grant won election after serving as the Union general who led the United States to victory over the Confederate States of America during the American Civil War. Grant supported African American rights, Native American policy, and civil service reform; additionally, he supported the creation of a transcontinental railroad. He also executed a successful foreign policy and was responsible for improving Anglo American relations.

grants-in-aid programs grants of federal money or other resources to States, cities, counties, and other local units

grass-roots pressures pressures on public officials from members of an interest group or the people at large

Great Leap Forward five-year plan for 1958 that was an attempt to modernize China quickly

gross domestic product total amount of goods and services produced in a country each year

Group of 8 (G8) forum formed in 1975 for eight of the world's most industrialized nations: the United States, Japan, Germany, France, Britain, Italy, Canada, and Russia

Guantanamo Bay, Cuba First leased by the United States from Cuba in 1903, Guantanamo Bay houses a naval base that has been in regular use ever since. Since January 11, 2002, the base has housed individuals captured by the U.S. military during the War on Terror. This detention center has been deeply controversial since it opened, and the fate of the prisoners housed there is hotly debated from both legal and moral perspectives.

H

Hamilton, Alexander Hamilton (1755 or 1757–1804) immigrated to North America in 1772 from the British West Indies. He entered the Continental Army in 1776 and served under General Washington. He held a number of positions in government, including as a member of the Continental Congress and the Constitutional Convention. He studied law and practiced in New York City. Hamilton was Secretary of the Treasury in President Washington's Cabinet. He was mortally wounded in a duel with Aaron Burr in 1804.

hard money contributions that are given directly to candidates for their campaigns, are limited, and must be reported to the government

hard-liners those who fight to maintain the status quo

Harrison, William Henry Elected as the 9th President in 1841, Harrison (1773–1841) was the first President to die in office. Born into an aristocratic Virginia planter family, he spent much of his time in the Northwest, obtaining title to Indian lands and leading efforts to repel Indian attacks. He contracted pneumonia and died after only four months in office.

heterogeneous of another or different race, family or kind; composed of a mix of elements

Hobbes, Thomas (1588–1679) English philosopher who felt that people and nations were in a constant battle for power and wealth. He thought that an absolute monarchy was the best government for England. He distrusted democracy, but thought that authorized representatives as the voice of the people would prevent a monarch from being unfair or cruel.

Holmes, Jr., Oliver Wendell (1841–1935) was a justice of the U.S. Supreme Court from 1902 to 1932 who was nicknamed the Great Dissenter.

Hoover, Herbert Hoover (1874–1964) graduated from Stanford as a mining engineer and began his career in China. He later served in various humanitarian posts abroad, including head of the American Relief Administration in Europe. He was elected the 31st President in 1928, just months before the 1929 stock market crash that sent the nation into a deep depression.

Hudson River a 315-mile long waterway that flows north to south through eastern New York State

I

ideological based on a particular set of beliefs—a comprehensive view of social, economic, and political matters

immigrants those people legally admitted as permanent residents of a country

impeach to bring formal charges against a public official

implied powers those delegated powers of the National Government that are suggested by the expressed powers set out in the Constitution; those "necessary and proper" to carry out the expressed powers

import quota limit put on the amount of a commodity that can be imported into a country

income tax a tax levied on the income of individuals and/or corporations

incorporation the process by which a State establishes a city as a legal body; the term comes from the Latin words *in* (into) and *corpus* (body)

incumbent the current officeholder

independent agencies additional agencies created by Congress located outside the Cabinet departments

independent executive agencies agencies headed by a single administrator with regional subunits but lacking Cabinet status

independent regulatory commissions independent agencies created by Congress, designed to regulate important aspects of the nation's economy, largely beyond the reach of presidential control

independents a term used to describe people who have no party affiliation

indictment formal complaint before a grand jury that charges the accused with one or more crimes

inferior courts the lower federal courts, under the Supreme Court

inflation general increase in prices throughout the economy

information formal charge filed by a prosecutor without the action of a grand jury

inherent powers powers the Constitution is presumed to have delegated to the National Government because it is the government of a sovereign state within the world community

inheritance tax tax levied on the beneficiary's share of an estate

initiative a process in which a certain number of qualified voters sign petitions in favor of a proposed statute or constitutional amendment, which then goes directly to the ballot

injunction court order that forces or limits the performance of some act by a private individual or by a public official

integration incorporating people of different races equally into society without separating the races from each other

interest charge for borrowed money, generally a percentage of the amount borrowed

interest group private organizations whose members share certain views and work to shape public policy

International Monetary Fund (IMF) organization formed in 1944 to oversee the international monetary system

interstate compacts formal agreement entered into with the consent of Congress, between or among States, or between a State and a foreign state

involuntary servitude forced labor

isolationism a purposeful refusal to become generally involved in the affairs of the rest of the world

Isthmus of Panama the narrow strip of land that lies between the Caribbean Sea and the Pacific Ocean in Panama; it is the location of the Panama Canal

item veto a governor may veto one or more items in a bill without rejecting the entire measure

J

Jackson, Andrew Known as "Old Hickory" for his toughness and aggressive personality, Jackson (1767–1845) was the seventh President of the United States, serving from 1829 to 1837. His political movement is known as Jacksonian Democracy because he believed that the common man should have a say in government. He is the only President to have fought in both the Revolutionary War, as a young teenager, and in the War of 1812, where he gained military fame; he is also the first President to come from west of the Appalachian Mountains.

Jackson, Robert H. Jackson (1892–1954) was a justice of the U.S. Supreme Court from 1941 to 1954. He is best known for his opinion in *West Virginia State Board of Education* v. *Barnette,* 1943, that expanded the scope of the 1st Amendment's freedom of speech guarantee.

Jamestown first permanent English settlement in North America; founded in 1607 in Virginia and named after King James I. The founding of Jamestown gave England an entry into the competition for the Americas, which Spain had dominated since the voyages of Christopher Columbus in the late fifteenth century.

Jay, John Jay (1745–1829) was a New York lawyer, president of the Second Continental Congress, diplomat, first Chief Justice of the United States, and governor of New York. His was a voice of moderation in relations with Great Britain before the Declaration of Independence. Jay favored strong centralized government and fought for ratification of the U.S. Constitution. He also helped draft the New York State constitution and served as the State's first Chief Justice. He helped negotiate and enforce liberal terms for peace with Great Britain and served as first Secretary for Foreign Affairs before George Washington appointed him first Chief Justice of the Supreme Court.

Jefferson, Thomas Jefferson (1743–1826) was the third President of the United States, serving from 1801 to 1809. He is known as the draftsman of the Declaration of Independence and for engineering the Louisiana Purchase.

Jim Crow laws category of laws that were drafted for the purpose of discriminating against African Americans

John, King John (1167–1216) was king of England from 1199 to 1216. Soon after John became king, war broke out between England and France. After several significant losses, taxes soared, and the monarchy became ruthless in its governing. This angered the barons, who forced John to sign the Magna Carta in 1215.

Johnson, Andrew Johnson (1808–1875) was the 17th president of the United States. As Abraham Lincoln's Vice President, Johnson became President when Lincoln was assassinated. He served from 1865 to 1869.

Johnson, Lyndon (1908–1973) the 36th president of the United States from 1963 to 1969. He was elected as Vice President and took over the presidency upon the assassination of President John F. Kennedy. In 1964, he signed the Civil Rights Act into law.

Johnson, Richard M. Johnson (1780–1850) was the nation's ninth Vice President, serving from 1837 to 1841 under Martin Van Buren. Johnson was the only Vice President chosen by the Senate.

joint committee legislative committee composed of members of both houses

joint resolution a proposal for action that has the force of law when passed; usually deals with special circumstances or temporary matters

judicial activism a judicial philosophy in which supporters believe that judges should interpret and apply provisions in the Constitution and in statute law in light of ongoing changes in conditions and values

judicial power the power to interpret laws, to determine their meaning, and to settle disputes that arise within the society

judicial restraint a judicial philosophy in which supporters believe that judges should decide cases based on the original intent of the Framers or those who enacted the statute(s) involved in a case, or on precedent

judicial review the power of a court to determine the constitutionality of a governmental action

jurisdiction the authority of a court to hear a case

jury a body of persons selected according to law who hear evidence and decide questions of fact in a court case

jus sanguinis the law of blood, which determines citizenship based on the citizenship of one's parents

jus soli the law of soil, which determines citizenship based on where a person is born

justice of the peace a judge who stands on the lowest level of the State judicial system and presides over justice courts

K

Kagan, Elena Kagan (born 1960) was the fourth woman appointed to the Supreme Court. President Obama nominated her to serve as the Solicitor General of the United States in 2009. After serving as Solicitor General for a year, she was nominated by President Obama as an associate justice of the Supreme Court in 2010, where she continues to serve.

Kennedy, John F. Kennedy (1917–1963) was the youngest person ever elected President. His inaugural address in 1963 urged citizens to "Ask not what your country can do for you, ask what you can do for your country." On November 22, 1963, Kennedy was assassinated in Texas.

Kerry, John Kerry (1943–) served in the military during the Vietnam War, earning a Silver Star, a Bronze Star, and three Purple Hearts. Despite his service record, he was an active member of Vietnam Veterans Against the War. Kerry served as a U.S. senator from Massachusetts between 1985 and 2013, becoming the Democratic nominee for President in 2004. In 2013, Kerry became secretary of state in the administration of President Barack Obama.

Keynes, John Maynard Keynes (1883–1946) was an influential British economist, known primarily for his revolutionary economic theory regarding the causes of extended unemployment. Keynes maintained that government had responsibility for stabilizing the economy through the use of fiscal policy (tax and spending programs). He believed that in periods of depression, the government should increase its spending, cut taxes, or do both to stimulate the economy.

keynote address speech given at a party convention to set the tone for the convention and the campaign to come

Khomeini, Ayatollah Khomeini (1902–1989) was an Iranian Shia (Muslim) leader and cleric. He led the revolution that overthrew the Shah (leader) of Iran in 1979. He later became the leader of Iran, dictating both political and religious law for ten years.

King, Jr., Martin Luther (1929–1968) African American clergyman, activist, and leader, King is best known for his role in the African American Civil Rights Movement where he advocated non-violent resistance to discrimination and segregation in the South.

L

labor union organization of workers who share the same type of job, or who work in the same industry, and press for government policies that will benefit its members

laissez-faire theory theory suggesting that government should play a very limited role in society

law of supply and demand law stating that when supplies of goods and services become plentiful, prices tend to drop; when supplies become scarcer, prices tend to rise

Leahy, Patrick (1940–) Democrat senator from Vermont; first elected in 1974. Elected president *pro tempore* of the Senate in 2012.

legal tender any kind of money that a creditor must, by law, accept in payment for debts

legislative power the power to make laws and to frame public policies

legitimacy the belief of the people that a government has the right to make public policy

Lenin, Vladimir (1870–1924) led the Bolshevik Revolution and was the architect of the Communist Party and its control over the Soviet Union. By the time of his death in 1924, the Soviet Union had become a one-party state in control of the country's social, political, and economic institutions.

libel false and malicious use of printed words

liberal constructionist one who argues for a broad interpretation of the Constitution's provisions, particularly those granting powers to the Federal Government

limited government basic principle of American government, which states that government is restricted in what it may do, and each individual has rights that government cannot take away; *see* constitutionalism, popular sovereignty

Lincoln, Abraham Lincoln (1809–1865) was elected 16th President of the United States, entering office in 1861 at age 52. He is known for issuing the Emancipation Proclamation, which declared that "all persons held as slaves... shall be then, thenceforward, and forever free..." He was assassinated in 1865.

line agency agency that perform the tasks for which an organization exists

line-item veto a President's cancellation of specific dollar amounts (line items) from a congressional spending bill; instituted by a 1996 congressional act, but struck down by a 1998 Supreme Court decision

literacy person's ability to read or write

lobbying activities by which group pressures are brought to bear on legislators, the legislative process, and all aspects of the public policymaking process

lobbyist person who tries to persuade public officials to do those things that interest groups want them to do

Locke, John (1632–1704) English philosopher who wrote about his theories concerning the natural rights of man, the social contract, the separation of Church and State, religious freedom, and liberty. Locke's theories influenced the American and French revolutions.

London capital of England; originally founded by the Romans circa a.d. 50. The time period during which many of the North American colonies were established was known as Stuart London. During this time, from 1603 to 1714, the city of London grew tremendously; also during this time London suffered two great disasters: the Plague of 1665 and the Great Fire in 1666.

Long, Huey Long (1893–1935) was the governor of Louisiana and a U.S. senator. He started a Share-the-Wealth Society for distributing housing and income to American families as an alternative to President Franklin D. Roosevelt's New Deal program. Long ran for President in 1935 but was assassinated before the election could take place.

M

Madison, James Madison (1751–1836) wrote several of the *Federalist Papers* and was a major figure in the movement to replace the Articles of Confederation. It is his *Notes on the Debates in the Federal Convention* that have given us a clear understanding of what occurred during those debates. During the convention, Madison was the main architect of the Virginia Plan and had a strong influence on the entire meeting. In fact, he has been referred to as the "Father of the Constitution." At that time, he favored a strong National Government but later saw the benefits of stronger State governments.

magistrate a justice who handles minor civil complaints and misdemeanor cases that arise in an urban setting

Magna Carta Great Charter forced upon King John of England by his barons in 1215; established that the power of the monarchy was not absolute and guaranteed trial by jury and due process of law to the nobility

majority leader the floor leader of the party that holds the majority of seats in each house of Congress

majority opinion the opinion on which the decision of the Court is based, which identifies the issues in the case and the reasons for the decision

majority rule in a democracy, the majority of the people will be right more often than they will be wrong, and will be right more often than will any one person or small group

mandate instructions or commands a constituency gives to its elected officials; the term *mandate* comes from the Latin *mandatum,* meaning "a command"

Mandela, Nelson (1918–2013) the first black president of South Africa from 1994 to 1999 in the country's first democratic election. Prior to that, he was a political prisoner in South Africa for more than twenty years. He also helped end racial segregation in his country, and he was awarded the Nobel Peace Prize in 1993.

Mao Zedong Mao Zedong (1893–1976) led the Chinese communist revolution and served as the country's chief of state from 1949 to 1959. He then served as the chairman of the Chinese Communist Party until his death. Mao is best remembered for the Great Leap Forward, his disastrous attempt to move China quickly toward improved agricultural and industrial production, and the Cultural Revolution that destroyed much of China's cultural heritage.

Marbury, William In 1803, Marbury (1762–1835) became the plaintiff in *Marbury* v. *Madison,* the Supreme Court case that established the power of judicial review. He was appointed by President John Adams to become a justice of the peace in the District of Columbia. As a result of the decision in *Marbury* v. *Madison,* Marbury lost his commission to become a judge.

Marshall, George C. Marshall (1880–1959) served as general of the Army and Army chief of staff during World War II. He later became secretary of state and then secretary of defense in the administration of Franklin Roosevelt. He was the author of a post-war European Recovery Program that became famously known as the Marshall Plan, for which he received the Nobel Prize for Peace.

Marshall, John (1755–1835) the fourth Chief Justice of the United States Supreme Court. He had strong opinions about the power of the Supreme Court to interpret the Constitution and his rulings have had a profound impact on American law to this very day.

Marshall, Thurgood Marshall (1908–1993) was the first African American appointed to the Supreme Court (in 1967) and served as associate justice until 1991. In 1954, while an attorney, he successfully argued the case of *Brown* v. *Board of Education* (which declared racial segregation unconstitutional in American public schools) before the U.S. Supreme Court.

Marx, Karl A German philosopher best known for his multivolume work on political economics, *Capital,* Marx (1818–1883) is considered the father of modern socialism and communism.

Mason, George Owner of Gunston Hall, and one of the richest planters in Virginia, Mason (1725–1792) framed Virginia's Declaration of Rights, which served as a model for Jefferson in writing the Declaration of Independence and was the basis for the U.S. Constitution's Bill of Rights. He was an influential speaker at the Constitutional Convention and worked to have the Bill of Rights and the 11th Amendment incorporated into the Constitution.

mass media means of communication that reach large audiences, especially television, radio, printed publications, and the Internet

mayor-council government the oldest, most widely used type of city government, which features an elected mayor as the chief executive and an elected council as its legislative body

McCain, John McCain (born 1936) is a Republican senator from Arizona and co-sponsor of the Bipartisan Campaign Reform Act of 2002. As the presidential nominee in 2008, he lost the presidential race to Barack Obama.

McKinley, William William McKinley (1843–1901) of Ohio served seven terms in the U.S. House of Representatives, where he championed tariffs (taxes on imported goods) as a way to protect American businesses. Elected President in 1897, he led the U.S. into the Spanish-American War, which ended with the victorious U.S. receiving territory in Guam, Puerto Rico, and the Philippines. McKinley also supported statehood for Hawaii. He was assassinated during his second term as President.

Medicaid a program administered by the States to provide medical insurance to low-income families

medium means of communication; something that transmits information

mercantilism an economic and political theory emphasizing money as the chief source of wealth to increase the absolute power of the monarchy and the nation

metropolitan area a city and the area around it

Milosevic, Slobodan Milosevic (1941–2006) was president of Serbia from 1989 to 1997. A radical nationalist, he instituted policies that led to the breakup of the socialist Yugoslav federation and instigated a series of bloody conflicts with other Balkan states, including Kosovo, Bosnia, and Croatia.

ministers cabinet members, most commonly of the House of Commons

minority leader the floor leader of the party that holds the minority of seats in each house of Congress

Miranda rule constitutional rights that police must read to a suspect before questioning can occur

misdemeanor a lesser offense, punishable by a small fine and/or a short jail term

Missouri Plan an approach to judicial selection that combines election and appointment; a nominating committee provides a list of candidates from which the governor can choose

monetary policy process through which the government can influence the nation's economy through changes in the money supply and the availability of credit

monopoly firm that is the only source of a product or service

Monroe, James Monroe (1758–1831) was President of the United States from 1817 to 1825. During his leadership, Monroe minimized partisan tensions leading to the "Era of Good Feelings." Monroe gained Florida from Spain in 1821 and declared that European action to colonize any part of the Americas would call for the intervention of the United States. Years later, this declaration formed the basis of the Monroe Doctrine, arguably the President's most significant contribution.

Montesquieu, Charles de Montesquieu (1689–1755) was a French political philosopher of the Enlightenment whose major work, *The Spirit of Laws,* was a major contribution to political theory. His theory of the separation of powers had a great impact on the Framers of the Constitution of the United States.

Moses According to the Book of Exodus in the Torah (the Jewish Bible) and the Old Testament of the Christian Bible, Moses was the leader of the Hebrew people who is said to have led them out of slavery in Egypt and into the desert to find freedom in the "promised land" of Canaan. While in the desert, according to the both the Torah, the Old Testament, and the Koran (the sacred text of Islam), Moses climbed to the top of Mount Sinai, where God presented him with clay tablets containing the Ten Commandments.

municipality an urban political unit within a township that usually exists as a separate governmental entity

N

national popular vote plan proposal for electing the President whereby each State's election laws would provide for all of the State's electoral votes to be awarded to the winner of the national popular vote and enter into an interstate compact agreeing to elect the President by national popular vote

NATO (North American Treaty Organization) an alliance formed to protect the freedom and security of its members through political and military action

naturalization the legal process by which citizens of one country become citizens of another

Necessary and Proper Clause the final clause of Article 1, Section 8 in the Constitution, which gives Congress the power to make all laws "necessary and proper" for executing its powers

New Jersey Plan plan that was presented as an alternative to the Virginia Plan at the Constitutional Convention; called for a unicameral legislature in which each State would be equally represented

Nixon, Richard (1913–1994) Richard Nixon was an attorney before entering politics to serve as a representative and senator from California. He was Vice President under President Eisenhower, before being elected the 37th president in 1968. He served from 1969–1974. As President, he ended the draft and instituted a broad environmental program. Facing impeachment due to his involvement in the Watergate scandal, Nixon resigned in August 1974.

nomination the process of candidate selection in an electoral system

nonpartisan elections elections in which candidates are not identified by party labels

Norris, George A U.S. representative and senator from Nebraska known as an independent thinker, Norris (1861–1944) championed legislation to create the Tennessee Valley Authority, to support labor union activity, and to add the "lame duck" 20th Amendment to the Constitution, reducing the time between a congressional election and the first meeting of the new Congress.

North American Free Trade Agreement (NAFTA) agreement that removed trade restrictions among the United States, Canada, and Mexico, thus increasing cross-border trade

O

Obama, Barack Barack Obama (1961–) was the 44th president of the United States from 2009 to 2014. The first African American president, Obama was awarded the Nobel Peace Prize.

O'Connor, Sandra Day (1930–) first woman appointed to the Supreme Court. Nominated by President Reagan in 1981, she served as associate justice of the Supreme Court until she retired in 2006. Known for her carefully researched opinions, she was considered a moderate conservative.

off-year elections congressional election that occurs between presidential election years

oligarchy a form of government in which the power to rule is held by a small, usually self-appointed elite

omnibus measure one bill that contains numerous issues and topics

open market operations processes by which the Federal Reserve buys or sells government securities from and to the nation's banks in order to alter the money supply

open primary a party-nominating election in which any qualified voter can take part

opinion leaders any person who, for any reason, has an unusually strong influence on the views of others

ordinance power power of the President to issue executive orders; originates from the Constitution and acts of Congress

original jurisdiction the power of a court to hear a case first, before any other court

oversight function review by legislative committees of the policies and programs of the executive branch

P

Packwood, Bob Packwood (1932–) was a United States senator from Portland, Oregon. He was elected to the Senate in 1968 and served until his resignation, under threat of expulsion, in 1995.

Panama Canal artificial waterway that cuts across the Isthmus of Panama in Central America and links the Atlantic and Pacific oceans

panic derived from the Latin *panicus,* meaning "terrified"; a sudden widespread alarm about the economy that often results in a depression

pardon release from the punishment or legal consequences of a crime, by the President (in a federal case) or a governor (in a State case)

parliamentary a form of government in which the executive branch is made up of the prime minister, or premier, and that official's cabinet; this branch is part of the legislature

parliamentary system a form of government in which the executive branch is made up of the prime minister, or premier, and that official's cabinet

parochial church-related, as in a parochial school

parole the release of a prisoner short of the complete term of the original sentence

partisans lawmakers who owe their first allegiance to their political party and vote according to the party line

partisanship the strong support of their party and its policy stands

party caucus a closed meeting of a party's house or senate members; also called a party conference

party government the direction and control of the processes of government by the party who has majority favor

party identification loyalty of people to a political party

passport a legal document issued by a state that identifies a person as a citizen of that state and permits travel to and from that state

patent a license issued to an inventor granting the exclusive right to manufacture, use, or sell his or her invention for a limited period of time

patricians rich upper class, landowning aristocrats of the Roman Republic

Patrick, Luther Luther Patrick (1894–1957) was born near Decatur, Alabama. He graduated from Purdue University and received his law degree from the University of Alabama. After serving in various judicial positions including assistant attorney general of Alabama, he served as U.S. representative from Alabama 1937 to 1943 and from 1945 to 1947.

patronage the practice of giving jobs to supporters and friends

payroll tax tax imposed on nearly all employers and their employees, and on self-employed persons, with the amounts owed by employees withheld from their paychecks

Pearl Harbor a U.S. naval base located on the island of Oahu in Hawaii

peer group people with whom one regularly associates, including friends, classmates, neighbors, and co-workers

Pelosi, Nancy Nancy Pelosi (1940–) graduated from Trinity College in Washington, D.C. As one of California's representatives beginning in 1987, Pelosi became the first female Democratic leader of the House, the first female Speaker of the House, and for the 113th Congress, served as the Minority Leader in the House.

Penn, William An English Quaker leader who advocated for religious freedom, Penn (1644–1718) came to North America in 1682 and established the colony of Pennsylvania as a haven for Quakers and other religious minorities.

perjury the act of lying under oath

Perot, Ross (1930–) a self-announced third party candidate for President who founded the Reform Party in 1995. He self-declared as a presidential candidate and used his wealth from founding Electronic Data Systems to fund his campaign. He lost elections in 1992 and 1996.

persona non grata an unwelcome person; used to describe recalled diplomatic officials

petit jury this jury hears the evidence in a case, decides the disputed facts, and very occasionally interprets and applies the law; also known as a trial jury

petition a citizen's right to bring his or her view to the attention of public officials by such means as written petitions, letters, lobbying, and marches

Petition of Right document prepared by Parliament and signed by King Charles I of England in 1628; challenged the idea of the divine right of kings and declared that even the monarch was subject to the laws of the land

Philadelphia the largest city in the Commonwealth of Pennsylvania

picketing patrolling of a business site by workers who are on strike

pigeonholed expression describing how most bills introduced in each session of Congress are buried, put away, or never acted upon

plaintiff in civil law, the party who brings a suit or some other legal action against another (the defendant) in court

platform a political party's formal statement of basic principles, stands on major issues, and objectives

plebeians the common folk in the Roman Republic

plurality the largest number of votes cast for the office

pocket veto a type of veto a chief executive may use after a legislature has adjourned when the chief executive does not sign or reject a bill within the time allowed to do so

police power authority of each State to act to protect and promote the public health, safety, morals, and general welfare of its people

political action committees (PACs) political arms of special-interest groups and other organizations with a stake in electoral politics

political efficacy one's own influence or effectiveness on politics

political party a group of persons who seek to control government through winning elections and holding public office

political socialization process by which people gain their political attitudes and opinions

political spectrum the range of political views

politicos lawmakers who attempt to balance the basic elements of the trustee, delegate, and partisan roles

poll books list of all registered voters in each precinct

poll tax special tax, demanded by some States, as a condition of voting; outlawed by the 24th Amendment

polling place place where the voters who live in a certain precinct go to vote

Pope, Alexander Pope (1688–1744) was a famous and financially successful poet who was also a satirist and translator. He was born in London and raised in a Roman Catholic family. He is most famous for his use of the heroic couplet.

popular sovereignty a government that exists only with the consent of the governed

Powell, Colin Powell (1937–) is a four-star general who served as chairman of the Joint Chiefs of Staff from 1989 to 1993. In 2001, he became secretary of state under George W. Bush; he served in that capacity until 2005. Powell was the first African American to hold either of these Cabinet-level positions.

precedent court decision that stands as an example to be followed in future, similar cases

precinct smallest unit of election administration; a voting district

preclearance provision mandated by the Voting Rights Act of 1965 in which no new election laws and no changes in existing election laws, could go into effect in certain States unless first approved by the Department of Justice

preliminary hearing the first step in a major criminal prosecution where the judge decides if the evidence is enough to hold the person for action by the grand jury or the prosecutor

presentment formal accusation brought by the grand jury on its own motion, rather than that of the prosecutor

president of the Senate the presiding officer of a senate; in Congress, the Vice President of the United States; in a State's legislature, either the lieutenant governor or a senator

president pro tempore the member of the United States Senate, or of the upper house of a State's legislature, chosen to preside in the absence of the president of the Senate

Presidential Election Campaign Fund money donated by taxpayers when they file their federal income tax returns, administered by the FEC, and used for the purpose of subsidizing pre-convention campaigns, national conventions, and presidential election campaigns

presidential government a form of government in which the executive and legislative branches of the government are separate, independent, and coequal

presidential primary an election in which the party's voters 1) choose State party organization's delegates to their party's national convention, and/or 2) express a preference for their party's presidential nomination

presidential succession scheme by which a presidential vacancy is filled

Presidential Succession Act of 1947 law specifying the order of presidential succession following the Vice President

preventive detention law that allows federal judges to order that an accused felon be held, without bail, when there is good reason to believe that he or she will commit yet another serious crime before the trial

prior restraint idea that government cannot curb ideas before they are expressed

privatization process of returning national enterprises to private ownership

Privileges and Immunities Clause Constitution's stipulation that all citizens are entitled to certain "privileges and immunities," regardless of their State of residence

probable cause reasonable grounds, a reasonable suspicion of crime

procedural due process concept that holds that the government must employ fair procedures and methods

process of incorporation the process of incorporating, or including, most of the guarantees in the Bill of Rights into the 14th Amendment's Due Process Clause

progressive tax type of tax proportionate to income

project grants one type of federal grants-in-aid; made for specific projects to States, localities, and private agencies who apply for them

property tax a tax levied on real and personal property

proportional plan proposal by which each presidential candidate would receive the same share of a State's electoral vote as he or she received in the State's popular vote

proportional representation rule applied in Democratic primaries whereby any candidate who wins at least fifteen percent of the votes gets the number of State Democratic convention delegates based on his or her share of that primary vote

proprietary organized by a proprietor (a person to whom the king had made a grant of land)

prorogue adjourn, as in a legislative session

protectionism practice of national governments trying to control imports to protect native industries from foreign competition

public affairs those events and issues that concern the people at large; for example, politics, public issues, and the making of public policies

public agenda public issues on which the people's attention is focused

public debt all of the money borrowed by the government and not yet repaid, plus the accrued interest on that money; also called the national debt or federal debt

public opinion complex collection of the opinions of many different people; the sum of all their views

public opinion polls device that attempts to collect information by asking people questions; *poll* comes from the old Teutonic word *polle,* meaning "the top or crown of the head," the part that shows when heads are counted

public policies all of the things a government decides to do

public policy all of the many goals that a government pursues in all of the many areas of human affairs in which it is involved

pundit expert in a particular subject or field who is frequently called on to give opinions about it to the public

purge a process of government purification by removing rivals

purging process of reviewing lists of registered voters and removing the names of those no longer eligible to vote; a purification

Putin, Vladimir (1952–) became president of the Russian Federation in 1999, taking over when Boris Yeltsin resigned at the end of that year. He won elections in 2000, 2004, and 2012. Putin was also prime minister from 2008 to 2012. During his leadership, presidential power has increased, and he has improved Russia's economy. At the same time, some argue that he is not a true democratic leader.

Q

quorum fewest number of members who must be present for a legislative body to conduct business; majority

quota percentage of a group necessary to fulfill an affirmative action requirement

quota sample sample deliberately constructed to reflect several of the major characteristics of a given population

R

random sample certain number of randomly selected people

ratification formal approval or final consent to the effectiveness of a constitution, constitutional amendment, or treaty

rational basis test test in which the Court asks whether the classification in a law has a reasonable relationship to the achievement of a proper governmental purpose

Reagan, Ronald Born in Illinois, Reagan (1911–2004) began his career as an actor, appearing in more than 50 films. Reagan later moved into politics, serving two terms as governor of California, before being elected the 40th President, serving from 1981 to 1989. Reagan was 69 when first elected President in 1980, making him the oldest candidate to win the office. During his presidency, he called for an era of national renewal and reduced reliance on government.

reapportion redistribute, as in seats in a legislative body

recall a petition procedure by which voters may remove an elected official from office before the completion of his or her regular term

recess a time when both houses of Congress temporarily suspend business

recession absence of economic growth

recognition the exclusive power of a President to legally recognize (establish formal diplomatic relations with) foreign states

record a transcript of proceedings made in trial court

redress satisfaction of a claim payment

referendum a process by which a legislative measure is referred to the State's voters for final approval or rejection

reformers those who work to change or reform government

refugee one who leaves his or her homeland to seek protection from war, persecution, or some other danger

regional security alliances treaties in which the US and other countries involved have agreed to take collective action to meet aggression in a particular part of the world

registration procedure of voter identification intended to prevent fraudulent voting

regressive tax tax levied at a flat rate, without regard to the level of a taxpayer's income or ability to pay

representative government system of government in which public policies are made by officials selected by the voters and held accountable in periodic elections; *see* democracy

reprieve an official postponement of the execution of a sentence

reservations public lands set aside by a government for use by Native American tribes

reserve requirement amount of money the Federal Reserve determines banks must keep in reserve with one of the Federal Reserve Banks

reserved powers those powers that the Constitution does not grant to the National Government and does not deny to the States

resolution a measure relating to the business of either house of Congress or expressing an opinion; does not have the force of law and does not require the President's signature

reverse discrimination discrimination against a majority group

Rice, Condoleezza Rice (1954–) served as foreign policy adviser for George W. Bush's presidential campaign. Once Bush was elected, she became the first woman to head the National Security Council. In 2005, Rice became the first African American woman to serve as secretary of state. Later, Rice returned to her position as a professor at Stanford University and is the author of numerous books.

rider unpopular provision added to an important bill certain to pass so it will "ride" through the legislative process

right of association the right to associate with others to promote political, economic, and other social causes

right of legation the right to send and receive diplomatic representatives

Roberts, John Roberts (born 1955) received his J.D. from Harvard Law School in 1979. He later worked as a law clerk at the Supreme Court, Associate Counsel to President Ronald Reagan, and in the White House Counsel's office from 1982 to 1986. He was nominated to the Supreme Court by President George W. Bush and was confirmed in 2005.

Roosevelt, Franklin D. (1882–1945) the 32nd president of the United States from 1933 to 1945. He was the only President to be elected to the office four times. He led the country through the Great Depression and World War II and developed the system of government programs and reforms together known as the New Deal.

Roosevelt, Theodore Roosevelt (1858–1919) was the 26th President of the United States, serving from 1901 to 1909. Nicknamed Teddy, he was a hunter, soldier, naturalist, and recipient of the Nobel Peace Prize who also secured the route for and began construction on the Panama Canal.

Roper, Elmo Roper (1900–1971) developed the first scientific poll for political forecasting using small samples. While working for *Fortune* magazine, Roper accurately predicted that Franklin Roosevelt would win the presidency in 1936, 1940, and 1944; these achievements brought him significant fame. In his later years, Roper continued in the polling industry and also wrote for newspapers and the *Saturday Review* magazine.

Rousseau, Jean Jacques A Swiss-born philosopher, writer, and political theorist, Rousseau's (1712–1778) treatises and novels inspired the leaders of the French Revolution. His famous work, *The Social Contract,* expresses his idea that humans are essentially free, but the progress of civilization has substituted subservience and dependence to others for that freedom. To overcome this, people must invoke their free will to reconstruct themselves politically along democratic ideals.

rule of law concept that the government and its officers are always subject to the law

runoff primary a primary in which the top two vote-getters in the first direct primary face one another

S

sales tax a tax placed on the sale of various commodities, paid by the purchaser

sample representative slice of the public

search warrant court order authorizing a search

secretary an official in charge of a department of government

Security Council a 15-member panel that bears the UN's major responsibility for keeping international peace

sedition crime of attempting to overthrow the government by force or to disrupt its lawful activities by violent acts

seditious speech advocating, or urging, an attempt to overthrow the government by force or to disrupt its lawful activities with violence

segregation separation of one group from another on the basis of race

select committee legislative committee created for a limited time and for some specific purpose; also known as a special committee

Selma, Alabama Southern city that came to symbolize the South's resistance to the civil rights movement during the early 1960s; the city was the scene of a large march for voting rights, led by several African American leaders, including the Rev. Martin Luther King, Jr.

senatorial courtesy an unwritten rule that is closely followed in the Senate

seniority rule unwritten rule in both houses of Congress reserving the top posts in each chamber, particularly committee chairmanships, for members with the longest records of service

separate-but-equal doctrine doctrine established by the Court in the case *Plessy* v. *Ferguson,* in which it ruled that segregation could be maintained if the separation treated separated races equally

separation of powers basic principle of American system of government that the executive, legislative, and judicial powers are divided among three independent and coequal branches of government

session period of time each year during which Congress assembles and conducts business

shadow cabinet members of opposition parties who watch, or shadow, particular cabinet members and would be ready to run the government

Shays, Daniel A young farmer with a flair for militia drill, Shays (1747–1825) became a captain in the 5th Massachusetts Regiment of the Continental Army in 1777 and gained a reputation as a courageous and competent officer. After the war, he returned to farming. Like many others, he struggled with debts in the severe post-war recession. Shays emerged as a local leader in the movement protesting high taxes and a lack of debt relief.

Shays' Rebellion a series of confrontations between debtor farmers and State government authorities in western Massachusetts in 1786–1787

Sherman, Roger Sherman (1721–1793) was a Connecticut lawyer and judge, Framer of the U.S. Constitution, and Congressman. An early supporter of American independence, he attended the First and Second Continental congresses and also helped draft the Articles of Confederation. At the Constitutional Convention, he proposed what became known as the Connecticut Compromise, which created a House of Representatives chosen by population and a Senate with the same number of representatives from each State.

shield laws law which gives reporters some protection against having to disclose their sources or reveal other confidential information in legal proceedings

single-issue parties parties that focus on a single public question

single-member district electoral district from which one person is chosen by the voters for each elected office

single-member districts electoral districts from which one person is chosen by the voters for each elected office

slander false and malicious use of spoken words

Smith, Adam Smith (1723–1790) was a Scottish philosopher whose ideas are credited with pushing forward the nineteenth-century era of free trade. His book *The Wealth of Nations* (1776) influenced many intellectual and political leaders of the time, and his theories continue to have credibility among modern economists.

socialism philosophy based on the idea that the benefits of economic activity should be fairly distributed

soft money money given to State and local party organizations, in unlimited amounts, for election-related activities

Sotomayor, Sonia Sotomayor (born 1954) was the third woman appointed to the Supreme Court. President Obama nominated her to serve as an associate justice of the Supreme Court in 2009, and she continues to serve.

sound bite short, sharply focused report that can be aired in 30 or 45 seconds

sovereign when a state has supreme and absolute power within its own territory and can decide its own foreign and domestic policies

sovereignty utmost authority in decision-making and in maintaining order of a state

Speaker of the House the presiding officer of the House of Representatives, chosen by and from the majority party in the House

special district an independent unit created to perform one or more related governmental functions at the local level

special session an extraordinary session of a legislative body, called to deal with an emergency situation

splinter parties parties that have split away from one of the major parties

split-ticket voting voting for candidates of different parties for different offices in the same election

spoils system the practice of giving offices and other favors of government to political supporters and friends

staff agency agency that supports the chief executive and other administrators by offering advice and other assistance in the management of an organization

Stalin, Josef Stalin (1878–1953) rose from poverty to become the totalitarian leader of the Soviet Union from 1929 to 1953. Under his reign, which was characterized by brutality, the former peasant society became an industrial leader and a military force to be reckoned with. Among the many sweeping reforms made by Stalin was the collectivization of farming.

standing committee permanent committee in a legislative body to which bills in a specified subject area are referred; see select committee

state a body of people, living in a defined territory, organized politically (that is, with a government), and with the power to make and enforce law without the consent of any higher authority

state-building the process where outside countries attempt to strengthen the governing institutions of a country

statutory law a law passed by the legislature

straight-ticket voting practice of voting for candidates of only one party in an election

straw vote poll that seeks to read the public's mind by asking the same question of a large number of people; the odd name comes from the fact that a straw, thrown up in the air, will indicate which way the wind is blowing

strict constructionist one who argues for a narrow interpretation of the Constitution's provisions, particularly those granting powers to the Federal Government

strict scrutiny test test in which the Court holds the classification in a law to a higher standard; the State or federal government must show that its law is not related to an ordinary governmental purpose, but to a compelling governmental interest

strong-mayor government a type of city government in which the mayor heads the administration and exercises strong leadership in making city policy and running the city's affairs
subcommittee division of existing committee that is formed to address specific issues
subpoena an order for a person to appear and to produce documents or other requested materials
subsidy a grant, usually from a government to help an organization
substantive due process concept that holds that the government must create fair policies and laws
successor a person who inherits a title or office
suffrage right to vote
Super PAC independent political action committees, unaffiliated with any political party, which are allowed to raise and spend unlimited amounts; they must reveal their donors and cannot work directly with a candidate's campaign independent political action committees; unaffiliated with any political party
supply-side economics assumption that tax cuts increase the supply of money in private hands and stimulate the economy
Supremacy Clause a provision of the U.S. Constitution that states that the Constitution, federal law, and treaties of the United States are the "supreme Law of the Land"
surplus more income than spending
Suu Kyi, Aung San (1945–) a politician and opposition leader of Myanmar, who was awarded the Nobel Peace Prize in 1991. She was placed under house arrest for many years for opposing the government's military rule but was later freed and elected to public office.
swing voters members of the electorate who have not made up their minds at the start of the campaign and are open to persuasion by either side
symbolic speech expression by conduct; communicating ideas through facial expressions, with body language, or by carrying a sign or wearing an armband

T

Taft, William Howard (1857–1930) the 27th President of the United States from 1909 to 1913. He later became the tenth Chief Justice of the United States, making him the only person to have served in both offices.
Taney, Roger B. Taney (1777–1864) served as U.S. Attorney General and was appointed Chief Justice of the Supreme Court in 1836. His majority opinion in *Dred Scott* v. *Sandford,* 1857, stating that African Americans could not be considered U.S. citizens, caused much contention on the eve of the Civil War.
tariff tax on imported goods
tax a charge levied by government on persons or property to raise money to meet public needs
term two-year period of time during which Congress meets
territory a part of the United States that is not a state and has its own system of government
terrorism the use of violence to intimidate a government or society
Thomas, Clarence Thomas (born 1948) was the second African American appointed to the Supreme Court. President George H.W. Bush nominated him as an associate justice of the Supreme Court in 1991 to replace Thurgood Marshall, and he continues to serve.
Three-Fifths Compromise an agreement reached at the Constitutional Convention that a slave would be counted as three-fifths of a person when counting the population of a State
Thurmond, Strom The governor of South Carolina and a U.S. senator for 48 years, Thurmond (1902–2003) was a staunch opponent of school desegregation and civil rights who ran unsuccessfully for President in 1948. He later switched party affiliation from Democratic to Republican.
Tocqueville, Alexis de (1805–1859) French political scientist and historian best known for writing *Democracy in America,* an analysis of the political and social system in the United States during the 1800s.
tort a wrongful act that involves injury to one's person, property, or reputation in a situation not covered by the terms of a contract
township a subdivision of a county
trade association interest group within the business community
trade embargo ban on trade with a particular country or particular countries
transients person living in a State for only a short time, without legal residence
treason betrayal of one's country; in the Constitution, by "levying war against the United States or offering comfort or aid to its enemies"
treaty a formal agreement between two or more sovereign states
Truman, Harry Harry Truman (1884–1972) was a Missouri farmer, a judge, a senator, and Vice President for a few months under President Franklin D. Roosevelt. He became the 33rd President on April 12, 1945 when Roosevelt suddenly died. During his presidency, from 1945 to 1953, Truman saw Victory in Europe Day and ordered atomic bombs dropped on Japan.
trustees lawmakers who vote based on their conscience and judgment, not the views of their constituents
Trusteeship Council UN council that monitors territories of other UN members; today, the council exists in name only as by 1994 all Trust Territories had achieved self-governing status
Tyler, John Virginia native John Tyler (1790–1862) served in the State legislature and as Virginia governor. As a U.S. senator, his strict interpretation of the Constitution led him to resign over what he viewed as illegal actions by President Andrew Jackson regarding nullifying acts of Congress. Vice President when President William Henry Harrison died in office, he succeeded to the presidency in 1841. During his term, he approved statehood for Texas and Florida, but fought bitterly with his own Whig party over a national bank system. All but one member of his Cabinet resigned. During the Civil War, he was elected to the Confederate House of Representatives, but he died before he could serve.

U

unconstitutional contrary to constitutional provision and so illegal, null and void, of no force and effect
uncontrollable spending spending that Congress and the President have no power to change directly

unicameral an adjective describing a legislative body with one chamber; *see* bicameral

unitary government a centralized government in which all government powers belong to a single, central agency

United Nations an organization with 193 members that accept the obligations of the United Nations Charter, a treaty drafted in 1945

universe term used in polling that refers to the whole population that the poll aims to measure

V

veto chief executive's power to reject a bill passed by a legislature; literally (Latin) "I forbid"

Virginia Plan plan presented by the delegates from Virginia at the Constitutional Convention; called for a three-branch government with a bicameral legislature in which each State's membership would be determined by its population or its financial support for the Federal Government

visa a permit to enter another country, obtained from the country one wishes to enter

W

Walesa, Lech (1943–) a labor activist who formed Poland's first trade union. Though he was arrested for his union interactions, he was awarded the Nobel Peace Prize in 1983 and served as the president of Poland from 1990 to 1995.

ward a unit into which cities are often divided for the election of city council members

warrant a court order authorizing, or making legal, some official action, such as a search or an arrest

Warren, Earl Warren (1891–1974) was a Republican but liberal justice appointed to the Supreme Court by President Dwight D. Eisenhower. Warren was Chief Justice of the Supreme Court from 1953 to 1969 and presided over some of the Court's most important public school desegregation cases.

Washington, George Washington (1732–1799) was the first President of the United States from 1789 to 1797 and a Founding Father. Prior to his presidency, he was a general and commander in chief during the American Revolution.

weak-mayor government form of city government in which the mayor shares executive duties with other elected officials

welfare cash assistance to the poor

whips assistants to the floor leaders in the House and Senate, responsible for monitoring and marshaling votes

William and Mary of Orange King William III (1650–1702) and Queen Mary II (1662–1694) ruled jointly as king and queen of England, Scotland, and Ireland from 1689 to 1702 (Queen Mary died in 1694, but William continued to rule until 1702). Mary was the daughter of King James II, which meant that her Dutch husband could become co-ruler of England after he overthrew James's government.

Wilson, James Born and educated in Scotland, Wilson (1742–1798) emigrated to North America, arriving in the midst of the Stamp Act agitations of 1765. He studied to become an attorney, going on to specialize in land law. He entered politics just prior to the Revolutionary War and had a pivotal position of influence in the Constitutional Convention.

Wilson, Woodrow Woodrow Wilson (1856–1924) was a graduate of Princeton and the University of Virginia School of Law, and president of Princeton in 1902. He was elected to be the 28th president in 1912. Wilson served from 1913 to 1921 and advocated for a "new freedom" which stressed individualism and States' rights.

winner-take-all an almost obsolete system whereby a presidential aspirant who won the preference vote in a primary automatically won all the delegates chosen in the primary

World Bank organization formed in 1944 to provide economic assistance to developing countries to reduce global poverty levels

World Trade Organization organization created in 1995 to increase trade

writ of certiorari an order by the Court directing a lower court to send up the record in a given case for review

writ of habeas corpus court order that prevents unjust arrests and imprisonments

writs of assistance blanket search warrant with which British custom officials had invaded private homes to search for smuggled goods

Y

Yeltsin, Boris (1931–2007) a Russian politician who became president of Russia in 1990. He became the first popularly elected politician in Russia's history in 1991.

Z

zoning the practice of dividing a city into a number of districts, or zones, and regulating the uses to which property in each of them may be put

A

absentee voting > voto en ausencia Medidas para que voten, el día de las elecciones, aquellas personas que no puedan hacerlo en su lugar habitual de votación.

acquit > absolver Determinar que alguien no es culpable de un delito.

act of admission > decreto de admisión Ley del Congreso mediante la cual se admite a un nuevo estado dentro de la Unión.

Adams, John > Adams, John (1735–1826) fue abogado en Massachusetts, legislador, diplomático y segundo Presidente de los Estados Unidos. Por su sentido de la justicia, defendió a los oficiales ingleses de la Masacre de Boston, pero luego encabezó la defensa de la independencia estadounidense en el Primer y Segundo Congresos Continentales. Fue el principal autor de la Constitución del estado de Massachusetts; ayudó a negociar un tratado de paz con Gran Bretaña después de la Guerra de Independencia, consiguió el reconocimiento diplomático de los Estados Unidos y estructuró el comercio libre con todas las naciones.

Adams, John Quincy > Adams, John Quincy (1767–1848) 6° Presidente de los Estados Unidos, de 1825 a 1829, y autor de la Doctrina Monroe. John Quincy era hijo del presidente John Adams (1797–1801). Antes de ser elegido presidente, Adams fue secretario de Estado. Fungió como congresista después de su presidencia, de 1831 a 1848, y luchó contra la esclavitud. En 1848, sufrió una apoplejía y cayó en el piso de la Cámara de Representantes. Murió dos días después.

Adams, Samuel > Adams, Samuel Uno de los Padres Fundadores, Adams (1722–1803) se convirtió en líder político en Boston por medio de sus textos. Fue delegado en el Primer y el Segundo Congresos Continentales y participó en la redacción del borrador para la Declaración de Derechos.

adjourn > aplazamiento Suspender, por ejemplo, una sesión del Congreso.

administration > administración Funcionarios del poder ejecutivo de un gobierno, así como sus políticas y sus principios.

administrative law > Ley de Administración Ley compuesta por las normas, ordenamientos y reglamentos emitidos por las autoridades ejecutivas federales, estatales o locales, que actúan bajo la autoridad constitucional y o legal apropiada.

affirmative action > acción afirmativa Política que exige que la mayoría de los empleadores lleven a cabo ciertas acciones para remediar los efectos de discriminaciónes pasadas.

Albany Plan of Union > Plan de Unión de Albany Proyecto propuesto por Benjamín Franklin en 1754 cuyo objetivo era unir a las trece colonias en cuanto a asuntos comerciales, militares, así como para otros propósitos; las colonias y la Corona rechazaron el plan.

Albright, Madeleine > Albright, Madeleine (1937–) fungió como embajadora estadounidense frente a Naciones Unidas de 1993 a 1997. Posteriormente, el presidente Bill Clinton la nombró como la primera mujer que ocuparía el cargo de secretaria de Estado de los Estados Unidos dentro del gabinete presidencial, cargo que ocupó de 1997 a 2001. A partir de entonces se ha desempeñado como oradora, consultora y escritora.

alien > extranjero Persona residente nacida en otro país o que no se ha nacionalizado.

aliens > extanjeros residentes Residentes nacidos en el extranjero o sin ciudadanía estadounidense.

Alito, Samuel > Alito, Samuel (1950–) Obtuvo su diploma en Derecho de la Universidad de Yale en 1975, donde fue editor del *Yale Law Journal*. Alito ocupó diversos puestos judiciales durante los mandatos de Ronald Reagan y George H. W. Bush. En 2005, el presidente George W. Bush lo nombró, y Alito asumió su puesto como juez de la Corte Suprema el 31 de enero de 2006.

ambassador > embajador Representante oficial designado por el Presidente para representar a la nación en asuntos diplomáticos.

amendment > enmienda Cambio o adición a la Constitución o a una ley.

amicus curiae brief > alegato *amicus curiae* Término legal latino que significa "amigo de la corte". Es un documento conformado por alegatos escritos que se presentan ante la corte para apoyar a alguna de las partes en disputa.

amnesty > amnistía Perdón general otorgado a un grupo de personas que han violado la ley.

Anti-Federalists > antifederalistas Aquellas personas que se opusieron a la ratificación de la Constitución entre 1787 y 1788.

appellate jurisdiction > jurisdicción de apelación Autoridad de una corte para revisar decisiones de cortes inferiores; ver original jurisdiction/jurisdicción original.

apportioned > prorrateados Distribuidos como, por ejemplo, los escaños de un cuerpo legislativo.

appropriate > asignar Destinar a un uso particular.

Aristotle > Aristóteles (384–322 a.C. Filósofo griego que consideraba que las vidas humanas individuales están conectadas en un contexto social. Escribió acerca de los diversos tipos de gobierno y las obligaciones individuales del ciudadano.

Arouet, François-Marie > Arouet, François-Marie También conocido como Voltaire, Arouet (1694–1778) fue un importante pensador y escritor de la Ilustración. La creencia de Voltaire en la razón, la ciencia y la libertad religiosa hallan eco en sus obras de teatro, poemas, novelas, ensayos y en sus trabajos sobre historia y ciencia. Voltaire pasó gran parte de su vida exiliado, lejos de Francia, escribiendo y hablando sobre su filosofía.

Arthur, Chester > Arthur, Chester 21er Presidente de los Estados Unidos, ocupó el cargo de 1881 a 1885, Arthur (1829–1886) asumió la presidencia luego del asesinato del presidente James Garfield. Arthur firmó el Acta Pendleton, que elimina el sistema de botines y establece el mérito como base para la contratación de empleados federales.

Articles of Confederation > Artículos de la Confederación Plan de gobierno adoptado por el Congreso Continental, después de la Independencia de los Estados Unidos; se enunciaron como "un vínculo firme de amistad" entre los estados, pero le delegaron pocos poderes importantes al gobierno central.

assemble > congregar Reunirse con otras personas para expresar puntos de vista sobre asuntos públicos.

assessment > valuación Proceso para determinar el valor de una propiedad que será gravada.

assimilation > asimilación Proceso mediante el cual las personas de una cultura se integran en otra y se convierten en parte de ella.

at-large > elección general Elección de un funcionario público por los votantes de una unidad gubernamental completa, en vez de por los votantes de un distrito o subdivisión.

attorney general > procurador general Funcionario más alto del Departamento de Justicia.

autocracy > autocracia Forma de gobierno en la que una sola persona tiene poder político ilimitado.

B

backbenchers > diputados de segundo rango Miembro de la Cámara de los comunes de Gran Bretaña que no es líder del partido.

bail > fianza Suma de dinero que se exige que el acusado o la acusada pague como garantía de que se presentará en la corte en la fecha señalada.

balance the ticket > designar al compañero de fórmula Acción que, para reforzar sus oportunidades de ganar las elecciones, un candidato presidencial lleva a cabo cuando elige a un candidato a la vicepresidencia con base en sus características ideológicas, geográficas, raciales, étnicas, de género o de otro tipo.

Balkans > Balcanes Los Balcanes, a veces llamada península de los Balcanes, es una región geográfica en Europa central que generalmente incluye a Eslovenia, Croacia, Bosnia y Herzegovina, Serbia, Kosovo, Montenegro; Macedonia, Albania, Bulgaria, Rumania y Moldavia. El término puede tener diferentes interpretaciones geográficas, culturales e históricas.

ballot > papeleta electoral Medio que los votantes utilizan para indicar su preferencia en una elección.

ballot fatigue > fatiga al votar Fenómeno que se presenta cuando los votantes marcan menos casillas hacia el final de la papeleta electoral.

bankruptcy > bancarrota Procedimiento legal mediante el cual los bienes de una persona se distribuyen entre las personas con las que tiene deudas.

battleground States > estados reñidos Estados donde los resultados de las elecciones indican que cualquier candidato podría ser el ganador.

BCRA > BCRA (por su sigla en inglés) La Ley Bipartidista de Reforma de Campaña de 2002 intentó cerrar la brecha de los fondos no fiscalizados en las leyes de financiamiento de las campañas anteriores.

bench trial > juicio ante judicatura Proceso en el cual sólo el juez escucha el caso.

bicameral > bicameral Adjetivo que describe un cuerpo legislativo formado por dos cámaras.

Biden, Joe > Biden, Joe (1942–) Senador demócrata por Delaware; elegido por primera vez en 1972. Fungió como 47° vicepresidente de los Estados Unidos desde 2009 bajo la presidencia de Barack Obama.

bill > proyecto de ley Propuesta de ley que se presenta ante un cuerpo legislativo para su consideración.

bill of attainder > Escrito de proscripción y confiscación Acto legislativo que inflige un castigo sin que haya un juicio ante un jurado.

Bill of Rights > Carta de Derechos Las primeras diez enmiendas a la Constitución.

bills > proyectos de leyes Propuestas de leyes que se presentan ante un cuerpo legislativo para su consideración.

bipartisan > bipartidista Apoyado por dos partidos.

Blackstone, William > Blackstone, William (1723–1780) Juez inglés que escribió los *Comentarios acerca de las leyes de Inglaterra,* una serie de cuatro libros que tuvo una profunda influencia en los autores de la Declaración de Independencia y la Constitución de los Estados Unidos. Blackstone, importante personaje de la Ilustración, creía en la protección de los derechos de los inocentes, y en sustentar los juicios en el derecho consuetudinario, es decir, en fallos previos sobre asuntos similares.

Blaine, James G. > Blaine, James G. (1830–1893), congresista por Maine y presidente de la Cámara de representantes de 1869 a 1875, no tuvo éxito como candidato a la presidencia en 1876 y 1880. Ocupó el cargo de secretario de Estado en 1881 y, de nuevo, de 1889 a 1892.

blanket primary > elecciones primarias generales Proceso de elección en el que los votantes reciben una papeleta electoral grande que contiene los nombres de todos los candidatos, independientemente del partido, y en el cual pueden elegir libremente.

block grants > subsidios en conjunto Tipo de subsidios públicos federales que se ofrecen para un área particular pero definida en términos generales.

Boehner, John > Boehner, John (1949–) Congresista republicano de Cincinnati, Ohio, elegido para la Cámara de Representantes de los Estados Unidos en 1990. Fue líder mayoritario en 2006 y líder minoritario de 2007 a 2011. Se convirtió en presidente de la Cámara de Representantes en 2011.

Boston > Boston La ciudad más grande y capital de la mancomunidad de Massachusetts.

Bradley, Joseph P. > Bradley, Joseph P. Nombrado por el presidente Ulysses S. Grant, Joseph P. Bradley (1813–1892) sirvió como juez asociado de la Corte Suprema de 1870 a 1892. Bradley fue uno entre varios jueces que redujeron las garantías que la entonces recién aprobada Decimocuarta Enmienda otorgaba a los afroamericanos.

Brennan, William J. > Brennan, William J. (1906–1997) Al igual que Earl Warren, William J. Brennan, Jr., fue nombrado para la Corte Suprema por el presidente Dwight D. Eisenhower y, como Warren, Brennan sería uno de los jueces más liberales en la historia de la Corte, por sus votos en muchos casos de protección igualitaria. Estuvo en funciones de 1956 a 1990.

brief > alegato Reseña detallada presentada ante la Corte antes de dar un argumento oral; declaración escrita que presenta la postura legal de un partido y cita datos relevantes y precedentes legales.

Bryce, James > Bryce, James (1838–1922) Fue un político británico, embajador en los Estados Unidos de 1907 a 1913. Se hizo muy popular después de publicar *La República Norteamericana,* que constituye un estudio favorable del gobierno de los Estados Unidos

budget > presupuesto Un plan financiero para el uso del dinero, el personal y la propiedad.

bureaucracy > Presupuesto estatal Plan financiero de un estado para el uso del dinero público, sus empleados y sus propiedades.

bureaucrat > burocracia Estructura administrativa grande y compleja que gobierna los negocios cotidianos de una organización.

Bush, George H.W. > Bush, George H.W. Después de graduarse de la Universidad de Yale, Bush (nacido en 1924) inició su carrera en la industria del petróleo de Texas. En dos ocasiones, fue diputado en el Congreso en representación de Texas, y luego fue nombrado embajador frente a Naciones Unidas y director de la CIA. Bush fue vicepresidente de Ronald Reagan y fue elegido como el 41er Presidente, y ocupó el cargo de 1989 a 1993.

Bush, George W. > Bush, George W. (1946–) se graduó de la Universidad de Yale y de la Escuela de Negocios de Harvard antes de regresar a Texas a trabajar en la industria petrolera. Primero ocupó la gubernatura de Texas y, más tarde, fue elegido como 43er Presidente; ocupó el cargo de 2001 a 2009. Su elección significó la segunda ocasión en la historia estadounidense en la que el hijo de un Presidente (George H. W. Bush) llegó a convertirse en Presidente.

Byrd, Robert C. > Byrd, Robert C. (1917–2010) Representante al Congreso por Virginia Occidental de 1953 a 1959, y senador de 1959 a 2010; estuvo en funciones por más tiempo que cualquier otro legislador en la historia estadounidense. Se consideraba a sí mismo "hijo de las minas de carbón de los Apalaches" y dedicó su carrera política a luchar contra la pobreza en Virginia Occidental.

C

Cabinet > gabinete Cuerpo consultivo del Presidente que tradicionalmente está formado por los funcionarios más altos de los departamentos ejecutivos y otros agentes.

Calvert, George (Lord Baltimore) > Calvert, George (Lord Baltimore) Un miembro del parlamento que fundó Maryland como un refugio para católicos. Calvert (1578 o 1579–1632) llegó a América del Norte en 1628 pero no fue aceptado a causa de su religión. Regresó a Inglaterra y solicitó una cédula real para establecer una colonia en la que pudiera practicar su religión. La cédula fue concedida en 1632, poco después de su muerte.

capital > burócrata Persona que trabaja en una organización burocrática.

capital punishment > capital Todos los recursos creados por el hombre que se utilizan para producir bienes y servicios.

capitalism > pena capital La pena de muerte.

Capitol Hill > Capitol Hill El Capitolio de los Estados Unidos se localiza en el distrito histórico y residencial llamado Capitol Hill, en Washington, D.C. Otros edificios en Capitol Hill son la Corte Suprema de los Estados Unidos y la Biblioteca del Congreso. *Capitol Hill* también es una figura retórica que simplemente significa "el Congreso".

Carter, Jimmy > Carter, Jimmy (1924–) fue el 39° Presidente de los Estados Unidos y ocupó el cargo de 1977 a 1981. Ex oficial de la marina y gobernador de Georgia, Carter obtuvo el Premio Nobel de la Paz en 2002 y es autor de veintisiete libros. Durante su presidencia, Carter creó el Departamento de Educación, expandió el sistema de parques nacionales y entabló relaciones diplomáticas con la República Popular China.

Castro, Fidel > Castro, Fidel (1926–) era el líder político dictatorial de Cuba de 1959 a 2008. Mediante tácticas revolucionarias, hizo de la nación isleña el primer estado comunista en el Hemisferio occidental.

categorical grants > capitalismo Sistema económico en el que individuos tienen la libertad de poseer los medios de producción y de aumentar sus ganancias.

caucus > subsidio categórico Tipo de subsidio público federal; proporcionado para un propósito específico y rigurosamente definido.

censure > junta de dirigentes En función de instrumento nominativo, grupo de personas que comparten la misma ideología y que se reúnen para seleccionar a los candidatos que apoyarán en una elección.

certificate > amonestación Pronunciamiento de una condena formal.

Charles I, King > Carlos I, rey (1600–1649) fue rey de Inglaterra, Escocia e Irlanda de 1625 a 1649. Gobernó con mano dura y sus disputas con el parlamento provocaron una guerra civil. En 1649, Carlos fue declarado culpable de traición fue ejecutado.

charter > certificación Resultado del proceso en el que una corte inferior consulta a la Corte Suprema para que certifique una respuesta a una pregunta específica, tal como un procedimiento o una regla.

Chávez, Hugo > Chávez, Hugo (1954–2013) Llegó a la presidencia de Venezuela en 1999; obtuvo el cargo mediante un atentado contra la élite política tradicional en ese país. Conocido por ser directo y controvertido, Chávez insistió durante toda su presidencia en que su revolución socialista beneficiaría a todos en Venezuela, pero en especial a los pobres

checks and balances > carta constitucional Ley básica de una ciudad, su constitución; concesión de autoridad escrita otorgada por el rey.

Chiang Kai-shek > Chiang Kai-shek (1887–1975) Fue un militar y hombre de estado chino. Fue líder del Gobierno Nacionalista desde 1928 hasta 1949.

chief administrator > sistema de controles y equilibrios Sistema en el cual se traslapan las autoridades del poder legislativo, el poder ejecutivo y el poder judicial para permitir que cada poder verifique las acciones de los otros dos.

chief citizen > administrador en jefe Nombre que se le da al Presidente por ser el jefe de la administración del gobierno federal.

chief diplomat > primer ciudadano Nombre que se le da al Presidente por ser representante del pueblo y trabajar por el interés público.

chief economist > diplomático titular Nombre que se le da al Presidente por ser el arquitecto principal de la política exterior y un vocero ante otros países.

chief executive > economista en jefe Termino para referirse al Presidente en tanto supervisor la situación económica del país.

chief legislator > primer mandatario Nombre que se le da al Presidente porque está investido con el poder ejecutivo de los Estados Unidos.

chief of party > legislador en jefe Nombre que se le da al Presidente por ser arquitecto de la política pública y por ser la persona que determina la agenda del Congreso.

chief of state > jefe del partido Nombre que se le da al Presidente por ser el líder de su partido político.

Churchill, Winston > Churchill, Winston (1874–1965) Estadista británico que ocupó el cargo de primer ministro del Reino Unido, de 1940 a 1945, durante la mayor parte de la Segunda Guerra Mundial, y de 1951 a 1955. Fue el primer ciudadano honorario de los Estados Unidos y obtuvo el premio Nobel de Literatura.

citizen > jefe de estado Nombre que se le da al Presidente por ser el funcionario ceremonial de los Estados Unidos, el símbolo de toda la gente de la nación.

civil case > ciudadano Miembro de un estado o nación por nacimiento o naturalización, que se beneficia de todos los derechos civiles y que le debe lealtad a ese estado o nación.

civil disobedience > caso civil Caso relacionado con un asunto no criminal, como un litigio por contrato o una demanda por violación de patentes.

civil law > ley civil Área de la ley que se relaciona con la conducta humana, con litigios entre entidades privadas, así como entre partes privadas y el gobierno, que no están cubiertos bajo la ley penal.

civil liberties > libertades civiles Garantías que protegen la seguridad, las opiniones y la propiedad de las personas de actos arbitrarios del gobierno; entre ellas están la libertad de expresión y la libertad de religión.

civil rights > derechos civiles Término que designa actos positivos del gobierno con el objetivo de hacer realidad las garantías constitucionales para todo el pueblo, por ejemplo la prohibición de la discriminación.

civil service > servicio civil Grupo de empleados civiles que desempeñan el trabajo administrativo del gobierno.

civilian > civil Que no es militar.

civilian tribunal > tribunal civil Corte que actúa como parte del poder judicial y que está separada por completo de la institución militar.

clemency > clemencia Misericordia o piedad que dispensa el Presidente a un delincuente.

Clinton, Bill > Clinton, Bill (1946–) William J. Clinton fue elegido gobernador de Arkansas en 1978, y 42° Presidente para los periodos de 1993 a 2001. Durante su administración, los Estados Unidos disfrutaron en gran medida de un periodo de paz y crecimiento económico. En 1998 se convirtió en el segundo presidente impugnado por la Cámara de Representantes, pero el Senado lo declaró inocente y conservó su cargo.

Clinton, Hillary Rodham > Clinton, Hillary Rodham (1947–) se convirtió en la Primera dama de los Estados Unidos cuando su esposo, Bill Clinton, ganó la presidencia en 1993. En 2001, Clinton se hizo senadora por el estado de Nueva York y, mientras ocupaba ese cargo, intentó sin éxito ser candidata a la presidencia. En 2009, Clinton fue seleccionada para el cargo de secretaria de Estado en la administración del presidente Barack Obama, puesto que ejerció hasta su renuncia en 2013.

closed primary > elección primaria cerrada Elecciones para una nominación de un partido en la que sólo los miembros declarados del partido pueden votar.

cloture > limitación del debate Procedimiento que puede utilizarse para restringir o terminar un debate verbal de un cuerpo legislativo, especialmente en caso de una obstrucción.

coalition > coalición Alianza temporal de varios grupos que se juntan para alcanzar el poder mayoritario y controlar el gobierno.

coattail effect > efecto de refilón Efecto que produce la presencia de un candidato fuerte en la parte superior de una papeleta electoral y que ayuda a atraer votantes hacia otros candidatos de su mismo partido.

cold war > Guerra Fría Período de más de 40 años en el que las relaciones entre las dos superpotencias (Estados Unidos y la Unión Soviética) fueron por lo menos tensas, y a menudo hostiles; época de amenazas y de desarrollo armamentista.

collective security > seguridad colectiva Conservación de la paz y el orden internacionales.

collectivization > colectivización Hacer colectivos o propiedad del estado los medios de producción.

colonialism > colonialismo Control que tiene una nación sobre tierras extranjeras.

command economies > economía dirigida Sistema en el cual los burócratas del gobierno planean y dirigen la mayor parte de la actividad económica.

commander in chief > comandante en jefe Nombre que se le da al Presidente por ser el comandante de las Fuerzas Armadas de la nación.

Commerce and Slave Trade Compromise > Avenencia de Comercio y Trata de Esclavos Acuerdo durante la Convención Constitucional que protegió los intereses de los dueños de esclavos, al negarle al Congreso el poder de gravar la exportación de bienes desde cualquier estado y el poder de actuar, durante veinte años, en contra de la trata de esclavos.

commerce power > poder mercantil Poder exclusivo que tiene el Congreso para regular el comercio interestatal e internacional.

commission government > junta municipal Tipo de gobierno de la ciudad que tiene de tres a nueve comisionados, electos por voto popular, para formar el Consejo de la ciudad y combinan los poderes legislativos y ejecutivos en un solo cuerpo.

committee chair > presidente de comisión Miembro que encabeza una comisión permanente en un cuerpo legislativo.

common law > derecho consuetudinario Ley que no ha sido sancionada por un juez y se ha desarrollado a lo largo de los siglos, con base en ideas generalmente aceptadas de lo bueno y lo malo que se han ganado un reconocimiento judicial.

communism > comunismo Ideología que exige la propiedad colectiva, o estatal, de la tierra y de otros medios de producción.

commutation > conmutación Poder de reducir la duración de una sentencia o el monto de la multa por haber cometido un delito.

compromise > transigencia Acuerdo intermedio entre principios o sistemas opuestos, al que se llega mediante la modificación de algún aspecto de cada uno de ellos.

concurrent jurisdiction > jurisdicción coincidente Poder compartido por cortes federales y estatales para atender ciertos casos.

concurrent powers > poderes concurrentes Aquellos poderes que el gobierno nacional y los estados poseen y ejercen.

concurrent resolution > resolución conjunta Enunciado de una opinión sobre un asunto utilizado por la Cámara de Representantes y el Senado al actuar conjuntamente; no tiene el poder de la ley y no requiere la firma del Presidente.

concurring opinion > opinion coincidente Explicación escrita de los puntos de vista de uno o más jueces quienes apoyan una decisión alcanzada por una mayoría en la corte, pero desean añadir o recalcar un punto que no se remarcó en la decisión mayoritaria.

confederation > confederación Unión de diversos grupos para un propósito común.

conference committee > comité de consulta Comité conjunto temporal formado para reconciliar cualquier diferencia entre las versiones de un proyecto de ley propuesto por las dos cámaras legislativas.

Connecticut Compromise > Acuerdo de Connecticut Acuerdo alcanzado durante la Convención Constitucional que estableció que el Congreso debería estar integrado por un Senado donde cada estado estuviera representado de manera equitativa, y una Cámara de Representantes en la que la representación estuviera basada en la población de cada estado.

consensus > consenso Acuerdo general entre diversos grupos sobre temas fundamentales; acuerdo general sobre asuntos públicos.

constituencies > circunscripciones electorales Las personas e intereses que un funcionario electo representa.

constituent power > poder constituyente Poder no legislativo de la elaboración de la Constitución y del proceso de enmiendas constitucionales.

constitutional law > ley constitucional Está basada en la constitución de los Estados Unidos, las constituciones de los Estados y las interpretaciones judiciales de esos documentos.

constitutionalism > constitucionalismo Principio básico que establece que el gobierno y los gobernantes deben obedecer la ley; el gobierno de la ley.

containment > contención Política basada en la creencia de que si se pudiera evitar la expansión del régimen comunista, éste colapsaría debido a la fragilidad de su estructura interna.

content neutral > voto neutral El gobierno no regulará a las asambleas en lo concerniente a lo que se expresará en ellas.

continuing resolution > resolución ininterrumpida Medida que permite que las agencias continúen funcionando basándose en de las asignaciones del año anterior.

continuous body > cuerpo legislativo ininterrumpido Organismo del Estado (el Senado de los Estados Unidos, por ejemplo) cuya totalidad de escaños nunca se remplaza al mismo tiempo.

contract > contrato Acuerdo jurídicamente vinculante en el que una de las partes se compromete a hacer algo con o para un tercero.

controllable spending > gasto controlable Monto fijado por el Congreso y el Presidente para determinar cuánto dinero se dedicará anualmente para distintos rubros gubernamentales, como programas para la protección del ambiente y apoyos a la educación, entre otros.

convene > *convene* Reunir, o convocar, la sesión inaugural de la legislatura.

copyright > derechos de autor El derecho legal exclusivo de una persona para reproducir, publicar y vender sus propias creaciones literarias, musicales o artísticas.

council-manager government > gobierno de consejo-superintendente Modificación de la forma de gobierno de consejo-alcalde, que consiste en un consejo electo vigorosamente, un alcalde débil, y un superintendente nombrado por el consejo.

county > condado Unidad importante de gobierno local en gran parte de los estados.

courts-martial > corte marcial Corte integrada por personal militar para juzgar a quienes han sido acusados de violar la ley militar.

criminal case > caso criminal Caso en el que se juzga al acusado por cometer un delito, tal y como éste se define de acuerdo a la ley.

criminal law > derecho penal Área de la ley que define los agravios públicos y que establece su castigo.

Cultural Revolution > Revolución cultural Mao Zedong, presidente del Partido Comunista chino, convocó a este proceso durante su última década en el poder (1966–1976) para renovar el espíritu de la Revolución china. Guardias rojos, jóvenes y entregados, atacaron e intimidaron a intelectuales y a aquellos que carecían de fervor revolucionario. Algunos fueron enviados a campos de trabajo para ser reeducados.

Cunningham, Randy "Duke" > Cunningham, Randy "Duke" (1941–) Fue un aviador estrella de la marina estadounidense en la Guerra de Vietnam y después miembro de la Cámara de Representantes por el Partido Republicano de 1991 a 2005. Fue encontrado culpable de aceptar $2.4 millones en sobornos de contratistas militares, y sentenciado a más de ocho años de prisión en 2006.

customs duty > derecho de aduana Impuesto sobre los bienes introducidos a los Estados Unidos; también se conoce como arancel, impuesto sobre importaciones o tasa sobre importaciones.

D

de facto > *de facto* La situación tal y como existe de hecho.

de jure > *de jure* De acuerdo con la ley.

defendant > acusado En un juicio civil, es la persona en contra de quien el demandante pide ejecutar una acción judicial; en un caso penal, es la persona acusada de un delito.

deficit > déficit Diferencia anual entre los ingresos y los egresos.

deficit financing > financiamiento del déficit Práctica que consiste en subvencionar al gobierno mediante préstamos, a fin de compensar la diferencia entre los gastos y los ingresos gubernamentales.

deflation > deflación Disminución general de los precios.

delegated powers > poderes delegados Poderes explícitos, implícitos o inherentes que la Constitución transfiere al gobierno nacional.

delegates > delegados Personas con autoridad para representar a otros en una conferencia o convención; representantes; miembros del Congreso que votan según los deseos de sus constituyentes.

demand-side economics > economía de demanda Teoría que establece que un alza de los empleos debido a préstamos del gobierno producirá un incremento en los ingresos tributarios.

democracy > democracia Forma de gobierno en la cual la autoridad suprema reside en el pueblo.

democratic consolidation > consolidación democrática Proceso mediante el cual se establecen los factores necesarios para el éxito de una democracia.

democratization > democratización Cambio de una dictadura a una democracia mediante elecciones libres y justas.

denaturalization > desnaturalización Proceso mediante el cual los ciudadanos naturalizados pueden perder su ciudadanía de manera involuntaria.

Deng Xiaoping > Deng Xiaoping (1904–1997) llegó al poder en China en 1977, justo después de la impopular Revolución cultural que Mao Zedong inició en 1966. Deng siguió con el estilo autoritario de su predecesor, pero abrió a China a una economía de mercado que sacó a millones de campesinos de la pobreza.

deportation > deportación Proceso legal mediante el cual se le pide a los extranjeros que abandonen los Estados Unidos.

détente > distensión Palabra francesa que significa "relajamiento de las tensiones."

deterrence > disuasión Política que consiste en convertir a los Estados Unidos y sus aliados en una fuerza militar tan poderosa que su fortaleza desaliente, o prevenga, cualquier ataque.

devolution > delegación Transferencia de la autoridad del gobierno central a los gobiernos regionales.

dictatorship > dictadura Forma de gobierno en la que los gobernantes no pueden hacerse responsables ante la voluntad del pueblo; forma de gobierno donde el líder ejerce poder y autoridad absolutos.

diplomatic immunity > inmunidad diplomática Atributo mediante el cual los embajadores no están sujetos a las leyes del estado en el que están acreditados; condición en la que un embajador no está sujeto a las leyes del estado anfitión.

direct primary > elecciones primarias Elecciones realizadas dentro de un partido para escoger a los candidatos del partido para las elecciones generales.

discharge petition > petición de exoneración Procedimiento que permite a los miembros reiniciar (después de 30 días; 7 días en el caso del comité de reglas) la discusión para considerar una propuesta de ley que se había suspendido en una comisión de debate.

discount rate > tasa de descuento Tasa de interés que debe pagar un banco que toma un préstamo del Banco de la Reserva Federal.

discriminate > discriminar Dar un trato a ciertos grupos de personas diferente del que se da a personas que forman parte de otros grupos.

discrimination > discriminación Prejuicio, injusticia.

disenfranchised > privación del derecho al voto Acción que consiste en negarle a alguien el derecho de votar.

dissenting opinions > opiniones disidentes Opinión escrita por un juez que explica por qué está en desacuerdo con la decisión de la Corte.

District of Columbia > Distrito de Columbia El Distrito de Columbia (D. C.) es la sede del gobierno de los Estados Unidos de América. Se localiza entre Maryland y Virgina, en el margen del río Potomac, y tiene una extensión de 68 millas cuadradas. La ciudad de Washignton, D. C. abarca la totalidad del Distrito de Columbia.

district plan > plan de distrito Propuesta para elegir a los electores presidenciales, mediante la cual se seleccionarían dos electores en cada estado, de acuerdo con el voto popular de todo ese estado, y los otros electores se elegirían de manera separada en cada uno de los distritos del Congreso de ese estado.

divine right of kings > derecho divino de los monarcas La creencia de que Dios otorga autoridad a los regímenes.

division of powers > división de poderes Principio básico del federalismo; estipulaciones constitucionales que establecen que los poderes gubernamentales están separados según la ubicación geográfica (en los Estados Unidos, entre el gobierno nacional y los estatales).

docket > agenda Lista de casos por atender en una corte.

domestic affairs > asuntos internos Todas las cuestiones no relacionadas con el campo de los asuntos exteriores.

double jeopardy > doble juicio Parte de la 5ª Enmienda que establece que no se puede poner en riesgo la vida de una persona o su integridad física dos veces. Una vez que se ha juzgado por un crimen a una persona, no puede volvérsele a juzgar por el mismo delito.

Douglas, William O. > Douglas, William O. (1898–1980) fue el juez que pasó el segundo mayor tiempo en funciones en la Corte Suprema. Nombrado como juez asociado de la Corte por el presidente Franklin D. Roosevelt en abril de 1939, mantuvo su cargo por 36 años, hasta su retiro en noviembre de 1975.

draft > reclutamiento Conscripción o servicio militar obligatorio.

due process > proceso legal establecido El gobierno debe actuar con justicia y de acuerdo con las reglas establecidas en todo lo que hace.

Due Process Clause > Cláusula del Debido Proceso Parte de la 14.ª enmienda que garantiza que ningún estado negará los derechos básicos a su pueblo.

duty > arancel Impuesto a las importaciones.

E

economic protest parties > partidos de protesta económica Partidos surgidos en tiempos de descontento económico, que carecen de una base ideológica bien definida, están insatisfechos por las condiciones presentes y exigen mejoras.

Eisenhower, Dwight > Eisenhower, Dwight Elegido como Presidente en 1953, Eisenhower (1890–1969) traía consigo el prestigio de haber sido comandante de las Fuerzas aliadas en Europa en la Segunda Guerra Mundial, la coronación de una larga carrera militar. Fungió como 34º Presidente de 1953 a 1961, abogó por la paz y apoyó la abolición de la segregación en la escuelas y en el ejército.

electoral college > colegio electoral Grupo de personas elegidas cada cuatro años en todos los estados y en el Distrito de Columbia a fin de elegir formalmente al Presidente y Vicepresidente.

electorate > electorado Todas las personas que tienen derecho a votar en una elección determinada.

eminent domain > dominio supremo Poder de un gobierno de expropiar la propiedad privada para uso público.

enabling act > ley de habilitación Ley del Congreso que orienta al pueblo de un territorio de los Estados Unidos para que redacte una propuesta de la constitución para el estado, como un paso hacia la admisión de dicho estado dentro de la Unión.

English Bill of Rights > Declaración Inglesa de los Derechos Documento redactado por el Parlamento y aceptado por William y Mary de Inglaterra en 1689, elaborado para evitar el abuso de poder por parte de los monarcas ingleses; constituye la base de gran parte del gobierno y la política estadounidenses actuales.

engrossed > transcrito Proyecto de ley impreso en su forma final.

entitlement > derecho Beneficio, establecido por una ley federal, que se debe pagar a todos los que cumplan los requisitos, por ejemplo: Medicare, los cupones de alimento y las pensiones para los veteranos.

entitlements > derechos Beneficio, establecido por una ley federal, que se debe pagar a todos los que cumplan los requisitos para ser elegibles, por ejemplo: el seguro médico, los cupones de alimento y la pensión para los veteranos.

entrepreneur > empresario Persona con el impulso y la ambición para combinar los recursos de la tierra, de la mano de obra y del capital para producir bienes u ofrecer servicios.

equal protection > protección equitativa Concepto según el cual las leyes nacionales o las de los estados deben tratar a cada individuo de la misma forma como se trataría a otros individuos que tienen condiciones similares o están en circunstancias similares.

equity > *equity* Una rama de la ley que complementa la ley común mediante la adopción de un enfoque preventivo.

espionage > espionaje Acto de espiar.

Establishment Clause > Cláusula del Establecimiento Forma parte de la Primera Enmienda de la Constitución y garantiza la separación de la Iglesia del Estado.

estate tax > impuesto testamentario Gravamen sobre los bienes de una persona que muere.

ex post facto law > ley ex post facto Ley que se aplica a un acto cometido con anterioridad a la aprobación de la ley.

excise tax > impuesto al consumo Gravamen sobre la manufactura, la venta o el consumo de bienes y/o al suministro de servicios.

exclusionary rule > regla de exclusión Regla de acuerdo con la cual la evidencia obtenida como resultado de una acción ilegal de la policía no puede utilizarse contra la persona arrestada.

exclusive powers > poderes exclusivos Poderes que sólo el gobierno nacional puede ejercer.

executive agreement > acuerdo ejecutivo Pacto establecido de manera directa entre el Presidente y otro jefe un estado extranjero; pacto internacional obligatorio que tiene el poder de una ley pero que no requiere, a diferencia de un tratado, de la aprobación del Senado.

Executive Article > Artículo del Ejecutivo Segundo artículo de la Constitución. Define la presidencia y le otorga el poder ejecutivo del gobierno federal al Presidente.

executive departments > oficinas del poder ejecutivo A menudo llamadas Oficinas del Gabinete; son las unidades tradicionales de la administración federal.

Executive Office of the President > Oficina ejecutiva del Presidente Organización compleja, que abarca diversas oficinas separadas, cuyo personal está integrado por los consejeros y asistentes más cercanos al Presidente.

executive order > orden ejecutiva Directiva, regla o reglamento expedido por un primer mandatario o sus subordinados, con base en su autoridad estatutaria o constitucional, y que tiene el poder de una ley.

executive power > poder ejecutivo Poder para ejecutar, administrar y obligar al cumplimiento de la ley.

executive privilege > privilegio ejecutivo Poder que tiene el Presidente para rehusarse a revelar información.

expatriation > expatriación Proceso legal mediante el cual ocurre la pérdida de ciudadanía.

expressed powers > poderes explícitos Aquellos poderes delegados del gobierno nacional que se señalan explícitamente en la Constitución; también se conocen como los "poderes ennumerados".

extradition > extradición Proceso legal a través del cual un fugitivo de la justicia de un estado se retorna a ese estado.

F

factors of production > factores de producción Recursos básicos que se utilizan para elaborar todos los bienes y servicios.

failed states > estados fallidos Países con un sistema de seguridad nulo, una economía muy deteriorada, sistemas de asistencia de salud y de educación en crisis y donde prospera la corrupción.

FECA > FECA (por su sigla en inglés) La Ley Federal de las Campañas Electorales de 1971 fue la primera ley federal en regular el uso del dinero en las campañas presidenciales y del Congreso.

federal budget > presupuesto federal Documento financiero detallado que contiene las estimaciones de las recaudaciones y gastos que anticipan los ingresos y egresos federales durante el año fiscal venidero.

Federal Election Commission (FEC) > Comisión electoral federal (FEC, por su sigla en inglés) Una agencia independiente en el poder ejecutivo que administra toda la legislación federal concerniente al financiamiento de las campañas.

federal government > Gobierno Federal Forma de gobierno en la que los poderes están divididos entre un gobierno central y diversos gobiernos locales.

federalism > federalismo Sistema de gobierno en el que una constitución escrita divide los poderes del gobierno, entre un gobierno central y diversos gobiernos regionales.

Federalists > federalistas Personas que apoyaron la ratificación de la Constitución entre 1787 y 1788.

Feingold, Russ > Feingold, Russ Senador demócrata por Wisconsin de 1993 a 2010, Feingold fue uno de los patrocinadores de la Ley Bipartidista de Reforma Electoral de 2002.

felony > felonía Un crimen grave que puede castigarse con una gran multa, la prisión o incluso la muerte.

feudalism > feudalismo Sistema relativamente organizado en el cual los grandes señores les concedían sus tierras a otros señores de menor autoridad.

filibuster > obstruccionismo Tácticas de demora en las que senadores monopolizan el pleno del Senado con discursos u otras dilataciones para que se evite una votación sobre algún proyecto de ley.

First Lady > Primera dama La esposa del Presidente.

fiscal policy > política económica Métodos varios que usa el gobierno para obtener y gastar dinero.

fiscal year > año fiscal Período de 12 meses utilizado por el gobierno y el mundo de los negocios para su contabilidad, presupuesto, recaudación de ingresos y otros propósitos financieros.

527 organizations > organizaciones 527 Grupos de activistas políticos registrados de acuerdo con la Sección 527 del Código Interno de Ingresos (Internal Revenue Code), que no están asociados a ningún partido político pero tratan de influir en sus políticas y están autorizados para recaudar sumas de dinero ilimitadas.

floor consideration > consideración de la sala Proceso mediante el cual la Cámara de Representantes o el Senado consideran y reaccionan a las leyes propuestas.

floor leaders > líderes de fracciones Partidistas miembros de la Cámara de Representantes y del Senado elegidos por sus partidos con el objeto de llevar a cabo las decisiones partidistas e impulsar la acción legislativa a fin de que se cumplan los propósitos partidistas.

Ford, Gerald > Ford, Gerald (1913–2006) fue Presidente de los Estados Unidos de 1974 a 1977. Cuando el presidente Nixon se vio forzado a dejar la presidencia en 1974 por el escándalo de Watergate, el vicepresidente Ford ocupó el cargo durante el resto del periodo de Nixon. Ford se empeñó en mantener el poderío estadounidense en el extranjero y se esforzó en evitar una nueva guerra en Oriente Medio. Ford perdió la presidencia en 1976 por los problemas económicos, los efectos de Watergate y haber otorgado el perdón al ex presidente Nixon.

foreign affairs > asuntos exteriores Relaciones de una nación con otros países.

foreign aid > ayuda extranjera Auxilio militar y económico a otros países.

foreign policy > política exterior Conjunto de políticas conformado por todas las posturas y acciones que una nación asume en cada uno de los aspectos de sus relaciones con otros países; todo lo que el gobierno de una nación expresa y hace respecto a los asuntos mundiales.

formal amendment > enmienda formal Cambio o adición que se convierte en parte del lenguaje escrito de la Constitución misma, mediante uno de los cuatro métodos enunciados de la Constitución.

Framers > redactores de la Constitución Grupo de delegados que esbozaron la Constitución de los Estados Unidos en la Convención de Filadelfia en 1787.

franchise > sufragio Derecho a votar.

franking privilege > exención de franquicia Beneficio otorgado a los miembros del Congreso que les permite enviar por correo cartas y otros materiales gratis.

Franklin, Benjamin > Franklin, Benjamin Escritor, inventor, diplomático y legislador estadounidense, Franklin (1706–1790) propuso el Plan de Unión de Albany, que preveía los beneficios de la unidad entre las Colonias. Más tarde, firmó la Declaración de Independencia y ayudó a elaborar la Constitución, al insistir a los delegados que cooperaran y firmaran el borrador final.

free enterprise system > sistema de libre empresa Sistema económico caracterizado por la propiedad privada o corporativa de los bienes de capital; inversiones que están determinadas por una decisión privada, en vez del control estatal, y están sujetas a un mercado libre.

Free Exercise Clause > Cláusula de la Libertad de Cultos Segunda parte de la garantía constitucional de libertad religiosa, que garantiza a todos el derecho de creer en lo que se escoja en cuestiones de religión.

free market > mercado libre Mercado en el cual los compradores y vendedores tienen la libertad de comprar y vender como lo deseen.

full faith and credit > Cláusula de Fe y Crédito Cabal Cláusula constitucional según la cual cada estado acepta los actos públicos, documentos y procedimientos judiciales de cualquier otro estado.

Full Faith and Credit Clause > Cláusula de entera fe y crédito Requisito constitucional según el cual cada estado acepta los actos públicos, documentos y procedimientos judiciales de cualquier otro estado.

fundamental laws > leyes fundamentales Leyes de importancia primordial y duradera que no se pueden cambiar con facilidad.

Gallup, George > Gallup, George (1901–1984) era un encuestador y estadístico que fundó la famosa Encuesta Gallup. Además de realizar encuestas y desarrollar nuevos métodos para garantizar la precisión de los sondeos, Gallup fue profesor y escritor. También fundó el American Institute of Public Opinion, el British Institute of Public Opinion y el Audience Research Institute, Inc.

Garfield, James > Garfield, James (1831–1881) fue el 20° Presidente de los Estados Unidos; ocupó el cargo de marzo a septiembre de 1881. Tiene el récord del segundo periodo más corto en el cargo. Ex general de división de la Guerra Civil y miembro de la Cámara de Representantes por Ohio durante nueve periodos consecutivos, el presidente Garfield recibió un disparo de Charles J. Guiteau en 1881 después de negarse a nombrarlo para un cargo diplomático.

gender gap > brecha de género Diferencias medibles entre las elecciones partidistas actuales de los hombres y las mujeres.

general elections > elecciones generales Elecciones programadas regularmente en las que los votantes hacen una selección final de los funcionarios públicos.

George II, King > Jorge II, rey (1683–1760) fue rey de Gran Bretaña de 1727 a 1760. La colonia de Georgia fue nombrada en su honor después de que firmó el decreto real que concedía la colonia a sus veinte fiduciarios en 1732. El rey Jorge consideró que la colonia sería una zona de defensa importante entre los territorios controlados por España al sur y el resto de las colonias inglesas al norte.

gerrymandering > demarcación arbitraria Establecimiento de los límites de los distritos electorales de modo que den ventaja a un partido.

gift tax > impuesto a las donaciones Gravamen sobre las donaciones hechas por una persona viva.

Ginsburg, Ruth Bader > Ginsburg, Ruth Bader (1933–) Fue la segunda mujer nombrada para la Corte Suprema. Fue nominada por el presidente Clinton para el cargo de jueza asociada de la Corte Suprema en 1993, y continúa en funciones.

globalization > globalización Interdependencia económica entre naciones del mundo.

Glorious Revolution > Revolución Gloriosa Los acontecimientos que, en 1688, llevaron al parlamento a invitar a Guillermo y María de Orange a remplazar pacíficamente al rey Jacobo II a condición de que reconocieran la autoridad del parlamento y los derechos individuales. Con la firma de la Carta de Derechos, la Revolución Gloriosa ayudó a calmar la lucha centenaria por la supremacía entre el monarca y el parlamento en Inglaterra.

Gorbachev, Mikhail > Gorbachov, Mijaíl Secretario general del Partido Comunista de la Unión Soviética de 1985 a 1991, Gorbachov (nacido en 1931) asumió la presidencia de la Unión Soviética en 1990. En un solo año, su empeño en democratizar el sistema político y descentralizar la economía llevó al colapso de la Unión Soviética. Gorbachov renunció a la presidencia en 1991. Recibió el Premio Nobel de la Paz en 1990.

government > gobierno Institución mediante la cual una sociedad lleva a cabo y hace cumplir sus políticas públicas.

government corporations > empresa de servicios públicos Instituciones del poder ejecutivo que están sujetas a la dirección y el control del Presidente, formadas por el Congreso para que realicen determinadas actividades de tipo empresarial.

grand jury > gran jurado Dispositivo formal a través del cual puede acusarse a una persona de un crimen serio.

Grant, Ulysses S. > Grant, Ulysses S. (1822–1885) fue Presidente de los Estados Unidos de 1869 a 1877. Ganó la elección tras haber sido el general de la Unión que llevó a los Estados Unidos a la victoria sobre los Estados Confederados de América durante la Guerra Civil estadounidense. Grant defendió los derechos de los afroestadounidenses, las políticas para los indígenas norteamericanos y la reforma al servicio civil. Además, apoyó la creación de un ferrocarril transcontinental. También puso en marcha una política exterior fructífera y consiguió mejorar las relaciones anglo–estadounidenses.

grants-in-aid programs > programa de subvención de fondos públicos Subvenciones de dinero o de otros recursos federales para los estados, sus ciudades, condados y otras unidades locales.

grass-roots pressures > presión popular Presión que los miembros de un grupo de interés o la población en general ejercen sobre funcionarios públicos.

Great Leap Forward > Gran Salto Adelante Plan quinquenal de 1958 que fue un intento de modernizar rápidamente a China.

gross domestic product > producto interno bruto Cantidad total de bienes y servicios producidos por un país cada año.

Group of 8 (G8) > Grupo de los Ocho Foro conformado, en 1975, por ocho de los países más industrializados del mundo: los Estados Unidos, Japón, Alemania, Francia, Gran Bretaña, Italia, Canadá y Rusia.

Guantanamo Bay, Cuba > Bahía de Guantánamo, Cuba Los Estados Unidos la rentaron a Cuba en 1903. En la bahía de Guantánamo se localiza una base naval que opera desde entonces. A partir del 11 de enero de 2002, la base retiene individuos capturados por el ejército estadounidense durante la Guerra contra el Terrorismo. Este centro de detención causa controversia desde su apertura, y la suerte de sus prisioneros se debate acaloradamente desde las perspectivas legal y moral.

H

Hamilton, Alexander > Hamilton, Alexander (1755 o 1757–1804) emigró a América del Norte en 1772 desde las Indias Occidentales Británicas. Se enroló en el Ejército Continental en 1776, bajo el mando del general Washington. Ocupó diversos cargos de gobierno, como el de miembro del Congreso Constitucional y de la Convención Constitucional. Estudió derecho y ejerció esa profesión en la ciudad de Nueva York. Hamilton fue secretario del Tesoro en el gabinete del presidente Washington. Fue herido de muerte en un duelo con Aaron Burr en 1804.

hard money > fondos fiscalizados Aportaciones de campaña, realizadas directamente a los candidatos, que deben ser restringidas y enteradas al gobierno; dinero de campaña que está sujeto a las regulaciones de la FEC.

hard-liners > radicales Los que luchan por mantener el status quo.

Harrison, William Henry > Harrison, William Henry Elegido como 9° Presidente en 1841, Harrison (1773–1841) fue el primer presidente muerto en funciones. Nacido en una familia aristocrática de terratenientes de Virginia, pasó mucho tiempo en el Noroeste, ganado títulos sobre tierras indígenas y dirigiendo esfuerzos para contener los ataques indígenas. Enfermó de neumonía y murió a sólo cuatro meses de haber asumido el cargo.

heterogeneous > heterogéneo De diferente raza, familia o especie; compuesto por una mezcla de elementos.

Hobbes, Thomas > Hobbes, Thomas (1588–1679) Filósofo inglés que consideraba que las personas y las naciones estaban en pugna constante por el poder y la riqueza. Pensaba que la monarquía absoluta era la mejor forma de gobierno para Inglaterra. Desconfiaba de la democracia, pero pensaba que representantes autorizados de la voz del pueblo podrían evitar que el monarca fuera injusto o cruel.

Holmes, Jr., Oliver Wendell > Holmes, Jr., Oliver Wendell (1841–1935) Fue un juez de la Corte Suprema de justicia de los Estados Unidos de 1902 a 1932, a quien se le daba el sobrenombre de "The Great Dissenter" (El gran disidente).

Hoover, Herbert > Hoover, Herbert (1874–1964) se graduó de Stanford como ingeniero minero y comenzó su carrera en China. Luego ocupó diversos cargos humanitarios en el extranjero, incluida la jefatura de la American Relief Administration en Europa. Fue elegido como 31er presidente en 1928; unos cuantos meses antes de la crisis de los mercados de 1929 que sumió a la nación en una grave depresión.

Hudson River > río Hudson Una vía fluvial de 315 millas de largo que corre de norte a sur en el este del estado de Nueva York.

I

ideological > ideológico(a) Basado(a) en un conjunto particular de creencias; lo ideológico constituye una concepción amplia de asuntos sociales, económicos y políticos.

immigrants > inmigrantes Personas que son admitidas legalmente en calidad de residente permanente de un país.

impeach > impugnar Presentar cargos formales en contra de un funcionario público.

implied powers > poderes implícitos Aquellos poderes delegados del gobierno nacional que se sugieren o están implícitos por los poderes explícitos establecidos en la Constitución; aquellos que son "necesarios y pertinentes" para realizar los poderes explícitos.

import quota > cuota de importación Límite sobre la cantidad de un producto que se puede importar a un país.

income tax > impuesto sobre la renta Gravamen sobre el ingreso de los individuos y/o corporaciones.

incorporation > incorporación Proceso mediante el cual un estado establece a una ciudad como un cuerpo legal; el término proviene de las palabras latinas *in* (dentro) y *corpus* (cuerpo).

incumbent > titular Funcionario público actual.

independent agencies > oficinas independientes Agencias adicionales creadas por el Congreso y que se ubican fuera de los departamentos del Gabinete.

independent executive agencies > oficinas ejecutivas independientes Agencias dirigidas por un solo administrador que tienen subunidades operativas regionales pero que carecen del estatus del Gabinete.

independent regulatory commissions > comisiones regulatorias independientes Agencias independientes cuya función es regular aspectos importantes de la economía de la nación, en su mayoría fuera del control y dirección del Presidente.

independents > Independientes Término usado para describir a las personas que no están afiliadas a un partido.

indictment > denuncia Queja formal que el fiscal expone ante un gran jurado, que incluye cargos al acusado por uno o más crímenes.

inferior courts > cortes inferiores Las cortes federales menores, que están por debajo de la Corte Suprema.

inflation > inflación Incremento general de precios en la economía.

information > acusación del fiscal Acusación oficial presentada por un acusador sin acción de parte del jurado.

inherent powers > poderes inherentes Aquellos poderes que, se presume, son delegados al gobierno nacional constitucionalmente, debido a que es el gobierno de un estado soberano de la comunidad mundial.

inheritance tax > impuesto sobre la herencia Gravamen sobre lo que hereda un beneficiario.

initiative > iniciativa Proceso en el que determinado número de votantes calificados firman peticiones a favor de una propuesta que se pasa después directamente a la papeleta electoral.

injunction > mandato Orden judicial que fuerza o limita el desempeño de determinado acto, mediante la intervención de un particular o un funcionario público.

integration > integración Proceso mediante el cual se ofrece a un grupo participación igualitaria dentro de la sociedad.

interest > Interés Cargo que se hace por el dinero prestado; por lo general es un porcentaje de la cantidad prestada.

interest group > grupo de interés Organizaciones privadas cuyos miembros comparten determinados puntos de vista y trabajan para dar forma a las políticas públicas.

International Monetary Fund (IMF) > Fondo Monetario Internacional (FMI) Organismo creado en 1944 para supervisar el sistema monetario internacional.

interstate compacts > pacto interestatal Acuerdo formal suscrito con el consentimiento del Congreso, entre dos estados o entre un estado y un estado extranjero, el cual está autorizado por la Constitución.

involuntary servitude > servidumbre involuntaria Trabajo forzado.

isolationism > aislacionismo Rechazo voluntario a verse involucrado, de manera general, en los asuntos del resto del mundo.

Isthmus of Panama > Istmo de Panamá La franja estrecha de tierra que se encuentra entre el mar Caribe y el océano Pacífico, en Panamá. En él se localiza el Canal de Panamá.

item veto > veto de artículo Un gobernador puede vetar uno o más artículos de una propuesta de ley, sin rechazar toda la medida.

J

Jackson, Andrew > Jackson, Andrew Conocido como "Old Hickory" (viejo nogal) por su dureza y su personalidad agresiva, Jackson (1767–1845) fue el séptimo Presidente de los Estados Unidos, y ocupó el cargo de 1829 a 1837. Se conoce a su movimiento político como Democracia Jacksoniana, porque creía que el hombre común debía ser tomado en cuenta por el gobierno. Es el único presidente que peleó tanto la Guerra de Independencia, en su adolescencia, como la Guerra de 1812, en la que ganó fama militar. También es el primer presidente procedente del oeste de los montes Apalaches.

Jackson, Robert H. > Jackson, Robert H. (1892–1954) fue juez de la Corte Suprema de justicia de los Estados Unidos de 1941 a 1954. Es conocido por su opinión en el juicio de la *Junta de Educación de Virginia Occidental* contra *Barnette,* de 1943, que amplió el alcance de la garantía de libertad de expresión contenida en la 1ª Enmienda.

Jamestown > Jamestown Primer asentamiento inglés permanente en América del Norte; fundado en 1607 en Virginia y nombrado en honor del rey Jacobo (James) I. La fundación de Jamestown marcó la entrada de Inglaterra en la competencia por las Américas, que España había dominado desde los viajes de Cristóbal Colón a finales del siglo XV.

Jay, John > Jay, John (1745–1829) Fue un abogado de Nueva York, presidente del Segundo Congreso Continental, diplomático, primer presidente de la Corte Suprema estadounidense y gobernador de Nueva York. Su postura era moderada frente a Gran Bretaña antes de la Declaración de Independencia. Jay apoyaba un gobierno centralizado fuerte y luchó por la ratificación de la Constitución de los Estados Unidos. También ayudó a preparar el borrador de la Constitución del estado de Nueva York y sirvió como primer presidente de la corte de ese estado. Ayudó a negociar y a poner en práctica términos liberales para la paz con Gran Bretaña y fue el primer secretario de Asuntos exteriores, antes de que George Washington lo nombrara primer presidente de la Corte Suprema de Justicia.

Jefferson, Thomas > Jefferson, Thomas (1743–1826) fue un firme defensor de la democracia y los derechos civiles, y escribió la Declaración de la Independencia y el Estatuto de Libertad Religiosa de Virginia. Fungió como secretario de Estado en la gestión de George Washington y como vicepresidente en la de John Adams, y fue el tercer Presidente de los Estados Unidos (1801–1809). Durante su presidencia, los Estados Unidos compraron a Francia el territorio de Luisiana, expandiendo su extensión 827,000 millas cuadradas al oeste del río Mississppi.

Jim Crow laws > Leyes de Jim Crow Categoría de leyes enunciadas con el fin de discriminar principalmente a los afroestadounidenses.

John, King > Juan sin Tierra, rey (1167–1216) fue rey de Inglaterra de 1199 a 1216. Poco después de ser coronado, estalló la guerra entre Inglaterra y Francia. Después de varias derrotas importantes, se dispararon los impuestos y el monarca se convirtió en un soberano implacable. Esto enfureció a los barones que obligaron a Juan a firmar la Carta Magna en 1215.

Johnson, Andrew > Johnson, Andrew (1808–1875) Fue el 17° presidente de los Estados Unidos. Como vicepresidente de Abraham Lincoln, Johnson asumió la presidencia cuando Lincoln fue asesinado. Ocupó el cargo de 1865 a 1869.

Johnson, Lyndon > Johnson, Lyndon (1908–1973) Fue el 36° Presidente de los Estados Unidos de 1963 a 1969. Fue elegido vicepresidente y ascendió a la presidencia al momento del asesinato del presidente John F. Kennedy. En 1964, promulgó la Ley de los Derechos Civiles.

Johnson, Richard M. > Johnson, Richard M. (1780–1850) Fue el noveno vicepresidente de la nación, ocupando el cargo de 1837 a 1841, durante la presidencia de Martin Van Buren. Johnson fue el único vicepresidente escogido por el Senado.

joint committee > comité conjunto Comité legislativo compuesto por miembros de ambas cámaras.

joint resolution > resolución conjunta Propuesta de acción que tiene el poder de una ley cuando se aprueba; a menudo tiene que ver con circunstancias especiales o asuntos temporales.

judicial activism > activismo judicial Filosofía judicial que argumenta que los jueces deberían interpretar y aplicar las condiciones de la Constitución y del derecho escrito considerando los cambios progresivos de condiciones y valores.

judicial power > poder judicial Poder para interpretar las leyes, determinar su significado y resolver las disputas que surgen dentro de la sociedad.

judicial restraint > restricción judicial Filosofía judicial que argumenta que los jueces deberían tomar decisiones sobre sus casos basándose en la intención original de los creadores de la Declaración de Derechos o los que promulgan los estatutos del caso, o en el precedente.

judicial review > revisión judicial Poder de una corte para determinar la constitucionalidad de una acción gubernamental.

jurisdiction > jurisdicción Autoridad de una corte para atender un caso.

jury > jurado Conjunto de personas seleccionadas de acuerdo con la ley para que escuchen la evidencia y decidan cuestiones de hecho en un caso de la corte.

jus sanguinis > *jus sanguinis* Ley de la sangre que define la ciudadanía con base en la ciudadanía de los padres.

jus soli > *jus soli* Ley del territorio que determina la ciudadanía con base en el lugar de nacimiento de la persona.

justice of the peace > Juez de paz Juez que está en el nivel inferior del sistema judicial estatal y preside las cortes de justicia.

K

Kagan, Elena > Kagan, Elena (1960–) Fue la cuarta mujer designada para la Corte Suprema. El presidente Obama la nominó para el cargo de Procurador general de los Estados Unidos en 2009. Después de un año en el cargo, el presidente Obama la nominó como jueza asociada de la Corte Suprema en 2010, y todavía ocupa ese cargo.

Kennedy, John F. > Kennedy, John F. (1917–1963) fue la persona más joven que se haya elegido como Presidente. Su discurso de asunción de 1963 exhortaba a los ciudadanos a "No (preguntarse) lo que su país puede hacer por ustedes, pregúntense lo que ustedes pueden hacer por su país". El 22 de noviembre de 1963, Kennedy fue asesinado en Texas.

Kerry, John > Kerry, John (1943–) sirvió en el ejército durante la Guerra de Vietnam, por lo que ganó una estrella de plata, una estrella de bronce y tres corazones púrpura. A pesar de esta historia de servicio, era un miembro activo de Vietnam Veterans Against the War. Kerry fue Senador de los Estados Unidos por Massachusetts entre 1985 y 2013, y fue el candidato demócrata a la presidencia en 2004 y 2013. Kerry ocupó el cargo de secretario de Estado en la administración del presidente Barack Obama.

Keynes, John Maynard > Keynes, John Maynard (1883–1946) fue un influyente economista británico, conocido principalmente por su revolucionaria teoría económica que se ocupa de las causas del desempleo prolongado. Keynes pensaba que el gobierno es el responsable de estabilizar la economía mediante el uso de políticas fiscales (impuestos y programas de gastos). Creía que en los periodos de depresión, el gobierno debía incrementar sus gastos, reducir impuestos o hacer ambas cosas para estimular la economía.

keynote address > discurso de apertura Alocución dada en una convención de partido para establecer el tono de la convención y de la futura campaña.

Khomeini, Ayatollah > Jomeini, Ayatola (1902–1989) fue un líder y clérigo iraní chiita (musulmán). Encabezó la revolución que derrocó al sah (líder) de Irán, en 1979. Más tarde, él mismo se convirtió en líder de Irán, e impuso tanto leyes políticas como religiosas durante diez años.

King, Jr., Martin Luther > King, Jr., Martin Luther (1929–1968) Hombre religioso, activista y líder afroamericano, King es conocido por su papel en el Movimiento Afroestadounidense por los Derechos Civiles, en el que defendía la resistencia pacífica frente a la discriminación y la segregación en el Sur.

L

labor union > sindicato laboral Organización de trabajadores que comparten el mismo tipo de trabajo, o que laboran en la misma industria y que busca impulsar políticas gubernamentales que beneficien a sus miembros.

laissez-faire theory > laissez-faire Teoría que sugiere que el gobierno debería desempeñar un papel muy limitado dentro de la sociedad.

law of supply and demand > ley de la oferta y la demanda Ley que establece que cuando los suministros de bienes y servicios son abundantes, los precios tienden a bajar; cuando los suministros escasean, los precios tienden a subir.

Leahy, Patrick > Leahy, Patrick (1940–) Demócrata por el estado de Vermont, Leahy fue elegido senador por primera vez en 1974 y luego presidente *pro tempore* del Senado en 2012.

legal tender > moneda de curso legal Cualquier moneda que un acreedor debe aceptar, por ley, como pago de una deuda.

legislative power > poder legislativo Poder para hacer una ley y redactar políticas públicas.

legitimacy > legitimidad Crencia que un gobierno tiene el derecho de crear políticas públicas.

Lenin, Vladimir > Lenin, Vladimir (1870–1924) Líder de la Revolución Bolchevique y arquitecto del Partido Comunista y de su control sobre la Unión Soviética. Para el momento de su muerte, en 1924, la Unión Soviética se había transformado en un estado con un régimen de partido único que controlaba las instituciones sociales, políticas y económicas del país.

libel > libelo Utilización falsa y maliciosa de la palabra impresa.

liberal constructionist > construccionista liberal Aquel que argumenta una amplia interpretación de las estipulaciones de la Constitución, en particular las que otorgan poderes al gobierno federal.

limited government > gobierno limitado Principio básico del sistema estadounidense de gobierno que establece que el gobierno tiene restricciones en cuanto a lo que puede hacer, y en el cual cada individuo tiene ciertos derechos que el gobierno no puede enajenar; *ver* constitutionalism/constitucionalismo, popular sovereignty/soberanía popular.

Lincoln, Abraham > Lincoln, Abraham (1809–1865) Fue elegido 16° presidente de los Estados Unidos en 1861, y asumió su cargo a los 52 años. Se le recuerda por haber promulgado la Proclamación de Emancipación, que decretaba que "toda persona en situación de esclavitud... debe ser, de ahora en adelante, y para siempre libre...". Fue asesinado en 1865.

line agency > agencia del ramo Oficina que desempeña las tareas para las que la organización existe.

line-item veto > veto de partida Cancelación presidencial de ciertas cantidades de dólares de una cuenta de gastos del Congreso; este veto se instituyó en 1996 mediante una ley del Congreso, pero la Suprema Corte lo derogó en 1998.

literacy > alfabetismo Capacidad de una persona para leer o escribir.

lobbying > cabildeo Actividades mediante las cuales los grupos ejercen presión sobre los legisladores, el proceso legislativo y sobre todos los aspectos de la elaboración de políticas públicas.

lobbyist > cabildero Persona que intenta persuadir a funcionarios a realizar cosas que ciertos grupos de interés quieren que se lleven a cabo.

Locke, John > Locke, John (1632–1704) Filósofo inglés que escribió sobre sus ideas acerca de los derechos naturales del hombre, el contrato social, la separación iglesia–Estado, la libertad religiosa y la libertad. Las teorías de Locke influyeron en la Guerra de Independencia estadounidense y en la Revolución Francesa.

London > Londres Capital de Inglaterra, fundada originalmente por los romanos alrededor del año 50 d. C. El periodo durante el que muchas de las colonias norteamericanas se establecieron es conocido como Stuart London. En esta época que va de 1603 a 1714, Londres creció enormemente, pero también sufrió dos grandes desastres: la Peste de 1665 y el Gran Incendio de 1666.

Long, Huey > Long, Huey (1893–1935) Fue gobernador de Luisiana y senador estadounidense. Creó la sociedad Share-the-Wealth para dar alojamiento e ingresos a familias estadounidenses como alternativa al programa Nuevo Trato del presidente Franklin D. Roosevelt. Long se postuló a la presidencia en 1935 pero fue asesinado antes de que se llevara a cabo la elección.

M

Madison, James > Madison, James (1751–1836) fungió como el 4° Presidente de los Estados Unidos, de 1809 a 1817. Fue un estudioso de la historia, el gobierno y las leyes, formó parte del Congreso Continental e hizo importantes contribuciones a la ratificación de la Constitución, coescribiendo el *Federalist.* Madison escribió varios de los ensayos de los *Federalist Papers* y fue un personaje fundamental en el movimiento para sustituir los Artículos de la Confederación. Sus *Notes on the Debates in the Federal Convention* nos han permitido una comprensión clara de lo que ocurrió en esos debates. Durante la convención, Madison fue el arquitecto principal del Plan de Virginia y tuvo una gran influencia en toda la sesión. De hecho, se le ha llamado el "Padre de la Constitución". En esa época abogaba por un gobierno nacional fuerte, pero más tarde vio los beneficios de los gobiernos estatales fuertes.

magistrate > magistrado Juez que atiende demandas civiles y delitos menores que surgen en un contexto urbano.

Magna Carta > Carta Magna Constitución que los barones impusieron al rey John de Inglaterra en 1215; estableció el principio de que el poder del monarca no era absoluto y garantizó derechos fundamentales como el de un juicio con jurado y procesos establecidos legales para la nobleza.

majority leader > líder mayoritario Portavoz del partido político que posee la mayor cantidad de escaños en cada cámara del Congreso.

majority opinion > opinión mayoritaria Llamada oficialmente Opinión de la Corte; anuncia la decisión de la Corte sobre el caso y describe el razonamiento sobre el que ésta se basa.

majority rule > gobierno por mayoría En una democracia, la mayoría de personas estarán en lo correcto con más frecuencia, y estarán en lo correcto con más frecuencia que una sola persona o un grupo pequeño.

mandate > mandato Las intrucciones u órdenes que un grupo de votantes da a sus funcionarios electos. El término *mandato* proviene del latín *mandatum,* lo que significa "una orden".

Mandela, Nelson > Mandela, Nelson (1918–2013) Primer presidente negro de Sudáfrica, de 1994 a 1999, elegido en las primeras elecciones democráticas de ese país. Previamente, fue prisionero político en Sudáfrica durante más de 20 años. También ayudó a terminar con la segregación racial en su país, y obtuvo el Premio Nobel de la Paz en 1993.

Mao Zedong > Mao Zedong (1893–1976) encabezó la Revolución comunista china y fungió como jefe de Estado en China de 1949 a 1959. Posteriormente, fue presidente del Partido Comunista Chino hasta su muerte. Mao es recordado por el Gran Salto Adelante, su intento desastroso de hacer a China avanzar rápidamente hacia una mejor producción agrícola e industrial, y por la Revolución Cultural que destruyó mucho de la herencia cultural china.

Marbury, William > Marbury, William (1762–1835) Fue el demandante en el caso *Marbury* contra *Madison,* en 1803, en el que la Corte Suprema estableció el principio de la revisión judicial. Fue designado por el presidente John Adams como juez de paz en el Distrito de Columbia pero, como resultado del fallo en Marbury contra Madison, Marbury perdió su nombramiento como juez.

Marshall, George C. > Marshall, George C. (1880–1959) fue general de ejército y jefe de Estado mayor durante la Segunda Guerra Mundial. Luego se convirtió en secretario de Estado y, posteriormente, en secretario de defensa en la administración de Franklin Roosevelt. Creó un programa de recuperación europea de posguerra, conocido con el nombre de Plan Marshall, por el que recibió el Premio Nobel de la Paz.

Marshall, John > Marshall, John (1755–1835) fue el cuarto presidente de la Corte Suprema de Justicia de los Estados Unidos. Tenía opiniones muy firmes sobre el poder de la Corte Suprema para interpretar la constitución, y sus fallos han tenido un gran impacto en la legislación estadounidense hasta el día de hoy.

Marshall, Thurgood > Marshall, Thurgood (1908–1993) Fue el primer afroamericano nombrado para la Corte Suprema (en 1967); fue juez asociado hasta 1991. En 1954, cuando trabajaba como abogado, llevó con éxito el caso de *Brown* contra la *Junta de Educación* (que declaró la segregación racial inconstitucional en las escuelas públicas estadounidenses) frente a la Corte Suprema del país.

Marx, Karl > Marx, Karl Filósofo alemán conocido principalmente por su obra en varios tomos sobre política económica, *Das Kapital;* Marx (1818–1883) es considerado el padre del socialismo y del comunismo modernos.

Mason, George > Mason, George Propietario de Gunston Hall, y uno de los terratenientes más ricos de Virginia, Mason (1725–1792) redactó la Declaración de Derechos de Virginia, que sirvió de modelo a Jefferson al escribir la Declaración de Independencia y fue la base para la Carta de Derechos de la Constitución de los Estados Unidos. Fue un orador influyente en la Convención Constitucional y se esforzó para que la Carta de Derechos y la 11ª Enmienda fueran incorporadas a la Constitución.

mass media > medios masivos de comunicación Aquellos medios de comunicación que llegan a grandes audiencias, sobre todo la radio, televisión, publicaciones impresas e Internet.

mayor-council government > gobierno de consejo-alcalde El más antiguo y más utilizado tipo de gobierno municipal que cuenta con un alcalde que se elige como presidente ejecutivo y un consejo como su cuerpo legislativo.

McCain, John > McCain, John (1936–) Es senador republicano por Arizona y copatrocinador de la Ley Bipartidista de Reforma de Campaña de 2002. Como candidato presidencial en 2008, perdió las elecciones frente a Barack Obama.

McKinley, William > McKinley, William (1843–1901), de Ohio, cumplió siete periodos en la Cámara de Representantes federal, donde defendió con fuerza los aranceles (impuestos a los productos de importación) como una forma de proteger a los negocios estadounidenses. Elegido Presidente en 1897, llevó al país a la victoria en la Guerra Hispano–Estadounidense, por lo que recibió los territorios de Guam, Puerto Rico y Filipinas. McKinley también apoyó la estadidad de Hawái. Fue asesinado durante su segundo mandato presidencial.

Medicaid > Medicaid Programa administrado por los estados para proporcionar seguro médico a las familias de bajos ingresos.

medium > medio Un medio de comunicación; algo que transmite información.

mercantilism > mercantilismo Teoría económica y política que destaca el dinero como la fuente primaria de riqueza para incrementar el poder absoluto de la monarquía y de la nación.

metropolitan area > área metropolitana La ciudad y el área que la rodea.

Milosevic, Slobodan > Milosevic, Slobodan (1941–2006) fue presidente de Serbia de 1989 a 1997. Nacionalista radical, instituyó políticas que llevaron a la ruptura de la Federación Socialista de Yugoslavia e instigó una serie de conflictos sangrientos con otros Estados balcánicos, como Kosovo, Bosnia, y Croacia.

ministers > ministros Miembro del gabinete, y más frecuentemente de la Cámara de los Comunes.

minority leader > líder minoritario Portavoz del partido político que posee la menor cantidad de escaños en cada cámara del Congreso.

Miranda rule > Ley Miranda Derechos constitucionales que la policía debe especificar a un sospechoso antes de que se le pueda interrogar.

misdemeanor > falta leve Delito menor que se castiga mediante una pequeña multa o un breve período de encarcelamiento.

Missouri Plan > Plan Missouri Enfoque de la elección de jueces que combina la elección y el nombramiento; un comité de nominaciones ofrece una lista de candidatos de la que el gobernador puede elegir.

monetary policy > política monetaria Proceso mediante el cual el gobierno toma decisiones que afectan a la economía del país mediante cambios en la oferta monetaria y la disponibilidad de crédito.

monopoly > monopolio Empresa que es la única fuente de un producto o servicio.

Monroe, James > Monroe, James (1758–1831) Fue presidente de los Estados Unidos de 1817 a 1825. Durante su mandato, Monroe minimizó las tensiones partidistas y trajo la "Era de los buenos sentimientos". Monroe tomó Florida de manos de España en 1821 y declaró que las acciones europeas para colonizar cualquier parte de las Américas implicarían la intervención estadounidense. Años después, estas palabras formaron la base de la Doctrina Monroe, posiblemente la contribución principal de este presidente.

Montesquieu, Charles de > Montesquieu, Charles de (1689–1755) Fue un filósofo político francés de la Ilustración cuya obra principal, *El espíritu de las leyes,* fue un aporte esencial para la teoría política. Su postulado de la separación de poderes tuvo gran impacto en los redactores de la Constitución de los Estados Unidos.

Moses > Moisés Según el libro del Éxodo en la Torá (la Biblia judía) y en el Viejo Testamento de la Biblia cristiana, Moisés era el líder del pueblo judío que lo habría liberado de la esclavitud en Egipto, al conducirlo a través del desierto hacia la libertad en la "tierra prometida" de Canaán. Mientras estaban en el desierto, según tanto la Torá como el Viejo Testamento y el Corán (el texto sagrado del Islam), Moisés subió a la cima del Monte Sinaí donde Dios le entregó las tabletas de arcilla con los Diez Mandamientos.

municipality > municipalidad Unidad política urbana dentro de una población que por lo general existe como una entidad gubernamental independiente.

N

national popular vote plan > plan para el voto nacional popular Propuesta para elegir al Presidente de la Nación mediante la cual las leyes electorales de cada Estado decretan que los votos electorales sean otorgados al ganador del voto popular nacional y que de esta manera se llegue a un acuerdo interestatal donde se elija al presidente por voto popular.

NATO > OTAN (Organización del Tratado del Atlántico Norte) Alianza formada para proteger la libertad y seguridad de sus miembros a través de medidas políticas y militares.

naturalization > naturalización Proceso legal mediante el cual los ciudadanos de un país se convierten en ciudadanos de otro.

Necessary and Proper Clause > Cláusula de Necesidad y Conveniencia Cláusula constitucional que otorga al Congreso el poder de expedir leyes "necesarias y pertinentes" para el ejercicio de sus poderes.

New Jersey Plan > Plan Nueva Jersey Plan presentado en la Convención Constitucional como una alternativa al Plan de Virginia; proponía una legislatura unicameral en la que cada estado estuviera representado de forma equitativa.

Nixon, Richard > Nixon, Richard (1913–1994) Richard Nixon era abogado, antes de entrar en la política como diputado y senador por California. Fue vicepresidente del presidente Eisenhower antes de ser elegido como 37° Presidente en 1968. Ocupó el cargo de 1969 a 1974. Como presidente, terminó el reclutamiento militar obligatorio e instituyó un amplio programa ambiental. Frente al juicio político debido a su participación en el escándalo de Watergate, Nixon renunció en agosto de 1974.

nomination > nominación Proceso de selección de candidatos en una democracia.

nonpartisan elections > elección no partidista Elección en la que los candidatos no están identificados por afiliaciones partidarias.

Norris, George > Norris, George (1861–1944) Representante y senador estadounidense, originario de Nebraska, reconocido como pensador independiente. Impulsó la legislación para crear la Autoridad del Valle de Tennessee, para apoyar la actividad de los sindicatos, y para agregar la 20ª Enmienda ("lame duck amendment") a la Constitución. La enmienda reduce el periodo entre la elección legislativa y el inicio de sesiones de la nueva legislatura.

North American Free Trade Agreement (NAFTA) > NAFTA (Tratado de Libre Comercio de América del Norte) Acuerdo que elimina las restricciones comerciales entre los Estados Unidos, Canadá y México, con lo cual se incrementa el comercio transfronterizo.

O

Obama, Barack > Obama, Barack (1961–) Fue el 44° presidente de los Estados Unidos, de 2009 a 2016. Obama, primer presidente afroamericano, recibió el premio Nobel de la Paz.

O'Connor, Sandra Day > O'Connor, Sandra Day (1930–) Primera mujer nombrada para la Corte Suprema. Nominada por el presidente Reagan en 1981, fue jueza asociada de la Corte Suprema hasta su retiro en 2006. Conocida por sus opiniones cuidadosamente documentadas, era considerada como una conservadora moderada.

off-year elections > elección intermedia Elección del Congreso que ocurre entre las elecciones presidenciales.

oligarchy > oligarquía Forma de gobierno en la que el poder de gobernar lo ejerce una elite pequeña y por lo general autonombrada.

omnibus measure > ***omnibus measure*** Proyecto de ley que contiene diversos asuntos y temas.

open market operations > operaciones de mercado abierto Proceso por el cual la Reserva Federal compra y vende valores del Estado a los bancos del país para controlar la cantidad de dinero en circulación.

open primary > elección primaria abierta Elección partidista de nominación en la que cualquier votante calificado puede tomar parte.

opinion leaders > líderes de opinión Personas que por alguna razón tienen una poderosa influencia en los puntos de vista de otras.

ordinance power > poder de decreto Poder del Presidente de emitir órdenes ejecutivas; se fundamenta en la Constitución y en los actos del Congreso.

original jurisdiction > jurisdicción original Poder de una corte de atender un caso antes que otra corte.

oversight function > función de vigilancia Revisión de las políticas y los programas de la rama ejecutiva por parte de los comités legislativos.

P

Packwood, Bob > Packwood, Bob (1932–) Fue un senador estadounidense de Portland, Oregón. Elegido al Senado en 1968, ocupó el cargo hasta su renuncia en 1995, bajo amenaza de ser expulsado.

Panama Canal > Canal de Panamá Canal artificial que pasa a través del Istmo de Panamá, en Centroamérica, y conecta los océanos Atlántico y Pacífico.

panic > pánico Del latín *panicus,* que significa "aterrorizado"; una alarma repentina generalizada en relación con la economía, que a menudo resulta en una depresión.

pardon > perdón exoneración que lleva a cabo el Presidente o el gobernador del castigo o de las consecuencias legales de un crimen

parliamentary > gobierno parlamentario Forma de gobierno en la que el poder ejecutivo está conformado por el primer ministro o por el jefe del gobierno, y el gabinete de dicho funcionario. Este poder es parte de la legislatura.

parliamentary system > sistema parlamentario Forma de gobierno en la que el poder ejecutivo está constituido por el primer ministro, o premier, y su gabinete.

parochial > parroquial Relacionado con la iglesia, como las escuelas parroquiales.

parole > liberación bajo palabra Libertad condicional de un prisionero poco antes de que termine el lapso de su sentencia original.

partisans > partidista Legislador que le debe fidelidad, en primer lugar, a su partido político, por lo que vota de acuerdo con la línea del partido.

partisanship > partidarismo Acción gubernamental basada en la vigorosa fidelidad a un partido político.

party caucus > junta de dirigentes de partido Reunión cerrada de los miembros de la Cámara de Representantes o del Senado; también se conoce como Conferencia de partido.

party government > gobierno de partido La dirección y el control de los procesos de gobierno por el partido que cuenta con la mayoría.

party identification > identificación con el partido Lealtad de la gente hacia un partido político.

passport > pasaporte Documento legal emitido por el estado que identifica a una persona como ciudadano de un país y le permite viajar al exterior y regresar.

patent > patente Licencia expedida a un inventor para garantizar el derecho exclusivo de manufactura, uso o venta de su invento, durante un tiempo limitado.

patricians > patricio Aristócrata propietario de tierras en la antigua Roma.

Patrick, Luther > Patrick, Luther (1894–1957) Nació cerca de Decatur, Alabama, se graduó de la Universidad de Purdue y obtuvo su título en Derecho de la Universidad de Alabama. Después de ocupar diversos cargos judiciales, incluido el de fiscal general de Alabama, sirvió como diputado federal por Alabama de 1937 a 1943 y de 1945 a 1947.

patronage > patrocinio Práctica de dar trabajo a los simpatizantes y amigos.

payroll tax > impuesto sobre la nómina Gravamen tasado a casi todos los empleadores y sus empleados, así como a las personas autoempleadas; cantidad debida por los empleados que se les descuenta de su salario.

Pearl Harbor > Pearl Harbor Base naval estadounidense que se encuentra en la isla de Oahu, en Hawái.

peer group > grupo de camaradas Gente con la que uno se asocia regularmente y que incluye a socios, amigos, compañeros de clase, vecinos y compañeros de trabajo.

Pelosi, Nancy > Pelosi, Nancy (1940–) Se graduó del Trinity College en Washington, D.C. Mientras era representante por California a principios de 1987, Pelosi se convirtió en la primera mujer en dirigir la banca demócrata en la Cámara de Representantes, la primera mujer presidenta de la Cámara y fue la líder minoritaria de la Cámara en la 113era legislatura.

Penn, William > Penn, William Líder cuáquero inglés que defendía la libertad de culto. Penn (1644–1718) llegó a América del Norte en 1682 y fundó la colonia de Pensilvania como un refugio para los cuáqueros y otras minorías religiosas.

perjury > perjurio Mentir bajo juramento.

Perot, Ross > Perot, Ross (1930–) Se anunció a sí mismo como candidato presidencial por un tercer partido, el Partido de la Reforma, que fundó en 1995. Se autoproclamó candidato presidencial y usó la fortuna que adquirió con la creación de Electronic Data Systems para financiar su campaña. Perdió las elecciones de 1992 y de 1996.

persona non grata > ***persona non grata*** Una persona que no es bienvenida; se utiliza para describir a los funcionarios diplomáticos destituidos.

petit jury > jurado ordinario Este jurado escucha la evidencia en un caso, decide los hechos en disputa, y muy de vez en cuando interpreta y aplica la ley; también conocido como jurado de juicio.

petition > petición Derecho de un ciudadano a presentar su opinión ante funcionarios públicos, por medio de escritos, cartas, cabildeo y marchas.

Petition of Right > Solicitud de Derecho Documento preparado por el Parlamento y firmado por el rey Charles I de Inglaterra en 1628; cuestionó la idea del derecho divino de los reyes y declaró que incluso el monarca está sujeto a las leyes de la tierra.

Philadelphia > Filadelfia La ciudad más grande en el estado de Pensilvania.

picketing > vigilancia Manifestación de los trabajadores en el sitio donde están en huelga.

pigeonholed > dar carpetazo Expresión que describe cómo proyectos de ley que se presentan ante el Congreso se olvidan, se ponen a un lado o nunca se llevan a cabo.

plaintiff > demandante En el derecho civil, la parte que entabla un juicio u otra acción legal contra otra en una corte.

platform > plataforma Un enunciado formal por parte de un partido político respecto a sus principios básicos, opiniones sobre cuestiones políticas importantes y objetivos.

plebeians > plebeyos Personas que pertenecían a la plebe en la República Romana.

plurality > mayoría En una elección, el número de votos que el candidato que va a la punta tiene de ventaja sobre su competidor más cercano.

pocket veto > veto indirecto Tipo de veto que el Presidente puede utilizar después de que una legislatura se suspende; se aplica cuando un Presidente no firma formalmente o rechaza una propuesta de ley, dentro del tiempo comprendido para eso.

police power > facultad policial Autoridad de cada Estado para proteger y promover la salud pública, la seguridad, la moral y el bienestar general de su pueblo.

political action committees (PACs) > comité de acción política Extensión política de grupos de interés especial, los cuales tienen un gran interés en la política pública.

political efficacy > eficacia política La influencia o eficacia individual en la política.

political party > partido político Grupo de personas que buscan controlar el gobierno mediante el triunfo en las elecciones y ejerciendo puestos públicos.

political socialization > socialización política Proceso mediante el que la gente obtiene sus actitudes y opiniones políticas.

political spectrum > espectro político Gama de perspectivas políticas.

politicos > políticos Legisladores que intentan equilibrar las responsabilidades de un agente, partidario político y delegado.

poll books > padrón electoral Lista de todos los votantes registrados en cada distrito.

poll tax > impuesto sobre el padrón electoral Gravamen especial, exigido por algunos estados como una condición para votar; fue derogado por la 24a Enmienda.

polling place > casilla electoral Lugar donde los votantes que viven en cierto distrito acuden a votar.

Pope, Alexander > Pope, Alexander (1688–1744) Fue un poeta famoso, escritor de sátira y traductor, que tuvo éxito económico. Nació en Londres, creció en una familia católica y se le conoce sobre todo por emplear el pareado heroico.

popular sovereignty > soberanía popular Principio básico del sistema estadounidense de gobierno que establece que el pueblo es la fuente de todos los poderes gubernamentales, y que el gobierno sólo puede existir con el consentimiento de los gobernados.

Powell, Colin > Powell, Colin (1937–) es un general de cuatro estrellas, que se desempeñó como Presidente del Estado Mayor Conjunto de 1989 a 1993. En 2001, fungió como secretario de Estado de George W. Bush y mantuvo el cargo hasta 2005. Powell fue el primer afroestadounidense en ocupar estos cargos dentro del gabinete.

precedent > precedente Decisión judicial que se toma como un ejemplo a seguir en el futuro para casos similares.

precinct > circunscripción Unidad mínima de la administración electoral; distrito de votación.

preclearance > preautorización Una de las disposiciones de la Ley de Derechos Electorales de 1965, de acuerdo con la cual ninguna ley electoral nueva ni cambio alguno a las vigentes puede entrar en vigor sin la previa aprobación del Departamento de Justicia.

preliminary hearing > audiencia preliminar El primer paso del procesamiento de un crimen mayor, en el que el juez decide si la evidencia basta para que la persona comparezca ante el gran jurado o ante el fiscal para ser sujeto de una acción.

presentment > declaración del jurado Una acusación formal hecha por el jurado de acusación en vez del fiscal.

president of the Senate > presidente del Senado Funcionario que preside un Senado; en el Congreso es el vicepresidente de los Estados Unidos; en la legislatura estatal, cualquier vicegobernador o un senador.

president pro tempore > presidente *pro tempore* Miembro del Senado de los Estados Unidos, o de la cámara superior de la legislatura estatal, elegido para ser presidente, en caso de ausencia del presidente del Senado.

Presidential Election Campaign Fund > Fondo para la campaña electoral presidencial Dinero donado por los contribuyentes al enviar declaración federal de ingresos. Administrado por la Comisión electoral federal (FEC, por su sigla en inglés), y empleado para subsidiar las campañas previas a las convenciones, las convenciones nacionales y las campañas presidenciales.

presidential government > gobierno presidencial Forma de gobierno en la que los poderes ejecutivo y legislativo del gobierno están separados, son independientes y están en la misma jerarquía.

presidential primary > elección presidencial primaria Elección en la que los votantes de un partido: eligen a varios o a todos los delegados de la organización partidista estatal para la convención nacional de su partido, y/o expresan una preferencia por alguno de los distintos contendientes para la nominación presidencial de su partido.

presidential succession > sucesión presidencial Plan mediante el cual se resuelve la vacante presidencial.

Presidential Succession Act of 1947 > Ley para la Sucesión Presidencial de 1947 Ley que especifica el orden para la sucesión presidencial, después del Vicepresidente.

preventive detention > arresto preventivo Ley que permite a los jueces federales ordenar que un acusado de felonía sea arrestado, sin derecho a fianza, cuando existen buenas razones para creer que cometerá otro crimen grave antes del juicio.

prior restraint > censura previa Concepto de acuerdo con el cual el gobierno no puede reprimir las ideas antes de que se expresen.

privatization > privatización Regresar las empresas nacionales a la iniciativa privada.

Privileges and Immunities Clause > Cláusula de Privilegios e Inmunidades Estipulación constitucional en que se conceden ciertos "privilegios e inmunidades" a los ciudadanos, sin importar su estado de residencia.

probable cause > causa probable Fundamentos razonables, sospecha razonable de un crimen.

procedural due process > procesos legales establecidos El gobierno debe emplear procedimientos y métodos justos.

process of incorporation > proceso de incorporación Proceso de integrar, o incluir, la mayor parte de las garantías de la Carta de Derechos en la Cláusula del Debido Proceso establecido de la 14ª Enmienda.

progressive tax > impuesto progresivo Tipo de impuesto que es proporcional con el ingreso.

project grants > subvención de proyecto Tipo de subvención de fondos públicos; proporcionada para proyectos específicos de los estados, las localidades y las oficinas privadas que la solicitan.

property tax > impuesto a la propiedad Gravamen sobre los bienes raíces y la propiedad personal.

proportional plan > plan proporcional Propuesta para seleccionar electores presidenciales, mediante la cual cada candidato recibiría la misma cantidad de votos electorales de un estado que recibió durante la votación popular del estado.

proportional representation > regla de la representación proporcional Procedimiento aplicado en las elecciones primarias del Partido Demócrata, en el cual cualquier candidato que gane al menos el 15% de los votos emitidos en una elección primaria, obtiene el número de delegados, para la convención estatal demócrata, que le corresponda en esa proporción de las primarias.

proprietary > propiedad Organizado por un propietario (una persona a quien el rey le ha otorgado un terreno).

prorogue > prórroga Aplazamiento, por ejemplo, de una sesión legislativa.

protectionism > proteccionismo Práctica en la que gobiernos nacionales tratan de controlar las importaciones para proteger a sus industrias de la competencia extranjera.

public affairs > asuntos públicos Aquellos acontecimientos y asuntos que importan al público en general, por ejemplo: la política, los temas públicos y la determinación de las políticas públicas.

public agenda > agenda pública Asuntos públicos sobre los cuales está enfocada la atención de las personas.

public debt > deuda pública Todo el dinero que ha pedido prestado el gobierno a lo largo de los años y que todavía no paga, además del interés acumulado sobre ese capital; también se conoce como deuda nacional o deuda federal.

public opinion > opinión pública Colección compleja de opiniones de diversas personas; la suma de todos sus puntos de vista.

public opinion polls > encuestas de opinión pública Dispositivos que intentan recolectar información interrogando a las personas. El término en inglés *poll* proviene de la palabra en alemán antiguo *polle,* que significa "la coronilla", la porción visible de la cabeza que se puede contar en una multitud.

public policies > políticas públicas Todo lo que un gobierno decide llevar a cabo.

public policy > política pública Todas las metas que un gobierno se fija, en las diversas áreas de asuntos humanos en las que éste se interesa.

pundit > experto Especialista en un asunto en particular o campo del conocimiento a quien frecuentemente se pide que dé su opinión de manera pública.

purge > purga Proceso de revisión de las listas de los votantes registrados y de la eliminación de los nombres que ya no son elegibles para votar; una depuración; proceso de purificación gubernamental en el que se elimina a los rivales.

purging > purga Proceso de revisión de las listas de votantes registrados para retirar los nombres de quienes ya no pueden ejercer su derecho al voto. Una purificación.

Putin, Vladimir > Putin, Vladimir (1952–) Fue el primer presidente de la Federación Rusa en 1999, al tomar el poder después de la renuncia de Boris Yeltsin a finales de ese año. Ganó las elecciones de 2000, 2004 y 2012. También fue primer ministro de 2008 a 2012. Bajo su mando, el poder presidencial se ha acrecentado y la economía rusa se ha fortalecido. Al mismo tiempo, algunos argumentan que no es un verdadero líder democrático.

Q

quorum > quórum Mínimo número de miembros que debe estar presente para que un cuerpo legislativo funcione; mayoría.

quota > cuota Porcentaje de un grupo con el que es necesario contar para cumplir un requisito de acción afirmativa; regla que requiere que determinado número de trabajos o ascensos se den a miembros de ciertos grupos.

quota sample > muestra de cuota Muestra deliberadamente recopilada para reflejar ciertas características importantes de una determinada población.

R

random sample > muestra aleatoria Determinado número de personas seleccionadas al azar.

ratification > ratificación Aprobación formal, consentimiento definitivo de la eficacia de una constitución, de una enmienda constitucional o de un tratado.

rational basis test > prueba de razonamiento básico Examen menos intenso que el examen judicial riguroso que implementa la Corte Suprema para tomar decisiones en casos de protección equitativa; el examen pregunta si hay una relación razonable entre la clasificación en cuestión y el logro de algún propósito gubernamental.

Reagan, Ronald > Reagan, Ronald (1911–2004) fue un actor que se convirtió en político: primero como gobernador de California y después como Presidente, de 1981 a 1989. En la contienda presidencial, derrotó de manera aplastante a Jummy Carter. Durante su gestión, Reagan actualizó las leyes del impuesto sobre la renta y negoció un tratado de eliminación de misiles con la Unión Soviética.

reapportion > reasignación Redistribución, por ejemplo, de los escaños en un cuerpo legislativo.

recall > destitución Proceso por el cual los electores pueden remover a funcionarios antes de terminar su periodo.

recess > receso Período en que ambas cámaras del Congreso suspenden actividades temporalmente.

recession > recesión Pérdida o reducción del crecimiento económico.

recognition > reconocimiento El poder exclusivo de un Presidente para reconocer legalmente estados extranjeros y consecuentemente establecer relaciones diplomáticas con ellos.

record > registro Transcripción de los procesos llevados a cabo en una corte tribunal.

redress > resarcir Satisfacer una queja, por lo general mediante un pago.

referendum > referendo Proceso mediante el cual una medida legislativa se consulta con los votantes de los estados para su aprobación o rechazo final.

reformers > reformistas Aquellos cuyas acciones están encaminadas a cambiar o reformar gradualmente el gobierno.

refugee > refugiado Persona que abandona su hogar para buscar protección contra la guerra, la persecución o algún otro peligro.

regional security alliances > alianzas regionales de seguridad Tratados mediante los cuales los Estados Unidos y otros países han acordado actuar colectivamente para enfrentar una agresión en una determinada parte del mundo.

registration > registro Procedimiento de identificación del votante para evitar votaciones fraudulentas.

regressive tax > impuesto regresivo Gravamen con una tasa invariable, sin considerar el nivel de ingreso de los contribuyentes o su capacidad para pagarlo.

representative government > gobierno representativo Sistema de gobierno en el que las políticas públicas están elaboradas por funcionarios elegidos por los votantes y que rinden cuentas en elecciones periódicas; *ver* democracy/democracia.

reprieve > suspensión Aplazamiento oficial de la ejecución de una sentencia.

reservations > reservación Terrenos públicos que un gobierno reserva para el uso de las tribus nativas estadounidenses.

reserve requirement > reserva obligatoria Cantidad de dinero que la Reserva Federal determina que los bancos deben mantener en reserva con uno de los Bancos de la Reserva Federal.

reserved powers > poderes reservados Aquellos poderes que la Constitución no otorga al gobierno nacional y no niega a los estados.

resolution > resolución Medida relativa al funcionamiento de cualquier Cámara, o una opinión sobre un asunto; no tiene la fuerza de una ley y no requiere la firma del Presidente.

reverse discrimination > discriminación inversa Segregación en contra del grupo mayoritario.

Rice, Condoleezza > Rice, Condoleezza (1954–) fue la asesora en política exterior de la campaña presidencial de George W. Bush. Cuando Bush fue elegido, se convirtió en la primera mujer en dirigir el Consejo de Seguridad Nacional. En 2005, Rice fue la primera mujer afroestadounidense en fungir como secretaria de Estado. Más tarde, Rice regresó a su puesto como profesora en la Universidad de Stanford y es autora de numerosos libros.

rider > cláusula adicional Provisión, poco probable de ser aprobada por méritos propios, que se agrega a un proyecto de ley importante de cuya aprobación se tiene la seguridad, por tanto, se dice que dicha cláusula "cabalga" por todo ese proceso legislativo.

right of association > derecho de asociación Derecho de asociarse con otros para promover causas políticas, sociales, económicas y de otra índole.

right of legation > derecho de legación Derecho a enviar y recibir representantes diplomáticos.

Roberts, John > Roberts, John (1955–) obtuvo su posgrado en Derecho de la Escuela de Leyes de Harvard en 1979. Más tarde trabajó como asistente legal en la Corte Suprema, y Consejero legal del presidente Ronald Reagan y en la Oficina del Consejero de la Casa Blanca de 1982 a 1986. Fue propuesto para la Corte suprema por el presidente George W. Bush y confirmado en el cargo en 2005.

Roosevelt, Franklin D. > Roosevelt, Franklin D. (1882–1945) El 32° Presidente de los Estados Unidos, de 1933 a 1945. Ha sido el único presidente en ser elegido para este cargo cuatro veces. Él condujo al país durante la Gran Depresión y la Segunda Guerra Mundial y desarrolló el sistema de programas gubernamentales y reformas que se conoce en conjunto como el Nuevo Trato.

Roosevelt, Theodore > Roosevelt, Theodore (1858–1919) Fue el 26° presidente de los Estados Unidos; estuvo en funciones de 1901 a 1909. Apodado Teddy, era cazador, soldado, naturalista y recibió el premio Nobel de la Paz. También logró asegurar la ruta del Canal de Panamá y comenzó su construcción.

Roper, Elmo > Roper, Elmo (1900–1971) desarrolló la primera encuesta científica que hacía predicciones políticas con muestras pequeñas. Mientras trabajaba para la revista *Fortune,* Roper predijo con precisión que Franklin Roosevelt ganaría la presidencia en 1936, 1940 y 1944; lo que le dio una fama considerable. En sus últimos años, Roper siguió dentro de la rama de los sondeos y también escribió para periódicos y para la revista *Saturday Review.*

Rousseau, Jean Jacques > Rousseau, Jean Jacques Filósofo, escritor y teórico político nacido en Suiza. Los tratados y novelas de Rousseau (1712–1778) inspiraron a los líderes de la Revolución Francesa. En su famosa obra, *El contrato social,* expone su idea de que los humanos son esencialmente libres, pero el progreso de la civilización ha reemplazado esa libertad con la servidumbre y la dependencia hacia otros. Para superar esto, la gente debe hacer uso de su libre albedrío y reconstruirse políticamente a sí mismos junto con los ideales democráticos.

rule of law > gobierno de la ley El concepto en que el gobierno y sus oficiales estan sujetos a la ley.

runoff primary > elección primaria complementaria Elección primaria en la que los dos candidatos con más votos en la elección primaria directa se enfrentan; el ganador de esa votación se convierte en el nominado.

S

sales tax > impuesto a las ventas Gravamen sobre las ventas de distintos bienes, el cual paga el comprador.

sample > muestra Una porción representativa del público.

search warrant > orden de allanamiento Autorización judicial para registrar algo.

secretary > secretario Funcionario a cargo de un departamento de gobierno.

Security Council > Consejo de Seguridad Panel de quince miembros de la ONU que tiene la máxima responsabilidad para la conservación de la paz internacional.

sedition > sedición Delito que consiste en intentar derrocar al gobierno mediante la fuerza, o de interrumpir las actividades legales por medio de actos violentos.

seditious speech > discurso sedicioso La convocatoria o el apoyo a un intento de derrocar al gobierno mediante la fuerza, o a la interrupción de actividades legales por medio de la violencia.

segregation > segregación Separación de un grupo respecto a otro.

select committee > comité selecto Comité legislativo creado por un tiempo limitado y para algún propósito específico; también se conoce como comité especial.

Selma, Alabama > Selma, Alabama Ciudad sureña símbolo de la reticencia del Sur frente al Movimiento de los Derechos Civiles de principios de la década de 1960. La ciudad fue escenario de una larga marcha por el derecho al voto, encabeza por varios líderes afroestadunidenses, incluido el reverendo Martin Luther King, Jr.

senatorial courtesy > cortesía senatorial Costumbre de que el Senado no aprobará una nominación presidencial, si esa designación no es aprobada por el senador del partido mayoritario de ese estado, en donde la persona designada habría de servir.

seniority rule > regla de antigüedad Regla no escrita de ambas Cámaras del Congreso, de acuerdo con la cual, los puestos más altos de cada una de ellas los ocuparán aquellos miembros que tengan un historial de servicio más antiguo; se aplica de forma más estricta a las presidencias de los comités.

separate-but-equal doctrine > doctrina de iguales pero separados Doctrina establecida por la corte en el caso *Plessy* contra *Ferguson,* en el cual se determinó que la segregación puede mantenerse siempre y cuando cada raza se trate de manera igualitaria; base constitucional para leyes que segregan a un grupo respecto a otro, con base en la raza.

separation of powers > separación de poderes Principio básico del sistema de gobierno estadounidense, según el cual los poderes ejecutivo, legislativo y judicial constituyen las tres ramas del gobierno independientes e iguales.

session > sesión Período regular durante el cual se reúne el Congreso para atender asuntos oficiales.

shadow cabinet > gabinete alterno Miembros de los partidos de oposición que vigilan, o supervisan, a un miembro particular del gabinete, y que estarían listos para ejercer el gobierno.

Shays, Daniel > Shays, Daniel Joven granjero con un don para los ejercicios paramilitares, Shays (1747–1825) se convirtió en capitán en el 5° Regimiento de Massachusetts del Ejército Continental en 1777 y se hizo una reputación de oficial valiente y capaz. Después de la guerra, regresó a la agricultura. Como muchos, tuvo problemas de deudas por la fuerte recesión de posguerra. Shays surgió como líder local en el movimiento de protesta contra los altos impuestos y la falta condonación de deudas.

Shays' Rebellion > Rebelión de Shays Una serie de enfrentamientos entre granjeros deudores y autoridades del gobierno estatal en el oeste de Massachusetts entre 1786 y 1787.

Sherman, Roger > Sherman, Roger (1721–1793) fue un abogado y juez de Connecticut, redactor de la Constitución de los Estados Unidos y legislador. Fue uno de los primeros defensores de la independencia estadounidense y asistió al Primer y Segundo Congresos Continentales. También ayudó a redactar el borrador de los Artículos de la Confederación. En la Convención Constitucional, propuso lo que se conocería como el Acuerdo de Connecticut, que creaba una Cámara de representantes conformada según la población y un Senado con el mismo número de representantes para cada estado.

shield laws > ley escudo Ley que ofrece a los periodistas cierta protección contra la revelación de sus fuentes o la publicación de otra información confidencial durante los procedimientos legales.

single-issue parties > partidos de un único asunto Partidos que se concentran en un solo aspecto de la política pública.

single-member district > distrito de un solo miembro Distrito electoral en donde los votantes eligen, en la papeleta electoral, una sola persona para cada cargo.

single-member districts > distritos uninominales Distritos electorales en los que los votantes eligen a una sola persona para cada cargo vacante.

slander > calumnia Utilización falsa y maliciosa del discurso hablado.

Smith, Adam > Smith, Adam (1723–1790) fue un filósofo escocés a quién se atribuye el avance de la era del libre comercio en el siglo XIX. Su libro *La riqueza de las naciones* influyó a muchos líderes intelectuales y políticos de su época, y sus ideas siguen gozando de credibilidad entre los economistas modernos.

socialism > socialismo Filosofía basada en la idea de que los beneficios de la actividad económica deben distribuirse de manera equitativa entre toda la sociedad.

soft money > fondos no fiscalizados Dinero otorgado a organizaciones partidistas estatales y locales, en cantidades ilimitadas, para actividades relacionadas con las campañas electorales.

Sotomayor, Sonia > Sotomayor, Sonia (1954–) Tercera mujer nombrada para la Corte Suprema. El presidente Obama la nominó como jueza asociada de la Corte Suprema en 2009, y continúa en el cargo.

sound bite > informe sucinto Informaciones breves y concisas que pueden despacharse en 30 ó 45 segundos.

sovereign > soberano Estado que posee poder supremo y absoluto dentro de su propio territorio y puede decidir sus políticas internas y hacia el exterior; no estar subordinado ni ser responsable ante ninguna otra autoridad.

sovereignty > soberanía Autoridad suprema para tomar decisiones y mantener el orden en un estado.

Speaker of the House > Vocero de la Cámara Funcionario que preside la Cámara de Representantes y que es electo por el partido mayoritario en la Cámara, al cual pertenece.

special district > distrito especial Unidad independiente creada para llevar a cabo una o más funciones gubernamentales relacionadas a nivel local.

special session > sesión especial Sesión extraordinaria de un cuerpo legislativo, convocada para tratar una situación de emergencia.

splinter parties > partidos de escisión Partidos formados por la fractura de uno de los principales partidos; la mayor parte de los partidos pequeños importantes en el ámbito político estadounidense son partidos de escisión.

split-ticket voting > voto diferenciado Votar, en la misma elección, por candidatos de distintos partidos para puestos diferentes.

spoils system > sistema de prebendas Práctica de ofrecer cargos y otros favores gubernamentales a los simpatizantes y amigos políticos.

staff agency > oficina de apoyo Tipo de agencia cuya función es dar respaldo al Presidente y a otros administradores, ofreciendo consejos y otro tipo de asistencia en la administración de la organización.

Stalin, Josef > Stalin, José (1878–1953) emergió de la pobreza para llegar a ser el líder totalitario de la Unión Soviética de 1929 a 1953. Durante su régimen, caracterizado por su brutalidad, la antigua sociedad campesina se transformó en un líder industrial y en una potencia militar. Entre las muchas reformas radicales de Stalin se cuenta la colectivización de la agricultura.

standing committee > comisión permanente Comité permanente de un cuerpo legislativo al que se presentan las propuestas de ley sobre una materia específica; *ver* comité selecto.

state > estado Conjunto de personas que viven en un territorio definido y que tienen un gobierno con el poder de legislar y de hacer cumplir la ley, sin tener el consentimiento de una autoridad superior.

state-building > *state-building* Proceso en el cual países extranjeros tratan de fortalecer las instituciones gubernamentales de algún otro país.

statutory law > ley estatuida Ley aprobada por los legisladores.

straight-ticket voting > votación de partido único Práctica de votar en una elección por los candidatos de un solo partido.

straw vote > encuesta pre-electoral Encuesta que pretende conocer la opinión de la gente haciendo simplemente la misma pregunta a una gran cantidad de personas.

strict constructionist > construccionista estricto Persona que defiende una interpretación estrecha de las estipulaciones de la Constitución, en particular las referentes al otorgamiento de poderes al gobierno federal.

strict scrutiny test > examen judicial riguroso Estándar más alto que la prueba de fundamento razonable que una ley debe honrar en casos de protección equitativa; el Estado o el gobierno federal debe demostrar que esta ley no se relaciona con un interés ordinario del gobierno, sino con uno imperioso e inaplazable.

strong-mayor government > gobierno de alcalde fuerte Tipo de gobierno de una ciudad en el que el alcalde encabeza la administración y ejerce un fuerte liderazgo al crear las políticas y dirigir los asuntos de la ciudad.

subcommittee > subcomité División de un comité existente que se forma para atender asuntos específicos.

subpoena > citación Orden para que se presente una persona o para que se presenten documentos u otros materiales solicitados.

subsidy > subsidio Una subvención en dinero, por lo general otorgada por un gobierno.

substantive due process > proceso legal duradero Concepto de acuerdo con el cual el gobierno debe crear políticas y leyes justas.

successor > sucesor Persona que hereda un título o un cargo.

suffrage > sufragio El derecho de votar.

Super PAC > Súper PAC (comités de acción política) Comités de acción política independientes, sin afiliación a partido político alguno, a los que se permite recaudar y gastar cantidades ilimitadas. Están obligados a dar a conocer a sus donadores y no pueden trabajar directamente con los comités de acción política independiente de la campaña de ningún candidato.

supply-side economics > economía de oferta Idea que supone que la reducción de impuestos aumenta el dinero de entidades privadas y estimula la economía.

Supremacy Clause > Cláusula de Supremacía Cláusula de la Constitución de los Estados Unidos que estipula que la Constitución, la ley federal y los tratados de los Estados Unidos son la "ley suprema del país".

surplus > superávit Cuando hay más ingresos que gastos.

Suu Kyi, Aung San > Suu Kyi, Aung San (1945–) Política y líder opositora de Myanmar (Birmania), que obtuvo el Premio Nobel de la Paz en 1991. Estuvo bajo arresto domiciliario durante años por oponerse al régimen militar; posteriormente fue liberada y electa para un cargo público.

swing voters > votantes indecisos Miembros del electorado que no han tomado una decisión al comienzo de una campaña y están dispuestos a inclinarse hacia cualquiera de los candidatos.

symbolic speech > discurso simbólico Expresión mediante la conducta; comunicación de ideas a través de expresiones faciales, lenguaje corporal o mediante el uso de un letrero o portando una banda en el brazo.

T

Taft, William Howard > Taft, William Howard (1857–1930) El 27° Presidente de los Estados Unidos, de 1909 a 1913. Luego se convertiría en el décimo presidente de la Corte Suprema federal, por lo que es la única persona que ha ocupado ambos cargos.

Taney, Roger B. > Taney, Roger B. (1777–1864) fungió como fiscal general federal y fue nombrado presidente de la Corte Suprema en 1836. Su opinión mayoritaria en el juicio *Dred Scott* contra *Sandford* de 1857, en la que declaró que los afroestadounidenses no podían ser considerados ciudadanos estadounidenses, causó mucha polémica en la víspera de la Guerra Civil.

tariff > arancel Impuesto que se aplica a las importaciones.

tax > impuesto Cargo gravado por el gobierno a las personas o propiedades, con el objeto de satisfacer las necesidades públicas.

term > término Lapso especificado de dos años durante el cual se desempeñará en el cargo un funcionario elegido.

territory > territorio Territorio de los Estados Unidos que no tiene calidad de estado y que tiene su propio gobierno.

terrorism > terrorismo El uso de violencia para intimidar al gobierno o a una sociedad.

Thomas, Clarence > Thomas, Clarence (1948–) Fue el segundo afroamericano nombrado para la Corte Suprema. Nominado juez asociado por George H.W. Bush en 1991, sustituyó a Thurgood Marshall y aún conserva su cargo.

Three-Fifths Compromise > Avenencia de las Tres Quintas Partes Acuerdo logrado en la Convención Constitucional respecto a que un esclavo debería contarse como tres quintas partes de una persona, para propósitos de determinar la población de un estado.

Thurmond, Strom > Thurmond, Strom Gobernador de Carolina del Sur y senador de los Estados Unidos durante 48 años. Thurmond (1902–2003) fue un opositor férreo del fin de la segregación en las escuelas y de los Derechos Civiles que se postuló sin éxito para la presidencia en las elecciones de 1948. Después, cambió su afiliación del Partido Demócrata al Republicano.

Tocqueville, Alexis de > Tocqueville, Alexis de (1805–1859) Científico político e historiador francés, famoso por haber escrito *La democracia en América,* un análisis del sistema político y social de los Estados Unidos durante el siglo XIX.

tort > acto ilícito civil Hecho injusto que incluye daño a la propiedad de una persona, su reputación o a la persona en sí en una situación que no está cubierta por un contrato.

township > municipio División de un condado.

trade association > asociación comercial Grupo de interés dentro de la comunidad de negocios.

trade embargo > embargo comercial Prohibición de comerciar con un país o varios países en particular.

transients > transeúnte Persona que vive en un estado sólo por un breve tiempo, sin residencia legal.

treason > alta traición Deslealtad hacia el país propio; en la Constitución, librar una guerra en contra de los Estados Unidos, proporcionar aliento u ofrecer ayuda a sus enemigos.

treaty > tratado Acuerdo formal entre dos o más estados soberanos.

Truman, Harry > Truman, Harry (1884–1972) Fue un granjero de Missouri, juez, senador y vicepresidente de Franklin D. Roosevelt por algunos meses. Se convirtió en el 33er presidente el 12 de abril de 1945, cuando Roosevelt murió repentinamente. Durante su presidencia, de 1945 a 1953, Truman vio el Día de la Victoria en Europa y ordenó que se lanzaran las bombas atómicas sobre Japón.

trustees > Independientes Legisladores que votan en cada asunto de acuerdo con sus conciencias y sus juicios independientes, sin considerar las opiniones de sus electores o de otros grupos.

Trusteeship Council > Consejo de Administración Fiduciaria de las Naciones Unidas Consejo de la ONU que vigila los territorios administrados por los Estados miembros. Actualmente, el Consejo existe sólo en papel ya que, para 1994, todos los territorios en fideicomiso habían alcanzado el autogobierno.

Tyler, John > Tyler, John Oriundo de Virginia, John Tyler (1790–1862) trabajó en la legislatura del estado y fue gobernador. Como senador, su interpretación estricta de la Constitución lo hizo renunciar frente a lo que consideró acciones ilegales del presidente Andrew Jackson, sobre la anulación de acciones del Congreso. Vicepresidente a la muerte del presidente en funciones, William Henry Harrison, Tyler tomó el cargo en 1841. Como Presidente, aprobó la estadidad de Texas y Florida, pero peleó fuertemente con sus compañeros del Partido Whig sobre el sistema bancario nacional. Todos los miembros de su gabinete menos uno renunciaron. En la Guerra Civil fue elegido para la Cámara de Representantes confederada, pero murió antes de asumir el cargo.

U

unconstitutional > inconstitucional Contrario a las estipulaciones constitucionales y, por lo tanto, ilegal, nulo e inválido, que no tiene fuerza ni efecto.

uncontrollable spending > gasto incontrolable Gastos que ni el Congreso ni el Presidente tienen el poder de cambiar de manera directa.

unicameral > unicameral Adjetivo que describe un cuerpo legislativo con una sola Cámara; *ver* bicameral.

unitary government > gobierno unitario Gobierno centralizado en el que los poderes ejercidos por el gobierno pertenecen a una única oficina central.

United Nations > Naciones Unidas Grupo de naciones compuesto por 193 miembros, que acepta las obligaciones de la Carta de las Naciones Unidas, tratado redactado en el año 1945.

universe > universo Término que se usa en asuntos de elecciones que se refiere a la población entera que se intenta medir mediante una encuesta.

V

veto > veto Poder del Presidente para rechazar un proyecto de ley aprobado por una legislatura; literalmente "Prohíbo".

Virginia Plan > Plan de Virginia Proyecto presentado por los delegados de Virginia en la Convención Constitucional; proponía un gobierno con tres poderes y una legislatura bicameral en la que la representación de cada estado estuviera determinada por su población o por su apoyo financiero al gobierno central.

visa > visa Permiso para entrar a otro país, otorgado por el país al cual se desea entrar.

W

Walesa, Lech > Walesa, Lech (1943–) Activista laboral fundador del primer sindicato en Polonia. Aunque fue arrestado por sus actividades sindicales, obtuvo el Premio Nobel de la Paz en 1983 y fue presidente de Polonia de 1990 a 1995.

ward > barrio Unidad en la que suelen dividirse las ciudades para la elección de los miembros del consejo municipal.

warrant > mandamiento Orden judicial que autoriza o hace legal alguna acción oficial, como la orden de allanamiento o la orden de arresto.

Warren, Earl > Warren, Earl (1891–1974) Fue magistrado republicano pero liberal, nombrado para la Corte Suprema por el presidente Dwight D. Eisenhower. Warren fue presidente de la Corte Suprema de 1953 a 1969 y presidió en algunos de los casos más importantes de la corte sobre la abolición de la segregación en las escuelas.

Washington, George > Washington, George (1732–1799) Ocupó el cargo de primer presidente de los Estados Unidos de 1789 a 1797 y fue uno de los Padres Fundadores de la nueva nación. Antes de ser presidente, fue general y comandante en jefe durante la Guerra de Independencia.

weak-mayor government > gobierno de alcalde débil Forma de gobierno de una ciudad, en la que el alcalde comparte las obligaciones ejecutivas con otros funcionarios electos.

welfare > beneficencia Ayuda en efectivo a los pobres.

whips > *whips* Asistentes de los líderes de las fracciones partidistas en la Cámara de Representantes y el Senado que son responsables de vigilar y ordenar los votos.

William and Mary of Orange > Guillermo y María de Orange El rey Guillermo III (1650–1702) y la reina María II (1662–1694) tuvieron un reinado conjunto como soberanos de Inglaterra, Escocia e Irlanda, de 1689 a 1702 (la reina María murió en 1694, pero Guillermo siguió reinando hasta 1702). María era hija del rey Jacobo II, lo que significaba que su marido neerlandés podría convertirse en corregente de Inglaterra después de derrocado el régimen de Jacobo.

Wilson, James > Wilson, James Nacido y educado en Escocia, Wilson (1742–1798) emigró a América del Norte y llegó en medio de las revueltas por la Ley del Timbre de 1765. Estudió para convertirse en abogado, especializado en derecho inmobiliario. Entró en la política poco antes de la Guerra de Independencia y su influencia fue fundamental en la Convención Constitucional.

Wilson, Woodrow > Wilson, Woodrow (1856–1924) Graduado de Princeton y de la Escuela de Leyes de la Universidad de Virginia; fue presidente de Princeton en 1902. Fue elegido como 28° presidente en 1912. Wilson ocupó el cargo de 1913 a 1921 e impulsó la Nueva Libertad, que enfatizaba el individualismo y los derechos de cada estado.

winner-take-all > el ganador se lleva todo Sistema casi obsoleto donde un aspirante presidencial que ganaba la preferencia del voto en las elecciones primarias, automáticamente obtenía el apoyo de todos los delegados elegidos en dichas elecciones.

World Bank > Banco Mundial Organismo fundado en 1944 para proporcionar asistencia económica a los países en desarrollo y reducir la pobreza en el mundo.

World Trade Organization > Organización Mundial del Comercio Organización creada en 1995 para aumentar el comercio.

writ of certiorari > auto de avocación o *certiorari* Orden emitida por una corte superior dirigida a una corte inferior para que remita el expediente de un determinado caso para su revisión; el significado en latín de la expresión es "tener mayor certeza".

writ of habeas corpus > auto de *habeas corpus* Orden judicial que evita arrestos y encarcelamientos injustos.

writs of assistance > auto de ayuda Orden general de allanamiento con la que los funcionarios aduanales británicos invadían los hogares privados en busca de bienes de contrabando.

Y

Yeltsin, Boris > Yeltsin, Boris (1931–2007) Político ruso que ocupó la presidencia de ese país en 1990. En 1991, se convirtió en el primer político elegido por voto popular en la historia de Rusia.

Z

zoning > zonificación Práctica de dividir a una ciudad en un número de distritos, o zonas, y de regular los usos que se le puede dar a la propiedad en cada uno de ellos.

A

B

C

D

E

F

O

P

T

Y

Z

[Photography]

002, f11photo/Shutterstock; **004,** Michael Flippo/Alamy; **005B,** Look and Learn/Bridgeman Images; **005T,** Jose Luis Magana/Reuters; **009,** GL Archive/Alamy; **010B,** Richard Drew/AP Images; **010T,** ANAM Collection/Alamy; **012,** Jayne Fincher.Photo Int/Alamy; **015,** Yonhap News/YNA/Newscom; **016B,** Ragnarock/Shutterstock; **016T,** Winslow Townson/ASSOCIATED PRESS; **018,** Obed Zilwa/AP Images; **019,** Trekandphoto/Fotolia; **020,** Bettmann/Corbis; **023,** CAGP/Iberfoto/The Image Works; **026,** Quint & Lox/liszt collection/Alamy; **027,** Mario Tama/Staff/Getty Images; **028B,** Bettmann/CORBIS; **028T,** Jim West/Alamy; **029,** Artley Cartoons; **030,** AF archive/Alamy; **032,** Niday Picture Library/Alamy; **035,** Artley Cartoons; **040,** Library of Congress; **042,** Barney Burstein/Corbis; **044,** Mary Evans Picture Library/The Image Works; **046B,** FALKENSTEINFOTO/Alamy; **046T,** MPI/Stringer/Archive Photos/Getty Images; **047,** Barney Burstein/Corbis; **048,** North Wind Picture Archives/Alamy; **050B,** Everett Collection/SuperStock; **050T,** North Wind Picture Archives; **051,** Niday Picture Library/Alamy; **053,** Library of Congress; **054,** GL Archive/Alamy; **057,** John Parrot/Stocktrek Images/Alamy; **058,** Library of Congress; **059B,** Old Paper Studios/Alamy; **059T,** North Wind Picture Archives/Alamy; **060,** SuperStock/Glow Images; **062,** SuperStock/SuperStock; **063L,** Dbimages/Alamy; **063LC,** World History Archive/Alamy; **063RC,** Stock Montage/Contributor/Getty Images; **063R,** US Capitol Visitors Center online exhibition/wikimedia.org; **063,** Richmond, Virginia, USA/The Bridgeman Art Library; **064,** Trekandphoto/Fotolia; **067T,** World History Archive/Alamy; **067B,** North Wind Picture Archives/Alamy; **069,** JT Vintage/Glasshouse Images/Alamy; **070T,** Stock Montage/Contributor/Getty Images; **070B,** Richmond, Virginia, USA/The Bridgeman Art Library; **072T,** Library of Congress; **072B,** Pictorial Press Ltd/Alamy; **074,** SuperStock/SuperStock; **078,** Larry1235/Shutterstock; **080,** Kumar Sriskandan/Alamy; **084,** Bettmann/Corbis; **083B,** Marcophoto81/Fotolia; **083T,** Bettmann/Corbis; **085B,** Artley Cartoons; **085T,** Ben Margot/AP Images; **086B,** Artley Cartoons; **086T,** Artley Cartoons; **087,** Artley Cartoons; **089,** Artley Cartoons; **092,** Tom Barlet/Seattle Post-Intelligencer/Museum of History & Industry; **094B,** Bettmann/CORBIS; **094T,** Library of Congress; **096,** Everett Collection/Newscom; **097B,** Dana Verkouteren/AP Images; **097T,** Kevin Dietsch/Upi/Newscom; **098B,** UPPA/Photoshot/Newscom; **098T,** AP Images; **099,** Library of Congress; **101,** McClatchy-Tribune Information Services/Alamy; **102,** SuperStock/Glow Images; **104,** Bettmann/CORBIS; **106B,** Bob Daemmrich/Alamy; **106T,** Matt Detrich/ASSOCIATED PRESS; **107B,** Anthony Dunn/Alamy; **107T,** Library of Congress; **108,** Scott Dorrett/Fotolia; **109,** North Wind Picture Archives/Alamy; **111,** KENNY TONG/Shutterstock; **112B,** Master Sgt. Mark Olsen/Dvids; **112T,** Library of Congress; **113,** Steve Schapiro/Corbis; **115B,** Lee Lorenz/Cartoonbank; **115T,** Wilfred Osgood/National Geographic Society/Corbis; **116B,** Jacquelyn Martin/AP Images; **116T,** Federal Highway Administration (FHWA); **118,** Jeffrey M. Frank/Shutterstock; **119,** Bettmann/Corbis; **120,** Katharine Andriotis/Alamy; **121B,** Randy Snyder/Ap Images; **121T,** Bettmann/CORBIS; **122,** Tony Waltham/Robert Harding Picture Library Ltd/Alamy; **123,** SuperStock/Glow Images; **125,** Artley Cartoons; **128,** Vlad_g/Fotolia; **130,** Epa european pressphoto agency b.v./Alamy; **131,** Jason Reed/REUTERS; **133,** Gary Williams/EPA/Newscom; **134,** Stefan Zaklin/epa/Corbis; **136B,** INTERFOTO/Alamy; **136T,** Reuters; **138,** Paul M. Walsh/AP Images; **139,** Jason Reed/REUTERS; **141,** North Wind/North Wind Picture Archives; **142,** NASA Earth Observatory/NOAA NGDC; **143,** Larry Downing/Reuters; **145,** Bernard Schoenbaum/Cartoonbank; **147,** Library Of Congress; **148,** Jason Reed/Reuters; **150,** Mike Theiler/Upi/Newscom; **153,** David Pollack/Glow Images; **155B,** Epa european pressphoto agency b.v./Alamy; **155T,** Bob Daemmrich/PhotoEdit; **156,** White House/AP Images; **157,** Health, Science and Space/Alamy; **158,** Matthew Johnston/Alamy; **159,** Bettmann/Corbis; **160B,** AP Images; **160T,** PF-sdasm4/Alamy; **161,** Charles Tasnadi/AP Images; **162,** Ap Images; **164L,** GL Archive/Alamy; **164R,** Stock Montage/Contributor/Getty Images; **165B,** Stus.com; **165T,** Art Directors & TRIP/Alamy; **168,** Lightroom Photos/Alamy; **170B,** Bill Pierce/Time Life Pictures/Getty Images; **170T,** Bettmann/Corbis; **173,** Wally McNamee/CORBIS; **174B,** Historical/Corbis; **174T,** Bill Clark/Roll Call Photos/Newscom; **175,** Harris & Ewing/Corbis; **176,** Susan Walsh/Ap Images; **177B,** Hejzlar Jaroslav/CTK/Alamy; **177T,** Susan Walsh/AP Images; **180,** J. Scott Applewhite/Ap Images; **184,** Cagle.com; **185,** Underwood & Underwood/Corbis; **186B,** JOHN TREVER/PoliticalCartoons.com; **186T,** Bettmann/CORBIS; **187,** Lawrence Manning/Corbis; **188,** Epa european pressphoto agency b.v./Alamy; **190,** Alan King engraving/Alamy; **191,** Brendan Hoffman/Getty Images; **192,** Chip Somodevilla/Staff/Getty Images; **196B,** Ron Sachs/CNP/Corbis; **196T,** Robert Ariail; **199L,** GL Archive/Alamy; **199R,** Stock Montage/Contributor/Getty Images; **202,** Tupungato/Shutterstock; **204,** Air Collection/Alamy; **205B,** Wally McNamee/Corbis; **205T,** STEPHEN JAFFE/AFP/Newscom; **206,** Larry Downing/Reuters/Corbis; **208,** Everett/Glow Images; **211,** Dennis Brack/Danita Delimont/Alamy; **212,** Brooks Kraft/Sygma/Corbis; **213,** Tom Fox/Dallas Morning News/Corbis; **215,** Everett/Glow Images; **216B,** Library of Congress; **216T,** Library of Congress; **217B,** Library of Congress; **217T,** Library of Congress; **218B,** Ed Maloney/AP Images; **218T,** whitehousehistory; **219,** Jim West/Alamy; **220,** Jason Vorhees/AP Images; **221,** Pete Souza/The White House/PSG/Newscom; **223,** Nast,Thomas/Cartoonstock; **224,** Topical Press Agency/Stringer/Getty Images; **225,** GL Archive/Alamy; **227,** Robert J. Matson; **228,** Yna Pool/EPA/Newscom; **229B,** World History Archive/Alamy; **229T,** Bettmann/Corbis; **230B,** North Wind Picture Archives/Alamy; **230T,** DIZ Muenchen GmbH,Sueddeutsche Zeitung Photo/Alamy; **231,** Library of Congress; **238,** Molly Riley-Pool/Getty Images; **240,** DAN LOH/AP Images; **241B,** Fran/Cartoon Stock; **241T,** Denis Poroy/AP Images; **242,** David Hume Kennerly/Getty Images; **246,** Chuck Kennedy/The White House/Getty Images; **247B,** Shawn Thew/EPA/Newscom; **247T,** Pete Souza/The White House/Rapport Syndication/Newscom; **250,** USDA Photo/Alamy; **252,** Bettmann/Corbis; **253,** Corbis; **254,** Ron Edmonds/AP Images; **255,** FRC Collection/Alamy; **257,** Joe Robbins/Getty Images; **259,** Library of Congress; **260,** Patti McConville/Alamy; **261B,** JOHN ANGELILLO/UPI/Newscom; **261T,** Bill Greenblatt/Upi/Newscom; **262,** Wuerker, Matt/Cartoonstock; **264,** Tom Brakefield/Getty Images; **265,** US Army Photo/Alamy; **266,** KYDPL KYODO/AP Images; **267,** Warren Miller/Cartoon bank; **268,** harpweek.com; **269,** Time & Life Pictures/Getty Images; **269T,** MPI/Stringer/Getty Images; **271B,** Maj. R. V. Spencer/DoD/Newscom; **271T,** PF-(aircraft)/Alamy; **273B,** Keren Su/China Span/Alamy; **273T,** World History Archive/Alamy; **274,** ZUMA Press, Inc./Alamy; **277,** AP Images; **278,** ITAR-TASS Photo Agency/Alamy; **284,** Chip East/REUTERS; **287,** Zhao Yishen/Xinhua Press/Corbis; **288,** David L. Moore/Alamy; **289,** USAF/Handout/Getty Images; **289B,** Jacquelyn Martin/AP Images; **292B,** The National Security Agency; **292T,** Jason Reed/Reuters; **294,** Robert Harding World Imagery/Corbis; **300,** Brian Jannsen/Alamy; **302,** Nsf/Alamy; **303,** Corbis; **304,** Danish Siddiqui/REUTERS; **306,** KEVIN DIETSCH/UPI/Newscom; **307,** Bettmann/Corbis; **309,** Rich Legg/Getty Images; **310,** Richard A. Bloom/Corbis; **312B,** Eliana Aponte/Reuters; **312T,** Everett Collection/Newscom; **313,** M. Bruckner, Secretary of the Army, et al./kamenypapers.org; **314,** Flickr; **317,** Epa european pressphoto agency b.v./Alamy; **321,** Kim Kulish/Corbis; **322B,** Jeff Parker/Cagle Cartoons; **322T,** Brennan Linsley/AP Images; **328,** Everett Collection Inc/Alamy; **330,** MixPix/Alamy; **331,** Bridgeman Art; **332,** Akg-images/Newscom; **333,** Niday Picture Library/Alamy; **333T,** Akg-images/Newscom; **335,** Library of Congress; **337,** DON EMMERT/AFP/Getty Images; **338B,** ZUMA Press, Inc./Alamy; **338T,** Philip Scalia/Alamy; **339,** Everett Collection/Newscom; **340,** Campbell, Martha/Cartoonstock; **341B,** Monika Graff/The Image Works; **341T,** Bettmann/Corbis; **342,** HARRY CABLUCK/AP Images; **343,** Scott R. Galvin/AP Images; **344,** Kevin P. Casey/Corbis; **345,** Jacquelyn Martin/AP Images; **346B,** Bettmann/Corbis; **346T,** North Wind Picture Archives/Alamy; **347,** North Wind Picture Archives/Alamy; **348,** Bettmann/Corbis; **349,** AP Images; **350,** Bettmann/Corbis; **351,** Mark J. Terrill/AP Images; **352,** Doug Mills/AP Images; **354,** Peter Casolino/Alamy; **355,** Manuel Balce Ceneta/AP Images; **357,** Edward Kitch/AP Images; **358,** Bettmann/Corbis; **359,** Juice Images/Alamy; **361,** Dennis MacDonald/Alamy; **362,** ZUMA Press, Inc./Alamy; **364,** Martin Shields/Alamy; **365B,** Bettmann/Corbis; **365T,** cah.utexas.edu; **366,** Bettmann/Corbis; **367,** North Wind Picture Archives; **368B,** Michael Ireland/Fotolia; **368T,** Stus.com; **370B,** Imago stock&people/Newscom; **370T,** Michael Dwyer/Alamy; **371B,** Charles Barsotti/Cartoonbank; **371T,** Peter Foley/EPA/Newscom; **373B,** Baldwin, Mike/Cartoon Stock; **373T,** hypojustice.com; **374,** Stephen Boitano/Polaris/Newscom; **375,** HENNY RAY ABRAMS/Reuters/Landov; **376,** fStop Images GmbH/Alamy; **377B,** Library of Congress; **377T,** Deborah Cheramie/Getty Images; **378,** Library of Congress; **380B,** Peter Casolino/Alamy; **380T,** Ferd Kaufman/Ap Images; **382,** Flip Schulke/Black Star; **384,** Nathan Martin/AP Images; **392,** Paul A. Souders/Corbis; **394,** Bob Daemmrich/Photo Edit; **397B,** Library of Congress; **397T,** Rob Verhorst/Redferns/Getty Images; **399,** MIKE BLAKE/Reuters/Corbis; **400,** Rick Friedman/Corbis; **401,** 2010 RJ Matson, The St. Louis Post Dispatch/Cagle Cartoons; **402,** Chuck Savage/Corbis; **404,** Library of Congress; **406,** Jashim Salam/Demotix/Corbis; **407,** Jashim Salam/Demotix/Corbis; **408,** Bill Clark/Getty Images; **409,** MARCY NIGHSWANDER/AP Images; **410,** Mark William Richardson/Shutterstock; **411,** Library of Congress;

412, Francis Miller/Contributor/Getty Images; **413B,** Deborah Cheramie/Getty Images; **413T,** Shen Hong/Xinhua Press/Corbis; **416,** Bob Adelman/Corbis; **417,** Bettmann/Corbis; **419,** WALT ZEBOSKI/AP Images; **420,** Spencer Platt/Staff/Getty Images; **422,** 2010 RJ Matson, The St. Louis Post Dispatch/Cagle Cartoons; **424,** Cartoonist Group; **426,** Lightspring/Shutterstock; **428,** Bettmann/Corbis; **429,** SuperStock/Getty Images; **430,** McD/AP Images; **431B,** Everett Collection/Newscom; **431T,** World History Archive/Alamy; **434B,** J. Scott Applewhite/Ap Images; **434T,** DAVE GRANLUND, POLITICALCARTOONS; **436,** Visar Kryeziu/AP Images; **437B,** Library of Congress; **437T,** The Protected Art Archive/Alamy; **439,** Bettmann/Corbis; **440,** PARKER/FLORIDA/Cagle Cartoons; **441,** Bob Adelman/Corbis; **442,** Paul Schutzer/Getty Images; **444,** Jae C. Hong/AP Images; **446,** Parspix/ABACA/Newscom; **447,** People and Politics/Alamy; **448,** Delgado Roy/Cartoonstock; **452B,** JONATHAN ERNST/Reuters/Corbis; **452T,** EMMANUEL DUNAND/AFP/Getty Images/Newscom; **453,** Epa European Pressphoto Agency b.v./Alamy; **454,** Rogelio V. Solis/AP Images; **455,** Eugene Tanner/AP Images; **457B,** Steve Ruark/Ap Images; **457T,** Henry Burroughs/AP Images; **458,** Gilder Lehrman Collection/Bridgeman Images; **459,** Library of Congress; **461,** Hagen, Ralph/Cartoonstock; **462,** Digital Vision/Getty Images; **463B,** Ed Andrieski/AP Images; **463T,** Nati Harnik/AP Images; **464,** Elise Amendola/AP Images; **465,** ZUMA Press, Inc./Alamy; **466B,** Eric Audras/ONOKY Photononstop/Alamy; **466T,** Reuters; **467,** Thomas E. Franklin/AP Images; **468,** Grizelda/Cartoonstock; **469,** Milwaukee Journal-Sentinel, Erwin Gebhard/AP Images; **470B,** Keystone-France/Getty Images; **470T,** W. Eugene Smith/Getty Images; **475,** Brooks Kraft/Corbis; **476,** North Wind Picture Archives/Alamy; **477B,** North Wind Picture Archives/Alamy; **477T,** Photri Images/Alamy; **478,** Pictorial Press Ltd/Alamy; **479B,** Justin Sullivan/Getty Images; **479T,** Harley Schwadron/jantoo/Cartoonstock; **483,** ITAR-TASS Photo Agency/Alamy; **484,** Steve Rhodes/Demotix/Corbis; **486,** Minnesota Historical Society; **486B,** George Eastman House/Getty Images; **486C,** Library of Congress; **486L,** Nara; **487B,** Prettyfoto/Alamy; **487T,** Bob Daemmrich/Alamy; **488,** A. Ramey/PhotoEdit; **491B,** Seav Gardner/Reuters/Landov; **491T,** Scott J.Ferrell/Congressional Quarterly/Newscom; **492,** Miller Wiley/Cartoonstock; **495B,** Seth Perlman/AP Images; **495T,** Hagen/Cartoonstock; **497B,** Wuerker Matt/Cartoonstock; **497T,** Ron Sachs/CNP/Corbis; **502,** The Protected Art Archive/Alamy; **504,** David R. Frazier Photolibrary, Inc/Alamy; **506,** Epa European Pressphoto Agency b.v./Alamy; **507B,** Charles Dharapak/AP Images; **507T,** Dirk Shadd/ZUMA Press/Newscom; **508,** Daniel Coston/Retna Ltd./Corbis; **509,** Grzegorz Knec/Alamy; **510,** Everett Collection/Newscom; **511B,** Ronald Karpilo/Alamy; **511T,** Thomas Nast/Harpweek; **515B,** Everett Collection/Newscom; **515T,** Paul Hennessy/Polaris/Newscom; **518,** Zach Boyden-Holmes/Staff/ZUMA Press/Newscom; **519B,** Kurt Fehlhauer/Alamy; **519T,** ZUMA Press, Inc./Alamy; **521,** Mark Hirsch/AP Images; **522,** Everett Collection/Newscom; **523B,** Keystone Pictures USA/Alamy; **523T,** Xinhua/ZUMApress/Newscom; **524,** World History Archive/Alamy; **525,** Joel Page/Reuters/Corbis; **526,** Stock Montage/Contributor/Getty Images; **527,** DARREN HAUCK/Reuters/Corbis; **528,** ZUMA Press, Inc./Alamy; **529B,** CJ GUNTHER/EPA/Newscom; **529T,** Hans Pennink/AP Images; **531,** MARY BETH SCHNEIDER/AP Images; **532,** Tampa Bay Times/ZUMAPRESS/Alamy; **535,** Glen Stubbe/ZUMA Press, Inc./Alamy; **537,** Milt Priggee/Cagle Cartoons; **538,** ZUMA Press, Inc./Alamy; **539,** KEYSTONE Pictures USA/ZUMAPRESS/Newscom; **540,** AP Images; **541B,** Bettmann/Corbis; **541T,** Joe Marquette/AP Images; **544,** Chip Somodevilla/Getty Images; **547,** Stocktrek Images, Inc./Alamy; **549,** Melpomen/Fotolia; **550,** AP Images; **551B,** Lauren Victoria Burke/AP Images; **551T,** Chris Fitzgerald/CandidatePhotos/Newscom; **552,** Wuerker, Matt/Cartoonstock; **554,** Cphoto/Fotolia; **555B,** Marmaduke St. John/Alamy; **555T,** Stahler, Jeff/Cartoonstock; **556B,** BRENDAN SMIALOWSKI/POOL/EPA/Newscom; **556T,** J.B. Handelsman/The New Yorker Collection/Cartoonbank; **558,** Bob Daemmrich/Alamy; **562,** MOVEON.ORG/AFP/Newscom; **564, 565,** Kristoffer Tripplaar/Alamy; **566,** Richard Ellis/Alamy; **568,** Blend Images/Alamy; **570,** Old Paper Studios/Alamy; **572,** Adoc-photos/Corbis; **576,** Catnap/Alamy; **577,** World History Archive/Alamy; **579,** MARIO TAMA/AFP/Newscom; **580,** Grizelda/Cartoonstock; **581,** Bettmann/Corbis; **584,** Bloomberg/Contributor/Getty Images; **585,** US National Archives and Records Administration; **588B,** AugustSnow/Alamy; **588T,** Max Faulkner/AP Images; **592,** Hellen Sergeyeva/Fotolia; **593,** Minnesota Historical Society/Corbis; **594,** Anthony Behar/AP Images; **602,** Nasa; **604,** Don Despain/Alamy; **606,** PRNewsFoto/Caterpillar/AP Images; **610,** SeongJoon Cho/Bloomberg/Getty Images; **616, 617,** Sue Ogrocki/AP Images; **618,** Albert Herter/Malegislature; **619,** Baloo -Rex May/Cartoonstock; **621,** Scott Keeler/AP Images; **622,** Artizans Entertainment Inc.; **624,** Ellen Isaacs/Alamy; **625,** Rich Pedroncelli/AP Images; **627,** Usda Photo/Alamy; **628,** Toby Talbot/AP Images; **629B,** Bob Daemmrich Photography/Alamy; **629T,** Carpenter, Dave /Cartoonstock; **631,** Steven Johnson/MCT/Newscom; **632,** Reuters; **633B,** WOLVERTON/Cagle Cartoons; **633T,** Tannen Maury/EPA/Landov; **634B,** Susan Montoya Bryan/AP Images; **634T,** Phil Sears/AP Images; **635,** gilya3/Fotolia; **639,** Alan Klehr/Getty Images; **642,** New York Times Co./Contributor/Getty Images; **643B,** Library of Congress; **643T,** Michael Maslin The New Yorker Collection/The Cartoon Bank; **645B,** Bob Daemmrich/PhotoEdit; **645T,** Prisma/SuperStock; **649,** Bill Stormont/Alamy; **652B,** Austinamericana.files.wordpress; **652T,** B Christopher/Alamy; **654,** North Wind Picture Archives; **655,** Poulides/Thatcher/Getty Images; **656,** AL MOUNT/Fotolia; **660,** LHB Photo/Alamy; **661B,** R. Krubner/ClassicStock/Corbis; **661T,** SuperStock/GlowImages; **662,** Jim West/Alamy; **664,** Mason Vranish/Alamy; **667B,** Eisenhower Library & Museum; **667T,** Larry W. Smith/EPA/Newscom; **673,** Brian Jannsen/Alamy; **674,** Ken James/Bloomberg/Getty Images; **678, 679,** Roberto Fumagalli/Alamy; **680,** Oliver Gerhard imagebroker/Newscom; **682,** Baloo -Rex May/Cartoonstock; **684,** Joerg Boethling/Alamy; **686,** Chris Jackson/AP Images; **689,** Lewis Whyld/AP Images; **690,** PA/PA Photos /Landov; **693,** Dmitry Lovetsky/AP Images; **695,** Frederique Lengaigne/Gamma-Rapho/Getty Images; **697B,** Sergei Karpukhin/Reuters; **697T,** Maxim Marmur/AFP/Getty Images; **700,** Hulton Archive/Stringer/Getty Images; **701,** Rafael Ben-Ari/Fotolia; **704,** Evan Vucci/AP Images

[Text Acknowledgments]

ABC News – Permissions Dept., Defending the Electoral College by George Will, November 2, 2000. Copyright © ABC News. Used by permission.; **Alfred A. Knopf,** The Negro Speaks of Rivers," and "My People" from THE COLLECTED POEMS OF LANGSTON HUGHES by Langston Hughes, edited by Arnold Rampersad with David Roessel, Associate Editor, copyright © 1994 by the Estate of Langston Hughes. Used by permission of Alfred A. Knopf, an imprint of the Knopf Doubleday Publishing Group, a division of Random House LLC. All rights reserved; **American Enterprise Institute,** Save the Filibuster! Copyright © The American Enterprise Institute. Used by permission.; **Brennan Center for Justice at New York University School of Law,** "Filibuster Reform: Curbing Abuse to Prevent Minority Tyranny in the Senate" by Senator Tom Harkin from the Brennan Center for Justice. Copyright © Brennan Center for Justice.; **CBS News,** To Save a City: The Berlin Airlift by Roger G. Miller and Pro R Miller, 1948-1949. Copyright © Texas A&M University Press.; **CBS News,** "President President Obama" by Steve Kroft, from 60 Minutes, March 20, 2009. Copyright © 2009 CBS News.; **Center for Individual Freedom,** Judical Activism by John Roberts. Copyright © Center for Individual Freedom.; **Center for Responsive Politics,** Lobbying Data. Copyright © Center for Responsive Politics. Used by permission.; **CNN,** "Russia, China and partners call for non-intervention in Syria, Iran" by Jaime A. FlorCruz from CNN June 7, 2012. Copyright © 2012 CNN.; **Council on Foreign Relations,** "Remarks by UK Prime Minister Cameron and Deputy Prime Minister Clegg" by David Cameron, and Nick Clegg, May 12. Copyright © 2010 Council on Foreign Relations.; **Doubleday,** Excerpts from "Diary of a Young Girl: The Definitive Edition" by Anne Frank, edited by Otto H. Frank and Mirjam Pressler, translated by Susan Massotty, translation copyright © 1995 by Doubleday, a division of Random House LLC. Used by permission of Doubleday, an imprint of the Knopf Doubleday Publishing Group, a division of Random House LLC. All rights reserved.; **Dover Publications,** How the Other Half Lives by Jacob Riis. Copyright © Dover Publications.; **Ending Spending,** Earmarks Map 2011 Requests. Copyright © Ending Spending.; **Featurewell.com,** "We Should Be Done with Earmarks" by Alexandra Booze, November 15 2003. Copyright © 2013 TheHill.; **FindLaw,** A Critique of the Top Ten Modern Arguments for the Electoral College. Copyright © FindLaw.com Used by permission.; **Governing Magazine,** "Clueless in Boise" by Alan Ehrenhalt from Governing Magazine. Copyright © eRupublic, Inc.; **Harold Ober Associates,** The Collected Poems of Langston Hughes by Langston Hughes edited by Arnold Rampersad with David Roessel, Associate Editor. Copyright © 1994 by the Estate of Langston Hughes. Used by permission of Harold Ober Associates Incorporated.; **Houghton Mifflin Harcourt Publishing Company,** Silent Spring by Rachel Carson. Copyright © Houghton Mifflin Harcourt.; **Institute of Islamic Knowledge,** English Translation of the Meaning of Al-Qur'an: The Guidance for Mankind translated by Muhammad

Farooq-i-Azam Malik. Copyright © 1997 The Institute of Islamic Knowledge. Used by permission.; **Liberty Fund, Inc.,** "A Pennsylvania Farmer" from Friends of the Constitution: Writings of the Other Federalists, 1787–1788 edited by Colleen A. Sheehan and Gary L. McDowell Copyright © 1998 by Liberty Fund. Used by permission of the publisher.; **Liberty Fund, Inc.,** "A Pennsylvania Farmer" from Friends of the Constitution by Colleen A. Sheehan, Gary L. McDowell. Copyright © 1998. Liberty Fund.; **Ludwig Von Mises Institute,** The Antifederalists Were Right by Gary Galles from Ludwig von Mises Institute, September 27, 2006. Copyright © Ludwig von Mises Institute. Used by permission.; **National Council of Churches,** "I Corinthians, Chapter 13" from Holy Bible: With the Apocryphal. Copyright © 1989 National Council of Churches of Christ.; **Navajivan Trust,** Hind Swaraj and Other Writings by M.K. Gandhi. Copyright © The Navajivan Trust. Used by permission.; **OpenSecrets.org,** "Number on Total Lobbying Spending, Number of Lobbyists, and Top Spenders" from opensecrets.org. Copyright © Center for Responsive Politics. Used by permission.; **Oxford University Press (UK) – Journals,** The Oxford History of the American People by Samuel Eliot Morison. Copyright © 1965 Oxford University Press.; **Penguin Books, Ltd. (UK),** "Freedom from Fear" from FREEDOM FROM FEAR AND OTHER WRITINGS, REVISED EDITION by Aung San Suu Kyi, edited by Michael Aris, copyright © 1991, 1995 by Aung San Suu Kyi. Used by permission of Viking Penguin, a division of Penguin Group (USA) LLC.; **Penguin Group,** "Freedom from Fear" from FREEDOM FROM FEAR AND OTHER WRITINGS, REVISED EDITION by Aung San Suu Kyi, edited by Michael Aris, copyright © 1991, 1995 by Aung San Suu Kyi. Used by permission of Viking Penguin, a division of Penguin Group (USA) LLC.; **Routledge Publishing, Inc.,** Ibn Battuta: Travels in Asia and Africa 1325–1354 by Ibn Battua and H.A.R Gibb (trans.). Copyright © 1986 Routledge.; **Slate Magazine,** In Defense of the Electoral College from Slate Magazine, November 12, 2012. Copyright © Slate Magazine. Used by permission.; **Texas Children's Health Plan,** Top 5 Reasons to Vote from Texas Children's Health Plan. Copyright © Texas Children's Health Plan. Used by permission.; **The American Presidency Project,** Dwight D. Eisenhower: "Address Recorded for the Republican Lincoln Day Dinners.," January 28, 1954. Online by Gerhard Peters and John T. Woolley, The American Presidency Project. http://www.presidency.ucsb.edu/ws/?pid=10008.; **The National Center for Public Policy Research,** "Magna Cart or, The Great Charter of King John Granted June 15, 1215." Copyright © The National Center.; **The New York Times Magazine,** Kennedy, John F. "To Keep the Lobbyist Within Bounds." by John F. Kennedy, 19 February 1956. Copyright © 1956 The New York Times Magazine.; **The Washington Post,** Why Both Parties Need to Filibuster by Ruth Marcus from The Washington Post, January 27, 2010. Copyright © The Washington Post. Used by permission.; **The Yale Law School,** Declaration of the Rights of Man, 1789. Copyright © Lillian Goldman Law Library.; **Thomas Nelson, Inc.,** Ghana: The Autobiography of Kwame Nkrumah by Kwame Nkrumah. Copyright © Thomas Nelson, Inc.; **United Nations Department of Public Information,** United Nations Millennium Development Goals. Copyright © United Nations Publications. Used by permission.; **United Nations Publications,** United Nations Millennium Development Goals. Copyright © United Nations Publications. Used by permission.; **University of North Carolina Press,** From THE POEMS OF PHILLIS WHEATLEY edited and with an introduction by Julian D. Mason Jr. Copyright 1966 by the University of North Carolina Press, renewed 1989. Used by permission of the publisher. www.uncpress.unc.edu; **USA Today,** "Some want earmarks back to help Congress pass bills" by Erin Kelly, October 29, 2013. Copyright © 2013 USA Today.; **USA Today Magazine,** Senator Susan Collins quoted in "GOP: Obama regulations are killing jobs" by David Jackson from USA Today, September 24, 2011. Copyright © 2011 USA Today.; **USA Today Magazine,** "GOP: Obama regulations are killing jobs" by David Jackson, Sep 24, 2011. Copyright © 2011 USA TODAY.; **Vital Speeches of the Day,** Glory and Hope Speech by Nelson Mandela, May 11, 1994. Copyright © Vital Speeches of the Day.; **W.W. Norton & Company, Inc.,** The Feminine Mystique by Betty Friedan. Copyright © W.W. Norton & Company.; **Writers House LLC,** "I Have a Dream" by Martin Luther King. Copyright © 1963 Dr. Martin Luther King, Jr. Copyright © 1991 Coretta Scott King. Used by permission.; **Writers House LLC,** "Letters From a Birmingham Jail" by Martin Luther King. Copyright © 1963 Dr. Martin Luther King, Jr. Copyright © renewed 1991 Coretta Scott King. Used by permission.